Dutch Art

Garland Reference Library of the Humanities (Vol. 1021)

Advisory Board

Dutch Art

An Encyclopedia

Edited by
Sheila D. Muller

Garland Publishing, Inc. New York & London, 1997

Library of Congress Cataloging-in-Publication Data

Dutch Art : an encyclopedia / edited by Sheila D. Muller.
         p.   cm. — (Garland reference library of the humanities ; vol. 1021)
    Includes bibliographical references and index.
    ISBN 0-8153-0065-4 (alk. paper)
    1. Art, Dutch—Encyclopedias.   I. Muller, Sheila D. (Sheila
D'moch)   II. Series.
N6941.D88   1997

                      96–35513
                      CIP

Cover photo: Piet Mondrian *Composition,* 1929. The Solomon R. Guggenheim
Museum, New York. Photography by David Heald. Reprinted by
permission of Solomon R. Guggenheim Foundation, New York.

Cover design: Lawrence Wolfson Design, New York

Interior art layout: Eric J. Brearton

Printed on acid-free, 250-year-life paper
Manufactured in the United States of America

Contents

Preface

In a conference keynote address to the Historians of Netherlandish Art in October 1993, Seymour Slive, Gleason Professor of Fine Arts Emeritus of Harvard University, surveyed the crowded Remus Auditorium of the Museum of Fine Arts, Boston, and reflected on the thriving field of study he had helped to introduce to higher education in the United States after World War II. The small group of colleagues employed in teaching Dutch art in the 1950s included another American, J. Richard Judson (at Smith College); Julius Held (at Barnard College) and Wolfgang Stechow (at Oberlin College), both of whom had come earlier from Europe; and Egbert Haverkamp-Begemann, who arrived in 1959 (and soon after was to teach at Yale University). The students they trained to become professors, curators, museum directors, and patrons continued to encourage interest until, in the 1990s, Dutch art is taught across the United States in college and university courses and is represented in many North American public and private collections.

A great deal of the attention in North America has been focused on Dutch seventeenth-century painting, which was contemporaneous with early European settlement of the continent and which fascinates today because of "Dutch Realism," a verisimilitude that has been shown to mean a great deal more than meets the eye. In the 1970s and 1980s, when many academic disciplines felt the strains of methodological and ideological discord, the study of Dutch art was enlivened by fresh investigations of seventeenth-century painting that led to different interpretations of, especially, genre painting. In the Netherlands, in addition to the study of the seventeenth century, there was also a renewal of interest in nineteenth-century art and nationalism, in twentieth-century avant-garde movements, and in contemporary art. The scholarly controversies that were at times generated by new theories and discoveries were frankly discussed in the art historical literature of the 1980s and 1990s, stimulating the interest of increasing numbers of graduate students and drawing experts from the humanities and social sciences to examine the issues raised by art historians. In the mid-1990s, the study of Dutch art is inter-national and interdisciplinary, with the consequence that it is also the focus of greater public awareness.

The present volume is the latest in the succession of general works in English on Dutch art that have appeared since the mid-1960s, when the field became an established part of the North American academic curriculum. Including the present volume, these works, discussed below, represent the state of research on Dutch art at specific times in the last half of the twentieth century, and together they show the evolution of the field as a result of a diversity of approaches, changing perspectives, and the posing of new questions. This volume—an encyclopedic overview of knowledge that has been growing ever since Professor Seymour Slive embarked on his career—covers a greater span of time and includes more artistic developments than any of its predecessors.

In 1966, Jakob Rosenberg, Seymour Slive, and E.H. ter Kuile, three distinguished scholars, published *Dutch Art and Architecture 1600–1800* in the "Pelican History of Art" series. This monumental achievement was an encapsulation of the renewed thinking on the subject in the twenty years following World War II. With separate sections for painting, sculpture, and architecture, the book has remained in print (it was issued in revised editions with an updated bibliography in 1972 and 1977 and reprinted in 1982 and 1993; the sections on painting, with some revisions, were also published separately by Yale University Press in 1993), functioning well both as a course text and a ready reference source. At heart, it is a book about the history of reputations. Dutch seventeenth- and eighteenth-century painters were more prolific and received more notice from contemporaries abroad than did Dutch sculptors and architects; therefore, the book begins with the history of painting. Rosenberg and Slive, the authors of the painting section, considered the comments made about Dutch painters by seventeenth- and eighteenth-century critics, theorists, and historians, and weighed that evidence together with patterns in the collecting of Dutch paintings in the nineteenth and twentieth centuries.

After the late seventeenth century, three Dutch painters

enjoyed an international reputation: Frans Hals, Rembrandt van Rijn, and Johannes Vermeer. To deal with the accumulation of fact and myth about these artists, each has a chapter in the book devoted to him. Dutch painters, on the whole, developed local reputations; the majority, therefore, are included in the chapters on towns and subject specializations. Selected for individualized treatment on the basis of their later reputation as the major masters of the Dutch School, Hals, Rembrandt, and Vermeer are allowed to retain a problematic status: They appear in the book as the exceptions to the national character of Dutch art, which was produced by minor masters in local schools.

Between 1966 and about 1980, the reaction to "Rosenberg and Slive" (as *Dutch Art and Architecture 1600–1800* was commonly called in academic circles where the primacy of painting in art history was taken for granted) could be gauged by the many monographs on painters from the local schools of Dutch art that were written as Ph.D. dissertations. Preparing *catalogues raisonnés* and other studies delineating the important contributions of minor masters to the overall character of the Dutch School had become a major academic exercise on an international scale.

The justification for the next two general works on Dutch art was the presentation of this revised image of the Dutch School. In The Netherlands, art historian, critic, and museum director R.H. Fuchs wrote *Dutch Painting,* published in English by Oxford University Press in 1978, in which he traced the course of development of a Dutch School of painting from its origins in the later fifteenth century in Haarlem to the 1970s. Individual artistic achievements are subsumed into the chronology and mostly into the subject categories of genre painting, history painting, portraiture, landscape, and still life, which developed local traditions and permitted the practice of naturalism and specialization for which the Dutch School is famous. The chapters on nineteenth- and twentieth-century painting are more loosely organized in accordance with the changing later perception: "Local" had come to be seen as merely provincial by many people at that time, and, as a consequence, individual achievements had to be made to stand out. A succinct introduction to its subject, Fuchs' *Dutch Painting* was reprinted in 1989; however, its central argument about Dutch Realism (as mock realism that functions to disguise meaning as metaphor) reflects a trend in art historical research from the 1970s, and the importance given to formal analysis recalls the method of earlier art criticism.

The Golden Age: Dutch Painters of the Seventeenth Century by Dutch writer Bob Haak was published in a double edition in English (New York: Harry N. Abrams) and Dutch (Amsterdam: Meulenhoff) in 1984. It is a longer and larger book than Fuchs' although covering a shorter time, and an even more monumental work than that of Rosenberg and Slive because it restores a balance by placing the emphasis on the reputation of local schools and identifying the major and minor masters in each. Haak relied on the monographic studies written in the 1970s and early 1980s, and his book includes good reproductions for comparing a wide variety of works. *The Golden Age* provides the cultural context for seeing the art of Hals, Rembrandt, and Vermeer within the Dutch tradition, and confirms that seventeenth-century Dutch painting was of high quality generally. The ample evidence that seventeenth-century artists also diverged from tradition in very particular ways is, however, distributed through the book, making this an unwieldy tool to use in a systematic study.

In the mid-1990s the trend is away from general surveys of art history. Information is disseminated through monographs, specialized studies, dissertations, journal articles, exhibition catalogs, conference papers, and even films and video; to interpret the diversity of viewpoints and topical treatments for general use requires an encyclopedia.

Between these covers, Dutch art means primarily painting, drawing, printmaking, architecture, and sculpture. Building on the foundation of the preceding three general works, the organization of art production in local schools and by subject categories is accepted as the traditional norm, and it is extended for the time covered by the encyclopedia in order to provide historical and critical perspectives on changes that have taken place. The history of reputations still plays a role: Rembrandt, Vermeer, Vincent van Gogh, Piet Mondrian, and Karel Appel are the subjects of entries that go beyond biography to an evaluation of the national and international attention each has received. The rationale for having biographical entries is to correct inaccuracies in previous research or to add information about early masters, to recover reputations for eighteenth- and nineteenth-century artists or to make them for notable twentieth-century artists. Biography as an approach, therefore, is a reflection of the monographic studies that are still basic to art historical research, but it does not always give the complete picture. Cross-referencing among the biographies and the thematic and topical entries closes the research gap between individual reputation and cultural history.

Other kinds of concerns, raised more often since the 1980s, are addressed in entries relating to social history, gender issues, the history of ideas, and the place of government, politics, and religion in the support and development of the arts. The definition of art has been made broader to include the material culture of houses, gardens, and personal adornment in clothing, paying attention to creative expression in these forms. The exchange of influences between the fine arts and the applied arts, ceramics, coins, film, photography, postage stamps, and tiles is also examined. Various ways of writing about art and artists—in lives, literature, art theory, art criticism, and art history—are subjected to scrutiny for what they have contributed to our understanding of art in the past. The public's taste, expressed through patronage, amateurism, patriotism, critical response, and displaying works of art, is also among the subjects of study.

Readers who think something is omitted should first consult the Index, where they may find references to what they are looking for; they should also remember that what is presented is a state of research involving a reappraisal of what has gone before. One manifestation of this rapidly growing field is that the authors have written entries that include knowledge that is changing and developing. For enlisting some potential authors this was a disadvantage, because their reluctance to digest their own works-in-progress could not be overcome. A few other scholars could not be enticed to revisit their former thoughts about a subject when they have since moved on in other directions; that work was then left to others, who brought their own perspectives to the task. The most satisfying results were when authors and editor agreed that the entries should do more than summarize knowledge in the field; they should also highlight what is most interesting and provocative about a subject and point the direction for new thinking and research. Like the mirror of the world to which early Netherlandish art is often compared, because it reflects but does not impose a fixed point of view on that which it surveys, this encyclopedia mirrors the state of our knowledge about Dutch art in the mid-1990s.

Acknowledgments

From the time I agreed to become general editor of this Garland encyclopedia in 1991, I have sought and received advice, support, and cooperation from many people. My appreciation goes to all of them. In the 1990s, the study of Dutch art and architecture is very specialized; organizing this knowledge encyclopedically for five centuries required decisions that I would not have made before consulting with certain people. I am especially indebted to the members of my international advisory board, Walter S. Gibson, Carel Blotkamp, Rudolf Dekker, and Nancy Troy, who generously shared their expert knowledge about the state of research and scholarly methodology in different aspects of the field, and who gave me invaluable suggestions regarding contributors and entries at the crucial formative stage of this project.

I am very grateful for the early expressions of support and networking assistance I received from Svetlana Alpers, Linda Stone-Ferrier, and Alison McNeil Kettering. Their friendly counsel and introductions to other scholars and students enabled me to proceed with efficiency and enjoyment in this project.

There are numerous people in the Netherlands I wish to recognize and thank. I am obligated to Ger Luijten, who in discussing the idea of the encyclopedia with me raised probing questions about the rationale for such a book; the present Preface owes a great deal to the discussion I had with Ger Luijten in Utrecht in 1992. Rudolf E.O. Ekkart, Reindert L. Falkenburg, and J.F. Heijbroek each took time to review the prospectus and the list of entries and to offer valuable suggestions; my sincerest thanks to them for helping me to clarify my thinking on some fundamental issues. I also acknowledge the contributions made by Evert van Uitert and Peter Schatborn, who individually took the time to review early versions of the list of entries and to give me frank and good advice.

I am indebted to many others who kindly met with me in the Netherlands to offer opinions about the sort of encyclopedia coverage they would expect to see of their respective areas of specialization: John Sillevis, Annemieke Hoogenboom, Eveline Koolhaas-Grosfeld, Geert Imanse, Ilja Veldman, Graham Birtwistle, Bert Sliggers, Charles Dumas, Jan Teeuwisse, Martha Op de Coul, Johannes H. Kraan, L.J. van der Klooster, Christina Wansink, and Fred Meijer.

A very warm and special thank-you to Rudolf Dekker and Florence Koorn, to Herman Roodenburg and Christien Smits, to Wim Denslagen and Tilly Maters, and to Lotte van de Pol, for the gracious hospitality they extended to me in the Netherlands while also giving their support to this project. Thank you very much to Marijke de Kinkelder for coordinating important meetings with individual scholars at the Rijksbureau voor Kunsthistorische Documentatie in The Hague. My sincere thanks as well to the institutions and staff of the Rijksprentenkabinet and the Rijksmuseum in Amsterdam, the Haags Gemeentemuseum in The Hague, the Teylers Museum in Haarlem, the Stedelijk Museum in Amsterdam, and the P.J. Meertens Institute in Amsterdam for the professional courtesies extended to me in the summer of 1992, and for allowing me to use their superior facilities for work and research.

To all of the encyclopedia contributors, who undertook the assignments to write the entries and produced outstanding work for slight compensation: I am tremendously grateful to you for generously sharing your expertise with the readers of this book. Among those who took a broad interest and helped with developing topics in an entire subject area, I am beholden to Ilja Veldman, Wim Denslagen, Cynthia Lawrence, Graham Birtwistle, Elizabeth Honig, Hans Rooseboom, Maristella Casciato, and Mariët Westermann. To Ann Jensen Adams, Stephanie Dickey, Andrea Gasten, and Valerie Lind Hedquist, whom I could, and did, call on many times for help, my heartfelt thanks.

I wish to thank and give credit to those who worked carefully to translate entries for the encyclopedia: Esther Arts Warner and Michael Arts for their translations of articles written in Dutch; Ursula Brinkmann Pimentel for translating the articles written in German; Sigrun Müller, Kennie Lyman, Flavia Stara, and Allison Brunvand for translating the articles written in Italian. I owe thanks also to Maria Dobozy for sharing her expertise in the philology of Germanic languages.

I have many institutions to thank for their support during the several years that it has taken me to complete this project. Foremost is the University of Utah, which awarded me a teaching grant in the summer of 1992 to travel to the Netherlands, and a faculty research grant in 1994–1995 to fund assistance with translations. I wish to acknowledge the outstanding help I received in various forms from art history graduate students Ursula Brinkmann Pimentel and Wendi Miller. My thanks, too, to the Undergraduate Research Opportunities Program (UROP) and to the then director, Peter L. Goss, at the University of Utah, who supported an undergraduate assistant, Stacey Lundberg, in 1992–1993. I am enormously grateful to my colleagues in the College of Fine Arts and in the Department of Art for their understanding, good humor, and unending generosity in giving me support in this project.

I thank the museums, research institutes, foundations, and individuals around the world who are named in connection with the illustrations in this book for giving special attention and courteous consideration to the encyclopedia when the contributors and I requested photographs of objects from their collections and the permission to reproduce them.

Finally, a warm and personal expression of gratitude to my family for their patience, love, and understanding on the many occasions when my obligations to this project seemed to take precedence over life and death.

Introduction

What is covered in an encyclopedia of Dutch art? There is no easy answer to that question. At the time that coverage begins, around the middle of the fifteenth century, and until nearly the end of the sixteenth century, it is art that comes from the Low Countries. From 1581 to 1795, the home of Dutch art is the Republic of the United Provinces of the Netherlands. Later, in the nineteenth and twentieth centuries, Dutch art comes from the Kingdom of the Netherlands. Along with changing political orders and national borders, frequent infusions of foreign influence had an effect on the local artistic production. A few historical facts and circumstances, as well as clarification of some basic terminology, will help to focus the question of what is included in this encyclopedia.

Dutch is an adjective used in English for describing the characteristics of the inhabitants, language, or country that in 1996 is the Kingdom of the Netherlands. Willem of Orange, son of Willem V, the last *stadholder* of the United Provinces, was recognized as the first king of the Netherlands in 1815 at the Congress of Vienna after the defeat of Napoleon Bonaparte at Waterloo. Willem I's Kingdom of the Netherlands included Belgium until the Belgians seceded in 1830 to become a separate kingdom. The date of Dutch national independence is, therefore, celebrated as 1831. After that date, the state institutions in the Netherlands responsible for the arts—museums, academies of art, schools of arts and crafts, and, later, the art history departments in the universities—began to make a distinction between old Dutch art (meaning art from around the time of the old masters in the fifteenth through the seventeenth centuries) and new Dutch art (meaning art from the nineteenth and twentieth centuries). This distinction continues in the titles of two important art journals published in the Netherlands: *Oud Holland* ("Old Holland"), founded in 1883, and *Jong Holland* ("Young Holland"), founded in 1985.

Napoleon made the Netherlands part of the French Empire in 1810, but, before that, in 1806, he had installed his brother Louis-Napoleon Bonaparte as king of Holland, whose capital was Amsterdam. Holland was only one of the provinces of the Netherlands, but its prosperous cities and political importance at the time of the Republic of the United Provinces gave it primacy—so much so that "Holland" is still a synonym for the Netherlands. (The old province of Holland was separated into the modern provinces of North and South Holland in 1840.) Louis-Napoleon's reign continued the French domination of the Netherlands that had begun in 1795 when a French revolutionary army invaded the region and created the short-lived Batavian Republic (so called in recognition of the ancient inhabitants, the Batavians, who had fought to resist conquest by the Roman Empire).

Dutch culture experienced many such injections of foreign influence, and artists from the Netherlands carried the reputation of Dutch art abroad. In the late fourteenth and fifteenth centuries, artists from the counties of Holland and Zeeland in the northern part of the Low Countries were employed in the county of Flanders and the duchy of Brabant in the southern part of the Low Countries, and in France, the Rhineland, and parts of Britain, while artists from the southern region came north to work in the duchy of Guelders (Gelderland) and in the cathedral city of Utrecht. Artists from Holland and Utrecht traveled and worked abroad, particularly in Italy and England, in the sixteenth and seventeenth centuries. Between 1625 and 1650 the noble House of Orange-Nassau tried to create a French-style court in The Hague, favoring for that purpose foreign over Dutch artists, and French fashions became generally popular with the Dutch after Louis XIV's armies invaded the United Provinces at the end of the seventeenth century. When Willem III, prince of Orange and *stadholder* of the United Provinces, married Mary II Stuart and the two reigned as king and queen of England from 1689 to 1702, the Dutch stylistic influences that began appearing in Britain were already mixed with a French aesthetic. French culture and taste were pervasive in the eighteenth century, and, in the nineteenth and twentieth centuries, many Dutch artists traveled, studied, and worked in France, Belgium, Germany, England, and the United States. Thus, Dutch artists' assimilation and reinterpretation of foreign influences have continuously made contributions to the art of the Netherlands.

Dutch, as in the widely used art historical term the Dutch School, has a more limited designation, referring to the style and subject matter that were practiced with prodigious success by Dutch artists in the seventeenth century—the Golden Age of the Republic of the United Provinces of the Netherlands. Dutch artists of the seventeenth century are regarded as having perfected a style of realism, painting portraits, landscapes, still lifes, and genre scenes in response to patronage by the middle class, who, in circumstances that were unique in Europe, were able to pursue their own inclinations in the thriving market economy of the United Provinces, free of interference from court or church.

In the nineteenth century, historians and critics began to look at the Dutch School as the cultural efflorescence of the Republic. They were responding to the fact that Dutch art in the seventeenth century was a brilliant burst of innovation and invention that cast its glow over the eighteenth century, survived the French domination, and, in an early nineteenth-century revival that was imbued with Romanticism, quickened nationalist sentiments. Significant foreign developments in painting, such as mid-nineteenth-century Realism in France and the landscapes of the French Barbizon School, were recognized as having been inspired by seventeenth-century Dutch art; consequently, in the 1870s and 1880s, when The Hague School artists (after seeing the works in France) began painting from nature the daily life of peasants and the landscape around them, they were praised not as followers of the French but as a rebirth of the Dutch School. In the late nineteenth and early twentieth centuries, scholars, critics, and museum curators were loath to acknowledge that the character of the Dutch School could have been formed from influences seen as extraterritorial, and they identified as early Dutch School "primitives" (in the sense of belonging to the early stage in the development of a style) the fourteenth- and fifteenth-century artists whom they discovered within the modern borders of the Netherlands.

In the twentieth century, a great deal has been written about the early modern history of the Netherlands that is directed at dismissing some of the notions of nationalism. That history begins with a revolt that started in Flanders and led to the Eighty Years' War (1568–1648) with Spain. At the time of the Revolt of the Netherlands (the term has become synonymous with the Eighty Years' War), Flanders (a part of modern Belgium) and the Netherlands had a language and culture in common as neighbors in the region of the Low Countries. (The Dutch name for the Netherlands, *Nederland,* means "low country," and the Latin name, *Belgium,* referred to the whole of the Low Countries before the Kingdom of Belgium was created in 1830.) In the Middle Ages, the Low Countries had been divided into many small states, but, beginning in the late fourteenth century, the dukes of Burgundy, relatives at odds with the kings of France, began acquiring territory and extending their influence over the region through a rich and flourishing court culture. Under the dukes of Burgundy, the Low Countries prospered and the towns,

their original charters recognized by the dukes, were free to develop their local characteristics.

In 1568, when the Revolt started, the Low Countries consisted of seventeen provinces (corresponding in area to modern Belgium, Luxembourg, the Netherlands, and a small part of northern France) that were under the rule of the king of Spain. The king, Philip II, a Hapsburg, had inherited the Low Countries in 1555 from his father, Charles I, who, as Holy Roman Emperor Charles V (1519–1555), had enlarged the domain of the Hapsburgs in the Low Countries by adding counties, dukedoms, and the bishopric of Utrecht to the territories he already controlled through an inheritance from his grandmother Mary, daughter of the last duke of Burgundy, Charles the Bold (died 1477).

The Revolt was preceded by a fury of iconoclasm in 1566 protesting the Inquisition started by Philip II in the Low Countries. The Protestant base of the rebellion was the city of Antwerp in Flanders, but, in 1572, rebels attacking by sea seized the provinces of Holland and Zeeland and brought the Protestant Reformation (unavoidably identified with opposition to Spanish rule) to the North. After Antwerp fell to Spanish troops led by the duke of Parma in 1585, the headquarters of the Protestant anti-Spanish cause was moved to the province of Holland, where its chief defenders were the Calvinists and the leaders of the army of the United Provinces, the princes of the House of Orange-Nassau. In 1585, Maurits of Nassau was leader of the army; his father, Willem I of Orange, also known as William the Silent (Willem de Zwijger), who raised the army of the Revolt in 1568 and became a hero of the Republic, was assassinated in Delft in 1584. Maurits died in 1625 and was succeeded by his brother Frederik Hendrik, who died in 1647.

As Spanish troops overran Flanders and occupied the southern part of the Low Countries, the seven provinces (Holland, Friesland, Groningen, Overijssel, Gelderland, Utrecht, and Zeeland) to the north of the confluence of the Rhine, Maas, and Waal rivers, which along with the islands of Zeeland afforded a natural defensive barrier, formed a federation in 1581, the United Provinces of the Netherlands. The United Provinces acknowledged their determination to continue the Revolt until they won independence from Spain. The Twelve Years' Truce (1609–1621) was a break in the Eighty Years' War during which the fluctuating wartime boundary between the southern provinces (called in this period the Spanish, or Royal, Netherlands) and the seven northern provinces was temporarily stabilized. The economy of the North thrived during the truce, emigration from the South and other areas continued, and demand was increased for the arts to play a vital role in supporting cultural identity and civic pride. The South languished in comparison, except that the arts were also well supported by the Spanish-dominated court and the Counter-Reformation Roman Catholic Church, whose religious orders commissioned many altarpieces. When the war resumed the United Provinces gained more territory, until their borders (basically the same as those of the Netherlands today) were fixed in 1648 by the Treaty of Münster-Westphalia. That treaty ended the Eighty Years' War and required Philip IV of Spain to recognize the independence of the United Provinces.

The government of the Republic of the United Provinces consisted of representatives, elected by the towns in each of the seven provinces, who served in a body called the States General. This body met in The Hague (the seat of the old counts of Holland), where it conferred with the prince of the House of Orange-Nassau, who commanded the army for the United Provinces and whose official title was *stadholder* (literally, "lieutenant"). In that way, the towns, governed by oligarchies of regents from wealthy merchant families, maintained a voice in the affairs of war and state that had an effect on peace and order on the local level. About the time of the Twelve Years' Truce, it became law that only Calvinists could hold public office, as others might be sympathetic to Spain and a risk to security. Nevertheless, several times in the seventeenth century, the opposition between political and religious factions turned violent and threatened the internal stability of the United Provinces. Opposing each other were the advocates of religious tolerance, who were for ending the war (these were the regents from Amsterdam, which had replaced Antwerp in wealth and power, and from other towns, who defended the right of autonomy for local authorities to protect prosperity), and the proponents of religious orthodoxy, who wanted the war to continue (they were the Calvinist clergy and the people who looked up to the *stadholders*, who hoped to centralize authority in a state church and a royal House of Orange).

From the standpoint of politics, religion, and class relationships, the Republic of the United Provinces of the Netherlands was not without internal strains and tensions in its Golden Age; these are often necessary conditions for great creativity, as the history of art demonstrates. For understanding how Dutch art developed, it is important to remember that both sides at the start of the Eighty Years' War wanted to preserve the Low Countries; although division took place, it was not until much of the old life of Flanders—including many artists—had moved North, leaving the South with a different set of challenges to meet. Some form of control has to be imposed upon a subject to study it: The way that art is often studied is with a limited focus on an individual artist, a single theme, a period, a school, or some other defining context. Reasons for the exclusions are not always given, and often what has been excluded from the study of the Dutch School is the problematic relationship with the art and artists of the Southern Netherlands.

That was not the case with the first book on art and the lives of artists published in the United Provinces: Karel van Mander's *Het Schilder-Boeck* (1604). Van Mander was from the Southern Netherlands; he moved North, like many others during the Eighty Years' War, and settled in the town of Haarlem in the province of Holland around 1580. Van Mander, who was a painter, is a major source of information at the beginning of the Golden Age about the history and theory of art in the Netherlands; however, he made no distinctions between Dutch and Flemish artists and did not mention the Revolt. (In this regard, he has much in common with the painters of the seventeenth-century Dutch School, who, for all their apparent realism, also had a tendency to gloss over the problems of the age.) What appears to have been important for van Mander, and the artists for and about whom he wrote, was elucidating the evolution to the level of perfection of a Netherlandish tradition of art, as if events had brought him and several others to Haarlem to accomplish that goal. Challenging the hegemony of Italian artists and art theory was incentive for van Mander, who was canny in adapting the arguments of his literary models, to insist that there had been a unity of purpose in the study of nature by Netherlandish artists for centuries. Later seventeenth- and eighteenth-century Dutch writers about artists and art theory followed van Mander's example, never suggesting, as is the modern tendency, that there were two schools of Netherlandish art, one Dutch and one Flemish.

The practice of seventeenth-century Dutch painters to describe in detail the appearance or surface of their world (a practice that, according to van Mander, originated with Jan van Eyck in Flanders in the early fifteenth century) is often compared to that of delineation in mapping, for which the Netherlands were also famous in the sixteenth and seventeenth centuries. Many of the maps made in the Netherlands during and long after the Eighty Years' War persisted in keeping the original outline of the Low Countries intact as a profile *Leo Belgica*, although the head of the lion might be depicted on the north (at Amsterdam) instead of on the south (at Antwerp). Sometimes the map of the region was enclosed in a border in which was depicted a series of views of the major towns. Correspondingly, writers of a contemporary and popular form of guidebook to Dutch towns, the *beschrijvingen* (literally, "descriptions"), took the civic perspective to be more encompassing than the regional one when they recounted the history of the Revolt and the Republic through the experiences of citizens and bolstered civic pride with accounts of buildings, institutions, and reputed masters in local schools.

Van Mander's motives for stressing the regionalism of art are clear to modern scholars, while those who read the town *beschrijvingen* as primary sources are handed down the popular notion of Dutch history and art viewed in terms of the microcosm of local experiences. Maps from the same period, which frequently appear in the backgrounds of genre paintings, acknowledge that it is possible to have both points of view. All are correctives to the interests of nineteenth-century nationalism when viewing the past. From the late Middle Ages to the twentieth century, the Dutch have had their own way of interpreting in their art and architecture the styles and movements that originated outside their borders; only in the later twentieth century have scholars attuned to international developments begun to identify this as richly problematic. At the same time, the contributions made by Dutch artists in the seventeenth century, as well as those by artists in the twentieth century to the movements of De Stijl (1917–1930) and Cobra (1948–1951), stand out more clearly when viewed on the international scene. The answer to the question, "What is covered in an encyclopedia of Dutch art?" is the complexity of facts and issues that confront anyone who studies Dutch art in the 1990s.

A Reader's Guide and Bibliographical Note

Readers who wish to follow an orderly procedure in using the *Encyclopedia* will find a way to begin with the asterisked (*) entries in the following lists. For those interested primarily in an introduction to or general survey of Dutch art, it is recommended that they read all of the asterisked entries from all the groupings, turning as they choose to any of the *See also* suggestions at the end of each entry. For those readers interested in concentrating on one or a small number of areas of Dutch art, it is recommended that they begin in a grouping with the asterisked entries and use the *See also* suggestions at the end of the entries to discover related topics where additional information or a different perspective may be found. For those wishing truly "encyclopedic" knowledge, it is recommended that they proceed through an entire grouping, reading the asterisked and nonasterisked entries and all of the *See also* suggestions. For follow-up on any topics of particular interest, readers are directed to the Index.

Biographies have not been asterisked, in the expectation that readers will find the most pertinent discussions of particular individuals and their works to be in the thematic and topical entries, and thus will be able to follow up among the selection of biographies. Readers are also directed to the Index for inquiries about individuals or subjects not covered by entries of their own.

The selected bibliography accompanying each entry suggests the best and most authoritative sources for further inquiry. Many of the titles are not in English, and some readers may wonder if and when they really need to consult these works. A few remarks follow on the state of publishing about Dutch art.

There is abundant literature on Dutch art in English, but what is available does not represent all periods and subjects. This is a reflection of the special or limited interests of scholars outside the Netherlands who study particular aspects of Dutch art and write in English; scholars in the Netherlands who study and write about the same aspects are more likely to have their works translated and published in English. More is being written and published in Dutch on the art of the

Netherlands by Dutch scholars, who are closer to collections, archives, and institutions, and who are encouraged by the national efforts in education and journalism to increase the public's knowledge of their heritage from all periods. If the bibliographies in this encyclopedia were restricted to published sources in English, there would be a significant number of entries for which, surprisingly, no research would appear to exist.

Since the 1970s, more of the research by scholars in the Netherlands has been translated into English. Government agencies and private foundations in the Netherlands have been generous in their support of translation projects for scholarly research, so that it is increasingly common to find monographs, conference papers, journal articles, and dissertations that, if not completely translated, are published in Dutch with a summary in English. Some of the summaries stick to the facts and do not capture the force of the author's argument; others are a model of succinctness in clarifying a complex point. English summaries, when known to exist, are noted for the items in the bibliographies. In addition, most art and art history journals from the Netherlands print articles that are written in English, and they often translate book and exhibition reviews and the significant discoveries of Dutch authors into English for an international readership.

Museum exhibition catalogs are valuable resources: The essays by experts present the latest scholarly findings and opinions on a subject, and they may extensively summarize past research; the bibliography is comprehensive and up to date; the plentiful photographs are generally of the highest quality and provide extraordinary opportunities for close study and visual comparison of works of art in reproduction. Dutch national and municipal museums that regularly mount major exhibitions frequently publish a catalog with the complete text in Dutch and English. Smaller museums in the Netherlands may have published little material in English, but their catalogs (even if one cannot read the Dutch text) can be important sources of picture reproductions, collection information, and additional bibliography. Many of the exhibition catalogs produced since 1980 have assumed the importance of standard references, and they are cited in the bibliographies. Readers in the United States with access to college and university libraries or to public libraries in the major metropolitan areas should have little or no difficulty obtaining items from the bibliographies, even those in Dutch. For materials not immediately available, interlibrary loans are a useful option. Fortunately, with computers and the Internet, perusing library catalogs and databases world wide is becoming routine and easy for many people. These resources can turn up other means of access and also lead to the discovery of new sources. Finally, publications on art and architecture from the Netherlands may be ordered directly from the publisher or through a North American distributor. Dutch museums have departments of photographic services that will answer questions about reproducing the works of art in their collections.

A Note about the Spelling of Names

The Dutch language is tolerant of minor variances in the spelling of proper names. Differences of opinion exist both about artists from earlier centuries, whose names appear unpredictably and often in varying forms in archival documents, as well as about twentieth-century artists, whose professional activity has coincided with the occasional "spelling reforms" that have been promoted by progressive groups intending to make the Dutch language more logical and simple to use. A history of foreign contacts and the many foreign scholars and writers who have reported on the culture of the Netherlands have also left their mark on how Dutch proper names are spelled. Thus the problem of whether the spelling of an artist's name is based on the preponderance of archival evidence or whether it is according to the old or new styles of spelling has been further complicated by the tendency of both Dutch and foreign authors to amend a name to make it conform to the conventions of language in force at any particular time.

Readers will find consistency in the way that an artist's name is spelled throughout the text of the Encyclopedia. Spelling decisions were made by the editor, guided by the way that a name most often appears in the standard sources in the field; this is also the way that most contributors approached the problem. The exception to this is when new research has demonstrated that a change or correction of the standard is warranted, and acceptance of the change or correction has already begun to appear in scholarly publications. In the instances where research is still poised on the question of artistic identity, variant spellings are given and discussed. Common alternative spellings in current use of an artist's name may appear in the titles of works listed in the bibliography after each entry.

Overview of Groupings

Architecture
Arts (see also **Architecture, Drawing, Painting, Photography, Printmaking,** and **Sculpture**)
Biography
Cultural History
Drawing, History of Drawing

Groups, Schools, Movements
Ideas, Concepts, Themes
Internationalism
Painting, History of Painting
Patronage
Photography, History of Photography
Printmaking, History of Prints
Sculpture, History of Sculpture
Writing about Art

Entries Grouped by Major Category

Architecture

Amsterdam School*
Architectural competitions
Architectural criticism, issues of style
Architectural restoration*
Classicism in architecture*
De Stijl
Functionalism in architecture*
Landscape architecture
Neo-Gothic*
North American art, Dutch influences
Postmodernism
Public housing*
Renaissance architecture
Town halls
Urban planning, before 1750
Urban planning, from 1750 to the present*
Wendingen

Arts

Applied arts*
Artists' initiatives
Atlas, atlases
Calligraphers and calligraphy
Cartography*
Ceramics*
Clothing, costume, fashion: early pictorial and historical evidence
Clothing, costume, fashion: nineteenth and twentieth centuries
Coins, medals
Contemporary art
Feminism, feminist issues
Films, filmmaking
Graphic design*
Manuscript illumination*
Postage stamps
Roundels
Stained glass*
Tiles
Women artists

Biography

Aertsen, Pieter
Alberdingk Thijm, Josephus Albertus
Allebé, August
Alma Tadema, Laurens
Andriesse, Emmy

Andriessen, Mari
Appel, Karel
Armando
Backer, Jacob Adriaensz.
Bakker Korff, Alexander Hugo
Bellaert, Jacob
Berckheyde, Gerrit Adriaensz.
Berckheyde, Job Adriaensz.
Berlage, Hendrik Petrus
Berssenbrugge, Henri
Bloemaert, Abraham
Blommers, Bernardus Johannes
Bol, Ferdinand
Bosboom, Johannes
Bosch, Hieronymus
Bramer, Leonaert
Brands, Eugène
Breitner, George Hendrik
Bronner, Jan
Brouwn, Stanley
Cats, Jacob
Chabot, Hendrik
Constant (C. A. Nieuwenhuys)
Coornhert, Dirck Volkertsz.
Corneille
Couzijn, Wessel
Cuyp, Aelbert
Daniels, René
De Hondecoeter, Melchior
De Keyser, Hendrick
De Klerk, Michel
De Kooning, Willem
De Wit, Jacob
De Zwart, Willem
Derkinderen, Antoon J.
Dewald, C.M.
Dijsselhof, Gerrit Willem
Dou, Gerrit
Dudok, Willem Marinus
Duiker, Johannes
Dumas, Marlene
Dupont, Pieter
Eggers, Bartolomeus
Engebrechtsz., Cornelis
Erasmus, Desiderius
Fernhout, Edgar R.J.
Flinck, Govaert
Fortuyn/O'Brien
Gabriël, Paul Joseph Constantin
Geertgen tot Sint Jans
Gestel, Leo
Goltzius, Hendrick
Gudmundsson, Sigurdur
Hals, Dirck
Hals, Frans
Hammacher, A.M.W.J.
Hertzberger, Herman

Herwig, Reinhardt Herman
Huizinga, Johan
Humbert de Superville, D.P.G.
Huygens, Constantijn
Israëls, Isaac
Israëls, Jozef
Jongkind, Johan Barthold
Karsen, Eduard
Kleyn, Pieter Rudolph
Knip, Josephus Augustus
Kobell, Jan Baptist II
Koch, Pyke
Koekkoek, B. C.
Koninck, Philips
Koninck, Salomon
Koolhaas, Rem
Kramer, Pieter Lodewijk (Piet)
Krausz, Simon Andreas
Kröller-Müller, Hélène E.L.J.
Kromhout, Willem
Krop, Hildo
Kruseman, Cornelis
Kruyder, Herman J.
La Fargue, Paulus Constantijn
Leyster, Judith
Lievens, Jan
Lucebert
Maes, Nicolaes
Maris, Jacob Hendricus
Maris, Matthijs
Maris, Willem
Master I.A.M. of Zwoll
Master of the Virgin among Virgins
Matham, Jacob
Mauve, Anton
Mendes da Costa, Joseph
Mesdag, Hendrik Willem
Metsu, Gabriel
Moesman, Johannes Hendricus
Molenaer, Jan Miense
Mondrian, Piet
Neuhuijs, Albert
Nuyen, W.J.J.
Olie, Jacob
Oosterhuis, Pieter
Ouborg, Pieter
Oud, Jacobus Johannes Pieter
Ouwater, Isaac
Pander, Pier
Post, Pieter
Pothoven, Hendrik
Potter, Paulus
Pronk, Cornelis
Quellinus, Artus I
Quinkhard, Jan Maurits
Raedecker, John
Regters, Tibout

Contributors

Ann Jensen Adams
University of California
Santa Barbara
Court and official portraiture
Group portraiture
History portraits
North American collecting
Portraiture
Rembrandt research

Ingrid C. Alexander
Smithsonian Institution
Technical investigations
Underdrawings, underpaintings

Gretchen D. Atwater
Independent Scholar
New Jersey
Marine painting
Trade, exploration, and colonization overseas

Jeremy D. Bangs
Independent Scholar
Massachusetts
Leiden

Jochen Becker
Universiteit Utrecht
Monuments to artists
Nationalism
Public monumental sculpure (1795–1990)

Shirley K. Bennett
Independent Scholar
Washington, D.C.
Atlas, atlases
Cartography
Vinckboons, David (1576–1632)

Herman van Bergeijk
Independent Scholar
Delft
Dudok, Willem Marinus (1884–1974)

Reita Bergsma
Vrije Universiteit Amsterdam
Amsterdam Impressionists
Breitner, George Hendrick (1857–1923)
Robertson, Suze Bisschop (1855–1922)
Van Looy, Jacobus (1855–1930)

Ellinoor Bergvelt
Universiteit van Amsterdam
Knip, Josephus Augustus (1777–1847)
State and municipal art collecting and collections

Ansje Beusekom
Independent Scholar
Amsterdam
Films, film-making

Graham Birtwistle
Vrije Universiteit Amsterdam
Appel, Karel (Christiaan Karel Appel) (born 1921)
Brands, Eugène (born 1913)
Cobra Movement (1948–1951)
Constant (Constant Anton Nieuwenhuys) (born 1920)
Corneille (Corneille Guillaume Beverloo) (born 1922)
Lucebert (Lubertus Jacobus Swaanswijk) (1924–1994)
Rooskens, Anton (Joseph Antoon Rooskens) (1906–1976)
Wolvecamp, Theo (1925–1992)
World Wars I and II

Saskia de Bodt
Independent Scholar
The Netherlands
Belgium
Roelofs, Willem (1822–1897)

Eugenie Boer
Independent Scholar
The Netherlands
Bloemaert, Abraham (1564–1651)
Genre painting, eighteenth century
Terbrugghen, Hendrick (1588–1629)
Troost, Cornelis (1696–1750)
Utrecht Caravaggists
Van Baburen, Dirck Jaspersz. (ca. 1595–1624)
Van Honthorst, Gerard (1592–1656)

Peter van den Brink
Rijksuniversiteit Groningen
Backer, Jacob Adriaensz. (1608–1651)
Pastoral

Els Brinkman
Independent Scholar
Amsterdam
De Branding (1917–1926)

Ton J. Broos
University of Michigan
Writers on art, eighteenth century

Edwin Buijsen
Mauritshuis
The Hague
Van Goyen, Jan (1596–1656)

Maristella Casciato
University of Rome Tor Vergata
Amsterdam School
De Klerk, Michel (1884–1923)
Duiker, Johannes (1890–1935)
Functionalism in architecture
Hertzberger, Herman (born 1932)
Koolhaas, Rem (born 1944)
Public housing
Wendingen (1918–1931)
Wijdeveld, Hendricus Theodorus (1885–1987)

Alan Chong
The Cleveland Museum of Art
Cuyp, Aelbert (1620–1691)
Landscape

Petra ten-Doesschate Chu
Seton Hall University
France

Rudolf Dekker
Erasmus Universiteit Rotterdam
Postage stamps
Tiles

W. F. Denslagen
Rijksdienst voor de Monumentenzorg
Zeist
Architectural competitions
Architectural criticism, issues of style
Architectural restoration
Neo-Gothic
Postmodernism
Town halls

Stephanie S. Dickey
Herron School of Art
New York
Flinck, Govaert (1615–1660)
Lievens, Jan (1607–1674)
Rembrandt School
Rembrandt van Rijn (1606–1669)
Self-portraiture
Van der Helst, Bartholomeus (1613–1670)

Charles Dumas
Rijksbureau voor Kunsthistorische Documentatie
The Hague
La Fargue, Paulus Constantijn (1729–1782)
Ouwater, Isaac (1748–1793)
Pothoven, Hendrik (1726–1807)
Pronk, Cornelis (1691–1759)
Ten Compe, Jan (1713–1761)

Rudolf E.O. Ekkart
Rijksbureau voor Kunsthistorische Documentatie
The Hague
Quinkhard, Jan Maurits (1688–1772)
Regters, Tibout (1710–1768)

Mary Francey
University of Utah
De Kooning, Willem (born 1904)
Van Gogh, Vincent: diverse views

Wayne Franits
Syracuse University
Women's worlds

Carol J. Fresia
Independent Scholar
New York
Quacksalvers, quack doctors

Karin Gaillard
Independent Scholar
The Netherlands
Applied arts

Andrea C. Gasten
Independent Scholar
Maarssenbroek
Symbolism, Symbolists
Van Gogh, Vincent (1853–1890)

Walter S. Gibson
Case Western Reserve University
Bosch, Hieronymus (ca. 1450–1516)
Flanders, Flemish School

Amy Golahny
Lycoming College
Literature, poetry: analogues with the visual

Steven Golan
Independent Scholar
North Carolina
Bol, Ferdinand (1616–1680)
Koninck, Salomon (1609–1656)
Roman history
Subjects, subject categories, and hierarchies
Van den Eeckhout, Gerbrand (1621–1674)

Jane ten Brink Goldsmith
Independent Scholar
Massachusetts
Bramer, Leonaert (1596–1673)
Delft
Vermeer, Johannes (1632–1675)

Frans Grijzenhout
Independent Scholar
Amsterdam
Reputation of Dutch art abroad

Maartje de Haan
Museum Boymans-van Beuningen
Rotterdam
Dupont, Pieter (1870–1911)
Prints, modern graphic arts 1840–1945
Prints, modern grapic arts after 1945
Van der Valk, Maurits Willem (1857–1935)

Barbara Haeger
Ohio State University
Emblems and emblem books
Genre painting, seventeenth century

Marlite Halbertsma
Erasmus Universiteit Rotterdam
Art history, history of the discipline

Ludo van Halem
Jong Holland
Brouwn, Stanley (born 1935)
Fluxus

Valerie Lind Hedquist
Central College
Churches
History painting
Metsu, Gabriel (1629–1667)
Pre-Rembrandtists
Religion of artists

Paul Hefting
PTT Nederland
Graphic design

Lee Hendrix
J. Paul Getty Museum
Natural history illustration

Julie Berger Hochstrasser
University of California
Berkeley
Gamepiece
Still life
Vanitas, vanitas still life

Els Hoek
Independent art historian, art critic, curator
Amsterdam
Contemporary art (1980–1990)
Dada
Van Doesburg, Theo (1883–1931)

Martha Hollander
New College at Hofstra University
Dou, Gerrit (1613–1675)
Frames, painted
Framing devices within pictures
House interiors
Housewives and maids
Illusionism
Maes, Nicolaes (1634–1693)
Paintings-within-paintings

Elizabeth Alice Honig
Tufts University
Aertsen, Pieter (1508/1509–1575)
Commerce and commercial life
Van Brekelenkam, Quirijn Gerritsz. (ca. 1620/1625–
  ca. 1668/1669)
Van de Velde, Jan II (1593–1641)

Anita Hopmans
Universiteit van Amsterdam
Avant-garde
Sluijters, Jan (1881–1957)
Van Dongen, Kees (1877–1968)
Verwey, Kees (1900–1995)

Ida Jager
Vrije Universiteit Amsterdam
Kromhout, Willem (1864–1940)
Rotterdam

Carol Janson
Western Washington University
Artists' confraternities and craftsmen's guilds
Dutch history
Gouda

Natalie Kamphuys
Independent Scholar
Amsterdam
Contemporary Art (1980–1990)
Van Doesburg, Theo (1883–1931)

Bram Kempers
Universiteit van Amsterdam
House of Orange-Nassau
Huizinga, Johan (1872–1945)
State patronage, public support

J.M. Kennedy
Independent Scholar
Kansas
Eighty Years' War
Soldiers
War and warfare
Wouwerman, Philips (1619–1668)

Alison McNeil Kettering
Carleton College
Ter Borch, Gerard (1617–1681)
Women artists

Pieter Jan Klapwijk
Noordbrabandts Museum
's Hertogenbosch
Coins, medals

Florence Koorn
Haarlem Archiefdienst
Archives

Harry Kraaij
Independent Scholar
Amsterdam
Israël, Isaac (1865–1934)
Karsen, Eduard (1860–1941)
Tholen, Willem Bastiaan (1860–1931)
Verster, Floris (1861–1927)
Veth, Jan (1864–1925)
Witsen, Willem (1860–1923)

Fransje Kuyvenhoven
Rijksdienst Beeldende Kunst
The Hague
Voogd, Hendrik (1768–1839)

Cynthia Lawrence
Temple University
Berckheyde, Gerrit Adriaensz. (1638–1698)
Berckheyde, Job Adriaensz. (1630–1693)
De Keyser, Hendrick (1565–1621)
Eggers, Bartolomeus (ca. 1630–before 1692)
Public monumental sculpture (ca. 1550–1795)
Quellinus, Artus I (1609–1668)
Sculpture, 1550–1795
Tomb sculpture: early modern and later sepulchral art
Verhulst, Rombout (1624–1698)
Xavery, Jan Baptist (1697–1742)
Xavery, Pieter (ca. 1647–traceable to 1683)

Kitty de Leeuw
Erasmus Universiteit Rotterdam
Clothing, costume, fashion: nineteenth and twentieth
*   centuries*

Janey L. Levy
Independent Scholar
New York
Active life, active virtues
Carnal life, carnal vices
Contemplative life, contemplative virtues
Devotional images
Didactic images
Donor portraits
Erasmus, Desiderius (died 1536)
Last Judgment
Religious orders and their patronage
Sins and punishments

John Loughman
University College Dublin
Display
Dordrecht

Anne W. Lowenthal
Independent Scholar
New York City
Italy
Mannerism, Mannerists

Roger Mandle
Rhode Island School of Design
Amateurs, art academies, and art associations before the
*   nineteenth century*
Bas-relief, painting

Cats, Jacob (1741–1799)
De Wit, Jacob (1696–1754)
Krausz, Simon Andreas (1760–1825)

Diane E. Cearfoss Mankin
University of Cincinnati
Architectural painting
Aristocracy and gentry
Conversation piece
Country houses and gardens
De Hondecoeter, Melchior (1636–1695)
Marriage and family portraits
Van der Heyden, Jan (1637–1712)
Van Ruisdael, Jacob (1628/1629–1682)
Vingboons, Philips (1607–1678)

Brigitte van Mechelen
Vrije Universiteit Amsterdam
Chabot, Hendrik (1894–1949)
Van Golden, Daan (born 1936)
Visch, Henk (born 1950)
Westerik, Co (born 1924)

Fred G. Meijer
Rijksbureau voor Kunsthistorische Documentatie
The Hague
Ruysch, Rachel (1664–1750)
Van Huysum, Jan (1682–1749)

Walter S. Melion
Johns Hopkins University
Calligraphers and Calligraphy (1550–1650)
Goltzius, Hendrick (1558–1617)
Van Mander, Karel (1548–1606)
Writers on art, sixteenth and seventeenth centuries

Jos de Meyere
Centraal Museum
Utrecht
Utrecht

Wendi Miller
Independent Scholar
Utah
Townscapes

Sheila Muller
University of Utah
Bakker Korff, Alexander Hugo (1824–1882)
Bergen
De Ploeg
Israëls, Jozef (1824–1911)

Robert S. Olpin
University of Utah
North American art, Dutch influences
North American painting, Dutch influences

Nadine Orenstein
Metropolitan Museum of Art
Bellaert, Jacob (active 1483–1486)
Master IAM of Zwoll (active ca. 1485)
Matham, Jacob (1571–1631)
Paper, used for prints
Prints, printmaking, printmakers, (ca. 1500–ca. 1900)
Prints, publishers
Watermarks

K.A. Ottenheym
Universiteit Utrecht
Classicism in architecture (1625–1700)
Post, Pieter (1608–1669)
Renaissance architecture (1500–1625)
Van Campen, Jacob (1595–1657)

Annemiek Ouwerkerk
Rijksuniversiteit Leiden
Alberdingk Thijm, Joseph Albertus (1820–1889)
Art criticism, critical issues in the nineteenth century

Franco Panzini
Independent Scholar
Rome
Landscape architecture

Hanna Pennock
Mesdag Museum
The Hague
Blommers, Bernardus Johannes (1845–1914)
Gabriël, Paul Joseph Constantin (1828–1903)
Hague School, The (1870–1890)
Maris, Matthijs (1839–1917)
Maris, Willem (1844–1910)
Mauve, Anton (1838–1888)
Mesdag, Hendrik Willem (1831–1915)
Neuhuijs, Albert (1844–1914)
Vosmaer, Carel (1826–1888)

Tineke Reijnders
Universiteit van Amsterdam
Artists' Initiatives, (1970–1990)

Herman Roodenburg
P.J. Meertens Instituut
Amsterdam
*Clothing, costume, fashion: early pictorial and historical
    evidence*
Gestures

Hans Rooseboom
Rijksprentenkabinet, Rijksmuseum
Amsterdam
Andriesse, Emmy (1914–1953)
Dewald, C.M. (1868–1923)
Herwig, Reinhardt Herman (1878–1959)
Nature photography

Oosterhuis, Pieter (1816–1885)
Photographers, anonymous
Photography, early (1839–1925)
Photography, modern and contemporary (1925–1990)
Van der Meer, Hans (born 1955)
Van Ojen, E.M. (1886–1964)
Verveer, Maurits (1817–1903)
Woldringh, Meinard (1915–1968)

Bart A. Rosier
Independent Scholar
Amsterdam
Prints, early printed book and Bible illustration

Peter de Ruiter
Rijksuniversiteit Groningen
Armando (born 1929)
Art criticism, critical issues in the twentieth century
Hammacher, A.M.W.J. (born 1897)
Nul-group (Nul-groep) (1961–1965)
Schoonhoven, J.J. (1914–1944)

Zsuzsanna van Ruyven-Zeman
Independent Scholar
Maastricht
Reverse painting
Roundels
Stained glass

Diane G. Scillia
Kent State University
Geertgen tot Sint Jans (Gheerkin van Leyden)
  (active ca. 1465–1485 or 1480–1495/1496)
Haarlem School, early (ca. 1450–1500)
Master of the Virgin among Virgins (active ca. 1480–1510)

Stacey Sell
Independent Scholar
Pennsylvania
Drawing clubs
Drawing practices and techniques
Drawing theory
Drawings, uses and collecting

Elise Lawton Smith
Millsaps College
Engebrechtsz. (or Engelbrechtsen), Cornelis (1468–1527)
Van Leyden, Aertgen (Aert Claesz.) (1498–1564)
Van Leyden, Lucas (ca. 1494–1533)

Christien F.W. Smits
Independent Scholar
Amsterdam
Ceramics

Alexandra W.M. van Smoorenburg
Vrije Universiteit Amsterdam
Allebé, August (1838–1927)
Berssenbrugge, Henri (1873–1959)
Bosboom, Johannes (1817–1891)
De Zwart, Willem (1862–1931)
Derkinderen, Antoon J. (1859–1935)
Dijsselhof, Gerrit Willem (1866–1924)
Gestel, Leo (1881–1941)
Japonisme
Jongkind, Johan Barthold (1819–1891)
Kleyn, Pieter Rudolph (1785–1816)
Kobell, Jan Baptist II (1778–1814)
Koekkoek, B.C. (1803–1862)
Kruseman, Cornelis (1797–1857)
Maris, Jacob Hendricus (1837–1899)
Nuyen, W.J.J. (1813–1839)
Olie, Jacob (1834–1905)
Rochussen, Charles (1814–1894)
Roland Holst, Richard N. (1868–1938)
Ronner-Knip, Henriëtte (1821–1909)
Schelfhout, Andreas (1787–1870)
Schwartze, Thérèse van Duyl (1851–1918)
Tavenraat, Johannes (1809–1881)
Thorn Prikker, Johan (1868–1932)
Van Konijnenburg, Willem (1868–1943)
Weissenbruch, Jan (1822–1880)
Weissenbruch, Jan Hendrik (1824–1903)

Roy Sonnema
Georgia Southern University
Music, musical instruments
Musicians, musical companies, musical performers

Barbara Maria Stafford
University of Chicago
Humbert de Superville, D.P.G. (1770–1849)

John Steen
Independent Scholar
Utrecht
Daniels, René (born 1950)
Dumas, Marlene (born 1953)
Fernhout, Edgar R.J. (1912–1974)
Koch, Pyke (Pieter Frans Christiaan) (1901–1991)
Kruyder, Herman J. (1881–1935)
Magic Realism
Moesman, Johannes Hendricus (Joop) (1909–1988)
Ouborg, Pieter (1893–1956)
Struycken, Peter (born 1939)
Surrealism
Tonny, Kristians (1907–1977)
Toorop, Charley (Annie Caroline Pontifex) (1891–1955)
Toorop, Jan (1858–1928)

Werkman, Hendrik Nicolaas (1882–1945)
Wiegers, Jan (1893–1959)

Nancy Stieber
University of Massachusetts
Boston
Berlage, Hendrik Petrus (1856–1934)
Oud, Jacobus Johannes Pieter (1890–1963)
Urban planning, from 1750 to the present

Katlijne Van der Stighelen
Katholieke Universiteit Leuven
Van Schurman, Anna Maria (1607–1678)

Linda Stone-Ferrier
University of Kansas
Horticulture
Textiles, textile industry

Shana Stuart
Independent Scholar
Iowa
Huygens, Constantijn (1596–1687)
Jews
Koninck, Philips (1619–1688)

Vern Grosvenor Swanson
Springville Art Museum
Alma Tadema, Laurens
*   (Sir Lawrence Alma-Tadema) (1836–1912)*

Frauke Syamken
Independent Scholar
Berlin
De Stijl (1917–1932)
Mondrian, Piet (1872–1944)

E. Taverne
Rijksuniversiteit Groningen
Urban planning, before 1750

Harry Tummers
Katholieke Universiteit Nijmegen
Sculpture, ca. 1400–ca. 1550
Tomb sculpture: medieval effigial monuments
Van Wesel, Adriaen (ca. 1417–ca. 1490)

Ilja M. Veldman
Vrije Universiteit Amsterdam
Allegorical traditions
Coornhert, Dirck Volkertsz. (1522–1590)
Humanism, humanist themes
Prints, collecting
Protestant Reformation

Grace A.H. Vlam
Salt Lake Community College
Exotica
Non-Western cultural influences

Mieke van der Wal
Drents Museum
Assen
Andriessen, Mari (1897–1979)
Bronner, Jan (1881–1972)
Couzijn, Wessel (1912–1984)
Krop, Hildo (1884–1970)
Raedecker, John (1885–1956)
Sculpture, (1795–1945)
Van Hove, Bart (1850–1914)
Van Pallandt, Charlotte (born 1898)

Amy L. Walsh
Independent Scholar
Los Angeles
Animal painting
Potter, Paulus (1625–1654)
Rural life and views

Christina J.A. Wansink
Rijksbureau voor Kunsthistorische Documentatie
The Hague
Schouman, Aart (1710–1792)
Terwesten, Mattheus (1670–1757)
Van der Aa, Dirk (1731–1809)

Dennis P. Weller
Metropolitan Museum of Art
Haarlem
Hals, Dirck (1591–1656)
Hals, Frans (1581/1583–1666)
Leyster, Judith (1609–1660)
Molenaer, Jan Miense (1609/1610–1668)

Mirjam Westen
Gemeentemuseum
Arnhem
Feminism, feminist issues

Geraart Westerink
Rijksuniversiteit Groningen
Fortuyn/O'Brien (formed 1982)
Gudmundsson, Sigurdur (born 1942)
Kramer, Pieter Lodewijk (Piet) (1881–1961)
Kröller-Müller, Hélène E. L. J. (1869–1939)
Mendes da Costa, Joseph (1863–1939)
Pander, Pier
Royer, Louis (1795–1868)
Van der Eijnde, Hendrik Albertus (1869–1939)

Visser, Carel (born 1928)
Zijl, Lambertus (1866–1947)

Mariët Westermann
Rutgers University
Comic mode, sixteenth and seventeenth centuries
Humor, satire
Laren (ca. 1870–ca. 1925)

Rhetoricians' chambers
Steen, Jan Havicksz (1626–1679)
Theater and theatricality

Roger S. Wieck
The Pierpont Morgan Library
New York
Manuscript illumination

Dutch Art
An Encyclopedia

A

Active life, active virtues

Traditional Catholic thought sanctioned two primary modes of existence in the world: the life of virtuous actions, and the life devoted to contemplation of the divine. Matthew 25:35–36 listed six acts required of Christians: care of the hungry, the thirsty, the stranger, the naked, the sick, and the prisoner. Theologians later made the list conform to sacred numerology by adding a seventh act, burial of the dead. These Seven Works of Mercy occupied an important place in art.

Because Scripture explicitly links the works of mercy with salvation at the Last Judgment, artists commonly depicted them within that larger context. Saints may play an exemplary role as dispensers of charity. Christ often appears among the recipients, since he identified himself with them.

Such images were especially appropriate for charitable institutions. Originally religious foundations that helped the donors achieve salvation through their acts, these institutions became increasingly secular in the sixteenth century. The imagery itself also became more secular, substituting portraits of institutional officials performing the works of mercy in place of exemplary saints.

This desire to honor individuals ultimately led, in the seventeenth century, to group portraits of the officials of charitable institutions. In the sixteenth century, it also affected individual portraits. Sitters were shown with attributes that attested to their life of virtuous acts.

The works of mercy also found a place in Protestant art, though their significance was altered. While rejecting the Catholic notion that salvation depended on good works, many Protestants believed that faith inevitably produced works. Protestant images might include only the biblical six acts of mercy, reflecting their stress on the authority of the Bible. Images such as these, along with the portraits, attest to the continuing importance of a virtuous life in Dutch culture.

Janey L. Levy

See also Carnal life, carnal vices; Contemplative life, contemplative virtues; Portraiture; Roman history

Bibliography

Harbison, Craig. *The Last Judgment in Sixteenth-Century Northern Europe: A Study of the Relation between Art and the Reformation.* New York: Garland, 1976.
Levy, Janey L. "The Last Judgment in Early Netherlandish Painting: Faith, Authority, and Charity in the Fifteenth Century." Ph.D. diss., University of Kansas, 1988.
Muller, Sheila D. *Charity in the Dutch Republic: Pictures of Rich and Poor for Charitable Institutions.* Ann Arbor, MI: UMI Research Press, 1985.

Aertsen, Pieter (1508/1509–1575)

Innovative painter of still-life and peasant genre scenes, Pieter Aertsen was born in Amsterdam, but he left for Antwerp as a youth. There he may have worked in the studio of Jan Mandyn before registering as a master painter in 1535. Although his first documented work is from 1545–1546 (the *Van der Biest Triptych;* Antwerp, Koninklijk Museum voor Schone Kunsten), he evidently ran a successful studio during his Antwerp years. During that time his pupil was Joachim Beuckelaer (ca. 1535–1574), nephew of his wife, Kathelijne. By 1557, Aertsen had moved back to Amsterdam. There he received prestigious commissions, including one for the high altar of Amsterdam's Nieuwe Kerk. He also had a special patron, the merchant Jacob Rauwaert, who bought many of his works. Aertsen died in 1575. It is likely that he had remained a Catholic. Three of Aertsen's sons became artists; one was the portrait and genre painter Pieter Pietersz.

Although Aertsen produced altarpieces for many important sites, his major religious works were destroyed during the Iconoclasm of 1567. Therefore he is better known today for his still-life and genre scenes. Aertsen's *Butcher's Stall* (1551; Uppsala University) is considered the first significant still life in European art. In its background, though, is a scene of the Flight into Egypt, and many of his other apparently nonreligious works include secondary religious motifs. In these "mixed genre" scenes, secular and sacred subjects are related on a metaphoric level. Aertsen also painted images of peasant festivity; his *Peasant Feast* (1550; Vienna, Kunsthistorisches Museum) is an important precedent to the work of Pieter Bruegel. And in works like *Peasants with Market Goods* (1569; Stockholm, Hallwyl Museum) he initiated the popular seventeenth-century genre of the market scene.

Elizabeth Alice Honig

See also Commerce and commercial life; Flanders, Flemish School; Still life

Bibliography

Filedt Kok, J.P. et al. *Kunst voor de Beeldenstorm: Noordnederlandse kunst 1525–1580*. The Hague: Staatsuitgeverij, 1986.

Kloek, Wouter, and Gerard Lemmens, eds. *Pieter Aertsen*. The Hague: Gary Schwartz/SDU, 1989.

Moxey, Keith P.F. *Pieter Aertsen, Joachim Beuckelaer, and the Rise of Secular Painting in the Context of the Reformation*. New York: Garland, 1977.

Alberdingk Thijm, Josephus Albertus (1820–1889)

As a fervent proponent of the Roman Catholic emancipation, Josephus Albertus Alberdingk Thijm attempted to propagate his convictions in cultural politics and the domain of art history and aesthetics. In conjunction with the architect P.J.H. Cuypers, who was his brother-in-law, and the government official Victor de Stuers, Thijm was the most important promoter of the Neo-Gothic style of art and architecture in the Netherlands. Through his magazine *Dietsche Warande* (medieval Dutch pleasure-grounds), published after 1855, he kept in touch with the international Neo-Gothic movement. Originally a merchant of canned foods, he developed close contacts with the Amsterdam art world through his wife, who was the stepdaughter of the sculptor Louis Royer. Although self-taught, he became by great diligence and perseverance a connoisseur of medieval art and architecture. This was recognized in 1876 when, after being active as a book dealer and a publisher, he was made a professor of art history and aesthetics at the Rijksacademie in Amsterdam.

For Thijm, the Middle Ages were an exemplary period when there was a unity of religious, social, and aesthetic ideals; in medieval art he recognized a union of good, truth, and beauty. He hoped to see this revived in his own time after the restoration of the episcopal hierarchy of the Roman Catholic Church in 1853. In the years following, when many Catholic churches were being built and decorated, Thijm formulated his ideas in *Over de kompozitie in de kunst* (On Composition in Art) in 1857, and *De heilige linie* (The Holy Line) in 1858. These works are of interest for the knowledge of Christian iconography as well as for influencing Neo-Gothic art. Thijm's love of medieval architecture also brought him into the field of monument restoration.

In numerous articles and polemics, Thijm professed his views about art theory and history, architectural restoration and preservation, art criticism, and artistic practice. He was the editor of several magazines: *Astrea*, *De Spektator*, the *Volksalmanak voor Nederlandsche Katholieken* (The People's Almanac for Dutch Catholics), and *Dietsche Warande*. Under one of his pseudonyms, Pauwels Foreestier, he published witty criticism of exhibitions of contemporary art. Thijm put his ideas into practice, especially, by lobbying for the statue (by Royer and Cuypers) of his literary idol, the seventeenth-century poet Joost van den Vondel (1587–1679), that was erected in Amsterdam in 1867; and by influencing development of a comprehensive program of decoration for the Rijksmuseum (opened in 1885) to complement the Neo-Gothic building designed by Cuypers.

Annemiek Ouwerkerk

Historical note on the Roman Catholic emancipation: After the revolt against Spanish occupation of the Netherlands in the sixteenth century, the Protestant faith was officially recognized as the state religion while the Catholic faith was tolerated. Only after the time of French rule was the Roman Catholic episcopal hierarchy reestablished in 1853, and Dutch Catholics were granted the same rights as the Calvinist citizens of the nation.

See also Architectural criticism, issues of style; Architectural restoration; Art criticism, critical issues in the nineteenth century; Art history, history of the discipline; Neo-Gothic; Royer, Louis

Bibliography

Alberdingk Thijm, Catharina. *Jos. Alb. Alberdingk Thijm in zijne brieven geschetst als christen, mensch, kunstenaar*. Amsterdam: Van Langenhuysen, 1896.

Deyssel, Lodewijk van (Karel Joan Lodewijk Alberdingk Thijm). *De wereld van mijn vader*. Edited by Harry G.M. Prick. Amsterdam: Rap, 1986. Revision of the 1893 edition.

Geurts, P.A.M. et al., eds. *J.A. Alberdingk Thijm, 1820–1889, erflater van de negentiende eeuw: Een bundel opstellen*. Baarn: Arbor, 1992.

Hellenberg Hubar, B.C.M. van. *Arbeid en bezieling: De visie op het artistieke scheppingsproces verbeeld en verwoord door P.J.H. Cuypers, J.A. Alberdingk Thijm, en V.E.L. de Stuers*. Ph.D. diss., Katholieke Universiteit Nijmegen, 1995.

Plas, Michel van der. *Vader Thijm*. Lannoo: Tielt, 1995.

Allebé, August (1838–1927)

August Allebé owes his renown largely to his position as professor (1870–1880) and later director (1880–1906) of the Rijksacademie in Amsterdam. His view of education, in which daily practical exercise and the aesthetic instead of the moral value of art were most important, formed for young artists an attractive alternative to both the more traditional education at The Hague Academy and the Impressionism of The Hague School. Allebé's objective attitude toward trends and individuals was so stimulating to his students that sometimes there was talk of the School of Allebé, or of the Amsterdam School. This school consisted of such very different visual artists as E. Karsen, W.B. Tholen, J. Veth, G.H. Breitner, I. Israëls, A. Derkinderen, J. Meyer de Haan, J. Voerman, and J. Toorop.

In his own work Allebé never rose above the academic level. He painted figure pieces, animal paintings, and still lifes with a detailed technique and realistic colors. The artist received his first drawing lessons from the painter P.F. Greive, who worked in a realistic style. After studying from 1854 to 1857 at the Royal Academy in Amsterdam, and in 1858 at the École des Beaux Arts in Paris, Allebé went again to study with Greive in 1860, this time to become better at painting. Not until 1868 was he successful in breaking away from this studio. He settled in Brussels, where he worked for himself for two years and became a member of the Société Belge des Aquarellistes. Back in Amsterdam, he produced few paintings because of the pressure of his responsibilities at the Rijksacademie and an increasing fear of failure. After 1900 Allebé sometimes took time off to paint and had several exhibitions, but in 1913 he permanently laid down his brushes.

Alexandra W.M. van Smoorenburg

See also Belgium; Breitner, George Hendrik; Derkinderen, Antoon J.; Israëls, Isaac; Karsen, Eduard; Tholen, Willem Bastiaan; Toorop, Jan; Veth, Jan

Bibliography

Bionda, Richard, and Carel Blotkamp, eds. *De schilders van Tachtig: Nederlandse schilderkunst van 1880–1895.* Zwolle: Waanders, 1991.

Loos, Wiepke, and Carel van Tuyll van Serooskerken, eds. *Waarde heer Allebé: Leven en werk van August Allebé, 1838–1927.* Zwolle: Waanders, 1988.

Allegorical traditions

Allegorical images were important in Dutch art from the sixteenth to the eighteenth century. The word allegory is derived from the Greek and means a symbolic representation or metaphor. The most common way of representing an allegory is a personification: A human figure portrays an abstract concept and is provided with qualifying attributes. Personifications were widely used in the sixteenth century to represent all kinds of abstract concepts: cosmic phenomena, virtues, vices, character traits, or other ideas that were difficult to depict in any other way. Popular allegories were Death (in the form of a skeleton), Time (an old man on crutches and with an hourglass), Transitoriness (a *putto* or cherub blowing bubbles), and Love (Venus and Amor). In the sixteenth century, allegories also became popular as a guide for daily living; the opposition between good and evil and warnings against money, ambition, and carnal pleasures were frequent moral allegorical themes.

At the end of the sixteenth century, handbooks of personifications were made for poets and visual artists. The *Iconologia* (1593) by the Italian writer Cesare Ripa was translated into Dutch with amplification and published by Jan Pietersz. Pers in 1644. The book had a great influence on Dutch art of the seventeenth century, vastly expanding the repertory of allegories. At first, these allegories appeared mainly in prints, but later they also turned up in painting. The personification of Faith with attributes in the *Allegory of Faith* (ca. 1670; [Fig. 115] Metropolitan Museum, New York) by Johannes Vermeer is interpreted, for example, with the help of the Dutch edition of Ripa. Allegories appeared more and more often in decorative ensembles like tapestries, ceiling paintings, architectural sculpture, and in all sorts of arts and crafts. The themes in history paintings depicting stories from the Old Testament or classical antiquity could also have a moral allegorical meaning, because they expressed in a symbolic way current norms and values or referred to contemporary events.

The foundation for allegorical traditions in the Netherlands was laid in the graphic arts of the sixteenth century. Collecting prints was a way of assembling a "visual encyclopedia" of the world. Series of prints with profane allegories were especially popular. Many of these themes were developed from pure allegories into genre or landscape scenes in the seventeenth century. What follows is an account of the development of the most important allegorical themes in Dutch art.

The Seven Vices and the Seven Virtues

The canon of seven capital sins, or vices, and seven virtues was compiled by Pope Gregory I (Gregory the Great) at the end of the sixth century. Gregory formulated a system of capital sins that all stemmed from the vice of Pride. The first was Pride (*Superbia)*, followed by Wrath (*Ira*), Envy (*Invidia*), Avarice (*Avaritia*), Sloth (*Accedia*), Gluttony (*Gula*), and Voluptuousness or Lust (*Luxuria*). Hieronymus Bosch, in the *Tabletop of the Seven Deadly Sins and the Four Last Things* (ca. 1470–1490; Madrid, Prado; Color Plate 1) ascribed to him, showed these seven sins with genre-like scenes in which men and women are portrayed sinning. The all-seeing eye of Christ in the middle, and the Four Last Things (Death, the Last Judgment, Heaven, and Hell) in the corners of the panel indicate that one should interpret the genre scenes as exhortations to avoid these sins in daily life. In the print series by Pieter van der Heyden after Pieter Bruegel the Elder (1558), the capital sins are portrayed as female personifications with animals as attributes. Pride has a peacock, Wrath a bear, Envy a turkey, Avarice a frog, Sloth a donkey, Gluttony a swine, and Voluptuousness a rooster. This series also concludes with a print of the Last Judgment. During the course of the sixteenth century, the context of the Last Judgment falls away, as demonstrated in a series of prints illustrating the capital sins by Hendrick Goltzius, whose personifications are also paired with animals that indicate their symbolic meaning.

The seven virtues were the counterparts of the capital sins. There are three theological virtues, Faith (*Fides*), Hope (*Spes*), and Charity (*Caritas*); and four cardinal virtues, Fortitude (*Fortitudo*), Temperance (*Temperantia*), Justice (*Justitia*), and Prudence (*Prudentia*). They were also portrayed in a print series after drawings by Pieter Bruegel the Elder (1559–1560) in which they appear as personifications with attributes. The attributes would later become conventions: Faith has a cross or a Bible, Hope an anchor, Charity a number of children; Fortitude has a pillar of strength, Temperance a horse's bit or a pitcher and a bowl, Justice a balance, and Prudence a mirror or a snake. Goltzius handled the virtues in this way in a series of prints that also include the capital sins. One can see the virtues depicted separately or in smaller groups; for example, there was a preference for Faith, Hope, and Charity, which are found in 1 Corinthians 13:13.

The Five Senses

The concept of the five senses (Sight, Hearing, Taste, Smell, and Touch) played an important role in Christian thinking, for example, in the late-medieval *summae confessorum*, the collection of penitential and devotional manuals for the clergy and the laity. The portrayal of the senses in the visual arts started in the sixteenth century. At first, it was limited to prints, but after 1600 the senses also appear in a genre-like form in painting. They remain a favorite subject in Dutch genre painting of the seventeenth century.

The basic iconographic formula was introduced in a series of prints by Cornelis Cort (1561) after designs by Frans Floris. Each of the senses is portrayed by a female figure with characteristic attributes and an animal. Since then, the attributes have had several variations, but in general the iconography is as follows: Sight (*Visus*) has a mirror, a rising sun, and an eagle or a lynx; Hearing (*Auditus*) has musical instruments and a deer; Taste (*Gustus*) has fruit or drink and a monkey; Smell (*Olfactus*) has flowers and a dog; Touch (*Tactus*) has a fisherman's net and a spider, a bird biting on a finger, a snake, or a turtle. In the North, Goltzius introduced the theme in two print series (ca. 1578, engraved by Philips Galle, and ca. 1586, engraved by Nicolaas Clock and Cornelis Drebbel; Fig. 1). In a series engraved by Jan Saenredam (ca. 1595–1596), Goltzius gave the theme an all-new form by portraying couples in contemporary clothing engaged in actions that were characteristic for the sense portrayed. This new iconographic type had great influence. Ca. 1600, Crispijn de Passe I made a series of the senses according to the old-fashioned model of personifications; however, after 1612 he made a print series of the senses in the form of couples. Somewhat later, some of the attributes were adjusted to fit modern time: Persons who symbolize Sight have glasses or binoculars; Smell (and sometimes also Taste) smokes a pipe; Touch is a kissing couple. Even more adapted to refer to daily life are peasant scenes that portray the senses—for example, the five paintings of the *Senses* by Jan Miense Molenaer (1637; The Hague). His Sight stares into an empty wine jug, Smell is changing a baby's diaper, Taste is boozing, Hearing is singing, and Touch is a peasant being hit by his wife with a slipper. In a series of etchings by Jan Both, the senses are also portrayed in genre-like scenes—Smell by children who are relieving themselves, and Touch by the painful operation of a dentist. References to the five senses can also be found in other guises in seventeenth-century paintings of merry companies or still lifes.

The Four Seasons

In the early sixteenth century the four seasons sometimes appear in the form of classical gods. Spring is portrayed by Flora or Venus, Summer by Ceres or Pomona, Autumn by Bacchus, and Winter by Aeolus or Janus. Another iconography was introduced in the prints of Philips Galle after designs by Maerten van Heemskerck (1563) that are based on the *Metamorphoses* by Ovid. There, the four seasons are described as male personifications with attributes: Spring with flowers, Summer with sheaves of wheat, Autumn with grapes, and Winter warmly dressed with a pot of fire. This scheme was copied with female figures in prints by Johannes Sadeler after Dirck Barendsz. (Fig. 2), and by Jacob Matham after Hendrick Goltzius (1589). Some years later, Goltzius developed this allegorical scheme into scenes from daily life: In two series (ca. 1597 and 1601), engraved by Jan Saenredam, he represents the seasons as child or adult couples engaged in typical seasonal activities. In four prints of the *Seasons* by Pieter van der Heyden after Pieter Bruegel the Elder and Hans Bol (1570), the four seasons are portrayed by labor on the land, after the medieval tradition of the labors of the twelve months. This iconographic type was the basis for the representation of the seasons by means of seasonal landscapes, a practice that would replace personifications in seventeenth-century prints and paintings.

The Planet Children

The seven planets that were known at the time (the Moon, Mercury, Venus, the Sun, Mars, Jupiter, and Saturn) were thought from antiquity to have great influence on one's health, character, and choice of profession. In the fifteenth century the compositional scheme for representation was created: The planets are portrayed as classical gods in the air, mostly sitting on chariots, while their "children" on the earth are portrayed in their characteristic activities. Prints by Harman Jansz. Muller after Van Heemskerck (ca. 1568) follow this pattern faithfully, as do several print series after Maarten de Vos (1586 and later). In 1596, Goltzius changed this iconographic scheme by portraying the planet gods as statues in a landscape, while their "children" are engaged in genre-like activities around them. After that, planet gods are found mainly in decorative ensembles.

The Four Temperaments

The doctrine of the four temperaments also originated in antiquity and was based on the four humors, or fluids, that are secreted by the human body—blood, phlegm, bile, and black bile. One spoke of people having a certain temperament or character according to which fluid was in excess in their bodies: Sanguine (cheerful people, having too much blood), Phlegmatic (slow people, having too much phlegm), Choleric (bad-tempered people, having too much bile), and Melancholy (sad people, having too much black bile). In the Middle Ages these four temperaments were represented by one or two persons who, by means of attributes or actions, refer to the temperament. This is also the case in the prints by Pieter de Jode I after Maarten de Vos. In prints by Harman Jansz. Muller after Van Heemskerck (1566) the scheme of the planet children has been incorporated: A classical deity, who controls the temperament, is driving in the clouds; below him are the people who are engaged in their characteristic behaviors and occupations. This theme lost popularity after 1600.

The Four Elements

The idea that the entire cosmos, including everything on Earth, is constituted of four elements—Earth (*Terra*), Water (*Acqua*), Fire (*Ignis*), and Air (*Aer*)—also stems from classical antiquity. A traditional way of portraying the four elements was with animals—for example, a mole for Earth, a fish for Water, a bird or chameleon for Air, and a lizard or phoenix for Fire. An iconographic scheme introduced from Italy portrayed the elements as classical gods: Cybele as Earth, Neptune as Water, Juno as Air, and Vulcan or Jupiter as Fire. One can find this in the prints by Philips Galle (1564) and by Johannes Sadeler after Dirck Barendsz. (1587). At first, Goltzius followed the scheme of the elements as personifications with attributes that had been established by Maarten de Vos. Around 1600, several artists stopped using personifications and started to portray the elements by different professions: a hunter (Earth), a fisherman (Water), a bird hunter (Air), and a cook (Fire). Examples of this are the prints by Jacob de Gheyn II after his own designs (ca. 1597).

The Ages of Man

The span of a human life was portrayed in series of four, seven, or ten images, each describing a different age. Early in the sixteenth century, the scheme of the "stairway of life" was introduced. The stairs went up from infancy until adulthood and down from old age until death. At the end of the sixteenth century, prints and paintings in which the ages were portrayed by couples, as in the work of Jan Miense Molenaer, became popular. In the print series by Adriaan Collaert after Maarten de Vos (1581), human life is separated into seven stages and associated with the seven planets. Prints by Crispijn de Passe I and Raphael Sadeler I after Maarten de Vos (1591) divide the ages into four stages: Youth concerns itself with love; the riper age with work; middle age enjoys power, status, and acquired wealth; old age merely waits for death.

The Four Parts of the World

The four parts of the world are most often portrayed as female figures with attributes. Their traditional iconography was introduced in prints after Maarten de Vos in the sixteenth century. *Europe*, as Queen of the World, wears a crown and carries a scepter and a horn of plenty; weapons and instruments of art and science account for her leading position. *Asia* is in the company of a camel most of the time; she is adorned with flowers and jewels, and she holds a censer as a symbol of Eastern scents. *Africa* has dark skin; her symbols are a scorpion, a lion, an elephant, or a snake. *America* wears feathers and carries a bow and arrows of the indigenous people; a caiman is the animal belonging to her. In this form, the personifications can often be found among the decorations on world maps.

The Four Times of Day

The theme of four time periods in a day—Morning (*Aurora*), Afternoon (*Meridies*), Evening (*Vesper*), and Night (*Nox*)—also belongs to tradition. In prints by Johannes Sadeler after Dirck Barendsz. (1582), and by Jacob Matham after Karel van Mander (1601), four times of day are portrayed by classical

gods in heaven, while on earth are shown human activities characteristic for the time of day. The prints by Jan Saenredam after Goltzius (ca. 1598–1599) are genre-like pictures of a family at different times of the day: In the Morning the children go to school, in the Afternoon the family is at work, in the Evening they eat and drink, and at Night they sleep. In the seventeenth century, the four periods of a day are represented as Morning, Afternoon, Evening, and Night landscapes.

The Four Winds

In a print series (ca. 1585) by Crispijn de Passe I after Philips Galle, the four winds were depicted for the first time as the classical figures *Eurus* (East Wind), *Zephyr* (West Wind), *Boreas* (North Wind), and *Auster* (South Wind) known from Ovid's *Metamorphoses*. In prints (ca. 1582–1587) by Johannes Sadeler after Maarten de Vos, mythological figures were added to the four winds. In a series (ca. 1600) by Crispijn de Passe I the four winds appear as classical gods in the clouds, while on Earth, the personifications of the four seasons and the four parts of the world are portrayed.

Ilja M. Veldman

See also Active life, active virtues; Carnal life, carnal vices; Contemplative life, contemplative virtues; Emblems and emblem books; Genre painting, seventeenth century; History painting; Landscape; Last Judgment; Prints, collecting; Sins and punishments

Bibliography

Nordenfalk, Carl. "The Five Senses in Flemish Art before 1600." In *Netherlandish Mannerism*. Edited by G. Cavalli-Björkman, 135–154. Stockholm: Nationalmuseum, 1985.

Sluijter, Eric J. "Venus, Visus en Pictura." *Nederlands Kunsthistorisch Jaarboek* 42/43 (1991/1992): 337–396. (English summary).

Veldman, Ilja M. "De macht van de planeten over het mensdom in prenten naar Maarten de Vos." *Bulletin van het Rijksmuseum* 31 (1983): 21–53. (English summary).

———. "Goltzius' Zintuigen, Seizoenen, Elementen, Planeten en vier Tijden van de Dag: Van allegorie naar genre voorstelling." *Nederlands Kunsthistorisch Jaarboek* 42/43 (1991/1992): 307–336. (English summary).

———. "Philips Galle: Een inventieve prentontwerper." *Oud Holland* 105 (1991): 262–290. (English summary).

———. "Seasons, Planets, and Temperaments in the Work of Maarten van Heemskerck: Cosmo-Astrological Allegory in Sixteenth-Century Netherlandish Prints." *Simiolus* 11 (1980): 149–176.

Alma Tadema, Laurens (Sir Lawrence Alma-Tadema) (1836–1912)

Sir Lawrence Alma-Tadema was one of the most renowned academic painters of late nineteenth century. Universally admired for his superb draftsmanship and "real to life" depictions of classical antiquity, he was much sought after by Victorian collectors, who intimately connected with his vision. He so embraced the aspirations of his day that when the idealistic illusions of his age were shattered by modernism and World War I his art fell from favor. Now as the reevaluation of that era is well underway, his reputation is rebounding.

Laurens Alma Tadema was born Friday morning, January 8, 1836, in the Frisian village of Dronrijp. Later the family moved to Leeuwarden, the capital of Friesland to the north of Holland. His earliest work dates from 1849 when the artist was thirteen years old and reflects his acquaintance with the work of Bartel van der Kooi, the most significant portraitist from Friesland. Because no Dutch school would accept him, Alma Tadema entered the Royal Academy of Art at Antwerp in 1852. There he studied with Baron Gustave Wappers and Joseph Dyckmanns, and later he was an apprentice to Baron Hendrick Leys. His work during this period followed the academic interior genre style typical of the Netherlands tradition.

He married in 1862, and while on his honeymoon to Italy he ventured to Pompeii where he became enamored with life in antiquity. He was "discovered" by the famous art dealer Ernest Gambart and, to further his career, moved to Brussels in 1866. His Continental career proceeded past the death of his wife in 1869 to 1870, when he was persuaded to move with his two daughters to London, where his work was finding buyers.

He remarried in 1871 to an English woman, Laura T. Epps, who became a fine artist in her own right. They bought a home, Townshend House, in Regents Park, and Lawrence Alma-Tadema became a naturalized citizen in 1874. The next year he became an associate of the Royal Academy, and in 1879 a full academician. In the 1880s he moved to a large and fashionable home in St. John's Wood in London. He became a permanent fixture in the major exhibitions of the day, not only in the Summer Exhibition of the Royal Academy but in the Grosvenor Gallery and later in the New Gallery and elsewhere.

His reputation increased until he became one of the most famous of European painters. He won recognition at the Paris Exposition Universelle in 1878, 1889, and 1900. He was knighted by Queen Victoria in 1900 and given the Order of Merit in 1905 by King Edward VII. Except for the critic Carel Vosmaer, Alma-Tadema's work was not appreciated in his homeland. The Rijksmuseum was given his *An Egyptian Widow* (1872), and the Fries Museum in Leeuwarden was bequeathed a number of works after his death.

Unlike many artists he was able to maintain high standards of quality in his art until his death. His last picture dates from June 1912, the month of his death. Alma-Tadema's *oeuvre* of more than four hundred paintings covers several phases of European art: from the mid-nineteenth-century Netherlands tradition, Egyptian and Merovingian subjects, to high Victorian classical narrative pictures, such as *Spring* (1894; Malibu, J. Paul Getty Museum) and *A Favorite Custom* (1909; London, Tate Gallery).

To a degree, Alma-Tadema's art was more a summation of nineteenth-century values than an influence on the major fine art "isms" of the twentieth century. His career did, however, have some influence on twentieth-century cinema.

Though influenced by the Pre-Raphaelite, Japonist, aesthetic, and Impressionist movements of his day, he was basically a bourgeois painter of archeologically correct pictures of Greek and Roman maidens on marble benches. His importance, as with most artists, lies in the quality and originality of his paintings. Considered one of the finest colorists of the classical subject painters, he incorporated many of the advancements in European art up to, but not beyond, Impressionism. He developed a unique system for cataloging his paintings by placing a separate *opus* Roman numeral on each one. This system made it more difficult for forgers to pass unauthentic work as original. His last "Op." was 408.

Vern Grosvenor Swanson

See also Belgium; Mesdag, Hendrik Willem; Vosmaer, Carel

Bibliography

Lovett, Jennifer Gordon, and William R. Johnston. *Empires Restored, Elysium Revisited: The Art of Sir Lawrence Alma-Tadema*. Williamstown, MA : Sterling and Francine Clark Art Institute, 1991.

Standing, Percy Cross. *Sir Lawrence Alma-Tadema, O.M., R.A.* London: Cassell, 1905.

Swanson, Vern Grosvenor. *Alma-Tadema: The Painter of the Victorian Vision of the Ancient World*. London: Ash and Grant; New York: Scribner, 1977.

———. *The Biography and Catalogue Raisonné of the Paintings of Sir Lawrence Alma-Tadema*. London: Garton, 1990.

Amateurs, art academies, and art associations before the nineteenth century

During the eighteenth century in the Netherlands, relationships among artists, collectors, and amateurs were close. Wealthy, educated Dutch people not only collected art, but became supporters of education in the arts, and also tried to become proficient in them as well. In many Dutch cities and towns, there was created a more or less public form of education in the visual arts. Many city governments attempted to give some support to these efforts. Traditional artists' guilds (the Guild of St. Luke in most towns in the Netherlands) also created learning opportunities in the arts.

The models for these academies were both Dutch and adaptations of other European models. In Haarlem after 1582 (although probably not until 1588), an art academy was begun by the artist/biographer/critic Karel van Mander, along with Hendrick Goltzius and Cornelis van Haarlem. In Utrecht at about the same time, Abraham Bloemaert created an influential workshop in which he had many pupils. In his fashion his pupils Gerard van Honthorst and Hendrick Uylenburgh (the art-dealing relative of Rembrandt) began their own academies. Rembrandt formed a workshop that functioned like a school for his assistants, most of whom eventually went off on their own. In Italy, the Carracci formed a similar academy for the teaching of drawing. During this period, the status of the artist became more professional than trade-like, and his/her acceptance as a peer in the upper ranks of society had been established. In 1623, a loose confraternity of artists from the North residing in Rome, known as De Bentvueghels, formalized their organization in opposition to the Roman accademia. In Amsterdam, the Brotherhood of Painters was formed in 1653, and similar organizations were created in The Hague and Dordrecht around the same time, in reaction to the rather confining traditions of the guilds in those cities.

At the end of the century, a more radical model of academy was created in Holland, on the lines of the French academy, whose members' art, writings, and teachings were dedicated to promoting French and classical style in Dutch art. Called *Nil Volentibus Arduum*, it was begun by Gerard de Lairesse, Lodewijk Meijer, and Andries Pels. In Dordrecht, the artists' organization included collectors, amateur artists, and *Kunstliefhebbers* (art lovers). Exhibitions and classes were held for the public. In Utrecht, artists broke away from the guild in 1639, and by 1696 had formed into a Schilderscollegie (painters' school), permitting amateurs to attend drawing classes and lectures.

In Amsterdam in the early years of the eighteenth century, a number of informal schools were formed by artists like Arnold Boonen, Cornelis Pronk, and others. Scores of draftsmen and painters got their start in these settings. In 1743, the Amsterdam Tekencollegie (drawing school) was formed by petition of leading artists such as Jacob de Wit, Anthony Elliger, Tibout Regters, Jan Maurits Quinkhard, and Jacobus Buijs. Cornelis Ploos van Amstel, a legendary intellectual and art lover, became the first director of the academy. Public classes and lectures were given, and competitions and prizes were awarded. In The Hague, the guild was reformed as Pictura, a formal organization tied to the court of the *stadholder* (the hereditary [after 1747] position of head of state), and a free drawing school was created. In Haarlem, the academy, called *Kunst Zij Ons Doel* (Art Is Our Purpose), was founded in 1772. The director was the great collector-amateur Teyler van der Hulst, in whose house the academy met until 1781, surrounded by the great drawings and scientific and natural specimens in his collection.

In Amsterdam in 1778, a group of artists and intellectuals formed an academy called Felix Meritis, devoted to the study of the arts and sciences. In spite of the concerns of the *stadholder*'s party and the clergy, in a few years the association had over 1,200 members and over one million florins in its treasury. These academies and less formal artists' studio schools are much like those in America today, serving as a focus for socialization and interaction among professionals and art lovers and encouraging development of new generations of artists and patrons.

Roger Mandle

See also Dordrecht; Drawing clubs; Haarlem; Rembrandt School; State patronage, public support; Utrecht; Van Mander, Karel

Bibliography

Alpers, S. *Rembrandt's Enterprise: The Studio and the Market.* Chicago: University of Chicago Press, 1988.

Bolten, J. *Dutch and Flemish Method and Practice: Drawing Books, 1600–1750.* Landau, Pfalz: Pfalzische Verlagsanstalt GmbH, 1985.

Bruyn, J. "Rembrandt's Workshop: Its Function and Production." In *Rembrandt, the Master and His Workshop*, 68–89. London: National Gallery, 1992; distributed by Yale University Press.

Hoogewerff, G., *DeBeutvueghels*, The Hague: M. Nijhoff, 1952.

Mandle, R. *Dutch Masterpieces from the Eighteenth Century: Paintings and Drawings, 1700–1800.* Minneapolis: Minneapolis Institute of Arts; Toledo: Toledo Museum of Art; Philadelphia: Philadelphia Museum of Art, 1971.

Montias, J.M. "The Guild of St. Luke in Seventeenth-Century Delft and the Economic Status of Artists and Artisans. *Simiolus*, 9 (1977): 267–287.

Niemeijer, J.W. "Some Aspects of Dutch Eighteenth-Century Art." In *Dutch Masterpieces from the Eighteenth Century: Paintings and Drawings, 1700–1800*, by R. Mandle, 13–20. Minneapolis: Minneapolis Institute of Arts; Toledo: Toledo Museum of Art; Philadelphia: Philadelphia Museum of Art, 1971.

Pevsner, N. *Academies of Art, Past and Present.* Cambridge University Press, 1940.

Amsterdam Impressionists

The term refers to a generation of young artists active in the second half of the 1880s and the beginning of the 1890s. They formed an important and innovative link between the painters of The Hague School and the Symbolists in the 1890s. Because of their close relationship with a group of writers beginning at the same time, *De Tachtigers* (the writers of the 1880s), it is usual to refer to "the movement of the 1880s" and "the painters of the 1880s" (*de schilders van tachtig*). George Hendrik Breitner and Isaac Israëls are the most famous representatives of the Amsterdam Impressionists, but an equally great contribution to the movement was made by the artists Jacobus van Looy, Marius Bauer, Jan Veth, Eduard Karsen, Willem de Zwart, Suze Robertson, Jan Voerman, W.B. Tholen, Floris Verster, and Willem Witsen.

A number of these painters came out of the milieu of The Hague School, a group that specialized in landscape painting and was shown appreciation at that time. Some, like Breitner, Israëls, Tholen, De Zwart, and Witsen, were strongly influenced by the older generation at first. Because the *Hagenaars* (artists of The Hague School) also used an Impressionist touch, Dutch Impressionism is generally considered to have a landscape type with The Hague School and an urban type with the Amsterdam artists. Amsterdam, which was the cultural center of the Netherlands and a rising modern city in the 1880s and 1890s, played an important role in the development of the Amsterdam Impressionists. This young group of artists replaced the landscape with timely, completely modern themes like city life, street life, and entertainment in the capital city. They also brought back forgotten genres like the flower still life, the self-portrait, and the nude, or they gave them new impetus. The great contribution of this generation was that, within a decade, it brought Dutch art up to the same level as art abroad.

Most of the Amsterdam Impressionists came from the Rijksacademie and had been students of the director, August Allebé. His liberal policy gave central importance to the free development of the individual. He stimulated his students in their development as painters, and soon they were noticed as an independent-thinking generation. During their time at the academy, Van Looy, Witsen, and Maurits Willem van der Valk founded the artists' society known as St. Lucas. It was a reaction and a form of protest against the sluggish atmosphere and the restrictions that prevailed in established societies like Arti et Amicitiae.

The Nederlandsche Etsclub was founded in 1885 for similar reasons. Artists like Veth and Witsen wanted to revive the art of etching and to increase the exhibition possibilities. Witsen played a central and stimulating role in bringing together painters and writers. He was a generous host who brought many young artists together in his studio located at the Oosterpark, and in his family's country house, Ewijkshoeve. Also with the help of his financial contribution, *De Nieuwe Gids* was founded in 1885 by Frederik van Eeden, Willem Kloos, and Albert Verwey, among others. This literary magazine, in which articles about literature, visual arts, politics, and different branches of science appeared, became the most important mouthpiece for the new generation of painters and writers.

The younger people strove for a new form of art expressive of mood (*stemmingskunst*), in which the senses and feelings played an important role. Their loudly exclaimed, collective credo was individualism and *l'art pour l'art*. The polemical pieces by the painters/critics Veth, Van der Valk, and Witsen would determine the views of Dutch art criticism for years. In them, they did away with the aesthetics of the older critics. According to them, one had to be a practicing painter to be able to evaluate art. Art did not have to be functional or be based upon a view that is shared by the world.

The thoughts of both writers and painters were focused abroad and were influenced by the writings of French authors like Flaubert, Zola, and the brothers De Goncourt. It is not known how familiar the Amsterdam painters were with the work of their French contemporaries in the 1880s. In comparison with the avant-gardists of the 1870s, the paintings of the Dutch are often darker in tone and heavier in touch. At first Breitner, Israëls, and Van Looy looked for their models on the streets or in cafés. In doing this they followed the naturalism of a writer like Emile Zola and the choice of subject of a French painter like Degas. Many paintings are snapshot-like views that show the peculiar cutoffs of the picture plane that is a noticeable influence from photography. The influence was not accidental; Breitner and Witsen would receive posthumous recognition for their contribution to the development of photography.

Soon a much stronger emphasis was placed on the process of painting, and brush strokes became more expressive. Breitner and Isaac Israëls recorded with just a few quick strokes in drawings, watercolors, and oil paintings their impressions of Amsterdam city life and the social pastimes of the city's inhabitants (Fig. 3). Light and movement played an important role in the work of the Amsterdam Impressionists; however, Breitner, Karsen, and Verster, for example, used natural daylight and artificial city lighting in totally different ways in their works.

The individualism of the 1880s created a diversity of style and opinion, which came to a head in the 1890s. Among both the writers and the painters there was a spiritual parting of ways. Many artists married, moved, or lived for short or long periods abroad. After an intense but short florescence, Amsterdam Impressionism would be replaced by the new trends in the avant-garde—an individually evaluated Symbolist art and a socially engaged art of community. The work of Witsen and Karsen went the direction of a more inner form of the art of mood, which balanced their art on the border of Impressionism and Symbolism. The same was true for some of the works by Floris Verster and Marius Bauer. Breitner and Isaac Israëls continued in the way they were going and developed into Dutch Impressionists of preeminence.

Rieta Bergsma

Bibliography

Bionda, Richard, and Carel Blotkamp, eds. *The Age of Van Gogh: Dutch Painting, 1880–1895.* Zwolle: Waanders, 1990–1991.

Brom, G. *Hollandse schilders en schrijvers in de vorige eeuw.* Rotterdam: W.L. and J. Brusse, 1927.

Hammacher, A.M. *Amsterdamsche Impressionisten en hun kring.* Amsterdam: Meulenhoff, 1941.

Marius, G.H. *Dutch Painters of the Nineteenth Century.* 1903. Translated by Alexander Teixeira de Mattos. Edited by Geraldine Norman. Woodbridge, Suffolk: Antique Collectors Club, 1973.

Winkels, P.J.A. et al. *Ten tijde Van de Tachtigers: Rondom de Nieuwe Gids, 1880–1895.* The Hague: Nijgh and Van Ditmar, 1985.

Amsterdam School

The term Amsterdam School refers to an Expressionistic and Romantic tendency in composition that emerged from a group of young architects in that city during the first two decades of the twentieth century. These architects shared several characteristics: They were mostly born in the decade of the 1880s; they were engaged in the debate over introducing innovations to the academic tradition; they worked principally on designs for public housing commissioned by the municipalities and the building societies, according to the regulations of the *woningwet* (housing law). This sharing of a cultural milieu, clients, and design themes gave birth to a similarity of formal language that, if it did not constitute a true movement, determined nonetheless a mode of expression with a completely recognizable identity that profoundly marked the face of the city between the two World Wars.

The designation Amsterdam School was coined in 1916 by Jan Gratama (1877–1947) after the appearance in the city of the first new buildings inspired by a modern and imaginative Romanticism, all with vibrant façades in brick that were clearly inspired by a similar expressiveness of form. But this was not a real school. Without a precise ideological identity or a recognized leader, the architects of the so-called Amsterdam School acknowledged that their own identity was exclusively in the bond of friendship and professional custom. Their journal, *Wendingen,* started by H.Th. Wijdeveld (1885–1987), played a major part in promoting the new architectural language as well as in backing up the creative choices of the young designers. The journal was always a place for open discussion and never assumed a precise ideology.

The first building to show this unedited architectural vocabulary of Romantic Expressionism and formal excesses was the Scheepvaarthuis (1912–1916; Fig. 4), an office building commissioned by six Dutch shipowning companies. The commission was given to Johan van der Mey (1878–1949) and the younger participating designers, Michel de Klerk (1884–1923) and Piet Kramer (1881–1961). The three were acquaintances from the studio of Eduard Cuypers, where they had received their professional training. The façade of the Scheepvaarthuis is completely in brick with an ascending fenestration that is crowned with a sequence of tympanums. But even more amazing than the plastic aspect is the narrative character of the architecture: A host of sculptures and signs—in stone, iron, wood, or brick—makes it look like a sort of grand monument to the Golden Age of the Dutch Navy. The Expressionist energy of the form, the rich exuberance of the details, the alliance between architecture, sculpture, and the industrial arts had a profound effect at the time, especially because of the difference it posed to the figurative manner of H.P. Berlage, the recognized master of the period.

Together with its richness of form, the Scheepvaarthuis emblematized another characteristic of the Amsterdam School: the intensely creative approach of the designers to their work. This concept, deeply felt and seen, of the architect as an artist burst forth in the debates held in the cultural society Architectura et Amicitiae, to which many Dutch architects belonged and where social theories, new figurative experiences, and the role of architecture were discussed. In this setting, the young architects of the Amsterdam School defended the primacy of aesthetic values in the profession against the traditional image of the architect as a technician concerned with questions of construction and economics. Here, architects such as Cornelis Jonke Blaauw (1885–1947), Jan Frederik Staal (1879–1940), Piet Vorkink (1878–1960), and Wijdeveld joined Van der Mey, De Klerk, and Kramer.

In this "artistic" method of working, free from ideological and formal strictures, diverse references were gathered, such as exoticism, Japanese and Indonesian elements, or the taste for the aesthetic value of geometry, already experimented with by Berlage but enlarged upon in the writings and the works of the architect and theosopher Johannes Ludovicus Mattheus Lauweriks (1864–1932), who showed how it was possible to obtain harmonic proportions and spiritual content through respect for mathematical rules. Also included was the taste for organic and zoomorphic references. The architects were inspired by the conformation, at the same time geometric and

fantastic, of ocean shells and mineral crystals to seek a compromise between freedom of expression and interior order that could be applied to architecture in the same way that they arose from natural structures. Remembering his friend De Klerk, Kramer wrote in *Wendingen* VI: 9–10 (1924): "His buildings are the organisms of our time, beautiful and growing in a natural manner."

The hispid geometry of mineral crystals was transformed into the design for a chapel by Adolf Eibink and Jan Antoine Snellebrand (1915; Fig. 5) and into the competition design for a high-rise building by De Klerk (1915). The forms of marine mollusks or fossils even appear in the designs for country houses by Eibink and Snellebrand (1919–1920).

The imitation of natural forms reached its height in the resort village built between 1916 and 1918 at Park Merwijk, a coastal spot north of Amsterdam. This consisted of sixteen vacation houses (some of which have burned down), designed by Kramer, Guillaume Frédéric La Croix (1877–1923), Blaauw, Margaret Kropholler (1891–1966), and Staal, who was also responsible for coordinating the whole project. As a unit it has a strongly Romantic look, similar to the spirit of the Arts and Crafts Movement. Nearly all of the buildings have large, protective, sloped roofs, covered with straw thatch in picturesque shapes. The three Kramer houses, joined by a single façade, make up an angular slow-moving mass on the terrain. The houses by Kropholler, the first woman architect in the Netherlands, are a very imaginative rereading of the forms of traditional rural architecture and are distinguished by the feminine delicacy of their details. Staal's houses De Bark (The Ship) and De Ark (The Ark) take up literally the forms of naval architecture: main rooms like prows, terraces like lookout decks on the sterns.

Around 1920 opportunities for building public housing began to open up for the young architects of the school, following a strong commitment by the city of Amsterdam, which was then at the high point of its politics of social reform. The architecture, in its fertile inventiveness, united a solidity and constructive quality, imposed by the subject, that brought to maturity its expressive mode. The Amsterdam School, which is remembered above all for the large residential blocks that dot the city, was not the only group involved in this type of building. La Croix, De Klerk, Gratama, and Staal were among the first to deal with this new design theme; however, in view of the cultural priority given to this type of architecture by the Municipal Aesthetic Commission, the Schoonheidscommissie, which examined new projects, many other architects adapted themselves to its expressive modes, creating both a ring of new residential quarters around the city and an exceptional uniformity of urban design.

The Amsterdam School was the matrix for the buildings of the eastern housing projects of Transvaalbuurt and Indischebuurt, of the western projects in Mercatorplein and Spaarndammerbuurt, for housing in the south of Amsterdam carried out according to Berlage's ideal plan (Fig. 138), and for housing in north Amsterdam's scarcely populated areas. The language of the Amsterdam School, spreading out into many new areas, rooted itself deeply in the culture and taste of the urban classes. It flourished in the design elements of public places of entertainment and leisure. Business and urban décor also evinced an explicit debt to the school, winking at the formal models it had launched.

In 1923 De Klerk, who had been the preeminent creative mind of the school, died. At the same time, the liveliness that characterized the language of the group was exhausted in the repetition of schemes and in a generally new sense of architectural calm and severity. The opportunities for building public housing began to diminish because of the economic crisis in the mid-1920s, which caused the dwindling of state funds and the transition to private enterprise. In response to the different requirements of employers, the large residential blocks planned by the Amsterdam School became more sober, more regular, and more alert to the needs of a rationalized production. The so-called Second Amsterdam School was born. These were the years of the despicable façade architecture, which was the laughingstock of critics of the time, who labeled it "apron architecture" and "masked buildings." Private contractors did not ask architects to project the entire residential building (the distributive scheme of which was normalized by this time for economic reasons) but only its external façade in order to pass the test of the Municipal Aesthetic Commission, which still wanted the new constructions built according to the formal language of the Amsterdam School.

In the second half of the 1920s, the vitality of the school and its peculiar characteristics were definitely exhausted, although in the work of some architects there still remained signs of the former language. Evidence of this can be seen in the De Telegraaf building (1927–1930) by Staal and the University Laboratories (1932) by Berend Tobia Boeyinga (1886–1969), both in Amsterdam.

The formal language of the school was not restricted to Amsterdam but was propagated throughout the country by the Rijksgebouwendienst, the State Office for Construction. Signs of the school's formal language are visible in several post offices designed by Joseph Crouwel (1885–1962), the Veterinary Laboratory in Utrecht, also by Crouwel, and the laboratory of the School of Agriculture by Blaauw in Wageningen. Many other architects who had studied in Amsterdam, or merely sympathized with what the school had given rise to, were able to reuse that language in different localities. Significant examples include the bridge and the police station in Utrecht, the work of the Municipal Technical Office (1926–1928); some of the schools in Groningen constructed by the Office of Municipal Public Works at the end of the 1920s; and the first residential quarters by Willem Marinus Dudok (1884–1974), who was from 1915 the director of public works in Hilversum.

Maristella Casciato

See also Applied arts; De Klerk, Michel; Dudok, Willem Marinus; Kramer, Pieter Lodewijk; Public housing; *Wendingen*; Wijdeveld, Hendricus Theodorus

Bibliography

Bergvelt, Ellinoor et al. *Nederlandse architectuur, 1910–1930: Amsterdam School.* Amsterdam: Stedelijk Museum; Zaandam: Huig, 1975.

Casciato, Maristella. *De Amsterdamse School.* Rotterdam: 010, 1991.

———. *The Amsterdam School,* revised edition. Rotterdam: 010, 1996.

Searing, Helen. "Berlage or Cuypers? The Father of Them All." *In Search of Modern Architecture: A Tribute to Henry Russell Hitchcock.* Edited by Helen Searing, et al., 226–244. New York: Architectural History Foundation, 1982.

———. "Housing in Holland and the Amsterdam School." Ph.D. diss., Yale University, 1971.

Wit, Wim de, ed. *The Amsterdam School: Dutch Expressionist Architecture, 1915–1930.* New York: Cooper-Hewitt Museum; Cambridge, MA: MIT Press, 1983.

Andriesse, Emmy (1914–1953)

Emmy Andriesse, as well as most other members of the so-called GFK (*Vereniging van Beoefenaars der gebonden kunsten* [Federation of Applied Arts Practitioners]) in Amsterdam after World War II, recorded the daily lives of men and women with unadorned realism. But form and content were kept in balance, and the documentary photographs of this group are not without aesthetic qualities.

After World War II, photographs began to occupy a more important place in newspapers and magazines than ever before as an increasing number of editors realized that photography had the ability to summarize events or feelings that would have taken many words to describe. In addition, the "photobook" had come of age in the Netherlands: Photographers collaborated with graphic designers on books illustrated by photography and, in the process, became more than the suppliers of raw pictorial material. Events like jubilees, commemorations, or the publication of an industry's annual report became increasingly an occasion to commission a photographer.

In 1951, Emmy Andriesse was commissioned by an Amsterdam publisher to make the photographs for *De wereld van Van Gogh* (The World of Van Gogh). Most of her photographs are counterbalanced by a reproduction of a drawing or painting by Van Gogh, accompanied by excerpts from his letters. The lyrical quality of Andriesse's photographs is partly conjured up by the use of Mediterranean light found in the south of France (Fig. 6). This series is one of the best examples of how the artistic use of photography can surpass its use as merely documentary.

Hans Rooseboom

See also Photography, modern and contemporary

Bibliography

Boom, Mattie, Frans van Burkom, and Jenny Smets, eds. *Foto in omslag: Het Nederlandse documentaire fotoboek na 1945 / Photography between Covers: The Dutch Documentary Photobook after 1945.* Noordbrabants Museum, Den Bosch. Amsterdam: Fragment, 1989.

De Wereld van Van Gogh. Photographed by Emmy Andriesse. Amsterdam: Bert Bakker, 1951.

Leijerzapf, Ingeborg Th., ed. *Geschiedenis van de Nederlandse fotografie*. Alphen aan den Rijn/ Amsterdam: Samson/Voetnoot, 1984– .

Andriessen, Mari (1897–1979)

Mari Silvester Andriessen worked for a while in the studio of sculptor Jan Bronner after finishing elementary school in Haarlem. From 1912 until 1916, he studied at the Kunstnij- verheidsschool (School of Arts and Crafts) in Haarlem, and in 1917 he went to the Rijksacademie in Amsterdam, where Bronner, in the meantime, had become a professor. After vis- its to Paris and Chartres (1920) and a short study at the Acad- emy in Munich (1922), he completed his education with Bronner in 1923. Three years later, he won the silver medal of the Prix de Rome.

In the beginning, Andriessen worked primarily for the Catholic Church. His sculpture *St. Genoveva* (St. Genevieve) received a Grand Prize at the World Exhibition in Paris in 1937. That same year he received his first big secular commission for a sculpture of *Prudentia* (Prudence) for the restored town hall of Bergen op Zoom. In the same period, he made one of the six statues of lawyers from history, *Johannes Voet* (1937), for the building of the Hoge Raad (Supreme Court) in The Hague and ten panels (1937–1942) for the entrance doors to the *raadzaal* (council hall). The three huge sculptures, *Phoenix*, *Veiligheid* (Safety), and *Snelheid* (Velocity), that he made for the Central Station in Utrecht (which are no longer there) date from 1939.

After World War II, Andriessen, who was active in the resistance, produced a number of war monuments that do not honor heroes but depict the experiences and the deprivations of ordinary people. The most important of these monuments are in Haarlem (1949); Putten (1949–1950); Amsterdam, *De Dokwerker* (The Dockworker, 1950–1952); Enschede (1946– 1953); Rotterdam (1957); Nijmegen (1959); Scheveningen (1963–1966); and Amsterdam, *Anne Frank* (1975–1977). The most famous of these is *De Dokwerker*, erected in com- memoration of the February strike of 1941 in Amsterdam. In addition, he made more than twenty other public statues, such as *Cornelis Lely* (1953–1954; Den Oever), *Albert Plesman* (1958; The Hague), and *Queen Wilhelmina* (1967; Utrecht). Andriessen also made many portraits, small-scale sculptures, and medallions through the years. His works can be found in the collections of the Rijksmuseum Kröller-Müller in Otterlo, the Frans Hals Museum in Haarlem, and the Centraal Mu- seum in Utrecht.

Mieke van der Wal

See also Public monumental sculpture (1795–1990); Sculpture (1795–1945); World Wars I and II

Bibliography

Beek, Marius van. *Mari Andriessen*. Amsterdam: Meulenhoff, 1964.

Mulder, Theo. *Mari Andriessen: 80*. Haarlem: Frans Hals Museum, 1977.

Tilanus, Louk. *De beeldhouwer Mari Andriessen*. Weesp: De Haan, 1984.

Animal painting

The appearance of animals as independent subjects in Dutch art during the seventeenth century reflects a new attitude to- ward nature, which encouraged the study of animals. This shift was sponsored by empirical science as well as by the Calvinist Church, which considered the study of nature as a way to know God. Knowledge of nature, especially animals, was also viewed as morally instructive by seventeenth-century Neo-Stoic writers, who saw man as having been corrupted by society. Animals appear in Dutch art as objects of scientific study but also as natural inhabitants of the countryside, and, at times, as political allegory.

Prior to the sixteenth century, interest in animals had focused on their spiritual significance. The bestiary, an illus- trated collection of Christian allegories and pseudoscientific information, remained the primary handbook of knowledge concerning animals during the Middle Ages. In the thirteenth century, the translation of Aristotle's *History of Animals* into Latin transformed zoology into a science of observation and inspired encyclopedic treatises on animals, which summarized the knowledge of the Greeks. Fables and beast satires com- mented on society.

Renaissance exploration stimulated scientific interest in animals. Travelers described new and familiar animals, which they had actually seen, as well as fantastic beasts and races mentioned in Pliny, which they had expected to see. This blend of empirical knowledge with fantasy characterized con- temporary collections and the study of natural science. Thus, in *Historiae Animalium* (1551), Conrad Gesner repeated de- scriptions by Aristotle and Pliny and stiff images of real and fantastic beasts but also added his own text and more-natu- ralistic illustrations of animals he had personally studied.

Roelandt Savery was the first true animal painter in the Northern Netherlands. In his popular paintings of Paradise, birds and beasts dominate a thickly forested landscape, in which Adam and Eve, Noah, or Orpheus often assume sec- ondary roles. Savery made numerous sketches of animals *naer het leven* (after life). He derived most of the animals included in his paintings, however, from secondary sources—prints, stuffed animals and birds, as well as sculptures—contributing to the stiff, decorative quality of the often-profiled animals, which appear as additions to the landscape rather than as in- tegral parts of it. Like his contemporary Joris Hoefnagel, Savery gave his animals a more naturalistic "appearance" by reference to actual animals. In his chapter on animals in *Den grondt der edel vry schilder-const*, which opens the Schilder- boeck (1604), Karel van Mander promoted a similar ap- proach, describing how to represent the horse and cow in terms of geometric forms but also recommending the study of nature.

Scientifically accurate drawings were an essential part of the empirical study of nature at the University of Leiden and elsewhere during the seventeenth century. After his move to Leiden in 1595, Jacob de Gheyn II rendered precise drawings of plants, insects, and animals, such as the study sheet with four views of a frog manipulated to reflect principles of anatomy, or another of a live mouse. At mid-century, Albert

Eckhout painted *Two Tortoises* (The Hague, Mauritshuis) for a commission by Johan Maurits van Nassau to document the fauna of Brazil, while Rembrandt, Lambert Doomer, and others sketched exotic animals in Dutch menageries. Maria Sibylla Merian's delicately rendered drawings of butterflies and insects and Aart Schouman's eighteenth-century illustrations of the animals and birds in the menagerie of Willem V were likewise prized possessions of collectors and scientists.

The cattle piece was a unique development of the Northern Netherlands, where cattle, traditionally emblems of fertility and earth, represented one of the primary economic resources. Under the influence of Venetian pastorals, Claes Cornelisz. Moeyaert and Abraham Bloemaert, among others, introduced monumental animals to their history and pastoral paintings. During the 1640s, Paulus Potter and Aelbert Cuyp developed a new genre in which domestic animals dominate Dutch landscapes, and human figures, where included, are secondary. Potter's emphasis on the naturalism of his rustic scenes reflects the Georgic tradition, whereas the more generalized animals and figures of Cuyp adhere more closely to the arcadian legacy of Virgil's *Ecologues*. Cuyp's paintings, and those of Adriaen van de Velde, are Dutch variations of the pastorals of Nicolaes Berchem, Karel du Jardin, and others, who suggested Arcadia by the diffused light, landscape, and shepherds of Italy. For both groups, as well as for artists such as Philips Wouwerman, the paintings and especially the series of prints (1636) of animals by Pieter van Laer were seminal. Van Laer's animal prints differed significantly from the model books by Crispijn de Passe I, Cornelis Bloemaert (after Abraham Bloemaert), and Jacob Gerritsz. Cuyp. Like Van Laer's series, which was dedicated to a humanist, those by Potter, Berchem, and others represented animals in natural postures and were probably appreciated as independent art objects.

Some paintings of horses, cattle, and dogs were conceived as portraits of specific animals. Paulus Potter's famous painting *The Bull* (1647; The Hague, Mauritshuis), the realistic naturalism of which distinguishes it from the 1564 painting of a prize bull (Amsterdam Historical Museum), may have represented a particular animal. A notation in a seventeenth-century inventory suggests that some paintings of horses may, however, have been interpreted as emblems of freedom. Likewise, dogs and other animals in characteristic postures of defense, such as the paintings of Melchior de Hondecoeter and prints by Hendrick Hondius, can be read as emblems of vigilance, a theme monumentally represented in Jan Asselijn's painting *The Angry Swan* (ca. 1653; Amsterdam, Rijksmuseum). Animals continued to serve as political metaphors. The lion of the Netherlands, the English dog, as well as the watchdog of Holland and the angry bull, were all familiar images in prints. Cornelis Saftleven in the *Trial of Johan van Oldenbarnevelt* (1663) and Paulus Potter in the *Life of the Hunter* (ca. 1651) employed the tradition of the "world upside down" for political satire in paintings.

The interest in animal painting declined in the late seventeenth century and was only revived a century later as an expression of the new Dutch nationalism. Many of the paintings that were produced by Jacob van Strij, Pieter Gerardus van Os, and Jan Baptist Kobell II were either imitations or copies of seventeenth-century prototypes, especially after Potter, Cuyp, and Adriaen van de Velde. Other artists, however, worked more independently. Josephus Augustus Knip, for example, painted cattle pieces in a Southern context. The Hague School viewed the Dutch *animaliers* through the Barbizon painters. The last significant cattle painter (Fig. 56) was Willem Maris, who died in 1910.

Amy L. Walsh

See also Cuyp, Aelbert; De Hondecoeter, Melchior; Exotica; Gamepiece; Hague School, The; Italy; Knip, Josephus Augustus; Kobell, Jan Baptist II; Landscape; Maris, Willem; Natural history illustration; Non-Western cultural influences; Pastoral; Potter, Paulus; Ronner-Knip, Henriëtte; Rural life and views; Schouman, Aart; Utrecht; Van Mander, Karel; Wouwerman, Philips

Bibliography

Bartsch, Adam von. *The Illustrated Bartsch.* Edited by Walter L. Strauss. Vol. 1. New York: Abaris, 1978.

Bestiaire hollandais: Exposition de tableaux, aquarelles, dessins, et gravures par des artistes hollandais des XVIIe–XVIIIe siècles, et d'un choix de livres de la meme periode. Paris: Instituut Néerlandais, 1960.

Boschma, C. et al. *Meesterlijk vee: Nederlandse veeschilders 1600–1900.* The Hague: Rijksdienst Beeldende Kunst; Zwolle: Waanders, 1988.

Gerson, Horst. *Meisterwerke der holländische Tiermalerei des 17. Jahrhunderts.* Essen: Girardet, 1967.

Müllenmeister, Kurt J. *Tierdarstellungen in Werken niederländischer Künstler.* 2 vols. Bremen: C. Schünemann, 1978–1981.

Appel, Karel (Christiaan Karel Appel) (born 1921)

Cofounder of the Dutch Experimental Group and the Cobra Movement in 1948, Karel Appel has been since the later 1950s the most celebrated Dutch artist of his generation. Though best known for his painting and sculpture, Appel has worked in many other free and applied techniques, including ceramics, stained glass, and stage design, and has also published poetry and recorded experimental music.

Appel was born in Amsterdam, took courses at the Rijksacademie during the war (1942–1944), and until 1945 underwent influences from artists such as Van Gogh, Matisse, and Picasso. From 1946 to 1948, he developed a primitive figuration in paintings, sculptures, and assemblages that linked him initially to Corneille (whom he had met at the Rijksacademie) and then to a widening circle of younger artists who in 1948 founded the Dutch Experimental Group and Cobra (Color Plate 16). In 1949, public hostility to his mural painting *Vragende kinderen* (Questioning Children), in the Amsterdam Town Hall, and to works in the Cobra/Experimental exhibition held at the Stedelijk Museum, gave Appel considerable notoriety in his native land. This negative publicity helped provoke a voluntary exile: Appel moved to Paris in 1950 and has subsequently lived mainly in France, Monaco, and New York.

Encouraged by Willem Sandberg, director of the Stedelijk Museum in Amsterdam, Appel returned to Holland to execute mural paintings in the museum in 1951 (the "Appelbar") and 1956 (the restaurant), and in 1956–1957 he designed stained glass windows for two new Protestant churches: the Kruiskerk at Geleen and the Paaskerk at Zaandam. From then on, designs (often for windows) in collaboration with prominent Dutch architects became a recurrent feature in Appel's career, and in 1983 he also designed windows for the Temple Sholom in Chicago.

By the mid–1950s, Appel's painting was drawing the attention of critics such as Michel Tapié in France and Herbert Read in the English-speaking world. In 1954, he won the UNESCO Prize at the Venice Biennale—many other international awards were to follow—and had his first New York exhibition at the Martha Jackson Gallery. He visited the United States and Mexico in 1957, by which time his characteristic emphasis on the material qualities of paint and the physicality of the act of painting had established him as a leading European "action painter." In subsequent years, Appel went on to explore different technical and stylistic possibilities, often by responding to the international developments of the day. During the 1960s, for example, his large, colorful constructions reflected the dominant Pop Art of those years, and after a phase in the 1970s in which a revival of Expressionism and a return to Van Gogh–like vibrant stripes was discernible, his paintings of the 1980s seemed to engage in dialogue with the ascendant New Painting of young Italian and German artists. His recent work, the sculpture shown in Paleis Lange Voorhout in The Hague in 1993, includes large *tableaux* of objects culled from many different cultures and links Appel to a postmodern ethos of cultural pluralism. The continuing transformations in his *oeuvre* demonstrate both Appel's desire and his ability to rejuvenate his art.

In spite of many publications on Appel's art—some of them extravagantly large—art-historical coverage of his *oeuvre* remains fragmentary.

Graham Birtwistle

See also Cobra Movement; World Wars I and II

Bibliography

Appel, Karel. *Karel Appel. 40 ans de peinture, sculpture en dessin.* Paris: Galilée, 1987.

Bax, Marty. "De Appelbar." *Jong Holland* 3:3 (1987) 4–13.

Josephus Jitta, Mariette. "Karel Appel: 'Ik rotzooi maar wat aan.' Enige opmerkingen over een uitspraak." In *Karel Appel: Werk op papier.* 5–18. The Hague: Haags Gemeentemuseum, 1982.

Ragon, Michel. *Karel Appel: Peinture, 1937–1957.* Paris: Galilée; Amsterdam: Meulenhoff/Landshoff, 1988.

Reinhartz-Tergau, E. "Het monumentale werk van Karel Appel." *Karel Appel.* The Hague: Gallery Nova Spectra, 1981.

Restany, Pierre, and Allen Ginsberg (texts). *Karel Appel: Street Art, Ceramics, Sculpture, Wood Reliefs, Tapestries, Murals, Villa El Salvador.* Amsterdam: Becht; New York: Abbeville, 1985.

Visser, Harriet de, and Roland Hagenberg, eds. *Karel Appel: The Complete Sculptures, 1936–1990.* New York: Edition Lafayette, 1990.

Applied arts

The quality and design of industrial products became a topic of discussion in Western Europe in the course of the nineteenth century, and after the 1860s in the Netherlands. This was the start of various measures to improve the crafts and industrial design, which led to an unprecedented revival of the applied arts around the turn of the century.

The Netherlands had been slower than other countries to industrialize, and the movement for innovation in the applied arts started later than abroad. The battle against tasteless, machine-made products and the loss of traditional crafts began in Great Britain, the cradle of mechanized industry. The World Exposition in 1851 in London, at which the low quality of Western products was revealed on a broad scale, is generally seen as the turning point. In the following years important reforms in instruction in the crafts were enacted in England. In several places new drawing and applied-arts schools opened with a curriculum that was oriented toward both theory and practice. To support instruction, collections of "good" industrial design, both old and modern, were formed in several schools, modeled after the collection of a museum that opened in South Kensington in 1852—the present-day Victoria and Albert Museum. The English Arts and Crafts Movement, supported by the ideas of John Ruskin (1819–1900), William Morris (1834–1896), and Walter Crane (1845–1915), would deeply influence developments on the Continent in both a direct and an indirect way in the last quarter of the nineteenth century.

Dutch participation in the World Exposition of 1851 was, qualitatively as well as quantitatively, extremely meager. But even though the first negative reactions were voiced in the Netherlands at that time, it would still be a full twenty years before criticism became general and initiatives were taken to raise the level of the applied arts. The numerous national applied-arts exhibitions that were held in the nineteenth century at the instigation of private-interest organizations like the Nederlandse Maatschappij voor Nijverheid en Handel (Dutch Society for Industry and Commerce) made an important contribution to this. In the considerations pursuant to these exhibitions the importance of good drawing instruction for workers as a basic of their aesthetic education was pointed out several times and with increased emphasis. Among progressive theoreticians and artists was a growing aversion to the historical styles and excessively naturalistic ornamentation that characterized Dutch products of that time, and this gave rise to a desire for a new self-identifying national style.

With the *Exhibition of Art Applied to Industry* (Tentoonstelling van Kunst toegepast op Nijverheid) held in Amsterdam in 1877, this development reached a decisive phase. One of the organizers of this event, the architect J.R. de Kruyff (1844–1923), was among the most important nineteenth-century advocates of reform in Dutch industrial design.

His ideas, recorded in 1876 in a brochure published before the exhibition, are representative of the innovative thinking then dominant in progressive circles. De Kruyff defined art (and thus also art applied to industry) as "the result of three forces: reason, fantasy, and the sense of beauty." For him, a well-designed article was, in the first place, useful, it was made correctly, and it was pretty. He called "fashion" and "naturalism" the foremost causes for the decline of the national applied arts. According to him, the public had an unseemly desire for novelties, causing new trends and fads to follow each other with increasing speed and bringing more and more absurd and strange products onto the market. The improper use of raw materials and techniques, such as fashionable imitations of materials like wood in papier-mâché, he found unacceptable. Naturalism in ornamentation—the reproduction of organic forms as accurately as possible as decoration—was without a doubt the greatest offense and, therefore, utterly objectionable. However, this did not mean the rejection of nature as a source of inspiration; decorative motifs taken from nature were preferred, but they should be stylized rather than portrayed realistically. Furthermore, it was important that the ornament not be applied arbitrarily—not be "pasted on," as it were—as so often happened, but that it do justice to the function of the article. To refrain from decoration altogether was still not a consideration in this period since the desire to decorate was believed to be inherent to the human race. In order for a new *national* style to develop, study of the arts and crafts especially from the Netherlands' glorious past in the sixteenth and seventeenth century—the Dutch Renaissance—was stimulated. The objective was not to copy old examples literally; the study should be assimilated in a style full of character and corresponding to modern times. Good vocational training and inspiring (museum) collections of industrial articles were essential in this, and their realization was also strongly advocated.

The negative opinion of Dutch applied arts and the pleas for improvement, such as in the essay by De Kruyff and several other documents of the time, were largely grafted upon foreign sources. In these first years of awareness, criticism, and cautious changes, the greatest influence did not come directly from England, but from Germany and Austria. The movement to renew the arts and crafts had already borne its first fruits there: In imitation of England, the first museums of industrial design with connected schools had been opened and vocational education had been radically revised. The driving force behind this was the German architect and art theoretician Gottfried Semper (1803–1879), whose ideas were shaped in England, where he had been involved in the World Exposition of 1851 and in the plans to reform education. In 1860–1863, he wrote his best-known and influential book, *Der Stil in den technischen und tektonische Künsten*, an analysis of the essence of art and style. Although there is some early evidence (1864) of a direct influence from Semper's work, his ideas entered the Netherlands at first mainly through the publications of his German and Austrian followers and through different German trade journals. Several Dutch architects and designers also became acquainted with his work while attending the Polytechnic School in Zurich, where Semper taught from 1855 until 1871, or at the industrial-design school in Vienna.

As a far-reaching consequence of the Amsterdam exhibition of 1877, the *government* became involved with the issues. For years the government had refrained from any interference in the arts, but this liberal posture ended with the establishment in 1875 of the Department of Arts and Sciences in the Ministry of Home Affairs. The key position in this was taken by Victor de Stuers (1843–1916), author of the sensational *Holland op zijn smalst* (1873), which questioned the indifference of the government with regard to art and the cultural heritage. De Stuers became the head of the new department, a position he would hold for over twenty-five years. As a result of the Amsterdam exhibition of 1877, De Stuers, who had been deeply involved in its organization, established a state committee with the goal of investigating the situation of Dutch industrial design and making recommendations for improvement. Partly on the basis of the committee's report, a state training program for teachers of drawing and a state school for industrial design were started in 1881; both were housed in the nearly completed Rijksmuseum in Amsterdam. De Kruyff, who as secretary of the investigative committee had a great influence on the report, became the head of the industrial design school; W.B.G. Molkenboer (1844–1915) became the director of the school for drawing teachers. In 1878 a separate Department of Decorative Arts was created at the Polytechnic School in Delft, with A. Le Comte (1850–1921) as an inspiring and influential teacher.

An important plan had been realized earlier on the side of *private* interest: In 1877 a museum of industrial design was opened in Haarlem on the initiative of the Society of Industry and Commerce. The museum was expanded with a school two years later. The director, F.W. van Eeden, followed a Semperian policy as did his successor E.A. von Saher (1849–1918). Several years later an industrial-design museum and school were also established in Utrecht (1884–1886). In Amsterdam a third new trade school was added to the two state schools, the Quellinus School of Applied Arts and Drawing, which developed from the workshop for apprentices following the medieval example that architect P.J.H. Cuypers (1827–1921) had started during the construction of the Rijksmuseum.

In addition to his work as the architect of the Rijksmuseum, the Centraal Station in Amsterdam, and a great number of churches, Cuypers stands as the most important harbinger of the new direction in Dutch architecture and industrial design. His great example was the French architect and theoretician E.E. Viollet-le-Duc (1814–1879), whose opinions about a Constructive-rationalist architecture he promulgated in the Netherlands. As a fervent Roman Catholic (this faith could again be practiced openly in the Netherlands after 1853), he chose the Gothic style for carrying out his ecclesiastical commissions because no other form of architecture so reflects the flourishing of Catholicism; in his secular architecture and interior designs, he would add some neo-renaissance elements. Cuypers' special importance for the revival of the applied arts was as a supporter and propagator of the

Gemeenschapskunst (communal art) concept: a connection of all art disciplines under the leadership of architecture in service to a higher social ideal. The idea of an all-inclusive design would continue after Cuypers on a nonreligious, social-ideological footing by a new generation of artists. The Amsterdam Stock Exchange (1898–1903) by architect H.P. Berlage (1856–1934) is one of the most famous examples of such a *Gesamtkunstwerk* (total work of art). Architecture, sculpture (Fig. 125), painting, and applied arts are woven into a masterly whole.

The increasing interest of artists and notably architects in the applied arts during these years was the result, on the one hand, of a changed opinion that the essence of architecture was that of a craft (Semper), and, on the other hand, of a strong social feeling. Of all of the arts, the applied arts were closest to the people, and by bringing the people into contact with beautiful, well-designed utilitarian and decorative objects, their aesthetic sense would become developed, which would eventually lead to a more beautiful, more civilized, and happier society. While the advocates of a new industrial design had cited nationalist and economic motives during the 1860s, 1870s, and 1880s, after 1890 social-aesthetic ideals were emphasized. The elevation of the people became the new credo. Now the English Arts and Crafts Movement had more influence, particularly the publications of the founders, which were translated into Dutch during this period. A Dutch version of Walter Crane's *Claims of Decorative Art* (1892) appeared in 1894 under the title *Kunst en Samenleving*; in 1900, John Ruskin's *Stones of Venice* (1853) and, in 1903, the critical lectures of William Morris on art and society were translated.

The *oeuvre* of the socialist Berlage, which is imbued with this new ideology, marks the transition between tradition and innovation. His earliest designs for architecture, interiors, and furniture in Renaissance-like style still have all of the characteristics of the then current art theories; but in the 1890s Berlage, a follower of both Semper and Viollet-le-Duc, knew how to leave nineteenth-century historicism permanently behind and to arrive at an original design in which appropriateness, uniformity in style, honest use of materials, a logical and solid construction, and a subordinated ornamentation that was enclosed in the form were the basic principles (Fig. 7).

In the beginning of the 1890s some young industrial artists who had graduated from the new Amsterdam vocational schools achieved a contemporary idiom based on the same rational principles, while simultaneously in The Hague and Delft a new trend caught on that, in contrast, served the decorative—the Dutch Art Nouveau was a fact. The so-called Amsterdam, or "constructive," direction was given the name Nieuwe Kunst (the Dutch translation of Art Nouveau), to indicate that it concerned work of a specifically Dutch character, and is clearly distinguished from The Hague, or "decorative," direction, which is more connected to the international, flowery Art Nouveau. Today the term Nieuwe Kunst is used for all Dutch industrial arts from around the turn of the century. Like the foreign Art Nouveau, the Nieuwe Kunst borrowed stylistic elements and decorative techniques from

distant and older cultures. In the Dutch applied arts of around 1900, Japanese, Egyptian, and Assyrian influences as well as techniques such as batik from the Dutch East Indies can be recognized.

One of the first branches of industry in which the new notions of art took shape was the pottery industry. In 1877 De Porceleyne Fles, the only surviving seventeenth-century Delft faïence factory, attracted A. Le Comte to become an artistic adviser, and in the 1880s and 1890s several new businesses were formed that produced useful and decorative ceramics in the new style. The Hague pottery Rozenburg (1883), for example, became internationally known through the remarkable designs of Th. Colenbrander (1841–1930) and graceful eggshell porcelain (Fig. 21). Amstelhoek (1897) and De Distel (1895) in Amsterdam made simpler earthenware with modest, geometrical decorations. New ceramics companies were started also in Utrecht, Gouda, and other places; there were more than twenty companies active in this field in the Netherlands by 1905.

Mindful of communal art, several architects and artists applied themselves to practically all of the disciplines within the applied arts. Berlage, as an industrial designer *avant la lettre*, made designs for furniture, wallpaper, textiles, glass, ceramics, metalworks, and graphics for mass consumption. Although many of these designs were entirely or partly made according to traditional methods, Berlage was not against machine production. If it meant that the articles became affordable for a broader public, this was also a step forward in the direction of the desired new society in which art would be naturally integrated.

Berlage also made an important link with the public in 1900 by establishing 't Binnenhuis, an undertaking with the objective of designing, making, and selling exclusively Dutch interior furnishings and articles. This Amsterdam firm, to which dozens of industrial artists contributed especially during the first year, seems to have been started initially to vie with the art gallery Arts and Crafts, which had opened two years earlier in The Hague under the artistic direction of Chr. Wegerif (1859–1920) and J. Thorn Prikker (1868–1932) and was strongly oriented toward Belgium (the designs of H. van de Velde) and England. But it was probably also established to counterbalance, although to a lesser degree, the workshop of Van Wisselingh en Co. in Amsterdam, where G.W. Dijsselhof (1866–1924), C.A. Lion Cachet (1864–1945), and Th. Nieuwenhuis (1866–1951) had the opportunity to execute extraordinarily luxurious and richly decorated furniture and interiors (Fig. 8). These artists endeavored just as much to achieve an all-inclusive design, but more from the point of view of merely aesthetics than from a social idealism, as was the case of the group around Berlage. Furniture made of expensive woods with laborious sculptural ornamentation and inlaid work was also made in the Atelier voor Architectuur, Kunstnijverheid en Decoratieve Kunst (Studio for Architecture, Industrial Art, and Decorative Art) in Amsterdam between 1895 and 1900. The studio was started by K.P.C. de Bazel (1869–1923) and J.L.M. Lauweriks (1864–1932). It is clear that this completely handmade furniture was only for an *élite*, but even the simpler designs by Berlage and his sympathizers appeared not to be reserved for ordinary people. Besides, the strictly functional character of the 't Binnenhuis style was not compatible with the taste of the masses, who desired luxury. The "civilizing work" to bring them around to it would be continued until far into the twentieth century, with exhibitions against bad taste, model homes, and publications about "responsible living," but on the whole it appears to have had little effect.

De Bazel and Lauweriks, both adherents of theosophy, were particularly important for the Amsterdam design movement with their introduction, around 1895, of designing using geometrical systems. Thanks to J.H. de Groot (1865–1932), who further worked out this method and published about it, systematic designing was applied by various colleagues. Designing according to geometric systems could lead to the well-balanced proportions in both composition and decoration that are characteristic of much of the Dutch applied arts from the period 1900–1910.

At the *First International Exhibition of Modern Decorative Arts* in Turin, Italy, in 1902, the Dutch entries scored a great success and won international fame. Even though the movement for innovation in industrial design had started relatively late in the nineteenth-century in the Netherlands, by the turn of the century the Dutch had completely caught up in an artistic sense and the applied arts from the Netherlands could compete with the best in Europe.

Karin Gaillard

See also Architectural criticism, issues of style; Architectural restoration; Berlage, Hendrik Petrus; Ceramics; Dijsselhof, Gerrit Willem; Display; Exotica; Graphic design; Japonisme; Nationalism; Neo-Gothic; Stained glass; Thorn Prikker, Johan; *Wendingen*

Bibliography

Bergvelt, Ellinoor, et al. eds. *Industry and Design in the Netherlands, 1850–1950*. Amsterdam: Stedelijk Museum, 1985–1986.

Braches, Ernst. *Het boek als Nieuwe Kunst 1892–1903: Een studie in Art Nouveau*. Utrecht: A. Oosthoek, 1973. (English summary).

Eliëns, Titus M. *Kunst, nijverheid, kunstnijverheid: De nationale nijverheidstentoonstellingen als spiegel van de Nederlandse kunstnijverheid in de negentiende eeuw*. Zutphen: Walburg, 1990. (English summary).

Gans, Louis. *Nieuwe Kunst: De Nederlandse bijdrage tot de Art Nouveau*. Utrecht: A. Oosthoek, 1966. (English summary).

Kruyff, J.R. de. *De Nederlandsche Kunstnijverheid in verband met den Internationalen wedstrijd bij gelegenheid van de in 1877 te Amsterdam te houden Tentoonstelling van Kunst toegepast op Nijverheid uitgeschreven door de Afdeeling Amsterdam der Vereeniging tot bevordering van Fabriek- en Handwerksnijverheid in Nederland*. Amsterdam, 1876.

Leidelmeijer, Frans, and Daan van der Cingel. *Art Nouveau en art deco in Nederland: Verzamelobjecten uit de vernieuwingen in de kunstnijverheid van 1890 tot 1940*. Amsterdam: Meulenhoff/Landshoff, 1983.

Martis, Jan Alexander. "Voor de Kunst en voor de Nijverheid: Het ontstaan van het kunstnijverheidsonderwijs in Nederland." Ph.D. diss., University of Amsterdam, 1990. (English summary).

Ramakers, Renny. *Tussen kunstnijverheid en industriële vormgeving: De Nederlandsche Bond voor Kunst in Industrie*. Utrecht: Reflex, 1985. (English summary).

Simon Thomas, Mienke. "Het ornament, het verleden en de natuur: Drie hoofdthema's in het denken over vormgeving in Nederland 1870–1890." *Nederlands Kunsthistorisch Jaarboek* 39 (1988): 27–60. (English summary).

Voorst tot Voorst, J.M.W. van. *Tussen Biedermeier en Berlage: Meubel en interieur in Nederland 1835–1895*. 2 vols. Amsterdam: De Bataafsche Leeuw, 1992. (English summary).

Architectural competitions

The best conditions for creating architecture would seem to be provided through architectural competitions: A patron has only to organize a competition and wait to select the design he likes. The competing architects must, of course, know the building requirements, the awards, and the names of the jury. This is how it should be, but in reality it is different. The results of architectural competitions are seldom satisfying, wrote the secretary of the Society for the Promotion of Architecture, W.H. Warnsinck, in 1844. The reason, he said, was that the best architects refrained from participating because the patrons were not obliged to assign the work to the winner of the competition. Patrons could use the designs and alter them as they wished without the consent of the architect who produced them.

Another problem in the nineteenth century was that competitions often led to unending quarrels among the members of the jury or—if they were public competitions—in the press. This happened in 1862 when a group of Amsterdam art lovers took the initiative to found a new museum that would be named after King Willem I. Nineteen architects responded to the call, but none of their designs could win the approval of the jury. The only thing that resulted from it was a prize for Ludwig and Emil Lange, architects from Munich. The museum was eventually built, but by a protégé of the man who had a powerful position in the Ministry of the Interior, Victor de Stuers.

Architects in the Netherlands began to set up some rules for competitions in 1883, but they had to wait until the next scandal to reach a general agreement. The scandal came in 1906 when the jury of the competition for the Peace Palace in The Hague appeared to have a preference for the Dutch Renaissance style of the sixteenth century but had omitted to mention it in their program. In reaction the architectural society Architectura et Amicitia took the initiative to propose a set of regulations at the International Congress of Architects in London. Architectura et Amicitia had organized competitions since its foundation in 1855, mostly for minor works. In 1856, for example, these were for a shelter for a night watchman, a hunting cabin, and a bridge on a country estate.

In 1910, the first regulations were set up in the Netherlands, becoming—at least in essence—the code for architectural competitions that still applies today. Among the new regulations were an assurance of anonymity through use of a motto, compensation to the winner in case of the work being assigned to someone else, protection of the design as the intellectual property of the architect, and standardization of the prizes. Sanctions were not applied to the regulations, however, so that inadmissible varieties of competitions have continued to occur.

The history of architectural competitions lies hidden in archives where a totally different world of architecture exists in designs that were rejected and thus remained unbuilt. This world is fascinating because it reveals the contemporary debate on architecture. The famous competition for the Stock Exchange in Amsterdam is a case in point. H.P. Berlage, who eventually designed the existing building on the Damrak (1903), did not succeed in his first attempt to win the prize. That was in 1885, when in cooperation with Th. Sanders he designed a Neo-Renaissance building. The winner then was L.M. Cordonnier, but his design turned out to be a close copy of the town hall of La Rochelle in France and had to be withdrawn.

A much-discussed competition took place in 1933. It was organized by the city of Amsterdam in order to find new ways to design inexpensive housing for the working class. Ninety-two architects responded, but none could satisfy the criteria set by the jury. The architectural profession, nevertheless, learned from the experience, and the energy spent on this "modern" question was not lost. In this case the profession at large was stimulated, but in most cases competitions led to endless quarrels. These may be interesting for historians, but they probably don't serve the cause of architecture when the result is a mere compromise. A notorious example is the competition for a new town hall in Amsterdam, which started in 1936 and ended in 1987 with a combined design. The winner of the latest competition, Wilhelm Holzbauer from Vienna, had to adapt his design in order to combine the town hall with an opera house, which had been designed by the Dutch architect Cees Dam.

Architectural competitions nowadays have gained a more important position in the world of architecture, most likely due to a heightened public interest in the built environment.

Wim Denslagen

See also Architectural criticism, issues of style; Architectural restoration; Berlage, Hendrik Petrus; Nationalism; Public housing

Bibliography

Beek, Marijke. "Kwaliteitsbevordering van werkverschaffing: Architectuurprijsvragen van 1880 tot 1920." *Wonen TABK* 12 (1982): 10–29.
Jong, Cees de, and Erik Mattie. *Architectural Competitions.* 2 vols. Cologne: Benedikt Taschen, 1994.
Nooit gebouwd Nederland. Weesp: Unieboek, 1983.
Schilt, Jeroen, and Jouke van der Werf. *Genootschap Architectura et Amicitia.* Rotterdam: 010, 1992.

Architectural criticism, issues of style

In the first decades of the nineteenth century, Neoclassicism—the style that had been preeminent throughout the Western world since the second half of the eighteenth century—seemed to have an unshakable standing in the architectural profession. But rationalism—another legacy of the century of the Enlightenment—produced a new way of looking at the fundamentals of building that came to disturb the complacency of the architectural world. The architectural profession in the Netherlands became deeply divided on the issue of style; the architecture of the nineteenth century bears the evidence of the debates. Honesty and sincerity were to become key concepts: Architecture should not follow the dictates of an academic aestheticism any longer; it must turn away from the uninspired prescriptions of the classical orders and pursue economy of means, convenient disposition, and tautness. These views prepared the way for twentieth-century functionalism.

The first architectural periodical in the Netherlands, by the Society for the Advancement of Architecture (founded in 1842 in Amsterdam), began in 1843 by launching an attack on the false aesthetics of Neoclassicism. A well-known supporter of the rationalistic approach was J.H. Leliman (1828–1910). According to this way of thinking, a building should not only be functional, it should also express its function; that gave it "character," which was the logical consequence of truth. Architecture not only had to serve its function adequately, but this function should also be recognizable. This notion about "character" prepared the way for later eclecticism, the free combination of historic styles.

Some architects, among them I. Gosschalk (1838–1907), believed that the advancement of architecture depended on the development of new construction techniques, particularly in iron. But when Cornelis Outshoorn (1812–1875) built the famous iron-and-glass Palace of Popular Industry in Amsterdam (1864), his colleague Leliman commented that iron was suitable only for temporary constructions like the Crystal Palace in London (Joseph Paxton, 1850), not for monumental architecture that should be built of more massive materials. In the eyes of many architects iron had only technical, not artistic, significance.

By the middle of the century, the battle over styles governed theoretical discussions of architecture. In 1854, the influential architect W.N. Rose (1801–1878) condemned the application of different historical styles, through which, for example, churches, palaces, and town halls in the Greek, Moorish, Gothic, and Renaissance styles would be erected adjacent and juxtaposed to one another. Rose searched for "underlying principles" in architecture such as truth, unity, order, relation, coherence, and proportion. What Rose built according to these principles—for example, the Colonial Ministry (1860) in The Hague (a huge, austere stuccoed block with row upon row of identical rectangular windows)—was, however, much criticized by his contemporaries. C. Muysken (1843–1922) wrote in 1884 that the search for a new style by those who ignored all historical style forms had led only to disappointments and failures. He himself was a professed defender of the Dutch Neo-Renaissance.

The battle that was ignited over styles was sometimes fueled by political controversies between Protestants and Catholics. A famous case was the project for the Rijksmuseum in Amsterdam: Protestants were strongly opposed to the Neo-Gothic design of P.J.H. Cuypers (1827–1921) and pushed to have accepted a Dutch Renaissance style, which they associated with the Protestant founding fathers of the Dutch Republic at the end of the sixteenth century. Cuypers' design, however, prevailed in the end.

In retrospect, those discussions of styles seem futile when considered against the explosive growth of new types of architecture in the second half of the nineteenth century—railway stations, factories, hospitals, prisons, schools, and housing. Nevertheless, style remained a very important issue, in particular after the middle of the century when Neoclassicism gave way to an eclecticism in which not only classical motifs were applied but also forms from the Italian Renaissance, French Empire, and even the Romanesque style. This eclecticism was strongly favored by members of the influential Society for the Advancement of Architecture. One of the first examples of this style, a new stone façade for the church of St. Francis of Assisi by Tétar van Elven M.G. (1803–1882) on the Rokin in Amsterdam (1844, destroyed in 1911), roused a fierce debate in the architectural journals. The design was condemned mainly because the outward appearance had nothing to do with the interior of the church, a fundamental mistake according to one of the critics. This condemnation voiced what the rationalists had so often pleaded for: honesty and logic in construction. It was also voiced by the champion of the revival of the Gothic style, J.A. Alberdingk Thijm (1820–1889), who subscribed to the ideas of E.E. Viollet-le-Duc that the only way to overcome "disgusting" stylistic pluralism was to study the logical and humane principles of the Gothic masters of the thirteenth century. This belief was a rejection of the position that stylistic pluralism had the strength to produce a new style in accordance with nineteenth-century life.

Eclecticism was an international architectural language, and that may have limited its influence in the Netherlands during the last quarter of the nineteenth century when there was a revival of the old Dutch style associated with the period around 1600. In a debate between some leading architects, published in the periodical *Bouwkundig Tijdschrift* in 1881, C. Muysken, president of the Society for the Advancement of Architecture, defended his use of the old Dutch style for the castle-like country house Oud Wassenaar in Wassenaar (1879). He pointed out that a lively silhouette in combination with the use of multicolored brick, stone, and slate were perfectly attuned to the surrounding landscape near the dunes. P.J.H. Cuypers defended the Gothic style by pointing out that its building system was the most logical consequence of the rationalistic approach. Others, like J.H. Leliman, argued that the alternative of "Renaissance or Gothic" was not the only possibility; an architect must design for his clients and, therefore, must be flexible in his choice of styles.

A perceived threat to the architectural profession were the engineers from the Polytechnic School in Delft, founded in 1864. H.P. Berlage (1856–1934) was convinced that mere technical work could never become art. In part responding to the challenge from the engineers, he devoted his career to breaking free from the grip of the neo-styles and finding new ways for the architectural profession.

Wim Denslagen

See also Architectural competitions; Architectural restoration; Classicism in architecture; Functionalism in architecture; Nationalism; Neo-Gothic; Postmodernism; Renaissance architecture; Urban planning from 1750 to the present

Bibliography
Bock, Manfred. *Anfänge einer neuen Architektur: Berlages Beitrag zur Architecktonischen Kultur der Niederlande im ausgehenden 19. Jahrhundert.* The Hague: Staatsuitgeverij, 1983.
Groot, A. de. "Rational and Functional Building, 1840–1920." In *Het Nieuwe Bouwen: Previous History*, 23–83. Delft: Delft University Press, 1982.
Rosenberg, H.P.R. *De 19de-eeuwse kerkelijke bouwkunst in Nederland.* The Hague: Staatsuitgeverij, 1972.

Architectural history
See Amsterdam School: Applied arts; Architectural competitions; Architectural criticism, issues of style; Architectural restoration; Berlage, Hendrik Petrus; Classicism in architecture; De Keyser, Hendrick; De Klerk, Michel; De Stijl; Dudok, Willem Marinus; Duiker, Johannes; Functionalism in architecture; Hertzberger, Herman; Koolhaas, Rem; Kramer, Pieter Lokewijk; Kromhout, Willem; Landscape architecture; Neo-Gothic; Oud, Jacobus Johannes Pieter; Post, Pieter; Postmodernism; Public housing; Renaissance architecture (1500–1625); Town halls; Urban planning, before 1750; Urban planning, from 1750 to the present; Van Campen, Jacob; Vingboons, Philips; *Wendingen;* Wijdeveld, Hendricus Theodorus

Architectural painting
Buildings have served as major elements in paintings, prints, and drawings since the sixteenth century in the Netherlands, particularly in the virtuoso perspective views of artists like Hans and Paul Vredeman de Vries. The golden age of this genre was the seventeenth century when artists such as Pieter Saenredam, Emanuel de Witte, Jan van der Heyden, and Job and Gerrit Berckheyde produced painstakingly detailed representations of actual and fantasy architecture as main subjects of compositions. The eighteenth century also had its great practitioners, including Cornelis Pronk, Jan Ten Compe, several members of the La Fargue family, and Hendrik Pothoven.

Various classifications exist within the architectural painting category: church interiors and exteriors, civic building interiors and exteriors, country house exteriors, palace interiors and exteriors, and townscapes. Within each of these categories a composition and its various parts can be topographically correct, imaginary, or a combination thereof. Architectural specialists such as Emanuel de Witte produced both pictures of identifiable church interiors and paintings of fictitious ones throughout their careers. The blending of fantasy and reality within one work is exemplified by Jan van der Heyden's painting in the National Gallery of London juxtaposing two accurately rendered buildings, Nijenrode Castle and the sacristy of Utrecht Cathedral, which are not located together in reality. The resulting work is an evocation of a Dutch urban setting that did not really exist. Architectural paintings of actual buildings in their own surroundings may commemorate a particular place, monument, and/or event. *The Fireworks Pavilion Erected in Honor of the Freedom of Aachen* by Jan Ten Compe is a 1749 painting in The Hague Historical Museum that does all three by recording the Dutch capital's contribution to celebrations of the end of the Wars of Austrian Succession.

Literature concerned with architectural painting usually centers on a particular subset of the genre, such as townscapes or church interiors. An exception is Bob Haak's basic introduction to the various forms of architectural painting in his 1984 survey of Dutch painting. The approaches to interpreting the genre are varied. Many works, including Rob Ruurs' book on Saenredam, and Arthur K. Wheelock's study of mid-century Delft painters, focus on the technical aspects of perspectival illusionism, including the manipulation of various methods of perspective and whether optic devices were used as aids. The 1977 Amsterdam and Toronto catalog grapples with how and why the *stadsgezicht* (townscape) developed, along with issues of topographical accuracy and the differences between the paintings, prints, and drawings of city motifs. Walter A. Liedtke in his 1982 study, traces the artistic and technical developments of church interior images from the Italianate perspectives of Vredeman de Vries, to the "realistic imaginary churches" of Dirck van Delen and others, to the influence of Pieter Saenredam, arriving at the main focus of his book: the flowering of church portraiture in Delft with Gerard Houckgeest (Fig. 42), Hendrik van Vliet, and Emanuel de Witte.

An exhibition catalog and a biography point to the wide diversity of opinion among scholars. *Perspectives: Saenredam and the Architectural Painters of the Seventeenth Century*, is the catalog published in conjunction with a 1991 exhibition held in Rotterdam. The exhibition organizers chose to include only works that fit their interpretation of the seventeenth-century inventory term, "perspective," or a painting whose main purpose was the demonstration of masterly perspective skills. Church interiors are the most numerous of the selections, while townscapes are excluded. The various essays explore the paintings in terms of their artistic development (Jeroen Giltaij and Walter A. Liedtke), the evidence contained in picture collection inventories concerning the artistic and socioeconomic value of "perspectives" (J.M. Montias), and the possible functions and meanings the works held for contemporaries

beyond being mere displays of technical and artistic excellence (Rob Ruurs). Ruurs suggests that an architectural painting may contain religious, social, and political symbolism, but he asserts "there is more to suggest that it was bought for its artistic rather than its spiritual value." As Montias points out, ". . . most of these paintings were owned by true collectors . . . interested in the purely artistic quality of their collections" (Ruurs, 1987: 50).

A very different conclusion is reached by Gary Schwartz and Marten J. Bok in their biography of Pieter Saenredam. They use extensive and varied archival material to "reconstruct" a "historical personality" of the artist. They also attempt to rediscover the perceptions and usage of the buildings rendered. Their goal is to better comprehend Saenredam's art and the issues surrounding its production and purposes, from a point of view as close to a Dutch seventeenth-century one as possible. They found that the paintings were significant to contemporary audiences for their "historical and religious overtones" in addition to their merits as technically superior portraits of buildings (Schwartz and Bok, 1989: 76). Further, they assert that "the main attraction of architectural paintings to their contemporary buyers lay in the buildings and their monuments" (247). What most of these scholars can agree upon is the need for further archival research to help establish a more accurate context for the artists and paintings.

Diane E. Cearfoss Mankin

See also Berckheyde, Gerrit Adriaensz.; Berckheyde, Job Adriaensz.; Delft; House interiors; Illusionism; La Fargue, Paulus Constantijn; Ouwater, Isaac; Pothoven, Hendrik; Pronk, Cornelis; Schouman, Aart; Ten Compe, Jan; Townscapes; Van der Heyden, Jan

Bibliography

Giltaij, Jeroen, and Guido Jansen. *Perspectives: Saenredam and the Architectural Painters of the Seventeenth Century*. Rotterdam: Museum Boymans-van Beuningen, 1991.

Haak, Bob. *The Golden Age: Dutch Painters of the Seventeenth Century*, 152–161. London: Thames and Hudson, 1984.

Liedtke, Walter A. *Architectural Painting in Delft*. Doornspijk: Davaco, 1982.

Macandrew, Hugh et al. *Dutch Church Painters: Saenredam's Great Church at Haarlem in Context*. Edinburgh: National Gallery of Scotland, 1984.

Ruurs, Rob. *Saenredam: The Art of Perspective*. Amsterdam: Benjamins/Forsten, 1987.

Schwartz, Gary, and Marten J. Bok. *Pieter Saenredam: The Painter and His Time*. Maarssen: Gary Schwartz/SDU, 1989.

Wattenmaker, Richard J. et al. *Opkomst en bloei van het Noordnederlandse stadsgezicht in de zeventiende eeuw/ The Dutch Cityscape in the Seventeenth Century and Its Sources*. Amsterdam: Amsterdams Historisch Museum; Toronto: Art Gallery of Ontario, 1977; distributed by Landshoff, Bentveld-Aerdenhout, Holland.

Wheelock, Arthur K. *Perspective, Optics, and Delft Artists around 1650*. New York: Garland, 1977.

Architectural restoration

Restoration of old buildings, meaning the repair of dilapidated parts or reconstruction after calamitous destruction, has always been part and parcel of the art of building. In the nineteenth century, however, restoration of old buildings acquired a special meaning under the influence of nationalistic sentiments. Restoring the remnants of the past was instrumental in the strengthening of national identity. People began to see the importance of medieval architecture, and feared that without some collective effort or governmental support much of this heritage was in danger of being demolished or disfigured by injudicious alterations.

The first to bring charges against the neglect of this heritage was J.A. Alberdingk Thijm (1820–1889) in 1848. Thijm was not alone in the struggle for the preservation of medieval art and architecture; support was also given by Christiaan Kramm, Jan Frederik Oltmans, W.C. Timmerman, F.N.M. Eyck van Zuylichem, Servaas de Jong, W.J. Hofdijk, and C. Leemans. They prepared the way for the triumph of the Gothic revival in the second half of the nineteenth century. The building of new churches in the Gothic style went hand in hand with the restoration of medieval buildings. Important work in this field was done by the architects Th. Molkenboer (1796–1863), H.J. van den Brink (1816–1883), L.C. Hezenmans (1841–1909), F.J. Nieuwenhuis (1848–1919), and Alfred Tepe (1840–1920), but the most influential architect was P.J.H. Cuypers (1827–1921). His friendship with Thijm, and later with the powerful Victor de Stuers (1843–1916), contributed enormously to the influential role he played in the restoration of medieval architecture.

De Stuers is famous for his article "Holland op zijn smalst" (Holland Most Narrow), which appeared in *De Gids* in 1873. It was this article—a fierce accusation against the widespread neglect of the national heritage—that brought about the first governmental involvement in restoration. De Stuers was to become the first appointed official for the preservation of monuments.

As far as the restoration of old buildings is concerned, De Stuers' and Cuypers' policies were authoritative between 1875 and 1916. Their attitude toward the restoration of medieval architecture was deeply influenced by the works and writings of the French architect and restorer E.E. Viollet-le-Duc. In this view, restoration meant the reconstruction of a building as it should have been in its original form. This original form could be discovered by searching for the inner logic of the building system—just as the renowned biologist Georges Cuvier (1769–1832) was able to do when reconstructing an extinct animal from a few bones. Cuvier, as Viollet-le-Duc admitted, was his great example in this scientific method. A dangerous consequence of this highly influential theory was that the actual substance and historic significance of the building was considered to be less important than the hidden rationale of its original builders. Restorations along these principles turned old buildings into new constructions of

nineteenth-century invention, cleared of later additions and decorations. As a result, much of Baroque art and architecture in the Netherlands was demolished and replaced by Neo-Romanesque or Neo-Gothic work. This optimistic attitude toward the past, combining a strong belief in a scientific approach and a dangerous bias toward the Baroque, drove some architects to rectify, enlarge, or reduce old structures in a way that startled a later generation.

Cuypers did not feel the slightest reluctance to add, in 1882, four bays to the town hall of Nijmegen in the style of Herman van Herengrave, who built it in 1555. His restoration of the Romanesque church of Our Lady at Roermond (1864–1879) ended in, among other things, construction of four new towers in the spirit of the original design. In Maastricht he tore down the Baroque west tower (1767) of the Saint Servatius church and redecorated the entire interior. The much-despised eighteenth-century style having been swept out of this church and replaced by splendid new mural paintings after designs by Cuypers, there was no need to repeat the attack on the same church in the twentieth century. But, unfortunately, Cuypers' contribution was also doomed to be destroyed during the last restoration in the 1980s. The history of restoration is full of this sort of repetitious iconoclasm.

The way that architects like Cuypers restored old buildings began to meet fierce opposition at the beginning of the twentieth century. There had been some isolated criticism before. In 1861 Alberdingk Thijm and the well-known man of letters Carel Vosmaer (1826–1888) had protested the project to replace the old braced collar roof of the Ridderzaal (the Knights' Hall) in The Hague by an iron Neo-Gothic construction. In 1866 the architect J. Gosschalk protested the completion of the medieval ruin of the Castle of Brederode in Santpoort. Victor de Stuers, head of the Department for Cultural Affairs since 1875, was severely attacked in 1879 by the judge J. VerLoren, who reproached him for supporting a method of restoration in which the point of departure was not the monument in its existing form but some more or less vague idea about how it could have been originally. What seemed most objectionable to VerLoren was the falsification of an old building by adding new parts in the same style—for instance, the projected addition of an imitation sixteenth-century tower to a city gate in Hoorn.

At the end of the nineteenth century comparable protest from writers in other countries like John Ruskin, William Morris, A.N. Didron, J.P. Schmit, and A. Leroy-Beaulieu nourished a new approach to the preservation of historic buildings. One could hear the voice of Ruskin echoing in the words of the Dutch architect A.W. Weissman (1858–1923) when he said in 1886 that "one should aim at conservation, not restoration."

The new generation of the twentieth century adopted a set of restoration principles that was published in 1917. A leading role in the preparation of these *Grondbeginselen* (Fundamental Principles) was played by the art historian Jan Kalf (1873–1954), who inherited the powerful official position from Victor de Stuers in 1918. Kalf could, in his position, rely on the sympathizing support of a newly founded State Commission with architects like H.P. Berlage, K.P.C. de Bazel, and J.Th.J. Cuypers, the son of P.J.H. Cuypers.

The new principles stated that, among other things, a restoration should respect the contributions of all periods, without any stylistic prejudice, and that missing parts should be rebuilt in the style of our own age. "To conserve is better than to renew" is the way Kalf summarized the new principles.

A weak spot in this new approach was the introduction of modern design in historic architecture. The stress the new generation laid on conservation was admirable, but in other respects the difference with the old method turned out to be a change in style—new design instead of imitation. This led to new discussions and, after several experiments with modern additions to old buildings, to uncertainties about the possibility of rendering life back to old architecture with the help of modern artists. The moderns also lacked the support of the general public; people did not like the incongruous modern forms. Restoration architects who believed in reconstruction based on historical research had far more success.

After World War II, Kalf was disillusioned by the fact that his principles of 1917 had lost their inspiration, so he took the initiative to form a new commission for the evaluation of the old principles. This commission of 1948 came to the conclusion that restoration architects should have the right to reconstruct the original design even when this could lead to the destruction of later additions, if the original design was of historic interest. The commission admitted that this principle had produced many mistakes in the past, but also a lot of pleasurable restorations. In that period of rebuilding when so much had been damaged during the war, there was no time to split hairs—work had to be done and one had to be pragmatic.

In the 1950s and 1960s, the decades of large-scale slum clearance, restorations were still limited to the more important monuments. This changed radically in the 1970s, when slum clearance was replaced by urban renewal. This change of policy, with financial support from the government, led to the revitalization of more than 13,000 houses in areas of historic interest between 1970 and 1985. In the 1970s and 1980s the restoration of the more important (listed) historic buildings was greatly intensified by considerable subsidies, so that in 1990 almost all major monuments had been restored (Fig. 9 and Fig. 10).

The spirit of the 1948 commission governed these restorations: Reconstruction of the original form was allowed if it contributed to the historical interest of the monument. A strange consequence of this attitude was that, for instance, the old center of Amsterdam appears older in aspect than thirty years ago. This is due to the replacement of much nineteenth-century detail by eighteenth-century reconstruction.

Wim Denslagen

See also Alberdingk Thijm, Josephus Albertus; Art history, history of the discipline; Nationalism; Neo-Gothic; Stained glass; State patronage, public support; Urban planning, from 1750 to the present; Vosmaer, Carel

Bibliography

Denslagen, Wim. *Architectural Restoration in Western Europe: Controversy and Continuity.* Amsterdam: Architectura and Natura, 1993.

Tillema, J.A.C. *Schetsen uit de geschiedenis van de Monumentenzorg in Nederland.* The Hague: Staatsuitgeverij, 1975.

Archives

The data collected in archives are an essential resource for researching the historical and cultural background of works of art, their makers, their patrons, and their uses. Public archival repositories in the Netherlands exist at three levels: central, provincial, and local. In The Hague the General State Archives (Algemeen Rijksarchief) contains the archives of the central government from 1576 onward. In all of the capitals of the modern twelve provinces of the country are State Archives for the Province (Rijksarchieven in de Provincie); in The Hague this is combined with the Algemeen Rijksarchief. Here the archives of the provincial States in the time of the Republic (sometimes also of the medieval government) and of the more recent provincial government are kept.

Many municipalities have their own archives or participate in joint ventures with other municipalities, the Regional Archives (Streekarchieven). Where these local archives exist, the registers of the local notaries from the late sixteenth century onward (before 1811 notaries did not function in all of the provinces), the local judicial archives to 1811, and the church registers of baptisms, marriages, and burials before 1811 can be consulted there. In other cases these records are transferred to the Rijksarchieven in de Provincie. The archives of the local municipal governments in some cases go back to the thirteenth century. In many municipal archives there are also records of abolished craftsmen's guilds (including the artists' Guilds of St. Luke) and convents.

Apart from the archives from public bodies, which since the Archives Law of 1962 are required to be transferred to public repositories, private archives are kept at all levels, as well as collections of maps, drawings, prints, photographs, and films. Records containing information for genealogical research, especially, are indexed, including the church registers of baptisms, marriages, and burials, and the notarial registers before 1811. In some cases not only names are indexed but also other subjects, such as professions. The most recent guide to the archives is the multivolume survey edited by L.M.Th.L. Hustinx and published between 1979 and 1992. The archives and collections in each repository in the Netherlands are listed, and it is indicated for each archive whether an inventory or an index exists.

The last volume of this guide gives information about other institutions that keep private archives, among them the Netherlands Architecture Institute (Nederlands Architectuurinstituut) in Rotterdam; the Central Register for Private Archives (Centraal Register van Particuliere Archieven) in The Hague, which collects the data of families, churches, and societies; and the Netherlands Economic History Archive

(Nederlandsch Economisch-Historisch Archief) in Amsterdam, which keeps records relating to companies and businesses.

Florence Koorn

See also Art history, history of the discipline; Rembrandt research; State patronage, public support

Bibliography

Hustinx, L.M.Th.L., ed. *Overzichten van de archieven en verzamelingen in de openbare archiefbewaarplaatsen in Nederland.* 14 vols. Alphen aan den Rijn: Samsom, 1979–1992.

Aristocracy and gentry

The United Provinces of the Netherlands were generally believed to be ruled exclusively by a wealthy, bourgeois regent class whose mercantile empires were centered in the major urban centers of Holland. In truth, the traditional nobility, whether members of the titled aristocracy or of the landed gentry, still wielded a great deal of power and influence—if not always directly in politics and economics, then certainly in art and culture.

Those individuals still considered part of the hereditary aristocracy and gentry in the seventeenth and eighteenth centuries were dwindling in number. By making a break with Spain and becoming a republic, the United Provinces had by 1609 severed ties to any monarch with claims of sovereignty, thus eliminating any possibility of new individuals and families entering the ranks of those already endowed with titles and/or lands by past Holy Roman emperors, Spanish kings, or dukes of Burgundy. According to Nierop, though titles and privileges to lands and jurisdictions could be bought by the affluent middle class, and knighthoods and titles could be bestowed by foreign monarchs, there were still legal and social distinctions between those who inherited their status and entitlements and those whose honors were newly acquired through other means (Nierop, 1993: 22–29).

The most visible members of the high nobility living in the United Provinces were the princes of Orange-Nassau and their relatives. Though they never ruled their home country, the princes at times served officially as *stadhouder*. They emphasized their role as military commanders-in-chief by having themselves depicted leading troops into battle or by merely dressing in armor in formal portraits. In times of crisis, their influence could be enormous, as during the conflicts with Spain in the first half of the seventeenth century and during and after the *Rampjaar* (1672–1673) struggles with France and its allies. At other times, as during the *stadhouderloos* period of 1650–1672, their influence was minimal.

Yet throughout the seventeenth and eighteenth centuries, titled and untitled members of the nobility were representatives in the States General and held local, provincial, and national offices. An example was Johan van Wassenaer van Duivenvoorde (1577–1645), a member of the hereditary gentry class who held several offices in The Hague and was listed as one of its twenty wealthiest residents. Two fine portraits by Jan Mijtens of Johan and members of his family still hang in his castle, Duivenvoorde. One of the portraits has the building itself depicted in the background.

The elegant, courtly works of artists such as Rubens and Van Dyck served as the basic models for representations of the nobility in the Northern Netherlands. This is particularly evident in images of Frederik Hendrik (1584–1647) and his wife, Amalia van Solms (1602–1675) (Fig. 32). They had grand pan-European dynastic ambitions, as evidenced by the arranged marriage between their son, Willem II, and Mary Stuart, daughter of Charles I of England, and by their ambitious building projects and royal art collections and commissions. The Oranjezaal of the Huis ten Bosch in The Hague, with its classicist architecture and elaborate painted interior glorifying the career of Frederik Hendrik, is one of the main extant examples of Orangist royal aspirations. Especially after his ascension to the British throne in 1689, Willem III (1650–1702), following the lead of Louis XIV of France, initiated elaborate building, remodeling, and redecorating projects at his numerous Dutch homes and collected and commissioned art works extensively. The royal palace of Het Loo, now open to the public, is a modest villa (compared to England's Hampton Court or France's Palace of Versailles) full of the accumulated treasures of the House of Orange over the centuries.

The traditional ideas of middle-class sobriety, simplicity, and frugality may have toned down slightly the degree of luxury openly demonstrated by the Dutch aristocracy and gentry as compared to noble families in the rest of Europe. Yet in the last half of the seventeenth century and into the eighteenth century, wealth and a taste for opulence increased among the middle-class elite of the United Provinces, making the differences between depictions of the aristocracy, gentry, and urban patriciate less and less apparent. Artists such as Jan Mijtens, Gerard van Honthorst, and Paulus Potter worked for both noble and bourgeois patrons, often using the same formats for both.

A particularly interesting example is Paulus Potter's 1653 *Equestrian Portrait of Dirk Tulp* in the Six Collection, Amsterdam. It is believed that the horse, body, and background (which includes the castle at Cleves) were originally painted for Johan Maurits van Nassau, relative of the Orange family and *stadholder* of Cleves. But when the hoped-for commission did not materialize, Potter was evidently able to sell the large canvas to Dirk Tulp, inserting that patron's head in the place of Maurits'. An elaborate inscription and heraldic shield on the right foreground tree honor this member of an important Amsterdam regent family. Traditionally reserved for the nobility, equestrian portraits, portraits with castles or country houses in the background (Fig. 31), and heraldry were adopted by middle-class patrons in the seventeenth and eighteenth centuries, often blurring the distinctions between classes, if only in art and not in reality.

No sources in English deal exclusively with depictions of the Dutch aristocracy and gentry as a whole, especially those of the eighteenth century. One needs, instead, to refer to articles and books addressing specific types of Dutch painting that may include depictions of members of the nobility, such as portraiture, images of warfare, or allegorical works.

Diane E. Cearfoss Mankin

See also Classicism in architecture; Country houses and gardens; Court and official portraiture; Eighty Years' War; Gamepiece; History painting; House of Orange-Nassau; Marriage and family portraits; Pastoral; Portraiture; State and municipal art collecting and collections; War and warfare

Bibliography

Boogaart, E. van den, ed. *Johan Maurits van Nassau-Siegen, 1604–1679*. The Hague: Johan Maurits van Nassau Stichting, 1979.

Brenninkmeyer-de Rooy, B. "Notities betreffende de decoratie van de Oranjezaal in Huis ten Bosch." *Oud Holland* 96 (1982): 133–190 (English summary: 186–190).

Fock, C. Willemijn. "The Princes of Orange as Patrons of Art in the Seventeenth Century." *Apollo* 110:214 (December 1979): 466–475.

Marshall, Sherrin. *The Dutch Gentry, 1500–1650: Family, Faith, and Fortune*. New York: Greenwood, 1987.

Nierop, H.F.K. van. *The Nobility of Holland, from Knights to Regents, 1500–1650*. Translated by Maarten Ultee. Cambridge: Cambridge University Press, 1993.

Raaij, Stefan van. *The Royal Progress of William and Mary: Houses and Gardens of Their Time*. Translated by A.P.K. Graafland. Amsterdam: D'Arts, 1988.

William and Mary and Their House. New York, Pierpont Morgan Library. New York: Oxford University Press, 1979.

Armando (born 1929)

The name Armando (Latin: "by arming oneself") is not a pseudonym but a new name that he acquired around 1950. With this name he has, since then, built a reputation as a versatile artist. Armando draws, paints, is a poet, writes prose, and is a sculptor, a journalist, a theater and television producer (together with Cherry Duyns), and an actor. The coordinating theme of his multifarious but unified work is his obsessive fascination with the past, with aggression and violence, and with the beauty of evil. He wrote a few short manifesto-like texts as a member of the Dutch Informal Group (1958–1960) and of the Nul-group (1961–1965).

Armando was born in Amsterdam and lived during the war (1940–1945) in Amersfoort, not far from the German *Durchgangslager* (transit camp). He witnessed the events in and around this camp (called by Armando "the spot") from nearby and they greatly impressed him and also had a great impact on his works of art. For example, his controversial collection of interviews, *De SS-ers* (1967), which he put together with Hans Sleutelaar, grew out of these experiences. He struggles continuously, in his poetry, prose, drawings, and paintings, with the past and deals with memories of World War II, which he often lifts out of the actual situation. The theme of the guilty landscape, which occupies a major place in his visual and literary works, is also a result of these early memories. He sees nature as an accomplice in what happened and calls it guilty because it grows undisturbed and erases all traces.

His early work, drawings from the early 1950s, are partially influenced by Pieter Ouborg and the Cobra group (especially Constant). Soon after, he painted semiabstract and abstract paintings, which he calls *Peintures criminelles, Paysages criminels*, and *Espaces criminels*; they have a rough and thick layer of paint and became monochromatic and austere in the late 1950s. The work of this period coincided with his membership in the Dutch Informal Group, whose members abandoned an expressionistic and emotional concept of art.

The changes in materials around 1960 were far-reaching but were in fact also an extension of the "informal period." As a member of the Nul-group he made works that lacked altogether subjectivity and expression. He presented fragments from reality, such as a wall of automobile tires, or six rectangular tinned plates, painted in red, all the same size, and attached with nails on chipboard.

After the breakup of the Nul-group in 1965, Armando ignored his artistic calling until 1967. He then made rough drawings that suggest landscapes. In the early 1970s he also began to use photography in his work, which reinforces his themes.

Since 1979 Armando has lived and worked in Berlin, the city of the "enemy," where he also started his international career. In the 1980s he regularly exhibited his work outside of Holland, in places such as Berlin, Düsseldorf, Paris, Milan, Venice (Biennale), Kassel (Documenta 7), and New York. Titles of large black and white paintings made in series in Berlin, such as *Feindbeobachting, Gefechtsfeld, Schuldige Landschaft, Fahnen, Preussisch,* and *Kopf* (Observation of the Enemy, Battlefield, Guilty Landscape, Flags, Prussian, and Head), leave no room for doubt about their subject matters.

There is an extensive literature on and by Armando, although a first serious interdisciplinary study about his visual and literary art has yet to be written. For his versatility, in 1985 he received the Jacobus van Looy Award, which is bestowed to crown one's entire *oeuvre*. In 1989 his novel *De straat en het struikgewas* (1988) was honored with the Multatuli Prize.

Peter de Ruiter

See also Cobra Movement (1948–1951); Constant; Nul-group; Ouborg, Pieter; Schoonhoven, J.J.; World Wars I and II

Bibliography

Armando. *Armando uit Berlijn*. Amsterdam: De Bezige Bij, 1982.

———. *De straat en het struikgewas*. Amsterdam: De Bezige Bij, 1988.

———. *Verzamelde gedichten*. The Hague: Nijgh and Van Ditmar, 1964.

———. *Voorvallen in de Wildernis*. Amsterdam: De Bezige Bij, 1994.

Armando. Catalog, Dutch Pavilion, no. 41. Biennale di Venezia, 1984. The Hague: Netherlands Office for Fine Arts, 1984.

Armando: 100 tekeningen. Rotterdam: Museum Boymans-van Beuningen, 1985.

Ferron, Louis, ed. *Armando schilder-schrijver*. Weesp: De Haan, 1985.

Gercken, Günther. *Armando: Die Berliner Jahre*. The Hague: SDU, 1989.

Art criticism, critical issues in the nineteenth century

Art criticism as the discussion and judgment of contemporary art in the public press began in the Netherlands in the first half of the nineteenth century. Not until around 1840 did an initially hesitant reporting develop into criticism in this sense.

For art criticism to begin, publicity must go two ways: A periodical press must exist, and exhibitions must be accessible to everyone. These conditions were met in 1808 with the first exhibition of contemporary art. In support was a series of institutions, created after the French model during France's control of the Netherlands (1795–1813), that were intended to give a structure to the art world. One of these institutions, which continued to exist after 1813, was the Koninklijk Instituut (Royal Institute). As a Dutch *académie*, it organized contemporary art exhibitions, modeled after the example of the French salon, that were held in a different location every two years. After the first quarter of the century, because of increased art production, these exhibitions took place more often and in various cities at the same time.

The criticism that appeared after the first exhibitions was still far from the standard of contemporary French art criticism. Dutch art criticism developed gradually, like that in other European countries. Although everything about the exhibitions was borrowed from the French, the criticism did not entirely hold with existing salon criticism. It went through the same phases as French art criticism after the middle of the eighteenth century.

During the first fifteen years, until about 1825, the reviews of the exhibitions were devoid of any critical judgment; they were merely enumeration and reporting, or, as it was termed, "impartial." Two regular exhibition reporters appeared particularly in this early period, the anonymous "B." and Jeronimo de Vries, art organizer of the city of Amsterdam. They wrote for the two large general-interest magazines, the *Algemeene Konst- en Letterbode* and the *Vaderlandsche Letteroefeningen*. The scrupulous restraint of these first apologetic critics is explained by good manners of the time and by a lack of experience with the genre. As soon as increasing art production made a keener art criticism desirable, "B." and De Vries could not and would not comply and stopped their work.

At that point, between 1825 and 1830, appeared the first art criticism written by literary men, distinguishing itself through a sharp, genuinely critical tone. Their criticism was not published in the well-known general-interest magazines but in a number of new, progressive journals published by young writers. In spite of the brief existence of these small magazines, their influence on art criticism was far-reaching and permanent. The best known of these critics were Jacob van Lennep, Adriaan van der Hoop, and Everard Potgieter, the publisher of the leading periodical, *Gids*. In this phase, art criticism was practiced on an ad hoc basis by various writers. It was, to be sure, a genre for which one could select from a range of forms, such as the letter, the dialogue, or the babbling scribbled impression (this sometimes being in the form of a parody). Not until after 1840 did a single literary man devote himself to art criticism over a longer period.

In the years 1830–1840 stronger reviews were also published in the topical magazines and in the newspapers, which until then had included only reporting pieces without any critical judgments. The increasing art production was certainly also responsible for this. The quantitative supersaturation of the market made a selective art criticism necessary. This was especially demanded on the part of the professional artists with respect to the growing group of exhibiting amateurs who threatened to ruin the market. Most, naturally, saw less necessity for professional criticism of their own work. The majority of critics in this period stayed with less strict judgments. They knew well that there must be distinctions within the enormous output of art, but they were also afraid of offending through strong judgments and condemnation or of doing harm to the artists' livelihood. Instead of criticizing the works of art, they turned against the public, denouncing its unworthiness and great stupidity.

At the end of 1830 magazines specializing in the fine arts were started. The most important were *De beeldende kunsten* (1839), *De Kunstkronijk* (1840), *De spektator* (1843), and *De Nederlandsche kunstspiegel* (1844). In these genuine art magazines, art criticism occupied an obvious place. It was well informed about what was happening abroad and practiced by a number of regular professional critics. With this, art criticism became institutionalized.

Not only was mediocrity exposed, the critics also took a position and often introduced considerations of a more art-theoretical or art-historical nature. They evidenced familiarity with the German (art) philosophical tradition and with French salon criticism, readily picking up on a change in French taste. From the period after 1840 must especially be mentioned the liberal-classicist writer Carel Vosmaer and the Catholic art zealot J.A. Alberdingk Thijm, who with much engagement, knowledge, and a broad cultural vision published numerous reviews.

As criticism became more formalized and critics more or less professional, a full discussion began over the question of how and by whom works of art ought to be judged. The age-old debate over "lay judgment" (are only artists competent to make judgments about art?) was in the first instance settled in favor of the well-informed non-artist. But around 1880 this discussion was once again stirred up. In existence then was a movement of young writers who, grouping themselves around the journal *De Nieuwe Gids*, turned against the old established cultural magazines such as the *Gids*, *De spektator*, and the *Dietsche Warande*—the magazines in which Alberdingk Thijm and Vosmaer, among others, published their art criticism. Coming to the front as critics were Maurits van der Valk, Willem Witsen, and Jan Veth, all painters as well as writers, who on the basis of personal appraisal judged individual works of art. They found that art criticism must not be written from a general cultural view or from ethical conceptions, such as was the case with Alberdingk Thijm and Vosmaer, respectively.

Their art criticism was not directed at the general public, being comprised of neither reporting nor judgment, but was intended for their artist colleagues; in this regard it is best to characterize it as *critique pour la critique* ([criticism for criticism's sake]; Blotkamp, 1990). It followed that their pieces were subjective, sometimes arrogant and, indeed, badly polemicized against the old guard, of whose skill, erudition, and humor they did not always have a good notion.

Around 1890, when both Vosmaer and Alberdingk Thijm were dead, the *Nieuwe Gids* writers acknowledged that their goal was achieved: Young talent was pushed to the forefront, and criticism was practiced with other standards. A leitmotif in nearly all nineteenth-century criticism was the reevaluation of the seventeenth century; for the writers of *De Nieuwe Gids* that was more an attempt to translate the vitality of the seventeenth century into a vitalism of their own. For that and for the great involvement with which artistic quality was propagated, the art critics of *De Nieuwe Gids* are important.

It is remarkable that the continuing discussion of who is competent to make judgments about art should blaze up again in the first decades of the twentieth century. It even went so far that artists' societies such as Arti et Amicitiae in Amsterdam and Pulchri Studio and the Nederlandsche Kunstkring (Netherlands' Art Circle) in The Hague took action against criticism in the press. No critics were admitted to the expositions and even (in 1927) a joint brochure was published that included, among other things, a recommendation to prohibit criticism by law and to keep critics out of exhibitions.

Annemiek Ouwerkerk

See also Alberdingk Thijm, Josephus Albertus; Art criticism, critical issues in the twentieth century; France; Nationalism; State patronage, public support; Van der Valk, Maurits Willem; Veth, Jan; Vosmaer, Carel; Witsen, Willem

Bibliography

Blotkamp, Carel. "Art criticism in *De Nieuwe Gids*." *Simiolus* 5 (1971): 116–136.

———. "Painters As Critics: Art Criticism in the Netherlands, 1880–1895. In *The Age of Van Gogh: Dutch Painting, 1880–1895*. Edited by Richard Bionda and Carel Blotkamp, 82–94. Zwolle: Waanders, 1990.

Hoogenboom, Annemieke. *"De stand des kunstenaars": De positie van kunstschilders in Nederland in de eerste helft van de negentiende eeuw*. Leiden: Primavera Pers, 1993.

Koolhaas-Grosfeld, Eveline, and Annemiek Ouwerkerk. "Bibliografie van vroeg negentiende-eeuwse Nederlandse kunstkritieken." *Oud Holland* 97 (1983): 98–111.

Ouwerkerk, Annemiek. "'Hoe kan het schoone geprezen, het middelmatige erkend en het slechte gelaakt worden?': Nederlandse kunstkritiek in de eerste helft van de 19de eeuw." In *Op zoek naar de Gouden eeuw: Nederlandse schilderkunst 1800–1850*. Edited by Louis van Tilborgh and Guido Jansen, 62–77. Zwolle: Waanders, 1986.

Art criticism, critical issues in the twentieth century

The history of Dutch art criticism in the twentieth century has yet to be written, which is not as strange as it seems. There has been hardly any research done at Dutch universities into the reception of twentieth-century art. Even the history of appreciation of developments within the period—artistic avant-gardes such as Cobra and the Nul-group movement or a trend such as Magic Realism—has never been systematically studied; hence, Holland still lacks a serious study such as the one by Stephen C. Foster on the reception of American Abstract Expressionism.

Neither is there a clear view of the art-critical *oeuvre* of the most prominent Dutch art critics. It is assumed that during the 1920s and 1930s Kasper Niehaus was a prominent art critic of the newspaper *De Telegraaf*, but there is still no overview of his critical art reviews, which makes it impossible to evaluate the status and influence of his work. Jan de Vries has made a serious contribution with his dissertation (1990) on the study of the art-critical views of four critics: Albert Verwey (1865–1937), Albert Plasschaert (1874–1941), Just Havelaar (1880–1930), and Theo van Doesburg (1883–1931). De Vries placed special emphasis in his study on the aesthetic, historical, and social basis for their art criticism and on the principal intellectual influences they had undergone. A future study should consider the reception of modern art from the perspective of a larger number of art critics. Such a study would also have to include the work of prominent prewar art critics, such as Willem Steenhoff, Maria Viola, Jan Engelman, Kasper Niehaus, A.M. Hammacher, Pieter Koomen, Henry van Loon, Jo Zwartendijk, and W. Jos de Gruyter. Only then will it be possible to make more-nuanced judgments about the image of the avant-garde that was forming in the periods 1900–1920 and 1920–1940.

The same goes for the postwar developments in the visual arts and the history of their reception. After 1945 several important critics made names for themselves. A.M. Hammacher wrote in the weekly paper *De Groene Amsterdammer*, and Cees Doelman also worked for this paper and for the *Nieuwe Rotterdamse Courant*. Other names are Hans Redeker, Lambert Tegenbosch, W. Jos de Gruyter again, Charles Wentinck, Mathilde Visser, George Lampe, Cor Blok, Rudi Fuchs, Carel Blotkamp, and Anna Tilroe. They have made important contributions to building up the image of modern art in Holland in daily papers and weekly magazines (and occasionally in professional journals). But, again, there is no overview of their work.

Major changes in art criticism in Holland occurred at the end of the nineteenth century; therefore, a study should first of all be written about this period. Between 1880 and 1900 a new generation of painters came to the forefront, the Amsterdam Impressionists. Some of them, such as Willem Witsen, Maurits van der Valk, and Jan Veth, also wrote art reviews in *De Nieuwe Gids* that differ significantly from what people were used to in Holland at the time (namely, the writings of J.A. Alberdingk Thijm). Witsen, for example, focused more than was earlier done on the analysis of a work of art and attached much importance to the task of the art critic to explain it. It is noteworthy that the younger critics were very much engaged with the newer developments in the visual arts, notably with the work of George Hendrik Breitner and Isaac Israëls.

The sense of lyricism that had been so much the hallmark of the *Tachtigers* (as the writers of the 1880s called themselves) continued to determine to an important degree the standard for art criticism well into the twentieth century. This is true, for example, of H.P. Bremmer (1871–1956), who played an important role as adviser to Helene Kröller-Müller about her art collection. It is true that Bremmer was not a critic *pur sang*, but his contributions in the magazine *Beeldende Kunst*, of which he was the editor, exerted a tremendous influence on entire generations of artists and art lovers and, therefore, ought to be part of any study of prewar art criticism.

A prominent art critic such as Albert Plasschaert was, in his reviews, often interested in the expression of the feelings of the artist. Plasschaert was, like Willem Steenhoff (1863–1931), very reserved about abstract art, although Steenhoff, who wrote for years in the weekly paper *De Amsterdammer*, was very much aware of the significance of Mondrian and the qualities of the work of Kandinsky and Picasso. But the emotional expressiveness of a work of art remained very important to him, and in this sense he does not really differ from the *Tachtigers*. This is also the reason he could not support wholeheartedly the most prolific avant-garde artists around 1910–1915; he found their work ultimately too cool, not passionate and intimate enough.

In the years directly following World War II and during the 1950s, the question of the right of abstract art to exist dominated Dutch art criticism. The policies of Willem Sandberg worked as a catalyst in this respect. The notorious Cobra exhibition near the end of 1949 in the Stedelijk Museum in Amsterdam acted as a starting signal for the many critical and often hostile reactions toward his exhibition policies. During the mid-1950s, artists such as Pieter Ouborg and Willem Hussem were still defending abstract art.

Conservatives, however, critically monitored the latest developments. It was of great importance to art critics such as J.M. Prange of the newspaper *Het Parool* to discredit the exposition policies of Sandberg as much as possible. Prange was, for example, very negative about an exhibition of Jackson Pollock (Amsterdam, Stedelijk Museum, 1958). He and others saw Pollock as the personification of America: superficial and amusing. Art reviews contain expressions such as *kwasterij* (smear), *klodders* (daubed), and *zinloze bezigheid* (senseless busyness).

The art reviews of the 1950s are, therefore, often very subjective and prejudiced. This was to some degree the result of the limited understanding of art critics of the newest developments abroad. The writings of those critics who were aware of these foreign developments—such as Hammacher, the director of the Rijksmuseum Kröller-Müller in Otterlo, and W. Jos de Gruyter—were much more balanced.

Around 1960 there was finally an extensive stream of information about the latest trends in the visual arts. Several art critics closely followed the art of the 1960s—Pop Art, Neo-Realism, Zero, Post-Painterly Abstraction, Hard Edge, and Minimal Art. Those art forms at the same time called for a more objective art criticism. The first signs of this were the reviews written by George Lampe for *Vrij Nederland*, a weekly magazine. Lampe, who is an artist himself, can best be described as a transitional figure between the subjective art critic and the objective critic who wants foremost to inform his readers. He believes that the critic has to use clear and simple language to describe the most recent developments. He considers it to be his task to explain clearly what the artists are doing, what motivates them, and how and why their work develops as it does.

The polemic caused by the 1966 exhibition *In het licht van Vermeer, vijf eeuwen schilderkunst* (In the Light of Vermeer, Five Centuries of Painting) in the Mauritshuis in The Hague was characteristic of the state of Dutch art criticism in the 1960s. The controversy was about whether the critic should first of all inform the public about the origin and historical context of the work of art, or whether he should first of all judge the quality of the work. The older generation opted for the latter. The younger generation—including many more art-historically trained academics—used the historical background of a work of art more and more in its artistic evaluation.

A few art critics in the 1960s, such as Rudi Fuchs, gained a reputation for making in-depth formal analyses of works of art. Fuchs' formal analyses as well as those by others—following, incidentally, Clement Greenberg, notable American critic of the mid-twentieth century who expanded formal analysis to formulate an explanation of Abstract Expressionism—went so far that the poet-critic K. Schippers noticed to his dismay in his own art criticism that language had taken the place of the actual works of art.

Art criticism of the 1970s continued along the same path of providing a more factual account to inform the public. Critics used the knowledge they acquired during their art-historical studies. They were able, therefore, more than ever before, to use the tradition of modern art to evaluate contemporary art. As a result, the qualitative appreciation of art has become secondary. This also explains the languor of art criticism in the 1980s and 1990s. The work of young artists, such as Marlene Dumas (Fig. 47), René Daniels (Fig. 29), and Henk Visch, no longer provokes the kind of fierce discussions as did, for example, the work of Pieter Ouborg in the 1950s. At most, critics agree that they are important artists. Burning issues often failed to materialize for that reason in the 1980s.

Peter de Ruiter

See also Alberdingk Thijm, Josephus Albertus; Amsterdam Impressionists; Art criticism, critical issues in the nineteenth century; Art history, history of the discipline; Avant-garde; Cobra Movement; Contemporary art; Daniels, René; Dumas, Marlene; Feminism, feminist issues; Hammacher, A.M.W.J.; Kröller-Müller, Hélène; Magic Realism; Nul-group; Ouborg, Pieter; State and municipal art collecting and collections; State patronage, public support; Van der Valk, Maurits Willem; Van Doesburg, Theo; Veth, Jan; Visch, Henk; Witsen, Willem; World Wars I and II

Bibliography

Broek, Corine van den, and Peter de Ruiter. "W.J. Steenhoff als pleitbezorger voor moderne kunst in het weekblad *De Amsterdammer, 1907–1914.*" *Kunstlicht* 1 (1993): 19–23.

Ebbink, Hans, and Peter de Ruiter, eds. "Kunstkritiek in Nederland, 1945–1985." *Metropolis M* 5/6 (1986): 25–129.

Heij, J.J. "Kritiek bekritiseerd: Kunstenaars contra critici, 1919–1932." *Nederlands Kunsthistorisch Jaarboek* 28 (1977): 105–126.

Visser, Martijn. "Mathilde Visser: Kunstcritica en markante persoonlijkheid." *Jong Holland* 3 (1988): 16–22.

Vries, Jan de. "Gemeenschap en wereld-ik, geheel op de wijze der kunst: Nederlandse kunstkritiek en moderne kunst circa 1900–1920: Albert Verwey, Albert Plasschaert, Just Havelaar, Theo van Doesburg." Ph.D. diss, University of Amsterdam, 1990.

Wintgens, Doris. "Reacties in de kranten op het beleid van het Stedelijk Museum." In *De doorbraak van de moderne kunst in Nederland de jaren 1945–1951.* Edited by Willemijn Stokvis, 93–106. Amsterdam: Meulenhoff/Landshoff, 1984.

Art history, history of the discipline

Art history became a professional and academic discipline in the Netherlands only after 1870. It was and is closely related with the world of museums and such national institutions as the Rijksdienst voor de Monumentenzorg (Government Office for Monument Preservation) and the Rijksbureau voor Kunsthistorische Documentatie (RKD) (Bureau for Art Historical Documentation). This has bred a preference for the study of the national heritage, and this is encouraged because Dutch museums do not have a great deal of foreign art.

Although from the beginning of the nineteenth century the Germans developed new forms of art historical writing in which archival, biographical, cultural historical, and art historical data have been integrated, the Dutch used only the biographical model until late in the nineteenth century. The first book in which Dutch art was presented as a survey and not a series of artists' lives was *Nederlands schilderkunst van de 14e tot de 18e eeuw* in 1874, by the literator J. van Vloten. The pioneers in the scientific exercise of the profession were Abraham Bredius (1855–1946) and Cornelis Hofstede de Groot (1863–1930), who coupled rigorous research in the archives with a great knowledge of works of art. They, indeed, put Dutch art on the map. Bredius, who was not academically educated and rooted in the tradition of connoisseurship, was director of the Royal Picture Gallery, also called the Mauritshuis, in The Hague from 1889 until 1909. Among his most important works are the *Künstler-Inventare: Urkunden zur Geschichte der holländischen Kunst des XVIten, XVIIten und XVIIIten Jahrhunderts* (1915–1922) and his *oeuvre* catalog of Rembrandt (1935). Hofstede de Groot, who was educated as an art historian in Leipzig, was the assistant director of the Mauritshuis from 1891 until 1895 and director of the Prentenkabinet (Print Room) in Amsterdam from 1895 un-

til 1898. Between 1907 and 1928 he put together the *Beschreibendes und kritisches Verzeichnis der Werke der hervorragendsten holländischen Meister des XVIIten Jahrhunderts.*

Hofstede de Groot was in museum service for only a short time and worked primarily as a free-lance writer of articles, books, and appraiser's reports for the art trade. His portrait from 1923, in which he is sixty years old, gives a good picture of his life as an independent scholar (Fig. 11). In his home in The Hague he had access to a great private archive with documents and visual material regarding Dutch art until 1700. He left this archive to the Dutch state when he died, and in 1932 it became the basis for the RKD in The Hague. As of 1993, the RKD possessed 3.5 million photographs and reproductions, including foreign art. The RKD is the largest institution of its kind in the world; the library, with 380,000 books, periodicals, and catalogs, is the largest art historical library in the Netherlands. The RKD is also the publisher of *Oud Holland,* the oldest Dutch art historical journal (begun in 1883).

Through their efforts, Bredius and Hofstede de Groot set the tone for the practice of art history in the Netherlands: Their activities arose from the need of museums for attributions and systematic cataloging of their collections. The beginning of architectural history as a practice was, in the same way, connected with the protection and systematic cataloging of Dutch buildings of the past. An important role in cataloging national monuments was played by the (Koninklijke) Nederlandse Oudheidkundige Bond (KNOB), which was founded in 1899. Before World War II especially, the KNOB (Royal Dutch Archeological Society), through its journal *Bulletin van de KNOB,* was one of the most important art historical forums in the fields of Dutch architecture, sculpture, and archeology. The agitation of the KNOB against the neglect of the national patrimony in the arts resulted in 1918 in the establishment of the Rijksbureau (after 1947, Rijksdienst) voor de Monumentenzorg, which took responsibility for making an inventory of the monuments and any connected restoration.

At the end of the nineteenth century, the only institution offering a higher education in art history was the Rijksacademie in Amsterdam, where the art critic J.A. Alberdingk Thijm was appointed professor of art history in 1876. At Dutch universities art history was not a separate field of study, but part of a much broader instructional program that also included aesthetics. The first teaching chair in this area was established at the Gemeenteuniversiteit (City University) of Amsterdam, but it was occupied only by classicists. At the beginning of the twentieth century, art history became an independent academic discipline, but the appointment of ordinary professors was limited for a long time to one, Willem Vogelsang, in Utrecht in 1907. Vogelsang, who was educated abroad and later connected with the Rijksmuseum, trained numerous Dutch art historians. Vogelsang's main interests were not in archival work or the art of the seventeenth century. He promoted the formal analytical approach of Heinrich Wölfflin and researched the still underdeveloped field of

Northern Netherlandish miniatures; he was also a specialist in the applied arts and sculpture.

At the other Dutch universities, only extraordinary professors or lecturers were appointed. In 1926 a specialist on the Netherlands was appointed for the subjects of aesthetics and art history in Nijmegen. Professorships of art history were created at the Universities of Amsterdam in 1917 (but this position was held by a classicist until 1928), Leiden in 1946, Nijmegen in 1955, and Groningen in 1952, and at the Free University (Vrije Universiteit) in Amsterdam in 1965. Special chairs were established in the fields of architectural history (the first one was in Utrecht in 1958), modern art (the first one at the University of Amsterdam, 1963), iconology (Utrecht, 1955), and applied arts (Leiden, 1964). The Dutch institutes in Rome (founded in 1903) and Florence (1955) function as art historical research centers.

In 1993 there were twenty-four art history chairs at Dutch universities, including the Technical Universities in Delft and Eindhoven and the Open University in Heerlen. In addition, seventeen university professors and sixty-eight associate professors have been appointed. They are mainly responsible for research and for the education of the estimated 2,500 students who have chosen art history as their major. In 1938 the Vereniging van Nederlandse Kunsthistorici (VNK) (Society of Dutch Art Historians) was founded.

Although Erwin Panofsky received his first honorary degree from the University of Utrecht in 1938, the iconological method started slowly in the Netherlands. The first iconologists and iconographers were G.J. Hoogewerff, John B. Knipping (*Iconografie van de Contra-Reformatie in de Nederlanden*, 1939–1940), Gerard Knuttel, and Hans van de Waal (*Drie eeuwen vaderlandsche geschieduitbeelding, 1500–1800: Een iconologische studie*, 1952). Van de Waal developed a classification system for pictorial material based on iconography called Iconclass. After the appointment in Utrecht of Vogelsang's successor, J.G. van Gelder, in 1946, and William S. Heckscher as a professor of iconology in 1955, the practice of iconology in the Netherlands began to correspond to the method of Panofsky. Panofsky's "disguised symbolism" became the starting point for the iconological interpretation of Dutch art of the seventeenth century by Van Gelder's and Heckscher's students, such as Joshua Bruyn, Jan Emmens, and Eddy de Jongh (*Zinne-en minnebeelden in de schilderkunst van de zeventiende eeuw*, 1967).

In the mid-1990s, the ideas of the so-called Utrecht School are the subject of discussion and revision. Younger iconologists such as Eric Jan Sluijter, Reindert Falkenburg, and Jan Bedaux employ methods of interpretation that do not so strongly emanate from the hidden moralistic meanings in realistic-looking works of art. They study the implications that existing pictorial traditions have for certain themes, and also the relation between the representation and the daily reality in which objects and people functioned.

Hoogewerff was also a pioneer in researching the social context of art production, as shown in his *De geschiedenis van de St. Lucasgilden in Nederland* (1947). Into the 1990s, this aspect enjoys an increasing interest—for example, in the research of Gary Schwartz, Annemieke Hoogenboom, Marten Jan Bok, and Bram Kempers. Social-scientific research into art production is also being done in the departments for cultural studies at several Dutch universities. The Boekman Foundation in Amsterdam is the most important archive for materials about the overlapping provinces of art, government, and society, particularly where Dutch art of the twentieth century is concerned.

The Rembrandt Research Project gave an important stimulus to strengthening the ties between art history and the restoration sciences (something that had existed longer within architecture history and was more obvious). In the scientific examination of art the Netherlands holds a unique place because of the application in the late 1960s of infrared reflectography by J.R.J. van Asperen de Boer in Groningen. With this method, drawings underneath the paint can be made visible, which allows a more accurate attribution.

In the field of architectural history, the Netherlands holds an important place internationally in research on urban planning and spatial planning, as it is done by Ed Taverne in Groningen and Auke van der Woud at the Free University in Amsterdam. The theoretical debate on architecture received new impetus with the appointment in the 1990s of Alexander Tzonis at the Technical University in Delft.

Until the 1950s, most professors in the Netherlands came from the museums or institutions like the RKD and the Rijksdienst voor de Monumentenzorg. There is still a close cooperation between the universities and the museums, more so than between departments themselves. Working committees or seminars (*werkgroepen*) of art history students prepare catalogs and exhibitions—for example, *Tot leering en vermaak: Betekenissen van Hollandse genrevoorstellingen uit de zeventiende eeuw*, shown in the Rijksmuseum in 1976 with the cooperation of the Kunsthistorisch Instituut (Art History Institute) of the University of Utrecht. This was the first museum exhibition of iconological research on seventeenth-century Dutch genre painting. Also in cooperation with Utrecht was the 1978 exhibition *Kunstenaren der Idee: Symbolistische tendenzen in Nederland* in The Hague's Gemeentemuseum, in which the spiritual backgrounds of the Dutch avant-garde around 1900 were examined. Since the 1970s, faculty members and students in the art history institutes of the Universities in Groningen and Leiden have been researching Italian art in Dutch collections. A recent publication in this area was the 1989 catalog *The Birth of Panel Painting: Early Italian Paintings in Dutch Collections*, produced by the exhibiting Groninger Museum, Groningen, and Bonnefanten Museum, Maastricht.

New chapters in Dutch art history have been written in the catalogs of several exhibitions: *Het Vaderlandsch Gevoel: Vergeten negentiende-eeuwse schilderijen over onze geschiedenis* (Rijksmuseum 1978, with the Art History Institute of the University of Amsterdam) examined forgotten nineteenth-century history paintings and the patriotic sentiments expressed in them; *Industrie en vormgeving in Nederland 1850–1950* (Stedelijk Museum Amsterdam 1985, with the art history departments of the Universities of Utrecht and Leiden) took a look at the relation between industrial and design changes from the mid-nineteenth to the mid-twentieth century; and, in a bulky publication, *Glas in Lood in Nederland 1817–1968* (a joint production of the State Office for Visual Arts, the Free University in Amsterdam, and Leiden University in 1989) opened the window on the history of stained glass. Dutch art historians are preeminently focused on researching Dutch art and, to a lesser degree, Italian art. Extraordinary, therefore, because of the non-Dutch subject was the exhibition *Entartete beeldhouwkunst: Duitse Beeldhouwers 1900–1945*, dealing with so-called degenerate art and artists in Germany, that was organized by students at the Art History Institute in Nijmegen; the exhibition traveled to several Dutch and German museums in 1991–1992.

Until the 1960s, Dutch art historians showed a happy diligence for writing surveys. A book cherished by the general public was *Kunstgeschiedenis* (1923; reprinted 1949) by E.H. Korevaar-Hesseling. Larger, with much attention to non-Western art, was the *Algemene Kunstgeschiedenis* (1941–1951) compiled by F.W.S. van Thienen. Also written by professional art historians and intended for a broad audience were the illustrated books in the series *De schoonheid van ons land*, volumes and monographs in the series *Heemschut* and *Palet*, and the loose-leaf publications of *Openbaar Kunstbezit*. In addition, several surveys and reference books on Dutch art were published, among them G.H. Marius' *De Hollandsche schilderkunst in de negentiende eeuw* in 1903 (translated as *Dutch Painters of the Nineteenth Century* in 1979); W. Martin's *De Hollandsche Schilderkunst in de zeventiende eeuw* (1936); G.J. Hoogewerff's *De Noord-Nederlandsche Schilderkunst* (1936–1947); G. Knuttel's *De Nederlandse schilderkunst van Van Eyck tot Van Gogh* (1938). The list continued to grow with H.E. van Gelder as editor of *Kunstgeschiedenis der Nederlanden van de Middeleeuwen tot onzen tijd* (1935, 2nd edition 1946); E.H. ter Kuile as editor of *Duizend jaar bouwen in Nederland* (1948–1957); Anne Berendsen's *Het Nederlandse interieur 1450–1820* (1950); and A.B. Loosjes-Terpstra's *Moderne Kunst in Nederland 1900–1914* (1959). Then, this activity decreased. Bob Haak's *The Golden Age: Dutch Painters of the Seventeenth Century* in 1984 was an exception to this. The academic world has left the popularizing of art history to the media, schools, and museums and is creating a distinct profile for itself through specialized studies.

The academic practice of art history in the Netherlands shows increasingly the tendency to concentrate on the national heritage and the foreign (that is, Italian) art connected with it. The research on sculpture and the applied arts takes a modest second place; the study of old inventories for information about houses and material culture (the so-called Rapenburg Project) being done in Leiden is exceptional as far as the scope and problems to be solved are concerned. The Nota Deltaplan Cultuurbehoud in 1990 (a government bill earmarking more future funding for the inventory, conservation, and restoration of objects of historical, art historical, and scientific value in Dutch museum collections) and the government's striving to cluster scientific research into larger contexts around some themes promote the concentration on

Dutch art. It is debated whether so strong a focus on Dutch art will serve a purpose in the long run or is desired in this international and multicultural age. The flourishing research and teaching traditions in the field of non-Western art (particularly Indian and Indonesian) at the Universities of Amsterdam and Leiden have come to an end because of government budget cuts during the 1980s.

The strong orientation to museum practice brings a certain one-sidedness to the method. Questions that are less concerned with the tangibility of objects, such as are current in the "New Art History," have received little attention in the Netherlands, though this is changing. Interest is growing in the history of the discipline, but there still does not exist a good article or book about the historiography of the history of art covering the period of the last hundred years.

Marlite Halbertsma

See also Alberdingk Thijm, Josephus Albertus; Architectural restoration; Archives; Emblems and emblem books; Feminism, feminist issues; Genre painting, seventeenth century; Rembrandt research; Reputation of Dutch art abroad; State and municipal art collecting and collections; State patronage, public support; Technical investigations; Van Gogh, Vincent: Diverse Views; Writers on art, eighteenth century; Writers on art, sixteenth and seventeenth centuries

Bibliography

Emmens, Jan, and S.H. Levie. "The History of Dutch Art History." In Jan Emmens *Verzamelde Werken: Kunsthistorische Opstellen II*, 35–40. Amsterdam: Van Oorschot, 1981.

Grijzenhout, Frans, and Henk van Veen, eds. *De Gouden Eeuw in perspectief: Het beeld van de Nederlandse zeventiende-eeuwse schilderkunst in later tijd*. Nijmegen: SUN, 1992.

Halbertsma, Marlite, and Kitty Zijlmans, eds. *Gezichtspunten: Een inleiding in de methoden van de kunstgeschiedenis*. Nijmegen: SUN, 1993. (German Translation, Berlin, 1995)

Hoogenboom, Annemieke. "De introductie van kunstgeschiedenis aan de Nederlandse universiteiten: De voorgeschiedenis van de leerstoel van Willem Vogelsang." In *De Kunstwereld: Produktie, distributie, en receptie in de wereld van kunst en cultuur*. Edited by Ton Bevers et al., 78–102. Hilversum: Verloren, 1993.

"Kunstgeschiedenis in Nederland: Vier pleitbezorgers." Theme volume. *Kunstlicht* 14 (1993).

"Kunsthistorische bibliotheken en beelddocumentatiesystemen." Theme volume. *Open: Vaktijdschrift voor bibliothecarissen, literatuuronderzoekers, en documentalisten* 24 (September 1992).

Meijer, B.W., and C.E. van Rappard. *Kunsthistorisch onderzoek in Nederland. Rapport van de Verkenningscommissie voor de Kunstgeschiedenis*. Zoetermeer: Ministerie van Onderwijs en Wetenschappen, 1993.

Scheller, Robert W. "From Meerman to Marrow: Two-Hundred Years of Miniature Studies." In *Masters and*

Miniatures: Proceedings of the Congress on Medieval Manuscript Illumination in the Northern Netherlands. Edited by Koert van der Horst and Johann-Christian Klamt, 3–18. Doornspijk: Davaco, 1989.

Art museums, exhibitions

See Art history, history of the discipline; State and municipal art collecting and collections

Art schools, education

See Amateurs, art academies, and art associations before the nineteenth century; Applied arts; Art history, history of the discipline; Feminism, feminist issues; Rembrandt School; Sculpture (1795–1945); State patronage, public support

Artists' confraternities and craftsmen's guilds

The origin of independent artists' guilds derives from the medieval trade guilds of which they were members. Such guilds had strong religious affiliations and duties. St. Luke, believed to have been a painter and to have made portraits of the Virgin Mary, became the patron saint of artists' guilds. For this reason, some artists' guilds functioned as religious confraternities as well as craftsmen's guilds. Early records for these organizations remain scarce, particularly for the period prior to the mid-fifteenth century, but the guilds' activities became increasingly divorced from their religious practices during the following century.

The development of these local civic guilds forms no uniform pattern in terms of which crafts and occupations were affiliated with the guild. At Utrecht, the Saddler's Guild (active already in 1304) also included manuscript illuminators, carvers, and painters. The use of similar materials or practice of related activities justified the affiliation. Painters, for instance, might polychrome leather shields. In other instances, the guild members' occupations were more closely aligned. Painters, glassmakers, carvers, printmakers, and embroiderers all belonged to the Gouda St. Luke's Guild authorized by the city government on January 31, 1487. The Gouda St. Luke's Guild also constituted itself as a religious confraternity with the permission of the pastor of the St. Jan's Church and established an altar dedicated to St. Luke in the church.

Although the Iconoclastic riots in the Netherlands destroyed such altars during the 1560s and 1570s, guild loyalties could remain active as was the case with a relic owned by the Haarlem St. Luke's Guild. Although the guild lost its altar in the St. Bavo Cathedral, it retained the relic of St. John the Baptist, which had been given to the guild by the painter Barthel Pons in 1517. By 1627 the St. Luke's deacon, the painter Frans Pieterz. de Grebber, gave the relic to a Dominican friar for safekeeping. Five years later, Salomon de Bray and his fellow guild administrators attempted to recover it from its new home in Brussels. They argued that the relic belonged to the guild, not the confraternity of St. Luke, and that it represented property of Haarlem. Such polemics might have disguised the pro-Catholic sentiments of some guild members.

Although the external factors of government control and the particular religious and political loyalties of members could differ, the internal organizational structure of the guilds did exhibit consistency. These guilds functioned to ensure the adequacy of the training that apprentices received, the quality of the work produced, and the welfare of the crafts. Their members consisted of guild brothers, or masters, who were judged competent to run their own shop, and their servants or apprentices, known as *knechts*.

The deacons, or administrators of the guild, were chosen from among the brothers and were subject to the power and authority exercised by the city government. In some instances, the city appointed the deacons, as at Delft, and provided quarters for the guild to meet. The guild bylaws (subject to the approval of the city authorities) identified the crafts and occupations appropriate to the guild, listed the means by which one could become a master in the guild, and regulated the relationship between master and apprentices. The extent to which local governments restricted importation of works of art from out of town or curbed the number of registered masters permitted within the guild indicates local policy toward the art market as much as did their own commissions from local or foreign artists.

Guilds commonly required that artists and artisans become members prior to selling their work or taking on apprentices in the city. This meant paying yearly dues and adhering to the guild regulations about such issues as number of apprentices. Within the guild structures various occupational hierarchies existed. At Delft, for instance, printers and booksellers were quite well-to-do, with painters and glassmakers falling in the next range, and furniture makers below. Thus, Montias suggests that membership in the Delft St. Luke's Guild is fairly typical of a medium-size artistic community under effective guild control with substantial continuity in its social organization during the sixteenth and seventeenth centuries.

The exigencies of the Dutch Revolt did disrupt the functioning of the St. Luke's Guild in some cities, forcing their reconstitution during the Twelve Years' Truce with Spain (1609–1621). Under the impetus of the guild members, it became the occasion as well for augmentation or revision of the bylaws. Attention was focused upon limiting and controlling the flow of goods from the South and closer regulations of artistic practice. In some cases by the seventeenth century, the painters in such guilds attempted to distance themselves and form independent confraternities or corporations. Thus, the painters from The Hague St. Luke's Guild, who successfully applied for independent status in October of 1656, preferred to call themselves a brotherhood or confraternity rather than guild. The drawing academy, Pictura, established in 1682 under their administration, exemplifies the members' efforts to professionalize the curriculum.

By government decree in December of 1798, all craftsmen's guilds were officially dissolved. The response of the city governments, guilds, and their members demonstrated a slow compliance and differing positions over their future. In the ensuing discussions about reformulation of the guilds during the next decade, the mandate for artists to be members of such guilds was discarded. A steady decline of the existing St. Luke's Guilds took place at Haarlem (1798), Amsterdam (1811), Leiden (1812), and Delft (1833). The philanthropic activities of the Rotterdam guild allowed its continued function until 1885.

The history of artists' confraternities and craftsmen's guilds has of necessity focused upon individual cases. Additional studies like Montias' socioeconomic study of the artists and artisans of Delft in the seventeenth century are needed, not only for an understanding of the structure of art markets and civic and private patronage, but also to reexamine the characterizations of the fine and applied arts.

Carol Janson

See also Amateurs, art academies, and art associations before the nineteenth century; Applied arts; Delft; Gouda; Haarlem; Leiden; Religion of artists; Religious orders and their patronage; Utrecht

Bibliography

Hoogewerff, G.J. *De geschiedenis van de St. Lucasgilde in Nederland.* Amsterdam: P.N. van Kampen and Zoon, 1947.

Montias, John Michael. *Artists and Artisans in Delft: A Socioeconomic Study of the Seventeenth Century.* Princeton, NJ: Princeton University Press, 1982.

Artists' Initiatives (1970–1990)

Artists' initiatives became an accepted phenomenon around 1980. Other expressions for the same phenomenon are *vrijplaats* (sanctuaries) and "the alternative circuit," and it was characterized as *fabriekskunst* (factory art) at a documentary exhibition in 1982 ('s Hertogenbosch, De Moriaan). What it means for the artists are spaces that they have entire control over, and over which they can set their own conditions for use in artistic expression. The initiatives differ from other artists' alliances or organizations in that a platform is made available to all artists, not only the founders of those initiatives. A characteristic feature is the experimental policy, which is focused on forms of art and methods of presentation that are often less accepted by museums. The Netherlands has many of these artists' initiatives. They are vital stimuli to the ambience of cities and have contributed to both the cooperation between artists and their headstrong attitude, which often becomes known only afterward through galleries and museums.

Many of the initiatives are housed in former factories. De Fabriek in Eindhoven derived its name from just such a factory. Several middle-size manufacturing companies were closed during the late 1970s because of economic recession, resulting in empty factory buildings. The existence of these were a sheer torment for young artists who had just left the academy and were looking for a studio. It was not uncommon at that time, with its prevailing Punk mentality (and a national housing shortage), for individuals to break into and occupy empty houses. At a certain point they also began to break into and occupy these larger empty spaces. This happened in several cities in the Netherlands, and always where there was an academy of fine arts. Once these empty spaces had been taken over, the idea of a mere studio was often abandoned for the

more idealistic notion of an exhibition location.

Artists' initiatives such as W139 in Amsterdam, the above-mentioned De Fabriek in Eindhoven, and Artis in 's Hertogenbosch were at first tolerated by their local governments, then legalized, and, subsequently, subsidized. But other places did not survive. Aorta began in Amsterdam in 1982 but was discontinued when the building was demolished in 1988. Oceaan in Arnhem was discontinued for the same reason, while Stichting Air in Amsterdam disappeared even when the state subsidy remained forthcoming. The Droparchief in Hoorn, named after the candy factory in which it was first housed, moved to a sixteenth-century church on De Achterstraat in the same city and kept its name. The address is often taken as a title of defiance or mockery and is sometimes kept after a move: V2 (Vuchterstraat 234) moved first to a different street address, and in 1994 to a different city (from 's Hertogenbosch to Rotterdam). Some initiatives have been stopped because the initiator wanted to pursue a different career.

When looking back at the last decades, it makes sense to call Agora Studio (Maastricht, 1972–1985), In-Out Center (Amsterdam, 1972–1974), and Corps de Garde (Groningen, 1976–1985) artists' initiatives although they were not called that at the time. The most important initiatives were De Zaak (Groningen, 1979–1988), Droparchief (Hoorn, 1979), HCAK (The Hague, 1980), De Fabriek (Eindhoven, 1980), Het Apollohuis (Eindhoven, 1980), Lokaal 01 (Breda, 1981), V2 ('s Hertogenbosch, 1981), W139 (Amsterdam, 1981), Stelling (Leiden, 1981), Aorta (Amsterdam, 1982–1988), Sponz (Amsterdam, 1982–1984), Makkom (Amsterdam, 1983–1988), Hooghuis (Arnhem, 1985), De Bank (Enschede, 1985), Oceaan (Arnhem, 1987–1991), Artis ('s Hertogenbosch, 1983), Air (Amsterdam, 1989–1993), Casco (Utrecht, 1990), and Het Wilde Weten (Rotterdam, 1992). But a full list would be longer. For a congress of artists' initiatives, organized by De Fabriek on March 26, 1994, eighty initiatives were contacted.

The expression "set their own conditions" means first of all a noncommercial goal, which makes a natural enemy of the art gallery as institution. The work process is often ranked higher than the work already made. It often happens that artists are given the opportunity to work for many days on a project, while the final project is shown only for a short time. The opening occurs only at the very end, or the whole project culminates in a single presentation on a Saturday evening. Although the initiatives cannot claim any exclusive rights for the installations, there is no doubt that more fire, more water, more earth, and more darkness have passed through their spaces than anywhere else.

It is mostly beginning artists who show in this circuit. The contacts are a result of friendships. The quality of the work, therefore, varies. An initiative is like a breeding ground where artists work together and discuss art, and where new points of view and new techniques take root. The initiatives from the 1970s were the cradle for performance, video, and communications art. When the In-Out Center in Amsterdam closed, the Stichting Apple (Apple Foundation), which itself is not an artists' initiative but has close affinities to them, took up the torch. During the first half of the 1980s, the new places were characterized by a burst of different activities—Aorta, especially, caused the art world to tremble. Besides exhibitions, there were also performances by bands and poets, presentations of films, auctions, occasional fashion shows, and debates and dinners. The euphoria of such a newly conquered and freely adaptable space provokes such a neo-Dadaistic frivolity.

During the second half of the 1980s the emphasis was on the question of presentation. The well-groomed look goes hand in hand with carefully designed printed materials and with attention to theory. Some places hardly show their "underground" anymore; they have fully developed into regular institutions that can hardly be distinguished from ordinary galleries. This distinction is, of course, more difficult to realize on the smaller scale of a former local store (De Bank, Enschede; Oranjerie, Rotterdam) than it is in a former cigar factory (De Fabriek, Eindhoven; Artis, 's Hertogenbosch), a former theater (W139, Amsterdam), or an old school building (Lokaal 01, Breda). Large buildings require a thorough answer to their spatial conditions, which promotes experimentation.

But the attitude of autonomy remains the same. The self-determination that such places provide enables the artist more than anywhere else to control the context and interpretation of his or her work, resulting in an integrity that is at times also enticing to more-established artists. Different generations of artists have conscientiously created an image that radically differs from the more common image of the subservient artist who is subsidized by the government. The irony is that such initiatives were initially supported by individual contributions of BKR-users (the Beeldende Kunstenaars Regeling—Regulation for Artists of Visual Arts—which existed until 1987) and, later, through subsidies from local and state government.

Many publications have appeared in this peculiar circuit: books that describe the course of activities, but also periodicals such as the handsome journal *Drukwerk de Zaak*, which was considered by De Zaak as an extension of its platform. While most artists have withdrawn themselves at one time or other from these organizations to work independently, the founders of De Zaak think of their Initiatives as a product of their artistry.

Tineke Reijnders

See also Contemporary art (1980–1990); State patronage, public support

Atlas, atlases

The word atlas refers to a collection of maps bound together. The term was first used by Gerard Mercator (Gerard de Kremer, 1512–1594) in his atlas that was published posthumously in 1595. Credit for creating the first atlas is, however, usually given to Abraham Ortelius (Abraham Ortels, 1527–1598), who conceived of a work in 1570 in which each map was engraved to conform to a uniform size and format. Antwerp led the world in atlas production during the late 1500s, but Amsterdam became dominant in the seventeenth century. Several types of atlases were produced: world, country, sea, and city or town atlases.

The need for atlases was fueled by burgeoning global exploration, scientific advances, and international trade. As sailors, merchants, and travelers collected new information, geographers and cartographers improved their maps. Binding maps into folio volumes provided ease in handling and kept groups of maps in order. The first maps were on vellum, but printed maps became increasingly popular. Maps engraved on copper plates could be modified easily by burnishing out incorrect information and adding new data. Although not as durable as vellum maps, printed maps were ideally suited for offices where merchants charted the safest routes for their ships and geographers instructed sea captains. Sumptuous atlases consisting of many volumes were designed as gifts for royalty and for the *kunstkammer* (private art collection) of the wealthy. Costly atlases contained maps that were highly decorative and often ornamented with designs by popular artists. The maps were watercolored and gilded by special artists, in Dutch *afsetter van caerten*, the most famous of whom was Dirck Jansz. van Santen. Such precious maps were then gathered together with decorative frontispieces and placed in costly bindings of moroccan leather or violet velvet. Bindings of the bookbinder Albert Magnus were considered the most precious. To personalize the atlas, an owner could have his coat of arms stamped in gold on the cover. Many collectors had special cases built to hold and display their atlases.

The first comprehensive world atlas was Ortelius' *Theatrum Orbis Terrarum*, published by the Plantin Press, Antwerp, in 1570. This atlas contained fifty-three maps. By 1612 it was a commercial success, having been reprinted in several languages and in over forty editions. In competition with Ortelius' atlas was that of Gerard de Jode, the *Speculum Orbis Terrarum* (Mirror of the World, 1578). De Jode bound sixty-five maps in his atlas, but his efforts were overshadowed by the popularity of Ortelius' work. Mercator, the famous geographer, prepared an atlas that appeared in 1595.

The first sea atlas was published by Lucas Jansz. Waghenaer in 1584, the *Spieghel der Zeevaert* (Mirror of Navigation). It was produced in French, Latin, and German and reprinted many times. In 1592 Waghenaer published a second sea atlas, *Thresoor der Zeevaert* (Treasure of Navigation).

Atlas production in Amsterdam during the seventeenth century was dominated by several families, the most famous being those of Hondius, Visscher, Blaeu, and De Wit. Jodocus Hondius (Josse de Hondt, 1563–1612) in 1604 purchased the plates to Mercator's atlas. Hondius added additional maps and commissioned Peter Montanus to write a text to accompany the maps. The atlas was published in several languages, and in 1607 a less expensive pocket edition was issued. After Hondius' death, his wife and sons, Jodocus II and Henricus, carried on the work Jodocus had begun, expanding the Mercator-Hondius Atlas to ten volumes by 1658.

Claes Jansz. Visscher (1587–1652) published an atlas of the Netherlands in 1623. After his death in 1652, Visscher's son, Nicolaes, and his grandson, Nicolaes II, published *Atlas Contractus* in 1657, *Atlas Minor* in 1682, and *Atlas Major* in 1702. The firm was dissolved after the death of Nicolaes II's widow. Many of the copper plates were purchased by Pieter

Schenk (1645–1715), who continued to publish them.

By 1630 atlas production reached an all-time high, with the atlases of Blaeu being the most highly prized. Willem Jansz. (1571–1638), who published under the name Blaeu after 1620, began as an instrument and globe maker. He had studied under the Danish astronomer Tycho Brahe, and from 1634 to his death he was the official cartographer to the Dutch East India Company. Blaeu is known for a sea atlas published in 1608, *Het Licht der Zeevaerdt* (The Light of Navigation), *Atlantis Appendix* published in 1630 with sixty maps, and *Atlas Novus* of 1635. Joan Blaeu (1596–1673), Willem Jansz.'s son, published a monumental world atlas containing six-hundred maps, *Atlas Major*, and also an atlas of town plans.

In the latter part of the seventeenth century, Frederick de Wit (1630–1706) produced elegant sea, world, and town atlases. The maps show high-quality engraving enriched by splendid color. In the eighteenth century the best known world atlases were those of Schenk and Valk and Covens and Mortier.

Several Dutch publishers are specifically known for their sea atlases: Jacob Colom (1600–1673), Anthonie Jacobsz. (1606/7–1650), and Pieter Goos (1615/6–1675). Johannes van Keulen (1654–1715) edited one of the most popular sea atlases, *De Nieuwe Groote Lichtende Zee-fakkel* (The New Great Sea Torch), which was revised and expanded well into the eighteenth century.

Shirley K. Bennett

See also Cartography; Exotica; Prints, collecting; Prints, publishers; Trade, exploration, and colonization overseas

Bibliography

Allen, Phillip. *The Atlas of Atlases*. New York: Harry N. Abrams, 1992.

Amsterdam Historical Museum. *Gesneden en gedrukt in de Kalverstraat: De kaarten-en atlassendrukkerij in Amsterdam tot in de 19e eeuw*. Utrecht: HES, 1989.

Koeman, C. *Atlantes Neerlandici: Bibliography of Terrestrial, Maritime, and Celestial Atlases and Pilot Books, Published in the Netherlands up to 1880*. 5 vols. Amsterdam: Theatrum Orbis Terrarum, 1967–1971.

———. *Collections of Maps and Atlases in the Netherlands: Their History and Present State*. Leiden: E.J. Brill, 1961.

Vries, Dirk de. "'Chartmaking Is the Power and Glory of the Country': Dutch Marine Cartography in the Seventeenth Century." In *Dutch Marine Art of the Seventeenth Century*. Edited by George S. Keyes, 60–76. Cambridge: Cambridge University Press, 1990.

Vrij, Marijke de. *The World on Paper*. Amsterdam: Theatrum Orbis Terrarum, 1967.

Avant-garde

If avant-garde is defined as that which is ahead of its time and rejects conventional thinking, then it is proper to speak of a Dutch avant-garde at the beginning of the twentieth century. Amsterdam Impressionism and Symbolism, however modern, did not contend against the traditional in art. It is true that George Hendrik Breitner had a reproduction of Manet's *Olympia* hanging in his studio as an illustration of his modernity, but he himself never painted a similar commentary on the art of the past.

Jan Sluijters committed the first public assault on academic principles in 1907. His inducement was the withdrawal (on the grounds that he had made Fauvist work in Paris) in December 1906 of a four-year Prix de Rome (a national grant) that had been awarded to him earlier by the Rijksacademie. In reaction, Sluijters in 1907 purposely entered his most controversial canvases in the members' exhibition of the conservative art association in Amsterdam. Because they, too, were rejected, he launched a public battle between supporters and opponents of modern art. Among those supporting him were Piet Mondrian and the critic Conrad Kickkert. From the interaction between the work of Mondrian and Sluijters, and the orientation in the art of Vincent van Gogh, there next arose in 1908–1909 a revitalizing, strongly coloristic, disciplined way of painting—still after nature. This so-called luminism was termed Amsterdam luminism by Loosjes-Terpstra (1959) on account of its further diffusion among the artists belonging to the St. Lucas society in that city in 1908–1910. The appellation supposed, however, more homogeneity than there really was: Mondrian was already working with a concept of art formed by theosophy, while Sluijters tended toward a general expressionism.

In 1910 Kickkert, Mondrian, Sluijters, and Jan Toorop founded the Moderne Kunstkring (Modern Art Circle) with the objective of organizing exhibitions of exclusively contemporary artists and showing them in the context of the international avant-garde. It is obvious after the events that the foreign art exhibitions of the Kunstkring (at the Amsterdam Stedelijk Museum, 1911–1913) were definitive for the character of the ensuing mainstreams in Dutch modern art.

The first exhibition (1911), with entries from Braque, Picasso, and Le Fauconnier among others, was inducement for Mondrian to move to Paris. His study of Picasso's and Braque's Cubism led to later Neo-Plasticism and the ideas of De Stijl group. For the following two Kunstkring exhibitions, works were selected primarily from the Cubists of Montparnasse (especially from Henri La Fauconnier), together with works of Futurism—even then represented in the Netherlands—and the early works of Wassily Kandinsky, which were an influence on the stylistic "laggards" such as Jan Sluijters and Leo Gestel. This foreign art formed the basis for later abstractionist, partly nonfigurative, essentially expressionist conceptions of art represented in groups like Het Signaal (1916) and De Branding (1917) and the Bergen School (ca. 1913–1935). In a general sense, this expressionism is further evident as a dominant concept in a large part of Dutch modern art during the interwar period, and it was also responsible for the return to figuration at this time.

Anita Hopmans

See also Bergen; Breitner, George Hendrik; De Branding; De Stijl; Gestel, Leo; Mondrian, Piet; Sluijters, Jan; Toorop, Jan

Bibliography

Adrichem, Jan, van. "The Introduction of Modern Art in Holland, Picasso as *Pars pro Toto.*" *Simiolus* 21 (1992): 162–211.

Hopmans, Anita. *Jan Sluijters, 1881–1957: Aquarellen en tekeningen.* 's Hertogenbosch: Noordbrabants Museum; Zwolle: Waanders, 1991.

Ligthart, Arnold. "Le Fauconnier en de Europese Avant-Garde." In *Henri Le Fauconnier: Kubisme en Expressionism in Europa*, 13–65. Haarlem: Frans Hals Museum; Bussum: Thoth, 1993.

Loosjes-Terpstra, A.B. *Moderne Kunst in Nederland, 1900–1914.* 1959. Reprint. Utrecht: Veen/Reflex, 1987.

B

Backer, Jacob Adriaensz. (1608–1651)

Jacob Backer was born in 1608, the son of a Mennonite baker, Adriaen Dircksz., in Harlingen in Friesland. Three years later, after the death of his mother, Jacob and his father moved to Amsterdam, where his father remarried. Around 1625 Jacob returned to Friesland to study with Lambert Jacobsz. in Leeuwarden. The reason he did not stay in Amsterdam for his artistic training may have been personal: Lambert Jacobsz. was Mennonite like the Backers, and he was probably well acquainted with them. Jacobsz., who had started his career in Amsterdam, had other pupils besides Backer in those years. The much younger Govaert Flinck (born 1615) studied alongside him, and both young men traveled to Amsterdam around 1632 to launch their painting careers. Flinck continued his studies with Rembrandt, but Backer set himself up as an independent painter, although he must have been connected, as was Rembrandt, with Hendrick Uylenburgh's academy. Uylenburgh, too, was a Mennonite. That Jacob Backer had a successful start as a portrait painter is clearly shown by the commission he was honored to receive in 1633 from the regentesses of the Amsterdam Orphanage to paint their group portrait (Amsterdam Historical Museum).

Like that of most of the younger painters in Amsterdam between 1630 and 1640, Backer's work of the 1630s shows a strong influence from Rembrandt, who was the most prolific painter in Amsterdam at the time. This influence is clearly seen in Backer's earliest history paintings—for example, *John the Baptist Admonishing Herodes and Herodias* from 1633 (Leeuwarden, Fries Museum)—and in his portraits, an outstanding example of which is the *Portrait of Johannes Wtenbogaert* from 1638 (Amsterdam, Rijksmuseum). Nevertheless, Backer's style of painting differs strongly from Rembrandt's. Already in the 1630s his brushwork was far more fluid than most Dutch painters and was more dependent on the work of Flemish contemporaries such as Gonzales Cocques or Jacob Jordaens. A possible reason for this might have been a visit he made to Antwerp around 1638.

From 1640 until his death in 1651, Backer was held in high esteem. He was particularly successful as a portrait painter. In 1642 he finished his group portrait of the *Company of Captain Cornelis de Graeff* for the Kloveniersdoelen, the meeting hall of Amsterdam's musket-shooting civic guards. Among the other painters given highly important commissions to paint group portraits for the same location were Rembrandt and Bartholomeus van der Helst. In 1645 Backer was commissioned to paint an allegorical painting of the Dutch Republic for the *stadholder*, Frederik Hendrik, for his castle in Buren. Backer's portraits in the 1640s clearly fit in with the currently fashionable "van Dyckian" court style. This elegant and decorative portrait type suited him extremely well. In his history paintings, which show a tendency for Arcadian subjects, he was even more sublime (Fig. 12). As one of the originators of classicism, his influence on other history painters in Amsterdam, like Jacob van Loo, Abraham van den Tempel, Johannes van Noordt, and Jan van Neck, was enormous.

Peter van den Brink

See also Pastoral; Rembrandt School

Bibliography

Bauch, K. *Jacob Adriaensz. Backer, ein Rembrandtschüler aus Friesland.* Berlin, 1926.

Brink, P. van den et al. *Jacob Adriaensz. Backer.* Forthcoming. (1997).

Sumowski, W. *Gemälde der Rembrandt-Schüler.* Part I. Landau, Pfalz, 1983.

Bakker Korff, Alexander Hugo (1824–1882)

A native of The Hague, Alexander Hugo Bakker Korff was educated as a history painter in Antwerp before settling in Leiden in 1856 to work almost exclusively as a genre painter. His admiration for the seventeenth- and eighteenth-century Leiden *fijnschilders* is apparent in his preference for highly finished, small paintings of middle-class domestic life in which there is a careful rendering of textures and surfaces. His depictions of elderly women in genteel, bourgeois surround-ings—modeled on his two spinster sisters and the house that he shared with them—are often presented with gentle humor and a touch of irony as reflected in the chosen titles. An ex-ample is *Under the Palms* (1880; Amsterdam, Rijksmuseum) in which two elderly ladies admire a potted palm on a stand and, are titilated by thoughts of an exotic paradise. Bakker Korff's work enjoyed a great popularity with the nineteenth-century art-buying public, and he frequently made different versions and copies of his paintings as well as watercolors and drawings (sometimes made after a painting and recording the name of the purchaser). Abroad, his work was compared to that of Meissonnier.

Sheila D. Muller

See also Leiden

Bibliography

A.H. Bakker Korff. Leiden: Stedelijk Museum De Lakenhal, 1958.

Bionda, Richard, and Carel Blotkamp, eds. *The Age of Van Gogh: Dutch Painting, 1880–1895.* Zwolle: Waanders, 1991.

Bas-relief painting

Named in the Netherlands in the eighteenth century and known thereafter as *witjes*, as a play on the perfector of this subject, Jacob de Wit, these grisaille paintings were designed as part of a decorative room scheme to give the illusion of sculpture in marble, plaster, or stucco. The inventor of these large-scale paintings is not known, but the illusion was cer-tainly developed in Italian, French, and Flemish art before the seventeenth century and followed the fashion for the classi-cal decoration. The device was used by Dutch artists of that period to augment their decorations with the illusion of sculp-ture since this art form was less prevalent on a grand scale than in neighboring countries.

In the art of European Mannerists, sculpture was de-picted in paintings, and also in porcelain, tapestries, and other decorative arts. From the sixteenth century, Dutch painters specialized in paintings of architecture, including church in-teriors, carefully creating the effects of light on sculpture shown in these spaces. The increase in scale to life-size painted representations of sculpture by Dutch painters, in works whose sole purpose was sculptural illusion in architectural settings, satisfied the requests of patrons who wished to em-bellish their houses with sculpture without the necessary cost or space. Further, these paintings fused with and extended the architectural space and decorative schemes of the rooms.

As the Royal Court in The Hague during the early sev-enteenth century had a preference for Flemish painting, the influences of Rubens, Jordaens, and others on some Dutch artists of the time was significant. In the work of these paint-ers can be found bas-relief and other sculptural illusions. Moses van Uyttenbroeck is given credit for introducing bas-relief paintings into the scheme for the palace of Frederik Hendrik at Honselaarsdijk in 1638, according to Staring. For

the Huis ten Bosch, which was built in 1645, the architect and painter Jacob van Campen and Constantijn Huygens created a decorative scheme that included paintings imitating stucco reliefs in the ceiling of the Oranjezaal.

In the eighteenth century, Jacob de Wit's paintings of bas-relief sculpture in white and gray helped unify the decorative elements of the architecture and the illusionistic wall and ceiling paintings of the rooms. De Wit's decorations incorpo-rated grisaille paintings as overmantels (also known as chimneypieces), overdoor panels, and as inserts bordering ceiling panels. He made *witjes* for the Huis ten Bosch in 1738 and in 1749 and incorporated grisaille borders in his Amsterdam Town Hall mural work. Some of his most beau-tiful grisailles for domestic settings were for the house at Herengracht 168, Amsterdam. Few of his *witjes* remain in their original settings. Not many Dutch eighteenth-century paint-ers continued De Wit's grisaille painting format. Two who did were Dirk van der Aa (1731–1809) and Hendrik Willem Schweickhardt (1746–1797), both of whom were equally fac-ile at room decoration, animal and miniature paintings, and landscapes.

Roger Mandle

See also De Wit, Jacob; House of Orange-Nassau; Huygens, Constantijn; Illusionism; Van der Aa, Dirk

Bibliography

Fremantle, Katherine. *The Baroque Town Hall of Amster-dam.* Utrecht: Haentjens, Dekker, and Gumbert, 1959.

Gelder, J.G. van. "De schilders van de Oranjezaal." *Nederlands Kunsthistorische Jaarboek* 2 (1948–1949): 118–164.

Mandle, R. *Dutch Masterpieces of the Eighteenth Century: Paintings and Drawings, 1700–1800.* Minneapolis: Minneapolis Institute of Arts; Toledo: Toledo Museum of Art; and Philadelphia: Philadelphia Museum of Art, 1971.

Staring, A. *Jacob de Wit, 1695–1754.* Amsterdam: P.N. van Kampen, 1958.

Belgium

The countries of Belgium and the Netherlands experienced numerous artistic crosscurrents in the nineteenth and twen-tieth centuries. In 1815, after the defeat of Napoleon, the Northern and the Southern Netherlands were declared a con-stitutional unity. After 1830, when Belgium separated from the Kingdom of the Netherlands and established its own monarchy, the two countries grew apart in terms of their na-tional politics, religion, and economies. This also had conse-quences for the visual arts. In the second half of the nineteenth century the relationship between representatives of the for-merly closely related painting schools generated a fruitful in-teraction. On the one hand, old characteristics were confirmed and strengthened; on the other hand, the seeds for essential innovations were able to germinate. Since the 1840s both Dutch and Belgian painters sought to make their fortune in the neighboring country. Broadly speaking, the Dutch interest in Belgium was more of a profit-seeking sort at first. Dutch artists went there for their education or for the art market, which was brisker in the South than in the North. Until World War I, the picturesque aspect of Holland was important to Belgian painters: Adolf Dillens, Xavier Mellery, and Theodoor Verstraete came mainly for the traditional clothing and the old towns; a few others, among them Franz Courtens, came for the landscape.

In the nineteenth century, when the art of both the Northern and the Southern Netherlands was measured against the standard of the Golden Age of the seventeenth century, the old differences in character between the schools was an important aspect of art criticism. In fact, the old controversy involving Rembrandt versus Rubens (or realism versus idealism, introversion versus extroversion, Calvinism versus Catholicism) was in this respect still the model for discussion. Typical "Dutch" realism set an important standard for the Dutch school, more than did idealizing history painting, which was a less thriving affair in the North. Painters like Jan Willem Pieneman, H.A. van Trigt, and H. Egenberger were unable to get beyond a literal representation of the subject. In Belgium, however, history painting became very popular in the nineteenth century. "Grand art" visualizing poetry and allegories was produced under the direction of the great coryphaei Gustave Wappers, Nicaise de Keyser, Antoine Wiertz, Louis Gallait, and Henri Leys. Belgian art received international acclaim for the first time at the World Exposition of 1855 in Paris. The work of Henri Leys made an especially strong impression, while the Dutch school made a poor showing.

In the 1830s and 1840s the most successful painters of genre and landscape in the North as well as the South (for example, B.C. Koekkoek, Andreas Schelfhout, Petrus van Schendel, Eugène Verboeckhoven, and Louis Verwée) remained trapped in their imitations of the seventeenth century. In reaction to this, a new generation at the end of the 1840s started to look with new eyes—that is to say, their own eyes— at nature. From the moment that innovation and personal vision started to play a greater role, the specific characteristics of both schools were given more profound consideration and exploited in art criticism.

The French critic Théophile Thoré (alias William Bürger), who lived as a political refugee in Brussels between 1849 and 1860 and regularly visited and wrote about the Dutch museums, was one of the earliest to call attention to the parallels with the situation in the seventeenth century. In an article on the International Exposition in London in 1862, he gave examples of the cultural connections between the Southern and Northern schools in the Golden Age: Jacob Jordaens went to The Hague to carry out a prestigious project for the *stadholder* Frederik Hendrik; Adriaen Brouwer moved from Haarlem to Antwerp; and the great Frans Hals was a *flamand hollandisé* ("Dutchified Fleming"). The friendly exchange between the two countries had continued, wrote Thoré, and he gave contemporary examples: the popular painter Adolf Dillens from Ghent searched for his subjects in

Zeeland; and the Dutchman Willem Roelofs painted his landscapes of the surroundings of Dordrecht while living in Brussels. But, Thoré emphasized, the distinctive characters of both schools had *not* changed.

The nationalism apparent in Dutch and Belgian art criticism reached its peak in the 1870s. Since the 1860s cultural relations between North and South had awakened feelings of nationalism, and the question of whether or not nationalism in the arts existed dominated the discussions at cultural gatherings. A perspective on Belgian–Dutch cultural relations at the end of the nineteenth century is complicated by the Flemish self-consciousness that more and more played a role in it. Belgium is often seen (not least of all by the inhabitants themselves) as a border area between two cultures, Germanic to the north and Latin to the south. With this view, Flanders' chances of becoming the epicenter of a clash in the last decade of the nineteenth century increased. From an artistic perspective, the situation from about 1850 until World War I is as follows: Brussels stands for everything that is oriented toward France and the avant-garde; in contrast, Antwerp is called the center of idealism and the old-fashioned German romantic tradition. In addition, the tradition of Flemish realism from Jan van Eyck to Pieter Bruegel is another line of artistic and cultural demarcation that continues to today. The modern Belgian artist Roger Raveel, for example, still derives his references to reality from this tradition. Exactly these qualities have been related to the Flemish movement for some time. The pan-Germanic, even fascistic, consequences of this, which are often generalized by Dutch historians and art historians, are only partly valid here. The issue is a historical and cultural one that has its origin not so much in a pro-German as in an anti-French attitude. The form of realism that is sustained by the search for a distinctive Flemish identity is the same realism that since the 1890s has been persistently used to connect with the Northern Netherlands in the cultural domain.

The Dutch who moved to Belgium to get an education in the nineteenth century settled in either Antwerp or Brussels. The reason for this was not only that the education was free in Belgian academies while it was not in the Netherlands (the argument that is often cited in the literature), even though this surely played a role, as did the fact that Antwerp was geographically in a favorable position to the Netherlands. More important was that the Antwerp academy, which was the favorite of the Dutch into the 1880s, enjoyed an outstanding international reputation due to the great Belgian history painters who taught there: Wappers, De Keyser, and later Karel Verlat. In principle it was not the landscape painters but the genre painters who came to study in this bastion of romanticism, even though some of them, like Jacob Maris and Jan Voerman, later developed in the direction of landscape. Some of the most famous Dutch students at the Antwerp academy were Laurens Alma Tadema, Jacob and Matthijs Maris, Albert Neuhuijs, Otto Eerelman, and August Allebé, who later became director of the Rijksacademie in Amsterdam. Jacob Smits from Rotterdam, who took part of his education at the academy in Brussels, settled in Belgium in 1889 and became influential as a teacher at the Antwerp academy. Smits created a furor with his expressionistic scenes with religious content. He is one of the few Dutch painters in Belgium for whom the concept of a "Dutch school" begins to have less meaning after a time.

A unique case is Vincent van Gogh, who studied for a very short time—from December 1880 until April 1881—at the academy in Brussels. In January 1886, after he painted his *Potato-Eaters* in North Brabant, Van Gogh entered the academy in Antwerp, but he left within two months. In retrospect it is clear that his stay at the academies in Belgium was not very successful.

In the 1840s, Brussels became the site of a more settled Dutch artists' colony than Antwerp, where the interest of painters did not extend beyond the academy. In Brussels, they came for more than an academic education, even though more than two-hundred Dutch students registered between 1842 and 1884. With the exception of the brothers David and Pieter Oyens, and Jacob Smits, who registered in 1860 and 1875, respectively, it was the artists who entered the Brussels academy only at the beginning of the 1880s, Jan Toorop and Antoon Derkinderen, who are the most interesting for the history of Dutch art.

The landscape painters worked mainly outside of official circles. Willem Roelofs was an important magnet during his forty-year stay in Brussels. He advised P.J.C. Gabriël, H.W. Mesdag, C.N. Storm van's Gravesande, and others. Because of his relatively early familiarity with the ideas of the *plein-air* painters of the Barbizon School and their application in his own work, Roelofs has been viewed as a founder of The Hague School in the Netherlands (Fig. 58). He is also considered an innovator in Belgian art. In 1880, reflecting on fifty years of art in Belgium, the influential Belgian critic Camille Lemonnier identified Roelofs, Théodore Fourmois, Francois Lamorinière, and Martinus Kuytenbrouwer, another Dutchman, as the first artists to create the personalized landscape through their painstaking observation of nature.

Described as *"Parijs in het klein"* (a smaller version of Paris) by the Dutch landscape painter Gerald Bilders, Brussels was, for Dutch painters, even more attractive as a cultural capital than as an educational center. Thanks to the presence of many French exiles (Thoré-Bürger, Victor Hugo, and Charles Baudelaire, among others) who took refuge in Brussels, an erudite atmosphere prevailed. Moreover, power in Belgium was strongly centralized, with Brussels as the nucleus. Nobility, court, government—in short, a rich clientele—greatly contributed to a flourishing art trade. After 1850, the same French paintings that could be seen at the Paris salon were often seen at the salons held every three years in Brussels. In the Netherlands during those years, foreign participation at the exhibitions was limited to a great number of representative Belgian painters and a more modest delegation from Düsseldorf and Munich. The large quantity of Belgian entries to the Dutch exhibitions obviously indicates that there was considerable knowledge of the Southern school in the Northern Netherlands. The contacts with Belgian painters were mainly a result of personal efforts by some artists. For example, Johannes Bosboom, who later became very influen-

tial as a painter of church interiors, was an industrious intermediary between both schools of painting in the beginning of the 1840s. He visited the Belgian exhibitions yearly and was current in his knowledge of the Brussels art world. We know from his correspondence that he moved in Freemasonry circles in Antwerp, along with many local artists, and that he acted as a go-between for entries to the exhibitions.

Especially interesting with regard to the development of Dutch art are the different initiatives from the progressive artists in Brussels in the second half of the nineteenth century. Laurens Alma Tadema, Willem Roelofs, and C.N. Storm van 's Gravesande were members from the onset of the Société Libre des Beaux-Arts (Independent Society of Fine Arts) that was founded in Brussels in 1868. The theorist, painter, and follower of Baudelaire Louis Dubois, the painter and graphic artist Félicien Rops, and a great many realist landscape painters belonged. H.W. Mesdag was also a member at the beginning of his career and found his own style in this milieu. Important for the conception of The Hague School of painters, for whom a loose brushstroke became increasingly crucial, was the Brussels-based Société Belge des Aquarellistes (Belgian Society of Watercolorists), cofounded by Willem Roelofs in 1855, where many Dutch artists could exhibit. In the Netherlands, separate societies for exhibiting watercolors and drawings were not founded until more than twenty years later in 1876.

Roelofs, who was especially important in connection with the development of realism and its continuation in Impressionism, left Brussels in 1887 to settle in The Hague among his old friends from The Hague School. Meanwhile, in the Belgian capital, a next "generation" of Dutch artists was occupied in playing the role of the avant-garde of that time. Jan Toorop passed through a development from Impressionism to Symbolism to Pointillism in Brussels under the influence of Henry van de Velde, William Degouve de Nuncques, and Théo van Rijsselberghe. Toorop was also an important connection between the Belgian and the Dutch artists. Because of his friendship with poet and theorist Émile Verhaeren and with novelist Maurice Maeterlinck, many of the Belgian Symbolist theories made their way directly into the milieu of Dutch *fin de siècle* artists. Toorop was also a friend of Octave Maus and Edmond Picard, the spiritual forces behind the progressive Belgian artists' group Les Vingt (The Twenty), and as an adviser he helped Dutch artists establish many contacts with this circle and vice versa.

Around the turn of the century and certainly during World War I, Brussels lost its position as the center of the avant-garde. At the same time, the cultural separation between Flanders and the more French-directed part of Belgium widened. It was then that Flanders, whether or not under the influence of a conception of a Greater Netherlands, began to enter into cultural contacts with the Netherlands. Thus, one of the oldest Belgian art magazines, *De Vlaamse School* (The Flemish School), which was written in Dutch, was continued after 1902 as a joint Flemish and Dutch production with the title *Onze Kunst* (Our Art), published by J.E. Buschmann in Antwerp and L.J. Veen in Amsterdam. During World War I, the Netherlands became a haven for Belgian refugees. Three great Belgian Impressionists and Symbolists, Frits van den Berghe, Gustave de Smet, and Rik Wouters, made the transformation to Expressionism in the Netherlands between 1914 and 1921 under the influence of figures such as Le Fauconnier, Jan Sluijters, and Heinrich Campendonk. Back home during the 1920s, as members of the so-called School of Sint-Martens-Lathem, they would form the nucleus of what is considered to be Belgium's most important contribution to modern art: Flemish Expressionism. To show something of the complexity of the history of Flemish art in relation to Dutch art: In Belgium, the fact that the Flemish Expressionists had not opposed the German invasion was seen by some to be a form of collaboration. Even today there are some Flemish authors who want to connect Expressionism to the Germanic ideal of *blut und boden* (blood and soil), an unfairly reductive way to characterize a movement with an international orientation that had its Dutch parallel in the Bergen School.

Saskia de Bodt

See also Allebé, August; Alma Tadema, Laurens; Bergen; Bosboom, Johannes; Derkinderen, Antoon J.; Flanders, Flemish School; France; Gabriël, Paul Joseph Constantin; Hague School, The; Hals, Frans; History painting; Maris, Jacob Hendricus; Maris, Matthijs; Mesdag, Hendrik Willem; Nationalism; Neuhuijs, Albert; Roelofs, Willem; Sluijters, Jan; Symbolism, Symbolists; Tholen, Willem Bastiaan; Toorop, Jan; Van Gogh, Vincent; World Wars I and II

Bibliography

Bionda, Richard, and Carel Blotkamp. *De schilders van Tachtig*. Amsterdam: Rijksmuseum Vincent van Gogh, 1991.

Bodt, Saskia de. "Hendrik Willem Mesdag en Brussel." *Oud Holland* 95 (1981): 59–87.

———. *Halverwege Parijs. Willem Roelofs en de Nederlandse Schilderskolonie in Brussel 1840–1890*. Ghent: Snoeck-Ducaju, 1995. (English Summary)

Buyck, Jean. "Traditie en vernieuwing in het Antwerpse kunstleven omstreeks 1900: Preliminairen tot een receptiestudie." In *Antwerpen 1900: Schilderijen en tekeningen 1880–1914*. Antwerp: Koninklijk Museum voor Schone Kunsten, 1986.

Gerards, Inemie, and Evert van Uitert. "Jan Toorop: Een 'fabuleuze bevattelijkheid': Het symbolistische scheppen." *Jong Holland* 5 (1989): 2–17.

Hefting, Victorine et al. *Jan Th. Toorop: De jaren 1885 tot 1910*. Otterlo: Rijksmuseum Kröller-Müller, 1978.

Lemonnier, Camille. *Histoire des Beaux-Arts en Belgique: Cinquante ans de Liberté*. 3 vols. Brussels: M. Weissenbruch, 1880–1882.

Thoré, T. (Théophile). *Les Salons, études de critique et d'esthétique*. 3 vols. Brussels, 1893.

Uitert, Evert van. "Het oog wil ook wat: Over het beeld van de negentiende-eeuwse schilderkunst." *De Negentiende Eeuw: Documentatieblad Werkgroep 19e Eeuw* 16 (1992): 41–53.

Venema, Adriaan. *De ballingen: Frits van den Berghe, Gustave De Smet en Rik Wouters in Nederland 1914–1921*. Baarn: Wereldvenster, 1979.

Bellaert, Jacob (active 1483–1486)

Jacob Bellaert was one of the earliest publishers of illustrated books in Haarlem; he may have been a native of Zierikzee. His earliest book, dated 1483, makes use of the lettertype and woodcuts that had belonged to his fellow publisher Gerard Leeu of Gouda. Many of the woodcut illustrations to Bellaert's books were designed and cut by an artist known as the Bellaert Master and his workshop. The Bellaert Master is best known for his full-page illustrations to Bellaert's most sumptuous publication, Bartholomaeus Anglicus' *De Proprietatibus Rerum* (1485), which includes some of the earliest Netherlandish landscape representations.

Nadine Orenstein

See also Haarlem; Prints, printmaking, and printmakers (ca. 1500–ca. 1900)

Bibliography

Hind, Arthur. *An Introduction to a History of Woodcut*. Vol. 2, 574–578. London: Constable, 1935.

Holtrop, J.W. *Monuments Typographiques des Pays-Bas au Quinzième Siècle*, 37–40. The Hague: Nijhoff, 1868.

Snyder, James. "The Bellaert Master and *De Proprietatibus Rerum*." In *The Early Illustrated Book: Essays in Honor of Lessing J. Rosenwald*. Edited by Sandra Hindman, 41–61. Washington, DC: Library of Congress, 1982.

Berckheyde, Gerrit Adriaensz. (1638–1698)

The architectural painter Gerrit Berckheyde studied with his brother Job prior to being admitted to the Haarlem Guild of St. Luke in 1660. Although Job is frequently credited with the figures in his brother's pictures, it is more likely that he was one of a number of staffage specialists (including Johan van Huchtenburg, Nicolas Guerard, Dirck Maas, and Johannes Lingelbach) employed by Gerrit. Although Berckheyde had no students or shop, his works influenced eighteenth-century specialists such as Timotheus de Graaf, Jan ten Compe and Isaac Ouwater. A member of the De Wijngaartranken, a Haarlem rhetoricians' society, as well as a guild official, he drowned in a Haarlem canal on his way home from a party shortly after his sixtieth birthday.

During his long career, which coincided with the rise and decline of the genre of the Dutch town view, Berckheyde painted pictures of the country's major cities that are among the most evocative images of urban life produced in the Netherlands during the second half of the seventeenth century (Fig. 13). Just as his church interiors, these works depend on the presentation, topographical accuracy, and crisp draftsmanship of Pieter Saenredam's "building portraits." Following Saenredam's practice, Berckheyde would establish a structure as a scene's dominant motif, placed in isolation by his manipulation of space and light, slightly exaggerated in scale, and impervious to the potential distractions of the staffage and foliage. To some degree this explains his preferences for scenes set on open squares or broad canals that offer unobstructed vistas. Although Berckheyde's pictures were executed in his studio, they are based on sketches he made at the site, or on drawings or prints by other artists in his collection.

Berckheyde's response to the demands of the town view indicates his distinctive artistic personality as well as his original conception of the subject; it also distinguishes him from his contemporaries in the field, especially Jan van der Heyden, who produced views that are, on the whole, conceived in more pictorial terms. While Berckheyde's closely observed depictions of familiar landmarks evoke a sense of period ambience, his analytical approach to composition, his geometric expression of forms, his stylized patterns of light and shadow, and his apparent detachment from his subject create an impression of abstraction that strikes the twentieth-century eye as modern. Although the majority of his works are topographically accurate, his introduction of composite views in his German scenes reveals an unexpected talent for imaginative reconstruction. Berckheyde also maintained a keen interest in period styles in architecture, and in how they might be used (alone or in contrast) to achieve a nostalgic or symbolic effect.

Throughout his career, Berckheyde continued to appropriate new subjects, thereby indicating his response, both as artist and as entrepreneur, to the growing Dutch market for town views. While his earliest works depict the landmarks of his native Haarlem, his later pictures indicate increased demand for scenes of Amsterdam from the later 1660s, and of The Hague from the 1680s. At the same time, shifts in Berckheyde's *oeuvre* also suggest the public's interest in views of German cities (primarily Cologne) as well as Italianate landscapes, pastoral subjects, and hunting scenes.

Cynthia Lawrence

See also Architectural painting; Berckheyde, Job Adriaensz.; Commerce and commercial life; Country houses and gardens; Haarlem; Ten Compe, Jan; Townscapes

Bibliography

Lawrence, C. *Gerrit Berckheyde, 1638–98: Haarlem Cityscape Painter.* Doornspijk: Davaco, 1991.
Liedtke, W. *Architectural Painting in Delft.* Doornspijk: Davaco, 1977.
Walsh, J., Jr., and C.P. Schneider. "The Nieuwezijds Voorburgwal with the Flower Market in Amsterdam." In *A Mirror of Nature,* 8–11. Los Angeles: Los Angeles County Museum of Art, 1981.
Wattenmaker, R., ed. *The Dutch Cityscape in the Seventeenth Century and Its Sources.* Amsterdam: Stadsdrukkerij van Amsterdam, 1977.

Berckheyde, Job Adriaensz. (1630–1693)

The son of a Haarlem butcher, Berckheyde was apprenticed in 1644 to Jacob Willemsz. De Wet whose influence is apparent in his first dated canvas, *Christ Preaching to the Children* (1662; Schwerin, Staatliches Museum). During the 1650s Job traveled in Germany with his younger brother Gerrit, his only

recorded student: Although legends that Job was the superior artist, and that he contributed the staffage to Gerrit's canvases have been discounted, the Berckheydes' professional relationship remains unclear. Although the brothers' German journey may predate Job's entry into the Haarlem Guild of St. Luke in March 1654, it more likely occurred during the second half of the decade. The Berckheydes stopped in several cities along the Rhine before reaching Heidelberg where Job painted portraits and hunting scenes at the court of the Elector Palatine. However, according to Arnold Houbraken's biographical sketch, the brothers found it difficult to adjust to court life and requested permission to return to the Netherlands. Once back in Haarlem, the Berckheydes, who never married, shared a house (and perhaps a studio). In addition to producing pictures, Job occasionally served as an appraiser (for example, of the Van der Meulen collection, Amsterdam, 1680). He was elected an officer in the Haarlem rhetoricians' society, De Wijngaartranken, and, during the 1680s and 1690s, he assumed a position of influence in the guild. The financial records of his interment indicate that he was a wealthy man at the time of his death.

Job Berckheyde's *oeuvre* includes a number of genre scenes, some of which have been recently reattributed, painted in the manner of Adriaen van Ostade and Jan Steen. Among these is *The Baker* (ca. 1681; Worcester, Worcester Art Museum; Fig. 14), one of several depictions of bakers or bakery shops attributed to him that include his self-portrait as well as the "signature" arch motif that occurs in works by both brothers. In addition to depictions of professions or pastimes (for example, artists, card players, musicians), Job also painted rustic scenes that may be based on sketches he and Gerrit made during a trip along the Oude Rhine between Leiden and Utrecht; these drawings may account for the brothers' later inclusion of similar figures and motifs in their pictures.

Job Berckheyde is better known for his architectural subjects, which date from the later 1660s. These include views of the Amsterdam Stock Exchange (Amsterdam, Amsterdam Historical Museum) and the interior of the church of St. Bavo in Haarlem (Haarlem, Frans Hals Museum); the latter group, which recalls similar pictures by Gerrit, raises questions, in yet another context, about the brothers' mutual influence or even their involvement in each other's works. While the composition and meticulous delineation of Job's views of St. Bavo indicate his debt to Pieter Saenredam, his introduction of lusher atmospheric effects suggests that he, like his brother, was influenced by the church interiors of Emanuel de Witte.

Cynthia Lawrence

See also Architectural painting; Berckheyde, Gerrit Adriaensz.; Commerce and commercial life; Haarlem; Townscapes

Bibliography

Biesboer, P. "Schilderijen over de Kerk." In *De Bavo te Boek,* 96–104. Haarlem: J. Enschedé, 1985.
Bogendorf-Rupprath, C. von. "Job Berckheyde." In *Masters of Seventeenth-Century Dutch Genre Painting.* Edited by Peter Sutton, 8–9. Philadelphia: Philadel-

phia Museum of Art, 1984.

Fleischer, R. "Quirijn van Brekelenkam and the Artist's Workshop in the Hermitage Museum." In *The Age of Rembrandt: Studies in Seventeenth-Century Dutch Painting.* Edited by R.E. Fleischer and S.S. Munshower, 70–93. College Park, PA: Pennsylvania State University Press, 1988.

Houbraken, A. *De Groote Schouburgh der Nederlantsche Konstschilders en Schilderessen.* 3 vols. Amsterdam: By the Author, 1718–1721 (Vol. 3, 189–197).

Liedtke, W. *Architectural Painting in Delft.* Doornspijk: Davaco, 1977.

Welu, J. "Job Berckheyde's *Baker.*" *Worcester Art Museum Bulletin* (1977): 1–9.

Bergen

The North Holland village of Bergen, picturesque site of an old castle, has supported an active colony of artists since the early twentieth century. Their artistic interests have always been diverse, but from around 1910 until 1935, the artists who gathered in Bergen were united in responding to the stimulus and challenges of modernism. Among those who worked in and around Bergen for varying amounts of time were Gerrit Willem van Blaaderen (1873-1935), Dirk H.W. Filarski (1885-1964), Leo Gestel (1881-1941), Jan Sluijters (1881-1957), Charley Toorop (1891-1955), Piet Wiegman (1885-1963), and John Raedecker (1885-1956). For artists like Van Blaaderen, who followed the example of the old Dutch masters Jacob van Ruisdael and Meindert Hobbema and sought out the picturesque in landscape, and for Wiegman, who made the focus of his art the formal order and painterly expression he could bring to a still life of everyday objects, the challenges of modernism were seen to come from Cézanne and from French and German Expressionism. For Charley Toorop whose penetrating observations of people marked by their environment are the continuation of the spirit of Jozef Israëls and Vincent van Gogh, the modernist ideal of productive human labor provided a stimulus. Toorop's *Cheese Porters at the Cheese Market in Alkmaar* (1932-1933; Amsterdam, Stedelijk Museum; Colorplate 15) has been called "the *Potato-Eaters* of the twentieth century" (Fleischer et al., 1993: 15).

Gestel, whose residence in Bergen was interrupted by travel that brought him into contact with the movements of the avant-garde, and Henri Le Fauconnier (1881–1945) from France, who lived in Holland during World War I and was looked upon by the Dutch as a major representative of international modernism, brought an air of artistic innovation to the quiet country village. Both used the Cubist style in the paintings entered in the first modernist exhibition mounted in Bergen in the summer of 1913.

Whether this variety of artistic activity constituted a true "Bergen School" in the period before World War II is still a question. The Museum Kranenburgh in Bergen opened in 1993 with an exhibition and catalogue devoted to an examination of the role played by painters and sculptors in Bergen in interpreting international modernist movements in the Netherlands. Bergen along with the other places where local modernist groups were active—De Branding in Rotterdam, De Ploeg in Groningen—are subjects for further study in relation to the better-known pursuits of the members of the Moderne Kunstkring (Modern Art Circle) in The Hague and the Onafhankelijken (Independents) in Amsterdam during the same period. The Museum Kranenburgh has an important collection of works by artists who at one time or another worked in Bergen. The Kunstnaars Centrum Bergen (Bergen Artists' Center) has, since 1947, held regular exhibitions of the work of artists living in Bergen.

Sheila D. Muller

See also Avant-garde; Gestel, Leo; Israëls, Jozef; Raedecker, John; Sluijters, Jan; Toorop, Charley (Annie Caroline Pontifex); Van Gogh, Vincent

Bibliography
Fleischer, Alette, Nicoline Koek, and Peter Saal, eds. *Rond het "Oude Hof": schilders en beeldhouwers in Bergen 1910–1940.* Bergen: Stichting Museum Kranenburgh. Venlo: Van Spijk, 1993.

Gezicht op de "Bergensche School," 1910–1935. Bergen: Noordhollands Kunstcentrum Bergen, 1967.

Klomp, D. A. *In en om de Bergense School.* Amsterdam: Strengholt, 1943.

Welling, Dolf. *The Expressionists: The Art of Prewar Expressionism in the Netherlands.* Amsterdam: Meulenhoff, 1968.

Berlage, Hendrik Petrus (1856–1934)

The leading Dutch architect of his generation, H.P. Berlage profoundly influenced the development of twentieth-century architecture in the Netherlands and Europe. He envisioned a modern architecture of structural rationalism and monumentality, defined by space and geometry, imbued with social commitment. Although his architectural design retained the heavy masonry and mural emphasis associated with the nineteenth century, his distillation of historic styles abandoned imitation in favor of invention. The only Dutch member of his generation to participate in CIAM, the international congress of modern architects, Berlage promoted a rational, functional, and aesthetic architecture that would serve the community as well as express its nature.

Berlage forged a syncretic theory of architecture derived from the most advanced architectural theorists of late-nineteenth-century Europe. During his architectural training in Zurich, he came under the influence of Gottfried Semper's approach to materials, craft, and style. From E.E. Viollet-le-Duc he adopted the principles of structural rationalism. Working in an era of rapid social change, he embraced the social consciousness of John Ruskin and William Morris. Berlage's architectural position bridged tradition and modernity, craft and industry, the picturesque and the monumental. He recognized parallels in the work of Frank Lloyd Wright and played a pivotal role in the introduction of Wright's work to the Netherlands and Europe.

Berlage's career was long, prolific, and varied. His most important early commission was the Amsterdam Stock Exchange (completed in 1903), a building that takes full advantage of Viollet-le-Duc's theories of proportional systems. While its plan and façades are regulated by governing geometries, the building's masses are picturesquely composed to contribute to the urban skyline. Viewed by some contemporaries as cold and mechanistic, its uncompromising revelation of masonry and iron construction places it among the first buildings of the twentieth century to manifest a consistent modern rationality. Simultaneously, the building's iconographic program, interpreting the history of Amsterdam, allowed progressive painters, sculptors (Fig. 125), and craftsmen to explore modern expression in an architectural context. A similar collaboration occurred at the headquarters for the Diamond Workers' Union in Amsterdam (1897–1900), where monumentality and calm expressed the dignity of the workers' struggle. At a number of office buildings, notably Holland House in London (1916), Berlage treated materials and building techniques sensitively and rationally while exploiting the expressive potential of architecture. Toward the end of his career, increasingly influenced by the more abstract geometries of his younger contemporaries, he designed two important buildings in The Hague, the First Church of Christ, Scientist (1925–1926), and the Gemeentemuseum (1927–1935), both of which exemplify Berlage's mastery of spatial composition in the service of collective spirit.

Berlage was also active in the design of mass housing, urban design, and town planning. In Amsterdam, he designed several sober but distinguished housing projects; he defended standardization as necessary to the design of urban housing, citing aesthetic as well as economic justifications. His most important urban project was the plan for the South of Amsterdam. The first, unexecuted, plan of 1904 reflected the medievalizing influence of Camillo Sitte; the final plan of 1915, influenced by A.E. Brinckmann and W.C. Behrendt, abandoned the asymmetrical squares and street patterns of the first with sweeping boulevards and vistas that encouraged large-scale housing design of entire streets and city blocks (Fig. 138).

Berlage's great stature in the Netherlands led to many public positions and honors. Without his precedent, the much-vaunted contribution to modern architecture by the next generation of Dutch architects is inconceivable. He influenced not only the functionalists of Het Nieuwe Bouwen (The New Construction) who heeded his call for standardization, rationalism, and geometry, but also the Expressionist architects of the Amsterdam School who learned from his embrace of the representational means of architecture and from the scope of his urban vision.

Nancy Stieber

See also Amsterdam School; Architectural competitions; Architectural criticism, issues of style; Functionalism in architecture; Urban planning, from 1750 to the present

Bibliography
Polano, Sergio, ed. *Hendrik Petrus Berlage: Complete Works*. New York: Rizzoli, 1988.
Rovenelli, H.P. "H.P. Berlage and the Amsterdam School, 1914–1920: Rationalist as Expressionist." *Journal of the Society of Architectural Historians* 43 (October 1984): 256–264.
Searing, Helen. "Berlage and Housing: 'The most significant modern building type.'" *Nederlands Kunsthistorisch Jaarboek* 25 (1974): 133–179.
———. "Berlage or Cuypers? The Father of Them All." In *In Search of Modern Architecture*. Edited by H. Searing, 226–244. Cambridge, MA: MIT Press, 1982.
Singelenberg, Pieter. *H.P. Berlage: Idea and Style, the Quest for Modern Architecture*. Utrecht: Haentjens, Dekker, and Gumbert, 1972.

Berssenbrugge, Henri (1873–1959)

Henri Berssenbrugge was educated to be a draftsman and decorative painter at the Rotterdam Academy of Visual Arts and Technical Sciences. In 1901 he switched to photography, a technique that he taught himself and in which he acquired a name. Initially, he photographed in an impressionistic way, putting the atmosphere of the moment first. Later, around 1910, he grew dissatisfied with this and tried to give his work spiritual value as well. His first Symbolist portraits were created in 1913. With the help of bromide oil, bromide dye, and the gum print technique, he found methods to remove too much detail in the picture and to work in a flatter style. With the gum print technique he was able to get rid of the halftones, which sometimes made his photographic portraits look almost like woodcuts. During the 1920s, Berssenbrugge tried to achieve a greater abstraction under the influence of De Stijl. A famous work is the almost geometrical portrait of *Cesar Domela Nieuwenhuis* (Leiden, Prentenkabinet). Despite the great appreciation that Berssenbrugge found both in the Netherlands and abroad, some of his colleagues accused him of being too dependent on, and borrowing too much from, painting. It was thought that he denied the specific qualities of photography in doing this. However, through his great desire to experiment, Berssenbrugge gave an important stimulus to the development of photography as an independent art form.

Alexandra W.M. van Smoorenburg

See also De Stijl; Herwig, Reinhardt Herman; Photography, early

Bibliography
Leijerzapf, Ingeborg Th., ed. "Henri Berssenbrugge." Vol. 18, part 1, *Geschiedenis van de Nederlandse Fotografie*. Alphen aan de Rijn: Samsom, 1992.
Scheffer, H.J. *Portret van een fotograaf: Henri Berssenbrugge, 1873–1959*. Leiden: Sijthoff, 1967.

Bible, Bible illustration

See History painting; Manuscript illumination; Pre-Rembrandtists; Prints, early printed book and Bible illustration; Rembrandt van Rijn

Bloemaert, Abraham (1564–1651)

This leading history painter spent most of his life in Utrecht, where he led a flourishing studio with numerous talented students, including Hendrick Terbrugghen, Gerard van Honthorst, Jan van Bijlert, Cornelis van Poelenburch, Jan Both, and Jan Baptist Weenix. His students developed distinctive styles. Bloemaert also had many sons, four of whom—Hendrick, Adriaen, Cornelis, and Frederick—studied with him.

Influenced by international Mannerism, he followed this trend without falling into extremes. Bloemaert's style was elegant and graceful and his work remained easily accessible, as evidenced in a painting like the *Adoration of the Magi* (1624; Utrecht, Centraal Museum). In the course of his career, he also followed other stylistic currents with success.

Although he had never been to Italy himself, Bloemaert encouraged his students to undertake the journey. Several of them experienced the influence of Caravaggio and his followers. Bloemaert had no difficulty responding to Italian influence through his students. In 1620, after the return of Van Honthorst to Utrecht, Bloemaert applied Van Honthorst's Caravaggistic dramatic *chiaroscuro* to his own work; Bloemaert's *Supper at Emmaus* (1622; Brussels, Museés Royaux des Beaux-Arts; Fig. 68) is a good example of his work from this period. For Bloemaert, the Caravaggistic influence was not lasting, and after four years he went back to the style of late Mannerism. During his long and productive life, he created an elaborate and varied *oeuvre* for which others were willing to pay high prices. Besides mythical and biblical subjects in which landscape often plays an important role, Bloemaert painted portraits, still lifes, and genre scenes. It is to his credit that, along with the preservation of the Netherlandish tradition, he knew how to connect with the latest artistic developments.

Eugenie Boer

See also Italy; Mannerism, Mannerists; Terbrugghen, Hendrick; Utrecht; Utrecht Caravaggists; Van Honthorst, Gerard

Bibliography

Huys Janssen, P. *Schilders in Utrecht, 1600–1700*. Utrecht: Matrijs, 1990.

Nicolson, B. *Caravaggism in Europe*. 2nd ed. rev. and enl. Turin: Allemandi, 1990.

Roethlisberger, M.G., and M.J. Bok. *Abraham Bloemaert and His Sons: Paintings and Prints*. Doornspijk: Davaco, 1993.

Blommers, Bernardus Johannes (1845–1914)

During his lifetime Bernard Blommers was considered one of the foremost representatives of The Hague School. There was an extensive market abroad for his work, especially in the United States, England, and Scotland.

Blommers was initially trained as a lithographer in the print shop of his father. He also took lessons at The Hague Drawing Academy and at the studio of the genre painter Christoffel Bisschop. In 1865 he made a study trip along the Rhine with his friend Willem Maris, with whom he would later share a studio. In 1870 he visited Paris, where he stayed with Jacob Maris. Blommers was friendly with most painters of The Hague School; for example, Anton Mauve and Hendrik Willem Mesdag were witnesses at his marriage in 1871. As an active member of the artists' society Pulchri Studio and the Hollandsche Teeken-Maatschappij (Dutch Watercolor Society) he was in close contact with his colleagues. He was friends with Jozef Israëls from 1865 when his first painting hung next to Israëls' at the exhibition of living masters in The Hague. He was influenced by Israëls especially as far as subject matter was concerned.

Blommers worked in Scheveningen and later at Zandvoort and Katwijk. He painted genre scenes from the lives of fishwives and their children. His own wife, who came from Scheveningen, was often his model. In his studio Blommers had one corner completely set up as an inner courtyard of a house from Scheveningen. His early work, painted in a fine, detailed style (Fig. 15), consisted mostly of interiors that displayed domestic happiness. His later paintings and watercolors are more often beach scenes, often with children playing in the surf. His later work is more vigorous in touch. He was at the height of his fame in the beginning of the twentieth century. In 1904 he made a trip to the United States where he was received by Theodore Roosevelt.

Hanna Pennock

See also Hague School, The; Maris, Jacob Hendricus; Maris, Willem; Mesdag, Hendrik Willem

Bibliography

Gruyter, Jos de. *De Haagse School*. Rotterdam: Lemniscaat, 1968–1969. Reprint. 2 vols. in 1. Alphen aan den Rijn: Atrium, 1985. (English summary).

Leeman, Fred, and Hanna Pennock. *The Mesdag Museum: Catalogue of Paintings and Drawings*. Zwolle: Waanders, 1996.

Leeuw, Ronald de, John Sillevis, and Charles Dumas, eds. *The Hague School: Dutch Masters of the Nineteenth Century*. London: Royal Academy of Arts, in association with Weidenfeld and Nicolson, 1983.

Liefde-van Brakel, Tiny de. *B.J. Blommers, 1845–1914*. Katwijk: Katwijks Museum, 1993. (English summary).

Scheen, Pieter A. *Lexicon Nederlandse Beeldende Kunstenaars 1750–1880*. The Hague: Pieter Scheen, 1981.

Bol, Ferdinand (1616–1680)

A prolific Amsterdam history and portrait painter, Ferdinand Bol produced the majority of his dated works from 1641 to 1669. Born in Dordrecht, Bol moved to Amsterdam around 1636 to study under Rembrandt. Although Bol probably learned the fundamentals of painting in Utrecht under Jacob Gerritsz. Cuyp (1594–1651), he readily absorbed Rembrandt's style as evidenced by the formal qualities of his earliest dated paintings. Bol broke with Rembrandt's style after 1650, developing a brighter palette and more energetic line.

Although portraits constituted a significant portion of Bol's *oeuvre*, history painting was his most important contribution to seventeenth-century Dutch painting. Given the status of the history subject at the time as the most respectable of all possible categories of painting, it is not surprising that Bol devoted most of his artistic output to representing deeds and stories from the Bible, mythology, and ancient history. Amsterdam in the seventeenth century provided a wealth of opportunity for such commissions for Bol and other artists.

Bol's contribution to history painting is best understood in the context of the intellectual milieu in which he lived and worked. Many of Bol's most important commissions were created for Amsterdam's leading social and political organizations and reflect an underlying concern with promoting specific messages about such patrons. For example, while subjects from Republican Roman history, including *Pyrrhus and Fabricius* (1656) for the new Amsterdam Town Hall and *Titus Manlius Torquatus Decapitates His Son* (1663) for the Amsterdam Admiralty, depict on one level the deeds of two Roman consuls, they also provided a visual reminder to both the important city officials and the Amsterdam public of the discipline required for proper and virtuous civic leadership. The messages of steadfastness and military discipline as exemplified by Pyrrhus and Torquatus, respectively, can be traced to an earlier Italian humanist tradition, which used figures from ancient history as models of behavior for a city's public servants and citizens. Such a didactic humanist tradition was prevalent in Amsterdam in the seventeenth century and is a source for a deeper understanding of publicly commissioned art.

Although Bol was one of the most important history painters in Amsterdam during the seventeenth century, much of his work has not received the extensive scholarly investigation it deserves. While there has been some excellent and extensive scholarship devoted to the meaning and function of Bol's history paintings for public buildings, there is still lacking a comprehensive investigation of Bol's other mythological, allegorical, religious, and portrait paintings in the context of Dutch culture and visual tradition.

Steven Golan

See also Dordrecht; Drawing practices and techniques; History painting; History portraits; Rembrandt School

Bibliography
Blankert, Albert. *Ferdinand Bol, 1616–1680: Rembrandt's Pupil*. Doornspijk: Davaco, 1982.

Blankert, Albert et al. *Gods, Saints, and Heroes: Dutch Painting in the Age of Rembrandt*. Washington, DC: National Gallery of Art, 1980.

Brown, Christopher et al. *Rembrandt: The Master and His Workshop, Paintings*. New Haven: Yale University Press, 1991.

Bosboom, Johannes (1817–1891)

Johannes Bosboom is known as *the* painter of nineteenth-century church interiors. B.J. van Hove, painter of townscapes and stage scenery, pointed him in that direction when the twelve-year-old Bosboom began studying with him. From 1831 to 1835 Bosboom took lessons at The Hague Drawing Academy. Afterward he took various trips to Germany and Belgium. At first Bosboom painted in a Romantic style and with a rather exact technique, but around 1865 his touch became looser, his tone more subdued, and his compositions grander and more austere. Although the painter continued to fill his churches with figures dressed in seventeenth-century clothing, he was an example to his younger colleagues because of his "modern" technique. In addition to the respect that he earned as a painter, Bosboom acquired a great reputation as a watercolorist. Already by 1856 he was made an honorary member of the Société Belge des Aquarellistes. From the 1870s on he used this technique more and more. From the time that the Hollandsche Teeken-Maatschappij (Dutch Watercolor Society) was founded in 1876, he annually participated in its exhibitions with great success. Bosboom's work, together with that of Jozef Israëls, formed the basis for the painting of The Hague School.

Alexandra W.M. van Smoorenburg

See also Architectural painting; Drawing clubs; Hague School, The

Bibliography
Bionda, Richard, and Carel Blotkamp, eds. *The Age of Van Gogh: Dutch Painting, 1880–1895*. Zwolle: Waanders, 1990.

Gruyter, Jos de. *De Haagse School*. Vol. 1, 15–29. Rotterdam: Lemniscaat, 1968.

Leeuw, Ronald de, John Sillevis, and Charles Dumas, eds. *The Hague School: Dutch Masters of the Nineteenth Century*. London: Royal Academy of Arts in association with Weidenfeld and Nicholson, 1983.

Bosch, Hieronymus (ca. 1450–1516)

A painter of religious subjects and moral allegories, Hieronymus Bosch expressed the fears and concerns of the late Middle Ages in images of unsurpassed originality. He had many imitators and his paintings were avidly collected throughout Europe. The meaning of his often enigmatic art preoccupied his earliest critics and continues to challenge modern scholars.

Bosch was born into a family of painters active in 's Hertogenbosch since the early fifteenth century. Their surname "van Acken" suggests their origin in Aachen. Bosch is first mentioned in a record of 1474, but his date of birth is unknown. His portrait in the Arras Codex, although of uncertain authenticity, shows a man of advanced age, and this is generally accepted as proof that he was born around 1450. Sometime before 1480–1481, he married Aleyt Goyaerts van Meervenne, a wealthy woman perhaps some years his senior. There is no evidence that she came from a family of pharmacists, as is sometimes supposed. No children are recorded from their marriage.

Bosch was a member of the Brotherhood of Our Lady, a religious confraternity that maintained a chapel in St. John, the chief church of the city. He executed a number of commissions for this group, including a pair of shutters depicting David and Abigail, painted ca. 1488–1492 for a sculptured altarpiece completed by Adriaen van Wesel in 1476–1477, and a design in 1492 for a stained glass window. Later sources indicated other works painted for St. John: an *Epiphany*, scenes from the stories of Judith and Esther, and a *Creation of the World* on two shutters for a carved altarpiece above the main altar. His paintings were also acquired by highly placed members of the church and aristocracy. In 1504 he was paid for a huge *Last Judgment* triptych ordered by Philip the Fair, duke of Burgundy. Other pictures were owned by Queen Isabella of Spain; Margaret of Austria, regent of the Netherlands; and Philip of Burgundy, bishop of Utrecht. Three pictures were in the palace of Cardinal Domenico Grimani at Venice before 1521. Count Hendrik III of Nassau may have commissioned Bosch's *Garden of Earthly Delights*, recorded in his palace at Brussels as early as 1517.

It has been suggested that Bosch worked in Italy between 1499 and 1503; this claim is based on a triptych by Bosch now in Venice, often thought to depict the martyrdom of St. Julia, whose relics were preserved in Brescia. This identification of the subject in the Venice triptych has been disputed, however, and there is no conclusive evidence that Bosch ever traveled beyond his native city. He seems to have been unusually prosperous; tax records place him among the wealthiest citizens of 's Hertogenbosch. He died sometime before August 9, 1516, when the Brotherhood of Our Lady conducted a funeral mass in his memory.

None of Bosch's surviving works bears a date or is securely documented, nor is the presence of his name on a painting or drawing a guarantee of its authenticity. Hence the attributions and chronology of his *oeuvre* are based chiefly on stylistic analysis, a task complicated by the many existing copies of his paintings. Earlier scholars, such as De Tolnay and Baldass, attributed thirty to fifty paintings to Bosch himself, and nineteen to twenty-four drawings. Since the mid-1960s, however, these numbers have been considerably reduced through a careful examination of the works traditionally attributed to him, especially the study of his underdrawings by means of reflectography. In the latest catalog of Bosch's *oeuvre* (1980), Unverfehrt lists only twenty-five paintings and fourteen drawings. Around this core can be grouped a number of putative copies of lost works and a small number of paintings that may have been produced in Bosch's immediate workshop.

The lack of dated and documented works makes it equally difficult to trace Bosch's stylistic development. Scholars generally divide his career into three periods. To his early activity (ca. 1470–1490) are assigned such paintings as the *Epiphany* (Philadelphia, Museum of Art, Johnson Collection), *Christ Carrying the Cross* (Vienna, Kunsthistorisches Museum), *Ecce Homo* (Frankfurt, Städelsches Kunstinstitut), and the *Tabletop of the Seven Deadly Sins and the Four Last Things* (Madrid, Prado; Color Plate 1). There is considerably less agreement on which works belong to the middle and late phases of Bosch's career. Bosch's drawings have received less attention, and there is little consensus concerning their chronology and function.

Bosch's art ranges in subject from christological scenes and images of the saints to complex allegories depicting sinful humanity and its fate in the afterlife. While some of his religious pictures are traditional in concept, such as the *Crucifixion* (Brussels, Musées Royaux des Beaux-Arts), most of his work shows a remarkable inventiveness in form and treatment, culminating in *The Last Judgment* (Vienna, Akademie der Bildenden Künste), *The Haywain* (Prado, Madrid), *The Garden of Earthly Delights* (Prado, Madrid), the *Temptation of St. Anthony* triptych (Lisbon, Museu Nacional de Arte Antiga), and *Christ Carrying the Cross* (Ghent, Musée des Beaux-Arts). This same inventiveness is equally apparent in many of his drawings. Bosch's view of humanity is basically pessimistic, relieved by occasional flashes of humor. His artistic virtuosity is especially apparent in his scenes of Hell with their proliferation of devils and torments (see Color Plate 1, where Hell is shown as one of the Four Last Things). While his visual imagination was nourished by many forms of late Gothic art, including prints and manuscripts, he was equally heir to the realistic tradition of early Netherlandish painting. It was this tradition that also enabled him to paint some of the finest landscapes of the period, such as appear in *The Wayfarer* (Rotterdam, Museum Boymans—van Beuningen) and the *St. John on Patmos* (Berlin, Staatliche Museen).

Bosch probably trained with his father, but very little is known about earlier painting in 's Hertogenbosch, and his artistic origins are obscure. His earliest works show affinities with the art of the Northern Netherlands, especially illuminated manuscripts, and it is occasionally suggested that Bosch studied in Utrecht, then a major center of manuscript painting. If so, this might explain the "archaizing" tendencies that have been discerned in his work, including his bright colors and flatly modeled forms. The early paintings show fairly elaborate underdrawings, but in the pictures of his maturity, the underdrawing is often quite summary, indicating only the major outlines of the composition. Bosch also frequently deviated from his original design, introducing sometimes major changes during the course of painting. This mode of execution suggests that Bosch did not work according to a predetermined and detailed iconographical program, as is so often assumed. It is possible that he improvised some of his imagery as he worked.

A detailed account of Bosch's posthumous fortunes appears in Gibson (1983); its main points may be summarized here. Even while Bosch was alive, engravings very much in his spirit and possibly reflecting his inventions were made by the local designer-architect Alart du Hameel. Bosch also had many followers who copied his paintings and composed new pictures in his style. The center of this activity was Antwerp, led by Pieter Huys, Jan Mandyn, and, above all, Pieter Bruegel the Elder, hailed by his contemporaries as a "Hieronymus Bosch reborn."

The paintings and prints by Bosch's followers undoubtedly contributed to his widespread reputation as a *fazeur de diables* (maker of devils), whose creations were as empty of significance as the fashionable grotesque ornament of the period. There are a few exceptions, especially among the Spanish. Felipe de Guevara (ca. 1550) insisted that Bosch had painted the workings of the human soul, and José de Sigüenza (1605) esteemed his paintings as "books of great wisdom." These opinions must have been shared by Philip II of Spain, who acquired many of Bosch's paintings, among them *The Tabletop of the Seven Deadly Sins and the Four Last Things* (Madrid, Prado; Color Plate 1), which he installed in his bedroom in the Escorial.

When the scholarly study of Bosch emerged in the late nineteenth century, no one doubted that his art was basically Christian in content, and writers often turned to medieval accounts of Hell and other religious literature to determine the sources of his art. With few exceptions, this unanimity of opinion persisted until after World War II, when it gave way to the greatest diversity of interpretations. These can be divided into three major groups. Some critics, already beginning in the 1920s and 1930s, analyze Bosch's imagery in terms of modern psychoanalysis, in order to probe the mental state of the artist himself. Other scholars claim that Bosch belonged to some medieval heretical or gnostic sect or was an adept of one or more of the occult sciences. Tapping sources largely ignored by earlier writers, they turn to astrology, alchemy, Rosicrucianism, and other hermetic teachings to explicate his imagery. The third group of scholars reasserts the traditional view of Bosch as an orthodox Christian whose art reflects the ordinary religious and social concerns of his day. A recent variant of this approach is represented by Vandenbroeck, who suggests that Bosch's secular subjects express the ethos of the urban middle class to which Bosch himself belonged.

It is doubtful that these various trends in current Bosch scholarship will ever be reconciled. Nevertheless, a deeper understanding of the artist's milieu should enable us to evaluate more precisely the many theories and interpretations that continue to flourish around Bosch's person and art.

For a bibliography on Bosch before 1982, see Gibson. The other titles below include standard earlier works and some important recent publications.

Walter S. Gibson

See also Allegorical traditions; Comic modes; Devotional images; Didactic images; Erasmus, Desiderius; Last Judgment; Prints, printmaking, and printmakers (ca. 1500–ca. 1900); Sins and punishments

Bibliography

Baldass, Ludwig van. *Hieronymus Bosch*. New York: Harry N. Abrams; London: Thames and Hudson, 1960.

Blondé, B., and Vliege, H. "The Social Status of Hieronymus Bosch." *Burlington Magazine* 131 (1989): 699–700.

De Tolnay, Charles. *Hieronymus Bosch*. [New York:] Reynal and William Morrow, 1966.

Gibson, Walter S. *Hieronymus Bosch*. London: Thames and Hudson; New York: Praeger, 1973. Reprint. London and New York: Thames and Hudson, 1991.

———.*Hieronymus Bosch: An Annotated Bibliography*. Boston: G.K. Hall, 1983.

Marijnissen, Roger H., and Ruyffelaere, Peter. *Hieronymus Bosch: The Complete Works*. Antwerp: Mercator Fonds, 1987.

Jheronimus Bosch. English ed. 's Hertogenbosch: Noordbrabants Museum, 1967.

Unverfehrt, Gerd. *Hieronymus Bosch: Die Rezeption seiner Kunst im frühen 16. Jahrhundert*. Berlin: Gebr. Mann, 1980.

Vandenbroeck, Paul. *Jheronimus Bosch: Tussen volksleven en stadscultuur*. Berchem: EPO, 1987.

Bramer, Leonaert (1596–1674)

Leonaert Bramer was a leading artist in Delft through the late 1660s. He was a painter of night scenes and one of the few Dutch artists to practice the Italian art of fresco painting in the Netherlands. While his frescoes have all vanished, the approximately one hundred sixteen easel paintings that are known reveal a highly eccentric artistic personality. Bramer was also prolific as a draftsman; most of his drawings belong to large sets of illustrations. His drawings illustrating classical and popular literary texts (*The Aeneid*, Ovid's *Metamorphoses*, *Lazarillo of Tormes*, Quevedo's *Sueños*) provide an interesting link between the visual arts and Dutch literary culture of the period.

Nothing is known about Bramer's artistic activity before his departure for France and Italy in 1614. It was once thought possible that he received his early training from the Middleburg painter Adriaen van de Venne, but his trip to Italy and his connections there strongly suggest a training in the Utrecht workshop of Abraham Bloemaert. He traveled first through France; in 1616 he was in Aix-en-Provence, a major cultural center at the time. Here he inscribed his name in the *album amicorum* of Wybrand de Geest II (1592–1667), a Dutch painter from Leeuwarden, who appears to have studied with Bloemaert. Bramer is first recorded in Italy in 1619 and is last recorded there in 1627. He spent most of these years in Rome but is also reported to have visited other artistic centers. In Rome Bramer was a member of the Bentveughels ("Birds of a flock": the colony of Dutch and Flemish artists living in Rome) and worked for eminent patrons such as the Marchese Vincenzo Giustiniani and Don Camillo Pamphilij, nephew of Pope Innocent X. Outside of Rome his patrons included the wealthy Flemish merchant Gasper Roomer in Naples and Prince Mario Farnese in Parma. Bramer's pictures on slate produced in Italy also connect him with the circle of Cosimo II, grand duke of Tuscany.

While Bramer signed most of his paintings, only nine paintings are dated. Almost all of the twenty-six extant paintings from Bramer's Italian period are night scenes; about half of these deal with New Testament themes, while the rest represent the types of low-life subjects that were then becoming popular in Rome (soldiers, street people). Bramer's earliest signed and dated painting is the tiny picture on slate depicting *Soldiers Resting* (1626; The Hague, Bredius Museum; Fig. 40). The artist also appears to have depicted "sea tempests" while in Italy (*Shipwreck on a Rocky Coast*, Hamburg, Kunsthalle). Thematically and stylistically, works from

Bramer's Italian period may be connected with the work of Adam Elsheimer, Agostino Tassi, Caravaggio, Pieter van Laer, and Gerard van Honthorst.

Returning to Delft in 1628 with knowledge of the latest trends in Italian painting, Bramer specialized in the depiction of small histories staged in eerie nocturnal settings with unsettling phosphorescent light effects. His wraith-like figures and the ornate metal utensils that litter his works are other distinguishing features of his art. Bramer's preference was for scenes from the New Testament; his favorite subject appears to have been the circumcision of Christ. Works such as *The Epiphany* (ca. 1631–1632; Detroit, Detroit Institute of Art) reflect his Italian experience and the influence of Elsheimer, Van Honthorst, and Leonardo da Vinci. Other paintings such as *The Circumcision of Christ* (signed and dated 1631) demonstrate the impact of the young Rembrandt on his art.

The disappearance of most of Bramer's decorative paintings, many of which were done in the fresco technique, has obscured one of the most interesting facets of his seventeenth-century accomplishment. In the late 1630s Bramer provided decorative paintings for the *stadholders'* palaces of Honselaarsdijk and Rijswijk. In the 1650s he appears to have ceased doing easel paintings, turning his attention to large-scale decorative projects for public and private patrons in the town of Delft. His public commissions include frescoes for the municipal garden house and militia company, a ceiling painting for the St. Luke's Guild, a ceiling painting and wall paintings for the main hall of the Prinsenhof and a sign board for the Delft horse market. Of Bramer's numerous decorative paintings only a large canvas depicting *Music-Making Figures Before a Palace* (1660s) and the ceiling painting in the Prinsenhof remain. A small triptych in the Prinsenhof also appears to contain the designs for Bramer's wall paintings for the Delft militia company, and a set of drawings in Amsterdam depicting *The Siege of Leiden* may be designs for tapestries.

In the early twentieth century E.W. Bredt first exposed Bramer's lively wit and humor in the publication of Bramer's illustrations for *Tyl Eulenspiegel*, *Lazarillo de Tormes*, and Quevedo's *Sueños*. Subsequently, in an article on Bramer's illustrations for *The Aeneid* (1984), Jane ten Brink Goldsmith demonstrated a connection between Bramer and the Dutch poet Vondel and Dutch literary culture of the seventeenth century. Bramer's literary illustrations, not intended for reproduction in prints, appear to have been produced for private patrons, including Dutch artists such as Caspar Netscher and the Delft faïence manufacturer Abraham de Cooge. These illustrations offer a humorous and highly individualistic interpretation of popular literary texts of the period

Jane ten Brink Goldsmith

See also Delft; Italy; Utrecht Caravaggists

Bibliography

Barnes, Donna, and Jane ten Brink Goldsmith. *Street Scenes: Leonaert Bramer's Drawings of Seventeenth-Century Dutch Daily Life*. Hempstead, NY: Hofstra Museum, 1991.

Goldsmith, Jane ten Brink. "From Prose to Pictures: Leonaert Bramer's Illustrations for *The Aeneid* and Vondel's Translation of Virgil." *Art History* 7:1 (March 1984): 21–37.

———— et al. *Leonaert Bramer, 1596–1674: Ingenious Painter and Draughtsman in Rome and Delft*. Zwolle: Waanders, 1994.

Hofrichter, Frima Fox et al. *Leonaert Bramer, 1596–1674: A Painter of the Night*. Milwaukee, WI: Patrick and Beatrice Haggerty Museum, Marquette University, 1992.

Montias, J. Michael. *Artists and Artisans in Delft: A Socioeconomic Study of the Seventeenth Century*. Princeton, NJ: Princeton University Press, 1982.

————. "A Bramer Document about Jean Ducamps, Alias Giovanni del Campo." In *Essays in Northern European Art Presented to Egbert Haverkamp-Begemann on His Sixtieth Birthday*, 178–181. Doornspijk: Davaco, 1983.

Plomp, Michiel. "Een merkwaardige verzameling Teekeningen door Leonaert Bramer." *Oud Holland* 100 (1986): 81–153.

Wichmann, Heinrich. *Leonaert Bramer, Sein Leben und Seine Kunst*. Leipzig: K.W. Hiersemann, 1923.

Brands, Eugène (born 1913)

A member of the Dutch Experimental Group and the Cobra Movement from 1948 to 1949, Eugène Brands is a painter and artist in diverse media. Brands was born in Amsterdam, studied advertising art at the Rijksschool voor Kunstnijverheid (National School of Arts and Crafts) there (1934), and from the later 1930s to the mid-1940s made Surrealist photomontages and drawings. Contact in 1946 with Karel Appel, Corneille, and Anton Rooskens led to his membership in the Experimental Group a month after its formation in July 1948. As an Experimental artist, Brands made assemblages as well as paintings based on magical signs and wrote texts for both issues of the group's journal, *Reflex*. One of these, "Authentic Folk Music" (1949), revealed his deep interest and expertise in the field of ethnomusicology. Never a convinced group member, he withdrew from the movement after the turbulent Cobra exhibition at the Stedelijk Museum, Amsterdam, in November 1949. Through the 1950s, Brands' symbolic-figurative paintings continued to evoke mystery and magic and to maintain Surrealist accents, but by the early 1960s his painting was becoming more obviously a lyrical variant of Abstract Expressionism. Since then, apart from returning occasionally to the art of assemblage, Brands has mainly concentrated on developing a characteristic painterly style in which soft-edged, cloud-like color patches predominate and fluidity rather than structure shapes the compositions. A recurrent theme in Brands' thought and art is that of the universe in flux, formulated by the ancient Greeks as *Panta Rei*.

Graham Birtwistle

See also Cobra Movement; Surrealism

Bibliography

Brands, Eugène. "De beet van cobra." In *Eugène Brands*. Rotterdam: Galerie Delta, 1964.

Stokvis, Willemijn. "Het poëtische universum van Eugène Brands." In *Eugène Brands*, 7–22. The Hague/Amsterdam: Galerie Nouvelles Images, 1979.

Wingen, Ed. *Eugène Brands*. The Hague: SDU, 1988.

Breitner, George Hendrik (1857–1923)

The painter George Hendrik Breitner has become well known mainly because of his city views. He grew up in Rotterdam where his talent for drawing was soon recognized by the artist Christoffel Neurdenberg (1817–1906) and the history painter Charles Rochussen (1814–1894). From 1876 until 1880, Breitner was educated at the Art Academy in The Hague. After he became licensed to teach drawing, he spent some time as an instructor at the evening academy Ars Aemula Naturae in Leiden. Floris Verster was one of his students.

In 1880 Breitner obtained a place in the studio of The Hague School painter Willem Maris. While in The Hague he created a number of flower still lifes, landscapes, and self-portraits, although the military figure piece was especially attractive to him in those years. With Vincent van Gogh he worked in the working class neighborhoods of The Hague observing and painting the residents. In 1883 they painted in the province of Drenthe. He also worked for some time with the painter Willem de Zwart.

In 1884 Breitner left for Paris for six months. There he took drawing lessons from the liberal salon painter Fernand Cormon (1845–1924), who was teaching Henri de Toulouse-Lautrec at the time. Little is known about Breitner's stay in Paris, and his work does not show a direct influence from the French Impressionists.

In 1886 Breitner moved to Amsterdam and became the leading painter of the Amsterdam Impressionists. He took lessons at the Rijksacademie, and from 1888 until 1891 he shared with Isaac Israëls the studio–living quarters belonging to the painter Willem Witsen. His wish to be a history painter who painted the history of his own time was fully realized in his watercolors, drawings, and paintings from around this period; in a manner unlike anyone else, he portrayed the urban life of Amsterdam and its people (*The Rokin in Amsterdam at Night*, ca. 1895; Amsterdam, Stedelijk Museum; Fig. 3). Light and movement play an important role in his work. He had a quick, sketchy manner of painting, a special handling of color, and he often chose conspicuous ways of cutting off the picture plane. Undoubtedly this had everything to do with his interest in photography. Breitner was an inspired photographer, but his photographs served, like his drawings, mainly as helpful means for making his paintings.

Around 1893 he took a short period to reflect on his work. Quiet compositions of reclining and standing girls in kimonos replaced the daring and life-size nudes from the earlier period (*The Red Kimono*, ca. 1893; Amsterdam, Stedelijk Museum). In the second half of the 1890s, he concentrated again on the dynamics of the city and created many scenes of demolitions, dike burstings, and excavated building sites in Amsterdam.

Together with Witsen and Marius Bauer, Breitner took a trip to London in 1897, and in 1900 he went to Norway. From 1899 until 1914 he had a studio with the painter Cees Maks. In 1901, Breitner, who was then forty-four years old, married Marie Jordan. In that same year a large exhibition in his honor was organized by the artists' society Arti et Amicitiae; this is considered a turning point in his career, as it is thought that the quality of his art declined dramatically afterward and that he did not develop further. In 1908–1909 Breitner traveled to Pittsburgh as a member of the committee for the International Exhibition of Oil Paintings, which was organized by the Carnegie Institute. He also visited Philadelphia and New York. Only one painting is known from this period. After 1914 his productivity declined. Breitner died in 1923 and was buried in the New East Cemetery in Amsterdam next to Witsen. The Rijksmuseum and the Stedelijk Museum in Amsterdam and the Gemeentemuseum in The Hague own large collections of his work.

Rieta Bergsma

See also Amsterdam Impressionists; Hague School, The; Israëls, Isaac; Photography, early; Townscapes; Verster, Floris; Witsen, Willem

Bibliography

Bergsma, Rieta, and Paul Hefting, eds. *George Hendrik Breitner, 1875–1923: Schilderijen, tekeningen, foto's*. Bussum: Thoth, 1994. (English Summary).

Bionda, Richard, and Carel Blotkamp, eds. *The Age of Van Gogh: Dutch Painting, 1880–1895*, 110–118. Zwolle: Waanders, 1990–1991.

Hefting, Paul H. *G.H. Breitner in zijn Haagse Tijd*. Utrecht: Haentjes, Dekker, and Gumbert, 1970.

———. *De foto's van Breitner*. The Hague: SDU, 1989.

Bronner, Jan (1881–1972)

From the age of thirteen, Jan Bronner worked in different sculptors' and painters' workshops in Haarlem, where he also took evening lessons at the Kunstnijverheidsschool (School of Arts and Crafts) from 1894 to 1897. Between 1907 and 1912, he studied at the Rijksacademie in Amsterdam under Bart van Hove. In 1912 he visited Paris where the work of Auguste Rodin made a strong impression on him.

His reputation was immediately established in 1914 by his winning design for a Hildebrand monument for Haarlem. Under this pseudonym, Nicolaas Beets (1814–1903) had written his popular book, *Camera Obscura*. Bronner's design consists of an octagonal fountain basin with eight personages from the book on the rim, and the figure of the narrator, Hildebrand himself, at a short distance from them. This design made such a great impression that, in the same year, Bronner was appointed professor of sculpture at the Rijksacademie as the successor to Van Hove.

The execution and placing of the monument took almost another fifty years. During this time, the form of the figures evolved from anecdotal and narrative to sober and stylized, so that they acquired greater unity of form with the architectural part of the fountain. The final models were ready in 1948, but the monument was not unveiled in the Haarlem Wood until 1962. Because the limestone statues were repeatedly damaged, they were replaced by copies in freestone. Since 1990, the original statues have been arranged in the garden of Museum 't Nijenhuis in Heino.

Bronner's relatively small *oeuvre* includes mainly small-scale sculptures, portrait busts, and several medals. Because he was a professor at the Rijksacademie until 1947, teaching sculpture to more than 140 students (many of whom would become famous), he had little time for his own work. Therefore, his significance lies primarily in the great influence he had on his students, whom he taught to think in volumes and to cut straight the stone themselves.

Mieke van der Wal

See also Andriessen, Mari; Coins, medals; Couzijn, Wessel; Public monumental sculpture (1795–1990); Sculpture (1795–1945); Van Hove, Bart

Bibliography

Bomans, Godfried, H.M. Wezelaar, Mari Andriessen, and Charles Leplae. *Het Hildebrand monument van Prof. J. Bronner*. Amsterdam/Brussels: Elsevier, 1948.

Hammacher, A.M. *Beeldhouwkunst van deze eeuw en een schets van haar ontwikkeling in de negentiende eeuw.* Amsterdam: Contact, 1955.

Neelissen, Ton, and Josine de Bruyn Kops. *Een beeld van Bronner 1881–1971*. Haarlem: Frans Hals Museum, 1971.

Brouwn, Stanley (born 1935)

Since the early 1960s, the Surinam-born conceptual artist Stanley Brouwn has concentrated on the human experience of space and movement as concretized in direction, dimension, and distance. Although his work is widely recognized, there is hardly any information available about Brouwn as an artist. He considers his work the vestige of just a "man walking on planet Earth" and seeks the anonymity that sustains this universal theme. Therefore, he refrains from giving any biographical information about himself.

Brouwn's official *oeuvre* starts with a small body of works from ca. 1960–1964 that has as its basis the concept of direction. Most of his early works that did not relate to this concept were destroyed or rejected by him. The most important work from this period is the *This way Brouwn* series, which is considered to be an early example of conceptual art. It originated from a series of Fluxus-like actions he performed in the streets, not making himself known as an artist. In this case he asked passersby to note down how he would get from point A to point B. Sheets of paper that he carried with him for this purpose were stamped "This way Brouwn" afterward.

From the early 1970s, Brouwn has been counting and measuring his footsteps, following the conclusion that One Step—the title of many of his works—is the shortest form of direction. As the basic element with which distances are covered and space is experienced, the footstep might be seen as fundamental to human existence. His ongoing activity of counting and measuring led to a large and still growing body of work, centering on the reciprocity of length and distance, that is presented in the form of drawings, artists' books, file cabinets, sheets of paper or aluminum, measuring rods, and temporary installations. In the 1980s, surface areas and architectural elements that relate to body measurements, such as doors, were introduced as new motifs in this exceptionally consistent *oeuvre*.

Ludo van Halem

See also Contemporary art (1980–1990); Fluxus

Bibliography

Brouwn, Stanley. *This Way Brouwn 25–2–61 26–2–61*. Cologne and New York: Verlag Gebr. König, 1971.

Graevenitz, Antje von. "The Artist As a Pedestrian: The Work of Stanley Brouwn." *Dutch Art + Architecture Today* 1 (1977): 2–11; reprinted in Dutch as "Stanley Brouwn: 'Je loopt op de planeet aarde.'" *Metropolis M* 6:2 (May–June 1985): 38–45.

Halem, Ludo van. "De stilte rond Stanley Brouwn." *AkT over kunst* 13:2 (September 1989): 2–12.

———. "Elementaire belevenissen: Het vroege werk van Stanley Brouwn." *Jong Holland* 7:3 (1991): 10–25. (English summary: 60).

Stanley Brouwn: La Biennale di Venezia 1982. Introduction by Jan Debbaut. Amsterdam: Visual Arts Office for Abroad, 1982.

C

Calligraphers and calligraphy (1550–1650)

Personified by Karel van Mander, the Flemish art theoretician, as the "tenth Muse" and "sister to Pictura," *schrijfconst* (the art of fine writing) originated in the Southern Netherlands, where calligraphers headed the so-called French schools, teaching their art within a curriculum that inculcated commercial skills. Schoolmasters, many of whom migrated to the Northern Netherlands after 1580, established their reputation through the publication of three types of calligraphic manual: the typographical writing book, comprising maxims printed in *civilité*, the letterpress version of the Gothic running hand, and decorated with richly ornamented initial letters; the capital-letter book, composed of ornate capitals printed in alphabetical order on otherwise blank folios, which the books' owners would complete by inscribing texts of their choice; and, for advanced students and connoisseurs, the costly *materie-boecken* (copy-books), also known as *exemplaer-boecken*, which consisted of short texts written in various *handelinghen* or *handen* (hands), the formal and informal variants of the national scripts—Dutch, English, French, German, Italian, and Spanish—as well as Latin. By 1600 the production of such books had shifted northward, and Dutch calligraphers became famous throughout Europe for their copy-books, which displayed unparalleled mastery of diverse hands, often embellished by flourishes, curved strokes of the pen that elaborate upon letterforms. In many cases, the flourishes expand into *pennetrekken*, continuous lines that loop and coil into images, which playfully allude to the kinship of *schrijfconst* and *schilderconst*, the arts of writing and picturing.

Published in Amsterdam in 1594, the first Dutch copy-book is the *Theatrum artis scribendi* (Theater of the Art of Writing), compiled, engraved, and issued by Jodocus Hondius, who had recently moved from Antwerp. Following a short instructional text on writing, Hondius assembles exempla by the greatest masters of his day: among others, the Frenchman De Beauchesne, the Italian Curione, the Englishmen Bales and Martin, and the Netherlanders Van Sambix, Henrix, and Van den Velde, who had placed first, second, and

third, respectively, in the great writing competition held in Rotterdam in January 1590, the contest for the Prix de la Plume Couronnée (Prize of the Crowned Quill). In addition to the seven European hands, Hondius includes specimens of Greek and Hebrew.

Cornelis Boissens, born in Enkhuizen in 1569, is the first Dutchman to have designed and engraved a copy-book, the *Promptuarium variarum scripturarum* (Handbook of Various Scripts), published in Amsterdam ca. 1594. Like Hondius, Boissens demonstrates his command of the seven hands, but he prefaces his specimens with a short text on Italian letterforms, and he includes *fondementen*, alphabets that diagram how individual letters are formed.

Both Boissens and Hondius based their copy-books on the innovative publications of the schoolmaster Clemens Perret, who was born in Brussels in 1551. His first and most important manual is the *Exercitatio alphabetica* (Alphabetical Exercise, 1569), whose full title, emphasizing that calligraphy is a pictorial art, claims that Perret's letterforms are novel, varied, and beautiful in their rare ornamentation, relief, and depth derived from painting and architecture. The *Exercitatio alphabetica* established the format used in later Dutch copy-books: the first calligraphic manual engraved entirely from copperplate and bound as an oblong folio volume, it was also the first to include the seven European hands. Applying the rhetorical principle of decorum, Perret inscribed Dutch texts in a Dutch hand, French texts in a French hand, and so forth. Moreover, he underscored the affinities of writing and picturing, surrounding his texts with strapwork frames that play upon the spatial ambiguities of convex and concave letterforms. These innovations derive, in turn, from two earlier books on writing—Erasmus' *De recta latini graecique sermonis pronuntiatione* (On the Correct Pronunciation of Latin and Greek Speech, 1528), which includes an excursus on the affinity of drawing and writing, and Gerard Mercator's *Literarum latinarum* (Latin Letters, 1540), a manual on italic script, which encourages the use of a Latin hand for Latin text.

Born in Antwerp in 1569, Jan van den Velde I became

the most celebrated writing master of his day. Perhaps trained by Van Sambix, he may have followed his master to Delft, there securing a position as assistant to the French schoolmaster Caspar Becq, himself a renowned calligrapher. He was resident in Rotterdam by 1592, having been appointed writing master at the city's Latin school, and he simultaneously ran a French school from his home. Collaborating with the master engravers Gerard Gauw and Simon Frisius, Van den Velde produced a series of copy-books, among them the *Deliciae variarum insigniumque scriptuarum* (Delights of Various and Distinguished Scripts) and the *Spieghel der schrijfkonste* (Mirror of the Art of Writing), both issued in 1605, which consolidated his reputation as an incomparable penman skilled at every inflection of letterform, flourish, and *pennetrek* (Fig. 16). The *Spieghel*, for example, contains masterful examples of every hand then in use in Western and Southern Europe. Part 1 demonstrates Van den Velde's command of Dutch, French, German, and English hands, focusing especially on *gemeyne* (common) and *loopende* (running) scripts, the so-called common forms of running hand, favored by merchants, notaries, and secretaries who needed to record information quickly and precisely. Part 2, subtitled *Thresor literaire* (Literary Treasure), displays facility at cursive hands, the Latin, Italian, and Spanish in particular, which Van den Velde identifies with the *snel-lichte* (quick-effortless) usage of a noble and learned calligrapher. Part 3, the *Fondement-Boeck* (Book of Fundamentals), by turns handbook and treatise, offers a theory of the art of writing that is unique in its ambition and scope. Van den Velde assembles sixteen plates of *fondementen* covering the hands essayed in Parts 1 and 2, but, more important, he explains the calligrapher's aims. In doing so, he extends the argument of his first publication, the *Lettre défensive* (Letter of Defense) of 1599, issued to contravene Martin Wentsel, whose arithmetical primer of 1599 contained an attack on the educational value of calligraphy.

Van den Velde argues in the *Lettre* and *Spieghel* that he seeks to conform to a distinctive, yet universal, standard of imitation. Just as an arithmetician cannot rely on two or three rules only, but must know all numerical rules, and a French instructor cannot know only fragments of the language, but must grasp it thoroughly to render it cogently, so too the master penman cannot rely simply on one hand or two, but must command multifarious hands—the precious and highly wrought, the fleet and swift—in order to fulfill all functions and appeal to all readers. What confers distinction on the calligrapher, then, is not the promulgation of new letterforms, for the European hands have been strictly codified, but rather the ability to impersonate many penmen and to subsume one's hand into many hands. Following this logic, Van den Velde, instead of exploring new scripts in Part 2 of the *Spieghel*, has imitated variations on the italic hand perfected by Italian writing masters of the sixteenth century, renewing their accomplishments by accommodating his hand to theirs. This approach to imitation, which casts penmanship as a mode of impersonation, provided an alternative to the paradigm of emulation set forth in texts on rhetoric and poetry, which argue that the imitator must strive to surpass and transform the object of imitation, rather than simply translating it.

There was a great proliferation of writing manuals between 1605 and 1650, although none achieved the theoretical sophistication of the *Spieghel*. Having engraved the *Spieghel* for Van den Velde, Frisius himself executed a copy-book, the *Lust-hof der schrijf-konste* (Pleasure Garden of the Art of Writing), issued in 1610. Born in Harlingen ca. 1575, Frisius first settled in Paris, where he served the French calligraphers De Beaugrand, Le Gangneur, and Vignon, engraving a series of writing manuals on the Italian hand. After moving to Amsterdam ca. 1600 and then to The Hague ca. 1611, he pursued a successful career as a merchant, commercial agent, calligrapher, and etcher-engraver. Famed for his ability to translate the penman's ductile line into the resistant medium of copperplate, Frisius exemplified the paradigm of imitation set forth in Van den Velde's *Fondement-Boeck*. Besides engraving in the manner of writing, he also etched in the manner of engraving; the *St. Jerome* (1624), a large drawing in bister on linen, demonstrates that he could draw, too, in the manner of engraving. For David Roelands, the most accomplished calligrapher resident in Zeeland, Frisius engraved *t'Magazin oft' pac-huys der loffelycker penn-const* (Storehouse or Warehouse of the Praiseworthy Art of the Pen, 1617), which rivals Van den Velde's *Spieghel* in its variety of hands, ornamental flourishes, and intricate *pennetrekken*.

Born in 's Hertogenbosch in 1577 and trained by her father, the French schoolmaster Caspar Becq, as well as by Van Sambix and Van den Velde, Maria Strick became famous as a master of the Italian hands. She managed her father's school in Delft after his death in 1606, but ca. 1615 she moved to Rotterdam, where she opened a French school. Collaborating with her husband, the engraver Hans Strick, she produced four copy-books, the first of which, *Tooneel der loflijcke schrijfpen* (Theatre of the Praiseworthy Writing Pen), appeared in 1609. In the writing competition held in The Hague in 1620, she won second prize, beating the first-prize winner, George de Carpentier, French schoolmaster of Hoorn, in the execution of Italian scripts. Like Van den Velde, Boissens, and other calligraphers, she relied on the agency of a reproductive engraver to broadcast her virtuosity. In a contract signed by Hans Strick and the Rotterdam publisher Hendrick Crijnsz. Volmarijn, we learn that Strick received thirty-eight Flemish pounds in yearly installments of five pounds for engraving twenty-three plates after writing specimens by his wife.

Dutch towns vied for the services of the most renowned calligraphers, who were engaged by the municipalities as French or Latin schoolmasters and occasionally as town clerks. Among these masters were Anthoni Smyters, French schoolmaster in Amsterdam and author of the *Schryfkunst boeck* (Book on the Art of Writing, 1613); Samuel de Swaef, French schoolmaster in Bergen-op-Zoom and author-engraver of the *Proef-stuck van de schryf-konste* (Demonstration of the Art of Writing, 1619); Abraham van Overbeke, French schoolmaster to a series of towns in Zeeland and author of the *Beque der schrijfkonste* (Font of the Art of Writing, 1630); and Henry Lancel, French schoolmaster in Zierikzee and coauthor with De Swaef of the *Gedichten van verscheijde poëten* (Poems by

Various Poets, 1630). These and other calligraphers continued to demonstrate their facility in multifarious hands, long after popular usage had begun to favor the italic hand above local cursives. Yet the criteria of penmanship promoted in their texts remained pertinent to draftsmen, engravers, and all other artisans who aimed to delineate with a sure and supple hand.

Walter S. Melion

Bibliography

Croiset van Uchelen, Anthony R.A. "Abraham van Overbeke, an Early-Seventeenth-Century Writing Master from Zeeland." *Quaerendo* 2 (1972): 278–289.

———. *Deliciae: Over de schrijfkunst van Jan van den Velde*. Haarlem: J. Enschedé, 1984.

———. "Dutch Writing Masters and the Prix de la Plume Couronnée." *Quaerendo* 6 (1976): 319–346.

———. "The Mysterious Writing Master Clemens Perret and His Two Copy-Books." *Quaerendo* 17 (1987): 3–44.

———. *Nederlandse schrijfmeesters uit de zeventiende eeuw*. The Hague: Rijksmuseum Meermanno-Westreenianum, 1978.

——— "Samuel de Swaef and Henry Lancel, *Gedichten van verscheijde poëten*: An Early-Seventeenth-Century Schoolmasters' Combine." *Quaerendo* 4 (1974): 291–316.

De la Fontaine Verwey, Herman. "The Golden Age of Dutch Calligraphy." In *Miniatures, Scripts, Collections: Essays Presented to G.I. Lieftinck 4*. Edited by J.P. Gumbert and M.J.M. de Haan, 69–78. Amsterdam: A.L. van Gendt, 1976.

Melion, Walter S. "Memory and the Kinship of Writing and Picturing in the Early-Seventeenth-Century Netherlands." *Word and Image* 8 (1992): 48–70.

Osley, Arthur S. "A Check-List of Sixteenth- and Seventeenth-Century Writing Books." *Philobiblon* 15 (1971): 183–206.

Worthen, Amy N. "Calligraphic Inscriptions on Dutch Mannerist Prints." In *Goltzius Studies: Hendrick Goltzius 1558–1617*. Edited by Reindert Falkenberg, Jan Piet Filedt Kok, and Huigen Leeflang, 261–306. Zwolle: Waanders, 1993.

Carnal life, carnal vices

Although the fifteenth-century tradition of the Seven Deadly Sins also appears in the sixteenth century, this rigid doctrinal method generally gave way to a broader approach in the pictorial treatment of vice. Under the impact of humanism, artists turned to moralizing secular images, biblical narratives, and, occasionally, the lives of saints before their conversion.

Satirical and moralizing secular subjects include the *Ill-Matched Pair* (ca. 1515; Washington, DC, National Gallery of Art) by Quinten Massys and the *Card Players* (ca. 1515; Wilton House, Salisbury, Collection Earl of Pembroke) by Lucas van Leyden and other versions by his followers. Many scholars see these works as concerned with the folly of sexual desire and its consequences. The images thus belong to a larger group of literary and visual works dealing with folly in a variety of forms.

The market and kitchen scenes of Pieter Aertsen and Joachim Beuckelaer also address the carnal life. These works fill the foreground with a rich, sensual array of produce and meat; a secondary scene—often a biblical episode—occupies the background. Though these images have generated a lively scholarly debate, many art historians see them as moralizing commentaries on the temptations of the flesh and point to both Christian and humanist ideas informing the images.

In the realm of religious subjects, narrative images of biblical stories such as the prodigal son and the Israelites' dance around the golden calf have been seen as commentaries on sensual pleasures. Similar interpretations have been made of images such as those depicting the sinful life of St. Mary Magdalene before her conversion. The Magdalene, of course, also appeared frequently as a penitent hermit saint, as did St. Jerome and St. Anthony. With their emphasis on asceticism and denial, these latter images present the other side of the coin in the depiction of carnal life.

Janey L. Levy

See also Aertsen, Pieter; Bosch, Hieronymus; Commerce and commercial life; Humanism, humanist themes; Sins and punishments; Van Leyden, Lucas

Bibliography

Irmscher, Günter. "*Ministrae voluptatum*: Stoicizing Ethics in the Market and Kitchen Scenes of Pieter Aertsen and Joachim Beuckelaer." *Simiolus* 16 (1986): 219–232.

Silver, Larry. *The Paintings of Quinten Massys, with Catalogue Raisonné*. Montclair, NJ: Allanheld and Schram, 1984.

Smith, Elise Lawton. *The Paintings of Lucas van Leyden: A New Appraisal, with Catalogue Raisonné*. Columbia, MO: University of Missouri Press, 1992.

Cartography

The map as a work of art reached its quintessence in the Northern Netherlands during the seventeenth century. This development resulted from the felicitous confluence of three great achievements of this tiny land: critical advances in navigation and cartography, unparalleled growth and excellence in the pictorial arts, and affluence based in large part upon maritime commerce.

The rising prosperity of a large and literate middle class created a burgeoning market for lavishly decorated and geographically accurate maps. These were available as individual sheets, colossal wall maps, multivolume atlases, folios, and globes. Although it was possible for one craftsman to produce a map in its entirety, the production of maps in the late sixteenth and the seventeenth century grew into an industry that relied upon workers with specialized skills: cartographers, engravers and etchers, printers, publishers, artists to design the decorative motifs, and illuminators to paint and gild the decoration. Many of the artists selected for map production were already well known and respected for their works on canvas or prints. The quality of the art on many of the maps rivaled the geographic content as the *raison d'etre* of the work.

The pictorial motifs added to the maps varied considerably in type and content. Decoration was placed within the map proper or in borders. Subjects within the map included ships, monsters, allegorical figures, and portraits of navigators, cartographers, or rulers. Cartouches containing titles, dates, and textual information were usually embellished with portraits or genre-type scenes. The borders, which often were printed separately, contained strips or blocks of graphic works showing city views; costumed figures; allegorical scenes, such as the continents, seasons, and months; or encyclopedic-like collections of animals of the world. Secular scenes occurred more often than biblical ones on country or world maps. Scenes depicting stories of the Bible were used to ornament maps that were bound with the Dutch Bible.

To underwrite the enormous expense involved in publishing a new map, publishers looked for wealthy patrons, the usual ones being heads of government, affluent burghers, or royalty, who used maps as gifts. To repay the generosity of a patron, or to flatter a patron into supporting the publication of a map, a publisher included a laudatory dedication.

Antwerp dominated world map production in the sixteenth century, laying a firm foundation upon which seventeenth-century publishers built. Accuracy and fame of maps published in Antwerp were due in large part to the expertise of two giants in cartography, Gerard Mercator (1512–1594) and Abraham Ortelius (1527–1598). Mercator was trained as a mathematician, land surveyor, and instrument maker; he is remembered for the projection that bears his name. He also drew, engraved, colored, and published his own maps. Ortelius was an antique dealer who initially entered mapping as a buyer and illuminator of maps. He is most noted for his world atlas, *Theatrum Orbis Terrarum,* which was a collection of the best maps available. Among the famous printmakers who engraved or etched maps for Ortelius were Frans and Abraham Hogenberg, Jan Wierix, Jan van Doetecum, and his two sons, Baptista and Jan the Younger.

To decorate a map, an engraver often drew upon already published prints. Ortelius' maps were ornamented with motifs taken from print series by Hans Vredeman de Vries and Jacob Floris. One map by Ortelius, *The Abraham Map* of 1586, was ornamented with twenty-two biblical scenes drawn especially for the map by his friend, the esteemed Antwerp artist Maerten (Fig. 17). The coloring, or illuminating, of Ortelius' maps was done by his sisters. Another artist who worked closely with Ortelius was Joris Hoefnagel, who contributed city views to Braun and Hogenberg's *Civitates Orbis Terrarum* (1572–1618).

After 1585 Antwerp declined as the center for map production. Cartographers and artists alike fled Spanish oppression, flocking to the Northern Netherlands. There they provided an influx of talent into the expanding city of Amsterdam. Mapmaking flourished and the ornamentation on maps became more elaborate, requiring skilled engravers. Some of the engravers who worked for Amsterdam publishers were Baptista van Doetecum, Jan Saenredam, Jacob

Matham, Salomon Savery, Claes Jansz. Visscher, Jan Visscher, Abraham Blooteling, Pieter Goos, Jodocus and Henricus Hondius, and Philibertus Bouttats. These engravers often copied motifs from prints after the work of Flemish artists, such as Maarten de Vos, Frans Pourbus I, Jan van der Straet (Stradanus), Marcus Gheeraerts, and Hans Bol. Designs were also taken from the work of artists born or working in the Northern Netherlands, such as Hendrick Goltzius, Jacob de Gheyn II, Jan van Scorel, Dirck Barendsz., and Cornelis Ketel.

Publishers also commissioned a great number of well-known artists to draw models for specific maps. One can find drawings that are mirror images of the printed map designs and were indented when copied by the engraver onto the copper plate. In 1604 the cartographer and theologian Petrus Plancius (1552–1622) edited a set of five maps of the Holy Lands that were bound with a new edition of the Bible published by Jan Evertsz. Cloppenborch, an Amsterdam printer, publisher, and bookseller. These maps were ornamented with sixty-one vignettes showing biblical scenes drawn by the Amsterdam landscape and genre artist David Vinckboons (1576–1632) (Fig. 18). Today five of Vinckboons' drawings used for the map prints are known. A few years later, Vinckboons provided the decoration for another Plancius map, a world map of 1607. For this map, Vinckboons contributed border illustrations showing contemporary rulers receiving their subjects. Two of Vinckboons' drawings for these prints are extant. This artist also provided decorative motifs for a large wall map of the world of 1605 published by Willem Blaeu. Although only the cartouche decoration can be traced to Vinckboons, it is likely that he supplied models for much of the other ornamentation as well.

A drawing in Leiden by Adriaen van de Venne (1589–1662) matches a print on a map that depicted Frederik Hendrik and his well-trained troops relieving the besieged city of 's Hertogenbosch in 1629. This map was published by Balthasar Florisz. van Berckenrode and engraved by Salomon Savery.

Another artist who drew motifs for maps was Frans Post (1612–1680). Post spent seven years in Brazil between 1637 and 1644 drawing the people, animals, flowers, and landscape for the Dutch governor of Brazil, Johan Maurits van Nassau. Some of these designs were used to ornament a map of Brazil drawn by Georg Marcgraf and published by Joan Blaeu in 1647.

Nicolaes Berchem (1620–1683), son of the still-life painter Pieter Claesz., contributed a great many designs for maps. He provided allegorical scenes of the elements for the corner decoration of a 1658 world map published by Nicolaes Visscher. Berchem's drawn models are today in Vienna. This artist also drew decorative motifs for a map of America and a map of Asia published by Visscher. Berchem's drawing for the America map is in Windsor Castle; that for the Asia map was with a Paris dealer in 1984. The engraver of these maps was Jan Visscher. Together with Abraham Blooteling, Jan Visscher also engraved five maps ornamented with twenty biblical vignettes designed by Berchem. These maps were commissioned as illustrations for *La Sainte Bible* published by Louys and Daniel Elzevier in 1669. Nine of Berchem's original drawings used by the two engravers are known today.

Adriaen van de Velde (1636–1672), the Italianate landscape painter, drew the four continents that decorate a map of Amsterdam published by Frederick de Wit. Van de Velde's models for the map prints are in a private Amsterdam collection.

The late seventeenth-century painter and art theoretician Gerard de Lairesse (1641–1711) prepared cartouche decorations and title plates for maps by Nicolaes Visscher I and Nicolaes Visscher II. Lairesse's vignettes are in the classical style he favored for his history painting. A cartouche on a map of Brabant depicts a river god and Ceres with her horn of plenty. Lairesse's drawing for this is in Amsterdam. The map of the Archbishopric of Trier shows Diana with bow and arrow. Two drawings for this are known: A sketch is in the Rijksmuseum Kröller-Müller in Otterlo and a more developed design is in the Musée du Louvre in Paris. Gilliam van Gouwen was the engraver of Lairesse's map prints.

Another artist known primarily for his theoretical writings, Arnold Houbraken (1660–1719), also helped decorate maps. A 1712 map of Delfland by Jacob and Nicolaes Kruikius shows vignettes by Houbraken (engraved by Pieter Sluyter) in which there are figures clad in classical garb, *putti* emptying an overflowing horn of plenty, and *putti* playing with dogs. A cartouche is ornamented with two satyrs.

In addition to the painters who designed motifs for maps, a few painters drew the entire map. Such was the case with Pieter Saenredam (1597–1665) and Jacob de Gheyn II (1565–1629). Saenredam drew three maps that were engraved by Jan van de Velde and Willem Akersloot to illustrate Samuel Ampzing's description of Haarlem published in 1628. In constructing his maps, Saenredam copied from older maps and also made his own sketches of the area. He used artistic license in depicting the relative size of objects, such as ships and St. Bavo's church. De Gheyn engraved and designed *Siege of Geertruidenberg*, which was commissioned by the Amsterdam City and Board of Admiralty to immortalize Prince Maurits's feats in battle. De Gheyn engraved the map on two copper plates showing the river, the city, the city's defenses, and the approach and positions of the armies. De Gheyn also drew and engraved in 1597 a plan and view of the city of Schiedam for the Town Council. In 1598 he engraved and etched a plan of the court and village of The Hague that showed streets and buildings. At the front, he placed figures in contemporary dress who stroll across the map, a device he copied from Joris Hoefnagel's maps in the Braun and Hogenberg atlas of cities.

Although the Dutch continued to publish lavish maps well into the eighteenth century, accuracy and quality began to decline in the 1680s. Later publishers, such as Schenk and Valk, reused plates from the Visschers and Blaeu, turning out maps for those who wanted eye-catching wall decorations or magnificent atlases. For accurate maps, customers turned to French publishers. A new era was beginning in which the decorative qualities of maps would play an increasingly ancillary role.

Shirley K. Bennett

See also Allegorical traditions; Atlas, atlases; Coins, medals; Matham, Jacob; Prints, early printed book and Bible illustration; Prints, publishers; Vinckboons, David

Bibliography
Bennett, Shirley K. "Art on Maps, 1585–1685: Themes and Sources." Ph.D. diss., University of Maryland, 1990.
———. "Drawings by David Vinckboons as Models for Ornamenting Bible Maps." *Hoogsteder—Naumann Mercury* 10 (1989): 15–25.
———. "Drawings by Maerten de Vos: Designs to Ornament an Ortelius Map." *Hoogsteder Mercury* 11 (1990): 5–13.
———. "Nine Religious Drawings by Nicolaes Berchem: Designs to Ornament Maps in a 1669 Bible." *Hoogsteder Mercury* 13/14 (1992): 60–73.
Kunst in Kaart: Decoratieve aspecten van de cartografie. Edited by J.F. Heijbroek and Marijn Schapelhouman. Utrecht: HES, 1989.
Rees, Ronald. "Historical Links between Cartography and Art." *Geographical Review* 70 (1980): 62–78.
Schaar E. "Zeichnungen Berchems zu Landkarten." *Oud Holland* 71 (1956): 239–243.
Schilder, Günter. "Some Decorative Maps of Holland, 1569–1610." *Map Collector* (December 1978): 21–28.
Welu, James. "The Sources and Development of Cartographic Ornamentation in the Netherlands." *Art and Cartography.* Edited by David Woodward. Chicago and London: University of Chicago Press, 1987.
Zandvliet, Kees. *De Groote Waereld in 't Kleen Geschildert.* Alphen aan den Rijn: Canaletto, 1985.

Cats, Jacob (1577–1660)

See Emblems and emblem books; Genre painting, seventeenth century; History painting; Van Schurman, Anna Maria

Cats, Jacob (1741–1799)

One of the most accomplished and revered landscape draftsmen and watercolorists of the eighteenth century, Jacob Cats moved from his birthplace of Altona, Germany, to Amsterdam with his book-dealer father and began work for a cloth merchant. Soon after, Cats worked for a short time for a bookbinder, then began to take lessons in engraving from Abraham Starre. He studied drawing with Pieter Louw for three-and-a-half years, then became a pupil of the landscape painter and stencil maker Gerard van Rossum and worked in the wallpaper factory of Troost van Groenendoelen. Cats decided to create his own wallpaper business and was assisted financially by a relative, Willem Writs, and two friends from the art world, Johannes Goll and Jan de Bosch. Active in Cats' factory was the youthful Egbert van Drielst, who became an important painter and watercolorist in his own right. Cats collaborated with Van Drielst, painting the figures for his landscapes. Cats also gave drawing lessons at his factory; his best-known student is now considered a minor artist, Jan Evert Grave.

As Cats' wallpaper business declined, he gravitated toward his first love, which was drawing landscapes and topographicals. His preparation in the large format of wall decoration helped Cats maintain a coolness and lush interpretation of the towns he drew. His drawings were presumably inventions as much from memory as from the necessity he felt to alter the scenes for dramatic effect. He became one of the most sought-after artists of his genre; one of his most popular subjects were night townscapes. His drawings appealed through their atmospheric clarity and sense of actuality. His scenes are populated with figures engaged in everyday activities, yet they are never trite. While his work relies on the style of his predecessors Jan van der Heyden and Gerrit Berckheyde, his drawings are infused with an intimacy and actuality that surpass their art, making Cats one of the finest draftsmen in Europe of his time.

Roger Mandle

See also Berckheyde, Gerrit Adriaensz.; Townscapes; Van der Heyden, Jan

Bibliography

Mandle, R. *Dutch Masterpieces of the Eighteenth Century: Paintings and Drawings, 1700–1800.* Minneapolis: Minneapolis Institute of Arts; Toledo: Toledo Museum of Art; Philadelphia: Philadelphia Museum of Art, 1971.

Niemeijer, J.W. *Eighteenth-Century Watercolors from the Rijksmuseum Printroom, Amsterdam.* Alexandria, VA: Art Services International, 1993.

Ceramics

At different times the Netherlands has been the site of a thriving ceramics production. During the seventeenth century, the Dutch earthenware industry in Delft was one of the most important in Europe. After 1750 Delftware began to decline, and by 1800 there were few innovations. In the course of the nineteenth and twentieth centuries, other kinds of ceramics were developed, which created new vitality in the art.

The Origin and Decline of Delftware

Around 1500 the earthenware products in the Netherlands were mainly simple utilitarian pieces in addition to floor tiles and bricks. The objects were thrown in little potteries using locally found red and, sometimes, yellow clay. Decorations often were applied with the help of white engobe, or coating, made from the silt of white clay, and a layer of clear shiny lead glaze was applied over it to make the objects waterproof. A number of the shapes and decorations of this so-called folk earthenware remained unchanged for centuries, and some are even used today. Research on Dutch tableware has been done mainly by archeologists until recently. The Museum Boymans-Van Beuningen in Rotterdam has assumed an important role in this, establishing a separate wing in 1991 for the collection of findings from the digs. The many ceramic objects in this collection are the subject of several extensive research projects, in which the focus is on the cultural context. The results have been reported in a number of exhibitions and accompanying publications.

Shortly after 1500, the production of a more refined sort of earthenware was started in Antwerp after the arrival of several Italian potters, who introduced the techniques, shapes, colors, and decorations of Italian tin-glazed earthenware, or majolica. Plates, ointment jars, syrup jugs, and pitchers, as well as tiles, received a thin layer of clear white tin glaze, on which decorations were painted with metal oxides in different colors. On top of this a layer of shiny lead glaze was applied for protection. The Italian model is easily recognizable in the shapes and decorations of these Antwerp majolica. They include stylized flower and leaf motifs and exotic fruits, grotesquery, and reproductions of portraits, allegorical, religious, mythological, or biblical scenes. Geometric patterns were also copied from the Spanish-Moorish ceramics that were often traded in the Netherlands. Decorations with tulips and family coats of arms are a typical Dutch invention. Around 1550 the production of majolica was started in the northern provinces. Especially after the fall of Antwerp in 1585, a result of the rebellion of the Netherlands against the Spanish king, many majolica makers from Antwerp moved north and contributed to the development of prospering potteries in Haarlem, Amsterdam, Delft, and Rotterdam.

Of great consequence for the ceramics industry was the introduction of blue-painted Chinese export porcelain on the Dutch market around 1600. The porcelain possessed a refinement of material and decoration that was unknown to the Dutch. Majolica potters soon copied the blue decorations and the shapes of Chinese porcelain in a simplified form. The porcelain inspired some potters to improve their material; new methods were developed to purify and mix the clay better, the body became thinner and lighter in color, and the white layer of tin glaze was applied to not just the front but also the back of plates. Porcelain clay was found in Europe only after 1709, so making real porcelain was not possible in Europe during the seventeenth century. But the painting of earthenware did become more precise. To compete better with porcelain, Chinese patterns were not imitated on this finer earthenware, but attractive European decorations such as biblical stories, landscapes, and family coats of arms were applied. This new Dutch product was called *Porceleyn* during the seventeenth century, but nowadays it is called faïence. The coarser majolica was still made for a long time, but on a smaller scale, and it held its own mainly in specialized products like apothecary jars, which experienced no competition from Chinese porcelain.

The tile industry felt no competition at all and was even able to expand quite a bit with the increase of construction activity in the seventeenth century. After 1650 the Dutch tile industry was concentrated in Rotterdam, even though some production of tiles, as well as old-fashioned majolica, continued in Harlingen and Makkum in Friesland. In houses usually built of brick, tiles were a practical and decorative protection for floors and walls. After 1625 it became fashionable to paint them in blue and white. Gradually the motifs became less busy, and many tiles even remained completely white. In the eighteenth century a new color to decorate tiles became fashionable—

manganese purple. Pictures made up of different tiles as well as large tile plates with refined paintings were made exclusively for prosperous private patrons and institutions.

When a change of dynasty in China in 1647 nearly ended the importing of porcelain from Asia, the new faïence was able to answer an important part of the demand for luxury ceramics. At this time, Delft already had seventy workplaces and the production of tin-glazed earthenware soared so rapidly that the name Delftware has become synonymous with the term faïence in art historical literature. After the blue-and-white Chinese porcelain disappeared from the market, beautiful imitations of it were made in Delft (Fig. 19); and when colorful kinds of porcelain were imported from Japan and China after 1670, these were imitated as well. Around the year 1700, figurines were made in Delft after Chinese models; this selection was soon expanded with European figures and especially small sculptures of cows that were very popular.

In 1709 Johann Friedrich Böttger discovered porcelain clay in Saxony. The result was the establishment of porcelain factories in different places in Europe in a short time after the founding of the royal porcelain factory of Meissen in Saxony. In spite of the labor-intensive and expensive process of making European porcelain, it became a source of inspiration as well as of challenging competition for the faïence producers. Delft earthenware factories made fine and cheaper imitations, but their position in the market was already becoming more difficult after 1750. Then creamware came on the European market—high-fired earthenware with a cream white body, of high quality, and for a reasonable price. It was developed by factories in Staffordshire, England, among them the one of Josiah Wedgwood, who improved the method of making earthenware, refined the division of labor, and replaced the manual work by machines wherever possible. The Delft earthenware factories, with their old-fashioned methods, could not compete, and within a short time many went out of business. Only a few were left around 1800.

Art historical research on Dutch majolica and Delft faïence began in the nineteenth century, and it is not yet completed. Until 1920 the emphasis was on collecting data in the archives about different workplaces and masters. An attempt was made to develop a chronology and to ascribe groups of pottery to identified workplaces by comparing styles. An effort also was started to study the technical procedure. Given that stylistic criteria alone appeared to be a limited means of providing a balanced and complete picture of earthenware production, C.H. de Jonghe published an extensive study in 1947, in which she gave attention not only to the technique and new data from the archives but also to recent archeological finds. J.D. van Dam, curator of ceramics at the Rijksmuseum in Amsterdam, built upon this method in 1982 in an article about the development of majolica and faïence between 1560 and 1660; in addition to the archival, stylistic, technical, and archeological evidence, he also used economic and cultural historical facts.

In 1987 the Dutch Delftware Foundation (Stichting Delfts Aardewerk) was founded with the objective of preparing a publication in English about the tin-glazed earthenware that was made in Delft between 1560 and 1860, exclusive of tiles. To get a coherent picture of Delft production, many archival discoveries and much art historical data have to be organized and compared with the archeological finds. Furthermore, it is desirable to make an inventory of all dated and marked pieces, and all technical developments in the production process must be placed in order. The different stylistic influences on the decoration, the influence of Delft on the earthenware industry elsewhere in Europe, and the use and distribution of the products also have to be addressed.

Porcelain

For a short time in the eighteenth century, porcelain of a high quality was made in the Netherlands, but this was in difficult economic circumstances. Lacking the patronage of monarchs customary in other places in Europe, the Dutch also had costs that were higher because materials, porcelain painters, and technical specialists were brought in from abroad.

In the little city of Weesp, in the province of Utrecht, in 1757 the first Dutch porcelain factory was established. Here the ware produced was painted in different colors with flowers, animals, and rural scenes. Fourteen years later, in 1771, the inventory of this factory was sold to the clergyman De Mol from Oud-Loosdrecht, a nearby village. The clergyman hoped that his porcelain factory would fight the great unemployment in this area and consequently decrease the distressing poverty. In an eight-year period, between 1774 and 1782, many fine pieces were made here. In the beginning, a number of unfired pieces from Weesp were also decorated in Loosdrecht and, besides ware for table service, beautiful ornamental vases (Fig. 20), figurines, and plaquettes were made. Very characteristic are the monochromatic scenes of landscapes, bouquets, and birds in *encre de Chine*, beet red, red-orange, and sepia. The factory changed hands again and was moved in 1784 to Ouder-Amstel, then in 1809 to the nearby Nieuwer-Amstel, both on the outskirts of Amsterdam. Here tasteful, fashionable products were made, but because of the poor economic circumstances the factory had to be finally closed down in 1820.

Dutch porcelain can be found chiefly in Dutch collections, and until recently mainly articles and small catalogs have been written about these collections. Important research has been published about Loosdrecht porcelain, in a book that came out on the occasion of an exhibition at the Rijksmuseum in 1988. Besides surveying the shapes, scenes, and marks on Loosdrecht porcelain, the authors also paid attention to the function, uses, and marketing of the porcelain, and to the social-economic situation.

Industrial Earthenware

Around 1800 there was little left of the Delft earthenware industry. In 1836, Petrus Regout was the first to stand up to the English competition by starting a ceramics factory in Maastricht called De Sphinx, where English creamware was copied. The products he made were not different or finer, but because he was closer to the buyers in Europe, he could compete with the factories in Staffordshire and his company was able to grow into a thriving industry, which, in a modified form, is still in business.

Industrial Art Pottery

After 1850, when many technical improvements had changed the ceramics industry, more criticism could be heard in Europe about the leveling off of artistic quality. This was partly due to the new techniques by which shapes and decorations had been copied indiscriminately. To improve the artistic quality of the products, some companies brought in artists to make the designs. Furthermore, there was a movement to go back to decorating by hand. These new ceramics, designed by artists and hand-decorated were called "art pottery," and they were produced only in small numbers.

In the Netherlands, the new formula for art pottery caused a great number of new earthenware factories to be established. The only remaining factory in Delft, De Porceleyne Fles, was the first to respond and appointed architect Adolf Le Comte as a designer in 1877. He based his first drawings on the old patterns of Delft blue earthenware, but soon after he made new scenes with, among other things, town views or copies of famous paintings. Some years later, a faïence pottery known as the Plateelbakkerij Rozenburg was started in The Hague where Theodoor A.C. Colenbrander, also an architect, made sensational designs between 1885 and 1889. His shapes and scenes were inspired by nature and strongly influenced by art from the Middle East (Fig. 21). Around 1900, Rozenburg brought the very thin ware of eggshell porcelain onto the market under the direction of manager J. Juriaan Kok. It was painted with asymmetrical scenes of animals and flowers that were inspired by Japanese art. This porcelain made the factory world famous, and the scenes were copied by many new art potteries. This happened, for example, in the faïence factory Zuid-Holland in Gouda, but it soon also made ornamental and tableware after designs by its own artists.

Industrially produced ceramics had a difficult time in the Netherlands during the 1930s and 1940s. They revived for a brief time afterward, but the phenomenon of industrial art pottery had disappeared. In the years between 1950 and 1970 many wares of modern design were introduced on the market; however, most Dutch companies eventually lost the fight with cheaper competitors from Eastern Europe and West Germany and had to close down. Since 1969 only a few ceramics factories have been active in the Netherlands. Remarkably, one of them is the old Delftware factory of De Porceleyne Fles.

Art Pottery and Crafts

Some artists rejected on principle the methods of the industry, thus giving new life to the nearly lost craft of folk earthenware. The graphic artist Willem C. Brouwer, following ideas of William Morris, leader of the English Arts and Crafts Movement, started his own pottery in Leiderdorp in 1901. Here with several workmen, he made his Art Nouveau designs in small series entirely by hand. After several years of applying the decorations on the form with colored clay or carving in the clay, he later used colorful liquid glazes exclusively in the decoration of his forms. Brouwer's work had much success, especially because it appeared to be very suitable for modern flower arrangements. During the 1920s, several other potteries were started that worked in the same way as Brouwer did—those of Zaalberg father and son, Pieter Groeneveldt, the Mobach brothers, and Gerrit de Blanken. The craft of ceramics has been able to hold on in the form of small potteries, and it survives mainly on making dishes, pots, and flower vases.

Ceramics As Art

Going a step further than Brouwer, Chris Lanooy established himself as the first Dutch ceramic artist in 1907. Inspired by the work of French ceramic artists, he made by hand unique pieces that he considered to be an expression of his personal feelings and equal to the fine arts. Like the French, he was inspired by Japanese and Chinese ceramics and used only colorful glazes as decoration. Several other ceramic artists followed. In 1918 the first course in ceramic art was offered at the Quellinus School for arts and crafts in Amsterdam under the direction of Bert Nienhuis. Lea H. Halpen was one of the students who gained international fame after 1930. Until 1940 practically all ceramic artists decorated their work exclusively with colorful glazes.

After 1945 ceramic art experienced a great efflorescence; young potters looked for new styles and experimented with old and new techniques. They found different sources of inspiration and pursued internships in factories and with potters abroad. The use of colored glazes for decoration remained, but the style changed. The Englishman Bernard Leach, who chose his models from the coarser kinds of Asian ceramics, had an especially great influence. Dirk Hubers was one of the first to apply abstract graphic designs on his objects. Since the 1960s the boundary between sculpture and ceramic art has become blurred. Utilitarian objects like vases, bowls, and dishes are still made, but many abstract and figurative forms are also modeled. A contemporary ceramic artist whose work is well received is Geert Lap. His work has special sculptural value through the proportions, which are strengthened by the marvelous colored engobes covering the forms (Fig. 22).

A great deal of research has already been done on Dutch ceramics after the nineteenth century, although there are still possibilities in this area as well. The rise of ceramic craftsmen and artists after 1900 has been described by Mieke Spruit-Ledeboer, who has also written about handmade Dutch ceramics between 1975 and 1985. Evert van Straaten expanded on this research in a survey of the Dutch earthenware industry since 1876. Much information about factories, potteries, and ceramic artists can be found in catalogs of exhibitions and articles in Dutch art periodicals. However, there are still several companies and artists that have not been sufficiently studied. Among the latter are Lea H. Halpern and Marguérite Wildenhain-Friedländer, who because they were Jewish fled to the United States when World War II threatened. Also urgently in need of research are Franz Wildenhain and Dirk Hubers, who emigrated to the United States shortly after 1945.

Christien F.W. Smits

See also Applied arts; Delft; Exotica; *Japonisme*; Non-Western cultural influences; Tiles

Bibliography

Blaauwen, A.L. den et al. *Loosdrechts porselein, 1774–1784.* Zwolle: Waanders, 1988. (English summary).

Dam, J.D. van. "Geleyersgoet en Hollands Porceleyn: Ontwikkelingen in de Nederlandse aardewerk-industrie 1560–1660." *Mededelingenblad Nederlandse Vereniging van Vrienden van de Ceramiek* 108 (1982). (English summary).

Jonge, C.H. de. *Delft Ceramics.* Translated by Marie Christine Hellin. New York: Praeger, 1970.

———. *Oud-Nederlandsche majolica en Delftsch aardewerk: Een ontwikkelingsgeschiedenis van omstreeks 1500–1800.* Amsterdam: Scheltema and Holkema, 1947.

Ruempol, A.P.E., and A.G.A. van Dongen. *Pre-industrial Utensils, 1150–1800.* Amsterdam: De Bataafsche Leeuw, 1991.

Singelenberg-van der Meer, M. *Nederlandse keramiek-en glasmerken, 1880–1940.* 3rd ed. Lochem: De Tijdstroom, 1989.

Smits, C. "'Zich opofferen aan het Godenvak': De invloed van Oostaziatische glazuren op de nederlandse keramiek, 1890–1940." *Mededelingenblad Nederlandse Vereniging van Vrienden van de Ceramiek* 133 (1989). (English summary).

Spruit-Ledeboer, M.G. *Nederlandse keramiek, 1900–1975.* Amsterdam/Assen: Van Gorcum, 1977. (English summary).

———. *Nederlandse keramiek, 1975–1985.* Amsterdam: Allert de Lange, 1985.

Straaten, E.J. van. "Dubbelgebakken: Aardewerknijverheid in Nederland, 1876–1945." *Mededelingenblad Nederlandse Vereniging van Vrienden van de Ceramiek* 85 (1976). (English summary).

Chabot, Hendrik (1894–1949)

Born in a small town in North Brabant, the painter and sculptor Hendrik Chabot gained recognition primarily for his figure pieces such as *De Voetballer* (ca. 1936) in the Rotterdam soccer stadium. As a painter Chabot kept himself busy with, among other things, the penetrating representation of the affliction of war, of prisoners and their oppressors. He portrayed the bombardment of Rotterdam during World War II. In addition, he painted many landscapes in which the stress lay on color and use of material through which earth and sky make a sculptural impression. The misshapen bodies this Expressionist painted were appropriately called "degenerate."

Chabot's art was generally admired as a monument to the war, but with this the art itself was slighted. He worked until 1940 as a restorer, yet already by 1922 he had made his first sculptures. In that year he also joined the artists' group De Branding, founded in Rotterdam in 1915. After 1930 painting got the upper hand. After a meeting with Charley Toorop in 1933, Chabot joined the group R33. In this phase, he mainly painted the sea, the daily lives of farmers, and horses. Before his studio was destroyed during the aerial bombing in 1940, Chabot made large wooden sculptures. He also worked on a large painting for the *De Nieuw Amsterdam*, a ship of the Holland–America Line. During the war Chabot chose a darker palette for the horrors that are the subject of his art. Later, his use of color became less somber, and Chabot devoted himself to new themes such as the physiognomy of the laugh or mother and child.

In 1993 a private museum dedicated to Hendrik Chabot was opened in the Museum Park in Rotterdam. This is a response to the renewed interest in this artist, which has partially coincided with the growing appreciation for figurative art. The museum promises to have changing exhibitions of Chabot, along with kindred spirits such as Ossip Zadkine and Ernst Ludwig Kirchner.

Brigitte van Mechelen

See also De Branding; Rotterdam; Toorop, Charley (Annie Caroline Pontifex)

Bibliography

Vollemans, Kees, and Maarten Beks. *Henk Chabot: Concerterende landscappen.* Deurne: Gemeentemuseum de Wieger; Zwolle: Waanders, 1989.

Churches

The Dutch Reformed Church and dissenting religious groups, such as the Roman Catholic Church, the Lutherans, the Mennonites, and the Remonstrants, have played important roles in the history of Dutch art and architecture. In recent years, national and regional organizations and universities in the Netherlands have dedicated entire research divisions and budgets to studies regarding the arts and Dutch churches of all denominations. This research has unveiled information regarding the extensive art collections of the Roman Catholic Church, the important architectural contributions of the Mennonites and Lutherans, and significant insights into the way art and ornamentation have functioned in the Dutch Reformed churches. The notion that the stereotypical Dutch Protestant churches of the Golden Age of the seventeenth century were whitewashed and barren of any interior ornamentation, as the paintings of Pieter Saenredam show, has been laid to rest. Although it is true that the nineteenth- and early-twentieth-century Reformed interiors were very stark, research now indicates that the Calvinist interiors of the seventeenth and eighteenth centuries were conservatively decorated with religious and secular works of art.

When the Calvinists took over Roman Catholic churches in 1572, they purged the church interiors of a sumptuous array of liturgical objects, sculpture, and paintings of God the Father, Christ, and the saints. Although purified of extravagant ornamentation, the Calvinist Church still required furniture and objects that served religious and public functions. Simple, dignified pulpits, baptistery screens, baptismal fonts, organ shutters, brass chandeliers, and other suitable liturgical and civic objects replaced the papist articles in the Calvinist Church interiors.

In the newly acquired church sanctuaries, Roman Catholic devotional altarpieces were supplanted by painted texts of the Ten Commandments, the Articles of Faith, the Our Father, the Psalms, and biblical verses, in particular Deuteronomy 28:1 ("And if you obey the voice of the Lord your God, being careful to do all his commandments which I command you this day, the Lord your God will set you high above all the nations of the Earth") and Leviticus 26:1 ("You shall make for yourselves no idols and erect no graven image or pillar, and you shall not set up a figured stone in your land, to bow down to them; for I am the Lord your God"). Provided by community members, these painted boards were hung in the church for the edification of the faithful.

Prayers and epitaphs to the dead were painted on so-called memory boards and carved on elaborate tombstones, mausoleums, and memorials in Dutch Reformed Church interiors. Political champions, fatherland figures, and naval heroes, in particular, were especially venerated by these religious/secular objects. Hendrick de Keyser produced two well-known secular monuments for Dutch Reformed churches: the Monument to William of Orange (1614–1621) in the Nieuwe Kerk in Delft (Fig. 34) and the Epitaph of Jacob van Heemskerk (1609) in the Oude Kerk in Amsterdam (Fig. 33).

Guilds, which had previously supported opulent altars dedicated to their patron saints in Roman Catholic churches, now commissioned guild boards, often with biblical verses, in the Protestant Reformed churches. Stained glass windows, which had been considered *gruwzame monumenten uit het pausdom* (horrible monuments of the papacy) when they depicted papist imagery such as the Virgin Mary and saints, were replaced by colored glass windows celebrating baptisms, births, and marriages in Calvinist churches. Windows also depicted family heraldry and extolled the virtues of church administrators, church councils, regents and regentesses, as well as public officials such as burgomasters and governors.

The organ continued to play an important role in the church interior. Although organ music was not allowed by early Reformed Synods, by the 1630s and 1640s, many Dutch cities, such as Leiden and Delft, allowed organ accompaniments to the Psalms and secular organ concerts before and after the church service. Organ shutters, such as the great shutters by Caesar van Everdingen produced in 1643–1644 for the Grote Kerk in Alkmaar, were one of the few painted embellishments allowed by church and city officials in the Reformed Church interior. Scenes from the life of King David, traditionally considered a musician and author of the Psalms, decorated many of the organs rehabilitated or rebuilt by the Reformed Church during the seventeenth century.

Since war and fire destroyed many medieval Roman Catholic structures, the Dutch Reformed community also designed new buildings specifically suited for Protestant worship. Previously, church interiors had focused on the altar, where the sacrament of the Real Presence of the Eucharist was celebrated. The primary liturgical center of the Reformed Church, on the other hand, was the pulpit, around which the congregation was seated in concentric circles. The Reformers lavished their resources on fine pulpits with large sounding boards hanging overhead to amplify the words of the speaker. Fine extant examples include the new pulpit of 1642 in the Oude Kerk in Amsterdam by the sculptor Jan Pietersz.

Kistenmaker and the Nieuwe Kerk pulpit built after the fire of 1654 by Albert Jansz. Vinckenbrinck. Among the pews surrounding the pulpit were beautifully carved wooden seats for magistrates, such as the seats for city magistrates and the Prince of Orange in the Oude Kerk in Amsterdam. Delicate brass chandeliers provided illumination near the pulpit and also in areas, such as the converted chancel in old churches, where communion was celebrated at movable tables. These portable furnishings, such as altar tables and baptismal fonts, were less richly ornamented than the important pulpit. Long, simple wooden tables would temporarily extend down the naves and the aisles so the congregation could be seated for communion. The baptismal font was also of relative insignificance. It was generally movable and was usually placed by the pulpit as baptism welcomes the child into the community of believers who gather around the pulpit for public worship.

Since the pulpit is the liturgical center of the Calvinist Church, the Dutch Reformers often favored central-plan buildings for worship. The pulpit is placed against one side in octagonal churches, such as the oldest example, the Willemstad Church (1596–1607), as well as the Marekerk in Leiden (1649) and the Oostkerk in Middleburg (1667). Square buildings also occur, with the pulpit standing in the center of one side; this plan is apparent in the Nieuwe Kerk in Haarlem (1649) and in the Oosterkerk in Amsterdam (1671). The Greek Cross plan was also adopted—for example, in the Noorderkerk in Amsterdam (1623), where the pulpit is located in one of the corners. By the mid-seventeenth century, large, rectangular churches, called gallery churches, predominated. In these long halls with galleries on three sides in two tiers, the pulpit was placed along the fourth, bare wall.

Along with the Calvinist churches, other Protestant denominations, such as the Lutherans, Mennonites, and Remonstrants churches, also built churches and decorated their interiors. Mennonites and Remonstrants, following the precedents of the Dutch Reformers, built gallery churches in the seventeenth century. The Mennonite interiors were completely undecorated and were often more austere than the Dutch Reformed churches. No painted boards, grave monuments, stained glass, or heraldic devices alleviated the simplicity of the Mennonite interiors. Lutheran churches, on the other hand, contained paintings, sculpture, and liturgical objects, such as communion chalices and patens. The Lutheran appreciation of ecclesiastical art was closely related to the Roman Catholic attitude about the function of religious art and architecture. An example of a well-known Lutheran commission for paintings is the series of three parables painted by Barent Fabritius in 1661 for the Lutheran Church in Leiden.

During the seventeenth century, Roman Catholic churches were relegated to the clandestine rooms of domestic settings and attics of abandoned warehouses. Despite the vexing problems of inadequate worship space and official interference, the Roman Catholic Church continued to commission works of ecclesiastical art in the Netherlands. In the hidden churches of the seventeenth century, devotional paintings hung above richly decorated altars. Silver and gold eucharistic vessels, such as chalices, patens, and monstrances, joined the illuminated devotional and liturgical texts on the altar. Tapestries and marble provided a sumptuous backdrop for sculptural works and paintings.

The eighteenth century realized the separation of church and state in the Netherlands. The resulting freedom of religion allowed all denominations to worship openly. In some areas, churches that had been seized and conferred to the Dutch Reformed communities during the late sixteenth and early seventeenth century were returned to Roman Catholic parishes. For the most part, however, Roman Catholics and other dissenting religious communities looked forward to building new worship centers. In the nineteenth century, the government, under the authority of the Rijkswaterstaat (department of waterways), supervised the building of churches for Roman Catholics and some Protestant groups. Severe neoclassical façades characterize these so-called *waterstaatskerken* (waterways churches). Ecclesiastical building continued until the end of the nineteenth century when tastes turned to Neo-Gothic and Neo-Renaissance styles. Architects, such as P.J.H. Cuypers and A.C. Bleijs, planned and executed a number of these "revival" buildings for Roman Catholic parishes, including the Dominicuskerk on the Spuistraat and the Posthoorn in Amsterdam by Cuypers, and the Sint Nicolaaskerk by Bleijs.

The dilemma of the Dutch Reformed Church in the nineteenth and twentieth centuries has been the inability to maintain the grand medieval churches it had acquired in the seventeenth century. During the modern period, many of the old Reformed churches have been entirely secularized or sold to other denominations.

Valerie Lind Hedquist

See also Classicism in architecture; De Keyser, Hendrick; History painting; Leiden; Neo-Gothic; Protestant Reformation; Religion of artists; Renaissance architecture; Sculpture (ca. 1400–ca. 1550); Sculpture (1550–1795); Stained glass; Tomb scupture: early modern and later sepulchral art; Utrecht

Bibliography

Blokhuis, Marco, Peter van Dael, Guus van den Hout, and Jos Sterk. *Vroomheid op de Oudezijds: Drie Nicolaaskerken in Amsterdam*. Amsterdam: De Bataafsche Leeuw, 1988.

Dirkse, Paul. *Kunst uit oud-katholieke kerken*. Utrecht: Rijksmuseum Het Catharijneconvent, 1989. (English summary).

Eck, Xander van. "From doubt to conviction: Clandestine Catholic churches as patrons of Dutch Caravaggesque painting." *Simiolus* 22 (1993/1994): 217–234.

Evenhuis, R.B. *Ook dat was Amsterdam*. Amsterdam: W. Ten Have, 1966.

Haak, Bob. "The Patrons: The Church." In *The Golden Age: Dutch Painters of the Seventeenth Century*, 36–38. New York: Harry N. Abrams, 1984.

Haeger, Barbara. "Barent Fabritius' Three Paintings of Parables for the Lutheran Church in Leiden." *Oud Holland* 101 (1987): 95–114.

Lawrence, Cynthia. "Hendrick de Keyser's Heemskerk Monument: The Origins of the Cult and Iconography of Dutch Naval Heroes." *Simiolus* 21 (1992): 265–295.

Meischke, R. "Amsterdamse Kerken van de Zeventiende Eeuw." *Nederlandse Oudheid Kundige Bond Bulletin* 12 (1959): 85–130. (English summary).

Peet, Corjan van der and Guido Steenmeijer, eds. *De Rijksbouwmeesters: Twee eeuwen architectuur van de Rijksbouwendieust en zijn voorlopers*. Rotterdam: 010, 1995 (English summary).

Swigchem, C.A. van, T. Brouwer, and W. van Os. *Een huis voor het Woord: Het Protestantse kerkinterieur in Nederland tot 1900*. The Hague: Staatsuitgeverij, 1984.

Zijp, R.P. *Protestants Kerkinterieur 16de–19de Eeuw*. Utrecht: Rijks Museum Het Catharijneconvent, 1986.

Classicism in architecture (1625–1700)

Dutch architecture from 1625 to 1675 is characterized by a strong feeling for measured proportions and the use of classical orders after the example of Italian architectural treatises by Vignola, Palladio, and Scamozzi. While in other towns the style of Hendrick de Keyser and his followers was still leading, a few artists from Haarlem, among them Salomon de Bray and Jacob van Campen, developed a more classical building style during the 1620s. They limited ornament to the known classical orders and fit it into a mathematical pattern that was also followed in the proportions of walls and windows. In contrast with the working method of the previous generation, the decoration by Van Campen was more in accordance with the structure of the entire building and was no longer considered more or less independent of it. The orders of the pilasters that were used to accentuate the division of bays were correctly executed according to the Italian treatises, instead of applying increasingly new variations and inventions. The great source of inspiration for this new way of building was the classicism of Vignola, Palladio, and Scamozzi from the north of Italy. Their treatises, originally published in 1562, 1570, and 1615, respectively, found their way to the Northern Netherlands in the first half of the seventeenth century. The works of Vignola and Scamozzi, especially, were published in Dutch several times. In addition, developments in France, where there was a strong interest in the same classical tradition of architecture, were important for architecture in the Netherlands.

This style in the Dutch Republic is called Baroque classicism or Dutch classicism. The rise of this style, which was more severe and less picturesque than those of previous decades, is connected with increasing wealth in some circles in the Netherlands. This wealth was the foundation of a new, more stately lifestyle adopted by prominent citizens. The new classicism was more reserved and aloof in character and, because of this, more impressive than the exuberant and playful architecture from the beginning of the seventeenth century. With this combination of aloofness and grandness, the Baroque version of classicism became the suitable setting for the dignified life in the Golden Age.

The court of the *stadholder* Frederik Hendrik in The Hague was the center of this development. Frederik Hendrik was reared in France, and, in contrast with his half-brother Maurits, whom he succeeded in 1625, he had a great interest in embellishing and refining the court culture. Because of this he was a great stimulating force for culture in the Republic. The most important promoter of classicism at the court was Constantijn Huygens (1596–1687), secretary to the *stadholder*, diplomat, poet, and composer, who as an ambassador had already seen much of the world—Venice and London among other places. Besides being secretary, he was the cultural adviser to Frederik Hendrik, charged with attracting painters and architects. Through Huygens, Jacob van Campen and Pieter Post were introduced to the court. Although Van Campen had designed his first buildings in the 1620s in Amsterdam, he received the opportunity in The Hague to show a full, ripe classicism during the 1630s. In 1633 he designed the Mauritshuis for Johan Maurits van Nassau-Siegen, and in 1634 he began the building of Huygens' house on the Plein, also in The Hague. In both undertakings, the Haarlem-born Pieter Post was Jacob van Campen's assistant. With the completion of the Mauritshuis, Baroque classicism became the accepted style for noblemen, class-conscious regents, rich merchants, and administrative boards. It had a pure symmetrical design, clear division of the façade by "correct" pilasters, and a projecting center crowned with a pediment. It was not a direct copy of Italian architecture, but a correct implementation of the theories from the Italian treatises. The French influence is especially clear in the division of the interior into two mirror-image apartments.

The masterpiece of Jacob van Campen and the masterpiece of Dutch classicism is the Town Hall of Amsterdam (today the Royal Palace on the Dam), which was built in the period 1648–1655. This monumental building, 200 x 280 feet, is articulated in different building blocks such as corner pavilions and projecting centers. The front and rear façades are provided with Composite and Corinthian pilasters following the instructions in the treatise by Scamozzi.

The spread of Dutch classicism was principally the work of two former colleagues of Jacob van Campen—namely, Pieter Post and Philips Vingboons. Pieter Post worked mainly for patrons from circles in The Hague and for different administrative boards, while Vingboons worked for prominent regents and merchants in Amsterdam. In Leiden, it was the town architect Arent van 's Gravesande who helped shape the preference for purely proportioned classical architecture in private homes as well as civic buildings—for example, the Cloth Hall (Lakenhal) and the octagonal Marekerk (both ca. 1639–1640).

From the beginning, classicism in practice meant not only façades with pilasters but also façades without pilasters where the measured rhythm could be read only in the placing of the windows. During the 1660s the use of pilasters decreased noticeably. In the late work of Post and Vingboons from these years, there is an extreme tightening of the lines of the façade, while at the same time the use of classical ornaments is reduced drastically, even on buildings with an acknowledged function of being representative. This tightening and sobering can be seen as the perseverance of the same mentality that had led to classicism in the beginning of the seventeenth century. The lifestyle of the more prominent citizens, more dignified and more reserved, led in architecture to houses with a more serene exterior and a richer interior. At the same time that the wall space was becoming barer and more taut, what decoration remained was concentrated on the middle bay around the main entrance and the window above it. The last phase of Dutch classicism, during the last three decades of the seventeenth century, is, therefore, also called the taut style *(de strakke stijl)*.

The essence of the taut style is a new aesthetics whereby not only is the plastic quality of the façade decreased but the monumentality of the façade is strengthened at the same time by the tense rhythm of the corner accents, entrance bay, and sharply cut-out windows without frames. The new front façade of the Deventer Town Hall from 1693 by Jacob Roman (1640–1715) shows this new ideal with unprecedented severity and distinction. Roman became the *stadholder*'s architect in 1689. In the country houses that were built during this time by the King and *stadholder* Willem III and his nobles, the mathematical foundation of the designs was emphasized. Magnificent examples of this brick architecture in cubic simplicity are Castle Amerongen (1673–1678), Castle Zeist (1676–1686, architect Jacob Roman), and Castle Middachten (1695, architects Jacob Roman and Steven Vennekool).

K.A. Ottenheym

See also Country houses and gardens; House of Orange-Nassau; Huygens, Constantijn; Post, Pieter; Renaissance architecture; Town Halls; Van Campen, Jacob; Vingboons, Philips

Bibliography

Fremantle, K. *The Baroque Town Hall of Amsterdam.* Utrecht: Haentjes, Dekker, and Gumbert, 1959.

Huisken, J., K.A. Ottenheym, G. Schwartz, eds. *Jacob van Campen: Het Klassieke ideaal in de Gouden Eeuw.* Amsterdam: Architectura en Natura, 1995. (English summary).

Ottenheym, K.A. *Philips Vingboons, 1607–1678: Architect.* Zutphen: Walburg, 1989. (English summary).

Slothouwer, D.F. *De Paleizen van Frederik Hendrik.* Leiden: Sijthoff, 1945.

Swillens, P.T.A. *Jacob van Campen: Schilder en bouwmeester, 1595–1657.* Arnhem: Gysbers and Van Loon, 1979.

Terwen, J.J., and K.A. Ottenheym. *Pieter Post, 1608–1669: Architect.* Zutphen: Walburg, 1993. (English summary).

Vermeulen, F.A.J. *Handboek tot de geschiedenis der Nederlandsche bouwkunst.* Vol. 3, *Barok en klassicisme.* The Hague: Nijhoff, 1941.

Clothing, costume, fashion: early pictorial and historical evidence

It is fair to say that the history of clothing is a neglected field in the Netherlands. Since 1950 no book-length study has been published on the period before 1800; apparently the subject is of little interest both to historians and art historians.

Unfortunately the monographs written before 1950 (De Jonge, 1916, 1919; Der Kinderen-Besier, 1926, 1933, 1950) have all concentrated on "technicalities." Basing their observations on the many portraits preserved from the sixteenth, seventeenth, and eighteenth centuries, the authors wrote a history of Dutch fashion in which numerous articles of clothing were treated with meticulous care. Their pages tell us about the *zieltje*, the *portefraes*, the *vlieger* or the *fardegalijn*, names that have long since vanished with the garments themselves. Much of the charm of these older studies derives from the fact that the authors, in tracing all of these costumes, breathe new life into these long-forgotten names and into the many paintings and prints described as well. Our attention is drawn to an overwhelming variety of style, not only in the garments but also in the hats, shoes, stockings, collars, cuffs, and gloves.

Since these monographs were written long before the onslaught of social and economic history, they have their limitations. Of course, most of the portraits painted in the early-modern period show us the *élite*: a powerful Amsterdam burgomaster, a local regent from a small town such as Hoorn or Medemblik, or a member of the landed nobility in the provinces such as Gelderland, Friesland, or Groningen. Still, many of these portraits were never mentioned in the studies, as the authors were not interested in a history of clothing in general, but only in a history of fashion. As a consequence, large segments of the upper classes were simply ignored; living too far away from the centers of power and prestige and having less money to spend, they followed the new fashions only at a distance. They are as absent from these studies as the popular classes living in the cities and the countryside.

But even as a portrait of the most fashionable circles in the seventeenth and eighteenth centuries, the picture given by these authors seems a bit too festive and too summery. As many of the portraits on which these histories of fashion were based hung in reception rooms, and would be passed on to future generations, the sitters were nearly always portrayed in their most elegant and expensive clothes. Moreover, as only a minority sat in their furs and winter clothes, we may surmise that the fashions described in these older studies were mostly worn during the summer months of the year. To complicate matters even more, the assumption that the garments depicted in these portraits were actually worn is far from a safe one, as Irene Groeneweg (1987) has argued. Especially between 1670 and 1730, it was highly unusual for Dutch women to have themselves portrayed in period fashion, preferring instead a rather timeless "portrait costume" called *à la antique*: a Van Dyckian style of clothing, leaving out any head-covering, showing a deep décolletage, and having fabrics draped around the shoulders and arms. At this stage we can only formulate the urgent need for a less naïve history, not only of fashion but of clothing in general, that would allow systematically for the many iconographical conventions involved.

Clearly such a new history of clothing would profit greatly from the recent interest that Dutch historians and art historians are taking in probate inventories and related documents. But the most promising results are probably to be expected from a joining of forces by microsociologies on the presentation of self (Erving Goffman, *The Presentation of Self in Everyday Life*, 1959), and, especially, cultural histories of manners (Norbert Elias, *The Civilizing Process*, 1978), with research on hygiene and smells (Alain Corbin, *The Foul and the Fragrant: Odor and the French Social Imagination*, 1986), the body and the nude (Hollander, 1978), posture and gesture (Roodenburg 1991, 1993, and Bremmer and Roodenburg, 1992), and even color (Groeneweg, 1995).

Herman Roodenburg

See also Clothing, costume, fashion: nineteenth and twentieth centuries; Gestures; Genre painting, eighteenth century; Genre painting, seventeenth century; Portraiture; Theater and theatricality

Bibliography

Bremmer, Jan, and Herman Roodenburg, eds. *A Cultural History of Gesture from Antiquity to the Present Day*. Ithaca, NY: Cornell University Press, 1992.

Groeneweg, Irene. "Kanttekeningen bij een 18de-eeuws Nederlands vrouwenportret in 'antique kleeding.'" *Leids Kunsthistorisch Jaarboek* 4 (1987): 415–436.

———. "Regenten in het zwart: Vroom en deftig?" *Nederlands Kunsthistorisch Jaarboek* 46 (1995): 198–251.

Hollander, Anne. *Seeing through Clothes*. New York: Viking Press, 1978.

Jonge, C.H. de. "Bijdrage tot de kennis van de kleederdracht in de Nederlanden in de XVIe eeuw." *Oud Holland* 37 (1919): 1–70, 129–168, 193–214.

———. "Bijdrage tot de kennis van de Noord-Nederlandsche costuum-geschiedenis in de eerste helft van de XVIe eeuw." Ph.D. diss., Universiteit Utrecht, 1916.

Kinderen-Besier, J.H. der. *De kleeding onzer voorouders, 1700–1900: De kostuumafdeling in het Nederlandsche Museum voor Geschiedenis en Kunst te Amsterdam*. Amsterdam: Van Looy, 1926.

———. *Mode-metamorphosen: De kleedij onzer voorouders in de zestiende eeuw*. Amsterdam: Querido, 1933.

———. *Spelevaart der mode: De kleedij onzer voorouders in de zeventiende eeuw*. Amsterdam: Querido, 1950.

Roodenburg, Herman. "Over korsetten, lichaamshouding en gebaren: Een cultuurhistorische verkenning van de 'nieuwe fatsoenen' tussen ruwweg 1580 en 1630." *Textielhistorische Bijdragen* 31 (1991): 20–38.

———. "Over scheefhalzen en zwellende heupen: Enige argumenten voor een historische antropologie van de zeventiende-eeuwse schilderkunst." *De Zeventiende Eeuw* 9 (1993): 153–168.

Clothing, costume, fashion: nineteenth and twentieth centuries

Clothing can be seen as an important expression of the cultural standards and the social differentiation of a society. In the nineteenth and twentieth centuries, two main patterns of clothing can be distinguished in the Netherlands: dressing in local costume and after fashion. Fashionable clothing gradually became dominant, while local costume waned in popularity.

Local Costume

There are good reasons the term "local costume" is preferable to "traditional costume." First, this type of clothing varied from region to region so that every village or town had its own version. Second, it indicated communal identity—community of birth and status within the community. Third, the adjective "traditional" suggests that the costume was static. However, each new generation renewed its local costume by changing sizes, fabrics, or decorations of the existing garments and accessories or by thinking of new ways to wear them. Sometimes elements from city fashions were adopted.

At least until the first decades of the nineteenth century, local costume was worn by gentlemen farmers, tradespeople, ship owners, and even nobility (in Friesland), as well as plain farmers and fishermen. It was found all over Europe. Typical for the Netherlands was the great variety of local costume within a small territory, due to economic, cultural, and religious differences between regions and communities and their mutual competition.

Within communities there was differentiation, too. First, the costume reflected wealth. The rich wore expensive fabrics like silk, doeskin, damask, and lace, mostly imported from abroad. Their golden jewelry was beautifully worked, often encrusted with precious stones. The less well-to-do used plain woolen and linen cloth, initially homemade. They possessed silver or copper jewelry; the poor had none at all. In women's costume, the headdress (bonnet and jewelry) was the chief demarcator of wealth: The coastal provinces especially were famous for their head brooches and lace caps (Fig. 23). In men's clothing, buttons, buckles, and implements like knives and tobacco pouches played that role. Dressing above or beneath one's station was highly disapproved of and censured with laughter, gossip, and social isolation. In heterogeneous communities, local costume varied with occupational group (upper class, tradespeople, farmers, fishermen, and workers had their own versions) and with religion (Protestants and Catholics differed in attire). Details of women's costume showed whether they were married or not. Finally, the costume changed with age. Children's clothing differed from the adults' costume. The elderly wore outdated versions.

What exactly was worn in Dutch villages and provincial towns would make an extensive study. Still, it is important to mention that wooden shoes (*klompen*), often seen as typical of Dutch local costume, were not worn all over the country, although they became more widespread after 1850. Moreover, these were work shoes. When going out, especially to church on Sundays, people dressed in their best clothes, including other shoes, except for the very poor, who could not afford them.

Modernization affected community life greatly; better transportation and communication diminished isolation; and individual economic possibilities increased. As a result, dependency on neighbors disappeared and community ties weakened. Where feelings of community identity were strong—in either a village or an occupational group—and modernization was seen as reprehensible, people tended to cling to tradition, including local costume, in a defensive reaction. In some places (Staphorst, Scheveningen, and the countryside around Middelburg), the local costume can be seen today, though worn only by elderly women. Elsewhere, people adopted a "modern" lifestyle that included fashionable clothing between 1840 (Groningen, Friesland, Holland) and 1930 (Brabant, Twente). Transition took time, often several decades. Local elites first changed their costume for made-to-measure fashionable clothing, followed by tradespeople. Industrial workers came next; they generally bought ready-to-wear clothes. The same was true for farmers, fishermen, and agricultural workers—the last to turn their backs to local costume. Young adults took the lead in this process, followed by boys and girls (their children). Elderly people generally wore local costume until death. Men had more contacts outside the community where local costume made them feel like "bumpkins." Women were closely tied to their immediate vicinity and kept the local costume much longer. Women of all social classes found it hard to abandon their headdresses. Usually they combined fashionable garments with local caps for several decades.

Clothing after Fashion

During most of the nineteenth century, fashionable clothing was the privilege of the aristocracy, patricians, and the upper-middle class. It was expensive, not so much because luxurious fabrics and precious jewelry were used—the same was true for the local costumes of rich farmers and tradesmen—but because new clothes should be bought regularly. Outdated clothes were given to servants, collected by charity organizations to distribute among the poor, or sold to secondhand shops in the cities, where they were bought by middle- and lower-class people. Fashionable clothes were made to measure by Dutch tailors or seamstresses or ordered from their colleagues in Brussels, Paris, and London.

Middle-class women often sewed clothes for themselves. This was seen as a virtue; it reflected bourgeois values such as domesticity, solidity, and economy. As Dutch society was dominated by bourgeois culture, extravagance in fashion was rare. Women followed Parisian and men London fashions moderately and with some delay. Empire dresses, for example, that elsewhere had a transparent and flowing effect, often looked like stiff cocoons on Dutch women because they chose opaque material and wore underskirts underneath. Foreigners who visited the Netherlands thought the Dutch badly dressed: They lacked taste, refinement, and elegance, and many were behind fashion. Only in the court city of The Hague did a more modish and worldly way of life prevail among the elite and upper-middle class.

Toward the end of the nineteenth century, standards of living began to rise and chances for upward social mobility increased. At the same time cheap ready-to-wear clothes became available on a large scale, at first mostly imported from Germany. After 1880 production centers developed in Amsterdam and Groningen. To dress after fashion became a social and financial possibility for a growing part of the population. Differences in class and wealth could only be read from clothing details like fabric, cut, and accessories, and from the volume of wardrobes.

Modernization changed daily life thoroughly. New forms of transportation—in the Netherlands the bicycle became very popular—and better indoor heating necessitated less voluminous garments. The Vereeniging voor Verbetering van Vrouwenkleeding (Association to Improve Women's Dress) was founded in 1899 and had a large following. Its aim was to adapt clothing to modern ideas of health and hygiene: garments should be washable and light, enabling the skin to breathe and the body to move. Girls' and women's corsets were attacked as the source of many diseases. Reform clothing did not necessarily make a woman look ugly, as opponents argued. Liberty dresses, imported from England, and *haute couture* reform gowns designed by Madame La Vroye in The Hague were elegant, although expensive.

During the nineteenth century and the first decades of the twentieth century, bourgeois values spread to the other social classes. This coincided with tendencies in the Protestant and Catholic churches to purify both religion and daily life. The pillarization of Dutch society from 1900 to 1965 (a period when the churches were disunified and their function was divided among denominational–political interest groups) reinforced these bourgeois influences. Chastity was highly valued, especially for women. Decent women should avoid wearing men's garments and provocative clothing such as sleeveless dresses, low necklines, short skirts, and transparent fabrics. Newspapers avoided provocation even in their advertising (Fig. 24). Decency and economy prevailed over sexual attractiveness and elegance. Dutch middle-class and working-class women preferred big shopping bags and flat, sturdy shoes and showed little sensitivity for tasteful combinations of colors and garments. Unmarried young women, however, wore fashionable and sometimes "shocking" clothes that were sharply criticized by parents and church authorities.

In the second half of the 1960s de-pillarization and the second feminist wave changed the ideology toward women. Some turned to sexy clothing, while others attacked old concepts of femininity and adopted men's clothes. Youth cultures had great impact on fashion and brought, for example, American T-shirts and jeans into any fashionable wardrobe. Rising standards of living also lessened economy: Fashionable clothes were bought to last only one or two seasons. Today the Dutch dress in a more up-to-date manner, but they still have no reputation for elegance—they prefer casual wear. On average, they spend less on clothing and cosmetics than do their neighbors in Germany and Belgium.

Since the late 1930s there have been Dutch couturiers: Max Heymans, Dick Holthaus, Frans Molenaar, Edgar Voss, Frank Govers, and Fong Leng. Shoe designer Jan Janssen achieved an international reputation, as did some brands of ready-to-wear clothes, such as Soap Studio (Frits Klarenbeek), Orson and Bodil, and Oilily. Academies of arts have trained aspiring fashion designers artistically and technically, and commercial institutions like the Wool Secretary, the Cotton Institute and the Confection Center in Amsterdam have promoted Dutch design and industrial products.

Historiographic Note

Dutch local costumes have been described in travel reports (Ortigao) and portrayed in drawings, paintings, and photographs. Artists (Antoon Molkenboer, 1872–1960) and journalists around 1910 were the first to record the disappearing local costumes. Scientific interest rose after 1930, as art historians (F.W.S. van Thienen, Fea Livestro-Nieuwenhuis), museum conservators, and social scientists began to deal with the subject. A study center, located at the Nederlands Openluchtmuseum (Netherlands Open-Air Folklore Museum) in Arnhem, combines the efforts of scientists and amateurs.

Dutch fashionable clothing was studied by art historians (Christine Frowein, Ietse Mey) and fashion journalists (Pauline Terreehorst, among others). Most Dutch research, however, did not focus on the Netherlands but dealt with fashion in general.

Research has been usually concerned with either fashion or local costume. Only a few authors (Van Thienen, De Leeuw) discuss both. The Nederlandse Kostuumvereniging voor Mode en Streekdracht (Dutch Costume Association for Fashion and Local Costume), founded in 1980, unites scientists, conservators, private collectors, and amateur historians. Its annual journal, *Kostuum* (with summaries in English), offers a platform to all. An inventory of archives, museums, libraries, and their collections for the study of clothing in the Netherlands has been published in *Textielhistorische Gids* (1991).

Kitty de Leeuw

See also Portraiture

Bibliography

Jansen, F.L. "Distribution of Ready-Made Clothing in the Twentieth Century in the Netherlands." *Textile History* 24 (1993): 105–115.

Leeuw, Kitty de. "Local Costume in the Netherlands, 1800–Today: An Out-of-Date Position or a Collective Stand?" *Economic and Social History in the Netherlands* 3 (1991): 61–80.

Leeuw, K.P.C. de (Kitty). *Kleding in Nederland, 1813–1920: Van een traditioneel bepaald kleedpatroon naar een begin van modern kleedgedrag.* Hilversum: Verloren, 1992. (French summary).

Livestro-Nieuwenhuis, Fea. *Nationale Klederdrachten.* Zutphen: Terra, 1987.

Mey, Ietse. *Frans Molenaar, haute couture.* De Bilt: Cantecleer, 1986. (In Dutch and English).

Ortigao, Ramalho. *Holland 1883.* Translated by M. de Jong. Amsterdam: Van Campen, 1948.

Schnitger, C. "Women's Dress Reform in the Netherlands." *Textile History* 24 (1993): 75–89.

Terreehorst, Pauline. *Modus: Over mensen, mode en het leven.* Amsterdam: De Balie, 1990.

Textielhistorische Bijdragen. Enschede: Stichting Textielgeschiedenis, 1959– . (English summaries).

Textielhistorische Gids: Collecties bij Nederlandse achiefdiensten, bibliotheken en musea. Amsterdam: Nederlandsch Economish-Historisch Archief; Enschede: Stichting Textielgeschiedenis, 1991.

Thienen, F.W.S. van. *Kabinet van mode en smaak: Het Nederlands Costuum-Museum.* The Hague: Stichting Vrienden van het Nederlands Costuum Museum, 1955. (Dutch, French, and English text).

Cobra Movement (1948–1951)

The term refers to an international movement founded in 1948 as a flexible alliance of Experimental artists' and writers' groups in Denmark, Belgium, and Holland. The name Cobra was an acronym formed from the first letters of Copenhagen, Brussels, and Amsterdam, the "A" being represented by the Dutch Experimental Group (leading artists: Karel Appel, Constant, and Corneille). With its emphasis on free experimentation and collaborative (including artist/writer) production, its injection of low-art elements into the avant-garde, and its aggressively socialist and internationalist stance, Cobra gave rise to a characteristic and potent blend of primitivistic art and Marxian theory. The movement was officially disbanded in 1951, but in subsequent years the high profile and continuing collaborative activities of former members—for example, in new movements such as the Situationist International (founded 1957)—helped keep its name and identity alive. Cobra is now widely regarded as the second major movement of the century (after De Stijl) in which Dutch art has had a considerable international impact.

On November 8, 1948, at the close of a Surrealist-organized international artists' congress in Paris, six disenchanted delegates—Danish painter Asger Jorn, Belgian writers Christian Dotremont and Joseph Noiret, and Dutch painters Appel, Constant, and Corneille—withdrew to a café, agreed on a joint statement, and effectively started a new movement. The statement, signed by the six on behalf of the Revolutionary-Surrealist Center in Belgium and the Danish and Dutch Experimental Groups, rejected theoretical wrangling in contemporary Surrealist circles in favor of a "dialectical" and "organic" collaboration between their national groups. The name Cobra, which Dotremont shortly afterward invented for the new alliance, established links with biomorphic and irrationalist artistic traditions; as an acronym it clearly signaled a shift in orientation away from the hegemony of Paris and toward the participants' own Northern European centers. It was to the northernmost of these centers that attention turned initially. Only weeks after the founding of Cobra, Dotremont, Appel, Constant, and Corneille were in Copenhagen, where the Dutch Experimental artists exhibited as guests of the Danish Høst (Harvest) Experimental Group from November 19 to December 6, 1948. It was also in Copenhagen, and at

Jorn's instigation, that the first issue of the journal *Cobra* was published in March 1949.

Though Jorn was the only Danish artist present at the founding of Cobra, his role had been a decisive one. In 1946, on a visit to Paris to establish international contacts, Jorn had met Constant and the Algerian-French painter Jean Michel Atlan, through whom he was later introduced to Dotremont and other Belgian Surrealists. These meetings opened up lines of communication that were to lead to the formation of Cobra in 1948, but even before Cobra began Jorn was bringing news of recent Danish developments in art and theory to interested parties in other lands. In the late 1930s and early 1940s, Danish artists such as Ejler Bille, Carl Henning Pedersen, Egill Jacobsen, and Jorn himself had developed an art of "spontaneous abstraction" that was influenced by the work of Klee, Miró, Kandinsky, and Picasso but also drew directly on folk traditions, medieval Scandinavian art, tribal art, and child art. Their primitivizing artistic methods went hand in hand with progressive theories. In the pages of their magazine, *Helhesten* (Hell-Horse, 1941–1944), which was published under German occupation, these Danish artists countered Nazi racism and cultural repression by embracing non-Western tribal art and modern *entartete Kunst* (degenerate art), brought a sharp socialist critique to bear on classically informed "bourgeois" art and culture, and argued a theory of natural, unrepressed artistic expression on the basis of a dialectical-materialist worldview. Shaped and honed in wartime Denmark, these artistic developments and attitudes were mediated by Jorn to a wider circle after the war, and in 1948 they formed the cutting edge of the emerging Cobra Movement.

By early 1949, however, the southernmost Cobra center was active. At Brussels, Dotremont established the secretariat of the movement, published the first *Le Petit Cobra* (a stenciled bulletin) in February and the second *Cobra* journal in March, and from March 19 to 27 he organized the small exhibition *La Fin et les Moyens* (The End and the Means) under the joint names of Cobra and the Revolutionary-Surrealist Group. With the latter, Dotremont maintained the identity of the Brussels-based group (and magazine) *Le Surréalisme Révolutionnaire* he had initiated in 1947, and as editor-in-chief of the *Cobra* journals he helped to maintain a distinctly Belgian Surrealist presence in the new movement.

Many of the Cobra artists spent at least part of the summer of 1949 in Denmark, where from mid-August to mid-September the first Cobra congress—dubbed "Les Rencontres de Bregnerød" (the encounters of Bregnerød) by Dotremont—was held and murals were painted collectively. In November 1949, attention turned to Amsterdam, where the second Cobra congress coincided with the opening of a major Cobra exhibition at the Stedelijk Museum: the *Exposition International d'Art Expérimental*. In terms of scale and publicity, this exhibition can lay claim to representing the most memorable achievement of the Cobra Movement—and, more specifically, of the Dutch Experimental Group.

From its inception, the Dutch Experimental Group reflected international as well as national concerns. Constant had known Jorn since 1946, but it was the winter of 1947–1948 before he was introduced to Appel and Corneille. In the course of 1948, Constant, Appel, and Corneille established contact with the painters Theo Wolvecamp and Anton Rooskens, and together with Jan Nieuwenhuys (the brother of Constant) these artists founded the Dutch Experimental Group on July 16, 1948. Shortly afterward, Eugène Brands joined them, to be followed by three young poets: Jan G. Elburg, Gerrit Kouwenàar, and Lucebert, who were subsequently to become known in the literary context of De Vijftigers (Poets of the Fifties). One of the earliest products of the group was its magazine, *Reflex*, the first issue of which (September/October 1948) antedated Cobra by just a few weeks and prefigured the new movement by announcing the intention to combat bourgeois naturalism, sterile abstraction, and pessimistic Surrealism, and to work closely with other experimental groups in Copenhagen and Paris to free the way to a new kind of creativity. Along with several lithographs, poems, and short articles, the first issue of *Reflex* contained Constant's lengthy "Manifesto," a text that closely followed Jorn's example in criticizing Western, classical culture from a Marxist standpoint. In the second and final issue of *Reflex*, which came out in February 1949, several months after Cobra had begun, graphic works, articles, and a major early poem by Lucebert were accompanied by another theoretical text by Constant, entitled "Culture and Counterculture." Though Cobra activities were by now preoccupying the group, February 1949 also brought a rare opportunity for the Dutch Experimental artists to exhibit together in Holland: The location was De Bijenkorf, the department store in Amsterdam where they had already shown briefly in the summer of 1948.

But the group also had plans for a more ambitious exhibition. Willem Sandberg, director of the Stedelijk Museum in Amsterdam, had responded positively to a letter written to him in December 1948 by Constant (as secretary of the group) suggesting an exhibition in which the Dutch Experimental artists would be accompanied by their new-found Danish colleagues. By the spring of 1949 the plan had taken on a broader international sweep, and when the exhibition finally opened on November 3, 1949, the catalog (included as an insert in the fourth issue of *Cobra*, the Dutch issue) listed artists from Britain, America, Germany, France, Sweden, Switzerland, and Czechoslovakia, as well as from Denmark, Belgium, and Holland (Fig. 25). The works were spread over seven rooms in the Stedelijk Museum and hung in startling fashion—some high on the walls, some very low—by the designer of the exhibition, the architect Aldo van Eyck. In the week after the opening, the Dutch national press had a field day. Almost unanimously, critics ridiculed Experimental art and condemned the policy of Sandberg in giving it museum space. There were also sensationalist reports of a riot in the museum, since Dotremont's speech at a poetry evening on November 5 had led to a misunderstanding and to fisticuffs between artists and poets. As a result, Experimental and Cobra artists were portrayed by the press as charlatans and dangerous subversives—a notoriety that was to mark public reception of their work for many years. And, unfortunately for

the Dutch Experimental Group, the fracas at the poetry evening exacerbated existing internal tensions and provoked the resignations of the remaining literary members as well as the painters Brands, Rooskens, and Wolvecamp.

In the months following the Amsterdam exhibition, internal tensions also threatened the Cobra leadership. Socialist Realism, the official art program of international Communism, had become the subject of virulent polemics among left-wing European artists, and in the course of 1950 disagreements on this issue flared up within Cobra. Constant, who was not a party member, espoused the cause of Socialist Realism (in theory, at least), while Dotremont, who was then a Communist, took the opposite line. Dotremont accused Constant of encouraging artistic dictatorship, tried to enlist Jorn and others in refuting Constant's ideas, and effectively blocked the publication of a text by Constant on realism in the fifth *Cobra* (a German issue, produced by Karl-Otto Götz at Hannover). These ideological differences, as well as diverging personal and artistic concerns among the Cobra participants, meant that the impetus of the movement slowed in 1950 and 1951. In 1950, however, the fifteen monograph booklets of the *Bibliothèque de Cobra* canonized the leading artists of the movement, and Dotremont continued to edit further issues of *Cobra*, though an intended Danish double-issue (8/9) never reached publication. In 1951, the tenth *Cobra*—by now more a glossy art magazine than an experimental journal—contained the catalog for the second *Exposition Internationale d'Art Expérimental*, organized at Liège in October/November of that year by the (Belgian) Royal Society of Fine Arts and Cobra. This exhibition was the swan song of the movement, and *Cobra 10* anounced itself as the last issue. By then, both Jorn and Dotremont were seriously ill with tuberculosis, and not only the will but the energy to continue Cobra had dissipated.

Formed in an act of secession from postwar attempts to revive Surrealism, Cobra came to resemble a Surrealist movement perhaps more than its founders initially intended. Cobra's primitivizing, spontaneous approach to experimental painting and writing was inspired by automatic techniques long practiced by Surrealists; the leading Cobra theorists (Jorn, Constant, and Dotremont) were, much as the Surrealist initiator André Breton had been, dialectical materialists seeking to change both art and society; and in the end Cobra was not spared the kind of ideological infighting that had marked the history of Surrealism and its splinter groups. Moreover, in spite of Cobra's Northern European accents, the shift in geographical orientation turned out to be neither complete nor lasting; by 1950, leading Cobra artists such as Appel, Constant, Corneille, Dotremont, and Jorn had in fact returned to work in Paris. But the ironies of its history may not detract from recognition of the unique corpus of artworks created by Cobra: collectively painted murals, small poet–painter booklets, writings by painters and paintings by writers, and substantial early paintings by pioneers of an emerging postwar style (Color Plate 16). These works demonstrate an informality and vitality quite distinct from the products of Surrealism and (with the exception of Jean Dubuffet) contemporary Parisian art. What is more, the ideological concerns of Cobra by no means engendered a recoil into Surrealism; as a movement with left-wing sociocultural ideals, Cobra can be seen, with hindsight, to have provided a stepping stone between an older Surrealism and newer developments such as the Situationist International of the later 1950s and 1960s, in which Jorn and Constant were once again to join forces.

Evaluation of the achievements of Cobra is not, however, a settled matter. Historiography of the movement, which began in earnest in the mid-1960s, has aroused controversies in which the Dutch art historian Willemijn Stokvis, the former Cobra artists Dotremont and Constant, and the French writer Jean-Clarence Lambert have been the main participants. Stokvis helped organize the retrospective exhibition *Cobra 1948–51* at the Boymans-van Beuningen Museum, Rotterdam, in 1966, and went on to write a published Ph.D. dissertation on Cobra (Stokvis, 1974, reprint 1990) in which she maintained that the major achievement of the movement had been a painterly one: A "Cobra language" comprising spontaneous techniques and an iconography of fantasy creatures, developed first by Danish and then largely by Dutch artists (Appel, Constant, Corneille), and only years later adopted by the Belgian painter Pierre Alechinsky. For Stokvis, Cobra had thereby created an important Northern European variant of international postwar Abstract Expressionism. But neither Dotremont nor Constant agreed with Stokvis' assessments of Cobra. After the 1966 exhibition, Dotremont published a list of complaints—they chiefly concerned inadequate attention for the Belgian contributions and for the innovative, interspecialist character of Cobra—while in various speeches and texts Constant maintained that the real achievement of Cobra lay not in any painterly style but in its liberated, experimental attitude. (Jorn, who died in 1973, kept aloof from the controversy, though Danish writers have tended to present Cobra as an international variation on a basically Danish theme.) After Dotremont's death in 1979, his cause was taken up by Lambert in a major new book on Cobra (Lambert, 1983), which in turn was sharply criticized by Stokvis for overemphasizing the Belgian contribution. National interests have played a part in these polemics, but so too have differing conceptions of how a movement such as Cobra relates to the history of modern art. Stokvis has evaluated Cobra in the conventional art-historical terms of stylistic and iconographic development, while her opponents have pointed instead to the unorthodoxy of Cobra's cross-specialization and to its role in the history of critical, left-wing avant-garde groups. It has been argued, however, that none of these perspectives can claim sovereignty, since the movement itself was marked by internal polemics and by unresolved conflicts between artistic and ideological motivations (Birtwistle, 1988).

The last word has certainly not been said on the history of the Cobra Movement, but scholars considering entry into this field need to be aware that literature available in English as of the mid-1990s presents only a very limited view of the subject. The most substantial art-historical study on the movement (Stokvis, 1974, 1990) is in Dutch (Stokvis, 1988, though in English, is a much shortened and popularized account), and for a study of primary sources and relevant documents—including those reissued in facsimile by Van Gennep and Editions Allia—a working knowledge of French, Dutch, Danish, and German is necessary.

Graham Birtwistle

See also Appel, Karel; Brands, Eugène; Constant; Corneille; Lucebert; Rooskens, Anton; Wolvecamp, Theo; World Wars I and II

Bibliography

Berreby, Gérard, ed. *Documents relatifs à la fondation de l'Internationale Situationniste*. Paris: Editions Allia, 1985.

Birtwistle, Graham. "Terug naar Cobra: Polemiek en problemen in de historiografie van Cobra." *Jong Holland* 4 (1988): 10–20, 39–40.

Cobra, 1948–1951. Amsterdam: Van Gennep, 1980.

Cobra, Forty Years After: Collection J. Karel P. van Stuyvenberg. The Hague: SDU, 1988.

Flomenhaft, Eleanor. *The Roots and Development of Cobra Art*. Hempstead, NY: Fine Arts Museum of Long Island, 1985.

Lambert, Jean-Clarence. *Cobra*. London: Sotheby, 1983.

Shield, Peter. "'Les Rencontres de Bregnerød': Cobra Myth and Cobra Reality." *Jong Holland* 8 (1992): 30–44.

Stokvis, Willemijn. *Cobra: Geschiedenis, voorspel en betekenis van een beweging in de kunst van na de tweede wereldoorlog*. Amsterdam: De Bezige Bij, 1974. Reprint. Amsterdam: De Bezige Bij, 1990.

———. *Cobra: An International Movement in Art after the Second World War*. New York: Rizzoli, 1988.

Coins, medals

Numismatics (from the Latin *nomisma*, meaning coin) includes the study of the history of money as well as of the development of the art of designing medals. This distinction is essential: Medals are decorative or commemorative pieces; coins, on the other hand, are legal tender. Both categories, however, show inevitable points of contact.

Medal Art

Until late into the twentieth century, medals were made exclusively for the commemoration of a historical event or a specific person. The art of medals, then, cannot be seen as separate from the historical and social context in which it was developed. Only in the twentieth century have medal designs also become the domain of artists who see in the making of medals a possibility of bringing their artistic skill and convictions into expression.

The prototype of the medal as we now know it was made in 1439 by the Italian painter Pisanello, establishing the connection of medal design with other branches of art already in the Renaissance. Medals from this period show a portrait likeness on the obverse and an allegorical representation with symbolic meaning on the reverse. Medals from this period were intended for a small circle of intimates of the (mostly princely) patron; a historical context is not yet extant.

Inspired by Italian examples, the painter Quinten Massys from Antwerp was the first artist in the Netherlands to design medals. The development of medal artistry soared in the course of the seventeenth century through, among other things, the invention of the screw press, by which medals could be struck instead of being cast. Just as with the other branches of the fine and applied arts, the patrons were—in conformity with social relations in the Republic—to be found mainly in the circles of local and provincial governments and important persons. History medals and portrait medals also formed the most important genres in medal art in this period. Governments had medals struck to recall important historical events. The Eighty Years' War (1568–1648) and the expansion of the Republic as an important economic power, with its attendant necessary clash of arms, furnished them with plentiful subjects. These medals shaped the reaction to the growing self-consciousness of the young Republic. Many historical works in the seventeenth and eighteenth centuries were based on surveys of the historical facts in connection with struck medals, such as Joachim Oudaens' *Medalische Historie der Republyk van Holland* from 1688 and Gerard van Loon's *Beschrijving der Nederlandsche Historie-penningen* from 1723–1731, the most important source for medal art in the Netherlands for the period 1555–1716.

The commissions for portrait medals came especially from the circles of the well-to-do middle class, who with the rise of commerce and the growing prosperity connected with it became an important power in the Republic. In contrast to the situation in the surrounding countries, the role of the court was much less prominent in giving commissions and stimulating the development of art. In this period of flourishing medal art, the only significant role played by the court of the *stadholder* involved the realization of a series of medals of the *faits et gestes* of the king and *stadholder* Willem III, which served as a counterpart for the *Histoire Métallique* of the French Sun King Louis XIV.

Portrait medals were frequently based on painted or engraved portraits. History medals attest to having close ties with cartography and topography: Many medals bear depictions of towns that are borrowed from cartographic representations, such as ground-plans, townscape profiles, and bird's-eye views.

The production of medals in the eighteenth century did not reach the level of quality of the preceding era, yet it cannot be called a period of decline. Medalists such as members of the Holtzhey family in the North (Amsterdam, Middelburg, Harderwijk) and the Van Berckel family in the South ('s Hertogenbosch, Brussels) turned out a considerable number of medals of decent artistic quality. In both families, the manufacture of medals was combined with mastery in making coins. All sorts of organizations in the fields of commerce and industry joined the categories of patrons from the seventeenth century with commissions for medals.

In the nineteenth century, the reduction bench was introduced. This instrument, by which reliefs could be reduced, determined to a considerable degree the character of medals: The graphic aspect predominated over the sculptural.

Medal art in the Netherlands has undergone a number of important developments in the twentieth century. In the first decades of the century, the decorative artist Christiaan Johannes van der Hoef, under the influence of Art Nouveau, gave Dutch medal art a new stimulus through the application of stylized forms and a gradual raised relief.

The sculptor Jan Bronner and his pupil and follower Piet Esser were seen by many as the founders of the new Dutch medal art. As professors at the Rijksacademie voor Beeldende Kunst in Amsterdam, they had numerous students who gained renown as sculptors and medalists. Bronner encouraged his students to carve their medals full-size and to keep a close relation between the obverse and the reverse. On the basis of his influence, the role of the Amsterdam Rijksacademie became viewed by some as all-dominant in the development of modern medal art in the Netherlands. The ideas developed by Bronner and Esser should be, according to this view, passed on by them via their respective students to generation after generation to be developed further. Others found the influence of Bronner and his kind overrated and placed clearly in connection with the artistic trends in the twentieth century, which had also permeated Dutch medal art.

Not only sculptors but also graphic artists and industrial designers applied themselves to designing medals. Some medalists, in the spirit of Renaissance medals, attempted to find a maximum of expression within the traditional limitations—form, thickness, choice of materials—of medal art. Others strove to break through the limitations of the medium and, in the extension of the modeling technique, to cross the boundary into plastic art.

The choice and handling of materials also appeared less bound by convention than earlier: Designers no longer executed their medals exclusively in bronze but also in clear plastic, soapstone, or glass, as well as enamel, using applied techniques such as hot-pressing or casting. The last technique was a return to the beginnings of medal art; before the struck medal, the cast medal had prevailed for more than two-and-a-half centuries. The discussion of whether such objects can be considered medals is still unresolved. A general judgment cannot be passed on this question, so much the more because in the course of time the criteria themselves change. So, in the meantime, it also became generally accepted to call heavier cast medals from only decades ago *paardevijgen* (horse dung).

With the sculptural conception of medals and the free use of materials, Dutch medal art in the twentieth century has moved to the artistic forefront internationally. The role of the Vereniging voor Penningkunst (Society for Medal Art), established in 1925, should not go unmentioned. This society annually gives commissions to one or more artists to make medals and has strongly contributed to the developments described.

The important role of Dutch medal art is also acknowledged on the international level. The sculptor and medalist Jos Reniers won a prize in 1992 at the congress of the Fédération Internationale de la Médaille (FIDEM), and in 1994 the prestigious American prize, the J. Sanford Saltus Award for Signal Achievement in the Art of the Medal, was given to the medal designer Marianne Letterie.

Coins and Bank Notes

Until French domination of the Netherlands, the striking of coins was not only by province but, in a number of cases, also organized on the municipal scale. The provincial and municipal mints stood under the authority of the sovereign lord, respectively the municipal authority. The mint masters of the coin workshops were frequently, in addition, active as medalists. Only after the establishment of the Batavian Republic (1795) was there talk of a serious improvement of the monetary system. Designs for the heads on the coins were supplied by medalists such as Johan George Holtzhey and David van der Kellen Jr.

Since 1980, much has happened within the limitations that currency brings with it in size, weight, and design. The coins with traditional portraits are being replaced by a new series by Bruno Ninaber van Eyben. In these coins, there is a conscious departure from the current coin type, inspired by Italian Renaissance medals with a profile portrait encircled by a legend, that has been struck in the Netherlands since the sixteenth century.

In this case, it is an industrial designer who has captured the standard from a sculptor (L.D. Wenckebach) and a medalist (J.C. Wienecke), who respectively had designed the coins with the portraits of Queen Juliana (1948) and Queen Wilhelmina (1919). Besides this currency, incidental design commissions were given to Dutch artists for occasional coins (ten- and twenty-guilder pieces).

Artists are also connected with the history of the Dutch bank note. Although their progressive designs for a long time did not meet with enthusiastic reception in the rather conservative circles of patrons and printers, noted artists such as C.A. Lion Cachet, Leo Gestel, and more recently the designer R.D.E. Oxenaar have provided designs that have enabled the Netherlands to build up a reputation in this area that is wholly its own as well.

Pieter Jan Klapwijk

See also Bronner, Jan; Dutch history; Nationalism; Sculpture (1795–1945); State patronage, public support

Bibliography

Bolten, J. *Dutch Banknote Design.* Amsterdam: De Nederlandsche Bank; Dordrecht: Kluwer Academie, 1988.

Chijs, P.O. van der. *De munten [van Nederland] van de vroegste tijden tot de Pacificatie van Gent (1576).* 9 vols. Haarlem: Erven F. Bohn, 1851–1866.

De Nieuwe munten van Nederland. The Hague: Ministerie van Financien, 1982.

Gelder, H. Enno van. *De Nederlandse munten.* Utrecht: Spectrum, 1980.

Jacobi, Hans, and Bert van Beek. *Geld van het Koninkrijk.* Amsterdam: Pampus Associates, 1988.

Loon, G. van. *Beschrijving der Nederlandsche Historie-penningen.* 4 vols. The Hague: Christiaan van Lom, 1723–1731. Reprint. Amstelveen: AMNU, 1986.

Meer, G. van der. *A Survey of Numismatic Research, 1978–1984.* International Association of Professional Numismatists, Special Publication No. 9. London, 1986.

Tilamus, Louk. "Vorm en ruimte in de Nederlandse penningkunst." *De Beeldenaar: Tweemaandelijles tijdschrift voor numismatick en penningkunst in Nederland en Belgie* 15:6 (1991): 457–464.

Wessem, J.N. van. *Nederlandse penningkunst.* The Hague: SDU, 1988.

Comic modes, sixteenth and seventeenth centuries

During the sixteenth century, comic representation in the Northern Netherlands was largely restricted to prints and small paintings of marginalized types and peasants. After 1600, comic works became more ambitious in thematic scope and pictorial strategies, and some artists became more self-conscious about their comic projects.

Early accounts of Hieronymus Bosch, Adriaen Brouwer, and Jan Steen emphasize the comic character of their works. The interpretation of their comic modes remains an unresolved challenge. To understand which images were comic and how they were meaningful, themes and strategies of comic literature can be compared with analogous visual means, and comic depictions can be compared with related "serious" images. This survey discusses some iconographic and formal means of comic representation and suggests how specific comic images may be seen historically.

Comic imagery, widely present on the margins of medieval art, in the sixteenth century assumed a more central position in art production, stimulated by an expanding print culture and by the uncertain status of religious images under Reformed attack. Prints, with their largely anonymous audience, allowed their makers new freedom of themes. Reformed rhetoric against devotional images, and the shrinkage of the market for them, also encouraged experimentation with secular themes. Sixteenth-century comic works could take the allegorical theme of the seven sins, for example, but represent it more concretely. On a tabletop designed by Bosch, peasants and burghers engage in these sins in household settings (ca. 1470–1490; Color Plate 1). The gullibility of dupes in his compositions *The Conjuror* and *The Stone Operation* (ca. 1470–1490) and the revelry of passengers aboard his *Ship of Fools* (ca. 1495–1500) are secular follies with equivalents in comic texts.

Printmakers developed similar comic material. A large, anonymous woodcut from Leiden (ca. 1525–1530) of the embarkation of an ill-equipped vessel on a *Pilgrimage to Sint Reijnuut* (Saint Cleaned-Out, a.k.a. Saint Broke) celebrates the drunks, beggars, and clergy who will visit the saint of the penniless. The group of pilgrims and Bosch's *Ship of Fools* resemble the literary "guilds" of fringe figures, frequently represented as setting off on a pilgrimage to lands of the dissolute. Texts and images alike orchestrate a symbolic removal of nonproductive types from urban, early capitalist society. Adriaen van de Venne's *Sint Reynuut* (engraving and poem, 1635) suggest the theme's continuing efficacy for a seventeenth-century public. Steen's paintings of drunken homecomings by boat updated its meanings by limiting the transgressions to burghers in rustic settings (1650s–1660s).

In a common "World Upside Down" process, these representations rely on the inversion of preferred societal structures and behavior, such as the guild, the pilgrimage, and modest conduct, for their comic effect. By representing the inversion as laughable, these images underscored the obvious correctness of the usual order while providing imaginary relief from it. Like comic texts of the period, they ridicule financial mismanagement and its results, an urgent issue in the early capitalist centers in which they were produced. Lucas van Leyden and the Amsterdam printmaker Cornelis Anthonisz. represented exemplars of irresponsible living, including gamblers, beggars, drunks, and prostitutes (ca. 1510–1545). The rather serious character of these prints makes them primarily didactic rather than comic in type.

The World Upside Down principle could help construct or maintain gender identities. In anonymous prints narrating the *Struggle for the Trousers*, a sturdy woman forces her husband to hand over his attire, including his underpants. In the seventeenth century, cheap, single-leaf woodcuts elaborated this theme into *The Life of Jan de Wasser* (John the Launderer). Lucas produced more than a dozen prints on *The Power of Women*, in which historic seductresses reduce heroic suitors to "feminine," or nonrational, actions and even to death. Through the mockery of bystanders or through the physical characterization of wanton women and foolish men, some of the prints indicate that these reversed relations are funny but inappropriate. In *The Poet Virgil Suspended in a Basket* (1525; Fig. 26), Lucas caricatured the laughing spectators themselves, suggesting that such power upsets are no laughing matter. These images thus may have neutralized common anxieties about female sexual power.

Professional conduct was another favorite comic theme. No type was ridiculed more consistently than the doctor, whether quack, as usual in the sixteenth century, or outmoded physician, as represented by Steen and Frans van Mieris. Quacks are identified by outlandish dress, signifying their foreign origins just as garbled dialects do in texts. Doctors wear old-fashioned dress and are as unable to diagnose lovesickness or pregnancy as their literary counterparts. But the patients of these false or stupid professionals come in for as much laughter from painted or actual viewers, whether they are fools allowing professional misconduct to persist, or lovesick maidens controlled by libido rather than reason.

Artists could indicate the victim's responsibility for his or her folly by bodily signs for stupidity. Bosch's stone sufferer and Lucas' dental patient (1523), for example, are rotund peasants, notorious in satire for gullibility. The ambiguous peasant remained a central comic figure for the next century and a half. Although the inflections of peasant imagery varied, peasants in comic images appeared as fundamentally "natural" creatures, essentially different from the civilized, rational, urban citizens represented in contemporary portraits. By contrast to these physically and morally upright beings, peasants appear round, hunched, even neckless, with simplified limbs; they rarely sit straight and customarily shout, guzzle, dance, make love, vomit, or fight.

These physical peasants can be seen as raw sexual beings (Lucas); drunken, belligerent boors (Brouwer); coarse, impoverished louts (Van de Venne); uninhibited revelers (David Vinckboons); or, uncomically, as sincere and harmless persons of few and simple needs (late pictures by Adriaen van Ostade and paintings of *Prayer before the Meal* by Jan Steen, 1660s). For urban viewers, natural peasants may have embodied unstated fears about lack of rational control, and they may have acted out mute desires for a simpler, pleasurable life. So effective was this peasant figure that Steen and others borrowed its body and the compositions and spaces in which it lived for the transgressions of their own middle class, in paintings of taverns, dissolute households, and family celebrations of censored festivals (1650s–1670s).

By then middle-class comic figures had begun to upstage the peasant, in farces as in images. From the 1610s, Willem Buytewech, Esaias van de Velde, and Dirck Hals represented merry companies of the children of the newly prosperous Dutch Republic, living the unproductive high life in foppish dress, overly colorful and beribboned. Steen mined this comic vein in monumental paintings of peasants and burghers carousing together and of fine interiors whose inhabitants squander their means.

For all of these themes, images use markers to signal the comic genre to which they belong, such as the costume and body conventions mentioned. The most pervasive characteristic of comic representations, however, is their insistent "realism." Comic theorists since antiquity had emphasized that comedy was "an imitation of life, a mirror of customs, an image of truth." In practice, this requirement involved thematic concerns with "common" people and with basic biological needs such as procreation and bodily intake and elimination. It also demanded a full range of pictorial realist strategies, such as apparently random compositions and disorderly spaces to suggest the accidentality of life, the presence of a "witness" in the image to guarantee truthfulness, and an apparently selective representation of persons and objects, in sufficient detail to suggest high fidelity to the originals.

Much comic representation relied on facial and gestural conventions, either by exaggerating them to render a character comic (the swaggering, the earnest, the boorish), or by misappropriating them to comic effect (polite gestures used by seductresses). But the most specific comic sign is the laughing face in the image, frequently directed at the beholder. Like similar laughing prompts in texts and plays, the laughers encourage the viewer to respond in kind. The prompt is especially common in seventeenth-century art, and its absence in earlier representations of comic themes makes their interpretation more ambiguous. Comic representation in general became more deliberate and varied after 1600. Judith Leyster, Brouwer, Van de Venne, and Steen (Fig. 119) may have been especially self-conscious comic artists, portraying themselves in comic roles or producing mostly comic works.

But how to interpret even the obvious laughter of seventeenth-century protagonists? Comic texts and images had the stated aim of entertaining and edifying their audiences by presenting an unedited image of reality, exposing foibles to be avoided. The thematic and formal means of comic images, however, also imply unarticulated functions of comic modes. Most comic material must have been produced by and for a prosperous urban middle class, from the artisan to the patrician, and could have served the changing needs of its members for self-definition, by ridiculing other groups or follies that might destabilize its preferred social order and supporting beliefs, or by representing the temporary upset of "normal" behavior and power structures as comic.

While comic paintings may have bolstered tenets of dominant middle-class ideology, they did not do so conspiratorially. Moreover, their repetitive detailing of social transgressions may have served vicarious interest in those foibles as well. Comic modes, so heavily dependent on lifelike description of indulgence and deceit, allowed beholders an imaginary courting of disorder not possible in carefully regimented life. Because comic representations displaced transgressions onto laughable others, viewers could enjoy them free of moral charge.

Mariët Westermann

See also Bosch, Hieronymus; Commerce and commercial life; Humor, satire; Leyster, Judith; Quacksalvers, quack doctors; Rural life and views; Steen, Jan Havicksz.; Theater and theatricality; Van Leyden, Lucas; Vinckboons, David

Bibliography

Alpers, Svetlana. "Realism As a Comic Mode: Low-Life Painting Seen through Bredero's Eyes." *Simiolus* 8 (1975/1976): 115–143.

Bol, Laurens J. *Adriaen van de Venne: Painter and Draughtsman*. Doornspijk: Davaco, 1989.

Jacobwitz, Ellen S., and Stephanie Loeb Stepanek. *The Prints of Lucas van Leyden and His Contemporaries*. Washington, DC: National Gallery of Art, 1983.

Leuker, Maria-Theresia. *'De last van 't huys, de wil des mans. . . .': Frauenbilder und Ehekonzepte im niederländischen Lustspiel des 17. Jahrhunderts.* Münster: Verlag Regensberg, 1992.

Miedema, Hessel. "Realism and Comic Mode: The Peasant." *Simiolus* 9 (1977): 205–219.

Raupp, Hans-Joachim Raupp. "Ansätze zu einer Theorie der Genremalerei in den Niederlanden im 17. Jahrhundert." *Zeitschrift für Kunstgeschichte* 46 (1983): 401–418.

———. *Bauernsatiren: Entstehung und Entwicklung des bäuerlichen Genres in der deutschen und niederländischen Kunst ca. 1470–1570.* Niederzier: Luca-Verlag, 1986.

Renger, Konrad. *Adriaen Brouwer und das niederländische Bauerngenre 1600–1660.* Munich: Hirmer Verlag, 1986.

Vandenbroeck, Paul. *Beeld van de andere, vertoog over het zelf: Over wilden en narren, boeren en bedelaars.* Antwerp: Koninklijk Museum voor Schone Kunsten, 1987.

Westermann, Mariët. "How Was Jan Steen Funny? Strategies and Functions of Comic Painting in the Seventeenth Century." In *A Cultural History of Humour from Antiquity to the Present*. Edited by Jan Bremmer and Herman Roodenburg. Cambridge: Polity Press, 1996.

Commerce and commercial life

During the seventeenth century, when the Dutch Republic was at the center of European economic activity, the imagery of commercial life assumed an important place in its artistic production. The Dutch were proud of their character as a nation of traders, and it is no surprise to find this reflected in their art. However, as with other genres of painting, the imagery of commerce and commercial life was highly circumscribed in its content. Pictures of the great international trade, of merchants and bankers, are rare. Instead, interest focused on small-scale trade: the purchase of foodstuffs and the maintenance of domestic economy. The commercial life of the family or the city served to represent, in microcosm, the commercial pride of the nation.

Market scenes, the most common form of commercial imagery, had developed in the Southern Netherlands during the sixteenth century. The originator of the genre was Pieter Aertsen, who, although mostly active in Antwerp, was an Amsterdam native and spent the last years of his life there. Nevertheless, the tradition of market painting that stemmed from his work prevailed largely in the South: These were large-scale scenes of market stalls in which attention was lavished on the goods displayed for sale. In the Dutch Republic, what became at mid-century the dominant mode of representing markets had its origins not in painting but in the graphic arts. In the 1620s and 1630s, Jan van Goyen and Gerard Ter Borch depicted city marketplaces in many drawings. Already, however, they were following a paradigm set in the 1610s by two engravers, Jan van de Velde II of Haarlem and Claes Jansz. Visscher of Amsterdam.

An engraving designed by Van de Velde and executed by Visscher establishes the form and context that Dutch market imagery was to take (1616; Fig. 27). It shows an urban square where the business of marketing takes place. A glimpse of the Sint Bavokerk (Saint Bavo's Church) provides a topographical reference point—the city of Haarlem. While the hustle and bustle of the market is conveyed by indistinct figures at the far side of the square, the foreground is dominated by one large market stall. There, two women in market-sellers' dress do business with housewives who wear the cloaks of burgher shoppers. The print served as a title page for a series of landscape images; therefore, celebrating the provisioning of the urban population through the abundance of the Dutch countryside is a crucial motive behind early market imagery. This city commerce is linked to specific local sites and is carried out entirely by women.

The urban nature of the market is an essential component of its imagery. Holland's powerful cities were able to legislate a constant flow of foodstuffs into their centers, where market sale became a highly visible and regulated activity. When the new literary genre of city description books arose during the seventeenth century, markets were among the sites described and, often, illustrated. Certain types of markets were housed in elaborate, centrally located buildings. The completely enclosed Meat Halls did not attract painters; but the semi-open Fish Halls, with their rows of stone benches covered by roofs supported on slender columns, were a favorite subject. Gerrit and Job Berckheyde often painted the Haarlem Fish Halls, which wrapped around the side of the Sint Bavokerk on the city's center square; they and other artists also depicted Amsterdam's Fish Halls, located just off the Dam square. Leiden's less elaborate wooden fish stalls were the subject of works by Quirijn van Brekelenkam and Jan Steen. Van Brekelenkam focused his works on a single stall, while the other painters gave general views of the market environment.

Fruit and vegetables were sold at temporary stalls in open marketplaces, either alongside canals or in squares. Images of such markets are less likely than fish market paintings to be topographically accurate, but some do depict specific sites. As in Van de Velde's early print, the painters usually concentrate our attention on the transactions at one stall while also conveying some sense of the broader activities in the market. Perhaps the most accomplished painter of this kind of scene is Hendrick Martensz. Sorgh of Rotterdam, himself a sometime market-bargeman. His works include not only fruit and vegetable markets, but fish and poultry ones as well; some are topographically accurate, while in others recognizable elements are used within a fictive setting. The focus is often on a conversation, as buyer and seller discuss the price of the food to be exchanged. Gabriel Metsu's *Vegetable Market at Amsterdam* (ca. 1661–1662) shows a market in that city where bargaining, argument, and flirtation occur; this painting may refer to a theatrical market scene from *Moortje*, a popular comedy by Gerbrand Adriaensz. Bredero.

While most artists showed trade in large cities, a few made a specialty of markets in villages. Barend Gael's paintings of poultry markets are one example; Floris van Schooten's modest produce stalls are another. Despite the simplicity of his characters, Van Schooten sometimes provides a lavish still-life display. This was uncommon among Dutch painters but does occasionally occur, the most famous example being a collaborative work in which Frans Hals painted the fruit-seller attending a stall whose wares are beautifully rendered by the still-life specialist Nicolaes van Heussen (1630).

Certain forms of provisioning took place, albeit sometimes illegally, outside official markets. Goods might be sold door-to-door: Gabriel Metsu, Frans van Mieris the Elder, and Nicolaes Maes are among the artists who depicted women peddling fish or produce along the streets. However, the commodity most often shown as sold in this fashion is milk. Women carry the milk in brass vessels or wooden tubs hanging from a yoke; in most paintings, we see money changing hands after milk has been poured into the buyer's earthenware pot. Several works by Maes depict this moment with a solemn stillness, very different from the lively banter that takes place in market squares.

Commercial life moves further into the home in "threshold" commerce scenes. In these pictures, the viewpoint is *from*

the interior of the house *to* the doorway where a seller of fruit or seafood has arrived. The domestic interiors shown in these works are often very elegant, and the artists explore the nuances of class-determined interaction between customers and vendors. In Jacob Ochtervelt's *Fish Seller* (ca. 1669), the richly clad owner of the house teases the old peddlar woman standing well below him on the front steps, while a kneeling housemaid looks on in amusement. Conversely, in Van Brekelenkam's *Fish Seller* (1666) a barefoot fishwife stands impassively, looking down at the wealthy housewife as she kneels to inspect the fish. In other images of this domestic economy, contact between fine housewife and crude vendor is avoided altogether: Brekelenkam and Pieter de Hooch often show a maid bringing wares from the peddler to the seated housewife so she can make her choice.

The transactions discussed thus far are ones that occur more or less directly between producers and consumers of goods. However, the seventeenth century also saw the growth of another type of commerce: that which took place in shops, where the storekeeper brought in a variety of goods and re-sold them to customers. Depictions of these locales are rare in Dutch art with one important exception: the works of the Leiden *fijnschilders* (fine painters, specialists in painting fine details). Beginning with Gerrit Dou's *Grocery Shop* (1647), Leiden fine painters took up the subject with enthusiasm; indeed, their exploration of this genre outlasted the vogue for market scenes, continuing in popularity into the eighteenth century with the works of Willem van Mieris (Fig. 51) and Frans van Mieris the Younger. Shop paintings virtually always take the format of a view through a stone window or "niche"; this internal frame mediates our viewing of the retail shop's mediated exchange. Dou's London *Poulterer's Shop* (ca. 1660–1665; Fig. 28) is typical of the genre. A *trompe l'oeil* structure frames our view into the shop's interior. Directly behind it, a girl with a market pail gestures toward her desired purchase, a hare held up by the old shopkeeper. Dead poultry are neatly arrayed across the ledge of the window. Beyond this highly lit and finely detailed surface scene we see the dim, cavernous interior of the shop where a second transaction occurs.

If the shops of the *fijnschilders* represent the height of artifice in the imagery of commerce—both in their subject matter and in their facture—then Italianate market scenes represent the epitome of "naturalness." These works portray a natural marketing, entirely the opposite of the highly regulated practices of the Dutch Republic. The scene is frequently set in the Italian countryside. Peasants have set up a produce stall beside a road; a city woman has ventured out with her servants to buy goods from them. Hendrick Mommers was the most prolific practitioner of this genre, producing dozens of roughly drawn paintings that are variations on the theme. These Italianate market scenes are no more "real" than the stone windows of the *fijnschilders'* shops: Each type of work reflects an ideal of how a certain form of commerce does, or could, function, building both its aesthetic and its iconography on that ideal.

Like most Dutch genre painting, market scenes have been interpreted as containing moralizing messages based on concerns voiced in emblem books or hortatory tracts. The question of moral or message in these scenes is best looked at in the context of their general cultural functions and meanings. An important factor to keep in mind is that all of these pictures are ones of domestic economy, images in which commerce occurs between women. This reflects but also magnifies the actual conditions of marketing in Dutch cities. While official sellers—fishwives, applewives—and their customers were all women, men did play a part in carrying goods and selling wares from barrows along the streets. The pictured market is, however, a decidedly female realm, its status precariously balanced between the "public" sphere and the domestic one. Moralists like Jacob Cats singled out wise marketing as one of the duties of the virtuous housewife; yet fishwives were notoriously vulgar, and the market could be a site fraught with temptations both sexual and economic. Thus, the market genre as a whole served to represent the good wife's ability to successfully negotiate the perils of the market, as well as to negotiate the commercial deals that would maintain her household's economy.

That said, it should also be admitted that the city market was a site loaded with significance to Dutch society: It carried connotations of civic pride, economic virtue, and proper behavior in social intercourse. It is, therefore, not surprising that it should sometimes have been made a locus for the expression of specific social and moral concerns. The illustrators of Jacob Cats' moralizing texts frequently invented market scenes as ways of illustrating his more abstract points. Proverbs and jokes could also be situated in a market setting. These verbal expressions arose from the same interests that motivated the makers and buyers of market scenes; less frequently, they directly informed individual paintings. Joachim Wtewael's *Fruit and Vegetable Seller* (1618) refers to the proverb "one rotten apple spoils the whole basket": a girl is shown learning this behavioral lesson at the same time that she learns good shopping techniques from her mother. Gabriel Metsu's *Old Man Selling Poultry to a Young Woman* (1662) draws upon standard erotic jokes about "birding" and old men's lust for younger women. In both instances, the "moralizing" or "emblematic" element is merely a variation of the basic social concerns that inform all market imagery.

The large-scale commercial activity of men took place in different environments than the small trade among women and was rarely depicted by artists. For instance, the great Amsterdam Beurs, or Exchange, was situated almost adjacent to the Fish Halls, and yet its elegant, arcaded courtyard designed by Hendrick de Keyser was seldom a subject for paintings. One work by Emanuel de Witte shows the crowd of merchants gathered there at trading time, Dutch burghers mingling with Portuguese Jews and turbaned visitors from the Levant (ca. 1650). The nearby Grain Exchange, another important commercial site, was never depicted in paintings at all. Also fairly unusual are images of livestock markets, at which the expensive exchanges took place between men. Unlike food markets, livestock fairs occurred only a few times a year and in certain cities. Sybrand van Beest produced several paintings of the swine market in The Hague, while Philips

Wouwerman often depicted the Valkenburg horse fair.

As unusual commercial occasions for which people might travel great distances, some livestock markets assumed a festive character that distinguished them from the mundane daily food markets. In this sense they were akin to a final type of commercial activity in the Dutch Republic, the free market of the *kermis,* or fair. Every sizable town held such a fair once a year, and some larger cities had two yearly fairs. At fairs, the normal rules of commercial activity were suspended, and the free exchange of goods was allowed. For example, guild regulations normally prohibited the sale of paintings by artists not locally registered, but during fairs artists from other towns and even other countries could market their wares freely. The carnivalesque character of certain fairs was famous, attracting visitors from far and wide. One of the most notorious was The Hague's *kermis,* described in Adriaen van de Venne's book *Tafereel van de Belachende Werelt* (Image of the Comical World, 1635). Van de Venne also produced large grisaille paintings of The Hague *kermis,* showing a mixture of gentry, burghers, bumpkins, beggars, ballad singers, and peddlers celebrating together just outside the Binnenhof (this location was the inner courtyard of the old castle and the center of the *stadholders'* court).

In sixteenth-century Netherlandish art, the revelry of the *kermis* had been associated with the rude, uncivilized behavior of farmers and villagers, and early artists had taken care to distinguish their boorishness from the gentility of proper city folk. In the early years of the Dutch Republic, David Vinckboons, a Flemish immigrant, continued this tradition in his *kermis* images. However, as the century progressed, the undertones of condemnation or even of social distancing seem to decrease. Paintings of towns' *kermissen* by Jan Miense Molenaer, Jan Victors, or Jan Steen are comical without basing that comedy on the difference between city and country folk, "us" and "them." Other images, like those of Van de Venne in The Hague or Gerrit Lundens in Amsterdam, give topographically correct portrayals of their city's *kermissen,* now granted pride of place in the city's identity as markets had been. The festive meeting of social groups *in* the city, rather than their differentiation *outside* the city, is what interests these artists. As behavioral restrictions as well as economic ones were eased at the fairs, flirtation and street dancing are also frequently depicted.

Trade and exchange played defining roles in Dutch cultural practice and identity; likewise, they held an important place in the artistic imagery that culture produced. Both the proper exchange of daily marketing and the topsy-turvy world of the *kermis* provided artists with the opportunity to explore social ideals and norms. Personal behavior and interaction as defined by gender and socioeconomic class are primary concerns worked through in these contexts. As Dutch ascendancy in world trade declined toward the end of the seventeenth century, so the imagery of commerce declined as a part of artistic output; apart from the occasional stylized shop scene, it had vanished altogether by the beginning of the eighteenth century.

Elizabeth Alice Honig

See also Aertsen, Pieter; Berckheyde, Gerrit Adriaensz.; Berckheyde, Job Adriaensz.; Dou, Gerrit; Emblems and emblem books; Framing devices within pictures; Genre painting, eighteenth century; Genre painting, seventeenth century; Haarlem; Housewives and maids; Leiden; Maes, Nicolaes; Metsu, Gabriel; Molenaer, Jan Miense; Prints, printmaking, and printmakers (ca. 1500–ca. 1900); Steen, Jan Havicksz; Still life; Townscapes; Trade, exploration, and colonization overseas; Van Brekelenkam, Quirijn Gerritsz.; Van de Velde, Jan II; Vinckboons, David; Women's worlds

Bibliography

Freedberg, David, and Jan de Vries, eds. *Art in History, History in Art: Studies in Seventeenth-Century Dutch Culture*. Santa Monica, CA: Getty Center for the History of Art and the Humanities; distributed by the University of Chicago Press, 1991.

Joachim Beuckelaer: Het markt-en keukenstuck in de Nederlanden 1550–1650. Ghent: Museum voor Schone Kunsten, 1986.

Kistemaker, Renée et al. *Amsterdam Marktstad*. Amsterdam: Dienst van het Marktwezen, 1984.

Schneeman, Liane. "Hendrik Martensz. Sorgh As a Painter of Market Scenes." In *The Age of Rembrandt: Studies in Seventeenth-Century Dutch Painting*. Edited by Roland E. Fleischer and Susan Scott Munshouwer, 171–187. Papers in Art History from Pennsylvania State University, vol. 3. University Park, PA: Pennsylvania State University Press, 1988.

Stone-Ferrier, Linda. "Gabriel Metsu's *Vegetable Market at Amsterdam* and Its Relationship to a Bredero Farce." *Artibus et Historiae* 25 (1992): 163–180.

———. "Gabriel Metsu's *Vegetable Market at Amsterdam*: Seventeenth-Century Dutch Market Paintings and Horticulture." *Art Bulletin* 71:3 (September 1989): 428–452.

Constant (Constant Anton Nieuwenhuys) (born 1920)

Painter, constructionist, and theorist, Constant was a leading member of the Dutch Experimental Group/Cobra Movement (1948–1951) and the Internationale Situationniste (Situationist International, founded 1957). Constant was born in Amsterdam, took courses at the Rijksacademie (1939–1940), and went on to paint in a Cézannesque/Cubist manner during the war. On a visit to Paris in 1946 he met the Danish artist Asger Jorn, who introduced him into international avant-garde circles. During the following three years, Constant developed a free, primitivistic approach to painting (Fig. 25) that brought him into association with other Dutch Experimental and Cobra artists, and published articulate Marxian theories in the journals *Reflex* and *Cobra* (1948–1949). But in 1950–1951 he diverged from mainstream Cobra practice by promoting Socialist Realism and painting almost solely on the theme of war. His war *oeuvre* gave rise in 1952–1953 to simplified images, then to experiments in "Spatial Colorism" with the architect Aldo van Eyck and to a short phase of geo-metrical-abstract painting. By 1954 Constant had begun to make metal and plexiglass constructions, and in the years 1958–1960 his constructions and theories concerning a new urban environment played a central role in the Internationale Situationniste. Constant left that group in 1960, but throughout the 1960s he continued his urban project—a series of maquettes, plans, and theories sketching a technologically advanced infrastructure for the *homo ludens* of post-revolutionary society—under the name New Babylon. Since 1974, when a major exhibition in The Hague marked the end of the New Babylon project, Constant has resumed painting and reaffirmed classical and romantic themes and traditional craftsmanship in oils and watercolors.

Graham Birtwistle

See also Cobra Movement

Bibliography

Birtwistle, Graham. "The Language of War Art: Constant and Picasso." *Jong Holland* 7 (1991): 28–47.

Constant schilderijen 1940–1980. The Hague: Haags Gemeentemuseum; distributed by Staatsuitgeverij, 1980.

Lambert, Jean-Clarence. *Constant: Les trois espaces*. Paris: Editions Cercle d'Art, 1992.

New Babylon. The Hague: Haags Gemeentemuseum, 1974.

Sussman, Elisabeth, ed. *On the Passage of a Few People through a Rather Brief Moment in Time: The Situationist International, 1957–1972*. Cambridge, MA: MIT Press, 1989.

Contemplative life, contemplative virtues

The story of Christ in the house of Martha and Mary (Luke 10:38–42) established the precedence of the life devoted to contemplation of the divine. Later theologians developed elaborate doctrines concerning the practice of the contemplative life. The process traditionally follows three steps, from meditation through speculation and finally to contemplation itself. The highest stage should be imageless—pure, abstract consideration of invisible things. But writers generally recognized that most of the faithful needed images to assist them.

Art reflects devotional practices in various ways. Small, intimate diptychs satisfied the growing demand for images for private use. Narrative elaboration of subjects such as the Passion, and formats such as the "dramatic close-up," answered in pictorial form the desire for more detailed and intimate knowledge of the experiences of the sacred figures, a desire answered in similar ways by devotional literature. Hermit saints who renounced the world and devoted themselves to prayer and contemplation became common subjects in art. The contemplative process itself seems to have received visual expression in works that show a praying donor, unaccompanied by a patron saint, in the company of divine figures such as the Virgin and Child. The lack of a patron saint and the unfocused gaze of the donor have caused scholars to interpret these scenes as concrete visualizations of visions.

The contemplative life received special promotion in the Netherlands through the activities of the Devotio Moderna and the Beguines, lay movements whose members lived communally in ways similar to the monastic orders but did not take vows. The Brothers and Sisters of the Common Life who composed the Devotio Moderna particularly stressed the *Imitatio Christi* (Imitation of Christ). The modes of piety promoted by these movements spread far beyond their members to influence the culture profoundly.

Janey L. Levy

See also Active life, active virtues; Devotional images; Donor portraits; Manuscript illumination; Religious orders and their patronage

Bibliography

Harbison, Craig. "Visions and Meditations in Early Flemish Painting." *Simiolus* 15 (1985): 87–118.

Marrow, James. *Passion Iconography in Northern European Art of the Late Middle Ages and Early Renaissance: A Study of the Transformation of Sacred Metaphor into Descriptive Narrative.* Brussels: Van Ghemmert, 1979.

Ringbom, Sixten. *Icon to Narrative: The Rise of the Dramatic Close-Up in Fifteenth-Century Devotional Painting.* Åbo: Åbo Akademi, 1965.

Contemporary art (1980–1990)

Contemporary art in the Netherlands is directly connected with international developments. Against the background of postmodernism arose a new attitude toward reality. The past, present, and future were no longer obviously linearly related. The history of art was seen as a reservoir of images that could be reused. The abandonment of the idea of progress resulted in a renewed appreciation for the art of painting. During the first three years of the 1980s, there was a tidal wave of figurative expressionistic paintings. After 1983, sculpture and the new media (photography, video, the computer) joined in. Besides Expressionism, Surrealism, and abstract-geometric art, the postwar movements such as Pop Art, Minimal Art, and Conceptual Art were also reinterpreted. Other features of the period 1984–1990 were the mixing of high and low art, the blurring of the boundaries between media, and a great attention to art in a spatial environment.

During the 1970s, artists such as Jan Dibbets (born 1941), Lydia Schouten (born 1948), and Peter Struycken (born 1939) used photography, video, and the computer, respectively, to order reality in a new way. But painting was still practiced. In 1975 the Stedelijk Museum in Amsterdam organized the exhibition *Fundametele Schilderkunst* (*Fundamental Painting*). In addition to artists such as Robert Ryman, Agnes Martin, and Gerhard Richter, others, among them Kees Smits (born 1945), Toon Verhoef (born 1946), and Rob van Koningsbruggen (born 1948), exhibited abstract paintings with a main theme being the motion and transformation that resulted from the act of painting itself. Both aspects, motion and transformation, were essential for the art of painting in the 1980s. Moreover, artists using photography and combined techniques were also of importance. While a key word for the fundamental painters was objectivity, Carel Visser (born 1928,

Fig. 147), Ger van Elk (born 1941), Daan van Golden (born 1936), and Pieter Laurens Mol (born 1946) worked with associations. They created their own iconography and expressed a personal world of experience.

The impulse for the so-called *Wilde Schilderen* (*Wild Painting*) came from abroad. At the end of 1980 the *Jonge Italianen* (the *Young Italians:* Chia, Cucchi, Clemente) could be seen in the Stedelijk Museum in Amsterdam. Regardless of the differences in their works, they combined a whole list of different styles and borrowed motifs from the history of art. In 1981 the Groninger Museum in Groningen presented the group Mülheimer Freiheit from Cologne with Walter Dahn, Georg-Jiri Dokoupil, and others. The raw expressionistic style of the Germans found followers among the young Dutch artists, as did Dahn's and Dokoupil's practice of painting together and making music that broke through the proverbial isolation of the visual arts. Thus Maarten Ploeg (born 1958) painted and worked together with Peter Klashorst (born 1957) in this way. With artists' initiatives such as Aorta, W139, and V2, the joint project was more important than the individual contributions.

The exhibition *Westkunst* (Cologne, 1981) was important for the reinterpretation of the history of art. The neglected period of the 1930s and unknown portions of the *oeuvre* of the great avant-gardists (the later Picasso, Picabia, De Chirico, and the *periode vache* [cow phase] of Magritte) were expatiated. In the publication *Hunger nach Bildern* (Hungering for Images) by Wolfgang Max Faust and Gerd de Vries, the explosive increase of figurative images was placed in the context of the categorically ignored postwar German art of painting (Georg Baselitz, Sigmar Polke, Anselm Kiefer, Gerhard Richter).

The Dutch hunger for images at the beginning of the 1980s must also be seen in the context of four postwar figurative painters: Reinier Lucassen (born 1939), Alphons Freymuth (born 1940), Pieter Holstein (born 1934), and, from Belgium, Roger Raveel (born 1921). In the Netherlands the burden of guilt and morals was not as heavy as in Germany, but here the idea that the postmodern society would not let itself be guided (and that the artist, therefore, did not have the task of leading the way) was also felt as a liberation.

In the midst of the sometimes uncontrolled explosion of painting, there were artists who knew how to preserve the balance between gesture and concept. For René Daniels (born 1950), one of the most important painters from this period, painting is never done for its own sake. Neither is there mention of arbitrary citations or mere personal expression of feelings. His now completed *oeuvre* is characterized by a continuity not bound by time. Every time the same themes reoccur in different ways. Every painting can be seen as the next step in a chronological artistic development, as well as an "interference" *(stoorzender)* that adjusts and changes older work (Fig. 29).

Marlene Dumas (born 1953) has also from the beginning let herself be guided by what personally affects her—the image of the woman in art and society—without falling into strict particulars. In the beginning, she worked out her themes with collages in which drawn and photographed images were combined with text. After the mid-1980s, Dumas applied herself to classical genres such as the portrait and the (nude) figure (Fig. 47). She makes paintings, drawings, and gouaches.

Sculpture also had been mostly figurative and painterly in the early eighties. Henk Visch (born 1950) makes fanciful sculptures; in the work of Alexander Schabracq (born 1957) Western and non-Western elements combine into contemporary magic realism; and the sculptures of Peer Veneman (born 1952) are only at first sight abstract. They use a range of materials (copper, feathers, wood, plastic, velvet), and all three have literally crossed the limits between painting and sculpture. Painter Aldert Mantje (born 1954) and sculptor Harald Vlugt (born 1957) have for some time combined their forces in blackened landscapes full of electronics and dead animals.

An important exhibition for further developments in sculpture was *Groene Wouden* (*Green Forests*) at the Rijksmuseum Kröller-Müller in Otterlo in 1983, with work by Robert O'Brien (1951–1988), Niek Kemps (born 1952), and Arno van der Mark (born 1949). The key word was "reflection," a word that can be connected with the keep-off/artificial appearance of the sculptures as well as with the necessity to stand still before art and artistry. After 1983, O'Brien and Irene Fortuyn (born 1959) made sculptures that neither the form, material, nor technique makes clear what they are: pedestals, furniture, architecture, art? (Fig. 30) For Kemps, the surface of a sculpture is essential. His perfectly finished, gleaming, or partially transparent sculptures literally give up reflections and make it impossible for the viewer to grasp the world (captured by photographs) that is behind the surface. In the work of Arno van der Mark, perception and the need to get hold of reality through perception are also important themes.

Rob Scholte (born 1958) began his career in the Amsterdam artists' initiative W139. Together with Sandra Derks (born 1960) he made a painting based on multiple copies of the same coloring book. Since that time reproduction versus originality and the combination of art and popular images have become elevated as themes. Scholte has an extensive archive of images that form the source of his paintings. The artist, who believes that the more often an image is reproduced the better it can convey meaning, is not afraid to play with the market mechanics in art. Scholte emphasized the profile of himself as the artist of the '80s: business-like and involved in mass media.

After the conception of an avant-garde at the head of a linear cultural tradition had given way to the realization that everything was possible, Dutch artists focused on the question of the place of art and artists in the network of forces that is called society. To exorcise arbitrariness, it was necessary to channel the postmodern freedom and to choose a point of view—even if it is a changeable one. While prior to 1984, the heroism of the beginning of modern art was reflected in a precious mirror image, artists later based their artistic position on postwar trends. There has been talk of Neo-Pop, Neo-Minimal and Neo-Conceptual Art, but there was never a revival in the traditional sense. What was at issue was not style but a vision that, interpreted from a personal point of view, could accept a wide range of manifestations.

Looking back, René Daniels, Marlene Dumas, and Henk Visch also searched for an ahistorical point of view. However, Fortuyn and O'Brien, Kemps, Van der Mark, and Scholte openly distanced themselves from the personal signature, from the unity of form and content, from the distinction between high and low culture—in short, from all of those things that had been so important in the traditional appreciation of art. The peculiar way in which Scholte gave new life to Pop Art has also been crucial for the new look of Dutch art after 1985. The sculptors of *Groene Wouden* also succeeded in shifting the attention from gesture to concept, not so much through lack of outward appearance, but by involving the beholder in the enticing game of frivolous appearances.

While Scholte's archive of images contains a wide diversity of material, other artists have chosen specialization. The artists' group After Nature makes realistic paintings in the historic genres of still life, portrait, and landscape—all under the pretext of the craftsmanship of painting, but in reality in order to go to extremes, just as Scholte does, in the disclosure of mechanics and conventions. Those who belong to After Nature are Peter Klashorst, Bart Domburg (born 1957), Jurriaan van Hall (born 1962), Ernst Voss (born 1959), and the brothers Gijs (born 1964), Justus (born 1966), and Aad (born 1967) Donker. Philip Akkerman (born 1957) even goes a step further and makes only self-portraits. Within this genre he subjects all painting styles and methods, according to a preset plan, to conscientious examination.

The opposite of After Nature is Capital Gains, a casual group of artists who make a case for art as a social reality and who prefer to use domestic techniques such as embroidery, braiding, and macramé. They are Berend Strik (born 1960), Arnout Mik (born 1962), Paul Perry (born 1956), Jorgen Leijenaar (born 1957), and Hans van Houwelingen (born 1957). In this context should also be mentioned Guido Geelen (born 1961), who uses the more common practice of hobby ceramics to make vases and monumental sculptures, and Joep van Lieshout (born 1963), who, using the minimalist idea of standardized measuring, began to pile up paving stones and beer crates, and later developed bright-colored polyester sculptures that can serve as furniture or even as complete living quarters.

The mix of disciplines is what unites Dutch sculpture in the late 1980s: sculptural design and interior decorating, as with Van Lieshout; sculpture and architecture, such as in the recent "dwellings" of Jan van de Pavert (born 1960); and sculpture, design, and painting as with Rob Birza (born 1962). This mix goes hand in hand with an increased interest in art as a theatrical experience, partly mental, partly sensory. Aside from the work itself, the environment is also a factor to consider. Artists such as Mirjam de Zeeuw (born 1959), Roos Theeuws (born 1957), Lidwien van de Ven (born 1963), and Mark Manders (born 1968) prefer to build an installation on the spot rather than work in a studio. Seymour Likely also builds installations, but this imaginary artist—the brainchild of Aldert Mantje, Ido Vunderink (born 1955), and Ronald Hooft (born 1962)—does not see the concept of environment architecturally but socially, with historical and political overtones. The work of Seymour Likely varies from clothing printed with bank notes for a basketball team to the exploitation of a disco bar. The theatrical experience of art is the point of departure of the art of the 1990s.

Els Hoek
Natalie Kamphuys

See also Artists' Initiatives; Brouwn, Stanley; Daniels, René; Dumas, Marlene; Feminism, feminist issues; Fortuyn/O'Brien; Photography, modern and contemporary; Postmodernism; Prints, modern graphic arts after 1945; State patronage, public support; Struycken, Peter; Van Goldén, Daan, Visch, Henk; Visser, Carel

Bibliography

Cooke, Lynn. *Contemporary Art from the Netherlands.* Chicago: Museum of Contemporary Art, 1982.

Dumas, Marlene et al. *Miss Interpreted: Marlene Dumas.* Eindhoven: Stedelijk Van Abbemuseum, 1992.

Edelkoort, Lidewij. *Fortuyn/O'Brien: Marble Public.* Amsterdam: Stedelijk Museum, Artist Publication, 1991.

Groot, Jacob de et al. *Henk Visch.* The Hague: Netherlands Office for Fine Arts, 1988.

Hoek, Els. *René Daniels.* Vienna: Raum Aktueller Kunst, 1983.

Kremer, Mark et al. *Niek Kemps at the Biennale di Venezia, Padiglione di Fiandra e Olanda.* Rijswijk: Ministry of Welfare, Health, and Cultural Affairs, 1993.

Lamoree, Jhim et al. *Six Dutch Artists: Marlene Dumas, Rob Scholte, Han Schuil, Alexander Schabracq, Peer Veneman, and Henk Visch.* Edinburgh: Fruitmarket Gallery, 1989.

Ottevanger, Alied. "The Image as Mask: Recent Developments in the Visual Arts." *Dutch Art and Architecture Today* 11 (1982): 2–12.

Scholte, Rob. *Rob Scholte: How to Star.* Rotterdam: Museum Boymans-Van Beuningen, 1988.

Sinderen, Wim van. *Seven Dutch Artists: Aldert Mantje, Willem Sanders, Rob Scholte, Ton van Summeren, Peer Veneman, Harald Vlugt, and Martin van Vreden.* Rotterdam: Art Finance, 1991.

Sizoo, Hans. "New Painting in Holland." *Flash Art* 107 (1982): 39–42.

Tuyl, G. van. "A New Direction in Dutch Sculpture." *Dutch Art and Architecture Today* 17 (1985): 18–25.

———. *Young Dutch Sculptors.* The Hague: Netherlands Office for Fine Arts, 1988.

Conversation piece

The term is specifically used to denote a particular subset of portraiture, defined by Adolph Staring as "a portrait-group of a family, [with] small-scale figures seen in the natural setting of their own home or garden, and behaving as people normally do when amongst good friends, i.e., naturally and simply" (Staring, 1956: 57). This category of painting has had great international popularity from the seventeenth century on and is particularly associated with eighteenth-century England. In the Netherlands, especially during the seventeenth century, this portrait format was fashionable for families across the social spectrum, from shopkeepers and craftsmen, as illustrated by Rembrandt's innovative *Shipbuilder and His Wife* (1633; London, British Royal Collection), to patricians, as seen in *The Portrait of Jeremias van Collen and Susanna van Uffelen and Their Twelve Children* (attributed to Pieter van Anraedt, ca. 1661; Amsterdam, Rijksmuseum; Fig. 31).

In their separate monographs on the subject, scholars Mario Praz and Ralph Edwards concentrate on discussing and presenting the possible antecedents and subsequent development of the conversation piece in various countries and time periods. Both suggest Jan van Eyck's *Portrait of Giovanni Arnolfini and Giovanna Cenami* (1434; London, National Gallery) as a likely prototype. Just as most modern interpretations of the painting indicate that it is not merely a glimpse into the bedroom and private life of this Italian couple living in Flanders, neither are the casually staged seventeenth- and eighteenth-century conversation pieces only "entertaining and faithful documents of domestic life," as Adolph Staring suggests in reference to Dutch examples (Staring, 1956: 57).

More recently, art historians such as E. de Jongh, Hans Joachim Raupp, and David R. Smith have explored complex issues concerning patronage, artistic choice and convention, social and moral custom, the differences between "biographical" and "rhetorical" truth in portraiture (Raupp, 1986: 259), and hidden and overt symbolism. *The Portrait of the Ruychaver-van der Laen Family* attributed to Jan Miense Molenaer (ca. 1630; Amsterdam, Van Loon Museum) richly illustrates the coming together of these various factors. Though the likenesses of the family members may be fairly true to life, and the activities seem to be quite ordinary, the figures are actually illustrating the five senses and the four ages of man. The elderly couple at the far right in the painting died in 1626, before the painting was executed, further demonstrating that the composition is not a reenactment of an actual or typical afternoon of the family at home (De Jongh, 1986: 215–217). The work raises questions on more than one level as to why these easily recognized symbolic traditions were chosen, and what this painting really tells us about the people and the images of themselves they wished to convey, both individually and as a family.

More typical of conversation pieces are poses, gestures, and symbols that are less programmatic. For instance, *The Portrait of Jeremias van Collen and Susanna van Uffelen and Their Twelve Children* exudes affluence and status, embodied in the elegant poses, rich clothing, and classicizing surroundings of the figures, and in the unambiguous symbol of high socioeconomic standing: the family's very own country villa, Velserbeek, behind them.

These images of specific people are easily confused with *gezelschap* (merry company) or other daily-life scenes with their generic figures or types, since the portraits and genre works are often similar in appearance. *Company in a Garden* (1661) by Barent Graat in the Rijksmuseum, Amsterdam, illustrates the easy confusion. This may be a conversation piece, since the figures shown in a garden setting may be specific but still unidentified members of a family depicted in a portrait; yet the traditional title implies it is a genre work. As Raupp has suggested (Raupp, 1986: 260), this confused boundary between genre and portraiture is a fertile topic for further research.

Diane E. Cearfoss Mankin

See also Allegorical traditions; Aristocracy and gentry; Country houses and gardens; Genre painting, eighteenth century; Group portraiture; House interiors; Marriage and family portraits; Molenaer, Jan Miense; Musicians, musical companies, musical performers; Portraiture; Rembrandt van Rijn; Subjects, subject categories, and hierarchies; Troost, Cornelis

Bibliography

Edwards, Ralph. *Early Conversation Pictures from the Middle Ages to about 1730: A Study in Origins.* London: Country Life Limited, 1954.

Franits, Wayne. Review of *Portretten van echt en trouw. Oud Holland* 102 (1988): 249–256.

Jongh, E. de. *Portretten van echt en trouw: Huwelijk en gezin in de Nederlandse kunst van de zeventiende eeuw.* Haarlem: Frans Hals Museum; Zwolle: Waanders, 1986.

Praz, Mario. *Conversation Pieces: A Survey of the Informal Group Portrait in Europe and America.* University Park, PA: Pennsylvania State University Press, 1971.

Raupp, Hans Joachim. "Review of *Portretten van echt en trouw.*" *Simiolus* 16 (1986): 254–262.

Smith, David R. *Masks of Wedlock: Seventeenth-Century Dutch Marriage Portraiture.* Ann Arbor, MI: UMI Research Press, 1982.

Staring, Adolph. *De Hollanders Thuis: Gezelschapstukken uit drie eeuwen.* The Hague: Nijhoff, 1956. (English summary).

Coornhert, Dirck Volkertsz. (1522–1590)

Dutch poet, prose writer, and moral philosopher, D.V. Coornhert's importance for the art of printing is not solely due to the fact that he worked in etching and engraving, but also that he devised the subjects for many prints, although he did not draw them himself. From 1547 until 1559 he was the most important etcher/engraver of drawings by Maerten van Heemskerck in Haarlem. In addition, he engraved after Frans Floris, Lambert Lombard, and Willem Thibaut. In 1560 Coornhert temporarily stopped engraving to give all of his attention to the writing, translating, and printing of books and to politics. In 1567 he was suspected of sedition and arrested by the Spanish authorities then occupying the Netherlands. After he was released on bail, he fled in 1568 to the Rhineland, where he stayed in exile until 1576. There he engraved prints after designs by Adriaan de Weert, an exile from Brussels, and the young Hendrick Goltzius became his student. When Coornhert was allowed to return, Goltzius followed him to Haarlem.

Coornhert, through his strong personality, must have made an impression on the ideas and choice of subjects by the artists whose drawings he rendered into prints. This can be seen when comparing prints engraved by Coornhert with his literary work. The majority of Van Heemskerck's prints that can be viewed as lessons for daily life go back to ideas of Coornhert. The same is true of the religious and political allegories that Coornhert collaborated on with Adriaan de Weert, as well as the work of the young Goltzius.

Ilja M. Veldman

See also Goltzius, Hendrick; Gouda; Haarlem; Humanism, humanist themes; Prints, early printed book and Bible illustration; Prints and printmaking, printmakers (ca. 1500–ca. 1900); Writers on art, sixteenth and seventeenth centuries

Bibliography

Veldman, I.M. *De wereld tussen Goed en Kwaad: Late prenten van Coornhert.* The Hague: SDU, 1990.

———. "Leerzame dwaasheid. De invloed van het *sotten schip* (1548) op zottenvoorstellingen van Maarten van Heemskerck en Willem Thibaut." *Nederlands Kunsthistorisch Jaarboek* 37 (1986): 195–224. (English summary).

———. *Maarten van Heemskerck and Dutch Humanism in the Sixteenth Century.* Amsterdam/Maarssen: Gary Schwartz, 1977.

Corneille (Corneille Guillaume Beverloo) (born 1922)

Cofounder of the Dutch Experimental Group and the international Cobra Movement in 1948, Corneille is one of the major lyrical artists of his generation. Born in Liège (Belgium) of Dutch parents, Corneille studied drawing and printmaking at the Rijksacademie, Amsterdam (1940–1943), where he met Karel Appel. A stay in Budapest in 1947 brought influences from Surrealism and Paul Klee that remained visible in the linear accents and poetic fantasies typical of Corneille's work in the later 1940s. In association with Appel and Constant he helped lead the Experimental Group, whose journal *Reflex* bore a Corneille lithograph on the cover of its first number (September 1948). From 1950 on, the French-speaking Dutchman made his base in Paris, but his extensive travels— for example, in Africa (1948, 1949, 1951, 1956) and Central and South America (first visit 1957–1958)—were decisive in his artistic development and gave rise to an extensive collection of ethnographic art. Semi-abstract paintings and graphics from the 1950s are related to landscapes seen in the Sahara or symbols on Ethiopian tombs, while from the mid-1960s on Corneille has developed a colorful primitive figuration to evoke tropical and increasingly erotic themes. From his early days a poet as well as a draftsman-painter, Corneille has associated closely with writers throughout his career and made graphic portfolios together with poets such as Christian Dotremont and Octavio Paz. Since the later 1970s, repetitious paintings and prints for the popular-art market have considerably diluted his *oeuvre*.

Graham Birtwistle

See also Cobra Movement

Bibliography

Birtwistle, Graham, and Patricia Donkersloot-Van den Berghe. *Corneille: The Complete Graphic Works, 1948–1975.* Amsterdam: Meulenhoff, 1992.

Gribling, Frank. *Corneille.* Amsterdam: Meulenhoff, 1972.

Kerkhoven, Ronald. *Het Afrikaanse gezicht van Corneille.* The Hague: Museon, 1992; distributed by Uniepers Abcoude.

Laude, André. *Corneille, Le Roi-Image.* Paris: Editions SMI, 1973.

Country houses and gardens

Ownership of a country house and garden was a matter of great social, political, and economic importance and prestige to the wealthy Dutch patriciate during the seventeenth and eighteenth centuries. The country estate was idealized as a place of retreat from the very real ills and pressures of city life. This idealization stems from ancient Roman concepts, expressed by such poets as Horace and Virgil, about the superior quality of the life led by the gentleman farmer. Practically speaking, the patriciate of this mostly urban nation considered country houses and gardens as status symbols with many personal benefits. Dutch seventeenth-century tastes in rural retreats were at first modest. The character, size, and number of properties and homes were small, especially when compared with those found in England or France. By the end of the seventeenth century, and into the eighteenth century, however, the size and level of luxury of these properties became grander and more ostentatious, and the number of villas and gardens in several areas of the Netherlands grew tremendously.

The country houses and estates of the early modern Netherlands developed from two sources: (1) remodeled castles and manor houses and their surrounding lands, and (2) newly established properties and villas. The former were founded by members of the nobility and gentry from medieval times through the sixteenth century. After separation from Spain, many, though not all, of these lands were abandoned, and the homes either went into ruins or were bought by members of the ascending urban middle-class patriciate. Only a few aristocratic and gentry families, including the House of Orange, retained their wealth and properties. Members of the Dutch burgher elite usually were the ones who developed *buitenhuizen* (country houses and estates) on new sites. These were often located in areas surrounding major cities or along rivers such as the Vliet, Amstel, and Vecht.

Typical Dutch country-house owners still considered their stately townhouses lining the major urban canals their primary residences. Their political and economic power rested in the cities. This is atypical of the European ruling classes in general. For instance, during this same period of history, British authority remained with the aristocracy and gentry, whose country houses were their main homes. Much of the power and wealth of the English ruling classes originated in the vestigial feudal system of inheriting or buying and controlling vast tracts of land. Even when Dutch children inherited from their parents, country properties were only a small portion of the total wealth. Individual holdings remained small relative to British estates. Besides the fact that less land was available in the Netherlands, all children of wealthy families, male and female, received portions, keeping each of their holdings fairly modest. British eldest sons inherited virtually everything and thus kept large estates intact.

Most of the country houses built in the seventeenth-century Netherlands were executed on a scale appropriate to the modest size of the grounds. The stark classicizing style inspired by the townhouse and villa designs of the sixteenth-century Venetian architects Andrea Palladio and Vincenzo Scamozzi appealed to Dutch sensibilities. Native architects, such as Jacob van Campen, Pieter Post, Philips Vingboons, and their followers, took their inspiration from the architectural books of these influential Italians in creating the Dutch classicist style. Van Campen's 1628 remodeling of the Huis ten Bosch (now the town hall) in Maarssen, near Utrecht, is probably the earliest example of a still-extant country house demonstrating clear Palladian design elements such as the two-story Ionic-order temple front superimposed on a one-story building. For the most part, however, country-house designs followed the innovations made by these architects in townhouse constructions. The Huygens House in The Hague (destroyed), jointly designed by Van Campen and its owner, Constantijn Huygens, and the neighboring Mauritshuis, started by Van Campen and completed by Pieter Post, are prime examples of the austere, hipped-roof, cubic form that was the urban and rural architectural design preferred by the patrician class in the Netherlands during most of the seventeenth century.

In the late seventeenth century and throughout the eighteenth century, the more elaborate French architectural forms and decorations of the Louis XIV and Rococo styles superseded the compact buildings, planar surfaces, and restrained adornment of the Scamozzian and Palladian aesthetic. For instance, the Huis ten Bosch in The Hague, the country retreat built by Pieter Post in 1645 for Frederik Hendrik and Amalia van Solms, was originally an austere central-plan villa surrounded by a late Renaissance-style garden. In the eighteenth century, the house was transformed into a larger, more lavishly decorated palace with wings and a grand and extensive Baroque garden and park.

The tradition in Netherlandish genre and landscape art of depicting the castles and country homes of the rich and famous dates back at least to the early fifteenth century with the Limbourg Brothers' calendar pages in *Les Très Riches Heures du Duc de Berry*. Images of medieval and Renaissance-style villas and palaces appear early in the seventeenth century in open-air *gezelschap* (merry company) scenes, as in David Vinckboons' *The Garden Party* (ca. 1610), in the Rijksmuseum, Amsterdam. In landscape art depicting the native Dutch countryside, castles and ruins appear in the works of Claes Jansz. Visscher, Willem Buytewech, Jan van Goyen, and Salomon van Ruysdael, to name a few. Elegant villas in the more sober Dutch classicizing style join medieval buildings in the panoramic paintings of Philips de Koninck and others from the 1650s on, while the new architecture is featured in works such as *A Park with Fountains and a Country House* (late 1670s; Washington, DC, National Gallery of Art) by Jacob van Ruisdael. In high-life genre works of the 1660s and 1670s, such as *Skittles Players in a Garden* by Pieter de Hooch (Waddesdon, UK, James A. de Rothschild Collection, Waddesdon Manor), cubic classicizing villas are important background elements that add to the aura of leisurely sophistication in such pictures.

"Portraits" of identifiable country houses in prints and drawings appear throughout the seventeenth century, from the ground-level works of Claes Jansz. Visscher early in the century, to the bird's-eye views of Romeyn de Hooghe and Daniel Stopendaal at century's end. Intriguing examples in between are the over two hundred topographically accurate drawings of castles and villas executed by Roeland Roghman around 1647 and 1648. (See the English summaries in W. Th. Kloek.) Exactly why they were made remains a mystery, but clearly it is a manifestation of the popularity of architectural imagery and the impetus to document a particular place at a particular time in Dutch culture. Most of the painted portraits of country houses date to the 1660s and 1670s and were executed by landscape and cityscape painters, such as Jan van der Heyden and Gerrit Berckheyde. Van der Heyden alone painted about thirty portraits of known country houses and their gardens, including at least five of Goudestein (Amsterdam *burgomeester*, Joan Huydecoper's home and grounds near Maarssen), and seven extant images of the Huis ten Bosch and its gardens in The Hague.

By the end of the seventeenth century and into the eighteenth century, two types of large printed series of actual country-estate images were published. One type involved sets of various views of a particular house and estate, usually belonging to King Willem III or to one of his courtiers. For example, four large engravings and forty small etchings of different views of Zorgvliet (formerly Jacob Cats' estate), were commissioned in the 1690s by then owner Hans Willem Bentinck, friend and adviser to Willem III. The second type of printed series, such as *De Zegepralende Vecht* (The Praiseworthy or Triumphant Vecht, 1719) and *Hollands Arcadia* (Dutch Paradise, 1730), illustrated numerous estates and villas in particular areas where there were high concentrations of country retreats, such as along the banks of the Vecht and Amstel rivers.

Many patrons chose to have likenesses of themselves and their families portrayed in a park, garden, or terrace setting with their own country house or an imaginary one in the background. The *Portrait of Jeremias van Collen, His Wife, Susanna van Uffelen, and Their Twelve Children*, with their house and estate, Velserbeek, in the background, attributed to Pieter van Anraedt, is a document (ca. 1661), now hanging in the Rijksmuseum, Amsterdam, of a known family and their country residence (Fig. 31). A painting by Barent Graat, *Company in a Garden*, from the same approximate time and located in the same museum, is possibly a portrait of an unidentified family in an idealized estate setting. These individuals probably wanted to demonstrate their wealth, prestige, and good taste.

Celebrations of country-house life were not restricted to the visual arts. A whole poetry genre devoted to particular country estates and their owners thrived in the seventeenth-century Netherlands. The *hofdicht*, the Dutch version of a literary form found throughout Europe, hearkens back to ancient Roman prototypes. Though generally translated as "country house poem" in English, the *hofdicht* consistently omits references to the house itself or its architecture. Instead, the park and gardens are praised as orderly reflections of God and his beneficence. Often the contents of the house are lovingly described as they relate to the ideal of a recreational and/or scholarly retreat afforded by a place in the country. Two of the earliest and most influential *hofdichten* were written by the statesmen Constantijn Huygens and Jacob Cats about their own retreats from civic life, Hofwijck and Zorgvliet, respectively.

Diane E. Cearfoss Mankin

See also Aristocracy and gentry; Classicism in architecture; Group portraiture; House of Orange-Nassau; Huygens, Constantijn; Landscape; Literature, poetry: analogues with the visual; Post, Pieter; Rural life and views; Van Campen, Jacob; Van der Heyden, Jan; Vingboons, Philips

Bibliography

Ackerman, James S. *The Villa: Form and Ideology of Country Houses*. London: Thames and Hudson, 1990.

Guillermo, Jorge. *Dutch Houses and Castles*. London: Taurus Parke Books, 1990.

Kloek, W. Th. *De kasteeltekeningen van Roelant Roghman*. Vol. 2. Alphen aan den Rijn: Canaletto, 1990. (English summaries).

Kuyper, W. *Dutch Classicist Architecture: A Survey of Dutch Architecture, Gardens, and Anglo-Dutch Architectural Relations from 1625–1700*. Delft: Delft University Press, 1980.

Mankin, Diane E. Cearfoss. "Dutch Seventeenth-Century Images of Palaces and Villas inside the Netherlands." Ph.D. diss., University of Kansas, in progress.

Raaij, Stefan van. *The Royal Progress of William and Mary: Houses and Gardens of Their Time*. Amsterdam: D'Arts, 1988.

Schwartz, Gary. "Jan van der Heyden and the Huydecopers of Maarsseveen." *J. Paul Getty Museum Journal* 11 (1983): 197–220.

Wijck, H.W.M. van der. "Country Houses in the Northern Netherlands: The Way of Life of a Calvinistic Patriciate." *Apollo* 96 (November 1972): 406–415.

Court and official portraiture

From miniatures to larger-than-life figures, portraits of monarchs, the nobility, and members of their courts are produced to impress, to claim social and political power for the individuals portrayed. When bestowed as gifts they cement family relationships and political ties, and they were even circulated as proxies for such official events as betrothals and marriages. Claims to power and affiliation are made by these images both through asserting hereditary ties and through personal traits and the objects associated with rulership.

The earliest court portraits were frequently painted for

religious settings. Individuals might be embedded in pictorial genealogies—a series of portraits that includes images of the subject's powerful ancestors both living and dead—such as the seventeen members of the Van Swieten family kneeling at the foot of the Virgin and Child (mid-fifteenth century, lost; copy dated 1552, Leiden, Stedelijk Museum De Lakenhal). Or they might appear individually on wings flanking an altar such as the full-length standing portraits of Philip the Fair and Joanna the Mad painted around 1500 (Brussels, Musées Royaux des Beaux-Arts).

Until 1579, official court portraiture in the Netherlands was comprised of portraits of Hapsburg monarchs, frequently in versions or copies after paintings by Titian and especially Antonis Mor. The former originated, and the latter promulgated, what came to be recognized as the international state portrait format: a full-length standing figure accompanied by such symbols of power and office as a column, swagged curtain, and throne or table on which lay a crown or helmet. By the early seventeenth century this was a favored format for portraits of the aristocracy, such as Everard van der Maes' portraits of *Johan van Duivenvoorde*, later lord of Voorschoten, and his wife, *Maria van Voerst*, of 1608 (Duivenvoorde castle), and for the Princes of Orange and members of their extended families. Royal portraits were painted both individually and in series to hang in royal palaces, castles of the nobility, and town halls by such artists as Michiel van Mierevelt—the leading painter of the *stadholder*'s court—Jan van Ravesteyn, Gerard and Willem van Honthorst, Adriaen Hanneman, Jan Mijtens, and at the end of the century Jan de Baen and Caspar Netscher. The full-length format was also the prototype for such double portraits as that of *Frederik Hendrik and Amalia van Solms* painted by Gerard van Honthorst in about 1637 for Constantijn Huygens (The Hague, Mauritshuis; Fig. 32), and of their son *Prince Willem II and Princess Henrietta Mary Stuart* by Anthony van Dyck of 1641 (Amsterdam, Rijksmuseum). The originals of these portraits of nobility as well as of popular military heroes served as models for literally hundreds of copies produced for private homes of the middle class in three-quarter formats, bust lengths, and print series after them. For the latter patrons, such images advertise and thus help create political affiliations.

The equestrian portrait is the second important and long-lived format employed for Dutch royalty. Originally representing leadership on the battlefield during war and the privileges of the hunt in peace, this format later came to connote rulership more generally through the parallels drawn between the ability to govern a horse and the ability to rule a people. Examples range from the series of woodcuts depicting the *Procession of the Counts and Countesses of Holland* by Jacob Cornelisz. van Oostsanen in 1518, and the series of eight tapestries known as the *Nassau Genealogy* designed around 1530 by Bernard van Orley (destroyed), through the *Ancestors and Relatives of Prince Maurits* by Adriaen van de Venne in 1621 (Darmstadt, Heissisches Landesmuseum), to such individual equestrian portraits as *Frederika Sophia Wilhelmina of Prussia*, dated 1789, by Tethart Philip Christiaan Haag (Amsterdam, Rijksmuseum).

The persistence of these two portrait formats and their associations, which continue to be employed for Dutch court portraiture, lies in the power and importance of symbolic continuity in the face of changing governmental forms and the vicissitudes of royal power. T.P.C. Haag and Philip van Dijk were court painters to Princes Willem IV and Willem V, while Johan Tischbein was also popular at the *stadholder*'s court at the end of the eighteenth century. Joseph Paelinck employed these formats for portraits of King Willem I and Queen Wilhelmina early in the nineteenth century, as did Jan Kruseman in representations of Kings Willem I and Willem II and their relations, and Nicolaas Pieneman for Kings Willem II and Willem III. While more informal royal portraits are created today, both painted and photographed official portraits of Queen Beatrix and her family continue more or less to follow conventions established at the end of the sixteenth century.

Pastoral themes by such artists as Gerard van Honthorst were also popular for royal children during the seventeenth century, and an unusual history portrait of *Sofia Hedwig, Duchess of Braunschwieg Wolfenbuttel, with Her Children as Caritas* by Paulus Moreelse of 1621 should be noted (Apeldoorn, Palace Het Loo). The contemporary history painting is a portrait genre that became particularly popular in the nineteenth century, in themes that originated in the seventeenth. Examples include Pauwels van Hillegaert's *Prince Frederik Hendrik at the Siege of 's Hertogenbosch, 1629*, Cornelis Kruseman's *H.R.H. the Prince of Orange at the Battle of Boutersem, 1831* of 1839, and Otto Erelman's *Frederiksplein, Amsterdam, during the Entry of Queen Wilhelmina, 1898*.

Ann Jensen Adams

See also Devotional images; Donor portraits; History portraits; House of Orange-Nassau; Kruseman, Cornelis; Manuscript illumination; Portraiture; Nationalism; State and municipal art collecting and collections; State patronage, public support; Van Honthorst, Gerard; War and warfare

Bibliography
Jenkins, Marianna. *The State Portrait: Its Origin and Evolution.* New York: College Art Association of America, 1947.

Couzijn, Wessel (1912–1984)
One of the first Dutch sculptors to use abstract forms on a monumental scale, Wessel Couzijn, who was born in Amsterdam, was three years old when his family moved to New York. In 1926 he attended a summer course at the Art Students League. In 1930, after returning to Amsterdam, he was accepted at the Rijksacademie, where he took lessons from Jan Bronner. He won the Prix de Rome in 1936, which enabled him to live in Rome until 1938. In 1939–1940 he was in Paris, studying at the Académie Ranson, where Aristide Maillol was an instructor.

With the outbreak of World War II, Couzijn, who was Jewish, left again for the United States, where he met Ossip Zadkine and worked for him for a short time. At the end of 1946, Couzijn returned to Amsterdam. In his work at this time the relation between matter and space became a more independent premise and he started to use abstract forms in monumental sculpture. An important example of this is his design for a (never-executed) *National Monument to the Merchant Navy* in Rotterdam (1951), which is constructed from open, loose elements. (In 1968 Couzijn himself had this work executed in stainless steel, and in 1974 it was placed in Vlissingen.) Related to it is his submission in the competition of the Institute of Contemporary Arts in London for a *Monument to the Unknown Political Prisoner* (1952), which received honorable mention. In 1953–1954 he designed a series of twenty-four reliefs relating to the Battle of Arnhem for the Provinciehuis (Province House) of Gelderland in the city of Arnhem.

Contacts with Jacques Lipchitz and Shinkichi Tajiri led him to experiment with all sorts of unusual ways to cast bronze in the mid–1950s. In 1960 the Dutch pavilion at the Venice Biennale was practically devoted to his work—this was his international breakthrough. His preliminary study for one of his most famous works was shown there: *Corporate Entity* (1959–1963; Rotterdam, Unilever Building). In the 1960s, Couzijn often used real implements in his compositions; he used two iron fire screens in *Auschwitz* (1966–1967; Otterlo, Rijksmuseum Kröller-Müller). During the 1970s, stainless steel became a favorite material in his work.

Couzijn was also a graphic artist (dry point and lithography, mainly around 1960) and made drawings (mostly in the 1970s). In 1963 he was one of the founders of Ateliers '63 in Haarlem, a training school where beginning artists could work under the direction of experienced artists. In 1966 he received the David Röell Prize; in 1967, the Dutch National Prize for Visual Arts and Architecture. From 1945 until 1978, he was married to the sculptor Pearl Perlmuter (born 1915 in New York). Couzijn's works can be found in the collections of the Stedelijk Museum in Amsterdam, the Stedelijk Van Abbe Museum in Eindhoven, the Gemeentemuseum in The Hague, and the Rijksmuseum Kröller-Müller in Otterlo.

Mieke van der Wal

See also Bronner, Jan; Public monumental sculpture (1795–1990); Sculpture (1795–1945)

Bibliography

Boelema, Ida, ed. *Couzijn, beeldhouwer sculptor*. Weesp: Stichting Openbaar Kunstbezit, 1986.

Hammacher, A.M. *Beeldhouwkunst van deze eeuw en een schets van haar ontwikkeling in de negentiende eeuw*. Amsterdam: Contact, 1955.

Schuurman, K.E. *Wessel Couzijn*. Amsterdam: Meulenhoff, 1967.

Cuyp, Aelbert (1620–1691)

Aelbert Cuyp came from a family of artists; early in his career he occasionally collaborated with his father, Jacob Gerritsz. Cuyp, a Dordrecht portraitist and history painter. Aelbert Cuyp's earliest works, dated 1639 and 1640, mix an eclectic range of styles, but by 1641 Cuyp was closely imitating the yellow-and-brown impasto favored by Jan van Goyen. Cuyp's pictures were frequently based on drawings of the rivers and inlets around his native Dordrecht. He also made several sketching trips to Utrecht and, in 1652, to Nijmegen, Cleves, and Elten. A remarkable number of paintings are based on his observational drawings and retain the original freshness of their being recorded from nature.

Even early in his career, Cuyp was interested in intense lighting effects—brilliant sunshine, inclement weather, lightning storms, or moonlight. In the late 1640s, Cuyp took up the techniques and imagery of Italianate landscape painters, especially Jan Both. The clear blue skies and golden light of Both's art are the most important source for Cuyp's mature landscapes of the 1650s. Cuyp portrayed his native Dordrecht in this grand, dramatic style, occasionally depicting important maritime ceremonies. He also painted several views of Nijmegen, the citadel famed in the seventeenth century as the seat of Claudius (or Julius) Civilis, leader of the ancient Batavian revolt that was celebrated as the prototype for Dutch nationhood. The artist also developed a sophisticated type of equestrian hunting portrait that displayed his magnificently attired patrons in elegant settings. Nearly all of Cuyp's late landscapes include aristocratic horsemen and were laden with specific references that were recognizable and reassuring to his clients. The synthesis of naturalistic landscape techniques with the Italianate landscape imagery resulted in Cuyp's own "Dutch classical" style distinct from any of the artist's sources.

Alan Chong

See also Dordrecht; Landscape; Reputation of Dutch art abroad; Rural life and views; Van Goyen, Jan

Bibliography

Chong, Alan. "Aelbert Cuyp and the Meanings of Landscape." Ph.D. diss., New York University, 1992.

———. "New Dated Works for Aelbert Cuyp's Early Career." *Burlington Magazine* 133 (1991): 606–612.

Reiss, Stephen. *Aelbert Cuyp*. London: Zwemmer, 1975.

D

Dada

In the Netherlands, Dada was not an artistic movement like it was in Zurich, Paris, or Berlin. Individual artists—the painter-couple Otto and Adya van Rees, Paul Citroen, De Stijl artists Theo van Doesburg and Vilmos Huszár, and the poets Antony Kok and Til Brugman—were infected with the enthusiasm for Dada in one way or another, but none of them was a full-blooded Dadaist. Van Doesburg could have been one; he had a volatile personality, a talent for networking, and the energy to attack relentlessly. But he was in Leiden instead of Zurich; he met Piet Mondrian, Vilmos Huszár, and the architect J.J.P. Oud (instead of Hugo Ball, Richard Huelsenbeck, and Tristan Tzara) and founded the magazine *De Stijl*. Van Doesburg was the driving force behind *De Stijl*, but Mondrian, who was beginning to write down his theory at the time *De Stijl* and Dada were originating, was the spiritual leader. Instead of "Nothing! Nothing! Nothing!" the starting point for artistic debate in the Netherlands was Mondrian's self-conscious theorizing as formulated in *"De Nieuwe Beelding in de schilderkunst"* (Neoplasticism in Painting), which appeared in installments in *De Stijl* in 1917–1918, as well as the formal solutions he suggested in his canvases. When Van Doesburg, as the editor of *De Stijl*, learned about Dada in 1920, he devised a Dadaist alter-ego: I.K. Bonset.

According to Tristan Tzara in the *Dada Almanach* of 1920, Otto (1884–1957) and Adya van Rees (1876–1959) were at the cradle of Dada. They lived in Zurich in 1915–1916, were friends with Hans Arp, and showed their painted, pasted, and embroidered abstract compositions at the Cabaret Voltaire. Instead of Dadaist, one would have to characterize these works as either a harsh version of Orphism or an esoteric interpretation of Cubism. So, despite their presence at all of the first important manifestations of the new movement, and although they undersigned Huelsenbeck's 1918 and 1919 Dada manifestos, neither Adya nor Otto van Rees was a Dadaist. After 1919, when they were involved in a train accident and lost their thirteen-year-old daughter, their life and work moved away from the mainstream.

In Berlin, the young Paul Citroen (1896–1983) was in the right place at the right time to experience the birth of the movement. In 1916, Citroen worked in Herwarth Walden's Der Sturm (The Storm) bookshop and attended the Café des Westens, where the future Berlin Dadaists (Grosz, the Herzfelde brothers, Mehring, Hausmann, Baader, Blumenfeld) met regularly. In 1917, Citroen left Berlin to represent Der Sturm in Amsterdam, which means that he was not involved when Dada conquered the Café des Westens. After World War I, Erwin Blumenfeld came to Amsterdam. From 1919 onward Citroen made Dadaist collages and photomontages, of which only a few have survived. In May 1920 Citroen wrote to Huelsenbeck in a letter that was published in the *Dada Almanach* reporting on the reception of Dada in the Netherlands: There are only three men who visit all the Chaplin films, he said, and who therefore can be called true Dadaists—himself, Blumenfeld, and a certain "Sieg von Menk." Two years later Citroen started at the Bauhaus; in his later work (mainly portraits) there is not even a trace of Dada's spirit.

In 1915 Theo van Doesburg (1883–1931) was familiar with Expressionist and Futurist literary theory, which means that despite all differences, the artistic developments in the two neutral countries during the war, the Netherlands and Switzerland, were rooted in similar ideas. Still, he would not be able to know Dadaist literature before the end of 1919. In February 1920 he traveled to Paris and, during his stay in the French capital, grew enthusiastic about Dada through his encounter with the paintings of Francis Picabia. Back in the Netherlands, he began to build his Dada network and wrote an article on Dada in *De Nieuwe Amsterdammer* of May 8, 1920. Even so, it took some time before he was informed properly about its origin and nature. In June 1920 he began corresponding with Tzara; he promised to send newspaper clippings for the Dada archive. Van Doesburg rapidly understood that he had better not openly adhere to Dada. His ideas about painting and architecture as propagated in *De Stijl* would no longer be convincing and, on the other hand, he would not be considered a whole-hearted Dadaist either. At the end of spring 1920, I.K. Bonset (from "*ik ben sot*," meaning "I am foolish") was born.

In the spring of 1921 (from March 28 until April 9), Van Doesburg visited Paris, where he met with Tzara and admired the exhibition of works by Suzanne Duchamp and Jean Crotti in the Galerie Montaigne. During this stay the idea to publish a second, Dadaist, magazine—*Mécano*—came to him. Tzara was helpful in collecting material. Three issues of *Mécano* appeared in 1922 and the fourth in the spring of 1923.

In April 1921 Van Doesburg settled in Weimar, Germany. While establishing a bond with Paris Dada, he also corresponded with the Berlin artists Hans Richter, Raoul Hausmann, and Hannah Höch, as well as with Kurt Schwitters from Hannover. Although in 1922 there was no longer a real Dada movement in Paris or Berlin, for Van Doesburg Dada had only just started. He organized a Constructivist congress and invited the Dadaists, too. On September 25, 1922, Hausmann, Schwitters, Arp, and Tzara performed in Weimar and on September 26 and 27, in Jena. Two days later, after Hausmann and the Parisians left, Schwitters, Van Doesburg, and his girlfriend, Nelly van Moorsel, were in Galerie von Garven in Hannover. These small and intimate soirées, attended only by friends, colleagues, and Bauhaus students, were tryouts; Van Doesburg wanted to organize a Dada tour through the Netherlands.

The idea of a Dada tour came from De Stijl painter Vilmos Huszár, a Hungarian who had settled in the Netherlands. Huszár visited Weimar in August 1922 and returned in a Dadaist mood. Van Doesburg contacted Schwitters, Hausmann, Tzara, and, through the latter, Arp, and Georges Ribemont-Dessaignes. Apart from the program (including music, dance, decoration) and the publicity (Van Doesburg proposed sandwich men), finances were an important point of discussion in the correspondence of the next few months. On December 4, Van Doesburg left Germany to stay with Huszár in Voorburg near The Hague and arrange things personally. The poet Antony Kok, who had enjoyed his friends' interest in Dadaism from the start and who better than anyone else understood Van Doesburg's eagerness to "to wake up the stuffy, tedious, sleepy Holland with a crashing Dada tour," paid for the leaflet that accompanied the tour. Until the last moment, Van Doesburg tried to persuade Tzara to come. But the tour started without him or any of the other important Dadaists. Contributors were Huszár and Van Doesburg (who were De Stijl artists), Schwitters (who called his art *Merz*), and Nelly van Moorsel, who in September in Weimar was proclaimed "the indispensable Dadaist musical instrument of Europe."

The first soirée was held in the Haagse Kunstkring (The Hague Art Circle) on January 10, 1923. After The Hague, the performance was repeated in Haarlem (January 11), Amsterdam (January 19), Delft (January 22), 's Hertogenbosch (January 25), Leiden (January 26 or 27), and again The Hague (January 28), Utrecht (January 29), Rotterdam (February 6), and in one or two more cities. From the many reviews that were written, the evening can be fairly precisely reconstructed.

Van Doesburg read his pamphlet *What Is Dada?* which was published by *De Stijl*. During this lecture, Schwitters, who was sitting in the back of the room, regularly barked, cooed, croaked, crowed, and made other kinds of animal sounds. After a short break, Schwitters mounted the stage to alternately roar, whisper, and shout out loud the text of his "Ursachen und Beginn der grossen gloriereichen Revolution in Revon" (The Origins and Beginning of the Big, Glorious Revolution in Revon). While Schwitters was reading, Huszár, who from 1916 onward had been particularly interested in the idea of movement in painting, started a shadow play with his *Mechanisch dansende figuur* (Mechanical Dancing Figure). Nelly van Moorsel concluded the first half of the evening on the piano playing music by the Italian composer Vittorio Rieti. During the intermission the audience could buy Dadaist literature.

The second half of the evening started with Rieti's music, after which Schwitters read several of his poems, among them "An Anna Blume" (To Anna Blume). At the end, Nelly played "Ragtime" which Eric Satie had composed for *Parade*, and which Van Doesburg had christened "Rag Time Dada" on the program. Although all performances were based on the above proceedings, each city got its own version of Dada.

In the last issue of *De Stijl* Schwitters vividly recalled the evening in Utrecht. While he was reading his "Big, Glorious Revolution," some men climbed onto the stage and presented him with a huge bouquet (made of cabbage leaves, rotten flowers, and soup bones) and a laurel wreath that obviously was found at the cemetery. One of them sat down at Van Doesburg's little table and read from a huge Bible. Instead of welcoming the incident as Schwitters had expected, Van Doesburg furiously pushed the bouquet into the orchestra pit, after which the audience rose and started a tumultuous fight over its remnants.

In his letters to Tzara, Van Doesburg boasted about his success. He continued to believe that the small soirées were like an appetizer; for the "real Tour" the "real Dadaists" had to come to the Netherlands in the winter of 1923. Alas, this tour never took place.

In May, Theo and Nelly van Doesburg settled in Paris. In addition to organizing the exhibition of De Stijl architecture in the Galerie L'Effort Moderne, Theo was still in touch with Tzara. Tzara was organizing *La soirée du coeur à barbe* (The Evening of the Bearded Heart) on July 6 and 7 at the Théatre Michel, at which his *Coeur à Gaz* (The Heart Running on Gas) would be restaged. The prospectus mentions "Téo van Doesburg" as the stage designer for the dancer Lizica Codréano, but in the final program his name no longer appears. Since no traces of these designs are contained in the Van Doesburg archives, he probably did not contribute them after all. But Nelly "Petro" did contribute to the performances: She played the piano while Sheeler and Strands' *Fumées de New York* (Fumes of New York) was being shown, interpreting compositions by Jacob van Domselaer and her favorite animal marches by Vittorio Rieti.

Van Doesburg wrote an eyewitness account that describes the legendary evening—marking the end of Dada and the beginning of Surrealism—as a fight between stage-Dadas (in allegiance to Tzara) and hall-Dadas (in allegiance to André Breton, Paul Éluard, and Louis Aragon). Before the intermission, the hall-Dadas had been removed by the police, but with the help of wigs, beards, and glasses, they had succeeded in again mingling with the audience. Physically the victory was for the stage-Dadas, according to Van Doesburg, but since the hall-Dadas refused to leave and kept interrupting, "they had accomplished what they wanted to do: to close down Tzara's play. At twelve-thirty, the most elegant automobiles began arriving at the door of the Théatre Michel. No passerby would have suspected that this stylish audience just had witnessed an uproar."

Els Hoek

See also De Stijl; Van Doesburg, Theo; World Wars I and II

Bibliography

Beckett, Jane. "Dada, Van Doesburg, and De Stijl." In *Dada: Studies of a Movement*. Edited by Richard Sheppard. Chalfont St. Giles, England: Alpha Academic, 1980.

Dachy, Marc. *The Dada Movement, 1915–1923*. New York: Rizzoli, 1990.

Forde, Gerard. *Paul Citroen, Erwin Blumenfeld, 1919–1939*. London: Photographers Gallery, 1993.

Huelsenbeck, Richard. *Dada Almanach*. Berlin: Erich Reiss Verlag, 1920. Reprint. New York: Something Else Press, 1966.

Schippers, K. "Dada Holland." In *Dada in Europa: Werke und Dokumente*. Frankfurt am Main: Städtiche Galerie im Städelschen Kunstinstitut, 1977–1978.

Straaten, Evert van. *Theo van Doesburg, Painter and Architect*. The Hague: SDU, 1988.

———. "'Tzara Was Almost Beaten to Death!' Theo van Doesburg an Eyewitness of the *Soirée du Coeur à Barbe*." *Jong Holland* 4 (1987): 61–62.

Daniels, René (born 1950)

From 1972 to 1975, René Daniels received an education at the Royal Academy of Art and Design in 's Hertogenbosch where his teachers were Edgar Fernhout and Sipke Huismans. In 1976–1977 he started with drawings and paintings in which objects like books, phonograph records, cameras, and such were created by rhythmic repetition of equal forms. In addition to early abstract figurative work, he produced lyrical works like *La Muse Vénale* (1979), inspired by the poetry of Charles Baudelaire. Daniels' method approaches the psychic automatic activity of the Surrealists. His work underwent influences from Francis Picabia, René Magritte, and Marcel Duchamp, particularly in regard to the relation between art and life; language is also an essential part. His *oeuvre* forms the repercussions of Daniel's personal life and artistry. The same motifs, often with multiple meanings, return again and again, which gives the body of works a strong unity (Fig. 29).

Recurring themes are his travels (*Historia Mysteria*, 1982), the art trade (*Academia*, 1982; *Paleis des Boos-Aards*, 1983), and art criticism (*Apollinaire*, 1984).

After 1984 his paintings of exhibition spaces were created from more or less abstract perspective forms, which also appear as satellites, bow ties, and microphones. From 1985 on, Daniels used transparent colors, as in *Painting on the Flag* (1985). In several paintings from the series *Lentebloesem* (Spring Blossom; 1986–1987), he reproduced his *oeuvre* by means of trees, of which the branches carry the written titles of the paintings. From 1984 until 1987 he worked as a teacher at Ateliers '63. His *oeuvre* has been considered cut off since 1987 as the result of an injury resulting in brain damage. He participated in the exhibitions *Westkunst* (Cologne, 1981), *Documenta* 7 (1982) and 9 (1992), *Zeitgeist* (Berlin, 1982), and *The Broken Mirror* (Vienna, 1993).

John Steen

See also Contemporary art; Fernhout, Edgar R.J.; Surrealism

Bibliography

Debbaut, Jan. "A Short Introduction to the Work of René Daniels." *Dutch Art and Architecture Today* 13 (May 1983): 2–7.

Debbaut, Jan, and Arno Vriends. *René Daniels: Paintings and Drawings, 1976–1986*. Eindhoven: Stedelijk Van Abbemuseum, 1986.

De Branding (1917–1926)

In September 1917, a number of painters set up De Branding (The Surf), the first organization of modern artists in Rotterdam, which existed until 1926. The primarily young artists were dissatisfied about the lack of possibilities for exhibiting in their own city; the modern work they produced was not commercially attractive to Rotterdam's art dealerships, and the Boymans Museum had no section for modern art. By presenting themselves as a group, the Branding painters hoped to draw attention to their isolated situation.

In contrast to their famous contemporaries, the artists of De Stijl, the group of De Branding did not acquire an identifying signature. The work of the members was too diverse and the composition of the group was too changeable. Besides, fellow artists from other cities were invited to join the exhibitions. No program was established for the art of De Branding. As a collaboration for the purpose of creating opportunities, the activities of the group were virtually limited to holding exhibitions.

As a result of the heavy bombardment of Rotterdam in World War II, comparatively little of the group's work is left. The art of the Branding painters is scarcely collected by Dutch museums. For these reasons, research on the group has been largely frustrated.

In time, De Branding became known as a group of occult-oriented, abstract artists. This characterization, evolving because the painters with interests in esoteric sciences such as theosophy and anthroposophy were initially in the forefront of the group, is only partly true. Of the thirteen artists who can be considered members, four worked in a style in which a recognizable representation played an important role: Herman Bieling, Marius Richters, Wim Schuhmacher, and Willem Smit. With these painters there is no question of occult influences. So, too, with Piet Begeer, who made completely abstract paintings alongside his expressionistic work. He applied the predominantly geometric forms as self-sufficient image material. In this his abstract work differed from that of the remaining eight Branding painters—Geert Adegeest, Bernard Canter, Gerlwh (pseudonym of Ger Ladage), Bernard Toon Gits, Laurens van Kuik, Jan Sirks, Johannes Tielens, and Georges Robèr—in which an inward representation perceived by an astral, meditative, visionary, or introspective means is represented, giving expression as such to something lying outside the work itself. Through its bond with mystical content and the limitation or even the exclusion of figurative elements, this work is characteristic of the transition from Symbolism to Abstract Modernism. De Branding held its eleventh and last exhibition in January 1926. In the nearly nine years of the group's existence, the Branding painters had confronted their fellow Rotterdammers not only with the city's own contemporary art, but also with the work of more than 120 Dutch and foreign artists. In the Branding exhibitions, works could be seen that otherwise would seldom or never have been shown in Rotterdam, such as those of Theo van Doesburg and Piet Mondrian. Through cooperation with Herwarth Walden, a Berlin art dealer and leader of Der Sturm (The Storm), one of the most important movements in modern art at that time, De Branding could exhibit work by, among others, Paul Klee, Franz Marc, Alexander Archipenko, Albert Gleizes, Marcoussis, Johannes Feiniger, Iwan Puni, and Diego Rivera. The widely traveled leader of the group, Herman Bieling, made it possible through exhibitions of De Branding for Rotterdam to be the host city for the premiere showing in the Netherlands of the work of Kurt Schwitters and Constantin Brancusi.

Although the goal of having a municipal art space was never reached, De Branding made itself credible through the exceptional standards of its exhibitions. For a long time the name of the group has been synonymous with modern art in Rotterdam.

Els Brinkman

See also Avant-garde; Rotterdam

Bibliography
Boelema, Ida. "De Branding." *Museumjournaal* 17:5 (1972): 254–261.

Brinkman, Els. *De Branding, 1917–1926*. Rotterdam: Stichting Kunstpublicaties Rotterdam, 1991.

Imanse, Geurt. "De jaren 1915–1918: Het ontstaan van De Branding en De Stijl." In *Van Gogh tot Cobra: Nederlandse schilderkunst 1880–1950*, 135–178. Utrecht: Centraal Museum, 1980.

———. "Van Sturm tot Branding." In *Berlijn-Amsterdam 1920–1940: Wisselwerkingen*, 251–264. Amsterdam: Querido, 1982.

De Hondecoeter, Melchior (1636–1695)

This late-seventeenth-century artist specialized in painting accurate depictions of exotic and domestic birds in elegant park-like settings. He also produced a few common barnyard scenes and gamepieces, and, more rarely, depicted other animals such as dogs and horses. Born in Utrecht, he was trained by his father, Gijsbert Gillisz. de Hondecoeter, and his uncle, Jan Baptist Weenix, both of whom were also bird and landscape painters. Melchior worked for four years in The Hague before settling permanently in Amsterdam.

His paintings reflect the Italianate and classicizing tastes of the Dutch elite of the time. He was patronized by wealthy burghers such as the Amsterdam confectioner Adolf Visscher and by royalty and aristocracy, as evidenced by his commission from Willem III to paint the exotic menagerie the king kept at his palace, Het Loo. Two paintings now in the Pinakothek in Munich can be documented as belonging to Visscher, while the Mauritshuis in The Hague houses the portrait of the royal zoo.

To date, no *catalogue raisonné* of the works of Melchior de Hondecoeter exists. His name and art appear in still-life monographs and exhibitions, but since he concentrated on depicting live birds, and only occasionally painted gamepieces, treatment of this artist in such publications is cursory and incomplete. He is often briefly introduced in general surveys of seventeenth-century Dutch painting. Since his extant works are plentiful and are included in many major collections, entries about specific paintings and brief biographies of the artist occasionally surface in exhibition catalogs and catalogs of collections.

Diane E. Cearfoss Mankin

See also Animal painting; Gamepiece; Utrecht

Bibliography
Bergstrom, Ingvar. *Dutch Still-Life Painting in the Seventeenth Century*. Translated by C. Hedstrom and G. Taylor. London: Faber and Faber, 1956.

MacLaren, Neil. *National Gallery Catalogues: The Dutch School*, 176–178. London: National Gallery Publications, 1960.

Sullivan, Scott A. *The Dutch Gamepiece*. Montclair, NJ: Allanheld and Schram, 1984.

Sutton, Peter C. *Northern European Paintings in the Philadelphia Museum of Art from the Sixteenth through the Nineteenth Century*, 124–128. Philadelphia: Philadelphia Museum of Art, 1990.

De Keyser, Hendrick (1565–1621)

Little is known about the versatile artist Hendrick de Keyser, who trained in the Utrecht studio of Cornelis Bloemaert, before he was named town sculptor and stonemason of Amsterdam in 1595. His activity in the capital, both as an architect and as a sculptor, coincided with its rapid expansion and the corresponding increase in demand for new structures and for architectural and monumental sculpture. As Salomon de Bray's *Architectura Moderna* (1631), a thinly disguised monograph

1. Hieronymus Bosch, Tabletop of the Seven Deadly Sins and the Four Last Things, *ca. 1470-1490.*
Oil on panel, 120 cm. × 150 cm. Museo Nacional del Prado, Madrid.

2. Hendrick de Keyser. Westerkerk, Amsterdam, 1621-1631. *(Photo: David Lawrence.)*

3. Dirck van Baburen. The Procuress, *1622. Oil on canvas. 101.5 cm. × 107.6 cm.*
M. Theresa B. Hopkins Fund. Courtesy of the Museum of Fine Arts, Boston.

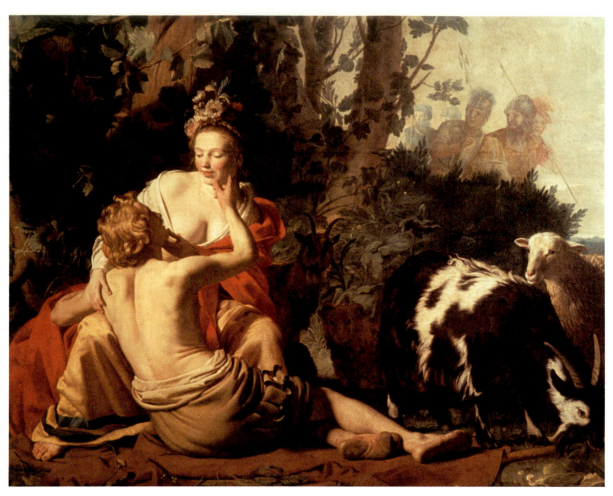

4. Gerard van Honthorst. Granida and Daifilo, *1625. Oil on canvas, 145 cm. × 178.5 cm. Centraal Museum, Utrecht.*

5. Rembrandt van Rijn. The Militia Company of Capt. Frans Banning Cocq and Lt. Willem van Ruytenburch
(The Nightwatch), *1642. Oil on canvas, 363 cm. × 437 cm. Rijksmuseum, Amsterdam.*

6. *Jan van Goyen*, View of Leiden from the Northeast, *1650. Oil on panel, 66.5 cm. × 97.5 cm.*
Stedelijk Museum De Lakenhal, Leiden.

7. Nicolaes Maes. The Eavesdropper, *1657. Dordrechts Museum, Dordrecht.*

8. Gerrit Dou. The Young Mother, *1658. Mauritshuis, The Hague.*

9. Rombout Verhulst and Willem de Keyser. Tomb Monument of Maerten Tromp,
1658. Delft, Oude Kerk. (Photo: Cynthia Lawrence.)

10. Anton Mauve. A Dutch Road, ca. 1880. Oil on canvas, 50.5 cm. × 36.8 cm. The Toledo Museum of Art, Toledo, Ohio; Gift of Arthur J. Secor.

11. Vincent van Gogh. The Loom, *1884. Oil on canvas. Kröller-Müller Museum, Otterlo.*

12. Gerrit Th. Rietveld. Rietveld Schröder House, *1924. Utrecht, The Netherlands.*
Copyright © 1995 Estate of Gerrit Rietveld/Licensed by VAGA, New York, NY.
(Photo: Centraal Museum, Utrecht/Ernst Moritz.)

13. Jan Wiegers. Landscape with Red Trees, *1924. Wax on canvas, 70 cm. × 70 cm. Stedelijk Museum, Amsterdam.*

14. Carel Willink. Job's Tidings, *1932. Stedelijk Museum, Amsterdam.*

15. Charley Toorop. Cheese Porters at the Cheese Market in Alkmaar, *1932-1933. Oil on canvas, 150 cm. × 178 cm. Stedelijk Museum, Amsterdam.*

16. Karel Appel. Two Birds and a Flower, *1951. Oil on canvas, 115 cm. × 120 cm. Collection Clos Pegase Winery, Napa Valley, California.*

on De Keyser's *oeuvre,* indicates, in his architectural commissions De Keyser forged a transition between the imaginative decorative style of Northern Renaissance artists, such as Hans Vredeman de Vries, and the vocabulary of international Mannerism more generally, and that of later classicists, such as Jacob van Campen.

De Keyser's first major architectural commission was the Zuiderkerk (1603–1611; tower to 1614), the earliest large Protestant church built in the Netherlands. His continuing experimentation with the requirements of the Protestant cult (which necessitated a shift in focus from the choir to the nave) appears in his later plans for the Noorderkerk (begun in 1620), which employs a central plan radiating from the pulpit, and for the more assured Westerkerk (1621–1631; Color Plate 2), the largest Protestant church in Europe before the completion of St. Paul's in London, which marks De Keyser's emergence as a classicist. His other Amsterdam projects included his design for the Stock Exchange (1608–1611); his renovation of the city's historical monuments (such as the medieval Mint Tower; the Jan Roodenpoort; the Haarlemmerpoort, ca. 1615–1618; and the Reguliers Tower), and his plans for private houses, built in red brick, with pointed gables either stepped or flanked by consoles. De Keyser's most notable architectural commissions outside Amsterdam include the cupola (1612–1613) on the tower of the church of St. Lebuinus in Deventer and the restoration of the façade of the town hall in Delft (ca. 1620). He also obtained patents for several of his inventions, including his design for a bridge that allowed ships to pass under without lowering their mast (1596) and his formula for imitation marble (1612).

During the first quarter of the seventeenth century, De Keyser was also the country's most important sculptor. To a certain degree, his figures and ornamentation remain rooted in the traditions of the sixteenth century; unlike contemporary Dutch Mannerist sculptors, such as the international figure Adriaen de Vries, De Keyser remained a more provincial artist. Although little is known of his early activity, by 1595 De Keyser was employed by the Amsterdam admiralty to carve insignias for its ships, and he had set up a private workshop where he executed works in marble, bronze, and wood. Among his earliest commissions are a group of realistic portrait busts (ca. 1606–1608; Amsterdam, Rijksmuseum) in painted terra-cotta and marble that reveal his feeling for characterization. De Keyser was also responsible for several sepulchral monuments, including the epitaphs of *Petrus Hogerbeets* (1601, formerly Hoorn, Grote Kerk); *Jacob van Heemskerk* (completed 1609; Amsterdam, Oude Kerk; Fig 33), and *Joseph Justus Scaliger* (ca. 1618; formerly Leiden, Pieterskerk). He also executed the elaborate canopied table tomb of *Willem I of Orange* (1614–1621; Delft, Nieuwe Kerk; Fig. 34), based on Italian and French examples (for example, Primaticcio's monument for Henri II in St. Denis), with its double effigy (maquettes, Amsterdam, Rijksmuseum) and bronze figures of the four virtues. De Keyser was also responsible for a number of monumental figures, including *St. John the Evangelist* (1613) for the rood screen of the Sint Janskerk in 's Hertogenbosch (London, Victoria and Albert Museum), for

which he was reprimanded by the Dutch Reformed Church; the memorial to *Erasmus* (1618; Rotterdam, Marktplein), the only public statue produced under the Republic; and the figure of *Justice* (ca. 1620) for the Delft town hall. Among his projects for architectural sculpture in Amsterdam are the figures and relief (ca. 1603–1604) for the portal of the Tuchthuis, a house of correction (which he also designed, ca. 1595); the relief (ca. 1609) on the portal of the Spinhuis; and decorative gable stones.

Several artists trained or worked in De Keyser's studio, including the English sculptor Nicholas Stone (1586–1647), his son-in-law, who eventually returned to London; and Gerard Lambertsz., his chief apprentice (ca. 1619) who was later active at Elseneur (Denmark). In the Netherlands, De Keyser was succeeded by his three sons. Pieter de Keyser (Amsterdam, 1595–1676), an architect and sculptor much influenced by Flemish art, who produced realistic portraits (such as the effigy of *Piet Hein,* ca. 1626; Delft, Oude Kerk) as well as several notable monuments (the tomb of *Willem Lodewijk of Nassau,* based on a design by the elder De Keyser, now destroyed; and the *Soop* monument, 1637, Skara, Sweden), and architectural sculpture in Amsterdam. Willem de Keyser (Amsterdam, 1603–1674), an Amsterdam architect and sculptor who was also active in London and The Hague, is best known for the reliefs of naval battles he executed for monuments of *Jan van Galen* (ca. 1654; Amsterdam, Nieuwe Kerk) and *Maerten Tromp* (ca. 1655–1658; Delft, Oude Kerk; Color Plate 9). Hendrick the Younger (Amsterdam, 1613–1665) relocated to England by 1633 where he worked in the shop of his brother-in-law.

Cynthia Lawrence

See also Churches; Classicism in architecture; Public monumental sculpture (ca. 1550–1795); Renaissance architecture; Sculpture (1550–1795); Tomb sculpture: early modern and later sepulchral art; Utrecht

Bibliography

Jimkes-Verkade, E. "De ikonologie van het grafmonument van Willem, I, prins van Orange." In *De Stad Delft, cultuur en maatschappij van 1572 tot 1667,* 214–230. Delft: Culturele Gemeenschap van Delft, 1981.

Kuyper, W. *Dutch Classicist Architecture.* Delft: Delft University Press, 1980.

Leeuwenberg, J., and W. Halsema-Kubes, eds. *Beeldhouwkunst in het Rijksmuseum,* 223–233. The Hague: Staatsuitgeverij, 1973.

Neurdenburg, E. *De zeventiende eeuwsche beeldhouwkunst in de Noordelijke Nederlanden. Hendrick De Keyser, Artus Quellien en Rombout Verhulst en tijdgenoten.* Amsterdam: Meulenhoff, 1948.

———. *Hendrick de Keyser, beeldhouwer en bouwmeester van Amsterdam.* Amsterdam: Scheltema and Holkema, 1930.

Rosenberg, J., S. Slive, and E.H. ter Kuile. *Dutch Art and Architecture, 1600–1800.* Baltimore: Penguin, 1966.

Six, J. *Hendrick de Keyser als beeldhouwer.* Amsterdam:

Koninklijk Oudheidkundig Genootschap, 1910.

Troost, W. "Hendrick de Keyser als scheepsdecorateur."
  Ons Amsterdam 11 (1971): 350–352.

Weissman, A.W. *Hendrick de Keyser*. Amsterdam:
  Koninklijk Oudheidkundig Genootschap, 1887.

De Klerk, Michel (1884–1923)

Michel de Klerk was born into a humble and rather large family in Amsterdam, where he lived and worked all of his life. In little more than a decade, before his sudden death, he created several public-housing complexes in which the most salient characteristics of the style of the Amsterdam School are manifest. Although he never assumed the role of leader within the group, his contemporaries considered him as such, and as many as five issues of the journal *Wendingen* were dedicated to him after his death.

At the age of fourteen, Michel de Klerk entered the studio of Eduard Cuypers to begin a long professional apprenticeship, which was interrupted only twice by travel. One of these trips—to Scandinavia—became very important in his formation. In 1911 De Klerk designed a sober apartment building on the Johannes Vermeerplein for the developer Klaas Hille, who a few years later gave him the commission for his first residential block in the Spaarndammerbuurt northwest of Amsterdam. An architecture of solid wall masses, the Hillehuis (Hille's House) shows many signs of De Klerk's creativity, such as the refinement of details and the articulated rhythms of the façade.

The three public-housing projects in the Spaarndammerbuurt, a workers' quarter on the outskirts of Amsterdam, synthesize many of the peculiar characteristics of the young designer's formal vocabulary, rich in Romantic values and a wide range of symbolic references. Furthermore, they are among the most appreciated results deriving from application of the *woningwet* (housing law). The first block was completed for Hille in the period 1913–1915; the other two, for the *woningbouwvereniging* (housing society) Eigen Haard (One's Own Hearth) between 1914 and 1921. From the beginning, critics were divided about the treatment of architecture as sculpture with strong plastic characteristics; they recognized its vitality, playfulness, and popular appeal, but they also feared the threat of individualism and unmotivated transgression inherent in these works.

In the triangular block at Spaarndammerbuurt (Fig. 35), called Het Schip (The Ship) by the tenants, De Klerk offered the most convincing evidence of his designing process. He conceived of architecture on the scale of a housing project perfectly placed within the urban context, rich and varied in its forms unfolding according to intrinsic logic, mysterious and at the same time plausible, free from recognizable references but capable of evoking limitless suggestions. The building has been compared to a medieval manor house, a ship, a locomotive. With one hundred two apartments, a post office, a small house for tenant meetings in the courtyard, and a school, the building exemplifies the model of a new type of construction—the "workers' palace." The exterior walls of brick, in warm tones of red-orange and red-brown, curve and curl as if under a light breeze, accentuating the rhythm of the openings. Furthermore, like a medieval cathedral, the building is decorated with a myriad of small-scale figures and details that are almost hidden in the texture of the brickwork: A group of pelicans sits on the left corner of the post office; near the window jambs there are postal horns, arrows, and windmills; and there are little winged horses on the front of the school.

The apartment complex that De Klerk designed in collaboration with Piet Kramer for the building society De Dageraad (The Dawn) dates from 1920–1923. It is situated in Amsterdam South in an area planned by H.P. Berlage. De Klerk and Kramer worked harmoniously together, although De Klerk's contribution is evident in the surprising variety of solutions. The unmistakable mark of his rich formal imagination, charged with symbolic associations, may be noticed in the apartment blocks in the form of big "houses" that close one side of the two symmetrical open squares of the complex (Fig. 36). The buildings, entirely of brick, are distinguished by an extremely lively use of color: The roof tiles are orange; the wall bricks are rose-colored; the basement level is brown.

In Amsterdam South, De Klerk also created one section of the apartment blocks constructed by the Amstels Bouwvereniging (Amstel Building Society). Along the Vrijheidslaan, he designed a severe façade skillfully animated by rows of protruding balconies linked at various levels by small cylindrical volumes. On the posterior façade, on the ground floor, are two curved volumes containing shops that form an ideal entrance to the central area of the complex.

De Klerk left a testament to his rich imagination and extraordinary talents as a draftsman in a vast collection of drawings done in pastels, charcoal, and colored inks. These include portraits capturing the character of his family and friends, sketches for furniture and interior decoration, and especially architectural drawings. The latter consist mainly of sketches for building details and rapid recordings of spatial and formal ideas relating to realized buildings, imagined projects, or projects never carried out. Of this last type, two submitted for competitions stand out for the peculiarity of their architectural vocabulary and because they won him second prize: the design for a funeral chapel at a public cemetery (1910), and the design for the Rijksacademie voor Beeldende Kunsten (National Academy of Arts) in Amsterdam (1917–1918). The cemetery design, submitted to the competition with the motto Reincarnatie (Reincarnation), was much admired for the happy union of symbolic significance and monumental character (Fig. 37). The national academy design, with the motto Groot Amsterdam (Great Amsterdam), was acknowledged even by the most critical of judges to contain an artistic spirit capable of matchless virtuosity.

Maristella Casciato

See also Amsterdam School; Architectural competitions; Berlage, Hendrik Petrus; Kramer, Pieter Lodewijk; Public housing; *Wendingen;* Wijdeveld, Hendricus Theodorus

Bibliography

Frank, Suzanne Shulof. *Michel de Klerk, 1884–1923: An Architect of the Amsterdam School.* Ann Arbor, MI: UMI Research Press, 1984.

———. "Michel de Klerk's Design for Amsterdam Spaarndammerbuurt, 1914–1920." *Nederlands Kunsthistorisch Jaarboek* 22 (1971): 175–213.

Searing, Helen, E. "Eigen Haard: Workers' Housing and the Amsterdam School." *Architectura* 2 (1971): 150–152.

Wit, Wim de, ed. *The Amsterdam School: Dutch Expressionist Architecture, 1915–1930.* New York: Cooper-Hewitt Museum; Cambridge, MA: MIT Press, 1983.

De Kooning, Willem (born 1904)

Affiliated with the first generation of the New York School, Willem de Kooning made a singular contribution to the transformation of American art in the years immediately following World War II. However, his early training in disciplined academic practice is rarely acknowledged in analyses of the role De Kooning played in the emergence of Abstract Expressionism. In fact, De Kooning's work alone, within the formation of this modern avant-garde movement, is an observable response to academic tradition in Western painting. Furthermore, it was De Kooning who moved European figural tradition into the realm of late modern abstraction. Reasons for his resolute resistance to the imperative of pure abstraction are found in the early academic training he received in Rotterdam.

Born on April 24, 1904, in Rotterdam, De Kooning (his surname is a variant of *de koning*, "the king") began his training as an artist at the age of twelve when he left grammar school to apprentice with the commercial arts and decorating firm of Jan and Jaap Gidding. Because he demonstrated exceptional aptitude, Jaap Gidding advised him to enroll for the full course of evening courses offered by the Academie voor Beeldende Kunsten en Technische Wetenschappen (Academy of Fine Arts and Techniques) in Rotterdam where he studied until 1921. He left the Giddings in 1920 to work for art director Bernard Romein through whom he learned about Jugendstil De Stijl, Piet Mondrian, Theo van Doesburg, and French modern art while continuing his classes at the academy.

Inaugurated in the seventeenth century, Dutch academies differed from European academies, which flourished under royal patronage. In contrast, the Dutch established institutions for art education that combined both guild and academy disciplines and made no distinction between fine and applied arts. Therefore, students learned lettering and commercial sign painting along with traditional cast drawing, perspective and life drawing, first from the male, then the female figure, and regularly attended lectures in art theory and history. The rigors of this training instilled in young De Kooning a respect for craftsmanship and an awareness of popular arts that added a further dimension to his training in traditional Western high art which would be discernible in every phase of his subsequent artistic development. He completed his studies at the academy in 1924 after traveling for a year in Brussels and Antwerp.

Determined to seek employment as a commercial artist in the United States, De Kooning immigrated illegally in 1926 by working in the engine room of the SS *Shelley* bound for Norfolk, Virginia. He was next hired by a coaler bound for Boston, where, upon landing, he obtained the necessary landing papers to allow him to live and work in the United States. He took up temporary residence at the Dutch Seaman's Home in Hoboken, New Jersey, working as a house painter while looking for a commercial art job. When he found such employment he discovered it paid less than house painting and continued doing that while working as a free-lance commercial artist.

Living and working in New York during the 1930s was stimulating for De Kooning, who, even as a newcomer, was comfortable in the ethnic and cultural diversity of the city (unlike his countryman, Vincent van Gogh, who was socially alienated within the artistic and intellectual milieu of Paris when he moved there in 1886). New York in the 1930s was a rich mixture of nationalities that included American artists and intellectuals as well as European expatriate or immigrant artists, writers, musicians, and photographers. Present were Hans Hoffmann from Germany, Arshile Gorky from Armenia, John Graham (born Ivan Dabrowski) from Russia, André Breton (the "pope of Surrealism") and Fernand Léger from France, fellow Dutchman Piet Mondrian, and American "colonial Cubist" Stuart Davis, all of whom De Kooning credits with having a significant influence on his early career. During this period he became friends with painter Franz Kline and critic Harold Rosenberg who, along with Clement Greenberg, interpreted Abstract Expressionism for a perplexed and confused reading public.

Although still an illegal immigrant in 1935, De Kooning was awarded several commissions by the Works Projects Administration's Federal Art Project, which, in its earliest days, did not enforce a citizenship requirement. Through Burgoyne Diller he obtained a commission for one ninety-foot section of a three-part mural, *Medicine*, for the Hall of Pharmacy at the 1939 World's Fair. This commission, and murals he painted for the Williamsburg Federal Housing Project in Brooklyn (now lost), served to convince De Kooning that his life should be devoted to painting. When citizenship was declared mandatory for Federal Art Project workers in 1936, De Kooning resigned. He did not become a naturalized citizen until March 1962. He married Elaine Fried in 1943, and, although they separated in 1956, she returned in 1979 when his illness had progressed to a stage requiring constant care. When she died in 1989, De Kooning's daughter Lisa (born in 1956 to Joan Ward) and his lawyer, John L. Eastman, petitioned the New York State Supreme Court to appoint them conservators of the De Kooning estate.

In 1944 the De Koonings moved to Carmine Street in Greenwich Village, where he had a studio large enough to accommodate the large scale of his current work. In 1948 he moved to a loft studio at 88 East Tenth Street, and in 1961 he designed a studio to be built at 182 Woodbine Drive, Springs, Long Island, adjacent to the cottage he purchased that year. Construction of this studio, partly subsidized by Joseph H. Hirshorn, was supervised by architect Otto Winkler, who had it ready for occupancy in 1964. Although he stopped painting in 1990, the artist still lives in the cottage.

Although De Kooning mastered the complexities of various forms of abstraction that were prominent in New York during the 1930s, he continued to explore the challenges of modernist figural representation. De Kooning was always intrigued with the concept of the American banal; the works in the *Women* series are parodies of the ubiquitous American sex symbol prevalent in advertising during the 1950s and 1960s. The long sequence of magisterial *Women* began with the first series in 1938 that culminated with *Pink Lady* (ca. 1944; American private collection). This evolved over the next two series to include the troublesome *Woman I* (1950–1952; New York, Museum of Modern Art), which required hundreds of studies, drawings, and oils before the fragmenting, isolating, and merging of parts of the figure acquired the desired figural monumentality through an unconventional process. That the figures are often described as ferocious and menacing may be due to the gaping and grinning mouths in skull-like faces, especially evident in the vampire-like *Woman V*, 61 × 44.5 inches (1952–1953; New York, Whitney Museum of American Art), and *Woman and Bicycle*, 76.5 × 49 inches (1951–1953; New York, Museum of Modern Art), who wears a toothy grin as a necklace.

The mouths make the *Women* of the 1950s terrifyingly vociferous; they speak of social values that included repressive ideals of a stereotyped feminine sexuality that characterized the climate of the decade. Reminiscent of World War II pin-ups, they are products of American popular culture rendered in visual language that connects them with European figural tradition. Devoid of narrative content, they are in the tradition of Western representation of woman as object of the viewer's gaze, but their confrontive aggression converts a voyeuristic spectator into an active participant. In contrast, the following series, painted during the 1960s, portrays females as more seductive and appealingly pulchritudinous. For example, *Two Standing Women*, 29.125 × 23.25 inches (1963–1964; Washington, DC, Hirshorn Museum, gift of Joseph H. Hirshorn), and *Clamdiggers* (1964; American private collection), more playfully rendered in luminous tones, are denizens that inhabit a more serene environment. Less flagrantly sexual, these figures, while still overpowering, convey a sense of self-assurance, casting the figures from the 1950s in an archaic frame. The final two series of *Women* occupied De Kooning from 1960 through 1965, after which his work included a number of abstracted landscapes.

Leaving the figural motif temporarily, De Kooning was occupied with lithography and sculpture from 1970 until 1975 when he attempted an unsuccessful return to the figure that had, by now, become so totally dismembered that only faint traces of the authority of the earlier figures remained. His work in the 1980s contains references to nature, less to figure, yet he has never achieved pure abstraction and has continued to explore the figural motif although it becomes increasingly elusive in his later search for pastoral content, as in

Untitled XIX (1977; American private collection). The sculptural figures, particularly, seem indecisive and unresolved, unable to detach themselves from the limitations of the material.

Most of the written information about De Kooning's life and work is found in exhibition catalogs of one-person and group shows. Essays by Judith Zilczer and others in the catalog of the 1993 Hirshorn Museum exhibition of forty-two De Kooning works, included in Joseph H. Hirshorn's gift of his art collection to the Smithsonian Museum, discuss De Kooning's contributions in light of critical perspectives of the 1990s. Bennett Schiff discusses De Kooning's work as a whole, describing it as a persistent search for the elusive transfiguration he may never have found and about which he can never enlighten us. A 1988 monograph by Diane Waldman includes a comprehensive chronological listing of events in the artist's life and career and notes the impact of Surrealism, brought to New York by Max Ernst, André Breton, Yves Tanguy, and André Masson, on De Kooning's artistic development. The catalog of the 1983 Whitney Museum exhibition yields important information about De Kooning's rarely mentioned drawings by Paul Cummings, about his late sculpture by Clare Stoullig, and a further investigation of paintings by Jörn Merkert. Sally Yard's dissertation, published in 1986, offers detailed information about De Kooning's first twenty-six years in New York. The catalog by Thomas B. Hess of the 1968 Museum of Modern Art exhibition of De Kooning's work contains well-written formal interpretations of drawings and paintings that were also shown in Amsterdam, London, New York, Chicago, and Los Angeles. Brian O'Doherty's essay, written during the artist's most productive period, concludes that De Kooning expressed a European idea that could be experienced and discovered only in America. De Kooning's work, he asserts, expressed the combined hope and memory reborn in every immigrant.

Mary F. Francey

See also Mondrian, Piet; North American painting, Dutch influences

Bibliography

Auping, Michael et al. *Abstract Expressionism: The Critical Developments*. New York: Harry N. Abrams, in association with Albright-Knox Gallery, 1987.

Feaver, William. "The Incomparable de Kooning." *ARTnews* 93:5 (May 1994): 148–151.

Hess, Thomas B. *Willem de Kooning*. New York: Museum of Modern Art; Greenwich, CT: New York Graphic Society, 1968.

O'Doherty, Brian. *American Masters: The Voice and the Myth*. New York: Random House, 1967.

Schiff, Bennett. "Any Style of Painting Is a Way of Living Today." *Smithsonian* 25:1 (April 1994): 108–118.

Seitz, William C. *Abstract Expressionist Painting in America*. Washington, DC: National Gallery of Art; Cambridge: Harvard University Press, 1983.

Tuchman, Maurice et al. *New York School: The First Genera-*

tion: *Paintings of the 1940s and 1950s*. Los Angeles: Los Angeles Museum of Art; Greenwich, CT: New York Graphic Society, 1965.

Waldman, Diane. *Willem de Kooning*. New York: Harry N. Abrams, in association with the National Museum of American Art, Smithsonian Institution, 1988.

Willem de Kooning: Drawings, Paintings, Sculpture. New York: Whitney Museum of American Art, 1983.

Yard, Sally. *Willem de Kooning: The First Twenty-Six Years in New York*. New York: Garland, 1986.

Zilczer, Judith. *Willem de Kooning: From the Hirshorn Museum Collection*. Washington, DC: Hirshorn Museum and Sculpture Garden, Smithsonian Institution; New York: Rizzoli, 1993.

De Ploeg

The Groningen art circle De Ploeg (The Plow) was given its name by Jan Altink (1885–1971), one of the cofounders, because the field of art in Groningen needed breaking up, as with a plow. The group was started in March 1918 as a reaction to an exhibition held by the local art society Pictura that had been disappointing in several ways: A number of younger professional artists had their works rejected while amateurs' works were accepted, and few paintings were sold. Looking back after twenty years, Johan Dijkstra (1896–1978), a cofounder who became secretary in June 1918 and wrote the most about the group, claimed that the real disappointment of the exhibition was the absence of art displaying a Groningen dialect; instead, the common inflection was a borrowed Impressionism from The Hague School.

According to Adriaan Venema, who has studied the phenomenon and the group's diverse and changing membership during its brightest years, De Ploeg was not an art movement but a period between 1918 and 1930 in the capital of the Northern province of Groningen when artists, rooted in the traditional, routine, and easygoing in art, set out in search of new forms that would free them. Coming together just one year after De Stijl, the revolutionary Dutch modernist movement, the first members of De Ploeg were mostly nonprofessional painters whose primary interest in starting the group was, as outlined in the articles of their association, to bring artists into closer social contact and create opportunities for their work to be seen. Dijkstra would later cast those events in a revolutionary light and assert that De Ploeg was created to show Groningen what Groningen art should be: "something that is blazing, uninhibited, cruel, alarming, and liberating" like the open, windy Northern land of Groningen itself, "with its strong, local colors" (Venema 1978: 5). Implicit in his characterization of the Groningen group is the identification of some of the members with the spirit and color of German Expressionism, especially the art of Ernst Ludwig Kirchner, and their desire to be separated from the art of mood and tonalism of The Hague School painters of the late nineteenth century.

Given the freedom to experiment that they were seeking (art should have "the right of intuition, spontaneity, improvisation," wrote Dijkstra [in Venema 1978: 5]), the association of the members would remain casual and loose and the occasions for social contact stimulating. To break from the tonal grays in the landscapes of The Hague School, Dijkstra, Altink, and others found the "ideal open-air studio" in the country setting of Blauwborgje, where among the red-brick farmhouses with blue tiled roofs, white window frames, and green doors, and protected from the wind by a sloping dike, they tested their ideas of art in nature. Their favorite gathering spot in the city was a café, Bodega Dik, which these self-styled bohemians called Chez Dicque, where during the 1920s the original group, including Jan Wiegers (1893–1959) (Color Plate 13) and George Maartens (1894–1931), were joined by the artist, printer, and publisher Hendrik Nicolaas Werkman (1882–1945), and by writers, journalists, university students, and Herman Poort, a minor poet and major personality. To a great extent the energy of De Ploeg, which was spent in trying to change the provincialism of their art world, was built up during those evenings at Bodega Dik.

The second objective of the members of De Ploeg, to exhibit their work as a Groningen group, was realized as early as February 1919 when members and supporters filled the rooms of Pictura with their own paintings, watercolors, and drawings; a newspaper critic noted at the time the great number of Groningen landscapes included in the exhibition. The energy of the group was felt through regular exhibitions thereafter, increasing in frequency during the early 1920s when the works included the graphic and applied arts. In 1920 the group sponsored a series of lectures on modern art, modern architecture (inviting H.P. Berlage to speak), and Near and Far Eastern art. A number of publications were also launched that were aimed at reaching beyond Groningen—most notably, the nine issues of the avant-garde magazine *The Next Call* (1923–1926) by Werkman with contributions of text and graphic art by individual members of De Ploeg.

De Ploeg arranged for the works of other modern artists from the Netherlands and Europe to be exhibited in Groningen; among these were Vilmos Huszár and Theo van Doesburg in 1922, Georg Grosz in 1923, and Paul Signac, André Derain, Raoul Dufy, and Henri Matisse, among others, in a collection of French art exhibited in 1925. After 1924, Dijkstra, Wiegers, Jan Jordans (1883–1962), Henk Melgers, and Jan van der Zee, all members of De Ploeg, submitted works that were exhibited with De Onafhankelijken (The Independents) in Amsterdam. In April 1930, just twelve years after its founding, the new ground that De Ploeg had hoped to break so that its Groningen roots could grow stronger had proved to be immensely fertile: In April the work of Werkman, who had made a trip to France with Wiegers the year before, was included in an exhibition of Cercle et Carré in Paris, and the Groningen group exhibited together at the Stedelijk Museum in Amsterdam, the principal showcase of the modern movement in the Netherlands.

Sheila D. Muller

See also Avant-garde; Prints, modern graphic arts 1840–1945; Werkman, Hendrik Nicolaas; Wiegers, Jan

Bibliography

Boonstra, R. *De Ploeg*. Dordrecht: Dordrechts Museum, 1976.

Petersen, A.J. "De Ploeg." Ph.D. diss., Rijksuniversiteit Groningen, 1958.

Venema, Adriaan. *De Ploeg, 1918–1930*. Baarn: Wereldvenster, 1978.

De Stijl (1917–1932)

The Dutch journal *De Stijl* (The Style), published in the period 1917–1932, disseminated an idea of art that first influenced Dutch artists and later had great international influence. By having all areas of the visual arts collaborate, a social utopia of universal harmony was supposed to be realized, based on a geometrically abstract, Constructivist formal language. The best-known Dutch artists of this movement, also known as De Stijl, were the editor of the periodical, the painter and architect Theo van Doesburg, the painter Piet Mondrian, the architect Jacobus Johannes Pieter Oud, the furniture designer and architect Gerrit Rietveld, the Belgian sculptor Georges Vantongerloo, and the Italian painter Gino Severini, who lived in Paris.

De Stijl was not a fixed group with a homogeneous principle, but rather a joint enterprise. Goals and principles did not have the same validity for all, and the connection between many artists was loose because many did not know each other, and there was only one joint exhibition. Well-known examples of art by De Stijl members are the abstract paintings of Mondrian (Fig. 86), the *Red and Blue Chair* (1918–1923; Fig. 39) and the Schröder House in Utrecht (1924; Color Plate 12) by Rietveld, and the colorful axonometric architectural designs by Cornelis van Eesteren and Van Doesburg (1923). Women also participated: Nelly van Doesburg organized exhibitions and Dada events under the pseudonym Petro van Doesburg; Sophie Taeuber-Arp collaborated from 1926 to 1928 on the interior design of the Café Aubette in Strasbourg; and Truus Schröder-Schräder was a colleague of Rietveld and designed large portions of the Schröder House.

A richly detailed chronology of the history of the journal and an analysis of the religious and philosophical background is provided by Hans L.C. Jaffé, who wrote one of the first books about De Stijl as a movement. Since the 1980s, the normative, often idealized picture of a uniform group with a coherent principle has been corrected. The turning point was the opening of archives and the exhibition *De Stijl: Visions of Utopia* in 1982. The most authoritative recent publication, which includes an extensive bibliography, is a monograph by Paul Overy that explains the historical context and the stylistic and formal principles.

A collection of biographies of the founding fathers, by Carel Blotkamp and others, shows the changing relationship between the artists in the first years of De Stijl and the different backgrounds of the architects Jan Wils, Robert van 't Hoff, Oud, and Rietveld, and the painters Bart van der Leck, Vilmos Huszár, Mondrian, and Van Doesburg himself.

The first issue of *De Stijl*, dated October 1917, and with a cover design by Huszár, appeared in November 1917 in Delft and Leiden (Fig. 38). The editor and publisher, Van Doesburg, was the central figure in the history of the journal. The periodical appeared for the last time in 1932 as a commemorative issue after Van Doesburg's death. Like many other avant-garde magazines, *De Stijl* had a small circulation and often suffered financial difficulties. It never sold more than a few hundred copies. During its first years, one of the major functions of *De Stijl* was to distribute pictures of key works, to point out stylistic commonalities, and to strengthen them. The collaborators showed their work and wrote about each other and about their artistic concepts.

The foremost notion of *De Stijl*'s artistic theory was known as *nieuwe beelding* (new forming). Mondrian, known as "the father of *nieuwe beelding*," was, next to Van Doesburg, the first author to formulate this idea in a series of articles called "De Nieuwe Beelding in de Schilderkunst" (Neo-Plasticism in Painting) (*De Stijl*, 1917: 1–12). Mondrian derived this term from the vocabulary of the theosophist Matthieu H.J. Schoenmakers and translated the term into French as *Neo-Plásticisme*, later into English as Neo-Plasticism, meaning something like "new image forming" or "new structure." The gist is the concept of a utopian worldview that unites art and life. Individualism and external appearance were supposed to be superseded by a universal harmony. Art, as an immediate universal expression, was assigned the role of changing society. In order to achieve harmony and balance, the formal and stylistic means were strictly geometric–abstract: an orthogonal (horizontal–vertical) system of lines and rectangular areas in primary colors (red, yellow, blue) and noncolors (black, white, gray). The single, independent element and the composition of elements into a whole were supposed to symbolize the relationships between the individual and the community and were meant to give rise to an ethical and aesthetic change in consciousness. Nevertheless, the concept changed, depending on the artist who utilized it. With the exception of Mondrian, no one belonging to the De Stijl movement ever considered all aspects of this concept as binding. In 1925, Van Doesburg expanded the concept dynamically and formulated the new theory of Elementarism. In architecture, other formal elements were included: a dissolution of the closed form, renunciation of any ornamentation, and construction of the building from geometrically formed individual elements. Retained were, above all, the orthogonal principle, the geometrical formal language, and the predominant use of primary colors.

The first manifesto of De Stijl in 1918 proclaimed the radical break with tradition; nonetheless, De Stijl is rooted in Dutch tradition. The typical formal language has several roots: the functional architecture of Rotterdam, a city flourishing because of industrialization; the model provided by the architect Hendrik Petrus Berlage and his socialist-utopian ideals; and the opposition against the Symbolist-Expressionist architecture of the Amsterdam School. The utopian art concept has its roots in Calvinist principles and in other spiritual trends, especially theosophy, which was widely disseminated around the turn of the century.

The common basis for artists of the first years was the

endeavor to break out of the isolation the country had experienced by remaining neutral during World War I and to seek an international dialogue with other artists. To a great degree, the Dutch artists were engaged in socialism, anarchism, or Communism. However, the striving toward equality within the movement and the ideal of "unity in plurality" superseded politics, in contrast to other Constructivist movements that had political goals. Most designs and works of art were not intended for mass production but were single works, despite the universal goals. Most of the commissions executed by De Stijl artists were for private homes and for medium-size businesses. Pictures, too, were purchased by private collectors. Only a few larger, but also more conventional, designs commissioned by government were intended for lower-income classes and publicly financed housing—for example, the Spangen block of apartment buildings by Oud (1919).

During the first years, Van Doesburg, Mondrian, and Oud were the leading personalities, theoretically as well as artistically. Most of the first contributors left *De Stijl* between 1920 and 1925—that is, they ceased to write for the journal because working with Van Doesburg was difficult and ideas about art differed considerably. Mondrian's official break with *De Stijl* in 1925 was preceded by a lengthy difference in opinion with Van Doesburg, not over diagonals, as is often mentioned, but over dynamics and depictions of a fourth dimension. In contrast to Mondrian's static, eternally unchanging, worldview of harmony and equilibrium stood Van Doesburg's ideal of dynamics and constant change—his belief in progress. Artists like Vantongerloo and Severini, as well as Van Doesburg, paid great attention to new theories from the natural sciences—not just the theory of relativity, but also the idea of a fourth dimension that expressed a higher order. Van Doesburg used these theories as a basis from which to develop a new architectural theory in which weightlessness and dynamics played a large part. Space and time were supposed to be experienced simultaneously. In contrast, Mondrian's architectural concept was of a multitude of plane surfaces to be connected intellectually.

From the mid-1920s onward, the history of De Stijl is no longer the history of a group of Dutch artists, but the history of an idea that was disseminated in all of Europe by Van Doesburg. In 1920 he began years of traveling through Europe to establish contact with many artists and movements. He gave classes at the Bauhaus in Germany and became acquainted with the German architects Walter Gropius and Ludwig Mies van der Rohe.

De Stijl, like Bauhaus—which existed almost at the same time—and other Constructivist movements, had the general goal of uniting painting, sculpture, the applied arts, architecture, and design. However, the principles of De Stijl were opposed by the craft ideal in design and functionalism in Bauhaus architecture, which—after an initial phase of rapprochement—led to later differences.

During his stay in Weimar and Berlin, Van Doesburg met artists from Eastern Europe. He was enthusiastic about their social and artistic ideals. In *De Stijl* of 1922, Van Doesburg included art by Soviet artists like Kasimir Malevich as well as Hungarian artists. The series of paintings entitled *Von Zwei Quadraten* (Of Two Squares) by the Russian avant-garde artist El Lissitzky appeared in a special edition (*De Stijl*, 1922: 10–11). *De Stijl* became an important platform for the dissemination of Eastern European avant-garde art in Western Europe.

In 1922 Van Doesburg participated in the congress of the Union Internationaler Fortschrittlicher Künstler (Union of International Progressive Artists) in Düsseldorf, where he joined a particularly radical group of Constructivist artists, whose manifestos he printed in *De Stijl*. The most important demands were those for creating anti-individualistic, anti-Expressionist art of political and social relevance. The artists met in Weimar in September 1922 for the Konstruktivistische Internationale (Constructivist International), organized with the help of Van Doesburg. Dada artists, including Hans Arp and Tristan Tzara, also participated in this meeting. Despite its irrationality, Van Doesburg valued Dada because of its destructionist and anticonventional trends that were—like abstract art—opposed to existing traditions.

From 1921–1923 onward, *De Stijl's* literary orientation was influenced by Dada and Futurism. Experimental poems in great typographic variation were written by the Dutch poet Antony Kok (one of the signers of the first De Stijl Manifesto), the German Dada painter Kurt Schwitters, and Van Doesburg himself. The height of this activity was a Dada tour through Holland in 1923.

Unlike Eastern Europe, France saw De Stijl predominantly as an architectural movement. The first and only exhibition in which De Stijl artists presented themselves as a group occurred in 1923—even though the group did not exist any longer by this time—at the gallery of Léonce Rosenberg in Paris, where the group exhibited architectural designs and models. Even though Mondrian also lived in Paris during the years 1920–1938, his work experienced little success because abstract artists were an ignored minority in a Paris occupied with Surrealism.

De Stijl appeared less and less often between 1923 and 1928. Reasons were dwindling finances and Van Doesburg's participation in other projects. In an anniversary issue published in 1928, Van Doesburg once more conjured up the general idea. After this date, *De Stijl* appeared only three more times: a commemorative issue for Dada artist Hugo Ball; an issue about the extension of the Café Aubette in 1928; and a last commemorative issue in 1932 after Van Doesburg's death in 1931. Contributions for this issue were written even by artists who had distanced themselves for some time from the journal and the movement.

De Stijl painting is often discussed only in terms of Mondrian's mature abstract work with its broad horizontal and vertical lines on a white background with colored rectangles. Less consideration is given to other artists: Van der Leck was the first to use geometric elements in primary colors in his paintings; Huszár created the first logo of *De Stijl*; and Cesar Domela Nieuwenhuis, who did not join De Stijl until 1924, used diagonals in a manner similar to Van Doesburg. Especially questions about the relationship between abstract art and visible reality played a considerable role. Using Analytical Cubism as a point of departure, Mondrian had banned any figurative reference in his pictures from 1918 onward. Other artists arrived at their geometrical compositions through a step-by-step abstraction, but used a motif as their starting point, as did Huszár and Van der Leck, for example. Vantongerloo used the titles of his sculptures and pictures to suggest that they were the result of mathematical operations, but it is not possible to replicate them. Colors used were not necessarily always primary. Many painters, like Van Doesburg, for example, were architects or designers as well; or sculptors like Vantongerloo; or typographers like Huszár and Domela. De Stijl artists later joined other groups in Paris: Van Doesburg founded Art Concret (Concrete Art) in 1930 and was cofounder of Abstraction-Création (1931); Mondrian and Vantongerloo belonged to Cercle et Carré (1929).

The first buildings, which still included traditional elements, designed by Oud, Wils, and Van 't Hoff were strongly influenced by Frank Lloyd Wright and the Arts and Crafts Movement. The ideal of collaboration between painters and architects—to create a completely abstract environment and to combine all arts in constructive harmony—had already been formulated in theory during the first years by Van der Leck, Oud, and others. The urban setting was meant to be changed into an abstract, balanced environment. Painters played a subordinate role until the beginning of the 1920s and created architectonically predetermined areas, often windows. Around the middle of the 1920s, painters and architects discovered the constructive power of color and planes of color which transformed every wall and every piece of furniture into an independent composition. At the same time, the interaction with other elements created a new type of abstract spatial experience. Examples are the axonometric designs of Van Doesburg and Van Eesteren (1923) as well as the room by Rietveld and Huszár for an exhibition in Berlin in 1923. A chair belonging in this room, the "Berliner Stuhl" by Rietveld, shows how sculpture and furniture are integrated and through their construction make a part of the room a visual as well as a physical experience. The Schröder House is the best embodiment of De Stijl's architectural principles, but it demands a great degree of adjustment by the inhabitants to the architecture. Most of the time, the architecture remained in the design stage. Realized designs required compromises that gave rise to conflicts between painters and architects. Toward the end of the 1920s, architects began to orient their work toward practical social problems. They combined the principles of De Stijl with functional elements of the International Style. Painters returned again to abstract aesthetic considerations. During the mid-1920s, Van Doesburg had begun a dynamic reworking of the architectural and painterly formal language in order to create a new space-time concept. Variations of the abstract space-time concept are Van Doesburg's interior design of the Café Aubette (1926–1928); the Cité dans l'espace (1925), an installation of metal bars by the Austrian Frederick Kiesler; and the abstract films and animations of the Swedish artist Viking Eggeling and the Germans Hans Richter and Werner Graeff.

The anarchistic and, in part, romantic enthusiasm of many De Stijl artists for technology can be traced back to influences from Futurism and the machine aesthetics of Wright. On the one hand, there is the striving for clear forms and the perfection of intellectual values; on the other hand, a few artists collaborated with Dada artists in order to abolish tradition that much quicker by employing destructionist elements. The ideal of a stable universal utopia, a mixture of rationalistic design and spirituality, was typical not only of De Stijl, but also of other avant-garde groups of this time. But the ideal contains an unsolvable contradiction: It is at the same time a reflection of rational systems as well as a self-referencing network of formal, abstract relationships. Because the utopia of an aesthetic, new environment failed in the face of practical demands, an absolute abstract art was not possible. Nonetheless, the stylistic principles and the striving toward a *Gesamtkunstwerk* (total work of art) developed by De Stijl continue to have great influence on Dutch and international art.

Frauke Syamken

See also Applied arts; Art criticism, critical issues in the twentieth century; Avant-garde; Berlage, Hendrik Petrus; Dada; France; Functionalism in architecture; Graphic design; Kröller-Müller, Hélène E.L.J.; Magic Realism; Mondrian, Piet; North American painting, Dutch influences; Oud, Jacobus Johannes Pieter; Public housing; Sculpture (1795–1945); Van Doesburg, Theo; World Wars I and II

Bibliography
Blotkamp, Carel et al. *De Stijl: The Formative Years, 1917–1922.* Cambridge, MA: MIT Press, 1986.
Finkeldey, Bernd et al. *Konstruktivistische Internationale, 1922–1927: Utopien für eine europaeische Kultur.* Stuttgart: Hatje, 1992.
Friedman, Mildred, ed. *De Stijl, 1917–1931: Visions of Utopia.* New York: Abbeville, 1982.
Jaffé, Hans L.C. *De Stijl, 1917–1931.* Cambridge, MA: MIT Press, 1986.
McNamara, Andrew. "Between Flux and Certitude: The Grid in Avant-Garde Utopian Thought." *Art History* 15 (1992): 60–79.
Overy, Paul. *De Stijl.* London: Thames and Hudson, 1991.
Peterson, Ad, ed. *De Stijl, 1917–1932.* 2 vols. Reprint. Amsterdam and The Hague: Athenaeum, Bakker, Van Gennep, 1968.
Troy, Nancy. *The De Stijl Environment.* Cambridge, MA: MIT Press, 1983.
Vink, H.J. "Ruimte en tijd in de geschriften van Severini, Vantongerloo, Mondriaan en Van Doesburg." *Jong Holland* 2 (1990): 2–13, and 3 (1990): 2–16.
Warncke, Carsten-Peter. *De Stijl, 1917–1931.* Cologne: Taschen, 1991.

De Wit, Jacob (1696–1754)
Born in Amsterdam of Catholic parents and educated from the age of nine in the tradition of grand salon decoration and large-scale religious painting, Jacob de Wit emerged as the

most sought-after creator of these types of work in Holland during his time. His first teacher was Albert Spiers, now regarded as a minor painter of wall murals. In 1708, De Wit's uncle in Antwerp, the art collector and dealer Jacob de Wit, virtually adopted him, enrolling him in the studio of Jacob van Hall. It was in Antwerp that De Wit absorbed the art of Rubens, Van Dyck, and their followers, which became the most important influence on his style.

Returning to Amsterdam, De Wit was immediately favored with important commissions for the Catholic Church, beginning with the Moses and Aaron Church decorations in 1716. His greatest impact on the art of his time was through his decorative commissions for the ruling class in Amsterdam, Paris, London, and perhaps in other European cities. He was a facile and graceful painter of ceiling and wall decorations, and of *witjes*, or gray-white paintings in imitation of stucco wall reliefs. For his paintings, many dispersed from their original sites, there exist many lovely drawings, which he usually inscribed with information about the commission.

His most important secular commission was for the Amsterdam Town Hall, now the Royal Palace, in 1735–1737, which included an enormous scene of *Moses Choosing the Seventy Elders*, accompanied by *witjes*. De Wit had several pupils, including the engraver-illustrators Jan Punt and Jan Stolker. He was, by some accounts, one of the highest-paid painters of his day in the Netherlands.

Roger Mandle

See also Bas-relief painting

Bibliography

Mandle, R. *Dutch Masterpieces of the Eighteenth Century: Paintings and Drawings, 1700–1800*. Minneapolis: Minneapolis Institute of Arts; Toledo: Toledo Museum of Art; and Philadelphia: Philadelphia Museum of Art, 1971.

Niemeijer, J.W. *Eighteenth-Century Watercolors from the Rijksmuseum Printroom, Amsterdam*. Alexandria, VA: Art Services International, 1993.

Staring, A. *Jacob de Wit, 1695–1754*. Amsterdam: P.N. van Kampen, 1958.

———. *Jacob de Wit: The Titan of the Amstel*. Amsterdam: Koninklijk Paleis, 1986.

De Zwart, Willem (1862–1931)

From 1877 to 1880 Willem de Zwart worked in the studio of Jacob Maris in The Hague, where he also learned to paint. In the evenings he took drawing lessons at The Hague Academy (1876–1880). De Zwart painted animal studies, landscapes, townscapes, figure pieces, and still lifes with a technique that, at least until around 1894, was in between that of Jacob Maris and George Hendrik Breitner. In 1883 he was awarded a royal subsidy. From 1884 until 1886 De Zwart painted tiles for the Rozenburg faïence factory in The Hague to earn some extra money. In 1886 he lived with some other artists, including the graphic artist Ph. Zilcken, in the Kleine Loo in The Hague. He gained a reputation quickly with the etchings that he made during this time.

De Zwart's early work appears to be rather melancholy. After his marriage in 1889 this changed; he started using larger formats and his palette became lighter, especially after his move to the Gooi region in 1894. From 1900 to 1905 De Zwart lived in Amsterdam, after that in Bloemendaal (1905), then in Scheveningen (1906), and a year later he moved to Leidschendam (1907–1917). After 1905 De Zwart suffered from severe depressions, which required his being in an institution from 1906 to 1907. In this period his colors became increasingly burnt in tone.

In 1911 De Zwart's wife divorced him. After his move to The Hague in 1917 he lapsed into variations on old themes and created almost nothing of real interest. Exceptions to this are the room screens with exotic birds or nudes, and the drawings and pastels on plywood, also mostly of birds. Another work, curious and typical, is *De Kwelgeesten* (The Tormentors) from 1924, in which he depicts himself on the top of a hill, surrounded by ghostly faces. He donated the work to The Hague Gemeentemuseum.

Alexandra W.M. van Smoorenburg

See also Japonisme; Laren; Maris, Jacob Hendricus

Bibliography

Bionda, Richard. *Willem de Zwart, 1862–1931*. Haarlem: J. Enschedé, 1984.

Delft

In his classic study of art and culture in Delft, published in 1923, Max Eisler characterized the citizens and art of this Dutch city as having "dignity, restraint, and stateliness." Recently what have been regarded as the "courtly" qualities of Delft painting have been connected with a broader regional tradition in the South of Holland (Liedtke, 1992). Delft first emerged as an artistic center in the fifteenth century. From the fifteenth through the seventeenth century the art of painting flourished in Delft, reaching its peak in the 1660s in the work of Johannes Vermeer. In the seventeenth century Delft also became famous for its tin-glazed pottery, known as Delftware. Following Vermeer's death in 1675, Delft's importance as an artistic center quickly declined. However, its tin-glazed pottery continued to earn the city fame through the eighteenth century.

In the last years of the fourteenth century and in the beginning of the fifteenth century many cloisters, chapels, and houses of God, such as the convent of St. Agatha, the Holy Hospice, and the Chapel of St. Cornelis, were founded in Delft. A Gothic church (the Oude Kerk) had been constructed in the thirteenth century, and another large church (the Nieuwe Kerk) was completed in the closing years of the fourteenth century. Most of the paintings produced in Delft during this early period were connected with the flowering of religious institutions; the only secular types of works to be produced were portraits. It has been suggested that the Guild of St. Luke, which included painters, was founded around 1434–1435.

During the fifteenth century Delft was an important

center of manuscript illumination. The history of Delft manuscript illumination begins in the early part of the century with the Master of the Morgan Infancy Cycle. Manuscripts produced in Delft display distinctive types of miniature and border decoration, and the so-called Delft grisailles, produced about 1440–1460, appear to be a local peculiarity. The identities of the individuals who produced manuscript illuminations in Delft are not known.

Larger religious paintings and portraits were also produced in Delft during the fifteenth century. The identity of the anonymous engraver known as the Master of the Virgin among Virgins is based on a panel depicting *The Virgin Mary Surrounded by Virgins* in the Rijksmuseum in Amsterdam. About twenty works on panel, some of which are big, have been attributed to this artist, who appears to have favored scenes from the Passion and the Crucifixion of Christ. His early paintings are quite primitive, while his later works display a highly expressive style. His masterwork is a *Lamentation* (ca. 1500; Liverpool, Walker Art Gallery), and his best known portrait is *Hugo de Groot* (1451–1509), pastor of the Nieuwe Kerk (Chapel Hill, Ackland Art Gallery). Another artistic figure, known as the Master of Delft, began as a designer for woodcut illustrations for books printed in Delft. His personality is less clear than the Master of the Virgin among Virgins. However, his religious paintings are characterized by their frequent inclusion of homey details. His largest and most ambitious painting is a triptych of *The Crucifixion* (ca. 1510; London, National Gallery) in which the Nieuwe Kerk can be seen in the background.

A major event affecting artistic production in sixteenth-century Delft was the fire that partly destroyed the Nieuwe Kerk on May 3, 1536. In the first twenty years after the fire, work on the Nieuwe Kerk and other edifices created a great bustle of artistic activity. Many of the leading works produced during this period were by artists from other Dutch artistic centers. Anthonie Blocklandt of Montfoort, who had studied with Frans Floris in Antwerp, worked in Delft between 1553 and 1572 producing altarpieces for local religious institutions. The Haarlem painter Maerten van Heemskerck produced an altar panel of *The Three Magi* for the St. Agatha Church (1550), and it is likely that another painting he produced was for the Chapel of St. Luke in the Nieuwe Kerk (1549). An artist from The Hague, Cornelis van Scheveling, came to Delft in 1548 to paint the insides and the exterior of the doors of the great organ in the Nieuwe Kerk. These paintings, executed in watercolor, depict scenes from the life of King David. The Utrecht painter Jan van Scorel was also contracted by the Nieuwe Kerk to provide a high altar that was expected to exceed the magnificence of the one he produced for the Utrecht cathedral. One of the few Delft painters to contribute to the local milieu was Cornelis Jacobsz. He received numerous commissions from the city, including one to record an iceberg that drifted into Delfshaven in January 1565. The latter painting is the first known landscape by a Delft painter.

In the summer and fall of 1566 Delft was affected by the Iconoclast riots that swept through the Netherlands. Calvinist extremists wreaked havoc in the churches, defacing or destroying all of the "graven images" they could reach. Commenting on this event a century later, the Delft historian Dirck van Bleyswijck bewailed the loss of altarpices by such noted masters as Pieter Aertsen, Anthonie Blocklandt, Frans Floris, and Maerten van Heemskerck that had graced the Nieuwe Kerk in the sixteenth century. The social and political upheaval was followed by the great "Alteration" (*alteratie*) in July 1572 whereby Delft became a Protestant city. Following this event religious art underwent a gradual decline, and painters in the Delft St. Luke's Guild were superseded and outnumbered by glassmakers.

In the wake of the political and religious turmoil that beset the Netherlands in the late sixteenth century the Dutch court relocated from The Hague to Delft. In 1573 Willem I of Orange took up residence in the St. Agatha convent (now the Prinsenhof), and he was assassinated there in 1584. In the last years of the century Delft emerged as a leading center of courtly portraiture. Jacob Willemsz. Delff I, born in Gouda, worked as a portrait painter in Delft from 1582 until his death in 1601. Two of his sons became painters; the third, Willem Jacobsz. Delff, developed into one of the most talented engravers of the period. In addition to courtly portraits, Jacob Willemsz. Delff I produced impressive civic guard pieces, one of which, dating from 1592, still hangs in the Delft Town Hall. In 1590 the Antwerp painter Hans Jordaens I became active in Delft, producing genre scenes and histories in the manner of Frans Francken II.

In the opening years of the seventeenth century Delft continued to be a leading center for the production of courtly portraits. The most successful and productive portraitist in Delft around the turn of the century was Michiel van Mierevelt, who was praised by Constantijn Huygens in the 1620s for the naturalness and simplicity of his paintings. Van Mierevelt's patrons included members of the Orange-Nassau court and the wealthy burghers of Delft and The Hague, such as Jacob Cats. Many of his portraits were reproduced in engravings by his son-in-law, Willem Jacobsz. Delff.

Other secular genres, such as still-life painting and the depiction of architectural interiors, began to flourish in Delft in the opening years of the seventeenth century. Cornelis Jacobsz. Delff, son of the portrait painter, produced kitchen scenes in the manner of the Flemish painter Pieter Aertsen. His style may be distinguished by the glow of the copper vessels often included in his works. The Flemish painter and architect Bartholomeus van Bassen was active in Delft from 1613 to 1622. He painted imaginary architectural interiors closely related to the prints of the Leeuwarden printmaker and architect Hans Vredeman de Vries.

One of the principal industries in Delft at the start of the seventeenth century was tapestry weaving, which was first established with the arrival of François Spiering, a Flemish refugee. About 1604 Spiering was joined by Karel van Mander the Younger, whose father had designed cartoons for the factory and whose own involvement in the tapestry business continued until his death in 1623. Spiering died in 1630, but his factory was continued by his sons, Aert and Pieter, and, after 1635, by Maximiliaen van der Gucht, albeit on a more modest scale. The first decades of the century also witnessed the rapid growth, starting from a couple of small masters' shops, of the faïence industry, which was to bring fame and fortune to the makers of tin-glazed pottery of Delft in the later years of the century.

In the second quarter of the seventeenth century painting in Delft began to acquire a more diversified character. Van Mierevelt continued to paint courtly portraits until his death in 1641; Willem van Vliet produced portraits in Delft in Van Mierevelt's style. In still life, Cornelis Jacobsz. Delff continued to produce kitchen scenes until 1638; another kitchen-scene painter was Pieter Cornelisz. van Rijk. The Middelburg artist Balthasar van der Ast came to Delft in 1632 and worked in the manner of the Flemish painter Ambrosius Bosschaert the Elder. Jacob Woutersz. Vosmaer, who may have been a student of Jacob de Gheyn I, painted flower pieces during this period in the Flemish tradition. Harmen Steenwijck and Pieter Steenwijck painted *vanitas* still lifes related to the works of Pieter Claesz. and Willem Heda in Haarlem. Landscape painting emerged in the work of Jacob van Geel, who worked in Delft from 1626 until 1632 painting outdoor scenes in the Flemish tradition. His fantasy views, almost always small in size, include trees of erratic growth, with branches and half-rotten trunks overgrown by moss and ivy. The Rotterdam artist Simon de Vlieger worked in Delft from 1634 until 1637; he specialized in the depiction of ships tossed about in stormy seas conceived in a manner closely related to the work of the Haarlem painter Hendrick Vroom.

Genre painting, which flourished in Haarlem in the opening years of the seventeenth century, found a proponent in the work of the Delft painter Anthonie Palamedesz., who studied with Van Mierevelt. Palamedesz. specialized in the production of interiors with merry-making figures and guardroom scenes similar to the works of Amsterdam painters Pieter Codde and Willem Duyster. His younger brother, Palamedes Palamedesz., was his student and specialized in cavalry battles related to the work of the Haarlem painter Esaias van de Velde.

A key figure in the Delft artistic milieu between 1626 and the late 1660s was Leonaert Bramer. This Delft-born painter left for France and Italy in 1614 and returned home in 1628. His early works produced in Italy (Fig. 40) and his Delft paintings of the 1630s reflect a wide range of artistic influences. Bramer specialized in the depiction of histories enacted by small, eccentric figures in nocturnal settings rendered in phosphorescent light effects. While his paintings were inspired by such notable figures as Elsheimer, Tassi, Feti, and Jacopo Bassano, the artist displays a strikingly individualistic artistic personality difficult to classify within his own milieu or in relation to Italian art. Between 1632 and 1641, the Haarlem painter Jacob Symonsz. Pynas also produced small histories in Delft. Pynas, too, had spent time in Italy earlier in the century and was strongly affected by Elsheimer.

The Delft painter Pieter Anthonisz. van Groenewegen was in Rome from about 1615 to 1623 and belongs to the first generation of Netherlandish artists who specialized while in Italy in the production of landscapes. His small paintings of Roman ruins reflect the influence of two other Dutch painters of Rome at the time, Cornelis van Poelenburch and Bartholomeus Breenbergh. Another Delft painter to spend time in Italy, Christiaen van Couwenberg, returned to Delft in 1630. The decorous and substantial figures in his paintings are closely related to the works of his Utrecht contemporaries, such as Gerard van Honthorst and Jan van Bijlert. The Delft still-life painter Willem van Aelst also spent time in France and Italy before settling in Delft in 1645. He produced flower and gamepieces in the manner of the Utrecht artist Jan Davidsz. de Heem.

A notable feature of painting in Delft prior to 1650 is the extent of Flemish influence evident in works by both native and nonnative artists. Another key feature is the extent to which local artists, whether native or nonnative, produced works that in subject matter and style reflected currents prevalent elsewhere. Within this spectrum, Leonaert Bramer emerges as the most innovative personality of the period. In contrast to the crafted and polished images produced by his Delft contemporaries, Bramer produced paintings that display a remarkable technical crudeness accompanied by an astonishing expressive vitality.

It is generally acknowledged that in the years around 1650, Delft emerged as a more innovative presence within Dutch art. At about this time painters active in Delft began to display a radically new conception of pictorial space and light. This concern—evident in the depiction of church interiors, domestic interiors, outdoor courtyards, and the Delft townscape—is thought to have been grounded in an underlying interest in perspective and optics. The motivating force behind this new development is thought to have been Carel Fabritius, a Rembrandt pupil who was active in Delft starting in 1650. His career was tragically cut short by his death in the massive explosion of the Delft gunpowder magazine in 1654. The optical and spatial distortions evident in Fabritius' famed *View of Delft with a Musical Instrument Seller's Stall* (signed and dated 1652; London, National Gallery; Fig. 41) have suggested the use of the *camera obscura*, a mechanical recording device and early forerunner to the modern-day camera.

The spatial and optical concerns evident in the work of Fabritius make their way into Delft architectural painting at mid-century. Gerard Houckgeest, a student of Bartholomeus van Bassen, came to Delft in 1635 and remained there until 1652. Around mid-century he began producing "realistic" church interiors, most notably interior views of the Oude Kerk and the Nieuwe Kerk in Delft (Fig. 42). Emanuel de Witte also painted "realistic" church interiors in Delft between 1650 and 1652, focusing again on the Oude Kerk and Nieuwe Kerk. In the early 1650s the Delft painter Hendrick Cornelisz. van Vliet began producing architectural interiors based on the works of Houckgeest.

The Rotterdam painter Pieter de Hooch was active in Delft from about 1653 to 1660; his specialty was the depiction of the domestic world of women and children in sunlit interiors and outdoor courtyards. Like Fabritius, he was interested in light and perspective. His *Courtyard of a House in Delft* (signed and dated 1658; London, National Gallery; Fig.

43) exemplifies his style as well as the artistic orientation of Delft painting at mid-century. The artist Hendrick van den Burch, who belonged to the St. Luke's Guild in Delft between 1649 and about 1655, may be considered a follower of Pieter de Hooch. The Delft painter Cornelis de Man, who later produced decorative works with Bramer for the St. Luke's Guild in Delft, also painted portraits, figure pieces, church interiors, and some marine views.

The concern with optics and perspective evident in Delft painting at mid-century is also present in the work of Leonaert Bramer, still a major force in the Delft artistic milieu of the 1660s. During this period the artist ceased producing small histories and turned his attention to large decorative commissions. This shift in his artistic orientation was made possible by the refurbishing of the Delft townscape following the gunpowder explosion of 1654. All of Bramer's decorative commissions, many of which were carried out in the Italian fresco technique, were for key civic buildings—the headquarters of the Delft militia company, the residence of the St. Luke's Guild, the municipal garden house, and the Prinsenhof. With the exception of a ceiling painting depicting *Christ Surrounded by Music Making Angels* (1667–1669) in the main hall of the Prinsenhof, all of these civic commissions by Bramer have disappeared.

The developments that occurred in Delft painting in the mid-seventeenth century are thought to have culminated in the paintings of Johannes Vermeer, who began his career when the tide of innovation had already subsided. When Vermeer reached maturity in the 1660s the only other major force within the Delft artistic milieu was Bramer. Vermeer paintings such as *View of Delft* (ca. 1658–1660; The Hague, Mauritshuis; Fig. 145), *The Street in Delft* (ca. 1660; Amsterdam, Rijksmuseum), and *The Music Lesson* (ca. 1664; London, Buckingham Palace) retrospectively capitalize upon the lessons to be found in the works of Fabritius and De Hooch. The exemplary craftsmanship and quiet restraint that inform Vermeer's paintings are also in some sense a survival of qualities that have been noted as peculiar to paintings produced in Delft. The decline in Delft painting following the death of Vermeer in 1675 suggests that this type of perfection was impossible to sustain; at the same time, it is part of a broader picture connected with widespread economic decline in the Netherlands in the closing years of the century.

The notion of a Delft "school" of painting has been questioned in recent years and is thought to be a modern invention. In the fifteenth century Delft painting was largely derivative of prevailing styles in other artistic centers in the Netherlands. While some native figures contributed to the artistic production of the sixteenth century, the most significant works during this period were produced by artists from other Netherlandish artistic centers. In the closing years of the sixteenth century Delft became home to a form of courtly portraiture exemplified in the paintings of Van Mierevelt, but this development was short-lived and did not affect other artistic genres. Leonaert Bramer emerged upon the scene in the late 1620s as a curious aberration who managed to catch the fancy of many local collectors. Meanwhile, a wide range of

artistic trends prevalent in the Netherlands found exponents in the native milieu in the first half of the seventeenth century. For a short period around mid-century a common concern with optics and perspective appears to have informed artists active in Delft. Notably, however, the artists affected were all outsiders, with the exception of Bramer and Vermeer.

While the concerted developments that occured in Delft painting at mid-century do not translate into a Delft "school" of painting, there is a more fundamental way in which these developments obtain a meaningful coherence within the broad spectrum of art in Delft from 1500 to 1700. The refurbishing of the Delft townscape following the gunpowder explosion of 1654 was accompanied by an emerging sense of civic pride and civic awareness. This development is epitomized in the publication of the first full-scale history of the city by the local historian Dirck van Bleyswijck in 1667. The publication of this volume coincides with the completion of Bramer's wall murals and ceiling painting for the main hall of the Prinsenhof, not only a major civic building, but also a monument to the Dutch resistance against Spain and the birth of a Dutch Republic. Notably, much of Van Bleyswijck's discussion revolves around famous public buildings in the town of Delft, many of which were decorated by Bramer.

Paintings by Fabritius, De Hooch, Houckgeest, and Vermeer consistently embody an interest in the local scene. The numerous paintings by Houckgeest that depict the tomb of Willem I of Orange in the Nieuwe Kerk speak to Delft civic pride within a broader Dutch context (Fig. 42). Vermeer's *Art of Painting* (ca. 1661; Vienna, Kunsthistorisches Museum) combines the notions of fame, history, and the Dutch achievement in particular. Civic awareness in Delft just after mid-century is coupled with Dutch awareness, just as developments in Delft painting from 1400 through 1700 are closely bound up with broader developments in Dutch painting. More specifically, however, the "dignity, restraint, and stateliness" recognized in Delft art by Max Eisler are part of a broader regional picture.

Jane ten Brink Goldsmith

See also Architectural painting; Bramer, Leonaert; Ceramics; De Keyser, Hendrick; Manuscript illumination; Master of the Virgin among Virgins; Prints, early printed book and Bible illustration; Townscapes; Vermeer, Johannes

Bibliography

De Stad Delft: Cultuur en Maatschappij tot 1572. 2 vols. Delft: Stedelijk Museum Het Prinsenhof, 1979.
De Stad Delft: Cultuur en Maatschappij van 1572 tot 1667. Delft: Stedelijk Museum Het Prinsenhof, 1981.
Eisler, Max. *Alt Delft: Kultuur und Kunst.* Amsterdam: Elsevier, 1923.
Liedtke, Walter. "The Delft School, Circa 1625–1675." In *Leonaert Bramer, 1596–1674: A Painter of the Night.* Milwaukee, WI: Patrick and Beatrice Haggarty Museum, Marquette University, 1992.
Montias, J. Michael. *Artists and Artisans in Delft: A Socio-economic Study of the Seventeenth Century.* Princeton, NJ: Princeton University Press, 1982.

Wheelock, Arthur K. *Perspective, Optics, and Delft Artists around 1650.* New York: Garland, 1977.

Derkinderen, Antoon J. (1859–1935)

Antoon Derkinderen is considered to be the founder of the monumental direction in Dutch art that is also called *Gemeenschapskunst* (communal art). His ideal was a sensible integration of architecture, painting, and sculpture, a derivative of the idea of *Gesamtkunstwerk* (total work of art). From 1878 until 1880 Derkinderen studied at the Royal School of Applied and Visual Arts in his birthplace of 's Hertogenbosch. His attendance at the Rijksacademie in Amsterdam from 1880 until 1885 was interrupted by a year of study at the Royal Academy in Brussels in 1882–1883 (together with Jan Toorop). Engaged as he was, Derkinderen was closely involved in the founding of the artists' society St. Lucas in 1881 and the Dutch Etching Club in 1885. For the first time, in 1887, he saw frescoes by Giotto in Italy and by Puvis de Chavannes in France. The fairly flat, hieratic style of these artists inspired him in his monumental commissions to paint frescoes in, among other places, the Begijnhofkerk in Amsterdam (1884–1888), the town hall in 's Hertogenbosch (1889–1891 and 1893–1896), and the Amsterdam Stock Exchange building (1898–1903) by H.P. Berlage. He deemed the two-dimensional character of his representations in agreement with their place on the wall. For the Amsterdam Stock Exchange, Derkinderen also designed stained-glass windows. From 1903 until 1906 he had his own studio for stained-glass art, De Zonnebloem in Laren. After his appointment to succeed August Allebé as the director of the Rijksacademie in 1907, he no longer realized any large projects; however, his influence on monumental art could be felt far into the 1920s.

Alexandra W.M. van Smoorenburg

See also Applied arts; Belgium; Berlage, Hendrik Petrus; Laren; Stained glass; Toorop, Jan

Bibliography

Bionda, Richard, and Carel Blotkamp, eds. *The Age of Van Gogh: Dutch Painting, 1880–1895*, 122–124. Zwolle: Waanders, 1990.

Hammacher A.M. *De levenstijd van Antoon der Kinderen.* Amsterdam: H.J. Paris, 1932.

Trappeniers, Maureen. *Antoon Derkinderen, 1895–1925.* 's Hertogenbosch: Noordbrabants Museum, 1980.

Devotional images

Religious images for public and private devotion dominated the art of the Netherlands in the late fifteenth and early sixteenth centuries. These works ranged from monumental altarpieces to intimately scaled diptychs and single images. They were placed in churches, charitable foundations, guild halls, private homes, and even inns. They included works on panel and canvas, carved altarpieces, manuscripts, and prints. Subject matter in some ways represented a continuation of late medieval iconographic traditions, with Passion scenes, the Last Judgment, Infancy scenes, and images of the Virgin. But this period also witnessed the emergence of a number of new devotional subjects, a phenomenon that needs more study.

Some new themes grew out of traditional ones. The Rest on the Flight into Egypt, for example, expands the Infancy cycle. Since images of this usually show a seated Virgin and Child dominating the foreground, they also represent a variation on traditional *Andachtsbilder* (devotional images) of the Virgin and Child, as Reindert L. Falkenburg notes. Other new subjects, such as the Virgin with the Bowl of Milk, fall into this same category. Some depictions of the Virgin and Child incorporate Joseph, transforming the subject to the Holy Family. The growing cult of Joseph helped give character to these images, as that of St. Anne, the Virgin's mother, did to representations of the extended sacred family known as the Holy Kinship. Other important subjects focusing on the Virgin include the Assumption and the Seven Sorrows. The former owed at least part of its popularity to the defense of it in a letter attributed at the time to St. Jerome, who himself enjoyed great admiration during the period.

Newly popular images of Christ included numerous depictions of the Holy Face. Netherlandish artists also began to elaborate the life of Christ, adding scenes from his public life to the existing Infancy and Passion cycles. Some of these subjects already formed part of traditional cycles in manuscripts such as books of hours, but they had not previously been treated as independent subjects in large-scale artworks. Examples include miracles, such as the Marriage at Cana and the Feeding of the Five Thousand, and parables, such as the Prodigal Son. Perhaps the most frequently depicted scene from Christ's public life was the event that marked the beginning of it, his Baptism (Fig. 67).

Depictions of the Baptism of Christ may reflect in part a growing cult of St. John the Baptist and the increasing stature of the Knights of St. John of Jerusalem. Numerous images of the Baptist preaching, as well as small round devotional panels of his head on a platter, suggest such a possibility. In general, religious imagery reveals a growth in the cult of saints during this period. Saints began to appear not only as patrons but also as the primary subjects of an increasing number of paintings. Many saints enjoyed this new prominence; the most popular were St. Anthony, St. Jerome, and St. Mary Magdalene. All three spent time living in the wilderness, and all were exalted as exemplars of asceticism and penitence.

One final category of new subject matter must be mentioned. Increasingly, Old Testament episodes became the principal focus of religious paintings. This seems to correspond to a renewed interest in the Bible itself on the part of both humanists and reformers.

Numerous factors formed part of the vast artistic/cultural/historical dialogue engaging devotional art. They include the examples and standards set by the first generation of Early Netherlandish artists from the Southern Netherlands, particularly Jan van Eyck and Rogier van der Weyden, which continued to exert a powerful authority with artists and their patrons until well into the sixteenth century. This influence seems to have been particularly strong in works produced for export to foreign markets.

The large, anonymous, often foreign, market for which works were mass-produced on speculation had a profound impact on all aspects of art, including stylistic features, compositions, iconography, and technique and working methods. Both painted and carved altarpieces displayed this impact.

Economic factors could also influence the choice of support for a painting. At least some paintings on canvas appear to have been executed on fabric because it was less expensive than panel. But the choice of support could also be tied to function. Some paintings on canvas originally served as processional banners, others provided lightweight organ doors.

The demands of function also affected the format and iconography of devotional art. Scholars have explored extensively the Eucharistic imagery of altarpieces and the ways the works answered the liturgical requirements of the mass. But they have paid little or no attention to the relation of art to other sacraments such as penance, characterized by Steven Ozment as the centerpiece of institutional piety during the period. Penance served the Church as a means to reinforce its authority and control in response to both internal and external challenges. The stress on the sacrament resulted in a proliferation of written and pictorial penitential guides, intended for both the clergy and the laity. Hieronymus Bosch's *Tabletop of the Seven Deadly Sins and the Four Last Things* (ca. 1470–1490; Madrid, Prado; Color Plate 1) provides an excellent example of this. The concern with penance may also have contributed to the rise in popularity of images of penitential saints.

The growth in the cult of saints as a whole may owe something to the Church's need to assert its authority and doctrines. At the same time, the depictions of saints may also have served the deeply felt need of many faithful for a meaningful personal connection with the divine. This need resulted in expanded practice of the contemplative life and emotional, empathic private devotion, which encouraged intimate half-length images and rich narrative pictorial elaboration, particularly of Passion scenes.

Both penitential and other images of St. Jerome spoke to other cultural forces beyond those already noted. The saint enjoyed the support and promotion of the Devotio Moderna and the humanist Erasmus, two influential forces in Netherlandish culture. Similarly, other broad cultural forces contributed to the rise of other subjects in art. The importance of preaching among both Catholics and Protestants, for example, presumably informs the numerous depictions of St. John the Baptist preaching.

One final aspect of devotional art requires comment. That is the emotional response of the viewer to the image, or, to be more precise, the transformational *experience* that takes place in the interaction between viewer and work of art. This issue lies at the heart of any profound understanding of the art, but art historians have begun to explore it only recently, and only with great difficulty. The often obscure language in the writings of scholars such as David Freedberg and Craig Harbison reveals just how hard it is to approach this topic. We lack the language to discuss such issues; indeed, to the extent that language shapes the view of the world, our conventional language may impair our ability clearly to perceive such experiences. But the efforts must continue, in order to retrieve some sense of the power the art once had.

Janey L. Levy

See also Bosch, Hieronymus; Churches; Contemplative life, contemplative virtues; Flanders, Flemish School; History painting; Last Judgment; Protestant Reformation; Utrecht Caravaggists

Bibliography

Falkenburg, Reindert L. *Joachim Patinir: Landscape as an Image of the Pilgrimage of Life*. Translated by Michael Hoyle. Amsterdam and Philadelphia: Benjamins, 1988.

Freedberg, David. *The Power of Images: Studies in the History and Theory of Response*. Chicago: University of Chicago Press, 1989.

Friedländer, Max J. *Early Netherlandish Painting*. Translated by Heinz Norden. 14 vols. Leiden: Sijthoff; Brussels: Éditions de la Connaissance, 1967–1976.

Harbison, Craig. "The Northern Altarpiece as a Cultural Document." In *The Altarpiece in the Renaissance*. Edited by Peter Humfrey and Martin Kemp. Cambridge: Cambridge University Press, 1990.

Ozment, Steven. *The Age of Reform, 1250–1550: An Intellectual and Religious History of Late Medieval and Reformation Europe*. New Haven: Yale University Press, 1980.

Panofsky, Erwin. *Early Netherlandish Painting: Its Origins and Character*. 2 vols. New York: Harper and Row, 1971.

Wolfthal, Diane. *The Beginnings of Netherlandish Canvas Painting, 1400–1530*. Cambridge: Cambridge University Press, 1989.

Dewald, C.M. (1868–1923)

Associated with the pictorialists (*picturalisten*) of late-nineteenth and early-twentieth-century photography, C.M. Dewald stands out as one who did not share all of the artistic pretensions of that movement. Whereas a fellow pictorialist like W.H. Idzerda (1873–1938) was convinced of the artistic possibilities of photography, Dewald was hesitant about using the expression "artistic photography." He thought the "territory" of photography was not equal to that of the arts, and he considered Idzerda's ideas foolish pretensions. The question of whether photography could be an art provoked much polemical writing, especially in the first decade of the twentieth century, a time when several important photographic exhibitions were being held. Idzerda and Dewald seem to have agreed, at least, upon the place where portraits should best be made: Not in the photographer's studio, full of stereotypical props, but in the sitter's own surroundings. Thus, the painter Jozef Israëls was photographed in his own studio by Dewald around 1904. Characteristic of both pictorialist portraiture and the high esteem in which Israëls was held is the fact that Dewald has depicted him in a respectful manner, in a pensive mood, and holding his brushes in hand (Fig. 44).

No one but Isaac Israëls, Jozef's son, could have taken greater liberty and photographed the old painter fallen asleep in a chair, his feet up, one hand supporting his head, with his hat on his legs. Though Isaac Israëls may have used a camera only a few times, his picture has the same nonchalance and casual charm as those by George Hendrik Breitner and Willem Witsen, whose photographs are better known.

Very little attention has been paid to C.M. Dewald in the literature on Dutch photography. His *Portrait of Jozef Israëls* is a rare example of his work.

Hans Rooseboom

See also Israëls, Jozef; Photography, early (1839–1925)

Didactic images

The Catholic Church, on the authority provided by St. Gregory the Great in the sixth century, justified religious art on the basis of its ability to educate the faithful, particularly the illiterate. St. Thomas Aquinas and St. Bonaventura reiterated the argument in the thirteenth century. The Church still relied on it in the face of Protestant attacks, citing it in the decree on images issued by the Council of Trent in 1563. But the Protestant attacks underscore the complexity of the issue regarding religious images. Whatever instructional possibilities they might possess, some images—particularly cult images—might also be the objects of idolatrous worship.

The scholar Sixten Ringbom outlines two approaches in image theology, a didactic one and a theological one, which he believes correspond to two types of sacred images, narrative representations and cult images. He also identifies a third approach, which he calls empathic, in which the concern is with the beholder's experience of profound emotion. Significantly, he notes that individual images could fulfill all three functions. This, of course, is why zealous reformers were not swayed by Catholic arguments regarding the educational uses of art.

All religious images, then, can in a broad sense be viewed as instructional. But some works are more explicitly so than others, and it is worth drawing attention to them briefly. Several highly diagrammatic late-fifteenth- and early-sixteenth-century works carry didactic inscriptions, often accompanied by a compartmentalized organization. Hieronymus Bosch's *Tabletop of the Seven Deadly Sins and the Four Last Things* (ca. 1470–1490; Madrid, Prado; Color Plate 1) is the best known. Like many other such images, it can be related to instructional writings such as catechetical and penitential texts.

Humanism and the Reformation changed the character of didactic art. Moralizing secular subjects and biblical narratives replaced the earlier doctrinal imagery.

Janey L. Levy

See also Bosch, Hieronymus; Churches; History painting; Humanism, humanist themes; Protestant Reformation

Bibliography

Freedberg, David. "The Hidden God: Image and Interdiction in the Netherlands in the Sixteenth Century." *Art History* 5 (1982): 133–153.
Ringbom, Sixten. *Icon to Narrative: The Rise of the Dramatic Close-up in Fifteenth-Century Devotional Painting*. Åbo: Åbo Akademi, 1965.

Dijsselhof, Gerrit Willem (1866–1924)

Gerrit Willem Dijsselhof played an important role in the renewal of Dutch handicrafts in the 1890s under the influence of, among other things, Walter Crane's 1892 book, *The Claims of Decorative Art* (translated into Dutch by J. Veth in 1894), and Japanese art. He did pioneering work in his search for a new, natural, yet decorative design, and he looked for new production techniques in the area of the applied arts. In this way he and C. A. Lion Cachet were the first in the Netherlands to employ batik (1890); he also experimented with the old-fashioned graphic technique of woodcut because of his interest in book decoration and typography. Dijsselhof's drawings of fish and flowers particularly were at first clearly in the service of his decorative art. His greatest interest was designing room screens, wall decorations, lamps, and furniture (Fig. 8).

After a number of years of studying at The Hague Academy (1882–1885), the Rijksnormaalschool voor Teekenonderwijs (State Normal School for Drawing Education) in Amsterdam (1884–1886), and the Rijksschool voor Kunstnijverheid (State School for the Applied Arts) in Amsterdam (1886), Dijsselhof joined with Theo Nieuwenhuis, Lambertus Zijl, and Joseph Mendes da Costa to establish the applied-arts society Labor et Ars in 1886. After an inspiring trip to Berlin, Dresden, Prague, Vienna, Munich, and Paris, which he made in 1888 with Nieuwenhuis, Dijsselhof threw himself into the fight against the currently dominating neo-styles by taking nature itself as the basis for his designs. Fifteen years later, in 1903, Dijsselhof abandoned interior design because of his lack of financial success and devoted himself entirely to painting in a naturalistic style.

Alexandra W.M. van Smoorenburg

See also Applied arts; *Japonisme*; Mendes da Costa, Joseph; Zijl, Lambertus

Bibliography

Bionda, Richard, and Carel Blotkamp, eds. *The Age of Van Gogh: Dutch Painting, 1880–1895*, 125–126. Zwolle: Waanders, 1990.
Braches, E. *Het boek als Nieuwe Kunst, 1892–1903: Een studie in Art Nouveau*, 43–50. Utrecht: A. Oosthoek, 1973.
Vries, R.W.P. de. *G.W. Dijsselhof*. Amsterdam: Elsevier, 1912.

Display

While some art theorists in the seventeenth and early eighteenth centuries made recommendations on how paintings should be arranged in numbers and by subject in the various rooms of the domestic dwelling, there is little evidence that such advice gained a widespread currency. For the most part, the owners of paintings seem to have dispensed with strict principles of display, and their collections were hung according to personal taste.

The most comprehensive account in Northern Europe of an ideal program of hanging was given by Sir William Sanderson in his *Graphice* (London, 1658). He was adamant that pictures should be hung to their best advantage and in a decorous manner. Different categories of painting were regarded as more appropriate to certain rooms. For instance, representations of peasants, shepherds, and milkmaids were suitable for front halls; landscapes, hunting scenes, and histories "of notable actions," for the great chamber. These preferences reflect the thinking of some Italian theorists: Giovanni Battista Armenini, Gian Paolo Lomazzo, and Giulio Mancini had all earlier advised that scenes of magnificence and virtue be placed in the most public areas of a house.

In the Northern Netherlands, in the last quarter of the seventeenth century, Gerard de Lairesse devised a similar blueprint for subject suitability. However, his comments are mostly directed to artists involved in furnishing a complete purpose-made decorative scheme for an individual patron, consisting of large painted wall hangings, overmantels, overdoors, grisaille murals, and painted ceilings; many of his observations, nonetheless, agree substantially with those of Sanderson and the others. In the main reception room he urged the placing of "tapestries or paintings with life-size figures of magnificent events which took place in closed rooms or palaces," and in the kitchen, "images of kitchen equipment and the spoils of the hunt, the picture of some maid, servant, dog, or cat."

However, the evidence of household inventories suggests that most collections were hung with apparent disregard for subject. Religious or mythological representations, landscapes, still lifes, and portraits were placed in close proximity to each other. "Kitchens" or "kitchenpieces" were just as likely to be hung in the *voorhuis* (front hall) as in the *keuken* (kitchen) where food was usually consumed. It is important to remember that room functions were not as sharply defined in this period as they were later to become; for example, most chambers had sleeping facilities, and it was only after about 1700 that independent bedrooms generally emerged. Room headings in inventories allude instead to relative location within the house, or the predominant color scheme, or the wall coverings and other decorative materials.

There are some indications that family portraits were treated differently when locating paintings in different parts of the house. This practice is related to the phenomenon of increasing divisions between private and public spaces. There is a clear pattern in richer inventories after 1650 of placing large numbers of these family images in a single chamber, with privileged access, usually an upstairs rear room. Such a process of "privatization" reflects the growing appreciation by relatives of family portraits as personal heirlooms, establishing their genealogical lineage and commemorating the lives and appearances of deceased loved ones. Such resonances were lost when a family portrait was introduced into a more impersonal environment. There is also a visual justification of elite status in these rooms, which appropriate the royal and aristocratic tradition of the family portrait gallery.

Contemporaries seem also to have distinguished between family portraits intended for the selective consumption of family members, and others that were directed toward a broader audience. Certainly *portraits historiés* (history portraits or role-playing portraits), were nearly always hung in the main reception rooms and could be easily admired by guests. Also, large-scale, more formally posed portraits, in which the sitter presents his public self-image, must also have inhabited these communal spaces.

A second consideration a collector faced when distributing his paintings among different apartments was in what quantities they should be clustered. Sanderson was of the opinion that pictures should be arranged sparingly and advised owners against clutter. Most seventeenth-century inventories show that paintings were not amassed in a single room but were evenly dispersed throughout the house; in the earlier decades of the century, the majority of paintings were located in the *voorhuis* and *keuken*, but this situation changed as larger, more multiroomed houses were built.

There was a tendency in the later seventeenth century, especially among the wealthier owners with high-quality paintings, to bring together their best works in one place, which often resulted in a disproportionately high concentration of works. These rooms, usually referred to as the *grote* or *beste kamer* or as the *zaal* or *salet,* were lavishly furnished and generally located on the ground floor. With their ostentatious displays of luxury, they were among the most publicly accessible spaces. This greater propensity toward accumulating pictures in a single room may also be linked to an important change in interior decoration. Until around 1670, most reception rooms in well-to-do Dutch homes had wainscoting that ran to three-quarters the height of the walls; in the period that followed, the walls were covered with linen painted mostly with landscape or mythological scenes and known as *kamerbehangsels.* This reduced the number of rooms in which paintings could be displayed. Rooms like these are embryonic art cabinets, although they still contained a considerable amount of other furnishings and objects; it was only in the 1740s that rooms almost entirely devoted to the display of paintings came into existence among collectors.

How were paintings hung on the walls of individual rooms? De Lairesse urged that landscapes should be hung at a height where their horizons were equal with eye level, otherwise the artistic objectives of "naturalness and deception" would be lost. In the same vein, portraits that are hung high should have a low horizon although he admits that such considerations are often wasted as the hanging positions of portraits were altered with great regularity and without taking into account the artist's original intentions.

From reading an inventory, it is not easy to get an impression of how paintings would have been arranged on the walls. Inventories have little consistent information to offer on the way pictures were hung or how they related to other room contents. A location that is more frequently indicated and appears to have been reserved for the most highly prized works was the area above the fireplace. The paintings that hung here were not restricted to any particular subject category. Sometimes they are specifically designated a *schoorsteenstuk* (chimney piece) and were set into the paneling of the chimney breast or enclosed within a frame that exactly fitted the dimensions of this space.

The most important source for the hanging of pictures are representations of the domestic interior. Despite their apparent documentary quality, this visual source has to be handled with great care: It is impossible to know the extent to which the painter may have manipulated the interior space for some iconographic or aesthetic end or as the result of artistic convention. Examples of "pictures within pictures" providing thematic support for the main picture are numerous.

The most striking feature about the hanging patterns of most "pictures within pictures" is their almost obsessive concern with symmetry. This mode of hanging conforms well with the historical system known as the "picturesque," or decorative, hang, which was the dominant pattern during the eighteenth and nineteenth centuries, both with Continental princely collections and with those of smaller English country houses. An aspect of this approach is "skying," or the placement of paintings high on the wall. That this, too, was common in the Netherlands during the seventeenth century can be seen in works such as Pieter Janssens Elinga's triangular perspective box in the Bredius Museum, The Hague. On opposite walls of a *voorhuis*, single rows of paintings are hung in parallel elevated positions above open doorways. Complementary subjects, media, the scale of the figures represented, and perhaps also the style are shown to be just as important factors in composing a picturesque hang as size and format.

The compulsion to symmetry and skying are a signal of how many owners must have viewed their collections. In a decorative hanging system, the individuality of the art work is supplemented by the desire for overall uniformity. Additionally, it is to be doubted whether some of the detail in pictures that were hung at high levels could be fully comprehended. Certain kinds of paintings appear to lend themselves to being hung at a height—for instance, large-scale "tonal" landscapes and church interiors with low viewpoints. Other works were cantered forward to allow them to be seen from below.

In domestic interiors where paintings are hung in tiers, it is usually the case that smaller pictures are hung at a lower level, inviting the spectator to stand near the wall. Pictures by Leiden *fijnschilders* (painters who specialized in fine details), with their quality of detail and small dimensions, must have been displayed at close quarters.

Apart from promoting paintings to the status of overmantels, there was another way of breaking the restrictions on individuality posed by a decorative hang and the monotony of densely accumulated paintings. The attachment, using hooks and eyes, of a metal curtain rail and curtain to a picture frame not only protected the work from smoke, dust, and light, but also conferred a sense of mystique and uniqueness to the now-concealed image. Pictures with curtains also occur in representations of the domestic interior, like Gabriel Metsu's *Portrait of the Valckenier Family* (1657; Berlin, Staatliche Museen). The

first curtained paintings are found in Antwerp gallery paintings from the 1620s, suggesting that the practice of covering paintings may have been of Flemish import.

Besides creating a demand for large "impressionistic" paintings that could be hung at height, the need for significant quantities of paintings with comparable dimensions and formats had several consequences for the art market. Whether the decorative hang was fueled by the movement toward standardization in the manufacture and commercial provision of panels, canvases, and frames, or whether it helped instigate these practices is difficult to determine. The inventories of dealers abound with references to panels and canvases of fixed sizes usually based on their monetary value. There are also documented references to frame sizes that use the same terminology.

Another by-product of the picturesque hang was that it encouraged artists to produce pendants and even series of pictures. The phenomenon of paired paintings is among the most characteristic aspects of Dutch art in the seventeenth century. Besides the most prevalent of these—pendant portraits of husbands and wives—a wide range of other contrasting themes is found in inventories. Among suites of paintings frequently encountered are the Four Seasons, the Four Parts of the Day, the Four Elements, the Four Evangelists, and the Five Senses. A common portrait series consists of representations of the Twelve Roman Emperors, which were also collected as antique coins and marble busts.

The visual evidence would suggest that paintings were hung chiefly for their decorative possibilities. However, this is not to say that they were merely regarded as other furnishings and did not impinge in some way on the sensibilities of their owners. In many instances, paintings were arranged on walls with regard for their scale and degree of finish: large, loosely painted works at height, and smaller, more finely executed ones lower down. Within the tightly controlled system of the decorative hang, individual highly prized works were singled out for special attention by placing them above a fireplace or covering them with a curtain.

John Loughman

See also Allegorical traditions; Archives; Court and official portraiture; History portraits; House interiors; Illusionism; Marriage and family portraits; Paintings-within-paintings; Portraiture; Subjects, subject categories, and hierarchies

Bibliography

Fock, C.W. "Kunstbezit in Leiden in de 17de eeuw." In *Het Rapenburg: Geschiedenis van een Leidse gracht*. Edited by Th.H. Lunsingh Scheurleer, et al. Vol. 5a, 3–36. Leiden: Kunsthistorisch Instituut, 1991.

Lairesse, G. de. *Het Groot Schilderboek*. Amsterdam: Willem de Coup, 1707.

Muizelaar, Klaske, and Ernst van de Wetering. "Kunst in het 17de-eeuwse binnenhuis." *Kunstschrift* 36 (November–December 1992): 14–21.

Muller, Jeffrey M. "Private Collections in the Spanish Netherlands: Ownership and Display of Paintings in

Domestic Interiors." In *The Age of Rubens*. Edited by
P.C. Sutton, et al., 195–206. Boston: Museum of Fine
Arts; Ghent: Ludion Press, 1994.

Vandenbroeck, Paul. "De 'salette' of pronkkamers in de
17de-eeuwse Brabantse burgerhuis: Familie-en
groepsportretten als iconograpfische bron." *M en L:
Monumenten en Landschappen* 9:6 (1990): 41–62.

Waterfield, Giles. "Picture Hanging and Gallery Decoration." In *Palaces of Art: Art Galleries in Britain, 1790–
1990*. Edited by G. Waterfield, et al., 49–51.
Dulwich: Dulwich Picture Gallery; London: Lund
Humphries, 1991.

Donor portraits

Works ranging from large public altarpieces to small private
devotional diptychs commonly included portraits of the patrons. Such importance attached to the inclusion of the donor that even when purchasing works from an artist's stock,
people might commission portrait wings to add to the central panel. Donor portraits functioned on a variety of levels:
as expressions of pious devotion; as testimony to the patron's
wealth and status; and as memorials honoring individuals,
families, and groups.

Certain conventions characterize these portrayals. The
donors kneel, sometimes before *prie-dieux*, their hands clasped
in prayer. Male figures occupy the space on the viewer's left—
that is, the right, or favored, side of the divine figure at the
heart of the image. Female figures in the same image are then
relegated to the less preferred side. But these general guidelines permit considerable flexibility.

On occasion, a sacred scene may displace female donors
from their traditional location. In such instances, women
appear on the side with the men, but subordinate to them and
farther from the divine subject.

Donors and sacred figures often occupy separate realms,
with the donors relegated to the wings in triptychs. Patron
saints commonly act as intermediaries. Usually the name
saints of the donors appear, but variations occur. The saints
may reflect the dedication of the site, or the general function
of the foundation (such as a hospital). Sometimes the factors
determining their selection elude modern scholars. Male saints
may accompany women, and, more rarely, female saints may
present male donors. On occasion the saint appears only symbolically, as, for example, an image in a stained-glass window.

The donors might be husband and wife, without other
family members. Often, however, children accompany the
couple, arrayed behind their parents according to gender. If
deceased at the time of the painting, small crosses above their
heads often indicated their status. Occasionally, name saints
of the children might also appear.

Deaths of spouses might occasion some unusual iconography. An altarpiece might include, for example, the deceased
wife as well as the present wife of the male donor.

Coats of arms often accompanied the donors and help
modern scholars identify them. Occasionally, the coats of arms
completely replaced the donors.

In addition to families, donors might be members of a
community such as a confraternity or a religious order. Sometimes only a few members of the group took part in the commission and thus appeared as donors. In other instances, the
entire community was involved. In such circumstances, the
portraits might include only the officers, or the complete
group.

Sometimes the donors appear without the benefit of
patron saints. This occurs less often in altarpieces of the fifteenth century, more often in the sixteenth century. It is standard in the popular half-length devotional diptychs.

Sometimes little distinction separated secular and sacred
realms. Donors on wings, for example, might inhabit the same
landscape as the divine figures in the center. Donors also sometimes invaded the central panel, both with and without patron
saints. Where the donor kneels before a traditional devotional
grouping such as the Lamentation or the Virgin and Child,
some scholars have interpreted the images as visualizations of
visions experienced by the praying donors rather than an au-
dacious intrusion into the divine realm. But the donor might
also appear as an actual participant in the sacred drama. Such
unaccompanied donor-participants occur particularly in
works commissioned by organizations (Fig. 62). But they seem
largely to have disappeared in the sixteenth century, perhaps
viewed as improper in turbulent religious times.

However, donors continued to invade the sacred sphere
in one notable group of works—*memorietafels* (memorial
paintings), such as the *Last Judgment* (1506) by Jan Provost for
Isabel de Malefiance (Fig. 73), a work from the Southern
Netherlands that was a model for Northern works as well.
Pieter Pourbus' *Soyer van Male Epitaph* (1578) illustrates the
extent to which pictorial memorialization of the family became
the dominant concern. The large family fills the central space,
displacing the Resurrected Christ (now relegated to the right
edge of the painting) before whom they kneel.

Much work remains to be done on donor portraits. No
broad study providing a general overview of the subject exists.
Some recent scholarship has suggested that examination of the
history of the family may provide insights into representations
of families. Many other aspects also demand exploration, including the relationship, spatial and psychological, of the
donors to the divine subject; the role of accompanying saints;
the setting for the figures; teachings of the Church relevant to
the depiction of donors in sacred images; and the impact of
change in social organization and class structure.

Janey L. Levy

See also Contemplative life, contemplative virtues; Devotional
images; Geertgen tot Sint Jans; Last Judgment; Manuscript
illumination; Marriage and family portraits; Portraiture;
Stained glass

Bibliography

Blum, Shirley Neilsen. *Early Netherlandish Triptychs: A
Study in Patronage*. Berkeley and Los Angeles: University of California Press, 1969.

Hughes, Diane Owen. "Representing the Family: Portraits
and Purposes in Early Modern Italy." *Journal of Inter-*

disciplinary *History* 17 (Summer 1986): 7–38.

Huvenne, Paul. *Pierre Pourbus, Peintre brugeois, 1524–1584.* Bruges: Memling Museum; Bruges: Crédit Communal, 1984.

Snyder, James. *Northern Renaissance Art: Painting, Sculpture, the Graphic Arts, from 1350 to 1575.* New York: Harry N. Abrams, 1985.

Dordrecht

Strategically situated on an island at an important juncture of the Maas and the Waal rivers, the principal estuary of the Rhine, Dordrecht had developed in the thirteenth and fourteenth centuries into the most vibrant trading center in Holland. This expansion was actively encouraged by the counts of the province and largely facilitated by their granting of monopolies on staple goods (particularly German wine and lumber), which enforced their sale at Dordrecht. During the sixteenth century, however, the town suffered from economic malaise, and by 1620 the decline had become absolute; the old staple rights now operated only as a tax on products traveling to the larger markets of Rotterdam and Amsterdam. Its concentration on river traffic led Dordrecht to neglect the more lucrative sea trade in commodities like Baltic grain; the restrictive practices of the guilds stilted competition. While its population expanded between 1600 and 1700 by around forty-five percent (from fifteen thousand to twenty-two thousand), by 1750 Dordrecht's population had fallen to sixteen thousand. Estimated taxable income in 1742 was below the average per capita for Holland as a whole, placing it among lesser towns like Gouda, Hoorn, and Leiden.

Despite such unfavorable conditions, Dordrecht managed to sustain a small but vibrant community of artists for most of the seventeenth century. It is difficult to estimate the number of artists working in the town throughout the century; the entire archives of the confraternity of painters (founded 1642) have vanished. Of the eighty-seven people who enlisted prior to 1642 in the Guild of St. Luke as "painters" or paid their enrollment costs to the "painters' guild," only twenty can be identified with certainty as *fijnschilders* (literally, fine painters or artist-painters); the remainder would appear to be mostly *kladschilders* or *grofschilders* (literally, rough painters or decorator-painters), who applied paint to buildings and furniture.

The social origins of Dordrecht painters were in general relatively humble. They tended to be born into the lower-middle-class families of tradesmen, artisans, and small merchants. Their economic position was not a strong one, and many had to supplement their income through other activities. Only four painters appear in the seventeenth-century tax registers of those liable for payment of the "200th penny" tax (that is, residents with assets of one thousand guilders or more in immovable goods and paper investments like bonds, annuities, and shares), and all are at the lowest rate of assessment: Jan Olis (ca. 1610–1676), Jacob Gerritsz. Cuyp (1594–1651/1652), Cornelis Bisschop (1630–1674), and Nicolaes Maes (1634–1693).

While it is surely an oversimplification to speak of city schools when confronted with the broad and interwoven spectrum of seventeenth-century Dutch art, certain stylistic and thematic patterns emerge for Dordrecht. The most important figure working in the first half of the century was J.G. Cuyp. Not only was he the most fashionable portraitist, but he also painted still lifes, genre scenes, and histories. His influence was felt as a teacher, and among his pupils were his half-brother Benjamin (1612–1652) and son Aelbert (1620–1691), Adriaen Verveer (?–1680), and probably also Paulus Lesire (1612–1654/1656) and Ferdinand Bol (1616–1680). The last-named was also the first of a long succession of local painters to spend a period of training in Amsterdam with Rembrandt. Indeed, J.G. Cuyp may be called the instigator of the Dordrecht "Rembrandt School" as he employed the two styles that had most influenced Rembrandt: Utrecht Caravaggism and the early Amsterdam history-painting tradition (the so-called pre-Rembrandtists). Bol was followed into the studio of Rembrandt by Samuel van Hoogstraten, Nicolaes Maes, Jacobus Leveck (1634–1675), and Aert de Gelder. The mysterious Abraham van Dijck, who is believed to have studied with Rembrandt around 1650 and whose art is closely related to that of Maes, may also have been a Dordrechter: an "Abram van Dijck, bachelor, painter" was buried in the town in August 1680. Other painters like Lesire, Benjamin Cuyp, and Pieter Verelst (ca. 1618–1671) were also influenced by Rembrandt, although there is no evidence that they studied with him. The history paintings of Bisschop also reveal the impact of the Amsterdam master, but his knowledge of Rembrandtesque exemplars was gained during his apprenticeship with Bol in Amsterdam.

There were other aspects of figural painting at Dordrecht. During the 1640s, Olis and Jacob van der Merck (ca. 1610–1664) produced high-life "companies" and guardroom scenes in the manner of Anthonie Palamedesz. and Pieter Codde. In contrast, Benjamin Cuyp and Abraham Diepraem (?–after 1677) painted representations of peasants in a broad, painterly style. Around Maes, a group of genre painters came to the fore who were heavily influenced by his depiction of figures, usually engaged in domestic activity and placed in a clearly defined spatial setting (Color Plate 7). The best known of these are Bisschop and Reinier Covijn (ca. 1636–1681).

Dordrecht's peak as a center of art production occurred during the two decades after mid-century. The number of painters working in the town during the years that followed appears to have dwindled. Nevertheless, a strain of painting emerged, now termed *fijnschilderen* (verb: to paint in a fine or refined manner), distinguished by its highly polished surfaces. Its main exponents in the town were Godfried Schalcken (1643–1706), Arnold Verbuys (1673–1717), Arnold Boonen (1669–1729), and Arnold Houbraken (1660–1719). The interest of Schalcken and Boonen in depicting nocturnal scenes lit by candlelight was taken up with great gusto in the late eighteenth and early nineteenth centuries by Michiel Versteegh (1756–1843) and Johannes Rosierse (1818–1901).

During the first half of the eighteenth century, the most important painters working in Dordrecht were Adriaan van der Burg (1693–1733) and Aart Schouman (1710–1792).

Not only did both artists produce easel paintings, but catering to the new taste in interior decoration, they also painted large-scale wall hangings, overdoors, and overmantels.

Among the few still-life painters active in Dordrecht was the precocious Johannes Bosschaert (1610/1611–1628), an influential flower and fruit painter; many of his compositional ideas were borrowed by the highly productive Bartholomeus Assteyn (1607–1669/1677). A more versatile artist was Abraham Susenier (?–1666/1672), who painted combined fruit and flower pieces, shells, fish, *vanitas* objects, and open-air still lifes.

Landscape painting at Dordrecht was dominated by Aelbert Cuyp (1620–1691). His views of the surrounding countryside bathed in golden Italian sunlight had a profound impact; to judge by the number of works in his style that were painted by contemporaries, Cuyp must have had a number of pupils and imitators, but the name of only one of these, Abraham van Calraet (1642–1722), has come down to us. Cuyp's influence lived on into the early nineteenth century in the work of Abraham van Strij (1753–1826) and, to a lesser extent, in the bright manner and saturated colors of Adrianus van der Koogh (1796–1831) and Willem de Klerk (1800–1876). Our knowledge of other currents in Dordrecht landscape painting during the Golden Age is fragmentary, with the names of many, like Barend Bisbinck, a pupil of Jan Both, known to us only through documents. One of the earliest landscapists to work in the town was Jacob van Geel (1584/1585–1638 or later), who is recorded in Dordrecht during the 1630s and painted woodland scenes in the Flemish Mannerist tradition. The following decade, Johannes Ruisscher (ca. 1625–after 1675) was resident in Dordrecht and provides another link with Rembrandt; while little of his painted *oeuvre* survives, his drawings and prints show him to have been a close follower of Rembrandt, and also of Hercules Segers, with whom he is sometimes confused. Although Dordrecht failed to foster any townscape, church interior, or seascape specialists during the seventeenth century, this situation was somewhat remedied with the later advent of the marine painters Martin Schouman (1770–1848) and J.C. Schotel (1787–1838).

In 1642, the painters broke from the Guild of St. Luke (also known as the Guild of the Six Trades), which also included glassmakers, tinsmiths, plasters, potters, and lantern makers, and formed themselves into a new brotherhood. The romantic notion that the painters demanded independence as a result of growing awareness of the superior artistic value of their occupation cannot be entirely accepted. Surviving documentation suggests that the painters were primarily motivated by economic considerations. By forming themselves into a separate entity they could maximize their profits and, above all, control the art market from which they earned a living. Although Houbraken gives the impression that the new brotherhood was a unified body of artist-painters, it also included decorator-painters. Indeed, the relationship between the two groups was an unhappy one, and by 1695 internal strife had reached such levels that it was decided that each should go his separate ways. Even after this secession there

continued to be disputes between artist-painters and decorator-painters over their respective work areas, in particular whether the former should be allowed to participate in the painting of decorative elements on ceilings. This squabbling is another indication that the market for easel paintings had contracted during the closing decades of the century, something that is confirmed by the decision of major artists like Maes, Schalcken, and Boonen to move more or less permanently to the more prosperous centers of Amsterdam and The Hague. In the eighteenth century other artist organizations like the St. Luke Brotherhood (established 1735) came into being; however, these were mostly composed of dilettantes and were dedicated to the reception rather than the practice of art.

There is no evidence that the seventeenth-century Dordrecht brotherhood ever established an academy where young artists could collectively draw after the nude model as The Hague confraternity did in 1683. Artistic education resided solely in the master–apprentice system. In 1735, the artists Cornelis Greenwood and Aart Schouman, tiring of drawing from plaster casts, decided to band together with some amateurs in order to sketch the human figure. This was, however, an informal arrangement, and it was only with the foundation of the Pictura Drawing Society in 1774 that a more established institution dedicated to the practice of drawing and the discussion of art came into being at Dordrecht.

Only a handful of Dordrecht painters like Van Hoogstraten could hope for occasional corporate patronage, and then mainly for group portraits from the Mint and a few charitable institutions. All of the important commissions from the town government went to nonresident artists like Adam Willaerts, Christiaen van Couwenberg, and Johannes de Baen. Local artists had to rely instead on the open market. Paintings were sold at the twice-yearly sales held by the brotherhood, at auctions of the chattels of deceased persons carried out by the *slagroede* (municipal auction house), or through the services of art dealers. Restrictions imposed by the Guild of St. Luke, and later the brotherhood, on the import of paintings from outside the town appear to have been largely successful. A survey of almost three hundred fifty inventories of paintings drawn up between 1620 and 1749 indicates that Dordrecht homes were overwhelmingly hung with the work of local masters. By comparison with other Dutch towns, most collections were small, and few (only twenty-eight in the sample) had more than eighty paintings. While some prominent Dutch contemporaries (Rembrandt, Van Poelenburch, Terbrugghen, for example) were represented, examples by much more expensive Italian and sixteenth-century Flemish artists are a rarity. Inventories reflect the actual artistic situation in Dordrecht; in a town where there were few landscapists, it is not surprising that landscapes in inventories increased between 1620 and 1700 at a rate below that for Delft and Leiden inventories. Many large collections were dispersed in the late eighteenth century, including that of Johan van der Linden van Slingeland, which numbered seven hundred paintings.

Although something of a backwater in economic terms, Dordrecht had a small but vibrant community of artists for most of the seventeenth century. Declining opportunities after 1670 compelled many of the most talented to move away; Johan van Gool's comment made in 1750, that Dordrecht was "a rich soil to cultivate painters, but not in the long term to nourish them," appears justified.

John Loughman

See also Amateurs, art academies, and art associations before the nineteenth century; Bol, Ferdinand; Cuyp, Aelbert; Drawing clubs; Genre painting, eighteenth century; Landscape; Maes, Nicolaes; Portraiture; Rembrandt School; Schouman, Aart; Still life; Town halls; Writers on art, eighteenth century

Bibliography

Bol, Laurens. *Aart Schouman, 1710–1792*. Doornspijk: Davaco, 1991.

Erkelens, J., et al. *Tussen Zonnegoud en Kaarslicht, Dordtse Meesters 1780–1840*. Dordrecht: Dordrechts Museum, 1986.

Loughman, John. "Paintings in the Public and Private Domain: Collecting and Patronage at Dordrecht, 1620–1749." Ph. D. diss., Courtauld Institute of Art, London, 1993.

Loughman, John, et al. *De Zichtbaere Werelt: Schilderkunst uit de Gouden Eeuw in Hollands oudste stad.* Dordrecht: Dordrechts Museum; Zwolle: Waanders, 1992.

Dou, Gerrit (1613–1675)

Born in Leiden, Gerrit Dou studied with several artists including his father, a glass engraver, before becoming Rembrandt's first student at the age of fifteen. When Rembrandt left for Amsterdam in 1631, Dou established himself as an independent painter. He began his career as a portraitist, then in the 1640s came to specialize in small-scale genre scenes, usually with one or two figures. In 1648, he was active along with Jan Steen and others in founding the painters' guild, the Guild of St. Luke, in Leiden. Dou was renowned for the meticulous detail and high finish of his work (Color Plate 8), which owed much to his early training as an engraver. This talent earned him the praise of his peers, the patronage of wealthy connoisseurs, and some of the highest prices on the market. He also had many pupils and followers, known as the *fijnschilders* (fine painters, specialists in painting fine details), who imitated his style well into the eighteenth century. Dou never married and rarely left his native city.

Dou's pictures are displays of erudition and virtuosity. He often adapted the symbolic vocabulary of emblems for his genre scenes and also favored illusionistic devices that displayed his formidable skill. In a typical picture from the 1640s, *Self-Portrait with Book and Pipe* (Fig. 45), a painted curtain is drawn back to reveal the artist leaning out of an illusionistic stone archway. The dark background scene shows an artist's studio—two men next to an easel, grinding pigments for paints—which contrasts with the intellectual activity represented by the painter's book. During the nineteenth century,

his precision and smooth finish were considered stiff and labored, and his reputation declined. While Dou is recognized as a major figure today, no full-scale monograph on him exists in published form. Current assessments of his work focus on his complex iconographic schemes.

Martha Hollander

See also Commerce and commercial life; Emblems and emblem books; Genre painting, eighteenth century; Genre painting, seventeenth century; Illusionism; Leiden; Quacksalvers, quack doctors; Rembrandt School; Women's worlds

Bibliography

Baer, Ronni. "Gerard Dou." Ph.D. diss., New York University, 1990.

Hecht, Peter. *De Hollandse Fijnschilders: Van Gerard Dou tot Adriaen van der Werff.* Amsterdam: Rijksmuseum; Maarssen: G Scwartz/SDU, 1989–90.

Sluijter, Eric J. et al. *Leidse Fijnschilders: Van Gerrit Dou tot Frans van Mieris de Jonge.* Leiden: Stedelijk Museum Het Lakenhal; Zwolle: Waanders, 1988. (English summary).

Drawing clubs

After their appearance during the seventeenth century, drawing clubs and societies continued to gain popularity over the next century, not only in large art centers like Amsterdam but in many small towns as well. These clubs provided Dutch artists and amateurs with the opportunity to meet in order to practice and discuss art in congenial, often informal, surroundings.

Drawing clubs probably had their origins in the small, informal "academies" that Dutch artists encountered in their trips to Italy. These groups, often run by a master artist like Guercino, came together several times a week to draw from the nude model. Both students and established artists could come to practice and receive or offer instruction. As drawing from the nude model became more widely accepted in the North during the course of the seventeenth century, similar groups were established by Dutch artists. Drawings of models from different points of view by different artists and, more rarely, documentary evidence reveal that masters and students gathered in groups to draw from life. The details of their activities, such as precisely who attended these sessions, how often they met, or what other exercises they might have practiced, are in many cases unknown. Willem Goeree's description of the typical *geselschap* or *Kollegie* (society or College) described them mainly in terms of their place in the education of young artists, but Goeree also emphatically recommended attendance for accomplished artists, who could continue to benefit throughout their lives by practicing life drawing. Goeree noted that students profited both from the opportunity to draw the live model and the chance to learn from their peers (Goeree, 1974: 72–73; 80). Although these groups seem to have consisted mainly of artists and students early in the century, amateurs took an increasing interest in their activities and, by the later seventeenth century, were joining or forming their own clubs, giving the groups a more widespread impact on Dutch culture.

Drawing clubs flourished during the eighteenth century, gaining additional popularity from the Dutch enthusiasm for clubs and societies devoted to all branches of knowledge and from the presence of a large and well-educated middle class. Drawing clubs afforded their members the opportunity to practice in the company of others and, as amateurs became increasingly active participants, the chance for professional artists and art lovers to come together. This was considered especially beneficial for the latter, who could improve their taste and their sensitivity to beauty through frequent contact with professional artists. Although amateurs were considered perfectly capable of learning about art simply by learning the rules and theory so important to classicist thought, a professional practiced these rules daily, constantly improving his or her judgment far beyond the capabilities of a dilettante. Amateur artists and collectors could, in turn, benefit from this improvement by mingling with professionals. While learning to draw had long been considered useful in the education of laymen as well as painters, it took on a new significance during the eighteenth century. Training in drawing could have moral benefits and ultimately even patriotic significance, a concept borrowed from French theory. In turn, a drawing club could introduce an artist to a network of potential patrons.

Drawing clubs varied in size and formality, ranging from groups of a few interested people to large and highly visible societies with permanent quarters, but most shared similar activities. Most clubs met several evenings a week in order to practice drawing and discuss art. Smaller groups often met in members' homes or coffeehouses: The Amsterdam club Pax Artium Nutrix, for instance, met in the tavern De Zon, where their models included one another as well as one of the servants. In some clubs, members contributed toward hiring a model from outside the group. Drawing from life formed a major part of the activities not only of smaller clubs but also of well-established societies like Felix Meritis, another Amsterdam group. The drawing department was only one part of this society, which also included branches devoted to areas like natural sciences, literature, and music. Members of Felix Meritis met in elaborate permanent facilities, and their activities included drawing both clothed and nude models, copying casts and other objects, and sponsoring lectures on art theory. While not all drawing clubs featured formal lectures as part of their activities, most included discussions of art or theory by members or visitors. Members often brought in compositions of their own creation or portfolios from their collections for their companions to examine and criticize.

By the end of the eighteenth century, nearly every Dutch city had a drawing club. The groups were not only part of a larger cultural pattern of fondness for clubs and societies but also helped make Dutch collectors among the most knowledgeable in Europe.

As the end of the century approached, the activities of some clubs became increasingly regulated and formalized. Among the more successful measures of this type were annual drawing competitions. Felix Meritis, which had almost one hundred members by the early nineteenth century, began to hold these contests in 1799 and was followed by some of the other large clubs, including the Leiden group Ars Aemula Naturae. These large, well-organized societies did not completely phase out the informal, small clubs, however: In Amsterdam alone there were several such groups coexisting with Felix Meritis. The club Zonder Wet of Spreuk, whose name means "Without Law or Motto," exemplifies these groups. Active in early-nineteenth-century Amsterdam, this club continued to mix amateurs and artists and to focus on life drawing as a primary activity. The practices of many of the members, who used their studies of clothed models directly in their finished paintings or prints, were closely related to those of their seventeenth-century counterparts.

The trend toward regulation, brought about in part by the influence of French academic thought, continued throughout the early part of the century. The most striking result of this pattern was the separation of amateurs and professionals. Artists gravitated toward academies intended for professional instruction, while dilettantes preferred the less structured clubs. Some overlap remained between the two types of groups: Amateurs sometimes served as administrators in academies, while a few artists continued to enjoy the informal companionship of the amateur groups. These groups had lost their central place in drawing practice and education, however, and after the early nineteenth century the role of the drawing club in Dutch art had changed permanently.

Stacey Sell

See also Amateurs, art academies, and art associations before the nineteenth century; Haarlem; Hague School, The; Rembrandt School

Bibliography

Goeree, Willem. *Inleyding tot d'Algemeene Teyckenkonst.* 1967. Reprint. Soest: Davaco, 1974.

Jellema, Renske E. *Herhaling of vertaling? Natekeningen uit de achttiende en negentiende eeuw.* Haarlem: Teylers Museum, 1987.

Knolle, Paul. "Dilettanten en hun rol in 18de-eeuwse Noordnederlandse tekenacademies." *Nederlands Kunsthistorisch Jaarboek* 5/6 (1986/1987): 289–301. (English summary).

———. "Het Departement der Tekenkunde van Felix Meritis." *Dokumentieblad werkgroep achttiende eeuw* 15 (1983): 141–196. (English summary).

Niemeijer, J.W. "Het voortleven der Zon-sireen." *Nederlands Kunsthistorisch Jaarboek* 38 (1987): 256–264. (English summary).

Rijdt, R.J. te. "Figuurstudies van het Amsterdamse particuliere tekengenootschap 'Zonder Wet of Spreuk' (ca. 1808–1819)." *Bulletin van het Rijksmuseum* 38 (1990): 223–244. (English summary).

Schatborn, Peter. *Dutch Figure Drawings.* Amsterdam: Rijksmuseum; The Hague: Government Printing Office, 1981.

Drawing practices and techniques

The drawing methods and practices of Dutch artists remained in some ways remarkably constant for centuries. Although there were variations according to factors like the discovery of new materials or foreign influences, artists made and used drawings in many of the same ways from the sixteenth through the nineteenth centuries.

During the early sixteenth century, draftsmen maintained a number of traditional techniques. Extensive underdrawing remained a common practice for some artists. Workshops continued to keep books or portfolios of drawings, usually copied from other works of art, in the tradition of medieval model books. Students, assistants, or the master could consult these stores of motifs as needed in their own paintings.

As the century progressed, however, the growing influence of Italian practices had a profound impact on the way Dutch artists made and used their drawings. Some Dutch artists adopted the elaborate series of preparatory drawings developed in Central Italy, which included rough compositional sketches, detailed figure studies, and finished compositional drawings or cartoons. Many others, however, used only one or two components of the process. The figure study, for instance, gained popularity later in the century both as preparation for a specific painting and as general practice. Hendrick Goltzius was among those to make chalk-figure studies from a nude model, a practice that was not yet common in the Netherlands. In addition to his drawings of the live model, Goltzius studied the human figure by drawing classical sculpture during a trip to Italy, a popular pilgrimage for Northern artists during this time.

Most of the techniques and media used by draftsmen throughout the next four hundred years were already in use during the sixteenth century. Pen and ink, often combined with wash, were common in both rough sketches and meticulously hatched finished drawings. Goltzius and his followers made some of the most famous virtuoso pen drawings, using a system of swelling and tapering lines that imitated the modeling system of his engravings. Both red and black chalk were in use, but they became more popular in the following century. Relatively few metalpoint drawings survive from the sixteenth century, suggesting that this traditional medium was not used as habitually as it had been during the previous century. Some artists, however, probably continued to use silverpoint on a prepared tablet in a traditional way that explains the relative rarity of such drawings. After the drawing had served its purpose, the artist could cover it with another preparatory layer and use the surface again.

Seventeenth-century artists continued to use these types of preparatory drawings, with dozens of personal variations on the procedures. Some left large numbers of drawings, allowing reconstruction of their working methods. In Adriaen van de Velde's case, the process included drawings after life made both on walks in the countryside and in the studio as well as compositional sketches. As in the previous century, however, the use of preparatory drawings apparently varied greatly according to the habits of individual artists. Some painters, such as Johannes Vermeer, Frans Hals, and Jan Steen, left few if any securely attributable drawings, giving little indication as to whether they worked without preparatory sketches or their drawings simply did not survive. Only a few of Rembrandt's vast number of known drawings seem to have been direct preliminary sketches, and the extensive changes he made during the course of executing many of his paintings suggest that he worked without drawings much of the time.

Drawing from life took on greater importance during the seventeenth century, both in preparation for specific paintings and as general practice. The chalk-figure drawing continued to gain popularity, and artists grouped together to draw nude models. Govaert Flinck and Ferdinand Bol, for instance, formed part of one of these groups, leaving a number of figure drawings in black and white chalk on blue paper. Several members of this group were former pupils of Rembrandt, who sometimes drew nude models with his students. The figure studies of Rembrandt and many of his followers, however, are rough pen and ink sketches very different in appearance from most figure drawings of the time. Artists also drew after studio props, which included sculpture, casts, and mannequins. Posable wooden mannequins were particularly useful for detailed drapery studies, made either for practice or for direct use in a painting. In addition, drawing from the imagination remained important, and many of the narrative sketches of Rembrandt and his pupils were probably made in part to exercise the imagination (Fig. 116).

The techniques already in use during the sixteenth century remained those most in favor during the seventeenth century. The main difference was the growing popularity of watercolor, which was used mostly for highly finished drawings intended as works of art in themselves. Chalk was one of the most common materials for many types of drawings. Artists sometimes made counterproofs of their chalk drawings: A dampened chalk drawing could be pressed facedown on a clean sheet of paper, leaving a reverse image. This prevented smearing of the original and gave the artist a reversed variant of a pose for possible use in a painting. Although most artists drew on paper, a few continued to prefer parchment.

Classicist theory and practice, much of it imported from France, shaped some aspects of drawing practices in the eighteenth century. Many drawings from the Neoclassical era exhibit a linear clarity and precision partly inspired by the work of British sculptor and draftsman John Flaxman (1755–1826). Figure drawing formed a crucial part of academic training, and artists left hundreds of meticulous chalk drawings after nude male models. Artists also made highly finished, elaborate drawings for annual competitions at academies and drawing societies, and detailed finished drawings were also popular with collectors of the time. One of the most common types of drawing in the eighteenth century was the topographic view, a finished work intended for a collector. The artistic pilgrimage to Rome, first popularized in the sixteenth century, had become less common early in the eighteenth century but regained importance in the last decades of the century, and many young artists made drawings after classical and Italian art, ruins, and landscapes. As the century progressed, both style and subject matter were also influenced by the renewal of interest in the art of the seventeenth century. In addition to their growing popularity as independent works of art, drawings continued to function as crucial tools in the preparatory methods of most artists.

In drawing techniques, the eighteenth century is marked by a widespread interest in color of all types. As they had in the previous century, artists frequently added color to black-and-white drawings by executing them on tinted paper, and watercolors were extremely popular. As in the seventeenth century, watercolor was applied over a detailed chalk or pencil drawing, giving the work a meticulous and linear appearance. Draftsmen used pastel much more frequently than they had in the previous century, and collectors prized pastel portraits like those by Cornelis Troost. This craving for color extended to the habit of reworking etchings with watercolor and other materials to create works that were a blend of print and drawing. Draftsmen often combined gray and brown wash with chalk, ink, or other materials to create a wide range of tonal values.

The styles and techniques of nineteenth-century drawings are notable for their variety: Academic training continued to flourish, resulting in meticulous figure drawings after live models and sculpture, but many artists broke away from this classicist style later in their careers. Although the drawings of the early part of the century were conservative in appearance, the landscape draftmanship of the later years was characterized by a greater freedom and variety. The chalk or charcoal drawings of many of The Hague School painters, including Willem Roelofs and Anton Mauve, were expressive, abbreviated, and painterly. Pen drawings range from the detailed nature studies by Albert Bilders to the rougher sketches by Vincent van Gogh, who often used the broad strokes created by a reed pen in a way that recalls his brushwork. Watercolor sketches, particularly those of The Hague School, were often made with minimal underdrawing, giving them a greater spontaneity and a more luminous quality than earlier watercolors. Pencil and sepia were more widely available and in greater demand during the nineteenth century than they had been earlier.

Perhaps the most striking change in drawing practices during this time is the diminishing role of the preparatory sketch. As many artists deliberately turned away from academic practices, some rejected the lengthy series of preliminary drawings that had become so much a part of the methods of many of their predecessors. Of course, many artists continued to use preparatory drawings of some type: The rough sketch from nature was particularly useful to many landscape painters.

Certain elements of drawing practice and technique, then, remained crucial for artists throughout four centuries. Foreign influences, particularly French and Italian, shaped some practices, but Dutch artists of all periods were selective in their adaptations of foreign methods. The preferences of individual artists gave rise to dozens of variations on common practices even within any given era, resulting in a wide range of personal adaptations of even the most established aspects of drawing practice and technique.

Stacey Sell

See also Calligraphers and calligraphy; Goltzius, Hendrick; Hague School, The; Laren; Rembrandt School; Technical investigations; Troost, Cornelis; Underdrawings, underpaintings

Bibliography

Hand, John Oliver, et al. *The Age of Bruegel: Netherlandish Drawings in the Sixteenth Century.* Washington, DC: National Gallery of Art; New York and London: Cambridge University Press, 1986.

Jonker, M., and M. Kersten. "De functie van het blad: Tekenen in Nederland, 1765–1800." In *Edele Eenvoud: Neoclassicisme in Nederland, 1765–1800.* Edited by F. Grijzenhout, et al., 187–257. Haarlem: Teylers Museum; Zwolle: Waanders, 1989.

Leeuw, Ronald de, John Sillevis, and Charles Dumas. *The Hague School: Dutch Masters of the Nineteenth Century.* London: Royal Academy of Arts, in association with Weidenfeld and Nicolson, 1983.

Mandle, Earl Roger, and J.W. Niemeijer. *Dutch Masterpieces from the Eighteenth Century: Paintings and Drawings, 1700–1800.* Minneapolis: Minneapolis Institute of Arts, 1971.

Meder, Joseph. *The Mastery of Drawing.* 2 vols. Translated and revised by Winslow Ames. New York: Abaris, 1978.

Niemeijer, J.W. "Academies and Other Figure Studies from Jean Grandjean's Roman Period." *Master Drawings* 12 (1975): 351–358.

Robinson, William W. "Rembrandt's Sketches of Historical Subjects." In *Drawings Defined.* Edited by Walter Strauss and Tracy Felker, 241–257. New York: Abaris, 1987.

Robinson, William W., and Peter Schatborn. *Seventeenth-Century Dutch Drawings: A Selection from the Maida and George Abrams Collection.* Amsterdam: Rijksmuseum; Lynn, MA: Zimman, 1991.

Schatborn, Peter. *Dutch Figure Drawings.* Amsterdam: Rijksmuseum; The Hague: Government Publishing Office, 1981.

Wolk, Johannes van de, Ronald Pickvance, and E.B.F. Pey. *Vincent van Gogh: Drawings.* Otterlo: Rijksmuseum Kröller-Müller; New York: Rizzoli, 1990.

Drawing theory

Dutch drawing theory from the early seventeenth century onward was heavily influenced by foreign art theory, first by Italian Renaissance art literature and later by French classicism. Both of these, in turn, were shaped partly by classical literature about art and rhetoric. Despite this influence, Dutch theory and its relationship to practice remained distinct in many ways.

The earliest Dutch writers of this period already discussed the central importance of *teykenkonst* (also spelled *teyckenconst*). Although a literal translation of *teykenkonst* would be "drawing," most seventeenth-century theorists imbued the term with a more complex meaning. Karel van Mander referred to it as the "father of painting" and noted that it was the artist's means of expression of hidden meanings and ideas: More than just marks on a paper, a drawing was the link between the painter's imagination and the outside world. Before making a drawing on paper, Van Mander advised, the artist should make a compositional sketch in the imagination (Van Mander 1973, 2: 3). Some writers distinguished between *tekenen* (to draw) and *schetsen*, to sketch. Although a *schets* could mean, as in English, a rough, unfinished drawing, Samuel van Hoogstraten seems to have associated it with the physical act of drawing rather than with the "drawing" in the artist's imagination (Van Hoogstraten, 1678: 27). In their belief that *teykenkonst* was closely linked to the image or idea in the artist's mind, both authors articulated a major theme in drawing theory. Although many of Van Mander's comments on *teykenkonst* are adaptations of Giorgio Vasari's discussions of *disegno*, or drawing, Van Mander differed in one important respect. While Vasari's writings reflected his Central Italian belief that drawing is the basis of all art and that successful painting cannot exist without extensive preparatory drawing, Van Mander's view was less emphatic. His view that painting directly without preparatory drawings is the mark of an accomplished and daring artist has counterparts in seventeenth-century artistic practice. A number of artists, including Rembrandt, evidently worked without the series of preliminary steps embraced by many Central Italian artists, though certainly many Dutch artists did make extensive preparatory drawings.

As the basis of art and the "father of painting," *teykenkonst* played a crucial part in the education of a young artist. Some writers, including Willem Goeree, compared learning to draw to learning to write the alphabet (Goeree, 1974: 17). This comparison not only reinforced the point that drawing provided a student with the tools necessary for a career in painting, it also adhered to a convention in art theory in which painting is compared to poetry. In both art and literature, students learned through imitation; in keeping with this idea, copying formed a major part of a young painter's education. Most theorists from the seventeenth century onward advocated a system of learning to draw that involved a series of steps, beginning with the easiest tasks and ending with the most difficult and important. A pupil began to learn to draw by copying other drawings and prints, including model books or drawing books, which were compiled especially for this purpose and usually concentrated on the human figure. After this, the student moved on to drawing after paintings, progressed through drawing after casts or sculpture, and finally was ready to draw after life. In actual practice, most students probably followed a less structured program than this, working on more than one step at once or skipping one entirely.

Both early in a painter's education and throughout his or her career, constant practice in drawing was a matter of great importance. Van Mander, for instance, commented that perfection in *teykenkonst* could be achieved only through good understanding, which in turn could be earned only by a combination of practice and inborn talent (Van Mander 1973, 2: 3). This combination of practice and talent, or *exercitatio* and *ingenium*, was standard in artistic training through much of

the seventeenth century, and treatises urge young artists to be diligent in practicing their drawing skills not only as students but throughout their lives. As classicism took root in the Netherlands, however, students were expected to study theory, or *ars*, as well. By the end of the century, writers like Gerard de Lairesse placed increasing stress on the theory, or the rules, of art, until *ars* became as important as practice and more important than natural talent.

Theorists from the early seventeenth century onward stressed the necessity of drawing *naer het leven*, or "after life." Van Mander noted that only the artist who had drawn from life could work from the imagination, because in drawing from life the student would be able to learn all things, including expression, movement, contour, and modeling (Van Mander 1973, 2: 13). In some cases, drawing *naer het leven* meant drawing the live nude model. While a number of seventeenth-century writers, including Crispijn de Passe II, discussed the benefits of this practice at length, the extent to which Dutch artists actually studied the nude model at the time is difficult to determine. Certainly some of them gathered together in small groups to do so throughout the century, and by the eighteenth century drawing after the live model was a major part of academic training.

Working *naer het leven* had a broader meaning than simply drawing the nude figure, however. Roelandt Savery's drawings of peasants labeled *naer het leven* are examples of other types of figure studies made from life that were used in finished works, a procedure that became more common in the seventeenth century than it had been earlier. The term could also describe drawing from nature of any type, including landscapes or animals. The subject of the drawing did not, in fact, even need to be alive in a sketch made *naer het leven*: It could be, for example, a cast or a sculpture. Rembrandt's inventory, for instance, lists drawings *naer het leven* of people, animals, and statues. In some cases, then, the meaning of *naer het leven* is closer to "from reality" than "after life." Some, like the eighteenth-century artist Jan Hulswit, even used the term to describe landscape drawings that he considered particularly close to reality though they were not made on the site (Elen, 1987: 258–259). While *naer het leven* was one vitally important way of drawing, another was *uit den gheest* (sometimes *inventor*), or "from the imagination." The artist's imagination was one of his or her most highly valued faculties. Artists often worked in a way that combined the two methods, making sketches *naer het leven* that were later combined in a composition developed in the imagination, or using the knowledge they had gained from working after life to create a work from the imagination.

One of the types of drawings most closely linked to the artist's imagination was the rough sketch. Italian Renaissance writers, in particular Leonardo da Vinci and Vasari, were responsible for reviving Pliny's beliefs about the value of the rough sketch. The quick sketch was the means of recording the artist's first thoughts, and as such it gave evidence of the creative furor that seized him or her. Moreover, the tangled lines of the rough sketch could serve as further inspiration for an artist, who could visualize new images within them. Although these ideas were most widespread among Italian artists and theorists, they were also familiar to many Northerners, including Franciscus Junius, author of *De Pictura Veterum* (The Painting of the Ancients, 1634), and Van Hoogstraten.

The rise of classicism at the end of the seventeenth century and the later popularity of Neoclassicism corresponded to changes in drawing theory and practice. Theory itself became more important: According to classicist ideas, the rules of art were both learnable and teachable, and lectures in art theory became a standard part of education in drawing. In the hierarchy of the genres, history painting was the noblest type of painting, making mastery of the human figure a necessity for aspiring artists. Accordingly, life drawing and drawing from casts played increasingly major parts in artistic education. Although the study of ancient sculpture had been encouraged for centuries, Neoclassical theorists gave it a new relevance. They held that classical artists and their Renaissance followers, like Raphael, had studied nature and selected the most beautiful aspects of it; therefore, studying and drawing these types of art exposed the student to the best of nature. The study of life and classical art were combined in life classes, where students often drew live models in poses borrowed from ancient sculpture. Sometimes they compared their drawings to a cast of the statue from which the pose had been borrowed, a step that allowed them to correct the unavoidable flaws of nature in their life drawings and to better learn the ideal of true beauty.

Neoclassical theory associated the study of classical art with moral improvement. Johann Winckelmann, a German whose writings helped shape Dutch drawing theory of the time, linked the nobility of Greek art with moral virtue. Similarly, the clarity of contour of much Neoclassical draftsmanship had moral associations. Among the inspirations for the emphasis on pure contour were Greek vase painting, a desire for formal and narrative clarity, and the belief, as in earlier periods, that drawing was the basis of all art.

Although some aspects of Dutch drawing theory changed throughout the centuries, then, the basic conviction remained that drawing was essential for all forms of art. This belief affected many aspects of drawing practice, among them the education of young artists. In addition, as was the case with artistic practice, Dutch art theorists remained open throughout the centuries to influences from international sources, particularly France and Italy, to contribute to their beliefs about drawing.

Stacey Sell

See also Drawing practices and techniques; Drawings, uses and collecting; Van Mander, Karel; Writers on art, sixteenth and seventeenth centuries

Bibliography

Elen, Albert J. "'Met Eenigen Verandering naar 't leven': Compositionele herhaling met variaties in het tekenkunstig oeuvre van Jan Hulswit (1766–1822)." In *Achttiende–eeuwse kunst in de Nederlanden*, 241–267. Leids Kunsthistorisch Jaarboek, no. 4. Delft: Delftsche Uitgevers Maatschappij BV, 1987. (English summary).

Emmens, J.A. *Rembrandt en de regels van de kunst*. Amsterdam: Van Oorschot, 1979. (English summary).

Goeree, Willem. *Inleyding tot d'Algemeene Teyckenkonst*. 1697. Reprint. Soest: Davaco, 1974.

Grijzenhout, F. et al., eds. *Edele eenvoud-Neoclassicisme in Nederland 1765–1800*. Haarlem: Teylers Museum; Zwolle: Waanders, 1989.

Held, Julius S. "The Early Appreciation of Drawings." In *Acts of the Twentieth International Congress of the History of Art*. Vol. 3, 72–93. Princeton, NJ: Princeton University Press, 1963.

Hoogstraten, Samuel van. *Inleyding tot de Hooge Schoole der Schilderkonst*. Rotterdam: Fransois van Hoogstraeten, 1678.

Mander, Karel van. *Den Grondt der edel vrij schilderconst*. Edited and annotated by Hessel Miedema. 2 vols. Utrecht: Haentjens, Dekker, and Gumbert, 1973.

Robinson, William W., and Peter Schatborn. *Seventeenth-Century Dutch Drawings: A Selection from the Maida and George Abrams Collection*. Amsterdam: Rijksmuseum; Lynn, MA: Zimman, 1991.

Schatborn, Peter. *Dutch Figure Drawings*. Amsterdam: Rijksmuseum; The Hague: Government Printing Office, 1981.

Drawings, uses and collecting

Although they were popular with collectors from the seventeenth century onward, drawings had many functions for artists and amateurs alike. Artists were among the most avid collectors, and their uses for drawings were particularly varied.

Before 1600, there were evidently very few amateur collectors of drawings in the Netherlands. The growing interest in collecting drawings was influenced by Italian writers and collectors, who believed that sketches displayed the creative furor and workings of the artist's mind. Unlike many of their Italian counterparts, however, Dutch collectors for most of the seventeenth century strongly preferred finished drawings to rough sketches. Many artists made meticulously finished drawings specifically for purchase by collectors, and the survival of so few rough sketches from the seventeenth century may be due as much to the preferences of collectors as to the practices of artists. Amateurs collected drawings by both Dutch and foreign artists, but the precise contents of most seventeenth-century collections are unknown: Inventories and sales records often list drawings by the book rather than by individual work, usually giving few details even when an artist's name is mentioned. For the most part, drawings were stored in books or folios, organized by artist or by subject matter and occasionally by technique, but they were sometimes framed for hanging. Although drawings formed the major part of some collections, in others they were a small part of a cabinet of curiosities, or *kunstkammer*, which included natural as well as man-made wonders. Some collectors, including Jan Six, kept an *album amicorum*, an album in which friends and acquaintances left verses or mottoes, samples of their elaborate calligraphy, and drawings. Rembrandt was among the artists to draw in Six's album. Six, Reynier van der Wolf, and Gerard and Jan Reynst were only a few of the many seventeenth-century collectors who took an interest in drawings, although they collected other types of art as well.

Artists as well as amateurs were avid collectors of drawings. A large collection of drawings had a practical purpose in an artist's studio: The drawings could serve as a source of motifs or compositions and would also be useful in teaching students how to draw. Copying the drawings of other artists was one of the earliest and most important steps in learning to draw; it was also an activity that many artists continued throughout their lives both in order to learn from the styles of others and to record compositions for possible later use. Among the collections held by artists were those of Rembrandt and the Ter Borch family; a large portion of Rembrandt's collection was in turn purchased by Jan van de Cappelle.

Drawings were, of course, intended for many purposes other than collections. They had an important place in the preparatory methods of most seventeenth-century painters and served as models for the projects of other artists. Drawings functioned as designs for, among other things, metalwork, tapestries, and prints. Hendrick Goltzius, for example, supplied his followers with detailed drawings from which to make engravings. Drawings for this purpose are usually highly finished, with clear indications of modeling to guide the engraver. In addition, a finished drawing of a proposed painting was useful in allowing the patron to inspect the work and specify changes. Artists also made drawings without any ultimate purpose in mind, simply for the exercise of the hand and imagination. They also kept sketchbooks of drawings from life or the imagination with the idea that the motifs might be useful at some later date.

Collectors sought drawings even more eagerly during the eighteenth century. During the early part of the century, topographical scenes increased dramatically in popularity. Although these detailed studies of local landscapes and townscapes were made by artists in other countries as well, they were particularly highly regarded by Dutch collectors, who bought them singly or in sets, sometimes commissioning entire series. Some collectors assembled atlases consisting of hundreds of topographical drawings and prints, which they sometimes supplemented with related portraits and historical scenes. These drawings also sometimes served as designs for prints or models for oil paintings: Egbert van Drielst was among those who kept portfolios of landscape drawings for display to his patrons, who could choose to have a finished drawing or painted version made of one of the available designs. Jan Hulswit used his sketches after nature for similar purposes, making many different versions of some designs, including both highly finished copies and simpler rough sketches for sale to collectors. Copies of old-master paintings by eighteenth-century draftsmen were also an important source of income for many artists.

One of the most famous drawing collections of the eighteenth century was that of Cornelis Ploos van Amstel, who owned more than five thousand drawings. His collection included works by both contemporaries and old masters, and was arranged by subject matter, with larger categories split into "colored" and "noncolored." Although he owned drawings by both Dutch and foreign artists, he had far more of the former—in direct contrast to some collectors of the time who sought mainly Italian drawings. He also owned an extensive atlas and a large number of watercolor copies after paintings. In addition to his collection, he is known for his project of publishing a series of print facsimiles of drawings, which made collections of old-master "drawings" available to those of lesser means. Ploos van Amstel may have had altruistic motives for collecting in addition to the typical reasons: He believed that an art collection was useful and enriching for students as well as the owner.

Drawings continued to function in many of the same ways that they had during the seventeenth century, although some shifts occurred as fashions changed. The eighteenth-century taste for painted wall decoration led to a need for design drawings for these projects and consequently provided employment for many artists, including Jurriaen Andriessen (1742–1819). There was also a growing demand for designs for book illustrations and for series of topographical prints. Artists living or studying in Rome could also sell drawings of the local scenery and art to tourists as an additional source of income.

Like their earlier counterparts, nineteenth-century collectors prized finished drawings made as independent works of art. Drawn copies of paintings still formed an important part of many collections. While in the eighteenth century the most important aspect of a copy was its aesthetic quality, during the following century collectors valued fidelity to the original. Some painters, such as Jozef Israëls, made watercolor copies of their own paintings as less expensive versions for collectors. Israëls also accepted commissions for portrait drawings.

Nineteenth-century collectors, like those before them, deeply admired old-master drawings as well as those by their contemporaries. One of the major Dutch collectors of the time was King Willem II, who owned an impressive number of Italian Renaissance drawings, including hundreds of sketches by Fra Bartolommeo. In contrast, the painter Hendrik Willem Mesdag was an avid collector who concentrated on the artists of his own century, particularly members of The Hague and Barbizon Schools. Collectors began to seek rough sketches, including the abbreviated chalk and charcoal sketches of The Hague School artists, more seriously than they had in earlier centuries. Although collectors continued to buy directly from artists or each other, art dealers played an increasingly important role in the art market from the mid-nineteenth century onward. Drawings had a valued place in the market, because dealers were able to sell them quickly and more easily than more expensive paintings.

By the end of the nineteenth century, drawings played a smaller part in the preparatory process than they had in earlier centuries. Instead, some artists made them largely as independent works of art. Vincent van Gogh, for instance, though a prolific draftsman, evidently made very few preparatory drawings. Artists continued to keep sketchbooks, and quick studies after nature formed a large part of the *oeuvres* of many artists like Anton Mauve. Some of these sketches later formed the basis for paintings or other drawings. Despite their spontaneous appearance, some of these sketches were carefully observed: Some drawings by Willem Roelofs, for instance, include notations by the artist about the correct proportions or appearance of the scene he was drawing.

The most striking trend in the evolution of drawing functions, then, is the growing interest in drawings as works of art in their own right. Finished drawings were already made for collectors in the sixteenth and seventeenth centuries, but later collectors developed enthusiasm for sketches as well. Throughout the centuries, drawings continued to function as aids to artists in their work, as preparatory tools, designs for craftsmen, and sources of useful compositions and motifs.

Stacey Sell

See also Amateurs, art academies, and art associations before the nineteenth century; Atlas, atlases; Exotica; Hague School, The; Israëls, Jozef; Mauve, Anton; Mesdag, Hendrik Willem; Roelofs, Willem

Bibliography

Broos, Ben. "'Notitie der Teekeningen van Sybrand Feitama': De boekhouding van drie generaties verzamelaars van oude Nederlandse tekenkunst." *Oud Holland* 98 (1984): 13–39. (English summary).

Elen, Albert J. "'Met Eenigen Verandering naar 't leven': Compositionele herhaling met variaties in het tekenkunstig oeuvre van Jan Hulswit (1766–1822)." In *Achttiende-eeuwse kunst in de Nederlanden*, 241–267. Leids Kunsthistorisch Jaarboek, no. 4. Delft: Delftsche Uitgevers Maatschappij BV, 1987. (English summary).

Gelder, J.G. van, and Ingrid Jost. *Jan de Bisschop and His Icones and Paradigmata*. Doornspijk: Davaco, 1985.

Held, Julius S. "The Early Appreciation of Drawings." In *Acts of the Twentieth International Congress of the History of Art*. Vol. 3, 72–93. Princeton, NJ: Princeton University Press, 1963.

Jellema, Renske E. *Herhaling of vertaling? Natekeningen uit de achttiende eeuw*. Haarlem: Teylers Museum, 1987.

Kettering, Allison McNeil. *Drawings from the Ter Borch Studio Estate*. The Hague: Staatsuitgeverij, 1988.

Laurentius, Th., J.W. Niemeijer, and G. Ploos van Amstel. *Cornelis Ploos van Amstel, 1726–1798, Kunstverzamelaar en prentuitgever*. Assen: Van Gorcum, 1980. (English summary).

Schatborn, Peter. "Van Rembrandt tot Crozat, Vroege verzameling met tekeningen van Rembrandt." *Nederlands Kunsthistorisch Jaarboek* 32 (1981): 1–54. (English summary).

Dudok, Willem Marinus (1884–1974)

Willem Marinus Dudok is considered to be one of the most remarkable twentieth-century architects in the Netherlands. His major works were built during the period between World

Wars I and II. Although he never intervened in the discussions about modern architecture in the 1920s, he is regarded in retrospect as an important transitional figure between modern and traditional building. Dudok is especially known for the outstanding quality of his work in Hilversum, where he arrived after a short career in the army and a position as city engineer for the city of Leiden. During his period in Leiden, he not only did work on commission from the city but also collaborated on projects with J.J.P. Oud. Together they built public housing in Leiderdorp (1914–1915) and the office for the newspaper *Leids Dagblad* (1916–1917), which shows an expressive use of brick. The two men remained lifelong friends.

From 1915 until 1954 Dudok was in charge of the Public Works Council of Hilversum. As such, he was responsible for the design of many public buildings, including schools, slaughterhouses, cemeteries, and police stations. Due to his work on these buildings and on many residential quarters in Hilversum, he defined the future townscape to a great extent. He advocated a closely concentrated city with restrained growth and limited extension; therefore, bound in form. He considered the possibility of indefinite growth only as a potential planning nightmare.

Dudok designed several recognized and exceptional buildings, such as the Dutch Student House at the Cité Universitaire of Paris (1927–1939) and the department store De Bijenkorf, with its expansive glass walls, in Rotterdam (1928–1930, destroyed). Yet his name is attached most often to one outstanding building, the Town Hall of Hilversum (1915–1931). With this work the architect achieved international renown. This building's complex articulation of volumes, the moderate architectural language in which functionalism is combined with Romanticism, and the use of brick (the famous yellow Dudok brick) as the traditional building material are features that characterize much of Dudok's later architecture. The initial ideas for the Town Hall date back to 1915; he began by making designs in the style of H.P. Berlage and the Amsterdam School. In 1923 he reached the definitive solution for this building, which was to become a mecca for many young architects. In many ways Dudok tried to arrive at an architecture that retained characteristics of the Amsterdam School, Neo-Plasticism, and functionalism.

Dudok had the opportunity to plan and build in many other cities besides Hilversum. However, attention focused on the Hilversum Town Hall has tended to eclipse these other projects. The columbarium at Westerveld (1925–1926), the HAV-Bank in Schiedam (1931–1935), the office for *De Nederlanden* in Arnhem (1937–1939), and the City Theater in Utrecht (1937–1941) are all works that were crucial to his development before 1940 and that are hardly taken into consideration today. Yet, undoubtedly, they constitute masterworks in Dutch architectural history. Another aspect of his work that deserves more attention is town planning. Dudok was asked to develop proposals for Hilversum (from 1915 onward), The Hague (1934–1942; 1945–1952), Alkmaar (1942–1943), Velsen (1945–1952), and Zwolle (1948–1953). Although his plans were rarely executed, they left their imprint on the work of many of the architects and planners who followed. Furthermore, for Dudok, the relationship between urban planning and architecture was always integral, as most of his projects demonstrate. In the principles of urban planning, Dudok was influenced by visual planners Camillo Sitte (*Der Städtebau*, 1889) and Raymond Unwin (*The Garden City*, 1905). His working method followed from the large to the small scale. The first sketches of a building were typically perspectives, made to address the visual effect of a built object within the cityscape. Inversely, in an interior walk through the Town Hall of Hilversum the sensation of going through a city is felt, because Dudok also adhered to the principle of fifteenth-century Renaissance architect Leon Battista Alberti that a house should be a small city and a city a large house.

From the period after World War II are buildings that have hardly been acknowledged: the administration building for the Royal Dutch Steelworks at Velsen (1947–1951), with its extraordinary glass bridge over the street, and the Town Hall of Velsen (1949–1965). At the end of his career, after leaving his position in Hilversum, Dudok worked on a large number of projects for a real-estate developer. The tension that characterized his prewar architecture is often lacking due to a search for a clarifying simplicity. Although the quality of these projects remained high, especially compared to the architectural poverty of the Netherlands at that time, they never had the innovative character of his work before the war.

Herman van Bergeijk

See also Amsterdam School; Berlage, Hendrik Petrus; Functionalism in architecture; Leiden; Oud, Jacobus Johannes Pieter; Public housing; Town halls; Urban planning, from 1750 to the present

Bibliography

Bergeijk, Herman van. *Willem Marinus Dudok, 1884–1974: Architect-stedebouwkundige*. Naarden: V + K Publishing, 1995.
Magnée, Robert, ed. *Willem M. Dudok*. Amsterdam: Van Saane, 1954.

Duiker, Johannes (1890–1935)

A civil engineer, born in The Hague, Johannes Duiker was one of the protagonists of the functionalist tendency promising to renew architecture and addressing the moral character of building. During a prolific career, interrupted by his sudden death, he worked for about twenty years with Bernard Bijvoet (1889–1979), a fellow student from his university days. His activity as a designer was coupled with intense work as a writer; in 1930 he published *Hoogbouw* (High-Rise Building), a successful pamphlet in defense of high-rise residential construction. He was one of the founders and the first editor of the magazine *De 8 en Opbouw*, the voice of groups in favor of the *Nieuwe Zakelijkheid* (New Objectivity), meaning an efficient functionalism in architecture and aesthetics.

Duiker and Bijvoet were enjoying their first professional success in 1919 when they participated in the competition to design a Rijksacademie voor Beeldende Kunsten (National Academy of Arts) to be constructed in the new area of urban expansion, Amsterdam South. Their entry, richly influenced by Frank Lloyd Wright, won first prize. The project was never realized, however, because, due to various uncertainties, the idea to construct the academy was abandoned. In this early phase of the search for a professional identity, the two young engineers also entered a design in the international competition for the *Chicago Tribune* building (1922); their project still had the flavor of Wright but also recalled studies for buildings by Ludwig Mies van der Rohe.

Between 1924 and 1930, Duiker designed and built several very important buildings that have become landmarks of Dutch modern architecture. These were a farm house in Aalsmeer (1924–1925); the Zonnestraal (sun ray) sanatorium complex in Hilversum; the Nirwâna Flats in The Hague, a collaboration with the engineer Jan Gerko Wiebenga (1886–1974); and the Open-Air School in Amsterdam.

The commission for the Zonnestraal came from an aid association of the diamond-cutters' union; the site chosen was a wooded area near Hilversum, approximately fifty kilometers east of Amsterdam. The passwords in the fight against illness were light, air, and sun; these requirements shifted from therapy to construction in the buildings' designs and became general rules for all good architecture. The geometric simplicity of the volumes, the clearness of the construction emphasized by the use of thin walls of reinforced concrete and glass, the exposure of all external and internal spaces to full sunlight, and the careful design of the interior for promoting hygiene were the new architectural rules that Duiker consistently applied in all of his work.

The plan of the complex is symmetrical: The communal services are in a building in the center and on both sides are the patients' residence pavilions, placed obliquely to encourage exposure to the sun. Thus, the sanatorium did not follow the custom of being a single building but instead was conceived as a small village around a large green courtyard. Construction began in January 1927; the next June the central building and one of the pavilions were opened. The second pavilion was completed in 1931.

After completing the sanatorium, Duiker was dedicated for more than a decade (1919–1931) to architecture that combined innovative therapeutic requirements, typological innovation, and aesthetic quality.

The project for the Zonnestraal sanatorium coincided with a decisive period in Duiker's research, which was directed toward evaluating the expressive quality of the new technology used in construction. This research continued with the creation of the Open-Air School in Amsterdam South (1927–1930; Fig. 46), a surprising quadrangular building, apparently simple in shape, which is, however, the result of a profound study of the character of an organism spatially capable of absorbing full light and air. Once again, the aim of the architect was to encourage free circulation of air and direct sunlight.

Classrooms and service areas are housed in a cubic volume, built on a grid of reinforced concrete pillars with walls almost entirely of glass, which contains the school as a single body. Classrooms are fully transparent and share an outdoor veranda. On the top of the building there is a terraced roof with space for lessons in the open air. The pillars are placed inside the structure leaving the glass corners completely unobstructed, while the structural cage of reinforced concrete, fully visible, is turned with respect to the volume that contains it. This creates, though starting with a simple volume, a complex and dynamic spatial geometry consisting of planes and lines that interact and intersect with each other.

In the last years of his activity, Duiker reduced the use of strict geometry in the organization of his compositions and experimented instead with a freer, softer effect. Deriving from this new sensibility toward the fluidity of space were his plans for movie theaters in Amsterdam as well as his last work, the Grand Hotel Gooiland in Hilversum, completed after his death. In this evolution toward richer forms, architecture continued to exhibit a very clear and sincere character—in other words, it did not lose that principle of the ethics of construction on which the entire experience of Duiker was based.

Maristella Casciato

See also Architectural competitions; Functionalism in architecture

Bibliography

Casciato, Maristella. "Johannes Duiker: Functionalist Architect." *Casabella* 562 (1989): 61–63.

Jelles, E.J., and C.A. Alberts. "Duiker, 1890–1935." *Forum voor architectuur en daarmee verbonden kunsten* (Genootschap Architectura et Amicitia) 5/6 (1972): 1–144.

Molema, Jan. *Ir. J. Duiker.* Rotterdam: 010, 1989.

Vickery, Robert. "Bijvoet and Duiker." *Perspecta* 13/14 (1971): 130–161.

Dumas, Marlene (born 1953)

Born in Kaapstad, South Africa, Marlene Dumas attended the University of Kaapstad from 1972 to 1975, graduating with a B.A. degree in Visual Arts. During her education at Ateliers '63 in Haarlem in the years 1976–1978, her work became figurative. Early works are abstract sculptures, sometimes combined with photographs and drawings on paper, pasted, stapled, glued, or spelled with magazine photographs, photocopies, and other paper. In 1979–1980, she studied psychology at the University of Amsterdam. Since 1982 she has painted—using pictures of herself and persons from her surroundings—situations into which she projects her own emotions, as in the series of portraits *Martha* (1984), *The Jewish Girl* (1984), *The Space Age* (1984), and *The Occult Revival* (1984). In addition, there are works with a more art theoretical character, such as *The Futility of Artistic Confession* (1983).

She calls herself more of a sensualist than a stylist. "My best works are erotic displays of mental confusion (with intrusions of irrelevant information)," she said in 1985. Since 1987 she has created group portraits and nudes (Fig. 47), sometimes in combination, as in the series *Snowwhite* (1988). Since 1989 her portraits have included many mothers, children, and babies, sometimes in combination, sometimes in groups. Black and white and color play an important role in graphics, such as *Black Drawings* (1991–1992), and paintings like *The Blonde, the Brunette, and the Black Women* (1992). Works like *Straightjacket* (1993) were created on her visits to the patients in a psychiatric institution.

Dumas regularly publishes short art theoretical texts, in which she discusses the function of art, the meaning of works of art for herself, and the interpretation by others. A teacher at the Rijksacademie in Amsterdam, she has participated in group exhibitions such as *Documenta* 7 (1982) and 9 (1992), *Bilderstreit* (Cologne, 1989), and *The Broken Mirror* (Vienna, 1993). She also has had solo exhibitions, including *The Eyes of the Night Creatures* (Amsterdam, 1985), *Miss Interpreted* (Eindhoven, 1992), *Marlene Dumas/Francis Bacon* (Malmö/Turinø, 1995), and *Models* (Salzburg, Frankfurt am Main 1995).

John Steen

See also Contemporary art; Feminism, feminist issues

Bibliography

Dumas, Marlene, et al. *Marlene Dumas.* Bonn: Bonner Kunstverein; London: Institute of Contemporary Arts, 1993.

Schaffner, I. "Erotic Displays of Mental Confusion: Marlene Dumas in the Van Abbemuseum." *Kunst en Museumjournaal* 3 (1991/1992): 26–35.

Dupont, Pieter (1870–1911)

Pieter Dupont obtained a teaching credential in 1891 from the Rijksnormaalschool voor Tekenonderwijs (National Normal School for Drawing Teachers). Dissatisfied with teaching, he enrolled at the Rijksacademie in Amsterdam from 1889 until 1893. There he learned about the graphic arts, although the training he received concentrated on the reproductive function of graphic processes rather than on the production of original graphic art. The artist Maurits Willem van der Valk introduced Dupont to free graphic expression. On Van der Valk's recommendation Dupont went to Paris (1896–1900), where he discovered one of his most important themes—the horse. The workhorses on the banks of the river Seine captured his attention (Fig. 106); at first, he made a number of etchings with them as the subject. Later, he went further, using the almost-forgotten technique of copperplate engraving, a time-consuming graphic technique he learned in 1898 from the artist Carel Helweg. Dupont stayed on in France until 1903, living in Nogent-sur-Marne and Auvers-sur-Oise as well as Paris.

Once back in the Netherlands, he did portrait engraving and, among other things, also engraved stamps and banknotes for the Dutch government. From 1903 until his death in 1911, he held the position of professor of engraving at the Rijksacademie. Dupont created new interest in copperplate engraving in the Netherlands, and a number of graphic artists after him, among them Kuno Brinks, Debora Duyvis, and Engelina Reitsma-Valença, continue to work in this technique.

Maartje S. de Haan

See also Prints, modern graphic arts 1840–1945; Van der Valk, Maurits Willem

Bibliography

De Vries, R.W.P., Jr. *Nederlandsche grafische kunstenaars uit het einde der negentiende eeuw en het begin van de twintigste eeuw*. The Hague: Oceanus, 1943.

Dupont, W.F. *Pieter Dupont, een Nederlandsch graveur, zijn leven en werken*. Oisterwijk: Oisterwijk, 1947.

Kersten, Michiel. *De Nederlandse Kopergravure, 1900–1975*. The Hague: SDU, 1989.

Dutch history

How cultures account to themselves for their past has been a long-standing area of interest within the study of Dutch art. Johan Huizinga's essays on Dutch civilization in the seventeenth century and the large private collections of historical prints assembled during the nineteenth century (Amsterdam, Rijksmuseum, Muller collection) are representative of these interests among Dutch scholars. In the seventeenth century, Dutch artists, theorists, and collectors used the term history painting more broadly to define a highly valued category of art. Biblical or religious scenes, mythology, classical history, and literature, as well as allegorical subjects or histories, define its themes. Within that category, biblical scenes represented the largest component in Dutch seventeenth-century painting.

Within the extant paintings of the seventeenth century, representations of history are a small component. At Delft, the twelve hundred inventory records for 1610–1670 analyzed by John Michael Montias, show that no more than five percent of the recorded paintings fall in the category of "histories and allegories" for any one decade. Within the larger category of history painting, the same inventory studies show a steady reduction in numbers from one-third of all paintings recorded (1610–1619) to one-sixth by 1670. Although the Delft study represents only one city, the general decline in the larger category of history painting seems consistent with Dutch art as a whole.

It is important to recognize, however, that Dutch representations of history frequently occurred in other media (prints, coins, stained glass, pageantry). The categorization of these artists and media within the minor arts has left them relatively understudied, yet they are critical to an understanding of how history functioned in Dutch society. For instance, these alternative media have particular value for visualizing the experiences of the Dutch Revolt against Spain (1568–1648), where the economic costs and the destructive forces of warfare limited the potential for monumental art. Large-scale paintings for public or private buildings developed in the later seventeenth century after the conclusion of peace with Spain.

Civic pageantry, commemorative coins and prints, and stained glass often shared their pictorial language. The messages intended for Dutch communities vary, however, with the context in which they are presented. This pictorial language helped develop the conceptual models for the monumental art of the later seventeenth century. The visualized and verbalized theatrical language of the nonprofessional chambers of rhetoricians (*rederijkers*) provides another key to understanding

Dutch history and art. These groups consisted of nonprofessional playwrights, poets, and actors, who participated in civic festivals and competitions. Artists were often active participants within these organizations as well. The construction of narrative, the identification of characters (both historical and allegorical), the choices of language and audience all offer valuable points of comparison. Since their productions functioned primarily for a public and civic forum, they provide important documentation about contemporary Dutch society across classes.

The portrayal of the past brought its own difficulties for the Renaissance and Baroque artist. During the Renaissance, the artist's audience frequently operated out of a typological framework of historiography. This resulted in indirect references to contemporary events based, for instance, on biblical analogies. For instance, when Leiden donated a stained-glass window to the Gouda St. Jan's Church in the 1590s, the city fathers chose to represent the Spanish Siege of Leiden as the Siege of Bethulia. The visual message for the viewer conveyed the continuity of history through God's providence, not unlike the texts of Dutch city histories.

Representation of historical events unfamiliar to the artist through personal observation required using familiar visual traditions, as did the need to ensure the audience's comprehension. This suggests why traditions and conventions played such an important role for the depiction of history in art, and it allows a reconsideration of the role of artistic innovation within this genre. The retention of visual conventions formed a necessary control for the message's comprehension, and it often paralleled the image's message of historical continuity. Thus, the contexts and usage of the work of art formed a critical component in its interpretation and visualization.

The Dutch Revolt against Spain lasted for eighty years and spanned nearly half of the sixteenth and seventeenth centuries. Although monumental art referencing these events was relatively slow to develop for the reasons mentioned earlier, a variety of means were used to express these experiences, beginning with the sieges and battles of the 1570s. A few examples will demonstrate these relationships.

The visual convention of using personifications to represent provinces, such as the Dutch Maid, or Liberty, appeared during the 1570s in coins and prints. Coins used as counters in government offices, as commemorative medals marking an important treaty among the provinces, or as paper coins of necessity during sieges portrayed a seated maid in an enclosed garden, not unlike medieval Marian iconography. Civic or provincial coats of arms, identifying texts, or attributes (a hat for Liberty) gradually distinguished the figures. Familiarity with the images developed from the repetition and codification of motifs across the arts.

Key political figures like Willem I of Orange, considered to be the father of the country by many Dutch citizens, became associated with these personifications in monumental art. Thus Hendrick de Keyser's tomb of this assassinated leader (1614–1621; Delft, Nieuwe Kerk; Fig. 34) combines details of his lying-in-state with personifications of his ambitions for his country and his qualities as statesmen (Liberty and Justice, among others).

The linking of political narrative with the House of Orange was not the only means to represent the changing issues of political autonomy. By the mid-seventeenth century, for instance, images of Liberty appeared in relation to trade. The municipal government of Leiden ordered paintings from Abraham van den Tempel for the governor's room of the Lakenhal (Cloth Hall) in 1648. The themes represent the flourishing of the manufacture of *laken* (refined wool) at Leiden under the new conditions of peace. The Leiden City Maid, Wisdom (Minerva), and Cloth (Laken) Manufacture appear in the paintings to narrate the message of coming economic prosperity and civic pride.

The Dutch Revolt represents only one example of how history is portrayed within Dutch culture, but it exemplifies the conceptual issues that framed Renaissance and Baroque culture, which in later centuries was defended as the national heritage. Issues of artistic conventions and traditions, and the difficulties of identifying and codifying the past, suggest that the researcher must use inclusive resources that negate traditional boundaries between art, literature, and history to better clarify the relationships between artist, audience, and object.

Carol Janson

See also Coins, medals; Eighty Years' War; History painting; History portraits; House of Orange-Nassau; Huizinga, Johan; Nationalism; Prints, printmaking, and printmakers (ca. 1500–ca. 1900); Public monumental sculpture (ca. 1550–1795); Public monumental sculpture (1795–1990); Rhetoricians' chambers; Roman history; Stained glass; Tomb sculpture, early modern and later sepulchral art; Tomb sculpture, medieval effigial monuments; Town halls; War and warfare

Bibliography

Blankert, Albert. *Gods, Saints, and Heroes: Dutch Painting in the Age of Rembrandt*. Washington, DC: National Gallery of Art, 1980.

Huizinga, Johan H. *Dutch Civilization in the Seventeenth Century, and Other Essays*. New York: Harper and Row, 1969.

Montias, John Michael. *Artists and Artisans in Delft: A Socioeconomic Study of the Seventeenth Century*. Princeton, NJ: Princeton University Press, 1982.

Waal, H. van de. *Drie eeuwen vaderlandsche geschieduitbeelding 1500–1800: Een iconologische studie*. 2 vols. The Hague: Nijhoff, 1952. (English summary).

E

Eggers, Bartolomeus (ca. 1630–before 1692)

Perhaps the most prominent native Netherlandish sculptor of the second half of the seventeenth century, Bartolomeus Eggers received numerous civic, court, and private commissions. A self-avowed disciple of Artus I Quellinus (according to Nicolas Tessin's interview of 1687), he was also influenced by his major competitor, Rombout Verhulst. The lists of maquettes included in the three inventories of his studio (1681, 1687, and 1692) provide important documentation for the later years of his career.

Eggers, who was born in Amsterdam, may have studied (ca. 1646/1647) with Pieter Verbruggen the Elder in Antwerp. He later joined Quellinus' workshop (which included Verhulst) at the Amsterdam Town Hall, where he and his brother Jacob, also a sculptor, witnessed Quellinus' will in 1654. Eggers remained in Amsterdam, where he married in 1662 and became a member of the Guild of St. Luke in 1663. By 1665 he was resident in The Hague, producing garden sculpture for Johan Maurits van Nassau in a workshop located in the Mauritshuis. His most important commission from this period is the memorial for the admiral Jacob van Wassenaar-Obdam (completed 1667; The Hague, Grote Kerk), executed after sketches by the local painter Cornelis Monincx. In comparison with contemporary monuments for naval heroes by Verhulst, Eggers' mausoleum, which is based on that of Willem I of Orange in Delft, is artistically and iconographically uninspired. The contrast between the two sculptors is even more pronounced in Verhulst's monument (completed by 1669) for Carel Hieronymus, Baron van In en Kniphuisen and his wife, to which Eggers added a standing effigy of her second husband (before 1692). Eggers also executed sculpture for the façade of the *waag* (weigh house) in Gouda (completed 1669), and that of the stock exchange in Amsterdam (1670). From 1662 he received numerous commissions from Count Friedrich Wilhelm of Brandenburg, including series of busts of emperors (1674), figures of empresses (1682), and alabaster figures of the counts of Brandenburg (1686–1688), as well as garden sculpture (such as his *Rape of Proserpina*, ca. 1680) for the palace in Berlin.

Cynthia Lawrence

See also Quellinus, Artus I; Sculpture (1550–1795); Tomb sculpture: early modern and later sepulchral art

Bibliography
Leeuwenberg, J., and W. Halsema-Kubes, eds. *Beeldhouwkunst in het Rijksmuseum*, 321–322. The Hague: Staatsuitgeverij, 1973.

Neurdenburg, E. *De zeventiende eeuwsche beeldhouwkunst in de Noordelijke Nederlanden: Hendrick De Keyser, Artus Quellien en Rombout Verhulst en tijdgenoten.* Amsterdam: Meulenhoff, 1948.

Eighty Years' War

In 1568 the seven provinces of the Northern Netherlands entered into a conflict with Spain that ended in 1648 with the recognition of the Dutch Republic as an independent nation. Images generated during this revolt reflected not only the violent aspects of war, but also the more routine. The length of the war—eighty years—and the changes in warfare implemented at the time brought about transformations in the way society and the military interacted, ultimately influencing representation in art. Although the war fought mainly on land did not usually touch the daily lives of people in the maritime provinces of the Northern Netherlands, exposure to the art produced in the major cities in the seventeenth century did constantly impress upon citizens of the United Provinces the ongoing circumstances of the conflict. In addition to the more established subjects of battles, skirmishes, and plundering, Dutch artists focused on the intimate and leisurely activities of the soldiers encamped before a siege.

The Eighty Years' War was primarily a conflict involving long sieges marked by limited skirmishes, ambushes, and raids with few major battles. Despite the fact that battles were a rarity, a popular subject for artists such as Pauwels van

Hillegaert in the early part of the seventeenth century was the famous Battle of Nieuwpoort in 1600. Surprisingly, the inconsequential battle between Bréauté and Lekkerbeetje on Vucht Heath in the same year was depicted in an extraordinary number of prints and paintings by various artists. Prints, pamphlets, and illustrated histories helped disseminate information about sieges and battles, even though they were not always the most decisive events of the war. These images are typical small-scale battle scenes in which the general confusion of fighting between cavalry forces is conveyed using a large number of figures in a landscape.

Early in the war, extreme animosity toward the Spanish took the form of the Black Legend, which greatly affected written histories. Generated by the supposed atrocities against the Dutch army and civilians in Haarlem, Maastricht, Oudewater, and Naarden, this anti-Spanish propaganda possibly influenced the images of plundering and violence of the countryside that came to be known as *boerenverdriet* (peasant sorrow). The Dutch army was also guilty of committing brutal acts early in the war. While artists in Flanders depicted the theme in fairly violent terms, the artists of the Northern provinces produced subdued versions. By the time the subject was depicted by Esaias van de Velde and Joost Cornelisz. Droochsloot after the Twelve Years' Truce (1609–1621), the war had moved farther south and the situation of war had changed. Plundering and ransoming were still a legitimate part of warfare, but early in the war, Prince Maurits had instituted severe military codes to limit excessive behavior. In the paintings, soldiers of unspecified allegiance display booty or take prisoners, but the violence has diminished. Although the memories of former cruelties may have inspired such images, the realities of a more controlled, disciplined, and organized army moderated the conception of the theme for Northern artists.

Discipline was especially crucial during the Eighty Years' War because extended sieges meant long, tedious periods of waiting for the troops. Civilians were most familiar with these soldiers in guardrooms and encampments who amused themselves with gambling, drinking, and smoking. In the many siege paintings produced by artists such as Van Hillegaert, and the related depictions of generic encampments by Philips Wouwerman later in the century, the ordinary activities of camp life with the soldiers, their families, and the numerous camp followers became commonly represented (Fig. 152).

What characterizes many of these intimate views of camp life as well as depictions of skirmishes, plundering, and raids is their tendency to be only generalized references to warfare. Instead of representing actual events from the Eighty Years' War, artists were more often motivated by news of the events and the presence of soldiers to produce small cabinet pieces portraying contemporary conflict of an unspecified nature.

Although there is an extraordinary amount of historical research dealing with the Eighty Years' War, scholarship concerning artistic responses to it has been neglected. A few dissertations have covered selected artists who specialized in painting soldiers or smaller themes related to the war, but many other areas still need to be studied.

J.M. Kennedy

See also Dutch history; Soldiers; War and warfare; Wouwerman, Philips

Bibliography

Fishman, Jane Susannah. *"Boerenverdriet": Violence between Peasants and Soldiers in Early Modern Netherlands Art.* Ann Arbor, MI: UMI Research Press, 1982.

Groenveld, S., and H.L.P. Leeuwenberg. *De bruid in de schuit: De consolidatie van de Republiek 1609–1650.* Zutphen: Walburg, 1985.

Groenveld, S. et al. *De kogel door de kerk? De Opstand in de Nederlanden en de rol van de Unie van Utrecht 1559–1609.* Zutphen: Walburg, 1979.

Emblems and emblem books

Emblems, which consist of a motto, a picture, and a subscript that together convey the meaning of the whole, became the rage in Europe in the sixteenth century and remained extraordinarily popular for well over one hundred fifty years. The production of emblem books, which after 1535 was the greatest in Germany and the Netherlands, reached flood-like proportions and it has been estimated that six hundred authors creating two thousand titles produced a million volumes. In addition, emblematic devices appeared in stained-glass windows, tapestries, jewelry, paintings, architecture, theatrical props, and street processions.

One of the reasons that emblems became so popular is that they responded to a fascination with the hermetic and a taste for riddles, puzzles, word plays, and other exercises for one's ingenuity. In principle, the meaning of the emblem was not to be immediately accessible but was to be arrived at only after the viewer/reader had grasped the significance of the interplay between the motto (*lemma, inscriptio*), the image or picture (*pictura*), and the subscript (*subscriptio*). Exactly what each part consists of and how it relates to the others is the subject of dispute among scholars. Heckscher and Wirth (1967), for example, state that the motto and image, when viewed together, must create an enigma that can be resolved only by the subscript. Albrecht Schöne, on the other hand, avoids a narrow definition of each part and allows for a flexible interrelationship among the three parts in creating the meaning. As Daly (1979) explains, Schöne asserts that any part may participate in either or both of the emblem's dual functions of representation and interpretation, description and explanation. Thus, the motto or inscription, which is often a proverbial statement or maxim, may name the object represented in the image, and the subscript, the primary purpose of which is interpretive, may also include a representative function.

The first emblem book was Andrea Alciati's *Emblematum liber*, which was initially unillustrated but which was subsequently provided with images in several editions, the first being the Augsburg edition of 1531 issued (without Alciati's approval) by Heynrich Steyner. Steyner added the prints in order to assist the less well-educated reader and thus created the acknowledged model for the emblem book. The first emblem book printed in the Netherlands and printed in Dutch was *Tpaleys der gheleerder ingienen*, a translation of G. De la

Perrière's *Le théatre des bons éngins*. This book, described by its author as one hundred moral figures, was printed in Antwerp in 1554 and played an important role in the development of Netherlandish emblem literature. Moreover, the French origin of the work and the fact that it was translated by a *rederijker* (rhetorician) make it indicative of the early phase of emblem production in the Netherlands, during which the influence was from France and the first enthusiasts were printers and *rederijkers*. Emblems appealed immediately to the latter, who already had a predilection for pictorial as well as verbal puzzles and for word and image interplay. The commercial interest of the printers caused the rapid proliferation of emblem books, and some, like Christopher Plantin, were personally interested. Porteman (1977) notes that Plantin and the humanist circle around him already showed a concern for the less-learned reader and a preference for the moralizing aspirations of the genre, two factors that were to be of great significance for the later evolution of emblem literature in the Netherlands.

The first distinctively Netherlandish genre, the love emblem, however, was more elitist than popular. Emblem books focusing on the theme of love originated early in the seventeenth century and flourished, especially in the Northern Netherlands where they contributed to the renewal of literature in Amsterdam and Leiden during the first two decades of the century. A collaboration of fine artists, such as Jacob de Gheyn II, Crispijn de Passe I and his sons, and Adriaen van de Venne, with virtually all who achieved literary fame at the time (Pieter Cornelisz. Hooft, Gerbrand Adriaensz. Bredero, Daniel Heinsius, Hugo Grotius, Otto van Veen) produced works of high quality. Many of the books, like Hooft's *Emblemata amatoria* (1611), were printed in several languages, to appeal to an international market. It is worth noting that books by Heinsius and Van Veen had an impact on *galant* (elegant) cultural life and that their emblems appear as wall decorations in France and Germany, a circumstance that supports Porteman's contention that this is one of the few periods when Netherlandish literature can be considered international. Hooft's *Emblemata amatoria*, while appealing to an international audience, also contains elements that lead toward a distinctively Dutch character. It moves away from the more classical mode favored by Van Veen toward a modernization and, if one may use the term, Hollandization of the emblem that reached fruition in the work of Jacob Cats. Cats' *Silenus Alcibiadis Sive Proteus*, printed in 1618, includes each emblem three times, and each time it is given a different meaning. The first is about love, the second is moralizing, and the third is religious. Subsequent editions united all three meanings under one image to stress that the reader is to progress from the love association, through the moralizing, to the religious, which is the ultimate goal. This conception reflects Cats' moralizing orientation. The emphasis on the moralizing element along with the increasingly realistic manner of representation in the plates paved the way for the flowering of the realistic emblem.

Both the emphasis on moral instruction and the interest in being accessible to a broad and less educated audience char-acterize the realistic emblem book that flourished in the Northern Netherlands in the seventeenth century. Indeed, the realistic variant of the vein of didactic emblem literature can be considered a Dutch contribution. These works generally draw their material not from mythology or ancient history but from daily life and ordinary experience, and their plates usually present familiar things in a believable way. These books are also distinguished by the unusually high quality of the prints, images created by artists like Claes Jansz. Visscher and Adriaen van de Venne. The first of these books is Roemer Visscher's *Sinnepoppen*, printed in Amsterdam in 1614. Visscher's images are presented directly and simply but not all of the subjects are familiar nor are all of the meanings easily determined. Other works in this category include Johan de Brune's *Emblemata of zinnewerk*, printed in 1624, and Jan van der Veen's *Zinnebeelden oft Adams Appel*, printed in 1642. By far the most popular author, however, was Cats, who produced numerous books, among them *Spiegel van den ouden ende nieuwe tijdt*, which was printed in 1632. Cats' works combined Renaissance learning and popular intelligence, and, in this way, they speak to all. While the subscripts of verse and/or prose text are often long, involved, and bear witness to Cats' somewhat pedantic erudition, the pictures sometimes present the meaning of the whole by themselves or occasionally function as mere illustrations to the text. Thus, the meaning of Cats' emblems is often readily accessible, a trait that they share with others in this category and that leads some to consider them a degenerate form of emblem. Cats' works were reprinted repeatedly and remained popular into the eighteenth century.

The high point of the works produced during the last half of the seventeenth century are the pietistic emblem books of Jan Luyken, who, with his son Caspar, continued to produce emblems into the eighteenth century. The high quality of these books is exceptional during this period. After the middle of the seventeenth century the texts become increasingly derivative, indicating the beginning of a decline. In the eighteenth century, the habit of associating meaning with objects of experience, the emblematic mode of thought, gave way because it was not suited to the prevailing view of the world and reality.

The thought grew out of both Neo-Platonism and traditional forms of biblical exegesis. Emblematists applied medieval techniques of biblical exegesis to all objects of history and creation, thus making all things carriers of meaning. Moreover, they continued to give things a variety of meanings, both positive and negative. To what degree, however, the method of giving meaning and the relationship between the veiled meaning of the emblem and the medieval conception of creation as containing a hidden message for man reflect the persistence of a medieval world view is another matter. Some see seventeenth-century Dutch culture as the end, the last flowering, of the medieval tradition and cite as evidence the propensity for seeking out deeper meaning in everyday things or using such things as vehicles for ready-made ideas. They assert that the concept of *ut pictura poesis*, which likens painting to poetry, was central to the culture and that a great many paintings function like emblems; their true meaning is veiled and not immediately accessible.

In order to discover the meaning of seventeenth-century Dutch paintings, especially genre scenes, Eddy de Jongh, who along with Jan Emmens pioneered this approach, argues that the works must be decoded. Toward this end, he has examined paintings in the context of contemporary language, prints with inscriptions, and literature—especially emblem books—and thus has greatly enriched our understanding of these works. However, this approach is not without its problems, one of which is the way in which emblem books are used in deciphering paintings. Among the dangers is the risk of losing sight of the work as a whole and considering it as an assemblage of objects, all of which are of equal importance and all of which have meanings that can be uncovered by matching them with emblems. Moreover, when one finds the various objects reproduced as emblems, one must then determine which of the often contradictory meanings presented by various emblems or within the same emblem are relevant to the work. To minimize error, De Jongh (1967) explains, one must pay attention to the calculated position of the emblematic objects within the work (being alert to anything that is unnatural) and consider them in relationship to both a complete program and a fixative element, which determines how the work, and hence the various features within it, are to be read. The last does not always exist, and then the viewer is left with a choice of interpretations. One also must compare the work to similar works ("Pearls of virtue, pearls of vice," *Simiolus* 8 [1975/1976]: 69–97). Nonetheless, however the method is applied, problems inherent in the broader implications of the approach remain.

The vast majority of seventeenth-century Dutch paintings were destined for an anonymous public. Therefore, it is unlikely that an artist would create a work whose meaning could be deciphered only by those familiar with particular emblems. Moreover, this approach fails to consider sufficiently that paintings convey meanings differently from both prints with inscriptions and emblems, and it seeks the key to the meaning of the work outside of the painting, which can lead to the application of meanings not intrinsic to the work. For example, as Bedaux (1990) points out, Jan van Bijlert's *Merry Company* (ca. 1630–1635; Utrecht, Centraal Museum) does not warn of the transience of life nor refer to man as being caught between God and the devil, despite the close resemblance between the detail of the two hands pulling on a pretzel and the picture of Johan de Brune's emblem that conveys this message. The scholar interpreting the work in this way was looking for the meaning of the work in a text and thus failed to perceive that it is visually evident in the painting. The woman pulls the pretzel with two fingers, while her male companion uses only one. The artist indicates that this detail is significant by including a man who holds up a pretzel with two fingers and looks directly at the viewer, thus drawing attention to himself and the way that the pretzel is held. The woman who holds the pretzel with two fingers is cheating at the game, and this establishes women's wiles, not the plight of the human soul, as the theme of the picture (Bedaux, 1990: 76).

Clearly, one must remember that paintings construct

meaning very differently from emblems and prints with inscriptions. These meanings must be sought in the visual presentation of the material, the visual traditions and conventions with which the subject of the work is related, and the context of the whole. Emblems, like other forms of literature, language, and prints with inscriptions, can play an important role in interpretation by providing a cultural context. These forms of evidence attest to the currency of particular maxims, metaphors, and attitudes and thus help support arguments about the kind of association that the work was intended to evoke in the mind of the viewer.

The emblematic mode of thought was still much in evidence in seventeenth-century Dutch culture, and one should be attuned to the possibility that paintings may include elements that are to be understood metaphorically and that they may allude to things outside themselves. However, one must remember that paintings are visual constructs, not realized abstractions, and that, intended for an anonymous audience, the associations they evoke are likely to be general rather than specific, readily accessible (to those familiar with the culture and the traditions) rather than arcane.

Barbara Haeger

See also Allegorical traditions; Art history, history of the discipline; Genre painting, eighteenth century; Genre painting, seventeenth century; Humanism, humanist themes; Literature, poetry: analogues with the visual; Rhetoricians' chambers

Bibliography

Bedaux, Jan Baptist. *The Reality of Symbols: Studies in the Iconology of Netherlandish Art, 1400–1800.* The Hague and Maarssen: Gary Schwartz/SDU, 1990.

Daly, Peter M. *Emblem Theory: Recent German Contributions to the Characterization of the Emblem Genre.* Nendeln/Liechtenstein: KTO Press, 1979.

Dickey, Stephanie S. "'Judicious Negligence': Rembrandt Transforms an Emblematic Convention." *Art Bulletin* 68 (1986): 253–263.

Heckscher, W.S., and K.A. Wirth. "Emblem, Emblembuch." In *Reallexikon zur Deutschen Kunstgeschichte.* Vol. 5, cols. 85–228. Stuttgart: Alfred Druckenmuller Verlag, 1967.

Henkel, Arthur, and Albrecht Schöne. *Emblemata: Handbuch zur Sinnbildkunst des XVI und XVII Jahrhunderts.* Stuttgart: J.B. Metzlersche Verlagsbuchhandlung, 1978.

Jongh, E. de. *Zinne- en minnebeelden in de schilderkunst van de zeventiende eeuw.* Amsterdam: Nederlandse Stichting Openbaar Kunstbezit, 1967.

Landwehr, John. *Emblem Books in the Low Countries, 1554–1949.* Utrecht: Haentjens, Dekker, and Gumbert, 1970.

Porteman, K. *Inleiding tot de Nederlandse Emblemataliteratuur.* Groningen: Wolters-Noordhoff, 1977.

Praz, Mario. *Studies in Seventeenth-Century Imagery.* Rome: Edizioni di Storia e Letteratura, 1964.

Renger, Konrad et al. *Die Sprache der Bilder: Realität und Bedeutung in der Niederlandischen Malerei des 17.*

Jahrhunderts. Brunswick: ACO Druck GMBH, 1978.

Engebrechtsz. (or Engelbrechtsen), Cornelis (1468–1527)

A painter active in Leiden, Cornelis Engebrechtsz. was notable for his development of a refined late-Gothic style and for his establishment of a painting workshop in the early sixteenth century. His mature works exhibit a distinctive blend of native Dutch narrative interests and the rhythmic energy of Antwerp Mannerism.

Some scholars have suggested that he was a pupil of the Brussels painter Colijn de Coter, but the extension of Engebrechtsz.'s *oeuvre* back into the 1490s with works such as the *Crucifixion* (Amsterdam) makes it possible to characterize his earliest style as clearly Dutch, without the Flemish influence that appears somewhat later in his career.

Two of the four works described in the seventeenth century by Van Mander (1936), the *Lamentation* and *Crucifixion* triptychs in Leiden, are still extant in their entirety and formed the basis for later attributions. There has been disagreement about dating, but the *Lamentation* was probably painted ca. 1508 in what Gibson (1977) calls the first phase of Flemish influence on Engebrechtsz.'s career (ca. 1500–1510). The interweaving of surface patterns, thick, weighted drapery, and quiet yet emotionally intense poses suggests an awareness of the school of Rogier van der Weyden in Brussels, where Engebrechtsz. might have traveled ca. 1500–1505.

Another stylistic shift took place in the 1510s, under the influence of Antwerp Mannerism, and continued through the 1520s. In the Leiden *Crucifixion* (ca. 1510–1520) the composition is more complex and fluid than in the earlier *Lamentation*, and the figures are more graceful and active in their emotional display. The decorative details of costume and setting, which also can be seen in *Constantine and Helena* (ca. 1517; Munich), further underscore Engebrechtsz.'s relationship with Antwerp Mannerism, although his concern for organizational clarity distinguishes him from the cluttered turbulence of many Antwerp paintings.

Engebrechtsz.'s workshop helped establish Leiden as one of the most important artistic centers of the early sixteenth century in the Northern Netherlands. According to Van Mander, his pupils included Lucas van Leyden and Aertgen van Leyden as well as Engebrechtsz.'s three sons, Pieter, Cornelis, and Lucas Cornelisz.

Elise Lawton Smith

See also Flanders, Flemish School; Leiden; Van Leyden, Aertgen (Aert Claesz.); Van Leyden, Lucas

Bibliography

Bangs, Jeremy D. *Cornelis Engebrechtsz.'s Leiden*. Assen: Van Gorcum, 1979.

Friedlander, Max J. *Early Netherlandish Painting*. 14 vols. New York: Praeger, 1967–1976.

Gibson, Walter. *The Paintings of Cornelis Engebrechtsz.* New York: Garland, 1977.

Hoogewerff, G.J. *De Noord-Nederlandsche Schilderkunst*. 5 vols. The Hague: Nijhoff, 1936–1947.

Mander, Carel van. *Dutch and Flemish Painters*. Edited and translated by Constant van de Wall. New York: McFarlane, Warde, McFarlane, 1936.

Erasmus, Desiderius (died 1536)

Though the Dutch humanist Desiderius Erasmus did not, like his contemporary Martin Luther, break with the Catholic Church, the religious climate of his day troubled him deeply. The concerns he shared with the German monk and other reformers included the use of religious images. But like Luther, Erasmus never penned a single comprehensive statement of his views on images; instead, discussions of the subject occur as aspects of larger topics in his work.

While references to art appear in numerous writings by Erasmus, three works in particular contain substantial passages: his treatise on marriage (*Instituto christiani matrimonii*, 1526), that on prayer (*Modus orandi Deum*, 1524), and, finally, his response to both sides of the Reformation debates (*Liber de sarcienda Ecclesiae concordia*, 1533). Important passages also occur in the *Enchiridion militis christiani* (1504) and in *Praise of Folly* (1511). In these texts, Erasmus reveals that he was not an iconoclast. But he sharply criticizes many contemporary practices regarding images.

Erasmus believed that art could serve religion well as a means to educate and to inspire piety. He was even willing to tolerate some works and practices he found questionable, such as carrying statues of saints in processions, because he believed that their elimination would cause more problems than their continued use. But he condemned idolatry and superstitious belief in the magical properties of images; devotion given to images and saints more properly belonged to Christ. Erasmus also attacked certain subjects and modes of depiction as unacceptable.

In particular, the Dutch humanist denounced subjects such as the Seven Falls of Christ and the Seven Swords (or Sorrows) of the Virgin as human fabrications not founded on Scripture. He abhorred contemporary images of biblical subjects such as David and Bathsheba, and the Dance of Salome, that presented them in a lascivious manner, maintaining that all Christian subject matter is chaste by nature. He similarly objected to images that portrayed saints as drunks or whores. In addition, Erasmus objected to detailed depictions of Heaven and Hell that emphasized the physical nature of torments and joys, presenting them in concrete, everyday terms that trivialized the notions of damnation and blessedness (Color Plate 1).

Scholars have also seen Erasmus' religious writings as influential for contemporary art in a broader sense. The numerous depictions of the Calling of St. Matthew may echo his call for Christians to renounce material wealth. The art of his friend Quinten Massys in particular seems to interpret visually many of the ideas associated with the humanist and his circle. Erasmus' discussions of the Virgin's humility, St. Jerome's meditation on Death, and St. Mary Magdalene's identity and character appear to inform Massys' depictions of those figures. The artist's secular paintings seem to share with

Praise of Folly an interest in instruction through ridicule.

The learned Dutchman's writings also reveal the importance of portraits for himself and other Northern humanists. Scholars have observed that such portraits, commonly exchanged among Northern humanists, helped strengthen the web linking members of the far-flung intellectual community. These portraits often depart from earlier portrait conventions in ways that reflect humanist concerns. Thus Erasmus and his circle helped establish new approaches to portraiture.

Janey L. Levy

See also Humanism, humanist themes; Nationalism

Bibliography

Collected Works of Erasmus. Toronto: University of Toronto Press, 1974–[ca. 1995].

Panofsky, Erwin. "Erasmus and the Visual Arts." *Journal of the Warburg and Courtauld Institutes* 32 (1969): 200–228.

Silver, Larry. *The Paintings of Quinten Massys, with Catalogue Raisonné.* Montclair, NJ: Allanheld and Schram, 1984.

Vlam, Grace A.H. "The Calling of St. Matthew in Sixteenth-Century Flemish Painting." *Art Bulletin* 59 (1977): 561–570.

Exotica

The exotic in Dutch art refers to (1) the presence in Dutch painting of non-Western objects, including flora, fauna, even human beings; and (2) the conscious acceptance and application of non-Western stylistic elements and techniques. These two aspects do not necessarily go hand in hand; in the history of Dutch art, exotic object-possession preceded by several centuries the more philosophical possession of non-Western artistic vision and/or technique.

Exotic object-possession is rooted in the desire to know all about God's creation. This encyclopedic attitude was already cultivated throughout the Middle Ages in the compilations of such authors as Pliny the Elder, Isidore of Seville, and Vincent of Beauvais, as well as in *herbaria* (books of plants), *bestiaria* (books of animals), and *lapidaria* (books of gems). In the sixteenth century—the age of global discovery—the encyclopedic attitude expanded to embrace the spectacular new discoveries in the world, and found tangible expression throughout Europe in a fury of collecting exotica preserved in *Kunstkammern* and *Wunderkammern* (collections of art and curiosities). These collections included *naturalia* (shells, flora, and fauna), antiquities and man-made creations, and *ethnographica* (artifacts of other cultures), and were amassed by European royalty. This fury of collecting did not as yet have the stigma of vanity attached to it, for the royal princes considered it their duty to gather and study the riches of the earth. They found ecclesiastical precedence for it in the frequently depicted topos of the Adoration of the Magi. It is in paintings of this subject that some of the first exotica appear. Royal collectors employed painters (for example, Joris Hoefnagel) to depict as accurately as possible such *naturalia* of limited life

span as live animals and plants. Even some artists became collectors (Albrecht Dürer in Germany, Jacob de Gheyn II, Rembrandt van Rijn in the Netherlands). In this manner painters developed their own encyclopedic view of the world.

Appetite was whetted by oral accounts and published illustrated travel descriptions of non-European places (Jan Huyghen van Linschoten's *Itinerario* of 1592), which, accompanied by exotic specimens, stimulated trade and acquisition.

After its declaration of independence from Spain (1579), the Northern Netherlands established its own trade routes and commerce connections in Asia and America. Consolidation of individual enterprises led in 1602 to the founding of the Dutch East India Company (V.O.C.) with markets in India, Persia, the Moluccas, Java, China, and Japan; in 1621 the West India Company began trading in the Caribbean and Brazil. A flood of exotic *naturalia*, artifacts, and *ethnographica* entered Dutch ports, flowing immediately into the subject matter of much seventeenth-century Dutch painting. Regarded with scientific curiosity, these exotic objects became integrated into a cohesive epistemological system, at the forefront of which stood still-life painting. Still lifes can be considered small-scale, "instant" *kunstkammern* for Dutch citizens, who had adopted the collecting habits of sixteenth-century monarchs, as they enjoyed a high standard of living (Fig. 90). Besides still-life painting, genre painting was the second most popular category in the seventeenth century. It frequently included *exotica*, even into the eighteenth century. Also included in this encyclopedic epistemology are the "scientific" landscapes by Dutch painters visiting Brazil and Indonesia (Frans Post, Albert Eckhout).

The interest in and study of *exotica* continued into the eighteenth century, where it is best expressed in scientific-book publications, illustrated with engravings that combine art and science. Furthermore, *exotica* were applied to interior decoration of the Dutch home (wallpapers, ceramic tile, upholstery, and furnishings).

In more than three hundred years of exposure to exotic products and Oriental art, Dutch artists, with the exception of Rembrandt, were never inclined toward adoption and/or adaptation of non-Western ways of seeing and composing. This did not begin to happen until the last two decades of the nineteenth century, after the Japanese woodcut had become widely known in Europe. However, its influence, called *Japonisme*, was mainly operative in France, where Vincent van Gogh experienced and embraced it. His contemporaries in the Netherlands had much less exposure to Japanese woodcuts, mainly in the 1890s, and absorbed Japanese stylistic elements indirectly through the works of Degas, Gauguin, and Bernard, or the Art Nouveau applied arts. Through the international Art Nouveau style, *Japonisme's* impact on artistic expression continued in early-twentieth-century ceramic, graphic, and commercial art, and in women's fashions. As public consciousness and appreciation of exotic cultures were raised through the establishment of ethnological museums in Leiden, Amsterdam, and Rotterdam, and artists became more personally involved with Asiatic philosophies and cultural practices, such as Zen, absorption of Oriental style and technique became more widespread and was more convincingly expressed in the latter part of the twentieth century.

Grace A.H. Vlam

See also Applied arts; Ceramics; *Japonisme*; Natural history illustration; Non-Western cultural influences; Still life; Trade, exploration, and colonization overseas

Bibliography

Bergvelt, E., and R. Kistemaker, eds. *De wereld binnen handbereik: Nederlandse kunst- en rariteitenverzamelingen 1585–1735.* 2 vols. Amsterdam: Amsterdams Historisch Museum; Zwolle: Waanders, 1992.

Freedberg, David, and Jan de Vries, eds. *Art in History, History in Art: Studies in Seventeenth-Century Dutch Culture.* Santa Monica, CA: Getty Center for the History of Art and the Humanities, 1991.

Lach, Donald F. *Asia in the Making of Europe.* 3 vols. Chicago: University of Chicago Press, 1965–1992.

Montias, J.M. "Review of *De wereld binnen handbereik: Nederlandse kunst- en rariteitenverzamelingen 1585–1735.*" *Simiolus* 22 (1993/1994): 99–105.

Wichmann, Siegfried. *Japonisme: The Japanese Influence on Western Art in the Nineteenth and Twentieth Centuries.* New York: Harmony Books, 1981.

F

Feminism, feminist issues

Vrouwenkunstbeweging (**Women in the Arts Movement**)
In the wake of the women's movement at the end of the 1970s, a flourishing Women in the Arts Movement developed in the Netherlands. In criticism of the established cultural institutions with their one-sided policies set up for men, women artists organized numerous initiatives and women art historians arranged exhibitions in alternative spaces—in women's center bookstores, and cafés. A number of organizations and institutions played a conspicuous role in this: the Amsterdam Foundations Amazone (Amazon) and Stichting Vrouwen in de Beeldende Kunst (Foundation for Women in the Visual Arts); the Stedelijk Museum in Gouda; and the Gemeentemuseum in Arnhem.

Amazone, founded in 1977 in Amsterdam, regarded art as a means to individual growth and self-reflection. Besides offering legal and psychological assistance, cultural workshops and lectures, the foundation organized exhibitions in which themes such as housekeeping, menstruation, femininity, and part-time work were illuminated through works of art and photographs. In the first years, especially, the foundation was concerned with raising consciousness about the social position of women; after 1985 the emphasis was on the presentation of theme exhibitions about women and culture, such as female choreographers, *Women in Dada, Myths, Women and Design,* and autobiographies by women artists.

One of the most important driving forces in the Dutch women's art movement is the Stichting Vrouwen in de Beeldende Kunst (SVBK). The SVBK was established in 1977 in answer to the poor socioeconomic position of women artists and the underrepresentation of their work in exhibitions and public collections. By means of exhibitions, conferences, a library, an extensive archive, the publication of the topical, bilingual art magazine *Ruimte* (since 1983), and awarding the Judith Leyster Prize (since 1987), the SVBK has made known the work and the problematic position of female artists. In 1978 the foundation published the report *Een leuke hobby heb je* (A Fun Hobby You Have) that contained the first concrete

information about the professional position of contemporary women artists. The report, based on an investigation, laid bare the prejudice against the professionalism of women artists. It was followed, in 1985, by *Het 'kleine verschil' in het beeldende kunstbedrijf* (The "Little Difference" in the Visual Arts Business), a publication about their socioeconomic position.

The organization moved up to the firing line with the controversial two-part exhibition and publication *Feministische Kunst Internationaal* (Feminist Art International) in 1978–1979, in which forty European and American women artists took part with well over ninety works. The selection committee (Liesbeth Brandt Corstius, Josine de Bruyn Kops, Marlite Halbertsma, Rosa Lindenburg, Din Pieters, Margriet van Boven, Wies Smals, and the artist Wies de Bles) reemphasized the importance of the content side of art as a reaction to the masculine approach, which would be much more directed toward the form. Three themes were central: the social division of sex roles; inquiry into the feminine self; and utopias and fantasies. Moreover, existing opinions about what art ought to be and the boundary line between art and life were put to discussion. The selection committee presented films, videos, and performances in the Foundation de Appel (by the Americans Betsy Damon and Mary Beth Edelson, the Germans Ulrike Rosenbach and Valie Export, and the Dutch artist Lydia Schouten, among others). The second part of the exhibition, consisting of sculpture, drawings, photographs, and installations (by Miriam Cahn, among others), traveled after 1979 to six museums. These noteworthy exhibitions provoked vehement discussions—something any curator in the engaged 1990s would only be jealous of. The attempt to stretch the existing notion of art and the plea for the revaluation of female creativity were nevertheless stifled in the press, which criticized the feminist message and the quality of the art works.

The criticism affected in a negative way the image of the SVBK, which since then has been associated—wrongly—only with "feminist art" and navel-staring. With this excuse, many critics and curators could bring criticism in sex-specific terms that included judgments of quality, and ignore the disproportionate representation of female artists.

In 1987 the SVBK reopened public discussion on this subject with the international symposium *The Art Machine: Exposure on the Art Scene* and a number of exhibitions of historical and contemporary art. The symposium, on the occasion of the tenth anniversary of the foundation, did not shun critical dialogue: Opponents were invited as members of the forum and as guest speakers. The symposium took place in, among other spots, the Stedelijk Museum in Amsterdam, ironically the same museum that was the first target "stormed" with balloons by the SVBK in 1979 on account of a discriminatory museum poster. The topic of the symposium was the position of the female artist in the established art world. Statistical research into the acquisitions and exhibition policies (from 1977 to 1987) of five large modern-art museums in the Netherlands gave the lie to the general opinion that female artists had at last penetrated the established cultural institutions.

Despite all of the public discussions, exhibitions, and publications, the Women in the Arts Movement was received with many of the same opposing arguments as in other countries: It was working to "ghetto-ize" art and to harm so-called autonomous judgments of artistic quality. This is not preventing Amazone and the SVBK, together with other women's organizations dedicated to film, literature, or music, from opening in 1995 the Landelijk Centrum voor Vrouwen in de Kunsten (National Center for Women in the Arts). The center, located in Amsterdam, will organize exhibitions, symposia, and classes.

Forming Collections

Two museums have distinguished themselves through their preferential policy with regard to the work of female artists. Josine de Bruyn Kops, on becoming director (1976–1986) of the municipal museums in Gouda, initiated a preferential policy for female artists; the Stedelijk Museum in Gouda has ninety percent of its acquisitions budget reserved for the purchase of contemporary works by women artists. The collection of mainly Dutch artists contains works by Marjolein van den Assem, Helen Frik, Hieke Luik, and Elizabeth de Vaal.

The director of the Arnhem Gemeentemuseum (now the Museum of Modern Art), Liesbeth Brandt Corstius, has also applied a quota in exhibitions and collection policies since her appointment in 1982: At least fifty percent of the participants in exhibitions are women and a same percentage of the acquisitions budget for the contemporary-art collection is set aside for work by female artists. The international collection is built up around the theme of art and reality and includes works by, among others, Alice Aycock, Ania Bien, Barbara Bloom, Miriam Cahn, Marlene Dumas (Fig. 47), Fortuyn/O'Brien, Kinke Kooi, Maria Roosen, Lydia Schouten, Lily van de Stokker, and H.W. Werther.

Research: Images of Women and Individual Women Artists

Stimulated by the stream of feminist art-historical publications from the United States, England, and Germany, the first seminars on women's studies/art history were organized in Dutch universities in 1977, most of them initiated by the students. The emphasis in women's studies/art history lay not so much on research about "versatile" women artists, their work and/or the social-historical context as it did in the analysis of the image of woman in the work of male artists within particular movements or periods. A systematic research program was lacking, however, until, in an interdisciplinary context, the theme of women and culture was made part of the syllabus that was developed in women's studies literature under the leadership of Professor Rosi Braidotti at the University of Utrecht.

Research into the representation of women and femininity in Dutch art resulted in the publication of Debora Meijers' *De Vrouw een godin, de kunst een god: Over vrouwenstudies en het symbolistisch vrouwbeeld* (Woman a Goddess, Art a God: On Women's Studies and the Symbolist Image of Women) (Den Helder: Talsma and Hekking, 1980), and in theme exhibitions in museums and accompanying publications, such as *De kunst van het moederschap: Leven en werk van Nederlandse vrouwen in de 19e eeuw* (The Art of Motherhood: The Lives and Work of Dutch Women in the Nineteenth Century) by Liesbeth Brandt Corstius and Cora Hallema (Haarlem: Frans Hals Museum, 1981).

In *Romantische liefde: Een droombeeld vereeuwigd* (Romantic Love: A Vision Immortalized) (Marjan Rinkleff, ed., Arnhem: Gemeentemuseum; Nijmegen: SUN, 1985), the ideal of romantic love and marriage was analyzed on the basis of eighteenth- and nineteenth-century Dutch art. The shift in the late-medieval image of woman and, especially, the moralizing view in the fifteenth and sixteenth centuries were central in *Tussen heks en heilige: het vrouwbeeld op de drempel van de moderne tijd* (Between Witch and Saint: The Image of Woman on the Threshold of Modern Time) organized by Petty Bange, et al., with catalog by Ellen Muller (Nijmegen: Nijmeegs Museum Commanderie van Sint Jan, 1985) as well as in *Helse en hemelse vrouwen: Schrikbeelden en voorbeelden van de vrouw in de christelijke cultuur* (Hellish and Heavenly Women: Images of Evil and Exemplary Women in Christian Culture) (Marlies Caron, ed., Utrecht: Rijksmuseum Het Catharijneconvent, 1988).

Though in all these analyses the image of woman was related to the social-historical context, and in this sense was a criticism of the current art-historical knowledge, the approach became at the same time characterized by a rather static presentation of woman as mother versus woman as whore. In more recent studies there is more attention to multiple interpretable layers of meaning in images of women, such as in *Bruiden des doods* (Brides of the Dead), about *fin-de-siècle* images of women, by Ulrike Weinhold (1989). In *Contact en controle: Over het vrouwbeeld van de Stichting Goed Wonen* (Contact and Control: The Image of Women by the Goed Wonen Foundation, 1992), Wies van Moorsel analyzed the image that emerged from the ideology of the Goed Wonen (Good Living) Foundation (1946–1968); the foundation drew on the movement of Het Nieuwe Bouwen and combined the objective of improvement of interior design with traditional family-mindedness. Dissertations underway in the 1990s in the Netherlands analyze the construction of femininity and masculinity in the *Andachtsbilder* of Anselm Feuerbach (by Miriam van Rijsingen) and the relationship between nature, femininity, and art in German Romantic theory (by Paulien Kintz).

Investigation into the work, the reception, and the position of twentieth-century women artists got started comparatively late in the Netherlands. Notable publications and accompanying exhibitions include the monographs *Charley Toorop* by Marja Bosma (Utrecht, Centraal Museum, 1982) and *Lou Loeber: Utopie en werkelijkheid* by Marente Bloemheuvel (Laren, Singer Museum, 1993).

In *Een beeld van een vrouw: Nederlandse beeldhouwsters uit de school van Bronner,* edited by Jane van Balen-Swets (Amsterdam: Dekker, 1988), interviews and analyses of art criticism are the basis for focusing on the work and the position of nine female sculptors from the Rijksacademie in Amsterdam in the 1920s and 1930s. The women, including Nel Bakema, Corinne Franzén, Nel Klaassen, and Loeki Metz, formed part of a class taught by Jan Bronner, who stressed the relationship between sculpture and architecture. The investigation goes into the significance of the traditional working method of the female sculptors with respect to their position: They had to fight against the idea that women would be too weak or not creative enough for the profession of sculptor. This made them especially motivated to show that they had really mastered the craft. The choice of a traditional working method had to do with this, for in this tradition distinct criteria for quality existed.

In *Bloemen uit de kelder* (Flowers from the Cellar), edited by Anneke Oele, Miriam van Rijsingen, and Hesther van den Donk (Arnhem: Gemeentemuseum, 1989), a light was shined on the reception and the work of nine female painters active around 1900: Maria Bilders-van Bosse, Lucie van Dam van Isselt, Anna Julia de Graag, Sina (Sientje) Mesdag-van Houten, Coba Ritsema (who belonged to the group of women artists in Amsterdam known as De Joffers), Suze Bisschop Robertson, Margaretha Roosenboom, Thérèse Schwartze, and Maria Vos. In the series *"Was getekend . . ."* ("Signed . . ."), edited by Nio Hermes (Amsterdam: Stichting Amazone, 1990), autobiographical statements by Charley Toorop and Jacoba van Heemskerck, among others, were analyzed.

The work of female artists who were active after World War II has been published, especially, in the form of *oeuvre* and exhibition catalogs. These include *Theresia van der Pant* by Riet van der Linden, Roos van Put, et al. (The Hague: SDU, 1989); *Else Berg* by M. Hoogendonk, et al. (Haarlem: Frans Hals Museum, 1989); *Ferdi Tajiri* by Alexander von Grevenstein and Hans Janssen (Maastricht: Provincie Limburg, 1991); *Loes van der Horst* by Roos van Put et al. (Amsterdam: Judith Leyster Stichting, 1991); and *Pearl Perlmuter* by Mirjam Western and Brigitta vaan Blitterswijk (Amsterdam: Meulenhoff-Landshoff, 1988). The art magazine *Ruimte* (editor Riet van der Linden), published in Dutch and English, offers much current information about contemporary women

artists. Also appearing in its issues are considerations of such themes as multiculturalism, art and technology, and the body.

Mirjam Westen

See also Art history, history of the discipline; Artists' initiatives; Dumas, Marlene; Fortuyn/O'Brien; Leyster, Judith; Robertson, Suze Bisschop; Schwartze, Thérèse van Duyl; State and municipal art collecting and collections; State patronage, public support; Toorop, (Charley) Annie Caroline Pontifex; Women artists

Bibliography

Buikema, R., and A. Smelik, eds. *Vrouwenstudies in de Cultuurwetenschappen.* Bussum: Coutinho, 1993.

Halbertsma, Marlite. "Vrouwenstudies kunstgeschiedenis: Een paradigmatische wending?" *AKT: Aktueel Kunsttijdschrift* 14 (1990): 3–15.

Hollema, C. "Talent alleen is niet genoeg." *Jaarboek voor Vrouwengeschiedenis* 3 (1982): 11–35.

Linden, Riet van der. "Vrouwenbeweging en beeldende kunst." In *Vrij Spel: Nederlandse kunst, 1970–1990.* Edited by Willemijn Stokvis and Kitty Zijlmans, 239–261. Amsterdam: Meulenhoff, 1993.

Top, Titia. *Art and Gender.* Groningen: Universiteit van Groningen, 1993.

Venema, A. *De Amsterdamse Joffers.* Baarn: Wereldvenster, 1977.

Westen, Mirjam. "Kunsthistorikerinnen und Künstlerinnen in den Niederlanden: Forschung, Projekte, Politik." *Kritische Berichte* 18 (1990): 85–92.

Vries, Maud de, ed. *Publieke vrouwen: Zinnebeelden in de openbare ruimte.* Amsterdam: Amazonereeks/In de Knipscheer, 1994.

Fernhout, Edgar R.J. (1912–1974)

Edgar Fernhout grew up surrounded by famous Dutch artists such as Jan Toorop, Charley Toorop, Gerrit Rietveld, and John Raedecker. He started drawing and painting while still very young and was self-taught. On the advice of art critic H.P. Bremmer (1871–1956), he concentrated on still life. In 1930–1931 he was in Paris, in the midst of an international avant-garde movement. Piet Mondrian had a lasting influence on his work. In 1932 Fernhout settled in Amsterdam and had his first solo exhibition at art dealer Carel van Lier's gallery.

Already in his early work, Fernhout combined abstraction and realism. Light, color, and space perform an essential function in his work. His *oeuvre* developed thematically from the studio to nature; it also includes self-portraits as a painter. From 1936 to 1939 Fernhout was in Italy, but he returned to the Netherlands at the beginning of World War II in September 1939. He survived the war partly because of portrait commissions. In 1954 he stopped doing self-portraits and studio still lifes. After the death of his mother, Charley Toorop, in 1955, he moved to De Vlerken in Bergen and began drawing and painting the natural surroundings of the studio: woods, polder, dunes, beach, and sea. Although his work became gradually more abstract, the observation of nature remained essential. In the beginning he reproduced objects, as in *Stronken en net* (Tree Stumps and Net, 1957). After 1958 he produced a yearly cycle of paintings entitled *Voorjaar, Zomer, Herfst*, and *Winter* in which the alterations of light, color, and space are represented in the changing of the seasons. In 1967 he became a teacher at Ateliers '63 in Haarlem, and in 1968 he was active in the students' protest. His works since 1968 are square monochrome canvases on which rectangular color blocks glitter in a special way, partly because of the simultaneous color contrast.

John Steen

See also Mondrian, Piet; Raedecker, John; Toorop, Charley (Annie Caroline Pontifex); Toorop, Jan

Bibliography

Berk, A. van der et al. *Edgar Fernhout: Schilder/painter.* The Hague: SDU; Amsterdam: Nederlandse Stichting Openbaar Kunstbezit, 1990.

Cammelbeeck, G.J.P. *Edgar Fernhout.* Amsterdam: Meulenhoff/Landshoff, 1969.

Films, filmmaking

It was only after World War II that a permanent moving-picture industry was established in Holland. During World War I, a number of major films were released by the Hollandia Film Company. Competition from abroad became too fierce after the war, however, and Hollandia foundered in spite of the favorable reception of its films among the Dutch people. Hollandia's history proved that the domestic market was too small to provide a profitable base of operations.

From 1927 onward the Dutch Film League (De Nederlandsche Filmliga) promoted avant-garde films from France, Germany, and the former Soviet Union, and these inspired Joris Ivens (1898–1989) and others to make documentaries. The Netherlands acquired international renown for this genre of film, which was less expensive to make and for which it was easier to find sponsors. Since 1956 government subsidies have provided funds for the sponsoring of film productions. However difficult and discouraging the system of subsidies is at times, it, in principle, provides filmmakers the opportunity to work out a project. Although every film is, therefore, highly personal, Dutch motion pictures have some things in common. Most subjects depicted, such as life in and after World War II, are adapted from modern Dutch novels by Jan Wolkers, Willem Frederik Hermans, Harry Mulisch, Gerard Reve, and Hugo Claus. Often encountered is a preoccupation with mortality, individual human nature, personal identity, and ethical responsibility, although such themes are, of course, not exclusively Dutch. A touch of Surrealism is to be found in the more recent Dutch films.

Before World War II

The film industry in Holland began much like it had in many other countries: at fairgrounds or in vaudeville theaters, where self-made "documentaries" were shown by their makers. Anton Nöggerath Sr. produced one of the first Dutch feature films known at present: *William III Visits the Amsterdam Vondel Park* (1899). He also filmed the festivities surrounding the coronation of Queen Wilhelmina in Amsterdam in 1898. Willy Mullens, made the fictional *The (Mis)Adventures of a French Gentleman without his Trousers on the Beach at Zandvoort* in 1905.

In 1912 Maurits Binger founded the Hollandia Film Company in Haarlem. Before World War I, his studio, which had a big staff, produced a large number of short subjects, the so-called wooden shoe-and-windmill films. During World War I, the Netherlands retained its neutral status and Dutch films received popular acclaim. Binger, influenced by the French Film d'Art, started directing and producing longer films, with Annie Bos as his preferred star. He and the other directors—Johan Gildemeijer (who made the remarkable opera-film *Gloria Transita* in 1917) and Theo Frenkel Sr. (*The Wreck in the North Sea*, 1917)—had high hopes for the future of the Dutch film industry once the war ended. In 1918 Hollandia released *The Good Hope*, based on a well-known Dutch play by Herman Heijermans. Within Holland it was considered the best Dutch film until then.

After the war, however, the export of Dutch films did not match the expectations of the producers. Foreign investments did not return the expected profits, and the domestic market was too small to cover expenses. As a result the Hollandia Film Company nearly went bankrupt in 1919. The less expensive but important documentary department, which had produced *The State Mines* (1917), became independent. The motion-picture department fused with an English production firm. This Anglo-Hollandia Film Company continued to produce films until 1923 but never attained the level of the old Hollandia. Apart from documentaries by Willy Mullens, Otto van Neijenhoff, and Polygoon (the documentary department of the former Hollandia Film Company), very few films were made until 1929.

In 1927 the Dutch Film League was founded to promote film as an autonomous art. Unlike the owners of the large movie houses and the entertainment industry, the Film League imported avant-garde films from Germany and France, as well as Soviet productions other than those by Sergei Mikhailovich Eisenstein and Vsevolod Pudovkin, whose work was already shown, or planned to be exhibited, in the big cinemas. Eisenstein, Pudovkin, and Dziga Vertow visited the Film League, however, to introduce their work personally. Among its founders were Joris Ivens and Mannus Franken, who showed their first films, *The Bridge* (Ivens, 1928), *Rain* (Franken/Ivens, 1929), and *Le Jardin du Luxembourg*, (Franken, 1929) to the members of the Film League. The Film League triggered a significant number of Dutch documentaries, characterized by a rhythmic montage and made in a realistic documentary style inspired by an internationalist consciousness. Also screened by the Film League were such "scientific" movies as *Crystals* (*Uit het rijk der Kristallen*, 1927) by J.C. Mol. Outside the Film League, Max de Haas and his production company, Visie, made several documentaries according to the same avant-garde principles, such as *Torchlight Procession* (1932). Jan Hin shot his *Turn of the Tide* (*Kentering*, 1932) and other documentaries commissioned by Catholic organizations from a Roman Catholic perspective.

The film critics who promoted the film as art form supported these documentaries; because they feared that the primacy of the image would be undermined, they also continued to promote the silent film after the first sound films came to the Netherlands in 1929. A few filmmakers continued to produce silent documentaries long after this date. Ivens and Lou Lichtveld were, however, among the first to take a chance with sound and made *Philips Radio* as early as 1931.

A revival of the Dutch feature film can be discerned after about 1934, due to the introduction of sound and the arrival of German film directors who had fled the Hitler regime. The Dutch public had become more and more aware that there were none of the new sound films that were made in their own language. This was one of the causes of the revival. Another was the arrival of German immigrants, who actually directed the best Dutch feature films produced during this period. Kurt Gerron (*Mystery of the Moonlight Sonata*, 1935), Max Ophüls (*A Comedy about Money*, 1936), Ludwig Berger (*Pygmalion*, 1937), and Detlef Sierck (Douglas Sirk) (*Boefje* [*Scoundrel*], 1939) showed themselves equal to Dutch directors, like Gerard Rutten (*Dead Water*, 1934) and Charles Huguenot van der Linden (*Young Hearts*, 1935). These films were much appreciated by their audience, who nevertheless also liked the minor Dutch comedies such as *De Jantjes* (*The Bluejackets*, 1934) and the so-called Jordaan films—named after a working-class neighborhood in Amsterdam. All of these activities ended when the Germans occupied Holland in May 1940.

During the war the "Film Guild" was installed, and the former documentarian and director of *William of Orange* (1934), G.J. Teunissen, became head of this department of the "Chamber of Culture." Every filmmaker who wanted to continue to work legally was required to be registered with this organization. The Jewish population of Holland was not allowed to stay in business, and later was largely deported to the German concentration camps. Among them was the most important prewar theater owner, Abraham Tuschinski. Dutch filmmaking during this period was controlled by the German Universum Film Aktiengesellschaft (UFA).

Documentaries

After the war, the devastated Dutch film industry had to start all over again. Ivens was *persona non grata* because he had sided with the Indonesian cause in making *Indonesia Calling* (1946). He lived abroad afterward and was not rehabilitated until 1985. His apprentice John Ferno (*Sky over Holland*, 1967) and filmmakers Henk van der Horst (*Faja Lobi*, 1960) and Charles Huguenot van der Linden (*Big City Blues*, 1962) continued to work in the Dutch documentary tradition, each in his own manner. Bert Haanstra learned the trade abroad, and his documentaries are considered the best of their type: *Mirror of Holland* won the Cannes Grand Prix in 1951 in the short-film category and *Glass* (1957) became world-famous after winning an Academy Award in 1960. Haanstra's human touch imbues all of his work with a distinctive quality that is also to be seen

in his feature films. Jan Vrijman (*The Reality of Karel Appel*, 1962) was the *enfant terrible* of the postwar documentary. In his 1964 release *Blind Child*, Johan van der Keuken revealed his personal approach to the world as a perplexed observer of reality, a viewpoint developed progressively in his later work, including *Face Value* (1991). He and Bert Haanstra are considered the most important Dutch makers of the documentary film. Documentaries made for television by Cherry Duyns, Hans Keller, and Emile Fallaux, however, equal cinematic quality.

From 1987 onward, Amsterdam has been host to the International Documentary Festival (IDFA), which aims to bring the documentary back to the cinema and has installed the Joris Ivens Award. It also allows young talents to show their work and to take part in workshops supervised by prominent Dutch documentary filmmakers.

Major Motion Pictures

It was some time after World War II before the first Dutch motion pictures were released. Ironically, the first films brought out were directed by Germans (for example, Wolfgang Staudte, *Ciske de Rat*, 1955). In 1955 Bert Haanstra made *Fanfare;* Fons Rademakers, who was also trained abroad, made his debut with *Village on the River* in 1958. Also in 1958, the Dutch Film Academy (NFA) was founded. Its first students formed the Dutch *nouvelle vague*, or, "First Wave." The magazine *Skoop*, which they founded in 1964, published their manifesto: "We need continuous motion-picture production."

Frans Weisz (*Illusion Is a Gangster Girl*, 1965), Nikolai van der Heijde (*A Morning of Six Weeks*, 1966), Pim de la Parra (*Obsessions*, 1968), Wim Verstappen (*The Less Fortunate Return of Josef Katusz to the Land of Rembrandt*, 1966), and Nouschka van Brakel (*Sabotage*, 1967) were influenced by the French *nouvelle vague* of Jean-Luc Godard, François Truffaut, and the criticism of the French film industry published in the journal *Cahier du Cinema* in the 1950s. They breathed new life into the Dutch film industry. Their roughly framed and cut films with improvised acting based on constantly changing scripts—or no script at all—were dismissed by conservative film critics who still used criteria rooted in prewar Film League ideology. With the exception of the work of Adriaan Ditvoorst (*That Way to Madras*, 1965; *Paranoia*, 1967), which earned awards at several international festivals, these films remained unknown outside of Holland.

Pim de la Parra and Wim Verstappen, who founded their own production company, Scorpio Film (1965–1976), created jobs in filmmaking and provided opportunities to learn the trade by producing a large number of low-budget movies, filmed with hand-held cameras on location, in accordance with their motto: "Ten bad movies are preferable to no movies at all." Their trademark was nudity; in 1971 they released *Blue Movie*, which incensed Dutch morality and at the same time constituted a turning point in the popularity of the Dutch film.

From the 1970s on, there has been a professionalized mainstream, a "producers' cinema." Many of the names associated with it can be traced back to the First Wave cinema. The

1970s were dominated by films produced by Rob Houwer, Matthijs van Heijningen, and Rob du Mée, who collaborated with successful directors and stars like Willeke van Ammelrooy, Monique van der Ven, Rutger Hauer, Peter Faber, and Jeroen Krabbé. Fons Rademakers made *Mira* (1972) and *Max Havelaar* (1977). In 1973 Paul Verhoeven made *Turkish Delight*, the biggest Dutch box-office success ever. Verhoeven earned international renown with *The Fourth Man* (1983) and became a successful Hollywood director, responsible for such productions as *Robocop* (1987) and *Basic Instinct* (1992). He was not a graduate of the Dutch Film Academy and despised art films and the atmosphere surrounding them. His experience was mainly in television work: the serial *Floris*, a Dutch *Ivanhoe*. Frans Weisz (*The Burglar*, 1972), Nikolai van der Heijde (*Help, the Doctor Is Drowning!*, 1974), Nouschka van Brakel (*The Debut*, 1977), and Wim Verstappen (*Pastorale 1943*, 1978, starring Renée Soutendijk, "the face of the Eighties") also rejected the idiom of French *nouvelle vague* and turned to the commercially more successful sex star and action formula. Adriaan Ditvoorst (*The Blind Photographer*, 1972) did not embrace commercial success and remained an individualistic outsider until the end; his last film was *White Madness* (*De Witte Waan*, 1984). Jos Stelling, who was self-taught, suddenly appeared on the scene with the impressive *Mariken from Nieumeghen* (1974), based on a play written in the Middle Ages and performed exclusively by amateurs. René van Nie made his *Anna, Child of the Daffodils* in 1974; in 1975 Herbert Curiël made *Cancer Rising*, which was produced by George Sluizer, who released *Twice a Woman* (1979) himself.

Although the 1970s were the first time that Dutch films had been more popular with the public than foreign films, the Dutch critics still gave them a cold shoulder. Critical opinion finally changed in the 1980s with Frans Weisz's *Charlotte* (1981), at a time when theater audiences were again on the wane. In 1980 Dutch Film Days were founded as a festival to promote the Dutch film and at which Golden Calf Awards are given in various categories. After 1980 an increasing number of films combining quality and popularity appeared in the theaters. More female directors entered the field: Marleen Gorris' *A Question of Silence*, Annette Apon's *The Waves*, Lili Rademakers' *Minuet*, and Mady Saks' *Dreamland* all date from 1982. New names like Pieter Verhoeff (*The Dream*, 1985), Ben Verbong (*The Girl with the Red Hair*, 1981), Ate de Jong (*A Flight of Whimbrels*), Orlow Seunke (*A Taste of Water*, 1982), Leon de Winter (*The Border*, 1984), Rudolf van den Berg (*Bastille*, 1984), Theo van Gogh (*A Day at the Beach*, 1984), and Alex van Warmerdam (*Abel*, 1986) made their films in very individual styles and with varying success. Jos Stelling altered his style in *The Illusionist* (1983). Pim de la Parra returned to his "no-budget" concept of what he calls "Minimal Movies." Dick Maas (*The Elevator*, 1983; *Flodder*, 1986) also founded his First Floor Productions during the 1980s. Guido Pieters made remakes of *Ciske de Rat* (1984) and *The Good Hope* (1986). Also in 1986, Fons Rademakers, the first Dutch motion-picture director after the war, won an Academy Award for the Best Foreign Film, *The Assault*. In

1988 George Sluizer directed *The Vanishing* after a story of Tim Krabbé; in 1992 it was badly remade in Hollywood. Although not all Dutch films meet these international standards, continuous production has been achieved and will not likely disappear.

Animation and Experimental Cinema
The development of Dutch animated films took another course than that of the feature film: from commercial studio-oriented production to an individual mode of production, from entertainment to art, instead of the other way around. Prior to World War II, Georg Pal had already made commercials. His work was carried forth by the Toonder Studio, which dominated the industry after the war until 1973. In that year Holland Animation was founded, an organization representing the independent makers of animated films at festivals abroad and at a biennial festival in the Netherlands. Ronald Bijlsma (*Brainwash*, 1973), Paul Driessen (*The Writer*, 1988), and Börge Ring, whose *Anna and Bella* won an Oscar in 1984, belong to the best animation artists. In 1983 the first full-length animation feature was released: *If You Know What I Mean*, after Marten Toonders' cartoons.

Between 1968 and 1971 Frans Zwartjes produced twenty-three short films, including *Eating* (1971). In 1976 he made *It's Me*, a close observation of actress Willeke van Ammelrooy. His *Pentimento* (1979) and *In Extremo* (1981) are full-length features, but no less extreme in conception. Lacking any formal training, Zwartjes developed a completely independent style, influenced by performance art instead of film conventions. His experiments in developing also resulted in powerful images. Eric de Kuyper, both a filmmaker and a film theoretician, made his debut with *Casta Diva* of 1983. Although highly intellectual, his films can be considered a very personal tribute to Hollywood melodrama.

Art Houses and International Festivals
When during the 1970s Dutch film production grew more professional, the second generation of students of the Dutch Film Academy focused on the "alternative circuit" of noncommercial modes of film production and distribution. Ideologically they were supported by the magazine *Skrien*, founded by students of the NFA in 1968. In the Free Circuit, noncommercial and political movies and videos were encouraged and members strove to establish theaters independent of the commercial distribution system. The Free Circuit activities (later known as the Association of Dutch Film Theaters, ANF) have undermined the "closed shop" system of distribution and screening.

Huub Bals, who was the initiator of art houses and the Rotterdam International Film Festival (1972–), initially found himself caught between the commercial and more rigid noncommercial circuits. He was not especially preoccupied with the Dutch film as such or with any ideology other than that of the "good" film. He altered the history of Dutch film culture by having introduced, since 1960, over two hundred cineasts and their films from all over the world into the Netherlands. Bals died in 1988; since 1990 his work at the Rotterdam Film Festival has been carried on by Emile Fallaux. The festival also sponsors young talents who work in the Netherlands, such as Alessandro Agresti (*Secret Wedding*, 1989) and Peter Greenaway (*Drowning by Numbers*, 1988).

Ansje van Beusekom

See also Rotterdam; Toorop, Charley (Annie Caroline Pontifex); World Wars I and II

Bibliography

Beerekamp, Hans, and Jan Heys. *Netherlandscapes: Eighty-Five Years of Dutch Filmmaking.* New York: Amsterdam Foundation for Cultural Exchange [between] The Netherlands-USA, in association with the International Film Circuit, 1989.

Cowie, Peter. *Dutch Cinema: An Illustrated History.* London/New York/The Hague: Tantivy Press, A.S. Barnes. Ministry of Culture, Recreation, and Social Welfare, 1979.

———, ed. *Variety International Filmguide.* London/Hollywood: Andre Deutch, Samuel French (published annually).

Dibbets, Karel. *Sprekende films: De komst van de geluidsfilm in Nederland 1928–1933.* Amsterdam: Otto Cramwinckel, 1993.

Dibbets, Karel, and Frank van der Maden, ed. *Geschiedenis van de Nederlandse film en bioscoop tot 1940.* Weesp: Wereldvenster, 1986.

Dittrich, Kathinka. *Achter het doek: Duitse emigranten in de Nederlandse speelfilm in de jaren dertig.* Weesp: Wereldvenster, 1987.

Donaldson, Geoffrey N. *Filmography of Dutch Silent Fiction Film.* Amsterdam: Nederlands Filmmuseum, 1996.

Gelder, Henk van. *Holland's Hollywood.* Amsterdam: Luitingh/Sijthoff, 1995.

Hogenkamp, Bert. *De Nederlandse documentaire film 1920–1940.* Amsterdam: Stichting Film en Wetenschap and Van Gennep, 1988.

Stevens, Matthew. *Directory of Contemporary Dutch Films and Filmmakers.* Trowbridge UK: Flicksbooks, 1990.

Vincendeau, Ginette, ed. *Encyclopedia of European Cinema.* New York: Facts on File, 1995.

Flanders, Flemish School

The complex and changing artistic relationships between the Northern and Southern Netherlands have yet to be adequately studied. In general, between 1400 and about 1585, Dutch painters and printmakers sought inspiration, and often employment, in the artistic centers of the South. In the decades around 1600, however, many Flemish artists emigrated northward, where they interacted with native artists to create the Dutch Golden Age.

Any survey of this subject must begin with a definition of the geographical areas involved. The North comprises what is now the Kingdom of the Netherlands; the South is equated with modern Belgium. Originally the Netherlands consisted of a heterogeneous collection of provinces, of which the most powerful were Flanders, Brabant, and Holland, that only gradually came under the control of the dukes of Burgundy and their Hapsburg successors. This region was split by the Eighty Years' War (1568–1648) into an independent, largely Protestant United Provinces dominated by Holland and including part of Brabant, and a Catholic Southern Netherlands ruled by Spain and later by Austria.

Until this separation, the major political, cultural, and commercial centers of the Netherlands lay in the Southern provinces of Flanders and Brabant; here also were the largest centers of artistic production and patronage, drawing many artists from the North. Jan van Eyck, for example, began his career at the court of Holland at The Hague, but entered the service of Duke Philip of Burgundy in 1425 and moved south, ultimately settling in Bruges. It was a fateful move. Not only did Van Eyck join Robert Campin and Rogier van der Weyden to found the fifteenth-century Flemish school of painting, but through his associations with the Burgundian court and its international connections, Van Eyck's art entered the mainstream of European painting.

Further discussion of Dutch–Flemish artistic relationships is complicated by attempts to discern a characteristically "Dutch" style in fifteenth-century Northern painting, especially in Haarlem. Petrus Christus, born in Baerle, near the present Belgian–Dutch border, worked in Bruges from 1442 on, as the chief successor to Van Eyck. Dirck Bouts, born in Haarlem, settled in Louvain in 1447–1448. Christus cannot be considered "Dutch," but because he and Bouts show stylistic affinities with Albert van Ouwater of Haarlem, it is sometimes assumed that Christus and Bouts trained in Haarlem and, together with Van Ouwater, form an "early Haarlem School," displaying "Dutch" sensibilities, particularly in the handling of space and landscape, qualities that Christus and Bouts later introduced into Flemish painting. This primacy of Haarlem is rejected by Geyl (1959) and other scholars who insist that the "Haarlem" style, including the work of Van Ouwater, was actually derived from Flemish sources (Van Eyck, Van der Weyden), and that efforts to isolate specifically "Dutch" qualities at this early date are anachronistic. But while the existence of a fifteenth-century "Dutch" style is thus disputable, significant differences can nonetheless be observed between Flemish and Dutch painting even this early. Flemish painters show a somewhat greater stylistic uniformity; Dutch painters tend to exhibit more individual characteristics, although very often influenced by the Southern Netherlands. An example is Geertgen tot Sint Jans, a pupil of Van Ouwater. Even if he was not the "Gheerken de Hollandere" registered in 1475 in the manuscript illuminators' guild at Bruges, his highly distinctive style was nevertheless influenced by Van der Weyden and particularly Hugo van der Goes. The Master of the Virgin among Virgins, who conducted a sizable workshop at Delft, shows stylistic connections with Joos van Ghent (Joos van Wassenhove), and it is suggested that he worked in Ghent before coming north. More problematic is the Master of the Tiburtine Sibyl; although related stylistically to Bouts at Louvain and the Haarlem artists, his connection with both places is unclear. The case of Hieronymus Bosch is even more complicated. His native town, 's Hertogenbosch, was then in the Duchy of Brabant, but Bosch displays many affinities of style and expression, particularly in his earlier work, with Utrecht and the Northern Netherlands in general, and he is rightly considered a Dutch artist. Nevertheless, his later paintings show his familiarity with Flemish art, especially that of Hugo van der Goes.

It is occasionally suggested that Bosch traveled to Southern Brabant and Flanders, but he may have seen Flemish models closer to home. Indeed, certain Flemish compositions must have circulated in the North fairly soon after their creation. Thus Campin's *Descent from the Cross* (ca. 1428–1430) inspired a miniature in the *Hours of Catherine of Cleves*, executed only a few years later by the unknown master illuminator of the book.

How these and other compositions were transmitted we can only guess, but this does suggest how Gerard David might have encountered Flemish art before he left his native Holland to settle in Bruges in 1484. His earliest works, presumed by some scholars to have been painted in Haarlem, show Geertgen's strong influence combined with reminiscences of Campin, Van Eyck, and Van der Weyden. In Bruges, where he succeeded Hans Memling, David fused the tradition of Van Eyck and Memling with his own Haarlem manner to create what has been called a perfect balance of "Dutch" and "Flemish" qualities.

In the early sixteenth century, Antwerp quickly became the major center of Flemish painting, influencing many artists from the North. Among the Dutch painters emerging around 1500, both Jacob Cornelisz. and Jan Mostaert developed Geertgen's style into a decorative, occasionally overwrought, Mannerism that in their later work rendered them susceptible to the stylish elegance of the so-called Antwerp Mannerists, active from about 1505 on. No visit south is recorded for Cornelisz., but Mostaert worked as a portraitist for Margaret of Austria, governess of the Netherlands, between 1516 and 1526. What time, if any, he spent at Margaret's court in Mechelen, we do not know, and we can only guess why she favored Mostaert over the more fashionable painters of the South. Cornelis Engebrechtsz. was the Dutch artist of this generation most responsive to Flemish art. His essentially Dutch early style was first modified by the art of Colijn de Coter, with whom he may have worked in Brussels. His later paintings show the pervasive influence of Antwerp, especially the Antwerp Mannerists, perhaps through the mediation of an artist erroneously identified as Jan Wellens de Cock, who more plausibly was one of Engebrechtsz.'s sons.

For Lucas van Leyden, Engebrechtsz.'s most famous pupil, two trips to the Southern Netherlands, in 1521 and 1527–1528, proved decisive. Not only was he introduced to Flemish painting, especially that of Gossaert, his traveling companion on his second trip, but he also encountered the art of Raphael, available in the prints of Marcantonio Raimondi and particularly in the Vatican cartoons, then in Brussels. Raphael's compositional methods influenced his late works, and in this respect, Lucas' two Flemish excursions served as substitutes for the Italian journeys of his two Dutch contemporaries Jan van Scorel and Maerten van Heemskerck.

Some Dutch painters settled more or less permanently in Antwerp in the early decades of the sixteenth century. They include Jan Mandyn from Haarlem and two artists from Amsterdam, Pieter Aertsen, who became a pupil of Mandyn, and Jan van Amstel (also known as the Brunswick Monogrammist), possibly Aertsen's brother. What "Dutch" qualities these artists brought with them cannot be determined; Van Amstel's art, in fact, has been linked with that of the Bruges manuscript painter Simon Bening. However, it is likely that Antwerp's international art market encouraged these Dutch expatriates to specialize in subject matter that would not have been feasible at home. Mandyn produced pictures in the style of Bosch, and Van Amstel painted biblical and tavern scenes teeming with small, well-articulated figures. Aertsen earned fame for his still lifes, market scenes, and pictures of peasant revelries. Returning to Amsterdam in the mid-1550s, Aertsen and his sons continued to paint the subjects he had introduced in Antwerp.

The two major Dutch painters of the mid-century, Van Scorel and Van Heemskerck, were oriented toward Italy almost to the exclusion of current Flemish art. Even though Van Scorel was briefly Gossaert's pupil in Utrecht (1517) and in 1550 collaborated with the Bruges painter Lanceloot Blondeel in cleaning the *Ghent Altarpiece*, Flemish influence is restricted chiefly to his spacious background vistas, which occasionally reflect the landscapes of Joachim Patinir and his followers at Antwerp (Fig. 67). Van Heemskerck's connections with Antwerp were more crucial. Many of his designs were engraved at Antwerp by printmakers in the employ of Hieronymus Cock, the most important print publisher in Northern Europe. Other Van Heemskerck designs were engraved or etched at Haarlem by Dirck Volkertsz. Coornhert. While Coornhert seems to have published some of these plates in Haarlem, others were shipped south to Cock. Especially through his association with the Antwerp book publisher Christopher Plantin, Cock had access to foreign markets probably not readily available to Haarlem. Indeed, Antwerp's international contacts undoubtedly attracted earlier Dutch printmakers such as Cornelis Bos, active there between 1540 and 1544, when he was exiled on religious grounds, and Cornelis Cort, who worked for Cock before departing for Italy around 1565. After Cock's death in 1570, his major successor in Antwerp was Philips Galle of Haarlem. Antwerp's virtual monopoly in print publishing was broken only after 1582, when Hendrick Goltzius founded his own enterprise at Haarlem. He was followed by many other Dutch print publishers, including his own stepson, Jacob Matham, and, above all, Claes Jansz. Visscher, whose family dominated the print trade in Holland for most of the seventeenth century.

By the later sixteenth century, traditional artistic ties between North and South were changing radically as a result of the Eighty Years' War, especially after the fall of Antwerp to Spanish troops in 1585. In search of employment no less than religious freedom, many Flemish artists emigrated to Holland, either directly or after a period of activity elsewhere. To cite only a few major names, they included Hans Roelandt

Gillis van Coninxloo, both from Antwerp; Roelandt Savery and his brother Jacob the Elder, natives of Courtrai; and Jacob de Gheyn II, whose father had left Utrecht a generation earlier to work as a painter in Antwerp. Many Flemish emigrés ultimately settled in Amsterdam and The Hague, but almost every Dutch city had its Flemish contingent.

The contributions of these Flemish emigrants to Dutch art cannot be underestimated. The architect Lieven de Key of Ghent, for example, became the town architect of Haarlem, where he designed a number of buildings. Karel van Mander, born near Courtrai, composed his *Schilder-Boeck* (Book on Picturing, 1604) and his theoretical treatises on art while living in Haarlem and Amsterdam. But the most pervasive Flemish influence was exerted on Dutch painting. The influx of so many painters during a fairly short period undoubtedly encouraged an increasingly affluent Dutch public to acquire pictures on a large scale, and the Flemish artists offered this public a dazzling array of secular subjects: landscapes, still lifes, flower pieces, genre scenes, and the like. Most of these subjects had long been the staple of the Antwerp painters, but, with the exception of Aertsen's kitchen scenes, they were relatively rare in earlier Dutch painting. The Flemish probably also introduced their Dutch colleagues, who were often their students, to the advantages of specializing in certain subjects, a practice seldom encountered in sixteenth-century Holland, except perhaps among the portraitists.

Flemish artists played an important role in transmitting international Mannerism into Holland. Thus, about 1584, Van Mander introduced Goltzius and Cornelis Cornelisz. van Haarlem to the art of Bartholomeus Spranger, a Flemish artist working at the court of Rudolph II at Prague. Savery also worked in Prague before finally settling in Holland. This Mannerist style in its various aspects influenced many Dutch painters, but others, especially younger artists, embraced a more realistic style, to which Flemish artists also contributed. Genre scenes in the tradition of Pieter Bruegel the Elder were introduced into Holland by David Vinckboons, a native of Mechelen. Another Bruegel follower was Adriaen Brouwer, who resided for six to eight years at Haarlem; there, under the influence of Frans Hals (himself of Flemish origin), he created a type of low-life genre that was carried on by Adriaen van Ostade and influenced other Dutch artists, including Jan Steen and Rembrandt. After Brouwer's return to Antwerp in 1631–1632, his genre scenes were emulated by David Teniers the Younger.

After 1630, the influx of Flemish artists significantly declined and contacts between North and South became more sporadic. Dutch artists occasionally went to Antwerp, like Jan Lievens, resident there between 1636 and 1644; his study of Rubens and Van Dyck is reflected in the work he produced after his return to Holland. Jan Davidsz. de Heem, born in Utrecht, lived most of his life in Antwerp, where he painted sumptuous still lifes imitated by artists both in Holland and in the Spanish Netherlands.

Flemish painting in its more Baroque manifestations was much favored by aristocratic and patrician circles in Holland. The *stadholder* Frederik Hendrik owned a number of Flem-

ish paintings, and he commissioned still others from Rubens. This taste may have been encouraged by the humanist-statesman Constantijn Huygens, a fervent admirer of Rubens. Frederik's widow, Amalia van Solms, summoned Jacob Jordaens and other Antwerp painters to execute the murals of the Oranjezaal in the Huis ten Bosch. Dutch collaborators in this project included Theodor van Thulden and Pieter Soutman, both former Rubens assistants.

After the death of the Dutch sculptor Hendrick de Keyser, sculpture in Holland was dominated by Flemings. Chief among them was Artus I Quellinus of Antwerp. After working for Frederik Hendrik, he was commissioned in 1647 to execute the sculpture for the new town hall of Amsterdam. There he spent fourteen years, assembling a studio of Flemish and Dutch assistants to complete the project. Quellinus returned to Antwerp in 1665, but one of his Flemish assistants, Rombout Verhulst, remained in Holland, where he became the leading sculptor of the later seventeenth century.

Note
Bibliographical note: Flemish immigration to the Northern Netherlands in the wake of the Eighty Years' War and its impact on all aspects of Dutch culture is discussed by Briels (1978) with further literature. Briels (1987) explores in detail the contributions of Flemish artists to seventeenth-century Dutch painting. No comparable survey exists of North–South relationships in other periods, but useful discussions of the "early Haarlem school" occurs in Panofsky (1953), Snyder (1960), Chatelet (1981), and Geyl (1937). Riggs (1977) provides a good account of Hieronymus Cock and his influence, while Filedt Kok (1993) discusses Goltzius as a print publisher. The standard literature should be consulted for other artists mentioned in this essay.
Walter S. Gibson

See also Aertsen, Pieter; Belgium; Bosch, Hieronymus; Coornhert, Dirck Volkertsz.; Engebrechtsz., Cornelis; Haarlem School, early; House of Orange-Nassau; Humanism, humanist themes; Huygens, Constantijn; Italy; Mannerism, Mannerists; Manuscript illumination; Prints, early printed book and Bible illustration; Quellinus, Artus I; Sculpture (1550–1795); Van Leyden, Lucas; Van Mander, Karel; Verhulst, Rombout; Vinckboons, David

Bibliography
Briels, Jan. *Vlaamse schilders in de Noordelijke Nederlanden in het begin van de Gouden Eeuw, 1582–1630.* Antwerp: Mercator Fonds, 1987.
———. *Zuid-Nederlandse immigratie 1572–1630.* Haarlem: Fibula-Van Dishoeck, 1978.
Chatelet, Albert. *Early Dutch Painting: Painting in the Northern Netherlands in the Fifteenth Century.* Translated by Christopher Brown and Anthony Turner, 53–92. New York: Rizzoli, 1981.
Filedt Kok, Jan Piet. "Hendrick Goltzius: Engraver, Designer and Publisher, 1582–1600." In *Goltzius-Studies: Hendrick Goltzius, 1588–1617.* Edited by Reindert

Falkenburg, Jan Piet Filedt Kok, and Huigen Leefland, 159–218. Zwolle: Waanders, 1993.

Geyl, Pieter. "De haardleerheid der (of sommige) kunsthistorici." *Bijdragen voor de geschiedenis der Nederlanden* 14 (1959): 217–226.

———. "Heeft het zin een Noord-Nederlandse school van primitieven te spreken?" In *Kernproblemen van onze geschiedenis: Opstellen en voordrachten, 1925–1936,* 23–28. Utrecht: A. Oosthoek, 1937.

Panofsky, Erwin. *Early Netherlandish Painting: Its Origins and Character.* Vol. 1, 319–330. Cambridge: Harvard University Press, 1953.

Riggs, Timothy A. *Hieronymus Cock, 1510–1570: Printmaker and Publisher at the Sign of the Four Winds.* New York: Garland, 1977.

Snyder, James. "The Early Haarlem School of Painting." *Art Bulletin* 42 (1960): 39–55, 113–132.

Flinck, Govaert (1615–1660)

Govaert Flinck, born on January 25, 1615, to a well-to-do Mennonite family in Cleves, was one of the most important pupils of Rembrandt van Rijn and, like him, was an accomplished painter and draftsman who specialized in historical subjects and portraiture, but also produced landscapes, genre scenes, and figure studies. His career in Amsterdam was marked by continuous success until his death in 1660 at the age of forty-four.

According to Arnold Houbraken (1718–1721), Flinck's father tried to dissuade him from becoming an artist until, around 1629, the Mennonite preacher, painter and art dealer Lambert Jacobsz. visited Cleves and convinced Flinck's parents to let Govaert study with him in Leeuwarden. Around 1633 Flinck moved from Leeuwarden to Amsterdam and joined the workshop run by Hendrick Uylenburgh, also a Mennonite and an associate of Jacobsz. There he studied with Rembrandt and, in 1636, signed his first independent paintings. When Rembrandt moved on, Flinck took over as manager of the Uylenburgh studio and later worked independently. Flinck was the favorite painter of the poet and playwright Joost van den Vondel, who dedicated many poems to his works, and was on cordial terms with Joan Huydecoper, Jan and Pieter Six, Jan Wtenbogaert, and other prominent collectors. His only known pupil was Johann Spilberg (1619–1690) from Düsseldorf.

Houbraken states that Flinck learned Rembrandt's manner of painting so well that his works were sometimes mistaken for those of the master, and, indeed, some are only now being recognized. A large canvas depicting *The Sacrifice of Abraham* (ca. 1636; Munich, Alte Pinakothek), based on a painting of the same theme by Rembrandt (St. Petersburg, Hermitage), was signed as "retouched by Rembrandt" but has been attributed to Flinck (Von Moltke, 1965).

After about 1645, Flinck developed a brighter, clearer, and more decorative approach to color and brushwork. His portraits became more superficial and elegant, introducing such elements as classical architecture and landscape backgrounds, under the influence of the newly fashionable Flemish Baroque style epitomized by Van Dyck. Flinck painted large-scale history paintings and group portraits and received the plum commission of the age: the series of twelve paintings detailing the exploits of the Batavians, inhabitants of the Netherlands in Roman times, for the newly built Amsterdam Town Hall. On February 2, 1660, Flinck died just as his work on the Batavian series was taking shape, and the commission was divided among several other artists, including Jurriaen Ovens, Jan Lievens, Jacob Jordaens, and Rembrandt.

Among Flinck's principal works are *Isaac Blessing Jacob* (1638; Amsterdam, Rijksmuseum), *St. Paul in His Study* (ca. 1637; Vienna, Kunsthistorisches Museum), *The Militia Company of Capt. Albert Bas and Lieutenant Lucas Conijn* (1645; Amsterdam, Rijksmuseum), *Portrait of a Gentleman* and *Portrait of a Lady* (1646; Raleigh, NC, Museum of Art), *The Amsterdam Civic Guard Celebrating the Peace of Munster* (1648; Amsterdam, Rijksmuseum), *Amalia van Solms Mourning Stadholder Frederik Hendrik* (1654; Amsterdam, Rijksmuseum), and *Marcus Curius Dentatus and the Samnites* (1656; Amsterdam, Royal Palace).

Stephanie S. Dickey

See also Drawing practices and techniques; Group portraiture; History painting; Portraiture; Rembrandt research; Rembrandt School; Rembrandt van Rijn; Roman history; Van der Helst, Bartholomeus

Bibliography

Dudok van Heel, S.A.C., "Het schilderhuis van Govaert Flinck en de kunsthandel van Uylenburgh aan de Lauriergracht te Amsterdam." *Jaarboek Amstelodamum* 74 (1982): 70–90.

Houbraken, A. *De groote schouburgh der Nederlantsche konstschilders en schilderessen.* 3 vols. Amsterdam: A. Houbraken, 1718–1721.

Sumowski, Werner. *Drawings of the Rembrandt School.* Vol. 4, 1883–2166. New York: Abaris, 1981.

———. *Gemälde der Rembrandt-Schüler.* Vol. 2. Landau, Pfalz: Edition PVA, 1983–[1994].

Von Moltke, J.W. *Govaert Flinck.* Amsterdam: Menno Hertzberger, 1965. (In English).

Fluxus

Generally described as a mentality, or as a network of like-minded artists opposing the traditional, heroical art work, Fluxus originated from failing attempts by the American artist George Maciunas (1931–1978) to found a magazine for the so-called Newest Music, or "Neo-Dada in Music, Theater, Poetry, Art," as he at first called the interdisciplinary art form in which visual, theatrical, and musical elements were combined. In June and September 1962, Maciunas organized several festival events in Western Germany that brought together many artists working in different media. Only a few months after these festivals, Fluxus appeared for the first time in the Netherlands. The occasion was the vernissage of an exhibition by the German artist Wolf Vostell (born 1932) on October 5, 1962, at the Monet art gallery in Amsterdam where a program of the Newest Music was performed by chiefly German and American artists.

Willem de Ridder (born 1939) soon became the pivotal figure of Fluxus in the Netherlands through his contacts with these artists. In his gallery, Amstel 47, he presented their work; through his Fluxshop, and later the European Mail-Order Warehouse, the Fluxus multiples that were produced by Maciunas in New York were sold (the remaining stock is in the Gilbert and Lila Silverman Fluxus Collection in Detroit, Michigan). Together with Wim T. Schippers (born 1942), De Ridder organized a series of Fluxus festival events in Amsterdam, The Hague, Scheveningen, and Rotterdam in 1963–1964, in which they both also acted as performers.

Whereas De Ridder acted chiefly as an organizer, Schippers made himself known as an artist with a wide range of talents. Gifted with a peculiar sense of humor and a preference for unusual themes like boredom or confusion, he started as a visual artist but soon extended his activities to drama and the electronic media. His pouring out of a bottle of lemonade in the sea near Petten in North Holland for the television program *Signalement* in 1963 was a performance that had clear associations with events typical for Fluxus: everyday acts that are performed in an alienating context. The absurdity of these Fluxus-related pieces is mirrored in Schippers' 1986 stage play, entitled *Going to the Dogs*, in which six German shepherds are the sole actors. Some of Schippers' television comedies and soap operas for VPRO television, such as the *Fred Haché Show* (1971), are now collected by Dutch museums as a form of video art. Not taking any rules for granted and overtly attacking morals and authorities, these programs represent progressive tendencies in Dutch society of the late 1960s and 1970s.

Other important Dutch artists working in the spirit of Fluxus were Stanley Brouwn (born 1935) and Pieter Engels (born 1938). Brouwn joined some German Fluxus performances in 1964, but he had started doing anonymous actions in the streets, like measuring bricks or asking the way, as early as 1960. Although Brouwn's working methods are related to Fluxus, Engels' subject matter is more in line with the goals of Fluxus. For instance, making the *Weight of Modern Art Piece* (1968) the subject of a work, Engels mocked the status and value that is traditionally attributed to a work of fine art.

As the avant-garde grew rapidly more acceptable in the Netherlands in the 1960s, a younger generation of artists took art not as seriously as they might have done in the conservative 1950s; they tried to undermine preconceived ideas about art in order to create new possibilities. Many activities were performed that are related to Fluxus, although they cannot be designated as such. These activities are well documented, but they still have not been studied in connection with each other.

Ludo van Halem

See also Artists' Initiatives; Brouwn, Stanley; Graphic design

Bibliography
Beeren, Wim et al. *Actie, werkelijkheid en fictie in de kunst van de jaren '60 in Nederland.* Rotterdam: Museum Boymans-van Beuningen; The Hague: Staatsuitgeverij, 1979.
Haks, Frans. "Over Fred Haché, Barend Servet, Fluxus en Wim T. Schippers." *Museumjournaal* 18 (1973): 246–251.
Halem, Ludo van. "Parallele Aufführungen neuester Musik: Een Fluxusconcert in kunsthandel Monet." *Jong Holland* 6:5 (1990): 19–27. (English summary, 39–40).
Hendricks, Jon. *Fluxus Codex.* New York: Harry N. Abrams, 1988.
Levy, William, and De Ridder, Willem. *De Ridder Retrospective.* Groningen: Groninger Museum, 1983.
Ruhé, Harry. *Fluxus, the Most Radical and Experimental Art Movement of the Sixties.* Amsterdam: "A," 1979.
———. "Muziek voor Piano en Hartige Hapjes: Fluxus in Nederland." *Museumjournaal* 24 (1979): 106–110.

Fortuyn/O'Brien (formed 1982)

Irene C. Droogleever Fortuyn (born 1959) and Robert O'Brien (1951–1988) after 1982 produced works of art together that are presented as the work of an independent third person under the name Fortuyn/O'Brien. O'Brien had formerly made artificial ruins in which material estrangement was an important aspect. Fortuyn had not been previously active as an artist. After O'Brien's death, she continued working under the same name and from the same mentality so that no break in style can be detected.

Fortuyn/O'Brien works from a theoretical substructure that has important consequences for the composition of the work. Fortuyn/O'Brien is occupied with the position of the sculptor and sculpture within current society and the cultural Establishment. She asks questions about the viewer's position and examines the validity of the traditional way of looking at and presenting art. The work of art reacts to the outcome of this theoretical inquiry.

Fortuyn/O'Brien calls attention to a confusion growing between the art disciplines that is caused by an estrangement in the materials used and the techniques chosen. The mass media play an important role in this; many objects cannot be traced back to any origin. Therefore, the basis for a traditional conception of art has been taken away, and the balance between content/meaning and outer form has been tipped to the advantage of the latter. Within art a sort of "associative incest" is created. In reaction to this, Fortuyn/O'Brien wants to make art that stands detached from the context determined in the late eighteenth and nineteenth centuries that serves as the basis for the current testings and interpretations of the visual arts, and the automatic weighing and estimation deriving from that. Important for this is letting go of illusion, applying estrangement, and striving for a conscious lack of content.

In the outward appearance of form the work is made striking by both emptiness and elegance (Fig. 30). Most pieces consist of several loose elements. Fragile wooden constructions, stretched with transparent materials like silk, are used. Most pieces have a clear relation to defined spaces like rooms and gardens. Through the applied formal language, associations are made with architecture and design. Material estrangement remains important. Titles of the pieces seem rather arbitrary. The quoting from the past that Fortuyn/O'Brien abhors cannot always be avoided, which immediately demonstrates one of the weak points of the work; theory and practice do not always connect.

Geraart Westerink

See also Contemporary art (1980–1990); Feminism, feminist issues

Bibliography

Fortuyn/O'Brien. *Bon Voyage Voyeur: Gedachten Over Sculptuur*. Amsterdam: privately published, 1984.

————. *Marblepublic*. Amsterdam: Stedelijk Museum, 1991.

————. *The Twenty-Four Men in White*. Saint-Etienne: Maison de la culture et de la communication Saint-Etienne, 1988.

Melchers, Marisa. "Ongekende ontwikkelingen in de beeldhouwkunst." In *Vrij Spel: Nederlandse kunst 1970–1990*. Edited by Willemijn Stokvis and Kitty Zijlmans, 79–100. Amsterdam: Meulenhoff, 1993.

Frames, painted

One of the illusionistic devices adopted by Netherlandish artists to enhance the lifelike quality of their pictures was a painted frame or arch appearing to surround the scene. It originated in fourteenth- and fifteenth-century manuscript and panel painting as an illusionistic church portal, revealing the religious scene beyond it. Alluding to the symbolism of a doorway or threshold, the painted arch functioned as a demarcation between a sacred subject and the viewer's space, and hence as a metaphor for transition between modes of being. This useful and provocative motif, isolating and revealing an imaginary three-dimensional world beyond it, was also adapted for secular subjects. For example, the fifteenth-century Flemish artist Jan van Eyck, and his follower Petrus Christus, occasionally included an illusionistic stone ledge, complete with inscriptions, in portraits. During the sixteenth century, artists continued to use the illusionistic window or ledge, now free of references to ecclesiastical architecture, to set off and ennoble the figures of their sitters.

Seventeenth-century painters, eager to cultivate illusionistic effects, found the painted frame was particularly appealing because it called attention to the physical presence of the painting itself. Furthermore, it alluded to the stone ledges in portraits by Leonardo and Titian. During the 1620s and 1630s, Gerard van Honthorst and other Utrecht followers of Caravaggio popularized a genre derived from Italian sources of single half-length figures, usually drinkers or musicians, appearing to lean out of painted windows. Throughout the 1660s, Gerrit Dou adopted a similar format with a number of genre scenes enclosed in stone niches (Fig. 28). Dou was the most notable seventeenth-century practitioner of this illusionistic device. With the niche, he was able to construct endless variations of iconographically rich imagery within a single format and display his great mimetic skill. Another related device is the mock doorway, illustrated by Samuel van Hoogstraten's *View into a Corridor* (1663).

Artists occasionally imitated the ebony frames used for framing paintings in the seventeenth century, but usually only when including in their illusionistic schemes a painted curtain drawn across a rod. Like the frame, this curtain had its origins in religious painting as a vehicle for divine revelation. In Hugo van der Goes' *Nativity* (ca. 1480), a prophet in the foreground pulls back a curtain from a rod to reveal the Christ Child. Curtains had other associations. During the sixteenth century they had come to be used on the theatrical stage, pulled open to reveal inner scenes such as rooms or landscapes. In households, curtains were often kept over pictures to protect them from dust. Along with the painted archway, the curtain in the seventeenth century became a popular motif for fostering the deliberate confusion of actual and fabricated objects. Rembrandt, in his *Holy Family* of 1646, painted a curtain dawn back on a rod to reveal the serene domestic scene behind it. His former student Dou painted a similar drawn curtain in his *Self-Portrait with Book and Pipe* of about 1647 (Fig. 45). In the dark background there are two men next to an easel, grinding pigment. This little *tableau*, which identifies the setting as an artist's studio, is framed by a second curtain that drapes across the interior arch of the niche. Other genre painters such as Nicolaes Maes and Johannes Vermeer, along with the architectural painters Emanuel de Witte and Gerard Houckgeest, also experimented with the drawn curtain. The painted frame, with or without a curtain, was one of the more playful demonstrations of seventeenth-century painters' commitment to illusionism.

Martha Hollander

See also Dou, Gerrit; Framing devices within pictures; Genre painting, eighteenth century; Genre painting, seventeenth century; Illusionism; Utrecht Caravaggists

Bibliography

Birkmeyer, Karl M. "The Arch Motif in Netherlandish Painting of the Fifteenth Century." *Art Bulletin* 43 (1961): 2–16.

Moffitt, John F. "Rembrandt's Revelations and Calvin's Curtains." *Gazette des Beaux-Arts* 113 (1989): 175–186.

Reutersvärd, P. "Tavelforhänget: Kring ett motiv i holländst 1600—tafelsmalerei." *Konsthistorisk Tidskrift* 25 (1956): 97–113. (English summary).

Sluijter, Eric Jan. *De lof de schilderkunst. Over schilderijen van Gerrit Dou (1613–1675) en een traktaat van Phillips Angel uit 1642.* (Zeven Provincïen Reeks, 7.) Hilversum: Verloren, 1993.

Thiel, P.J.J. van and C.J. de Bruyn Kops. "Prijst de Lijst: Een onderzoek naar form en functie van de Hollandse schilderijlijst in de zeventiende eeuw." *Prijst de Lijst: De Hollandse Schilderijlijst in de zeventiende eeuw.* The Hague: Rijksmuseum Amsterdam en Staatsuitgeverij, 1984.

Framing devices within pictures

Dutch painters, particularly in the seventeenth century, frequently composed their pictures out of two or more separate vignettes within a single scene. This use of multiple images is typical of the Netherlandish tradition of encyclopedic, detailed description. In addition to making pictures more visually engaging, these secondary images were vehicles for enriching genre scenes, architectural views, histories, and portraits with symbolic meaning or commentary. Painters made inventive use of architectural details such as windows, doorways, and arches to frame their ancillary scenes.

The use of framing devices has a long history in Netherlandish art. In fifteenth- and sixteenth-century religious and mythological scenes, artists often used small background scenes to represent past or future events. In the sixteenth century, small background scenes appeared in portraits as attributes and in religious scenes as anecdotal details (Fig. 63). Such devices for opening pictorial space are closely related to stage design. The sixteenth-century Netherlandish stage consisted of a two-story triple arch divided into several smaller frames or arches in which various characters could appear simultaneously. At important moments, curtains would be pulled back to reveal scenes—simulated rooms or landscapes—within the frames. This canonical design, surviving well into the seventeenth century, had a strong influence on painting.

The opening of pictorial space was first codified in 1604 by Karel van Mander in his treatise on painting, *Schilder-Boeck* (Book on Picturing). In his chapter on composition, he refers to this device, which he calls *doorsien* ("looking through"), as a generic means of drawing the viewer into a scene: "Our composition should enjoy a fine quality, for the delight of our senses, if we allow there a place of penetration or a vista . . . into which the eye can plunge."

As seventeenth-century painters explored the expressive potential of perspective and optical effects, they began to acknowledge the capacity of the ancillary space to enrich their scenes of contemporary life. Landscape painters often constructed their views of the Dutch countryside around a distant view (Color Plate 6). Pieter de Hooch, with his talent for perspective and geometric precision, constructed his quiet scenes of domestic life in houses and courtyards, transforming everyday settings into complex configurations of indoor and outdoor spaces (Fig. 43). Architectural painters such as Pieter Saenredam, Emanuel de Witte, and Gerard Houckgeest created off-center compositions of church interiors, exploiting the characteristic vast Gothic vaults and broad columns to create views into multiple spaces (Fig. 42).

A popular version of the *doorsien* is the view into another room, common in interior scenes from the 1640s on. Nicolaes Maes' *The Eavesdropper* of 1657 displays one of the century's most inventive and influential uses of multiple views (Color Plate 7). The picture space is divided into several distinct areas, while the figures are isolated in separate contrasting groups; meanwhile, the eavesdropper is poised between the public and private territories of dining area and corridor. By reconfiguring a single interior as a cluster of vignettes, Maes creates an ironic anatomy of the household, exposing the desires and conflicts of its members.

Some artists manipulated space for an explicitly illusionistic effect, surrounding entire scenes with painted windows or archways to play on the relationship between actual and fictive frames. During the 1620s, Gerard van Honthorst and other Utrecht Caravaggists created a genre of drinkers and revelers shown in half-length, leaning out of painted windows or archways. Three decades later, Gerrit Dou and his followers, the Leiden *fijnschilders* (fine painters), adopted a similar motif for their small-scale, iconographically complex genre paintings (Fig. 28). By the end of the century, such experiments with space had been abandoned for variations on already established compositional formulas.

Martha Hollander

See also Display; Dou, Gerrit; Frames, painted; History painting; House interiors; Illusionism; Paintings-within-paintings; Theater and theatricality

Bibliography

Hollander, Martha. "Structures of Space and Society in the Seventeenth-Century Dutch Interior." Ph.D. diss., University of California at Berkeley, 1990.

Kernodle, George R. *From Art to Theatre*. Chicago: University of Chicago Press, 1944.

White, John. *The Birth and Rebirth of Pictorial Space*. Icon editions. New York: Harper and Row, 1967.

France

Though the French have had a long-lasting love affair with seventeenth-century Dutch painting, it was by no means love at first sight. On the contrary, the French contemporaries of the Dutch masters, steeped in the classicist art theories of the Italian Renaissance, reproached the artists from the seven United Provinces for their emphasis on faithful imitation, at the expense of beauty, harmony, and decorum, as well as for their exclusive preoccupation with ordinary, even vulgar, subject matter rather than lofty historical subjects derived from the Bible, classical mythology, or ancient history. Charles Alponse du Fresnoy, in his *L'Art de la peinture* (The Art of Painting) of 1668, emphasized that true art requires the creation of an idealized image of reality, based on the standards of perfection established by the classical Greek sculptors. Among modern artists he praised the Italian Renaissance masters, notably Raphael, who better than any artist had been able to translate the classical sculptural example into the new "idiom" of oil painting. It was Raphael's style, transmitted by the seventeenth-century French painter Nicolas Poussin, that was the supreme model at the Académie des Beaux-Arts, founded under Louis XIV to uphold the lofty standards of French art.

Among the first French art theorists to have a less negative view of Dutch painting was Roger de Piles, who, writing at the end of the seventeenth century, praised some aspects of Rembrandt's work (his *chiaroscuro* and originality of conception) though he still blamed the artist for the excessive and vulgar realism of his paintings. Yet, it was neither art theorists nor critics who were ultimately responsible for the increased interest in Dutch painting that developed in France in the course of the eighteenth century. Instead, it appears that the art market was the primary cause of this dramatic change in taste. Ironically, it was a scarcity of the much-admired paintings of the Italian school at the end of the seventeenth century that prompted art dealers to promote Dutch art, which was in ready supply at the time. And they clearly were successful. From the 1740s onward, sales catalogs show that considerable numbers of Dutch paintings were changing hands and that prices were on the rise. Around the same time, albums reproducing the holdings of important collections began to show a dramatic increase of prints after works by the Dutch masters. These reproductive prints, whether distributed in albums or sold separately, did much to popularize the taste for Dutch pictures. Indeed, by the middle of the eighteenth century, the reputation of the Dutch school was firmly established in France. Paintings by Rembrandt and his school, the Bamboccianti and the Italianate landscape painters (notably Nicolaes Berchem), the Leiden *fijnschilders* (fine painters), the rural landscapists (Paulus Potter, Adriaen van de Velde, Jan Wijnants, and Philips Wouwerman), and the decorative flower painters (Jan van Huysum, Rachel Ruysch) seem to have been in particular demand. However, since it was obviously to the advantage of the dealers to continuously expand the canon of Dutch art, ever new artists were added to it. By the end of the century, the stock of the great art dealer Jean-Baptiste Lebrun included works by Meindert Hobbema, Jacob van Ruisdael, Pieter Saenredam, and even Johannes Vermeer.

The new enthusiasm for Dutch paintings and their rising market value prompted young French painters to take the Dutch school more seriously than the Academy had taught them to do. Since the beginning of the century, artists in need of money produced copies and pastiches of Dutch paintings, notably by Rembrandt and his school. While the names of many of these *pasticheurs* are forgotten today—a Robert Tournières (1668–1733), a Jean Raoux (1677–1734), or an Alexis Grimoux (1678–1733)—even better-known artists like Antoine Coypel (1661–1722) followed this practice.

Did Dutch painting set eighteenth-century French art on the course toward intimacy, cultivation of ordinary subject matter, and a tendency toward realism? Or, did the French become more receptive to Dutch painting because there was an inevitable anticlassicist backlash after the death of Louis XIV in 1715? It is the kind of "chicken-or-egg" question that is difficult to answer. Perhaps it is safest to say that Dutch pictures served as points of reference for the young artists of the early Rococo period who sought to free themselves from the stranglehold of the Academy in order to create a new art, less formal and less formidable than the work of their classicist predecessors.

All of the major French Rococo painters appear to have been intimately familiar with the Dutch tradition, but the way that familiarity manifests itself in their work is often quite different. Jean-Antoine Watteau (1684–1721), the first eigh-

teenth-century French painter of note, is known to have copied works by Dutch and Flemish artists in his youth. Later in life he had ample opportunity to study Dutch paintings in the collection of his friend and patron, Jean de Jullienne. His famous *fêtes galantes* (elegant parties) may be related to the works of Adriaen van de Venne (one of whose paintings he copied) as well as to those of later painters of merry companies, notably Jan Steen.

The interiors of Jean-Baptiste-Siméon Chardin (1699–1779) and Jean-Baptiste Greuze (1725–1805) at first glance seem more closely related to Dutch painting than the work of Watteau. But though they show a general affinity with the works of such bourgeois genre painters as Gabriel Metsu and Gerard Ter Borch (sharing with them, for example, a tendency to teach moral lessons appropriate for a middle-class clientele), the similarity remains for the most part limited to content and there is little in the way of formal resemblance. The same may be said for Chardin's still lifes, which, though comparable to the works of a Pieter Claesz. or Willem Claesz. Heda in their simple arrangements of foodstuffs and ordinary implements, in reality show little resemblance to the works of the Dutch still-life painters.

From a purely formal point of view, the paintings of Jean-Honoré Fragonard (1732–1806) often come closer to Dutch art, particularly to the works of Hals and Rembrandt. Fragonard is known to have copied paintings by Rembrandt in his youth, and he may even have visited Holland. The artist's bravura brushwork, most notable in his portrait studies, is reminiscent of some of the genre heads of Frans Hals, while the warm tones and *chiaroscuro* of some of his interior scenes call to mind the works of Rembrandt and Nicolaes Maes.

The taste for Dutch art continued throughout the Revolutionary and Napoleonic periods, despite a new wave of classicism that swept across France with the onset of the Neoclassical period in the mid-eighteenth century. In the French national museum in the Louvre, created during the Revolutionary period, the Dutch school occupied an important place, and it continued to do so under Napoleon when the museum's director, Dominique Vivant Denon (himself an avid collector of Dutch art), added considerably to the holdings through monetary acquisitions and by way of "war booty" (which had to be returned after 1815).

Bourgeois genre painting in the Dutch manner remained popular in France throughout the later part of the eighteenth and early nineteenth centuries as the works of Martin Drölling (1752–1827), Léopold Boilly (1761–1845), and Marguérite Gérard (1761–1837) attest. Unlike their Rococo predecessors, these painters tended to compose their pictures in a sober classicist fashion that is more closely related to David than to the Baroque compositions of seventeenth-century Dutch interior painters. Meanwhile, the early nineteenth century saw the development of a new type of narrative history painting (namely, *peinture troubadour*) that showed scenes from the intimate life of historical figures in interiors resembling those of Metsu, Dou, or Frans van Mieris. It is not surprising that Vivant Denon, with his love of Dutch art, promoted this type of painting—practiced by such artists as Fleury Richard

(1777–1852) and Pierre Révoil (1776–1842)—among collectors, even recommending it to the Emperor and his first wife, Joséphine.

Around the turn of the eighteenth to the nineteenth century, the taste for Dutch landscape painting underwent a dramatic change. While earlier on it was primarily the sundrenched landscapes of the Italianate and idyllic landscape painters that had been appreciated by art lovers and collectors, now a new interest developed in the darker, often slightly melancholic, woodland scenes of Van Ruisdael and Hobbema. The art dealer Lebrun, at the end of the eighteenth century, had a considerable number of works by Van Ruisdael and Hobbema in his stock, and to meet the new demand for the works of these artists, he hired a contemporary painter, Georges Michel (1763–1843), to copy them. Michel was also employed by Vivant Denon to restore Dutch paintings in the Louvre, where the artist became enamored with the works of Rembrandt and his followers. In the course of his long career, Michel produced a considerable number of early Romantic landscapes that, while highly personal, show an affinity with the landscapes of Van Ruisdael, Rembrandt, and the latter's followers Philips Koninck and Hercules Segers.

While the taste for Dutch painting continued throughout the Revolutionary and Napoleonic periods, it was clearly a cultural undercurrent vastly outdone by the overwhelming preoccupation with classical and Renaissance art. By the 1830s, however, a renewed interest in seventeenth-century Dutch painting began. Arsène Houssaye (1815–1896), one of the foremost critics under the July Monarchy (1830–1848) regularly wrote articles about Holland and Dutch painting for *L'Artiste*, a widely read magazine of which he was the editor-in-chief. He also published, in 1844, a major book on Flemish and Dutch painting. Even more crucial to the revival of interest in Dutch painting were the writings of Théophile Thoré (1807–1869), a committed Republican journalist and critic, who lived in exile from 1849 to 1858. During these nine years, Thoré spent much time in Belgium and Holland, making a special study of Dutch paintings. Using the pseudonym William Bürger, he published several books and articles on Dutch painting, most importantly a two-volume work on the museums in Holland. Thoré, whose views were strongly colored by his political convictions, admired Dutch painting as the artistic expression of the society and culture of the Dutch Republic. He contrasted the naturalism of the art of the Dutch Republic with the "mystical art of the Middle Ages" and the "allegorical and aristocratic art of the Renaissance." Thoré is often held responsible for the revival of interest in Johannes Vermeer and Frans Hals. The former, indeed, had been mostly forgotten until Thoré's pioneering article in the *Gazette des Beaux-Arts* in 1866; the latter owed the renewed fascination with his work in the first instance to the opening of the Frans Hals Museum in Haarlem in 1862, which made available to the public the majority of the large group portraits by Frans Hals, which until then had been hardly known. It was Thoré's merit to have alerted the French to the existence of this museum and to the new aspects of Hals' art that it revealed.

A third critic who did much to spark the interest in Dutch painting, particularly during the later part of the nineteenth century, was Eugène Fromentin (1820–1876). Unlike Houssaye and Thoré, Fromentin was not a critic but a painter and a novelist, who approached Dutch painting in a highly personal manner. It is precisely the subjective aspect of his writings and their high literary quality that made Fromentin's *Maîtres d'autrefois* (Masters of Past Times) a classic text on Dutch art, still reprinted and read today.

Dutch painting was an important source of inspiration for the first major landscape school to originate in France, the school of Barbizon. The careers of the Barbizon artists—Narcisse Diaz (1808–1876), Jules Dupré (1811–1889), Théodore Rousseau (1812–1867), among others—began for the most part around 1830, at the time when Georges Michel was in his late sixties and totally forgotten by his contemporaries. (It was not until 1845, two years after Michel's death, that Thoré wrote the first article about his art.) Like Michel, the Barbizon artists preferred the painters of the Dutch scene over the Italianate landscape painters. Influenced by the growing nationalism that developed in the wake of the Revolution of 1830, these artists saw great merit in the depiction of the artist's native countryside no matter how simple and unassuming it was. Working in Barbizon, a small village in the Fontainebleau Forest not far from Paris, they painted the type of mixed woodland and agricultural landscape that had been favored by Van Ruisdael, Hobbema, and the landscape painters of the Rembrandt school.

Closely linked to the Barbizon school were several artists who specialized in the painting of landscapes with cattle, a genre in which Dutch artists—notably Aelbert Cuyp, Paulus Potter, and Adriaen van de Velde—had excelled. Among French cattle painters, Jacques-Raymond Brascassat (1805–1867), Constantin Troyon (1810–1865), and Charles Jacque (1813–1894) were particularly attracted to Dutch painting, which played a crucial formative role in their development.

Dutch art was an important inspiration as well to those nineteenth-century artists who, like the Rococo painters before them, wanted to move away from academic classicism to create an art depicting ordinary life. The most important nineteenth-century artists to do so were the mid-nineteenth-century Realists, led by Gustave Courbet (1819–1877) and Jean-François Millet (1814–1875). Both painters were intimately familiar with Dutch painting. Courbet traveled to Holland as a young artist (1846) and wrote to his parents that "a trip like this teaches you more than three years of work." The works he admired most in the Dutch museums were not the landscapes or the genre paintings of the *petits maîtres hollandais* (little Dutch masters) but rather the monumental group portraits of Rembrandt and Bartholomeus van der Helst (those by Hals were not publicly accessible until the opening of the Frans Hals Museum in 1862). Courbet's major works, the *Burial at Ornans* (1849), showing a gathering of French nineteenth-century bourgeois not unlike the "burghers" in *The Nightwatch* (1642) by Rembrandt (Color Plate 5), as well as the *Painter's Atelier* (1854–1855) were clearly conceived with Dutch group portraits in mind. The same may be said for the gatherings of artists, poets, and musicians painted by Courbet's follower Henri Fantin Latour (1836–1904), which resemble the regents' portraits of a Hals or Van der Helst in their simple, straightforward compositions and sober coloring.

While Courbet was inspired in first instance by Dutch group portraiture, other Realists such as Millet and François Bonvin (1817–1887) were attracted instead to genre painting. Millet appears to have been most interested in the work of Rembrandt and Adriaen van Ostade, while Bonvin looked at such interior painters as Pieter de Hooch and Pieter Janssens Elinga. The young Édouard Manet (1832–1888), who, due to his marriage to a Dutch wife, traveled to Holland more than once, also made some references to the Dutch tradition in his work. Intimate pictures such as *Madame Manet at the Piano* (1867–1868; Paris, Musée d'Orsay) recall the works of Dutch interior painters like Metsu and Ter Borch, while the famous *Bon Bock* (Philadelphia, Philadelphia Museum of Art) of 1873 is a nineteenth-century rephrasing of the work of Frans Hals.

While the Impressionists seem to have been little interested in Dutch painting (with the possible exception of the young Degas), among the Symbolists Odilon Redon (1840–1916) expressed a profound admiration for the work of Rembrandt. This is not altogether surprising, for Redon's teacher, the etcher Rodolphe Bresdin (1822–1885), had closely studied the graphic work of Rembrandt and his followers. Redon's own lithographs often show a strong affinity with Rembrandt's etchings, particularly in their mysterious *chiaroscuro* effects.

Dutch art remained popular in France during the early twentieth century. Widely available in French museums, and a subject of study by several French art historians, it became in a way a part of France's cultural patrimony. Twentieth-century artists in France continued to show an interest in Dutch art, but more eclectically than before. While previously the taste for particular genres of Dutch painting had set in motion specific movements in French art, now individual artists studied different aspects of Dutch painting in an entirely personal and idiosyncratic manner. Thus Henri Matisse (1869–1954) in his youth copied a large still life by Abraham van Beyeren; Joan Miró (1893–1983) based his Dutch interiors on genre paintings by Hendrick Martensz. Sorgh and Jan Steen; and Pablo Picasso (1881–1973) had Rembrandt on his mind when he made many of his late etchings. While the works of all three artists were, in one way or another, inspired by Dutch art, they no longer shared a common denominator.

Petra ten-Doesschate Chu

See also Belgium; Drawing theory; Flanders, Flemish School; Genre painting, eighteenth century; Hague School, The; *Japonisme*; Nationalism; Prints, collecting; Reputation of Dutch art abroad; State and municipal art collecting and collections; Utrecht

Bibliography

I. PRIMARY SOURCES

Blanc, Charles. *Histoire des peintres de toutes les écoles: École hollandaise.* 2 vols. Paris: Vve Jules Renouard, 1861.

Bürger, W. [Théophile Thoré]. *Musées de la Hollande.* 2 vols. Paris: Vve Jules Renouard, 1860.

———. "Van der Meer de Delft." *Gazette des Beaux-Arts.* 1st ser., 21 (1866): 297–330; 458–470; 542–575.

Fromentin, Eugène. *The Old Masters of Belgium and Holland. (Les Maîtres d'autrefois.* 1875.) New York: Schocken Books, 1963.

Houssaye, Arsène. *L' Histoire de la peinture flamande et hollandaise.* Paris: J. Hetzel, 1844.

Lebrun, J.B. *Galerie des peintres flamands, hollandais, et allemands.* Paris/Amsterdam: 1792.

Thoré, Théophile. "Petit Guide des artistes en voyage, Hollande." *Annuaire des artistes et des amateurs* 1 (1860): 247–256.

II. SECONDARY SOURCES

Atwater, V.L. "A Catalogue and Analysis of Eighteenth-Century French Prints after Netherlandish Baroque Paintings." Ph.D. diss., University of Washington, 1988.

Banks, Oliver T. *Watteau and the North: Studies in the Dutch and Flemish Baroque Influence on French Rococo Painting.* New York: Garland, 1977

Carpenter, Richard B. "The Dutch Sources of Fragonard." Ph.D. diss., Harvard University, 1955.

Chu, Petra ten-Doesschate. *French Realism and the Dutch Masters.* Utrecht: Haentjens Dekker and Gumbert, 1974.

———. "Nineteenth-Century Visitors to the Frans Hals Museum." In *The Documented Image: Visions in Art History.* Edited by G.P. Weisberg and L.S. Dixon, 111–144. Ithaca, NY: Syracuse University Press, 1987.

Cohen, Janie. *Picasso Rembrandt Picasso: Prenten en tekeningen van Picasso geïnspireerd door werken van Rembrandt.* Amsterdam: Museum het Rembrandthuis, 1990.

Fried, Michael. "Manet's Sources." *Artforum* 7:3 (March 1969): 28–82.

Gerson, Horst. *Ausbreitung und Nachwirkung der holländischen Malerei des 17. Jahrhunderts.* 1942. Reprint. Amsterdam: B.M. Israel, 1983.

Haskell, Francis. "The Old Masters in Nineteenth-Century French Painting." *Art Quarterly* 34 (1971): 55–85.

Heppner, A. "Thoré-Bürger in Holland." *Oud Holland* 55 (1938): 17–34; 67–82; 129–144.

Jowell, Frances Suzman. "Thoré-Bürger and the Revival of Frans Hals." *Art Bulletin* 56 (1974): 101–117.

Mirimonde, A.P. de. "Les Opinions de M. Lebrun sur la peinture hollandaise." *Revue des arts* 6 (1956): 207–214.

Samis, Peter S. "Aemulatio Rembrandti: The Nineteenth-Century Printmaker Flameng and His Prises/Crises de Conscience." *Gazette des Beaux-Arts.* 6th ser., 116 (1990): 243–260.

Theroux, Alexander. "The Sphinx of Delft: The Strange Correspondence between a Dutch Master and His French Disciple (Vermeer and Proust)." *Art and An-*

tiques II (December 1988): 84–89.

Tuin, H. van der. *Les vieux peintres des Pays-bas et la critique en France de la première moitié du XIXe siècle.* Paris: Nizet, 1953.

———. *Les vieux peintres des Pays-bas et la littérature en France de la première moitié du XIXe siècle.* Paris: Nizet, n.d.

Verbeek, J. "Bezoekers van het Rijksmuseum in het Trippenhuis." *Bulletin van het Rijksmuseum* 6 (1958): 59–72.

Weisberg, Gabriel P. "François Bonvin and an Interest in Several Painters of the Seventeenth and Eighteenth Centuries. *Gazette des Beaux-Arts.* 6th ser., 76 (1970): 359–366.

Functionalism in architecture

The celebrated work *Bouwen/Bauen/Bâtir/Building—Holland* was written by the architect Johannes Bernardus van Loghem (1881–1940) and published in 1932. A volume of just one hundred forty pages with numerous black-and-white illustrations, it can be reasonably considered the most complete expression of the style of architecture most often associated with the designation Het Nieuwe Bouwen (The New Construction). The "new builders," whose collective desire for renewal is represented in the concept of Het Nieuwe Bouwen, were, above all, motivated by a strong moral conviction that would manifest itself in a functional architecture: an architecture that was antidecorative, flexible, light, transparent, and with thought expanded toward health and hygiene. These design goals would be achieved through the rational use of new technologies and materials, such as reinforced concrete, iron, and, first and foremost, glass.

Their peaceful revolution began to take shape in a manifesto made public in 1927 in the pages of the journal *i 10*. It was revealed that the "new builders" shared the same ideals as those held by radicals in other artistic disciplines. The manifesto was signed by a group of architects who had organized in Amsterdam during the same year; their leader and spokesman was Benjamin Merkelbach (1901–1961). In accordance with the prevailing avant-garde trend, the architects, who would come to be known as De 8, would often utilize numbers and/or letters in the titles of journals, notices, and all other forms of communication. The group was initially comprised of only six members: B. Merkelbach, H.E. van de Pauwert, P.J. Verschuyl, J. van den Bosch, J.H. Groenewegen, and Ch.J.F. Karsten, but by 1928 they had added three new members. The first supporters were Albert Boeken (1891–1951), Johannes Duiker (1890–1935), and Jan Gerko Wiebenga (1886–1974), all of whom became, during the next two years, apostles who preached the religion of functionalism.

The principal achievement of the architects of De 8 was in elevating the status of the functional building by making it the central theme of their designs. The slogans expressed in the manifesto were the result of the radicalization of the role of the architect, a process that had begun in the early 1920s in response to a changing socioeconomic climate. Battling the narrow traditionalism that they believed had rendered their colleagues' ideas sterile and resulted in the repetition of pre-established design schemes, the group, motivated by a strong

pragmatism, declared that they were in favor of designs that emphasized a "useful" function even if the end result appeared "ugly." It was in their search for the "rational" that they became modern architects. The members of De 8 wrote proudly of "working more towards the science of construction than the art of construction."

In the early 1930s, "internationalists" sincerely believed in cultural cooperation. These were also the years in which many Dutch intellectuals, among them several architects, adopted progressive ideals. Designers such as Martinus Adrianus Stam (1899–1986) and Van Loghem moved to the Soviet Union to join colleagues from France, Germany, and Switzerland who were assisting in the construction of the new urbanism. For many the temporary move was motivated by a desire to experience the reality of Communism, a political system that reflected many of their own views. Also, the acceptance of De 8 at the CIAM (Congrès International d'Architecture Moderne) was interpreted as recognition given for the validity and necessity of architectural reform, and a defense of the ideals of modernity conducted at the European level.

A group of architects located mainly in Rotterdam embraced the same principles as De 8 and had been operating from a milder kind of dogmatism since 1920. Opbouw (Edification) was founded by Willem Kromhout (1864–1940), a designer (Fig. 71) of the same generation as H.P. Berlage, one of the originators of modern architecture in the Netherlands. The Rotterdam group was guided by a shared social commitment that was, in the words of Van Loghem, "based on economic and technical renewal." Joining Opbouw were architects who, through their work, contributed to the eradication of obsolete construction practices and realized a form of architecture that was objective and, at the same time, strongly allusive and rich in imagination. Among the members were Leendert Cornelis van der Vlugt (1894–1936); Johannes Andreas Brinkman (1902–1949); Jacobus Johannes Pieter Oud (1890–1963); Stam; Willem van Tijen (1894–1974), the designer of the Bergpolder Flats, the first high-rise apartment building with an iron framework (1933–1934; Fig. 48); Van Loghem; Huig Aart Maaskant (1907–1977); and Johannes Hendrik van den Broek (1898–1978).

Many of the factories, hospitals, movie theaters, swimming pools, sports complexes, hotels, silos, dams, office buildings, homes, and schools that were built during the period 1925–1940 displayed their designers' common yearning for technological experimentation with a strong analogy of language. The result was the birth of an aesthetic of functionalism or of the Nieuwe Zakelijkheid (New Objectivity).

The definition was born in Germany, where since the mid-1920s Neue Sachlichkeit referred to the new realism that was mixed with socialist sentiment. This realism resulted from objectivity toward form and materials and resisted investing them with ideal implications. The anti-Expressionist attitude present in the arts translated into an architecture whose characteristics were the result of an empirical engineering. Buildings were designed to function like mechanical parts and to possess both spatial beauty and symbolic significance. For Van Loghem and others in the Netherlands, the *sachlich* attitude that inspired the

Nieuwe Zakelijkheid carried within it the nucleus for the future because the art that was created emanated from sound human relationship (van Loghem, 1932: 50).

The unity of thought that guided Het Nieuwe Bouwen forged, in the final years of the 1920s, a stronger union between the Opbouw group from Rotterdam and the De 8 group from Amsterdam. This union resulted in a collaboration that gave birth to a journal that documented the achievements and developments of both groups. Entitled *De 8 en Opbouw*, the new publication first appeared in January 1932 and ended its publication run in 1943. The journal became the primary forum for discussions regarding the aesthetics of the Nieuwe Zakelijkheid and for the dissemination of knowledge and experimentation related to new technologies. It also provided ample space for illustrations of international modern architecture.

To provide a profile of the journal is by no means a simple task, since an examination of the eleven volumes would reveal strong ideological differences. This is due in large part to the fact that the publication did not serve as the mouthpiece for the director or the editorial staff, but rather as a sounding board for the ongoing debate occurring at the center of both groups. The two groups never attempted to establish an official party line. The initial years of the journal were dominated by Duiker, editor-in-chief from the first issue until his unexpected death in 1935. The contributions of Cornelis van Eesteren, Van Loghem, Merkelbach, and Van Tijen were certainly no less important, but it should be noted that Duiker's strong personality influenced the cultural climate of the period as well as the work of colleagues. Perhaps his two most influential designs were the Zonnestraal Sanatorium near Hilversum and the Open-Air School in Amsterdam (Fig. 46). According to Duiker's colleagues these works illustrated one of the essential characteristics of Het Nieuwe Bouwen: openness. Duiker embodied the functionalist ideal of "dissolving the artistry in the engineer's mind," to use Boeken's definition; he was an engineer who produced culture.

The topics discussed in *De 8 en Opbouw* were those that both groups considered essential to daily living: art, science, technology, construction, industry, fragments of a real life that looked toward the future. The articles revealed that both groups shared a strong social commitment. It was, therefore, with great passion that the journal tackled the theme of the "Functional City," a topic at the center of debate during the fourth CIAM (1933), and documented the birth of an urban science that departed from mere aesthetic exercise.

The spirit of the avant-garde found throughout the pages of *De 8 en Opbouw* inspired the most intrinsic principles of the Nieuwe Zakelijkheid: freedom, spontaneity, and a sense of community. Often illustrations in the journal consumed an entire page and featured collage or photomontage techniques. Such illustrations facilitated communication and represented a formidable instrument of persuasion.

Generational and philosophical differences eventually led to a disagreement between De 8 group, now referred to as "the old 8," and Group 32, led by Boeken and Arthur Staal (1907–1993) who joined the ranks of *De 8 en Opbouw* determined to restore to it the objectives of the founding year, 1932. The explicitly apolitical Group 32 suggested that, in deference to a conservative trend within the political culture, articles in *De 8 en Opbouw* promoting a political agenda unrelated to architecture should be removed from the journal. After 1935 the journal altered its course, and contributors returned to writing articles on style, aesthetics, the harmony of nature, and other qualities of architectural composition. In broadening its horizons and silencing those with idealistic motivations, the journal gained a larger and more international audience. Then, in the late 1930s when external conditions (economic crisis, the rise of Fascism, the threat of war in Europe) degenerated further, *De 8 en Opbouw* lost the ground that had nourished it and retreated completely into neutral territory and conventionality. Indeed, *De 8 en Opbouw* was the only avant-garde periodical that, after the "heroic period" of the modern movement (ca. 1925–1935) in architecture, continued to follow its development and offer criticism throughout the 1930s.

A building that had served as a catalyst for the principles of the Nieuwe Zakelijkheid was, without a doubt, the Van Nelle Factory in Rotterdam (Fig. 49). It represents the successful marriage of a strong intellectual tension with an inexhaustible will for the resurrection of architecture's primordial values. The project of Van der Vlugt and Brinkman, the factory was constructed between 1926 and 1931 with the assistance of Stam and Wiebenga (it was the latter who performed the structural calculations necessary for the use of reinforced concrete). The building was commissioned by Kees van der Leeuw, the young owner of Van Nelle and an intellectual theosopher whose objective was to experiment with new methods of organization in factory architecture, following in the wake of new developments in the United States.

The end result was an extraordinary block, given character by a façade comprised completely of windows whose transparency echoed the water in the canal that ran parallel to the building. The architecture was endowed with space: Angled ramps were stretched to different levels of the main structure; the detached smokestack was both a visual and a functional signal; the cylindrical mass that rose from the outline of the building simulated a captain's tower on the bridge of a ship. The form has a mechanical accent, but in its unity the building speaks the language of progress, modernity, and utopian idealism. Indeed, from the close collaboration of client and designers resulted an anti-ideological building and, at the same time, an exemplary product of the culture that characterized the architecture of the Nieuwe Zakelijkheid.

Maristella Casciato

See also Architectural criticism, issues of style; Berlage, Hendrick Petrus; Duiker, Johannes; Kromhout, Willem; Oud, Jacobus Johannes Pieter; Public housing; Urban planning, from 1750 to the present

Bibliography
Bernini, Beatrice, and Timo de Rijk. *Het nieuwe Wonen in Nederland, 1924–1936*. Rotterdam: 010, 1990.

Bock, Manfred, ed. *De 8 en Opbouw, 1932–1943: Periodical of New Architecture.* Translated by John Kirkpatrick. Amsterdam: Van Gennep, 1989.

Bosma, Koos, and Liesbeth Crommelin, eds. *Het Nieuwe Bouwen: Amsterdam, 1920–1960.* Translated by Elizabeth Crocker et al. Amsterdam: Stedelijk Museum; Delft: Delft University Press, 1983.

Het Nieuwe Bouwen in Rotterdam, 1920–1960. Rotterdam: Museum Boymans-van Beuningen; Delft: Delft University Press, 1982.

Loghem, J.B. van. *Bowen/Bauen/Batir, Building—Holland.* Amsterdam: Kosmos, 1932.

Molema, Jan et al. *The New Movement in the Netherlands 1924–1936.* Rotterdam: 010, 1996.

Rebel, Ben. "Het nieuwe bouwen: Het functionalisme in Nederland, 1918–1945." Ph.D. diss., Rijksuniversiteit Utrecht, 1983. (English summary).

Furniture

See Applied arts

G

Gabriël, Paul Joseph Constantin (1828–1903)

Paul Gabriël is considered one of the foremost representatives of The Hague School, although he did not count himself as part of the group. He was also a landscape painter but resisted the gray tonality of his colleagues.

Gabriël was a son of the sculptor Paul Joseph Gabriël from Amsterdam. He received his first drawing lessons at the Rijksacademie in Amsterdam and from the architect L. Zocher. In Cleves in Germany he took lessons from the landscape painter Barend Cornelis Koekkoek. Through Haarlem, where he met Anton Mauve, he went to Oosterbeek in Gelderland. In this artists' colony amid wooded surroundings, he painted *en plein air*. After three years he returned in 1856 to Amsterdam. His work did not sell very well, which made him decide to take his chances in Brussels. In the twenty-four years he lived in Belgium he developed into an accomplished landscape painter. He became friends with Willem Roelofs, who had an important influence on his work.

Gabriël painted outdoors as much as possible; nature and its continual study were for him the best training. He went to the Netherlands every summer to paint polder landscapes. His subject was the expansiveness of the Dutch land decorated with a single windmill, a peat boat, or the nesting baskets for ducks that hang on thin poles.

In 1884 he settled in Scheveningen, near the art center of The Hague. He gave lessons to Willem B. Tholen, among others. Only at the end of his life did he receive the recognition that he deserved.

Hanna Pennock

See also Belgium; Mauve, Anton; Roelofs, Willem; Tholen, Willem Bastiaan

Bibliography

Bionda, Richard et al. *The Age of Van Gogh: Dutch Painting 1880–1895.* Zwolle: Waanders, 1990.

Gruyter, Jos de. *De Haagse School.* 2 vols. Rotterdam: Lemniscaat, 1968–1969. Reprint. 2 vols in 1. Alphen aan den Rijn: Atrium, 1985. (English summary).

Leeman, Fred, and Hanna Pennock. *The Mesdag Museum: Catalogue of Paintings and Drawings.* Zwolle: Waanders, 1996.

Leeuw, Ronald de, John Sillevis, and Charles Dumas, eds. *The Hague School: Dutch Masters of the Nineteenth Century.* London: Royal Academy of Arts, in association with Weidenfeld and Nicolson, 1983.

Gamepiece

Pictures featuring dead game—hare, deer, boar, or birds, from a string of small finches to larger fowl such as swan or peacocks—became popular in the Netherlands around 1650, relatively late in the development of the newly emergent genre of still life. Deriving from sixteenth-century kitchen scenes by Pieter Aertsen and Joachim Beuckelaer, early gamepieces of the 1640s piled game with other food and kitchen utensils. They soon evolved toward more elegant displays, alluding to the privileged social status surrounding the hunt, and survived into the eighteenth century in a more grandiose form.

The first Dutch works were mostly small, simple compositions in the monochrome style then prevalent. Early specialists included Elias Vonck (ca. 1605–1652), his son Jan (1631–1663), and Matthijs Bloem (active early 1640s–1666), though many other artists numbered a few gamepieces among their *oeuvres*. Rembrandt did several in the 1630s, predating any other Dutch examples, while Philips Angel (1616–ca. 1683), Harmen Steenwijck (1612–after 1656), and Michiel Simons (active 1669–1673) included game in their still lifes.

Around 1650 Willem van Aelst (1625/1626–after 1683) introduced a more elegant form of the gamepiece. In place of the rough kitchen surroundings, he arranged the game on a polished marble table or in an elegant stone niche, surrounded by elaborate accoutrements of the hunt: velvet game bags or brocaded hunting jackets, rifles and powder horns, nets and decoy whistles or falconry gear. Van Aelst had worked for some years as the court painter for Ferdinand II de Medici before settling in Amsterdam; many painters of the gamepiece were indebted to him, including William Gowe Ferguson (1632/ 1633–ca. 1695), a Scotsman who spent most of his life in Holland, and Hendrick de Fromantiou (1633–1694), who became court painter for Frederick William the Great Elector in Berlin.

With this shift in the character of the gamepiece, production increased. As the Netherlands enjoyed growing prosperity, more people were finding time for hunting as a leisure pursuit. More important, it had always been a status symbol: Since the Middle Ages, falconry had been the domain of royalty, greyhounds were reserved for privileged classes, and access to hunting grounds had been restricted. These new gamepieces met a growing demand by wealthy burghers for pictures that could display their own rising social positions: Whether or not one actually hunted, a painted gamepiece could suggest suitably aristocratic allusions.

The centers now were Amsterdam, where the wealthy burgher class was growing rapidly, and The Hague, where the court and state officers provided ample patronage. The Hague's most important game painter was Cornelis Lelienbergh (1626–after 1676); one of the more prolific specialists, Jacobus Biltius (1633–1681), who was born in The Hague, went from there to Amsterdam and Maastricht. Dead birds also appeared within *vanitas* still lifes by artists such as Petrus Schotanus (1601–ca. 1675), while a whole separate subgenre was the *bedriegertje* (*trompe l'oeil*, or fool-the-eye illusionistic painting) of hunting gear, popularized by Anthonie (1631–1673) and Johannes (1633–1688) Leemans and others.

Many painters who produced gamepieces were better known for other things: Utrecht-born Melchior de Hondecoeter (1636–1695), a third-generation painter, was known principally for his live-bird scenes; he studied with his father before entering the studio of his uncle through marriage, Jan Baptist Weenix (1621–1660/1661). Weenix, best known for his Italianate landscapes, painted only a few gamepieces, but his son Jan was the finest and most celebrated of all Dutch game painters.

Jan Weenix (1640–1719) began painting genre scenes under his father, switching to still life in the 1680s to focus on works such as this for the remainder of his career (Fig. 50). In the early years of the eighteenth century he worked for Johann Wilhelm, Elector Palatine, in Düsseldorf and Bensberg, producing over one hundred thirty paintings, mostly gamepieces. His greatest achievement was the cycle of twelve huge canvases he painted as wall decorations for the Elector's castle at Bensberg. Weenix's only known pupil was Dirk Valkenburg (1675–1721); with their deaths the last major practitioners of the genre were gone.

The late gamepiece, after 1680, had become larger, more colorful, and more dramatically lit, often animated with live animals such as hunting dogs. This development was inspired by artists such as Frans Snyders and Jan Fyt in the Southern Netherlands, where the gamepiece was the most important type of still life in the seventeenth century. French taste showed in the park-like landscape settings with classical buildings, urns, and statues; but, in turn, the technical achievements of the Dutch painters had an important influence upon French game painters in the early eighteenth century such as Jean-Baptiste Oudry and Jean-Baptiste-Siméon Chardin. Gamepieces remained popular throughout the eighteenth century in Germany as well.

Julie Berger Hochstrasser

See also Aertsen, Pieter; Aristocracy and gentry; De Hondecoeter, Melchior; Still life; Utrecht; *Vanitas, vanitas* still life

Bibliography

Sullivan, Scott. *The Dutch Gamepiece*. Montclair, NJ: Allanheld and Schram, 1984.

Gardens

See Country houses and gardens; Horticulture

Geertgen tot Sint Jans (Gheerkin van Leyden) (active ca. 1465–1485 or 1480–1495/1496)

Recent research has supported the latter dating of his career. According to Karel van Mander (in *Schilder-Boeck*, 1604), Geertgen was a student of Albert van Ouwater and he died young, at about the age of twenty-eight. He was a *famulus et pictor* (servant and painter) at the Commandery of the Knights Hospitalers of St. John (the Johanniters) at Haarlem and his one authenticated altarpiece was made for that order's chapel. The surviving wing panel of this ensemble shows *The Lamentation of Christ* on the interior and *Julian the Apostate Ordering the Burning of the Bones of St. John the Baptist* on the exterior (both in Vienna, Kunsthistorisches Museum; Fig. 62). Geertgen's style derives from that of Hugo van der Goes, whose *Montfort Altarpiece* he seems to quote in his *Lamentation*. Other influences include Rogier van der Weyden. The backgrounds of the Vienna panels may preserve Van Ouwater's landscape style.

Several panels attributed to Geertgen exhibit a mysticism akin to Rhenish art—for example, the *Man of Sorrows* (Utrecht), the *Night Nativity* (London), and the *St. John the Baptist in the Wilderness* (Berlin). The *Madonna of the Rosary* (Rotterdam), the *Holy Kinship*, and the *Tree of Jesse* (both in Amsterdam) demonstrate the influence of rosary imagery fostered by the Dominican Order at Cologne from about 1475 onward.

Later scholars also include Geertgen as one of the founders of the Leiden School.

Diane G. Scillia

See also Devotional images; Donor portraits; Flanders, Flemish School; Haarlem School, early; History painting; Religious orders and their patronage.

Bibliography

Chatelet, A. *Early Dutch Painting: Painting in the Northern Netherlands in the Fifteenth Century.* Translated by Christopher Brown and Anthony Turner. New York: Rizzoli, 1980.

Friedlander, M.J. *Early Netherlandish Painting.* Translated by Heinz Norden. Vol. 5. New York: Praeger, 1970.

Snyder, J.E. *Northern Renaissance Art: Painting, Sculpture, the Graphic Arts from 1350 to 1575.* New York: Harry N. Abrams, 1985.

Genre painting, eighteenth century

It is a generally accepted view that Dutch painting of the eighteenth century was in great measure tributary to the seventeenth century. Genre painting is no exception; particularly before 1750, it relies on the motifs of the seventeenth century. With the continuation of familiar motifs (music-making groups, female fish sellers, bubble-blowing children) there is, however, a certain spirit lacking. The great attention to outward perfection does not make up for it. For a while, the moralizing content remained present in the composition as a whole, but it was produced less and less in a concealed way through emblematic details. In the representation of figures, there was often a certain amount of coldness and stiffness. Even though the Amsterdam artist Cornelis Troost cannot always be claimed to be free of awkwardness, he was still the most skillful and lively painter of the first half of the eighteenth century. Like no other, he knew how to breathe new life into the conventional themes. However, Troost had few students, and he did not start a school.

Philip van Dijk (1680–1753) was trained, like Troost, by Arnold Boonen (1669–1729). Much more than Troost, van Dijk focused on surface refinement and smoothness in painting. This same striving for outward refinement also characterizes a number of painters who were called the Leiden *fijnschilders* (fine painters) after the town in which they lived. They were well-paid masters, who specialized in making cabinet paintings of extremely careful workmanship. Because of their virtuosity and the echo from the past, their paintings were sought-after objects for (princely) collectors in the Netherlands and abroad. The careful technique of Frans van Mieris the Elder and, especially, the delicate brushwork of Gerrit Dou (both seventeenth-century artists) formed the example for the Leiden *fijnschilders*. Their subjects were also borrowed from the seventeenth century. The arched window opening, into which the action of the figures is set, comes back again and again in their compositions. This was an invention from the seventeenth century attributed to Dou (Fig. 28); his shining polished copper pans, his famous still lifes of dressed poultry and game, of carrots and other root vegetables, and the gathered-up curtain were also popular motifs with the eighteenth-century *fijnschilders*. One of the most famous Leiden *fijnschilders* is Willem van Mieris (1662–1747), son of Frans van Mieris the Elder. Willem's son, Frans van Mieris the Younger (1689–1763), was also part of the Leiden group. They both continued the pictorial tradition and the extremely refined painting style of Frans van Mieris the Elder. Willem van Mieris is known for dozens of shop and kitchen scenes, framed most of the time by an arched window (Fig. 51). The stereotypic eroticism of the images, suggested by the poses and the looks of the personages and by the objects like fish and eggs, is still present at the beginning of the century, but it decreases in meaning in the course of the eighteenth century.

In this context the conversation piece also merits some attention. Strictly speaking, it is a part of portraiture; however, it is not always possible to draw a hard line of demarcation between a genre scene with a number of figures in domestic surroundings and a conversation piece, which deals with people whose names are (or were) known. The rapprochement reached between the categories has to do with a development that was taking place in the eighteenth century; both in the area of portraiture and genre painting, the deeper meanings were gradually being lost. The formal composition and the weighty symbolism that were part of group portraiture in the seventeenth century made way for a more informal representation. Surrounded by favorite objects, elegantly dressed persons were portrayed in their comfortable living environment. Neither the symbolism nor the identity of the persons are of decisive interest. An example of the coming together of genre painting and the conversation piece is a painting by Nicolaas Muys (1740–1808), with the title *De Kunstbeschouwing*, (*Contemplating Art,* 1779; Rotterdam, Museum Boymans-Van Beuningen). Muys portrayed himself, his brother, and his sister in a living room, surrounded by art objects and open books on the table.

The indisputable master of both the conversation piece and the genre scene was Cornelis Troost, but Tibout Regters (1710–1768) and Hendrik Pothoven (1726–1807) should also be mentioned. Even though their style is somewhat stiff and awkward, they still give a superb picture of the life of the rich citizens of the eighteenth century. Pothoven, who was a student of Philip van Dijk, was highly praised in his time for his rendering of smooth satin, lace, and carpets.

In the second half of the eighteenth century, there is a discernible change in the art. The more or less mechanical continuation of seventeenth-century achievements makes way for a more conscious reorientation to the art of the great masters from the Golden Age. The quest for a sublime material expression, which made painters earlier in the century use virtuoso brushstrokes, was no longer the main motivation. Without falling into sentimentality, the accent moved to the human aspect of the picture—a writing boy, a reading couple. The tendency for deeper meanings to fade away continued; the moral implications in a genre scene moved into the background, if they did not disappear altogether. A rotten apple in a basket was nothing more than a rotten apple, whereas a century earlier such an apple would have served as a symbol for bad company.

In the work of Hendrik Schweickhardt (1746–1797) the motifs of Adriaen van Ostade, David Teniers the Younger, and Cornelis Dusart reappear in civilized form. The once-quarreling farmers, whose intemperate behavior hid a warning about the sin of anger, have become refined country people who are engaged in innocent pleasure in front of their houses. *A Writer Sharpening His Pen* (1784; Amsterdam, Rijksmuseum; Fig. 52), by Jan Ekels the Younger (1759–1793), shows a simplicity of conception and clarity of form that relate to the atmosphere created by Johannes Vermeer in his interiors a century earlier.

From the beginning of the nineteenth century, Adriaan de Lelie (1755–1820) and Wybrand Hendriks (1744–1831) should be mentioned. Both painters gave back to genre painting the integrity that was missing from it for most of the early eighteenth century. Despite the inspiration they received from the preceding century (from Vermeer, Gabriel Metsu, and Gerard Ter Borch), the works of De Lelie and Hendriks are a sincere expression of their own time.

Eugenie Boer

See also Conversation piece; Dou, Gerrit; Genre painting, seventeenth century; Group portraiture; Humor, satire; Leiden; Portraiture; Pothoven, Hendrik; Regters, Tibout; Troost, Cornelis

Bibliography

Fuchs, R. *Dutch Painting*. London: Thames and Hudson, 1978.

Hecht, P. *De Hollandse fijnschilders*. Maarssen: Gary Schwartz/SDU, 1989.

Knoef, J. *Tusschen Rococo en Romantiek*. The Hague: Stols, 1943.

Mandle, R. *Dutch Masterpieces from the Eighteenth Century: Paintings and Drawings, 1700–1800*. Minneapolis: Minneapolis Institute of Arts, 1971.

Rosenberg, Jakob, Seymour Slive, and E.H. ter Kuile. *Dutch Art and Architecture, 1600–1800*. Baltimore: Penguin, 1966.

Sluijter, E.J. "Hendrik Willem Schweickhardt, 1746–1797: Een Haagse schilder in de tweede helft van de achttiende eeuw." *Oud Holland* 89 (1975): 142–212.

Staring, A. "De beeldende kunst in de achttiende eeuw." In *Kunstgeschiedenis der Nederlanden*. Edited by H.E. van Gelder et al. 3 vols. 3rd ed. Utrecht: De Haan, 1954–1956.

Genre painting, seventeenth century

It is important to note that the term "genre," denoting scenes of everyday life, was not employed in the seventeenth century. Pictures that today are called genre scenes were then referred to more specifically. Commonly cited types included the *buitenpartij* (outdoor party), *bordeeltje* (brothel scene), and *boerenkermis* (peasant fair). The word "genre" acquired its current meaning in France toward the end of the eighteenth century and became widespread only in connection with the evolution of nineteenth-century genre painting. As a result, the term carries with it connotations of the nineteenth-century concept of realism, which do not apply to seventeenth-century Dutch genre paintings. Nonetheless, due to the lack of a satisfactory alternative, the term "genre" continues to be used. Consequently, it is important to recognize that it is a problematic term and that it does not signify a coherent category. The fact that there was no all-encompassing term or phrase employed to characterize these works in the seventeenth century should be a constant reminder to us today of the risks involved in making generalizations about the nature and content of such a diverse body of images.

Seventeenth-century Dutch artists produced paintings in record quantities, including an unprecedented number of images that presented what, at first glance, may appear to be simply scenes of people in the activities of daily life: skating, drinking, gambling, dancing, fighting, courting, caring for their homes and children, and earning their livings. The variety of subjects and the convincing rendition of "reality" seemed to nineteenth-century admirers to indicate that Dutch painters had provided an accurate record of their lives and surroundings. While seventeenth-century Dutch genre paintings continue to amaze and delight viewers with their re-creations of reality, they are no longer considered to be accurate recordings of daily life. Despite the great variety, the range of subjects is not encyclopedic. Some situations, professions, and activities appear again and again, while others are neglected or overlooked entirely. Moreover, the costumes, settings, and situations do not always reflect normal practices, reminding the viewer that the pictures themselves are artificial constructions whose structures and motifs are artistically arranged to create a particular effect, and in which conventions and patterns can be perceived.

To what effect are the pictures constructed? Scholars do not agree, and their disagreement relates, in part, to their different perceptions of seventeenth-century Dutch culture. For example, Eddy de Jongh, the foremost proponent of the iconological approach, sees a marked propensity for seeking out the meaning inherent in everyday things and occurrences, and for using them as vehicles for ready-made ideas, as one of the most notable characteristics of the Dutch in the seventeenth century. He argues that many medieval modes of thinking and expression, among them the visual metaphor, persisted for seventeenth-century artists and viewers. De Jongh was the first to assert that the realistic appearance of seventeenth-century Dutch genre paintings is a *schijnrealisme* (pseudorealism) that conceals beneath its surface the true meaning of the picture (De Jongh, 1971). According to this approach, everything that is depicted in the work is a potential carrier of meaning. Considered in this way, the pictures function much like emblems and provide the viewer with the pleasure of deciphering their meanings and, more often than not, a moralizing message. De Jongh uses seventeenth-century language, literature (especially emblem books), and inscribed prints to uncover the hidden messages in particular pictures and to support the presence of didactic content, witticisms, and other veiled meanings in genre painting in general. He argues that seventeenth-century Dutch art and literature were judged by the same standards—conforming to a prevailing belief in *ut pictura poesis* (painting is like poetry)—and that both were intended to instruct as well as give pleasure.

Svetlana Alpers, on the other hand, argues that Dutch picture-making is not tied to texts for meaning in the same way that contemporary Italian pictures are, and she examines the way in which Dutch images are part of a specifically visual mode of understanding the world. Alpers sees seventeenth-century Dutch culture not as a last flowering of a medieval thought system in which ordinary things are regarded as corporeal metaphors for the spiritual, but as the beginning of empiricism, attested to by a fascination with optics and optical devices as aids to learning. Experimental science, she contends, confirms the making of pictures as a way to a new and certain knowledge of the world. The senses are not dangerous but the path to understanding, and sight is the preeminent sense. Seeing is a way of knowing, she explains, and picturing is a way of recording knowledge; moreover, as a form of language, picturing is a way of acquiring knowledge. The meaning of a picture is not what lies beneath its surface but what one sees there.

The differences between these two influential scholars' approaches can be demonstrated by examining their interpretations of Gerrit Dou's *The Quacksalver* (1652; Rotterdam, Museum Boymans-van Beuningen; Fig. 114). Both state that the theme of *The Quacksalver* is deception, as is characteristic of the representation of quack doctors—for example, Jan van de Velde II's print after Willem Buytewech, which bears an inscription saying that people want to be deceived. However, their interpretations differ significantly. The catalog *Tot lering en vermaak* (For Instruction and Amusement), written by De Jongh with his students, connects various figures, activities, and objects in Dou's painting to emblems depicting the same or similar things and uses the accompanying texts to explain the quack's deceiving his audience as a warning against sensual seduction and choosing the carnal life, the basest of the three life alternatives. The highest choice is the contemplative life, which is exemplified by the artist in the painting, a self-portrait of Dou, who is contrasted to the quack. The artist and the quack are contrasted for an additional purpose, and this, the catalog contends, is to reveal the elevated nature of the art of painting, an art that by virtue of its literary content is equal to poetry. In contrast to the quack, whose work is stupid *naaperij* (aping, mimicry), a concept underscored by the presence of an ape, the artist's work is based on a rational foundation; painting appeals to reason because it contains a moralizing message (De Jongh, 1976: 87–89).

According to Alpers, however, Dou's work celebrates the mimetic aspect of painting so frequently praised in seventeenth-century Dutch writings about art, as, for example, when Samuel van Hoogstraten compares a perfect painting to a mirror of nature that deceives the eye in a praiseworthy manner. Focusing on what is visually presented to the viewer, Alpers does not deal with the texts of the emblems to which the figures and motifs in the painting have been connected, but considers only that the latter exemplify popular maxims and proverbs. She refers to them as pictorial quotations and states that the result can be considered taxonomic, a catalog of human behaviors visually presented. The picture is, thus, not prescriptive but descriptive, and the artist's skill at describing is stressed. Alpers notes that both the artist and the quack deceive a willing audience, and Dou, who shows himself looking directly at the viewer, captures the viewer's eye and thus draws attention to the painterly deception, to the masterly illusionism of his craft (Alpers, 1983: 116).

Like Alpers, Eric Jan Sluijter interprets the picture as a celebration of the painter's mimetic skills and focuses on what is visible. He contends that Dou, like other Dutch artists working for an anonymous public whose knowledge of specific emblems could not be assumed, used common motifs that would prompt the viewer to make the appropriate associations. For example, Sluijter explains the dead tree in the painting not as part of an emblem about the anxiety of choice, or a pictorial quotation of a maxim, but as a motif alluding to the fruitlessness of the activity portrayed. Dou, he points out, employs several such motifs in underscoring the characteristically negative qualities associated with the quack and his audience, who, according to pictorial convention, exemplified deceit and stupidity, respectively. Compared and contrasted to the quack and his audience are the artist and the viewer. As Sluijter explains, the quack deceives his silly, gullible audience with pretty words, while the artist turns to the viewer, who is above such ploys but who is deceived in a praiseworthy way by Dou's painting. Like the quack, Dou earns his living by deceit; however, the deception that he practices as a painter causes not material and personal loss but pleasure and delight and is highly prized (Sluijter, 1990: 28–33).

Like many scholars, Sluijter has been influenced by aspects of the approaches of both De Jongh and Alpers. He states that although the iconological approach has greatly enriched our understanding of seventeenth-century art, one must always be careful with a method that (as Alpers argues) was developed for fifteenth- and sixteenth-century Italian art, an art that is closely connected with texts and often is intended for particular contexts. Sluijter urges those who wish to comprehend how pictures were understood at the time to consider the work in broad cultural context, including examining the implications of things such as the dress of the figures. He notes that all types of literature should be consulted, not to discover sources for pictures or to pinpoint limited meanings, but to help demonstrate what metaphors were current and what kinds of associations a given activity or thing would likely evoke in the mind of the viewer. He stresses that paintings were created for an anonymous audience; therefore, the visual means through which they must communicate must make connections with the recognizable and familiar, such as stereotypes and other things drawn from the world of experience. Thus, the most profitable way to investigate a work is in light of the pictorial tradition. Sluijter's method of investigation emphasizes comparison and analysis: To understand why certain subjects were popular and appealing, they must be studied not only with similar subjects, but also with similar types, and the pictorial conventions involved must be accurately analyzed. One must comprehend their origin and development and perceive how particular painters transformed, adapted, or diverged from these conventions. In this way, and with the use of all possible cultural and historical sources, one can begin to recover the "how" and "why" of certain subjects and can explore the meaning that pictures had for artists and the public. In addition, Sluijter underscores the importance of remembering that paintings are not reality but artificial constructions, and that the viewer's experience of them is not open-ended but determined to a great extent by the artist's presentation.

In formulating his method for examining genre paintings, Sluijter also takes into account seventeenth-century Dutch writings about art, noting that, while they say nothing meaningful about genre images and nothing about didactic content, they emphasize the mimetic aspect of painting and its ability to delight and deceive the eye (in Freedberg, 1991: 175–208). Like Alpers, Sluijter uses Samuel van Hoogstraten's comparison of the perfect painting to a mirror in *Inleyding tot de hooge schoole der schilderkonst* (Introduction to the Elevated School of Painting) in 1678 as a basis for a more extended rumination on the character of seventeenth-century Dutch painting. However, whereas Alpers focuses on the imitative aspect of the mirror metaphor and the attention it brings to the surface aspect of painting, Sluijter, prompted by Van Hoogstraten's evocation of vain and transient beauty in his discussion of Narcissus and the origin of the art of painting, adds another element. He states that a great many paintings present a deceptively real image and, at the same time, confront the viewer regarding them with associations of beauty, pride, vanity, transience, and self-knowledge—like a mirror. Thus, while moralizing meanings are not obviously implied, he states, they are not excluded either.

Peter Hecht makes seventeenth-century writings about art the cornerstone of his argument that many genre pictures convey no moralizing meaning. He contends that the *fijnschilders* (literally, fine painters; artists active in the second half of the seventeenth century, mainly in Leiden) selected subjects for representation and included objects for their pictorial potential rather than for any associations they might evoke in the viewer's mind. He notes that Philips Angel in *Lof der schilder-konst* (Praise of Painting), published in Leiden in 1642, claimed that painting is superior to sculpture due to its ability to imitate nature in a lifelike way. Hecht argues that in order to make the same point, Gerrit Dou in his *Kitchen Maid* (Karlsruhe, Staatliche Kunsthalle), painted ten years later in Leiden, contrasts the convincing representation of a carrot leaf with the stiff and stylized vine portrayed in a sculptural relief. Moreover, the fish, fowl, and hare in the same picture could have been included by Dou because they gave him the opportunity to display his artistic virtuosity in representing the differing textures of scales, feathers, and fur rather than because of their erotic connotations. (Hecht, 1992: 86). Hecht opposes the iconological approach and rejects the idea that all Dutch art was meant to be read symbolically, in part because there is no evidence for such a reading in the relevant texts. He proposes that what one encounters in these pictures is the notion that the subject is simply a vehicle for the form. Although Hecht considers only genre works by the *fijnschilders*, he places his conclusions within the broader context of seventeenth-century Dutch painting, and thus it is unclear to what degree he sees the concept of "art for art's sake" as applying to the wider body of works.

While Van Hoogstraten and Angel, the authors of the only relevant texts on art published in the seventeenth-century (Karel van Mander's *Schilder-Boeck* (Book of Picturing) being published in 1604 and thus too early to be helpful), make no mention of the didactic content of art, the popular writer Jacob Cats (1577–1660) does, as Sluijter notes (in Freedberg, 1991:196–197). In his discussion of the rival merits of painting and poetry, Cats observed that paintings could confront people with their faults, an observation Angel chose

to omit when he drew upon Cats' text, "De beschryving van de op-komste van Rhodopis" from *Proef-steen van de Trou-Ringh* ("Description of the Rise of Rhodopis," from Touchstone of the Wedding Ring) of 1637. Simon Schama argues that this is one of the functions of seventeenth-century Dutch painting. He states that there is a combination of enticement and admonition in Dutch art, which reflects the dualistic nature of the culture, and that the viewer confronted with an image of sensual transgression can choose to either "luxuriate in its license or ruminate on the wages of iniquity" (Schama, 1979: 109). Other scholars, perceiving changes in genre painting in the course of the seventeenth century, assert that works of the first decades often present clear moralizing messages, while the frequency of such messages and the clarity of presentation diminishes as the century progresses. Linda A. Stone-Ferrier compares this move toward increasingly descriptive genre images to a waning interest in emblems and notes that, at the same time, history painting declined in Delft and there was a sharp growth in the already expanding categories of still life, landscape, and genre painting (Stone-Ferrier, 1983: 24). Lyckle de Vries (in Freedberg, 1991: 209–244), the first to explore this change in some detail, states that by the 1630s questions of style began to receive increased attention and that this interest in aestheticism was accompanied by an iconographic erosion, a gradual loss of understanding of the subject matter's original didactic content. He attributes the practice of not explicitly indicating how a painting was to be interpreted to both a mass production of pictures, accompanied by a mindless repetition of traditional motifs, and the growing distance between artist and collector. De Vries suggests that the declining interest in explicit didactic content may be related to the rise to power of the middle class, who in the second half of the sixteenth century felt the need to distinguish themselves from others and employed Christian humanist ethics to do so. As their identity was established and position gained, the need to chastise those who failed to adhere to the rules may have diminished and didacticism declined. De Vries also notes that the lack of explicitness places the burden of interpretation on the viewer. Those who, after 1650, purchased a genre painting by Gerard Ter Borch or Frans van Mieris the Elder, for example, could either see it as a painted sermon or focus on its painterly refinement while acknowledging its moralizing with a disinterested nod.

While questions about symbolic content and moralizing meanings no doubt will continue to be debated, the increased attention that has been given to the way pictures are constructed visually is raising other issues. For example, some scholars like Sluijter and Celeste Brusati (Brusati, 1993) are focusing on the erotic content of paintings in which women are presented as objects of desire, often insistently framed and voyeuristically viewed. Others are exploring the way viewers of different genders and eras relate to the works (Kettering, 1993). Still others are addressing the ways that genre imagery can express ideas about national identity, civic pride, and horticultural innovation (Linda Stone-Ferrier in Freedberg, 1991: 29–58). Clearly, one today is confronted with a host of different approaches, generated not only by the differing attitudes toward method and toward the Dutch culture that produced these works, but also by the extraordinary diversity of the images themselves.

Barbara Haeger

See also Allegorical traditions; Art history, history of the discipline; Carnal life, carnal vices; Contemplative life, contemplative virtues; Didactic images; Dou, Gerrit; Emblems and emblem books; Gestures; Humanism, humanist themes; Illusionism; Literature, poetry: analogues with the visual; Quacksalvers, quack doctors; Subjects, subject categories, and hierarchies; Ter Borch, Gerard; Writers on art, sixteenth and seventeenth centuries

Bibliography
Alpers, Svetlana. *The Art of Describing: Dutch Art in the Seventeenth Century.* Chicago: University of Chicago Press, 1983.

Bock, Henning, and Thomas W. Gaehtgens, eds. *Hollandische Genremalerei im 17. Jahrhundert, Symposium Berlin 1984.* Berlin: Gebr. Mann Verlag, 1987.

Brown, Christopher. *Scenes of Everyday Life: Dutch Genre Painting of the Seventeenth Century.* London and Boston: Faber and Faber, 1984.

Brusati, Celeste. *Johannes Vermeer.* New York: Rizzoli, 1993.

Freedberg, David, and Jan de Vries, eds. *Art in History, History in Art: Studies in Seventeenth-Century Dutch Culture.* Santa Monica, CA: Getty Center for the History of Art and the Humanities, 1991.

Hecht, Peter. "Dutch Seventeenth-Century Genre Painting: A Reassessment of Some Current Hypotheses." *Simiolus* 21 (1992): 85–95.

Jongh, E. de. "Realisme en schijnrealisme in de Hollandse schilderkunst van de zeventiende eeuw." *Rembrandt en zijn tijd.* Brussels: Musées Royaux d'Art et d'Histoire, 1971.

Jongh, E. de, et al. *Tot lering en vermaak.* Amsterdam: Rijksmuseum, 1976.

Kettering, Alison McNeil. "Ter Borch's Ladies in Satin." *Art History* 16 (1993): 95–124.

Schama, Simon. "The Unruly Realm: Appetite and Restraint in Seventeenth-Century Holland." *Daedalus* 108 (1979): 103–123.

Sluijter, Eric J. "Hoe realistisch is de Noordnederlandse schilderkunst van de zeventiende eeuw? De problemen van een vraagstelling." *Leidschrift* 6 (1990): 5–39.

Stone-Ferrier, Linda A. *Dutch Prints of Daily Life: Mirrors of Life or Masks of Morals?* Lawrence, KS: Spencer Museum of Art and Allen Press, 1983.

Sutton, Peter C. *Masters of Seventeenth-Century Dutch Genre Painting.* Philadelphia: Philadelphia Museum of Art, 1984.

Gestel, Leo (1881–1941)

After having set out to be a drawing teacher, Leo Gestel finally decided in 1904 to become an independent artist. Meanwhile, he had acquired the elementary certificate in freehand drawing (1897–1899), passed through the Rijksnormaalschool voor Teekenonderwijs (National Normal School for Drawing Education, 1900–1903), and taken evening classes at the Rijksacademie (1900–1904), the last two in Amsterdam. In 1904, together with Jan Sluijters, Gestel visited various places in Belgium and Paris, where he was very impressed by the "new" French art. Among the Dutch artists who inspired him were primarily Vincent van Gogh, Jan Toorop, Floris Verster, and Kees van Dongen. From 1904 until 1914 Gestel experimented, as did Sluijters and Piet Mondrian, with all sorts of styles: there exist Impressionist, divisionist, luminist, and Cubist landscapes, figure pieces, and flower still lifes. Gestel exhibited with the modern artists' society St. Lucas (1907–1911) and the Moderne Kunstkring (Modern Art Circle, 1911–1914). In 1915 he founded with others the Hollandsche Kunstenaarskring (Dutch Artists' Circle) and exhibited his works done in Mallorca. After 1915 Gestel worked a great deal in Bergen, an important artists' center in North Holland at that time. There he changed to an Expressionist way of painting. During trips to Germany, Italy, and Belgium in the 1920s, Gestel gained many new impressions. In Belgium he had contact with Gustave de Smet and Frits van den Berghe. After a fire in his studio in 1929, he settled in Blaricum, where he lived until his death. His late Expressionist work shows a continuing simplification and emits a fairly melancholy spirit.

Alexandra W.M. van Smoorenburg

See also Avant-garde; Belgium; Bergen; Coins, medals; Sluijters, Jan

Bibliography
Estourgie-Beijer, M.E.Th., and E. Heuves. *Leo Gestel: Schilder en tekenaar.* Zwolle: Waanders, 1993. (English summary).

Loosjes-Terpstra, A.B. *Leo Gestel als modernist; werk uit de periode 1907–1922.* 's Hertogenbosch: Noordbrabants Museum, 1983.

———. *Moderne Kunst in Nederland, 1900–1914.* 1959. Rev. ed. Utrecht: Veen/Reflex, 1987.

Gestures

If God is to be found in the smallest detail, as Flaubert and Panofsky put it, then art historians—from Vasari to Morelli, Panofsky, and so many others—have amply written about God. In fact, gestures have always received attention, from one scholar after another.

Unfortunately, this attention has hardly been of a systematic kind. Though valuable monographs have been written on antiquity and the Middle Ages (Brilliant, Garnier), on the early-modern period there is not much more than J.J. Tikkanen's outdated but still interesting *Die Beinstellungen in der Kunstgeschichte* (1912). As for the study of gestures in Dutch seventeenth-century art, one of the reasons for its neglect may be found in the tendency of all iconologists (including the Dutch school of Eddy de Jongh and its followers) to restrict their symbolic universe to the "great tradition," to the world of high art and high literature (for example, emblem books). At the same time, historians have not been very helpful either. Even though the "new social history," as defended by Peter Burke and others, has stressed the place of symbolism in everyday life and has concentrated on apparently trivial routines and rituals in reconstructing the rules implicit in a given culture, in "reading" its "grammar," the historian's interest in gesture is still quite meager. Contacts, however, have been made. In fact, a joining of forces of art historians, historians, and also literary historians may turn the study of gesture into one of the most promising fields of the last few years. Its practitioners can also learn from sociologists, such as Erving Goffman and his "dramaturgical approach," from anthropologists, sociolinguists, and semiologists. No less important is the work done on nonverbal communication, in particular on kinesics (the study of body movements).

For the moment it seems prudent to define the concept rather loosely, drawing no rigid lines between "gesture" (of the hands and limbs) and "posture" (the whole carriage and deportment of the body). The range of sources, apart from the visual material itself, is considerable. Even though treatises that were entirely devoted to the subject, such as *L'arte de'cenni* (1616) by Giovanni Bonifacio or John Bulwer's *Chirologia: or the Naturall Language of the Hand* (1644), may have been less known in the Dutch Republic, numerous data on gesture may be found in the "civility books," a tradition beginning more or less with Castiglione's *The Courtier* (1528) or Erasmus' *De civilitate morum puerilium* (1530), but persisting well into the eighteenth century. No less important is the vast literature on public eloquence (going back to Aristotle, Cicero, and Quintilian), on clothing, dancing, acting, fencing, and the like. On actual behavior much is to be gleaned from such personal sources as letters, diaries, and memoirs, and from such administrative sources as judicial, notarial, and church records. These sources can inform us concerning the social aspects of gesture (class, gender, ethnicity) and moral aspects, such as honor and shame. Though mostly overlooked by iconologists, much of this material contains valuable information on the routines and rituals of everyday life, including gesture and posture.

Herman Roodenburg

See also Emblems and emblem books; Genre painting, seventeenth century; History painting; Portraiture; Theater and theatricality

Bibliography

Bolten, J. *Positur: Gaan en staan in de beeldende kunst van de 16de en 17de eeuw.* Leiden: Rijksuniversiteit Leiden, 1991.

Bremmer, Jan, and Herman Roodenburg, eds. *A Cultural History of Gesture from Antiquity to the Present Day.* Ithaca, NY: Cornell University Press, 1992.

Brilliant, R. *Gesture and Rank in Roman Art: The Use of Gestures to Denote Status in Roman Sculpture and Coinage.* New Haven: The Academy, 1963.

Garnier, F. *Le langage de l'image au Moyen Age: Signification et symbolique.* 2 vols. Paris: Leopard d'or, 1982–1989.

Roodenburg, Herman. "Over scheefhalzen en zwellende heupen: Enige argumenten voor een historische antropologie van de zeventiende-eeuwse schilderkunst." *De Zeventiende Eeuw* 9 (1993): 153–168.

Tikkanen, J.J. *Die Beinstellungen in der Kunstgeschichte: Ein Beitrag zur Geschichte der künstlerischen Motive.* Helsingfors: Akademische Buchhandlung, 1912.

Goltzius, Hendrick (1558–1617)

Engraver, draftsman, painter, and print publisher, Hendrick Goltzius became known as the Dutch Proteus, famed for his powers of imitation, which he demonstrated in new and surprising ways. Praised in Karel van Mander's *Schilder-Boeck* (Book on Picturing, 1604) as a paragon of *teyckenconst* (also spelled *tekenkonst;* drawing or the art of delineation), Goltzius disseminated his prints and drawings widely, aiming to broadcast his achievements throughout Europe. For his efforts he twice received a gold chain, the mark of courtly favor, awarded by Duke Wilhelm V of Bavaria and Cardinal Federico Borromeo, and his works entered major collections, such as the *kunstkammer* (art and curiosity cabinet) of Emperor Rudolf II.

Born to a family of painters in the Rhenish village of Mühlbracht in 1558, Goltzius first studied with his father, the glass painter Jan Goltz. Resident in Duisburg from 1561, he came to know the engraver Dirck Volkertsz. Coornhert, exiled in nearby Xanten, with whom he engaged to study the art of engraving around 1575. By 1576 Goltzius had become known as Coornhert's *discipele* (disciple), his apprentice but also a follower of his controversial religious views. He followed his master to Haarlem in 1577, collaborating with him as had the draftsmen Maerten van Heemskerck and Adriaan de Weert. Like them, Goltzius translated Coornhert's allegorical conceits into pictorial images, converting *aerdighe sin-rijcke beduytselen* (pleasing allegories, rich in meaning) into drawings, which then served as models for prints.

Between 1577 and 1582 Goltzius executed plates for Antwerp print publishers such as Philips Galle, engraving his own designs, as well as those by Maarten de Vos, Johannes Stradanus, and Anthonie Blocklandt. By 1582, however, he had himself begun publishing prints, and between 1582 and 1584 he issued ambitious plates after Blocklandt and Dirck Barendsz., Northern epigones of Parmigianino and Titian, respectively. In the allegorical series *Ways and Means to Fortune* (1582), he set forth his aims as engraver-publisher, averring that *ars* (the theory or the rules of art) and *usus* (the practice of art), being inextricably linked, result in honor and wealth that lead, in turn, to peace of mind. Goltzius began to engrave designs by the imperial painter Bartholomeus Spranger in 1585, having studied drawings owned by Van Mander. In order to translate Spranger's serpentine figures, he modified his burin-hand (use of the burin), engraving long sinuous lines that undulate with the body's contours, rising and falling in concentric series of swelling and tapering hatches. By 1587 he was actually collaborating with Spranger, who sent a large drawing of the *Nuptials of Cupid and Psyche*, engraved by Goltzius with a dedication to Wolfgang Rumpf, the imperial chamberlain. Along with the *Roman Heroes* of 1586, dedicated to Rudolf II, the *Nuptials* is an early example of Goltzius' ambition to consolidate his fame by entering into a fiction of courtly service. Based in Haarlem, he retained commercial control of his plates, even while claiming to have placed his skill at the disposal of the emperor and his court. In the plates after Spranger, and even more in the *Great Hercules* of 1589, whose ostensible theme is the hero's *virtus* (martial virtue), Goltzius' central theme is his own virtue, which has mastered burin and copper plate, overcoming intractable materials to produce a distinctive manner of line that signals the engraver's virtuosity.

Goltzius embarked on a trip to Italy in 1590, traveling to Venice, Bologna, Florence, Rome, and Naples, where he studied ancient statuary and Italian masters famed for their *colorito* (coloring), returing to Haarlem in 1591 with vivid memories of paintings by Raphael, Titian, Correggio, and Veronese, among others. He now relied on former students such as Jacob Matham and Jan Saenredam to engrave his designs, devoting himself to the production of a few demonstration plates such as the *Life of the Virgin* (1593–1594), a series of six prints, each of which distills the pictorial manner of an Italian painter or Northern engraver. Rather than displaying his own manner of line, Goltzius aimed to impersonate masters whom he assembled into a cross-cultural canon, not only imitating their distinctive pictorial manners, but even inventing images as they would have. For his skill at impersonating masters as varied as Albrecht Dürer, Lucas van Leyden, Federigo Barocci, and Jacopo Bassano, Goltzius received the epithet Proteus, for he, like the ancient sea god, had succeeded at transforming himself into that which he imitated.

Granted an imperial privilege in 1595, Goltzius continued to issue prints until 1601, but he had virtually ceased to engrave by 1598, having transferred control of his print workshop to his stepson Jacob Matham. Yet his burin-hand remained central to his greatest achievements as draftsman, the innovative *penwercken* (works of the pen), drawn in the manner of engraving on primed canvas. Portraying *Venus Receiving the Gifts of Bacchus and Ceres* (ca. 1599–1602; Fig. 53), a theme that had fascinated Goltzius since 1588, the first *penwerck* layers traditional media in unprecedented ways, combining glue sizing, black ink, and oil colors within a continuum of pictorial means that shifts from painting to drawing, drawing to engraving, and engraving to painting. These ambiguities are typical of the *penwercken*, which certify Goltzius' command of *inventie* (technical invention). In another *penwerck*, the immense *Venus, Bacchus, and Ceres* of 1606, Goltzius portrays himself at the altar of Venus, offering pairs of burins held in both hands to show that his love of art and command of artisanship issue from his burin-hand.

Impressed by his experience of Italian masters, Goltzius turned to painting around 1600, pursuing the principles of *wel verwen* (coloring well) until his death in 1617. Along with Cornelis Cornelisz. he introduced the use of large canvases, preferring to coat the surface before painting with a colored gray ground instead of the white ground traditionally associated with panel painting. Many of his images reflect upon the nature of the art of painting, the most spectacular being the *Danaë*, painted for the collector Bartholomeus Ferreris in 1603. Goltzius' theme is the power of painting to seduce the eyes, as the beauty of Danaë seduced Jupiter, compelling him to shower her with gold, just as the viewer pours gold upon the painter to procure his work (E.J. Sluijter, in Falkenburg, Filedt Kok, and Leeflang, 1993: 376–378). Like the *penwercken* rendered in the manner of engraving, the prints that distill the manner of Italian and northern masters, and the prints that translate Spranger's inventions, the *Danaë* indulges Goltzius' predilection for the topic of imitation, allowing him once again to explore the means and ends of art as his crucial theme.

Walter S. Melion

See also Allegorical traditions; Coornhert, Dirck Volkertsz.; Drawing practices and techniques; Drawing theory; Flanders, Flemish School; Haarlem; Humanism, humanist themes; Italy; Landscape; Mannerism, Mannerists; Matham, Jacob; Prints, printmaking, and printmakers (ca. 1500–ca. 1900); Prints, publishers; Roman history; Van Mander, Karel; Writers on art, sixteenth and seventeenth centuries

Bibliography

Falkenburg, Reindert, Jan Piet Filedt Kok, and Huigen Leeflang, eds. *Goltzius Studies: Hendrick Goltzius 1558–1617.* Zwolle: Waanders, 1993.

Ginneken, Lily van, ed. "Goltzius als schilder." Theme volume. *Openbaar Kunstbezit* 29 (1985).

Melion, Walter S. "Love and Artisanship in Hendrick Goltzius' *Venus, Bacchus, and Ceres* of 1606." *Art History* 16 (1993): 60–94.

———. "Piety and Pictorial Manner in Hendrick Goltzius' *Early Life of the Virgin.*" In *Hendrick Goltzius and the Classical Tradition.* Edited by Glenn Harcourt, 44–51. Los Angeles: Fisher Gallery, 1992.

———. *Shaping the Netherlandish Canon: Karel van Mander's "Schilder-Boeck."* Chicago: University of Chicago Press, 1991.

Nichols, Lawrence W. *The "Pen Works" of Hendrick Goltzius.* Bulletin no. 88. Philadelphia: Philadelphia Museum of Art, 1991.

Reznicek, Emil K. J. *Hendrick Goltzius Zeichnungen.* 2 vols. Utrecht: Haentjens, Dekker, and Gumbert, 1961.

Riggs, Timothy, and Larry Silver, eds. *Graven Images: The Rise of Professional Printmakers in Antwerp and Haarlem, 1540–1640.* Evanston: Mary and Leigh Block Gallery, 1993.

Sluijter, E.J. "Venus, Visus en Pictura." In *Goltzius Studies: Hendrick Goltzius 1558–1617.* Edited by Reindert Falkenburg, Jan Piet Filedt Kok, and Huigen Leeflang, 337–396. Zwolle: Waanders, 1993.

Strauss, Walter L. *Hendrik Goltzius, 1558–1617: The Complete Engravings and Woodcuts.* 2 vols. New York: Abaris, 1977.

Gouda

According to its initial charter granted on January 31, 1487, the Gouda St. Luke's Guild included painters, sculptors, glassmakers, printers, and embroiderers as members. By the sixteenth century, the glassmakers took on a prominent role. The Crabeths, Dirck (died 1577) and Wouter (died 1589), represent the most noted artists in this arena, and their work influenced subsequent generations. The number of glassmaking ateliers at Gouda during the next two centuries (eighteen in 1621) indicate that it remained a viable field.

The Gouda St. Jan's Church, where the Crabeths and subsequent generations of glassmakers worked, was admired and visited for its stained glass during the seventeenth century and beyond. The church wardens' purchase of the window cartoons and a subsequent plan to publish prints of selected windows affirm the recognition of their merit. Small pamphlets published at Gouda since the 1680s functioned as guides for the visitor.

The St. Jan's Church is a major site for the study of Northern Renaissance stained glass. It contains the pre-Reformation Catholic stained-glass commissions, as well as the earliest and largest surviving cycle of post-Reformation stained glass in a Dutch Reformed church. Many churches suffered destructive waves of Iconoclastic riots during the 1560s and 1570s, leaving no visual traces of their earlier contents when they were converted to Protestant usage. The survival of these scarce works enables a comparison with contemporary painting and prints. They also permit an examination of the relationship between the iconography of the cycles and the changes in patronage (noble to civic) of their donors during the second half of the sixteenth century.

The Crabeths began designing windows for the choir, dedicated to the life of Christ and St. John the Baptist, after a fire devastated the St. Jan's Church in 1552 (Fig. 126). Dirck received other commissions for church windows in The Hague, Amsterdam, and Utrecht, and he also created designs for tapestries and small-scale windows for private dwellings. His early work shows the influence of Jan Swart, a printmaker, who may have trained Adriaen Crabeth, the older brother of Dirck and Wouter, during a proposed residency in Gouda (1530s).

The political turmoil of the 1560s and 1570s led to disruption of the city's artistic life. Cornelis Ketel (the Crabeths' brother-in-law) fled to London. However, the prominent Haarlem draftsman, printmaker, and philosopher Dirck Volkertsz. Coornhert spent his remaining years at Gouda (1588–1590). The post-Reformation *Freedom of Conscience* window in St. Jan's may have been influenced by his writings.

The post-Reformation windows designed by artists from the donating cities celebrated historical themes of civic pride. The Crabeth's successor, Adriaen Dircksz. de Vrije, did not play as critical a role in the post-Reformation work. Later in the seventeenth and eighteenth centuries, Gouda glassmakers visually recorded and repaired the St. Jan windows in drawings and watercolors. The city historians, church wardens, and artists focused upon the recognition of Gouda's historic moment in the tradition of glassmaking.

Carol Janson

See also Ceramics; Coornhert, Dirck Volkertsz.; Protestant Reformation; Roundels; Stained glass

Bibliography

Bogtman, R.W. *Glans Der Goudse Glazen*. Gouda: Fonds Goudse Glazen, 1990. (English summary).

Filedt Kok, Jan Piet et al. *Kunst voor de beeldenstorm*. The Hague: Staatsuitgeverij, 1986. (English translation of introductory essays).

Janson, Carol. "Preserving the Word: Wtewael's *Freedom of Conscience* Window at Gouda." *Konsthistorisk Tidskrift* 57 (1988): 18–29.

Graphic design

During the last hundred years, graphic design has become an indispensible part of Dutch culture. Closely connected with developments in modern and contemporary art and architecture, this professional field has also experienced the rivalry between traditionalism and experimentation.

Little attention has been paid to this graphic discipline, and not unreasonably so. In the Calvinistic Netherlands of the nineteenth century, publishers and readers were often primarily interested in the edifying contents of the book and not in its outward appearance. In spite of the typographical tradition (with important contributions from, among others, the printing family of Joh. Enschedé), Dutch printed matter from the nineteenth century was characterized by a neglect of aesthetics and dominated by a stuffy sensibleness.

The renewal began around 1890, simultaneously with the birth of youthful impetuousness in the arts and crafts in Europe: The Jugendstil from Austria and the Art Nouveau from France also had their effect in the Netherlands. In graphic design the inspiring example came especially from the English Arts and Crafts Movement. The writings of Lewis F. Day, William Morris, and Walter Crane were translated into Dutch. Their ideas about the social function of art and design, and about good form in society, were then mixed with a fascination for stylized forms, for the inner structure (geometry) of nature, for the ornaments of other cultures—Egypt, Arabia, the Dutch Indies—and for the symbols of theosophy, in which many artists had a great interest. Everywhere new form sources were explored and applied in every conceivable way. Graphic design was not yet a "profession" in those days, and graphic designers as well as visual artists and architects designed hardcover books, posters, covers for magazines, and calendars. Examples can be found among the architects H.P. Berlage (1856–1934), K.P.C. de Bazel (1869–1923), J.L.M. Lauweriks (1864–1932) and H.Th. Wijdeveld (1885–1987), who published the well-known and, through his efforts well-designed, magazine *Wendingen* from 1918 until 1931. Among the artists who carried out commissions for graphic work during the first decade of the twentieth century were A.J. Derkinderen (1859–1935), Richard N. Roland Holst (1868–1938), Jan Toorop (1858–1928), J. Thorn Prikker (1868–1932), Willem van Konijnenburg (1868–1943), and Jan Sluijters (1881–1957).

The climate for innovation in this area has always been

favorable in the Netherlands. There were many clients from the business world, mostly managing directors with some cultural baggage, who through their commissions underwrote the new ideas about art and society. One can see this in the graphic expressions, sign posters, advertisements, or packing materials used by companies like the Gist en Spiritus Fabrieken (Yeast and Methylated Spirits Factories) in Delft and the Netherlands' PTT (the postal and telecommunications service—especially in their stamps). These examples are some of the best of what was produced in the field during that time. In addition, there were many printers, publishers, and cultural institutions (museums, theaters) that stimulated the new developments in graphic design.

In the fields of architecture, fine arts, and applied arts, the professional societies that were founded at the time played an important role in promoting the Nieuwe Kunst. The Nederlandse Vereniging voor Ambachtkunst en Nijverheidskunst (VANK) (Dutch Society for Trades and Applied Arts), established in 1904 to promote the applied arts, was able to obtain commissions for its members. The VANK published yearbooks and, in contrast with the rigid theory of William Morris, made an effort to bring about the "harmonic connection between artistic professionalism and mechanized technique." In graphic design of the first decade after 1900, one can distinguish two directions: the "decorative, ornamental" and the "rational, constructive." The first one took the liberty to express itself in the beauty of the decoration; the other strived to be functional and organized to the last particular and to have only modest ornament. These two directions (the free and the more constructive) have always played a role in the developments of Dutch graphic design, even though it has been with different insights and with different objectives in every period. Designers from the first years, such as C.A. Lion Cachet (1864–1945), Th. Nieuwenhuis (1866–1951), Theo van Hoytema (1863–1917), G.W. Dijsselhof (1866–1924), and Chris Lebeau (1878–1945), can be called the ornamentalists, while, for example, Berlage, De Bazel and Th. Molkenboer (1871–1920) can be called rationalists. A third directional line was formed by the letter designers, like the purist J. van Krimpen (1893–1958), S.H. de Roos (1877–1962), and J.F. Van Royen (1878–1942), who gave a new élan to the tradition of Dutch lettering from the seventeenth and eighteenth century.

The Nieuwe Kunst remained in all possible variations present in graphic design until far into the 1920s, while after 1917 the first reactions to this individual aesthetic appeared in a new graphic imagery by Theo van Doesburg (1883–1931) and Vilmos Huszár (1884–1960), who were part of the movement of De Stijl (Fig. 38). After 1917, the need for a new world in a political perspective had its correlation in functional and objective aspects in architecture, the visual arts, and typography. Expressive and personal creativity was rejected; the search was for geometric, pure elementary forms. Some years later this was further developed in graphic design by Piet Zwart (1885–1977), Paul Schuitema (1897–1973), and Gerrit Kiljan (1891–1968), who in their work and their teaching defended the use of forms that were created out of mate-

rials and industrial techniques from their own time: They were the first to use phototypography in the Netherlands. As an individual, the artist and printer H.N. Werkman (1882–1945) contributed to this new design in an original way with his magazine *The Next Call*, which was circulated throughout Europe. These innovations were partly fed by the Revolution and the Constructivist art from Russia after 1917, by the German Bauhaus but also, as a contrast, by Dada. Artists like El Lissitzky, Moholy Nagy, Kurt Schwitters, and the typographer Jan Tschichold visited the Netherlands and left their marks. There were many international contacts with similar groups, for example, in Poland. In the 1920s clients were also willing to integrate these experiments in their businesses, like the Van Nelle factory (Jac. Jongert, 1883–1942) and Van Berkel (Paul Schuitema) in Rotterdam, the PTT, and the Dutch Cable factory in Delft (Piet Zwart).

During the economically bad period of the 1930s, objectivity in design was increasingly flanked by freer and more visual and illustrative possibilities, which here and there were influenced by Surrealism. Examples are the work of Raoul Hynckes (1893–1973), Dick Elffers (1910–1990), Willem Sandberg (1897–1984), and the immigrants Stefan Schlesinger (1896–1942) and Henri Friedlaender (born 1904), which had their effect through the 1950s. World War II was a period of standing still; however, printing work done illegally during the German occupation (Willem Sandberg, Jan Bons [born 1918]) produced marvelous examples from that time.

After 1945, Willem Sandberg (printing for the Stedelijk Museum in Amsterdam), Jan Bons, Otto Treuman (born 1919), Dick Elffers, and younger people like Jurriaan Schrofer (1926–1990) and Wim Crouwel (born 1928) prepared the way for the design of the last forty years.

Since 1960, a time of economical prosperity, the faith in progress has been expressed in a new functionalist and objective design, clear and subservient to businesses and cultural institutions. The first large design agencies were established to meet the growing demand for house styles. Alongside, the rising discontent and protest against existing social relations are expressed in the provocative design of Anthon Beeke (born 1940), Swip Stolk (born 1944), and, to a lesser degree, Gert Dumbar (born 1940). Theirs is not objective, rigid design but open, ironic, and challenging with a direct relation to daily life. Here the new art trend Fluxus played a role. One can find the rising political engagement in the design of Jan van Toorn (born 1932) and his students (the group Wild Plakken). In these developments there are always loners who manage to remain independent and have their own style. Gielijn Escher (born 1945) is a clear example of this with his colorful and pictorial posters.

Since the 1980s, graphic design seems to have become "institutionalized," an accepted fact for clients. The number of designers has increased sharply, and idealism or ethics decreased. Agreed-upon standards in the field are left behind and, in the new freedom, everything is allowed: all existing typographic and visual means, from medieval lettering to television images, from classic book typography to staged photography for illustration. With this freedom the group Hard Werken (Working Hard) created a profile for themselves, but the method was soon copied by many young people. The reaction was expressed in a classic design, which has a clear example in the work of Walter Nikkels (born 1940), who avoids every fleeting and superficial element. The tradition of Dutch letter design is, next to this noisy multiformity, continued by Gerrit Noordzij (born 1931) and Gerard Unger (born 1942), and lately many younger people have dedicated themselves to this specialized part of the profession, including Max Kisman (born 1953) and Erik van Blokland (born 1967). New techniques, the arrival of the personal computer, and the growing stream of designers have all led to a graphic design of good but average quality; only a few succeed to rise above that line of demarcation today.

Characteristic of graphic design in the Netherlands is the relatively great autonomy, the strong relation with the visual arts (academies of art offer courses in the field), the stimulating effects of yearly retracing "the fifty best books" and such, the willingness of clients to experiment, and the great interest in this trade by printers. Even though mainly connected with advertising and commercial interests in other countries, graphic design in the Netherlands constitutes a different category of art.

Paul Hefting

See also Amsterdam School; Applied arts; Berlage, Henrik Petrus; Contemporary art; Dada; De Ploeg; De Stijl; Derkinderen, Antoon J.; Fluxus; Functionalism in architecture; Photography, modern and contemporary; Postage stamps; Prints, modern graphic arts (1840–1945); Prints, modern graphic arts after 1945; Sluijters, Jan; Symbolism and symbolists; Thorn Prikker, Johan; Toorop, Jan; Van Konijnenburg, Willem; *Wendingen;* Werkman, Hendrik Nicolaas

Bibliography

Brattinga, Pieter, and Dick Dooijes. *A History of the Dutch Poster, 1890–1906.* Amsterdam: Scheltema and Holkema, 1968.

Broos, Kees. "Dutch Design for the Public Sector." *Graphis* 35 (1979/1980): 478.

———. "From De Stijl to a New Typography." In *De Stijl, 1917–1931: Visions of Utopia.* Edited by Mildred Friedman, 147–165. New York: Abbeville, 1982.

Broos, Kees, and Paul Hefting. *Dutch Graphic Design, 1892–1992.* London: Phaidon, 1993; Cambridge, MA: MIT Press, 1993.

"The Dutch Issue." Theme volume. *Print* (November/December, 1991).

Graphic Design and Typography in the Netherlands: A View of Recent Work. New York: Herb Lubalin Study Center of Design and Typography/Cooper Union and Princeton Architectural Press, 1992.

Purvis, Alston W. *Dutch Graphic Design 1918–1945.* New York: Van Nostrand Reinhold, 1992.

Group portraiture

In representing individuals in the same space and—in at least the portrait's terms—the same time, group portraits create for the viewer imaginative connections among those portrayed. At the same time, by associating individuals and their group with locations and objects that convey specific associations, these portraits can richly endow their subjects with—and may reinforce for their viewers—communally held ideals. Group portraits depict two types of subjects: families and sometimes friends, and members of institutions. Both share many visual traditions, compositional conventions, and narrative devices.

Until Catholics and their altars were displaced from their churches at the end of the sixteenth century, portraits of families frequently appeared as praying donor figures on altars, commemorative panels, or stained-glass windows. Often several generations are portrayed: a donor or donor couple with their parents and children as, for example, the *Commemorative Panel of the Bam Family* attributed to Pieter Pietersz. (1573; Kalkar, Sankt Nicolai Kirche). Such images identify the individual as a member of a lineage. Although increasingly rare in the seventeenth century, the tradition continued in private altarpieces, such as the wings by Thomas de Keyser, dated 1628, representing a man and his son on one side and his wife and their daughter on the other (destroyed; formerly Berlin, Kaiser Frederich Museum). While such genealogical portraits are less common in the secular sphere, Gerrit Pietersz. Schaep commissioned in the first half of the seventeenth century a unique variant in a series of copies of portraits of his maternal and paternal ancestors that he assembled on two single panels (Amsterdam, Amsterdam Historical Museum). Jan Miense Molenaer's *Musical Company* (ca. 1640; Haarlem, Frans Hals Museum; Fig. 87) is a more usual version of the multigeneration secular portrait in representing as painted portraits the ancestors and relatives of the family portrayed.

It was more customary in the seventeenth century, however, for individuals to be portrayed with their immediate nuclear family, particularly with their children, rather than with their ancestors. Their settings and narratives associate family members both individually and as a group with a variety of qualities of character, meanings that have been extensively investigated by Eddy de Jongh, most recently in an exhibition of 1986. Maerten van Heemskerck's *Family of Pieter Jan Foppesz.* (ca. 1530; Kassel, Staatliche Kunstsammlungen) is seated at a table bearing a Eucharistic still life. Emanuel de Witte's *Family Portrait* (1678; Munich, Alte Pinakothek) depicts a father holding toward his daughter a bunch of grapes, which De Jongh has shown represents an admonishment of chastity. Frans Hals represented *Isaac Massa and Beatrix van der Laen* (ca. 1622; Amsterdam, Rijksmuseum; Fig. 59) seated at the base of a tree around which climbs ivy, clinging to the tree with the same firmness as the couple are attached to each other. Cornelis de Graeff and his family are shown before his country estate at Soestdijk in a painting by Jacob van Ruisdael, the figures in which are attributed to Thomas de Keyser (ca. 1660; Dublin, National Gallery of Ireland). The De Graeffs are linked with their country estate and the prestige of its ownership, as well as with the pastoral ideals attached to country life. In 1645 Dirck van Delen portrayed a couple and their two children standing before the tomb of Willem I in the Nieuwe Kerk, Delft (Amsterdam, Rijksmuseum). The family members were no doubt asserting patriotic sentiments toward the father of their country and the House of Orange. Such paintings are prototypes for the larger category of the "conversation piece" (whose figures are not necessarily related), a term that appears as early as 1661 in Flemish writer Cornelis de Bie's *Het Gulden Cabinet van de edele vry schilder-const* (The Golden Cabinet of the Noble Free Art of Painting). The tradition continued through the eighteenth and nineteenth centuries in works by Cornelis Troost, Jan and Julius Quinkhard, Wijbrand Hendriks, and Adriaan de Lelie, as, for example, the latter's *Family of the Silversmith Adrianus Bonebakker* of 1809.

While most of these images appear to portray a nuclear family—couples alone or with their children—the relations of those included may be surprisingly complex. A number of portraits by Jan Mijtens, for example, depict a couple in a landscape with a group of children, some of whom were by that time deceased. His *Family of Jacques Martini* (1647; New Orleans, New Orleans Museum of Art) includes the deceased first wife with several deceased children peering at her husband, their children, and second wife from the edge of a cloud. Other family portraits may include cousins, maiden aunts, or additional in-laws—depending no doubt on which family member originated the commission. Rather than demonstrating that the nuclear family suddenly emerged in the seventeenth century or that affective ties suddenly bloomed (historians have shown that both appeared long before), these images suggest that the cultural function of the portrait had changed; that individuals were less concerned to request prayers from the viewer for their soul after death than to identify themselves in life with valued traits of character and contemporary familial networks.

Many of these compositional themes were also used for individuals who were related not by family ties but by membership in cultural or social institutions. In 1527–1528, Jan van Scorel portrayed a group of men who had made a pilgrimage to Jerusalem (Utrecht, Centraal Museum). Lined in bust length across a narrow panel, each carries a palm branch and is identified by his coat of arms. A large proportion of group portraits represent the leaders of various civic institutions. They range from guild deacons—as, for example, the *Six Wardens of the Amsterdam Drapers' Guild* attributed to Pieter Pietersz. (1599; Amsterdam, Rijksmuseum) or the *Officers of the Silversmith's Guild* dating from 1627 by Thomas de Keyser (destroyed; formerly Strasbourg, Musée des Beaux-Arts)— through bodies responsible for the control of the quality of the products of guilds, such as Rembrandt's *Syndics of the Drapers' Guild* (1662; Amsterdam, Rijksmuseum), to the *Regents of the Amsterdam Rasphuis* (House of Correction) by Cornelis van der Voort (1618; Amsterdam, Amsterdam Historical Museum). Among the largest of these genres were regents of charitable institutions such as orphanages, hospitals, and leper asylums. Perhaps the best known of this type are the pendant canvases by Frans Hals representing the *Regents* and *Regentesses of the Old Men's Almshouse* (1664; Haarlem, Frans Hals Mu-

seum). While the majority of such group portraits customarily show their subjects seated around a table—often with objects representing their financial activities—a few, like Werner van den Valckert's panels of the *Members of the College of Aalmoezeniers* (1626–1627; Amsterdam, Amsterdam Historical Museum), are an unusual combination of narrative and allegory. Shortly after the turn of the seventeenth century, surgeons began to commission group portraits of themselves seated around a dissection or an anatomy lesson. Rembrandt's *Anatomy Lesson of Dr. Tulp* (1632; The Hague, Mauritshuis) is the best-known example of the genre painted also by Aert Pietersz., Thomas de Keyser, and Nicolaes Eliasz Pickenoy. Most of these genres continued to be painted through the eighteenth century in works by Jan Quinkhard, Troost, De Lelie, and others.

The earliest surviving Dutch shooting-company portrait, representing officers and members of city militia, is the *Shooters of the Kloveniersdoelen* (1529; Amsterdam, Rijksmuseum) attributed to Dirck Jacobsz.; its most famous follower is Rembrandt's *Nightwatch* (1642; Amsterdam, Rijksmuseum; Color Plate 5). This genre represents its sitters in settings ranging from the simple two-row lineup of Jacobsz.'s work, through the full-length gesturing figures of Rembrandt's painting, to sharing a communal meal as in Frans Hals' well-known portraits of the civic guards of Haarlem (Haarlem, Frans Hals Museum) painted between 1616 and 1639.

The first and still only large-scale study of the Dutch group portrait is that by Alois Riegl first published nearly a century ago. Riegl was concerned primarily with the formal qualities of these works and their psychological relationship with, and impact upon, the viewer. Characterizing individuals' relations with each other and their world through three attitudes—will, feeling, and attention—Riegl observed that the coherence of Dutch group portraits is indebted to the latter: the attention of the depicted figures directed toward each other and the viewer and the reciprocated attention of the viewer required to complete the work. He traced the group portrait through three stages or solutions to the problem of unifying what he believed to be essentially democratic groups: from rows of figures holding symbolic attributes of their corporate membership (for example, the shooters' portrait by Dirck Jacobsz.); through a "closed internal coherence" created by a general activity that brings them together (for example, the civic guard portraits of Frans Hals); to an "external coherence" produced by a dramatic narrative that both subordinates the figures within the group and relates them to the viewer (for example, in Rembrandt's *Nightwatch*). While Riegl attributed ethical traits—humility and healthy self-esteem—to this attention, his concern for the viewer's subjectivity has generated several studies of his works among scholars currently investigating the subjective dimension of image production and reception.

While he sought to define cultural traits through Dutch group portraits, Riegl consciously refused to link them with specific events. In contrast, recent investigations of Dutch shooting-company portraits—most notably an exhibition held in 1988—both locate these images within their cultural context and seek to identify the events that may have prompted their commission. Important formal and iconographic studies of individual group portraits by Rembrandt have also been undertaken. What has been little considered, however, is the cultural function of these paintings for their subjects and viewers. The circumstances and associations of some group portraits seem clear, such as Gerard Ter Borch's *Oath of the Treaty of Munster, 1648* (London, National Gallery). However, while most appear to portray a specific and complete group—the officers of a guild for a single year, for example—even such a well-known painting as Rembrandt's *Anatomy Lesson of Dr. Tulp* represents a group of surgeons only two of whom were wardens of the guild in the year in which it was painted. The kinds of circumstances that may have prompted a group of individuals to commission a portrait, and the larger meanings of such portraits for their viewers, have yet to be identified for most of these images. Nonetheless, in characterizing a variety of relationships between individuals, such portraits may have helped to define—and in the process construct—social relationships and cultural institutions.

Ann Jensen Adams

See also Active life, active virtues; Conversation piece; Devotional images; Donor portraits; Hals, Frans; Geertgen tot Sint Jans; Genre painting, eighteenth century; History portraits; Marriage and family portraits; Pastoral; Quinkhard, Jan Maurits; Rembrandt research; Rembrandt van Rijn; Troost, Cornelis

Bibliography

Carasso-Kok, M., et al., eds. *Schutters in Holland: Kracht en zenuwen van de stad.* Haarlem: Frans Hals Museum; Zwolle: Waanders, 1988.

Haak, Bob. *Regenten en Regentessen, Overlieden en Chirurgijns: Amsterdamse gorepsportretten van 1600 tot 1835.* Amsterdam: Amsterdam Historical Museum, 1972.

Jongh, E. de. *Portretten van echt en trouw: Huwelijk en gezin in de Nedelandse kunst van de zeventiende eeuw.* Zwolle: Waanders, 1986.

Muller, Sheila D. *Charity in the Dutch Republic: Pictures of Rich and Poor for Charitable Institutions.* Ann Arbor, MI: UMI Research Press, 1985.

Praz, Mario. *Conversation Pieces: A Survey of the Informal Group Portrait in Europe and America.* University Park, PA: Pennsylvania State University Press, 1971.

Riegl, Alois. "Das Holländische Gruppenporträt." *Jahrbuch der Kunsthistorischen Sammlungen in Wien* 23 (1902): 71–278. Reprint. 2 vols. Vienna: Osterreichischen Staatsdruckerei, 1931.

Smith, David R. *Masks of Wedlock: Seventeenth-Century Dutch Marriage Portraiture.* Ann Arbor, MI: UMI Research Press, 1982.

Gudmundsson, Sigurdur (born 1942)

This artist, born in Iceland, settled permanently in the Netherlands in 1970. In the period 1970–1980, he made mostly photographs of staged situations in which he himself was a figure. Since 1980 he has also made three-dimensional works, for interior and exterior spaces, that have been created autonomously and as the result of commissions. In addition, he has occupied himself increasingly with the production of drawings and graphics in a pictorial language that is related to his three-dimensional work. Since 1985 his work has shown a reduction of form.

Sigurdur Gudmundsson calls himself a conceptual artist who occupies himself with giving form to the ideas that come bubbling up from his sensory world. His feelings are determined by the associative power of particularly natural elements within the visible reality. He calls his works solidified memories, in which he transforms spirit to matter. Reasoning is subordinated in the creative process. Because of this, there is little hierarchy reigning in the choice of material in Gudmundsson's work. He is not fascinated by formal problems; technical skills or the lack of them do not determine the concept.

Iceland, his birthplace, plays a role as catalyst of emotions, influencer of material and formal choice, and determiner of a poetic undertone. Themes occurring in his work are estrangement, balance, harmony, the confrontation between nature and culture, and the relationship between matter and spirit; he often uses irony.

Geraart Westerink

See also Contemporary art (1980–1990); Public monumental sculpture (1795–1990)

Bibliography

Eyck, Zsa Zsa, ed. *Sigurdur Gudmundsson.* Venlo: Van Spijk, 1991.

Hefting, Paul. *De Eigen Ruimte: Beeldhouwkunst in Nederland na 1945.* Amsterdam: Elsevier, 1986.

H

Haarlem

Haarlem, situated on the Spaarne River just a few miles west of Amsterdam and near the dunes along the North Sea, was the most important and innovative artistic center in the Northern Netherlands during the sixteenth and first half of the seventeenth century. Already noted for the accomplishments of its painters in the fifteenth century, it became by the early seventeenth century one of the most creative centers for painting and graphics in all of Europe. At precisely the time that artists were abandoning Mannerist vocabulary in favor of greater naturalism, they found a growing and receptive market for their production in Haarlem. Innovations by the city's painters and draftsmen appeared in a number of genres, particularly landscape. Long before the end of Holland's Golden Age, however, Haarlem's position as the most important artistic center in the Netherlands passed to Amsterdam. Since then Haarlem has played a secondary role in the artistic life of Holland, as its artists have generally followed trends developed elsewhere.

The example provided by Geertgen tot Sint Jans (active ca. 1465–1485 or 1480–1495/1496) and other fifteenth-century painters continued with the next generation of Haarlem artists. Chief among them was the Haarlem native Jan Mostaert (ca. 1475–1555), probably one of Geertgen's pupils. He became a master in the city by 1500. In addition to continuing earlier traditions, he excelled as a portrait painter and infused a greater objectivity into his religious scenes. Mostaert and his contemporaries found in Haarlem an environment rich in commission opportunities. For example, civic and guild organizations, religious orders and confraternities, and the city's churches, including the recently completed Saint Bavo's Church, provided artists with numerous commissions until the time of Iconoclasm. In the following century painters also competed for major commissions from the city's civic guard companies, charitable institutions, the new town hall, and even altarpieces for clandestine Catholic churches. Unfortunately, the loss of documents has hindered research regarding the specific nature of many of these important Haarlem commissions.

While Haarlem did not measure up to Antwerp in terms of artistic importance during most of the sixteenth century, a number of its artists, including Mostaert, attempted to rival Antwerp's most innovative painter, Quinten Massys (1465/1467–1530). For example, aspects of Massys' Mannerist vocabulary and his experimentation in subject matter prompted Haarlem artists to make their own contributions to Northern figure painting. The most important of these was Maerten van Heemskerck (1498–1574). After completing his training in the late 1520s with Jan van Scorel (1495–1562) in Haarlem, Van Heemskerck developed a nervous and energetic Mannerist style closely linked with humanistic themes. Elements of his early style appear in his large and imposing *St. Luke Painting the Virgin* (1532; Haarlem, Frans Hals Museum). Dedicated to his guild prior to his leaving for Italy, it is one of the masterpieces of sixteenth-century Northern painting.

According to Karel van Mander, Jan Sanders van Hemessen (ca. 1500–ca. 1560) was active in Haarlem by midcentury after moving from Antwerp. In addition to his religious imagery and portraits, Van Hemessen's paintings of proverbs, parables, and satirical subjects were very influential. They brought secular subjects popularized in Antwerp by Massys and Marinus van Reymerswaele (active ca. 1509–died after 1567) to Haarlem and, in a number of instances, served as precursors to the "rise of realism" that defined Haarlem's importance as an art center during the following century.

A number of late-sixteenth-century events in the history of Haarlem and its environs had a direct bearing on the development of its art during the next century. After the Iconoclasm that took a terrible toll on the art produced up to this time, the Spanish siege of the city from December 1572 to July 1573, and a catastrophic fire in 1576, destroyed much of the city, its economy, and its art market. In many instances the organizations that had previously commissioned artworks were now outlawed. When Antwerp fell to the Spanish in 1585, however, mass immigration to Haarlem brought dramatic change for the city. Population grew from eighteen thousand at the time of the siege to forty thousand by 1622.

Craftspersons, including a number of innovative artists, brought their skills to Haarlem from the Southern Netherlands. By the end of the century, textiles, brewing, and trade contributed enormously to the city's new prosperity. This prosperity meant a market for artists experimenting in a range of new styles and subjects.

Among the new arrivals to Haarlem late in the century were the draftsman and engraver Hendrick Goltzius (1558–1616) and the writer and artist Karel van Mander (1548–1606). According to Van Mander they joined with the painter Cornelis Cornelisz. van Haarlem (1562–1638) to form an academy "to study from life." While this academy probably existed more in theory than in actual practice and must date no earlier than 1588, it, nevertheless, came at a time when fundamental changes came to Haarlem's artists' community. In abandoning their Mannerism for more naturalistic and classical styles, these artists turned to *naer het leven* (after life) from *uyt den gheest* (from the imagination).

Goltzius, in particular, exerted enormous influence on the following generation of artists, especially its printmakers. Among his pupils were Jacob Matham (1571–1631), Jacob de Gheyn II (1565–1629), and Jan Saenredam (1565–1607). Goltzius' engraved portraits and his portrait and landscape drawings, unlike his late Mannerist paintings, are striking examples of a new aesthetic. Around 1610, subject specialization appeared in Haarlem, and the city would take its place as the cradle of a new, more realistic art. Haarlem quickly became a magnet for a younger generation of innovative artists who shared their ideas with others. In addition to the role played by the Guild of St. Luke and various social organizations, artists were linked through family connections and marriage, by teacher-and-pupil relationships, and in their roles as collectors, art dealers, and experts often called upon to offer opinions regarding attributions.

As the city grew and prospered during the first quarter of the seventeenth century, artists were at first hard pressed to satisfy the growing demand for pictures and prints. Although the city's militia companies and other civic organizations still commissioned group portraits, and the completion of Haarlem's new town hall generated other commissions, an open art market supported by a broad spectrum of the population gave artists the best opportunity to sell their works. Guild regulations sought to guarantee quality and professionalism within its membership.

One of the first of the new genres introduced in Haarlem was marine painting. The careful observation found in Hendrick Vroom's (ca. 1566–1640) paintings of ships and coastal scenes is symptomatic of the new art. Like his contemporaries who developed the naturalistic landscape, his choice of subject matter may have been related to a nationalism stemming from the ongoing struggle by the Dutch to win their freedom from the Spanish (Fig. 80).

Nearly all of the major developments in seventeenth-century Dutch landscape took place in Haarlem. Beginning with Goltzius and his naturalistic drawings, a number of landscape innovators were active at least briefly in the city in the 1610s. The group included Hercules Segers (1589/1590–ca.

1633/1638), Willem Buytewech (1591/1592–1624), Esaias van de Velde (1587–1630), Jan van de Velde II (1593–1641), and Jan van Goyen (1596–1656). Initially limited to drawings, etchings, and print series based on direct observations from nature, painted landscapes by Esaias van de Velde and Jan van Goyen appeared in the 1610s. The realism and simplicity of their views are in sharp contrast to the more colorful and complex Flemish landscape examples. In the next decade Haarlem landscape painters such as Pieter de Molijn (1595–1661) and Salomon van Ruysdael (1600/1603–1670) further contributed to the genre through the use of tonalist palettes.

Unlike landscape, where printmakers made early contributions to the new art, still life was linked to the accomplishments of its painters. Innovations by Nicolaes Gillis (ca. 1580–after 1632), Floris van Dyck (1575–1651), and Floris van Schooten (active ca. 1610–1655) share a similarity to examples by their Flemish counterparts. The "spread" still lifes pioneered by these artists emphasize high viewpoints and carefully rendered foods and objects spread across tabletops. The next generation of still-life painters, including Pieter Claesz. (1597/1598–1661) and Willem Claesz. Heda (1593/1594–1680/1682) and their many followers, developed a new type of still life, the *ontbijtje* (breakfast piece). By dropping the viewpoint and overlapping objects, their monochrome breakfast pieces, *vanitas* still lifes, and later banquet pieces strike a note of immediacy while suggesting a sense of moderation (Fig. 127).

Haarlem could also claim innovations in a traditional genre, portraiture. Frans Hals (ca. 1582/1583–1666) was one of the most original portrait painters of his generation, breathing life into the sitters of his single and group portraits (Fig. 59). His remarkable virtuosity in brushwork and his use of animated poses and lively expressions found quick acceptance among the leading citizens of Haarlem beginning in the 1610s. One of his followers, Johannes Verspronck (1597–1662), came close to his genius, but without his spontaneity.

Hals also painted a number of genre scenes of engaging half-length figures prior to 1635. In them he showed his awareness of the Caravaggesque tradition active in Utrecht. Haarlem genre painting, however, developed in the direction of small-scale pictures of full-length, finely detailed figures in interiors and garden settings. The often indulgent behavior displayed by these figures may have served as warnings to the viewer. Beginning with Willem Buytewech's rare examples painted early in the century, this tradition was continued by Dirck Hals (1591–1656); Judith Leyster (1609–1660), whose work also comes close to examples by Frans Hals; and Jan Miense Molenaer (1609/1610–1668). Of the three, Molenaer was the most inventive, and prior to his and Leyster's move to Amsterdam in 1636, he had begun to explore peasant imagery. Peasant scenes were another Haarlem contribution to Dutch painting, as Adriaen van Ostade (1610–1684) and, earlier, Adriaen Brouwer (ca. 1605/1606–1638), who spent part of the 1620s in Haarlem, made significant contributions to low genre. Van Ostade's earliest peasant scenes detail unsavory behavior, while his later works assume a more positive and accepting view of the lower classes. Among his followers in

Haarlem were Cornelis Bega (1631/1632–1664) and Cornelis Dusart (1660–1704). Van Ostade's brother, Isaack (1621–1649), specialized in village scenes with a sophisticated unity between the landscape and figures. About the same time, Philips Wouwerman (1619–1668) further explored the potential of figures within landscapes. His technical skills are characteristic of most of Haarlem's painters after mid-century.

Innovation surfaced in a number of the other genres in Haarlem painting and graphics during the first half of the century. Pieter Saenredam (1597–1665), for example, specialized in architectural subjects painted with a clarity and simplicity lacking in works by church painters active in Delft at mid-century. He, in turn, influenced fellow Haarlemers Job (1630–1693) and Gerrit Berckheyde (1638–1698) (Fig. 13).

As might be expected, history painting in seventeenth-century Haarlem followed a more conservative course, due in part to the requirements of its patrons. The most important painters in this genre are known as the Haarlem classicists. They include Pieter Soutman (1580–1657), Salomon de Bray (1597–1664), Pieter de Grebber (ca. 1600–1652/1653), and Jan de Bray (ca. 1627–1697). Their classicizing manner identifies them as the true heirs of Goltzius and his emphasis on a more intellectual approach to art. Salomon de Bray had studied with Goltzius and Cornelis van Haarlem after moving from Amsterdam, and in addition to his importance as a painter, he was largely responsible for the reorganization of the Haarlem Guild of St. Luke in 1631. Members of the Haarlem classicists often received commissions from outside of Haarlem, including examples from the Huis ten Bosch near The Hague. Oriented toward a more sophisticated audience, their works tend to display a wider range of influences.

During the second half of the seventeenth century a number of important artists were active in Haarlem for at least part of their careers. For example, Gerard Ter Borch (1617–1681) joined the guild there in 1635, and Jan Steen (1625/1626–1679) worked in the city in the 1660s. Compared to the activity from earlier in the century, however, Haarlem no longer exerted the influence it once had. Technical proficiency seemed to overtake innovation. Only Haarlem's landscape painters continued to contribute to Holland's Golden Age. Landscape had developed from early realism, through tonalism, to a classical phase just after mid-century. This development is evident when comparing works by Salomon van Ruysdael and his nephew Jacob van Ruisdael (1628/1629–1682), before the latter moved to Amsterdam about 1656. During his long career Van Ruisdael depicted an unmatched range of landscape subjects. He effectively transformed the views of his immediate environment into monumental, even romantic, scenes quite different from those depicted by the previous generation of Haarlem landscape painters.

Van Ruisdael's reinvention of his native landscape stands in contrast to views of Italy and other foreign lands depicted by a number of his contemporaries. Nicolaes Berchem's (1620–1683) landscapes inspired by Italy, views of Brazil by Frans Post (1612–1680), and images resulting from Allart van Everdingen's (1621–1675) travels in Scandinavia all enriched the landscape tradition in Haarlem.

Long before the end of the third quarter of the seventeenth century Haarlem had lost its position as the most important artistic center in the Netherlands. During the early eighteenth century the majority of Haarlem artists either responded to the elegant Rococo style developed elsewhere or continued to reflect upon the accomplishments of Dutch painters from the previous century. With the spread of the style of Louis XV, larger decorative schemes with an abundance of stucco and wood decoration came into vogue. Gerrit van Heerstal (ca. 1690–1746) and Jan van Logteren (1709–1745), among other artisans active in Haarlem, did make significant contributions in this area. French influence continued to exert itself on Haarlem later in the eighteenth century, especially during a prosperous period from about 1750 to 1775. A number of elegant Louis XVI–style villas built in Haarlem at this time still stand along the Nieuwe Gracht (New Canal). For much of the last two centuries, Haarlem's reputation as an art center has come as a consequence of its museums, especially Teylers Museum, founded late in the eighteenth century, and the Frans Hals Museum, which opened to the public in 1913. Both have been leaders in the acquisition and exhibition of works of art and in museum education. A visit to the Frans Hals Museum, with its seventeenth-century setting, has long been a highlight for visitors to the Netherlands. Not only do its collections document the glories of Haarlem painting of past centuries, but its contemporary exhibitions speak to the city's continuing contributions as an art center.

Dennis P. Weller

See also Amateurs, art academies, and art associations before the nineteenth century; Berckheyde, Gerrit Adriaensz.; Berckheyde, Job Adriaensz.; Commerce and commercial life; Drawing theory; Flanders, Flemish School; Geertgen tot Sint Jans; Goltzius, Hendrick; Haarlem School, early; Hals, Dirck; Hals, Frans; History painting; Humanism, humanist themes; Landscape; Leyster, Judith; Mannerism, Mannerists; Manuscript illumination; Marine painting; Matham, Jacob; Molenaer, Jan Miense; Prints, printmaking, and printmakers (ca. 1500–ca. 1900); Rhetoricians' chambers; Rural life and views; Steen, Jan Havicksz.; Still life; Ter Borch, Gerard; Townscapes; Van de Velde, Jan II; Van Goyen, Jan; Van Mander, Karel; Van Ruisdael, Jacob; *Vanitas, vanitas* still life; Wouwerman, Philips

Bibliography

Ackley, Clifford. *Printmaking in the Age of Rembrandt.* Boston: Museum of Fine Arts, 1980.

Blankert, Albert et al. *Gods, Saints, and Heroes: Dutch Painting in the Age of Rembrandt.* Washington, DC: National Gallery of Art, 1981.

Haak, Bob. *The Golden Age: Dutch Painters of the Seventeenth Century.* New York: Harry N. Abrams, 1984.

Hofrichter, Frima Fox. *Haarlem: The Seventeenth Century.* Rutgers: State University of New Jersey; Jane Voorhees Zimmerli Art Museum, 1983.

Kloek, W.Th. et al. *Art before the Iconoclasm.* Amsterdam:

Rijksmuseum; The Hague: State Printing Office, 1986.

Mander, Karel van. *Het Schilder-Boek*. 1604. Reprint. Utrecht: Davaco, 1969.

Snyder, James. *Northern Renaissance Art*. New York: Harry N. Abrams, 1985.

Taverne, E. "Salomon de Bray and the Reorganization of the Haarlem Guild of St. Luke in 1631." *Simiolus* 6 (1972/1973): 50–69.

Haarlem School, early (ca. 1450–1500)

According to Karel van Mander (in *Schilder-Boeck*, 1604), Albert van Ouwater was the leading artist at Haarlem "as far back in time as the Van Eycks." Only the *Raising of Lazarus* (ca. 1460; Berlin) stands as evidence of Van Ouwater's talents. The figures and landscape in this panel are remarkably like those found in Dirck Bouts' paintings. Van Mander relates that Bouts (active 1450–1475) was born in Haarlem and may have worked there prior to his move to Louvain. No paintings by Bouts are dated before 1462, but several panels attributed to him are placed stylistically midway between his later works and Van Ouwater's panel—for example, the *Infancy Altarpiece* panels (Madrid), considered to be among Bouts' early works. Bouts' role in the Haarlem School has been examined by Schoene, Snyder, and Chatelet, but his ties to van Ouwater remain unclear. Bouts left Haarlem before 1457.

Very little is known of Van Ouwater and his production, only what Van Mander tells us: He was a fine painter; his *Raising of Lazarus* was much admired by Maerten van Heemskerck; he was the inventor of the first and best manner of painting landscape; and Geertgen tot Sint Jans was his pupil. Van Mander further described two of Van Ouwater's major commissions: the *Raising of Lazarus* and the *Altar of the Roman Pilgrims*. By Van Mander's time, the *Raising of Lazarus* had been carried off to Spain "fraudulently and without paying," but he had studied a grisaille copy and described the composition so well that there is no doubt the Berlin painting is Van Ouwater's original. The second work, the Roman Pilgrims' altarpiece, is lost. This "had an interesting landscape in which one saw several travelers or pilgrims, some on their way, others resting, eating, and drinking." Two copies exist and although they differ in details, they agree in placement of the figures in a landscape constructed of staggered coulisses. Such copies undoubtedly reflect a common source.

Van Mander also gave the earliest account of Geertgen tot Sint Jans. Geertgen's activity lasted only about ten to fifteen years. If he was still alive close to 1500 (as Snyder [1971] convincingly argued), then he began working around 1485. Chatelet (1980) believed Geertgen died around 1485. Geertgen lived with the Commandery of the Knights Hospitalers of St. John at Haarlem and painted the *Triptych with a Crucifixion* for that order. This altarpiece was already partly destroyed by Van Mander's time. Only one wing with the *Lamentation of Christ* and a "miracle or unusual event" on the other (Fig. 62) survived. This had been sawed in two and was hung in the Commandery's new building, where Van Mander saw them. Snyder (1960) argued that this altarpiece

was probably executed around 1490.

No extant paintings by Van Ouwater fill in the twenty- to twenty-five-year gap between the execution of his *Raising of Lazarus* and Geertgen's earliest activity. Scholars have suggested several other works, by other artists, to complete those missing years. The panels by the Master of the Gathering of the Manna are among these. Recently, Marrow and others (1990) identified a number of manuscripts as having been executed in Haarlem between 1465 and 1485.

According to Van Mander in the second edition of the *Schilder-Boeck* (1618), Jacob Jansz. van Haarlem painted a *Crucifixion Altarpiece* for the grain carriers of that city in 1474. Jacob Jansz., who has been identified as the Master of the Brunswick Diptych (active ca. 1480–1500), is considered a follower of Geertgen, but Snyder holds that he was either a contemporary whose career parallels Geertgen's or that he was slightly older than Geertgen and may have trained the younger artist. Scholars notice stylistic affinities between early panels by Gerard David (active ca. 1480–1523) and those by Geertgen and have assumed the two artists worked together or may have trained together. David, born in Oudewater, entered the Painters' Guild in Bruges as a "free master" in January 1484, which argues against his knowing Geertgen's works directly. The similarities between their panels can be explained if the Master of the Brunswick Diptych (Jacob Jansz.?) was active about 1475–1485. The Master of the Tiburtine Sibyl (active 1480–1490) is usually considered a follower of Bouts or Geertgen: His *Emperor Augustus and the Sibyl* (Frankfurt) exhibits Boutsian characteristics, while his *Raising of Lazarus* (Mexico City) seems to derive from Geertgen's panel in Paris. His paintings bear some affinity to the woodcut illustrations in books published by Jacob Bellaert in Haarlem between 1484 and 1487. Jan Mostaert was active from 1498 to 1555 and trained Albert Simonsz., who told what he knew about the earlier activity in Haarlem to Van Mander. Chatelet (1980) discusses additional artists before 1500 from whom no works survive.

Diane G. Scillia

See also Bellaert, Jacob; Devotional images; Flanders, Flemish School; Geertgen tot Sint Jans; Haarlem; Religious orders and their patronage; Van Mander, Karel

Bibliography

Chatelet, A. *Early Dutch Painting: Painting in the Northern Netherlands in the Fifteenth Century*. Translated by Christopher Brown and Anthony Turner. New York: Rizzoli, 1980.

Friedlander, M.J. *Early Netherlandish Painting*. Translated by Heinz Norden. Vols. 3, 5, 14. New York: Praeger, 1967–1972.

Hoogewerff, G. J. *De Noord-nederlandsche Schilderkunst*. 5 vols. The Hague: Nijhoff, 1936–1947.

Marrow, J.H. et al. *The Golden Age of Dutch Manuscript Painting*. New York: George Braziller, 1990.

Scillia, D.G. "Three New Paintings by the Master of the Tiburtine Sibyl." *Oud Holland* 94 (1980): 1–10.

———. "Van Mander on Ouwater and Geertgen." *Art Bulletin* 60 (1978): 271–273.

Schoene, W. *Dieric Bouts und seine Schule*. Berlin: Verlag fur Kunstwissenschaft, 1938.

Snyder, J.E. "The Early Haarlem School of Painting, I–II." *Art Bulletin* 42 (1960): 39–55, 113–132.

———. "The Early Haarlem School of Painting, III." *Art Bulletin* 53 (1971): 444–458.

Hague School, The (1870–1890)

The Hague School is a collective name for a large group of artists who painted landscapes and genre paintings after nature and who all lived at one time or another in The Hague. The group flourished in the years 1870–1890, but in the three decades after that their works sold for very high prices. The most important representatives were Bernardus Blommers, Johannes Bosboom, Paul Gabriël, Jozef Israëls, Jacob and Willem Maris, Anton Mauve, Hendrik Willem Mesdag, Albert Neuhuijs, Willem Roelofs, and Jan Hendrik Weissenbruch.

The Hague School was first mentioned in 1875 when the art critic J. van Santen Kolff wrote a four-part article in the journal *De Banier* on an exhibition of living masters. At these annual exhibitions, which were held, in turn, in The Hague, Amsterdam, and Rotterdam, the public could take note of the latest developments in contemporary art. In that year Van Santen Kolff made explicit mention in his review of a new movement in the art of painting that was centered in The Hague. He called the movement a "school," comparable to the schools of Düsseldorf, Weimar, or Munich. These German cities were at the time important centers with many artists whose paintings had all more or less the same subject matter. They were mostly romanticized landscapes or scenes from daily life of the local people, clothed in traditional dress. Analogous to such a Düsseldorfer School, Van Santen Kolff observed in The Hague a thriving new genre of "sea-village life" (*zeedorpsleven*). The village concerned was Scheveningen, situated by the North Sea, near The Hague. The "master of pity *par excellence*" of this Scheveningen genre was Jozef Israëls, who represented in dark colors the gloomy events of fishermen's lives (Fig. 54). Others, who showed the sunnier side, were Bernardus Blommers (Fig. 15), David Artz, and Philip Sadée. As Van Santen Kolff pointed out, the market in genre paintings was at the time filled with scenes of Scheveningen, often of poor quality. He noticed, however, in the work of these painters a joyful amalgamation of "healthy realism" and poetry. By realism he meant: inspired by the actual observation of reality and based on authentic feelings. These painters were able to create a true mood and move away from conventional, romanticized, and often sentimental imagery.

Van Santen Kolff noticed not only in the genre but also in the landscape painting "ultra-radical" innovation. These two branches of the art of painting, genre and landscape, formed the very heart of The Hague School. The reproduction of the landscape was, according to the reviewer, also healthily realistic, simple but true, and, moreover, typically Dutch. These artists knew how to reproduce nature in their paintings the way they saw and felt it (Color Plate 10). They strove toward conveying the mood and poetry of the landscape, giving preference to a "dark" day rather than to a "boring 'bright-blue' sky." They did not use strong light effects nor strong colors but painted with shades of gray. For this reason The Hague School is at times also called the Gray School, and the work a mood-producing art (*stemmingskunst*). Not only was the vision of these painters new but also their way of painting, which was broad and forceful. Van Santen Kolff mentioned among the masters of these landscape painters Mauve, Mesdag, Jacob and Willem Maris, Roelofs, and Gabriël. Their renewed force was that they had liberated themselves from the ruling conventions in the art of painting.

The image that Van Santen Kolff sketched in 1875 of The Hague School corresponds with the image we have today. However, the innovations of the group of painters in The Hague had not just dropped from the sky. Already by the 1850s some painters were living and working *en plein air* in Oosterbeek, a village in the wooded surroundings of Arnhem. Gerard Bilders, before he died young, worked there and by 1860 had already written about a "fragrant, warm gray" and the "sentiment of the gray." He sought a tonalistic way of painting with colors that express a mood. Such ideas must already have been prevalent at the time and must have been discussed by those who worked at one time or another in nature: the Maris brothers, J.W. Bilders and his son Gerard, Roelofs, Gabriël, Mauve, and Mesdag. The contacts between the later members of The Hague School were made in the 1860s.

An important model for the painters of The Hague School was the Barbizon School which flourished around 1830. French painters such as Corot, Daubigny, Diaz, Millet, Rousseau, and Troyon worked *en plein air* in the forest of Fontainebleau in the village of Barbizon, not far from Paris. They sought inspiration in Dutch painting of the seventeenth century, which was very popular in France in those years. For that reason The Hague School was considered a continuation of the Dutch Golden Age.

A few Dutch painters knew Barbizon from their own observation. Already in 1849 Roelofs wrote in a letter that he was very curious about "those new French landscape painters. Some of my acquaintances who have seen much in Paris are very much impressed by them." In the early 1850s Roelofs traveled three times to Barbizon and Fontainebleau. The impressions he gained there greatly influenced his work. Israëls and Jacob Maris also knew Barbizon firsthand. Others could, since the 1840s, see the works of French painters at exhibitions, such as at the expositions of living masters. In later years their paintings were made available in art dealers' galleries, first only sporadically but later more frequently. Collectors acquired many paintings from Barbizon; by 1880 Mesdag had built a nice collection, including many works by the painters of Barbizon. His museum could be visited by appointment.

The beginning of The Hague School can be dated around the year 1870 when several painters, more or less accidentally and from different points of the compass, settled in The Hague. Mesdag, from Groningen, was the first. He had decided later in life to become a painter and had traveled via Oosterbeek to Brussels to take lessons from Roelofs and Laurens Alma Tadema. During a vacation to the German island of Norderney he had discovered the sea as a subject for painting. This made him decide in the spring of 1869 to settle in The Hague, where his favorite subject was at hand. An additional reason was that his brother-in-law, Samuel van Houten, had become a member of the Dutch Lower House. The Mesdags moved next door to the Van Houtens. Mesdag made his breakthrough in 1870 when he won a gold medal with his large painting *Les Brisants de la Mer du Nord*. He would paint the sea for the rest of his life (Fig. 84).

In 1871 Israëls came from Amsterdam to The Hague. He was also from Groningen and a good friend of Mesdag, who might have suggested that Israëls come to The Hague. Israëls became famous for his scenes of fishermen's lives. In the same year Mauve settled in The Hague after having moved countless times. His work consists mainly of silver-gray shadowy landscapes, often bedecked with animals. Jacob Maris returned in 1871 from a stay of a few years in Paris where he had painted best-selling "Italian folk types." In The Hague he dedicated himself to landscapes, especially those directly around his own studio (Fig. 55). He also painted townscapes and imaginary combinations of elements from different Dutch cities. His work is painted with a forceful brushstroke and with thick layers of paint. Jacob's brother Matthijs also left in 1869 for Paris, never to return to his hometown of The Hague. His dreamlike compositions have little to do with the works of The Hague School, although they are similar in that both are a mood-producing art. He is usually counted among the members of The Hague School.

Other artists already lived in The Hague. Willem Maris had made several trips but, unlike his brothers, had not settled abroad for long periods. He had worked in nature from an early age and preferred ducks near a ditch or cows in a pasture (Fig. 56). Blommers also traveled but always painted genre scenes in the fishing villages of Scheveningen, Zandvoort, and Katwijk. Bosboom, the oldest of the group, had already lived and worked for a long time in The Hague. He specialized in painting church interiors, and in the 1870s he also made beach and sea views at Scheveningen. Jan Hendrik Weissenbruch also belonged to the older generation and was born and reared in The Hague. He painted expansive landscapes with high skies. His works often look very modern because of the tight manner in which he treats color surfaces (Fig. 57). Roelofs and Gabriël lived in Brussels and came to Holland during the summers to paint polder landscapes (Fig. 58). They both eventually settled, in 1887 and 1884, respectively, in The Hague. The name "Hague School" is derived from the fact that most artists lived in this city; however, they painted not only around The Hague but also in other places in Holland: in Drente (Fig. 81), Gelderland, Brabant, and in the polders of North Holland.

The reasons most painters moved to The Hague are barely known. There are, however, ample reasons why The Hague was an attractive city. It is officially the capital of the Netherlands; the government is seated in The Hague. The allure that the city has because of this can be detected not only in the wide streets and town squares, stately homes and luxurious hotels, but also in the people themselves, who included nobility, artists, and literary critics. The Royal Cabinet of Paintings (the Mauritshuis), with its collection of seventeenth-century Dutch art, was an important source for the study of old masters. Moreover, the art dealership of Goupil (later called Boussod, Valadon and Company) had been established in The Hague since 1861, a branch of thriving Goupils in Paris. It would sell much of the art of The Hague School.

More important for the painters, certainly, must have been the great variety in the surroundings of The Hague. It was situated amid large pastures, polders, and canals, while the city's west side is a characteristic dune landscape. The North Sea and the wide beach of sand give the city its silver-gray sky the painters loved so much. In the 1870s the life at the beach became popular, and the climate at the coast was praised for its healthy fresh air. Moreover, there was also Scheveningen, which, although it was situated very close to The Hague, had still kept its own character and simplicity. It was a closed community, totally dependent upon fishing. The painters were unaware of the harsh living conditions of the people of Scheveningen; they only saw the picturesque aspects of life in a fishing village. In the 1880s a harbor was built at Scheveningen; prior to that time the flat fishing boats were dragged by horses onto the beach.

Prior to 1870 the world of art was already flourishing in The Hague. There lived and worked many artists who could teach the younger generation. The younger artists copied the works of seventeenth-century masters in the Royal Cabinet of Paintings and learned at the academy to draw in the traditional way, using antique statues and draped models. It is noteworthy that all painters of The Hague School enjoyed a classical training. The movement—contrary to, for example, French Impressionism—cannot be called avant-garde. The painters of The Hague School chose the same subjects as their predecessors: landscapes, livestock, town views, interiors, and genre scenes. They differ only in their observation of reality—without any romantic or literary connotations. Also, the tonalistic and loose, unconventional effects were actually different. Moreover, the first painters of The Hague School were not young anymore, and they differed rather greatly in age: Bosboom, for example, was born in 1817; Roelofs in 1822; Mesdag in 1831; Mauve in 1838; and Blommers in 1845.

An important and binding influence in the world of art in The Hague was the painters' society Pulchri Studio. It was founded in 1847 by, among others, Bosboom, Roelofs, and Johannes and Jan Weissenbruch. The name was coined in Latin, like those of other art societies at the time, and means "in the practice of the beautiful." The society consisted of working members (artists) and art-loving members (amateurs), mostly from well-to-do families. Artists had the opportunity to draw from a dressed model and later also from a nude model, and at set times they held gatherings in which they would review art. This was an extraordinary opportunity to see each other's work and to get to know each other's ideas. Sometimes a collector would show portfolios of drawings from his collection, and later the art dealer Goupil would also send over works of art. Often works were sold at these gatherings, and a five percent commission went to the society.

At first, people were seated at these art-review gatherings and works of art were passed around for commentary. When the attendance grew, the gatherings changed from "sitting" to "walking" art reviews, whereby the drawings could be seen for one evening in frames against the wall. When Pulchri obtained larger accommodations in 1887, it became possible to organize real exhibitions. The paintings and drawings of working members were available for sale, but older works were also exhibited. When a member died, a retrospective of his work was held, such as in 1890 for Mauve, and in 1891 and 1892 for Bosboom. Pulchri also exhibited foreign works in the possession of Dutch collectors: In 1890, for example, there was an exhibition of paintings by Charles François Daubigny; in 1892 a presentation of works by Jean-François Millet; and in 1897 and 1902 two large expositions of paintings and pastels by the Italian painter Antonio Mancini were organized. Pulchri also took care of collective shipments to foreign expositions.

An important aspect of the artists' society were the social meetings that were organized by a special committee. Members showed *tableaux vivants* on such evenings, which were accompanied by music or poetry. Even comedies were performed. Everything was always completely organized by the members themselves. The preparations and the decorations were done very professionally; when they wanted to perform *The Raft of the Medusa* by Géricault, Matthijs Maris in Paris received a request to make a watercolor painting of the original in the Louvre so the participants could faithfully follow its colors. Birthdays and jubilees of members were cause for lively dinners and parties. All of those activities strengthened the already close mutual bonds.

The flourishing of Pulchri Studio in the years 1870–1900 was closely connected with the flourishing of The Hague School. It is also true the other way around: The activities and exhibitions the society organized contributed in a significant way to the fame and dissemination of the work of The Hague School. Mesdag was a central figure who had become a member immediately after his arrival in The Hague in 1869. He was chairman from 1889 until 1907; under his vigorous leadership the society prospered as never before. He would even provide, when necessary, major financial support.

Mesdag played in many other ways an important role in the art world of The Hague. In 1881 he painted, with the help of his wife, Sina (Sientje), and Blommers, George Hendrik Breitner, and Theophile de Bock, the large panorama of Scheveningen by the sea. The phenomenon of a panorama, "a painting without borders," was at the time a popular combination of the art of painting and spectacle. Mesdag painted Scheveningen and surroundings, seen from on top of a dune, as it appeared before the construction of the harbor. This famous painting has certainly contributed to the reputation of The Hague School. Mesdag's private collection was a source of information for The Hague's artists. He owned many works by the Barbizon School, The Hague School, and Italian artists. It is noteworthy that his personal taste ran to oil sketches and studies for paintings,

because in studies the hand of the artist is clearly revealed.

In 1876 Mesdag decided, with Jacob Maris and Mauve, to found the Hollandsche Teeken-Maatschappij (Dutch Watercolor Society). The example they had in mind to follow was the Société Belge des Aquarellistes (Belgian Society of Watercolorists) in Brussels. The appreciation of watercolor paintings (at the time often called drawings) was not based solely on artistic grounds but also on financial reasons. The rather small works of art had a high artistic and decorative value, and the price was significantly lower than for paintings. For these reasons it was an attractive medium for the artist as well as for the buyer. The organization of a Teeken-Maatschappij (Watercolor Society) was, therefore, financially interesting. During the first years membership was by invitation; later one could be recommended for membership by submitting two or three watercolors. Only artists residing in The Hague were members; everyone outside of The Hague, including foreigners, became honorary members. A big exhibition sale was held annually.

The painters of The Hague School sold much of their work at exhibitions of the Hollandsche Teeken-Maatschappij and Pulchri Studio as well as at exhibitions abroad. However, the largest part found its way through the international art market. Collectors in England, Scotland, Canada, and the United States created large collections of works by The Hague School. The English railroad magnate James Forbes, for example, owned a collection of thirty-two hundred paintings and watercolors, a third of which were by The Hague School. Their popularity increased, especially after 1890, to such a degree that prices skyrocketed. These works were still selling at very high prices well into the beginning of the twentieth century.

The artistic high point of The Hague School was in the 1870s and 1880s. At the end of the nineteenth century most of the artists were well on in life; they remained true to their themes, and repetitions were not uncommon. In the wake of members of The Hague School was a large group of minor artists who also participated in exhibitions and were successful, such as Louis Apol, Taco Mesdag, Sina Mesdag-van Houten, Alexander Mollinger, Pieter ter Meulen, Geo Poggenbeek, and Willem Cornelis Rip. A few young persons grew up in the tradition of The Hague School; painters such as George Hendrik Breitner, Vincent van Gogh, Isaac Israëls, Willem Tholen, and Willem de Zwart soon found their own way. Eventually The Hague had to give up its leading role in the world of art to Amsterdam, where a new generation concentrated on very different matters.

Hanna Pennock

See also Amsterdam Impressionists; Blommers, Bernardus Johannes; Bosboom, Johannes; Breitner, George Hendrik; De Zwart, Willem; France; Gabriël, Paul Joseph Constantin; Israëls, Isaac; Israëls, Jozef; Laren; Maris, Jacob Hendricus; Maris, Matthijs; Maris, Willem; Mauve, Anton; Mesdag, Hendrik Willem; Nationalism; Neuhuijs, Albert; Roelofs, Willem; Tholen, Willem Bastiaan; Van Gogh, Vincent; Weissenbruch, Jan; Weissenbruch, Jan Hendrik

Bibliography

Bodt, Saskia de. "Pulchri Studio: Het imago van een kunstenaarsvereniging in de negentiende eeuw." *De negentiende eeuw* 14 (1990): 25–42.

Gruyter, Jos de. *De Haagse School.* 2 vols. Rotterdam: Lemniscaat, 1968–1968. Reprint. 2 vols. in 1. Alphen aan den Rijn: Atrium, 1985. (English summary).

J.K. (J. van Santen Kolff). "Een Blik in de Hollandsche Schilderschool onzer Dagen." *De Banier: Tijdschrift van "Het jonge Holland"* 2 (1875): 258–271; 306–337; 3 (1875): 43–73; 157–203.

Leeman, Fred, and Hanna Pennock. *The Mesdag Museum: Catalogue of Paintings and Drawings.* Zwolle: Waanders, 1996.

Leeuw, Ronald de, John Sillevis, and Charles Dumas, eds. *The Hague School: Dutch Masters of the Nineteenth Century.* London: Royal Academy of Arts, in association with Weidenfeld and Nicholson, 1983.

Marius, G.H. *Dutch Painters of the Nineteenth Century.* Edited by G. Norman. Woodbridge, Suffolk: Antique Collectors Club, 1973.

Sillevis, John et al. eds. *De Haagse School: De collectie van het Haags Gemeentemuseum.* The Hague: Haags Gemeentemuseum, 1988.

Hals, Dirck (1591–1656)

Dirck Hals, a younger brother of Frans Hals (ca. 1582/1583–1666), was a native of Haarlem. Most of his colorful merry-company scenes reveal fashionably dressed figures in interiors or park-like settings. Possibly owing to the uneven quality of his *oeuvre*, Dirck Hals' importance to Haarlem genre painting in the 1620s and 1630s is not well understood or fully appreciated.

Even though he did not join the Haarlem Guild of St. Luke until 1627, paintings by Dirck Hals date before 1620. He probably trained with his brother prior to this, as his lively oil sketches on paper from the late 1610s and 1620s have much in common with Frans Hals' art. Dirck Hals' painted compositions, however, show the influence of Esaias van de Velde (1587–1630) and particularly Willem Buytewech (1591/1592–1624). While Dirck Hals' figures often appear to be stiff and doll-like, many of his best works exhibit a skillfully applied and smooth brushwork.

Documents place Hals in Leiden during much of the 1640s, as courts there confiscated his property in 1643 and 1649 for rent arrears. He was buried May 17, 1656, in Haarlem's Begijnhof Church. Prints after works by Hals were executed by a number of Haarlem artists, including Cornelis van Kittensteyn (ca. 1600–after 1638) and Jacob Matham (1571–1631). In addition to exerting influence on Jan Miense Molenaer (1609/1610–1668) and Judith Leyster (1609–1660), both of whom may have been active in his workshop, Hals provided the figures for architectural paintings by Dirck van Delen (1605–1671).

Dennis P. Weller

See also Haarlem; Hals, Frans; Leyster, Judith; Molenaer, Jan Miense

Bibliography

Sutton, Peter C. et al. *Masters of Seventeenth-Century Dutch Genre Painting.* Philadelphia: Philadelphia Museum of Art, 1984.

Welu, James A. et al. *Judith Leyster: A Dutch Master and Her World.* Worcester: Worcester Art Museum; Zwolle: Waanders, 1993.

Hals, Frans (ca. 1582/1583–1666)

Frans Hals, the son of a cloth-worker from Mechelen, was born in Antwerp during the early 1580s. Sometime after Antwerp's fall to the Spanish in 1585, his parents moved their family to Haarlem. During Hals' long career he became one of the most gifted and innovative portrait and genre painters of his age. His vigorous and free brushwork gave such vitality to his figures that, according to one contemporary historian, "they seem to live and breathe" (Schrevelius, 1648: 383). After receiving commissions from many of Haarlem's most important families and civic organizations, Hals, like many of his contemporaries, was forgotten soon after his death. A new appreciation for his genius surfaced in France in the 1860s, as the Realists and then the Impressionists marveled at the vitality of his brushwork and his surety of touch. Since the time of Hals' rediscovery scholars have continued to debate questions regarding attribution, with *oeuvre* catalogs ranging from just over one hundred extant works to nearly three hundred.

Little is known about Hals prior to 1610, the year he entered the Haarlem Guild of St. Luke and married Anneke Harmensdr. (1560–1615). A posthumous 1618 second edition of the *Schilder-Boeck* by Karel van Mander (1548–1606) states that Hals had trained with the author. This training would have occurred prior to 1603 when Van Mander left Haarlem, but neither Hals' style nor choice of subject matter reflects Van Mander's influence. Following the death of his wife in 1615 and a brief trip to Antwerp in the summer and fall of 1616, he remarried in February 1617. For the next few years Hals was associated with one of Haarlem's rhetoricians' chambers and he was a member of the Saint George Civic Guard.

Hals' earliest known picture dates to 1611, and with the completion of the *Portrait of Isaac Massa and Beatrix van der Laen* (ca. 1622; Amsterdam, Rijksmuseum; Fig. 59) a decade later, many of the qualities that define Hals' mature style are evident. Detached and broken brushwork, a light tonality, and beautifully detailed costumes bring life to the sitters of this rare double portrait. Hals showed a willingness to experiment even more in his portrait-like genre pictures of merrymaking children and young adults and in his *troniën* (individual bust or figure studies) from the same period. These works, which show Hals' awareness of the Utrecht Caravaggists, are brilliant in execution. The painter's detached brushwork defines form in a way that suggests little more than a fleeting impression of the model. Hals combined these elements with his mastery of composition in the many large and imposing civic guard group portraits he painted between 1616 and 1639.

The largest number of Hals' extant paintings are single-figure portraits of many of Haarlem's most important citizens. While Hals often took a more conservative approach in his early portrait commissions, by the 1640s he had abandoned this manner for the bolder brushwork and *alla prima* techniques found in his earlier genre scenes. By the end of his career Hals' brushwork had acquired a more expressive, economical character, and his palette darkened. These elements are best seen in his two late group portraits of the *Regents* and the *Regentesses of the Old Men's Almshouse* (ca. 1664; Haarlem, Frans Hals Museum).

Hals' last years found him on public assistance and exempt from paying his guild dues. Financial troubles had plagued the painter throughout his lifetime, for even in years when commissions were plentiful he had appeared in court for nonpayment of bills. These occurrences and other documented events prompted Arnold Houbraken to question the character of Hals and his family. The painter died on August 29, 1666, and was buried in the choir of Saint Bavo's Church in Haarlem on September 1.

Only his son-in-law Pieter Gerritsz. van Roestraeten (1630–1700) and Vincent Laurensz. van der Vinne (1629–1702) are documented as Hals' pupils. Houbraken cited others, however, including Adriaen Brouwer (ca. 1605/1606–1638), Dirck van Delen (1605–1671), Philips Wouwerman (1619–1668), Adriaen van Ostade (1610–1684), and many of his sons. Hals also influenced his brother Dirck Hals (1591–1656), Jan Miense Molenaer (1609/1610–1668), and Judith Leyster (1609–1660). It is uncertain whether they were his pupils or merely shared a studio. Many of the attribution questions that have plagued scholars are undoubtedly related to the activity of his workshop.

Dennis P. Weller

See also Group portraiture; Haarlem; Hals, Dirck; Leyster, Judith; Molenaer, Jan Miense; Underdrawings, underpaintings

Bibliography

Bode, Wilhelm von, and W.J. Binder. *Frans Hals: His Life and Work.* 2 vols. Translated by M.W. Brockwell. Berlin: Photographische Gesellschaft, 1914.

Grimm, Claus. *Frans Hals: The Complete Works.* Translated by Jürgen Riehle. New York: Harry N. Abrams, 1990.

Hofstede de Groot, Cornelis. *A Catalogue Raisonné of the Works of the Most Eminent Dutch Painters of the Seventeenth Century.* Translated by Edward G. Hawke. Vol. 3, 1–139. London: Macmillan and Co., 1910.

Houbraken, Arnold. *De Groote Schouburgh der Nederlantsche konstschilders en schilderessen.* Vol. 1, 90–95. Amsterdam, 1718.

Schrevelius, T. *Harlemias.* Haarlem, 1648.

Slive, Seymour. *Frans Hals.* 3 vols. New York and London: Phaidon, 1970–1974.

Slive, Seymour et al. *Frans Hals.* London: Royal Academy of Arts, 1989.

Valentiner, Wilhelm R. *Frans Hals.* Stuttgart and Berlin: Deutsche Verlags-Anstalt, 1921.

Hammacher, A.M.W.J. (born 1897)

Abraham Marie Wilhelmus Jacobus Hammacher, born in Middelburg (Zeeland), is an art critic and art historian of great merit in the field of nineteenth- and twentieth-century art. Hammacher gained international renown as director of the Rijksmuseum Kröller-Müller in Otterlo (1947–1963) and as a versatile writer of studies of Van Gogh, Jacques Lipchitz, Barbara Hepworth, Marino Marini, Henry van de Velde, and René Magritte. His book on the international art of sculpture, *The Evolution of Modern Sculpture* (1969; second, enlarged edition published in 1988) is generally recognized as a standard work. *Phantoms of the Imagination* (1981) reveals his deep-seated interest in the fantastic in the visual arts. From 1952 until 1968, Hammacher was professor of art history at the Technical University in Delft. In 1958 he received an honorary degree from the University of Utrecht. In 1990 Hammacher became *Commandeur des Arts et des Lettres*, receiving a prestigious French cultural award.

Before World War II, Hammacher had combined his work as a writer with an administrative job at the Postal Service, but in 1919 he began a career as art critic for the newspaper *Utrechtsch Dagblad*. In 1927 he switched to the *Nieuwe Rotterdamsche Courant*, where he worked until 1934. During the same time he traveled regularly to Italy (Florence, Siena) and France and published articles on late-nineteenth-century and modern painting and sculpture. His first book, *De Levenstijd van Antoon der Kinderen,* appeared in 1932. During the same years, in which he developed into one of the foremost Dutch writers on the visual arts, he also laid the basis for his artistic views. Partly due to the influence of his friendships with the philosopher G.J.D.C. Stempels (1879–1927) and the communal artist Richard N. Roland Holst (1868–1938), he placed works of art in his studies in a broad cultural and historical context, without losing sight of the intention of the artist and the quality of his or her work. This is clearly shown, for example, by his contributions on Charley Toorop, with whom he became friends in 1930.

After World War II, from 1945 until 1947, Hammacher was head of the Department of Visual Arts and Architecture in the Ministry of Education, Arts, and Sciences in The Hague. His most important feat as director of the Kröller-Müller Museum—which gave it its international standing—was the construction of the sculpture garden. His collection policy was to give special attention to acquiring sculptures and the drawings of sculptors.

His friendships with, among others, Barbara Hepworth, Ben Nicholson, Jacques Lipchitz, and Marino Marini, and his contacts with the international art world (Giulio Carlo Argan, Douglas Cooper, Charles Mauron, Adrian Stokes, Paul Hodin, Jean Cassou, and Michel Seuphor) enabled him more than any one else in Holland to write with a keen understanding of the creation process and the specific problems of the modern painter and sculptor.

After retirement, Hammacher moved to Brussels with his wife, Renilde Hammacher-van de Brande, former conservator of the Museum Boymans-van Beuningen in Rotterdam. He remained active as an author and art critic, however. His study of French painter Georges Seurat was published in 1994.

Peter de Ruiter

See also Art criticism, critical issues in the twentieth century; Roland Holst, Richard N.; State and municipal art collecting and collections; Toorop, Charley (Annie Caroline Pontifex)

Bibliography

Hammacher, A.M. *Charley Toorop.* Rotterdam: W.L. and J. Brusse, 1952.

———. *De Levenstijd van Antoon der Kinderen.* Amsterdam: H.J. Paris, 1932.

———. *The Evolution of Modern Sculpture: Tradition and Innovation.* New York: Harry N. Abrams, 1969.

———. *Magritte.* New York: Harry N. Abrams, 1973.

———. *Phantoms of the Imagination: Fantasy in Art and Literature from Blake to Dali.* New York: Harry N. Abrams, 1981.

———. *Silhouette of Seurat: Essays on Georges Seurat (1859–1891).* Translated by Mary Charles. Otterlo: Kröller-Müller Museum, 1994.

Hammacher, A.M., and Renilde Hammacher-van den Brande. *Van Gogh: A Documentary Biography.* London: Thames and Hudson, 1982.

Kooten, Toos van. "A.M. Hammacher en het Rijksmuseum Kröller-Müller, 1947–1963." *Jong Holland* 1 (1987): 38–47.

Ruiter, Peter de. "A.M. Hammacher als kunstcriticus: Zijn Utrechtse en Haagse jaren 1917–1927." *Jong Holland* 4 (1992): 19–34.

Hertzberger, Herman (born 1932)

European architecture in the early 1960s, in professing to be antimonumental, sought to develop design ideas that would free it from the rigid aesthetic of the International Modern. In this widespread climate of intellectual revision, several Dutch architects concentrated on exploring concepts that derived from the structuralist language and the anthropological and ethnographic studies of Claude Lévi-Strauss. In architecture, structuralism became an alternative formula whose password was "labyrinthine clarity," meaning a nonhierarchic relationship among spaces with the objective of creating organisms capable of stimulating freedom of choice and of behavior. In contrast to a neutral functionalist ordering, architectural space was articulated in a flexible way, introducing the ideas of "territorial zoning" and "public domain" that shifted the accent of the form depending on the manner in which it was used.

Herman Hertzberger was one of the most prominent exponents of structuralism in architecture. He graduated from the Technical University in Delft in 1958 and the following year joined the editorial staff of *Forum*, the journal of the society Architectura et Amicitia in Amsterdam, working alongside Aldo van Eyck (born 1918) and Jacob Berend Bakema (1914–1981). Van Eyck and Bakema were the two Dutch members of Team 10, the group engaged in revising *Forum*

in response to the need to remodel the relationship between the disciplines of architecture and urban planning, not only on the basis of quantitative parameters but with a cultural and creative approach.

For the young Hertzberger, the editorial meetings had the same stimulating effect as had his encounter with two buildings: the Maison de Verre in Paris (1928–1932), the work of Pierre Chareau (1883–1950) and Bernard Bijvoet (1889–1979); and the Children's Home in Amsterdam (1955–1960) by Aldo van Eyck. During the *Forum* years (1959–1963), Hertzberger intensively participated in the common effort to give form to a Neo-Humanistic architecture in which the quintessence of the confrontation between man and his space is expressed, which in more diverse cultures is based on the concept of "place," and which experiments with the physical and psychological significance of the "threshold," "intermediate space," and continuity between the private and public worlds.

During these years, Hertzberger concentrated on designing three-dimensional modular grids and published a series of photographic collages superimposed on match boxes to show, not the formal structure of architecture, but the system of human associations that it generates. Two buildings are the most eloquent result of the research on grids as the generator of spaces that guarantee the identity of the users: the extension of the LinMij Laundry in Amsterdam (1962–1964) and the Montessori School in Delft (1960–1966).

In Hertzberger's professional activity, the design of the school building—both kindergarten and elementary school—constituted a recurring theme and became a means for experimenting with the valences of an architectural space in which the relationships between early childhood development and the activity of learning are formed and stored. In the first Montessori School, and later in the Apollo Schools (1980–1983) and in the De Evenaar School (1984–1986), both in Amsterdam, as well as in the most recent elementary school at Almere (1991–1993), the architect developed an alternative to the traditional sequence of classroom units lined up along a corridor by articulating the spaces on the basis of an open and continuous system; intermediate areas cross and are superimposed on the primary grid of classes with the objective of offering individuals every occasion to participate in and confront the products of the collective imagination. The architecture has been conceived in the materials and the colors of a big playhouse; the plans show a preference for clustered groupings around a central communal nucleus.

If the plans for schools have been a leitmotif for Hertzberger, he has also confronted many other architectural themes during his more than thirty-year career, without ever reneging on his initial purpose to create spaces that give the individual the security "that you are somebody living somewhere." He has designed many dwellings, single-family residences and collective housing for students (Students' Residence, Amsterdam, 1959–1966) or the elderly (De Overloop Home for the Elderly, Almere, 1980–1984). He has built influential structures such as the Vredenburg Music Center in Utrecht (1973–1978) and the Library/Institute for Art Education in Breda (1990–1994). He has participated in many competitions for urban design, some of them international.

The building that has received the greatest international acclaim is the headquarters of the Centraal Beheer insurance company (Fig. 60) in Apeldoorn (1967–1972), being extended in the mid 1990s by Hertzberger himself. The point of departure for the designer is that of redefining the relationship between the functional aspects of the office as a workplace and the psychological-behavioral aspects of the community of individuals who daily inhabit it. The form that resulted is the "office landscape": a disposition of the spaces in which the individual work units (office islands) maintain their autonomy while gaining a sense of collectivity from the constructed form. The plan of the Centraal Beheer building consists of a regular grid-like structure, where each unit is at the same time an area of work, part of the collegial system, and a marginal element to the empty central space that cuts vertically through the interior of the complex. On this modular framework are grafted, according to the principle of flexibility, a myriad of variations that cooperate, nevertheless, in the objective of creating an identity of place "where everyone would feel at home." Seen from the outside, the Centraal Beheer building looks like a little city placed against the side of a hill, a refined play of volumes and of colors, with gray used for the concrete facing and red for the fixtures.

A similar plan can be found in the gigantic complex of the Ministry of Social Welfare and Employment (1979–1990) built near The Hague. In this case, however, each unit is composed of about thirty offices linked to spaces for communal activity, subdividable in turn. The monumental character of the building is accentuated by the rigorous symmetry of the plan and the structural value provided by many vertical linkages. The result is an interior space less informal and multivalent than that of the Centraal Beheer. The play of fragmentation is, in part, belied by the outside, which has the character of a turreted bastion, accentuated like the Centraal Beheer by the uniformity of the gray color of the concrete facing, and skillfully concealed by the closed slits of the windows.

In the early 1980s Hertzberger's activity was much more consistent outside the Netherlands. In Germany he designed isolated buildings, including residences, artists' studios, and offices in the Media-Park in Cologne (1990). He also participated in many competitions, among them the one for the new Gemäldegalerie (1986) and another for the Esplanade Film Center (1986–1991), both near the Kulturforum in Berlin. He received first prize for the design of Accumulata, a complex of offices and facilities in Munich (1993). In these projects and those for new sports centers in the Netherlands, Hertzberger abandoned the modular idea that had guided him in the preceding decades in order to assign greater weight to linear images and to emphasize the form of the roof.

Hertzberger's work has received a great deal of recognition, even internationally: from the architectural prize of the city of Amsterdam (1968) to the A.J. van Eyck Prize (1980) for the Vredenburg Music Center in Utrecht; and from the Richard Neutra Award for Professional Excellence (1989) to the European Prize for Architecture for his complete *oeuvre*. Since 1991 Hertzberger has been an Honorary Fellow of the Royal Institute of British Architects. Along with designing, Hertzberger has always been intensely involved in teaching, both in Europe and in the United States. In 1990 he founded the Berlage Institute in Amsterdam, an international postgraduate program in architecture, urban design, and landscape architecture. The Berlage Institute, with Hertzberger as its initial chairman, has found its most natural location in the above-mentioned Children's Home by Aldo Van Eyck.

Maristella Casciato

See also Functionalism in architecture; Postmodernism

Bibliography

Herman Hertzberger: Recent Works. The Hague: Rijksdienst Beeldende Kunst, 1990; distributed by *ARCHIS*, NAI Rotterdam.

"Hertzberger, Herman." Theme number. *Architecture and Urbanism (A+U)*. (April 1991).

Hertzberger, Herman. *Lessons for Students in Architecture*. Rotterdam: 010, 1991.

Reinink, Wessel. *Herman Hertzberger, Architect*. Rotterdam: 010, 1990.

Herwig, Reinhardt Herman (1878–1959)

The schoolteacher Reinhardt Herman Herwig traveled the Dutch countryside extensively in the first quarter of the twentieth century. Although Herwig did not scorn picturesque compositions, as his *View of the Limburg Village of Waelwylre* (Fig. 61) demonstrates, the character of his photographs of life on the land is primarily documentary. His photographs are an important visual source for those interested in how the Dutch countryside used to be.

Herwig's photographs are examples of the naturalistic photography that began about 1890. Until recently not much attention has been paid to this school in the research that has been done on the history of Dutch photography. Richard Tepe, C.E. Mögle, Jacob Olie, Geert Jannes Landweer, and, initially, Henri Berssenbrugge belonged to the naturalistic school as well.

Many of Herwig's photographs appeared in booklets and in the Dutch magazine *Buiten*, a modest equivalent of the British *Country Life*. The illustrations in *Buiten* were of relatively good quality. In the years around 1905 Herwig wrote several small travel guides that were illustrated with his own photographs—for example, the *Geïllustreerde Gids voor de Groninger Veenkoloniën* (Illustrated Guide to Groningen's Peat Colonies, 1905). These were printed in the relatively new autotype technique that "translated" the original photographs into dots of ink of various sizes, small enough to give the impression of a coherent picture. As autotype pictures were rather crude at first, they were met with criticism. As late as 1925, one critic spoke of the limp halftones and expressed preference for a "pithy print" like a woodcut. Autotype has, however, given the final blow to illustrations in non-photographic techniques. Moreover, thanks to this printing technique, photography gained access to the popular, mass-produced magazines and books.

Hans Rooseboom

See also Photography, modern and contemporary

Bibliography

Met de camera van Reinhardt Herman Herwig door Drenthe,
1900–1925. Assen: Drents Museum, 1989.

History painting

The term refers to images of unique, nonrecurring events based on religious, classical, literary, or allegorical sources. Since history painting typically relates ennobling or instructive narratives, it differs from the general, repeatable occurrences of daily life that appear as genre imagery during the Golden Age of Dutch art in the seventeenth century. In addition to artistic skill, painters of history scenes must have intellectual insight, which has led critics since antiquity to regard history painters as the most praiseworthy practitioners of art. This attitude was instituted by the great seventeenth-century academies in Italy and France and was also promulgated by native art theorists in the Netherlands. In writings such as Karel van Mander's *Schilder-Boeck* (1604), Philips Angel's *Lof der Schilder-konst* (1642), Pieter de Grebber's one-page leaflet (1649), and Samuel van Hoogstraten's *Inleyding tot de Hooge Schoole der Schilder-konst* (1678), history painting was promoted as the noblest profession for Dutch artists.

The development of history painting in the Northern Netherlands in the late fifteenth and early sixteenth centuries laid the groundwork for seventeenth-century artists of elevated themes. In the art of the Haarlem painters Albert van Ouwater (active 1450–1480) and Geertgen tot Sint Jans (active ca. 1465/1485 or 1480–1495/1496), Van Mander recognized the beginning of a Dutch school of history painting in which narrative realism replaces the static, symbolic style of traditional devotional works. Although still lacking the active, engaging gestures, expressions, and poses of mature history painting, Van Ouwater's *Raising of Lazarus* (ca.1455–1460) and Geertgen's *Julian the Apostate Ordering the Burning of the Bones of St. John the Baptist* (ca. 1490; Fig. 62) exhibit clear spatial compositions in which intelligible arrangements of figures relate the essence of religious texts. In these paintings, the Northern Netherlandish interest in contemporary settings and costumes, which heightens the immediacy of the scene, also emerges.

Both Hieronymus Bosch (1450–1516) in 's Hertogenbosch and Jan Mostaert (ca. 1475–1555), a successor to Geertgen tot Sint Jans in Haarlem, expanded the iconographic and stylistic possibilities for Dutch history painting in the sixteenth century. In addition to Old Testament proverbs and biblical parables, popular moralizing literature, such as the *Ars Moriendi* and the *Ship of Fools*, served as textual sources for Bosch, while Mostaert illustrated scenes from Ovid and contemporary accounts of New World explorations. Although Bosch's bizarre, imaginative scenes vex modern scholars who search for specific interpretations of his works, Bosch's contemporaries and immediate successors admired the Dutch painter's unidealized figures, the immediate physical action and reaction of his characters, and the convincing landscape settings of much of his narrative imagery. In his history paintings, Mostaert also adopted landscape backgrounds for many of his unusual subjects, such as Coronado's journey in the American Southwest, in which nude figures predominate.

Perfecting the organization of monumental figures in landscape compositions, another Dutch artist, Lucas van Leyden (ca. 1494–1533), earned international praise for his prints and altarpieces. Both the Italian Renaissance writer Giorgio Vasari and Van Mander recognized Lucas as a genius in representations of history subjects. In his well-known *Ecce Homo* engraving from 1510, Lucas modernized biblical history by placing Christ and Pilate in a contemporary Leiden setting (Fig. 63). Secondary figures and anecdotal details underscore the prosaic, human dimensions of the religious drama. This Northern approach to historical themes influenced Lucas' seventeenth-century successors, including Rembrandt van Rijn.

In addition to his prints, Lucas also painted large-scale altarpieces in which classical figures, rhetorical gestures, and controlled compositions reveal his indebtedness to the Italian Renaissance. Lucas' contemporary, Jan van Scorel (1495–1562), however, is recognized by Van Mander as the first artist to bring Italianate narrative modes to the Northern Netherlands. Van Scorel traveled extensively and returned to Utrecht and Haarlem with a thorough understanding of the High Renaissance figural and compositional styles of Michelangelo and Raphael and the Venetian use of color perfected by Titian (Fig. 67). Van Scorel's student, Maerten van Heemskerck (1498–1574), made extensive studies of antique sculpture and monuments while in Rome before returning to Haarlem. In his drawings, engravings, and paintings, Van Heemskerck's classical instruction surfaces in the figures and settings of his religious and pagan subject matter (Fig. 77).

The patrons for fifteenth- and sixteenth-century depictions of history scenes came from religious and secular spheres. Bishops and religious orders, regents and guilds, intellectual humanists and sophisticated collectors commissioned works of history and promoted the production and development of narrative themes. The circumstances for patronage in the Northern Netherlands during the seventeenth century, however, inhibited history painting and encouraged Dutch artists to specialize in painting nontextual genre imagery.

Traditional patrons for history painting, such as royalty, nobility, and the Roman Catholic Church, played a negligible role during the 1600s. Among the small group of royal and aristocratic patrons were the Dutch leaders, or *stadholders*, who decorated their modest, by European standards, residences with grand mural decorations in the international Baroque style. For example, Prince Frederik Hendrik, who held the position of *stadholder* from 1625 to 1647, commissioned history works from a small number of Dutch and Flemish masters for his palaces at Honselersdijk and Ter Nieuburgh in South Holland and at Noordeinde and Huis ten Bosch in The Hague. Later in the century, the *stadholder* and king of England, Willem (William) III, who reigned from 1672 to 1702, embellished his hunting palace, Het Loo, in Soestdijk with historical themes. Despite these large-scale commissions, the *stadholder* and his court did not actively collect the history paintings of native artists, preferring, instead the works of

Pieter Paul Rubens and his Flemish contemporaries.

In addition to the decline of royal patronage, the repression of Roman Catholicism in the Northern Netherlands resulted in the absence of an important patron for religious imagery. Although the official Dutch Reformed churches permitted stained-glass windows and the decoration of organ shutters, in general, places of worship were not ornamented with imagery. Some religious groups tolerated by the Calvinists, such as the Lutherans, Mennonites, and Remonstrants, incorporated somber religious imagery into their worship settings. However, these institutional patrons for religious art did not replace the important role previously held by the Roman Catholic Church. The overall production of altarpieces and devotional works was greatly diminished in the Northern Netherlands during the seventeenth century, although some artists continued to paint for hidden Roman Catholic congregations or for private Roman Catholic patrons. With the conventional means of patronage interrupted, artists of history painting looked elsewhere for customers.

Dutch painters could still produce history pieces for public places, such as town halls, guild halls, and charitable institutions, and for the upper classes, who favored historical themes for their stately homes. Images from the Bible, classical history, mythology, and contemporary history, as well as allegorical works, are well represented among the inventories of upper-class Dutch seventeenth-century collectors. The middle class, however, wanted depictions that more closely mirrored their own surroundings. Burghers buying art on the open market fostered the representation of scenes from everyday life, such as landscape, seascape, townscape, still life, portraiture, and genre depictions. Artists, accordingly, mastered a particular kind of realistic subject matter and left scholarly themes of history to a small number of Dutch painters.

The general transition in content from history to genre during the seventeenth century resulted in a new approach adopted by history painters for their subject matter. An interest in naturalism and the commonplace encouraged Dutch artists to transform distant history into contemporary incidents, resulting in classical and biblical scenes that take place in Dutch settings. In many seventeenth-century Dutch history works, the obscure characters of the past become the modern Dutch man or woman wearing contemporary costume. At times the shift toward realism in history painting, notably the inclusion of contemporary figures and settings, results in *portraits historiés*, or historicized portraiture. For example, in his *Banquet of Anthony and Cleopatra* (1669) and *Ulysses and Penelope* (1668), the Haarlem artist Jan de Bray (ca. 1627–1697) painted contemporary Dutch couples acting out episodes from classical sources. Dutch artists embraced the modernization of history in order to accentuate its direct appeal to the contemporary viewer.

This careful attention to narrative realism does not mean Dutch history painters ignored original textual sources. For the most part, Dutch artists depended on texts that had been translated into Dutch for their initial ideas regarding a history theme. For religious imagery, the illustrated Vulgate Bible and the Lutheran Bible, both in Dutch translation, were popular.

In addition, Protestant and Roman Catholic print Bibles and devotional works also contributed to the visual and textual resources available to artists of all denominations. The distinctive influence of the official Dutch Reformed *Statenbijbel* (1637) emerges around mid-century, particularly in Rembrandt's paintings of the patriarchs Abraham, Isaac, and Jacob. Another popular source for Old Testament imagery were the translated writings of the Jewish historian Flavius Josephus (ca. 37–100).

A wide range of nonreligious sources also provided textual and visual information for the Dutch history painter. Allegories were based in large part on Cesare Ripa's *Iconologia*, which was available in Dutch translation in 1644. For mythological themes, artists consulted Ovid's *Metamorphoses*, as explained by Karel van Mander in his *Schilder-Boeck* of 1604, which served as a general source for classical history as well. When artists wished to depict scenes from Roman history, they considered Joachim Oudaen's *Roomsche Mogentheyt of Naewkeurige Beschrijving* (1664). In addition, foreign and native literature also influenced the subject matter and the interpretation of narrative themes. Dutch artists favored the Italian writers Torquato Tasso (1544–1595), Ludovico Ariosto (1474–1533), and Giovanni Battista Guarini (1538–1612) and contemporary Dutch authors such as Gerbrand Adriaensz. Bredero (1585–1618), Jacob Cats (1577–1660), and P.C. Hooft (1581–1647).

In the first decades of the century, the Dutch public supported history painters such as Salomon de Bray in Haarlem and Pieter Lastman in Amsterdam. As the century progressed, however, history scenes, which were often the more expensive paintings in Dutch collections, became less of the total artistic output as painters turned to everyday scenes in order to earn a living. Only late in the century, with the political and social triumph of France, did history painters, such as Gerard de Lairesse (1640–1711), author of *Grondlegginge der Teekenkunst* (1701) and *Het Groot Schilderboek* (1707), and Adriaen van der Werff (1659–1722), once again receive prestigious commissions for history painting.

The dominance of Dutch genre painting in the seventeenth century has overshadowed the role of history painting as a major force in Northern Netherlandish art at this time. Despite the popularity of Rembrandt, who was first and foremost a painter of histories, scholars disregarded the significance of history painting until the 1980–1981 exhibition, *Gods, Saints, and Heroes*. In the exhibition catalog, images of history are divided into categories that roughly correspond to various schools of Dutch painting. Religious history painting, mythological themes, and scenes from classical history occur in the art of the late Dutch Mannerists, the Utrecht Caravaggists, the Pre-Rembrandtists, Rembrandt and his followers, and in the works of classicists working in Haarlem in the first half of the century (1614–1670) and classicists working in the latter part of the century when the Netherlands was under the influence of France (1674–1700). A small number of history painters fall outside these designations. For example, Jan Steen (1625/1626–1679), an artist who lived and worked in Leiden, The Hague, Delft, Warmond, and Haarlem during his career, is classified in the category reserved for independents and eccentrics.

The first three generations of history painters in the Northern Netherlands were Roman Catholics who trained in Italy. These include the Mannerists who were active in Haarlem, Utrecht, and Amsterdam; the Pre-Rembrandtists in Amsterdam; and the Caravaggist painters in Utrecht. In Haarlem, the theoretician Karel van Mander (1548–1606) introduced the Mannerist style of Bartholomeus Spranger (1546–1611), which he had learned in Italy, to his contemporaries Hendrick Goltzius (1558–1616) and Cornelis Cornelisz. van Haarlem (1562–1638). These three Haarlem artists formed an academy of sorts in their hometown where they emphasized life drawing. Historical scenes that included nude figures were preferred for their paintings and prints. In biblical scenes, such as the Flood, or in depictions of classical couples, such as Venus and Adonis (Fig. 64), nude male and female figures are given central position in the foreground of the pictorial space. Elongated and arranged in contorted poses, these figures act out the historical narratives in exaggerated, active ways, underscoring the artists' abilities in figural representation.

Van Mander's writings regarding the theory and practice of art were published in 1604 and emphasized the importance of depicting the human figure in scenes from classical and biblical history. His publications also spread the interest in these themes as expressed by the Mannerist style. In Utrecht, with the paintings of Abraham Bloemaert (1564–1651) and Joachim Wtewael (1566–1638), and in Amsterdam under the direction of Lastman's teacher, Gerrit Pietersz. Sweelinck (1566–ca.1628), Mannerist history painting proliferated.

Lastman (ca. 1583–1633), brought history painting into the seventeenth century, most notably by teaching Rembrandt. Most of Lastman's paintings are religious; half of his *oeuvre* represents Old Testament themes, while paintings of the New Testament and classical subjects also occur. Lastman's compositions are derived from sixteenth-century print series, Bible illustrations and drawings, revealing his stylistic dependency on his Northern predecessors (Fig. 76).

Contemporary with the painting developments of the Pre-Rembrandtists in Amsterdam is the Caravaggist movement in Utrecht. Gerard van Honthorst (1590–1656) and Hendrick Terbrugghen (1588–1629) were greatly influenced by the art of Caravaggio while they studied in Italy. This affection for the flamboyant Italian Baroque painter determined the style and content of art in Utrecht after the return of Terbrugghen in 1614 and Van Honthorst in 1620. Like Caravaggio, these artists emphasized the naturalism of large-scale figures in sharply illuminated interiors (Figs. 131 and 140).

Rembrandt's role as painter and teacher dominated the direction of Dutch history painting for much of the rest of the seventeenth century. In emulation of the international artist Pieter Paul Rubens, Rembrandt and his contemporary Jan Lievens (1607–1674) embraced the respected subject of history for their art as a means of gaining social prestige and important commissions. In the beginning of their careers, both artists were recognized by Constantijn Huygens (1596–

1687), secretary to Frederik Hendrik and an influential patron and connoisseur. According to Huygens, Rembrandt and Lievens captured what Van Mander enumerated as the primary intent of history painting, the "passions, desires, and suffering" of historical protagonists. In particular, Huygens praised Rembrandt's paintings from the 1630s for their ability to convey universal truth through particular details, which Rembrandt ably expressed by psychological and physical details in works such as *Judas Returning the Thirty Pieces of Silver* (1629). In fact, Huygens argued that Rembrandt brought classical perfection in history painting to the Northern Netherlands.

Most scholars would agree with Huygens that Rembrandt's art represents the highest achievements in seventeenth-century Dutch history painting. According to research by Christian Tümpel and others, Rembrandt first consulted the textual account of the historical event. After reading the biblical, classical, or mythological narrative, Rembrandt determined the crucial moment of transition in the story when the characters react to a specific action. If necessary, Rembrandt deviated from the text in order to heighten the drama of the scene. In his later paintings, such as *Jacob Blessing the Sons of Joseph* (1656; Fig. 118), Rembrandt dropped anecdotal details and focused on basic human emotions, often emphasizing internal decision making rather than externalized action. By reducing the range of colors and limiting the number of figures, Rembrandt concentrated the viewer's attention on the psychological component of the event. These characteristics, along with his masterful use of *chiaroscuro*, established Rembrandt's personal style as the archetype of Dutch history painting in the Golden Age.

In commentaries on Rembrandt's history paintings, many late-seventeenth-century critics accused the Dutch master of following nature too closely and ignoring the rules governing proportions, anatomy, and perspective. Since Rembrandt often debased elevated historical subject matter and deviated from the narrative accounts, experts claimed his approach lacked decorum and respect for the original text. Writing in 1681, in *Gebruik en misbruik des toneels* (Use and Misuse of the Stage), Andries Pels (1631–1681) called Rembrandt "the first heretic in painting."

Despite these condemnations, Rembrandt's influence prevailed as he trained the majority of Dutch history painters in the seventeenth century. After studying in his workshop, some students followed his stylistic features and iconographic content, while others turned to different themes or different styles. Students such as Ferdinand Bol (1616–1680), Gerbrand van den Eeckhout (1621–1674), and Aert de Gelder (1645–1727) closely followed Rembrandt's definitive style throughout much of their careers; however, changing patterns of patronage and style at mid-century encouraged some artists to abandon Rembrandt's approach. After a period producing paintings after Rembrandt, Nicolaes Maes (1634–1693) turned to portraiture, and Govaert Flinck (1615–1660) embraced international classicism. By the late seventeenth century, only De Gelder continued to work in what, by then, was considered the old-fashioned style of Rembrandt.

As an alternative to the earthy, unrefined imagery of Rembrandt and his students, decorous, idealized scenes from history appear in the works of a wide range of Dutch painters, including the so-called Haarlem classicists Pieter de Grebber (ca. 1600–1652/1653); Salomon (1597–1664) and Jan de Bray (ca. 1627–1697); and Caesar van Everdingen (ca. 1617–1678), who lived and worked in Alkmaar but is closely associated with the Haarlem School; and the Utrecht artist Cornelis van Poelenburch (1594/1595–1667). In accordance with the dictates of the international classical style as promulgated by the French Academy of Sculpture and Painting (1648) and exemplified by the paintings of Nicolas Poussin (1593/1594–1665), Dutch artists increasingly adopted a restrained, controlled style for their depictions of history at midcentury. In decorations for the Oranjezaal in the Huis ten Bosch in The Hague, De Grebber, Salomon de Bray, and Everdingen, among others, provided works with monumental, idealized figures, balanced compositions, and restrained pure colors. Precise contour lines and an overall hard-edged quality characterize these paintings glorifying the *stadholder* Frederik Hendrik.

Although initial patronage for classicism came from the court of Orange in The Hague, by the last quarter of the seventeenth century, many artists were producing history scenes in emulation of classical stylistic conventions. In collaboration with the Amsterdam intellectuals who founded the literary society Nil Volentibus Arduum (nothing is difficult for those with the will), which introduced French literary theories into Dutch society, artists such as Gerard de Lairesse promoted the French academic taste in painting by depicting edifying scenes in an elegant, formal manner. De Lairesse later codified the theoretical underpinnings of classical history painting in his book *Het Groot Schilderboeck*, which remained an authoritative source for history painters until the nineteenth century. Like his French counterpart, Roger de Piles, De Lairesse created a ranking system of art in which the international classical style of history painting was ranked as dignified and wellsuited for the aristocracy, while the Dutch realist style of genre imagery was intended for the lower and middle classes.

As might be expected, De Lairesse produced easel paintings and wall and ceiling paintings as interior decorations for influential sophisticated patrons, most of whom were Amsterdam intellectuals and businessmen. De Lairesse's contemporary in Rotterdam, Adriaen van der Werff, (1659–1722) also enjoyed the patronage of wealthy merchants and royalty. In his *Groote Schouburgh der Nederlantsche konstschilders en schilderessen* (Great Theatre of Netherlandish Painters and Paintresses) of 1721–1723, Arnold Houbraken called Van der Werff the greatest of all Dutch painters. His cabinet pieces reveal his training as one of the *fijnschilders*, or fine-painters, but his mature style exhibits the classical grace of idealized figures, clear contours, and delicate colors of late Dutch classicism. In terms of history painting, Van der Werff's influence extended well into the nineteenth century.

History painting declined considerably in the Netherlands in the eighteenth and nineteenth centuries. During this period, artists reverted to the realistic genre imagery so strongly associated with the Golden Age of Dutch painting in the seventeenth century, or they adopted the contemporary French style found in conversation pieces. By 1807, the Teylers Society in Haarlem invited contributions regarding the state of Dutch history painting, and the results were published in 1809 under the title "Treatises . . . Setting out the Reasons for the Small Number of Dutch History Painters and the Means of Making Good This Lack." Despite the good intentions of the Haarlem society, history painting continued to play only a minor role in Dutch art after the death of Adriaen van der Werff.

In survey texts of Dutch painting, only two history painters of these later centuries are generally mentioned, Jan Willem Pieneman (1779–1853) and Charles Rochussen (1814–1894). Both artists depicted Dutch history in patriotic scenes emphasizing the realism of the events. Arguably, their art is recognized more for its content than for its artistic strengths.

The eighteenth and nineteenth centuries are the least studied in terms of history painting. Very little has been published on the period or on individual painters. This is not the case when considering seventeenth-century history painters. In particular, Rembrandt and his followers have received an abundance of scholarly attention. Insightful stylistic information and iconographic explanations are found in catalogs published in 1992 during Netherlands-wide exhibitions that reported the results of investigations undertaken by the Rembrandt Research Project. For lesser-known painters of the period, such as the classicists working in Haarlem, Utrecht, and Amsterdam, updated biographies and *catalogues raisonnés* are needed, although good sources of information regarding the minor masters are often published during small exhibitions in regional museums.

Valerie Lind Hedquist

See also Bol, Ferdinand; Bosch, Hieronymus; Churches; Dutch history; Flinck, Govaert; France; Geertgen tot Sint Jans; Haarlem; History portraits; House of Orange-Nassau; Huygens, Constantijn; Italy; Literature, poetry: analogues with the visual; Mannerism, Mannerists; Nationalism; Pastoral; Pre-Rembrandtists; Rembrandt School; Rembrandt van Rijn; Roman history; State and municipal art collecting and collections; Subjects, subject categories, and hierarchies; Utrecht Caravaggists; Van den Eeckhout, Gerbrand; Van Leyden, Lucas; Writers on art, eighteenth century; Writers on art, sixteenth and seventeenth centuries

Bibliography

Blankert, Albert et al. *Gods, Saints, and Heroes: Dutch Painting in the Age of Rembrandt.* Washington, DC: National Gallery of Art, 1980.

Broos, Ben. *Intimacies and Intrigues: History Painting in the Mauritshuis.* The Hague: Mauritshuis, 1993; distributed by Martial and Snoeck.

Cavalli-Björkman, Görel. "History Painting in the Age of Rembrandt." In *Rembrandt och hans tid, Människan i Centrum/Rembrandt and His Age, Focus on Man,* 21–

31. Stockholm: Nationalmuseum; Uddevalla: Bohus-läningens Boktryckeri, 1992.

Fuchs, R.H. "Classic Histories: History Painting in the Seventeenth Century." In *Dutch Painting*, 62–80. London: Thames and Hudson, 1985.

Haak, Bob. "Something to Paint: History Painting and the Depiction of Contemporary Events." In *The Golden Age: Dutch Painters of the Seventeenth Century*, 77–85. New York: Harry N. Abrams, 1984.

Kirschenbaum, Baruch D. *The Religious and Historical Paintings of Jan Steen*. New York: Abner Schram, 1977.

Mandle, R. *Dutch Masters from the Eighteenth Century*. Minneapolis: Minneapolis Institute of Arts, 1977.

Marius, G.H. *Dutch Painters of the Nineteenth Century*. Woodbridge, Suffolk: Antique Collectors Club, 1973.

Snyder, James. *Northern Renaissance Art, Painting, Sculpture, the Graphic Arts from 1350 to 1575*. Englewood Cliffs, NJ: Prentice-Hall, 1985.

Tümpel, Christian et al. *Het Oude Testament in de Schilderkunst van de Gouden Eeuw*. Amsterdam: Joods Historisch Museum; Zwolle: Waanders, 1991.

History portraits

While displaying enough identifying features to be recognized as a portrait of its contemporary subject, the history portrait also depicts that individual at the same time in the guise of an earlier religious or historical figure. The association between the portrayed individual and the historical figure in whose guise he or she is represented relies on typology, an established verbal and literary device of theology. The portrayed individual is represented with his or her own physiognomy and/or other identifying features and, at the same time, linked with a figure from the past through costume or auxiliary objects—often codified by the visual tradition through their relation to other figures, particularly in a narrative—or through the setting in which the figure is located. This typological link should be distinguished from allegory and symbolism, both of which may also figure in the image. Contemporary figures who are portrayed as themselves merely viewing a historical event are not history portraits in the strict sense, unless such viewing is an identifying feature of their antecedents.

The genre seems to have originated toward the end of the fifteenth century. It was most popular in the sixteenth and seventeenth centuries, the same period in which the use of typological associations in literature—which relied on the same kinds of associations—reached its height. In being associated with a historical figure, the portrayed individual is accorded the traits—usually of character—of the figure in whose guise he or she appears. It is thus an inventive solution to the problem of visually representing character, which, by the seventeenth century, was no longer believed to be literally written in the body.

A pan-European genre, the history portrait was particularly popular for representing the power and virtue of monarchs and aristocrats. Within the Northern Netherlands, Willem I was portrayed as St. George in an etching by Marcus Gheeraerts of 1577, an apparently unique association of the prince with that saint. In the next century, Jacob Cuyp represented Frederik Hendrik as the triumphant David in a painting that celebrated the prince's triumph at 's Hertogenbosch in 1629 ('s Hertogenbosch, Gemeentehuis). In the latter image, the recognizable face of Frederik Hendrik and the town of 's Hertogenbosch in the background make literal contemporary references, and typological reference to David is produced through the decapitated head of Goliath at David's feet. As in many Dutch history portraits, however, more than simple typology functions within the latter image to convey meaning. The seven provinces of the Netherlands are represented allegorically as six young women and one older one playing music and singing to a text drawn from Psalm 98: "He has accomplished a wondrous deed by his hand." A *putto* holds a symbolic laurel wreath above Frederik Hendrik/David's head and a banderole that reads, "Gloria Excelsis."

Family portraits, however, dominate the genre in the Northern Netherlands. Inhabitants of the Northern Netherlands readily identified themselves with both the chosen people of Israel, and with the Roman Republic in contemporary texts; these identifications also appear in their history paintings. In 1574–1575 Maerten de Vos represented members of the family of Peeter Panhuys—his wife, Margarita van Eicklenberg, their children, and relatives—as members of the Israelite people in an image depicting *Moses Showing the Tablets of the Law to the Israelites* (The Hague, Mauritshuis). Gerbrand van den Eeckhout several times portrayed patrons as the Celto-Iberian family of Aluccius, his captive fiancée, and her parents in the *Continence of Scipio* (Toledo, Toledo Museum of Art [Fig. 120]; The Hague, Dienst Verspreide Rijkskollekties).

Favored subjects for a man and his wife were couples from both the Old Testament and mythology. Ferdinand Bol portrayed Erasmus Scharlaken and his wife, Anna van Erckel, as *Isaac and Rebecca* in a painting now in Dordrecht (ca. 1648; Dordrechts Museum), and Van den Eeckhout represented another couple as *Isaac and Rebecca before Abraham* in 1665 (The Hague, Mauritshuis). Bol portrayed a husband, his wife (with one breast bared), and their nearly nude child as *Paris Offering the Golden Apple to Venus, with Cupid* (1656; Dordrecht, Dordrechts Museum, on loan from Dienst Verspreide Rijkskollekties), and Jan de Bray represented at least two couples as *Ulysses and Penelope*, once in 1668 (Louisville, Kentucky, J.B. Speed Art Museum) and a second time in 1677 (Haarlem, Frans Hals Museum).

Not all history portraits appear at first glance to flatter their subjects. De Bray portrayed himself, his parents, his siblings, and his spouse in more than one version of the scene *Cleopatra Betting Antony that She Can Spend More than Ten Million Ducats on a Meal* (1652 and 1656 [or 8], Hampton Court, Collection of Her Majesty the Queen; 1669, Manchester, New Hampshire, Currier Gallery of Art); Caesar van Everdingen's *Diogenes Searching for an Honest Man* of 1652 shows the aged Diogenes with a cart of his favorite food, turnips, and holding a light at midday seeking an honest man among a family portrayed standing in a Dutch town square

(The Hague, Mauritshuis).

The German art historian Alois Riegl observed that Dutch group portraits invite the psychological participation of the viewer. We might extend this observation to the history portrait, and then consider the psychological effect that participation may have on changing the viewer. While not necessary for their meaning, such portraits may have provided an opportunity for viewer identification with the portrayed individuals, and an occasion for applying to themselves morals or lessons associated with the biblical or historical subjects.

Ann Jensen Adams

See also Bol, Ferdinand; History painting; Literature, poetry: analogues with the visual; Marriage and family portraits; Pastoral; Roman history; Van den Eeckhout, Gerbrand

Bibliography

Polleross, Friedrich. "Between Typology and Psychology: The Role of the Identification Portrait in Updating Old Testament Representations." *Artibus et Historiae* 24 (1991): 75–117.

Riegl, Alois. "Das Holländische Gruppenporträt." *Jahrbuch der Kunsthistorischen Sammlungen in Wien* 23 (1902): 71–278. Reprint. 2 vols. Vienna: Osterreichischen Staatsdruckerei, 1931.

Wishnevsky, Rose. "Studien zum 'portrait historié' in den Nederlanden." Ph.D. diss., Ludwig-Maximilians Universität, 1967.

Horticulture

In the seventeenth century, Dutch horticulture had attained a national and international importance through the cultivation of new vegetables, exports, and horticultural writings. The subject of horticultural gardening, however, was not depicted by Dutch painters. Instead, an unprecedented group of paintings of vegetable markets was produced by Dutch artists from those cities that had become internationally famous for their horticulture and marketing of vegetables.

In the sixteenth century, horticultural activity had not been economically important or vital. The cultivation of vegetables, fruits, and other plants took place only in the private gardens of well-to-do citizens or in the immediate surroundings of Leiden and a few other cities. At the turn of the sixteenth century, however, the areas surrounding Leiden and Delft in particular had become centers for the cultivation of vegetables.

Although Leiden remained the most important horticultural center in the seventeenth century because of the large surrounding area and the intensity of cultivation, other areas in North and South Holland developed as significant regions for horticulture, such as Beverwijk, Heemskerk, the Langendijk (north of Alkmaar), and the Streek (an area between Hoorn and Enkhuizen). After mid-century, other areas that became known for their cultivation of vegetables were in the Westland (that stretch of land behind the dunes between The Hague and the Hoek van Holland) and surrounding the Oude en Nieuwe Wetering, Haarlem, the Beemster, Purmer,

Dordrecht, Rotterdam, Gouda, and immediately around Amsterdam. Many vegetable growers, especially in Leiden, grew rich on the intense cultivation of the soil.

Seventeenth-century Dutch literary interest in their famous horticulture took various forms, including botanical books or herbals, which were first published in the sixteenth century; country-house poetry in which gardens were described; and books of husbandry. Throughout the seventeenth century, illustrated herbals were published repeatedly in Dutch rather than Latin, which testifies to the lay person's general interest in botanical information. The illustrations for herbals provide reliable visual information and reflect a scientific interest in the description of herbs, plants, and vegetables. On the other hand, some of the accompanying texts offer confusing information, referring, for example, to different images of plants by the same name.

The paintings of vegetable (and sometimes fruit) markets appeared suddenly after the middle of the seventeenth century. Gerrit Dou, Jan Steen, and other artists of the Leiden school created the prototypes for such paintings. Gabriel Metsu, Jan Victors, Nicolaes Maes, Hendrick Martensz. Sorgh, Quiringh van Brekelenkam, Emanuel de Witte, Michiel van Musscher, Jacob Toorenvliet, and others continued the pictorial tradition in Amsterdam, Rotterdam, and Delft. The vegetables in such paintings, which were represented with great attention to detail, were often those produced or traded in the communities depicted. Unlike earlier mid-sixteenth-century paintings with large displays of vegetables, such as Pieter Aertsen's *Christ in the House of Martha and Mary* (1553), the mid-seventeenth-century market paintings depict the vegetables with scientific accuracy. Such paintings satisfied a demand for pictorial celebrations of the horticulture and vegetable marketing that had become internationally famous by the middle of the seventeenth century.

Linda Stone-Ferrier

See also Commerce and commercial life; Exotica; Leiden; Natural history illustration; Rotterdam; Rural life and views; Still life

Bibliography

Kistemaker, Renée, M. Wagenaar, and J. van Assendelft. *Amsterdam, marktstad.* Amsterdam: Dienst van het Marktwezen, 1984.

Sangers, W.J. *De ontwikkelingen van de Nederlandse tuinbouw tot het jaar 1930.* Zwolle: N.V. Uitgevers-Maatschappij W.E.J. Tjeenk Willink, 1952.

Stone-Ferrier, Linda. "Gabriel Metsu's *Vegetable Market at Amsterdam:* Seventeenth-Century Dutch Market Paintings and Horticulture." *Art Bulletin* 71:3 (September 1989): 428–452.

House interiors

During the 1660s, the market for subject matter reflecting contemporary society and family life was expanding greatly, and artists were seeking to make their representations of space more realistic and detailed. During this period of innovation in subject matter and technique, plausible house interiors replaced the imaginary palaces that had been typical settings since the late sixteenth century. The domestic interior became a canonical setting for portraits and genre scenes. The popularity of this setting was also due to the profound significance of the house in Dutch culture as a symbol of family solidarity and social status.

Interior scenes evolved from a number of printed sources: Adriaen van de Venne's illustrations of proverbs and the emblem books of Jacob Cats and Johan de Brune; proverbs by Claes Jansz. Visscher; and especially the architectural pattern books of Flemish printmaker and designer Jan Vredeman de Vries. These albums of imaginary halls, staircases, and courtyards provided standard compositions, as well as solutions to problems of perspective, that painters could adapt and alter as they chose. Also influential were the vignettes of elegant Parisian life by the French engraver Abraham Bosse, which were widely disseminated in the Netherlands.

Early-seventeenth-century artists such as Bartholomeus van Bassen and Dirck van Delen specialized in fanciful, ornate architectural settings that owed much to De Vries' imaginary designs. These were succeeded in the 1620s and 1630s by extremely plain interiors, painted in the monochromatic palette fashionable until the mid–1640s. By 1650, artists experimenting with perspective had begun to depict the domestic environment in greater detail. Until the middle of the eighteenth century, rooms in Dutch houses generally did not have specialized functions; they were used indiscriminately for eating, sleeping, socializing, and storage. Interior scenes, illustrating this transition from the traditional practices of communal living to the emerging notion of privacy, would show a single room filled with accoutrements: beds, still lifes, cabinets, sculptures, pictures, and maps. Artists used these elements, often invested with symbolic meanings, to enrich and clarify the subjects. Nicolaes Maes' *The Eavesdropper* (1657; Dordrecht, Dordrechts Museum), which shows a young housewife eavesdropping on the seduction of her maid, takes place in the stairway and corridor of a rather grand house, between a dining party upstairs and a kitchen at the right (Color Plate 7). The map on the wall, which has associations of worldliness, and the classical head of Juno, the Roman goddess of marriage, provide a tacit commentary on this comic scene of seduction and secrecy.

The richly appointed middle-class interior that had evolved by the 1660s would be widely imitated in the succeeding centuries, though the use of symbolic elements eroded. Toward the end of the century, settings became more opulent as French taste influenced interior design and decor. In the eighteenth century, artists such as Cornelis Troost used large, elegant interiors filled with antique sculpture as settings for fashionable "conversation pieces": group portraits in a social setting, showing the sitters at work or leisure in their familar surroundings. These images satisfied the demand for portraits in the English manner of Sir Joshua Reynolds, whose works were widely circulated in prints. In contrast, Jan Ekels the Younger, Wijbrand Hendriks, and other artists of the late eighteenth and early nineteenth centuries responded to a vogue

for reviving the intimate genre scenes of the past (Fig. 52). Recent studies of material culture in seventeenth- and eighteenth-century Holland can allow current scholarship to supplement the art-historical issue of stylistic conventions with a consideration of the relationship between the domestic interior depicted in art and the actual conditions of the household.

Martha Hollander

See also Applied arts; Architectural painting; Bakker Korff, Alexander Hugo; Conversation piece; Display; Genre painting, eighteenth century; Hague School, The; Israëls, Jozef; Maes, Nicolaes; Musicians, musical companies, musical performers; Paintings-within-paintings; Textiles, textile industry; Troost, Cornelis; Women's worlds

Bibliography

Hollander, Martha. "Structures of Space and Society in the Seventeenth-Century Dutch Interior." Ph.D. diss., University of California at Berkeley, 1990.

Liedtke, Walter A. "Toward a History of Dutch Genre Painting." In *De Arte et Libris: Festschrift Erasmus 1934–1884*, 11–22. Amsterdam: Erasmus Antiquariaat en Boekhandel, 1984.

Liedtke, Walter A. "Toward a History of Dutch Genre Painting II." In *The Age of Rembrandt: Studies in 17th-Century Dutch Painting.* Roland E. Fleischer and Susan S. Munshower, eds. State College, PA: Pennsylvania State University Press, 1988.

Lunsingh Scheurleer, T.H., C.W. Fock, and A.J. van Dissel. *Het Rapenburg: Geschiedenis van een Leidse Gracht.* 11 vols. Leiden: Rijksuniversiteit Leiden, 1986–1992.

Thornton, Peter. *Seventeenth-Century Interior Design in England, France, and Holland.* New Haven: Yale University Press, 1978.

Zumthor, Paul. *Daily Life in Rembrandt's Holland.* Translated by S.W. Taylor. New York: Macmillan, 1963.

House of Orange-Nassau

Members of the royal House of Orange have played important, although not always leading, roles as patrons and collectors of art. From the sixteenth to the end of the eighteenth century, they built and consolidated their position of authority, and after an interruption between 1795 and 1815, when the Netherlands were under French rule, they returned to power as kings. In more recent times, their female descendants have been able to hold their own through a series of adjustments within a constitutional monarchy.

From the Waning of the Middle Ages until the Revolt

During the fifteenth century, the most influential patronage in the Low Countries came from other families, in particular the dukes of Guelders, the counts of Holland, and the dukes of Burgundy. The Nassau family did not leave its mark on the waning culture of the Middle Ages. The grave monument that Hendrik III, count of Nassau and lord of Breda (1504–1538), had placed in the Great Church of Breda for his uncle Engelbert II is one of the oldest preserved testimonies to the widely branching Nassau patronage in the Netherlands (Fig. 134). An uninterrupted tradition of painted portraits was begun with Engelbert in 1487. Inside the fortifications of Breda, which the Nassaus helped financially to construct, the family had a residence that, under Hendrik, was enlarged and appointed with paintings, tapestries, and other valuables.

The connection between Nassau and Orange was established through the marriage (ca. 1517–1518) of Hendrik III with Claudine of Chalon, the only daughter of Jean, who was prince of Orange in the region of Provence. Hendrik had a part in the election in 1519 of Prince Karel (Charles I of Spain, who inherited the Netherlands in 1515) as Holy Roman Emperor; he accompanied Karel (Charles V as emperor) to Italy, and the emperor made him *stadholder* (leader) of Holland. He was succeeded by his son René, the first count of Nassau who was also prince of Orange. In 1559, René was succeeded as lord of Breda by his young cousin Willem, whose family castle was in Dillenburg in Germany. Around 1545, they were both portrayed on horseback in a series of colored prints.

Willem I of Orange also had at his disposal a residence in Brussels. Among his possessions were coins, antiques, silver and gilded-silver plates and vessels, jewels set with diamonds, tapestries (some of which depicted illustrious ancestors and the history of Hannibal), and a small collection of paintings, including a peasant fair, or *kermis*, Old and New Testament histories, landscapes, and soldier scenes. The hanging over the mantle in the Great Gallery was a work that Willem had inherited: Hieronymus Bosch's *Garden of Earthly Delights* triptych (ca. 1510–1515).

The Revolt of the Netherlands against Spanish rule that began in 1568 and the Reformation were turning points for both the Netherlands and the House of Orange-Nassau. First, the prince had to pawn a part of his Brussels valuables to pay for the war; later he was forced to leave behind the rest, and Bosch's painting passed into Spanish ownership. When Willem of Orange joined the rebels in the North, he moved to Delft and into the modest Prinsenhof, where he was assassinated in 1584. The portrayals of Willem of Orange from this time were sometimes commissioned by him, as, for example, the portraits in the church windows in Gouda, but more often they were commissioned by people from his entourage. In pamphlets and other printed matter he was represented as a reasonable, moderate, freedom-loving, and religiously devout prince, in contrast to the tyrant, the duke of Alva, who, as the representative of King Philip II of Spain in the Netherlands, had became the target of satire. The heroic role of Willem of Orange in the Revolt and his move to the Northern Netherlands were sanctioned by the States General after his death through their commission of a great tomb monument in the Nieuwe Kerk in Delft, which was completed in 1621 (Fig. 34).

Stadholders in the Republic of the United Provinces of the Netherlands

Maurits, eldest son and successor of Willem I of Orange, consolidated the authority of the family in the Northern Netherlands. He had the *stadholder*'s quarters in The Hague enlarged and redecorated with portraits of his army's leaders by Jan van Ravesteyn, which were made between 1611 and 1625, the year of his death. The militarily successful Maurits also commissioned works from Jacob de Gheyn II, and laid the foundation for a court patronage that flourished under his brother and successor, Frederik Hendrik, when The Hague became the center of government of the Republic (Fig. 32).

Art was also commissioned and acquired by other members of the family. Johan Maurits of Nassau-Siegen (1604–1697), grandson of Willem's brother, held a high position in the West India Company. In Brazil he built forts and villas and had plants and animals documented in drawings and paintings. He commissioned construction of the Mauritshuis, which, together with the elegant townhouses built for Constantijn Huygens and others, gave The Hague the allure of royalty. Many of the paintings and drawings that he commissioned dealing with his "scientific" interests were conveyed as gifts to German, French, and Danish monarchs. Of long standing, but modest, was the patronage of the family branch of Nassau-Dietz, who as the *stadholders* of Friesland resided in the Prinsenhof in Leeuwarden.

In the course of the seventeenth century, the power of the *stadholders* increased and their patronage occurred on a larger scale. They bought and expanded the palaces of Noordeinde, Honselersdijk, Huis ter Nieuwburg, and Huis ten Bosch—all in and around The Hague—and provided them with gardens and decorated them with paintings. They did the same with the castle in Buren, where a gallery was devoted to the portrayal of military victories. The images show that they strove for a coherent pictorial program in which the thematic emphasis was on the military power of the Oranges as the leading family in the Northern Netherlands. These dynastic portrayals culminated in the monumental paintings that Amalia van Solms commissioned for Huis ten Bosch in memory of her husband, Frederik Hendrik, who died in 1647. The Flemish painter Jacob Jordaens and Dutch artists, among whom were Jacob van Campen and the court painter Gerard van Honthorst, decorated the central room, the Oranjezaal, with scenes that glorify the *stadholder* as triumphant.

Amalia van Solms inherited the assets of the *stadholder*, among which were paintings (not the most precious of the furnishings) by Flemish artists Paulus Bril, Jan Bruegel, Rubens, and Van Dyck, and also by contemporary Dutch painters like Van Poelenburch, Roelandt Savery, Moreelse, Terbrugghen, Van Baburen, Herman Saftleven, Lievens, and Rembrandt. Together with portraits by Van Honthorst, these paintings were inherited by her daughters, and, through them, most of the *stadholder*'s collection of paintings passed into the collections of German princes, and afterward into the museums in Berlin and Dessau. The Oranges had in their palaces many portraits of family members and of members of great European dynasties, with whom they were connected by marriage and diplomatic ties. Despite the parceling out of the art collection, such series of portraits, in which Willem I of Orange always preceded Maurits and Frederik Hendrik as the patriarch, continued to define and fix the image of the Northern Netherlands—not least because houses and government buildings were also decorated with them.

The short reign of Willem II (1647–1650) and the two periods (1650–1672 and 1702–1747) without *stadholders*, when anti-Orange supporters of the Republic controlled the towns and the States General, were not conducive to a magnificence of patronage by the Oranges. Willem III, who in 1672 acquired the position of *stadholder* and after 1689 combined it with being king of England, could, however, afford a great show. After 1685, he commissioned in different phases the palace, garden, fountains, and statues at Het Loo, originally a small hunting castle. In England, he was active in the palaces of Hampton Court and Kensington. He ordered drastic renovations to be made to the *stadholder*'s quarters in The Hague, to the palace that his father had purchased in Honselersdijk in Dieren, to the castle in Breda, and to the estate near Soestdijk, where Gerard de Lairesse and Melchior de Hondecoeter carried out his commissions. Willem III brought paintings with him from England. Among them were two paintings by Lucas van Leyden (Piero di Cosimo, it was determined later), *The Young Mother* by Gerrit Dou (bought by the States General and offered to Charles II in 1660 as one of the gifts from the Dutch on the occasion of the restoration of the Stuarts in England; Color Plate 8), as well as *Man with a Falcon* and the *Portrait of Jane Seymour* by Hans Holbein the Younger. With works by Van Dyck, Bassano, and Veronese, the *stadholder*-king Willem III gave the Orange collection a more international cachet than his ancestors had done. This cosmopolitan orientation did not last because, again, many works disappeared through inheritance, and because the hard-pressed widow of Johan Willem Friso van Nassau-Dietz, cousin of the childless Willem III (who died in 1702), auctioned the paintings in Het Loo in 1713. Thus one cannot speak of a consciously gathered and, as a whole, top-quality painting collection. The Oranges could not, despite their beautifully decorated palaces, which formed the nucleus of court life, measure up against the leading *connoisseurs* and *collectioneurs* of the seventeenth and eighteenth centuries.

A new collection was built up by the *stadholders* Willem IV (son of Johan Willem Friso and raised at the court in Friesland), who became the first hereditary *stadholder* in 1747, and Willem V, who succeeded his father as hereditary *stadholder* in 1766. Both were also active overseeing the construction of new palaces and the renovation of existing ones. This was well-timed because Noordeinde and Honselersdijk, which had been repurchased from German princes in 1754, were much neglected. Radical renovations were made to Huis ten Bosch, which received two wings, a new façade, and decoration in the French court style with two new chimneys, ornaments, and painted work in 1733. Willem IV bought Rembrandt's *Simeon in the Temple* at an auction in 1733 and acquired works by Dou, Willem van Mieris, Godfried Schalcken, Philips Wouwerman, and Adriaen van der Werff. In 1749 he bought *The Bull* by Paulus Potter, which along with about thirty other paintings was given a place in the *stadholder*'s quarters. Most of paintings were hung in the gallery and the neighboring rooms of the palace Het Loo, along with possessions brought from the court in Leeuwarden.

Willem V crowned his career as a collector in 1771, when he was still only twenty-three years old, at the auction of the Amsterdam merchant Gerrit Braamkamp, whose catalogue records three hundred thirteen items. His first purchases had been three works by Jan Steen at the Lormier auction in 1763. A year later he acquired *View of the Tomb of Willem I of Orange in the Nieuwe Kerk in Delft* by Gerard Houckgeest (Fig. 42), one of the many paintings of the monument that was erected in honor of Willem of Orange. Then the *stadholder* bought another Steen, a *Battle* by Wouwerman, a very precious Schalcken, and, from the art dealer Pieter Yver, two works by the contemporary French painter Vernet. In 1768, Willem V became the owner of the whole cabinet—an exquisite collection of forty-one paintings—of Govert van Slingelandt, the receiver-general of Holland and West Friesland, who had trained himself as a *connoisseur*. In his younger years the *stadholder* visited several collections (like the one of the bishop of Rotterdam) and auctions (like those of the widow of Allard de la Court in Leiden and the king of Poland). His purchases are characterized by the usual interest in pictures that have a relation with the Oranges and that play a principal part in Dutch art, supplemented by a few works by the famous Italian, Flemish, German, and French old masters. The prominent place of the Dutch *fijnschilders* (fine painters) among the *stadholder*'s acquisitions fits in with a general appreciation of their work by experts in the eighteenth century after a period of declining interest. According to the judgment of contemporaries, the slight international character of the collection was a weakness, but the quality of the Dutch masters was praised. In 1773, Willem V moved the painting cabinet from the *stadholder*'s quarters in the Binnenhof (the inner courtyard of the old castle), where at the time the most important works from Het Loo could also be found, to a specially created gallery in the Buitenhof (the outer courtyard) that was accessible to the public on certain days. After that he commissioned a few works, mainly from painters in The Hague and Antwerp, and he received some more works as gifts. His collection, in addition, consisted of a renowned zoological garden at Het Loo, described in a publication from the director of the menagerie, and a nature cabinet. This was regarded as one of the most important in the world, and from this part of his collection the *stadholder* took the most important pieces with him when he fled to England in 1795.

Kings and Queens

The French, who overran the country in 1795 and occupied it until 1814, had the paintings of the *stadholder* transported to Paris to be included in a great public museum. The works of art from the Oranjezaal in Huis ten Bosch in The Hague were the starting point for the first national art museum (Nationale Konst-Gallerij) that was founded there in 1798 on the initiative of the agent of finances, I.J.A. Gogel, and opened on May 31, 1800. The reign of Louis Napoleon Bonaparte, the brother of Napoleon, as king of Holland (1806–1810) was important for royal patronage in the Netherlands through the substantial purchases and the introduction of numerous institutions. Among the institutional changes were the establishment of the Koninklijk Instituut van Wetenschappen, Letterkunde, en Schone Kunsten (Royal Institute of Sciences, Literature, and Fine Arts), a plan for a Koninklijke Academie (Royal Academy), and the transformation of the Nationale Bibliotheek (National Library) from the Batavian Republic—the government of the Netherlands from 1795 to 1806—into the Koninklijke Bibliotheek (Royal Library). During this period the town hall of Amsterdam became the Koninklijk Paleis (Royal Palace), and Het Loo, which had been used as a hospital in 1795, was remodeled to serve as a royal summer residence.

Willem I, who returned to the Netherlands in 1813 and was crowned king in 1815, bought several paintings, commissioned some others, and maintained the framework for cultural institutions. In 1830, Willem I promoted the purchase of paintings on behalf of museums, when the institutions or the ministry did not have enough means themselves. Moreover, in 1816, several new museums were founded, among them the Koninklijk Kabinet van Schilderijen (Royal Cabinet of Paintings), today known by the name of the building in which it has been housed since 1822, and which was bought shortly before for that purpose: the Mauritshuis in The Hague. The public collection was strengthened with the addition of some important pieces: in 1822, the *View of Delft* by Johannes Vermeer (Fig. 145), and in 1828, the *Anatomy Lesson of Dr. Nicolaes Tulp* by Rembrandt. Willem I contributed chiefly to the formation of the national collection by not reclaiming the property of his grandfather and of his father, a large part of which was returned from Paris after difficult negotiations. Furthermore, the king supported the formation of the Koninklijk Kabinet van Zeldzaamheden (Royal Cabinet of Rarities), in which the collection of portrait miniatures was placed, the Koninklijk Penningenkabinet (Royal Cabinet of Coins and Medals), and the Koninklijke Bibliotheek (Royal Library). He also gave a boost to art education as a part of economic policy.

Willem II, who came to the throne in 1840, brought to an end the buying of art for national collections, but he put together an exquisite private collection in which were represented Flemish paintings from the fifteenth century (Jan van Eyck and Hans Memling) and Italian paintings and drawings from the sixteenth century (Perugino, Leonardo da Vinci, Andrea del Sarto). As a young crown prince in his twenties, he had begun buying art, and after 1842, the collection, which had been brought over from Brussels, could be seen in the new Gothic Room of the unpretentious Kneuterdijk palace in The Hague, which had been bought by his father. Besides being a selective collector, Willem II was also interested in architecture, with a preference for the Neo-Gothic style then flourishing in England, as his palace in Tilburg shows. Furthermore, he supported the erection of an equestrian statue of Willem I of Orange across from the palace at Noordeinde. In 1850, a year after his death, the collection, which had been given as collateral to the Russian czar for loans received, was auctioned. Only some of the pieces passed into the possession of Willem III, who did not make a name for himself as a collector and patron. He supported several young artists, was a great lover of music and theater, and received increasing criticism in pamphlets, magazines, and newspapers, which denounced his liberal morals. His first wife, Sophie, expanded the collection of portrait miniatures considerably by purchases and inheritance. Queen Wilhelmina, who was crowned after the regency of Emma, Willem III's second wife, in the Nieuwe Kerk in Amsterdam in 1898, had a great interest in this collection. She was herself a painter and had Het Loo completely remodeled between 1911 and 1914. However, the continuing decline of royal patronage was unmistakable, and remained so after she abdicated in 1948.

The modernizing of media and image making progressed during the time of Queen Juliana (1948–1980), who is known primarily through photographs of the royal family together at Soestdijk palace and on bicycles. The image of the monarchy became more bourgeois, more domestic, and less martial. At the same time, symbolism and the emphasis on tradition became more important, as witnessed in rituals such as Prince's Day, Queen's Day, coronations, and the placing of the remainder of the family's collection in museums. A part of the Orange collection was transferred in 1972 to the Stichting Historische Verzamelingen van het Huis Oranje-Nassau (Foundation for the Historical Collections of the House of Orange-Nassau), and then into a museum in the renovated palace of Het Loo.

The palace of Soestdijk, expanded with wings in the meantime, was reputed to be private, not the least because of a notion in Dutch society about the "secrecy of Soestdijk" that was not supposed to be made public. The public image of the monarch's home was carefully controlled, and political cartoonists, photographers, journalists, intellectuals, and historians respected this. Only some left-wing publications gave voice to a revival of republican thinking around 1966. But the dominant image of the royal household that could be seen in photographs and later also on television was a happy family without financial worries, led by a sensible queen who was above all political parties. This did not allow for major commissions or the building of a special art collection. The areas in which the royal family gave in to luxury expenditures they kept to themselves as much as possible, with the exception of the sports cars of Prince Bernhard, who, according to a statement that has been attributed to Juliana, knew the Ferrari factory near Modena better than any other place in Italy.

Queen Beatrix, who was crowned April 30, 1980, has given the monarchy a higher cultural respect than her parents did, and she has used the possibilities of new means of communication more effectively. Her reputation among the intelligentsia is also very favorable. The private life of the family is generally respected. Beatrix's public image is as an expert administrator and a hard worker who is above all of the political parties and who fosters an interest in culture. Outstanding examples of the way the monarchy uses public relations are two films that were broadcast on television in 1988. One was a portrait of the queen in which she is shown at work as a sculptor, and in which she shows to the people all of the modern art of Noordeinde Palace, which was completely renovated between 1977 and 1986. The other is a documentary with six artists' portraits that were presented to the queen as a gift to the nation. The queen herself did not play a leading role in the commissions. The Council of State, the province of Limburg, the town of Kampen, and other institutions have portraits of the monarchs made, and the responsibility for restoration and redecoration of palaces lies with the nation's government.

Conclusion

The contribution to the arts by members of the House of Orange in what is now known as the Netherlands consisted of commissioning and purchasing works of art with the aim of decorating a series of palaces that were again and again renovated. Characteristic of this family is the continual parceling out of possessions to heirs. Their collections did not stay together through inheritance by the oldest son or inside one territorial state. Discontinuity in possession and royal magnificence in moderation were reinforced because the Oranges inside the Republic did not have the position of sovereign monarchs with a great court. Next to a continually restrained family patronage stood an influential "passive patronage"— that is, the opportunity to form an image that was provided regularly and systematically through the initiative and means of others. This is being continued in a well-planned and effective public relations policy regarding the monarchy. The result is that the Oranges as a dynasty, after a long history, are a prominent and yet reserved presence in Dutch society.

Bram Kempers

See also Architectural restoration; Aristocracy and gentry; Bas-relief painting; Country houses and gardens; Court and official portraiture; Eighty Years' War; Flanders, Flemish School; France; History painting; History portraits; Huygens, Constantijn; Nationalism; Post, Pieter; Public monumental sculpture (ca. 1550–1795); Public monumental sculpture (1795–1990); Rembrandt van Rijn; State and municipal art collecting and collections; State patronage, public support; Tomb sculpture: early modern and later sepulchral art; Tomb sculpture: medieval effigial monuments; Trade: exploration and colonization overseas; Utrecht Caravaggists; Van Campen, Jacob; Van Honthorst, Gerard; War and warfare

Bibliography

"The Anglo-Dutch Garden in the Age of William and Mary." Theme Volume. *Journal of Garden History* 8:2–3 (April–September 1988).

Drossaers, S.W.A., and T.H. Lunsingh Scheurleer. *Inventarissen van de inboedels in de verblijven van de Oranjes en daarmee gelijk te stellen stukken.* 3 Vols. The Hague: Rijks Geschiedkundige Publicatieën, 1974–1976.

Fock, C.W. "The Princes of Orange as Patrons of Art in the Seventeeth Century." *Apollo* 110 (1979): 466–475.

Fock, C.W., and B. Brenninkmeyer-de Rooij. "De schilderijengalerij van prins Willem V op het Buitenhof te Den Haag." *Antiek* 11 (1976): 113–176.

Hinterding, E., and F. Horsch. "'A Small but Choice Col-

lection': The Art Gallery of King William II of the Netherlands, 1792–1849." *Simiolus* 19 (1989): 5–122.

Kempers, B. "Vermogend en toch matig: Vijf eeuwen kunst van Oranje." *Amsterdams Sociologisch Tijdschrift* 16 (1898): 71–107.

Mauritshuis: The Royal Cabinet of Paintings: Illustrated General Catalogue. The Hague: Government Printing Office, 1977.

Schaffer-Bodenhausen, K.E., and M.E. Tiethoff-Spliethoff. *Portrait Miniatures in the Collection of the House of Orange-Nassau.* Zwolle: Waanders, 1991.

Sluijter-Seiffert, Nicolette, et al. *Mauritshuis: Illustrated General Catalogue.* Amsterdam: Meulenhoff, 1993.

Housewives and maids

Maids had an assertive presence in daily life in Holland during the seventeenth century. The majority of household servants in Holland, only one or two to a household, were women, and they were often treated as members of the family. Maids and their mistresses thus had an unusually close relationship, as many foreign travelers noted. This relationship became one of the most popular and enduring themes in Dutch genre painting. The appeal of the subject also had its origins in the later sixteenth century. The upheaval of the Reformation led to considerable debate about the proper domain for women, and the theme of feminine vice and virtue became a popular subject for Netherlandish printmakers. While the ideal role for women was that of wife and mother, the negative archetype was Eve, trickster and temptress. During the seventeenth century, the good woman/bad woman dichotomy survived in didactic manuals on household and family management, in which women's anarchic potential was thought to be controlled through industry and docility. While the housewife continued to be a paragon of femininity, her maid, considered naturally lazy and immoral, was presented as her foil.

In the seventeenth century, when genre scenes began to proliferate, the piquant combination of housewife and maid, embodying these opposite poles of feminine behavior, became a popular subject for artists. The good and bad female stereotypes expressed in didactic literature, however, were often undercut and parodied in art, presented with varying degrees of subtlety and tone. The maid plays many roles in portraits and genre paintings. She can be a neutral, subsidiary figure, standing in the background of a formal family portrait or entering with a tray in a scene of men and women idly socializing. Sometimes she is shown as lazy, falling asleep over her work. Sometimes she gets into mischief, acting as a spy or pickpocket. Nicolaes Maes devoted a series of satirical pictures to the subject of maids and their employers eavesdropping on one another. In a typical example from the series, *The Eavesdropper* of 1657, he ostensibly depicts a virtuous housewife coming down the stairs and overhearing the flirtation of her neglectful maid (Color Plate 7). Yet Maes comments ironically on this traditional contrast by making the housewife smiling and conspiratorial rather than stern and condemnatory, and places her between the formal dining party above and the scene of seduction below. She is caught between public decorum and the private sexual license of her maid.

The maid is also a willing domestic helper. Pieter de Hooch's domestic scenes often visualize an ideally serene, orderly world where servant and mistress engaged together in domestic tasks (Fig. 43). Yet this tacit harmony between mistress and maid also occurs in images of other feminine activity, such as the popular scenes of women reading or writing love letters, where the maid becomes an ally for her mistress' flirtations. The close relationship of women without men, at work and play alike, suggests a feminine association that cuts across social boundaries. Thus there are two aspects to the servant–mistress relationship in seventeenth-century Dutch art: The two women are distinguished by their class and behavior but sometimes linked through the presumed charms and weaknesses of their gender.

Martha Hollander

See also Commerce and commercial life; Genre painting, seventeenth century; Maes, Nicolaes; Marriage and family portraits; Women's worlds

Bibliography

Franits, Wayne. *Paragons of Virtue: Women and Domesticity in Seventeenth-Century Dutch Art.* Cambridge: Cambridge University Press, 1993.

Hollander, Martha. "The Divided Household of Nicolaes Maes." *Word and Image* 10:2 (April 1994): 138–152.

Kloek, Els, Nicole Teeuwen, and Marijke Huisman, eds. *Women of the Golden Age: An International Debate on Women in Seventeenth-Century Holland, England and Italy.* Hilversum: Verloren, 1994.

Robinson, W. "*The Eavesdroppers* and Related Paintings by Nicolaes Maes." In *Holländische Genremalerei im 17. Jahrhundert: Symposium, Berlin 1984.* Edited by H. Bock and T.W. Gaehtgens, 283–313. Berlin: Mann, 1987.

Schama, Simon. "Wives and Wantons: Versions of Womanhood in Seventeenth-Century Dutch Art." *Oxford Art Journal* 3 (1980): 5–13.

Huizinga, Johan (1872–1945)

In his own country and abroad Johan Huizinga is known as the most famous and important historian from the Netherlands. He made a name for himself not only as a cultural historian, but also as a cultural critic and a cultural philosopher. In each of these three roles, the visual arts have a central place. Huizinga represents the culmination of a respectable tradition of historical reflections in which pictures were used as historical sources. Visual experiences were of great importance for the development of Huizinga's thinking. The way in which he has assimilated them also makes clear what a difficult task it appears to be for historians to use art in an adequate manner in their research.

In Huizinga's visual history writing, four facets can be distinguished: the visual arts as the motive for research; art as a source in research; the status of artists as a theme; and art as being the best way to characterize a society in a certain time. The point of departure in writing *The Waning of the Middle Ages* (*Herfsttij der middeleeuwen,* 1924; a new translation in 1996 is more accurately entitled *The Autumn of the Middle Ages*) was, in his own words, "to arrive at a genuine understanding of the art of the brothers Van Eyck and their contemporaries . . . to grasp its meaning by seeing it in connection with the entire life of their times." Seeing the works of the fifteenth-century Flemish painters at a retrospective exhibition in Bruges formed the starting point for this book, which has become so influential. Remarkable, however, is the fact that in the course of the story only very few concrete examples of paintings are used to understand the society under scrutiny. It is typical, too, that only the later editions were illustrated. The level of abstraction remains high, and the information about iconography, social position of artists, and patrons is limited.

In *Dutch Civilization in the Seventeenth Century* (1941), Huizinga has become much more careful. Rembrandt, Pieter Saenredam, and Vermeer have here taken the role of Van Eyck and Gerard David, but the metaphor is much less pronounced, and everywhere there appears to be doubt whether this art can provide a good insight into the society of the Republic. Huizinga makes it clear that in this society the big patrons did not set the tone, but that painters relied on numerous, mostly small, collectors and buyers. Partly because of this, Huizinga expresses his doubts in the fifth chapter, which is entirely devoted to the visual arts, about the role of the artist as a prime witness to the society of which he is a part. With this, "realism" becomes central, as in it lies that which is "typically Dutch" for Huizinga.

As a cultural critic, Huizinga cast his light on contemporary art through many short articles. He did not like abstract art (Wassily Kandinsky, Odilon Redon), and he worked for the preservation and renewal of figurative-symbolic art. He was co-organizer of an exhibition of the work of Vincent van Gogh (1895–1897), published a monograph on his friend Jan Veth (1927), and occupied himself intensively with monumental art in public buildings, in particular the work of his friend Richard N. Roland Holst.

Huizinga's thoughts as a cultural philosopher concern images as a key to comprehension in learned reflection. From an oration in 1905 to an article of 1941, he tried to put into words in a series of reflections fundamental opinions about "historical aesthetics," "morphology of the past," "*historiebeeld,*" and variants of these. Most have not been translated, just like the cultural critical contributions on art and in opposition to historical studies, but this side of his work has not played a very large role in the Netherlands either.

Bram Kempers

See also Flanders, Flemish School; Nationalism; State patronage, public support

Bibliography

Haskell, F. *History and Its Images: Art and the Interpretation of the Past.* New Haven: Yale University Press, 1993.

Huizinga, J. *Briefwisseling*. Edited by L. Hanssen, W. Krul, and A. van der Lem. 3 vols. Utrecht: Veen, 1989–1991.

———. *Dutch Civilization in the Seventeenth Century (1941), and Other Essays*. Translated by Arnold J. Pomerans. New York: Harper and Row, 1969.

———. *Verzameld Werken*. 9 vols. Haarlem: Willink, 1948–1953.

———. *The Waning of the Middle Ages: A Study of the Forms of Life, Thought, and Art in France and the Netherlands in the Fourteenth and Fifteenth Centuries*. Garden City, NY: Doubleday, 1924.

———. *The Autumn of the Middle Ages*. Translated by Rodney J. Payton and Ulrich Mammitzch. Chicago: University of Chicago Press, 1996.

Kempers, B. "De verleiding van het beeld: Het visuele als blijvende bron van inspiratie in het werk van Huizinga." *Tijdschrift voor geschiedenis* 105 (1992): 30–50.

Lem, A. van der. *Johan Huizinga: Leven en werk in beelden en documenten*. Amsterdam: Wereldbibliotheek, 1993.

Humanism, humanist themes

Italian humanism, which from the end of the fifteenth century had influence in the Netherlands, was an intellectual movement concerned with the study of the humanities: literature, history, and philosophy. Following the ancient philosophers, the humanists imagined an ideal type of human being that had to be strived for through development and education, and in this regard they put great value on the mental, moral, and religious capabilities of man.

Since humanism considered antique culture exemplary, it brought about a revival of ancient art and philosophy. Even though this ancient culture was not entirely lost during the Middle Ages, the later humanists endeavored to bring the spirit of the antique into accordance with their own world of thinking and culture. The didactic character of ancient culture was already apparent as far back as the works of the late-antique moral philosophers Cicero, Seneca, and Boethius, whose writings were also known in the Netherlands. Furthermore, it was thought during the Renaissance that the mythological stories were meant allegorically and that they could be explained in a moral, modern way. Such an interpretation of the ancient myths can be found in Italian writings on mythology: Giraldi's *De deis gentium* (1548), Conti's *Mythologiae sive explicationis fabularum* (1551), and Cartari's *Le imagini colla sposizione degli dei degli antichi* (1556). These handbooks were also used by artists in the Netherlands as a source of reference. In this manner Conti's book was the reference for Karel van Mander's *Wtleggingh opden Metamorphosis Pub. Ovidij Nasonis* (Interpretation of the *Metamorphoses* by Ovid) of 1604, which inspired many seventeenth-century Dutch artists in their representation of mythologies.

It was typical of humanism in the Netherlands that it began in the monasteries, rather than in the towns, courts, and universities where it had begun in Italy. The *studia humanitatis* promoted interest in the original sources of texts, and for that reason one of the greatest Dutch humanists, Erasmus of Rotterdam, made new translations of the Bible from the original language. Furthermore, Dutch humanists wanted schooling and education for the population of the Netherlands, which prompted Erasmus to write the *Enchiridion militis christiani* (Instructions for the Christian Knight) in 1504 for that purpose. It became a popular moral tract, full of quotations from the Bible and ancient writers. Another means of education were the Latin school plays by Dutch humanists such as Gnapheus and Macropedius that were centered around themes from the Bible or from ancient times. Because most writers were clergy or schoolmasters, the neo-Latin literature had a strong moralistic tendency in the Netherlands: Humanistic studies were not considered an objective in themselves, but a way to improve theological studies and Christian life. That is why Dutch humanism is also called Christian, or biblical, humanism. This also had its effect on the visual arts because many classical subjects had a moral meaning to them.

The court of Philip of Burgundy (1465–1524), who after 1517 was the bishop of Utrecht, was also an important humanistic center. Philip gathered a circle of scholars and artists, among whom was Jan Gossaert, who decorated the castle in Wijk bij Duurstede in "antique style." Philip took Gossaert to Rome (1508–1509), where the artist made drawings after ancient sculpture. After his return, Gossaert made several paintings with mythological subjects for Philip—for example, *Venus and Amor* (1521; Brussels, Musées Royaux des Beaux-Arts) and *Neptune and Amphitrite* (1516; Berlin, Staatliche Museen). The paintings were given frames with moralizing inscriptions in Latin on them that were composed by Philip's court humanist, Gerrit Geldenhauer.

Through the travels of Dutch artists to Italy, and through the influence of imported Italian prints and translations of Italian literature, soon all sorts of themes taken from classical antiquity or Italian humanism were introduced to Dutch art. Besides many mythological subjects, this included the *Triumphs of Petrarch*, which is based on a sonnet cycle by the fourteenth-century Italian poet Petrarch. It consists of a succession of triumphs or glorifications, of Love, Chastity, Death, Fame (Fig. 65), and Time, in which the main character or personification in each scene is dethroned in the following scene of triumph by a stronger force of nature or a stronger moral, with the exception of Christ, who, in the sixth print in the series, is the ultimate victor. Its portrayal goes back to the scheme of the ancient triumphal march (*triumphus*) of a general after his victory, a motif that recurs again and again in the visual arts of the sixteenth and seventeenth century.

Humanists also played a role in the creations of artists in the later sixteenth century. The humanist Hadrianus Junius, who lived in Haarlem, was a friend of Maerten van Heemskerck and Philips Galle. The text of an emblem by Junius appears on Van Heemskerck's painting *Momus Criticizing the Works of the Gods* (1561; Berlin; Staatliche Museen), and he probably also provided the information for the series of prints called *The Seven Wonders of the World* (1572) by Galle after Van Heemskerck. Van Heemskerck was one of the first

Dutch artists who made mythological works on a large scale like *Venus and Cupid in Vulcan's Forge* (1536; Prague, Narodni Museum) and the *Concert of Apollo and the Muses on Mount Helicon* (1565; Norfolk, VA, Chrysler Museum; Fig. 77). During his stay in Rome (1532–1536) he got to know the ancient monuments and sculpture well and came to understand the way in which ancient classical culture had been integrated into Italian contemporary art. After him, it was Hendrick Goltzius (who visited Italy in 1591) and Cornelis Cornelisz. van Haarlem who extensively depicted themes from antiquity, especially in their prints made around 1600. The graphic arts played a very important role in the Netherlands, and humanists often composed Latin verses that were engraved along with the prints as explanatory or ornate inscriptions. Hadrianus Junius wrote Latin verses for many prints by Van Heemskerck and Philips Galle between 1551 and 1572. Latin verses by the humanists in his circle are engraved on many of Goltzius' prints. The most important was the humanist Cornelius Schonaeus from Haarlem, whose verses appear on prints by Goltzius or his studio from 1587 until 1602. Other poets who made verses for prints by Goltzius were Franciscus Estius and Petrus Scriverius. Theodorus Schrevelius made verses for prints by Jacob Matham and Jan Saenredam during the first quarter of the seventeenth century. The famous scholar Hugo de Groot (Grotius) wrote Latin verses for prints by Karel van Mander.

Ilja M. Veldman

See also Allegorical traditions; Coornhert, Dirck Volkertsz.; Erasmus, Desiderius; Goltzius, Hendrick; Haarlem; Italy; Literature, poetry: analogues with the visual; Nationalism; Prints, early printed book and Bible illustration; Prints, printmaking, and printmakers, (ca. 1500–ca. 1900); Protestant Reformation; Urban planning, before 1750; Utrecht; Van Mander, Karel

Bibliography

Gelder, H.A. Enno van. *The Two Reformations in the Sixteenth Century: A Study of the Religious Aspects and Consequences of the Renaissance and Humanism*. The Hague: Nijhoff, 1964.

IJsewijn, Josef. "The Coming of Humanism to the Low Countries." In *Itinerarium Italicum: The Profile of the Italian Renaissance in the Mirror of Its European Transformations, Dedicated to Paul Oskar Kristeller on the Occasion of His 70th Birthday*. Edited by H.A. Oberman and Th.A. Brady, 193–304. Leiden: E.J. Brill, 1975.

McGee, Julie L. *Cornelis Corneliszoon van Haarlem, 1562–1638: Patrons, Friends, and Dutch Humanists*. Nieuwkoop: De Graaf, 1991.

Sterk, J. *Philips van Bourgondië, 1465–1524: Bisschop van Utrecht als protagonist van de Renaissance, zijn leven en maecenaat*. Zutphen: Walburg, 1980.

Veldman, Ilja M. *Maarten van Heemskerck and Dutch Humanism of the Sixteenth Century*. Amsterdam/Maarssen: Gary Schwartz, 1977.

Humbert de Superville, D.P.G. (1770–1849)

David Pierre Giottino Humbert de Superville's seminal work, *Essai sur les signes inconditionnels dans l'art* (1827–1832), is a major theoretical statement on the problem of judging from physical appearances. This Dutch artist, pro-French patriot, ardent Kantian, museum director, mythographer, semiologist, and cultural comparatist belongs to that international generation of polymaths growing up just prior to the French Revolution and continuing as teachers in the nineteenth-century academies and institutions spawned by that upheaval. Like Quatremère de Quincy, Ottley, Flaxman, Boullée, Bossi, Blake, Soane, Runge, and Goethe, he adhered to the idealistic educational goals emerging from Enlightenment humanism. Like these reform-minded artists, and thinkers such as Coudillac or Warburton, he wanted to construct a new formal language for the modern era. Rather than rely on classicism, however, he systematically forged an expressive vocabulary rooted in the experience of many intersecting antiquities: Egyptian, Chinese, Hindu, Polynesian, Greek, Roman, and medieval. A proponent *avant-la-lettre* of cultural studies, he sought to develop systematically a global theory of perception, based on variable human emotions, that would nonetheless avoid the pitfalls of mere subjective associationism as it had been developed in Britain by Hume, Alison, and Price.

Physiognomics had widespread currency in the intellectual and artistic life of the eighteenth century. Marivaux, Hogarth, Lichtenberg, and Lavater drew attention to the suggestive signs that marked the human face. Going beyond the practice of caricature in the formulation of stereotypes, Humbert wanted to create a new science of the legible body. Unlike Charles Le Brun's seventeenth-century attempts to anatomize the passions according to muscle movement, Humbert focused on their schematization, the geometrical vocabulary of diagrams that "unconditionally" and immaterially mapped the mind's motions on features and limbs.

It is not accidental that he was also the rediscoverer of the Italian "primitives." Working in Italy as part of Jean-Baptiste Seroux d'Agincourt's team of young artists illustrating the *Histoire de l'Art* (begun in 1782), Humbert rediscovered the fourteenth- and fifteenth-century frescoes at the Campo Santo in Pisa.

Journeying throughout Umbria and Tuscany with W.Y. Ottley in the 1790s, the Netherlander recorded works by Pietro Lorenzetti, Nicola Pisano, Taddeo Gaddi, Masolino, and Giotto in an abstract linear style reminiscent of "purist" allegories by Carsteus or Ingres. He even took the name "Giottino" to emphasize his love for Italian *trecentisti*. These archaic models not only infused his own graphic production (some fifteen hundred drawings), but also governed his view that the meaning of all phenomena, human or divine, could be discerned only in their cosmological, and even geological, origins. Because the Italian "primitives" were closer to the beginnings of Western art (that is, before its flowering during the Renaissance), he reasoned their works exhibited more clearly and in unsullied fashion the natural signs from which they had been constructed.

The never-completed *Essai*, whose truncated version

enchanted Charles Blanc, Charles Henry, Georges Seurat, and the French Symbolists, attempted to uncover first those pristine conditions in which worldwide myths, rites, and art had once arisen and from which its present-day manifestations measurably departed. Signs, both natural and artificial, pose a double problem to the hermeneuticist. They can have referents in two directions. The directional schemata traced on the faces and bodies of Egyptian colossi, Hindu gods, Greek herms, Eastern Island sculpture, or Giotto's saints evoke or provoke, on the one hand, the psychological condition felt by the observer who perceives them. On the other hand, they are also universal hieroglyphic symbols reflecting cosmic and historical events that transcend the sensorium of any individual.

Prescient of Saussure, Barthes, and Derrida, Humbert's sophisticated grammar of signs deconstructs works of art into pure and primitive signifiers. A rudimentary alphabet of primal lines and colors, abstracted from their material contexts, constitutes a basic *ars combinatoria* or visual language from which all forms of human, animal, plant, mineral, and artifactual communication might be deduced. Humbert's heroic and labyrinthine quest to find deep structural connections between natural and artificial domains continues to be pressing today. Steering between the poles of relativism and absolutism, nurture and nature, internal and external pressures, Humbert tried to establish a bioaesthetics in which the physical and moral dimension of human beings were inseparable from the material and cultural environment in which they originated and evolved.

Barbara Maria Stafford

See also Gestures; Italy; Leiden; Symbolism, Symbolists

Bibliography

Harrison, Andrew. "Review of *Symbol and Myth:* Humbert de Superville's Essay on Absolute Signs in Art." *Art International* 26 (1983): 62–64.

Lavin, Sylvia. *Quatremère de Quincy and the Invention of a Modern Language of Architecture.* Cambridge, MA: MIT Press, 1992.

Levitine, George, and Melinda Curtis. *Search for Innocence: Primitive and Primitivistic Art of the Nineteenth Century.* College Park, MD: University of Maryland Art Gallery, 1975.

Loyrette, Henri. "Seroux d' Agincourt et les origines de l'histoire de l'art medieval." *Revue de l'Art* 48 (1980): 40–56.

Michaud, Eric. "La fin de l'iconographie." In *Méthodologie Iconographique.* Edited by Gèrard Siebert, 125–136. Strasbourg: AECR, 1981.

Previtali, Giovanni. *La fortuna dei primitivi dal Vasari ai Neoclassici.* Turin: Einaudi, 1964.

Scheller, Robert. "The Case of the Stolen Raphael Drawings." *Master Drawings* 11:2 (Summer 1973): 119–137.

———. "Croep zuevenda Figuren D.P.G. Humbert de Superville 1770–1849." Theme volume. *Openbaar Kunstbezit* 113 (1969).

Stafford, Barbara Maria. "Arena of Virtue and Temple of Immortality: An Early Nineteenth-Century Museum Project." *Journal of Architectural Historians* 35 (March 1976): 21–34.

———. *Artful Science: Enlightenment Entertainment and the Eclipse of Visual Education.* Cambridge, MA: MIT Press, 1994.

———. *Body Criticism.* Cambridge, MA: MIT Press, 1991.

———. *Symbol and Myth: Humbert de Superville's Essay on Absolute Signs in Art.* Cranbury, NJ: Associated University Press, 1979.

Torrini, Annalisa. *Disegni di Humbert de Superville.* Milan: Electra, 1991.

Humor, satire

Humorous representations in the eighteenth and early nineteenth centuries encompassed a wider range of themes than previous comic art, including comic plays, historical parodies, polite society, political events, and the institutionalized arts. Although indebted to the seventeenth-century comic mode, this visual humor was cleaner, discarding earlier scatological and sexual motifs. It also lacked the visual acerbity of contemporary English satirists.

Cornelis Troost and his pupil Jacobus Buijs specialized in scenes from comedies. Their favorite comic types, articulated by costume and body, included the stiff Quaker suitor; the amply decolletéed adulteress; and the husband she has made a cuckold. Troost also used exaggerated postures and gestures to suggest military self-importance or to mock meetings of educated gentlemen at country houses such as in *Rumor Erat in Casa* (There was a Commotion in the House, 1740; The Hague, Mauritshuis; Fig. 66). Some of his history scenes parallel literary parodies of history. Troost and Dirk Langendijk were exceptional among genre painters in exploiting earthier comic motifs, including the display of naked buttocks; more explicit sexual motifs entered the domain of libertine pornography rather than comic art.

Most popular celebrations, fairs, and markets—traditionally sites of alcoholic, sexual, and scatological license—in the works of Johannes Prins, Jan Anthonie Langendijk, and others became pleasing town views, with peasants, small traders, and upper-class burghers going their harmonious ways. Plain burghers may be mocked, as in Isaak Ouwater's *Lottery Office* mobbed by gamblers (1779), but since the figures are usually subservient to the architecture, treatment is never harsh. These paintings gave élite collectors amusing images of popular community and thereby register a reform of popular culture, inherited from the seventeenth century, in which church and government attempted to sanitize communal events. In this civilizing process, the cultural gap between higher and lower societal layers became pronounced, the educated élite distancing itself from popular traditions. Pictorially, this class rarely interacts with lower rungs on the social ladder, except to dispense charity.

A pluriform, youthful audience remained, however, for cheap, single-leaf woodcuts with small pictures and simple rhymes, ridiculing targets from abnormal physiques to henpecked husbands and French fashions. Even the civilizing *Maatschappij tot Nut van het Algemeen* (Society for the Utility of the General

Community) adopted these prints to make educational points through comic themes. Satiric engravings for adults also retained older means, including allegorical figures, abundant captions, and identifications of targets with popular fools such as Don Quixote and Harlequin. Publishers frequently issued seventeenth-century plates with new texts, using those about the tulip trade, for example, for the stock speculation of 1720.

By the late eighteenth century, satirists began to employ simpler means, such as contour drawings and caricature. Pieter van Woensel mocked the French occupation in his periodical *De Lantaarn* (ca. 1800). From 1812, Napoleon's defeats spurred cartoons by Harmanus Fock and Wijnard Esser, in which apparently naive draftsmanship further disarms the general. The Belgian revolt against Dutch government yielded similarly light visual polemics (1830–1832). In internal affairs, Jacob Smies mocked the practices of polite society, including charity, the culture circuit, and classical education. He and others also ridiculed the new societies of art and the national exhibition of 1808.

Caricatural representations of a failed balloon trip (1804), the Dutch Trading Company (1824), a planned credit bank (1836), and a railway investment scheme (1845) show a hesitantly modernizing society, often through the modern medium of lithography. Widely available newspapers and lithographs had become the primary sites of comic discourse, as genre painters had begun to reinterpret the tradition of Johannes Vermeer rather than that of comic genre.

Mariët Westermann

See also Comic modes; Genre painting, eighteenth century; Theater and theatricality; Troost, Cornelis

Bibliography

Heurck, Em. van, and G.J. Boekenoogen. *L'Imagerie populaire des Pays-Bas.* Paris: Editions Duchartre and van Buggenhoudt, 1930.

Kunzle, David. *The Early Comic Strip: Narrative Strips and Picture Stories in the European Broadsheet from ca. 1450 to 1825.* Berkeley: University of California Press, 1973.

Kuyk, J. van. *Oude politieke spotprenten.* The Hague: Nijhoff, 1940.

Rijn, G. van, and C. van Ommeren. *Katalogus der historie-, spot- en zinneprenten betrekkelijk de geschiedenis van Nederland verzameld door A. van Stolk Cz.* Vols. 4–9, Amsterdam: Frederik Muller, 1900–1908. Vol. 10, The Hague: Nijhoff, 1931.

Veth, Cornelis. *Geschiedenis van de Nederlandsche caricatuur en van de scherts in de Nederlandsche beeldende kunst.* Leiden: Sijthoff, 1921.

Huygens, Constantijn (1596–1687)

A true Renaissance man for the seventeenth century, Constantijn Huygens had a career full of impressive accomplishments. He was a versatile linguist, a published poet, a gifted musician, and the composer of about eight hundred musical pieces. His education in the sciences, architecture, and painting enabled him to correspond with many notable scholars, scientists, and artists of the century, including Descartes, Galileo, Hooft, Vondel, Cats, Rembrandt, Rubens, Van Honthorst, Vossius, Lipsius, and Leeuwenhoek, among others. His middle-class family, which had emigrated from the Southern Netherlands, included his father, Christiaan, who served as the secretary to Prince Willem I of Orange; his mother, Susanna, who was the sister of the miniaturist Joris Hoefnagel; his brother, Maurits, who acted as secretary to the Council of State in The Hague; and his son, Christiaan (1629–1695), the renowned Dutch physicist.

One of Huygens' significant contributions to seventeenth-century Dutch art was his influence as an artistic adviser to the House of Orange. He served in this capacity from his appointment in 1625 as a secretary to Prince Frederik Hendrik (Fig. 99); he continued in this position with the prince's son, Willem II, and subsequently with Frederik Hendrik's widow, Amalia van Solms. Huygens' artistic tastes, which coincided with the patronage extended by his royal patrons, were first recorded in his unpublished autobiography of 1629–1631. In the section devoted to an extensive summation of the merits of many contemporary painters, Huygens did not differentiate between artists in the Northern and the Southern Netherlands, nor did he seem to have a preference for a particular style, but instead appreciated a variety of artists. Although he acknowledged the older generation of artists—Hendrick Goltzius, Michiel van Mierevelt, and Hendrick Vroom—his primary interest was directed toward the younger painters, including Jan Porcellis, Cornelis van Poelenburch, Moyses van Wtenbrouck, Jan van Goyen, Jan Wildens, Paul Bril, and Esaias van de Velde. Reflecting contemporary opinions, he most valued the works of the history painters, such as Gerard van Honthorst, Hendrick Terbrugghen, Dirck van Baburen, Anthony van Dyck, Abraham Janssens, Everard van der Maes, Pieter Isaaksz., Pieter Lastman, and Jacob Pynas. He singled out Pieter Paul Rubens, living in the Southern Netherlands, as the greatest contemporary painter, noting both the appeal and the revulsion evoked by his painting of *Medusa* (ca. 1616).

Significantly, Huygens reserved his highest accolades for Rembrandt and Jan Lievens, young painters from the Northern Netherlands, and he referred specifically to Rembrandt's painting of *Judas Returning the Thirty Pieces of Silver* (1629; England, private collection). Indicating in his discussion that he believed that they would surpass even Rubens, he marveled at their youth, their humble origins, and their innate talents, but he was critical of their insensibility to the merits of a trip to Italy to study the masterpieces. Huygens' comments indicate that he was the first major connoisseur to appreciate Rembrandt's talent, and it is not coincidental that at the height of Huygens' interest, Rembrandt received his commission for a series of Passion paintings for Frederik Hendrik.

After the mid 1630s, Huygens' taste, and that of his royal patrons, shifted to embrace the classical style in architecture and painting that was prevailing throughout Europe. Huygens continued to exert considerable influence on the style and decorations of the numerous royal palaces, enlisting the cooperation of the architect Jacob van Campen on several occasions. For the interiors, he considered artists such as Salomon de Bray, Caesar van Everdingen, Nicolaes Berchem,

Jacob Backer, Gerrit Bleecker, and Jacob van Loo to be suitably decorous. Artists who worked outside of the restrained classicism were seldom patronized by the House of Orange after the middle of the century, and, to a degree, that also affected the tastes of the Dutch middle classes.

Shana L. Stuart

See also Backer, Jacob Adriaensz.; Classicism in architecture; Flanders, Flemish School; House of Orange-Nassau; Italy; Lievens, Jan; Music, musical instruments; Portraiture; Post, Pieter; Rembrandt van Rijn; Van Campen, Jacob; Van Honthorst, Gerard; Writers on art, sixteenth and seventeenth centuries

Bibliography

Colie, Rosalie Littell. *"Some Thankfulnesse to Constantine": A Study of English Influence upon the Early Works of Constantijn Huygens.* The Hague: Nijhoff, 1956.

Lawrence, Cynthia. "Worthy of Milord's House? Rembrandt, Huygens, and Dutch Classicism." *Konsthistorisk Tidskrift* 54 (1985): 16–26.

Schwartz, Gary. *Rembrandt: His Life, His Paintings.* New York: Viking Penguin, 1985.

Slive, Seymour. *Rembrandt and His Critics, 1630–1730.* The Hague: Nijhoff, 1953.

Worp, J.A. "Constantijn Huygens over de schilders van zijn tijd." *Oud Holland* 9 (1891): 106–136.

I

Illusionism

A fundamental principle of realistic Western painting is a cultivated verisimilitude that suggests to the eye that the object depicted is real. The paradoxical appeal of illusionism is that it persuades the eye that an object is real rather than painted and, at the same time, permits the viewer to be aware of the fact that it is painted, thereby calling attention to the artist's mimetic skill. This manipulation of technique for the celebration of painting is central to the theory and practice of Dutch art.

From the fifteenth century onward, Netherlandish artists sought to create lifelike figures and settings to make their religious scenes as realistic as possible to encourage the viewer's involvement. They developed their use of perspective to create the illusion of three dimensions on a flat surface and refined the technique of oil painting to permit a high degree of surface detail. Artists such as Jan van Eyck, Dirck Bouts, and Hans Memling, and their imitators throughout the sixteenth century, strove to represent all of the surfaces of the world—skin, hair, fabric, grass, leaves, metal, stone—with an undiscriminating fidelity.

Illusionism had many appealing possibilities for seventeenth-century Dutch painters: precise articulation of three-dimensional space; depiction of surface textures, either by eliminating all traces of their brushwork or by building up layers of paint with the impasto technique; and capturing the more imprecise, evanescent effects of light, shadow, distance, and atmosphere. Furthermore, the cultivated illusion of a painted world's tangible presence had a commercial incentive. According to the painter Philips Angel, in his 1642 paper *Lof der Schilder-konst* (In Praise of Painting), excelling in the rendering of textures will entice the viewer's eye and help the painting sell better.

The mimetic ambition of painters was aided throughout seventeenth-century Europe by advances in the science of optics. Home to the lens-grinding industry and figures such as Anton van Leeuwenhoek, inventor of the microscope, the Dutch Republic was the leader in technological developments in optics. During this period, the use of optical devices was on the rise: glass frames squared with a grid, wide-angle lenses, convex mirrors, and the *camera obscura*. Artists often used such instruments to help them create the illusion of spatial depth on a flat surface.

Holland's first art theorist, Karel van Mander, writing in 1604, claimed that painting is superior to sculpture because it can represent the totality of the visible world. Accordingly, the power of painting to deceive the eye was given paramount importance in writings on art. All of the theoretical and practical treatises on art included stories about the wondrous skill of painters, a rhetorical tradition dating from antiquity. Pliny the Elder records the story of Zeuxis, whose painted grapes fooled birds who tried to eat them; and his rival Parrhasius, who painted over a picture a sheet so lifelike that Zeuxis himself tried to pull it aside. The sixteenth-century Italian theorist Giorgio Vasari relates a similar story about Giotto. In a contemporary version of this story, Samuel van Hoogstraten reports that his father painted a goat so realistically that the goat itself, enraged by the image, butted the canvas until it was destroyed.

The frequently used term *naer het leven* (after life) reveals the commitment, though variously expressed, toward realistic representation. For Van Mander, the phrase refers to the selective imitation of nature—that is, copying only the most aesthetically pleasing aspects of nature. He encouraged artists to supplement their recording of the world with equal study of antique sculpture and other great art of the past. Van Hoogstraten, however, in his treatise *Inleyding tot de hooghe schoole der schilderkonst* (Introduction to the Elevated School of Painting) of 1678, advocates the thorough study of nature over antique art; he writes that the artist must develop "a compass in the eye." Van Hoogstraten, one of the few Dutch artists who actually recorded his theories about painting, believed that a painting was "a science that represents all ideas and notions that the visible world can provide . . ." and, at the same time, "a mirror of nature" that makes things that do not exist seem to appear, and hence deceives the eye in an entertaining manner.

Nonetheless, van Hoogstraten's view of picture making as a science does not mean that pictures were meant to be strict reproductions of reality. The artist was required to be highly imaginative at composing the image as a whole. This combination of intense observation and creative reconfiguration is fundamental to Dutch art. Architectural painters, for example, would often change details of their church interiors to enhance effects of light and plunging perspective. Still-life painters would copy individual flowers that bloomed at different times of the year and then assemble them into an invented composition, complete with insects, nuts, berries, and assorted small objects, to create a desirable encyclopedic variety. The end result might, therefore, be a meticulous rendering of a composition that could not actually exist but would nonetheless be endowed with a persuasively tangible presence by the artist's mastery.

The architectural painter Pieter Saenredam was one of the earliest seventeenth-century painters to combine imaginative, representational talent with strict scientific rigor. His church interiors, based on measurements and preliminary drawings of actual buildlings, revolutionized the use of mathematical perspective. At the same time, he used his acute skills of observation to capture the atmospheric light in these vast spaces. Other architectural painters, such as Gerard Houckgeest and Emanuel de Witte, also pursued striking perspective compositions and effects of light, along with Job and Gerrit Berckheyde, who specialized in exterior views of cities (Fig. 13).

By mid-century, many artists were adopting perspective techniques as well as optical instruments for their city views and domestic interiors, though without Saenredam's precision. Instead, artists tended to favor a slightly tipped-up perspective for the sake of greater display. It is also a feature of Dutch landscape, which offers a "bird's-eye" view of huge vistas not easily seen in actual experience. The raised viewpoint was probably exaggerated by the use of curved lenses. Certain artists were fascinated by such lenses, such as Carel Fabritius. His *View of Delft with a Musical Instrument Seller's Stall* (1652; Fig. 41) shows a street viewed from a shop in the foreground that records the wide-angle distortion created by a double concave lens. Vermeer often copied a similar wide-angle effect in his interior scenes. Nicolaes Maes creates an unusually dramatic perspective effect in *The Eavesdropper* of 1657, dividing an interior into two plunging vistas of stairway and corridor ending in distant views: a room upstairs and a back garden (Color Plate 7).

Along with the illusion of extensive space, high finish in the Eyckian tradition was a major factor of illusionistic practice. Its most celebrated master was Gerrit Dou, who specialized in precisely detailed, small-scale genre scenes with a smooth, enamel-like surface (Color Plate 8). His careful rendering of textures and light effects, and the suppression of brushstrokes, was greatly valued by critics and patrons alike. Dou and his most famous pupil, Frans van Mieris the Elder, were not only highly praised but enjoyed commercial success. The followers of these two artists, the *fijnschilders* (fine painters), propagated Dou's style well into the eighteenth century.

Dou often enhanced his meticulously executed pictures with illusionistic devices. He often painted a simulated stone frame around his figures, and occasionally he included a curtain that appeared to hang on a rod across this frame. Rembrandt had used this motif in his *Holy Family* of 1646. This playful device was particularly effective because it simulated the curtains that were often hung over paintings in Dutch households to protect them from dust. Hence it suggested not only that the depicted object might be real, but that the painting itself is a physical object in its own right. De Witte and Houckgeest experimented with motif in their paintings of churches, as did Maes and Vermeer in their domestic interiors. Another kind of illusionistic curtain, especially favored by Dou and Jan Steen, was a theatrical drape pulled back from the front of the picture. Dou's *Self-Portrait with Book and Pipe* (ca. 1647), featuring both curtains, a second interior space behind, the painted stone niche, and ingeniously cast shadows, displays Dutch illusionism at its most complex (Fig. 45).

The painted curtain, calling attention to the painting itself as physical object, is an example of *trompe l'oeil*, a phenomenon in painting popular throughout Europe in the sixteenth and seventeenth centuries. *Trompe l'oeil* (fool the eye), the most dramatic example of illusionism, depends on a fixed viewpoint and uses the techniques of perspective and foreshortening to create the illusion of a real object inhabiting the same three-dimensional space as the spectator. The most spectacular examples of *trompe l'oeil* occur in the wall and ceiling decorations of antique and Italian Renaissance art, which created fictive extensions of actual interior space by placing painted objects and figures in illusionistic architectural details such as columns and moldings.

True *trompe l'oeil* is relatively rare in Dutch art, because the small size and portability of pictures would not permit a fixed view. Van Hoogstraten, with his passionate commitment to the illusionistic power of painting, came the closest. He created deceptive views through mock doorways and windows, and shallow still lifes such as letters pinned to false boards and dead game hanging from false walls. He was particularly fascinated by perspective boxes and constructed at least one himself. This unusual and entertaining object, originating in sixteenth-century Italy, was a large box with a hole at one end. Looking through the hole, the viewer was treated to a simulated three-dimensional scene. The perspective box represents the triumph of illusionism in its most extreme form. Yet it is clear that even within the context of easel painting, exploiting the medium of paint for the sake of optical persuasion was a powerful impulse in Dutch art. The appeal of these small pictures was the fact of picture making itself: The viewer's pleasure derived from seeing something apparently real while still knowing that it was, in fact, the product of the painter's mastery.

Martha Hollander

See also Architectural painting; Bas-relief painting; Dou, Gerrit; Frames, painted; Framing devices within pictures; Genre painting, eighteenth century; Genre painting, seventeenth century; Maes, Nicolaes; Magic Realism; Natural history illustration; Paintings-within-paintings; Still life; Van Mander, Karel; Writers on art, eighteenth century; Writers on art sixteenth and seventeenth centuries

Bibliography

Alpers, Svetlana. *The Art of Describing*. Chicago: University of Chicago Press, 1983.

Brusati, Celeste. *Artifice and Illusion: The Art and Writing of Samuel van Hoogstraten*. Chicago: Chicago University Press, 1995.

Kemp, Martin. *The Science of Art*. New Haven: Yale University Press, 1990.

Koslow, Susan. "De wonderlijke Perspectyfkas: An Aspect of Seventeenth-Century Dutch Painting." *Oud Holland* 72 (1967): 35–56.

Milman, Miriam. *Trompe l'Oeil Painting: The Illusion of Reality*. New York: Rizzoli, 1983.

Muylle, Jan. "Fascinatio. De betovering van en door het oog. Een 17de-eeuwse tonkast in trompe l'oeil." *De Zeventiende Eeuw. Culture in de nederlanden in interdisciplinair perspectief 8* (1992): 245-74.

Vries, Lyckle de. "The Changing Face of Realism." In *Art in History, History in Art: Studies in Seventeenth-Century Dutch Culture*. Edited by David Freedberg and Jan de Vries, 209–248. Santa Monica, CA: Getty Center for the History of Art and the Humanities, 1991.

Industrial design

See Applied arts

Israëls, Isaac (1865–1934)

The talent of Isaac Lazarus Israëls was revealed early. As the son of the renowned painter Jozef Israëls (1824–1911), he was exposed to art and literature at a young age, and at twelve he began taking lessons at the Academy for the Visual Arts in The Hague. Until he entered the Rijksacademie in Amsterdam in 1883, he concentrated on figure painting, portraits, history painting, and military subjects. In 1887, Israëls settled in Amsterdam and was accepted into the circle of the *Tachtigers* (the writers and artists of the 1880s) as an established artist. After 1888 he lived at the same time as George Hendrik Breitner in the "Witsenhuis," the studio living quarters in the Oosterpark belonging to the artist Willem Witsen. Breitner and Israëls influenced and inspired each other in their choice of motifs and use of color. During this period Israëls concentrated on making sketches and watercolors—a technique that lent itself extremely well to the rendering of figures in motion along the streets and to capturing life in the cafés, dance halls, and theaters of Amsterdam. He had great admiration for the paintings of Manet and Degas and for the novels by Émile Zola. After 1894 he focused on oil painting and exhibited more regularly. Around 1900 his palette lightened and he chose more elegant subjects, among them the models in fashion houses; Israëls came his closest to the style of French Impressionism during this period. Israëls was a cosmopolite: Until 1923 he lived alternately in Amsterdam, Paris, and London, and he painted in Italy. The works of Isaac Israëls are

in various museum collections in the Netherlands.

Harry J. Kraaij

See also Amsterdam Impressionists; Breitner, George Hendrik; Israëls, Jozef; Witsen, Willem

Bibliography

Bionda, Richard, and Carel Blotkamp, eds. *The Age of Van Gogh: Dutch Painting, 1880–1895*, 154–159. Zwolle: Waanders, 1990–1991.

Wagner, Anna. *Isaac Israëls*. Venlo: Lemniscaat, 1985.

Israëls, Jozef (1824–1911)

Jozef Israëls, one of the leading members of The Hague School and best known for his pictures of life in the fishing community of Scheveningen, was born into a poor Jewish family in Groningen, where he received his early training in drawing and painting at the Minerva Academy, the local art school. In 1842, through arrangements made by a Groningen art dealer, he entered the studio of Jan Adam Kruseman (1804–1862) in Amsterdam and took classes in the evenings with Jan Willem Pieneman (1779–1853) at the Rijksacademie. Through these channels, he was solidly prepared to work as an academic figure and history painter. Between 1845 and 1855, Israëls sought to enlarge on his academic training through travel to several of the centers of artistic activity at the time: He visited Paris (where he copied the works of Renaissance and Baroque masters and took lessons from Horace Vernet and Paul Delaroche at the École des Beaux Arts); Düsseldorf, then the focus of German Romanticism; and the Dutch *plein-air* artists' colony at Oosterbeek in the forest near Arnhem. However, Israëls' conversion to genre painting and realism occurred after his sojourns in 1855 and 1856 at the Dutch seaside villages of Zandvoort and Katwijk, where he observed and became captivated by the hard lives of poor fishermen and their families. *Passing Mother's Grave* (1856; Amsterdam, Stedelijk Museum), in which the theme is a tragic moment in the lives of a Zandvoort fisherman and his two children, marked a new direction for Israëls. For its monumental treatment of the commonplace, it has been called a milestone in nineteenth-century realism in the Netherlands, an event equal in impact to Gustave Courbet's *The Stone Breakers* (1849) in France (De Leeuw, Sillevis, and Dumas: 189).

After Israëls' *Fishermen Carrying a Drowned Man* (ca. 1860; London, National Gallery) was shown at the Paris Salon in 1861 and the next year in London at the International Exhibition, his reputation abroad was firmly established, and for the rest of his life he met the demand for his works by painting smaller versions and watercolors of his best-known and most popular paintings. His paintings were also reproduced in prints, and some were published with accompanying poems by Nicolaas Beets (1814–1903). Israëls' appeal lay in his preference for traditional themes (death and loss, motherhood, old age, courtship) set in the present in the lives of simple people (Fig. 54). In this regard, his art had a great influence on the young Vincent van Gogh. In contrast to the Romantic artists of a generation earlier, Israëls painted the quiet, tense, or meditative moments of fishermen's wives and families waiting on the dunes or grieving at home, away from the action and drama of shipwreck and death at sea. In 1878 he had a replica of a Scheveningen fisherman's cottage built in his studio in The Hague and posed his models there. The outdoor settings captured in his paintings are mostly gray and somber, reflecting the melancholy in the lives of his subjects.

Israëls kept in close contact with other artists and visited other locales. In the early 1870s, he was a summer resident in the village of Laren in the Gooi, which partly because of him became an artists' colony. He took his family (his son Isaac also became a painter) on a tour of European art centers in 1877, and every year after he took them to the Paris Salon. In the 1880s, he returned after many years to painting scenes of Jewish life that he sometimes observed in the Jewish quarter of Amsterdam; *The Jewish Wedding* (1903; Amsterdam, Rijksmuseum), thought to depict the wedding of his daughter, is a typical example of these later works.

In 1904, the year that he celebrated his eightieth birthday, Israëls sent several paintings to the Venice Biennale exhibition and also traveled to Venice. At home in the Netherlands, he was given the royal honor of an appointment as a Commander of the Nederlandse Leeuw (Order of the Dutch Lion). The same year, C.M. Dewald photographed the painter in his studio (Fig. 44).

Sheila D. Muller

See also Hague School, The; Israëls, Isaac; Laren; Prints, modern graphic arts 1840–1945

Bibliography

Leeuw, Ronald de, John Sillevis, and Charles Dumas, eds. *The Hague School: Dutch Masters of the Nineteenth Century.* London: Royal Academy of Arts, in association with Weidenfeld and Nicholson, 1983.

Italy

A reciprocal relationship between Italy and the Netherlands existed throughout the sixteenth and seventeenth centuries. Typically, Northerners traveled south, attracted by the fame of antique monuments and the achievements of Italian artists. Italian ideas were communicated to the North by Italians active there, returning Netherlanders, patrons, and works of literature and art. Several important phases of Dutch art were directly influenced by Italy; Netherlanders also left their mark there. Flemish artists took the lead in the fifteenth and early sixteenth centuries, but later Dutch artists became equally drawn to Italy and its culture.

A pattern of travel, influence, and patronage involving Italy and the North had been established in the fifteenth century. Rogier van der Weyden was in Rome probably in 1450 for the papal jubilee; several of his later works show Italian influence. In the 1470s, Tommaso Portinari, Bruges representative of the Medici, commissioned Hugo van der Goes to paint a large altarpiece for the Portinari Chapel in S. Egidio, Florence. It is unlikely that Petrus Christus traveled to Italy, but he was evidently familiar with Italian perspective theory,

perhaps stimulated by foreign patrons in Bruges. Several of Christus' later panels, such as his *Portrait of a Man* (ca. 1465), suggest an exchange of technical and formal ideas with Antonello da Messina in the North.

The pace of contacts with Italy quickened throughout the Netherlands in the early sixteenth century. In 1508, the Fleming Jan Gossaert traveled to Rome to study antiquity at the behest of his patron, Philip of Burgundy. Gossaert's drawings of ancient sculpture and monuments affected his own works long after he returned home. The Venetian artist Jacopo de'Barbari was a colleague of Gossaert's at the Burgundian court. Bernard van Orley, de'Barbari's successor as court artist in Brussels, supervised the production of the tapestries woven from Raphael's cartoons, which arrived in 1517, and subsequently adapted High Renaissance ideals in his own works.

When Adriaen VI became pope in 1522, he put his Utrecht compatriot Jan van Scorel in charge of antiquities in the Belvedere. His time there was short—the pope died in 1523—and Van Scorel returned north, imbued with the spirit of Italy. Study of Michelangelo's *Battle of Cascina* and Raphael's loggias informs the figures in Van Scorel's *Baptism of Christ* (1527–1529; Fig. 67); the landscape, however, recalls Joachim Patinir. Bramante's St. Peter's inspired the setting of Van Scorel's *Presentation of Christ in the Temple* (ca. 1530–1535). Van Scorel was also important as the teacher of Maerten van Heemskerck and Antonis Mor, both of whom shared their master's devotion to Italy. The characterization "Romanists" acknowledges these artists' commitment to the ideals and classical norms of antiquity and the Renaissance.

Van Heemskerck's study with Van Scorel in Haarlem in the late 1520s shaped the young artist's early style, as in the *Rest on the Flight into Egypt* (ca. 1530), with its Raphaelesque Madonna and Child. Another early work, *St. Luke Painting the Virgin* (1532), is permeated with humanist motifs and arcane symbolism. St. Luke's bench features an antique relief depicting the saint and his ox in the guise of Europa and the bull. His easel is a classical herm, and a torch-bearing angel reminiscent of a classical victory lights the models, again a Raphaelesque Madonna and Child. Thus, even before traveling south later in 1532, Van Heemskerck had embraced Christian humanism and Italian art. The meticulous sketchbooks he made in Rome between 1532 and 1536 are unparalleled records of the city and its monuments. When he settled in Haarlem, Van Heemskerck continued to draw on his Italian experience in works like the *Self-Portrait with the Colosseum* (1553).

Van Scorel's other brilliant pupil, Antonis Mor, was born in Utrecht. A portrait specialist, he emulated Titian, whose works he evidently studied in Brussels even before going to Italy in 1550. Mor's amalgam of Netherlandish and Venetian elements won him commissions at the Portuguese, Spanish, and English courts in the following decade.

Utrecht, a Catholic bishopric, was particularly receptive to Italian contacts. Anthonie Blocklandt, Utrecht's leading artist from 1577 until his death, in 1583, had developed a polished and influential style through study with Frans Floris in Antwerp and a trip to Italy in 1572. Synthesizing Italian and

French Mannerism, he helped prepare the way for the eruption in the 1580s of late Dutch Mannerism.

That phenomenon, too, had strong Italian roots. They took hold in Haarlem in 1583, when Karel van Mander introduced Hendrick Goltzius and Cornelis Cornelisz. van Haarlem to drawings by Bartholomeus Spranger, a Flemish colleague Van Mander had befriended in Rome in the 1570s. Spranger's Netherlandish version of Italian Mannerism, indebted to such artists as Parmigianino, Federico Zuccaro, and Marco Pino, proved a powerful goad to the Haarlemers. Goltzius' engravings after Spranger, notably *The Wedding of Cupid and Psyche* (1587), readily communicated the style. Cornelis van Haarlem, as designer, and Goltzius, as engraver, also imitated Spranger's boldly expressive manner, pervaded with eroticism, in such engravings as the *Disgracers* (1588), a subject that Titian had interpreted in paintings for the Spanish court. Other Dutch Mannerists, like the Utrecht artist Joachim Wtewael, would see Italy at firsthand and amalgamate ideas from Jacopo Zucchi, Correggio, and the Bassano with the Spranger style.

Cornelis Cornelisz. van Haarlem never went to Italy, but Goltzius' journey there in 1590 helped foster the development of a more moderate, classicizing current in his works. Goltzius' study of ancient monuments and Italian Renaissance sculpture, recorded in chalk drawings, was influential in the development of a classicizing trend in Dutch art. Cornelis Cornelisz. van Haarlem and the Utrecht artist Abraham Bloemaert were among those affected.

Evidence of north–south contact lies also in literary works such as Lodovico Guicciardini's *Descrittione di tutti i Paesi Bassi* (1567), an invaluable "description of all the Low Countries" as seen through the eyes of a Florentine based in Antwerp. Giorgio Vasari's *Vite* (1550; 2nd ed. 1568) was the source for Van Mander's understanding of Italian art theory and practice and a point of departure for Van Mander's *Schilder-Boeck* (Book of Picturing, 1604). Van Mander reshaped the Vasari paradigm in both the theoretical and the biographical sections of the *Schilder-Boeck* to argue a theory of Netherlandish art.

The Utrecht Caravaggists, who flourished in the 1620s, developed a compelling naturalism associated with Michelangelo Merisi da Caravaggio. His powerfully modeled figures, dramatic *chiaroscuro*, and intensely expressive realism inspired artists like Hendrick Terbrugghen, Gerard van Honthorst, and Dirck van Baburen, each of whom spent several years in Italy in the early seventeenth century. Each absorbed Caravaggio's style distinctively in both history and genre paintings. Terbrugghen, the first to return to Utrecht (1614), fused naturalistic modeling and strong *chiaroscuro* with lingering Mannerism—in the grotesque types and claustrophobic space—in his *Calling of St. Matthew* (1621; Fig. 131), a subject Caravaggio had made famous. The iridescent greens, pinks, and blues also recall a Mannerist palette, which Terbrugghen handled with characteristic delicacy. His quiet, internalized drama contrasts with Caravaggio's more theatrical interpretation. Van Honthorst, nicknamed Gherardo della Notte (Gerard of the Nights) because of his preference for nocturnal light effects, returned in 1620. Van Honthorst specialized in genre paintings depicting merry companies eating, drinking, playing games, and flirting, bathed in the golden light of one or more obscured candles. His candlelight variation on Caravaggio's *chiaroscuro*, which had precedents in earlier Netherlandish art, was widely imitated. When Van Baburen returned to Utrecht about 1621, he, too, painted genre subjects, such as *The Procuress* (1622; Color Plate 3), which features three robust figures engaged in an exchange of mercenary love. Here the light is clear and bright, but the naturalism and directness are the legacy of the Italian master. The format, with large half-length figures, was associated with one of Caravaggio's Italian followers, Bartolomeo Manfredi, who along with other Caravaggisti also influenced Netherlanders.

The Dutch Caravaggists' style spread to Netherlandish painters who never set foot in Italy. Bloemaert, the teacher of Terbrugghen, Van Honthorst, and Jan van Bijlert, another Caravaggist, in turn learned from his pupils in the 1620s. Bloemaert's *The Supper at Emmaus* (1622; Fig. 68), a candlelight scene with volumetric and dramatically expressive half-length figures, recalls Caravaggio's rendition of the same subject, which Bloemaert had never seen. Frans Hals' *Merry Drinker* (1628–1630) repeats the half-length format and spontaneity so popular in Utrecht. Rembrandt, too, adopted a Caravaggesque vocabulary in his early *Money-Changer* (1627), a half-length figure sheltering a candle that illuminates the surrounding darkness with exceptional subtlety. Johannes Vermeer surely was familiar with Van Baburen's *The Procuress*, since his mother-in-law owned it. Vermeer's early *Procuress* (1656) reflects knowledge of Van Baburen's, and the latter appears in the backgrounds of two of Vermeer's works from the 1660s and 1670s.

A group of Dutch painters called the *Bamboccianti* worked in Italy in the 1620s, specializing in scenes of street life and rustic landscapes, generally small-scale works with Caravaggesque genre elements. Their name acknowledges the leadership of Pieter van Laer, or *Bamboccio*, which means "clumsy doll" (he was a hunchback). In Rome from about 1625 to 1639, Van Laer was an influential member of the *Schildersbent*, or band of painters, known as much for parties as for paintings. A canvas of about 1660 (Amsterdam, Rijksmuseum) depicts an initiation ceremony, dominated by Bacchus amidst *Schildersbent* members dressed in classical togas. The *Bentvueghels*—or birds of the flock—included most of the Dutch painters in Rome at the time, and each had a nickname. Their works range from Cornelis ("Satyr") van Poelenburch and Bartholomeus ("Ferret") Breenbergh's sunny arcadian landscapes to Van Laer's darker street scenes teeming with low life.

Another generation of Dutch landscapists followed the path to Italy in the 1630s and 1640s. Most artists remained there only a few years, then returned north, where their luminous idylls disseminated the Italian idiom. Jan Both was the first to return to the Netherlands, about 1641. His scenes of tall, lacy trees and hills shimmering in limpid, golden light, like the *Southern Landscape with Travelers* (ca. 1645–1650), which depicts a rustic wooden bridge on the way from Rome to Tivoli, so successfully conjured up the Italian scene for Aelbert Cuyp that Cuyp was able to re-create it without traveling. Jan Asselijn, Jan Baptist Weenix, Adam Pijnacker, and Johannes Lingelbach each spent years in Rome before settling in the Netherlands for the rest of their productive lives. Weenix became Giovanni Battista Weenix upon returning home in 1647, after which even his depictions of Dutch mothers and children smack of life on the *campagna* (Roman countryside). Each artist naturally devised his own poetry—Pijnacker favoring sparkling highlights on tangled branches in the foregrounds of tranquil river scenes; Asselijn, silver-toned imaginary landscapes enlivened by genre figures reminiscent of Van Laer. Nicolaes Berchem, one of the most talented and prolific Italianate landscapists, probably also went south in the 1650s—perhaps with his pupil Karel du Jardin—but it was in the Netherlands that he painted most of his expansive scenes of sun-struck ruins peopled by picturesque cowherds and shepherdesses. The Italianates' range extended beyond landscape to portraits and still lifes as well as history and genre scenes.

Like other Dutch artists already mentioned, Rembrandt was deeply affected by Italian art without ever experiencing Italy itself. According to the diarist Constantijn Huygens, young Rembrandt and his colleague Jan Lievens decided not to go there since Italian art was readily available at home. Paintings like Rembrandt's *Self-Portrait* (1640; London, National Gallery) are prime evidence for the accuracy of their assessment. Rembrandt based the conception and pose on two sixteenth-century Italian portraits he saw in Amsterdam: Titian's *Portrait of a Man*, thought to represent the poet Ludovico Ariosto, and Raphael's *Portrait of Baldassare Castiglione*. Rembrandt had sketched the Raphael when it was auctioned in 1639, already introducing self-portrait elements. He developed his ideas in a self-portrait etching of 1639 and then in the painting of 1640, transforming himself into a poised, supremely confident Dutch counterpart of "Ariosto." A portrait of Rembrandt's wife, Saskia, as *Flora* (1641) was also based on a painting by Titian, which was, like the "Ariosto," in the Amsterdam collection of the Portuguese merchant Alfonso Lopez. Titian's "rough" style provided the model for Rembrandt's late technique, which contrasted with the *fijnschilders'* (fine painters') "smooth" style then fashionable in the Netherlands.

Adam Elsheimer's influence on Rembrandt exemplifies the complexity of Italo-Dutch exchange. Elsheimer, a German artist active in Venice and Rome, fused Caravaggesque and arcadian ideals in poetic small works on copper. Rembrandt's teacher Pieter Lastman was among the many artists affected by Elsheimer in Italy. Through Lastman, other Dutch artists in Rome before Elsheimer's death in 1610, and engravings by Count Hendrik Goudt after Elsheimer, Rembrandt, too, was affected by Elsheimer's lyricism, in landscapes as well as in paintings such as *Jupiter and Mercury Visiting Philemon and Baucis* (1658). Rembrandt also owned the copper plate for an etching of *Tobias and the Angel* by Hercules Segers after Elsheimer, which he reworked into a *Flight into Egypt*.

In Rome, according to Filippo Baldinucci, who wrote the first general history of the figurative arts in Europe (1681), Rembrandt was considered "spectacularly skillful in painting." This reputation stimulated commissions from the Sicilian nobleman Don Antonio Ruffo of Messina. Apparently in response to Ruffo's request for a painting of a philosopher, Rembrandt provided *Aristotle Contemplating a Bust of Homer* (1654). In 1661, Rembrandt shipped two more paintings to Ruffo, an *Alexander the Great* and a *Homer*. Finally, in 1669, Ruffo ordered one hundred eighty-nine of Rembrandt's etchings.

Rembrandt's interest in classic Italian art is recorded in a drawing of *Homer Reciting* that he contributed to his friend Jan Six's *album amicorum* (1652), inspired by Raphael's *Parnassus*, which he evidently knew through Marcantonio Raimondi's engraving. Rembrandt also collected Italian art, the 1656 inventory of his possessions listing paintings by such artists as Raphael, Giorgione, Palma Vecchio, and Jacopo Bassano. He also had an extensive collection of prints by or after Michelangelo, Raphael, Andrea Mantegna, the Carracci, Guido Reni, and Titian, among others.

The study of Italy and Dutch artists is a relatively neglected area. Art history's typical emphasis on national schools has created specializations that impede rather than encourage the broad inquiry that would lead to a nuanced and integrated assessment of developments north and south of the Alps. Theorists have challenged the binary thinking that underlies that north–south division, but the tendency persists. Another impediment is the limited linguistic facility that follows from focus on a single geographic area. The traditional Italo-centrism of art history has sometimes put Northern specialists on the defensive, which further militates against objective analysis.

Progress toward a deeper understanding of Dutch artists' contacts with Italy would seem to require fresh methodological approaches. There is also a need for more gathering of data and basic factual research—for example, on inventories of Italian art in Dutch collections. Italian archival records concerning Netherlanders have been inadequately explored. Paintings by Dutch artists probably go unrecognized in Italy. Thoroughgoing studies on the periods of foreign activity of both Netherlanders and Italians, emphasizing patronage, the scope of works executed abroad, influences, and contacts with foreign art and artists, are of fundamental importance, as are monographs on individual Dutch artists active in Italy.

Anne W. Lowenthal

See also Bloemaert, Abraham; Bramer, Leonaert; Classicism in architecture; Delft; Drawing theory; Flanders, Flemish School; Goltzius, Hendrick; Haarlem; History painting; Humanism, humanist themes; Humbert de Superville, D.P.G.; Huygens, Constantijn; Landscape; Literature, poetry: analogues with the visual; Mannerism, Mannerists; Pastoral; Pre-Rembrandtists; Rembrandt van Rijn; Renaissance architecture; Sculpture (1550–1795); Self-portraiture; Technical investigations; Terbrugghen, Hendrick; Utrecht; Utrecht Caravaggists; Van Baburen, Dirck Jaspersz.; Van Honthorst, Gerard; Van Mander, Karel

Bibliography

Art before the Iconoclasm: Northern Netherlandish Art, 1525–1580. The Hague: Staatsuitgeverij, 1986.

Berghe, E. H. van den. "Italiaanse schilderijen in Amsterdam in de zeventiende eeuw." *Jaarboek van het genootschap Amstelodamum* 84 (1992): 21–40.

Blankert, Albert, and Leonard J. Slatkes. *Nieuw licht op de gouden eeuw: Hendrick ter Brugghen en tijdgenoten.* Utrecht: Centraal Museum; Brunswick: Herzog Anton Ulrich-Museum; Brunswick: Limbach, 1987.

Briganti, Giuliano, Ludovica Trezzani, and Laura Laureati. *The Bamboccianti: The Painters of Everyday Life in Seventeenth-Century Rome.* Translated by Robert Erich Wolf. Rome: Ugo Bozzi, 1983.

Clark, Kenneth. *Rembrandt and the Italian Renaissance.* New York: New York University Press, 1966.

Duparc, Frederik J., and Linda L. Graif. *Italian Recollections: Dutch Painters of the Golden Age.* Montreal: Montreal Museum of Fine Arts, 1990.

Gerson, Horst. "Italien." In *Ausbreitung und Nachwirkung der holländischen Malerei des 17. Jahrhunderts,* 137–195. 2nd ed. Amsterdam: B.M. Israel, 1983.

Kettering, Alison McNeil. *The Dutch Arcadia: Pastoral Art and Its Audience in the Golden Age.* Montclair, NJ: Allanheld and Schram, 1983.

Meijer, Bert W. "Over kunst en kunstgeschiedenis in Italië en de Nederlanden." In *Nederland–Italië: Relaties in de beeldende kunst van de Nederlanden en Italië / Artistic Relations between the Low Countries and Italy, 1400–1750.* Edited by Jan de Jong, Dulcia Meijers, Hanna Pennock, and Victor Schmidt, 9–34. *Nederlands Kunsthistorisch Jaarboek* 44. Zwolle: Waanders, 1993.

Melion, Walter. *Shaping the Netherlandish Canon: Karel van Mander's Schilder-Boeck.* Chicago: University of Chicago Press, 1991.

J

Japonisme

The influence of Japanese art (*Japonisme*) on Western art took place after 1853, the year that American Commodore Matthew C. Perry persuaded Japan to open to the Western world. After that the export of fine and applied arts began on a large scale. Artists such as Édouard Manet, Edgar Degas, Henri de Toulouse-Lautrec, Vincent van Gogh, Paul Gauguin, and James McNeill Whistler adopted themes from Japanese art, particularly from prints, and were inspired by the alternative it offered for the representation of reality. What captivated them was another view of representing the illusion of space and movement, the flattened use of color, and the linear character of the image. With these elements, artists began to experiment.

Since the Netherlands was the only country with whom Japan had never broken off trade, the Dutch were more familiar with Japanese artifacts than people in other countries. In the eighteenth century, most of these artifacts were still in private collections, but after 1816 they were put on public display in the collection of Japanese *ethnographica* and porcelain in the Cabinet of Rarities in The Hague (in 1821 this was brought into the Mauritshuis). In 1837, Ph.F. von Siebold, formerly a physician at the trading post in Deshima, Japan, made his collection of Japanese objects available for viewing in his home in Leiden. In spite of this availability, the influence of Japanese art on Dutch art occurred later than in the surrounding countries—namely, at the end of the 1880s.

Moreover, the influence worked mainly indirectly, through modern French, English, and Austrian art and literature. This was particularly the case in painting. Painters who are said to show Japanese influence are Vincent van Gogh, George Hendrik Breitner, Willem de Zwart, G.W. Dijsselhof, Jan Toorop (although in his case Indonesian art probably had a greater influence), Theo Hoytema, and J.G. Veldheer. In the area of the applied arts, direct reception of things Japanese was greater. In the porcelain industry a fruitful exchange had existed since the end of the seventeenth century. Dutch lacquer ware, which was influenced by Japan, experienced a period of great efflorescence in the eighteenth century. A fine example is the Japanese room from 1790–1791 in Huis ten Bosch in The Hague, in which the woods, lacquers, and furniture were designed by M. Horrix and the textiles are possibly from Japan. Furthermore, "Japanese skirts" (kimonos) and Japanese rice paper enjoyed great popularity in the Netherlands.

When, at the end of the nineteenth century, the call for new designs was loudly sounded, Japanese industrial arts offered a starting point. In the field of ceramics, Rozenburg porcelain from The Hague became a particularly well-known name. Initially, there was copying of the external features and a noticeable imitation in the (whimsical) decoration. For this, Franco-Japanese pattern books such as Gillots' *Documents décoratifs Japonais* or Fraipont's *Le album Japonais* were used. Around the turn of the century, appreciation began to grow for the simple form and the open construction in Japanese designs. Potters such as Ch. Lanooy and B. Nienhuis took inspiration from completely glazed but undecorated Japanese earthenware. Ultimately around 1900, the artist-metalsmith J. Eisenlöffel designed a tea service that, on the one hand, can be linked to the austere designs by H.P. Berlage and yet, on the other hand, can also be traced back to a Japanese sake kettle.

Although in the nineteenth century one could still generally find direct sources of Japanese inspiration and see the influence particularly in the external appearance of art works, in the twentieth century the emphasis came to be placed on the influence of ideas and philosophies. Such an integration of forms has been achieved that it is possible to speak of Japanese influence only if the artist mentions it.

Alexandra W.M. van Smoorenburg

See also Applied arts; Breitner, George Hendrik; Ceramics; De Zwart, Willem; Dijsselhof, Gerrit Willem; Exotica; Non-Western cultural influences; Toorop, Jan; Trade, exploration, and colonization overseas; Van Gogh, Vincent

Bibliography

Gulik, W.R. van, J.L. Blussé, and Th. H. Lunsingh
  Scheurleer. *In het Spoor der Liefde: Japans-Nederlandse*

ontmoetingen sinds 1600. Amsterdam: De Bataafsche
Leeuw, 1986.

Rappard-Boon, Ch. et al. *Imitatie en Inspiratie: Japanse
invloed op Nederlandse kunst van 1650 tot heden.*
Amsterdam: D'Arts, 1991.

Jews

Although there are some references to Jews in the Netherlands
in the Middle Ages, their documentable history begins after
the Dutch proclaimed independence from Spain in 1581.
Many Jews were attracted to the Netherlands in the early seventeenth century by the promise of religious tolerance and the
thriving economy. While Amsterdam was their principal destination, they settled in cities throughout the Netherlands,
where they generally functioned in autonomous communities separate from Dutch jurisdiction.

Whereas the Jews benefited from the complete freedom
of worship, from the ability to acquire land for their synagogues and cemeteries, and from the lack of an enforced
ghetto or any restrictive dress, their prohibition from the
Dutch guilds ultimately relegated them to a ghetto-like existence of poverty and squalor. In 1796, after finally being
granted full rights as citizens of the Netherlands, the Jews of
the Israelitic community began their assimilation into the
Dutch society, making notable contributions in the political,
economic, and social arenas. Tragically, the Jewish community was decimated by the Nazis in World War II, and the
community today represents a fraction of its prewar strength
and vitality.

The Jews who found refuge in the Netherlands were victims of persecution, and the first group to arrive in the seventeenth century were Sephardic Jews who had fled from the
Inquisition on the Iberian peninsula. Identified as the Portuguese community, they were a cosmopolitan assembly headed
by an impressive contingent of merchants, doctors, diplomats,
rabbis, and scholars who interacted regularly with their Dutch
neighbors, including the House of Orange. This interaction,
and the very presence of the community, generated a variety
of images that documented their uniqueness and celebrated
their accomplishments: Emanuel de Witte and Romeyn de
Hooghe portrayed views of their synagogues, De Hooghe and
Jacob van Ruisdael depicted their cemetery, Bernard Picart illustrated a variety of Jewish rituals as did several Jewish artists, and Govaert Flinck, Constantijn Netscher, Jan Lievens,
and Rembrandt executed portraits of members of the community. Rembrandt, who lived in the area that was settled by
the Jews, even received several commissions from members of
the Portuguese community.

However, it was the members of the second group of
Jews, who began to arrive in the 1630s, that populated many
of Rembrandt's biblical paintings. These Ashkenazic Jews,
escaping the pogroms in Germany and Poland, were easily
distinguished from the Portuguese community by their dress,
their use of Yiddish, and their lack of integration with the
Dutch community. In addition to their perceived suitability
for the biblical scenes, aspects of the Ashkenazic community,
including their synagogues, their rabbis, and their religious

customs, were illustrated in prints by a variety of Dutch artists, frequently as a contrast to the Portuguese community.
Throughout the ensuing centuries, although some images
caricatured various aspects of the communities in anti-Semitic
propaganda, most depictions of the communities continued
to document their special ceremonies and their prominent
individuals. Additionally, many images of and for the community were produced by Jewish artists. In the seventeenth century, prints were executed by Salom Italia, Benjamin Senior
Godines, and Jacob Jehuda Leon, while the Impressionist
painters Jozef and Isaac Israëls illustrated scenes of the
community's life in the late nineteenth century. A substantial
amount of scholarship has been directed toward the images
relating to the Portuguese community of the seventeenth century, but much work remains to be done on the images of the
Ashkenazic community and the events of both communities
after the seventeenth century.

Shana L. Stuart

See also Artists' confraternities and craftsmen's guilds; Exotica;
Israëls, Isaac; Israëls, Jozef; Non-Western cultural influences;
Religion of artists; Rembrandt van Rijn; World Wars I and II

Bibliography
Gans, Moses. *Memorbook: History of Dutch Jewry from the
Renaissance to 1940.* Baarn: Bosch and Keuning, 1971.

Morgenstein, Susan W., and Ruth E. Levine, eds. *Jews in
the Age of Rembrandt.* Washington, DC: Judaic Museum of the Jewish Community Center of Greater
Washington, 1981.

Rubens, Alfred. *A Jewish Iconography.* London: Jewish Museum, 1954.

Stuart, Shana. "The Portuguese Jewish Community in Seventeenth-Century Amsterdam: Images of Commemoration and Documentation." Ph.D. diss., University of
Kansas, 1992.

Jongkind, Johan Barthold (1819–1891)

In 1836 Johan Barthold Jongkind began going to The Hague
Drawing Academy in the evenings and to Andreas Schelfhout's
studio during the day. In 1846 he left for Paris with a royal
scholarship to continue his studies with Eugène Isabey. In
France, Jongkind made contact with the Barbizon painters—
Ziem, Diaz, Lapito, Rousseau, Troyon, Daubigny, and Corot.
In 1854 he fled from Paris for financial and emotional reasons
and returned to his old place of residence, Rotterdam. In 1860,
however, his French colleagues enabled him to return to Paris
though the proceeds from the sale of works they had donated.
Jongkind was admitted into the artists' group Cercle Mogador,
which included the Barbizon landscape painters. Until 1869
he still went regularly to the Netherlands, and the Dutch landscape would never disappear from his *oeuvre.* In France he did
much painting at first on the Brittany and Normandy coasts;
after the mid-1870s his interest was transferred to the center
of France, especially the Loire region, and after 1878 to the
South of France, particularly the surroundings of La Côte-
Saint-André, where he settled.

Jongkind was a very original artist, who was also seen by his contemporaries as *the* forerunner of Impressionism. His vibrant loose style (possibly created as a result of his excessive use of alcohol) and his clear, but at the same time atmospheric, use of color were much appreciated by the younger generation of artists, among them Monet and Pissarro. The period 1860–1875 is generally viewed as the highpoint of his career; afterward his production decreased. Even so, he made fine watercolors and drawings during the 1880s. Partly because of his precarious health, Jongkind retreated more and more from the Parisian artistic circles during the last years of his life. Only after his death did he receive recognition in the Netherlands.

Alexandra W.M. van Smoorenburg

See also France; Rotterdam; Schelfhout, Andreas

Bibliography

Hefting, Victorine. *Jongkind: Sa vie, son oeuvre, son époque.* Paris: Arts et Métiers Graphiques, 1975.

———. *l'Univers de Jongkind.* Paris: Henri Scrépel, 1976.

Sillevis, J. et al. *Jongkind: Een Hollander in Frankrijk.* Zeist: Zeister Stichting voor Kunst en Cultuur, 1991.

K

Karsen, Eduard (1860–1941)

Johann Eduard Karsen painted mostly Amsterdam canals, views of villages, farms, farmyards, and gardens. He received his first painting lessons from his father, Kasparus Karsen (1810–1896), who was known as a painter of city and river views. During the time he studied at the Rijksacademie in Amsterdam, Eduard Karsen came in contact with a number of the important young painters and writers of the 1880s, the so-called *Tachtigers*—George Hendrik Breitner, Jan Veth, Willem Witsen, Floris Verster, and the poet Albert Verwey. He became a member of the Nederlandse Etsclub (Dutch Etching Club) and the artists' society, St. Lucas. Using a pen name, he occasionally wrote about art—for example, in the literary magazine *De Nieuwe Gids* (The New Guide).

In contrast with Breitner and Isaac Israëls, Karsen, during his period in Amsterdam, did not choose to paint the bustling activity of the big city. Often he portrayed merely a deserted canal, a single small house, or a gabled façade. His work breathes a dreamy, still atmosphere. Karsen's views of cities and his landscapes are not so much realistic portrayals of actual places as they are expressions of his inner state of mind. Thus, he once gave one of his paintings of a little house the title of *Self-Portrait*. He had a clear preference for the twilight of an early morning or a dusky evening. Karsen painted with subdued colors, and his work sometimes comes across as naive. After 1895, his works are more rigorously composed, and the motifs are dissected into a pattern of horizontal and vertical lines.

Harry J. Kraaij

See also Amsterdam Impressionists; Breitner, George Hendrik; Israëls, Isaac; Verster, Floris; Veth, Jan; Witsen, Willem

Bibliography

Bionda, Richard, and Carel Blotkamp, eds. *The Age of Van Gogh: Dutch Painting, 1880–1895*, 169–172. Zwolle: Waanders, 1990–1991.

Hammacher, A.M. *Eduard Karsen en zijn vader Kaspar.* The Hague: Daamen, 1947.

Kleyn, Pieter Rudolph (1795–1816)

Pieter Rudolph Kleyn belongs to the category of artists who made Dutch art around 1800. Educated by the brothers Jacob and Abraham van Strij in Dordrecht, and given further training at The Hague Drawing Academy, Kleyn received a scholarship in 1808 (at the age of thirteen) from King Louis Napoleon to study in Paris with Jacques Louis David. From Paris he went to Rome in 1809, where he continued his studies at the French Academy in the Villa Medici. As with his fellow students abroad—J.A. Knip, A. Sminck Pitloo, and A. Teerlink—the influence of French classicism is clear in Kleyn's work. Kleyn's landscapes are fairly monumental, mostly sparing in the use of figures, and light in tone—for example, *The Entrance to the Park St. Cloud, Paris* (1809; Amsterdam, Rijksmuseum).

There are few specific facts known about the artist. We do know that he was back in the Netherlands around 1813, and that he went into the service of King Willem I as a lieutenant in the Dutch National Militia shortly after. He was wounded in the Battle of Quatre Bras in 1815, and this eventually led to his death in 1816.

Alexandra W.M. van Smoorenburg

See also France; Knip, Josephus Augustus

Bibliography

Luttervelt, R. van. "Herinneringen aan de Bonapartes in het Rijksmuseum." *Publicaties van het Genootschap voor Napoleontische studiën* 13 (1961): 561–564.

Scheen, P.A. *Lexicon Nederlandse Beeldende Kunstenaars 1750–1880.* The Hague: Pieter Scheen, 1981.

Knip, Josephus Augustus (1777–1847)

Josephus Augustus Knip is the most important of a family of landscape, flower, and animal painters. Born in Tilburg, he received his initial training from his father and afterward went, in 1801, to Paris to work as an artist. However, his real artistic education started in 1808, when he received from Louis

Napoleon, king of Holland (1806–1810), the Prix de Rome in its Dutch version. For Knip this honor meant academic training in France as a landscape and animal painter and in Italy, where he studied every aspect of the landscape.

The numerous precise pencil or pen drawings, in most cases lightly worked up in subtle watercolors, that he made during his studies abroad belong to the best of Dutch Neo-classical art. After his return to the Netherlands in 1812, he used his drawings like the pieces of a jigsaw puzzle to compose paintings, in which he excelled. His models were seventeenth-century Dutch Italianate landscape paintings, as prescribed by the Dutch Prix de Rome regulations. So in the work of this middle period, Knip combined the revival of Dutch seventeenth-century art and Neoclassicism, both of which were the consequence of his Prix de Rome training.

His earlier and later work was more in the mainstream. As he was more successful in France, he lived there again after 1823. In 1826 he went back to the Netherlands, where he gave lessons to family members of the House of Orange and to his own children. In 1832 he became blind, after which he received a small allowance from King Willem I.

Ellinoor Bergvelt

See also Animal painting; Ronner-Knip, Henriëtte

Bibliography

Bergvelt, Ellinoor. "De élèves-pensionnaires van Koning Lodewijk Napoleon/Gli élèves-pensionnaires di Re Luigi Napoleone." In *Reizen naar Rome: Italië als leerschool voor Nederlandse kunstenaars omstreeks 1800/ Paesaggisti ed altri artisti olandesi a Roma intorno al 1800.* Edited by Eric Ebbinge, Johannes Offerhaus et al., 45–77. Haarlem: Teylers Museum, and Istituto Olandese di Roma; Rome: Fratelli Palombi Editori, 1984.

———. "J.A. Knip, 1777–1847: De werkwijze van een 19de-eeuwse landschapschilder in relatie tot de kunsttheorie in Holland en Frankrijk omstreeks 1800." *Nederlands Kunsthistorisch Jaarboek* 27 (1976): 11–71.

Bergvelt, Ellinoor, and Margriet van Boven. *J.A. Knip, 1777–1847.* The Hague: Staatsuitgeverij, 1977.

Kuyvenhoven, Fransje, and Ronald Peeters. *De familie Knip: Drie generaties kunstenaars uit Noord-Brabant.* Zwolle: Waanders, 1988.

Kobell, Jan Baptist II (1778–1814)

Jan Baptist Kobell came from a large family of artists. His father was a marine painter. At an early age, Kobell lost both of his parents and, as a result, was reared in an orphanage in Utrecht. It was there that he began studying with the animal painter Willem Rutgaart van der Wall. In 1805 Kobell became a member of the Utrecht painters' college, and in 1807 he and P.C. Wonder together led the Utrecht society Kunstliefde (Love of Art), which was established that year. From 1810 until 1812 Kobell worked in Paris, and in 1813 he settled in Amsterdam, where, shortly after, he died insane. Kobell was a painter of cattle pieces in the style of Paulus Potter, and his works had international fame in the nineteenth century.

Alexandra W.M. van Smoorenburg

See also Animal painting; Utrecht

Bibliography

Huebner, F.M. *De romantische schilderkunst in de Nederlanden, 1780–1840,* 52, 82–83. The Hague: Oceanus, 1942.

Immerzeel, J. *De levens en werken der Hollandsche en Vlaamsche kunstschilders, beeldhouwers, graveurs en bouwmeesters.* Amsterdam: J.C. van Kesteren, 1842–1843.

Knoef, J. *Een eeuw Nederlandse schilderkunst,* 30–31. Amsterdam: Querido, 1948.

Koch, Pyke (Pieter Frans Christiaan) (1901–1991)

In 1927, shortly before the end of his law studies in Utrecht, Pyke Koch became a painter in that city. He was self-taught and took advice from Erich Wichmann. His first exhibition of two paintings was with De Onafhankelijken (The Independents) in 1928. His early work shows the influence of Nieuwe Zakelijkheid (New Objectivity) and Surrealism. In a portrait like *Asta Nielsen* (1929), the influence of film and photography is felt in the striking sensation of light and darkness. He also used painterly techniques and motifs from the early Italian Renaissance and fifteenth-century Flemish painters. Between 1930 and 1933, he combined these influences to create female portraits such as *Mercedes of Barcelona* (1930), *Bertha of Antwerp* (1931), and *De Schiettent* (The Shooting Tent, 1931). After his marriage to H.M. de Geer in 1934, he lived for a year in The Hague.

From the beginning, Pyke Koch's *oeuvre* has contained a Freudian symbolism of eroticism and power. His sympathy for fascism, which can be seen in the *Self-Portrait with Black Belt* (1937), was confirmed during his stay in Italy from 1937 until 1939. In his work during this period the admiration for Andrea Mantegna and Piero della Francesca is also visible. Koch collaborated with the German occupation during World War II with the goal of realizing a national Greater Netherlands (the Netherlands and Flannders) political culture. In January 1941, with a group of Dutch artists, he visited Joseph Goebbels in Berlin. After April 1941 he was no longer a member of the Nationaal-Socialistische Beweging (National Socialist Movement), but he was a member of the Kultuurkamer, a public agency designed to influence art and cultural life during the German occupation of the Netherlands (1941–1945). After the war he created a series of portraits of *Jkrv. C.J. Van Boetzelaer* (1947–1954), as well as a number of sports and circus scenes like *De Cortorsoinniste* (The Contortionist, 1956–1958), and repetitions of old themes like *Vrouwen in de Straat* (Women in the Street, 1962–1964; Fig. 69). He also made drawings and paintings, stage scenery, graphic designs (postage stamps and bookplates), and accepted monumental commissions (lampposts for downtown Utrecht). He also published several short art theoretical and political texts.

John Steen

See also Magic Realism; Surrealism; World Wars I and II

Bibliography

Blotkamp, Carel. *Pyke Koch*. Amsterdam: De Arbeiderspers, 1972.

Tilborgh, Louis van. "Freudian Motifs in the *Oeuvre* of Pyke Koch." *Simiolus* 15 (1985): 131–150.

———. Pyke Koch: *Schijlderen en Tekeningen/Paintings and Drawings*. Rotterdam: Museum Boymans-von Beuningen. 1995.

Koekkoek, B.C. (1803–1862)

Barend Cornelis Koekkoek was the most famous painter of the Koekkoek family of artists. His moderately Romantic forest and winter scenes were very popular until the 1860s. Trained by his father and by Abraham Kraijestein, teacher at the Middelburg Drawing Academy, Barend went from Middelburg to the Royal Academy in Amsterdam in 1822. There he became skilled in figure drawing and, thanks to J.A. Daiwaille, he also learned the technique of lithography. After some domestic traveling, Koekkoek settled in 1834 in Cleves, just across the border in Germany, where he founded a drawing academy in 1841. In that same year his book *Herinneringen en Mededeelingen van eenen Landschapschilder* (Memories and Comments of a Landscape Painter) was published. In this book, which is actually a travelogue of an art trip taken with friends in the German Rhine region, the painter gave his Romanticist's opinions about beauty. He also used the opportunity to give technical advice to young colleagues. Koekkoek traveled often and with pleasure to inspire his painting; he visited Germany, Belgium, and Switzerland.

Koekkoek's career went splendidly; he was called the prince among Dutch landscape painters (Andreas Schelfhout was the monarch). He received numerous honors, both in his own country and abroad. He was also an honorary member of several academies and societies. The palace-like residence that he built for himself and his family in Cleves in 1847 was made the town's municipal museum in 1958. It was given the name of the earlier resident: Haus Koekkoek.

Alexandra W.M. van Smoorenburg

See also Amateurs, art academies, and art associations before the nineteenth century; Drawing clubs; Landscape; Schelfhout, Andreas

Bibliography

Bruyn Kops, C.J. de. "De Hollandse jaren van Barend Cornelis Koekkoek." *Bulletin van het Rijksmuseum* 11 (1963): 39–53.

Gorissen, F. *B.C. Koekkoek, 1803–1862*. Düsseldorf: Rheinland Verlag, 1962.

Koekkoek, Barend Cornelis. *Herinneringen en Mededeelingen van eenen Landschapschilder*. Amsterdam, 1841. Reprint. Schiedam: Interbook International, 1982.

Koninck, Philips (1619–1688)

Although his contemporaries admired his history paintings and his portraits, Philips Koninck's most lasting contributions to seventeenth-century Dutch painting were his naturalistic panoramic landscapes. Rejecting the imaginary landscape settings and architectural fantasies of his predecessors, Koninck, who lived all of his life in Amsterdam, excelled at bird's-eye views of vast expanses evocative of the Dutch countryside. Typically, his large paintings evenly balance the ground sloping away to the horizon with a sky filled with large, fleecy clouds. Depth in these extensive vistas is created with the aid of winding rivers and paths, buildings and trees that diminish in size, and Koninck's characteristic alternating strips of light and shadow. Human inhabitants in the landscape are insignificant before the vastness, serving only as an occasional narrative element or compositional foil to emphasize the expanses of unlimited space.

The unprecedented grandeur and the harmonious colors of Koninck's landscapes have been compared favorably with the contributions by Hercules Segers, Jacob van Ruisdael, and Rembrandt. Many of the motifs found in his three hundred drawings and eight etchings can be directly related to Rembrandt's work, but it is not clear how the association between the two men was defined. Prior to 1640, Koninck, who came from a family of artists and goldsmiths, studied with his brother Jacob in Rotterdam. After his return to Amsterdam, he pursued other occupational tracks, although his artistic work was widely appreciated. He continued, however, from the late 1640s until at least 1676, to produce his own unique landscapes, which stand as his contribution to seventeenth-century Dutch art.

Shana L. Stuart

See also Landscape; Rembrandt School; Rembrandt van Rijn; Van Ruisdael, Jacob

Bibliography

Broos, Ben et al. *Great Dutch Paintings from America*, 314–317. The Hague: Mauritshuis; Zwolle: Waanders, 1991.

Gerson, Horst. *Philips Koninck*. Berlin: Gebr. Mann, 1935.

Sutton, Peter et al. *Masters of Seventeenth-Century Dutch Landscape Painting*, 366–370. Boston: Museum of Fine Arts, 1987.

Koninck, Salomon (1609–1656)

An Amsterdam painter of history and genre scenes, the little-known Salomon Koninck, cousin of Philips Koninck, is traditionally associated with the school of Rembrandt, although he never formally studied with the master. Koninck became an ardent follower of Rembrandt in the 1630s, as evidenced by the formal qualities of the paintings he produced at this time. Koninck was sent to Amsterdam by his father, the Antwerp jeweler Peeter Coningh, to train under various painters, including David Colijn, Franchois Vernando, and Claes

Cornelisz. Moeyaert. Koninck joined the Painter's Guild in Amsterdam in 1630 after establishing himself as an independent painter following his apprenticeship with Moeyaert.

Although neglected by current scholarship, Salomon Koninck was recognized by his contemporaries as a significant artist. The Flemish notary and rhetorician Cornelis de Bie included a biography of Koninck in his 1661–1662 book, *Het Gulden Cabinet van der Edel Vry Schilderkonst* (The Golden Cabinet of the Noble Free Art of Painting). An updated assessment of Koninck's contribution to seventeenth-century Dutch painting should include an in-depth consideration of the overall stylistic evolution of the artist's work in addition to the influence asserted by Rembrandt. An even richer vein of inquiry lies in the subjects depicted by Koninck, including scenes from the Bible and ancient history, and single-figure compositions depicting gold weighers and scholars. Koninck's depictions of old men weighing gold have been interpreted as allegories of avarice, although further investigation is necessary to support or disprove such a conclusion. Additional scholarship should assess Koninck's general contribution to history painting in Amsterdam.

Steven Golan

See also History painting; Pre-Rembrandtists; Rembrandt School

Bibliography

Bie, Cornelis de. *Het Gulden Cabinet van de Edel Vry Schilderkonst.* 1661–1662. Reprint. Soest: Davaco, 1971.

Huys Janssen, Paul, and Sumowski, Werner. *The Hoogsteder Exhibition of Rembrandt's Academy.* The Hague: Hoogsteder and Hoogsteder, 1992.

Sumowski, Werner. *Gemälde der Rembrandt-Schüler.* Vol. 3. Landau, Pfalz: Edition PVA, 1983.

Koolhaas, Rem (born 1944)

"The image of the modern city, at least in the way it was foreseen, hasn't become a reality anywhere. The city we have to make do with today is more or less made of fragments of modernity. [It is] almost as if abstract formal or stylistic characteristics sometimes survived in the pure state, while the program's plan had been a flop." Thus Rem Koolhaas, one of the most brilliant personalities to appear on the international architectural scene in the last quarter of the twentieth century, advanced his criticism of the myth of the planned and orderly city in an interview conducted by the urban historian Bruno Fortier for the journal *L'Architecture d'aujourd'hui* 262 (1989), privileging the recognition of its fragmentation and the permanence, in this new chaos, of a web of "fragments of modernity" as the new reading of the urban environment itself.

A native of Rotterdam, Koolhaas spent part of his childhood in Indonesia. After a brief career as a journalist and scriptwriter, he studied architecture at the Architectural Association in London between 1968 and 1972. He transferred to the United States, thanks to a grant, and from 1973 to 1979 was a Visiting Fellow at the Institute for Architecture and Urban Studies in New York. He directed his research toward analyzing the impact of New York metropolitan culture on architecture. Together with Elia Zenghelis, he created his first theoretical plans of the city.

The drawings made for these plans are collected in his book *Delirious New York: A Retroactive Manifesto for Manhattan*, first published in 1978 and reprinted in 1994 to coincide with an exhibition of Koolhaas' designs at the Museum of Modern Art in New York. Koolhaas analyzed the architectural development of the island of Manhattan, introducing the idea of seeing it as a "Retroactive Manifesto." Starting with the ineffectiveness of so many of the cultural manifestos of the twentieth century, Koolhaas characterized the quality of the metropolitan environment as a built manifesto, produced from the heterogeneous sedimentation of real and fantasy plans, making a sort of a paradigm of the urban panorama of the end of the twentieth century. The drafting of the book, a collage that mixed together actual plans, comments, and allusions to the urban scene, exemplifies the typical planning method of Koolhaas: the reuse, after they have been extracted from the original context, of paradigmatic icons of modern architecture of this century, from the designs of the Soviet Contructivists to the functionalism of German and Dutch "new builders."

In 1975 Koolhaas founded in London, together with Elia and Zoé Zenghelis and Madelon Vriesendorp, the Office for Metropolitan Architecture (OMA), a professional group that turns its attention to both sides of the Atlantic, gravitating toward New York for theoretical research and toward Europe for professional work.

In 1978 Koolhaas, Elia Zenghelis, and Zaha Hadid shared first prize in the competition for the extension of the Dutch Parliament building in The Hague. The design became the first in a series of plans for the insertion of modern architecture into the complex context of historical European cities and made Koolhaas known in Holland. Therefore, in 1980 Koolhaas opened an office in Rotterdam, which became the principal seat of OMA. In the same year he received two important commissions for projects of an urban scope: the feasibility plan for the insertion of tall buildings on the Maas riverfront at Rotterdam (1980–1982), and the plan for the IJ-Plein quarter in north Amsterdam, within which the design of two residential blocks, a school, and a gymnasium were also assigned to OMA.

In successive years a consistent number of designs, widely published in the architectural press, has issued from OMA. Among the designs that have not been built, the following stand out: that for the Parc de la Villette in Paris (1982–1983; second-prize winner in an international competition), in which the green area is segmented into horizontal bands that create a rapidly changing atmosphere; the design for the city hall of The Hague (1986–1987), which simulated the silhouette of a little turreted city; and the design for Sea Trade Center at Zeebrugge (1989), in which an ovoid tower contained all of the public services for the ferry docking to England. In 1989 Koolhaas received important recognition for the design of paradigms of the modern city, presented at two international competitions: first prize in the competition for the Center for Art and Media Techniques at Karlsruhe, and special mention at the competition for the National Library of France in Paris. He encountered the same theme in later competitions for the Jussieu Library and the reorganization of the university campus in the Latin Quarter in Paris (1993; first prize shared with Jean Nouvel; the two designers have been asked to collaborate on elaborating a program for the execution for the work).

Among the built designs that are outstanding for their innovative quality are the mechanistical National Dance Theater in The Hague (1980–1987); the multifunctional Byzanthium in the center of Amsterdam (1985–1990), which contains residences, offices, shops, and a restaurant; the Villa Dall'Ava in Saint-Cloud, Paris (1985–1991); the residential complex Nexus World in Fukuoka, Japan (1991); the Kunsthal in Rotterdam (1990–1992; Fig. 70), which has galleries for changing exhibitions and an adjacent Museum Park, a green space connecting the various museums in the area; and the megastructure of Congrexpo at Lille (1991–1995).

To learn more about the architectural models that Koolhaas imagines for the future, to enter in depth into the concepts that he promotes as passwords—for example, the *tabula rasa* as a condition of the modern, or urbanism versus planning—to go beyond the etiquette and the too-popular deconstruction, the last word can be found in the monumental intellectual autobiographical work *S-M-L-XL (Small-Medium-Large-Extra Large)* that the architect published in 1995.

Maristella Casciato

See also Functionalism in architecture; Landscape architecture; Postmodernism; Rotterdam; Urban planning, from 1750 to the present

Bibliography

Dijk, Hans van. *Rem Koolhaas, Architect.* Rotterdam: 010, 1992.

Koolhaas, Rem. *Delirious New York: A Retroactive Manifesto for Manhattan.* New York: Oxford University Press, 1978. Reprint. New York: Monacelli Press, 1994.

Koolhaas, Rem, and Bruce Mair. *S-M-L-XL (Small-Medium-Large-Extra Large): Office for Metropolitan Architecture.* New York: Monacelli Press, 1995.

Lucan, Jacques, ed. *OMA—Rem Koolhaas: Architecture, 1970–1990.* New York: Princeton Architectural Press, 1991.

"Rem Koolhaas: Office for Metropolitan Architecture." Theme volume. *Architecture and Urbanism (A+U)* 217 (October 1988).

Zaera, Alejandro, ed. *Rem Koolhaas, OMA, 1987–1992.* El Croquis 53. Madrid: El Croquis Editorial, 1992.

Kramer, Pieter Lodewijk (Piet) (1881–1961)

Pieter Lodewijk Kramer belongs with Michel de Klerk (1884–1923) and J.M. van der Mey (1878–1949) to the first and most important group of architects of the Amsterdam School. All three worked in the architectural office of Eduard Cuypers

(1859–1927) and were involved in the building of the Scheepvaarthuis (Navigation House, 1912–1916; Fig. 4).

Kramer's first independently designed building was the Gebouw voor Minder Marinepersoneel (Building for Navy Enlisted Personnel) in Den Helder (1911–1913, destroyed in 1940), where already many elements of the Amsterdam School can be seen in rudimentary form. After 1911 Kramer worked in the Buildings and Bridges Section of the Public Works Service for the City of Amsterdam, first as an assistant to Van der Mey and, after 1919, in a more independent position. By order of the Buildings Section, Kramer worked with De Klerk on an apartment complex for the housing society De Dageraad (1919–1921) that is regarded as one of the most characteristic products of the Amsterdam School.

The approximately two hundred-twenty bridge designs that he carried out between 1917 and 1955 for the Bridges Section of the Service form the lion's share of Kramer's *oeuvre*. Most of them were brought about in cooperation with the engineer W.A. de Graaf, who took care of the construction, and the sculptor Hildo Krop. Kramer's bridges, with their application of sculpture and wrought iron and placment in the general urban scene, are a good example of the *Gesamtkunstwerk* (total work of art) ideal of the Amsterdam School. More so than other Amsterdam School architects, Kramer paid attention to the principal forms and the place of the individual building in the total municipal picture.

The *Gesamtkunstwerk* notion was also practiced by Kramer in interior design; especially during World War I and the years following, he designed complete establishments. The department store De Bijenkorf in The Hague (1925–1926) is the last important building by Kramer, and it is also the last genuinely total work of art of the Amsterdam School. Once he had developed his style, Kramer remained faithful to it his entire life, and, therefore, not many changes appear in his work.

Geraart Westerink

See also Amsterdam School; De Klerk, Michel; Krop, Hildo; Public housing; Toorop, Charley (Annie Caroline Pontifex); *Wendingen*

Bibliography

Boer, W.T. de, and P.J.H.P Evers. *Amsterdamse bruggen 1910–1950.* Amsterdam: Amsterdamse Raad voor de Stedebouw, 1983.

Nederlandse architectuur: Amsterdamse School, 1910–1930. Amsterdam: Stedelijk Museum Amsterdam, 1975. 2nd ed. Monografieën van de Stichting Architectuur Museum. Amsterdam: Van Gennep, 1979.

Retera, W. *Piet Kramer.* Vol. 2, *Nederlandsche Bouwmeesters.* Amsterdam: Van Munster, 1927.

Wit, Wim de, ed. *The Amsterdam School: Dutch Expressionist Architecture, 1915–1930.* Cambridge, MA: MIT Press, 1983.

Krausz, Simon Andreas (1760–1825)

Harbinger of a new generation of Romantic painters and draftsmen, Krausz developed a rough-hewn style that set him apart from the more formalist tradition of view painters and decorators who flourished around him in The Hague. From 1773 to 1774, he was a pupil of Leonard de France, a Belgian landscape, portrait, and history painter who had studied in Italy. In 1780 Krausz enrolled in the Akademie van Tekende Kunst (Drawing Academy) in The Hague, and in 1782 he was awarded a gold medal in the painters' confraternity, Pictura, by Prince Willem V. In 1785 he was listed as a master in Pictura. In 1786 he was married to Adriana Everdina Boers.

Because of his unconventional style of drawing, painting, and engraving, Krausz was given wide praise, including mention on a list published in 1806 as one of the most celebrated painters, draftsmen, and engravers in the Kingdom of Holland. He was a frequent exhibitor in The Hague, showing in 1811, 1817, 1821, and 1823. Krausz's drawings are more gestural and purposely crude than any other Dutch contemporary. In their supreme naturalism, they exude a strength and directness that anticipated artists such as Wouter Troostwijk (1782–1810), whom he outlived. Krausz's pupils were Hendrikus van de Sande Bakhuyzen (1795–1860) and F.L. Huygens (1802–1887).

Following Krausz's death, the contents of his studio were sold in The Hague; the inventory lists fifty-six paintings, almost none of which are known today. His drawings stayed together, and a number of them are in the Amsterdam Rijksprentenkabinet.

Roger Mandle

See also Amateurs, art academies, and art associations before the nineteenth century; Drawing clubs; Drawing practices and techniques

Bibliography

Bol, L.J. *Tekeningen van Simon Andreas Kraus 1760–1825.* Dordrecht: Dordrechts Museum, 1964.

Mandle, R. *Dutch Masterpieces from the Eighteenth Century: Paintings and Drawings, 1700–1800.* Minneapolis: Minneapolis Institute of Arts; Toledo: Toledo Museum of Art; Philadelphia: Philadelphia Museum of Art, 1971.

Niemeijer, J.W. *Eighteenth-Century Watercolors from the Rijksmuseum Printroom, Amsterdam.* Alexandria, VA: Art Services International, 1993.

Kröller-Müller, Hélène E.L.J. (1869–1939)

Through her collecting activities and role as patron of visual artists and architects, Mrs. Hélène E.L.J. Kröller-Müller made an important contribution to the development of the arts and the growth of public art collections in the Netherlands. Inspired by artist and art critic H.P. Bremmer (1871–1956) and having generous financial means available to her, she began to collect art systematically and autonomously around 1910. The point of departure was the interaction between realism and idealism (abstraction), to which she called attention.

The heart of the collection she created consists of a large number of works by Vincent van Gogh; other accents are on movements such as Neo-Impressionism, Symbolism, Cubism, and De Stijl, and on individual artists such as Georges Seurat, Odilon Redon, Bart van der Leck, and Juan Gris. A small collection of old masters serves as the basis. The collection is sometimes described as "Apollonian."

Under the personal motto "spirit and matter are one," Mrs. Kröller-Müller tried to achieve a unity between art, nature, and architecture. Architecture, particularly, served as a binding factor. Architects P. Behrens (1868–1940), L. Mies van der Rohe (1886–1969), H. van de Velde (1863–1957), and H.P. Berlage (1856–1934) served the family and firm. The center of the planned building activities lay on the wilderness lands of the private estate De Hoge Veluwe. Berlage, who was exclusively affiliated with the family firm from 1913 to 1919, built St. Hubert's hunting lodge on the estate (1915–1919). Berlage and Van de Velde both made plans for a museum to be built in this area that, because of the economic crisis, was never realized.

In 1935 the estate was put under the direction of a foundation. For the art collection legated to the state in that same year, Van de Velde built a temporary museum in 1938 that turned out to be permanent. It was expanded in 1977 with an annex designed by W.G. Quist. Under the director A.M. Hammacher, a sculpture garden was formed in 1961 that has been enlarged several times.

Geraart Westerink

See also Berlage, Hendrik Petrus; Hammacher, A.M.W.J.; Mendes da Costa, Joseph; State and municipal art collecting and collections; Symbolism, Symbolists; Van Gogh, Vincent

Bibliography

Deventer, S. van. *Kröller-Müller: De geschiedenis van een cultureel levenswerk.* Haarlem: Tjeenk Willink, 1956.

Kröller-Müller, Hélène E.L.J. *Die Entwicklung der modernen Malerei.* Leipzig: Klinkhardt and Biermann, 1925.

Oxenaar, R.W.D et al. *Kröller-Müller: Honderd jaar bouwen en verzamelen.* Haarlem: J. Enschedé, 1988.

Wolk, J. van der. *De Kröllers en hun architecten.* Otterlo: Rijksmuseum Kröller-Müller, 1992.

Kromhout, Willem (1864–1940)

Willem Kromhout was among the pioneers of modern Dutch architecture. The artistic conscience among Dutch architects, Kromhout spoke for architecture as an art. "Above all else an architect has to be an artist, meaning a sensitive human being" was Kromhout's basic attitude.

Kromhout established himself as an independent architect in Amsterdam in 1890. In the society Architectura et Amicitia, he turned out to be an advocate for emancipation of the architectural profession. A better education for architects was central in this. In 1908 his efforts resulted in the establishment of the Voortgezet en Hooger Bouwkunst Onderricht (Continued and Higher Architectural Instruction), the predecessor of the later academies of architecture.

Kromhout used Architectura et Amicitia—of which he was for years a board member and twice the chairman—as a

TACTVS

5 *Cornelis Drebbel fecit*   *Henr. Gol. inuen.* *Petrus Oaie: excud.*

Jllicito Cypriæ senſu moueâre caueto;   Sic tamen hæud fines Tactus tranſcendet honeſti,
Serpentis morſu nam magis ille nocet.   Si modus in reliquis senſibus aptus erit.

1. Cornelis Drebbel after Hendrick Goltzius. Tactus *(Touch), ca. 1586.*
Engraving. Rijksprentenkabinet/Rijksmuseum, Amsterdam.

AESTAS.

T. Ber. nei.

Longis procedit calidissima solibus Æstas,
  Fluctuat in grauido culmine Messis agro.

Nunc tempus pluustra ingemere, et componere nidos,
  Dum tellus proprios pandit amica sinus.

2. Johannes Sadeler after Dirck Barendsz. Aestas (Summer), ca. 1587.
Engraving. Rijksprentenkabinet/Rijksmuseum, Amsterdam.

3. *George Hendrik Breitner.* The Rokin in Amsterdam at Night, *ca. 1895.*
Oil on canvas, 80 cm. × 130 cm. Stedelijk Museum, Amsterdam.

4. J.M. van der Mey in collaboration with M. de Klerk and P.L. Kramer. The Scheepvaarthuis, *Amsterdam, 1912-1916. The tower corner on the Prins Hendrikkade and Binnenkant. Photograph ca. 1930. Collection Netherlands Architecture Institute, Rotterdam. (Photo: Retina.)*

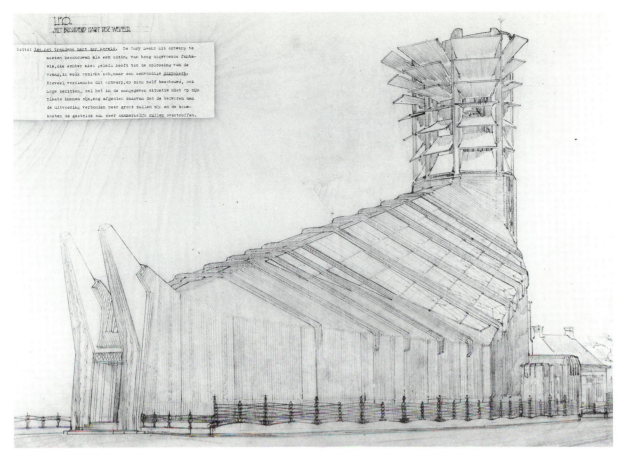

5. A. Eibink and J.A. Snellebrand. Competition design for a church in Elshout, 1915. Perspective. Collection Netherlands Architecture Institute, Rotterdam. (Photo: Retina.)

6. Emmy Andriesse. Saint-Rémy, for De Wereld van Van Gogh (Amsterdam, 1953). Silver gelatine print, 25.6 cm. × 23.7 cm. Prentenkabinet der Rijksuniversiteit, Leiden.

*7. Hendrik Petrus Berlage.
Dining Room (1890s) exhibited
at the First International Exhibition of Modern Decorative
Arts, Turin, Italy, 1902. Reproduced from* Dekorative Kunst
6, 1902/03, p. 42. *Courtesy of
the Library of the Technical
University, Delft.*

8. G. W. Dijsselhof. Dijsselhofkamer
(Interior with Furnishings), *ca.
1900. Collection Haags
Gemeentemuseum, The Hague.*

9. The Prinsenhof in Willemstad,
1623, partly destroyed in 1823.
(Photo: Rijksdienst voor de
Monumentenzorg, Zeist.)

10. The Prinsenhof in Willemstad,
after restoration in 1973 by
architect Jan Walraad.
(Photo: Rijksdienst voor de
Monumentenzorg, Zeist.)

11. Henk Meyer. Portrait of Cornelis Hofstede de Groot, *1923. Courtesy of the Groninger Museum, Groningen.*

12. *Jacob Adriaensz. Backer.* Granida and Daifilo, *ca. 1625. Oil on canvas, 8.9 cm. × 11.2 cm. Courtesy of the Museum Hannemahuis, Harlingen.*

13. Gerrit Berckheyde. The Market Place and Great Church of St. Bavo in Haarlem, *1674. Oil on canvas, 51.8 cm. × 67 cm. Reproduced by courtesy of the Trustees, The National Gallery, London.*

14. Job Berckheyde. The Baker, *ca. 1681. Oil on canvas, 63.5 cm. × 53 cm. Worcester Art Museum, Worcester, Massachusetts, Gift of Mr. and Mrs. Milton P. Higgins.*

15. *B.J. Blommers.* Where Are the Doves?, *ca. 1880s. Panel, 22 cm. × 16 cm. Mesdag Museum, The Hague.*

16. Title page to Jan van den Velde I, Spieghel der schrijfkonste *(1608 ed.). Engraving, approx. 21 cm. × 32 cm., by Jacob Matham, 1605, after design by Karel van Mander. Reproduced by courtesy of the Board of Trustees of the Victoria and Albert Museum, London.*

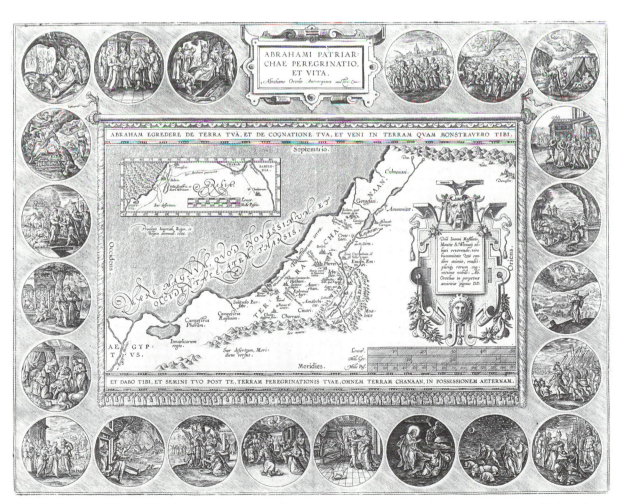

17. Abraham Ortelius. Abraham Patriarchae Peregrinatio et Vita *(Antwerp, 1586). Copperplate engraved map, 35 cm. × 45.5 cm., after designs by Maerten de Vos. Courtesy of the Library of Congress, Washington, D.C., Geography and Map Division.*

18. *Petrus Plancius*, Tabula Geographica, in qua Paradisus. . . . *(Amsterdam: Jan Evertsz. Cloppenborch, 1604).*
Copperplate engraving with watercolor, 29 cm. × 49.4 cm., by Baptista Doetecum after designs by David Vinckboons.
Bound with a Bible in the Koninklijke Bibliotheek, The Hague.

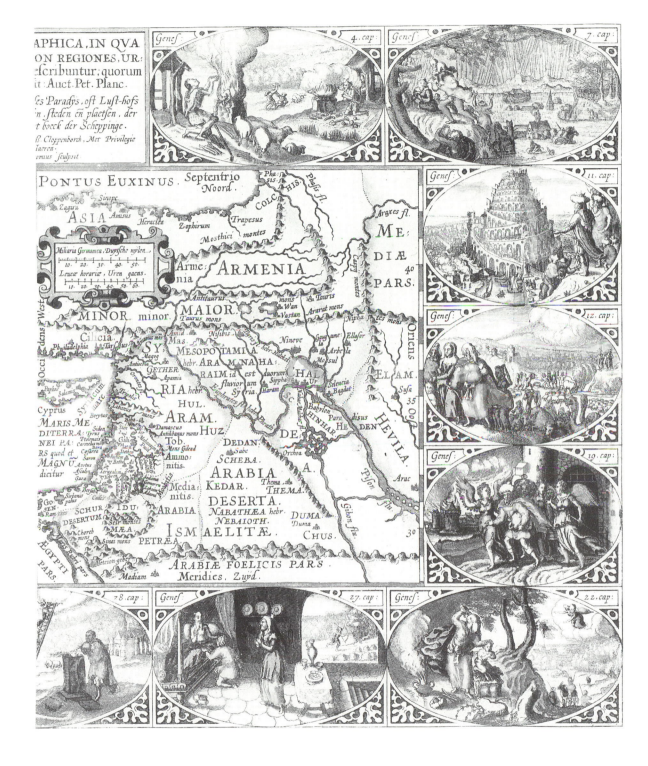

19. Delftware vase, fourth quarter of the seventeenth century. Collection Haags Gemeentemuseum, The Hague.

20. Cassolette, Loosdrecht, ca. 1780. Collection Haags Gemeentemuseum, The Hague.

21. *Theodoor A.C. Colenbrander. Four-part so-called "Day and Night" set, Rozenburg, 1885. Collection Haags Gemeentemuseum, The Hague.*

22. *Geert Lap. Bowl, 1980s. Collection Haags Gemeentemuseum, The Hague.*

23. Nineteenth-century local costumes worn by women from Vlaardingen and Maassluis. Reproduced from Valentijn Bing and J. Braet von Ueberfeldt, Nederlandsche Kleederdragten, naar natuur getekend (1857; reprint, Zutphen: Terra, 1978). Courtesy of the Netherlands Economic History Archive, Amsterdam.

24. Newspaper advertisements for women's lingerie, Vroom and Dreesmann Department Store. In the 1920s and 1930s, the advertisements that appeared in editions of the newspaper De Tijd *that were intended for the Catholic provinces of Brabant and Limburg showed the garments modified with sleeves and higher necklines. In other editions, the "immodest version" of the garments appeared. Reproduced courtesy of the Tilburg University Library.*

25. Constant. Barricade, *made especially for the Exposition Internationale d'Art Expérimentale, Stedelijk Museum, Amsterdam, November, 1949. Oil on canvas, 355 cm. × 283 cm. Stedelijk Museum, Amsterdam. Copyright © 1995 Constant/Licensed by VAGA, New York, NY.*

26. *Lucas van Leyden*. The Poet
Virgil Suspended in a Basket,
*1525. Engraving. National
Gallery of Art, Washington, D. C.,
Rosenwald Collection.*

27. *Jan van de Velde II*. Market
Scene, *1616. Engraving. Title
page to part 2 of a series of
Landscape prints published in
Amsterdam by Claes Jansz.
Visscher. Rijksprentenkabinet/
Rijksmuseum, Amsterdam.*

28. Gerrit Dou. A Poulterer's Shop, *ca. 1660-1665. Oil on panel. Reproduced by courtesy of the Trustees, The National Gallery, London.*

29. René Daniels. De revue passeren (Pass in Review), 1982. Oil on canvas, 130 cm. × 190 cm. Museum Boymans-van Beuningen, Rotterdam.

30. Fortuyn/O'Brien. Escargot, 1984. Wood, silk, color reproduction, goldleaf, oil paint, and lacquer, 165 cm. × 74 cm. × 109 cm. Stedelijk Museum, Amsterdam.

31. Pieter van Anraedt. Portrait of Jeremias van Collen and Susanna van Uffelen and Their Twelve Children in Front of Their Country House Velserbeek, *ca. 1661. Oil on canvas, 107 cm. × 155 cm. Rijksmuseum, Amsterdam.*

32. Gerard van Honthorst. Double Portrait of Frederik Hendrik and Amalia van Solms, *ca. 1637. Mauritshuis, The Hague.*

33. Hendrick de Keyser. Monument of Jacob van Heemskerk, 1609. Amsterdam, Oude Kerk. (Photo: Cynthia Lawrence.)

34. Hendrick de Keyser. Tomb Monument of Willem I of Orange, 1614-1621. Delft, Nieuwe Kerk. (Photo: Rijksdienst voor de Monumentenzorg, Zeist.)

35. Michel de Klerk. Housing project in the Spaarndammerbuurt. Third block near the Spaarndammerplantsoen on Zaanstraat, Oostzaanstraat, and Hembrugstraat, Amsterdam. Built for Eigen Haard, 1917-1921. View along Zaanstraat, photograph, ca. 1923. Collection Netherlands Architecture Institute, Rotterdam. (Photo: Retina.)

36. Michel de Klerk. Housing block on the Henriette Ronnerplein, Amsterdam South. Built for De Dageraad, 1921. Photograph, ca. 1930. Collection Netherlands Architecture Institute, Rotterdam. (Photo: Retina.)

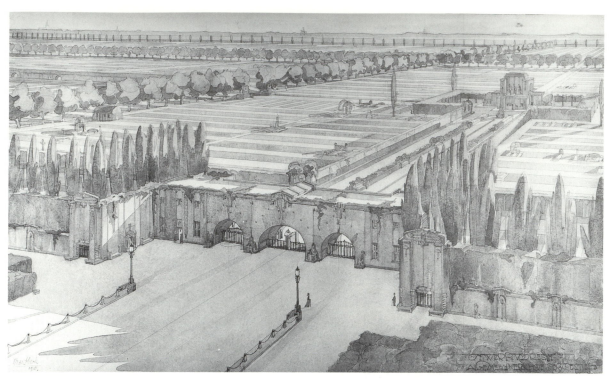

37. Michel de Klerk. Competition design for a cemetery with mortuary chapel, motto Reincarnatie *(Reincarnation),
1910. Bird's-eye view of the cemetery from the main entrance. Collection Netherlands Architecture Institute, Rotterdam.
(Photo: Retina.)*

*38. Vilmos Huszár. Design for
the cover of* De Stijl *1:1 (October
1917). (Photo: Frauke Syamken.
Courtesy of the Athenaeum
Publishers, Amsterdam.)*

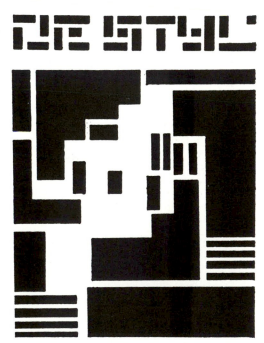

39. Gerrit Rietveld. Red and Blue Chair, *1918-1923. Stedelijk Museum, Amsterdam.*
Copyright © 1995 Estate of Gerrit Rietveld/Licensed by VAGA, New York, NY.

40. *Leonaert Bramer.* Soldiers
Resting, *1626. Collection
Bredius Museum, The Hague.*

41. *Carel Fabritius.* View of Delft with a Musical Instrument Seller's Stall, *1652.*
Reproduced by courtesy of the Trustees, The National Gallery, London.

42. Gerard Houchgeest. View of the Tomb of Willem I of Orange in the Nieuwe Kerk in Delft, *ca. 1650. Mauritshuis, The Hague.*

43. *Pieter de Hooch*. Courtyard of a House in Delft, *1658.*
Reproduced by courtesy of the Trustees, The National Gallery, London.

44. *C.M. Dewald*. Portrait of the Painter Jozef Israëls, *ca. 1904. Photogravure. Rijksprentenkabinet/ Rijksmuseum, Amsterdam.*

45. *Gerrit Dou*. Self-Portrait with Book and Pipe, *ca. 1647. Rijksmuseum, Amsterdam.*

46. Johannes Duiker. Open-Air School, *Amsterdam, 1927-1930. View from the courtyard entrance. (Photo: Collection NAI, Rotterdam.)*

47. Marlene Dumas. The Guilt of the Privileged, *1989. Oil on canvas, 110 cm. × 300 cm. Gemeentemuseum, Arnhem. Reproduced courtesy of the artist.*

48. J.A. Brinkman, L.C. van der Vlugt, and W. van Tijen. Bergpolder Flats, Rotterdam, 1933-1934. Photograph, ca. 1940. (Photo: Collection NAI, Rotterdam.)

49. J.A. Brinkman and L.C. van der Vlugt. Van Nelle Factory, Rotterdam, 1926-1930. View of the main façade. (Photo: Collection NAI, Rotterdam.)

50. Jan Weenix. Still Life with a Dead Hare, *1682. Staatliche Kunsthalle, Karlsruhe.*

51. *Willem van Mieris.* A Poulterer's Shop, *1714. Oil on panel, 42.5 cm. × 37.5 cm.*
Rijksdienst Beeldende Kunst, The Hague.

52. *Jan Ekels, the Younger.* A Writer Sharpening His Pen, *1784.*
Oil on panel, 27.5 cm. × 23.5 cm. Rijksmuseum, Amsterdam.

53. *Hendrick Goltzius.* Venus Receiving the Gifts of Bacchus and Ceres, *ca. 1599-1602.*
Mixed media on linen, 106.09 cm. × 80.77 cm. Philadelphia Museum of Art.

54. *Jozef Israëls*. Alone in the World, *ca. 1881. Oil on canvas,*
125 cm. × 200 cm. Museum Mesdag, The Hague.

55. *Jacob Maris.* Slatuintjes bij Den Haag *(Allotments near The Hague), ca. 1878.*
Oil on canvas, 62.5 cm. × 54 cm. Collection Haags Gemeentemuseum, The Hague.

56. *Willem Maris.* Four Cows Drinking from a Canal, *ca. 1885.*
Oil on canvas. Collection Haags Gemeentemuseum, The Hague.

57. *Jan Hendrik Weissenbruch*. Beach Scene, *1887. Oil on canvas.*
Collection Haags Gemeentemuseum, The Hague.

58. *Willem Roelofs*. Polder Landscape near Abcoude, *ca. 1865-1870. Oil on canvas.*
Collection Haags Gemeentemuseum, The Hague.

59. Frans Hals. Marriage Portrait of Isaac Abrahamsz. Massa (1586–1643) and Beatrix van der Laen (1592–1639), *ca. 1622.*
Oil on canvas. 140 cm. × 166.5 cm. Rijksmuseum, Amsterdam.

60. Herman Hertzberger. Head
Office of the Centraal Beheer
Insurance Company, Apeldoorn,
1967–1972. View of the interior,
ca. 1992. (Photo: Collection F.
Panzini, Rome.)

61. R.H. Herwig. View of the Limburg Village of Waelwylre, ca. 1900.
Modern print from original negative. Nederlands Openluchtmuseum, Arnhem.

62. Geertgen tot Sint Jans. Julian the Apostate Ordering the Burning of the Bones of St. John the Baptist, *ca. 1490.*
Kunsthistorisches Museum, Vienna.

63. Lucas van Leyden. Ecce Homo, *1510. Engraving. Kupferstichkabinett,
Staatliche Museen zu Berlin PK. (Photo: Jörg P. Anders.)*

64. Hendrick Goltzius. Venus and Adonis, *1614.*
Oil on canvas, 141 cm. × 191 cm. Alte Pinakothek, Munich.

Fama

Alex. Magnus

M.I.   C·Iuli·Cesar   4   Plato   Cato

PRÆPETIBVS PENNIS CAPVT INTER NVBILA CONDIT   MARMARICA INMANI QVAM CORPORE BELLVA DVCIT
FAMA LOQVAX, ACRIQVE TVBA LATE OMNIA COMPLET.   HAC VIVVNT VATES, ATQVE INCLITA CORPORA BELLO.

65. *Philips Galle after Maerten van Heemskerck.* The Triumph of Fame, *ca. 1565.*
Engraving. Rijksprentenkabinet/Rijksmuseum, Amsterdam.

66. Cornelis Troost. Rumor Erat in Casa *(There Was a Commotion in the House), 1740.*
Pastel, 56.5 cm. × 72.5 cm. Mauritshuis, The Hague.

67. Jan van Scorel. The Baptism of Christ, *1527-1529. Oil on panel, 121 cm. × 156.5 cm.*
Frans Hals Museum, Haarlem. (Photo: Tom Haartsen Studio, Oudekerk aan de Amstel.)

68. *Abraham Bloemaert.* The Supper at Emmaus, *1622. Panel. 145 cm. × 215.5 cm.*
Musées Royaux des Beaux-Arts de Belgique, Brussels.

69. *Pyke Koch*. Vrouwen in de Straat *(Women in the Street), 1962-1964. Oil on canvas, 115.5 cm. × 150 cm. Gemeentemuseum, Arnhem. (Photo: Gemeentearchief, Arnhem.)*

*70. Rem Koolhaas. Kunsthal,
Rotterdam, 1990-1992. View of
the entrance from the Museum
Park, ca. 1992. (Photo: Collection F. Panzini, Rome.)*

*71. Willem Kromhout. De
Noordzee Shipping Office,
Rotterdam, 1916-1919.
Destroyed 1940. Collection
Netherlands Architecture
Institute, Rotterdam.
(Photo: Retina.)*

72. J. Hoynck van Papendrecht. Anton Mauve in Laren, Painting in the Open Air, *1887.*
Drawing. Collection Haags Gemeentemuseum, The Hague.

73. Jan Provost, The Last Judgment with Isabel de Malefiance, *1506.*
Institut Royal du Patrimoine Artistique, Brussels. (Photo: Copyright A.C.L. Brussels.)

74. Lieven de Key. Town Hall, Leiden. 1593-1598. (Photo: Jeremy Bangs.)

75. *Judith Leyster. Self-Portrait, ca. 1630. Oil on canvas. National Gallery of Art, Washington, D.C. Gift of Mr. and Mrs. Robert Woods Bliss.*

76. Pieter Lastman. Paul and Barnabas at Lystra, *1614.*
Formerly Warsaw. (Photo: Muzeum Narodowe, Warsaw.)

77. Maerten van Heemskerck. Concert of Apollo and the Muses on Mount Helicon, *1565. Oil on panel, 103.5 cm. × 130.2 cm.*
The Chrysler Museum, Norfolk, Virginia, Gift of Walter P. Chrysler, Jr.

En van spele of tijtverdrijf der here of d'
vrouwen, daer men nochtan goede exem
pele bi mach verstaen ende leren.

At
mee
de
qua
et dat
een
heer
aen
hem
heb
ben
ma
ch is
als
hi go
des
niet

en ... ontziet, ende voir den menschen
hem niet en scaemt, voir gode zond' vrese
zondighet, en stoert die menschen mit on
daet van ongherechtighen leven, welke hen

78. *The Master of Dirc van Delf. King and Queen Playing Chess. From* Tafel van den Kersten Ghelove, *ca. 1400–1410.*
The Pierpont Morgan Library, New York, MS M. 691, f.131 v.

79. *The Master of Catherine of Cleves.* The Holy Family at Supper. *From* The Hours of Catherine of Cleves, *ca. 1440.*
The Pierpont Morgan Library, New York, MS M. 917, p. 151.

80. Hendrick Cornelisz. Vroom. The Return to Amsterdam of the Second Exhibition to the East Indies on July 19, 1599, *ca. 1600-1625.*
Oil on canvas, 110 cm. × 220 cm. Rijksmuseum, Amsterdam.

81. *Anton Mauve.* Bij Vries *(At Vries), ca. 1882. Canvas on panel. Mesdag Museum, The Hague.*

82. *Joseph Mendes da Costa.*
Monument to Christiaan de
Wet *in De Hoge Veluwe Na-
tional Park, 1922. Freestone,
H. 13 m. Kröller-Müller
Museum, Otterlo.*

83. *Joseph Mendes da Costa.*
Vincent van Gogh, *1908.*
*Bronze, H. 38 cm. Kröller-
Müller Museum, Otterlo.*

podium for his ideas about the question being asked by architects around the turn of the century: In what style should we build? In order to answer definitively within stylistic pluralism, the architect in 1891 in his lecture *Tout à l'égout* (All in the sewer) proposed running the repertory of historical styles through the sewer. As the head teacher of architecture at the Academy of Fine Arts and Technical Sciences in Rotterdam (1910–1915), Kromhout put his words into deeds by relegating the classical orders to the waste pile.

Kromhout would find a broadening of form possibilities in Eastern architecture, discovering in this his own strong tendency to the decorative. He could not, like his contemporary H.P. Berlage, find in rationalism the starting point for a new architectonic style. According to Kromhout, architecture was equal to "the modeling of cubic mass," in which brick served as the basic material. Given this starting point, he is often seen as the initiator of the Expressionism of the Amsterdam School.

Kromhout has gone down in history as the architect of the American Hotel (1902) in Amsterdam. After this building, the details of which show a strong relationship to Eastern architecture, he had still to create the major part of his *oeuvre*. Most of his work would be built in Rotterdam, where he was appointed head teacher of architecture in 1910. During his Rotterdam years, Kromhout became known as the architect of office buildings and villas for shipowners in that city. His much-discussed competition design for the Rotterdam Town Hall and an urban development design, the Blijdorp plan, remained unrealized. The shipping office of De Noordzee (Fig. 71) and the grand-café-restaurant Pschorr fell victim to German bombings in May 1940. Still surviving in Rotterdam are Kromhout's designs for the premises of the shipping union Scheepvaartvereeniging-Zuid, the printing office of Wyt and Sons, the trading firm Diepeveen and Company, the Diepeveen villa, and several residences in the Rotterdam neighborhood of Kralingen.

Ida Jager

See also Amsterdam School; Architectural criticism, issues of style; Berlage, Hendrik Petrus; Functionalism in architecture; Rotterdam

Bibliography

Bock, Manfred. *Anfänge einer neuen Architektur: Berlages Beitrag zur architektonischen kultur der Niederlande im ausgehenden 19. Jahrhundert.* Cahiers van het Nederlands Documentatiecentrum voor de Bouwkunst. Vol. 3. The Hague: Staatsuitgeverij; Wiesbaden: Steiner, 1983.

———. *Architectura, Nederlandse architectuur 1893–1918.* Amsterdam, Stedelijk Museum; Amsterdam: Van Gennep, 1975.

Jager, Ida. *Willem Kromhout Czn.* Rotterdam: 010, 1992.

Nederland bouwt in baksteen, 1800–1940. Rotterdam: Van Waesberge, Hoogewerff, and Richards, 1941.

Retera, W. *Willem Kromhout Czn.* Amsterdam: Van Munster, 1925.

Krop, Hildo (1884–1970)

The sculptor Hildebrand Lucien ("Hildo") Krop was a baker's son, born in Steenwijk, who was originally trained to be a baker. In 1907 he decided to apply himself fully to art and left for Paris, where he took lessons at the Académie Julian. Back in the Netherlands, he went to the Rijksacademie in Amsterdam (1908–1911), where he received instruction from Bart van Hove. In 1911 Krop won the silver medal in competition for the Prix de Rome; afterward he enrolled in the Kunstgewerbeschule (School of Applied Arts) in Berlin (1911–1912) and studied with Georg Kolbe. After a short stay in Rome, he left for Paris, where he most probably worked at the academy La Grande Chaumière, where Antoine Bourdelle was teaching. In Paris he also got to know Cubist sculptor Ossip Zadkine. Back in Amsterdam in 1914, Krop became the assistant of H.A. van den Eijnde in the execution of the sculpture for the Scheepvaarthuis (Fig. 4), designed by J.M. van der Mey, one of the most important architects of the Amsterdam School. Two years later he began working for the city of Amsterdam, which would remain his employer until his death. He made sculptures for a great many of the city's bridges and buildings (among them is the new wing of the Amsterdam Town Hall, 1922–1926) in his characteristic angular, Expressionistic style. He also made sculptures for several buildings in other cities, among them the department store De Bijenkorf in The Hague (1925).

Krop also produced seven grave monuments and about twenty public statues and memorials: Among these are reliefs for the *Belgian Monument* in Amersfoort (1917); the *Monument on the Afsluitdijk* (1933–1935); war monuments in Steenwijk (1946–1947), Amsterdam (in the Nieuwe Oosterbegraafplaats [New Eastern Cemetery], 1946–1948), and Kampen (1947–1948); and the statue of *H.P. Berlage* in Amsterdam (1956–1966). In addition, Krop made medallions and small three-dimensional works in several materials. He worked in ceramics: Around 1920 he was doing designing work for the ESKAF (Eerste Steenwijkse Kunst Aardewerk Fabriek/First Steenwijk Art Pottery Factory); later he made ceramics in his own kiln. He also made designs for furniture and interiors.

His work can be found in the Amsterdam Historical Museum and Stedelijk Museum in Amsterdam, in the Rijksmuseum Kröller-Müller in Otterlo, the Museum Boymans-van Beuningen in Rotterdam, and the Centraal Museum in Utrecht.

Mieke van der Wal

See also Amsterdam School; Public monumental sculpture (1795–1990); Sculpture (1795–1945); Van den Eijnde, Hendrik Albertus; Van Hove, Bart

Bibliography

Folkersma, E.W. "Hildo Krop en de Gemeente Amsterdam." In *Monumentale beeldhouwkunst in Nederland.* Edited by R.W.A. Bionda et al., 227–278. Weesp: Fibula-Van Dishoeck, 1984. (English summary.)

Lagerweij-Polak, E.J. *Hildo Krop: Beeldhouwer.* The Hague: SDU Uitgeverij Koninginnegracht; Amsterdam: Openbaar Kunstbezit, 1992. (English summary.)

Kruseman, Cornelis (1797–1857)

Cornelis Kruseman was trained by the portrait painters Ch. Hodges and J.A. Daiwaille in Amsterdam. Kruseman continued painting portraits, supplementing them with Italianate folk scenes, biblical subjects, and some history pieces. He painted in a very finished monumental academic style. In 1821 he made a study trip to Paris and Rome. He remained in Italy for four years, until 1825, returning to live there again from 1841 until 1848. In between he lived in the Netherlands, in The Hague and, after 1854, in Lisse. The notes that Kruseman made during his first trip to Italy were published in The Hague in 1826, followed by a German translation in Emden in 1831. Kruseman had many students, among whom were his cousin J.A. Kruseman and A.H. Bakker Korff.

Alexandra W.M. van Smoorenburg

See also Bakker Korff, Alexander Hugo

Bibliography

Knoef, J. *Van Romantiek tot realisme*, 13–40. The Hague: Stols, 1947.

Kruyder, Herman J. (1881–1935)

Originally a house painter, Herman Kruyder lived until 1898 in Baarn, where he received drawing lessons from H.C. van Dapperen (1863–1945). He was a student at the School of Arts and Crafts in Haarlem from 1899 until 1904. From 1904 to 1906 he was employed in the glass-painting business of the engineer J.H. Schouten in Delft. After that it was back to Haarlem, where he started to develop his true artistry. Until 1913 Kruyder's works were Impressionistic; later he experimented with Cubism and Expressionism in works such as *Paradijs I* (1913) and *Paradijs II* (1918). He made many watercolors during this period—still lifes, flowers, and a few landscapes—and created touching documentary drawings of the war. After his marriage in 1916, he settled in Heemstede. His first solo exhibition was in 1918 with J.H. de Bois in Haarlem. After 1922 he lived in Bennebroek, where he developed his own painting style with rich colors, as seen in well-known works like *De Brief* (The Letter, 1923–1927) and *De Varkensdoder* (The Pig Killer, 1926). His drawings and studies are remarkable for the large formats and the variations in technique.

In the beginning of 1926 he was hospitalized for psychiatric problems. After his release he made trips to Bruges, Houthem St. Gerlach (Limbourg), and Putten. From 1927 to 1934 he lived in Blaricum and painted Expressionistic works: *De Wagenmaker* (The Wagonmaker, 1932), *De Haan* (The Rooster, 1933) and *De Hond* (The Dog, 1934). The triptych *Pan* or *Lente* (Spring, 1933–1934), an ode to the senses, is more lyrical in character. At the end of 1934 Kruyder moved to Amsterdam. He was admitted to a psychiatric institution a short time later and died there in 1935. In addition to his paintings and drawings, he made sculpture and designed interiors.

John Steen

See also Avant-garde

Bibliography

Gruyter, W.J. de. "The Worlds of Herman Kruyder." *Delta* (Summer 1958): 18–25.
Kok, Arjen. *Herman Kruyder.* Zwolle: Waanders. 1996.
Reyne, P.C.J. *Herman Kruyder.* Amsterdam: Meulenhoff, 1963.

L

La Fargue, Paulus Constantijn (1729–1782)

Paulus Constantijn was the most talented and the most productive member of the La Fargue family of artists from The Hague; there were four brothers and one sister. Probably entirely self-taught, he applied himself at first to the making of *kamerbehangsels* (painted wall hangings), some of them commissioned by The Hague art dealer Gerard Hoet. Soon, however, he specialized in painting, drawing, and etching townscapes and landscapes with topographical elements. The sketches he made on site formed the source material on which he and his younger brothers Jacob Elias and Karel based their more elaborate paintings and drawings, sometimes after an interim of more than ten years. La Fargue's topographical work from the 1760s brought Rotterdam into the picture as well as The Hague. During the 1770s views in and around Delft, Leiden, Haarlem, and Amsterdam were added. While his paintings—mostly in a relatively small format and obviously influenced by seventeenth-century painters such as Jan van der Heyden—are rather static, his much more spontaneous drawings show greater originality. La Fargue's depictions are fairly reliable in a topographical sense, lively in color, and filled with charming little figures that create variety. In addition to townscapes, he is known to have represented actual events, portraits, and genre scenes. He also illustrated several almanacs and books. Even though this artist could count such important people as the French and English ambassadors among his patrons at the beginning of his career, his life was not easy, and he, his brothers, and sister were continually troubled by financial problems. La Fargue, who belongs to the group of better topographical artists of the second half of the eighteenth century, nevertheless derives his significance chiefly from the documentary value of his work.

Charles Dumas

See also Architectural painting; Display; Leiden; Prints, printmaking, and printmakers (ca. 1500–ca. 1900); Townscapes; Van der Heyden, Jan

Bibliography

Dumas, Charles. *Haagse stadsgezichten 1550–1800: Topografische schilderijen van het Haags Historisch Museum*, 429–492. Zwolle: Waanders, 1991.
———. *Het verheerlijkt Den Haag: Achttiende-eeuwse aquarellen en tekeningen door de familie La Fargue en haar tijdgenoten*. The Hague: Nijgh and Van Ditmar, 1984. (English summary.)

Landscape

In the seventeenth century the Netherlands produced an enormous variety of landscape subjects and styles. Dutch painters turned their attention to familiar surroundings, notably their rivers and native towns, as well as to more exotic locales that Dutch travelers encountered: the Rhine, Scandinavia, Italy, the Mediterranean, and even Brazil. Rivers, beaches, forests, mountains, castles, ruins, cities, farms, and roads were all commonly depicted. Painterly renderings of local scenery in monochromatic tones were produced at the same time as highly finished, brightly colored views of foreign places. Furthermore, landscape pictures were by far the most common, and least expensive, genre of painting in the seventeenth century. Explanations for such popularity can be sought in contemporary poetry and literature, which shows a moderate but by no means unusual interest in nature as a theme, or in the sense of national pride that arose in the new Dutch Republic.

Origins

The art of landscape in the United Provinces has its roots almost entirely in sixteenth-century Flanders since there had been few landscapists active in the North Netherlands in the 1500s. Pieter Bruegel the Elder established many subjects as well as compositional schemes, while his observational drawings also influenced later artists. The Revolt of the Netherlands starting in 1568 led to the flight of numerous artists from war-ravaged Antwerp. One of the most influential Flemish landscape painters to settle in Holland was Hans Bol (1534–1593). His carefully detailed, straightforward panoramas, usually depicting Antwerp, must be regarded as the very beginnings of Dutch landscape painting, although most of these were executed in Flanders. The wide vista, the slightly elevated viewpoint, and the subject of a familiar city would be prototypes for landscapes of the 1600s. Another emigrant from Flanders, the painter and writer Karel van Mander (1548–1606), brought with him a finely honed Mannerist style. Abraham Bloemaert (1564–1651) and his sons made large numbers of drawings and prints that employ international Mannerist devices. Most of Bloemaert's landscape paintings date from late in his career and seem anachronistic. Gillis van Coninxloo (1544–1607), influenced by the work of Jan Bruegel the Elder, concentrated on dense forest interiors. These highly finished renderings of dense thickets of trees inspired artists such as Roelandt Savery (1576/1578–1639), David Vinckboons (1576–ca. 1632), and Alexander Keirincx (1600–1652).

Sources of a New Naturalism

The legacy of Flemish sixteenth-century art was felt in other ways, particularly through the prints and drawings produced in Pieter Bruegel's circle. Bruegel's observational impulse was fully captured by Hendrick Goltzius' two drawings of 1603 depicting panoramas near Haarlem, but these sheets cannot have had much influence and are themselves unusual in the *oeuvre* of the artist. By 1607, Claes Jansz. Visscher (1587–1652) was producing refreshingly straightforward and simple drawings of the scenery around Haarlem. These were inspired directly by two series of prints made in 1559 and 1561 by Hieronymus Cock (after designs by the Master of the Small Landscapes), which Visscher himself reissued. Such simple, unpretentious views of villages and roads around Antwerp inspired generations of Dutch landscapists. Visscher made his own series of prints showing similar views, and Esaias van de Velde (1587–1630), Willem Buytewech (1591/1592–1624), and Jan van de Velde (1593–1641) soon followed with atmospheric drawings and prints. Esaias van de Velde also painted landscapes, including unembellished views of roads, village, and rivers.

In the early decades of the 1600s, a variety of specialists made innovative contributions to landscape painting. Many of the naturalistic techniques employed by Dutch landscapists had their roots in marine painting, in particular the work of Hendrick Vroom (1566–1640), whose attention to the effects of light and weather as well as to perspective had great resonance (Fig. 80). Vroom's depictions of important battles, state ceremonies, and city profiles greatly affected the development of landscape and cityscape. Painters of winter landscapes such as Hendrick Avercamp (1585–1635) and Adriaen van de Venne (1589–1662) were early practitioners of devices such as the low horizon and the wide panorama.

Esaias van de Velde's refreshingly straightforward views of the Dutch countryside greatly influenced a group of slightly younger painters, in particular the enormously prolific Jan van Goyen (1596–1656). Van Goyen began to favor quick, broken brushwork as well as a restrained monochromatic palette of browns, greens, and grays. Such paintings must have been produced relatively quickly; they sold for small sums in the seventeenth century. Only at the end of his life did he receive an important commission from the government of The Hague to paint a panorama of the town. Van Goyen's favorite subjects, such as roads, rivers, fields, beaches, and panoramas (Color Plate 6), were shared by the other "tonal" landscape painters, Pieter de Molijn (1595–1661), Pieter van Santvoort (1604/1605–1635), and Salomon van Ruysdael (1600/1603–1670). Van Santvoort's country landscapes are often broken by dramatic light and atmospheric effects, while Salomon van Ruysdael's later work becomes considerably brighter and more intense.

At the same time, Esaias van de Velde also inspired artists who preferred more saturated palettes and precisely painted forms. In particular, Cornelis Vroom (ca. 1591–1661) paid greater attention to trees, ruins, and compositional variety. Pieter Post (1608–1669) painted a few landscapes of remarkable intensity, but it was his brother Frans Post (ca. 1612–1680) who, after a trip to Brazil, made a name for himself as a landscape painter. His paintings made in Brazil have a startling freshness, while his more contrived later compositions done in Amsterdam had tremendous popular appeal.

Italian Views

It would be a mistake to assume that there was a characteristic Dutch landscape style or even mainstream subject matter given the immense variety of landscape types in the first half of the 1600s. Views of Italy were also very common in Holland and have a source in sixteenth-century Netherlandish painting. Paul Bril (1554–1626), a Fleming who had settled in Rome in the 1570s, had a profound influence on numerous Dutch landscape artists who ventured to Italy. Among the earliest painters from Holland to go to Rome in the 1600s were Jacob Pynas (ca. 1585–ca. 1656), Jan Pynas (1583/1584–1631), and Pieter Lastman (ca. 1584–1633), all of whom occasionally produced landscapes under the influence of Bril and Adam Elsheimer. The fresh drawings that Gerard Ter Borch the Elder (1584–1662) made in Rome anticipate the nature studies that Cornelis van Poelenburch (1594/1595–1667) and Bartholomeus Breenbergh (1598–1657) made in the same city. Van Poelenburch and Breenbergh, after returning to Holland, became highly successful history painters, integrating biblical and mythological staffage into luminous landscape settings. Indeed, the work of artists such as Bloemaert, Lastman, Van Poelenburch, and Breenbergh, as well Moyses van Wtenbrouck (ca. 1590–ca. 1647), who was influenced by both Van Poelenburch and Elsheimer, challenges the traditional division between figural and landscape painting, especially since they all appear to have commanded high prices and prestigious commissions because of their abilities in both genres.

Pieter van Laer (1592/1595–1642) became known in Rome as *Bamboccio* for his naive depictions of street life in that city, but many landscape painters took up the low-life figural imagery and the Roman atmosphere of Van Laer. Painters such as Herman van Swanevelt (ca. 1600–1655), Jan Both (ca. 1615–1652), Jan Asselijn (ca. 1615–1652), and Jan

Baptist Weenix (1621–1660/1661) worked in Rome at the same time as Claude Lorrain, the French painter of idyllic landscapes, and to a certain extent influenced each other. They also shared many of the same international clients. Van Swanevelt, Both, and Asselijn began as depicters of the Roman scene but quickly moved to the idealized scenery of the Italian countryside. After his return to the Netherlands, Jan Both influenced numerous other painters of Italianate landscapes, including Nicolaes (Claes) Berchem, Aelbert Cuyp, and Adam Pijnacker (ca. 1620–1673). Berchem (1620–1683) was a popular painter; his themes range from elegant hunting scenes to simple itinerant peasants and battle scenes, all set in misty countryside strongly reminiscent of Italy. Karel du Jardin's work includes glistening landscapes as well as highly refined Neoclassical figures set in equally academic settings.

Segers and Rembrandt

Rembrandt (1606–1669) produced a large number of drawings made in the outskirts of Amsterdam, as well as landscape prints and paintings. The paintings, mostly from the 1630s, are dramas of light and shadow, dependent on the mountainous landscapes of Hercules Segers (1589/1590–ca. 1633/1638). Rembrandt's pupils and followers also painted landscapes, principally Govaert Flinck (1615–1660), Philips Koninck (1619–1688), Roeland Roghman (1627–1692), and Gerbrand van den Eeckhout (1621–1674). Koninck specialized in large-scale, expansive panoramas, which are only rarely related to specific topographic motifs.

The principal successor to Jan van Goyen and Salomon van Ruysdael is Jacob van Ruisdael (1628/1629–1682), nephew of Salomon. Initially Van Ruisdael painted the simple farms and roads favored by earlier artists, but he soon turned his attentions to more dramatic landscape scenery, in large part influenced by the Scandinavian views done by Allart van Everdingen (1621–1675). Rugged mountains, waterfalls, and dense forests mark a departure from the familiar flat surroundings of Van Goyen, although such dramatic subjects recall earlier landscapes of the sixteenth century. More important perhaps, Van Ruisdael's paintings are filled with dark clouds, dramatic bursts of light, and a somber mood. Some works, such as *The Jewish Cemetery*, represent wholly new subjects in landscape painting and invite a symbolic or moralizing reading of Van Ruisdael's work. Meindert Hobbema (1638–1709) was Van Ruisdael's principal pupil. His landscapes are calmer and more peaceful and often show clearings or houses glimpsed through screens of trees. The term "classical" has sometimes been applied to the landscapes of Van Ruisdael, Hobbema, and Cuyp because of their bold, dramatic compositions, which often focus on a single landscape element, as well as strong contrasts of light and shade that appear to tie them to the international Baroque.

Landscape Painting at Mid-Century

In the middle of the seventeenth century, many landscape painters combined various trends in Dutch landscape painting, drawing equally from the "native" tradition of Van Goyen and Van Ruysdael and from the Italianate painters. The early landscapes of Herman Saftleven (1609–1685) are more Italianate tonally, while his later views of the Rhine valley, which proved extremely influential, combine Northern scenery with warm Italian light. The pictures of Aelbert Cuyp (1620–1691) also reveal a wide range of influences. Jan van Goyen's painterly landscapes were at first Cuyp's model, but later Jan Both formed his principal source. Cuyp sketched the Dutch landscape extensively; his paintings of Dordrecht, Nijmegen, and the Rhine valley are suffused with the golden afternoon sunlight of Jan Both. A parallel synthesis was achieved by Philips Wouwerman (1619–1668), although his precise sources are less clear. At first influenced by Van Laer, Wouwerman landscapes display an expansive silvery light, which probably has an Italianate source. The sandy roads and fallen trees painted by Jan Wijnants (1631/1632–1684) were inspired by Jacob van Ruisdael as well as by Wouwerman. Like Cuyp and Wouwerman, Adriaen van de Velde (1636–1672) and Paulus Potter (1625–1654) were strongly affected by the popular Italianate landscapes but managed to create a personal style. Potter's paintings of cattle and other farm animals, paralleled by some works of Cuyp, allude to political and literary associations of such animals.

Landscape painting increasingly encompassed a variety of forms and genres. Marine artists such as Simon de Vlieger and Jan van de Cappelle occasionally painted coasts, harbors, and beaches. City views, long a popular theme in the Netherlandish prints and drawings, arose as a distinct category of painting. Van Goyen, Van Ruisdael, Cuyp, and Johannes Vermeer (1632–1675) painted profiles of their native towns (Fig. 145), while Jan van der Heyden (1637–1712) and Gerrit Berckheyde (1638–1698) began to specialize in closer-up views of the buildings and public spaces of the Dutch cities (Fig. 13).

The end of the seventeenth century is remarkable for a shift in taste that came to favor more academic and classical landscapes, often employed as settings for mythological or historical subjects. Italianate landscapes increased greatly in popularity and prestige; the works of Jan Hackaert (1628–after 1685), Frederick de Moucheron (1633–1686), and Isaac de Moucheron (1667–1744) show increasing refinement and attention to upper-class subjects. The influence of Poussin and Gaspar Dughet from France, encouraged by the paintings and writings of Gerard de Lairesse, begins to be felt, especially in the landscapes of Albert Meyeringh (1645–1714), Johannes Glauber (1646–1726), and Jacob de Heusch (1656–1701). Gaspar van Wittel (1652–1736) took up residence in Rome and specialized in painting topographical views, introducing a landscape genre that would dominate eighteenth-century Italian landscape.

Reading Landscapes

Dutch landscape paintings are rarely solely about landscape elements. The figural elements provide a key to understanding the places depicted. Many landscape painters, such as Abraham Bloemaert, Cornelis van Poelenburch, Bartholomeus Breenbergh, and Karel du Jardin, devoted themselves equally if not more to figural paintings. Roelandt Savery, Paulus Potter, Aelbert Cuyp, and Adriaen van de Velde were skilled animal painters, and the meanings of their landscapes often depend on their handling of animals. Similarly, Potter, Wouwerman, and Berchem are sophisticated genre painters; the narratives of their pictures and the status of their figures greatly affect the interpretation of their landscapes. A few painters attempted to integrate portraits in landscape settings. Thomas de Keyser, Adriaen van de Velde, and Potter painted a few such portraits, but Aelbert Cuyp made a specialty of portraying upper-class horsemen in landscapes.

Early landscapes (those of the sixteenth and early seventeenth centuries) usually have a strong figural element, making a historical, mythological, or biblical connection unavoidable. Taking their cue from symbolic interpretations of Early Netherlandish painting as well as of seventeenth-century genre painting, some scholars have interpreted details in landscape pictures as having emblematic or moralizing meanings. Sunbeams could, therefore, represent the power of God; castles, the city of God; or travelers at an inn, the Prodigal Son. Whether these sorts of emblematic readings are possible without an explicit narrative subject or context is doubtful. Patronage and contemporaneous viewer reception can provide important clues to understanding Dutch landscapes. The frequency with which Dutch landscape painters depicted familiar or recognizable places is surely an indication of the meaning of paintings. Dutch cities loom constantly on the horizon; famed castles and country houses belonging to the *stadholder* are also common. Also encountered are ruins with celebrated connections to the Dutch wars of independence, such as the Huis te Kleef near Haarlem, or fortresses like Nijmegen, associated with the antiquity of the Dutch Republic. While these sites embody the seventeenth-century concept of the picturesque, or *schilderachtigheid*, in being pleasingly old and dilapidated, they also possessed political and social meaning.

Dutch landscape art also paralleled a new interest in nature poetry. Newly popular was the country-house poem, or *hofdicht*, a form based on Horace and Virgil, which delighted in country living. Even more Virgilian were agricultural handbooks and farm poetry, which lauded the economic productivity of the countryside. Perhaps more specifically relevant to individual Dutch landscapes are the countless poems and historical treatises that praised the Dutch cities and provinces, recounting tales of glory and providing detailed descriptions of local scenery. A few poems about specific paintings survive (namely, on works by Herman Saftleven and Adam Pijnacker), and these, too, evoke the delights of a specific, identifiable topography, whether the Rhine valley or the Italian countryside.

Alan Chong

See also Architectural painting; Country houses and gardens; Cuyp, Aelbert; Drawing theory; Flanders, Flemish School; Haarlem; Italy; Koninck, Philips; Literature, poetry: analogues with the visual; Marine painting; Pastoral; Prints, printmaking, and printmakers (ca. 1500–ca. 1900); Potter, Paulus; Rembrandt van Rijn; Rural life and views; Townscapes; Utrecht; Van Goyen, Jan; Van Mander, Karel; Van Ruisdael, Jacob; Vermeer, Johannes; Wouwerman, Philips

Bibliography
Duparc, F.J., and Linda Graif. *Italian Recollections: Dutch Painters of the Golden Age*. Montreal: Montreal Museum of Fine Arts, 1990.
Freedberg, David. *Dutch Landscape Prints of the Seventeenth Century*. London: British Museum Publications, 1980.
Haverkamp Begemann, Egbert, and Alan Chong. "Dutch Landscape and Its Associations." In *The Royal Picture Gallery, Mauritshuis*. New York: Harry N. Abrams, 1985.
Kettering, Alison McNeil. *The Dutch Arcadia: Pastoral Art and Its Audience in the Golden Age*. Montclair, NJ: Allanheld and Schram, 1983.
Stechow, Wolfgang. *Dutch Landscape Painting of the Seventeenth Century*. London: Phaidon, 1966.
Sutton, P. et al. *Masters of Seventeenth-Century Dutch Landscape Painting*. Boston: Museum of Fine Arts, 1987.

Landscape architecture

Landscape architecture of the late twentieth century has its origins in the achievements of the 1920s and 1930s, when the traditional nineteenth-century approach to urban planning was revolutionized. Equally influential for recent achievements in the Netherlands is taking into account the particular historical tradition in the formation of rural agricultural areas; the steps taken in past centuries to tame the region's harsh natural environment are being rediscovered and regarded as cultural values for contemporary landscape design.

Three large city parks marked the beginning of the modern period in the Netherlands: the Zuiderpark in The Hague (designed by P. Westbroek and Dirk Tersteeg, 1920–1923), the first Dutch park on a grand scale inspired by contemporary German public parks; the Kralingse Bos in Rotterdam (Marinus Jan Granpré Molière and others, 1924–1935), which introduced the application of functionalist tendencies into landscape parks; and the celebrated Amsterdamse Bos (Cornelis van Eesteren, Jacoba van Mulder, and others, 1929–1960), Amsterdam's woods. The avant-garde experiments in urban and land management that were being made in the expansion projects in Amsterdam in those years were used in the Amsterdamse Bos to create a large natural recreation area. Rightly considered the most significant example of a modern public park, the Amsterdamse Bos exhibits a new sensitivity toward ecological principles and environmental design through such modern urban-planning strategies as traffic separation and the zoning of special activities' areas.

In the years after World War II, the Netherlands became a leader in the organized application of the principles that derived from the urbanism of the 1930s, not only in city planning but in the more general planning of landscape areas. Ambitious schemes for redesigning the rural environment began to alter the appearance of the nation's landscape, especially in the polders, land areas originally under water that were being reclaimed for agricultural use. In these works, functionalist urban planning clearly shows the aesthetics of total manipulation of the environment and the landscape: Majestic tree-lined avenues connect the new agricultural villages and the various farms, while straight drainage canals are networked to form fields of strict geometric design.

The regulated organization of land areas of different scale produced exceptional results and truly manifested the new environmental aesthetics. An example is the village of Nagele on the Noord-Oostpolder (1948–1962), the project of a group of functionalist architects called De 8, where the experiment of integrating functionalist city planning with the historical arrangement of the agricultural land led to formation of a landscape that is an environmental continuity; there is no break between the urban and extra-urban spaces, and the total rationality of the organization achieves an aesthetic significance.

But it is not only in the new polder areas that the Netherlands has been successful in integrating the green and the built landscapes. Comparable quality of design can be found in the expansion of the major cities into the country. The Pendrecht quarter in Rotterdam, whose geometrically clear design was laid out in the late 1940s by Charlotte Stam-Beese with colleagues from the group Opbouw, is exemplary for introducing a complete system of gardens and green spaces that tie the new quarters to the countryside. Equally innovative are the four new western quarters of Amsterdam—Geuzenveld, Slotermeer, Slotervaart, and Oosdorp—arranged around the Sloterpark, an immense greenbelt with an artificial lake, modeled in naturalistic form, in its center. The achievement of this project by the Municipal Public Works Department began well before the war and continued through the 1950s. The result is an environment both natural and urban, a modern product of integrated planning.

One of the most famous small parks from this period is situated in the southern suburban part of Amsterdam—the Gijsbrecht van Amstelpark. It was designed in 1959 by Wim Boer, who created a landscape of green and water areas by constructing a strictly geometric weave of lines and right angles that is sublimely in character with the Dutch region. A rectilinear network of paths crosses three small rectangular islands, surrounded by canals, on which are placed a sequence of various types of landscapes: a playground, a tree-bordered common, and a flower garden.

In contrast to the rigorous landscape arrangements of the postwar period, the 1960s saw a tendency to Neo-Romantic inspiration, leading to the production of several landscape parks in which attention was returned to the scenic character of green areas with the intention of creating diverse and pleasant environments capable of stimulating the fantasy and interest of visitors. An example is the Rembrandtpark (designed by Doortje Haan-Wiegman and Janneke Theelen, 1969–1973) in Amsterdam. This park in the western part of the city is arranged around a number of water surfaces, formed and animated like a sequence of creeks that widen and narrow, with the effect of bringing to mind a picturesque garden. Similarly laid out is the Gaasperpark in Amsterdam (Pieter van Loon and Jan Willem van der Meeren, 1972–1981), enriched by spiraling spaces and intricate landscapes, designed to host

the 1982 Floriade, the international exposition of gardening that takes places every ten years.

The same Neo-Romantic approach is also evident in the vast nature and recreation areas of the Netherlands, such as the one in Rottemeren, north of Rotterdam (Klaas van Bergen and Hugo Nooteboom, 1956–1967). There, on the shores of the Rotte River, in a totally cultivated environment where nothing remains of the original natural landscape, an artificial landscape was created with woods, glades, and small winding lakes.

Contributing to the growing interest in the construction of natural landscapes was the emergence in the 1970s of the ecological movement and promotion of the construction of greenbelts, as well as continuation of the vigorous youth movement of 1968, which sought strongly to defend the quality of the urban and regional environment. The modern Dutch ecological experiment had deep roots, besides. It stems from experiments to create the great artificial forest in the Amsterdamse Bos, largely influenced by the biologist Jacob T. Thijsse, who promoted the first ecological gardens in the country in the 1930s. It was precisely with reference to these experiments that the first explicitly ecological public park was created in Amstelveen, south of Amsterdam—the Thijssepark (C.P. Broerse and J. Landwehr, begun 1939 and completed 1972). The park consists of a linear sequence of wooded glades crossed by watercourses, each producing a different environment; the composition assembles a great variety of habitats (among them turf and heath) and vegetation connected to a prevailing species (juniper, gentian, daisies).

Louis Le Roy, painter, teacher, and self-made ecological planner, was the central figure to emerge from the movement of 1968. From 1962 to 1968, in the residential suburb of Heerenveen in Friesland, he experimented with a controlled wilderness alongside a fast and busy street. This was the Kennedyplantsoen, an ecological garden distinctly spontaneous in character, consisting of a number of plant communities made up of thousands of trees, shrubs, weeds, herbs, and fungi. A path permitted access for enjoyment of this landscape designed with an aesthetic ideal of spontaneity.

Care for the natural environment was also expressed through respect for the existing landscape, seen as a cultural expression of human labor in the world. Several new parks along these lines were created during the 1970s: The ancient agrarian landscape undergoing transformation was used as an outline for redesigning the area. An example is the recreational area of Reeuwijkse Hout, in the province of South Holland (Han Lörzing and Ludo Leestmans, 1976–1980), where the ancient pattern of the fields, in narrow and parallel rectangular bands, is also maintained in the new park.

In the 1980s, the interest shifted again toward strong abstraction and inventiveness in landscape design. This change was due to the powerful influence felt in the Netherlands from contemporary new urban gardens in other European countries, particularly France and Spain. In these countries, discovery of the cultural role of the public garden—embellishment versus urban degradation—led to new meaning for landscape architecture, expressed through strong statements and sometimes a cerebral quality in the new parks' designs.

As a consequence, the Dutch changed their orientation, and a certain uniformity in the parks and gardens of the preceding decades—the result of the prevailing inspiration toward the creation of natural environments—was replaced in the 1980s by more creativity, emphasizing the artistic identity of each single project. The new gardens' characteristics are strong expressiveness of the design, attention to details, inventiveness in the arrangement of plants, and an eclectic composition combining the modern garden with quotations from the formal tradition of classic gardens. Geometry, which connects the garden space to the structure of the built city, is the common thread in all experiments.

An example is the park created in Zoetermeer to host the 1992 Floriade (Michiel den Ruijter, Ton Hinse, Geert Koning, Rob van der Ham, and Luc Vanderveke, 1981–1991). Located in the heart of the most urbanized area of the country, next to a major highway and railroad, the park reflects the new tendencies of the 1980s. Its strictly geometric layout recalls the "goose-foot" structure of historic French parks, while the interior of the regular design, defined by wide avenues, consists of various formal gardens in free juxtaposition.

The small Museum Park in Rotterdam (Rem Koolhaas, Office for Metropolitan Architecture, 1988–1993), built to connect the museums in the center of the city, derives its identity from the strong dissonance among the four zones into which it is divided. There is, in succession, an open square constructed in white mineral materials, lined by apple trees; a rectangular space of black asphalt used for traveling performances; a small, shady wooded area with a little lake and an island of flowers; and an irregular open space, partly paved and partly a meadow, in front of the Kunsthal (Fig. 70), an exhibition hall for exhibitions of contemporary art. An avenue crosses the entire area allowing the visitor to appreciate the different feelings caused by the contrast of environments and their totally diverse and discordant compositions, colors, and use of materials.

The same "collage" effect is the basis for the latest parks, such as Noorddijk Park in Groningen (Bart Brands and Nathieu Derckx of Bakker and Bleeker B.V., designed 1990), Overbos Park in Beverwijk (Ank Bleeker, designed 1990), and Kromhout Park in Tilburg (Bart Brands, Michael van Gessel, Jos Jacobs, designed 1991–1994). The motif of both parks was inspired by the juxtapositioning of different landscape passages. They display an entire collection of miniaturized landscapes, constructing an environment that is a metaphor for the multiform and fragmentary contemporary world.

Franco Panzini

See also Country houses and gardens; Functionalism in architecture; Koolhaas, Rem; Landscape; Urban planning, from 1750 to the present

Bibliography

Andela, Gerry. "The Public Park in the Netherlands." *Journal of Garden History* 4 (1981): 367–392.
Boersma, Tjeerd, and Gert ter Haar, eds. *Het nieuwe Stadspark.* Rotterdam: Nederlands Architectuur Instituut, 1991.
Lörzing, Han. *Van Bosplan tot Floriade: Nederlandse park-en landscapsontwerpen in de twintigste eeuw.* Rotterdam: 010, 1992.
Oranje Landschap. Aktuelle niederländische landschaftsarchitektur. Vienna: Planbox, 1994.
Rooijen, Maurits van. *De Groene Stad: Een historische studie over de groenvoorziening in de Nederlandse stad.* The Hague: Cultuurfonds van de Bank voor der Nederlandse Gemeenten, 1984.
"Stadspark en Buitenplaats." Theme volume. *Wonen/TABK* 9/10 (1977).
Vroom, Meto J., ed. *Outdoor Space: Environments Designed by Dutch Landscape Architects in the Period Since 1945.* Bussum: Thoth, 1992.

Laren (ca. 1870–ca. 1925)

In the half-century following its "discovery" in the 1870s, the North Holland village of Laren served as a retreat for dozens of artists from the Netherlands and abroad. The first painters to work there followed the aims of The Hague School, but by 1900 Laren artists represented local themes in a range of Realist and Post-Impressionist styles. Just before its decline as an art center in the 1920s, Laren saw its most innovative production by modernist artists.

Jozef Israëls, a leading painter of The Hague School, came to Laren in 1870 in search of a rural community unspoiled by the urbanization affecting the coast around The Hague. Laren was a village of two thousand peasant farmers, shepherds, and laborers in the weaving industry. The village's residents wore local costume, and its intimate farmhouses were surrounded by heather fields dotted with sheep. Transport to Laren was by postal coach, and visitors stayed in the modest coach inn. The situation must have appealed to Israëls, who in his work in The Hague had developed an idiom of the plain fisherman's life.

In the 1880s, at the encouragement of Israëls, Albert Neuhuijs and Anton Mauve moved from The Hague to Laren. Neuhuijs mostly painted still interiors with figures absorbed in domestic tasks or conversation. A broad application of brown and white pigments and a muted light thicken the ritual atmosphere of these works. Mauve, meanwhile, created defining images of Laren's lanes, moors, and sheep, applying his rich grey and brown tones with feathery strokes. These two Laren genres owe their themes and popularity to strong contemporary interest in painting of the seventeenth century. Both types of painting were highly regarded by Dutch and American collectors, and they became the stock in trade of followers such as Hein Kever. The development of this "Laren School" was facilitated by coach-inn owner Jan Hamdorff, who arranged models, rooms, and studios for the painters and encouraged visitors to buy their work.

As a retreat, Laren replaced more populous venues such as Oosterbeek and Scheveningen, which had served painters from the 1840s as Barbizon and Saint-Siméon did in France. In imagery and paint application, Laren artists remained close to their French and Dutch predecessors, but their commitment to *plein-air* painting may have been more pronounced as they completed large canvases outside (Fig. 72). This adherence to Realist practice had thematic limitations, however, as painters and collectors preferred nostalgic visions of Laren. The paintings of peaceful moors and family life rarely alluded to local economic hardships, and they included few of the references to modern life crucial to contemporary French painters. Exceptionally, the German painter Max Liebermann, who frequently visited Laren between 1884 and 1914, did represent working life in paintings such as *The Flax Barn* (1886).

Yet Laren was modernizing, in part because of the picturesque reputation it earned through its painters. In 1882 the village became accessible from Amsterdam by steam tram, and in 1905 Hamdorff reopened his coach inn as the luxury Hotel Hamdorff. Laren had become a favorite destination for tourists from Amsterdam and abroad, several of whom were to build summer villas there. Soon painters began to complain of the commercial motives of colleagues producing monotonous repetitions of Laren imagery.

Despite this conservative climate, several painters around 1900 experimented with Post-Impressionist innovations. Ferdinand Hart Nibbrig and Co Breman introduced Pointillist techniques and brighter palettes. Hart Nibbrig also used a broad brush to heroicize Laren peasants in portraits and genre scenes on the scale of history painting. Sigisbert Bosch Reitz produced strongly contoured scenes of religious events in Laren, which in their bright, flat patterning and folkloric themes recall works of the Pont Aven artists and the Nabis ("the Prophets," a group) active in France in the 1890s.

Early in the twentieth century, several modernist artists came to Laren, including Jan Sluijters, Piet Mondrian, Bart van der Leck, and Lou Loeber, the latter painting figurative themes in an idiom related to Mondrian's nonobjective principles. During World War I the Belgian exiles Gustave de Smet, Frits van den Berghe, and Jozef Cantré brought a fresh range of Expressionist works. These artists occasionally reinterpreted Laren themes, but their production was primarily informed by contacts with Expressionist artists in Amsterdam and Bergen.

By 1930 Laren had lost its importance as an artistic center. The village's role is commemorated in its Singer Museum (1956), which houses the Laren paintings and French Impressionist works collected by the American painter William Singer, as well as an increasing group of Dutch modernist works.

Mariët Westermann

See also France; Hague School, The; Mauve, Anton; North American painting, Dutch influences

Bibliography
Heyting, Lien. *De wereld in een dorp: Schilders, schrijvers en wereldverbeteraars in Laren en Blaricum 1880–1920.* Amsterdam: Meulenhoff, 1994.

Koenraads, Jan P. *Laren en zijn schilders: Kunstenaars rond Hamdorff.* Laren: Judi Kluvers, 1985.

Pol, J. van der. "De 'Larense School': Kunst voor de markt?" *Tableau* 7 (1984): 50–64.

Seumeren-Haerkens, M. van. "Kunstenaars rond Hamdorff." *Tableau* 8 (1985): 72–75.

Verboeket, Karin et al. *"Zij waren in Laren": Buitenlandsekunstenaars in Laren en 't Gooi.* Laren: Singer Museum, 1989.

Last Judgment

As the one event in religious history in which all humans take part, the end of the world occupies a special place in sacred thought and art. Its general features include Christ as Judge on a rainbow in the heavens; the Virgin and St. John the Baptist flanking him as Intercessors for humanity; a heavenly court surrounding the Judge; the dead emerging below to the sound of trumpets while St. Michael weighs souls; and the blessed entering heaven to Christ's right, while to his left the damned are cast into hell. But Last Judgment iconography exhibits rich variety, shaped by a range of factors.

Various texts inform the theme's depiction. Biblical sources include St. Matthew 25:31–46, St. John 5:27–30, and Revelation 20:11–14. In addition, a broad spectrum of literature shapes the image of heaven and hell. Scholars have cited St. Augustine's *City of God;* catechetical texts (which often include sections on the Last Judgment, heaven, and hell); accounts of the pilgrimage of life; and reports of journeys to hell and paradise such as the *Visions of Tondal* (or Tundale), which survives in numerous twelfth- to fifteenth-century manuscripts. In addition, the Last Judgment's concern with such larger issues as justice, authority, and the role of faith and works gave it a place in contemporary dialogues on these topics and resulted in its appearance in a variety of sites and pictorial contexts.

The theme appears on altarpieces, *memorietafels* (memorial paintings), panels for town-hall justice chambers, works for charitable organizations, and, occasionally, paintings for guild halls. Meaning shifts with form and context. Donor portraits might transform a *memorietafel* into a personal statement of hope for salvation (Fig. 73). Admonitory inscriptions on town-hall images draw explicit parallels between divine and human justice. Works for charitable institutions might reaffirm the foundation's goal: Acts of mercy earn salvation for the donor. The Last Judgment might also occur in expanded contexts, such as Hieronymus Bosch's penitential mirror, the *Tabletop of the Seven Deadly Sins and the Four Last Things* (ca. 1470–1490) (Color Plate 1), or woodcut Credo cycles.

In the sixteenth century, the new forces of humanism and the Reformation play important roles. Print series incorporate the Last Judgment in cycles devoted to humanist concerns. The influence of Erasmus leads to paintings of St. Jerome contemplating a manuscript image of the theme. Catholics and Protestants alike employ Last Judgment imagery in their doctrinal debates, though not always in expected ways, as Craig Harbison has shown.

Diverse portrayals of the dark, fiery realm of hell comprise one of the most fascinating aspects of Last Judgment scenes. Emphasis may focus on the damned or the demons. Frequently shown attacks on the clergy continue medieval tradition. Some images stress spiritual suffering; others, physical. Particular attention has been drawn to parallels with the *Vision of Tondal*, which like many images portrays hell as a vast landscape filled with horrific demons and individual scenes of gruesome physical torture. Some scholars have also attempted to associate punishments with particular sins.

Humanist interests and Reformation concern with other aspects of religious doctrine may have led to the de-emphasis on hell and heaven noted by Harbison in some sixteenth-century works. Humanism may also play a role in the revival of Boschian imagery and features such as the hellmouth (virtually abandoned by fifteenth-century painters, due at least in part to the value that was placed on their inventiveness). But the revival may also represent a desire to create "safe" images by using traditional pictorial language remote from ideological concerns. Only additional study can provide the answers.

Janey L. Levy

See also Active life, active virtues; Bosch, Hieronymus; Churches; Contemplative life, contemplative virtues; Devotional images; Didactic images; Donor portraits; Erasmus, Desiderius; Humanism, humanist themes; Manuscript illumination; Protestant Reformation; Sins and punishments; Tomb sculpture: early modern and later sepulchral art; Tomb sculpture: medieval effigial monuments; Town halls

Bibliography

Harbison, Craig. *The Last Judgment in Sixteenth-Century Northern Europe: A Study of the Relation between Art and the Reformation.* New York: Garland, 1976.

Kren, Thomas, and Roger S. Wieck. *The Visions of Tondal from the Library of Margaret of York.* Malibu, CA: Getty Museum, 1990.

Levy, Janey L. "The Keys of the Kingdom of Heaven: Ecclesiastical Authority and Hierarchy in the Beaune Altarpiece." *Art History* 14 (March 1991): 18–50.

———. "The Last Judgment in Early Netherlandish Painting: Faith, Authority, and Charity in the Fifteenth Century." Ph.D. diss., University of Kansas, 1988.

Leiden

Within the old town moat *(singel)* remarkably little has intruded on Leiden's seventeenth-century skyline. The chief medieval monuments rising above the city roofs are the Pieterskerk (ca. 1390–1565) and the Hooglandsekerk (ca. 1480–1500, nave incomplete), while the spires of the town hall (1599, rebuilt after a fire in 1929) and the Lodewijkskerk (spire of 1588, rebuilt in 1594) are joined by the dome of the Marekerk (built 1638–1659 by architect Aernt van 's Gravezande) and the tower of the Academiegebouw (added by Willem van der Helm to the fifteenth-century former convent building in 1670). Not far from the former location of the medieval Vrouwekerk is the Hartebrugkerk (by Th. Molkenboer, 1836–1837), with a modest cupola topping its squat tower. Leiden's most imposing building from the nineteenth century is the Stadsgehoorzaal (City Auditorium, by D.E.C. Knuttel, 1892). The town hall's fish market façade (by C.J. Blauw, 1935–1941) deserves praise for its unobtrusive modernism. The massive tower of the Petruskerk (by A.J. Kropholler, 1933–1935) dominates a neighborhood from the

same period to the south. The Merenwijk is a neighborhood on Leiden's northeast, representing a more livable version of town-planning ideas of the 1960s and 1970s that are better known from Amsterdam's suburb of Bijlmermeer. Also from the 1970s is a neighborhood northeast of the Hooglandsekerk that replaced what may have been the largest remaining concentration of seventeenth-century weavers' houses, only one or two of which have been preserved among the new. The new university buildings (Doelencomplex and University Library) represent architectural ideas of the 1980s.

The two medieval churches are moderately interesting architecturally. The transept façades of the Hooglandsekerk have an impressive unity of tracery incorporating the main doorways, tall windows, and the gables, very similar to the north transept at Goes. The Pieterskerk contains a magnificently carved pulpit and canopy (designed by Pieter Cornelisz. Kunst, 1532). Leiden's architectural treasures, however, date predominantly from the seventeenth and eighteenth centuries, beginning with the town hall *(stadhuis)*, designed by Lieven de Key and Luder van Benthem (1593–1598; rebuilt using the existing, restored façade, 1935–1941; Fig. 74). Strapwork ornament and a wealth of sculptural detail make this the most impressive town hall in the Netherlands built before that in Amsterdam. Connection with Van Benthem's other works in Bremen and the Weser area is apparent; thus the building reflects the international trading interests of Leiden's wool industry, one of whose major bankers, Daniël van der Meulen, a Flemish refugee, supervised the choice of architects and the course of construction. Also from this period is Lieven de Key's simpler Gemeenlandshuis van Rijnland (Communal-Lands House of Rhineland, 1598). Expansion along the north side of Leiden was carried out under city supervision, which resulted in the construction of the timber wharf *(stadstimmerwerf)* at the town's harbor in 1612, a beautifully preserved, stepped-gable brick-and-stone house and warehouse. Public buildings from the period include the Lakenhal (Cloth Hall, now the municipal museum) by Aernt van 's Gravezande (1639–1640); the weigh house and butter hall by Pieter Post, with collaboration by Willem van der Helm (1657) and sculptural decoration by Rombout Verhulst; the two remaining city gates, the Zijlpoort (1667, by Van der Helm, sculpture by Verhulst) and the Morschpoort (1668, by Van der Helm); and courtrooms added to the medieval prison (Gravensteen, now housing the university's law faculty) in 1671–1672 (by Van der Helm, with pediment sculpture by Pieter Xavery).

Among Leiden's thirty-five almshouses *(hofjes)* are several with architectural merit: the Annahofje (chapel from 1492–1509), the van Brouckhovenhofje (1640), the Jean Pesijnshofje (1683), and the Meermansburg (street façade by Jacob Roman, 1681, courtyard façade ca. 1750–1775). The Regents' Chamber of the Meermansburg contains an excellent collection of portraits by Willem Miereveld, Jacob Gerritsz. Cuyp, Jan de Baen, and others.

One of Leiden's stateliest buildings is the Bibliotheca Thysiana on the Rapenburg (by Van 's Gravezande, 1654–1655). Remarkably this private library foundation retains its interior furnishings, also designed by the architect, as well as its books, from the period of construction. The Rapenburg is the location of a grandiose sequence of seventeenth- and eighteenth-century house façades unequaled in the country. Noteworthy are Rapenburg 2,6,19,29–31,33,48, and 65. Several mansions have well-preserved interiors with ceiling and mantelpiece paintings, predominantly eighteenth-century plasterwork mantlepieces, ceilings and walls, and interior woodwork of the highest quality (for example, Rapenburg 2,8,19,67,69,70–74); and some retain large landscape paintings stretched like tapestries across entire walls, by painters including Dirk van der Aa, Dirk Kuipers, Pieter Hardimé, and Augustinus Terwesten.

Painting before the Reformation in Leiden was dominated by Cornelis Engebrechtsz. (1468–1527), Lucas van Leyden (1494?–1533), and Aertgen van Leyden (1498–1564). Works by the sons of Cornelis Engebrechtsz.—Cornelis Cornelisz. Kunst, Pieter Cornelisz. Kunst, and Lucas Cornelisz. de Kock—by Huygh Jacobsz. (Huych Jacopsz.) and Floris Jacobsz. (Jacopsz.) (Lucas van Leyden's father and uncle), and by Brother Tymanus (Cornelis Engebrechtsz.'s teacher) also have been tentatively identified. Three major altarpieces by Cornelis Engebrechtsz. and Lucas van Leyden's *Last Judgment* triptych are in the Stedelijk Museum De Lakenhal. Cornelis Engebrechtsz.'s work has been compared with that of Colijn de Coter of Brussels, although Cornelis' color is superior. The contact, if any, has not been adequately explained. Both Cornelis Cornelisz. Kunst and his brother Pieter traveled to Bruges in connection with Leiden's wool cloth trade, which may account for connections with the art of Gerard David. The series of Leiden drawings (for stained glass panels) with the initials "PC" are usually attributed to Pieter Cornelisz. Kunst, whose housemark monogram was, however, different; they may have been the work of Philips Claesz. van Zeyst, another Leiden artist, or the glass painter Pieter Hugenz. van Cloeting.

Little pre-Reformation sculpture remains, although archeological and documentary evidence indicates there was a lively production of pipe-clay statues. The *Madonna and Child* relief from Zoeterwoude (Utrecht, Rijksmuseum Het Catharijneconvent) and a similar relief depicting St. Nicholas are the best examples found in the area. Although tapestry weaving was a significant industry in the third quarter of the sixteenth century, only a few Leiden tapestries remain (Leiden, Stedelijk Museum De Lakenhal; Amsterdam, Rijksmuseum; and Leiden, Annahofje).

Leiden's gold and silversmiths produced excellent work. Early material is represented by a chalice of 1510 by Willem Dircxz. (now on loan to the Lakenhal) and a coconut cup from 1546 by Ghysbrecht Aerntsz. van Griecken (Lawrence, Spencer Museum of Art, University of Kansas), while numerous later pieces testify to high technical and design standards. The major silversmiths were Zacharias Cloot (died 1635); Johannes Fransz. de Maerschalck (1599–1665), maker of Leiden University's beadle's staff; Jacob Fortman (1682–1747), father of the silversmiths Hendrik, Abraham, and Dirk Fortman; Jacobus Kamphuis (1760–1829); and Hendrikus Johannes Schretlen (1788–1853). Johannes Schmeltzing (1639–1710) made numerous commemorative medals, many including portraits.

Leiden's painter-burgomaster Isaac Claesz. van Swanenburgh (1537–1614) taught Otto van Veen (1556–1629), who later was one of Rubens' teachers. Van Swanenburgh dominated Leiden art at the end of the sixteenth and the beginning of the seventeenth centuries. His series illuminating the activities of cloth production (now in the Lakenhal) offers excellent depictions of early industrial subjects. His widely traveled son, Jacob (1571–1638), was Rembrandt's first teacher. Militia portraits, as well as other subjects, were painted by Joris van Schooten (1587–1652), who received a commission in 1626 for six militia paintings (now in the Lakenhal). Artists such as Bartholomeus Dolendo, Willem Swanenburgh, and Jan Cornelisz. Woudanus contributed illustrations to scholarly works published in Leiden; the best work is seen in portrait engravings. Christian Hagen surrounded his large map of Leiden (1670) with detailed but rather dry views of important local buildings. The lively etchings produced by Rembrandt and Jan Jorisz. van Vliet did not affect typical scholarly publications. The presence of the university may have provided a market for paintings on the theme of the scholar in his study, as well as for *vanitas* still lifes, which became a Leiden specialty from the 1620s on. David Bailly (1584–ca. 1657) produced portraits and still-life paintings of this sort, as did Jan Lievens (1607–1674) and Rembrandt's pupil Gerrit Dou (1613–1675). Dou became famous for his finely painted, smooth-surfaced pictures (Color Plate 8), and he taught several others, now known as Lieden's *fijnschilders* (fine painters: Dominicus van Tol, Jacob Toorenvliet, Frans van Mieris the Elder, Pieter van Slingelandt, Godfried Schalcken, Karel de Moor, and Matthijs Naiveu). Gabriel Metsu's (1629–1667) work may be considered comparable, but Jan Steen (1625/1626–1679) and Jan van Goyen (1596–1656) did not participate in this aspect of Leiden's general artistic development. Van Goyen's landscapes (Color Plate 6) established conventions that seem to have been influential on the later painters of room-size wall coverings.

Seventeenth-century sculpture in Leiden is scarce but of high quality. The best examples are the monument to Johannes à Kerkhoven (Pieterskerk, 1663), the epitaph of Burgomaster Pieter Adriaensz. van der Werff (Hoogland-sekerk, 1661), and reliefs on the weigh house (1658–1662) and former plague hospital (Pesthuis, 1660) by Rombout Verhulst. Besides the pediment sculpture of the Gravensteen, Pieter Xavery also carved figures of Neptune and Mercury, flanking a bust of a Turk, for the pediment of the Gilded Turk (Het Vergulden Turk, in the Breestraat, no. 84). Several additional memorials in the Pieterskerk attract attention. Those of Johannes Cocceius (by I.D. Bleek, 1713) and Hermannus Boerhaave (by Anthony Wapperon, 1762) include good sculpture, as do those for Johan Luzac (1809) and Johan Meerman (1820, the mourning figure holding a portrait relief formerly had a gilt-bronze coronet of stars in her other hand).

Although organized in guilds before the Reformation and again in the seventeenth century, in 1694 Leiden's artists reorganized themselves in the Leiden Drawing Academy (Leidse Tekenacademie), where the tradition of Dou and Frans van Mieris the Elder was continued under the direction of Willem van Mieris (1662–1747) and his son Frans van Mieris the Younger. This group produced rather quiet local landscapes and portraits while discussing art theory. The Leiden watercolor views of Paulus Constantijn La Fargue belong to this world. Reorganization occurred again at the end of the century, when the still-existing club, Ars Aemula Naturae, was formed. Among its members was D.P.G. Humbert de Superville (1770–1849), who became its drawing teacher around 1813 and in 1825 director of the university's print room.

Hendrik Ringeling painted numerous Leiden church interiors around 1850, some with figures in seventeenth-century costume; these lack the drama of similar work by Johannes Bosboom, but Ringeling's grand church interiors with figures in contemporary clothing call to mind some English painters of modern life, such as William Powell Frith. Other mid-century painters of note were Chris de Windt, J.E. Kikkert, and Arend Jan van Driesten. Van Driesten was an excellent painter working in a style similar to that of the later Hague School. Alexander Bakker Korff painted numerous slightly humorous interiors, mostly depicting older middle-class women surrounded by their collections of century-old furniture. In 1878 George Hendrik Breitner became the drawing instructor for Ars Aemula Naturae; his student Floris Verster produced beautiful paintings and drawings around the turn of the century, some calling to mind the mist and mood of the English painter John Atkinson Grimshaw.

By that time "Ars" seems already to have reached its current semi-amateur "art guild" level. Theo van Doesburg, J.J.P. Oud, and Aart van Dobbenburgh attempted to move away from what they found stodgy, starting the art club The Sphinx and publishing from 1917 to 1932 the monthly *De Stijl*, whose editorial offices were in Leiden, wherever else its audience may have been.

With changes in society, transportation, and economics, Leiden has not remained a major center of artistic activity; the fashions of what is important first fluctuate elsewhere. Nonetheless, such artists as Jan and Charley Toorop, Pyke Koch, Kees Buurman, Albert Roskam, and Herbie Nijenhuis have worked in and around Leiden, and exhibitions of contemporary work are held at the Lakenhal from time to time and annually by the members of Ars Aemula Naturae.

Jeremy D. Bangs

See also Bakker Korff, Alexander Hugo; Breitner, George Hendrik; Classicism in architecture; Dou, Gerrit; Engebrechtsz., Cornelis; Genre painting, eighteenth century; Humbert de Superville, D.P.G.; Koch, Pyke; La Fargue, Paulus Constantijn; Lievens, Jan; Metsu, Gabriel; Oud, Jacobus Johannes Pieter; Post, Pieter; Rembrandt van Rijn; Renaissance architecture; Stained glass; Steen, Jan Havicksz.; Technical investigations; Toorop, Charley (Annie Caroline Pontifex); Toorop, Jan; Town halls; Urban planning, before 1750; Van der Aa, Dirk; Van Doesburg, Theo; Van Goyen, Jan; Van Leyden, Aertgen; Van Leyden, Lucas; *Vanitas, vanitas* still life; Verhulst, Rombout; Verster, Floris; Xavery, Pieter

Bibliography
Bangs, J. "The Leiden Monogramist PC and Other Artists' Enigmatic Fire Buckets." *Source* 1 (1981): 11–15.
———. "Lucas van Leyden's Uncle Floris Jacopsz.?" In *Tribute to Lotte Brand Philip Art Historian and Detective*. Edited by William W. Clark et al., n.p. New York: Abaris Books, 1985.
———, and G.D. Winius. "Daniël van der Meulen (died 1600): First Midas of Holland's Golden Age." In *Atti del Secondo Congresso Internazionale di studi storici Rapporti Genova-Mediterraneo-Atlantico nell'età moderna*. Edited by Raffaele Belvederi, 347–371. Genova: Universita di Genova, 1985.
Bangs, J.D. *Cornelis Engebrechtsz.'s Leiden: Studies in Cultural History*. Assen: Van Gorcum, 1979.
Boer, D.E.H. de, J.F. Heijbroek, and R.E.O. Ekkart. *Hutspot, haring en wittebrood: Tien eeuwen Leiden en de Leienaars*. 13 vols. Leiden: De Kler-Waanders, 1981–1982.
Familie Fortman, Zilversmeden te Leiden in de 18de Eeuw. Leiden: Stedelijk Museum De Lakenhal, 1972.
Kuile, E.H. ter. *De Provincie Zuidholland. Part 1: Leiden en Westelijk Rijnland*. Vol. 7, *De Nederlantsche monumenten van geschiedenis en kunst*. The Hague: Algemeene Landsdrukkerij, 1944.
Lunsingh Scheurleer, Th.H., C.W. Fock, and A.J. van Dissel. *Het Rapenburg: Geschiedenis van een Leidse Gracht*. 11 vols. Leiden: Rijksuniversiteit Leiden, 1986–1992.
Oerle, H.A. van. *Leiden binnen en buiten der stadsvesten: De geschiedenis van de stedebouwkundige ontwikkeling binnen het Leidse rechtsgebied tot aan het einde van de Gouden Eeuw*. Leiden: E.J. Brill, 1975.
Sluijter, E.J., M. Enklaar, and P. Nieuwenhuizen. *Leidse Fijnschilders: Van Gerrit Dou tot Frans Van Mieris de Jonge 1630–1760*. Leiden: Stedelijk Museum De Lakenhal; Zwolle: Waanders, 1988.
Wurfbain, M.L. *Catalogus van schilderijen en tekeningen*. Leiden: Stedelijk Museum De Lakenhal, 1983.

Leyster, Judith (1609–1660)

Judith Leyster, born in Haarlem and baptized in the Grote Kerk (Great Church) there on July 28, 1609, was one of that city's most accomplished genre painters. Her marriage to Jan Miense Molenaer (1609/1610–1668) in 1636 brought her career to an early end, and by the time of her death she was already forgotten as an artist. Since her rediscovery late in the nineteenth century, Leyster's reputation has continued to grow, fueled in recent decades with the rise of feminist studies. Unfortunately, her notoriety as a rare woman artist from the period has partly obscured consideration of her skills as a painter and a contributor to the development of Haarlem genre painting from the late 1620s.

Unlike many of her female contemporaries, Leyster did

not come from a family of artists. Her father, Jan Willemsz., was a small-ware weaver who tried his hand at running a brewery in 1618. He named it the *Ley-star* (lodestar) from a surname he had taken in 1603. The brewery failed, and a subsequent bankruptcy forced Leyster's parents in 1628 to leave Haarlem for Vreeland, a village near Utrecht. This move has fueled speculation that Leyster received early training in Utrecht, since her interest in nocturnes and the effects of artificial light can be traced to the Utrecht Caravaggists (Fig. 151). It is more likely, however, that she developed these interests in the Haarlem workshop of Pieter de Grebber (ca. 1600–1652/1653), where she may have been a fellow pupil with Maria de Grebber (ca. 1602–1680). Samuel Ampzing, a local historian, cited both women in his 1628 description of Haarlem.

Frans Hals (ca. 1582/1583–1666) probably played a role in Leyster's training in the late 1620s, as she imitated his virtuoso brushwork and favored similar subjects and compositions. Paintings once attributed to Hals are now convincingly placed within her *oeuvre*. By contrast, Leyster's small-scale genre interior scenes show a debt to Dirck Hals (1591–1656). It is likely that she, like Molenaer, either studied with him or was active in his workshop prior to joining Haarlem's Guild of St. Luke in 1633 as one of its first female members. By 1635 Leyster had established a workshop and had three students.

With the exceptions of tulip illustrations and possibly a painted still life, Leyster's pictures all date prior to the year of her marriage. Her *Self-Portrait* (ca. 1630; Washington, DC, National Gallery of Art; Fig. 75) showcases her abilities both as a portraitist and a genre painter. While the brushwork is not as broken and spontaneous as in examples by her that are closer to works by Frans Hals, she nevertheless pays a debt to him in the lively expression of her features.

Leyster and Molenaer may have shared a studio by the late 1620s, as identical motifs reappear in a number of their paintings. It is sometimes difficult to distinguish between their early works. After moving with Molenaer to Amsterdam in late 1636 Leyster seems to have largely abandoned painting in order to manage her husband's affairs and to assume the traditional roles of wife and mother. Leyster was buried in Heemstede on February 10, 1660.

Dennis P. Weller

See also Comic modes; Hals, Dirck; Hals, Frans; Haarlem; Molenaer, Jan Miense; Women artists

Bibliography

Harms, Juliane. "Judith Leyster: Ihr Leben und ihr Werk." *Oud Holland* 44 (1927): 88–96, 112–126, 145–154, 221–242, 275–279.

Hofrichter, Frima Fox. *Judith Leyster: A Woman Painter in Holland's Golden Age.* Doornspijk: Davaco, 1989.

Hofstede de Groot, Cornelis. "Judith Leyster." *Jahrbuch der königlich Preussischen Kunstsammlungen* 14 (1893): 190–198, 232.

Welu, James A. et al. *Judith Leyster: A Dutch Master and*

Her World. Worcester: Worcester Art Museum; Zwolle: Waanders, 1993.

Lievens, Jan (1607–1674)

Jan Lievens, born in Leiden on October 24, 1607, was a history painter, portraitist, and printmaker who also treated landscape and genre. His modern reputation rests primarily on his early association with Rembrandt van Rijn, but in his own time Lievens experienced a healthy measure of success, receiving commissions for public history paintings as well as portraits of Joost van den Vondel (etching), René Descartes (drawing, black chalk; Groningen, Museum voor Stad en Lande), and other prominent figures. Unlike Rembrandt, Lievens traveled beyond Holland to London and Antwerp.

A precocious talent, Lievens began his training before the age of ten with Joris van Schooten (1587–1652). From 1618 to 1621, he studied with Pieter Lastman in Amsterdam. He then returned to Leiden, where he worked closely with Rembrandt from 1625 to 1631. They treated many of the same subjects in both painting and etching, and their styles were so close that even contemporaries confused their works.

Lievens' mature style diverged from Rembrandt's under the impact of the Flemish painter Anthony van Dyck. Lievens may have met Van Dyck at the court in The Hague in 1631–1632. Both artists made portraits of the *stadholder*'s secretary, Constantijn Huygens, whose autobiography (ca. 1630) contains an early appraisal of Lievens' style and potential (Lievens' *Portrait of Constantijn Huygens*, ca. 1626–1627; Douai, Musée de la Chartreuse, on loan to Amsterdam, Rijksmuseum). In 1632 Lievens followed Van Dyck to the court of Charles I in London. By 1635 he was in Antwerp, joining the Guild of St. Luke and remaining there until 1644 in contact with Adriaen Brouwer, Lucas Vorsterman, and other Flemish painters and printmakers. In 1638 Lievens married Susanna Colyns, daughter of the sculptor Andries Colyns de Nole. Their son, Jan Andries, was born in 1644 and followed his father's profession (for example, *Portrait of Admiral Engel de Ruyter*, *Portrait of Capt. Jan van Gelder*, 1668; both Amsterdam, Rijksmuseum).

Jan Lievens' earliest paintings are somewhat garish versions of Lastman's history painting, but Flemish influence lends softness and clarity to his later brushwork and palette. His prints of biblical subjects and character types *(troniën)* are often close to those of Rembrandt (for example, *St. Jerome; The Raising of Lazarus* [ca. 1631]; and the so-called *Oriental Heads*, copied by Rembrandt in 1635). His refined portrait drawings and etchings combine Van Dyckian elegance with straightforward characterization (for example, *Andries de Graeff*, black chalk, 1657; Haarlem, Teylers Museum).

In Lievens' landscapes, executed in oil painting, chalk, pen and ink, and woodcut, human activity often takes second place to evocative studies of trees (for example, *Evening Landscape*, Berlin, Staatliche Museen; *Landscape with Trees*, woodcut). Rembrandt's inventory of 1656 includes landscapes by Lievens, suggesting that the two maintained some form of contact after their Leiden years.

In 1644, Lievens moved from Antwerp to Amsterdam,

where he lived off and on for the rest of his life (he was in The Hague 1654–1658). He was the only Dutch painter commissioned to provide history paintings for both the *stadholder's* summer palace in The Hague and the newly built Amsterdam Town Hall (*Allegory of the Birth of Frederik Hendrik; The Five Muses*, 1650, The Hague, Oranjezaal, Palace Huis ten Bosch; *Quintus Fabius Maximus Appearing before His Son*, 1656; *Brinio Elected Leader of the Canninefates*, 1661, Amsterdam, Royal Palace). He also traveled to Berlin and Cleves to work for the duke of Brandenberg.

In 1648, after the death of his first wife, Lievens married Cornelia de Bray; she died in 1668 leaving him with five small children. Financial hardship dogged him in the years before his death on June 4, 1674, in Amsterdam.

Other principal paintings include *St. Paul in His Study* (Bremen, Kunsthalle); *Portrait of an Old Man and a Boy (Eli and Samuel?)* (1631; Malibu, J. Paul Getty Museum); *Portrait of a Youth in a Gold Robe* (Edinburgh, National Gallery of Scotland); *Self-Portrait* (London, National Gallery); *Abraham and Isaac* (Brunswick, Herzog Anton Ulrich-Museum); *Allegory of Peace* (1652; Amsterdam, Rijksmuseum); *Portrait of Robert Kerr, First Earl of Ancram* (1654; Edinburgh, Scottish National Portrait Gallery).

Stephanie S. Dickey

See also Flanders, Flemish School; History painting; Huygens, Constantijn; Leiden; Literature, poetry: analogues with the visual; Prints, printmaking, and printmakers (ca. 1500–ca. 1900); Rembrandt research; Rembrandt School; Rembrandt van Rijn; Self-portraiture

Bibliography

Hollstein, F.W.H. *Leyster-Matteus.* Vol. 11, *Dutch and Flemish Etchings, Engravings, and Woodcuts, ca. 1450–1700.* Amsterdam: Menno Hertzberger, 1949.

Klessmann, Rüdiger et al. *Jan Lievens, ein Maler im Schatten Rembrandts.* Brunswick: Herzog Anton Ulrich-Museum, 1979.

Schatborn, Peter, and Eva Ornstein-van Slooten. *Jan Lievens: Prints and Drawings.* Amsterdam: Museum het Rembrandthuis, 1988.

Schneider, H. *Jan Lievens: Sein Leben und Seine Werke.* Supplement by R.E.O. Ekkart. Amsterdam: B.M. Israël, 1973.

Sumowski, Werner. *Drawings of the Rembrandt School.* Vol. 7, 3542–3933. New York: Abaris, 1983.

———. *Gemälde der Rembrandt-Schüler*, Vol. 3, 1764–1772. Landau, Pfalz: Edition PVA, 1983–[1994].

Vogelaar, Christiaan et al. *Rembrandt and Lievens in Leiden.* Zwolle: Waanders, 1991.

Weber, Gregor. "Dus leeft de dappre Graaf: Zu einem Bildnis Andries de Graeffs von Jan Lievens." *Oud Holland* 99 (1985): 44–56.

Literature, poetry: analogues with the visual

The interrelationships of text and picture in earlier centuries are complex. Generally, the study of these issues may be connected to the rapidly developing word-image field, which has broadened our conception of the interactions between visual and literary expressions, and our interpretations of the visual image which itself serves as a text. Fundamental to such studies is the analogy of poetry and painting, expressed by Plutarch, citing Simonides, and later embodied in Horace's phrase: *ut pictura poesis.* Horace's statement, often misquoted and taken out of its original context, may propose that poetry and painting share common values and purposes. In Dutch seventeenth-century literature about art, however, this proposal was invoked to give legitimacy to painting as an intellectual endeavor, to establish painting as a liberal art within both classical and contemporary traditions, and to provide a theoretical framework for its practice. In turn, Dutch seventeenth-century imagery often expresses these ideas through allusion to certain subjects and indication of allegorical levels of meaning. Analogues between the literary and visual arts within the period of Dutch Baroque involve nearly all categories of Dutch writing: lectures about art; poetry; illustrations in books; inscriptions on printed images, whether published singly or in series; poems on portraits; city descriptions; private diaries; plays; biographies of artists; instructional writing about art; and emblem books.

In practice, many specific analogues are closely associated with the social context of the making of pictures and related texts. For example, the celebrations in honor of St. Luke, patron saint of painters, brought together artists, writers, and collectors; the festivities often included recitation of texts that glorified the status of the arts, offered commentary upon actual paintings, or honored a prominent figure within the community of artists and writers. The feast of St. Luke held in Leiden, October 1641, featured a speech by Philips Angel, *Lof der schilder-konst* (Praise of Painting), that was published shortly thereafter; not only did this lengthy address set forth principles essential to the practice of painting, it also applied these tenets to known paintings, including several by Rembrandt van Rijn and Jan Lievens. At the feast of St. Luke held in Amsterdam, October 1653, the Dutch playwright Joost van den Vondel was honored; the festivities included texts proclaiming the union of painting and poetry, personified by Apelles and Apollo. At the 1654 Amsterdam feast, the entertainment included a play by Thomas Asselijn, in which the main characters were Apollo, Pallas, and Mercury—the three ancient gods considered most responsible for the prosperity of the arts.

Iconic poetry, generally defined as verse about actual works of art, provides the clearest demonstration of shared values between literature and the visual arts. During the 1640s, Vondel took up this kind of verse. His interest in it no doubt was encouraged by his friendship with the artist Joachim von Sandrart, who owned a number of Italian works of art that, along with works by Von Sandrart himself, served as the subjects for Vondel's earliest iconic verse. Other acquaintances guided Vondel in a similar vein. His playful celebration of the marriage of Willem Kalf and Cornelia Pluvier is also a demonstration of the aesthetically pleasing elements in a still life by Kalf himself. The collector Jan Six owned a painting upon which Vondel lavished his attention: Pieter Lastman's *Paul and Barnabas at Lystra* (1614; formerly Warsaw; Fig. 76). Written in 1647, Vondel's fifteen-stanza poem leads the viewer through the represented action and proposes interpretations about the biblical event, the painter's rendition of it, and the collector's possession of the picture. As told in Acts 14: 6–18, the apostles Paul and Barnabas are preaching in Lystra. After healing a cripple, they are mistaken for Jupiter and Mercury, and the priests and populace prepare a pagan sacrifice in their honor. As Christians, they reject the ceremony, and are stoned as they flee. Lastman followed the rules of narrative and pictorial clarity set forth in Karel van Mander's *Schilder-Boeck* of 1604; he also demonstrated knowledge of ancient sacrificial customs. Vondel's meticulous description of the action and apparatus in Lastman's painting is among the most sustained discussions of an image in Dutch literature. In 1718, Arnold Houbraken, who was not at all familiar with Lastman's work, quoted Vondel's poem as an authority for both Lastman's painting and its accurate depiction of a Roman sacrifice.

A painting belonging to Pieter Six, Pieter Paul Rubens' *Hero and Leander* (ca. 1604–1605; New Haven, Yale University Art Gallery) was the subject, first, of a madrigal (1619) by Giambattista Marino; second, of Vondel's Dutch variation (1650) on that Italian poem; and third, of a poem by Jan Vos (1662). Vos' forty-four-line stanza not only evokes the action as portrayed in the painting, but also refers to the classical literary sources, presents moralistic observations, and, finally, honors the collector. The study of Rubens' painting and the three *ekphraseis* (rhetorical responses; verbal evocations of the work of art) it inspired offer rare insight into the intricate relationships between imagery and poetic response.

Another work by Vos, *Strijd tusschen Doodt en Natuur, of Zeege der Schilderkunst* (Battle between Death and Nature, or Triumph of Painting, 1654), glorifies painting as the means of salvation and immortality and praises some artists then living in Amsterdam. The works of Rembrandt attracted many poets, among them Vondel, Vos, Jeremias de Decker, H.F. Waterloos, and Andries Pels; their writings, along with those by Von Sandrart, Jan de Bisschop, Samuel van Hoogstraten, Gerard de Lairesse, and others, chart the developments of Rembrandt's reputation and of the classicist critique. The town hall of Amsterdam, built and decorated by 1662, was a focus of significant literary attention, and its paintings received the versified praises of Vondel and Vos, among others.

Collaborations between authors and artists in the production of single volumes, often commemorative, form a significant component for study in the field of word–image relations. Among the most lavish volumes of cooperative ventures is that published on the occasion of Marie de' Medici's entry into Amsterdam in 1638. This folio consisted of poetic text by Caspar Barlaeus and prints after Claes Cornelisz. Moeyaert and others. It was shortly followed by a series of the Months, with poems by Barlaeus and Vondel and illustrations by Von Sandrart. Other illustrated publications, such as those with which Crispijn de Passe II, Romeyn de Hooghe, or Jan Luyken were involved, further demonstrate the close ties between the publication of a text and the production of images. Even modest print series indicate pervasive cooperation between publisher and designer, as demonstrated by prints in the various categories of landscape, genre, narrative, allegory, or portraiture. Narrative subjects, whether mythological, religious, or allegorical, often necessitated a textual element, perhaps merely a title identifying the figures portrayed; often such prints included a text that provided a moralistic interpretation. Portraits frequently were accompanied by verses that, inspired by classical models, elaborate upon the *topos* (type; a rhetorical or iconographic standard motif) of the speaking picture; such verses are indirect, rather than direct, expressions of asthetic appreciation.

Descriptions of cities often included biographies of local artists and mention of works of art that adorned buildings of extraordinary religious or civic importance. Examples include Jan Jansz. Orlers' *Leiden* (2nd ed., 1641), Samuel Ampzing's *Haarlem* (1628), and Melchior Fokkens' *Amsterdam* (1664).

Private diaries are rare, but a few offer insight into the visual arts. Foremost among them is the journal, kept around 1629–1631, by Constantijn Huygens, who eloquently praised Rubens, Gerard van Honthorst, and the young Leiden painters Lievens and Rembrandt. Aernout van Buchell, jurist and cleric, also kept a journal in the period 1628–1639 and wrote acutely interesting observations about Utrecht artists.

Biographical writing about artists and instructional texts for artists first appear in the Dutch language with Karel van Mander's *Schilder-Boeck* of 1604, which would form the model for subsequent writing about art in the Netherlands and Northern Europe. Those who emulated Van Mander include Von Sandrart, Van Hoogstraten, Wybrand de Geest, De Lairesse, Houbraken, and Jacob Campo Weyerman.

Current interpretive strategies for seventeenth-century paintings of landscape, genre, and still life are exploring the ways in which the image may be read as if its components convey a narrative. Paintings of biblical, mythological, theatrical, and pastoral themes relate generally to parallel categories of literature; analysis of such paintings indicates a highly developed appreciation for pictorial depictions of literary subjects. A number of artists were themselves poets, as, for example, Adriaen van de Venne, who composed images with texts in mind, even if they did not necessarily accompany his pictures. Occasionally paintings are inscribed with poems, so that the image itself contains an interpretive text. One notable example is Abraham Bloemaert's *Shepherdess Reading a Poem* (1628; Toledo, Toledo Museum of Art), which displays a pastoral text. Another is Von Sandrart's *Company of Cornelis Bicker* (1640; Amsterdam, Rijksmuseum), which includes the text of Vondel's poem in honor of the painting. In such pictures incorporating text, the roles of viewer and reader are inextricably bound with those of painter and writer. Even in many cases of paintings of landscape, genre subjects, and still life, the viewer becomes the "reader" of the elements within the image. This is an especially fruitful approach with respect to landscapes and seascapes, in which peaceful travel, calamitous shipwreck, or agricultural and industrial activity evolve within the drama of nature. Another approach, equally rewarding, would examine the relationship between literary theory and artistic practice. Documented analogues between word and image do not exhaust the subtle interdependencies, most certainly traceable, of Dutch seventeenth-century art and literature.

Amy Golahny

See also Allegorical traditions; Comic modes; Emblems and emblem books; Genre painting, seventeenth century; History painting; Landscape; Pastoral; Rhetoricians' chambers; Still life; Subjects, subject categories, and hierarchies; Theater and theatricality; Van Mander, Karel; Writers on art, eighteenth century; Writers on art, sixteenth and seventeenth centuries

Bibliography

Becker, Jochen. "Review of Gisbert Kranz. *Das Bildgedicht in Europe: Zur Theorie und Geschichte einer literarischen Gattung.* Paderborn: F. Schoening, 1973." *Simiolus* 8 (1975/1976): 26–30.

———. "Review of Gisbert Kranz. *Das Bildgedicht: Theorie, Lexikon, Bibliographie.* Cologne and Vienna: Böhlau Verlag, 1981." *Simiolus* 15 (1985): 225–230.

Freedberg, David, and Jan de Vries, eds. *Art in History, History in Art: Studies in Seventeenth-Century Dutch Culture.* Santa Monica, CA: The Getty Center for the History of Art and the Humanities, 1991.

Goedde, Lawrence O. *Tempest and Shipwreck in Dutch and Flemish Art: Convention, Rhetoric, and Interpretation.* University Park, PA: Pennsylvania State University Press, 1989.

Golahny, Amy. "Rubens' *Hero and Leander* and Its Poetic Progeny." *Yale University Art Gallery Bulletin* (1990): 21–39.

Kettering, Alison McNeil. *The Dutch Arcadia: Pastoral Art and Its Audience in the Golden Age.* Totowa, NJ: Allanheld and Schram; Montclair, NJ: distributed by A. Schram, 1983.

Porteman, Karel. "Geschreven met de linkerhand? Letteren tegenover schilderkunst in de Gouden Eeuw." In *Historische letterkunde: Facetten van vakbeoefening.* Edited by Marijke Spies, 93–113. Groningen: Wolters-Noordhoff, 1984.

———. *Joachim von Sandrart, Joost van den Vondel, Caspar Barlaeus: De Maanden van het jaar.* Wommelgem: Uitgeverij Den Gulden Engel, 1987.

———. "Zeventiende Eeuwse Nederlandse Poëzie op Schilderijen: Vondel over Willem Kalf." In *Handelingen Elfde Colloquium Neerlandicum: Colloquium van docenten in de neerlandistiek aan buitenlandse universiteiten,* 290–302. Utrecht: Internationale Vereniging voor Neerlandistiek, 1992.

Postma, Hugo, and Marjo Blok. "Duidelijkheid over de Amsterdamse St. Lukasfeesten in 1653 en 1654." *Oud Holland* 105 (1991): 32–38.

Schenkeveld, Maria A. *Dutch Literature in the Age of*

Rembrandt: Themes and Ideas. Amsterdam and London: Benjamins, 1991.

Slive, Seymour. *Rembrandt and His Critics, 1630–1730.* The Hague: Nijhoff, 1953.

Weber, Gregor J.M. *Der Lobtopos des "lebenden" Bildes: Jan Vos und sein "Zeege der Schilderkunst" von 1654.* Hildesheim, Zurich, and New York: Georg Olms Verlag, 1991.

Lucebert (Lubertus Jacobus Swaanswijk) (1924–1994)

Poet-member of the Dutch Experimental Group and the Cobra Movement from 1948 to 1949, Lucebert is also a draftsman and painter. Born in Amsterdam, he studied briefly at the Kunstnijverheidsschool (School of Arts and Crafts) in the late 1930s, and after the war he lived as a drifter, writing poems and making caricatural drawings. In 1948, he adopted his pseudonym, had his first exhibition, and associated with Gerrit Kouwenaar and Jan Elburg to form the poets' section of the Dutch Experimental Group. His poem "Love Letter to our Martyred Bride Indonesia" was published in the Experimental journal *Reflex* (March 1949). In November 1949, the poets left the Experimental Group, but by the early 1950s they achieved literary recognition as *de Vijftigers* (poets of the 1950s), and in 1953 Lucebert himself received the Poetry Prize of Amsterdam. Literary success gave Lucebert the financial means to paint in oils, which he has done consistently (alongside his literary work) since the later 1950s. His exploratory handling of paint and elementary figuration link him broadly with (former) Cobra artists such as Karel Appel, but his satirical and narrative tendencies also suggest affinities with the disturbing portraiture of Francis Bacon, the biting satire of Georg Grosz, and the visual wit of cartoonist Saul Steinberg. As the Netherlands' most celebrated contemporary poet and one of its most accomplished painters, Lucebert is studied both by art historians and literary scholars. Analyses have focused on his multilayered meanings and underlying gnostic themes, but easy correlations between his visual and literary works are usually discouraged, not least by Lucebert himself.

Graham Birtwistle

See also Cobra Movement

Bibliography

Elburg, Jan G., and others. *Lucebert schilder-dichter.* Amsterdam: Meulenhoff, 1991.

Jensen, Jens Christian, ed. *Der junge Lucebert: Gemälde, Gouachen, Aquarelle, Zeichnungen, Radierungen 1947 bis 1965.* Kiel: Kunsthalle der Christian-Albrechts Universität/Schleswig-Holsteinischer Kunstverein, 1989.

Pedersen, Ad, ed. *Lucebert in the Stedelijk: Catalogue of All the Paintings, Drawings, Gouaches, Watercolours, and Prints in the Collection.* Amsterdam: Stedelijk Museum, 1987.

M

Maes, Nicolaes (1634–1693)

Born in Dordrecht, the son of a merchant, Nicolaes Maes studied painting with Rembrandt in Amsterdam during the late 1640s. He was back in Dordrecht by 1653, when he married the widow Adriana Brouwers. His earliest works were religious scenes featuring the *chiaroscuro* effects that clearly reveal his debt to his teacher. In the mid-1650s he switched to genre subjects and created a number of domestic scenes featuring ambitious compositions and warm, bright colors. In the following decade, Maes made another, more dramatic shift in style and subject matter. He traveled to Antwerp, where he studied the works of Pieter Paul Rubens and Anthony van Dyck and visited Jacob Jordaens. On his return, he devoted the rest of his long career to portraiture in a light, elegant manner derived from his Flemish contemporaries, changing his reddish tonalities to a cool, grey palette. In 1673 Maes moved with his family to Amsterdam to broaden his circle of buyers; he remained there until his death.

Maes is best known for his genre scenes, although they make up only a small part of his *oeuvre*. In these depictions of domestic life—particularly of women at household tasks—he made bold experiments with illusionistic perspective and multiple views, a few years before Pieter de Hooch and Johannes Vermeer began achieving similar effects. His innovative approach to the domestic interior is best illustrated by a group of six comic scenes, done between 1655 and 1657, of maids and their employers eavesdropping on one another in different areas of a house. In a typical example, *The Eavesdropper* of 1657 (Color Plate 7), Maes breaks up the domestic space into isolated vignettes of public dining and private seduction, placing the eavesdropper at their boundaries. Through this ingenious manipulation of thresholds and viewpoints, the series provides a commentary on class conflicts within the household.

Martha Hollander

See also Dordrecht; House interiors; Housewives and maids; Rembrandt School

Bibliography

Marijnissen, Peter et al., eds. *De Zichtbaere Werelt: Schilderkunst uit de Gouden Eeuw in Hollands oudste stad.* Dordrecht: Dordrechts Museum; Zwolle: Waanders, 1992.

Robinson, W.R. "Nicolaes Maes As a Draughtsman." *Master Drawings* 27 (1989): 146–162.

Sumowski, Werner. *Gemälde der Rembrandt-Schüler.* Landau, Pfalz: Edition PVA, 1983–[1994] 5 vols.

Magic Realism

In the Netherlands, which had remained neutral during World War I, two tendencies developed among artists who worked in the Cubist style around 1917. Some of them gathered around the journal *De Stijl*, also the name of a movement whose members strove for a completely abstract art. Other Cubists decide to return to figuration, partly in imitation of Pablo Picasso. Some of them, like Charley Toorop and Bart van der Leck, were inspired by the opinions of Hendricus P. Bremmer, the adviser to the collector Hélène Kröller-Müller. While the artists of *De Stijl* rejected the physical part of nature and strove for the absolute spiritualization of art and life, Bremmer and his followers valued the natural and the individual in art. As early as 1916, Bremmer stopped his financial support of Piet Mondrian because of the artist's abstraction, which did not allow Bremmer to experience the individual emotion in the work of the artist. After *De Stijl* was first published, Charley Toorop immediately distanced herself from the philosophical basic assumptions of the journal: "To be part of the cosmic implies the acknowledgment of the natural element, which leads to animated *seeing.*" In 1918, Van der Leck, one of the founders of *De Stijl*, left abstraction, which he had achieved in his work in 1916, and again started making recognizable paintings. Several of the artists around *De Stijl*, among them Peter Alma and Chris Beekman, were led by political considerations, influenced by the Communist Revolution in Russia. Like the Communists they rejected complete abstraction because the people would not have any affinity with it. During the 1920s, this was true for a great number of social realists, among whom were Piet Begeer, Hendrik Chabot, Ger Gerrits, and Johan van Hell, who saw a paradigm in Van der Leck's work of 1913. They tried to give shape to a revolutionary art by adapting his angular styling and motifs from the lives of workers. A crucial year was 1924 when many artists left modernism to start working figuratively again.

In 1924 Wim Schuhmacher returned to figurative art after he saw the *retour à l'ordre* in the work of Georges Braque, Fernand Léger, Pablo Picasso, Albert Gleizes, Jean Metzinger, and Gino Severini in Paris. These painters also exhibited their work that year in the Hollandsche Kunstenaarskring (Dutch Artists' Circle) in the Stedelijk Museum in Amsterdam. Raoul Hynckes saw it there, and after this confrontation he destroyed his Impressionistic paintings to begin developing a more refined realism. Carel Willink, who enjoyed his education in Berlin from 1921 until 1923 and belonged to the Constructivist avant-garde there, returned to Amsterdam in 1924 and gradually began working figuratively again. Willink was guided by modern Italian painting, the work of Giorgio de Chirico, Carlo Carra, Achille Funi, and Felice Casorati that was exhibited in the Stedelijk Museum in 1928. Like them, Willink strove for a Neoclassicism after the break with Cubism and Futurism. This Neoclassicism was revived particularly in human figures in landscapes with classical architecture.

After 1926 there were surrealistic tendencies in the work of many Dutch painters. In the Netherlands, Surrealism became known mainly through literature and reproductions, with some exceptions like the exhibition of works by French and Belgian Surrealists in the Stedelijk Museum in Amsterdam in 1930. Kristians Tonny was the only Dutch artist who participated in the Surrealist Movement in Paris. Dutch Surrealism flourished particularly in Utrecht around Willem Wagenaar's art gallery, Nord, where, besides the well-known Surrealist Joop Moesman, other frequent visitors were Pyke Koch, Willem van Leusden, and Gerrit van 't Net. Pyke Koch, who started painting in 1927, tended toward the Verism of Georg Grosz and Rudolph Schlichter, as well as toward Constructivism and Surrealism. German painting, both the Neue Sächlichkeit and Magic Realism that started in Germany in 1924–1925 as a reaction to Expressionism, left visible marks in Dutch art.

The many realisms that came up during the 1920s—besides Magic Realism, the Nieuwe Zakelijkheid (New Objectivity), Neo-Realism, Verism, and Surrealism, one hears of social realism, populism, *pittura metafysica*, precisionism, and Neoclassicism—are often placed outside their original ideological, national, and artistic context in the Netherlands. In 1929, at the spring exhibition of De Onafhankelijken (The Independents) in the Stedelijk Museum in Amsterdam, when the latest developments in German realistic painting art were exhibited, Verism, which has a strong political strain, Magic Realism, and the Nieuwe Zakelijkheid, which places the accent mainly on technique, were all presented as Neue Sächlichkeit. In 1930, the Belgian V.E. van Uytvanck described Magic Realism as the French version of Neue

Sächlichkeit, and in 1933 Jacob Bendien connected the Nieuwe Zakelijkheid with Neo-Plasticism, for good reasons as both strive to have an objective form of expression for subjective feelings. In 1930, the term Magic Realism was used in art criticism to describe the work of Pyke Koch, Kor Postma, and Carel Willink, who jointly exhibited at P. de Boer's gallery in Amsterdam. On this occasion they did not present themselves as Magic Realists. Postma, who moved to Paris permanently in 1936, and who was influenced particularly by René Magritte and Max Ernst, was more of a Surrealist. Willink had always rejected the term Magic Realism as an adequate description of his work; he preferred the term "fantastic realism" (Color Plate 14); with Koch, who called himself a Neo-Realist during the 1930s and the 1940s, Willink considered issues of painterly technique exclusively. All three painters appeared to be concerned in both word and writings about abstract art, which, in this period, they rejected.

In 1937, in a work whose title translates as "Painters of Another Reality," S.P. Abas, an art historian, called Hynckes, Koch, and Willink Neo-Realists who had been purified by abstract art (Abas, 1937). They worked differently than the nineteenth-century realists, who held a mirror up to reality to portray it. In the construction of reality on the canvas, the Neo-Realists work according to a concept in which their means are used in a way that is "free from space, time, causality, and logic." In this manner they arrive at a magical condensed atmosphere, the one of the "painting I," according to Abas. He called Schuhmacher a "mystic realist," however, because he continued to experience reality as a unity, which can be portrayed as a whole. Besides Schuhmacher, Charley Toorop, Edgar Fernhout, and Dick Ket (1902–1940) continued to paint by using immediate observation; in contrast to the Magic Realists, they used no tools like photographs or their own imagination. Incidentally, before the war, Fernhout, Ket, Schuhmacher, and Charley Toorop were also often called Neo-Realists on the strength of abstract elements in their work.

At the beginning of World War II, Koch tried to gain appreciation from the Germans occupying the Netherlands for his work and the work of Ket, Schuhmacher, Fernhout, Charley Toorop, Hynckes, and Willink by labeling it Neo-Realism. During World War II, the paintings of some of them were regularly exhibited, some against their will, together with work of party members of the NSB (Nationaal-Socialistische Beweging/National Socialist Movement), at exhibitions of Dutch art in Germany.

Because of the preference of both fascists and Communists for realism, abstract art, which they banned, was seen as superior modern art by the Allies after 1945. In 1950, Willink protested in *De schilderkunst in een kritiek stadium* (The Art of Painting in a Critical Phase) against this odd occurrence. Membership in the Communist Party created problems for Charley Toorop at an exhibition at the Hammer Galleries in New York in 1954. Willem Sandberg, who preferred abstract art and the Cobra Movement after the war, had since 1954 exhibited the named realists in solo exhibitions in the Stedelijk Museum in Amsterdam. In 1960, the Gemeentemuseum in Arnhem organized the exhibition *The Frightening Thirties: Neo-Realism in*

Dutch Painting, in which works by Hynckes, Ket, Koch, Johan Mekkink, Schuhmacher, and Willink could be seen. However, in 1971, in the Koninklijk Museum voor Schone Kunsten in Antwerp, the work of Hynckes, Koch, and Willink was exhibited under the title *Magic Realism in the Netherlands*. In the catalog of this exhibition, Koch explained the difference between Magic Realism and Surrealism as follows: "Magic realism uses images which are *possible, but not probable;* surrealism uses *impossible, nonexisting* or *cannot exist situations*."

In 1979, Pyke Koch again defined the difference between Magic Realism and Surrealism; both exist by the grace of ambiguity, which arises when oppositions in reality are connected with one another on the canvas. The images that the Surrealists use are separated from reality with an axe, while the Magic Realists use a razor for this. The Magic Realists know how to connect fragments of reality without using any seams, so that the suggestion of reality is evoked (Fig. 69). Koch held the opinion that Magic Realism was as old as painting itself, and he gave as an example of a Magic Realist *avant la lettre* the fifteenth-century Italian painter Piero della Francesca, who connected opposite moods like suffering and extreme adoration with complete indifference, as, for example, in the *Flagellation of Christ*.

John Steen

See also Chabot, Hendrik; De Stijl; Koch, Pyke; Kröller-Müller, Hélène E.L.J.; Mondrian, Piet; Surrealism; Toorop, Charley (Annie Caroline Pontifex); World Wars I and II

Bibliography

Abas, S.P. *Schilders van een andere werkelijkheid: Raoul Hynckes, Pijke koch, Carel Willink*. The Hague: Leopold, 1937.

Blotkamp, Carel. "Charley Toorop on De Stijl." *Jong Holland* 6 (1990): 38–39.

Brand, Jan, and Kees Broos, eds. *Magisch realisten en tijdgenoten in de verzameling van het Gemeentemuseum Arnhem*. Zwolle: Waanders, 1992.

Eitner, Lorenz. "Magic Realism." *Delta: A Review of Arts, Life, and Thought in the Netherlands.* (Autumn 1960): 70–72.

———. *Paintings by Pyke Koch*. Minneapolis: Walker Art Center, 1960.

Koch, Pyke. "Declaration sur le réalisme magique: Définition des principes du réalisme magique pour un éditeur anglais, 1979." *Cahiers du Musee National d'Art Moderne* 7/8 (1981): 357.

———. In *Magisch Realisme in Nederland: Raoul Hynckes, Pyke Koch, Carel Willink*. Antwerp: Koninklijk Museum voor Schone Kunsten, 1971.

Marck, J.M.H. van der. *Neo-Realism in Painting*. Amsterdam: Meulenhoff, 1960.

Mannerism, Mannerists

Mannerism was a European stylistic trend that affected all artistic media in the sixteenth and early seventeenth centuries. It thrived in the Netherlands throughout that period, from its earliest manifestation in Antwerp about 1510 to an efflorescence generated in Haarlem in the 1580s. In painting, the graphic arts, and sculpture, Mannerists favored artifice and novelty, achieved, for example, with elongated or otherwise distorted figures in exotic poses, often with erotic overtones; with illogical spatial effects; and with unnatural, ornamental color. Mannerism is sometimes characterized as anticlassical and antinatural, but that view oversimplifies. Instability and ambiguity do supersede the classical norms of balance, clarity, and order, but imaginatively reworked classical motifs and subjects are common. Similarly, departures from naturalistic norms are the rule, but the interplay between art and nature is complex, with naturalistic elements sometimes used as a foil for artificial ones. Self-conscious of style, artists demonstrated virtuosity by changing modes at will. Through copying, imitation, and emulation, they sought to surpass their predecessors by dint of imagination.

The phenomenon of Italian Mannerism has been widely discussed, but fundamental questions about the origins and character of Netherlandish Mannerism remain. The style is adumbrated in the late fifteenth century in the works of Hugo van der Goes, whose altarpiece shutters depicting *The Trinity* and *Sir Edward Bonkil and Angels* (1473–1478) display an insistent verticality, confusing spatial effects, and an intense, private artistic vision, features that would later be associated with Mannerism. Soon after 1500, a style characterized by those qualities plus an opulent artifice became fashionable in Antwerp, the wealthiest commercial center in the Netherlands.

Italian, classical, and indigenous elements intermingle in Netherlandish Mannerism throughout the sixteenth century. Upon returning from a trip to Italy (1508–1509) to study ancient monuments, Jan Gossaert wittily employed a classical vocabulary, always with a Northern preference for naturalistic detail and dominant linearity, as in his *Neptune and Amphitrite* (1516). Bernard van Orley, Hapsburg court painter in Brussels, juxtaposed quotations from Raphael's tapestry cartoons with demons in his *Virtue of Patience* altarpiece (1521), combining Renaissance forms and Gothic fantasies.

The term "Romanist" is sometimes applied to Netherlanders such as Gossaert and Frans Floris who were devoted to the heroic figural ideal and the culture of the ancient world. Romanism and Mannerism are not, however, mutually exclusive. Indeed, those artists' reworkings of Italian and classical ideals could be quintessential Mannerist expressions. Floris' *Fall of the Rebel Angels* (1554), for example, translates Michelangelo's *Last Judgment* into a Northern idiom replete with fantastic monsters, a *horror vacui*, and convoluted forms. In the early 1520s, Jan van Scorel followed Raphael as keeper of the papal antiquities in Rome. The figures in paintings executed after Van Scorel's return to the Netherlands (1524) elaborate on classical ideals; the resulting exaggerations of pose and proportion typify Mannerism (Fig. 67). Van Scorel's pupil Maerten van Heemskerck also spent formative years in Rome in the 1530s. Van Heemskerck's *Concert of Apollo and the Muses on Mount Helicon* (1565; Fig. 77) owes much to Raphael's *Parnassus* and to Roman monuments Van Heemskerck had sketched, such as the marble Horses of Montecavallo, the source for his Pegasus.

Disjunction, seeming disorder, and evasiveness rule the composition. He teases by placing Apollo centrally but in the middleground, dwarfed by a sheet of music.

With the growing separation between the Northern and Southern Netherlands by the late sixteenth century, we can discuss Dutch developments apart from Flemish. The Northern city of Haarlem, Van Heemskerck's base, was the cradle of Dutch Mannerism, generated in the 1580s and influential into the next century. Its leaders in Haarlem were Karel van Mander, artist, theorist, and teacher; Hendrick Goltzius, engraver, draftsman, and later painter; and Cornelis Cornelisz. van Haarlem, primarily a painter. About 1583, Van Mander introduced his two younger colleagues to drawings by Bartholomeus Spranger, court painter to Hapsburg emperor Rudolph II. Spranger's sophisticated international Mannerist amalgam sparked a vibrant outpouring of designs like the four *Disgracers* by Goltzius and Cornelis Cornelisz. van Haarlem (1588), full of wit, eros, and virtuosity. Jacob de Gheyn II practiced his distinctive blend of fantasy and naturalism in neighboring cities. In Utrecht the chief exponents of Dutch Mannerism were Abraham Bloemaert and Joachim Wtewael. Wtewael, whose brilliant mythological scenes on copper exemplify the style, clung to Mannerist formulae throughout his career. Bloemaert's intensely Mannerist phase was short-lived, but he, too, used Mannerist color and formulae into the 1630s.

While Mannerism was a pervasive trend in the Netherlands, it coexisted with other approaches, such as forthright naturalism in portraits by Floris and Antonis Mor. Some major figures, notably Pieter Bruegel the Elder, were little affected by Mannerism.

Anne W. Lowenthal

See also Drawing theory; Engebrechtsz. (or Engelbrechtsen), Cornelis; Flanders, Flemish School; Goltzius, Hendrick; Haarlem; Italy; Utrecht; Van Mander, Karel

Bibliography
Cavalli-Bjorkman, Gorel, ed. *Netherlandish Mannerism: Papers Given at a Symposium in Nationalmuseum, Stockholm, September 21–22, 1984.* Nationalmusei Skriftserie n.s. 4. Stockholm: Nationalmuseum, 1985.

Kloek, W.Th., W. Halsema-Kubes, and R.J. Baarsen. *Art before the Iconoclasm: Northern Netherlandish Art, 1525–1580.* The Hague: Staatsuitgeverij, 1986.

Lowenthal, Anne W. "The *Disgracers:* Four Sinners in One Act." In *Essays in Northern European Art Presented to Egbert Haverkamp-Begemann on His Sixtieth Birthday,* 148–153. Doornspijk: Davaco, 1983.

———. *Netherlandish Mannerism in British Collections: A Loan Exhibition.* Doornspijk: Davaco, 1990.

Luijten, Ger et al. *Dawn of the Golden Age: Northern Netherlandish Art, 1580–1620.* Zwolle: Waanders, 1993.

Manuscript illumination
Between the late fourteenth and early sixteenth centuries illuminated manuscripts of such high quality were produced in the Northern Netherlands, by a variety of artists and in a variety of styles, that the period has been dubbed the "Golden Age of Dutch manuscript painting." While the work of French, Flemish, English, German, and Italian illuminators of this period has long been appreciated, widely published, and frequently exhibited, contemporaneous Dutch illumination has been relatively ignored. This manuscript painting often embodies a different esthetic, at times less elegant if more heartfelt, than that which typifies the work of other major European countries. Recent research, which has brought to light unknown manuscripts, coupled with late twentieth-century tastes more catholic than in previous generations, has brought Dutch manuscript illumination within the European canon.

One of the unmistakable influences on Dutch illumination of this period was the Devotio Moderna. This distinctly Dutch spiritual movement placed emphasis on personal faith, attaching great importance to meditation and prayer—especially the imitation of Christ and contemplation of his Passion. The movement's monastic and lay followers helped shape the appearance of Dutch manuscripts and their illustration. As part of this movement, the *Book of Hours,* the late medieval "best-seller," was translated by Geert Grote (died 1384) into Dutch as the *Getijdenboek.* It is a distinct feature of the period that, as opposed to the rest of Europe, *Books of Hours* from the Northern Netherlands are nearly always in the vernacular instead of Latin. In addition to *Books of Hours,* liturgical service books and Bibles comprise the most frequently commissioned manuscripts during this period of Dutch art history.

In the second half of the fourteenth century Albrecht, duke of Bavaria and count of Holland, Zeeland, and Hainaut (1358–1404), settled his court in The Hague. Around him, Margaret of Cleves (his second wife), and Albrecht's successor, William VI, a dynamic cultural life developed. The visual arts, architecture, literature, and music flourished. Patronage centered on the court of Guelders, as well as on the workshops in Utrecht, the largest and most important city in the Northern Netherlands, with a long artistic tradition.

The work of the first generation of Dutch illuminators, from about 1395 to 1415, can be divided between two styles: that of the Master of Margaret of Cleves and that of the Master of Dirc van Delf. The Master of Margaret of Cleves is named after the *Book of Hours* commissioned by Margaret, probably between 1395 and 1400 (Lisbon, Museu Calouste Gulbenkian). Its miniatures, all the work of one hand, are characteristic of the best of the European International Style: soft, muted colors and figures bearing fine features and clothed in gracefully falling drapery. Unusual at this time, however, is the artist's penchant for breaking the confines of the miniature's frame and placing figures in the margins of the page. The Master of Dirc van Delf receives his name from two different copies of the author's treatise, *Tafel van den Kersten Ghelove* (Table of Christian Faith), which Dirc, court chaplain at The Hague, dedicated to Duke Albrecht and his youngest son, John of Bavaria. Both manuscripts (Baltimore, Walters Art Gallery; and New York, Pierpont Morgan Library) date to the first decade of the fifteenth century. While still partaking of the elegance of the International Style, the work of the

Master of Dirc van Delf is more heartfelt, with figures with larger faces and drapery somewhat harder and more linear (Fig. 78).

The period from 1415 to 1425 was one of experimentation and growth. The painters of this second generation, while continuing the stylistic trends described above, expressed new concerns with narrative and domestic detail and highly innovative borders. Political troubles in Utrecht around 1415 forced many artists to flee the city, and artistic activity thrived in the west, in Delft, and farther east in the duchy of Guelders. The first leading artist of this period is the Master of the Morgan Infancy Cycle, who worked in Delft. Named after the inventive illustrations of Christ's Infancy in a *Book of Hours* datable to 1415–1420 (New York, Pierpont Morgan Library), this illuminator is known for his highly dramatic compositions and experimental juxtapositions of paint with washes. A second major illuminator is the Passion Master of Mary of Guelders, named after the cycle of miniatures he painted for the Hours of the Passion in the *Prayer Book* of Mary, duchess of Guelders and Jülich, shortly after 1415 (Berlin, Staatsbibliothek Preussischer Kulturbesitz). Extremely refined and subtle, the work of the Passion Master reveals his knowledge of current trends in Germany, France, and Flanders, and is among the most sophisticated Dutch illumination.

Dutch illumination in the second quarter of the century is characterized by a much broader style, with figures that have smooth, egg-shaped faces and thick, schematized drapery. The dominant artists are the "Masters" of Otto van Moerdrecht and the "Masters" of Zweder van Culemborg, terms used in the plural not so much to designate specific workshops, but more to refer to groups of artists working, often over disparate areas, in a common style. The Moerdrecht Masters are named after a group of manuscripts donated by Otto to the Carthusian monastery of Nieuwlicht in Utrecht in 1423. (Among these books was a three-volume commentary on the Old Testament by Nicolaus de Lyra, of which two volumes survive: Utrecht, Universiteitsbibliotheek.) The Zweder Masters are named after a missal made around 1425 for Zweder van Culemborg, bishop of Utrecht (Bressanone, Biblioteca del Seminario Maggiore). Their style, while still rather abstract, contains more pictorial naturalism, especially in atmospheric backgrounds, and detailed interiors than that of the Moerdrecht artists.

The Master of Catherine of Cleves, active from around 1430 to 1460, is, without question, the most gifted and original artist of this Golden Age of Dutch illumination. His masterpiece, the *Hours of Catherine of Cleves*, duchess of Guelders, was painted in Utrecht around 1440 and contains 157 miniatures; it represents the supreme achievement of Dutch illumination (New York, Pierpont Morgan Library). The richness of the Cleves Master's palette, his extraordinary powers of observation, in which the most minute details are captured, the everyday realism, and his complex iconography serve to rank him as one of the greatest of all illuminators (Fig. 79). Because the fourteen manuscripts to which he contributed illustrations date to a thirty-year period, it is possible to do something rare in the field of Dutch illumination: follow the artist's stylistic development. His early works are draftsmanlike and thinly painted, while in his mature phase, in which the *Hours of Catherine of Cleves* falls, figures and compositions are more harmonious and solidly painted. In the last phase the supple drapery becomes harder, more angular, and mannered.

In the fifteenth century Delft was a prosperous trading town. It had two parish churches and numerous monasteries, many of which had scriptoria producing illuminated manuscripts. Illuminators apparently included members of the religious communities as well as lay artists. Some of the workshops in Delft specialized in miniatures painted on single leaves that could be inserted in manuscripts according to a patron's taste or pocketbook. Delft manuscripts from 1430 to 1480 exhibit a number of recognizable characteristics: distinctive types of red and blue penwork, miniatures often painted in grisaille, and border decoration consisting of half-length angels, saints, and prophets. Typical Delft products are two *Books of Hours* (New York, Pierpont Morgan Library; and Baltimore, Walters Art Gallery) painted around 1440–1450 by artists called the Masters of the Delft Grisailles.

Utrecht, in the generation following the Master of Catherine of Cleves—that is, from 1460 to 1475—continued to be an important center for the production of illumination. The most important artist of this time, who was both an illuminator and a panel painter, is the Master of Evert Zoudenbalch, who painted miniatures around 1460 in the first volume of a Bible ordered by the canon of that city's cathedral, Evert Zoudenbalch (Vienna, Österreichische Nationalbibliothek). He was assisted by the Master of Gijsbrecht van Brederode, who is better known for his illuminated *Books of Hours*, especially the one commissioned in the late 1460s by the dean of the cathedral, Gijsbrecht van Brederode (Liège, Bibliothèque de l'Université). Both artists use bright colors and continue the naturalistic style of painting found in the works of their predecessors. In a political struggle over the bishopric of Utrecht, Gijsbrecht was imprisoned in 1470 and, fleeing the power of Duke Philip of Burgundy, his supporters left the city. Patronage for illumination in Utrecht evaporated.

Before the rise of Amsterdam in the sixteenth century, Haarlem was the cultural capital of Northern Holland and a major center for both illumination and panel painting (Albert van Ouwater, Dirck Bouts, and Geertgen tot Sint Jans worked there). Three quite different illuminators have been identified as working in Haarlem from 1445 to 1520. The work of the first, the prolific Master of the Haarlem Bible, can be found in more than twenty-five manuscripts dating from 1445 to 1474. Named after a three-volume Bible datable to the 1450s (Haarlem, Stadsbibliotheek), the Haarlem Master's style is notably linear, and his figures rather stiff, with drapery composed of large, wide folds. In a manner characteristic of other Dutch illuminators of this time, the Haarlem Master freely borrowed compositions from woodcuts. The Master of the London Jason is named after a *Historie van Jason* he illustrated with twenty lively pen-and-wash drawings between about 1475 and 1480 (London, British Library). Although known from only five manuscripts dating to the 1470s, this powerful, imaginative artist was the most gifted among his Haarlem colleagues. Finally, the third illuminator, active from around 1485 to 1519, is one of the few whose name is actually known from signed works: Spierinck. Although not as gifted at the two artists just discussed, Spierinck is interesting because his career can be followed over thirty years in at least fifteen manuscripts. Colorful and full of variety, Spierinck's works also borrow from contemporaneous panel painting, woodcuts, and engravings, as can be seen in a *Book of Hours* signed and dated 1488 by him (New York, Pierpont Morgan Library). The miniature of *Christ Washing the Feet of the Apostles* in this manuscript, for example, is derived from an engraving by Israhel van Meckenem.

During the second half of the fifteenth century, from 1460 to 1480, illumination in the eastern Netherlands was apparently restricted to Zwolle and perhaps Arnhem. In Zwolle, the followers of the Devotio Moderna, the Brethren of the Common Life, produced books for their own use and sale. The Masters of the Zwolle Bible are named after the monumental six-volume Bible they illuminated between 1464 and 1476 in Zwolle, a commission for the Chapter of St. Mary's in Utrecht (Utrecht, Universiteitsbibliotheek). Their sturdy style and many of their motifs are derived from prints, especially those in block books of the *Biblia Pauperum* and *Speculum Humanae Salvationis*. A second group of artists, the Masters of Margariet Uutenham, worked possibly around Arnhem. They are named after the decoration painted in the *Hours of Margariet Uutenham* around 1460 (United States, private collection). They, however, confined themselves to richly decorated borders and initials, preferring dark colors and highly burnished gold.

The important role played by Delft in Dutch illumination, second only to Utrecht, continued to the end of the fifteenth century. In style and composition the artists betray an awareness of Southern Netherlandish art. Both panel painting (particularly of such artists as Hans Memling, Gerard David, and Hugo van der Goes) and manuscripts from Flanders strongly affected the appearance of Dutch illumination during this period. Unquestionably the most important manuscript produced by these late fifteenth-century Delft painters is the *Breviary of Beatrijs van Assendelft* of about 1485, the collaborative effort of three illuminators (Utrecht, Rijksmuseum Het Catharijneconvent).

The final thirty years of Dutch illumination, from 1490 to 1520, were dominated by a group of artists collectively called the Masters of the Dark Eyes after their penchant for painting shadowy eyes on their figures. Although they worked in the country of Holland, the style itself was exported, and practitioners of the style can be found in both Flanders and England. A primary stylistic source for the group was the Ghent-Bruges school of illumination. By far the most important personality among these painters is the Master of the Bezborodko Hours. His name derives from a *Book of Hours* (The Hague, Koninklijke Bibliotheek) that was owned in the nineteenth century by the Russian count Nicolai Bezborodko. In addition to the dark, heavily shaded eyes that characterize this group as a whole, the Bezborodko Master's style is crisp

and linear, with complex compositions and elaborate borders. A second group of artists working in this period, and also influenced by Ghent-Bruges illumination, was the Masters of the Suffrages, named after a series of miniatures illustrating the Suffrages (short prayers to saints) in a *Book of Hours* in Vienna (Österreichische Nationalbibliothek). The Suffrages Masters borrow unabashedly from Flemish illumination, especially *trompe-l'oeil* borders of strewn flowers, while the baroque gestures, exaggerated forms, and caricature-like faces of their figures share similarities with the paintings of Northern Mannerists.

There are a number of reasons for the end of Dutch illumination around 1520, including the rise in inexpensive printing and the fall in popularity of *Books of Hours*, always a major vehicle for illumination. French illuminators continued to find work, mostly from courtly patrons, into the 1540s, and Flemish illuminators, too, worked until that time because of the continued export market for their products. But in the Northern Netherlands this was not the case, and the demise of manuscript painting can be detected somewhat earlier. By the middle of the sixteenth century, however, illumination ceased to be a viable art form across all of Europe.

Roger S. Wieck

See also Delft; Flanders, Flemish School; Prints, early printed book and Bible illustration; Utrecht

Bibliography

Byvanck, A.W., and G.J. Hoogewerff. *La miniature hollandaise dans les manuscrits des 14e, 15e et 16e siècles*. 3 vols. The Hague: Nijhoff, 1922–1926.

Defoer, Henri L.M., Anne S. Korteweg, and Wilhelmina C.M. Wüstefeld. *The Golden Age of Dutch Manuscript Painting*. New York: Pierpont Morgan Library, 1990; distributed by George Braziller.

Delaissé, L.M.J. *A Century of Dutch Manuscript Illumination*. Berkeley: University of California Press, 1968.

Gumbert, J.P. *The Dutch and Their Books in the Manuscript Age*. London: British Library, 1990.

Marrow, James H. *Descriptive and Analytical Catalogue of Dutch Illustrated Manuscripts of the Fifteenth and Sixteenth Centuries*. Doornspijk: Davaco. Forthcoming.

La miniature hollandaise: Le grand siècle de l'enluminure du livre dans les Pays-bas septentrionaux. Brussels: Bibliothèque Royale, 1971.

Oostrom, Frits Pieter van. *Court and Culture: Dutch Literature, 1350–1450*. Berkeley: University of California Press, 1992.

Pächt, Otto, and Ulrike Jenni. *Die illuminierten Handschriften und Inkunabeln der Österreichischen Nationalbibliothek: Holländische Schule*. 2 vols. Vienna: Verlag der Österreichischen Akademie der Wissenschaften, 1975.

Van der Horst, Koert, and Johann-Christian Klamt, eds. *Masters and Miniatures: Proceedings of the Congress on Medieval Manuscript Illumination in the Northern Netherlands*. Doornspijk: Davaco, 1991.

Marine painting

Marine painting is one of the largest, most diverse, and impressive categories of Dutch art, yet it is a subject upon which relatively little has been written. Monographs on only a few of the many marine specialists exist. Furthermore, most of the standard surveys are decades old and are almost exclusively concerned with stylistic analysis rather than considering the works in terms of their cultural background as well. A comprehensive exhibition in Minneapolis in 1990, *Mirror of Empire: Dutch Marine Art of the Seventeenth Century*, is a signal, however, that scholars are beginning to give this important aspect of Netherlandish art the attention it deserves.

Several characteristics of marine painting seem to have hindered scholars who might otherwise be interested in the topic. First, scholars have trouble defining marine painting—that is, they cannot decide whether to include it as a branch of landscape painting (hence, the seascape) or to categorize it separately. When art historians must deal with paintings containing ships and boats, they frequently do so only perfunctorily and sometimes seem uncomfortable covering the material at all. In their survey, *Dutch Art and Architecture, 1600–1800* (1966), Rosenberg, Slive, and Ter Kuile report that marine painting was popular through to the end of the eighteenth century, yet they devote only ten pages to the topic. Wolfgang Stechow states in the introduction to *Dutch Landscape Painting of the Seventeenth Century* (1966) that his decision to include seascapes was not made without "qualms" but was finally determined to be necessary to give a complete picture of the Dutch artists' visual response to nature. Marine painting follows the same basic trends as landscape painting and is intrinsically difficult to separate from landscape painting since the waters upon which ships and boats move are so intimately tied to the land. Thus, many scenes with shipping and pleasure boating are as much landscape as marine painting (Color Plate 6). The presence of ships or boats and water, however, does imbue paintings with meanings that are different from those of "pure" landscapes, and art historians need to find ways to address them adequately.

Second, the technical issues involved in discussing ships and boats are daunting. For example, the many varieties of vessels and the attendant sailing terminology are often confusing at best. It also sometimes seems necessary to be a meteorologist to understand the effects of the wind on ships and waves and to determine whether the artist is concerned with portraying weather accurately.

This leads to the third obstacle to studying marine paintings: Most modern scholars are unfamiliar with sailing and unaccustomed to living in a society with water-based commerce. Therefore, while many seventeenth-century art patrons must have known a great deal about the sea and rivers and the trade and pleasure they made possible, today scholars are less in tune with the sea. Perhaps this lack of understanding of the sea explains why art historians routinely repeat platitudes about the importance of the sea to the Dutch, but then do not often undertake any serious study of how such an important aspect of Dutch life influenced their art.

Instead, most scholarship to date has concentrated on surveying the stylistic changes found in Dutch marine painting. An understanding of these trends is certainly necessary, for without this foundation, new avenues of research are unlikely to present themselves. A brief survey of the basic developments in marine painting will, in fact, be helpful at this juncture.

Dutch strength in seafaring trade grew steadily during the sixteenth century, and Netherlanders made no secret of their pride in their seaborne power. By 1556, for example, Amsterdam's new weigh house had weather vanes of both Neptune and Fortuna on its roof, which alluded to the city's flourishing maritime trade. Reflecting the rise of many types of successful shipping, marine painting had just begun to develop as a new category of Dutch art by the end of the sixteenth century. It was in the seventeenth century that marine painting evolved into an important branch of Dutch art.

The expanding market for shipping scenes was closely tied to increased trade. As Karel van Mander explained in his *Schilder-Boeck* (Book of Picturing), first published in 1604, the new category of painting was popular with the Dutch as a direct result of their interest in shipping. Van Mander also reported that the artist Hendrick Cornelisz. Vroom (1566–1640) responded to the increased demand for painted shipping scenes by producing more of them.

Vroom, who worked in Haarlem, was the first European to specialize in marine painting. His favorite themes were large-scale representations of recent events, such as naval battles, the comings and goings of trading fleets and various dignitaries, as well as ships' portraits. *The Return to Amsterdam of the Second Expedition to the East Indies on July 19, 1599* (ca. 1600–1625) (Fig. 80) is typical of his style. Vroom's large painting shows the joyful conclusion of a trade voyage that not only established the underpinnings of Dutch trade and authority in the East, but also realized a return of 400 percent on the participants' initial investment, thus inspiring others to attempt the difficult journey. The painting's celebratory air manifests the pride of the Dutch in this exceedingly successful commercial venture. It is, however, believed to have been done some years after the fleet actually returned to its home port, probably within the first quarter of the seventeenth century. Thus, *The Return to Amsterdam* may have been a retrospective celebration of the successful voyages that led to the 1602 founding of the Dutch East India Company.

As in this example, Vroom's paintings usually have a raised viewpoint and a horizontal format without any lateral framing devices, which helps emphasize the expansiveness of the sea. Like those of other early marine artists, Vroom's compositions are multicolored and bright with a tendency to downplay atmospheric effects. His works are highly detailed and filled with lively activity.

Another early marine specialist, Adam Willaerts (1577–1664), was the leading marine painter in Utrecht. He worked in a style similar to Vroom's, executing highly detailed paintings in a bright palette, and was interested in many of the same subjects as Vroom. Willaerts, however, also painted beach scenes, sea storms, and shipwrecks, as well as religious subjects such as Christ preaching from the boat. Influenced by the landscapes of Roelant Savery (ca. 1576/1578–1639), he also painted works featuring mountainous coastlines.

The art of Jan Porcellis (ca. 1584–1632, active in Rotterdam, Middelburg, London, Antwerp, Haarlem, Amsterdam, and Zoeterwoude) marks a change from the detailed early style of Vroom and Willaerts toward the tonal phase of marine painting. Rather than lavish attention on the rigging and specifics of ships and boats, Porcellis used a limited palette and emphasized atmospheric effects. During the 1620s, his painting reveals an increased interest in the movements and interrelatedness of the sea, wind, and clouds. Furthermore, Porcellis, who was a capable sailor of Holland's inland waterways, preferred to feature sailboats in small compositions on panel instead of painting large works chronicling the enterprises of the great three-masted ships used in Dutch trade. Whatever type of vessel he portrayed, the sea and sky were of paramount importance to him. His art was highly influential for landscape painters such as Jan van Goyen and Salomon van Ruysdael, who worked in the monochrome phase of landscape painting from about 1630 to 1645. Another artist who owed a debt to Porcellis was Simon de Vlieger (ca. 1600–1653). De Vlieger's early works are closer to the style of Vroom, but later, like Porcellis, De Vlieger's main interest lay with atmospheric effects and re-creating the interplay of clouds, water, and sky. De Vlieger modified Porcellis' monochrome palette by adding a little more color. His range of subject matter is also broader than that of Porcellis and includes river and beach scenes as well as the theme of the "parade marine," in which vessels are anchored close together in a long line. De Vlieger's talent for rendering the moist atmosphere of the sea and rivers is combined with a greater attention to the ships and boats themselves than Porcellis demonstrated. De Vlieger's last works are serene and calm and point the way toward the art of Jan van de Cappelle.

As a wealthy dyer and merchant, Van de Cappelle (ca. 1624–1679) was a member of Amsterdam's patrician class. His wealth allowed him to amass a large collection of art works including, among other things, nine paintings and thirteen hundred drawings by De Vlieger. Van de Cappelle, who was apparently self-taught, expanded on the atmospheric effects of De Vlieger, and his art represents the zenith of tonal Dutch marine painting. In his hands, the air is filled with an almost tangible moisture that blurs the details of the vessels portrayed and acts as a unifying element. His early paintings tend toward a silvery tonality, while his later works are more golden. Van de Cappelle's subjects were shipping and boating as seen at the mouths of rivers, in harbors, and along the coast rather than on the open seas. He also painted some winter landscapes with his characteristic silvery tone. His luminous marine paintings are quiet scenes in which the reflective qualities of water play a major role. In order to exploit this reflectivity, the weather is calm or breezy at most.

Van de Cappelle painted in Amsterdam. By 1650, Amsterdam was the heart of the field of marine painting, and throughout the second half of the seventeenth century, marine painting is dominated by artists who worked in Amsterdam. The preeminence of Amsterdam's marine artists should come as no surprise since Amsterdam was by this time the busiest port as well as the home of the main chambers of the East and West India trading companies, the Admiralty, and many shipbuilding and ship repair enterprises. De Vlieger had lived in Amsterdam from 1638 to 1650, then he moved to Weesp, a small town nearby; all of the following artists worked in Amsterdam.

Willem van de Velde the Elder (1611–1693) and his son, Willem van de Velde the Younger (1633–1707), had flourishing careers in Amsterdam painting sea battles, war fleets, and ships' portraits. In 1672, however, England joined forces with France to attack the Netherlands, marking the turning point away from Dutch supremacy at sea, and the Van de Veldes moved to England in the winter of 1672–1673, although they returned periodically to the Netherlands. The market for paintings of naval battles had been high in the Netherlands when the Dutch ruled the seas, but in the third quarter of the seventeenth century when naval fortunes declined, so did the naval-battle art market. In many respects, this father and son duo returned to the themes, interest in detail, and the more colorful palette typical of Vroom and his contemporaries early in the century.

Van de Velde the Elder was an excellent draftsman who specialized in pen paintings *(pinseel schilderijen)*. These are paintings with minute detail executed on canvas or panel on a special white ground in such a way so as to look almost like an engraving. Van de Velde the Elder sailed with the fleets and sketched their activities as they happened at sea. His method of working was a departure from that of earlier artists, like Vroom, who often painted naval events years after they occurred. Van de Velde did not, however, merely document scenes. He felt free to change details, such as the placement of a ship in battle, in order to please his patrons. In England, the Van de Veldes worked primarily for Charles II and his brother James, Duke of York. Their 1674 contract with Charles II specifically states that Van de Velde the Elder was to be paid for making drawings of sea battles and that Van de Velde the Younger was to be paid for putting them into color.

The poetics of light and atmosphere completely escaped Van de Velde the Elder, but not his son. Van de Velde the Younger first studied with his father and then with Simon de Vlieger. From De Vlieger, Van de Velde the Younger learned to represent the light and atmosphere of the sea, but he did not do so to the exclusion of local color. Van de Velde the Younger was a versatile artist who painted precise ships' portraits, shipping on the seas, harbor and beach scenes, calms and storms, dignitaries at sea, and large naval history pieces, but is most famous for his naval battles.

Reinier Nooms (ca. 1623–1664), nicknamed *Zeeman* (Seaman), was also a talented draftsman and is especially well known for his marine prints. Nooms' paintings reveal his affinity for documenting ships and their activities, and his works are filled with a wide variety of accurately depicted vessels. Not only is shipping in Dutch harbors shown, but so are the businesses of shipbuilding and ship repair, which were important industries in Amsterdam. Probably a professional sailor,

Nooms seems to have been well traveled, as he also painted views of the Mediterranean and North Africa.

Ludolf Bakhuizen (1631–1708) was the leading marine artist in Amsterdam after the Van de Veldes moved to England. His paintings are dramatic, perhaps overly so, which may account for the low opinion of him held by many art historians in the past. Stechow dismissed him as a minor artist, but a recent exhibition (*Ludolf Bakhuizen*, 1985; Amsterdam, Nederlands Scheepvaart Museum) devoted to his art has helped rehabilitate his reputation. He, too, was a talented draftsman who used a strong color palette to depict a wide array of marine subjects, including naval battles, shipwrecks, and harbor scenes. His ships appear in calm and turbulent weather, but he preferred the drama of the latter.

This, then, is what the Dutch marine artists of the seventeenth century were painting. The question left to be answered is why they painted what they did. In addition to the usual monographs and surveys, more thematic approaches to Dutch marine painting are in order. Most surveys and studies note the importance of seafaring to the Dutch economy in their introductory remarks to the subject, but do little to carry the general remarks over to more specific examples. An understanding of why certain marine subjects were popular when they were is fundamentally lacking in art historical literature. The theme of tempests and shipwrecks has recently been treated (Goedde, 1989) as has the trade by Dutch East Indiamen (Atwater, 1991), but many more such topics could be explored. Although representations of Indiamen have been examined, the complexities of the depictions of trade on the inland waterways of the Netherlands and what they meant to the Dutch have not. Furthermore, many paintings of Dutch ships in battle are extant, yet no coherent study of them exists. Whaling and fishing vessels also appear with regularity in Dutch art but have not been studied. Also, the great shipbuilding and ship-repair enterprises of the Dutch form an important part of marine painting that cannot adequately be addressed in a monograph on an individual artist or in a landscape forum.

Marine painting is just beginning to be considered in depth by scholars in terms of its social and economic meaning. An almost overwhelming amount of primary-source material in Dutch on the shipping and trade industries is available. These sources need to be further examined to understand more fully what marine painting meant to the Dutch and why it was so popular, even after the Republic's maritime power declined in the eighteenth century. In the early nineteenth century, the artistic revival of the Golden Age brought an infusion of patriotic sentiment to marine painting as a category; later in the nineteenth and early twentieth centuries, the painters of The Hague School made their chief subjects the sea and the daily lives of the boatmen and fishermen's families who depend on it for their livelihood.

Gretchen D. Atwater

See also Haarlem; Hague School, The; Landscape; Literature, poetry: analogues with the visual; Rotterdam; Trade, exploration, and colonization overseas; Utrecht; Van Mander, Karel

Bibliography

Atwater, Gretchen D. "The Impact of Trade by the Dutch East India Company on Seventeenth-Century Netherlandish Art." Ph.D. diss., University of Kansas, 1991.

Bol, Laurens J. *Die Holländische Marinemalerie des 17. Jahrhunderts*. Brunswick: Klinkhardt and Biermann, 1973.

Boxer, C.R. *The Dutch Seaborne Empire, 1600–1800*. New York: Alfred A. Knopf, 1965.

Goedde, Lawrence O. *Tempest and Shipwreck in Dutch and Flemish Art: Convention, Rhetoric, and Interpretation*. University Park, PA: Pennsylvania State University Press, 1989.

Groot, Irene de, and Robert Vorstman, eds. *Sailing Ships: Prints by the Dutch Masters from the Sixteenth to the Nineteenth Century*. Translated by Michael Hoyle. New York: Viking Press, 1980.

Haak, Bob. *The Golden Age: Dutch Painters of the Seventeenth Century*. New York: Harry N. Abrams, 1984.

Keyes, George S. et al. *Mirror of Empire: Dutch Marine Art of the Seventeenth Century*. Minneapolis: Minneapolis Institute of Arts; New York: Cambridge University Press, 1990.

Preston, Rupert. *The Seventeenth-Century Marine Painters of the Netherlands*. Leigh-on-Sea: F. Lewis, 1974.

Maris, Jacob Hendricus (1837–1899)

Jacob Maris, the most important Dutch landscape painter of the last quarter of the nineteenth century, was in fact trained to be a painter of figures and interiors. His first teacher was J.A.B. Stroebel, a painter of interiors with whom he studied between 1849 and 1852. In the evenings Maris took drawing lessons at The Hague Academy (1850–1853). After 1853 he took painting lessons from the genre painter H. van Hove, with whom he moved to Antwerp in 1854. In Antwerp, Maris attended evening classes at the academy (1854–1856). He returned to The Hague in 1857 and worked with his brother Matthijs Maris from 1859 until 1861 on a series of portraits commissioned by the royal House of Orange. This enabled the brothers to work in the artists' colony in Oosterbeek in 1859 and in Wolfheze in 1860, and to travel through Germany, Switzerland, and France in 1861. Back in The Hague, Jacob Maris frequented the drawing evenings of the artists' society Pulchri Studio in 1861 because he could draw after live models there. In the end, as late as 1864, he began studying with the figure painter E. Hébert in Paris. After coming back from Paris in 1871 Maris changed unexpectedly to painting landscapes and townscapes. In them he expressed his admiration for the Barbizon School and for seventeenth-century Dutch masters such as Jacob van Ruisdael and Johannes Vermeer. With his confident broad touch and subdued use of color, he became one of the most important representatives of The Hague School (Fig. 55). Especially after 1890, Maris had enormous success in the Netherlands and abroad; like the other artists of The Hague School he sold many paintings to private collectors in Scotland and in the United States. Maris' most important students were his youngest brother, Willem Maris,

Bernardus Blommers, Willem de Zwart, and Th. de Bock. The last-named artist wrote the standard work on Jacob Maris that was published in 1903.

Alexandra W.M. van Smoorenburg

See also Belgium; Blommers, Bernardus Johannes; De Zwart, Willem; Hague School, The; House of Orange-Nassau; Maris, Matthijs; Maris, Willem; North American collecting; North American painting, Dutch influences

Bibliography

Bionda, Richard, and Carel Blotkamp, eds. *The Age of Van Gogh: Dutch Painting 1880–1895*, 179–181. Zwolle: Waanders, 1990.
Bock, Th. de. *Jacob Maris*. London: Maring, [1903].
Leeuw, Ronald de, John Sillevis, and Charles Dumas, eds. *The Hague School: Dutch Masters of the Nineteenth Century*, 200–215. London: Royal Academy of Arts, in association with Weidenfeld and Nicholson, 1983.

Maris, Matthijs (1839–1917)

Although he is always mentioned in connection with The Hague School, Matthijs Maris did not belong to it. Already by 1869 he had left The Hague forever, and his characteristic imaginative work holds a place of its own. In his early years, Matthijs spent a lot of time with his brothers, especially Jacob. They both had lessons at the Academy in The Hague and went on to the academy in Antwerp. Their early work shows many similarities. Matthijs traveled with Jacob to Oosterbeek and, in 1861, to Germany, Switzerland, and France. Important especially to Matthijs was the visit to Lausanne, with its castle, cathedral, and medieval center. These subjects returned often in his work. The reviews of his work in the 1860s were often critical, which is why he stopped exhibiting and withdrew into himself. In his paintings he began to concentrate more on the inner world and no longer on reality. In those years he was already painting to some extent symbolic paintings, long before there was any mention of Symbolism. However, he was forced to abandon this when, at Jacob's request, he settled with him in Paris in 1869. In the years that he lived in Paris, Matthijs painted figure pieces for commercial purposes, the so-called "potboilers," that he later equated with "suicide." Nevertheless, there are among these famous paintings, such as *Souvenir d'Amsterdam* (1871; Amsterdam, Rijksmuseum), a dreamlike, partly fantasized view of the city.

In 1877 Matthijs Maris left for London at the urging of the Scottish art dealer Daniel Cottier. Matthijs' suspicion of anything that had to do with money and commerce gradually caused him great conflicts with Cottier. Matthijs received help from his friend the Dutch art dealer Elbert van Wisselingh, who also lived in London. Van Wisselingh provided living quarters and financial security so that Matthijs could work at his leisure. He was, however, embittered and led a reclusive life. He worked for many years on his paintings, putting thin layers on top of each other. He painted almost exclusively monochromatic dream landscapes in those years. His most important works, and even then the most appreci-

ated, were already behind him: indistinct, poetic, and fantastic landscapes and figures of girls.

Hanna Pennock

See also Maris, Jacob Hendricus; Maris, Willem

Bibliography

Gruyter, Jos de. *De Haagse School*. 2 vols. Rotterdam: Lemniscaat, 1968–1969. Reprint. 2 vols. in 1. Alphen aan den Rijn: Atrium, 1985. (English summary.)
Leeman, Fred, and Hanna Pennock. *The Mesdag Museum: Catalogue of Paintings and Drawings*. Zwolle: Waanders, 1996.
Leeuw, Ronald de, John Sillevis, and Charles Dumas, eds. *The Hague School: Dutch Masters of the Nineteenth Century*. London: Royal Academy of Arts, in association with Weidenfeld and Nicholson, 1983.
Raad, Jacqueline de et al. *Maris: Een kunstenaarsfamilie*. Laren: Singer Museum; Zwolle: Waanders, 1991.

Maris, Willem (1844–1910)

Willem Maris lived his entire life in and around The Hague, where he was born the youngest of three artistic brothers. Willem was the first to become successful as a painter, but he was later overshadowed by the others because of his limited choice of subject matter. He began drawing and painting early, following instructions from his brothers Jacob and Matthijs. He took lessons at the Academy in The Hague and advice from the animal painter Pieter Stortenbeker, but for the rest developed independently. He copied old masters such as Paulus Potter and worked mainly after nature. In 1862 Maris made a trip to the artists' colony at Oosterbeek, where he met Gerard Bilders and Anton Mauve. He remained friends with the latter. In the same year he made his debut at an exhibition in Rotterdam with a painting entitled *Cows on the Heath*. He would paint such subjects his entire life; the trip along the Rhine that he took in 1865 with Bernardus Blommers and two later trips to Germany and Norway brought no change in that respect.

Willem Maris made studies after nature in The Hague and its surroundings and usually worked them up into paintings in his studio. He painted mostly landscapes with ducks at a water ditch and cows in a pasture (Fig. 56). He was especially fascinated by the effects of light and shadow. His preference was for pasture landscapes in hazy morning light. "I do not paint cows but light effects" is an often repeated quotation from the artist. While other painters of The Hague School tried to capture the mood of a landscape in shades of gray, Willem Maris set out to reproduce light and color. In his early work he painted with precision and delicacy. Around 1880 he changed to a broader touch and warmer colors. His style and subject matter were, however, quite constant, which increases the difficulty in the dating of his works. His paintings and watercolors sold well in the Netherlands and abroad, providing him a comfortable living.

Hanna Pennock

See also Blommers, Bernardus Johannes; Hague School, The;

Maris, Jacob Hendricus; Maris, Matthijs; Mauve, Anton; Potter, Paulus

Bibliography

Gruyter, Jos de. *De Haagse School.* 2 vols. Rotterdam: Lemniscaat, 1968–1969. Reprint. 2 vols. in 1. Alphen aan den Rijn: Atrium, 1985. (English summary).

Leeman, Fred, and Hanna Pennock. *The Mesdag Museum: Catalogue of Paintings and Drawings.* Zwolle: Waanders, 1996.

Leeuw, Ronald de, John Sillevis, and Charles Dumas. *The Hague School: Dutch Masters of the Nineteenth Century.* London: Royal Academy of Arts, in association with Weidenfeld and Nicholson, 1983.

Raad, Jacqueline de et al. *Maris: Een kunstenaarsfamilie.* Laren: Singer Museum; Zwolle: Waanders, 1991.

Marriage and family portraits

The family was the basic unit upon which the Dutch built their society during the seventeenth and eighteenth centuries. As a result, marriage and family portraits are particularly numerous in this period, appearing in a variety of forms, including pendant and double portraits of couples, betrothal portraits, and family group portraits. Within these basic categories, the sitters may be shown in contemporary dress in either formal or casual poses. Family groups are most often portrayed in the conversation-piece format, with the figures carefully posed to evoke the impression that the viewer has been made privy to a moment in the everyday life of the household, as in *The Portrait of Jeremias van Collen and Susanna van Uffelen and Their Twelve Children*, attributed to Pieter van Anraedt (ca. 1661; Amsterdam, Rijksmuseum; Fig. 31). In some instances, patrons chose to be depicted in *portraits histories* (historical portraits), in which they play mythological, biblical, pastoral, or historical figures (Figs. 94 and 120). Settings and backgrounds vary from indistinct ones, to domestic interiors, to exteriors often containing architectural, garden, and landscape elements. Activities can consist of sitting, standing, conversing and gesturing to one another, gathering around the dinner table, making music together (Fig. 87), walking out-of-doors, or returning from the hunt.

Very brief overviews of some of these types of Dutch marriage and family portraits, and the issues surrounding them, were written by William W. Robinson, in a 1979 *Apollo* article, and by William Wilson, in an exhibition catalog from 1980. However, during the mid-1980s, David R. Smith and E. de Jongh published more detailed and extensive studies regarding this important facet of Dutch painting. Seen as far more than straightforward records of the likenesses of a particular couple or family, these portraits were considered in light of the complex issues of patronage, artistic choice and convention, social and moral custom, the differences between "biographical" and "rhetorical" truth in portraiture (Raupp, 1986: 259), and hidden and overt symbolism.

Smith (1982) has focused much attention on identifying and decoding the visual vocabulary and rhetorical language of seventeenth-century Dutch marriage and family portraiture specifically. Sometimes ignoring biographical data that may be relevant to a particular couple or family, Smith has emphasized instead how portraits convey the socially accepted character, or *persona* (social façade), of an individual through artistic conventions, adapted by the Dutch from aristocratic court traditions to their own middle-class culture. The actions, attitudes, and settings combine into a "performance" of the subject's own role and status in society, which has been translated into a visual medium by the artist. He argues that the seventeenth-century attitude toward individual personality and character is based upon social identity, not inner psychological reality. The self is more of a theatrical projection than an innate being.

De Jongh approaches the interpretation of Dutch marriage and family portraiture in a different way. In the exhibition and catalog *Portretten van echt en trouw: Huwelijk en gezin in de Nederlandse kunst van de zeventiende eeuw* (Portraits of Matrimony and Faithfulness: Marriage and Family in Dutch Art of the Seventeenth Century), he sets stringent guidelines for interpreting portraiture based upon an iconological format. Relying heavily upon seventeenth-century literary evidence, particularly emblem books and treatises on social etiquette, De Jongh looks at the visual elements of each portrait and relates them to recorded dictums and metaphors, and to pictorial symbols and their captions, in order to decipher the meaning the portraits possibly had for the sitters and contemporary viewers. Rejecting any notions that the personality or individual attitudes of the sitters are projected, De Jongh instead contends that what we see is the reflection of society's standards of decorum. Often the personal histories of the sitters, as gleaned from documentary evidence, are used to explain the purposes of particular portraits, but only within the broader framework of the societal aims of such choices.

As both Wayne Franits (1988: 251–252) and Hans Joachim Raupp (1986: 258–259) have pointed out, one of the most obvious examples of the divergent approaches of De Jongh and Smith is the interpretation offered by each scholar of the Amsterdam Rijksmuseum double portrait of *Isaac Massa and Beatrix van der Laen* by Frans Hals (ca. 1622) (Fig. 59). As early as 1961, De Jongh, in conjunction with P.J. Vincken, interpreted this work as an innovative Dutch incorporation of emblematic symbols and pictorial traditions to create a unified composition exhibiting conjugal love and fidelity within the bonds of matrimony. Smith (1986) instead believes the portrait demonstrates Massa's personal (and Dutch bourgeois society's) antipathy to courtly society by contrasting the positive symbolism of the vine-covered tree, and the sensible dress and natural poses of the figures, with the negative—that is, courtly and erotic—motifs of the thistle and ivy, and the background love garden.

Questions remain: Whose interpretation is correct? What proofs do the literary and visual traditions really afford? What does the composition itself convey? Did Hals create a visual tension between the varying parts of the picture, or did he rather create a serenely unified whole? Aesthetic interpretation, as well as scholarly study, is still an important component in comprehending a work of art.

Within these varying possibilities for interpreting signs and symbols in Dutch portraiture lies the challenge for scholars in future studies. The meanings of particular poses, gestures, and attributes can often be ambiguous. As many aspects of the sociocultural context as can be discerned need to be utilized in interpreting portraits. Documentary evidence concerning societal attitudes and practices, and, when possible, personal history, must be considered. As more data on Dutch culture and individuals and their families is compiled, there is hope for greater insights into the people and their time. However, one must never overlook the fact that what determines anyone's interpretation of individual marriage and family portraits is one's own subjective frame of reference in trying to decipher the written and visual evidence.

Diane E. Cearfoss Mankin

See also Aristocracy and gentry; Conversation piece; Country houses and gardens; Court and official portraiture; Donor portraits; Emblems and emblem books; Genre painting, eighteenth century; Gestures; Group portraiture; Hals, Frans; History portraits; Pastoral; Portraiture; Van der Helst, Bartholomeus

Bibliography

Franits, Wayne. "Review of *Portretten van echt en trouw*." *Oud Holland* 102 (1988): 249–256.

Jongh, E. de. *Portretten van echt en trouw: Huwelijk en gezin in de Nederlandse kunst van de zeventiende eeuw.* Zwolle: Waanders, 1986.

Jongh, E. de, and P.J. Vinken. "Frans Hals als voortzetter van een emblematische traditie: Bij het huwelijksportret van Issac Massa en Beatrix van der Laen." *Oud Holland* 76 (1961): 117–152.

Raupp, Hans Joachim. "Review of *Portretten van echt en trouw*." *Simiolus* 16 (1986): 254–262.

Robinson, William W. "Family Portraits of the Golden Age." *Apollo* 110:214 (December 1979): 490–507.

Smith, David R. "Courtesy and Its Discontents: Frans Hals' *Portrait of Isaac Massa and Beatrix van der Laen.*" *Oud Holland* 100 (1986): 2–34.

———. *Masks of Wedlock: Seventeenth-Century Dutch Marriage Portraiture.* Ann Arbor, MI: UMI Research Press, 1982.

Wilson, William. *Dutch Seventeenth-Century Portraiture: The Golden Age.* Sarasota, FL: John and Mabel Ringling Museum of Art, 1980.

Master IAM of Zwoll (active ca. 1485)

The attribution of the twenty-six engravings signed with the monograms IAM, IA, or IM, and the word Zwoll (Fig. 103), often accompanied by a small drill used by medieval goldsmiths, has long been a subject of discussion. Recently, the prints have been seen as a collaboration between Johan van den Mijnnesten (active 1462–1504), the only major painter in Zwolle at that time, with a goldsmith there. The engravings are undated, but an early and late period can be distinguished on stylistic grounds. The prints are influenced by con-

temporary Flemish painting and German sculpture. Some served as sources for manuscript illuminations.

Nadine Orenstein

See also Prints, printmaking, and printmakers (ca. 1500–ca. 1900)

Bibliography

Dubbe, B. "Is Johan van den Mynnesten de 'Meester van Zwolle'"? *Bulletin van het Rijksmuseum* 18 (1970): 55–65.

Filedt Kok, Jan Piet. "Master IAM of Zwoll: The Personality of a Designer and Engraver." In *Festschrift to Erik Fischer: European Drawings from Six Centuries*, 341–356. Copenhagen: Royal Museum of Fine Arts, 1990.

Finkenstaedt, Elizabeth. "Some Notes on the Early Chronology of the Master IAM van Zwolle." *Simiolus* 1 (1986): 121–127.

Lehrs, Max. *Geschichte und Kritischer Katalog des Deutschen, Niederländischen und Französischen Kupferstichs im XV. Jahrhundert.* Vol. 2, 165–218. Vienna: Gesellschaft für Vervielfältigende Kunst, 1930.

Master of the Virgin among Virgins (active ca. 1480–1510)

This problematic Delft painter, named after the *Virgin among Virgin Saints* (ca. 1485–1490; Amsterdam, Rijksmuseum) has an idiosyncratic expressive style and unique color palette. Although there is a common thread among the works attributed to this artist, there is little stylistic consistency. Schretlen linked the Virgo Master's panels to a series of woodcuts attributed to Conway's Second Delft Cutter and some miniatures in manuscripts produced at Delft. Among the followers of the Virgo Master are the Master of Delft and the Master of the Spes Nostra, both active around 1500–1520.

Diane G. Scillia

See also Delft; Manuscript illumination

Bibliography

Boon, K.G. "De Meester van de Virgo inter Virgines." In *Oud Delft: Een serie historische publicaties over Delft en Delvenaaren.* Edited by B. van 't Hoff, F.W.N. Hugenholtz, and D.P. Oosterbaan. Vol. 2. Rotterdam: Nijgh and Van Ditmar, 1963.

Chatelet, A. *Early Dutch Painting: Painting in the Northern Netherlands in the Fifteenth Century.* Translated by Christopher Brown and Anthony Turner. New York: Rizzoli, 1980.

Conway, W.M. *The Woodcutters of the Netherlands in the Fifteenth Century.* Cambridge, 1884. Reprint. Hildesheim: Georg Olms Verlag, 1961.

Friedlander, M.J. *Early Netherlandish Painting.* Translated by Heinz Norden. Vol. 5. New York: Praeger, 1970.

Lemmens, G. Th. M. "Schilderkunst in Delft tot 1572." In *De Stad Delft: Cultuur en Maatschappij tot 1572.* Edited by I.V.J. Spaander and R.A. Leeuw, 143–147. Delft: Stedelijk Museum Het Prinsenhof, 1979.

Schretlen, M.J. *Dutch and Flemish Woodcuts of the Fifteenth Century*. London: Ernest Benn, 1925.

Scillia, D.G. "The Woodcut Designers of Delft." In *Masters and Miniatures*. Edited by Koert van der Horst and Johann-Christian Klamt, 413–424. Doornspijk: Davaco, 1991.

Matham, Jacob (1571–1631)

Jacob Matham, the prolific Haarlem engraver (Fig. 16) and print publisher, entered Hendrick Goltzius' workshop as a student in 1581, two years after his mother's marriage to Goltzius. After 1590 his name appears regularly on prints after Goltzius' Mannerist designs. Between 1594 and 1597, Matham traveled to Italy. He probably took over Goltzius' print publishing business as early as 1598, when his publisher's address begins to appear, but he only joined the artists' guild in 1600. In 1601 he received a print privilege from Rudolf II in Prague. His students included his sons, Adriaen, Jan, and Theodor, and Jan van de Velde II.

Nadine Orenstein

See also Goltzius, Hendrick; Haarlem; Prints, printmaking, and printmakers (ca. 1500–ca. 1900); Prints, publishers; Van de Velde, Jan II

Bibliography

Bartsch, Adam. *Le Peintre-Graveur*. Vol. 3, 131–243. Leipzig: J.A. Barth, 1854.

Filedt Kok, Jan Piet. "Hendrik Goltzius: Engraver, Designer, and Publisher, 1582–1600." In *Goltzius Studies: Hendrick Goltzius, 1558–1617*. Edited by R. Falkenburg, J.P. Filedt Kok, and H. Leeflang. Zwolle: Waanders, 1993.

Hollstein, F.W.H. *Dutch and Flemish Etchings, Engravings, and Woodcuts, ca. 1450–1700*. Vol. 11, 215–251. Amsterdam: Menno Hertzeberger, 1949–.

Strauss, Walter, ed. *The Illustrated Bartsch*. Vol. 4. New York: Abaris, 1980.

Widerkehr, Léna. "Jacob Matham Goltzij Brivignus: Jacob Matham graveur et ses rapports avec Hendrick Goltzius." In *Goltzius Studies: Hendrick Goltzius, 1558–1617*. Edited by R. Falkenburg, J.P. Filedt Kok, and H. Leeflang, 219–260. Zwolle: Waanders, 1993.

Mauve, Anton (1838–1888)

Together with Jozef Israëls, Jacob and Willem Maris, and Hendrik Willem Mesdag, Anton Mauve formed the heart of The Hague School. He grew up in Haarlem, where at a young age he became an apprentice to the animal painters Pieter Frederik van Os and Wouterus Verschuur. In the summer of 1858 he and his friend Paul Gabriël stayed for the first time in Oosterbeek. The picturesque landscape of the Veluwe and his contact with other painters working there, such as J.W. Bilders and his son Gerard Bilders, put him firmly on the track that would lead to The Hague School. He also got to know Willem Maris, who would remain his close friend. For ten years Mauve regularly went to Oosterbeek to work outdoors in nature. Here for the first time he painted excerpts from landscapes instead of predetermined compositions. This method would shape the future aspect of his *oeuvre*; for the rest of his life he made sketches *en plein air*. He went with his painter's kit outside, attached the canvas to the lid, and sketched the landscape. *Bij Vries* (At Vries), about 1882, is a good example; not only can we still see the holes from the thumbtacks, but we can also see an artist, probably Hendrik Willem Mesdag, at work in the same way (Fig. 81).

Mauve lived in different places in Holland before he settled in 1871 in The Hague. Other painters such as Jozef Israëls, Jacob Maris, and Mesdag had moved to The Hague around the same time, thus laying the basis for The Hague School. In 1872 Mauve married the niece of Vincent van Gogh; their honeymoon was spent in part with Paul Gabriël in Brussels.

In The Hague Mauve became actively involved in the artistic life. With Mesdag and Jacob Maris he founded the Hollandsche Teeken-Maatschappij (Dutch Watercolor Society) in 1876, and for a few years around 1880 he was active on the board of the painters' society, Pulchri Studio. He was a major influence on Van Gogh, who came to him in 1881 to ask his advice about art. Mauve encouraged Vincent to start painting instead of only drawing. Later they would disagree; nevertheless, for Van Gogh, Mauve remained one of his most beloved and admired painters.

In 1882 Mauve "discovered" the village of Laren, situated in a rural setting. In comparison with the urbanized environment of The Hague, Laren was pure, unadulterated nature. He spent the summers there with Albert Neuhuijs, and in 1885 he settled in the village and became Neuhuijs' neighbor (Fig. 72). Three years later Mauve died suddenly. He left an enormous *oeuvre* of paintings, watercolors, and sketches. His style can be called exemplary for The Hague School; he preferred gray, tonal landscapes beneath a dark cloudy sky (Color Plate 10). The dominating silver-gray tone is what gives the landscapes their subdued mood. Mauve's work is an outstanding example of mood-expressive art (*stemmingskunst*). His landscapes are always inhabited, whether by a flock of sheep, cows, or horses, or by rustic scenes of farm life that belong especially to the period he was in Laren and in which one can recognize the influence of Jean-François Millet. Mauve often worked on several paintings at a time. He painted quickly and with a loose touch. During the last years of his life, when he already enjoyed international renown, he produced a great deal for the art market, and much of his work was sold abroad. An illustration of the commercial side of his work was the way that his flock of sheep could be classified as either "sheep coming" or "sheep going." The rear view of the animals, which was easier to depict but provided a slightly less enjoyable scene, was naturally less expensive.

Hanna Pennock

See also Drawings, uses and collecting; Gabriël, Paul Joseph Constantin; Hague School, The; Israëls, Jozef; Laren; Maris, Jacob Hendricus; Maris, Willem; Mesdag, Hendrik Willem; Neuhuijs, Albert; Van Gogh, Vincent

Bibliography

Engel, E.P. *Anton Mauve, 1838–1888: Bronnenverkenning en analyse van zijn oeuvre.* Utrecht: Haentjens, Dekker, and Gumbert, 1967.

Gruyter, Jos de. *De Haagse School.* 2 vols. Rotterdam: Lemniscaat, 1968–1969. Reprint. 2 vols. in 1. Alphen aan den Rijn: Atrium, 1985. (English summary).

Heyting, Lien. *De wereld in een dorp: Schilders, schrijvers en wereldverbeteraars in Laren en Blaricum 1880–1920.* Amsterdam: Meulenhoff, 1994.

Leeman, Fred, and Hanna Pennock. *The Mesdag Museum: Catalogue of Paintings and Drawings.* Zwolle: Waanders, 1996.

Leeuw, Ronald de, John Sillevis, and Charles Dumas, eds. *The Hague School: Dutch Masters of the Nineteenth Century.* London: Royal Academy of Arts, in association with Weidenfeld and Nicholson, 1983.

Mendes da Costa, Joseph (1863–1939)

By reacting against the naturalism and academicism of the preceding period, Joseph Mendes da Costa stood, together with Lambertus Zijl, at the beginning of the revival of Dutch sculpture in the twentieth century. Starting from a manner related to Impressionism, he strove for an invigorated sense of form, more content, and less materiality. He was oriented toward the sculpture of archaic cultures and the Western European Middle Ages. In his free-standing monumental work and architectural sculpture, especially, this led to an increasing linear stylizing. These developments were promoted by the rise of industrial-design education and the repositioning of sculpture within architecture by, particularly, H.P. Berlage (1856–1934). In his long-term collaboration with Berlage, Mendes da Costa made architectural sculpture for a number of insurance offices and the Amsterdam Stock Exchange building (1898–1903). He also worked with K.P.C. de Bazel (1869–1923), making sculpture for the office of the Dutch Trade Society (1919–1926), and with A.J. Kropholler (1882–1973). Important autonomous monumental works are the monument to *Christiaan de Wet* (1922; De Hoge Veluwe National Park; Fig. 82) and the sculpture *De Raadsman*, both of which were commissioned by the Kröller-Müller family.

Of the great many independent works by Mendes da Costa, a large part consists of ceramic objects (often in stoneware), with folk imagery and Old Testament scenes as the most important themes, and decorated utensils. Interesting is an unfinished series of bronze figure sculptures of Vincent van Gogh (Fig. 83) and Francis of Assisi, among others. The independent work is equal in quality and quantity to the commissioned sculpture.

His striving for content in his work, which had a strong personal religious character, bordered on obsession as he grew older. He became estranged from his audience and isolated in his artistic position. The end of this development is his lifework, *Levensgang*, on which he worked for more than ten years and never finished.

Geraart Westerink

See also Applied arts; Berlage, Hendrik Petrus; Hammacher, A.M.W.J.; Kröller-Müller, Hélène E.L.J.; Public monumental sculpture (1795–1990); Sculpture (1795–1945); Symbolism, Symbolists; Zijl, Lambertus

Bibliography

Hammacher, A.M. *Mendes da Costa: De geestelijke boodschap der beeldhouwkunst.* Rotterdam: W.L. and J. Brusse, 1941.

Miranda, F. de. *Mendes da Costa, Jesserun de Mesquita: Nederlandse beeldende kunstenaars: Joden in de verstrooiing.* Wassenaar: Mirananda, 1978.

Roorda, T.B. *Mendes da Costa.* Amsterdam: Kosmos, 1929.

Mesdag, Hendrik Willem (1831–1915)

The sea painter Hendrik Willem Mesdag was a central figure in The Hague School. He was born, as was Jozef Israëls, another of the group in Groningen. His father was a banker but also an art lover and collector; an interest in art was, therefore, ingrained in him as he grew up. He began to work for his father and had a promising banking career ahead of him. In 1856 he married Sina (Sientje) van Houten, who, like him, came from a well-to-do family in Groningen; she would later become a painter of still lifes. When her father died in 1864, her inheritance made possible the fulfillment of a long-cherished wish: Mesdag, encouraged by Sientje, could now completely focus on the arts. They first moved in 1866 to the painters' village Oosterbeek, where Mesdag worked outside in nature. They then settled the same year in Brussels. With the recommendation of his cousin Laurens Alma Tadema, Mesdag received help and advice from the landscape painter Willem Roelofs. Alma Tadema also instructed him; he had an important influence on Mesdag's painting as well as on the development of his artistic taste.

During a vacation on the German island of Norderney in 1868, Mesdag discovered the subject that would become his speciality—the sea. Although his first paintings were very careful and detailed, he now developed a broader, more forceful touch. In 1869 he settled in The Hague, to be close to his favorite subject to paint. He made daily trips to Scheveningen to sketch the sea, whether outdoors or looking out from a hotel room. His breakthrough came in 1870 at the Parisian Salon, where he won a gold medal with his large painting *Les Brisants de la Mer du Nord.* From that time forward, even until very late in his life, he painted nothing but sea and beaches, sometimes with boats and figures, in all kinds of weather (Fig. 84). Eventually his work became rather a habit, he remained faithful to his subject matter and style without any innovation.

His most famous work is the *Mesdag Panorama,* which he painted in a little more than four months, assisted by his wife, Sientje, and the painters Bernardus Blommers, Theophile de Bock, and George Hendrik Breitner. It is an enormous, encircling painting that provides the viewer, who stands in the middle, with a suggestive view of the sea and the village of Scheveningen. It is one of the few panoramas that have survived from the nineteenth century.

Mesdag played an important role in the art world of The

Hague. He founded with Anton Mauve and Jacob Maris in 1876 the Hollandsche Teeken-Maatschappij (Dutch Water-color Society), which organized yearly exhibitions of water-color paintings. From 1889 until 1907 he was chairman of the painters' society, Pulchri Studio, which also organized many exhibitions of contemporary art.

Mesdag started collecting art in Brussels. His collection grew to such an extent that he built a house next to his own that he made into a museum. Visitors making an appointment could see an extensive collection of painters from the French Barbizon School, which Mesdag was the first to introduce to Holland. The same is true for a large number of paintings by the Italian Antonio Mancini (1852–1930), which Mesdag alone imported directly from the artist. Moreover, he owned many art objects and works of Dutch contemporaries, mainly members of The Hague School. The part of his collection he donated to the Dutch state can be seen at the Mesdag Museum in The Hague.

Hanna Pennock

See also Alma Tadema, Laurens; Belgium; Blommers, Bernardus Johannes; Breitner, George Hendrik; Drawings, uses and collecting; Hague School, The; Israëls, Jozef; Maris, Jacob Hendricus; Mauve, Anton; Roelofs, Willem

Bibliography

Gruyter, Jos de. *De Haagse School.* 2 vols. Rotterdam: Lemniscaat, 1968–1969. Reprint. 2 vols. in 1. Alphen aan den Rijn: Atrium, 1985. (English summary).

Leeman, Fred, and Hanna Pennock. *The Mesdag Museum: Catalogue of Paintings and Drawings.* Zwolle: Waanders, 1996.

Leeuw, Ronald de, John Sillevis, and Charles Dumas, eds. *The Hague School: Dutch Masters of the Nineteenth Century.* London: Royal Academy of Arts, in association with Weidenfeld and Nicholson, 1983.

Pennock, Hanna. "De levens van twee neven: Hendrik Willem Mesdag en Lourens Alma Tadema." *Jong Holland* 9 (1993): 8–19. (English summary).

Poort, Johan. *Hendrik Willem Mesdag, 1831–1915: Oeuvrecatalogus* [with bibliography]. Wassenaar: Stichting Mesdag Documentatie, 1989. (English summary).

———. *Hendrik Willem Mesdag: Oeuvrecatalogus: De Schetsen.* Wassenaar: Stichting Mesdag Documentatie, 1994.

Metsu, Gabriel (1629–1667)

Gabriel Metsu's paintings, in a diversity of themes and styles, date from the 1640s, when he was working in his birthplace of Leiden, to the 1660s, when he was living and working in Amsterdam. Biographical information is sparse, but Metsu is noted as one of the founding members of the Guild of St. Luke in Leiden in 1648. Records from the 1650s indicate that Metsu lived intermittently in Leiden until he moved to Amsterdam in 1657. The subject matter of his art extends from popular scenes of everyday life to religious history painting. He also depicted a small number of still-life images and portraits. Metsu's style changed from a broad, painterly execu-

tion found in large-scale works from the 1650s (*Dismissal of Hagar*, ca. 1653), produced in the manner of Nicolaus Knüpfer and Jan Baptist Weenix, to a refined, precise application of paint apparent in his Amsterdam paintings of the 1660s (*Vegetable Market at Amsterdam*, ca. 1661–1662), which resemble the works of Leiden *fijnschilders* (fine painters) such as Gerrit Dou. At the end of his career, Metsu's canvases became more monumental and less detailed, and reveal the influences of Johannes Vermeer and Pieter de Hooch (*The Sick Child*, ca. 1663–1664; Fig. 85).

Questions of style and connoisseurship regarding Metsu's *oeuvre* were addressed by Franklin W. Robinson in the mid-1970s. Since then there has been more consideration of Metsu's life, patrons, and iconography in individual works. Recent studies include investigation of the cultural contexts for his genre paintings (Stone-Ferrier, 1989 and 1992) and for his allegorical representation of Justice (Stone-Ferrier), and new research shows that his works of religious history and genre have close professional and personal ties to Roman Catholicism.

Valerie Lind Hedquist

See also Commerce and commercial life; Genre painting, seventeenth century; Leiden; Religion of artists

Bibliography

Broos, Ben et al. *Great Dutch Paintings from America.* The Hague: Mauritshuis; Zwolle: Waanders, 1991.

Gudlaugsson, S.J. "Kanttekeningen bij de ontwikkeling van Metsu." *Oud Holland* 83 (1968): 13–43.

Robinson, Franklin W. *Gabriel Metsu, 1629–1667: A Study of His Place in Dutch Genre Painting of the Golden Age.* New York: Abner Schram, 1974.

Stone-Ferrier, Linda. "Gabriel Metsu's *Justice Protecting Widows and Orphans*: The Meeting of Interests of Painter and Patron." In *The Tension between the Public and the Private in Dutch Culture of the Golden Age.* Dover: University of Delaware Press. Forthcoming.

———. "Gabriel Metsu's *Vegetable Market at Amsterdam* and Its Relationship to a Bredero Farce." *Artibus et Historiae* 25 (1992): 163–180.

———. "Gabriel Metsu's *Vegetable Market at Amsterdam*: Seventeenth-Century Dutch Market Scenes and Horticulture." *Art Bulletin* 71 (1989): 428–452.

Sutton, Peter C. et al. *Masters of Seventeenth-Century Dutch Genre Painting.* Philadelphia: Philadelphia Museum of Art, 1984.

Wessem, J.N. van, and Lucia Thyssen. *Gabriel Metsu.* Leiden: Stedelijk Museum De Lakenhal, 1966.

Moesman, Johannes Hendricus (Joop) (1909–1988)

Johannes Hendricus Moesman' born in Utrecht, was the son of J.A. Moesman (1859–1937), a calligrapher and lithographer. From 1919 to 1929 he took lessons in drawing from Jos Hoevenaar, Theo van der Laars, and Willem van Leusden. From 1923 to 1925 he was a student at the School for Graphic Trades in Utrecht. From 1925 to 1968 he worked as a lithographer and drew graphs for the Dutch Railway. In 1929, with others in the bookshop and art gallery Nord run by Willem Wagenaar, he came in contact with Surrealism through reproductions. Inspired by this, he combined the models in his academic drawing lessons with objects to create Surrealistic drawings. After 1930 these drawings become auxiliary studies that Moesman used to compose his Surrealistic paintings. He created his painting *oeuvre* in large part during his hour-and-a-half lunch breaks at work.

He exhibited for the first time in 1931 with De Onafhankelijken (The Independents) in Amsterdam. In 1933 and 1934 his work was removed from the Stedelijk Museum because of a perceived offensiveness in its character. The paintings that were created in the 1930s such as *Het Gerucht* (The Rumor, 1935–1941; The Netherlands, private collection) are the high point of his *oeuvre*. He painted little after the death of his father in 1937 and during World War II. As a calligrapher, he studied script after 1943 and, in 1962, developed the typeface Petronius; he also simplified Arabic script. After he was acknowledged as a Surrealist by André Breton in 1961, appreciation for his work grew. Some of his best paintings were created afterward, such as *Avonduur* (Evening Hour, 1962; The Netherlands, private collection). In 1963 his first retrospective was arranged by the graphic society De Luis. He wrote a number of articles on art criticism and art history after his retirement in 1965.

John Steen

See also Surrealism; Utrecht

Bibliography

Keers, Frits, and John Steen. *Moesman*. Zwolle: Waanders, 1996.

Molenaer, Jan Miense (1609/1610–1668)

The Haarlem painter Jan Miense Molenaer is best known for his iconographically rich genre scenes from the 1630s. He also executed genre-like portraits (Fig. 87) and a surprising number of religious pictures during the same period. After a move to Amsterdam late in 1636, Molenaer turned increasingly to peasant imagery painted in a looser manner with a limited palette. Considering the role that comedy and allegory play in his best works, Molenaer stands as a forerunner to Jan Steen (1625/1626–1679).

The son of a tailor, Molenaer was probably a Catholic. Documents concerning his training do not exist, but stylistic and compositional similarities with some of his early paintings and those by Frans Hals (ca. 1582/1583–1666) support arguments that he trained with this Haarlem master. Many of his early pictures also point to an association with Dirck Hals (1591–1656), with whom he and his wife, Judith Leyster (1609–1660), may have shared a studio. Signed paintings by Molenaer date from 1629, and by 1634 he was a member of Haarlem's Guild of St. Luke.

In spite of numerous court appearances, property speculation, and a range of other business dealings, Molenaer produced an enormous *oeuvre*. With the exception of a few signed and dated paintings from the years 1659–1662, his works after 1640 are largely disappointing. Attribution questions arose in Molenaer's lifetime, and pictures by his followers, including two of his brothers, Klaes (ca. 1629–ca. 1676) and Bartholomeus (ca. 1618–1650) and another Jan Jansz. Molenaer (1654–after 1684), continue to carry misattributions to Jan Miense Molenaer.

Dennis P. Weller

See also Comic modes; Haarlem; Hals, Dirck; Hals, Frans; Leyster, Judith; Music, musical instruments; Portraiture; Theater and theatricality

Bibliography

Sutton, Peter C. et al. *Masters of Seventeenth-Century Dutch Genre Painting*. Philadelphia: Philadelphia Museum of Art, 1984.

Weller, Dennis P. "Jan Miense Molenaer ca. 1609/1610–1668." Ph.D. diss., University of Maryland, 1992.

Welu, James A. et al. *Judith Leyster: A Dutch Master and Her World*. Worcester: Worcester Art Museum; Zwolle: Waanders, 1993.

Mondrian, Piet (1872–1944)

Piet Mondrian, known for his formally rigorous paintings, was one of the pioneers of geometrical-concrete art. For him, his abstract paintings were not only works of art, but also painterly expressions of the utopian ideal of combining art and life. He formulated this ideal in numerous writings and tried to realize it in his way of life. Pieter Cornelis Mondriaan (he later changed his name to "Piet Mondrian") was born March 7, 1872, in Amersfoort, the Netherlands, and died February 1, 1944, in New York.

Monographs published in the late 1980s and early 1990s concentrate on formal questions as well as biographical information. As of the mid-1990s, the best up-to-date bibliographies were in Blotkamp (1994), the catalog of the major international exhibition in The Hague, Washington, and New York (Bois et al., 1994), and thematically arranged, in the collected writings of Mondrian edited and translated by his heir, Harry Holtzman, in collaboration with art historian Martin S. James. Still valid is the catalog of works by the Belgian writer and friend of Mondrian during his Paris days, Michel Seuphor. Several essays by Herbert Henkels (in *Mondrian*, 1980) give an account of Mondrian's social and cultural milieu up to the time of his first journey to Paris in 1912 and describe the continuing influence of Dutch characteristics in his art.

Reared in a strict Calvinist, conservative environment, Mondrian went to Amsterdam in 1892 to study at the Rijksacademie. His early figurative work, such as *Windmill by the Water* (1900–1904; New York, Museum of Modern Art), was underestimated by most scholars, although it was appreciated by his peers at the beginning of the twentieth century. Henkels has described the social and cultural context for it, including the influence of Mondrian's father, a painter of political and religious histories whom Mondrian assisted, and the role of

Mondrian's uncle, a painter of Impressionist landscapes in the style of The Hague School. (Henkels, in *Mondrian*, 1980: 9–21; 219–285).

In approximately 1908, Mondrian began painting Symbolist works—for example, *The Red Tree* (1908–1910; The Hague, Gemeentemuseum). He came into contact with artists of the Dutch avant-garde, Jan Toorop, Conrad Kikkert, Jan Sluijters, and others, with whom he founded the *Moderne Kunstkring* (Modern Art Circle) in 1910. Early in the investigation of Mondrian, scholars considered the significance of his paintings; Robert P. Welsh and Robert Rosenblum saw Northern romantic influences in Mondrian's early landscapes and a mystifying atmosphere in his paintings of trees and windmills. Els Hoek and Carel Blotkamp investigated the meaning of symbolic images against the background of Mondrian's conversion to theosophy after 1900. According to Welsh, Mondrian's Symbolist paintings from the years 1908–1911 combine pictorial themes—human figures with uplifted faces and lonely towers and trees—with a construction of geometrically strict forms and strong, luminous colors, elements that continue in Mondrian's abstract works. These elements confer spiritual content on even the austerely geometrical paintings, like *Composition* (1929; New York, Solomon R. Guggenheim Museum; Fig. 86), which consist of rectangular areas in primary colors (red, blue, and yellow) and noncolors (white, black, and gray), separated by black horizontal and vertical lines (Welsh, 1966).

After seeing Pablo Picasso's and Georges Braque's works of Analytical Cubism for the first time in 1911, Mondrian moved to Paris in 1912 and began painting in a very abstract Cubist style. He dissected still lifes and church façades into a rhythmic structure of straight and curved lines with small areas of subdued colors. The iconography of the oval paintings as signs of a universal harmony between the male and female principle was worked out by Welsh (in *Piet Mondrian: Centennial Exhibition*, 1972). Taking a psychoanalytical approach, David Shapiro has found erotic connotations in Mondrian's flower paintings.

Due to World War I, Mondrian lived in Holland from 1914 to 1919. In close contact with other artists of *De Stijl*, the journal founded in 1917 under the editorship by Theo van Doesburg, Mondrian completed his passage to total abstraction. Hoek has shown how Mondrian, in contact with Vilmos Huszár, found his path to geometrical elements in his paintings. Under the influence of Bart van der Leck, these elements attained greater autonomy and a pure, almost primary, coloring.

Special attention has been paid to the relationship of Mondrian and Van Doesburg. They met in 1915 and were in close contact before Mondrian's move to Paris in 1919, as well as in the years that followed. Mondrian published his theory of the *Nieuwe Beelding* (Neo-Plasticism) in several series of articles in *De Stijl*. From 1924 onward, increasing disagreements led Mondrian to terminate his work with *De Stijl*. Later, he explained this by stating that Van Doesburg had introduced diagonal elements in painting. Scholars accepted this formal interpretation for a long time; however, by analyzing letters and theoretical treatises, Blotkamp and Nancy J. Troy have

each shown that the break was caused by incompatible differences in the interpretation of space and time in painting and architecture. Mondrian rejected any kind of motion as well as pseudomathematical elements of a fourth dimension in architecture and painting. Van Doesburg, on the other hand, accused Mondrian of rigidity and dogmatism and developed the new theory of Elementarism, based on Neo-Plasticism. Hoek has pointed out that Mondrian and Van Doesburg later renewed their association.

Mondrian lived in Paris from 1919 until 1938, and the greatest part of his so-called classical work originated there. He was in close contact with many artists, among them Fernand Léger, El Lissitzky, and Sophie Küpper, who established connections with Germany; with Joaquin Torres-García, the cofounder of the artists' group Cercle et Carré (Circle and Square); and with the American collector Katherine Dreier, who promoted his pictures in the United States from 1926 onward. He was a member of several artists' groups, including Cercle et Carré (1929) and Abstraction-Création (1931). Initially he experienced financial difficulties, but from 1925 onward his work was increasingly appreciated by buyers and collectors. While he remained in contact with Dutch artists through correspondence, the distance grew greater over the years. Mondrian's stylistic development and changes in compositional method during his time in Paris have been discussed extensively by Welsh and Hoek.

Mondrian did not only paint prolifically, he also wrote a lot. His most important writings include a series of articles that appeared in *De Stijl* (1917–1918): "De Nieuwe Beelding in de Schilderkunst" (Neo-Plasticism in Painting), published in a French translation in 1920 under the title *Le Neo-Plasticisme: Principe général de l'equivalence plastique* (Neo-Plasticism: The General Principle of Plastic Equivalence). He also wrote *L'Art réaliste et l'art superréaliste* (Realist and Superrealist Art), published in 1930 by Cercle et Carré; "Plastic Art and Pure Plastic Art" (1936) for *Circle: An International Survey of Constructive Art*; and his autobiography, *Toward a True Vision of Reality* (1941). In his writings he developed a utopian theory that was intended to embrace all areas of life. Within this intellectual framework, art as the precursor was given a central role. Blotkamp, Hoek, and Henkels have identified elements from the then widespread philosophy of theosophy, an idealistically interpreted natural science, and terminology attributed to the Christian theosophist M.H.J. Schoenmakers. The relationship between Mondrian's painted and theoretical work is still subject to discussion in the literature. Mondrian himself emphasized that his pictures resulted from artistic intuition and were not the result of a model or schema. But although he saw himself as an artist, he perceived his theories to be an important part of his life's work. Yves-Alain Bois and other scholars, who have examined the structural changes in his painterly *oeuvre*, have used Mondrian's writings to explain changes in his conception of formal elements.

Blotkamp and Troy have studied Mondrian's writings on architectural theory, which occupy an important position in his theoretical work. Blotkamp has pointed out that Mondrian's initial interest in architecture was affected by the influence of Bart van der Leck and J.J.P. Oud and that his theory changed over the years. As Troy wrote, Mondrian's architectural theory has a far-reaching utopian character because it is closely patterned after principles of two-dimensional painting and the attempt to exclude completely time and motion. Attempts at realization of the theory in the form of interior designs were not made. This was because, according to Troy, realization in Mondrian's studio could succeed only as a result of an intuitive, ongoing process.

Mondrian's studio fulfilled important functions in his ideal of the complete integration of art and life. Although at first Mondrian's New York studio was the only one known through documentation, Troy reconstructed the interiors of Mondrian's studios in Paris—the first studios of Neo-Plasticism—and their gradual changes over time. She has shown the public aspect of the studio, as a space for exhibitions, as well as a place where the artist engaged in a permanent process of self-reflection on his aesthetic principles. The principles of continuity between architecture and easel painting, which Mondrian also used in his unrealized interior designs, found their first realization in the studio. Henkels has discussed the function of the studio as a theoretical aspect of the creative process and as a testing ground and basis for paintings (Henkels, in *Mondrian*, 1980: 269). Blotkamp has pointed out the connection to the traditions of Romanticism, in which a studio can function as a temple for beauty and a reflection of the artist's personality.

Because of the threatening war in Europe, Mondrian moved to London in 1938 and to New York in 1940, where his work was greatly appreciated. He was a member of the artists' group American Abstract Artists and friends with artists Fritz Glarner, Carl Holty, Burgoyne Diller, and Charmion von Wiegand. In his late style, from 1932–1933 onward, he used double black lines, which, after 1939, he broke up into stripes of color fields, as in *Broadway Boogie Woogie* (1942–1943; New York, Museum of Modern Art). The grid-based early abstract paintings and the New York paintings have become subjects for formal-analytical investigations. Bois has examined the development of these pictures in terms of possible elimination of spatiality and has investigated the role of rhythm and repetition. Rhythm is an important concept in Mondrian's work. He believed jazz to be the music whose rhythm corresponded to the principles of Neo-Plasticism. As pointed out by Karin von Maur (in *Mondrian*, 1980), this is also manifest in his paintings.

Frauke Syamken

See also Avant-garde; Dada; De Branding; De Stijl; France; Hague School, The; Laren; North American painting, Dutch influences; Oud, Jacobus Johannes Pieter; Sluijters, Jan; Symbolism, Symbolists; Toorop, Jan; Van Doesburg, Theo; World Wars I and II

Bibliography

Blotkamp, Carel. *Mondrian: The Art of Destruction*. London: Reaktion Books, 1994.

Bois, Yves-Alain, Joop Joosten, Angelica Zander-Rudenstine, and Hans Janssen. *Piet Mondrian 1872–1944*. The Hague: Haags Gemeentemuseum; Washington: National Gallery of Art; New York: Museum of Modern Art; distributed by Leonardo Arte, Milan, 1994.

Hoek, Els. "Piet Mondrian." In *De Stijl: The Formative Years*. Edited by Carel Blotkamp et al. Cambridge, MA: MIT Press, 1986.

Mondrian: Drawings, Watercolors, New York Paintings. Essays by Herbert Henkels, Harry Holtzman, Joop M. Joosten, Robert Welsh, Karin von Maur. Stuttgart: Staatsgalerie Stuttgart, 1980.

Mondrian, Piet. *The New Art—The New Life: The Collected Writings of Piet Mondrian*. Edited and translated by Harry Holtzman and Martin S. James. Boston: G.K. Hall, 1986.

Piet Mondrian: Centennial Exhibition. Essays by M. Bill, N. van Doesburg, J. Joosten, T.M. Messer, M. Rowell, R.P. Welsh, and L.J.F. Wijsenbeek. New York: Solomon R. Guggenheim Foundation, 1972.

Rosenblum, Robert. *Modern Painting and the Northen Romantic Tradition: Friedrich to Rothko*. New York: Harper and Row, 1975.

Seuphor, Michel. *Piet Mondrian: Life and Work*. New York: Harry N. Abrams, 1956.

Shapiro, David. *Mondrian: Flowers*. New York: Harry N. Abrams, 1991.

Troy, Nancy J. *The De Stijl Environment*. Cambridge, MA: MIT Press, 1983.

Welsh, Robert P. *Piet Mondrian, 1872–1944*. Toronto: Art Gallery of Toronto, 1966.

Monuments to artists

With the exception of a few scattered grave markers, monuments to commemorate artists in the Netherlands were not created prior to the nineteenth century. Some of the exceptions are the monument for the canon Jan van Scorel in the Mariakerk in Utrecht (after 1562), an unusually early commemorative marker for Quinten Massys—who died in 1530, in Antwerp (1629), and a commemorative tablet at the gravesite of the poet Joost van den Vondel in the Nieuwe Kerk in Amsterdam (1772). Early, as well as noteworthy in the context of European public monuments, are the two civic monuments to genius: to Erasmus (Rotterdam; its present form by Hendrick de Keyser, 1622); and to Laurens Jansz. Koster, considered the inventor of printing with moveable type (Haarlem; first by Gerrit van Heerstal, 1722; later by Louis Royer, 1856).

After 1813, there were attempts to recall the exemplary achievements of the seventeenth century through its artists. In the 1820s, the first monument to an artist was created entirely in the spirit of the enlightening societies; it commemorated the moralizing poet Jacob Cats (Brouwershaven, Philippe Parmentier). A memorial to Ary Scheffer (1795–1858), who was particularly well known in France, was unveiled in 1862 (Dordrecht, J. Mezzara). Four years later, in 1866, a monument to Rembrandt was completed in Amsterdam (by Louis Royer); it was intended as a Dutch rejoinder to the monument to the Flemish master Rubens that was erected in Antwerp in 1840 (by W. Geefs). Later, a bust of Rembrandt was created in his birthplace of Leiden (T. Dupuis, 1906), but this was not until several years after a monument to Frans Hals was erected in Haarlem (T. Dupuis, 1900). Plans for a Netherlandish pantheon were only partly realized in the row of artists' effigies created for the exterior of the Rijksmuseum in Amsterdam (1885, various sculptors).

This figurative tradition continued with statues of Hieronymus Bosch ('s Hertogenbosch, A. Falise, 1930), of the architect Hendrik Petrus Berlage (Amsterdam, Hildo Krop, 1966), another Rembrandt monument (Amsterdam, Han Wezelaar, 1956), and a second monument to Van Scorel (Utrecht, H. Janzen, 1984). Striking in its formal expression is a memorial to Vincent van Gogh (Amsterdam, André Schaller, 1956) that uses Cubist-inspired shapes to show the painter seeking the sun above symbols of the dark earth. A double monument to the brothers Vincent and Theo van Gogh was created in 1964 by Ossip Zadkine (Zundert).

Among comparable statues to poets, the Vondel monument (Louis Royer and P.J.H. Cuypers, 1867) in Amsterdam, with allegorical figures in the four corners, follows an international trend. The sculptor Pier Pander created a remarkable monument to himself in his Temple (Leeuwarden, 1924), in which six symbolic figures are an attempt to represent the fundamental ideas of sculpture.

While the older type of memorial to an artist commemorates the great man, possibly accompanied by figures or allegories of his work (for example, the Vondel monument of 1867), the more recent monuments show the artist—more so in the Netherlands than elsewhere—just in his works. The most important Netherlandish example of this approach is the Hildebrand Monument (Haarlem, Jan Bronner, 1914–1918). Figures in Art Déco style representing characters from the novel *Camera Obscura* by Nicolaas Beets (pseudonym Hildebrand, 1814–1903) are placed around an octagonal fountain. The poet's memorial itself stands at a distance of 60 meters from the fountain in such a manner that it, too, has a view of the fountain. Prominent among the numerous, purely anecdotal monuments of this type are the poem *Wiltsangh* (Amsterdam, Sigurdur Gudmundsson, 1970) created by carving Morse code into three trunks, and a sculptural re-creation of Johannes Vermeer's *Milkmaid* (Delft, W.T. Schippers, 1976).

Jochen Becker

See also Architectural restoration; Bronner, Jan; De Keyser, Hendrick; Gudmundsson, Sigurdur; Krop, Hildo; Nationalism; Pander, Pier; Public monumental sculpture (1795–1990); Royer, Louis

Bibliography

Bionda, R.W.A. et al. *Monumentale beeldhouwkunst in Nederland*. Weesp: Fibula-Van Dishoeck, 1984. (English summary).

Music, musical instruments

The history of Dutch music between the sixteenth and eighteenth centuries comprises few notable composers or performers, mostly organists like Jan Sweelinck. Yet Dutch art from the same period includes a surprisingly large and diverse body of musical imagery. Music sheets, songbooks, and an extraordinary variety of musical instruments regularly appear in still-life paintings, genre scenes, pastoral landscapes, and history subjects. Such imagery, together with the many musical anthologies and popular songbooks that were published in Haarlem and Amsterdam, testify to a rich and varied musical life in the Dutch home, tavern, and church. Dutch paintings have long been regarded as valuable visual resources on the original appearance and use of old instruments. Recent scholarship has emphasized, however, that music and musical instruments sometimes function symbolically within Dutch art.

There are two broad categories of musical instruments in Dutch art: folk instruments, including bagpipes, hurdy-gurdies, fiddles, horns, simple flutes and pipes, rommel pots, and various other makeshift instruments; and the so-called fine art instruments, such as organs, harpsichords, virginals, lutes, citterns, guitars, viols, cornettos, and flutes. Yet except for the most expensive keyboard instruments and larger viols, which always indicate a refined context, the social identity of musical instruments can be highly ambivalent and problematic. Violins, for example, appear in representations of elegant *hausmusik* (chamber music) concerts as often as they are found in paintings of village taverns, and small bagpipes are acceptable among the wealthy elite in arcadian contexts. Furthermore, Dutch representations of music often disregard the classical antithesis between the "noble" stringed instruments and the "ignoble" wind instruments.

This is not to say that Dutch artists failed to avail themselves of the rich legacy of classical ideas about music and harmony perpetuated and expanded in Renaissance humanist thought. Thomas de Keyser's portrait of *Constantijn Huygens and His Clerk* at the National Gallery in London (Fig. 99), for example, shows the famous statesman seated in his study near a table that displays a celestial globe, a terrestrial globe, an architectural plan, and a large type of lute known as a chitarrone. These particular items are more than general references to Huygens' interest in the liberal arts and sciences. They illustrate the classic tripartite theory of harmony as originally defined by Boethius in ancient times: The two globes represent *musica mundana*, or the "music of the spheres," and its effects on the earthly elements; the architectural plan and chitarrone illustrate *musica instrumentalis*, or the physical manifestation of this cosmic harmony to the senses by means of mathematical proportion; and Huygens' act of receiving a letter refers to *musica humana*, or harmony among men, for as ambassador and secretary to the *stadholder* he was responsible for preserving and promoting political harmony.

Such abstruse and learned references were beyond the interests of most Dutch artists and their viewers, however. Musical allegories of harmony exist, but are represented in simpler terms more attuned to the domestic, middle-class values of Dutch society. The notion of harmony is thus found more often in portraits of musical families or dancing couples. Jan Miense Molenaer's family group portrait (ca. 1640) at the Frans Hals Museum in Haarlem (Fig. 87), for example, uses a musical concert as a familiar means for illustrating the idea of family concord. The concert in the foreground is made up of family members performing on a cello, lute, violin, and cittern, with a virginal visible behind to the left. One of the daughters sings from a part book as she beats the time, or *tactus*, with her right hand. Another part book inscribed *bassus* lies on the floor at the foot of the husband-father, signifying in musical terms his social role as the foundation of the family.

Reactionary Protestants developed more negative attitudes toward music. It was during this era that the old Pythagorean notion of music as the audible embodiment of a grand cosmic harmony was slowly being replaced by the modern empirical idea that music is really nothing more than pleasing vibrations in the ear. The new idea is best pictured in engraved and painted series of the five senses in which musical instruments or performing musicians now symbolize the sense of hearing. From the puritan point of view, music thus became the epitome of worldly vanity since it was a purely transitory, empirical experience that serves no practical function other than to please the senses. Indeed, during the early decades of the seventeenth century the Dutch Calvinists banned the use of the organ and other musical instruments during the church service.

Representations of music can refer to vanity in Dutch art in two closely related but distinct ways. On one level, music represents the sinful pleasures and pursuits of the world of the senses. *Vanitas* still-life paintings display bagpipes, flutes, lutes, violas, and sheaves of music piled alongside bags of money, armor, and other emblems of fame and glory as the vain preoccupations of earthly existence. On another level, music itself is likened to human life. The musical instruments piled in disuse and gathering dust on the tabletop, the songbooks with pages torn and weathered are, in this sense, metaphors of the human body after death. Like a corpse abandoned by its soul, so too the musical instrument, now broken and deteriorated, withers away in perpetual silence.

Because music can suggest so many different ideas—harmony, the sense of hearing, vanity, transience—it is often difficult to interpret the precise significance of musical instruments in a particular painting. Does a scene of an artist playing music in the studio, for example, illustrate the harmony of composition and color, or the vanity of time poorly spent? More important, not enough evidence exists to assume that all or even most Dutch representations of music and musical instruments are in some way symbolic of one or another of these ideas.

Roy Sonnema

See also Allegorical traditions; Genre painting, eighteenth century; Genre painting, seventeenth century; Group portraiture; Marriage and family portraits; Musicians, musical companies, musical performers; Portraiture; Still life; *Vanitas, vanitas still life*

Bibliography

Fischer, Peter. *Music in Paintings of the Low Countries in the Sixteenth and Seventeenth Centuries*. Amsterdam: Swets and Zeitlinger, 1975.

Moens, Karel. *Muziek en Grafiek: Burgermoraal en muziek in de zestiende en zeventi ende-eeuwse Nederlanden*. Antwerp: Hessenhuis Museum, 1994.

Raupp, Hans-Joachim. "Musik in Atelier; Darstellungen musizierende Kunstler in der niederlandischen Malerei des 17. Jahrhunderts." *Oud Holland* 92 (1978): 106–129.

Sonnema, Roy. "Representations of Music in Seventeenth-Century Dutch Painting." Ph.D. diss., University of California at Berkeley, 1990.

Winternitz, Emanuel. *Musical Instruments and Their Symbolism in Western Art*. New Haven: Yale University Press, 1979.

Musicians, musical companies, musical performers

Although some representations of music in Dutch pictures function intellectually for viewers—symbolizing specific ideas like harmony or vanity—in other pictures it is difficult or even impossible to assign the represented music a specific intellectual content. This is especially true for Dutch genre paintings of the sixteenth through eighteenth centuries, where the musical performance as a narrative event or experience often supersedes the simple display of musical instruments as symbolic markers. Many different kinds of musicians and musical performance may be found in Dutch genre painting, although the identity of these musicians and the contexts for their music are not always obvious to viewers today.

Paintings by the Utrecht Caravaggists Hendrick Terbrugghen, Gerard van Honthorst, and Dirck van Baburen frequently depict anonymous musicians singly or in small groups in large, half-length format (Color Plate 3). These musicians, usually playing lutes, violins, viols, flutes, and bagpipes, and dressed in antiquated festive costumes with boldly colored striped shirts and feathered caps, are presumably the professional tavern and brothel entertainers who were paid to attract and retain customers into the late hours of the night. Not only were they skilled musicians in the sense of producing pleasing renditions of popular songs and ballads on demand, but, like the medieval jesters of old, they could also recite drama (note that these musicians occasionally appear as pastoral characters, dressed as shepherds or shepherdesses) and tell witty stories and jokes. Accordingly, the paintings emphasize precisely this aura of entertainment—musicians smile, laugh, and pluck away energetically on their instruments as they turn to glance out of the picture, momentarily enticing the viewer to enter vicariously or become a part of this world of sensuous entertainment.

A very different kind of experience may be found in the musical paintings of artists like Judith Leyster, Jan Miense Molenaer (Fig. 87), Pieter Codde, Johannes Vermeer, Gerard Ter Borch, Gabriel Metsu, and Caspar Netscher. Elegantly dressed young men and women occupy well-appointed surroundings as they sing and play on virginals, lutes, guitars, viols, or flutes; eating, drinking, card playing, and other leisure entertainments may also be suggested. While it is possible some of these paintings, too, may represent taverns and brothels, more likely these are typical scenes of upper-middle-class Dutch *hausmusik* (chamber music). The concerts were intimate domestic gatherings at which family and friends would relax, socialize, and recreate with the music of fashionable motets and madrigals, popular songs, ballads, and even hymns. These domestic amateur concerts were also one of the primary occasions at which a young gentleman of leisure society could formally gain an introduction to and court a young lady. Many paintings thus depict intimate musical gatherings with overtones of love and romance. Such is the case with Ter Borch's *Music Party* (ca. 1675; Cincinnati, Cincinnati Art Museum; Fig. 88). Here a young gentleman and his friend are apparently paying a visit to the splendidly attired young lady, who sits across the table holding an expensive theorbo. There is a momentary pause in the concert, charged with psychic and emotional undercurrents. The gentleman looks up from his music and stares affectionately at his partner; she deflects his attentions by looking down blankly and reaching to turn the page in her own music album. Viewed in this way, the *hausmusik* concert in general provides a context for interpreting and experiencing the scene, while the music in particular functions as the narrative core that mediates human interaction.

Scenes of country weddings, *kermis* celebrations, and village tavern life also frequently represent musical performances. These subjects first appeared in the sixteenth century with Pieter Bruegel the Elder's magnificent scenes of village bagpipers and continued to be produced in seventeenth-century Holland by painters like Isaack van Ostade, Adriaen van Ostade, and Cornelis Dusart. Usually only one or two musicians perform, with others responding by dancing, singing along, clapping their hands, and stamping their feet. The primary instruments are typically anything that can carry a strong single melody—bagpipes, hurdy-gurdies, various fiddles, block flutes—often accompanied by rommel pots, tin pans, or anything else that can make noise. The music is presumably simple variations of local or popular folk songs. Provincial folk songs were sometimes included in popular music books for the use of wealthier city dwellers, and there are a small number of Dutch paintings that represent folk instruments in a wealthier *hausmusik* setting. While these paintings of musical amusements among the peasant class may have illustrated moral principles for some viewers, most people probably approached them as a form of comic entertainment.

A number of paintings exist in which the itinerant peasant musicians appear at a doorway playing bagpipes or hurdy-gurdies, as represented by Adriaen van Ostade and Jacob Ochtervelt and in a few etchings by Rembrandt. These musicians are the descendants of those represented by Bruegel who now are forced to beg from door to door because of the general decline in large peasant wedding and *kermis* celebrations.

Roy Sonnema

See also Comic modes; Music, musical instruments; Pastoral; Rural life and views; Ter Borch, Gerard; Utrecht Caravaggists; Van Baburen, Dirck

Bibliography

Alpers, Svetlana. "Bruegel's Festive Peasants." *Simiolus* 6 (1972/1973): 163–176.

Buijsen, Edwin, and Louis Peter Grijp. *Music and Painting in the Golden Age.* Antwerp: Hessenhuis Museum; The Hague: Hoogsteder and Hoogsteder; Zwolle: Waanders, 1994.

Fischer, Peter. *Music in Paintings of the Low Countries in the Sixteenth and Seventeenth Centuries.* Amsterdam: Swets and Zeitlinger, 1975.

Leppert, Richard. "Music, Representation, and Social Order in Early Modern Europe." *Cultural Critique* 12 (1989): 25–54.

Mirimonde, A.P. de. "Les sujets musicaux chez Vermeer de Delft." *Gazette des Beaux-Arts* 57 (1961): 29–52.

Sonnema, Roy. "Experiencing a Ruckers Virginal." *Southeastern College Art Conference Review* 12 (1992): 62–68.

N

Nationalism

The search for nationalism in art looks for a reflection of the specific national character, based on biological, geographical, climatic, social, or religious origins. Nationalism is expressed in a style thought of as typical of that nation, in a presentation of national themes, and in the discussion of art theory, art history, politics, as well as in the art market. In the separation of the nation's "own" and "the foreign," outsiders' opinions of the Netherlands (and its art) play an important role. They serve as an example to be surpassed as well as an inferior counterpart. Foreign art history and art theory preceded that of the Netherlands, and arguments presented in these writings often serve to determine Netherlandish discussion. The art of painting seems to have been considered a specific national product with specific characteristics, an approach probably only comparable to Italy.

A connection between climatic zones and national characteristics (discussed from antiquity onward, from Herodotus to Johann Joachim Winckelmann [1717–1768] as the reason for the perfection of nature in Greek art) relegates the Netherlands to a position at the perimeter of cultural creation. This position is determined by the cold, wet climate, a phlegmatic character, and assiduous narrowness. Netherlandish artists are given credit for exact imitation and seen as craftsmen able to produce pictures of a superior technical quality. Important content or compositions are reserved for French or Italian artists. The same applies to sculpture: The lack of a typical Netherlandish sculptural tradition is excused by the fact that the country lacks the materials (like ore or marble); the climate is not favorable for sculpture meant to be displayed outside; and the modest lifestyle does not lend itself to such testimony of fame and haughtiness.

In opposition to this, the Netherlands has been given the leading position in producing modern artists who deviated from the norm or were even revolutionaries, with Rembrandt as the most prominent heretic who deviated from all artistic norms. Everything not classical or idealized is subsumed into the "Dutch" category and discussed in art theory only as the forerunner of great art (for example, by Joshua Reynolds). Art theory sees the Dutch deviation into naturalness as freedom or simplicity, attributes that can be interpreted positively as well as negatively. This is the case also with the comprehensive concept of the middle-class (Huizinga, 1969). Thus for the Netherlands there is no antique tradition, but measurement by the norms of antiquity. The Netherlands emulates others but, even when rejecting others' norms, is still tied to them.

In the Netherlands, awareness of national art was based on historical, social, and political self-awareness. A specific Netherlandish political–social structure influenced development of lesser genres and delayed development of a strong national consciousness in comparison to other European countries. This national consciousness existed side by side with local patriotism and provincialism.

However, postulating national character in a young country like the Netherlands is questionable. Influences from the North as well as the South coexisted into the seventeenth century because the country only formally separated in 1648. The question of uniting these influences is still reflected today in the use of terms like great and small Netherlands (Geyl, 1946).

A lack of preliminary studies forces one to presume that the early and later United Netherlands formed an image composed of traditional motifs, revolutionary propaganda, and influences brought in by refugees from the South. This image is known to us through nineteenth-century eyes that tended to exclude historical facts like foreign ties, aristocratic trends, and the influence of regional and religious groups, and tended to discount—in terms of art history—the importance of Romanism, history painting, and *fijnschilderij* (fine painting, the technique of the fine painters). The concept of "typically Dutch" developed idealized associations that were later assumed necessary for historical and theoretical interpretations (as well as useful as a stylistic concept) of Netherlandish art, but certainly denoted no natural law.

The Sixteenth Century

Erasmus of Rotterdam formulated typical Dutch characteristics—honesty, simplicity, beauty and quality of household goods manufactured in the Netherlands, social thinking, business sense, courage, and education of the inhabitants. The people of the Netherlands formed these attributes themselves; they were not taken over from abroad. Erasmus referred to classical authors like Tacitus, who held up a mirror of the Batavians (the ancient inhabitats of the region of the Netherlands) as virtuous, freedom-loving examples for the Romans. The national character of simplicity originates here: It can be seen as an artistic mistake as well as a middle-class virtue in opposition to foreign courtly refinement. Both aspects are combined under the term "Primitivism." (The "addiction" to eating and drinking, for which Dutch as well as Germans were criticized, has its wellspring here and makes these nations an embodiment of *Gula*, or gluttony.)

Art literature in the Northern provinces was formed in emulation of Italian examples. The humanist and art lover Domenicus Lampsonius (1532–1599) included fifteenth- and sixteenth-century painters in a series of *Lives*. Painter and poet Lucas d'Heere (1534–1584) and historian M. van Vaernewijck, in 1568, praised the Ghent altarpiece (1432) by Hubert and Jan van Eyck as a local and national monument, comparable to the work of the greatly acclaimed ancient Greek painter Apelles and admired abroad. Supporting this admiration—even in Italy—are comments about the value of technical quality (in opposition to the traditionally more valued depiction of dramatic action and the *idea* of artistic invention) apparent in realistic portraits, landscapes, and still lifes (and later genre scenes); in other words, the "lower" categories in the hierarchy of subjects available to painters.

At the same time, the invention of oil painting by Jan van Eyck in the early fifteenth century was acknowledged to be the beginning of a national school of art. Like the invention of printing or the windmill, the development of a national school belongs in the catalog of *Nova Reperta* (modern inventions) meant to show the equal importance of the North in comparison to antiquity, and specific national cultural achievements. Art describing the countryside and city (including famous inhabitants of a city)—for example, Antwerp—resulted in praise of art as part of the praise of Netherlandish cities.

From the very beginning, historical accounts of the rebelling provinces included painters as examples of an independent cultural tradition. Hadrianus Junius' *Batavia* (first published in Leiden in 1588) includes a catalog of painters, from Jan Mostaert to Jan van Scorel and Maerten van Heemskerck up to contemporaries Philips Galle and Dirck Volkertsz. Coornhert. Painting and the graphic arts became a leitmotif and guarantee of national fame up to the present. At the same time, the characteristic themes and motifs were determined—middle-class virtues of simplicity (versus luxury) and industriousness, which for the art of painting could be criticized as simplemindedness, lack of ideas, and listless thoroughness. Freedom is a fundamental political and rhetorical theme, but this can also degenerate into disorderliness and licentiousness.

Already evident in Junius' work is the praise of the cow as a typical Netherlandish product, used—next to the heraldic lion—as a national symbol.

Typical of the humanistic tradition of history writing in the Netherlands is the early-seventeenth-century *Batavi Parallelon* by Hugo de Groot, Junius' successor in this field. De Groot singles out for praise the sculptor Willem Daniëlsz. van Tetrode (active in Delft, second half of the sixteenth century; died before 1588), who is less characteristic for the Netherlands but compares favorably with the sculptors of Italy and antiquity. Van Tetrode had permission (denied his Italian contemporaries) to complete and restore exemplary antique sculptures.

The Seventeenth Century

Stabilization of the new Dutch state resulted in connections drawn between tradition (antique models) and the emphasis on national qualities. At the beginning of the Golden Age, Karel van Mander wrote about art in his *Schilder-Boeck* (1604), modeling himself after Pliny the Elder and Giorgio Vasari. Besides antique and Italian models, meant to be emulated and surpassed, Van Mander considered the development of art in the Netherlands. At the beginning was Van Eyck's invention of oil paint. Northern artistic genealogy begins with Van Eyck, sees Italy with Van Scorel, and finds perfection in Hendrick Goltzius (a pattern similar to Vasari's tripartite division of stages reached by Giotto, Masaccio, and Michelangelo). Haarlem was important because Van Mander and Goltzius resided there and Albert van Ouwater had worked there as a landscape painter in the fifteenth century. For Van Mander the Netherlandish painters were leaders in landscape painting.

The traditional appreciation of landscape painting that in the second decade of the seventeenth century burgeoned in a series of local landscapes that express feelings of self-worth was also found in literature (L.J. Spieghel, *Hertspieghel*, 1614; C. Huygens, *Dorpen en Stedestemmen*, 1624–1625). Realistic landscape painting began with topographically correct views of the surroundings of Haarlem and Amsterdam that combine pride in national cultural achievements with nationalism, moral, and religious considerations. This applies to landscapes of Northern Holland as well as to views of Gelderland and Rhineland, and the depiction of the Dutch "own" national ruins, townscapes, single buildings, winter landscapes, and trade, such as the bleaching industry, mills, and animal breeding. Human mastery of nature (polders, tree-lined avenues, canals) was emphasized as well as specific national achievements and proficiencies (Freedberg, 1980). The details depicted in landscapes were also used to comment directly or indirectly on political events: marine battles from Hendrick Vroom to Willem van de Velde the Younger; pictures of the Amsterdam Town Hall; church interiors—especially the Nieuwe Kerk in Delft with the tomb of Willem the Silent (Fig. 42). Even dunescapes were reminders of older history when much of the land had yet to be reclaimed from the sea. In a higher style, history paintings treated Batavians and Romans as equals, often in series of large-scale propaganda pictures (Van de Waal, 1952). Finally, national and historical awareness is to be seen in the many prints of portraits that were collected in book form.

Art of the first half of the seventeenth century follows a formula, sometimes cunningly simple, close to nature, and modern. In the literature, simplicity, even bluntness, is praised as virtuous, in opposition to foreign pretensions (including South Netherlandish ones). Roemer Visscher's *Sinnepoppen* (1614) is an example, combining realistic images (after drawings by Claes Jansz. Visscher) and straightforward moralistic text, a prototype of Netherlandish emblem books.

Sculpture in the first half of the seventeenth century— for example, by internationally known Hendrick de Keyser— propagandizes for national heroes (Willem I of Orange, Erasmus, Burgomaster Van der Werff of Leiden); this is continued in the tombs of admirals. Contemporaries praised De Keyser's architecture as modern, as an accomplishment equal to that of antiquity and the Italians. Conspicuous in the Dutch adaptations of Palladio in architecture is the dominance of the Ionic Order, in contemporary theory a moderate position between the martial Doric and the ostentatious Corinthian Order. Corinthian columns were used on the Amsterdam Town Hall (by Jacob van Campen, 1648–1655) as an expression of a political goal to surpass antiquity as a new capital of Republican ideals. The contrast with the Antwerp Town Hall, built not quite one hundred years earlier, as well as with the recently created palaces of the *stadholder* was in this way made immediately clear.

The consciousness of living in a Golden Age seen in art literature and art politics was first in evidence in the foundation of Leiden University (1575). Consolidation of the political situation in 1609 resulted in prosperity and a desire for representation. Different cities responded by commissioning works of art: in Amsterdam, Hendrick de Keyser began his characteristic churches (Color Plate 2); Rotterdam commissioned him to restore his Erasmus sculpture; Haarlem gave commissions to several local artists (Goltzius, Cornelis Vroom, and Cornelis Cornelisz. van Haarlem); and the States General finally honored the founder of the Republic, Willem I of Orange (died 1584), with a grave monument (Fig. 34).

Emphasis on national art was also seen in the "Dutch Gifts," political gifts from the Republic to England. In 1618, Prince Henry received two paintings by Hendrick Vroom, *Sea Battle near Gibraltar against the Spanish Armada* (combining a national history theme with typical Netherlandish seascape), and *Storm at Sea*. In 1636, Charles I received two paintings by Geertgen tot Sint Jans, one by Aertgen van Leyden, and Jan Gossaert's *Adam and Eve*. This gift emphasized the importance of Dutch painting to one of the greatest patrons of the arts. In 1660, the gift to Charles II included Italian as well as Dutch paintings—Pieter Saenredam's *St. Bavo Church in Haarlem* and two genre scenes by Gerrit Dou (White, 1982) (Color Plate 8).

The Dutch consciousness of the seventeenth century as the golden century led to comparisons of their Republic, victorious over Spain, with Greece after victory over the Persians. Thus, most of the reasons for considering the seventeenth century *deze onse gulden eeuwe* ("this our golden age") were

political ones. Only in retrospect did Arnold Houbraken see the seventeenth century as "de Gulde Eeuwe voor de kunst" (*De Groote Schouburgh* 1718–1721, 2:237). In art literature, nationalism is vague (Houbraken considered Rubens and Van Dyck as contributing to Netherlandish fame), moderate, and intended foremost as a comparison with Italy.

It is of interest theoretically that Samuel van Hoogstraten (*Inleyding tot de hooge schoole der schilderkonst*, 1678) places the classical hierarchy of subjects side by side with technical virtuosity and the possibilities of modern "genre"; and, in doing so, emphasizes a traditional quality of Netherlandish art and opens the way to equality of different schools. He defends, as did Gerard de Lairesse (*Hat Groot Schilderboek*, 1707), the "low" taste of national art (in a comparison of cow and horse). For this even Constantijn Huygens and Van Hoogstraten found a theoretical educational journey to Italy superfluous for artists.

The Eighteenth Century

Eighteenth-century art relied to a great degree on the accomplishments of the previous century, as seen in painting as well as in the inventorying topographies—for example, *Tegenwoordige staat der Nederlanden* (Present-Day Condition of the Netherlands), 1758; *De Vechtstroom . . . verheerlijkt* (The Vecht Stream . . . Glorified), 1791—and national lexica of artists—for example, Houbraken.

Both art and art literature were strongly oriented toward the interests of the international art market. Contemporaries were aware of the stagnation and saw a decline in the separation of ideology and practice: The middle-class themes emphasized in the previous period were inadequate for the principles of French classicism. At the same time, Antoine Watteau followed these examples; and paintings from the Netherlands were interesting because their "low" style and everyday themes were seen (following Diderot) as a conscious effort to provide virtuous examples (for instance, in the captions of reproduced prints) or as undemanding decorations for intimate interiors in the style of Louis XV.

From the mid-eighteenth century onward bloomed a positive (self) image of the Golden Age—free, democratic, sensible, prosperous—as the national realization of an enlightened ideal. Its art read as realistic depiction of middle-class virtues and ideals. But again national character and national art had to be defended against foreign (especially English) criticism. Contrast between the *beau ideal* and simple "Realism," in practice already decided by collectors and the art market, continued as a theoretical problem into the nineteenth century (Koolhaas-Grosfeld, 1982).

The French Revolution declared higher ideals in art, but also encouraged nationalism in art directly or indirectly. In the Batavian Republic, official art reached back to examples of free Batavians as well as antiaristocratic and anti-English protagonists of the seventeenth century. Napoleon's looting of Dutch art in 1795 resulted in several things: worldwide fame for the works exhibited in Paris, concern and care for art remaining in the Netherlands, and, in 1800, the founding of a national art gallery, forerunner to the Rijksmuseum in Amsterdam. The bases of this collection were "national treasures" already returned by the occupiers of the Netherlands because they were—in the view of the classically oriented museum in Paris—worthless reminders of specific moments in Dutch history.

Government involvement in the arts (most of it only in the planning stage) was begun by the short-lived (1806–1810) king of the Netherlands, Louis Napoleon. He conferred a French model of centralist-national support for the arts on the Netherlands with an academy and periodic exhibitions of "living masters."

The forced international orientation of the political situation after 1800 strengthened national feeling, which in the following century, in an almost unique way, focused on national painting that was seen by a small, not very aggressive, nation as the indicator of national greatness. Perhaps this was so because this art was assured of international appreciation (more so than the little-understood Dutch language or controversial war deeds). In painting, a minified nation expressed its feeling for its great past.

The Nineteenth Century

Return of the art looted by France was taken to be a visible expression of freedom from French dominion. Art was seen—always in retrospect to the seventeenth century—as the noblest expression of national achievements. This led, on the one hand, to speculation that the newly won freedom would bring about a new Golden Age, and, on the other hand, to an overly optimistic belief that a Golden Age in art would engender a general Golden Age.

As art promotion followed Louis Napoleon's government support, so were stylistic means borrowed from French art, as, for instance, in the theme chosen by Jan Willem Pieneman in his *Battle of Quatre Bras on June 16, 1815* (1817–1818; Amsterdam, Rijksmusem). In the turn toward historical themes, classical heroes were often replaced with heroes from the nation's history or even with contemporary heroes. Landscape was rediscovered, initially as an expression of historical memories, and still lifes and genre scenes were painted praising civic spirit and family life of exemplary forebears. With these tendencies there also occurred in the course of the century a "purification" in which especially artists' biographies (for example, of Rembrandt and Jan Steen) were cleansed of (negative) anecdotes.

Enthusiasm turned to resignation after the 1830–1831 separation of the Kingdom of Belgium from the Kingdom of the (Greater) Netherlands, signifying that the Netherlands no longer had a leading role among European countries. Because of the stature of Rubens and an uninterrupted tradition of history painting and sculpture, Belgium was more successful in painting, architecture, and the applied arts; this was most apparent at international exhibitions. The failure of the North's hopes for a utopia were explained by the generally difficult times and lack of patronage, by weak government support, and a general loss of the characteristics that had made the seventeenth century great. This historical contrast was lamented by E. Potgieter, especially in a novella, *Het Rijksmuseum* (1844). It is an idealized description of a national museum with portraits and history paintings, a pantheon meant to serve as a school for the nation; its realization was delayed for four decades.

National history painting barely rose above the small-format theme catalogs created because of the initiative of Jacob de Vos Jacobsz. and the Amsterdam art group Arti et Amicitiae in *Historische galerijen* (1850–1863). Also found in these artificial galleries, as a stimulation and compensation for an underdeveloped tradition of sculpture, were statuettes of "famous men" *(Het Vaderlandsch gevoel, 1978)*. Such monuments as were actually executed were humble, and often only in the wake of competing Belgian efforts. Plans for the fusion of a national pantheon and a memorial to 1813 into a monumental encyclopedia of national history as art history were not realized until 1885 in P.J.H. Cuypers' design for Amsterdam's *Rijksmuseum* (Becker, 1985).

Central to the Rijksmuseum's program were Rembrandt and his work. Over the centuries, Rembrandt had been nationally and internationally elevated to a universal genius and leading national hero, as evidenced in 1884 by C. Busken Huet when he ended his magisterial art history *Het land van Rembrandt* with the sentence "Java en de *Staalmeesters* zijn eigenlijk onze beste aanbevelingsbrieven" (Java and the *Syndics* are truly our best letters of introduction). The accession of Queen Wilhelmina in 1898 was celebrated with an exhibition dedicated to Rembrandt, and Rembrandt's three-hundredth birthday in 1906 was celebrated across the country with festivities that this time included modern Dutch art.

In 1883 the Rembrandt Society was created to preserve and purchase national art treasures. This was a response to long-standing complaints about the neglect of art and monument preservation, pointedly commented on in 1873 by Victor de Stuers as a negative national trait in *Holland op zijn smalst* (Duparc, 1975).

Besides this slow formulation of national history in and with art, there were attempts by religious and political groups to formulate a "party line" through the medium of art. Questions were raised about the "picture worthiness" of historical persons as well as styles. The Hague's *National Memorial to 1813* (Fig. 124) created a flare-up of conflict between advocates of classicism and the Neo-Gothic contrasting liberal and Catholic views of history. The same conflict was renewed in the construction of the Rijksmuseum. This building was intended to be an expression of the national style, not only in content and decoration but also in the materials used. Increasing pressure from the Catholic faction, led by J.A. Alberdingk Thijm, resulted in a design that was scoffed at as a "monastery."

Meanwhile, a new generation saw a connection with typical national traits not in the depiction of history or imitation of a style, but in a fresh view of nature, as pursued by The Hague School of artists directly and indirectly—via influence of the French Barbizon School—seeking again the "spirit" of Dutch landscape painting of the seventeenth century.

The Twentieth Century

Traditional motifs of nationalism from the nineteenth century continued far into the twentieth century. The expansion of the image of Dutch art beyond the emphasis on sixteenth- and seventeenth-century realism was slow to occur and to acknowledge inclusion of Romanism, the Italianates, history painting, and the *fijnschilders* (fine painters)—all of which initially were seen as "antinational."

A general European interest in questions of national art and the effects of national geography on art was apparent in 1930 at an international art-historical congress in Stockholm. With international fascism, war, and the German occupation activating supposed national and popular features of Dutch art, its characteristics were discussed as "typically Germanic," in the way they had been formulated at the end of the nineteenth century by the German proselytizer for Rembrandt, Julius Langbehn (*Rembrandt als Erzieher von einem Deutschen*, 1890). In contrast, those who were persecuted and occupied politicized what they saw as traditional values in Dutch art and character: humility, independence, and tolerance.

The trend against historicism and programmatic internationalization of art in modern movements since World War I indicates a conscious turning away from traditional ideas and types. The national heritage is seen as repressive; after World War II, the Neo-Realists were suspected of fascism. The traditional motifs of Dutch art (windmill, cow, milkmaid, tulip) have been devalued in their use as advertisements for Dutch products, or have experienced abstract transformation by artists (Ger Dekkers, Jan Dibbets) or an ironic postmodern regeneration (Teun Hocks).

Jochen Becker

See also Alberdingk Thijm, Josephus Albertus; Architectural restoration; Art history, history of the discipline; Belgium; Classicism in architecture; Coornhert, Dirck Volkertsz.; Erasmus, Desiderius; Flanders, Flemish School; Hague School, The; History painting; Huizinga, Johan; Huygens, Constantijn; Landscape; Magic Realism; Monuments to artists; Neo-Gothic; Public monumental sculpture (ca. 1550–1795); Public monumental sculpture (1795–1990); Rembrandt research; Sculpture (1550–1795); Sculpture (1795–1945); State and municipal art collecting and collections; State patronage, public support; Town halls; Townscapes; Van Mander, Karel; World Wars I and II; Writers on art, eighteenth century; Writers on art, sixteenth and seventeenth centuries

Bibliography

Baneke, J. et al., eds. *Dutch Art and Character: Psychoanalytical Views on Bosch, Bruegel, Rembrandt, Van Gogh, Mondrian, Willink, Queen Wilhelmina.* Amsterdam: Swets and Zeitlinger, 1993.

Bank, J.Th.M. *Het roemrijk vaderland: Cultureel nationalisme in Nederland in de negentiende eeuw.* The Hague: SDU, 1990.

Becker, J. "'Ons Rijksmuseum wordt en tempel': Zur Ikonographie des Amsterdamer Rijksmuseums." In *Het Rijksmuseum: Opstellen over de geschiedenis van een nationale instelling.* Edited by E. de Jong, G.Th.M. Lemmens, and P.J.J. van Thiel, 227–326. Weesp: Fibula-Van Dishoek, 1985. (English summary).

————. "'Zoo praalt ook Nëerlands maagd in de achtbre rei der kunsten': Nationalisme in de Nederlandse kunst en kunstgeschiedschrijving in de 17de en 19de eeuw." In *Eigen en vreemd: Identiteit en ontlening in taal, literatuur, en beeldende kunst,* 171–180. Handelingen van het 39ste Nederlandse Filologencongres. Amsterdam: VU Uitgeverij, 1987.

————. "'Pictura nu wel Batavan soo jonstigh is': Zur Lebensbeschreibung Ouwaters in Karl van Manders *Schilderboeck.* In *Icon to Cartoon: A Tribute to Sixten Ringbom.* 41–53. Helsinki, 1995.

Becker, J., and A. Ouwerkerk. "De eer des vaderlands te handhaven: Costerbeelden als argumenten in de strijd." *Oud Holland* 99 (1985): 229–270.

Bizot, Pierre. *Histoire métallique de la république de Holland.* Amsterdam: P. Mortier, 1688–1690.

Carasso, D. "De schilderkunst en de natie: Beschouwingen over de beeldvorming ten aanzien van zeventiende-eeuwse Noordnederlandse schilderkunst, ca. 1675–1875." *Tijdschrift voor theoretische geschiedenis* 11 (1984): 381–408.

Duparc, F.J. *Een eeuw strijd voor Nederlands cultureel erfgoed.* The Hague: Staatsuitgeverij, 1975.

Freedberg, D. *Dutch Landscape Prints of the Seventeenth Century.* London: British Museum Publications, 1980.

Geyl, P. *Eenheid en tweeheid in de Nederland.* Lochem: De Tijdstroom, 1946.

Grijzenhout, F., and H. van Veen. *De gouden eeuw in perspectief: Het beeld der Nederlandse zeventiende-eeuwse schilderkunst in later tijd.* Nijmegen: SUN, 1992.

Het Vaderlandsch gevoel: Vergeten negentiende-eeuwse schilderijen over onze geschiedenis. Amsterdam: Rijksmusem, 1978.

Huizinga, J. *Dutch Civilization in the Seventeenth Century, and Other Essays.* New York: Harper and Row, 1969.

Jongh, E. de. "Real Dutch Art and Not-So-Real Dutch Art: Some Nationalistic Views of Seventeenth-Century Netherlandish Painting." *Simiolus* 20 (1990/1991): 197–206.

Judson, C.L. "The Birth of Dutch Liberty: Origins of the Pictorial Imagery." Ph.D. diss., University of Minnesota, 1982.

Koolhaas-Grosfeld, E. "Nationale versus goede smaak: Bevordering van nationale kunst in Nederland, 1780–1840." *Tijdschrift voor geschiedenis* 95 (1982): 605–636.

Tilborgh, L. van, and G. Jansen, eds. *Op zoek naar de gouden eeuw: Nederlandse schilderkunst 1800–1850.* Zwolle: Waanders, 1986.

Veldman, I. "Elements of Continuity: A Finger Raised in Warning." *Simiolus* 20 (1990/1991): 124–142.

Waal, H. van de. *Drie eeuwen vaderlandsche geschieduitbeelding, 1500–1800: Een iconologische studie.* 2 vols. The Hague: Nijhoff, 1952.

White, C. *The Dutch Pictures in the Collection of Her Majesty the Queen.* Cambridge: Cambridge University Press, 1982.

Natural history illustration

Natural history illustrations of plants, animals, and insects were widely produced by Dutch artists of the seventeenth and eighteenth centuries. This category of imagery is tied to the growth of empirically based natural science, in which Netherlanders showed a proclivity for botany and entomology. The Plantin-Moretus press in Antwerp and Leiden made a particular contribution to botany through its publication of treatises by Rembert Dodoens (1517–1585), Carolus Clusius (1526–1609), and Mathias Lobelius (1538–1616), who culled their illustrations from a pool of thousands of woodblocks commissioned by Christopher Plantin. Some artists became scientists in their own right, such as Jacob de Gheyn II (1565–1629), whose penetratingly observed watercolor studies of flowers, insects, and other small creatures point to the legacy of Joris Hoefnagel (1542–1601), one of the founders of entomological illustration. Dutch entomological illustration reached its apex in works by Maria Sybilla Merian (1647–1717), such as *Metamorphosis Insectorum Surinamensium* (1705; Amsterdam). The production of hand-painted nature illustrations flourished in Holland as a specialty of Herman Saftleven (1609–1685), Pieter Withoos (1654–1693), Johannes Bronkhorst (1648–1727), Herman Henstenburgh (1667–1726), and others and was fueled by the patronage of amateur naturalists and horticulturists such as Agnes Block (1629–1704). Natural history illustration, both printed and painted, intersects with many areas of Dutch art, such as the important pictorial genres of still life and animal painting, garden architecture, illustrated books, including emblem and fable books, ornamental design, and the decorative arts, particularly Dutch tiles.

Lee Hendrix

See also Country houses and gardens; Exotica; Horticulture; Non-Western cultural influences; Prints, publishers; Still life; Tiles

Bibliography

De Nave, F., and D. Imhof, eds., *Botany in the Low Countries (End of the Fifteenth Century–ca. 1650)*. Antwerp: Plantin-Moretus Museum and Stedelijk Prentenkabinet; distributed by Snoeck-Ducaij and Zoon, 1993.

Hendrix, Lee. "Of Hirsutes and Insects: Joris Hoefnagel and the Art of the Wondrous," *Word and Image* 11 (1995): 373–390.

Hendrix, Marjorie Lee. "Joris Hoefnagel and 'The Four Elements': A Study in Sixteenth-Century Nature Painting." Ph.D. diss., Princeton University, 1984.

Hopper, Florence. "Clusius' World: The Meeting of Science and Art." In *The Authentic Garden: A Symposium on Gardens*. Edited by Erik de Jong and L. Tjon Sie Fat, 13–36. Leiden: Clusius Foundation, 1991.

Schulz, Wolfgang. "Blumenzeichnungen von Herman Saftleven d.J." *Zeitschrift für Kunstgeschichte* 40 (1977): 135–153.

Segal, Sam. *Flowers and Nature: Netherlandish Flower Painting of Four Centuries*. Amstelveen: Hijnk International, 1990.

Nature photography

Nature photography has been usually overlooked in descriptions of the development of Dutch photography. It has received attention only when it forms part of the *oeuvre* of a professional photographer who is known for other subjects. Meinard Woldringh (1915–1968) and Martien Coppens (1908–1986) are two examples of this. Both made many landscape and nature photographs, but neither has ever been called a nature photographer. When the subject is landscape, there is no firm distinction between the work of men like Woldringh and Coppens on the one hand and nature photographers on the other. A significant and observable difference is that wildlife rarely appear in the works of those who are not mainly or exclusively photographing scenes from nature.

The quality achieved in nature photography cannot possibly be the cause for its neglect in photographic histories. The reason should rather be sought in the fact that nature photographers seem to have more in common with other lovers of nature than with professional photographers. Interest in nature is often the source of nature photography. It is an advantage, too, to have a profound knowledge of nature and its inhabitants—knowing where and when certain animals and flowers can be found heightens the chance of actually meeting or coming across them. Patience is an important quality in nature photographers, as often many days pass without seeing or coming near enough to the animal that is the subject of the search.

For a long time technical restrictions in photography (low-sensitivity plates and films, for instance) made photographing nature probably one of the most difficult specialties to master. Whereas buildings will stand still long enough, and people can be helped in doing so by inconspicuously supporting them, wildlife is less inclined to cooperate. Birds were, therefore, often photographed while brooding. Richard Tepe's book *De jacht met de camera* (Hunting with the Camera) of 1909 is witness to this. The earlier necessity of changing the plate after a picture had been made did not facilitate animal photography.

Traditionally, nature photography has served an educational goal. Illustrating books, magazines, and guides mostly required clear, sharp, even straightforward photographs. Widening technical possibilities enabled nature photographers to choose other settings. In due time a tendency to abstraction, out-of-focus adjustment, and other artistic liberties appeared. In some cases, clarity and beauty go together, as a photograph of *A Kestrel Picking at a Mouse* (ca. 1975) by Henk Tromp (born 1942) shows (Fig. 89).

Hans Rooseboom

See also Photography, modern and contemporary; Woldringh, Meinard

Bibliographic Note

There is no bibliography on the history of nature and wildlife photography in the Netherlands. Nature photography has been neglected by most scholars, who have tended to concentrate on the art-historical side of photography.

Neo-Gothic

The Neo-Gothic style in the Netherlands was introduced by King Willem II in 1840, when he built a gallery for his paintings in the garden of his palace on the Kneuterdijk in The Hague in remembrance of his stay in Oxford. In the next decade the new style became instrumental in the emancipation of the Roman Catholics. After the constitution of 1848, which gave Catholics full freedom of religion, most of the new churches were built in this style. The inspiration came then mainly from French and German Gothic architecture. A powerful encouragement to the revival of this style as the hallmark of the Roman Catholic Church came from the man of letters J.A. Alberdingk Thijm (1820–1889). However, the style was more than a vehicle for Roman Catholicism, it was also part of nineteenth-century historicism and suited the taste of those who were interested in the medieval past. Architects could use different historical styles, if asked. A. van Veggel, for example, designed a Neoclassicist church, St. Servatius, in Erp in 1843, and in 1852 he built the country house De Schaffelaar near Barneveld in Tudor style.

One of the more influential architects around the middle of the century was Theo Molkenboer (1796–1863), whose Neo-Gothic church on the Keizersgracht in Amsterdam (1854) was the first to be directly inspired by the French Gothic of the thirteenth century and the cathedral of Cologne. However, in this stage of the development of the Neo-Gothic style, most architects lacked the technical knowledge of the medieval masters. The vaults in the Amsterdam church were made of plastered wood.

The knowledge of Gothic constructions was greatly enhanced by the studies that resulted from the restorations of the major European cathedrals. Most influentual in the Netherlands was the work of the French architect E.E. Viollet-le-Duc (1814–1879). His theories were the basis for the restoration work of his Dutch counterpart, P.J.H. Cuypers (1827–1921), who restored several important medieval churches—for example, in Roermond, Rolduc, and Maastricht. After 1854 Cuypers worked closely with Alberdingk Thijm, who supplied him with the necessary theological and iconographical background for his church designs. In this period of his career, Cuypers sought his inspiration in the Île de France, as can clearly be seen in his church of St. Catharine in Eindhoven (1859–1867), where he applied a two-tower front, three porches as the western entrance, a two-aisled transept, an ambulatory with radiating chapels, and flying buttresses. Very different from the French examples was the building material: not stone, but brick. After 1865 he lived in Amsterdam, where he built six Neo-Gothic churches, the Rijksmuseum (1878–1885), and the Centraal Station (1885–1889).

The style was given new impetus by the founding in 1869 of the Guild of St. Bernulphus, a group of priests, artists, and architects whose aim it was to promote Christian art through the study of mainly late-medieval Dutch art. The most important architect in this group was Alfred Tepe (1840–1920), who had been trained with Vincenz Statz in the *Bauhütte* of the cathedral of Cologne.

P.J.H. Cuypers' work shows his development from an academic student of the high Gothic to a versatile designer. The impressive career of Tepe—he built seventy churches—did not show much variation. His brick churches are modest in their outside appearance but always lavishly decorated inside.

Several Neo-Gothic churches in the Netherlands were demolished in the twentieth century, and few of those remaining have kept their original interior decorations; nevertheless, today the appreciation of the style is widespread.

Wim Denslagen

See also Alberdingk Thijm, Josephus Albertus; Architectural criticism, issues of style; Architectural restoration; Churches; House of Orange-Nassau; Stained glass; Utrecht

Bibliography

Geurts, P.A.M., A.E.M. Janssen, C.J.A.C. Peeters, and Jan Roes. *J.A. Alberdingk Thijm, 1820–1889: Erflater van de negentiende eeuw.* Baarn: Arbor, 1992.
Peeters, C. "De neogotiek tussen nijverheid en kunst." *Tijdschrift voor Geschiedenis* 104 (1991): 356–380.
Rosenberg, H.P.R. *De 19de-eeuwse kerkelijke bouwkunst in Nederland.* The Hague: Staatsuitgeverij, 1972.

Neuhuijs, Albert (1844–1914)

Johannes Albert Neuhuijs, called Albert, belonged with Jozef Israëls, Bernardus Blommers, and Jacob Maris to the most important figure painters of The Hague School. Neuhuijs started out to become a lithographer in his hometown, Utrecht, where he also took lessons at a drawing academy. In 1869 he entered the academy in Antwerp. To earn a living, he made finely brushed genre paintings of ladies and noblemen, which were especially praised for their masterful reproduction of the silken robes. In 1871 he became financially independent because of a royal stipend. From 1872 until 1876 Neuhuijs lived in Amsterdam and regularly traveled to Nunspeet to paint the farmers. The many interior scenes do not show the poverty but rather a romanticized, joyful existence. In 1876 he settled in The Hague, where he became friends with painters of The Hague School and actively participated in the artists' societies. There he also painted scenes from the lives of farmers and fishermen.

In 1883 Neuhuijs moved to the village of Laren, where his friends Anton Mauve and Jozef Israëls had gone to work. He was one of the first to paint interiors. Like Blommers, who had a Scheveningen fisherman's house interior built in his studio, Neuhuijs had a Laren farmhouse interior set up in his studio. There he painted his sunny *tableaux* of mothers and children or a shoemaker with a baby in the crib by his side. His brushstroke became more forceful and his manner of painting less detailed.

After 1889 Neuhuijs moved several times and painted a great deal in Brabant. In later years he made many distant trips—for example, to America, where he was twice a jury member for the international exhibition in Pittsburgh. This request had everything to do with his fame, for in the years before World War I his work was much in demand and there was an extensive market for it, especially in England and the United States.

Hanna Pennock

See also Blommers, Bernardus Johannes; Hague School, The; Israëls, Jozef; Laren; Maris, Jacob Hendricus; Mauve, Anton

Bibliography

Heyting, Lien. *De wereld in een dorp: Schilders, schrijvers en wereldverbeteraars in Laren en Blaricum 1880–1920.* Amsterdam: Meulenhoff, 1994.

Leeman, Fred, and Hanna Pennock. *The Mesdag Museum: Catalogue of Paintings and Drawings.* Zwolle: Waanders, 1996.

Leeuw, Ronald de, John Sillevis, and Charles Dumas eds. *The Hague School: Dutch Masters of the Nineteenth Century.* London: Royal Academy of Arts, in association with Weidenfeld and Nicholson, 1983.

Nieuwe Bouwen

See Functionalism in architecture

Nieuwe Kunst

See Applied arts; Graphic design; Stained glass; *Wendingen*

Nieuwe Zakelijkheid, architecture

See Functionalism in architecture

Nieuwe Zakelijkheid, painting

See De Stijl; Magic Realism

Non-Western cultural influences

Representations of non-Western cultures entered the realm of Netherlandish art under the dual "sponsorship" of the encyclopedic frame of mind and expanding trade relations with foreign markets. Once established as an independent political entity, the Northern Netherlands, or United Provinces, also established sea routes independent of Spain and Portugal, and in 1602 founded the United East India Company (the VOC) followed in 1621 by the West India Company. Under the auspices of these two trade companies an extraordinary abundance of exotic goods and products from much of the Asiatic and American continents entered the ports of Amsterdam, Middelburg, Hoorn, and Enkhuizen, profoundly impacting Dutch society and culture. There was intense curiosity about the expanding world, so that, upon arrival in Holland, its exotica found immediate representation in Dutch painting, portrayed under minute scientific observation and with great artistic skill. This bond of art and science lasted far into the eighteenth century.

It had begun in the fifteenth century, where Oriental rugs are among the first non-Western goods to be depicted in painting, appearing on the floors of both sacred and secular interiors in the works of Jan van Eyck and Hans Memling, and in some illuminated manuscripts. In the seventeenth century, Turkish and, later, Persian rugs will leave the floor, and instead grace tables in still life, genre, and portrait painting, only to descend to the floor again in the eighteenth-century interiors. In may cases, realistic portrayal has made specific identification of rug and workshop possible. Exotic rugs are rarely lacking in the interiors painted by Johannes Vermeer (Fig. 115), Gerard Ter Borch, Gabriel Metsu, and Jan Steen.

The biblical subject of the Adoration of the Magi, so popular in the early sixteenth century, set a precedent for the ardent collection of exotica undertaken on an encyclopedic scale by so many European princes. It allowed painters of the subject to depict rare gifts as well as exotic human beings: The negro king becomes a standard feature among the Magi, as in the works of Geertgen tot Sint Jans and Hieronymus Bosch; the latter also introduced the Black generically in his *Garden of Earthly Delights* (ca. 1510–1515; Madrid, Prado). However, a mid-fifteenth-century Dutch manuscript Bible already had included the African Black in the story of King Solomon and the Queen of Sheba. Rembrandt and his pupils made this standard practice in their Old Testament paintings for the sake of realism and authenticity. Occasionally, the young, colored servant boy makes an appearance in the background or to the side of a family portrait, most likely of families who had lived in the Dutch East Indies and who had brought their servant(s) back to Holland with them. They are always dressed in Oriental costume to emphasize their ethnicity. At this point it is impossible to judge whether the exotic servants of some Dutch households set a precedent for popular Sinterklaas (Saint Nicolas) to bring with him a blackamoor servant, named Zwarte Piet (Black Peter), or the other way around.

A strong desire for realism and authenticity, coupled with his fascination with the exotic, led Rembrandt to study the Jewish community in Amsterdam and become a collector of exotica, including Mughal miniatures and Asiatic weapons. These peoples and objects were regularly incorporated into his *oeuvre*. Exceptionally, he also entered into the spirit of Oriental worlds of art, working at times with Japanese or Indian inks and papers and achieving a near-Oriental style in some of his drawings. Despite close Dutch trade relations with China and Japan, however, Far Easterners are rarely depicted. Although frequently copied from Chinese porcelain onto Delftware, Chinese figures appear but once in Dutch painting, in a work of Jan Asselijn.

The most abundant acceptance of non-Western culture is to be found in still-life painting, which may be viewed as being the Dutch burgher's miniature, "instant" *kunstkammer* (collection of rarities). Not that someone's specific collection was depicted, but still lifes reflected the collective taste and prosperity of the Dutch people and were painted for the open market (as were genre paintings and landscapes) by the millions. The earliest still lifes featuring exotica appear around 1600, right after the first Dutch ships returned with their cargoes from India and the Far East. The quantity of these imports gave seventeenth-century still-life painting an enormous boost and influenced its specialization.

Bulb flowers, such as tulips, hyacinths, lilies, and fritilaries, had come from Asia Minor in the sixteenth century and were ardently cultivated by Dutch horticulturists and illustrated in scientific *florilegia*. Bouquets of sometimes more than twenty varieties, often displayed in Chinese porcelain vases, fill the earliest still lifes. To these were quickly added insects and tropical butterflies from the West Indies and shells from the Caribbean and the Indian and Pacific oceans of incredible richness of form and color (see works of the Bosschaert family and Balthasar van der Ast). The flowers and shells were highly valued, fetching extraordinarily high prices; still lifes "immortalized" them. In two paintings by Hans Bollongier the "Viceroy" tulip is featured, for which bulb in 1637 the highest price ever was paid: forty-six hundred guilders. In the same year, the tulip market crashed. Of the shells, the Nautilus retained popularity throughout the seventeenth century, set in silver-gilt mountings or at times engraved.

Further additions to flowers and shells are many exotic fruits, such as apricots, grapes, peaches, citrus, melons, mulberries, almonds, olives, figs, and raisins; some of the earliest still lifes also contain sweets made from cane sugar, which came originally from India, and lengthwise-halved artichokes from Asia Minor (see works of Jacob de Gheyn II and Clara Peeters). The fruits of the sea were not forgotten; while oysters could be cultivated in Dutch sea grounds, red lobster could not, but both are featured in many banquet and *Pronk* still lifes as exotic delicacies. Banquet pieces of Willem Heda occasionally include pepper, the very spice that spurred people to find the sea routes to the "Indies," while in the *Vanitas* still life tobacco from America makes its appearance (tobacco was also exported from Japan). America further contributed melons, calabashes, pumpkins, cucumbers, pineapples, mangoes, coconut, green beans, and asparagus to the fruit and vegetable still lifes and paintings of market scenes. Nowhere else in Europe did the consumer have such a wide choice of food. In contrast, the Brazilian fruit and vegetable still lifes of Albert Eckhout catered to the scientific spirit of the age. With several other painters, he had accompanied Johan Maurits van Nassau, governor of Dutch Brazil, to that country to document its appearance, flora, fauna, and people.

Among the most popular of exotica to appear in still-life painting was Chinese porcelain. Interception of two Portuguese carracks by the Dutch in 1602 and 1603 brought a rich cargo of porcelain—called Kraak porcelain—to the auctions in Middelburg and Amsterdam. Of the Ming dynasty Wanli period (1573–1619), this porcelain in the form of vases, jars, dishes, bowls, platters, and cups immediately appeared in still-life painting and gradually entered Dutch households, as can be seen in genre painting. This expensive item is always coupled (in the still lifes) with the most exotic and richest of flowers, fruits, carpets, seafoods, and shells (Fig. 90). When in 1644 the Ming dynasty fell, the porcelain supply dried up temporarily, but the Dutch turned to Japan, which had begun to manufacture its own porcelain, and obtained Chinese imitation, as well as the Japanese colored ware (Arita), which also found an instant market in Holland. When trade with China could resume, even greater amounts of porcelain entered Dutch ports. Porcelain cabinets make their appearance in Dutch interiors at the end of the seventeenth century, while in the eighteenth century porcelain is used for interior decoration on chimney pieces and cupboards. Tableware was or-

dered in huge quantities, often after designs the Dutch supplied. Between 1729 and 1743, the VOC imported more porcelain into the Netherlands than during the entire seventeenth century.

The temporary shortage of Chinese porcelain in the middle of the seventeenth century had led in Holland to the production of cheaper imitation in ceramicware. The Delft faïence industry came up with a product that could hardly be distinguished from Chinese originals (Fig. 19). In the eighteenth century, with greater emphasis on interior decoration, ceramic tile and wallpaper took the place of paintings, while coffee, tea, and chocolate drinking became extremely fashionable. Although tea had been introduced to Holland in 1610, it was not until the 1670s that it became a social beverage, drunk from handleless cups as was (and is) customary in the Orient. Only chocolate cups had handles. The popularity of tea increased the need for porcelain services, utensils, and lacquered tea tables; for a Chinese ambience in which to enjoy the beverage, the home interior was furnished with Coromandel screens and Japanese folding screens, while in the garden tea pavilions built in "Chinese" style were erected (see paintings of Cornelis Troost).

The women who inhabit seventeenth- and eighteenth-century interiors are frequently dressed in silks (from Persia and China); men occasionally are depicted wearing a *japonsche rock* (kimono), as in the portraits of Jan Lievens and Caspar Netscher. A standard Shogunal gift to Dutch delegations, silk kimono, as well as cotton ones, were exported in large numbers from Japan in the seventeenth century. So was Japanese lacquerware, but it is rarely depicted in painting, except in a few still lifes of Willem Kalf. Persian turbans of silk become standard headgear for figures from the biblical past, and pearls from India adorn many Dutch women, as well as biblical heroines, lending them an authentic Oriental touch.

Dutch households included exotic pets, like parrots and monkeys, which had made their initial appearance already in still-life painting. While they at times acquire emblematic or symbolic meaning, most exotic animals and birds were studied for scientific reasons. They include the elephant (both African and Asian), the lion, the rhinoceros, the tortoise, the turkey, and the bird of paradise. This was an outgrowth of the sixteenth-century collecting habit of royalty, who employed numerous artists to scientifically depict and record their precious flora and fauna. Roelandt Savery repeatedly painted such animal collections under the guise of the earthly paradise, scenes to which Hieronymus Bosch already had applied the new faunal knowledge. Johan Maurits van Nassau, governor of Dutch Brazil in the period 1636–1644, brought artists and scientists with him to record the land, its resources, and culture, resulting in the landscape "publications" of Frans Post, the scientific still lifes of Albert Eckhout, and multivolume book publications to which both Post and Eckhout contributed illustrative material. Cartography and picture making are blended. That also occurred in the maps and atlases of Willem and Joan Blaeu. This bond between art and science will continue far into the eighteenth century, perhaps nowhere more perfectly than in Maria Sibylla Merian's *Metamorphosis*

Insectorum Surinamensium, published in Amsterdam in 1705. In the same year George Rumphius' *Amboinsche Rariteitkamer* was published with illustrations of crustaceans no less grand than the ones that appear in the still lifes of Willem Kalf, Jan Davidsz. de Heem, or Abraham van Beyeren.

As Brazil was relinquished to the Portuguese, and trade with the Far East gradually dwindled—the VOC was abolished in 1795 with Napoleon's takeover of the Netherlands, but the Japan trade continued in the hands of the Dutch government in Batavia—the impact of non-Western influences on Dutch life decreased. It was rekindled in Holland only toward the end of the nineteenth century, after the Japanese woodcut had become widely known and appreciated in Europe. Its influence, call *Japonisme,* was mainly felt in France, where Vincent van Gogh experienced and embraced it. With his brother Theo, he had amassed a considerable collection of Japanese prints, and his work (in France) strongly reflects the technical and stylistic influence of Hokusai, Hiroshige, Kuniyoshi, and others. In contrast to the seventeenth- and eighteenth-century artists (with the exception of Rembrandt), who only "collected" exotica in their paintings, Van Gogh also adopted an Oriental vision and manner of composing.

His contemporaries in Holland experienced *Japonisme* partly through direct exposure—George Hendrik Breitner owned a few prints, and in 1892 Pulchri Studio in The Hague held an exhibition of Japanese woodcuts—and secondarily via the work of French painters such as Edgar Degas, Paul Gauguin, and Émile Bernard and the international Art Nouveau. Breitner furnished the interiors of his *Girl in Japanese Kimono* series (1893–1894) with folding screens and Oriental carpets, aiming for two-dimensionality and surface pattern. In other works he experimented with Japanese painting formats and spatial arrangements. Others, in whose *oeuvre* Oriental vision was adopted or adapted, are Johan Thorn Prikker, Jan Toorop (who was born and raised in Indonesia), G.W. Dijsselhof, J. Voerman, Willem Witsen, Theo van Hoytema, and Piet Mondrian (works ca. 1901/1902). Travel to exotic places (the Middle East and Indonesia) inspired Marius Bauer to adopt Oriental subject matter, while exposure to and study of Oriental religions and philosophies further informed the work of Mondrian in the twentieth century.

Japonisme in Art Nouveau left its strongest impact on early-twentieth-century ceramic, graphic, and commercial art, as well as on women's fashions. The establishment of ethnological museums in Leiden (based on the encyclopedic collections of Japanese *naturalia* and *ethnographica* of Ph.F. von Siebold and J.H. van Overmeer Fisscher), Amsterdam (Tropenmuseum, focused on Indonesian cultures), and Rotterdam renewed public consciousness and appreciation for exotic art and culture. And as artists became more personally involved with Asiatic philosophies and cultural practices, such as Zen and *Zenga* (Zen painting), Oriental vision, style, and technique strongly informed, if not replaced, their innate Western manner. Calligraphic action painting is best represented in the *oeuvre* of Karel Appel; others in the latter part of the twentieth century imbued with Oriental vision and spirit are Mariet Numan, Kees Buurman, Loes van der Horst, and the potter Johnny Rolf.

Grace A.H. Vlam

See also Applied arts; Appel, Karel; Atlas, atlases; Bosch, Hieronymus; Breitner, George Hendrik; Cartography; Ceramics; Commerce and commercial life; Dijsselhof, Gerrit Willem; Exotica; France; History painting; Horticulture; Japonisme; Lievens, Jan; Mondrian, Piet; Natural history illustration; Onbong, Pieter; Rembrandt van Rijn; Rooskens, Anton; Still life; Thorn Prikker, Johan; Tiles; Toorop, Jan; Trade, exploration, and colonization overseas; Troost, Cornelis; Van Gogh, Vincent; *Vanitas, vanitas* still life; Vermeer, Johannes; Witsen, Willem

Bibliography

Bergstrom, Ingvar. *Dutch Still Life Painting in the Seventeenth Century.* New York: Hacker Art Books, 1983.

Bionda, Richard, and Carel Blotkamp, eds. *The Age of van Gogh: Dutch Painting, 1880–1895.* Zwolle: Waanders, 1991.

Bol, L.J. *The Bosschaert Dynasty: Painters of Flowers and Fruit.* 1960. Reprint. Leigh-on-Sea: F. Lewis, 1980.

Dutch Tiles. Philadelphia: Philadelphia Museum of Art, 1984.

Freedman, David, and Jan de Vries, eds. *Art in History, History in Art: Studies in Seventeenth-Century Dutch Culture.* Santa Monica, CA: Getty Center for the History of Art and the Humanities, 1991.

In the Wake of the Liefde: Cultural Relations between the Netherlands and Japan, since 1600. Rotterdam: Museum voor Volkenkunde Rotterdam; Amsterdam: De Bataafsche Leeuw, 1986.

Jörg, C.J.A. *The Geldermalsen: History and Porcelain.* Groningen: Kemper, 1986.

———. *Interactions in Ceramics: Oriental Porcelain and Delftware.* Hong Kong: Hong Kong Museum of Art, 1984.

King, Donald, and David Sylvester. *The Eastern Carpet in the Western World, from the Fifteenth to the Seventeenth Centuries.* London: Arts Council, 1983.

Segal, Sam. *A Prosperous Past: The Sumptuous Still Life in the Netherlands, 1600–1700.* The Hague: SDU, 1988.

North American art, Dutch influences

From the establishment in the early 1600s of the short-lived colony of New Netherland, the arts of Holland, whether directly or indirectly felt, have been a major source for the evolution of American realism and tonalism in painting and printmaking and for American architecture and applied arts. The Netherlands has also been a prime interactive partner in the development of American internationalism, modernism, and postmodernism in all of the visual arts. These important and complex connections have not been sufficiently studied by art historians over the years because of the overshadowing relationships American artists have also had with the arts of the British, Italians, Germans, and French; the arts of the Spanish and Dutch have always been separated into small and very distinct compartments away from the mainstream in typical histories of the American development.

Interspersed throughout the ongoing discussion have been

products of the American artist's and historian's intense desires to find elements absolutely "pure" in their "Americaness," almost as if success in such a search would calm the devils of cultural insecurity inherent to the field. But the America addressed here was at its outset and ever more a multicultural experiment in the New World. For example, "the Dutch enterprise" in America began when Henry Hudson, an English navigator in the employ of the Dutch East India Company in 1609, brought a mixed crew of about twenty Dutch and English sailors up the river that now bears his name.

Town Planning and Architecture

A fort was established five years later near Hudson's first landing site up river, and that place was in time surrounded by the community of Beverwyck, afterward Albany, New York. But Dutch colonization in America was always slow because the citizens of Holland were happy back home and comparatively few of them wanted to emigrate. So the new West India Company issued a charter of privileges and exemptions in 1629 under which members had the right to purchase extensive tracts of land from the native peoples. These grantees became known as *patroons* (protectors) because they were required to establish no fewer than fifty settlers on each tract and were thus created virtual barons over their feudal domains through an almost invited violation of the company's trade monopoly. In effect, this was the rapid creation of a new American aristocracy, and even after New Netherland had been New York for quite a long time, the British continued the practice.

Actually the West India Company had already relinquished its commercial monopoly in New Netherland back in 1638. This move was followed by an influx of English Puritan and French Huguenot colonists, along with others from many nations, who were all encouraged to increase the colony's population. Under director general Peter Stuyvesant, New Netherland's population grew from two thousand in 1647 to ten thousand residents on September 8, 1664, when Stuyvesant was forced to surrender New Amsterdam to a superior British force. By that time New Amsterdam, afterward New York City, had become New Netherland's center of society and administration, as well as a rather distinctive community.

In 1653 anxiety over the possibility of a land attack by native Americans and/or the British had led the burghers of Manhattan to build a wall across the island along the present Wall Street. However, the original crowding south of the wall was not really so much for protection as it was a transplanting of the compactness of old Amsterdam to its New World namesake. Indeed, as drawings and engravings of New Amsterdam show from 1651 on, the town was filled with "Hollandish" nostalgia from its stepped gables and occasional windmill to the Broad Street ditch, soon to become a canal named after old Amsterdam's Heerengracht.

Though a great fire of 1776 would destroy most of the original Dutch city, old New Amsterdam was to be remembered as a very convivial place where it was reputed that every other house was a tavern. Yet prominent within that setting was the five-story dignity of the old State House, at the center of the community's polyglot and lively commercial character, and of the line of two-and-a-half-story and three-and-a-half-story row houses of which it was a part. In many instances the heavy-timbered framing and construction of the buildings of New Netherland was not dissimilar to that of New England. Indeed, numerous structures throughout the colony were built of wood and stone.

On the other hand, the favored material in New Amsterdam was brick, which the Dutch considered superior to stone, for both dwellings and warehouses, all hemmed in by the Hudson (or North) River on one side and the East River on the other. Below Wall Street the close pattern of roads created the curves modern New York City has retained and, apart from the planned crowdedness others would have found difficulty liking, the Dutch settlement was quite attractive. Red, salmon, yellow, and purple bricks were laid in traditional and pleasing patterns. Meanwhile, Albany builders varied their end-gables of brick with the mouse-tooth pattern, along with patterns of brick over windows, and a decorative usage even of the iron wall-anchors holding their structures together.

Later such elements of initial Dutch-American building and decoration would make up only a small part of the very broad range of the American architectural eclecticism that burgeoned forth from the nineteenth century into the twentieth; interestingly, it was a descendant of early Dutch colonists of the more aristocratic sort who would author the most cutting critical surgeries in regard to the "nonprogressiveness" of such a stylistic potpourri.

A medievalist in the best engineering sense, Montgomery Schuyler of New York City's *Sun, Times,* and *World* (who also wrote articles in the 1880s for the *American Architect* and in the 1890s for the *Architectural Record*) was what might be called an eclectic of a most enlightened variety. He had no problem with the use of historical styles of architecture so long as the desired effect did not precede the cause; his enthusiasm was for those whose intent was ultimately to create the functional. Romanesque and Gothic cathedrals in particular had shown this historian-critic that engineering and art must not be divorced, and he was one of the first of an "Eastern Establishment" to praise the structural aesthetics of the Chicago School. More accurately, the writer found the organic functionalism of Louis Sullivan and Frank Lloyd Wright very hopeful work, in opposition to the rehash of admired solutions of the past in which there was no potential for progress.

Meanwhile, in the Netherlands, Hendrik Petrus Berlage, the first interesting architect in the formation of the structural rationalism that would lead to De Stijl and Het Nieuwe Bouwen, as Dutch functionalism was called, in designing his Amsterdam Stock Exchange (1898–1903) was indebted to a considerable extent to the work of the first great pioneer in the development of the Chicago School, Henry H. Richardson. The "Richardsonian Romanesque" had also been a tremendous influence in the development of both Sullivan and Wright as artists, and Berlage's approach to architecture was, in time, mightily impacted, too, by the design and philosophy of Wright in particular. He knew Wright's work through published accounts and then saw it on a trip to the United

States in 1911. The Dutchman was particularly taken with Wright's now destroyed Larkin Building of 1904. That design, once part of Buffalo, New York's, architectural tour, having obvious connections to his own Amsterdam Stock Exchange conception, Berlage saw in Wright's work more generally the American's rationality and mechanistic orientation—that is, the Wright whom Berlage found sought control and utilization of the machine in an exploration of new materials and techniques in the creation of a *new* culture.

Indeed, in no country of Europe were the designs of Frank Lloyd Wright studied earlier and with more interest than in the Netherlands; and Berlage was Wright's greatest admirer after his visit to the United States. Writing about the American's work in the "Wright issue" of *Wendingen* (no. 4, 1921), Berlage was additionally the initial critic to see certain of Wright's weaknesses, the Dutch architect's admiration of the American being the more impressive within the context of the critical.

So the formative influences on the architects of De Stijl and Het Nieuwe Bouwen were none other than Berlage and Wright. As numerous concepts that had been bubbling up everywhere in Europe before 1914 came to their first fruition in the Netherlands at this time, when those ideas were studied by architects everywhere the moment World War I was over, was it an "American-Dutch" or a "Dutch-American" influence working toward the creation of the so-called International Style? Yet, although the modernist directions of the International Style were presented in exhibitions and publications beginning in 1932 with a show at New York City's new Museum of Modern Art, designs in this style were not built in America until the late 1930s, when some of the architects themselves, fleeing the Nazi threat, came to the United States.

Indeed, even though it had been the architect Philip Johnson and historian Henry-Russell Hitchcock, back in a historical survey of the early 1930s, who were responsible for first coinage of "International Style" as a terminology, it had actually appeared as tangible building during the late 1930s, a time of great hesitancy toward the "non-American." After all, when the Americans Johnson and Hitchcock had paid tribute to the primary creators of the new style, including Walter Gropius and Mies van der Rohe of Bauhaus fame, France's Le Corbusier, and the Dutchman J.J.P. Oud, they had included only Wright as an American member of their modernist hierarchy. What everybody had forgotten at that time was that the International Style could not have developed in the same way without the influence—upon De Stijl and Het Nieuwe Bouwen and, therefore, also on De Stijl—of the Chicago School. But what those two old "Dutchmen," Berlage and Schuyler, had known around the turn of the century would again be known by everybody in 1940, with another "homecoming" of "The Style" in the person of new New York City resident Piet Mondrian of old Amsterdam.

Material Culture

Back in an era of "so long ago," inside the Dutch houses of New Amsterdam, one front room was frequently an office.

The remainder of the residence was divided into small rooms, and a garden in back provided shade in the summer as well as fruits and vegetables for the kitchen. The New Amsterdam home of Adam Roelantsen had a staircase entry, a built-in bed, and a pantry. Beside its portal were two benches, and its rooms were wainscoted. In short, if the rooms one sees in the interiors of Pieter de Hooch found only an approximation in New Netherland, it was not because the Dutch in America had not tried for more.

Wealthier men than Roelantsen owned turkey-work or Spanish leather chairs, kept their belongings in wooden chests and wardrobes (the Dutch *kast*, although commonly referred to in America as a *kas*) that were painted brightly with flower motifs, and ate from Delft china. For instance, the Hardenbergh bedroom, now preserved in the Henry Francis du Pont Winterthur Museum in Delaware, represents a 1760s Hudson River Valley interior, including an armchair and a side chair typical of that region, a small joined table, a bed with Oriental rugs, and an excellent example of the *kas* with turnip feet, a heavy cornice molding, and a grisaille fruit design painted in *trompe l'oeil*.

Meanwhile, the Philipse Manor at Yonkers, of about the same time, exhibits Dutch proportioning and simplicity of exterior detail, while the most distinguished of the manor interiors is that from the Van Rensselaer House in Albany, preserved by the Metropolitan Museum of Art to express the courtliness of life led by the leading Dutch families of Hudson River country. In truth, Dutch taste in colonial America in general was more sophisticated than that of Anglo-Americans simply because fashion was more advanced in the Netherlands than in England. The English looked to the Dutch for inspiration in matters of style, and often migrants from Holland brought fashions to the New World that had as yet not even become current in the British Isles.

That this was the case is perfectly understandable upon the basis of the general historical course of events in Europe during the time. The taste and style we know as "William and Mary" is Baroque in character, typified by dynamic, curved opposition and energy. In both furniture and silver, plasticity and a sense of depth and movement are achieved. For example, the so-called Spanish foot introduced with the advent of the eighteenth century, along with caning and chair backs with ballusters (turned split spindles), together with carved cresting rails, were all furniture elements that came to America via England from points of origin in the Low Countries and Spain. Afterward, the so-called Dutch foot (a round-pad termination for the cabriole leg) was a creation linked with the Queen Anne style (dominant in America until 1750).

From earliest days, colonial silversmithing had, of course, also been practiced. The principal centers for this in the seventeenth century were British Boston, Dutch New York and, to a lesser extent, British Philadelphia. For instance, the very robust quality of early New York pieces will not be confused with work done in New England. Old New Amsterdam, that convivial town, produced tankards especially, with rich engraved fronts and covers and foliated bands applied around heavily molded bases, and also large shallow drinking bowls with repoussé ornament, floral in motif and separated in paneled cartouches.

The most favored decorations for engraving were natural and stylized representations of flowers and animals, drawn from such wide-ranging sources as Oriental porcelain or a Dutch publication of poetic fables by Jacob Cats. The standard reeding technique (a set of small rounded moldings resembling a reed, in each case, and, together, a column shape) is found on some pieces, while chasing (embossing) occurs on a number of others, as the Dutch predilection for elaborate decorations continued to appear on silver from New York through the turn of the century. Also, regional differences are found in the globular shape of New York teapots versus the pear shape favored in Boston.

The New York colony, "old New Netherland," *was* different in many ways. For example, over thirty years after the Dutch had ceded the colony to the British, New Amsterdam–born Stephanus Van Cortlandt in 1697 received a royal grant from London for eighty-seven thousand acres just north of Manhattan. Van Cortlandt manor at Croton-on-Hudson was of a Dutch farmhouse style (long and low with thick stone walls) and richly furnished. Now restored as a museum, it would be joined by an even grander mansion built of gray stone in 1748 by John, nephew of Stephanus, in what is now Van Cortlandt Park, New York City's largest at 1,132 acres.

A portrait of this John Van Cortlandt is in the collection of the Brooklyn Museum today. Painted around 1730, the picture presents the wealthy young man dressed in his finest long waistcoat with numerous buttons, broad cuffs, and a long cravat. Indeed, colonial fashions in dress are frequently better read in paintings than from any actual garment retained from those formative days. Yet this is not to say that colonial crafts were not, in some cases, well developed at relatively early points. For instance, shoemakers are among the first craftsmen recorded at work in the colonies, and, by the early part of the eighteenth century, tailors were also numerous in cities like New York. Another anonymous portrait, of Thomas Van Alstyne (New York Historical Society), from around 1721 pictures that stalwart fellow in a no-nonsense style, in a no-nonsense suit probably, though not certainly, made up in the colonies of material created in either Europe or America.

One of the most notable aspects of the colonial Dutch, in contrast to English settlers, for example, was the genuine love of paintings they shared with their compatriots back home. This is manifest in various travelers' notes that comment on the profusion of pictures found in Dutch homes, a situation quite different from what was experienced in houses elsewhere in the colonies. Also, a number of Dutch estate inventories list paintings room-by-room, and a dozen or so titles in any given document of this kind is not unusual. In fact some late-seventeenth-century to early-eighteenth-century lists, like the thirty-nine pictures left by Cornelius Steenwyck, go much higher.

The initial paintings created in New Netherland are dated earlier—from the same period in the early to mid-seventeenth century as the first surviving colonial gravestones and woodcuts. Fragmentary data offers the student just a few known individuals who listed themselves as painters of one kind or another in the New Amsterdam area, among them Jacobus Strijcker, Augustine Herrman, Jan Dirckzen, Evert Duyckinck, and Hendrick Couturier. Of these, the first family of painters to be identified was that of Evert Duyckinck the First, who arrived in New Amsterdam with his father and brother in 1638. A glazier, the first Evert was also variously called, in documents of the time, a burner of glass, a painter of glass, a stainer of glass, a painter, and a limner. In short, this craftsman in glass seems to have manufactured and sold glass and then installed it and decorated it after his glass was in place in church houses and public buildings around the town and vicinity. But the elder Duyckinck's activities extended beyond such limited limning (namely, the act of illumination) to the painting of signs, coats of arms on fire buckets and coaches, and, finally it seems, to the making of portraits.

But the *real* painter in the family was Gerret Duyckinck, one of Evert's sons. In 1679, Gerret and Evert the First installed colored glass windows in the new church of the Labadist Fathers of Long Island. Then, on his own, Gerret painted portraits of himself and his wife (both New York Historical Society) that reveal more three-dimensional form through consistent *chiaroscuro* than anything done during the same period by the limners of New England.

Robert S. Olpin

See also Architectural criticism, issues of style; Berlage, Hendrik Petrus; Mondrian, Piet; North American collecting; North American painting, Dutch influences; Oud, Jacobus Johannes Pieter

Bibliography

Arnason, H.H. *History of Modern Art.* Rev. ed. New York: Harry N. Abrams, 1986.

Barker, Virgil. *American Painting: History and Interpretation.* New York: Macmillan, 1950.

Craven, Wayne. *American Art, History, and Culture.* Madison, WI: WCB Brown and Benchmark, 1994.

Hitchcock, Henry-Russell, and Philip Johnson. *The International Style: Architecture since 1922.* New York: Norton, 1932.

Karpel, Bernard, ed. *Arts in America: A Bibliography.* 4 vols. Washington, DC: Smithsonian/Archives of American Art, 1979.

Larkin, Oliver W. *Art and Life in America.* Rev. ed. New York: Holt, Rinehart, and Winston, 1964.

Mendelowitz, Daniel M. *A History of American Art.* New York: Holt, Rinehart, and Winston, 1970.

Pierson, William H., Jr., and Martha Davidson, eds. *Arts of the United States: A Pictorial Survey.* New York: McGraw-Hill, 1960.

Randel, William Peirce. *The Evolution of American Taste.* New York: Crown, 1978.

Schuyler, Montgomery. "The Point of View" and "An Architectural Pioneer: Review of the Portfolios Containing the Works of Frank Lloyd Wright." In *American Architecture and Other Writings*, 57, 316. New York: Atheneum, 1964.

North American collecting

With the exception of a few individuals, Americans collected little until shortly after the end of the Civil War. Early collectors were men of independent means who devoted their lives to travel and the pursuit of pictures, men like Richard and Charles Russell Codman in Boston, Luman Reed and John R. Murray of New York, Thomas Jefferson Bryan of Philadelphia, and Robert Gilmor Jr. of Baltimore. Reflecting an ethical rather than an aesthetic attitude toward the purposes and use of art, these men sought to create a visible history of civilization through the works of well-known painters. In such a context, copies were as acceptable as originals, and attributions were generous. Dutch art was appreciated for its apparent naturalism and secular subject matter: Its landscape and portraiture were highly appreciated, along with a few domestic genre scenes. Such paintings played a role in the self-conscious formation of a national identity as American collectors and commentators frequently viewed their own landscape through the eyes of Dutch artists. In 1834 New York merchant and collector Philip Hone, for example, found that the "mountains and the rich valies" of Northampton, Massachusetts, with the "spires of its numerous places of worship," brought to mind landscapes by Salomon van Ruysdael. American collectors themselves were identified with the social position of the original bourgeois owners of their paintings. A contemporary described Bryan in terms of a Rembrandt portrait, "a charming old gentleman with snowy hair and florid complexion, in picturesque robe and velvet cap, seated in an old-fashioned armchair in his gallery like a venerable burgomaster of Holland surrounded by his treasures."

The period between the Civil War and World War I witnessed the most extensive collecting of old-master paintings in the United States than either before or since. Dutch paintings were purchased primarily by a relatively small number of individuals with vast fortunes and high ambitions who relied to a great extent on dealers: Benjamin Altman, Henry B. Marquand, Andrew W. Mellon, William Clark, Charles and Annie Taft, Collis P. Huntington, Charles T. Yerkes, Henry Clay Frick, Mrs. Jack Gardner of Boston, William Elkins, Peter Widener, and John G. Johnson. Their collections formed the nucleus of many museums founded during this period: the Metropolitan Museum in New York, the National Gallery in Washington, DC, the Taft Museum in Cincinnati, the Isabella Stuart Gardner Museum in Boston, the Philadelphia Museum of Art, and the Detroit Institute of Arts.

Benjamin Franklin had voiced a commonplace when he wrote that "in love of liberty and in defense of it, Holland has been our example." In 1860 Théophile Thoré, the French art and social critic, described seventeenth-century Holland as "not unlike the young American society today, protestant and democratic." While authors put Dutch art and culture to political uses, the motivations for individual collectors were more personal. These self-made merchants and bankers sought to create collections rivaling those in eighteenth-century English country houses. They gravitated toward large paintings of sober tone with an emphasis on portraits or single-figure history paintings and landscapes.

The names of a handful of seventeenth-century Dutch artists appear with regularity—Rembrandt, Frans Hals, Jacob van Ruisdael, Salomon van Ruysdael, Meindert Hobbema, Johannes Vermeer, and, to a lesser extent Aelbert Cuyp and Gerard Ter Borch. Americans owned one hundred fifty-eight of the six hundred thirty-nine paintings attributed to Rembrandt in Abraham Bredius' catalog of 1936, and boasted of possessing nine of thirty-one paintings attributed to Vermeer.

Masterpieces of the fifteenth and sixteenth centuries also entered such American collections as that of John G. Johnson in Philadelphia during this period. Some members of this generation before World War I collected artists of The Hague School in paintings that accompanied their taste for seventeenth-century landscapes and Barbizon paintings: Jozef Israëls, Jacob Maris, and Anton Mauve, as well as the landscapes of Johan Barthold Jongkind.

In the period between the two World Wars American taste shifted away from dark rooms and Barbizon paintings to bright interiors and French Impressionism. Seventeenth-century Dutch art never went out of fashion—Andrew Mellon, Samuel Kress, and Jules Bache set salesroom records for Dutch art in the mid-1930s—but it was no longer collected in the large numbers of the previous period. At the same time, museums began to surpass individuals as collectors. A substantial number of masterpieces by Vincent van Gogh and Piet Mondrian, however, entered American collections.

A significant change has taken place since World War II in the sophistication of the private collector of old-master paintings, both in appreciation of quality and in knowledge. While J.P. Morgan first heard of Vermeer when he was offered a Vermeer painting in 1907, collectors today are well-informed specialists. As prices reach new heights, collectors recognize quality in less familiar artists and less popular genres such as history painting and Italianate works, although the Metropolitan Museum in New York found the resources to purchase Rembrandt's masterful *Aristotle Contemplating a Bust of Homer* in 1961. Important collections are still being created, including those of Linda and George Kaufman, the late Senator John and Theresa Heinz, Dr. and Mrs. Alfred Bader, and George and Maida Abrams. Parts of other important collections have been returned to the market, including those of Saul P. Steinberg, Gerald Guterman, and an anonymous private collector in Washington, DC. Southern California has become perhaps the most active region in the world for collecting Dutch art, in part through the collections assembled by Edward and Hanna Carter, the late Norton Simon, Armand Hammer, and the J. Paul Getty Museum in Malibu, California.

Ann Jensen Adams

See also Cuyp, Aelbert; De Kooning, Willem; Hague School, The; Hals, Frans; Israëls, Jozef; Jongkind, Johan Barthold; Maris, Jacob; Mauve, Anton; Mesdag, Hendrik Willem; Mondrian, Piet; Neuhuijs, Albert; North American art, Dutch influences; North American painting, Dutch influences; Rembrandt van Rijn; Ter Borch, Gerard; Van Gogh, Vincent; Van Ruisdael, Jacob; Vermeer, Johannes

Bibliography

Adams, Ann Jensen. *Dutch and Flemish Paintings from New York Private Collections.* Consulting curator Egbert Haverkamp-Begemann. New York: National Academy of Design, 1988.

Broos, Ben et al. *Great Dutch Paintings from America.* The Hague: Mauritshuis; Zwolle: Waanders, 1990.

Clark, Henry Nichols. "The Impact of Seventeenth-Century Dutch and Flemish Genre Painting on American Genre Paintings, 1800–1865." Ph.D. diss., University of Delaware, 1982.

Sutton, Peter C. *A Guide to Dutch Art in America.* Grand Rapids, MI: Eerdmans, 1986.

North American painting, Dutch influences

The Eighteenth and Nineteenth Centuries

Beyond New Amsterdam, Albany was a very active New Netherland painting center because the Dutch *patroons* not only wanted portraits of themselves and their family members, but certainly could afford them. Therefore, within that provincial realm, various groups of paintings constitute America's first "native" school of art.

Of these *patroon* paintings, one group is assigned to the "Wendell Limner," while the "Van Rensselaer Limner" worked farther south along the Hudson River. Another identifiable style appeared in the upper Hudson area at around the same time, and some believe its creator, the "Gansevoort Limner," was actually Pieter Vanderlyn, grandfather of the well-known Neoclassical painter John Vanderlyn of Kingston, New York.

Back along the colony's coast, a very active figure of the 1750s was the "De Peyster Limner," so called because of that artist's very engaging series of children's likenesses related not only to the De Peyster family, but also to the Van Cortlandts of Croton-on-Hudson. Among the best of these is the colorful and interesting portrait (ca. 1731) of Pierre Van Cortlandt that is now in the Brooklyn Museum. The subject was later a revolutionary leader and American statesman; he is shown in the painting as a boy of about ten years of age inhabiting a rather more elaborate Baroque setting than was the norm for most earlier examples. Some authentic Van Cortlandt settings were to be nice enough, for Pierre and his wife and child were to move in 1749 into the family mansion at Croton-on-Hudson, where he would have his portrait done again in 1810 (Sleepy Hollow Restorations) by the doggedly literal likeness painter John Wesley Jarvis. Though a comparison of the two paintings emphasizes the radical changes that had taken place in American art and life over the span of almost a century, they still may be linked to continued interest in America in the art of the Dutch seventeenth century, whether this was directly or indirectly pursued.

The still-life painting of Europe does not seem to have inspired any early involvement in the field in the New World. In New York and especially Pennsylvania, the home of a number of still-life specialists through the mid-1800s, one of the most interesting was Severin Roesin (active in America, 1848–1871). In his early works this artist showed a strong influence from the Dutch Baroque that he sharply and handsomely

interpreted upon the basis of a singular concentration upon each form. Another immigrant of the period was Arnoud Wydeveld (active 1855–1888), who did not only flower and fruit subjects, but also various piscatorial presentations. Certainly fish, fowl, or dead game in general had been central still-life subjects in Holland for a very long time. There was also the work of William H. Machen, who emigrated from Arnhem in the Netherlands to northwestern Ohio in 1847 to become a painter of many genres before he "caught a commission on a larger scale" (from the United States Fishery Commission late in the century); Machen would do a noted series of "ichthyographs" on canvas as the result.

America's leading still-life painter of the period, William Harnett, was an Irishman by birth who landed in Philadelphia with his family in 1849, when he was but one year old. Harnett's first still lifes (1875–1880) were based on the work of Americans James and Raphaelle, if not Rembrandt, Peale. Then, around 1880, he began to expand upon his painted objects' environments by way of paneling, cloth-covered tabletops, and carpets of elaborate patterning—supports that for the most part are not unlike so many props used by the greats of seventeenth-century Holland. Such were easily seen in London (his first European study stop), then in Frankfurt for six months, and finally in Munich before the end of 1881.

The first American artist to study in Munich after that city's initial international exhibition in 1869 was Frank Duveneck of Cincinnati. What Duveneck found was an amalgam of painting drawn from the blunt manner of Gustave Courbet, plus ingredients from the works of his artistic heroes from the 1600s: Frans Hals, Pieter Paul Rubens, and Rembrandt van Rijn, among others. All of this had then been Germanically interpreted by Wilhelm Leibl, the living, working leader of Leibl-Kreis, a loose confederation of artists then painting around the city in the "Munich Style." But for each Munich-based artist the "Munich Style" could be quite a different thing. For Duveneck it was a broad and brushy approach to technique that partook of planes and textures immediately created through an absolutely loaded application of what was often dark and resonant color in tar-based paint. At the time, in America, it would all be mistaken for vitality, of a "New" but "Old World" kind.

From time to time Americans have loved the facile brushwork of a Gilbert Stuart or a Thomas Sully; then later the fluidities of a Duveneck or a John Singer Sargent. But in between and throughout they have been sustained by "things," set in clarity and stillness. America as a republic had been born within the context of revived antimonarchical Greek- and Roman-inspired classicism. Among their compatriots many American painters shared the enthusiasms of their age. Yet this European-oriented "New World" was so remote from "Old World" centers of antiquarian delight that, among their fellows, only Benjamin West and John Vanderlyn became Neoclassical painters in the archeologizing, Greco-Roman revival-centered sense.

Vanderlyn was born in the Hudson River town of Kingston, New York, once called Wiltwyck by the Dutch, his appearance in the Vanderlyn family of painters occurring within the year that the American Revolution was ignited to the full fire of war. A consequence for Kingston was its sacking and burning by the British during the Revolutionary War, while a consequence for American art was John Vanderlyn's hatred of the nation responsible for that horrible act.

As a twenty-year-old noticed by the fascinating and ill-fated Aaron Burr, Vanderlyn was, with Burr's help, off to England very briefly before he settled into lessons in Paris under the Neoclassicist François-André Vincent. His friend in Europe and afterward was fellow American painter Washington Allston. Together these two became art students and tourists (England to Holland and Belgium and France) and then neighboring artists and comrades at work in Rome, sharing these very good experiences with such young writer friends as the British poet Samuel Taylor Coleridge and Vanderlyn's great fellow New Yorker, Washington Irving.

Today Washington Irving, who was a complex character, is best known as the humorist-historian, story writer, and general, gentle josher of life in "pre-British" New York, even though both of his most famous *Sketch Book* (1819–1820) stories—about "Rip Van Winkle" and the "Legend of Sleepy Hollow"—were based upon old German tales. Nevertheless, such charming Irving insights into his "native heritage" are still absolutely vivid, genre-inspiring and people-filled inventions of delight, and that is the way the extraordinary painter of many of that author's subjects, the enigmatic John Quidor of Tappan, New York, saw them, too.

Quidor began his career in a stodgy enough manner as a pupil of the ultraprosaic portrait painter John Wesley Jarvis. It made no difference. Not a portraitist, Quidor was to be the perfect illustrator of Irving's whimsical subjects (along with a few things by Cooper and Cervantes as well), with figures of great animation who live to this day in a world of consumingly warm *chiaroscuro*, as well as underpainted and glazed luminosity, and unusually broad painterliness of uncertain origins.

Quidor's one known student was the portraitist Charles Loring Elliott. More like Quidor's works are those of Alburtis De Orient Browere and David Gilmore Blythe, painters of anecdote known to have studied and borrowed pictorial aspects from the Dutch and Flemish of the seventeenth century. Yet neither Browere nor Blythe possessed the all-out "fire" of Quidor's originality or color.

The son of John H.I. Browere, the well-known maker of life masks of America's republican heroes, the younger Browere was born in Tarrytown, New York, and became known as a figure painter and landscapist before his death in Catskill, New York. David G. Blythe was known exclusively for his shadowy and exaggerated genre figure groups and has been called the "Adriaen van Ostade of Pittsburgh," Pennsylvania. But finally Blythe's and even Quidor's figures and settings find a more limited realm related to caricature when compared to the moderated humor of America's leading genre specialist, William Sidney Mount of Setauket, Long Island, New York.

At one point Mount admitted that a European visit might be "gratifying" to him, but then he noted his concern that the "splendor" of Europe's art could cause him to stay too long and thus lose his "nationality." So it seems that the painter may never have seen a real David Teniers or a Van Ostade, but he read that both of these seventeenth-century Netherlanders had accentuated their essentially brown and gray tones with spots of bright color. Then at another moment he commented that the most basic organization and usage of colors were to be discovered in the work of Aelbert Cuyp and Jan Both. The accumulation of such notations with sketches was Mount's pictorial "treasure," or at least part of it. Like others of his time the artist was interested in spiritualism. He participated in seances, read a spiritualist magazine called *The Sacred Circle*, and owned an 1855-published volume on "modern" spiritualism. Then on March 25, 1855, William Sidney Mount "received" in a "vision" some very good artistic advice in a letter from the great Rembrandt van Rijn himself, who was perhaps the best source Mount might think of, as to pictorial matters at least.

But in the real world of nineteenth-century American genre painting before the Civil War, only the works of the two Dutch-inspired Düsseldorf students, Richard Caton Woodville of Baltimore, Maryland, and the "Bruegelian" Missourian, George Caleb Bingham, can actually be placed alongside those of Mount in terms of quality and related influence. Beyond the war, a discussion of Eastman Johnson of Maine is interesting in the present context.

In fact had Johnson returned home after his two years at Düsseldorf, he could have remained the painter of hard and theatrical work not unlike that of Woodville or Bingham. But Johnson found Düsseldorfer painting especially weak in color and sought an enrichment of this kind in the art of The Hague School. There the Dutchman Jozef Israëls created a type of realism more like the painterly humanism of his French contemporary Jean-François Millet and, to some extent, Rembrandt, too. A hovery and melancholy *chiaroscuro* was Israëls' prime pictorial element, and his work was joined by that of the Maris brothers, Hendrik Willem Mesdag, and Anton Mauve, the leading painters in The Hague.

The American Johnson, too, was drawn to paint more like a painter in a Holland by then focused pictorially upon The Hague's new realist movement. But as an American and a "Victorian," Johnson also filled his interiors with "treasure," rooms full of furniture and other "things" in association with genre and/or portrait groups, or single figures who are absolutely silent in their social comment-without-comment within candid camera-like views.

A supposed "eye" of the camera was increasingly during that time what governed evaluations of any painting's believability. And that camera's "eye" became best understood in connection with what photographer Mathew Brady and his associates had been able to do within the context of the Civil War. "Actuality" there was—just plain, and even awful, fact, recorded in an unembellished, even laconic, manner. Brady had received his initial artistic training under the portrait and history painters William Page and Samuel F.B. Morse. But Morse, of course, was also the scientist-inventor of the telegraph, and it was "daguerreotypy," not painting, that Brady had learned from him.

For his part, Morse in April 1839 had called the photographic images of Daguerre "Rembrandt perfected," after having visited the Frenchman earlier in the year. To this Quidor's old student Charles Loring Elliott remarked that daguerreotypes had finally established "the truth" of that old master's "light and shade." And numerous French artists of the late nineteenth and early twentieth century felt much the same way—for example, various "photo-realists," a.k.a. "naturalist" followers after the painting of Jules Bastien-Lepage and others. But even in this context, the lure of the Netherlands' painting tradition was very powerful for Americans—that is, virtually all of the leading U.S. artists who were connected with the French-centered international phenomenon called "naturalism," from which some authorities exclude the Dutch realists (Weisberg, 1992: 210), also included art study, travel, and often residency in Holland as a part of that process.

As an example, Gari Melchers, the best known of the group, had gone to Düsseldorf first, then moved on to Paris to perfect his naturalist style, all before establishing a studio at Egmond-aan-Zee in Holland with fellow American advocate of French naturalism George Hitchcock. Walter MacEwen, another friend of Melchers, trained in Chicago initially, moved to Paris in the early 1880s, and developed a more personal form of naturalism there—such "divergence" not long after abetted by contact with the Dutch realism of Israëls. Other American naturalists of note during the time were William Norton and Elizabeth Nourse; each, in turn, discovered the new French naturalist reliance upon photographic descriptiveness and composition but then moved on to contact with Dutch art and life in their respective fashions.

Not surprisingly, much American naturalism was oriented to the somewhat larger spaces of field and pasture settings (often Dutch). After all, landscape had been, and would continue to be, a tradition in North America as crossings of the various "frontiers" of the "westward movement" were dreamed of and then achieved. Who painted America's first landscape? We do not know. An anonymous 1735 view of *Martin van Bergen's Farm at Leeds, Greene County, New York*, in Cooperstown's New York State Historical Association collection, has sometimes been called its colony's earliest "pure" painting of the kind.

The aforementioned painting is not a pure landscape presentation, and neither are the scenes of Francis Guy, who came from England in 1795 to paint people-inhabited cityscapes in the Manhattan and Brooklyn, as well as the Philadelphia and Baltimore, areas. Along with Guy, five other artists, among several more, were active as early recorders of the new American city: the Birches in Philadelphia and New York, the latter city's Robertson brothers (Archibald and Alexander), and Robert Salmon in Boston. And like Guy, all were influenced by Dutch cityscape prototypes.

William Birch and his son Thomas had arrived from England the year before Guy's appearance on American shores, and William was not only a painter, but, more importantly, an engraver and collector of seventeenth-century Dutch paintings. Works by Jan van Goyen, Willem van de Velde the Younger, Aert van der Neer, Aelbert Cuyp, and Jacob van Ruisdael were listed as being in the Robert Gilmor Collection in Baltimore, and a number of other private individuals up and down the coast were said to be owners of Dutch paintings at the time.

Thomas Doughty and Ashur B. Durand, the inventors of the Hudson River School style of panoramic "transcendentalism on canvas," are known to have been interested in the work of Van Ruisdael, while the collector Gilmor went so far as to travel to Holland himself, not only to add to his holdings, but also to sketch there some of the same scenes his artistic heroes had. In addition, such luminist masters as John F. Kensett, as well as the great arctic explorer and artist William Bradford, followed the lead of earlier marine specialists (Robert Salmon and Fitz Hugh Lane) with works of still, silent, and haunting light and precision. In Bradford's case, however, the 1845 arrival of the Dutch artist Albert van Beest modified his luminist approach toward a somewhat more painterly handling.

Even younger American tonalist landscapists such as George Inness and others were to be vitally influenced by the pre-Impressionist painting of both the French Barbizon School and related work centered at The Hague. An example is the early development of Henry Ward Ranger. His 1878 exposure to nearly a hundred paintings of the Barbizon masters in New York City, his immediate conversion to their mode of painting and subsequent independent study in France of the same artists' works, his discovery of Rembrandt in the Louvre and resulting departure for study with Mauve, Israëls, and Jacob Maris at The Hague Summer Colony at Laren— all constituted a classic American pattern of the time.

The Late Nineteenth Century

Though the phenomenon of Dutch influence upon American art during the late nineteenth century is not particularly well known today, in fact numerous articles regarding the art and life of Holland appeared from the 1880s into the early years of the twentieth century in such periodicals as *Century* and *International Studio*. Among American tonalists somehow "Dutch-connected" during those years, the foremost included George H. Bogert, Frank Boggs, Charles Warren Eaton, R. Swain Gifford, the Canadian Charles Paul Gruppe, William Henry Howe, Leonard Ochtman, and the Auburn, New York, artist Alexander Theobald van Laer.

James Abbott McNeill Whistler, as an expatriate American tonalist painter and printmaker, was a student of the etching of various Netherlanders of the 1600s. Indeed, from the early 1860s Whistler was enthusiastic about working in Holland and Belgium, and his first visit to the Netherlands in 1863 began a series of prints and watercolors added to on subsequent trips. A different, if not exactly reverse, geographical direction was taken by the Dutch expatriate printmaker Hendrick Dirk Kruseman van Elten; though he did not take up etching until he came to America in 1879, his prints reveal his Dutch origins not only via their subjects, but also through their creator's obvious interest in rendering tone and color beyond what was the norm in American landscape etching of the time.

When viewing the work of Henry Ward Ranger, the intent student of such painting can see similarities between his approach and that of the much more obscure Dutch-American landscapist William C.A. Frerichs, an artist with connections to The Hague School before his 1890s arrival in, and career carried out in various parts of, the eastern United States. Of course, America's tonalists do not represent America's mainstream into the new century any more than the mystical "tone poems" of Albert Pinkham Ryder do. But like the thickly impasted creations of Ryder, who in 1882 probably visited the studio of Matthijs Maris in London, those artists' canvases and prints provide a compelling and sensitive alternative to the flashy Munich Style of Duveneck and William Merritt Chase or the American Impressionism of the later Chase and others.

A *plein-air* painter and then Impressionist-inclined stylist as he grew older, Chase moved toward a much-changed palette and orientation through the turn of the century and beyond, and this, along with his authentic magic as a teacher, he passed on to the young Robert Henri, who had come to work early in the new century at Chase's New York School of Art. But Henri's truest mentor in a spiritual sense was the unique Philadelphian Thomas Eakins, whose truest mentor in every sense was Rembrandt of old Amsterdam, *not* Philadelphia. The power of Rembrandt van Rijn! It had, of course, been seen by so many over the years, to a point in the early twentieth century when numerous painted "examples of his work" (approximately eight hundred by the 1920s) were to be found in various collections throughout Europe, America, and elsewhere.

In the nineteenth century, any issue of authenticity in this regard tended to be overwhelmed by a prevailing notion of genius. But within a later period favoring the development of scientific connoisseurship, inevitable controversies over attribution would occur, and it is one of the major accomplishments of the American author and critic John C. Van Dyke, a New Jerseyite of Dutch lineage, that he in 1923 initiated with his study, *Rembrandt and His School*, a controversial-discussion-become-major-scholarly-pursuit that goes on to this day.

It was in the Rembrandts especially that Thomas Eakins had perceived the potency of truly compassionate realism and *chiaroscuro* based upon a uniquely resonant transparency of shadow—elements that would always remain conscious components of Eakins' own powerful American work. Indeed, Eakins' career was almost purely Philadelphia-based, with the exception of his European study during the 1860s. In Paris he studied with both J.L. Gérôme and Léon Bonnat, and from these academic masters the American derived his own factually based art expressed through a bold brush. Then of equal or even more import to Eakins was his opportunity in Europe to see the works of Rembrandt, Velazquez, and others of the world's very first artistic rank.

Meanwhile, the much more painterly John Singer Sargent singled out Frans Hals, along with Velazquez (for different reasons than Eakins), for particular study within his entirely cosmopolitan training experience. At about the same time, another portraitist and "the greatest living woman painter" (as William Merritt Chase called her), Cecilia Beaux, entered the Parisian classes of academician William Bouguereau along with those of naturalism's Tony Robert-Fleury, and also discovered the works of Rembrandt, Velazquez, and Titian in the museums of Europe.

Closer to home, talented Jean MacLane of Chicago learned a brushier form of second- or third-hand Netherlands-initiated traditional painting from Frank Duveneck in Cincinnati and then from Chase in New York, all such study coming at the outset of her long and admirable career as a professional painter of portraits in New York City. Margaret Foster Richardson was from Winnetka, Illinois, but studied and exhibited in Boston and Philadelphia until 1913, when she departed on a study tour of France, England, Austria, Germany, Belgium, and Holland. After she developed an early approach after two of her American teachers, Edmund C. Tarbell and Joseph De Camp (De Camp was an American who capitalized his "D"), her rather sedate manner found its ultimate inspiration in the work of Johannes Vermeer.

But overall and unfortunately, most American painting was similarly sedate as the twentieth century came into view. Surely a new artistic energy was needed to match the pulse of the nation's increasingly urban environment, and two directions would ultimately lead out of the impasse. The first way centered upon the artistic legacy of the realist Thomas Eakins, who had introduced living models into the practice of the Pennsylvania Academy of Fine Arts and had taught his students to "paint with the brush" in the way of Rembrandt. His traditionalist orientation had moved the work of Eakins and his best students away from the realm of painting as colored drawing. Most important, he had turned his students to their own surroundings in Philadelphia and then New York for subject matter.

The Twentieth Century

It was through Eakins' student Thomas Anshutz that the interest in painting contemporary genre was transmitted to Robert Henri and his friends, who made up what would be termed the Ash Can School. Of them Henri came from Duveneck's Cincinnati to Eakins' Philadelphia to study with Anshutz at the Pennsylvania Academy before sailing for Europe in 1888. Finding the original Rembrandts he needed to see in Paris, Henri found his interest in that master expanded to an enthusiasm for Hals and Velazquez during another stay in Europe in the 1890s.

George Luks, John Sloan, William Glackens, and Everett Shinn were all illustrators for the Philadelphia press. Back in early days, between about 1892 and 1896 or 1897, they had spent Thursday evenings at Henri's house talking about art and life and how these two pursuits might somehow be connected. Luks was of "Pennsylvania Dutch" stock and loved the work of Frans Hals and various distilleries equally. Like his friends, Luks had made early contact with the Eakins realist tradition through work with Anshutz at the Pennsylvania Academy. Following his training in Philadelphia he had studied further at Dusseldorf, Paris, and London—such experience solidify-

Then in 1896 Glackens, the grave but joyful Impressionist, and the realist Luks moved to New York. Shinn, who had created an equally broad painting style as that of Luks and Henri, followed the first two to Manhattan a year later. Thus when Henri arrived in the first year of the new century he found his old Philadelphia group virtually reassembled. Henri drew an old rebel against academic timidity, the fantasy painter Arthur B. Davies, into his circle soon afterward, as well as the Impressionist Ernest Lawson. In the fall of 1901 Maurice Prendergast, the Boston-based post-Impressionist, met Henri for the first time. Three years later when John Sloan, the most interesting urban genre specialist of them all, arrived from Philadelphia the stage was set for the formation of "The Eight."

The 1908 exhibition of The Eight represents in retrospect the first really direct look in America at its new urban environment—its immigrants, its commercial excitement, its high life and low. And it must be added here that these social realists did this not so differently from the way certain vital painters of Holland's seventeenth century had done—that is, within a previous age of great growth and energy—and on the site of "Old New Amsterdam" itself.

Meanwhile, America's other artistic road was a much more radical departure. At almost exactly the same time, some American artists made a leap from various forms of traditional realism or American Impressionism toward the formal language of European abstraction or the extreme distortions of Expressionism, without any real sense of transition.

Yet most of The Eight were involved in the International Exhibition of Modern Art held in New York at the Sixty-ninth Regiment Armory from February 17 to March 15, 1913. Held to compete with the traditional showings of the National Academy of Design in New York City, the Armory Show would present European works alongside the creations of the Association of American Painters and Sculptors, as opposed to the conservative pieces done by the membership of the old Academy of Design. A "success of scandal," the show drew more than seventy-five thousand people in New York, two hundred thousand in Chicago, and so on, which is not even to mention the exhibition's impact upon America's artistic community.

For example, in 1912 Marsden Hartley of Maine had gone to Paris with the help of the photographer-activist Alfred Stieglitz, who was the owner-operator of New York's famed 291 Gallery. Then in 1913, before a brief trip back to the United States to see the big show, Hartley went to Berlin, where he met members of the Blue Rider group of German Expressionists and let their artistic ways be absorbed into his initial creative intent as a modernist. It was on a much later trip (to Mexico during 1932–1933) that he discovered his late style, a consciously archaic manner inspired by the not so unlikely mutualities of vision found in works by Albert Pinkham Ryder, Vincent van Gogh, and Paul Gauguin, with the goal of expressing the tragic realities and higher moralities of simple folk, all finally found by "the painter from Maine" (as he called himself) mostly along the seacoasts of the northeastern United States and eastern Canada.

As with Hartley's work the creative development of many of America's most progressive modernists was halting through the 1920s and 1930s. One reason was a general American movement away from internationalism during these years toward further exploration of what was felt to be more "purely" American subject matter. The prime pioneer in this development was no doubt Edward Hopper. He had been to Paris early and experienced various modernist possibilities, but his great need to relate to a more familiar world in a realist context led him away from the purely experimental.

Hopper's compositions have been compared to those of Piet Mondrian, who was undoubtedly the most important abstract artist who came to America within the context of World War II. Around 1940 (the year of Mondrian's arrival in New York City), the tide turned again. The abstract art that had ebbed now rose in a spontaneous wave until it became, for the first time in America's history, a dominant movement. Impending war and then war itself finally broke through the last vestiges of isolationism in the United States. In the arts the new internationalism formed first through contact with certain European and expatriate American artists, who were forced across the Atlantic beginning in the late 1930s because of the changing social climate overseas.

As instances, an American look at Constructivism influenced Irene Rice Pereira, Balcomb Greene, and others, while the geometrical purities of Mondrian and the Dutch De Stijl movement cut a clean edge through the works of numerous artists in the United States. Essentially, the reason for this was a deep and peculiar receptivity to such concision actually within the earliest American artistic development. Going to London in 1938, Mondrian went on to New York City two years later and spent the remainder of his life there. He loved Manhattan's great vertical skyscrapers and the dynamism of the city. Dance halls, jazz bands, constant movement and change—all of these American urban elements drove the great Neo-Plasticist to alter the static calm of his earlier work radically. In short, his *Broadway Boogie-Woogie* (1942–1943; New York, Museum of Modern Art) and its like are not just the best "record jackets" ever created; they represent a huge influence upon American abstraction in not only painting but also sculpture and architecture—this last responding to the De Stijl influences that had already arrived in the United States during the 1930s.

Having originally been persuaded to leave London for New York by the American Neo-Plasticist Harry Holtzman, Mondrian had immediately been surrounded in the United States by an adoring circle of devotees, many of whom had been painting in his manner before he joined them. This group included Holtzman, Ilya Bolotowsky, Fritz Glarner, Albert Swinden, and Charmion von Wiegand.

The Mondrian exhibitions at New York's Dudensing Gallery continued to generate inspiration especially in the works of Bolotowsky, Glarner, and Burgoyne Diller; Mondrian's art was also conducive to the color experimentation goals of former Bauhaus artist Joseph Albers, and it has also been associated with the rigid verticality of the Color Field paintings of Barnett Newmann and the early work of Ad

Reinhardt. In the 1960s the Concrete Art of Max Bill and others was directly related to the art of Mondrian as well as his early colleague, Theo van Doesburg, and even the Pop artist Roy Lichtenstein has made free adaptations after reproductions of Mondrian paintings.

The California painter Richard Diebenkorn also used Mondrian as a primary source for his not really nonfigurative scenes, while William Bailey's still-life essences of the 1970s and beyond have additionally drawn upon Mondrian's geometrical rigor. So, too, has the 1970s New Image art of Jennifer Bartlett. Then in the 1980s postmodernist abstraction of Sherrie Levine one can find hand-painted watercolors and gouaches *after* art-book reproductions *after* Mondrian and others, these replete with printing flaws and the like. Such "rip-off" revivals actually working to revive the art it doesn't show, the influences of Mondrian go on within an ever-changing art world.

This is also very much the case with the Expressionist work of Willem de Kooning. A gigantic figure in the development of Abstract Expressionism in America, De Kooning, born in Rotterdam, arrived in the United States in 1926. This was a much earlier American beginning than that of Mondrian, and it was also much more an actual beginning. In fact, until the year Mondrian arrived (1940), this other Dutchman was essentially a figure painter and portraitist working in a style quite different from that for which he would become known in connection with his years of celebrity.

De Kooning did not even exhibit his work until 1948, and it was not until the next year that he began his famous series of "Woman paintings" presenting intense Expressionist images of often overpowering female figures, blatantly sexual and frequently menacing, sometimes only mildly erotic, but always strongly suggestive of a creature made by society who retains a kind of dynamic to be reckoned with by that same society.

De Kooning's astonishing achievement, which may be the last great example of European modernism energized by American contact, like the work of Mondrian, has influenced numerous artists in his adopted country to this day. Born on April 24, 1904, the painter was the subject of a celebration of his 90th birthday that centered upon a huge retrospective of his work at the National Gallery of Art in Washington, DC. There were the De Koonings among one of the world's great collections of the old masters and the not-so-old masters of the Old World and the New.

The American contemporary artist Pat Steir thinks that there is not much difference between the styles of the various historical periods; that despite the "alphabet" (colors) or "handwriting" (scale and space), it's all the same thing (in Arnason 1986: 631). For Steir, who was born in the same year Mondrian came to America, "strokes" for detail are what Rembrandt made; make them bigger and intensify the color, and the art-making ranges from Van Gogh to De Kooning. Finally it would appear that America's artistic connections to the Dutch have been more fundamental and timeless than we have perhaps ever known them to be.

Robert S. Olpin

See also De Kooning, Willem; De Stijl; Hague School, The; Laren; Mondrian, Piet; North American art, Dutch influences; North American collecting; Rembrandt van Rijn; Reputation of Dutch art abroad; Van Doesburg, Theo; World Wars I and II

Bibliography
Arnason, H.H. *History of Modern Art*. Rev. ed. New York: Harry N. Abrams, 1986.

Barker, Virgil. *American Painting: History and Interpretation*. New York: Macmillan, 1950.

Craven, Wayne. *American Art, History, and Culture*. Madison, WI: WCB Brown and Benchmark, 1994.

Eisenman, Stephen F., ed. *Nineteenth Century Art: A Critical History*. London: Thames and Hudson, 1994.

Gerdts, William H., and Russell Burke. *American Still-Life Painting*. New York: Praeger, 1971.

Gerdts, William H., Diana Dimodica Sweet, and Robert R. Preato. *Tonalism: An American Experience*. New York: Grand Central Galleries Art Education Association, 1982.

Karpel, Bernard, ed. *Arts in America: A Bibliography*. 4 vols. Washington, DC: Smithsonian/Archives of American Art, 1979.

Novak, Barbara. *American Painting of the Nineteenth Century*. New York: Praeger, 1969.

Rose, Barbara. *American Painting since 1900*. Rev. ed. New York: Praeger, 1975.

Weisberg, Gabriel P. *Beyond Impressionism: The Naturalist Impulse*. New York: Harry N. Abrams, 1992.

Wilmerding, John. *American Art*. New York: Penguin, 1976.

Nul-group (Nul-groep) (1961–1965)

The Nul-group was founded in 1961 and had four members: Armando (born 1929), Jan Henderikse (born 1937), Henk Peeters (born 1925), and J.J. Schoonhoven (1914–1994). The members lived in different cities and the informal contact they had with each other was the basis for the Nul-group. Its purpose was to strive for an objective art that must proceed from reality. The name of the group was chosen in imitation of the German group Zero, founded in 1958. The Nul-group grew out of the Dutch Informal Group (1958–1960), of which Kees van Bohemen was also a member.

Schoonhoven concisely expressed the basic assumptions of Nul: "Zero is, in the first place, a new conception of reality in which the individual role of the artist is limited to a minimum. The Zero-artist only chooses, he isolates parts of reality (materials as well as ideas derived from reality) and shows them in the most neutral way possible" (*De nieuwe stijl*, vol. 1, 1965: 118). This new conception of reality, which hardly fits his own work, began to dominate in the work of the members around 1960. The opposition to subjectivism, which had prevailed in the 1950s (Cobra and after), had then reached a high point. The members of the Nul-group confronted this subjectivism with a more impersonal, cooler approach to works of art. They considered Nul as a fresh start and expressed its basic assumptions in manifesto-like texts. The artists attached no value to a so-called original and unique work of art.

There was much diversity in the work of each of its members as well as in their thoughts about the idealistic character of the group. Peeters, the most important organizer, spokesman, and ideologist of the Nul-group, wanted to use his works to make the public aware of everyday reality and bridge the gap between art and society. His materials included plastic, nylon, cotton balls, foam rubber, and feathers—mostly soft materials that he ordered in a geometrical pattern so that any emphasis was avoided. The repetition principle also played a role in the work of Armando. But Armando chose hard materials: On a monochrome base he attached industrial products such as bolts and barbed wire. Schoonhoven made white reliefs and used the principle of repetition of seemingly identical hollows and concavities, which he called *Reihungen*. Henderikse, who felt a close affinity for the work of Armando, also applied the principle of repetition in his works, which were made, for example, out of cork. But he also made assemblages without any order whatsoever.

The work of the Nul-group was exhibited in the Stedelijk Museum in Amsterdam (1962, 1965) and in the Gemeentemuseum in The Hague (1964). The group also published a journal, *Nul = 0, 'tijdschrift voor de nieuwe konseptie in de beeldende kunst'* (Journal for a New Conception in the Visual Arts, 1961, 1963). Literary sympathizers with the Nul-group published in the journals *Gard-Sivik* (1956–1964) and *De nieuwe stijl* (1965–1966).

In the 1960s the art reviews were very critical. Most critics were negative with the exception of just a few, such as Lambert Tegenbosch, George Lampe, and the writers J. Bernlef and K. Schippers, who gave attention to Nul in the 1967 book *Een cheque voor de tandarts* (A Check for the Dentist). A comprehensive study of the Nul-group has yet to be made, although much art-historical research was done in the 1980s. Such a study would have to show the influence of the pioneering movement of the Nul-group on the visual arts of the 1960s and 1970s. Henk Peeters keeps personal custody of the valuable Nul archive.

Peter de Ruiter

See also Armando; Art criticism, critical issues in the twentieth century; Schoonhoven, J.J.

Bibliography

De nieuwe stijl: Werk van de internationale avant-garde. 2 vols. Amsterdam: De Bezige Bij, 1965–1966.

Faassen, Sjoerd van, and Hans Sleutelaar, eds. *De nieuwe stijl 1959–1966.* Amsterdam: De Bezige Bij; The Hague: Nederlands Letterkundig Museum en Documentatiecentrum, 1989.

Nul: Die Wirklichkeit als Kunst fundieren: Die niederländische Gruppe Nul 1660–1965. Esslingenam am Neckar: Galerie der Stadt Villa Merkel, 1993.

Nul: Negentienhonderd vijf en zestig. Amsterdam: Stedelijk Museum, 1965. (English text).

Peeters, Henk, ed. *Informele kunst in België en Nederland 1955–1960: Parallellen in de nederlandstalige literatuur.* The Hague: Haags Gemeentemuseum; Antwerp: Koninklijk Museum voor Schone Kunsten, 1983–1984.

Wesseling, Janneke. *Alles was mooi: Een geschiedenis van de Nul-beweging.* Amsterdam: Meulenhoff/Landshoff, 1989.

Wilbrink, Jos. "De Nul-beweging: Illusieloos idealisme: Een studie naar de opkomst van een kunstenaarsgroepering binnen het kunstenaarschap." In *Kunst en beleid in Nederland*, 167–215. Amsterdam: Boekmanstichting/Van Gennep, 1991.

Nuyen, W.J.J. (1813–1839)

Wijnand Nuyen began at age eleven to study with Andreas Schelfhout and, in addition, took lessons at The Hague Drawing Academy until 1829. As was the custom for artists in those days, Nuyen traveled a great deal in both the Southern and Northern Netherlands. In 1833 he took a trip to France with A. Waldorp and visited Southern Germany. Official recognition for the artist came rather late, in 1836, when he was selected to be a member of the Royal Academy in Amsterdam. In 1838 he married C.J. Schelfhout, the daughter of his teacher.

If one wants to speak of a Dutch Romantic School, only the painters Johannes Tavenraat and Nuyen can be properly considered as its representatives. After the academy, Nuyen very quickly developed his own view of landscape painting, inspired by developments in French and English Romantic painting. He was one of few Dutch who did not shun the dramatic aspect; he employed a colorful palette—also very non-Dutch—and painted with a loose, sketchy (for that time) stroke. With his fresh vision he gave Dutch painting an important impetus. Contemporaries both praised and heavily criticized him. Despite the limited time that was given him, Nuyen left a relatively large *oeuvre* of paintings, finished drawings, and lithographic illustrations.

Alexandra W.M. van Smoorenburg

See also Schelfhout, Andreas; Tavenraat, Johannes

Bibliography

Sillevis, J. et al. *Wijnand Nuyen: Romantische werken.* The Hague: Haags Gemeentemuseum, 1977.

Olie, Jacob (1834–1905)

Jacob Olie was an architect by profession, and later a teacher and principal of the technical school in Amsterdam. Photography was his hobby. His photographs are not so much of artistic as of historical importance. For example, he documented rather extensively the Amsterdam urban expansion that took place at the end of the nineteenth century. He was also interested in old architecture. The atmosphere in his photographs resembles the atmosphere in topographic paintings by his contemporary Cornelis Springer. His photographic *oeuvre* can be divided into two periods: From about 1860 to 1870, when he mainly took pictures in the city; and from 1890 to 1905, when he also went into the countryside and began taking photographs of landscapes. In the interim period he was too busy in his job as a principal (1876–1890) and as a father of seven children. During this time, he did draw and paint watercolors, in a Springeresque manner like his photographs.

Alexandra W.M. van Smoorenburg

See also Herwig, Reinhardt Herman; Photography, early

Bibliography

Boorsma, Annemarie, and Ingeborg Th. Leijerzapf, eds. "Jacob Olie." Vol. 5, part 3, *Geschiedenis van de Nederlandse Fotografie*. Alphen aan de Rijn: Samsom, 1979.

Koppens, Jan. "Jacob Olie fotografeerde roerig Amsterdam in alle rust." *Foto* 29 (1974): 51.

Wagner, Rolf D. "Olie und Berssenbrugge: Zwei Pioniere der Niederländische Sozialfotografie." *Tendenzen* 19 (1978): 18–22.

Oosterhuis, Pieter (1816–1885)

In addition to his role in photographing public works under construction in the nineteenth century, Pieter Oosterhuis is best known for the topographic cityscapes he made from the second half of the 1850s onward. Reproduced in three popular formats—as *cartes-de-visite* ("visiting cards," measuring approximately 9 x 6 cm), cabinet photographs (approximately 15 x 10 cm), or stereo photographs (Fig. 91)—these views were widely sold.

Stereo photography gained enormous popularity in the third quarter of the nineteenth century. Two pictures were made simultaneously, or shortly after each other, with an interspace equal to the human eyes. Mounted together on a card and seen through a viewer, stereographs gave an astonishing illusion of depth. The use of foreground setoffs hightened the effect, which Oosterhuis understood well. Stereo photography seems to have surprised the public as much as photography itself had done in 1839. "The delusion is truly perfect," an Amsterdam newspaper wrote in 1855. Soon, so the story goes, stereo viewers were part of many drawing rooms, and whole series of stereographs were viewed in the family circle.

Oosterhuis was the foremost Dutch stereo photographer of his time. His pictures were put into circulation by several publishers in the Netherlands. Topographic photography and photographic reproductions of works of art (also part of Oosterhuis' *oeuvre*) fit in well with the publishers' stock that consisted of topographic prints and art reproductions done in other techniques, travel accounts, and kindred subjects.

Hans Rooseboom

See also Photography, early

Bibliography

Boom, Mattie. "'Een waarlijk volkomen begoocheling': Stereofotografie in Nederland." *Jong Holland* 2 (1986): 2–13.

Veen, Anneke van. *Pieter Oosterhuis*. Amsterdam: Fragment, 1993.

Ouborg, Pieter (1893–1956)

From 1916 to 1938 Pieter Ouborg lived and worked in the Dutch East Indies, where he taught drawing and art history.

His early drawings reveal an influence from Van Gogh. Ouborg was self-taught as a painter. During his first leave in Europe in 1923–1924 he became aware of Cubism and Expressionism. Until 1930 he painted Indonesian landscapes in a Cubist style, and he was inspired by Indonesian models; moreover, he painted masks. In 1931, during his second leave in Europe, he came directly into contact with Surrealism through an exhibition of L'Art Vivant in Brussels; until then he had known of it only through literature and reproductions in magazines such as *Cahiers d'Art*. He showed Surrealistic work at his first solo exhibition at the Debois gallery in Haarlem; the criticism was generally negative.

His first Surrealistic period, from 1931 until 1940, was called the blue period. From 1932–1934 he created works that as far as the technique of *grattage* (scratching), themes, and figuration are concerned can be compared with those of Max Ernst. From 1934–1938 he painted still lifes, the so-called *opstellingen* (placements). In "automatic drawings" he experimented with automatic writing. Ouborg was, moreover, a collector and painter of Indonesian masks and *wajang* dolls. During the 1930s his work became more somber.

He returned to the Netherlands in 1938 and resided in The Hague until his death. In his second Surrealistic period the compositions are more spatial, as in the *tempelopstellingen* (temple placements) consisting of theatrical architecture in which the circumstances of war are assimilated with many symbols of transitoriness. In 1944 he began using abstract figuration. After 1945 his work explodes in an orgy of color. In 1949 he was invited to become a member of Cobra. In 1950 Ouborg received the Jacob Maris Prize, which, because of the experimental character of his art, created a public scandal. In 1953 he had an exhibition in the town hall of The Hague and, in 1954, in the Stedelijk Museum in Amsterdam.

John Steen

See also Art criticism, critical issues in the twentieth century; Cobra Movement; Surrealism

Bibliography

Duis, Leonie ten, and Annelies Haase. *Ouborg: Schilder = Painter*. The Hague: SDU, 1990.

Oud, Jacobus Johannes Pieter (1890–1963)

J.J.P. Oud won international recognition as a founder of Dutch functionalism, Het Nieuwe Bouwen (The New Construction), primarily through his housing design. The clean lines and plastic volumes of his mass housing have consistently attracted critical appraisal as humane and modern solutions expressing social as well as aesthetic values.

Educated at a crafts school in Amsterdam, Oud also attended classes at the Technische Hogeschool (Technical University) of Delft. His early work reflects the influence of H.P. Berlage, the leading Dutch rationalist at the turn of the century. In 1916, however, his orientation shifted upon acquaintance with the avant-garde artist Theo van Doesburg. Oud quickly absorbed the architectural implications of Cubism and Futurism. He became a frequent contributor to Van Doesburg's periodical, *De Stijl*, arguing forcefully for an architecture shorn of historical reference and responsive to mass production. In 1917–1918 Oud collaborated with Van Doesburg on two projects: a vacation home in Noordwijkerhout, De Vonk, and the Villa Allegonda at Katwijk aan Zee where the interlocking white cubes suggested a new formal vocabulary. Plastic geometric play was also evident in several unexecuted designs: housing along a beachfront (1917) and a factory (1919).

In 1918 Oud was appointed architect to the Housing Authority in Rotterdam. His first projects, brick housing blocks at Spangen (1918–1920) and Tusschendijken (1920–1923), display little of De Stijl's plasticity, but at the garden village of Oud-Mathenesse (1922–1923), he applied the movement's restrictive scheme of primary colors. The construction site office there and the café De Unie in Rotterdam (1925) are Oud's most vigorous De Stijl compositions.

At his most acclaimed projects, the housing row at the Hoek van Holland (1924–1927) and the housing complex at Kiefhoek in Rotterdam (1925–1929), Oud forged a synthesis of De Stijl Neo-Plasticism and the functional response to housing requirements. The low-rise housing at the Hoek van Holland extends in two ribbons of white, each culminating gracefully in matching curved storefronts. At Kiefhoek, individual housing units are subsumed in continuous white planes, the several blocks forming an abstract urban pattern (Fig. 113).

Acknowledged internationally as a proponent of modernism, Oud was invited in 1927 to participate in the Weissenhofsiedlung, a model housing exhibition in Stuttgart. Oud's project combined minimal housing plans with rhythmic white cubic massing. However, a series of factors curtailed Oud's further experimentation in Rotterdam. The decline of national support for public housing, the economic crisis of the 1930s, and personal difficulties contributed to a period of low productivity.

When Oud once again began to execute commissions, it was in a vein that apparently repudiated geometric purity. For the Holland-America Line (1937–1938), Oud designed ship interiors that released the fluid lines of his earlier work into decorative flourishes. More controversial was his design for the Shell Building in The Hague (1938–1946). Its monumental symmetry and decorative brickwork appeared to betray Oud's former allegiance to the ideals of Het Nieuwe Bouwen. Historicist reference entered into Oud's urbanism with the unexecuted design for the Hofplein in Rotterdam (1942–1943).

In the postwar period, Oud returned to the modernist vocabulary of industrial materials and abstract forms with the design of several large institutional projects, notably the Children's Convalescent Home in Arnhem (1952–1960) and the Convention Center in The Hague (1956–1969, completed posthumously by his son, Hans Oud). In recent years, his complex career has been reassessed, with growing appreciation for both his aberrations from the narrowly defined path of functionalism and the beauty of his housing design, as evidenced by the restoration of his most important works.

Nancy Stieber

See also Berlage, Hendrik Petrus; De Stijl; Functionalism in architecture; Public housing; Van Doesburg, Theo; Urban planning, from 1750 to the present

Bibliography

Esser, Hans. "J.J.P. Oud." In *De Stijl: The Formative Years, 1917–1922.* Edited by Carel Blotkamp et al., 123–151. Cambridge, MA: MIT Press, 1986.

Grinberg, Donald I. *Housing in the Netherlands, 1900–1940.* Delft: Delft University Press, 1977.

Jaffe, Hans L.C. *De Stijl.* New York: Harry N. Abrams, 1967.

Pommer, Richard, and Christian F. Otto. *Weissenhof 1927 and the Modern Movement in Architecture.* Chicago: University of Chicago Press, 1991.

Ouwater, Isaac (1748–1793)

The Amsterdammer Isaac Ouwater was the son of a painter of still lifes and landscapes who had the same name. New archival research has discovered his true birthdate to be 1748, not 1750. He was probably taught by his father. He painted and drew mainly townscapes, which show a strong influence from the seventeenth-century painter Jan van der Heyden, even though they are completely eighteenth century in atmosphere. They are reliable topographically and characterized by a crisp drawing. His body of works is not very large; dated works are known from the period 1776–1789. Besides working in Amsterdam, the artist was also active in the environs of that city, as well as in Utrecht, The Hague, Delft, Leiden, Hoorn, and Enkhuizen. Moreover, he also depicted some more rural subjects, like the country houses along the Vecht and in the province of Gelderland. In the paintings of Ouwater, all of the achievements of the eighteenth-century townscape are brought together: the clear and colorful palette, the refined light and the shadow play, the enormous amount of detail, and the lively and diverse decorations. The artist is rightly considered the grand master of this genre.

Charles Dumas

See also Humor, satire; Townscapes; Van der Heyden, Jan

Bibliography

Dumas, Charles. *Haagse stadsgezichten 1550–1800: Topografische schilderijen van het Haags Historisch Museum,* 566–580. Zwolle: Waanders, 1991.

P

Paintings-within-paintings

The use of paintings within an interior scene has its origins in Flemish allegorical pictures of the sixteenth and seventeenth centuries by artists such as Jan Bruegel the Elder. Such scenes illustrated the taste for private encyclopedic collections: Wealthy individuals would amass pictures, prints, books, natural objects, and curiosities in order to acquire the totality of information about the world. These scenes, abundantly displaying paintings of all subjects, often recorded actual collections and could represent allegories of painting or human knowledge. In the seventeenth century, when artists produced their work for the open market and people from all segments of society owned paintings, interior scenes often featured pictures on the walls, sometimes copies of known works (Fig. 115). Paintings also appeared in still lifes and pictures of artists' studios, where they not only advertised the artist's talent, but retained their traditional function as allegories of knowledge, skill, and artistic endeavor (Fig. 75).

Like maps—also common in Dutch homes—and views into other rooms, paintings often enhanced the subject matter, functioning as explanatory pictorial glosses on the main scene with varying degrees of subtlety. For example, in Pieter de Hooch's *Woman and Child in a Pantry* (ca. 1658), showing a woman fetching a drink for a little girl, a portrait of a man hangs on the wall in an adjoining room. As if standing in for the absent head of the household, the portrait anchors the intimate pair in a larger familial context. A more ironic commentary occurs in Eglon van der Neer's *Couple in an Interior* (ca. 1675), which portrays a soberly dressed couple seated beneath a large painting of a nude Venus.

Paintings within paintings often contained imagery borrowed from popular emblem books. One of the earliest examples occurs in two pictures by Dirck Hals from the early 1630s, one showing a smiling woman holding a letter, the other showing a woman tearing up a letter. Behind the smiling woman is a picture of a ship on calm seas, while behind the other woman is a storm-tossed ship. The paintings are based on an emblem comparing a lover to a ship at sea, re-

quited in love when the sea is calm and rejected when the ship capsizes in a storm. Marine paintings appear in two similar scenes of thirty years later, Gabriel Metsu's *Woman Reading a Letter* (ca. 1663) and Johannes Vermeer's *The Love Letter* (ca. 1670).

Vermeer was particularly fond of this device, sometimes using the same painting in different scenes. Two pictures of women at their music feature a painting of Cupid, while landscapes appear on the walls or decorate the open lids of virginals in several other interiors. Dirck van Baburen's *The Procuress* (1622; Color Plate 3), a picture that Vermeer himself owned, appears in two other scenes of music making, suggesting the bond between music and love expressed in emblem literature. A more problematic example is *Woman Holding a Balance* (ca. 1662), also by Vermeer, in which a Last Judgment scene hangs behind a woman holding an empty pair of scales. Scholars continue to dispute the connection between the religious painting and the serenely smiling woman.

Studies of estate inventories have documented the types of pictures actually owned by various households, and thereby the care with which artists chose the paintings depicted in their interiors. When contrived as iconographic cues, paintings within paintings are often difficult for modern art historians to interpret, due in part to twentieth-century distance from a culture familiar with emblems and other allegorical material. In some cases, however, the ambiguity of these secondary pictures may have been deliberately cultivated to suit the tastes of an increasingly sophisticated clientele.

Martha Hollander

See also Display; Emblems and emblem books; Framing devices within pictures; House interiors; Marriage and family portraits; Vermeer, Johannes

Bibliography

Fock, C.W. "Kunstbezit in Leiden in de 17de eeuw." In *Het Rapenburg: Geschiedenis van een Leidse Gracht*. Edited by T.H. Lunsingh Sheurleer, C.W. Fock, and A.J. van

Dissel, 3–36. Leiden: Rijksuniversiteit Leiden, 1990.

Goodman-Soellner, Elise, "The Landscape on the Wall in Vermeer." *Konsthistorisk Tidskrift* 58 (1989): 76–88.

Hedinger, Bärbel. *Karten in Bildern: zur Ikonographie der Wandkarte in holländischen Interieurgemälden des siebzehnten Jarhunderts.* Hildesheim/New York: Olms, 1986.

Keyszelitz, R. "'Das Bildim Bild' in *Der 'Clavis Interpretandi'* in der holländischen Malerei des 17. jahrhunderts." Ph.D. diss., Ludwig-Maximillians-Universität zu München, Munich, 1956, 54–72.

Loughman, John. "Paintings in the Public and Private Domain: Collecting and Patronage at Dordrecht, 1620–1749." Ph.D. diss., Courtauld Institute of Art, London, 1993.

Smith, David R. "Irony and Civility: Notes on the Convergence of Genre and Portraiture in Seventeenth-Century Dutch Painting." *Art Bulletin* 69 (September 1987): 407–430.

Stechow, Wolfgang. "Landscape Paintings in Dutch Seventeenth-Century Interiors." *Nederlands Kunsthistorisch Jaarboek* 2 (1960): 165–184.

Pander, Pier (1864–1919)

In the decade at the end of the nineteenth century and the beginning of the twentieth century, Pier Pander was the leading figure in Dutch sculpture. He was born in 1864, the son of a Frisian barge captain and his wife. Supported by a number of Frisian noblemen, the talented youth studied art in Amsterdam and Paris. In 1885 he won first prize in the sculpture competition of the Prix de Rome. That same year he was struck by illness and spent two years in bed. He was left with a crippled leg that hindered his mobility for the rest of his life, possibly contributing to a stronger development within his work. In 1890 he settled permanently in Rome, where his house became a meeting place for Dutch artists, among them the writer Louis Couperus (1863–1923), who describes his meetings with Pander in several works.

Pander's career went well from the start. He received many commissions for portraits, including the head of Queen Wilhelmina for a new coin in 1898. He was successful with his children's heads and medallions, which sold in large numbers. His work was generally admired, and in 1903 he received a royal decoration.

Pander's work is accessible, sensitive, and elegant, with a reserve in the kind of subjects selected and technical effect. It can be described as literary-symbolic in content with a Neoclassical composition founded upon academic principles (Fig. 92). Pander was influenced by theosophy and the philosophy of Dr. Carl Freiherr du Prel.

After he found his own style early, his work experienced hardly any further development, which often was (and is) the cause for criticism. His lifework was a little temple to art, with five sculptures entitled *Morning, Power, Awakening Feelings, Courage,* and *Rising Thought.* It was built in Leeuwarden in 1924, and in 1954, in fulfillment of the terms of his will, became a museum for his work. Since his death, the sculptor has fallen somewhat into oblivion.

Geraart Westerink

See also Sculpture (1795–1945)

Bibliography
Daalen, P.K. van. *Nederlandse beeldhouwers in de negentiende eeuw,* 70–73, 75. The Hague: Nijhoff, 1957.

Hammacher, A.M. *Beeldhouwkunst van deze eeuw,* 22–23, 49, 60. Vol. 14, *De schoonheid van ons land.* Amsterdam: Contact, 1955.

Klein, M. *Louis Couperus en Pier Pander: Teksten voor en over de beeldhouwer Pier Pander.* Baarn: Arethusa, 1985.

Wiersma, J.P. *Pier Pander: Een Friese beeldhouwer in Rome 1864–1919.* Drachten: Laverman, 1966.

Paper, used for prints

Prints from the fifteenth to the eighteenth century were primarily printed on laid paper. Laid paper was produced from a liquid pulp made of beaten cotton or linen rags. Fine "white" paper, used for printing, was made from the best clean rags, while coarser "brown" paper was made from lower-grade, dirtier rags. Some woodcuts were printed on coarse blue paper, produced from a pulp of blue textiles. A mold, a wood frame with brass wires stretched across the surface, was used to shape the paper—widely spaced wires, called chain wires, were crossed perpendicularly by narrowly spaced ones, called laid wires. An additional wire design was tied to the chain and laid wires to form the watermark. The traces of these wires can be observed when the sheet of paper is held against the light. The mold was plunged into a vat of pulp and filled. Once the water drained from the mold, the resulting paper was pressed between pieces of felt and then hung to dry. The paper could be sized with gelatine or glue to give the paper a hard surface and prevent ink from bleeding. Paper used for printing was generally more softly sized than writing paper because sizing could make the paper less pliable than necessary for taking impressions from a plate or woodblock.

Laid paper was produced in various sizes denoted by names such as *vierendeelen, halve folien, mediaen blad,* and *groote dubbel folien;* some larger sheets were called *dobbel lombarts blad, reael blad.* It is not clear whether there was any standardized system of nomenclature for paper sizes. Another type of paper, used most notably by Rembrandt, was imported Japan paper, made from a pulp of mulberry bark. Japan paper is a smooth, woven paper that shows no watermark or laid lines and bears a golden color that could heighten a print's tonal quality. Other, often more expensive, productions from this period were printed on other supports besides paper, such as silk, parchment, and linen.

The earliest paper mill in the Netherlands was established in 1405 in Hoey. Eventually, Antwerp became a great papermaking center during the sixteenth century. The earliest Northern Netherlandish paper mills date only from around 1586. The beginning of a Dutch papermaking business resulted from the flight of many of the Southern papermakers to Holland following the capture of Antwerp by the Spanish. Even so, Holland was not known for the production of quality paper until around 1685. Until then, Dutch mills produced mainly coarse "brown" paper, and Holland imported most of its fine-quality paper. The earliest printmakers in the Northern Netherlands used paper from Italy, France, Switzerland, and Germany. During the seventeenth century, some papers with Dutch watermarks were, in fact, made in France expressly for the Dutch market. Some print publishers found it profitable to invest in paper mills or even to act as agents between a number of foreign papermakers and local purchasers of paper.

Nadine Orenstein

See also Prints, printmaking, and printmakers (ca. 1500–ca. 1900); Prints, publishers; Watermarks

Bibliography

Churchill, W.A. *Watermarks in Paper in Holland, England, France, etc., in the Seventeenth and Eighteenth Centuries and their Interconnection.* Amsterdam: Menno Hertzberger, 1935.

Hunter, Dard. *Papermaking.* 2nd ed. New York: Knopf, 1967.

Krill, John. *English Artists' Paper: Renaissance to Regency.* London: Trefoil, 1987.

Robison, Andrew. *Paper in Prints.* Washington, DC: National Gallery of Art, 1977.

Pastoral

"Here make the udder milked along the green banks
Where Tytir delights in pipes and Amaryllis
His beloved, while they lie resting under the beech tree
And listen to the sweet tones of the herd."

With those words from his theoretical handbook *De grondt der edel-vry schilder const* (The Foundations of the Noble and Liberal Art of Painting), written in 1604, Karel van Mander articulated his feeling for the harmony between man and nature. A painter who must have felt attracted to Van Mander's words, and who most certainly read his book, was Pieter Lastman. Lastman's *concerts champêtres* (rustic concerts) already date from the 1610s and come remarkably close to the atmosphere Van Mander discloses. Lastman probably considered himself an heir to the great Venetian painters Jacopo Bassano, Giorgione, and Titian, who were his artistic predecessors. It is remarkable that Lastman's paintings did not have any impact on his followers. His type of pastoral proved to be a dead end.

The essence of Dutch pastoral painting lies in the world of the antique. This does not mean only the sculptural and architectural remnants of the Greek and Roman eras, or the idyllic Roman Campagna, which was known to all Dutch painters who visited Italy. The true essence lies in antique pastoral poetry, foremost in Theocritus' *Idylls* and Virgil's *Eclogues*, as well as in Ovid's *Metamorphoses* and Longus' shepherd prose from the third century, *Daphnis and Chloe*. The bucolic poetry of those ancient writers came to life again in the Renaissance, at first through the work of Petrarch and Boccaccio. Later it was of great significance for Jacopo Sannazaro (*Arcadia*, 1486) and especially Torquato Tasso's *Aminta* (1573) and Battista Guarini's *Il pastor fido* (The Faithful Shepherd), published for the first time in 1589. It was especially this pastoral play by Guarini that proved to be of immense interest, not only for Dutch literature but for painters as well.

Il pastor fido was first translated into Dutch in 1619 by Govert van der Eembd. This prose translation was based not on the original Italian text but on a French translation. Two years earlier the first edition of *Anna Rodenburgh's Trouwen Batavier* appeared, which was an adaption of the original play, written by the Dutch playwright Theodore Rodenburgh. He was not the only writer to become inspired; better known are Pieter Cornelisz. Hooft's *Granida* from 1615, and Joost van den Vondel's *Leeuwendalers,* which was written in 1647 to commemorate the end of the war with Spain that started in 1568. More translations and dramatizations of *Il pastor fido* would follow, although its popularity faded by the end of the seventeenth century.

The popularity of Guarini's pastoral-tragical comedy in the visual arts was much greater in the Netherlands than anywhere else. Even in Italy the subject did not gather that much attention in painting. Nevertheless, it is curious that it took until 1630 for the first painting depicting a scene from *Il pastor fido* to be made in the Netherlands. The creator was Anthony van Dyck from Flanders, and the canvas was a commission from the Dutch *stadholder* Frederik Hendrik for a chimneypiece for his residence in The Hague. Five years later, in 1635, Frederik Hendrik commissioned a cycle of four paintings with scenes from Guarini's play for his pleasure palace, Honselaarsdijk. The commission was given to four Utrecht painters, Abraham Bloemaert, Cornelis van Poelenburch, Herman Saftleven and Dirck van der Lisse. The four paintings were transported to Berlin in 1742, but became separated in 1830 when two of the paintings were transfered to the new Kaiser Friedrich Museum while the others stayed in Charlottenburg Castle.

The first Dutch painter who favored the subject was Bartholomeus Breenbergh. This interesting artist started out as a painter of Italianate landscapes, but after his return to the Netherlands he began a career as a history painter and portraitist in Amsterdam. He was especially fond of mythological themes and subjects taken from contemporary literature. He painted no fewer than six different scenes from *Il pastor fido,* the earliest dating from 1631. Other Amsterdam painters, like Jacob van Loo, Jacob Backer, Daniël Thievaert, and Jacob de Wet, also painted scenes from the play.

The only other pastoral play that could compete with *Il pastor fido* in popularity was Hooft's *Granida.* The popularity of Hooft's play was especially great in Amsterdam, where it was very successful on stage. It does not really come as a surprise, then, that there proved to be a market for paintings that depicted this subject. Three painters especially were fond of painting the initial meeting-scene from the first act: Jacob

Backer (Fig. 12), Gerbrand van den Eeckhout, and Jan van Noordt. Their compositions were all based on one prototype that dated from 1623. The painter of this prototype did not work in Amsterdam; he was Dirck van Baburen from Utrecht. Another Utrecht artist, Gerard van Honthorst, painted a later scene from the play, *Granida and Daifilo As Lovers* (1625; Utrecht, Centraal Museum; Color Plate 4), that should be regarded as one of the first classicizing paintings in the Netherlands. The painting was probably meant as a wedding gift for Frederik Hendrik and his wife, Amalia van Solms.

It is remarkable that other pastoral plays or poems could not inspire Dutch painters, although some of them isolated scenes from nonpastoral plays that possessed a strong pastoral flavor. Especially popular was the scene of Cimon and Iphigenia from Jan van Arp's *Chimon. Op de Reeghel: Door liefde verstandigh* (Cimon, or the Rule: Wise through Love) from 1639, which was based on one of the stories from Boccaccio's *Decameron*. Another popular scene for painters to depict was *The Meeting of Don Juan and Preciose* from the play *De Spaensche Heydin* (The Spanish Gypsy), by the Amsterdam playwright Mattheus Gansneb Tengnagel, that was performed on stage in 1644, one year after it was published. The play was inspired by a poem from 1637 by Jacob Cats. In all of the scenes mentioned, a confrontation or meeting takes place. Especially the meeting scenes between Granida and Daifilo and Don Juan and Preciose have, in most depictions, a pronounced stage-like setting. It would not be surprising if the actual theatrical performance played an important role in the artists' and viewers' conception of the depicted scene.

Of course, painted representations of a direct literary source played only a part, albeit a large one, in the increasing popularity of pastoral painting in the Netherlands. The roots of Dutch pastoral lie in Utrecht. Utrecht had a long traditional bond with Italy, and a trip to Rome was part of the education of Utrecht painters. Of the older generation of painters at the beginning of the seventeenth century, Paulus Moreelse felt much attracted to the pastoral genre. He was the first one to paint a half-length figure in pastoral attire (1617), and from 1622 onward he produced a long series of shepherds and shepherdesses at half-length, such as the so-called *Beautiful Shepherdess* (1630) in the Rijksmuseum in Amsterdam (Fig. 93). Others also painted such half-length figures, especially in Utrecht. Among them were Jan van Bijlert, Hendrick Terbrugghen, and Gerard van Honthorst. Outside Utrecht this type of painting never became very popular. After 1640 it lost its attraction to painters completely.

Paulus Moreelse can be regarded as a genuine specialist in pastoral painting. Not only did he introduce the first half-length shepherdess, he was the first Dutch painter to produce a pastoral portrait. In 1622—a remarkably early date—he painted a portrait of two children in pastoral dress; only after 1640 did this specific type of portrait become a specialization of Aelbert and Jacob Cuyp, Dirck Santvoort, and Gerbrand van den Eeckhout. Not only children were portrayed in shepherd's attire; women, too, identified with pastoral portraiture as the many portraits that Gerard van Honthorst and Jan Mijtens made at the *stadholder's* court attest. In contrast, single male portraits are rare in Dutch pastoral painting. Most men probably considered the pastoral role effeminate and preferred to be depicted as hunters, as is shown in Jacob Backer's *Portrait of a Boy As a Hunter and a Girl As Shepherdess* (ca. 1645). In large pastoral family portraits, a portrait type especially in demand in the Netherlands, men were often portrayed as hunters, which offered them a more commanding role amid their kin. A specific type of portraiture that needs to be mentioned here is the *portrait historié*, although one could consider every pastoral portrait as such. Hooft's *Granida*, for instance, appealed especially to the Dutch as a subject for a wedding portrait. In the 1660s Jan Mijtens painted a beautiful *Portrait of a Couple As Granida and Daifilo*, which hangs in the Rijksmuseum in Amsterdam (Fig. 94). Interesting as well are Bartholomeus van der Helst's *Self-Portrait as Daifilo* and its pendant, *Portrait of Anna du Pire As Granida*, from 1660.

Pastoral landscape as a category is more or less synonymous with Italianate landscape painting. It is important, however, that a distinction is made between the landscapes that we know from the so-called first and second generation of Italianate artists—Van Poelenburch, Breenbergh, Nicolaes Berchem, and Jan Asselijn—and the poetic fantasy landscapes, which do make us think much more about an unknown and distant Arcadia. This type of bucolic landscape, in which fantasy figures play an important role, we only know from Pieter Lastman and, later, from Moyses van Wtenbrouck an important painter at Frederik Hendrik's court. This type of landscape appealed much more to the taste of the French and the Italians. We have only to look at the fairy-tale landscapes of Claude Lorrain and Domenichino to verify this. Late in the seventeenth and in the beginning of the eighteenth century, the influence of these imagined heroic landscapes can be felt in the work of Johannes Glauber, Jan Frans van Bloemen, Hendrick Frans van Lint, and Isaac de Moucheron. In figural painting as well, this academic French taste is apparent, especially in the lazy pastoral love encounters painted by Caspar Netscher, Eglon van der Neer, Adriaen and Pieter van der Werff, and, of course, Gerard de Lairesse. But by then the Golden Age of Dutch painting had already faded, and the Netherlands was no more than a French province.

Peter van den Brink

See also Backer, Jacob Adriaensz.; Bloemaert, Abraham; Country houses and gardens; History portraits; Italy; Landscape; Literature, poetry: analogues with the visual; Portraiture; Rural life and views; Theater and theatricality; Utrecht; Utrecht Caravaggists; Van der Helst, Bartholomeus; Van Honthorst, Gerard; Van Mander, Karel

Bibliography

Brink, P. van den. *Het gedroomde land: Pastorale schilderkunst in de Gouden Eeuw.* Utrecht: Centraal Museum, 1993.

Brink, P. van den et al. *La pastorale olandese nel Seicento.* Rome: Istituto Olandese, 1983.

Budde, I. "Die Idylle im holländischen Barock." Ph.D. diss., Cologne, 1929.

Gelder, J.G.van. "Pastor fido-voorstellingen in de Nederlandse kunst van de zeventiende eeuw." *Oud Holland* 92 (1978): 227–263.

Gudlaugsson, S.J. "Representations of Granida in Dutch Seventeenth-Century Painting." *Burlington Magazine* 90 (1948): 226–230, 348–351; and 91 (1949): 39–43.

Kettering, Alison McNeil. *The Dutch Arcadia: Pastoral Art and Its Audience in the Golden Age.* Montclair, NJ: Abner Schram, 1983.

———. "Rembrandt's *Flute Player*: A Unique Treatment of Pastoral." *Simiolus* 9 (1977): 19–44.

Meyere, J.A.L. de. *"Granida en Daifilo" (1625) van Gerard van Honthorst.* Utrecht: Centraal Museum, 1988.

Photographers, anonymous

Signing photographs has not always been a custom. Up to forty percent of the nineteenth-century photographs made in the Netherlands are anonymous. A source of attribution can be stylistic distinctions or the development in a group of works or in a period. Often uncertainty remains since there are fewer ways to begin looking for signs of authorship in photographs than in paintings, drawings, or prints. The simple cause of this is the smaller proportion of handworkmanship in the genesis of photographs. Sometimes a photograph can be attributed fortuitously through secondary factors such as recognition of the setting used in a portrait.

The Dutch theologian J.J. Prins (1814–1898) has been identified as the sitter in one recently discovered nineteenth-century portrait photograph (Fig. 95). The photographer remains unknown for the present; however, considering Prins' apparent age in the portrait and his year of birth, the photograph should be dated between 1855 and 1865. It would then be a late specimen of the calotype or salted paper print process, one of the earliest photographic techniques. At the time this picture was made, the small *cartes-de-visite* (visiting cards) already dominated portrait photography. The conventions of this type of portrait—stiff poses and stereotypical settings of a chair, a table, or a pedestal on a carpet, photographed with crisp sharpness—are absent in Prins' portrait. On the contrary, it has all of the charm and somewhat clumsy manner of posing characteristic of the early calotype portraits. Only a table and part of the chair are visible; the rest of the surroundings are lost in a blur.

To limit the exposure time that the less light-sensitive calotype negatives required, the portrait was made outside or in a greenhouse, catching as much sunlight as possible. As a consequence of this, Prins' eyes are tightly shut. In a lithograph that J.H. Hoffmeister made after this photograph, the eyes are opened normally and the expression on the face is more relaxed. Due to the long exposure times required, sitting for a photographer was no easy and pleasant activity. People had to remain motionless by means of an invisible or inconspicuously disguised support. Many a nineteenth-century newspaper cartoon was devoted to the topic of sitters fallen asleep or causing their portraits to be out of focus by their having moved too much.

It is not certain whether the maker of Prins' portrait was an amateur or a professional photographer. Amateurs played an important role in early photography since they were not troubled by artistic conventions or restrictions that were the consequence of a need to profit from the medium. It is also possible that the portrait was made by a foreigner. Many French and German photographers traversed the Netherlands, and their contribution to early Dutch photography has been an important one; however, most of them did not work in the calotype process but in the rival daguerreotype. For a photographer to settle in a town was out of the question until the 1850s; most Dutch towns were medium-sized and held few inhabitants who could afford to have their portraits made at the then-current high prices. Moreover, the economy in the Netherlands was not flourishing in the 1840s. The pioneer photographers in the Netherlands have, therefore, remained somewhat elusive to history.

Hans Rooseboom

See also Photography, early (1839–1925)

Bibliographic note

The problem of the huge amount of anonymous photographs has not yet been adequately studied nor has a separate publication been devoted to the topic. Many photographic portraits from the nineteenth century remain in private hands and not in public collections.

Photography, early (1839–1925)

The invention of photography, announced by Louis J.M. Daguerre in Paris in 1839, was met with enthusiasm and astonishment as well as some distrust. How uncommon photographs were perceived to be is revealed by the absence of a special language to describe them. Instead, one finds many comparisons of photographs to the graphic techniques already in existence, and flowery descriptions like "the new art of generating drawings by sunlight." When the new invention was discussed in the nonillustrated press, engravings, etchings, mezzotints, and aquatints were all called upon more than once to elicit understanding. The words "sun," "sunlight," "nature," "drawing," and "generate" constitute the vocabulary in many variants of the sort of description given above. What is striking in all of them is the lack of any reference to the indispensable chemical part of the process. By not mentioning that human workmanship was involved, it was suggested that nature alone had caused the scenes to become fixed on paper or a metal plate.

The first photographers were required to be partly chemists due to the complexity of the photographic process. After about 1860, when some of the biggest technical problems had been solved—the long exposure times, for instance—difficulties decreased and prices dropped. Portrait photography became not only a means of support but even an "industry." Its general quality and originality did not benefit from this. Small 9 x 6 cm portraits in the format of *cartes-de-visite* (visiting cards) gained extraordinary popularity from about 1860 onward. Soon stereotypical settings, poses, and props, used irrespectively of the person depicted, dominated these small photographs in order to achieve a high production.

The low aesthetic quality of most nineteenth-century portraits, especially the *cartes-de-visite*, shows that photography met the public's demand for pictures without any artistic pretension. If early photography should be allotted a place among the arts, it would have to be next to the many engraved and lithographed portraits, topographical views, and other popular subjects in the same period. It would be unfair to compare the early portraits, many of them by photographers who are today anonymous, to the large-scale "grand" portraits painted in the Netherlands by Jan Willem Pieneman and Cornelis Kruseman. These artists were employed by people in much higher social and economic circles and they were paid proportionately. Photography in the same circumstances could only be seen, for example, following in the tradition of the lithographic portraits of well-known people produced by J.P. Berghaus and the albums containing lithographic views of country houses and landscapes compiled by P.J. Lutgers. Subjects, composition, and settings are comparable. Photographs distinguished themselves, however, from other graphic techniques by their texture and variety of gray tones. The mid-1850s saw a first peak of achievement with the landscapes by J.A. van Eijk, townscapes by Herman Bückmann, and portraits by Eduard Asser. Bückmann was the only professional photographer among them.

Both the painter's contribution to early photography and photography's influence on the course of painting are easily overestimated. Early photographers had a wide diversity of backgrounds, certainly not only as artists. Their profession stood on the border of art, handicraft, science, and trade, and belonged to none of these exclusively. It should be noted that many of the tendencies in painting that have been attributed to photography's influence had begun well before 1839. In addition, it would be incorrect to assign photography a place between the old theoretical poles of "idealism" and "realism." Photographic realism went far beyond that of paintings since it lacked the latter's well-considered and mostly invented compositions. It is, therefore, not of much use to speak of "photographic realism" in painting. Photography, much more bound to reality but less to artistic conventions, shows a wider variety of compositions and subjects.

Opinions of prominent Dutch painters concerning photography are not known. As in other countries, they may have been of the opinion that painting belonged to a distinctly other world, or they pretended it to be so. The long, careful, and laborious study of an artist after nature differed significantly from the way a camera perceived and recorded a scene. Besides, photography served all kinds of purposes from the beginning, not only artistic ones. This has certainly contributed to the insecure status it held during the nineteenth century. Professional jealousy (that is, economic motives) disguised as aesthetic arguments may have contributed to the painter's harsh criticism of photography, but it must not be forgotten that condemnations of superficial perception, com-

monplace subjects, an excessive amount of detail, and nonselective rendering of scenes had already been a topic in art theory well before 1839.

In contrast to the lukewarm attitude of artists toward photography is the fact that photographs have been the source of many drawings, paintings, and prints. To be sure, not only artists lacking imagination or drawing ability worked—whether occasionally or not—after photographs. It should be noted that photographs were used not only as a visual source but they were also copied using other techniques simply in order to print them. Photographs could not be reproduced in ink easily and cheaply until the end of the century.

While many photographers from around 1860 onward derived poses and settings from portrait painting and applied them without much refinement, the views that some of them made of bridges, canals, railways, and other public works under construction were much more original. For the first time photographers developed an aesthetic of their own, independent of what was being done in the arts. Julius Perger (Fig. 96), Pieter Oosterhuis, Jacobus van Gorkom Jr., and Johann Hameter had a preference for standing on or near the longitudinal axis of these public works, thereby giving their photographs a strong sense of depth. Such views are rare in nineteenth-century art. These monumental photographs give credit to the engineering works of the period; the people that appear in them only served as props or for the sake of scale. Most of these photographs were made from the 1860s to the 1880s.

Portrait photography was mainly considered a way of earning a living. Its general quality did not improve in the last quarter of the nineteenth century, although the work of Louis Wegner (1816–1864) is a favorable exception. This, and the rise of facile amateur snapshot photography from the 1880s onward, led to a reaction from the so-called pictorialists (*picturalisten*). At first, most of these were serious amateurs who strived for art. Especially after the turn of the century, Wieger Hendricus Idzerda (1873–1938) tried to raise the level of his profession by making pictures with much more care than had been previously done. Pictorialists took offense not only at the props used over and over again by professional portrait photographers but also at the enormous amount of retouching of the negatives. Scornfully, they said that this retouching made people look like "billiard balls" or "wax statues." The pictorialists thought other things also required attention: A shiny button attracting more attention than the sitter's face might be characteristic of the way a camera rendered things; it would not, however, definitely lead to "art in photography."

The pictorialists in the early twentieth century wanted to change all of this, and, indeed, their portraits are much more dignified. They were also printed in a better technique. Pictorialist pictures usually display a quiet atmosphere, largely due to the diffused incidence of light. This is visible not only in portraits but also in the other subjects favored by the pictorialists: fairyland-like avenues with tall birches, flocks of sheep returning to the fold, farmers sitting outside their houses, and workmen at their jobs (Fig. 97).

Above all, pictorialists expressed feelings of beauty. They were much closer to the epigones of The Hague School than to contemporary modernist painters like Jan Sluijters and Piet Mondrian. Besides being sincere in their aesthetic feelings, the pictorialists seem to have suffered from some kind of inferiority complex. As they thought that photography in itself could not be artistic, they ignored and even hid typical photographic properties like naturalism, sharpness, and the great amount of detail. Photography, being at the divide between art and handicraft, was claimed to be an art by the pictorialists on the condition that it was properly used. Idzerda, especially, propagated the idea of "artistic photography" and strove for its recognition. The plain objectivity and mechanical nature of camera-made pictures were not sufficient for creating works of art, he thought. To be works of art, photographs should not merely be the result of rays of light, a lens, a camera, and a plate sensitive to light. Art should not render the appearance of things or record one rather arbitrary moment out of a prolonged action. What art should express are the artist's feelings. This axiom defined the pictorialist attitude toward art and photography and the relationship between the two. Human workmanship—the hand of man—the absence of which had amazed so many people at the time of the invention of photography had to return. A photograph should bear the distinctive stamp of its maker, no matter how much time and effort that would require. Complex techniques and processes were used to improve upon the camera-made (that is, mechanically made) negatives. Preferring man to the machine, the eye to the lens, subjectivity to objectivity, and the human spirit to the photographic plate, the pictorialists paid much attention to the technical and chemical part of photography. Many times the resulting pictures resembled drawings, paintings, and prints. This resemblance was not felt to be dishonorable: It was not the means that mattered, only the results. All was well as long as the photographer could exercise his influence during the creative process from the making of the negative to finishing the photographic print. Henri Berssenbrugge (1873–1959) was the most inventive of the pictorialists, exploring the boundaries of photography and the other arts—at the price of being criticized for not using purely photographic means.

Improvements in optics in the twentieth century, stimulated greatly by the wide and diverse use of lenses in photography, were blamed for being a source of photography's degeneration. The "crude sharpness" of recently developed lenses was regarded as extremely unartistic. The bad taste of the public was another object of pictorialist complaint, as professional portrait photographers often catered to it. Those members of the public taking an easy-to-handle box camera in their own hands were judged just as harshly. Contrary to the intricate processes used by the pictorialists, handling a small box camera was all too effortless and only fostered laziness. Means, not results, did matter this time.

Amateur snapshots rarely had any artistic value; they were not meant to. What is striking about the pictorialists' statements on this subject is the exaggeration: One critic complained as early as 1892 that the mass of snapshot photographers had for a couple of years disturbed the calm at the beach. Idzerda fancied that serious amateur photography had been washed down the drain by the "democratization of photography." Comparable statements exist about museums getting overcrowded, politics becoming a matter of interest to just anyone, and rivers growing crammed with pleasure crafts. They breathe a reluctance to let common people partake in activities that had for a long time been the privilege of a small group. To be sure, things had changed quickly in photography. In no more than twenty-five years (the last quarter of the nineteenth century), photography had changed from a complicated, difficult, and expensive activity to one that was fit for children.

One senses a certain nostalgia in pictorialist pictures. Scenes of quiet life on the land constitute a substantial number of them. The concern felt for farmers, workmen, tramps, and gypsies was rather superficial, and they mainly served as picturesque motifs. The genre photographs of farm interiors and old people in hospital wards are often mannered or sentimental. Compared to pictorialist photographs, the snapshots that the painter George Hendrik Breitner made of Amsterdam city life stand out in their liveliness and directness. Their technical imperfection only adds to these qualities. Breitner used the snapshots, just as he did his sketches and drawings, only as preliminary material for his paintings. His photographs cannot have had any influence other than private, since the negatives and prints appeared only at the time of his death in 1923.

Hans Rooseboom

See also Berssenbrugge, Henri; Breitner, George Hendrik; Dewald, C.M; Herwig, Reinhardt Herman; Oosterhuis, Pieter; Photographers, anonymous; Verveer, Maurits; Witsen, Willem

Bibliography

Coppens, Jan. *Een camera vol stilte: Nederland in het begin van de fotografie, 1839–1875*. Amsterdam: Meulenhoff, 1976.

Coppens, Jan et al. "*. . . door de enkele werking van het licht . . .*": *Introductie en integratie van de fotografie in België en Nederland, 1839–1869*. Antwerp: Gemeentekrediet, 1989.

Evers, G.A. "Hoe de fotografie in Nederland kwam." *Lux* 25 (1914): 356–366, 420–425; and 26 (1915): 20–28, 171–174, 247–257, 295–299, 331–339, 384–394.

Leijerzapf, Ingeborg Th., ed. *Fotografie in Nederland 1839–1920*. The Hague: Staatsuitgeverij, 1978.

———, ed. *Geschiedenis van de Nederlandse fotografie*. Alphen aan den Rijn: Samsom, 1984–.

———, ed. *Het fotografisch museum van Auguste Grégoire: Een vroege Nederlandse fotocollectie*. Gouda: Catharina Gasthuis; The Hague: SDU, 1989.

Venetië, Robbert van, and Annet Zondervan. *Geschiedenis van de Nederlandse architectuurfotografie*. Rotterdam: 010, 1989.

Photography, modern and contemporary (1925–1990)

Photography came of age in the Netherlands in the second half of the 1920s. By then, photographers of a new generation—exponents of Nieuwe Fotografie (New Photography, the equivalent of American Straight Photography)—felt themselves independent from developments in the arts and acted accordingly. They no longer imitated paintings, drawings, and prints but opened up, whether or not it was prudent, two new fields for photography: advertising and journalism. They were helped in this by the widening possibilities of publishing photographs in newspapers, magazines, and books.

Thanks to the invention of the autotype printing technique in the 1880s, photographs and text no longer needed to be printed separately. Autotype quality was good enough for illustrations in cheap magazines and books. The beautiful collotype, woodburytype, and photogravure printing techniques had been too expensive to be used widely in other than well-executed editions. Even after the introduction of autotype printing, it took a long time before photographs definitely superseded hand-drawn illustrations in the press. Not until the 1920s is there an observable shift toward the utilization of photographs instead of drawings in newspapers. Besides, the number of illustrations in the press, especially newspapers, had always been very modest, and photographs mainly accompanied news accounts. Portraits, curiosities, and sites of calamities were the main subjects of photographs appearing in newspapers and magazines. Press pictures rarely gave a deeper insight.

At a time when the role of the machine—in both work and daily life—was not yet fully accepted and its influence on people was viewed with some anxiousness, mechanical devices were not considered inferior or objectionable in New Photography. On the contrary, the qualities inherent in photography (objectivity, sharpness, the amount of detail recorded) were welcomed as being useful to the goals the New Photographers had set themselves. Photographic realism could be utilized in a wide range of fields: science, advertising, and journalism. Artistic use was not the exclusive care of this group. Moreover, the axiom of what art should be had changed; functionality was thought to be more important than aesthetics. Therefore, hiding characteristic properties was no longer needed. On the contrary, Piet Zwart (1885–1977), who initiated New Photography in the Netherlands together with Gerrit Kiljan (1891–1968) and Paul Schuitema (1897–1973), thought photography to be superior to other graphic techniques because it comprised all gray tones between white and black. Kiljan, Schuitema, and Zwart took advantage of the possibilities photography offered and judged pictorialism as being not "true to material." As the pictorialists had done in their time, the New Photographers blamed their predecessors for being unnatural and deceptive.

Around 1932, Zwart photographed extensively in a woodworking industrial plant (Fig. 98). One senses that he was less interested in the employees than in the repetition of machine forms and products. The vocabulary of New Photography is constituted by repetition of forms, small

details of plain objects that had not been the subject of investigation through the lens before, and very high or low points of view. All was now viewed in a completely different way.

Not having a background as photographers but being art teachers and designers, Kiljan, Schuitema, and Zwart were particularly interested in applying photography in publicity. They treated photographs as full-fledged elements, fully incorporating them in their designs for advertisements, brochures, and booklets. All frills were left out of them. Trying to inform the public in a modern and honest way, Kiljan, Schuitema, and Zwart considered photographs very useful because of their truthfulness. They assembled photographs in photomontages and *fototypografie* collages in which photography and typography were mingled. Photographs were no longer mere illustrations to a text.

New Photography exercised its influence not only through the use of photographs in print. In 1930 Kiljan, soon accompanied by Schuitema, set up the first training course for photographers in the Netherlands. Before then, the trade had to be learned abroad or in a photographer's studio. Kiljan incorporated photography into the program of the Advertising Department at The Hague Academy of Arts and trained many photographers who would become well known. The program gave much attention to advertising, photography, and typography and to executing experiments with photographic means, trying to become acquainted with all possibilities within the range of the medium.

Kiljan, Schuitema, and Zwart had concentrated on the application of photography in advertising. In 1948 Zwart himself spoke out against human beings depicted only as "photographic things" as had been done in New Photography. After World War II, a younger generation of documentary photographers who had been rooted in New Photography and who had partly been trained by Kiljan and Schuitema, gave men and women a central place in their pictures. The documentary photographs made by Emmy Andriesse, Eva Besnyö, Carel Blazer, Cas Oorthuys, and other members of the photographers' branch of the GKF, the Vereniging van Beoefenaars der Gebonden Kunsten (Federation of Applied Arts Practitioners), are marked by a sincere humane compassion. World War II and its terrors—depicted illegally by some of them—may be held responsible for this. The GKF photographers preferred their pictures to be printed in books, magazines, and newspapers rather than framed and hung on the wall (Fig. 6). They were often employed by publishers to provide photographs for travel guides or by industries to supply photographs for annual reports and commemorative books. The appearance of New Photographs in print turned out to have been only a sign of what was yet to come. The growth of the picture press after 1945 was due to the interest that editors of both magazines and publishing firms had taken in photographs. Meanwhile, photographs had become more than just illustrations to a text. Documentary photographers were allowed more freedom than they had had before the war, which may explain why they did not experience a wide gap between their assignments and "free" work; the two were often mingled.

Aart Klein (born 1909), a member of the GKF photographers' section, succeeded in combining documentary photography with near-abstract beauty. Although the GKF photographers had renounced the sentimental, superficial, and genre-like depictions of other people's lives as made by the pictorialists, their own pictures of life on the land, rural trades, and costume still contained some sense of nostalgia. Klein broke with this—whether or not on purpose—by imposing a technical device upon his photographs that eliminated most gray tones. The resulting contrast and interplay of black and white give his pictures a graphic, if sometimes grim, quality.

As for photographs that panegyrized the Dutch landscape or in which a sense of nostalgia interfered, it should not be overlooked that publishers desired, or selected, photographs that fostered this feeling. A photographer like Kees Scherer seems to have become a victim of this. He is best known for his views of Amsterdam city life in the 1950s. Nearly all of them have been made in the early morning or late afternoon, as can be deduced from the ever-present skimming light. Much more variation, however, is to be found in the rest of his work.

Although television took over part of its task, documentary photography did not waver after the first period of its efflorescence in the 1950s and 1960s. An increasing quantity of magazines and newspapers employed photographers; however, much more attention has been given to artists' uses of photography since about 1970. In view of the nonphotographic background of most of these artists and their use of mixed media, not all of their works necessarily belong to photography in the first place. In some cases, however, photography perceptibly has had the greater part in the final result of blending different techniques. This domination has not been only of a physical and material nature. Jan Dibbets (born 1941), for example, made the camera's optical deformations the subject of many of his photographs. He has made kinds of construction-like drawings, as if an engineer caused the horizons and other straight lines to bend. In contrast to this, Ger Dekkers' (born 1929) sequences of stately, man-made Dutch landscapes are purely photographic: Five or seven photographs of orchards, dikes, lines of trees or flagstaffs, each of them taken from a slightly different point of view, are put side by side in series. This results in intriguing changes of composition and alterations of what is actually visible, or seen together, in each of the photographs.

While Dekkers' pictures are lucid, those taken by the postmodernists of the 1980s are obscure. The usual transparency of photographs, so much utilized for documentary and other purposes, has been replaced by complex, often highly symbolic, mostly staged, scenes. Ambiguity and artificiality being an important theme, these photographs are often difficult to "read." Gérald van der Kaap (born 1959) is one of the most important postmodernist photographers.

The antithesis to the trend in postmodernist photography is a most recent inclination in Dutch photography toward panoramic, thinly populated landscape photographs with no particular meaning. There even seems to be no other idea intended than showing a piece of commonplace reality. Whereas documentary photographers have always chosen significant moments or compositions (the meeting of persons or objects) to explain a certain situation or atmosphere, these symbols are now discarded. Hans van der Meer and Hans Aarsman, among others, realized that symbolic gestures or moments sometimes turned out to be pitfalls since other meanings could be imposed—consciously or not—upon a photograph that had, in fact, "frozen" only one brief moment. For this reason Aarsman tried to evade all too clear contents or meanings. The pictures from his series *Hollandse taferelen* (Dutch Scenes) of 1988–1989 show unimportant little absurdities and other unimpressive scenes that took place at common places. The landscapes that Wout Berger, another representative of this style, photographed for the series *Giflandschappen* (Poisoned Landscapes), published in 1992, do not show outwardly the poison they contain. Ton Broekhuis, Jannes Linders, and André-Pierre Lamoth have photographed landscapes in which quietness and emptiness predominate. Whereas the spectator is inclined to search for a meaning, trained in doing so after many years of viewing photographs published in newspapers, magazines, and books, he or she is now invited to look at all parts of the picture with equal attention instead of considering one object, person, look, or action as the main subject.

Bibliographical Remarks

The history of photography is a young field of scholarly research in the Netherlands. The amount of research done has not kept pace with the interest shown in photography by the public over the past two decades. The quantity of publications devoted to it is still very modest and is mainly of monographic character. These factors seem to have kept most historians of photography from systematic, comparative, and interdisciplinary investigations that go beyond the topic of the individual photographer. Such research, to be effective, should reveal more about subjects such as the relationship between photographs and popular prints of the nineteenth century; the decline of portrait photography in the years around World War II; the simultaneous rise of photography used for fashion, advertising, and magazine illustration; the training of photographers; and the role played by magazines and amateur and professional societies in the development of photography in the Netherlands. A consequence of the predominantly monographic character of the research so far is that while a whole group may be criticized for some reason or another, its members, being men and women of flesh and blood, will often be judged with much more sympathy.

Many important photographers from all periods await the first proper study devoted to them. The current view of nineteenth-century photography is especially for this reason provisional and somewhat obscured. The history of nineteenth-century photography also suffers most from the fact that nearly forty percent of all photographs cannot be attributed. In general, the photographer's *oeuvre* is much more comprehensive than that of other artists, while much less of it has been published. The ways that this disadvantages knowledge and understanding will be clear. Considering all of this, there is ample opportunity for discussing the course of Dutch photography: by adding new facts to existing knowledge, by posing new broad insights, and by rediscovering photographs and even lost photographers.

The most important public collections of photography in the Netherlands that provide access to scholars are in the Rijksprentenkabinet of the Rijksmuseum in Amsterdam, the Stedelijk Museum in Amsterdam, the Prentenkabinet of the Rijksuniversiteit Leiden, and the Nederlands Fotoarchief in Rotterdam.

Hans Rooseboom

See also Andriesse, Emmy; Applied arts; Graphic design; Nature photography; Photography, early (1839–1925); Van der Meer, Hans; Van Ojen, E.M.; Woldringh, Meinard

Bibliography

Barents, Els, ed. *Fotografie in Nederland 1940–1975*. The Hague: Staatsuitgeverj, 1978.

Bool, Flip, and Kees Broos, eds. *Fotografie in Nederland 1920–1940*. The Hague: Staatsuitgeverij, 1979.

Boom, Mattie, Frans van Burkom, and Jenny Smets, eds. *Foto in omslag: Het Nederlandse documentaire fotoboek na 1945 / Photography between Covers: The Dutch Documentary Photobook after 1945*. Den Bosch: Noordbrabants Museum; Amsterdam: Fragment, 1989.

Broos, Kees, and Flip Bool. *De Nieuwe Fotografie in Nederland*. Amsterdam/The Hague: Fragment/SDU, 1989.

Hollands dossier 1980–1990: Een decennium fotojournalistiek. Amsterdam/The Hague: Focus/SDU, 1990.

Leijerzapf, Ingeborg Th., ed. *Geschiedenis van de Nederlandse fotografie*. Alphen aan den Rijn: Samsom, 1984– .

———. *Het fotografisch museum van Auguste Grégoire: Een vroege Nederlandse fotocollectie*. Gouda: Catharina Gasthuis; The Hague: SDU, 1989.

Merlo, Lorenzo. *Hedendaagse fotografie in Nederland / New Dutch Photography*. Amsterdam: Kosmos, 1980.

Roodenburg, Linda. *Fotowerk: Fotografie in opdracht 1986–1992*. Amsterdam: Beurs van Berlage; Rotterdam: 010, 1992.

Roots and Turns: Twentieth-Century Photography in the Netherlands. Amsterdam: Stedelijk Museum; The Hague: SDU, 1988.

Portraiture

In 1604 Karel van Mander complained that the "outstanding" painter Michiel van Mierevelt was forced through economic necessity to practice the "side-road or by-way of art," that is, portraiture. Van Mander's complaint highlights two aspects of the genre throughout most of its history. On the one hand, portraiture ranked in relatively low esteem in art theoretical texts; on the other, patrons demonstrated their appreciation for the genre through widespread commissions and economic support. In spite of taking as its subject the human body—the noblest of God's creations—portraiture has been little esteemed because of its apparent restriction to mere transcription of that body; in the hierarchy of genres, portraiture ranked far below history painting, which also represents the body. History painting was seen to engage the creative imagination of the artist and convey universal moral truths and models for human conduct. In contrast, the most successful portraits were those judged to be the closest to their original, those to which the painter had added the least of his creative personality.

This fiction of portraits' naturalism is required and sustained by the power invested in portraits by society. Their functions range from a palpable reminder of loved or admired figures who are long deceased or live far away, to powerful manifestations of monarchs. Louis Marin, for example, has persuasively argued that in Louis XIV's France, the monarch's actual power resided not in his private body but in the public image of that body. Similarly, Nigel Llewellyn has demonstrated that in Tudor and Stuart England, funerary portraits served as imaginative holding vessels for the monarch's political body until the investiture of his successor.

Whether focused on its subject's visible body, or symbolizing invisible character, the study of Dutch portraiture has been directed by this trope of realism. It has barely moved beyond the paradigm established by Van Mander: Portraits are praised for their realism (painted "but as if their subject were alive"), examined for attribution, and annotated with a sketch of the sitter's biography. While the ostensible subject of investigations has changed in the twentieth century, these terms—or rather their inversion—continue to direct modern research. Portraiture's "realism" has been replaced by iconographic studies of portraits' rich symbolic content, and sitter's biographies have been supplemented by investigations of the conscious manipulation of these symbol systems in the fashioning of public images of self. Research in these areas has produced a wealth of important data. Eddy de Jongh's investigations of the iconographic codes employed by Dutch portraiture—most recently in an exhibition of 1986—and research in the Amsterdam archives by archivists I.H. van Eeghen and S.A.C. Dudok van Heel identifying sitters to Rembrandt and others are invaluable. In turn, H. Perry Chapman, Hans-Joachim Raupp, David Smith, and others have used this type of data to study the self-fashioning of Dutch artists and sitters. (Examples of the work of individual artists and their respective contributions to portraiture in these areas will be found in the bibliography cited at the end of this and related topics.)

An area that to date remains underinvestigated, however, is the psychological impact of the portrait on the individual viewer and the broader material and imaginative functions of the portrait in the culture at large. While the portrait as a subject has long been disparaged for its simplicity—ranking among the merely reproductive genres—in its production the portrait is, in fact, the most complex, for it potentially involves more individuals than any other: not only the artist and the patron, but also the sitter and the viewer. For each of these individuals, the portrait may be described as a site that structures meaning in two reciprocal areas. First, portraits endow individuals and groups with general qualities and distinctive features. Second, in doing so they help create the frames through which are understood and valued both concepts of identity for the individual and definitions of social relations within the culture. Portraits establish these frames by calling upon—and, in the process, structuring and restructuring—ideas or meanings in three areas: the sitter's perceived character and personal history, contemporary social structures and cultural issues, and the visual tradition. The portrait participates, then, in setting the terms through which perceptions about the individual are produced, in shaping the cultural discourses through which they are understood, and in defining the devices of, and associations with, the visual tradition through which they are presented.

Portraiture in the Netherlands flowered in a period and society in which ideas about what constitutes the individual were undergoing rapid and profound transformation. By the end of the seventeenth century, identity itself was being questioned: Was there a core component of an individual that remained constant throughout his or her life, or did the individual change from moment to moment with each new experience? If aspects of an individual remained the same even when the body changed, how was this to be conveyed in portraiture?

Late fifteenth- and sixteenth-century portraits frequently depict individuals praying, visually situated beside deceased ancestors on commemorative altarpieces. By the late sixteenth century, individuals are more frequently depicted in secular settings surrounded by members of their nuclear family. The shift may tell us less about changes in the affective family unit than about a changed function of the portrait, particularly for individuals who may not have been able to trace their lineages very far. Identity of these seventeenth-century sitters seems to be derived less from ancestors than from living relatives. As urban civic institutions began to replace the power of the landed aristocracy, individuals also began to commission portraits of themselves with fellow members: guild deacons, regents of charitable institutions, and shooting companies, for example. Some of these portraits, however, constitute what appear to be arbitrary subgroups of these institutions, suggesting that their imaginative function hovers somewhere between representations of the public institution and a private friendship portrait.

But it was in the area of the more direct representation of character that the Dutch portrait underwent the greatest change and demonstrated the largest variety. Character could be represented typologically, as in the history portrait. It might be represented symbolically, as in the sixteenth-century portrait of the banker, merchant, and humanist *Pompeius Occo* (ca. 1531; Amsterdam, Rijksmuseum) by the Amsterdam artist Dirck Jacobsz. Here the sitter's left hand rests on a skull while his right holds a flower, a pink, both traditional symbols of the transitoriness of life and resurrection and, by extension, the Christian contemplation of the sitter upon eternal life. Or it could be represented through an individual's contemporary activities. In what has come to be known as the

genre portrait, later the conversation piece, Dutch men, women, and children are represented in contemporary settings and in activities ranging from work, social service, and leisure to religion. This portrait genre first appeared toward the end of the 1620s in paintings by Thomas de Keyser and Pieter Codde, among others. De Keyser's portrait of *Constantijn Huygens and His Clerk* (1627; London, National Gallery; Fig. 99), for example, shows the secretary to Prince Frederik Hendrik in a study, seated at a desk on which lie a quill, inkpot, and paper that remind the viewer that Huygens translated Donne into Dutch and was a prodigious correspondent. The plans before him suggest plans for the prince's palace or a military campaign, on both of which he advised. He had played the chitarrone, or lute, in a command performance for King James I. On the wall in the background are a tapestry, apparently representing the Sultan of Egypt converting to Christianity, an allusion perhaps to his ambassadorial training, and a seascape by Jan Porcellis, referring no doubt to his collecting and early appreciation for the art of his contemporaries. Each of these and other iconographic referents suggest that his identity could be represented by his activities in the secular world. In their representation, such activities were being validated for both the sitter and viewer.

Character was even inscribed on the body itself in conventions that ranged from idealization by such artists as Gerard van Honthorst, Nicolaes Maes, or Caspar Netscher—who reflected the virtue and purity of the soul in a flawless body—to the close descriptions of such artists as Frans Hals and at times Rembrandt, in which the body is examined in minute detail for its individuality and very human deviations from idealized norms. Finally, motion—and immobility—were employed to depict character. As the urban middle class began to supplant the landed aristocracy in economic and political power, particularly after 1609, the year that the Twelve-Year's Truce was called in the War with Spain, they adopted in their portraits many of the conventions that had come to be associated with portraits of monarchs and aristocrats: the full-length or three-quarter-length life-size format, the static pose, and the impassive facial expression associated with the characterological ideal of neo-Stoicism.

A more complex issue in the study of portraiture is the psychological impact such images might have had on their viewers. Investigations of seventeenth-century beliefs about portraiture, using as a guide the language of twentieth-century object-relations theory, may prove fruitful.

Ann Jensen Adams

See also Active life, active virtues; Contemplative life, contemplative virtues; Conversation piece; Court and official portraiture; Donor portraits; Group portraiture; Hals, Frans; History portraits; Last Judgment; Marriage and family portraits; Monuments to artists; Pastoral; Rembrandt van Rijn; Roman history; Sculpture (1400–1550); Sculpture (1550–1795); Sculpture (1795–1945); Self-portraiture; Subjects, subject categories, and hierarchies; Tomb sculpture: early modern and later sepulchral art; Tomb sculpture: medieval effigial monuments; Van Honthorst, Gerard; Van Mander, Karel

Bibliography

Adams, Ann Jensen. *Portraiture and the Production of Identity.* Cambridge: Cambridge University Press. Forthcoming.

Blasse-Hegeman, H., E. Domela Nieuwenhuis, R.E.O. Ekkart et al., eds. *Nederlandse Portretten. Leidse Kunsthistorisch Jaarboek* 8. The Hague: SDU, 1990.

Campbell, Lorne. *Renaissance Portraits.* New Haven: Yale University Press, 1990.

Chapman, H. Perry. *Rembrandt's Self-Portraits: A Study in Seventeenth-Century Identity.* Princeton, NJ: Princeton University Press, 1990.

Drie Eeuwen Portret in Nederland. Amsterdam: Rijksmuseum, 1952.

Ekkart, R.E.O. "Painted Immortality: Portraits in the Mauritshuis." In *The Royal Picture Gallery, Mauritshuis,* 81–91. New York: Harry N. Abrams, 1985.

Grijzenhout, Frans, and Carel van Tuyll van Serooskerken, eds. *Edele eenvoud: Neo-Classicisme in Nederland 1765–1800.* Zwolle: Waanders, 1989.

Jongh, E. de. *Portretten van echt en trouw: Huwelijk en gezin in de Nederlandse kunst van de zeventiende eeuw.* Haarlem: Frans Hals Museum; Zwolle: Waanders, 1986.

Llewellyn, Nigel. *The Art of Death: Visual Culture in the English Death Ritual ca. 1500–1800.* London: Victoria and Albert Museum in association with Reaktion Books, 1991.

Marin, Louis. *Portrait of the King.* Translated by Martha Houle. Minneapolis, MN: University of Minnesota Press, 1988.

Marius, G.H. *Dutch Painters of the Nineteenth Century.* Edited by G. Norman. Woodbridge, Suffolk: Antique Collectors Club, 1973.

Raupp, Hans-Joachim. *Unterschungen zu Kunstlerbildnis und Kunstlerdarstellungen in den Niederlanden im 17. Jahrhundert.* Hildesheim: Georg Olms Verlag, 1984.

Schwartz, Frederic. "'The Motions of the Countenance': Rembrandt's Early Portraits and the 'Tronie.'" *RES* 17/18 (1989): 89–116.

Smith, David. *Masks of Wedlock: Seventeenth-Century Dutch Marriage Portraiture.* Ann Arbor MI: UMI Research Press, 1982.

Vries, A.B. de. *Het noord-nederlandsch portret in de tweede helft van de 16de eeuw.* Amsterdam: Enum, 1934.

Wassenbergh, A. *De Portretkunst in Friesland in de zeventiende eeuw.* Lochem: De Tijdstroom, 1967.

Wilson, William H. *Dutch Seventeenth-Century Portraiture: The Golden Age.* Sarasota, FL: John and Mable Ringling Museum of Art, 1980.

Post, Pieter (1608–1669)

Pieter Post was one of the most important classicist architects in the middle of the seventeenth century. Like his brother Frans Post, he began his artistic career as a painter in Haarlem. Known to be by him are some landscapes and battle scenes from the 1630s. After around 1635 he also worked as a draftsman for the building projects of Jacob van Campen in The Hague—the Mauritshuis and the house of Constantijn Huygens. He was active as an independent architect after 1639 (designs for the country house Vredenburg on the Beemster polder). Moreover, he was supervisor in 1640 of the large-scale renovation, designed by Jacob van Campen, of the Oude Hof (Noordeinde Palace) in The Hague. In 1645, following his appointment as court architect and in that capacity, he drafted the plan for enlarging the Huis Honselaarsdijk (demolished at the beginning of the nineteenth century) for Prince Frederik Hendrik. His master work he designed in 1645 for Princess Amalia van Solms: the Huis ten Bosch (The Hague) with a cross-shaped central hall, the Oranjezaal. However, Post had no direct influence over the decoration of the Oranjezaal with its well-known cycle of paintings honoring Frederik Hendrik; the program and coordination of the painters were in the hands of Van Campen and Constantijn Huygens.

Post also worked for various administrative bodies, such as the Great Water Board of Rhineland (Hoogheemraadschap van Rijnland) surveyors of the dikes, and the States of Holland. For the Rhineland he designed Huis Swanenburg in Halfweg (1645) and for Holland the new States Hall in the Binnenhof in The Hague (1652). In addition to palaces, government buildings, and representative residences, he also made designs for purely utilitarian buildings, such as the States General's gunpowder magazine in Delft (1662), the cannon foundry in The Hague (1665; destroyed 1945), and some austere but impressive village churches (for example, Woubrugge, 1652; and Moerkapelle, 1664). While Post initially excelled in the right application of the classical orders after Italian example, he changed to working with increasingly restrained and taut façade planes after the middle of the century. With plastic sculptural details like cartouches, acanthus leaves, *putti*, and coats of arms, he could still give something like a proper accent. In these sober brick blocks of cubic simplicity, the ideal of classicism finds direct expression; the essence of beauty lies always in the carefully considered proportions of the building, not in the ornamentation.

K.A. Ottenheym

See also Classicism in architecture; House of Orange-Nassau; Huygens, Constantijn; Leiden; Van Campen, Jacob

Bibliography

Terwen, J.J., and K.A. Ottenheym. *Pieter Post, 1608–1669: Architect.* Zutphen: Walburg, 1993. (English summary).

Postage stamps

No form of art is distributed on a larger scale than postage stamps. An example of this is a stamp designed by Peter Struycken that between 1981 and 1991 sold no less than one billion copies. The wide dissemination of this special type of graphic art makes its artistic, technical, and commercial history well worth studying.

Many Dutch artists have designed stamps. The first

Dutch stamp dates from 1852 and was based on a portrait of King Willem III by the then popular painter J.W. Pieneman. During the second half of the nineteenth century, stamps produced in the Netherlands were not noticeably different from those in other countries; the designs followed the traditional forms used for coins and medals. The first remarkable stamp was in 1906, designed by Antoon Derkinderen. It was an isolated issue, and the initiative came from outside the Dutch Post Office (PTT), from a society against tuberculosis.

Nevertheless, the success of this stamp made the PTT strive for better designs. In 1920 a contest was organized and ninety designs were submitted. The jury was disappointed by the results, and the first and second prizes were not awarded. However, the PTT, the public, and the artists had become aware of the specific problems surrounding this type of graphic design. In following years, the PTT tried to establish an artistic policy, although at first there was no clear direction. Two stamps by Jan Toorop in 1922 were attractive designs but rather old-fashioned. More modern were the photomontages by Piet Zwart in 1931 and M.C. Escher in 1935 (Fig. 100). The painter Pyke Koch designed stamps in the 1930s, among them a series with ancient Germanic symbols, issued under the German occupation. In the decade after 1945, consistently excellent designs for stamps were made by artists like Paul Citroen (1949) and Theo Kurpershoek (1953).

Great changes took place after 1960. Production techniques had until then restricted the designers and had required great skills from engravers. New printing techniques, such as offset, brought greater freedom. For the series of children's stamps (a yearly showpiece of the PTT), children's drawings were used more than once (1965, 1976, 1988). For this series, illustrators of children's books were also asked, like Wim Bijmoer (1967) and Dik Bruna (1969). Most remarkable—and humorous—were the cartoons by Joost Swarte in 1984. Other acclaimed designs were made by the Centrum voor Cubische Constructies (Center for Cubist Constructions; the architects William Graatsma and Jan Slothouber) in 1970. The computer designs made the same year by R.D.E. Oxenaar also opened new perspectives.

The greatest test for a designer are the everyday stamps. These have to be simple, yet they require a character of their own, such as can be seen in the series by Wim Crouwel that has been in use since 1976. The stamps designed by Peter Struycken—like the one that sold one billion copies—are another example. In recent years, the PTT has commissioned designs from foreign artists, which is quite unusual since most national post offices do not step outside the boundaries of their country.

The iconography of Dutch stamps is not very complicated. For more than a century they glorified the country and people of the Netherlands, usually depicting great men or important events of the national past. These are still the principal topics, although new themes and images are appearing. The children's stamps issued in 1985 were a warning against the dangers of traffic. The environment and pollution became the topics in a series of stamps made by Jaap Drupsteen in 1991.

The artistic policy of the PTT is at the moment progressive and adventurous, especially when compared to that of other countries. Stamps are now widely regarded as a form of art. There is a PTT Museum at Zeestraat 28 in The Hague. That until recently the designs should have come from the mainstream of Dutch art is understandable. Revolutionary artists have seldom been asked to contribute. A telling detail is that only in 1988 were stamps issued with works by Karel Appel, Corneille, and Constant; however, only already existing paintings by these founders of the Cobra Movement were reproduced. For that reason, these stamps are as traditional as ones on which works by Rembrandt (1930, 1956), Frans Hals (1962) or Van Gogh (1990) were used.

The development of Dutch stamps since 1965 has become increasingly influenced by commercial interests: The stamps must be sold. This influence is mainly positive: Stamps have to be attractive in order to counterbalance the use of postage meters and franking privileges. The PTT has taken more account of the wishes of stamp collectors both inside and outside the Netherlands. The PTT, which until 1994 was a state-owned institution, is now a private company, and the need for best-selling stamps is greater than ever. One can only speculate what effects this will have on this flourishing form of graphic art.

Rudolf Dekker

See also Graphic design

Bibliography

Boeraad, H.C., and P.H. Hefting, eds. *The Boundaries of the Postage Stamp: Marketing, Management, and Design.* Maastricht: Jan van Eyck Academie, Design Department; Amsterdam: De Balie, 1993.

Hefting, P.H. *Royal PTT Nederland NV: Art and Design, Past and Present: A Guide.* The Hague: Koninklijke PTT Nederland NV, 1990.

Moor, Christiaan de. *Postzegelkunst: De vormgeving van de Nederlandse postzegel.* The Hague: PTT Post, 1960.

Pro-fil: Informatieblad van PTT Post B.V. over nieuwe postzegeluitgiften en filatelistische onderwerpen. The Hague: PTT Post, 1989–. (Previously published as *Profil: Mededelingenblad van het Staatsbedrijf der PTT t.b.v. belangstellenden in de filatelie.* The Hague: PTT Post, 1975–1989.)

Postmodernism

Postmodernism in architecture is no new twentieth-century style, but a word to describe a new view of architecture and a new attitude. It means in general the rejection of the ideals of the Modern Movement, or what is supposedly built in its name. Postmodernism is less a movement than a—rather vague—concept, and that is perhaps why the word has encouraged so many minds to search for explanations and meanings.

The word *postmodern* was coined in the United States and reached Europe, like everything else, shortly afterward, in the second half of the 1970s. In that time modern building had developed a certain stylistic monotony, which could be interpreted as the legacy of functionalistic doctrines of the Modern Movement. This movement of the 1920s had produced brilliant architecture in the often white geometrical style of architects like Gerrit Rietveld (1888–1964; Color Plate 12), J.B. van Loghem (1881–1940), and Johannes Duiker (1890–1935; Fig. 46), but it had also paved the way for the austere functionalism of a lot of public housing and urban developments in the 1950s and 1960s. In spite of the sometimes well-ordered urban space, like Pendrecht in Rotterdam (1949–1952), designed by Charlotte Stam-Beese, the buildings themselves do look somewhat dull and uniform. One of the doctrines of the Modern Movement had been that the form of a building should be the result of functional solutions. A beautifully designed exterior should never be an aim in itself, because that was rejected as decadent aestheticism. Not all architects of the Modern Movement believed in those kinds of doctrines, but the austere moralism seemed to take root in the postwar reconstruction of the Netherlands.

Postmodern expresses the feeling that the well-meant moralism had to be overcome, because it had led to uninspired, monotonous buildings. Architects should be freed from moral restrictions and should be allowed to mock conventions in architecture. They may again use ornament—something that had been strictly forbidden by architect Adolf Loos (1870–1933) in the beginning of the twentieth century—and they may again draw from historical architecture, an offense of the highest order, according to the doctrines of the Modern Movement. Postmodern architects are no longer looking for eternal truths; they design for commercial clients. They are no longer led by their social conscience, but by trends and their own, now utterly free, creativity. This freedom produces buildings that look unfinished as if to ridicule the unfounded seriousness of the so-called high art of architecture. A fine example is the façade of the LOKV Building (Institute for Artistic Education) on the Ganzenmarkt in Utrecht by Mart van Schijndel (1984). The two pillars in the center of the façade, which under normal conditions ought to carry its weight, miss their upper-halves, so that the façade seems to soar. Other architects display an almost childish pleasure in playing with commonplace elements and banal associations. They might have been influenced by the ideas of the American architect Robert Venturi. One of them is Sjoerd Soeters. The roof of his Circus Theater in Zantvoort (1991) resembles circus tents, and the façade is partly built in the form of the streaming national flag of the Netherlands, including the white flagpole with the orange nob.

These examples illustrate the Postmodern attitude. It ridicules the codes of modernist architecture, ignores clarity in design, evades functionalism or social objectives. This attitude produces architecture of spectacle and surface glitter, architecture that is colorful and theatrical. Postmodern architecture is no longer the serious and autonomous profession based on the rigid morality of rationalistic and honest design; rather it has became commercialized and begun to cultivate glamour and luxury. Understandably, this has provoked opposition from people who had always believed in the right course of the Modern Movement, and who were shocked to see that architects were merely interested in outward appearances—or worse, in "cheap" design for the representativeness of the establishment. The German philosopher J. Habermas was the most eloquent opponent, but his influence in the world of architecture is limited.

Wim Denslagen

See also Art criticism, critical issues in the twentieth century; Artists' initiatives; Contemporary art; Functionalism in architecture; Photography, modern and contemporary; Public housing; Urban planning, from 1750 to the present

Bibliography
Graafland, Arie, ed. *De bevrijding van de moderne beweging: Een dialoog met de modernen.* Nijmegen: SUN, 1988.
"Postmodernisme: Het woord en zijn wankele betekenissen." Theme Volume. *Wonen/TABK* 6/7 (1985).

Pothoven, Hendrik (1726–1807)

Hendrik Pothoven, born in Amsterdam, became a student of the engraver Frans de Bakker at a young age. He afterward took lessons from Philip van Dijk, The Hague portrait, genre, and history painter. In the winters he stayed with his parents in Amsterdam, while he spent his summers with his teacher in The Hague. Around 1777 he would settle in The Hague permanently. Pothoven, who was a painter and a draftsman as well as a mezzotint engraver, made mainly portraits and conversation pieces. He excelled in rendering the material of the clothing of the persons he portrayed. After the death of Tibout Regters in 1768, he was one of the painters most in demand for conversation pieces. The portraits he made in The Hague are generally more powerful and more elegant, possibly because he was under the influence of a more French-oriented taste there. Figure studies for a great number of these paintings have been saved. In addition to portraits, Pothoven is known to have executed a pair of townscapes (of The Hague and Amsterdam) and a single interior (of the Ridderzaal [Knights' Hall] in The Hague). Moreover, he also drew numerous copies after paintings by seventeenth-century masters such as Frans Hals, Rembrandt, Jan Steen, and Bartholomeus van der Helst. From archival sources, it also appears that he took over the candle-making business of his father-in-law in 1777.

Charles Dumas

See also Architectural painting; Conversation piece; Genre painting, eighteenth century; Portraiture; Regters, Tibout; Townscapes

Bibliography
Dumas, Charles. *Haagse stadsgezichten 1550–1800: Topografische schilderijen van het Haags Historisch Museum,* 581–592. Zwolle: Waanders, 1991.
Rijdt, R.J.A. te. "Figuurstudies door Hendrik Pothoven." *Leids Kunsthistorisch Jaarboek* 8 (1989): 345–367.
Staring, A. *De Hollanders thuis.* The Hague: Nijhoff, 1956.

Potter, Paulus (1625–1654)

Best known for his monumental painting *The Bull* (1647) in the Mauritshuis in The Hague, Paulus Potter is better represented by his numerous carefully composed and delicately rendered cabinet paintings of cattle and rustic farm scenes. He was also an adept draftsman and etcher.

Paulus Potter was baptized in Enkhuizen on November 20, 1625, the son of Pieter Symonsz. Potter (1597/1600–1652) and Aechtie Pouwels. Bartsius. By May 1628, Potter lived in Leiden, where his father later became a headman of the glassmakers' guild and Paulus enrolled in the university. Pieter Potter turned to painting, producing still lifes, guardroom scenes, historical subjects, and landscapes. In late 1631, the family moved to Amsterdam. Paulus Potter was trained as a history painter, probably initially by his father. Early paintings, such as *Christ and the Woman of Samaria* (1641) and *Abraham's Return* (1642), show the influence of works by Claes Cornelisz. Moeyaert, with whom Pieter Potter was probably acquainted. In 1642 Paulus Potter became a student of the Haarlem history painter Jacob de Wet.

Potter's earliest rustic scenes of cattle in open landscapes and in farmyards date from 1643. The new naturalism in these works was inspired by contact with the work of Claes Bleker but ultimately depended on Pieter van Laer's paintings, especially his print series of animals (1636). In his mature paintings, such as *Cattle Going Out to the Fields* (1647), Potter, like Van Laer, placed animals at strategic points to direct the viewer through the composition. Animals partially hidden by a door jamb, or elsewhere by a hill, imply the continuation of space beyond the foreground. Light reflects off the ground onto the underbelly of a cow, as well as through the animal's translucent ears and along the brim of the farmer's hat.

Paulus Potter registered as a master painter in the painters' guild of Delft in 1646. The following year he produced the life-size painting *The Bull* in which cattle and sheep pose before a distant landscape. Potter's realistic description of the texture of the animals and the flies buzzing around the bull were a *tour de force* for a young artist and created a sensation when the painting was captured by the French and hung in the Louvre from 1795 until 1815.

In 1649 Potter joined the guild in The Hague, where he lived in a house owned by Jan van Goyen. The following year he married Adriana van Balckeneynde, the daughter of a court builder who lived next door. Potter's paintings became more elegant and often included horses, at times isolated as if a portrait, such as the *Gray Horse* (1653). In the *Great Farm* (1649) and the *Reflected Cow* (1648) sophisticated visitors pass a farmyard where farmers and cattle lead seemingly peaceful lives. Potter had sophisticated patrons; Arnold Houbraken noted in *De Groote Schouburgh* (1718–1721) that Potter painted the *Great Farm* for Amalia van Solms, wife of the *stadholder* Frederik Hendrik, who rejected it because of the prominent portrayal of a urinating cow. Houbraken also noted that Potter was often visited by Johan Maurits van Nassau, the Dutch governor of Brazil, and was convinced by Dr. Nicolaes Tulp, the surgeon portrayed in Rembrandt's anatomy lesson group portrait of 1632, to return to Amsterdam to paint.

In 1652 Potter moved to Amsterdam, where he died at the age of twenty-eight in 1654, the date of his elegant portrait by Bartholomeus van der Helst (The Hague, Mauritshuis). Potter's cabinet paintings influenced Karel du Jardin and Adriaen van de Velde, as well as Albert Klomp (ca. 1618–1688?). Shortly after Potter's death, Marcus de Bie used his drawings for series of etchings of animals, in some cases completing the series with his own designs. Potter's great popularity during the late eighteenth and nineteenth centuries resulted in numerous copies and imitations by both Dutch and foreign artists.

Amy L. Walsh

See also Animal painting; House of Orange-Nassau; Landscape; Rural life and views; State and municipal art collecting and collections

Bibliography

Bredius, Abraham. "Pieter Symonsz. Potter: Glaseschrijver, ooc schilder." *Oud Holland* 11 (1893): 34–46.

Walsh, Amy L. "Paulus Potter: His Works and Their Meaning." Ph.D. diss., Columbia University, 1985.

Walsh, Amy, Edwin Buijsen, and Ben Broos. *Paulus Potter: Paintings, Drawings, and Etchings.* Zwolle: Waanders, 1994.

Westrheene, T. van. *Paulus Potter: Sa vie et ses oeuvres.* The Hague: Nijhoff, 1867.

Pre-Rembrandtists

The term is used to describe artists, specializing in the painting of history subjects, who lived and worked in Amsterdam in the early decades of the seventeenth century. Rembrandt's teacher, Pieter Lastman (ca. 1583–1633), was the undisputed leader of this group, which included Claes Cornelisz. Moeyaert (1590/1591–1655); Jan Tengnagel (1584/1585–1635); Jan (ca. 1583–1631) and Jacob Pynas (ca. 1585–ca. 1656); and François Venant (1590/1591–1636). Moyses van Wtenbrouck (ca. 1590–ca. 1647), who worked in The Hague, also followed the stylistic and iconographic features associated with the Pre-Rembrandtists. With the exception of Venant, the Pre-Rembrandtists were Roman Catholics, which may partly explain their travels for artistic study to Italy, where they were influenced by the art of Adam Elsheimer and Paul Bril.

As a group, these artists preferred dramatic scenes from the Old and New Testaments, classical sources, mythology, and contemporary literature. Pivotal episodes of recognition and revelation, miracles and sacrifice, meetings and departures, in which dialogue figures prominently, were favored. In addition to representing narrative imagery derived from well-established themes, such as the New Testament subject matter of Christ's life and Passion, the Pre-Rembrandtists were also innovators in depicting unusual subjects, especially less familiar stories from abstruse classical texts and the Old Testament.

These little-known scenes appear in the work of Pieter Lastman, the group's foremost artist. Inspired by sixteenth- and seventeenth-century Bible illustrations by Lucas van Leyden, Maerten van Heemskerck, Matthäus Merian, and

Tobias Stimmer, Lastman depicted Old Testament narratives, such as the dramatic encounter between the angel and the ass in the Genesis account of Balaam (*Balaam and the Ass*, 1622) or the meeting of David and Uriah (1611 and 1619), which had not previously appeared in paintings. Lastman imparted this interest in unusual themes to his student, Rembrandt, who continued to paint uncommon biblical, classical, and historical subject matter well into the mid-seventeenth century.

For the Pre-Rembrandtists, both the choice and the interpretation of much of their subject matter depended on a precise reading of a literary source. By closely following a text, the Pre-Rembrandtists strove for iconographic and narrative clarity in the pictorial content of their art. According to Astrid and Christian Tümpel, this approach to history painting is particularly evident in the Pre-Rembrandtists' treatment of religious subject matter from the Old Testament, for which iconographic and stylistic solutions had not already been established in medieval and Renaissance altarpieces. Paradoxically, for their treatment of these unusual Old Testament subjects, the Roman Catholic Pre-Rembrandtists consulted biblical sources that reflected the changes brought about by sixteenth-century Protestant Reformers, such as John Calvin and Martin Luther. These illustrated texts emphasized the literal and historical significance of biblical stories, rather than typological or allegorical meaning, which had been the focus in the Middle Ages. The new Protestant emphasis on the literal explication of the text led to an increase in Bible illustrations that were sequential, narrative, and theatrical. These biblical depictions eventually influenced the Pre-Rembrandtists in their representations of Old Testament themes, in particular.

In pictorial terms, the paintings of the Pre-Rembrandtists are active, engaging scenes that take place in a historical context. In Lastman's version of *Paul and Barnabas at Lystra* (1614; Fig. 76), figures are arranged in the foreground, parallel to the picture, with attention given to easily understood expressions and gestures. Numerous attributes of place and time identify the characters and the specific historical episode. Settings are thoroughly delineated with architectural and landscape details that establish a convincing historical backdrop. These settings were inspired, in part, by the firsthand experiences of the Pre-Rembrandtists in Italy as well as by the popular textual source of historical authenticity, *The Antiquities of the Jews* by the Jewish historian Flavius Josephus.

Despite this attention to exhaustive detail, iconographic confusion sometimes arises when interpreting Pre-Rembrandtists' works. Since the Pre-Rembrandtists would often isolate a particularly dramatic episode from a story, which was not necessarily the most obvious or comprehensible one, and then infuse narrative features that precede and/or follow the depicted scene, the primary subject matter could be lost in a profusion of particulars. By returning to the literary source of the pictorial content, however, the subject matter can usually be established.

Scholarly interest in the Pre-Rembrandtists as a distinct group of history painters is a relatively modern development in Dutch art history. Early monographic studies on the leading painters of the movement date to the early twentieth century;

however, more specific analyses of style and iconography did not appear until the pioneering works of Christian and Astrid Tümpel in the 1970s. Astrid Tümpel has prepared *catalogues raisonnés* on both Pieter Lastman and Claes Cornelisz. Moeyaert. Her husband, Christian Tümpel, an art historian and theologian, has published extensively on interpretative issues regarding the Pre-Rembrandtists and their influence on Rembrandt. The Tümpels were instrumental in arranging the first exhibition dedicated to the works of Pieter Lastman at the Museum Het Rembrandthuis in Amsterdam held concurrently with the Rembrandt exhibition at the Rijksmuseum in Amsterdam in 1992. Although much of the stylistic and iconographic groundwork has been realized, research on issues of patronage and denominational iconographic decisions remains to be conducted. Future studies of the Pre-Rembrandtists' relationship with artistic predecessors, especially the importance of Italian art, could balance the present emphasis placed on their role as forerunners of seventeenth-century history painting and specifically the art of Rembrandt.

Valerie Lind Hedquist

See also Dordrecht; History painting; Italy; Literature, poetry: analogues with the visual; Prints, early printed book and Bible illustration; Religion of artists; Rembrandt van Rijn; Roman history; Writers on art, sixteenth and seventeenth centuries

Bibliography

Blankert, Albert et al. *Gods, Saints, and Heroes: Dutch Painting in the Age of Rembrandt.* Washington, DC: National Gallery of Art, 1980.

Broos, B.P.J. "Rembrandt and Lastman's Coriolanus: The History Piece in Seventeenth-Century Theory and Practice." *Simiolus* 8 (1975/1976): 199–228.

———. "Rembrandt en zijn eeuwige leermeester Lastman." *Kroniek van het Rembrandthuis* 3 (1972): 76–96.

Stechow, Wolfgang. "Some Observations on Rembrandt and Lastman." *Oud Holland* 84 (1969): 148–162.

Tümpel, Astrid. "Claes Cornelisz. Moeyaert Katalog der Gemälde." *Oud Holland* 88 (1974): 1–163, 245–290.

Tümpel, Astrid, and Peter Schatborn. *Pieter Lastman: Leermeester van Rembrandt.* Amsterdam: Rembrandthuis; Zwolle: Waanders, 1991.

Tümpel, Astrid, and Christian Tümpel. *The Pre-Rembrandtists.* Sacramento: E.B. Crocker Art Gallery, 1974.

Prints, collecting

The sixteenth and the seventeenth centuries were the flourishing periods of the Dutch art of printmaking. Thanks to a division of labor that became common around 1550, the art was practiced on a professional level. The designer made a drawing, the professional engraver made a print, and the print publisher took care of the production and the sales. The print publishers, who made larger editions than in the past, provided for the dissemination of Dutch prints throughout Europe. In this way they strongly promoted the collecting of prints.

Prints were sold as singles or in series. This was done on the street, in bookstores, or at auctions. They were also offered in the form of bound albums. Collectors hung prints on the wall, glued them in scrapbooks (which were often luxuriously appointed), or saved them in portfolios or in chests of drawers that were especially made for this purpose. Originally the prints were collected and saved according to subject rather than the name of the artist. This is clear from the requirements for an "ideal print collection" according to Samuel Quicchelberg (1565). He considered a collection of prints as an encyclopedia of the visible world. Print collections of the late sixteenth and early seventeenth centuries, like those belonging to the Spanish King Philip II in the Escorial; to Ferdinand, archduke of Tyrol, in Schloss Ambras; to the Amsterdam painter and art dealer Jan Basse de Oudere; and to the Amsterdam regent Michiel Hinloopen, were all organized by subject. This is also true for biblical print books, which were brought onto the market by the print publishers. Examples are the *Thesauris veteris testamenti* (1585) by Gerard de Jode, the *Theatrum biblicum* (1643) by Claes Jansz. Visscher, and the *Grooten Figuer-Bibel* (1646) by Jan Philipsz. Schabaelje. The few preserved print albums compiled by private collectors, like the "Heemskerck album" in the Rijksprentenkabinet in Amsterdam (ca. 1572), are based on the same principle. After the seventeenth century, prints were more often organized by the name of the artist. Before this, it happened only when the artist was extremely famous, as was Albrecht Dürer, whose works were placed in separate albums in the collection of Archduke Ferdinand of Tyrol.

As early as the middle of the sixteenth century, Dutch prints were known all over Europe. Giorgio Vasari, for example, describes in his *Lives* (*Le Vite de' più eccellenti Architetti, Pittori, et Scultori Italiani . . .*, 1568) a great number of prints by Maerten van Heemskerck, which were apparently circulated in Italy shortly after being made. On the other hand, the import of Italian prints into the Netherlands introduced the style and subjects of the Italian Renaissance. In the seventeenth century, the etchings of Rembrandt (not his paintings) established his reputation in Italy. In this way prints were an important tool for the distribution of knowledge about national schools of painting. Especially in the Netherlands, prints played a role in the collecting and the distributing of knowledge about almost every possible subject. In addition, people collected prints because of their aesthetic pleasure and to be able to admire the different styles of painters and engravers. Existing works of art (paintings, statues, frescoes) were also reproduced in prints—graphic reproduction in the original sense of the word.

Not just *liefhebbers* (amateurs) collected prints but also artists. Rembrandt, for example, had a large collection of prints as a part of his *kunstkammer*, where every now and again he received inspiration for his own work. The inventory of his possessions that was made in 1656 counted thirty-four *kunstboeken* (art books): prints that were mainly saved by the name of the artist, but also by subject. They contained all sorts of prints from the sixteenth and seventeenth centuries and also Italian prints. Other artists, like Caspar Netscher and Gerard Ter Borch, had their students practice by copying prints.

In the second half of the seventeenth century the number of prints on the market increased considerably. Some collections focused on a specific subject—for example, portraits of famous persons from the past. Slowly they lost their function as an educative part of an encyclopedic *kunstkammer* and were collected more and more often because of their artistic value. Many print albums were organized chronologically, according to artist. Thanks to the many reproduction prints that conveyed artistic developments in pictures, such collections could function as an illustrated history of art.

Ilja M. Veldman

See also Amateurs, art academies, and art associations before the nineteenth century; Allegorical traditions; Atlas, atlases; Exotica; Humanism, humanist themes; Prints, printmaking, and printmakers (ca. 1500–ca. 1900)

Bibliography

Bruin, A. de et al. "Conservatie, restauratie en onderzoek van een zestiende-eeuw prentenboek." *Bulletin van het Rijksmuseum* 38 (1990): 173–214. (English summary).

Hajos, E.M. "The Concept of an Engravings Collection in the Year 1565: Quicchelberg, *Inscriptiones vel tituli theatri amplissimi*." *Art Bulletin* 40 1958: 151–156.

Parshall, P.W. "The Print Collection of Ferdinand, Archduke of Tyrol." *Jahrbuch der Kunsthistorischen Sammlungen in Wien* 78 (1982): 140–184.

Robinson, W.W. "This 'Passion for Prints': Collecting and Connoisseurship in Northern Europe during the Seventeenth Century." In *Printmaking in the Age of Rembrandt*. Edited by Clifford Ackley, xix–xlvii. Boston: Museum of Fine Arts, 1981.

Waals, J. van der. *De prentschat van Michiel Hinloopen: een reconstructie van de eerste openbare papierkunstverzameling in Nederland*. Amsterdam: Rijksmuseum; The Hague: SDU, 1988.

Prints, early printed book and Bible illustration

Until the seventeenth century, the business of Dutch book illustration—the adorning of books printed with moveable type with woodcuts or copper engravings—was mostly carried out in Antwerp, the center for book production in the Southern Netherlands. At this time Dutch book illustration was also greatly indebted to German examples. In the early years the printers in the North played an important role, however, and Dutch *incunabula* (books printed before 1500) are anything but primitively illustrated.

Printing started in Louvain (Leuven) and Utrecht in the Netherlands in 1473, some twenty years after it was invented in Germany. Before that time (but not before the invention of moveable type) unknown "proto-typographers" printed the blockbooks of the *Biblia Pauperum* (Poor Person's Bible, 1465), the *Canticum Canticorum* (Song of Songs, 1466), the *Ars Moriendi* (Art of Dying, 1464), and the *Speculum Humanae Salvationis* (Mirror of Human Salvation, 1467). In 1477 print shops were established in several important Northern cities: Delft, Gouda, and Deventer. Leiden and Zwolle followed in 1478; Haarlem, in 1483.

The first woodcut book illustrations to be produced in the Northern Netherlands, in 1480 in Utrecht, were designed for a *Fasciculus Temporum* ("a bundle of time," a history of the world) printed by Jan Veldener. In fact, these prints were additional illustrations to a series that Veldener had used in an earlier edition of the same work when he was still working in Louvain in the South. They were copied after the illustrations in a book printed in Lübeck, Germany, by Lucas Brandis in 1475. Veldener produced some more illustrated books in the early 1480s, but of greater importance was Gheraert Leeu in Gouda, who was, indeed, the most prolific Dutch printer of his time.

Leeu had started his business in 1477 and produced his first illustrated book in 1480: the *Dialogus Creaturarum*, a moralizing fable book adorned with 121 woodcuts. The book was an instant best-seller and went through nine editions in Latin and in the vernacular, including one in French that probably was meant for the Flemish *élite*. The woodcuts were soon copied by German and Swedish printers, and over a century later their compositions still stood as a model for a series of sixty-five etchings for Moermannus' *Apologi Creaturarum*, an emblem book printed in 1584 by Christopher Plantin for Gerard de Jode.

Other illustrated books published by Leeu in Gouda are the *Seven Wise Mannen* (Seven Wise Men from Rome, before 1482) and the *Gesta Romanorum* (1481). In 1482 Leeu printed a Passion book adorned with thirty-two woodcuts. The series was extended to sixty-eight for a *Devote Ghetiden* (Book of Hours) in 1484. Leeu had these illustrations copied from a series of engravings by the German master Israhel van Meckenem (ca. 1445–1503), who, in his turn, had copied the woodcuts from a vernacular *Speculum Humanae Salvationis* and an adaption of the *Legenda Aurea* (Golden Legend) printed by Lucas Brandis in Lübeck in 1475 and 1478. Trade between the two major German cities of Cologne and Lübeck and the Northern Netherlands was so very lively, in fact, that the Cologne printer Heinrich Quentel had published a lavishly illustrated Bible in 1479 in a dialect that was spoken also in the eastern part of the Netherlands; thus the Bible was certainly meant for a Dutch market.

Leeu's *Devote Ghetiden* illustrations were subsequently used in several religious books by Leeu himself as well as by other printers. In 1485 Leeu moved his press to Antwerp, where he extended the series with new, larger woodcuts to serve as illustrations to a Dutch adaption of Ludolphus de Saxonia's *Vita Christi* (1487). After Leeu's death in 1492 the blocks returned to the North, where Pieter van Os in Zwolle and the Collaciebroeders (Collacie Brothers) in Gouda used them in a Life of Christ and a Book of Hours in 1495 and 1496.

Meanwhile, printers like Jacob Bellaert in Haarlem, Christian Snellaert in Delft, and the Collaciebroeders in Gouda adorned their books with several new series of woodcuts illustrating both the Life of Christ (mostly belonging to the same tradition as Leeu's series) and various secular narra-

tives. Among these are the *Historie van Jason* and the *Historie van Troyen* (both by Bellaert, Haarlem, 1485), the *Scaecspul* (Jacobus de Cessolis' allegory on the game of chess, printed by Jacob van der Meer in Delft in 1483), *Godevaert van Boloen* (the history of Godefroy of Boulogne, by Gerard van Os, Gouda, 1485) and *Le Chevalier Délibéré* (Collaciebroeders, Gouda, 1489; Fig. 101).

All in all, the last two decades of the fifteenth century in the Northern Netherlands saw an important output of first-class book illustrations. However, Antwerp in the meantime had established itself as the paramount center of book production. In the first decades of the sixteenth century few illustrations appeared in the North, and printers made use of rather old blocks for their religious books, many of them reminiscent of Leeu's *Devote Ghetiden* woodcuts. The most important printers of these early years were Jan Seversz. in Leiden, Hugo Jansz. van Woerden in Leiden, and Richard Pafraet in Deventer.

Up to this point the names of the persons who designed and cut the woodcuts are not known. In the past, art historians like Max J. Friedländer were tempted to attribute them to known artists like the Master of the Virgin among Virgins. Nowadays, however, it seems altogether safer to refer to these artisans by the names with which William Martin Conway labeled them: the First, Second, and Third Gouda woodcutter, and the Haarlem woodcutter, who worked, respectively, on the *Dialogus Creaturarum*, the *Devote Ghetiden*, *Le Chevalier Délibéré*, and the *Historie van Jason*. Yet in some cases Conway's attribution of a large number of works to a single woodcutter remains doubtful. Further research is inevitable and will be greatly helped by the comprehensive *catalogue raisonné* of the Dutch woodcuts of the fifteenth century completed in 1994 by Ina Kok, the librarian of the Deventer Athenaeumbibliotheek (Athenaeum Library in Deventer).

The first well-known Dutch artist to contribute designs for book illustrations was the painter and engraver Lucas van Leyden (1494?–1533). Jan Seversz. used some of these in his *Missale Traiectense* (Utrecht missal) of 1516. In the early 1520s another important painter, Jacob Cornelisz. van Oostsanen (ca. 1472–1533), designed a great number of woodcuts meant almost exclusively to be book illustrations for the Amsterdam printer Doen Pietersz., one of the first printers in the city (active from 1518; printing started in 1512 in Amsterdam). Among the books illustrated with woodcuts by Jacob Cornelisz. van Oostsanen the most significant is the *Passio Domini Nostri*, a Passion book by the humanist priest Alardus Amstelredamus (1523). In 1530 the series was extended from sixty-eight to eighty in the *Stomme Passie* (the "mute" passion—that is, without text).

Thus, some good book illustrations were produced, mostly in Amsterdam in the post-*incunabula* period (1500–1540), faintly echoing the output of single-leaf woodcuts. In Deventer, Albert Pafraet (the successor to Richard Pafraet in that city) illustrated his New Testament of 1525 with four portraits of the Evangelists after Hans Holbein the Younger. Jan Swart (ca. 1500–1560), an Italianate artist from Groningen (the most northern city of the Netherlands), designed a series of seventy-five illustrations to the Old Testament (Fig.

102); however, these woodcuts were a commission from the Antwerp printer Willem Vorsterman, who published them in his Bible of 1528, the second complete Bible in Dutch. Swart's illustrations (some compositions going back to Quentel's Cologne Bible and the block book *Biblia Pauperum*) rank among the best produced, equaling Holbein's contemporary cuts for the *Icones* (which appeared as a book only as late as 1538 in Lyons).

From 1550 to 1570, Dutch book illustration dwindled as a result of the general decline of book production in this period. Altogether the output of illustrated books in the North was modest and their execution simple, while their size rarely went beyond *octavo*. Moreover, practically none of the illustrations were original. Peter Jansz. in Leiden printed the illustrations in a New Testament (1532) with blocks belonging to the Antwerp printer Willem Vorsterman (including twenty-one Apocalypse illustrations after Holbein). Peter Warnersen in Kampen illustrated a Life of Christ (1565) with copies after the one hundred eighty-six woodcuts by Lieven de Witte (ca. 1503–after February 1578) from Ghent, which, since 1537, had appeared in various books and Bibles by Mattheus Crom in Antwerp, and were subsequently copied extensively by several other Antwerp printers. And Harmen Jansz. Muller in Amsterdam published Ovid's *Metamorphoses* in Dutch (1588), with woodcuts based on German copies after the illustrations by the Lyons artist Bernard Salomon.

A new impulse came from Christopher Plantin, who in 1583 opened a branch of his firm in Leiden, where he became printer to the university; the business was continued by his son-in-law Franciscus van Raphelingen until 1597. Plantin himself stayed only two years before returning to Antwerp, but during this period he published thirty books, including the combined *Emblemata* of Joan Sambucus and Hadrianus Junius (first editions: Antwerp, 1564–1565), with numerous woodcuts by Plantin's regular illustrators Geoffroy Ballain and Pieter Huys; and *Recht Ghebruyck ende Misbruyck van Tydlycke Have* (Right Use and Abuse of Temporal Goods, 1585) by the Dutch humanist Dirck Volkertsz. Coornhert, with twenty-five copper engravings by the Antwerp artist Jan Wierix.

One of the most remarkable productions of the Leiden period was the *Imagines et Figurae Bibliorum*, a picture Bible containing one hundred etchings by Pieter van der Borch (1545–1608) from Malines (Mechelen) with texts by Plantin's friend, the self-styled prophet Hiël (Hendrik Jansen Barrefelt), printed under a false name and address. The copper plates were used again and again in the seventeenth century in picture Bibles printed in Amsterdam by Claes Jansz. Visscher and others, and finally in 1717 by Izaak Enschedé in Haarlem. By this time, copper engravings and etchings, which had far greater artistic and painterly possibilities than the woodcut, had definitively started replacing the woodcut in book illustration. During his short time in Leiden, Plantin, who had made use of engravings in books ever since his polyglot Bible of 1568–1573, played an important role in the revival of book illustration in the North.

After 1578, when the Northern provinces became Protestant, an enormous increase in the production of Reformed Bibles took place; these had before been printed in Embden, Germany, by Dutch exiles since the late 1550s. But these "Biestkens" Bibles (named after their printer), "Liesveldt" Bibles (in which the text printed by Liesveldt from 1526–1542 was followed), and "Deux-aes" Bibles (named after a curious annotation in the margin next to Jeremiah 3) contained few illustrations or none at all.

The first Dutch Bible (containing only the Old Testament, including the Apocrypha but without the Psalms; and without illustrations) had been printed a century before in 1477 in Delft by Maurice Yemantsoen and Jacob Jacobsz. Except for Quentel's Cologne Bible of 1479 and the *Bible int Corte*, a history Bible published in Antwerp in 1516 and 1518 (with copies after the Cologne woodcuts), no Dutch Bibles were published until the 1520s. Only when Martin Luther's translation of the Bible was published in Germany (the New Testament appeared in 1521; the first three parts of the Old Testament followed in 1523–1524) did Dutch editions (translations of Luther's text) start to appear—mostly in Antwerp, but also in Delft and Amsterdam.

In Antwerp, around 1530 Jacob van Liesveldt printed the first complete Bible in Dutch (illustrated with forty-eight woodcuts, of which thirty-five were copied after the prints by artists from the workshop of Lucas Cranach the Elder in Luther's editions of the Old Testament). In later Antwerp editions, the number of illustrations grew to two hundred or more. With the exception of the woodcuts designed by Jan Swart and Lieven de Witte, no original Dutch work was produced. Instead, the printers made their woodcutters copy series by Holbein, Erhard Schön (who had designed illustrations for the Vulgate editions of the Lyons printer Jacob Sacon in 1518–1521), Hans Sebald Beham (whose picture book *Biblische Historien* appeared in 1533), and other German and also French artists, many of them unknown.

Of the more than one hundred twenty illustrated editions of the Bible printed in the Netherlands in the sixteenth century, only twenty-odd were produced in the North. And the greater part of these were the Reformed "Deux-aes" Bibles, only some of which contained just a few woodcuts copied from the illustrations in the French Protestant Geneva Bibles, which had as their ultimate source the copper engravings in Robert Estienne's Latin Bible of 1540.

Dutch book illustration made a good start in 1480, and the woodcuts adorning the Dutch *incunabula* stand on a high level when considered internationally. Soon afterward, however, Antwerp took the leading role in book production. The fact that Leeu moved his press from Gouda to the Southern metropolis is significant in this respect, as is the fact that Swart designed his woodcuts for an Antwerp printer. Yet, illustrated books of high quality were still being produced until the turn of the century. In the sixteenth century, book production and illustration were far more modest in the North, where Amsterdam—relatively late (1512) and initially only slowly—was beginning to rise as a center of printing. At the end of the era, from the beginning of the 1580s, copper engravings and etchings were beginning to take over the role of the woodcut in book illustration. Plantin's Leiden workshop was an important link in the introduction and development of this new medium.

Bart A. Rosier

See also Bellaert, Jacob; Coornhert, Dirck Volkertsz.; Gouda; Humanism, humanist themes; Prints, printmaking, and printmakers, (ca. 1500–ca. 1900); Protestant Reformation; Sins and punishments

Bibliography

Bohemen, Petra van et al. *Het boek in Nederland in de 16de eeuw.* The Hague: Rijksmuseum Meermanno-Westreenianum and Staatsuitgeverij, 1986.

Conway, William Martin. *The Woodcutters of the Netherlands in the Fifteenth Century.* Cambridge, 1884. Reprint. Hildesheim and Nieuwkoop: Georg Olms Verlag and De Graaf, 1970.

Delen, A.J.J. *Histoire de la gravure dans les anciens Pays Bas et dans les provinces Belges des origines jusqu'à la fin du XVIII siècle.* Paris: Les éditions d'art et d'histoire, 1924–1935.

Kok, C.H.C.M. (Ina). "De houtsneden in de incunabelen van de Lage Landen 1475–1500: Inventarisatie en bibliografische analyse." 2 vols. Ph.D. diss., Universiteit van Amsterdam, 1994. (English summary).

Kok, Ina. "A Rediscovered *Devote ghetiden* with Interesting Woodcuts (CA 1117)." *Quaerendo* 13 (1983): 176–190.

Nijhoff, Wouter. *L'art typographique dans les Pays Bas pendant les années 1500–1540.* The Hague: Nijhoff, 1926–1935.

Schretlen, M.J. *Dutch and Flemish Woodcuts of the Fifteenth Century.* London: Ernest Benn, 1925.

Stevenson, Alan. "The Problem of the Blockbooks." In *Blockbücher des Mittelalters,* 229–262. Mainz: Gutenberg-Gesellschaft und Gutenberg-Museum, 1991.

Strachan, James. *Early Bible Illustrations: A Short Study Based on Some Fifteenth- and Early-Sixteenth-Century Printed Texts.* Cambridge: Cambridge University Press, 1957.

Prints, modern graphic arts 1840–1945

In the first half of the nineteenth century, artists in Europe, particularly in France, developed a renewed interest in original graphic art. After the flourishing period of the seventeenth century, few graphic artists had practiced original printmaking, especially etching. Etching became used primarily as a technique for reproducing paintings. Inspired by the French painters of the Barbizon School, who collected seventeenth-century Dutch etchings and made a number of original etchings after nature, a group of artists from The Hague—among them Jan Weissenbruch (1822–1880), Reinier Craeyvanger (1812–1880), Lambertus Hardenberg (1822–1900), and Joseph Hartogensis (1822–1865)—also decided to make original prints with landscape as the subject. They took their small, easily handled etching plates and etching needles out with them into nature in order to record on the metal on the spot.

In 1848 they established De Haagse Etsclub (The Hague Etching Club). This was an informal circle of friends who exchanged their etchings. The prints were sketchy and printed in a great number of states, each very different from the other. It appears from this that experimenting with the etching technique came first for the members. They avoided confrontation with the public, publishing no etchings and holding no exhibitions. When their interest in etching faded, they abolished the etching club in 1860.

Only a few of the painters of The Hague School occupied themselves with etching. Jozef Israëls (1824–1911), etched mainly the poor interiors of the fishermen's families of Scheveningen. Willem Roelofs (1822–1897) etched landscapes, as did his student C.N. Storm van 's Gravesande (1841–1924). The last recorded in etching and lithography mainly the landscape of Holland but also that of the surrounding countries. Going further, Matthijs Maris (1839–1917) made some remarkable etchings in the style of his paintings in which he experimented with various inks and states.

Etching was still being taught in the academies in the Netherlands as a reproduction technique. In the 1890s, a number of students at the Rijksacademie van Beeldende Kunsten (National Academy of Arts) in Amsterdam resisted this, among them Jan Veth (1864–1925) and Willem Witsen (1860–1923). Following foreign example, they established in 1885 a club of *peintres-graveurs* that aimed to be a stimulus to original graphic art, particularly etching, and to bring it again to the attention of the public. The Nederlandsche Etsclub (Dutch Etching Club), as it was called, organized a number of exhibitions at which many foreign artists were also represented by graphic art. Almost annually the Dutch Etching Club published an album with the work of its members.

Many well-known artists were members and provided etchings for the albums. Jan Veth made some small etchings that, however, lag in importance behind his later lithographic work: portraits of contemporaries that appeared in the newspaper *De Groene Amsterdammer* and in *De Kroniek.* Willem Witsen experimented in the 1890s with a combination of various techniques. This is especially evident in his darker etchings of London (Fig. 105). Back in the Netherlands, Witsen primarily produced town views of Rotterdam, Dordrecht, and Amsterdam (Fig. 104), as well as various large etchings of farmers at work.

Philip Zilcken (1857–1930) was a graphic artist who practiced many techniques and genres and was a great admirer of contemporary English graphic art by, among others, Francis Seymour Haden (1818–1910) and James McNeill Whistler (1834–1903). He was also involved with the founding of the Dutch Etching Club and was represented in the albums and exhibitions with fine drypoints. Marius Bauer (1867–1932), inspired by his trips to the Middle East, set down numerous Arabian landscapes and street scenes on his etching plates in a fluent drawing style. Many members of the Dutch Etching Club were inspired by the landscape of Holland, among them Willem de Zwart (1862–1931) and Willem Bastiaan Tholen

(1860–1931). Both attempted to approximate a coloristic effect in their etchings. Maurits Willem van der Valk (1857–1935) was also inspired principally by the Dutch landscape; his early Impressionistic etchings gradually changed into more stylized landscapes with a great attention to detail (Fig. 142). Jan Toorop (1858–1928) was represented a few times in the albums of the Dutch Etching Club. He and Richard N. Roland Holst (1868–1938) represented in their lithographs the style of Art Nouveau in the albums. In 1896 this etching club was dissolved because the goals of stimulating original etching and making graphic arts exhibitions possible had been achieved. In 1898 there was an attempt to reestablish the Dutch Etching Club with the album *Hollandsche Prentkunst* (Dutch Prints), but this publication settled for any example of original printmaking and was not concerned about artistic quality. It had only one volume.

Fifteen years after the dissolution of the Dutch Etching Club, the graphic artists Simon Moulijn (1866–1948) and Johannes Veldheer (1866–1954) founded the Vereniging tot Bevordering der Grafische Kunst (Society for the Advancement of the Graphic Arts) in 1911. The Grafische (Graphic), as the society quickly came to be called, organized regular exhibitions of the work of its members. The most important graphic artists before World War II were members of this society.

Johannes Aarts (1871–1934) and, particularly, Pieter Dupont (1870–1911) are responsible for the revival of copper engraving in the Netherlands. Both had been teachers at the Rijksacademie in Amsterdam. Dupont, whom Van der Valk had inspired to make etchings, quickly shifted his interest to the laborious process of engraving. Using fine lines, he engraved numerous portraits and prints of his favorite subject, the workhorse (Fig. 106). Aarts' prints, worked from top to bottom, give an impression that is much less lively. Three pupils of Dupont and Aarts also applied themselves to engraving: Engelina Reitsma-Valença (1899–1981), Kuno Brinks (1908–1992), and Debora Duyvis (1886–1974). Reitsma-Valença made mostly engraved portraits; Brinks, Aarts' successor at the Rijksacademie, has a varied engraving *oeuvre;* and the engravings of Duyvis are characterized by a strong simplification and stylizing that show the influence of Cubism.

This international artistic trend is represented in intaglio printing only in the drypoints of Lodewijk Schelfhout (1881–1943). Cubism in the Netherlands is represented in the woodcuts of Herman Bieling (1887–1964), cofounder of the progressive artists' society De Branding in Rotterdam, and the independent Jacoba van Heemskerck (1876–1923). Among the De Stijl group, only Bart van der Leck (1876–1958) made a few lithographs. However, the designs and typography of Piet Zwart (1885–1977) and the Hungarian Vilmos Huszár (1884–1960) should also be considered in connection with De Stijl. Around 1912, Erich Wichmann (1890–1929) is one of the few who made abstract graphic art.

Realism continued to reign supreme in Dutch graphic art even after 1900. One of the most prominent artists from this period was the self-taught Antoon Derkzen van Angeren (1878–1962). His sketchy landscapes show the influence of Jongkind and Whistler. Derkzen van Angeren studied the prints of seventeenth-century masters and tried to approximate them as closely as possible. He mixed his own inks according to old recipes and tirelessly tracked down old Dutch-made paper. In 1917 he was appointed teacher of *vrije grafiek* (free graphic art) at the art academy in Rotterdam, where he gave lessons in engraving and etching and was a major impetus for Rotterdam's revival of the graphic arts after the war.

Andreas Schotel (1896–1984) took over from his teacher the striving for a craftsmanlike way of etching. He made his own ink and, with it, attempted to fill only the etched grooves. This produced single black etched lines on a spotless white paper. Schotel called his method *de schone druk* (pure, clean printing). A number of graphic artists went further with this printing method, among them Ap Sok (b. 1917), who was also a student of Derkzen van Angeren. Next to Derkzen van Angeren, many young artists owed their enthusiasm for graphic art, especially lithography, to Simon Moulijn, also a teacher at the Rotterdam academy. Moulijn worked in the lithographic technique depicting mostly dreamy gardens, parks, and portraits.

In the period 1900–1930, a number of graphic artists were impressed by the dreamy scenes of the French artist Odilon Redon (1840–1916), whose work was regularly exhibited in the Netherlands at the art gallery of dealer J.H. de Bois. The influence of Redon is clearly demonstrated in the portraits of Wout van Heusden (1896–1982) from Rotterdam. His later prints show influence from Surrealist artists such as René Magritte (1898–1967). Jacobus Prange (1904–1972) also derived his subjects, which he translated into lithography, from the Surrealists' dream world. With artists Willem van Leusden (1886–1974) and Joop Moesman (1909–1988), Utrecht became the center of Dutch Surrealism. Aart van Dobbenburgh (b. 1899) devoted himself almost entirely to the sacred lithography with very detailed nature studies and portraits.

Woodcut, long forgotten, became popular in the Netherlands at the end of the nineteenth century. K.P.C. de Bazel (1869–1923) and J.L.M. Lauweriks (1864–1932) used the technique especially for the design of vignettes and ornamental borders in books and magazines. The decorative element also returns in the elegant woodcuts of two Haarlem artists, Jacobus Veldheer (1866–1954) and Wijnand Nieuwenkamp (1874–1951). Nieuwenkamp, in particular, cut his decorative images in stylish lines. Among Veldheer's subjects were views of Holland's villages.

The woodcuts of members of the artists' society De Ploeg in Groningen, among them Jan Wiegers (1893–1959) and Johan Dijkstra (1896–1978), were clearly under the influence of Expressionism. Dijkstra made angular compositions of landscapes and other subjects. Wiegers, who had been in contact with German Expressionist Ernst Ludwig Kirchner (1880–1938), cut his landscapes in more flowing lines.

The woodcuts of Samuel Jessurun de Mesquita (1868–1944), with his strongly stylized figures, hold a special place. His student M.C. Escher (1898–1972) is also difficult to place within the history of Dutch graphic arts. Escher played in ingenious ways with the laws of perspective and gravity in his alienating fantasy architecture. His graphic puzzles show decorative, rhythmically ordered figures who flow into each other and again go their own way (Fig. 107).

Jeanne Bieruma Oosting (1898–1994), also a student of Jessurun de Mesquita, spent most of World War II in Paris. Her etchings from this period were initially characterized by Expressionism; later they became more influenced by Surrealism. After the war, her figurative work showed a greater simplification. During World War II, the graphic artist Hendrik Nicolaas Werkman (1882–1945) also was active. He disseminated his illustrated writings via his own printing shop, De Blauwe Schuit (The Blue Boat). Noteworthy are his so-called *druksels*, in which Werkman built up his nearly abstract images from stencils in fierce colors. His abstractions are an exception in Dutch graphic art before 1945, which consisted mostly of figurative works.

Maartje S. de Haan

See also Applied arts; De Zwart, Willem; Dupont, Pieter; Hague School, The; Maris, Matthijs; Roelofs, Willem; Roland Holst, Richard N.; Rotterdam; Tholen, Willem Bastiaan; Toorop, Jan; Van der Valk, Maurits Willem; Veth, Jan; Werkman, Hendrik Nicolaas; Witsen, Willem

Bibliography

Blom, Ad van der. *Tekenen dat het gedrukt staat: 500 jaar grafiek in Nederland.* Haarlem: Kosmos, 1978.

Boon, K.G. "De grafiek in Nederland na 1800." In *Kunstgeschiedenis der Nederlanden van het einde van de zestiende eeuw tot onze tijd in Noord-Nederland,* 575–599. Vol. 2 of *Kunstgeschiedenis der Nederlanden van de Middeleeuwen tot onze tijd.* Edited by H.E. van Gelder and J. Duverger. Utrecht: De Haan, 1955.

Bosch, Lodewijk. *Nederlandsche prentkunst sedert 1900.* Utrecht: De Branding, 1921.

Giltay, Jeroen. "De Nederlandsche Etsclub, 1885–1896." *Nederlands Kunsthistorisch Jaarboek* 27 (1976): 91–125.

Hall, H. van. *Repertorium voor de geschiedenis der Nederlandsche schilder-en graveerkunst sedert het begin van de eeuw tot het eind van 1932.* Vol. 1. The Hague: Nijhoff, 1936.

Moulijn, Simon. *De lithografische prentkunst.* Amsterdam: De Maatschappij voor goede en goedkoope lectuur, 1918.

Sluyter, Gerard. *De Moderne Grafiek in Nederland en Vlaanderen.* Amsterdam: Nederlandsche Uitgevers Maatschappij, 1928.

Vervoorn, A. J. *Nederlandse prentkunst, 1840–1940.* Lochem: De Tijdstroom, 1983.

Prints, modern graphic arts after 1945

The format of prints became increasingly larger after World War II. Small graphics, which could be held in the hand for viewing, gave way to larger sheets, which needed to be exhibited on the wall. This development, however, did not interfere with interest in the graphic arts. Under the influence of a further advancing democratization, artists wanted to bring their art closer to the people. This goal made it extremely appropriate to have prints that were affordable and, therefore, obtainable by everyone. To reach this goal, artists found various new places for their activity: graphic arts calendars; special editions of prints *(Prent 150);* and presentations of prints in a variety of newspapers (for example, *Vrij Nederland*). The Vereniging tot Bevordering der Grafische Kunst (Society for the Advancement of the Graphic Arts) organized regular exhibitions, and Dutch graphic artists showed their work at international expositions. For beginning graphic artists, who found that buying printing equipment was too expensive, *grafische ateliers* (workshops) were set up in different cities. These had etching and lithography presses with which, for a small fee, they could print their works.

The number of graphic artists who, besides printing their works themselves, put out to contract the laborious printing process has grown in recent years. On the other hand, more and more craftsmen's print shops are disappearing. Many artists use Piet Clement as their printer. Since 1984, he and others have organized *Grafiek Nu: Biënnale van de Nederlandse Grafische Kunst* (Graphics Now: Biennial Exhibition of Dutch Graphic Art), which attempts to give a representative overview of Dutch graphic arts. The large number of figurative and realistic prints in this exhibition is remarkable testimony to the great interest in this trend within Dutch graphic arts. More experimental prints are published by the artists' group Ink on Paper, which has also since 1984 sent prints, printed by the Amsterdam lithographic printing office, by mail to interested parties. A special gallery for modern graphic arts (Grafiekwinkel Inkt), where artists show their work to the public, has been established in The Hague.

The conflict that divided the Dutch art world into two camps after 1945 also had repercussions in the graphic arts: The moderate modernists, who wanted to hold on to figurative art and united in a group with the significant name Realisten (The Realists), opposed those on the side of abstraction and experimentation. The latter, who united under the name Vrij Beelden (Free Images), were supported by Willem Sandberg, director of the Stedelijk Museum in Amsterdam, the most important museum for contemporary art. The work of the members of Vrij Beelden anticipated the well-known postwar art movement, Cobra.

After the war, in the badly bombed city of Rotterdam, experimental color graphics thrived as never before. Antoon Derkzen van Angeren (1878–1962) and Simon Moulijn (1866–1948), teachers of graphic techniques at the Rotterdam Academy of Fine Arts and Technical Sciences, instilled enthusiasm in many young artists for the graphic arts. The younger generation of artists, including Wally Elenbaas (born 1912), Daan den Dikkenboer (1918–1979), and Jan Bezemer (born 1907), flung themselves into the medium of color lithography. It is more this technique that unites them than a clear relationship of style. Elenbaas never wholly abandoned the figurative;

man, bird, and sun turn up again and again in his work. For Bezemer, the animal holds a central place. In his early work, he rendered it in large color planes; later the animal vanishes behind a tangle of lines. Den Dikkenboer was inspired primarily by the port of Rotterdam. The coloring of his harmonious color lithographs shows a relationship with the work of the French artist Pierre Bonnard (1867–1947).

The figurative element that never entirely disappears in the Expressionist prints of the Rotterdammers also has an important role to play for a large proportion of the following generation of graphic artists. Klaas Gubbels (born 1934), a student of Elenbaas, concentrated on two elements: a coffee pot and a table. These objects brought him back to the most essential forms. Artists who are also occupied with figurative Expressionism include Fons Haagmans (born 1948), whose prints show a striving for simplified form similar to Gubbels'; Charlotte Mutsaers (born 1943), who provides her own books with comical illustrations; and Josien Brenneker (born 1950), whose lithographs lean toward Abstract Expressionism.

The art of Cobra was, of course, of major importance for the movement of Abstract Expressionism. The members of Cobra (Constant, Corneille, Lucebert, and Appel) were painters first of all; only later did they devote themselves to the graphic arts. Abstract Expressionism was especially popular in Dutch graphic arts during the 1960s—for example, in the work of Jef Diederen (born 1920) and Ger Lataster (born 1920). Lataster has held on to the expressive element while Diederen has turned increasingly toward a tighter design. The internationally known artist Martin Engelman (1924–1992) turned to this art form late and worked first in a figurative style. The work of Tom Thijsse (born 1945) and Reinier Lucassen (born 1939) developed out of Abstract Expressionism; they later allowed figurative elements into their work.

It is noteworthy that nonfigurative Constructivism in Dutch graphic arts was represented primarily by sculptors: Bob Bonies (born 1937), Dick Cassée (born 1931), and Carel Visser (born 1928). Visser has made a number of large woodcuts in black and white; Cassée uses small formats to make simple two-dimensional geometric figures in warm earth tints or in blind-stamping; and Bonies makes monumental multicolored compositions with large flat planes (Fig. 108). Bram Bogart (born 1921) also makes use of geometric figures but lets the lines consist of ragged edges in contrast to the tight planes of the preceding artists. Fon Klement (born 1930) also shows stylized flat planes in his prints, but he abandons the two-dimensional design through shadowing and overlapping planes with which he suggests space. Peter Struycken (born 1939) makes use of modern technology, including the computer, for his Constructivist graphics.

Even before World War II, Utrecht was known as the center of Dutch Surrealism through the paintings of Joop Moesman (1909–1988) and Willem van Leusden (1886–1974). Van Leusden intensively studied the works of Hercules Segers (ca. 1589/1590–1633/1638), and his own work became strongly influenced. Together with Moesman he was a member of the graphics society De Luis (The Louse) that was founded in the 1960s. Other members included Dirkje Kuik (born 1929),

whose urban ruins, animals, and strangely dressed people are more dreamy and fairy-like than Surrealistic; and Peter Vos (born 1935), who is mainly active as an illustrator and uses the world of birds as the source of inspiration for his witty, finely worked prints. Charles Donker (born 1940) is the member of De Luis who finally comes the closest to realism. He records nature almost undisturbed by man as accurately as possible in his thoroughly worked etchings.

Harry van Kruiningen (born 1906) is important for Dutch graphic art not only because of his beautiful prints inclining toward Surrealism (Fig. 109) but especially for his experiments with all kinds of graphic techniques, which he describes in his publications. His own work, which earlier often had a literary theme as the subject, has recently focused on images that he observes through the microscope, demonstrating that Van Kruiningen is particularly interested in the origins of life. He has passed on his experiments with techniques to a younger generation, among them Roger Chailloux (1931–1977), whose prints show monumental sculptures, and Ru van Rossem (born 1924), whose work is inspired by the prehistoric wall paintings in southern France. Anton Heyboer (born 1924) is another who experiments with the etching technique in his thoroughly worked prints. The human figure and symbolic texts have a central place in his prints.

Realism continues to play an important role in Dutch graphic art. Herman Berserik (born 1921) was one of the members of Realisten, the group of artists who opposed the nonfigurative art of Cobra and Vrij Beelden. Berserik's small prints show everyday subjects. His work is often mentioned in the same breath with that of Co Westerik (born 1924), but Westerik admits a striking alienation into his more poetic realism (Fig. 110). Toon Wegner (born 1926) can also be counted among the realists. Since these three artists live in The Hague, they are regarded as "The Hague figurativists." Realists can also be found in Utrecht (for example, Charles Donker) and in Amsterdam. Aat Verhoog (born 1933) creates a furor in the capital city with his realistic prints of love-making men, and women in advanced stages of pregnancy, which he prints in large editions using the cheap rotary press.

Realism mixed with cynicism and irony is to be seen in the work of Herman Gordijn (born 1932), who shows the deterioration of the human (mostly female) body; Sipke Huismans (born 1931), who quite rapidly mixes his figurative work with more abstract forms; and Pieter Holstein (born 1934), who draws inspiration for his work from film images of the 1940s and 1950s. Holstein was clearly influenced by Pop Art, which emerges even more in the prints of Jacob Zekveld (born 1945), Marte Röling (born 1939), and Hans Wap (born 1943). Realistic representations of the landscape can be found in the prints of Sees Vlag (born 1934) and Hans Heijman (born 1951). Laetitia de Haas (born 1948) shows primarily gardens and interiors, and Piet Klaasse (born 1918) is mainly interested in musicians and portraits.

Realism, which was always strongly represented in the work of Dutch graphic artists before World War II, continued to play an important role after 1945. Many graphic artists make a single excursion into abstraction but each time return to the figurative and realistic element.

Maartje S. de Haan

See also Cobra, Movement; Contemporary art; Graphic design; Moesman, Johannes Hendricus (Joop); Postage stamps; Rotterdam; Struycken, Peter; Surrealism; Visser, Carel; Westerik, Co

Bibliography

Blom, Ad van der. *Grafiek Nu: Hedendaagse prentkunst in Nederland.* Amsterdam: Elsevier, 1984.

Grafiek Nu 2–6: Biënnale van Nederlandse grafische kunst. 5 vols. De Bilt: Cantecleer, 1986–1994.

Jacobs, P.M.J. *Beeldend Nederland: Biografisch handboek.* Tilburg: P.M.J. Jacobs BV, 1993.

Stokvis, Willemijn. *De Doorbraak van de moderne kunst in Nederland, de jaren 1945–1951.* Amsterdam: Meulenhoff, 1984.

Stokvis, Willemijn, and Killy Zijlmans. *Vrij Spel: Nederlandse Kunst 1970–1990.* Amsterdam: Meulenhoff, 1993.

Prints, printmaking, and printmakers (ca. 1500– ca. 1900)

Three techniques dominated print production until the end of the seventeenth century: woodcut, engraving, and etching. During the early part of the fifteenth century, printmaking in the Northern Netherlands was characterized mainly by the production of blockbooks, woodcut books produced before the invention of moveable type in which text and image are combined. Blockbooks, such as the *Biblia Pauperum, Canticum Canticorum,* and the *Speculum Humanæ Salvationis,* are considered to have been designed and cut in the 1470s in the Northern Netherlands. During the 1480s, identifiable publishers based in Holland began to excel in the production of illustrated books with moveable type; among them were Jacob Bellaert in Haarlem, Gheraert Leeu in Gouda, Christian Snellaert in Delft, Pieter van Os in Zwolle, and Jan Veldener in Utrecht and Culemborg.

During the first decade of the sixteenth century, book illustration began to diminish in quality in the Northern Netherlands, while Dutch artists began to make strides in the production of individual prints. Many of these woodcutters were painters as well, such as Jacob Cornelisz. van Oostsanen, who made about one hundred sixty-six woodcuts, including a lively frieze depicting the Dukes and Duchesses of Holland on Horseback. Lucas van Leyden, one of the greatest printmakers of his century, made bold advances in the field of woodcutting in one hundred thirty woodcuts. Jan Swart from Groningen followed him in the 1540s with a number of woodcuts. In Amsterdam, Cornelis Anthonisz., who was not a painter, further developed the Renaissance character of the Dutch woodcut with his moralizing prints and broadsheets. He also pioneered in mapmaking with a twelve-sheet *Bird's Eye View of Amsterdam* in 1544. After the mid-sixteenth century, engraving gradually replaced woodcut as the primary technique for high-quality prints, and woodcut was relegated to the domain of popular prints. The technique briefly regained popularity in the 1590s and early 1600s when Hendrick Goltzius and his school cut a number of *chiaroscuro* woodcuts.

The most notable engravers during the last quarter of the fifteenth century in the Northern Netherlands were Alart du Hameel of 's Hertogenbosch, who produced a number of engravings after Hieronymus Bosch, and the Master IAM of Zwoll (Fig. 103). The early part of the sixteenth century was dominated by the work of one engraver, Lucas van Leyden. This first true *peintre-graveur* active in the Northern Netherlands earned an international reputation with his one hundred sixty-eight engravings and six etchings. Lucas's prints were particularly innovative in subject matter (Fig. 26); some of his genre subjects set a precedent for artistic themes that became popular in the seventeenth century.

By the 1550s, engraving in the Northern Netherlands had become stylistically and economically centered around activities in Antwerp. Several artists engraved plates for print publishers in Antwerp—for example, Harmen Jansz. Muller in Amsterdam and Dirck Volkertsz. Coornhert in Haarlem, whose works were published by Hieronymus Cock. Coornhert engraved about two hundred prints after designs by the painter Maerten van Heemskerck. Other printmakers in Holland were influenced by styles from farther abroad. The work of Allart Claesz., an individualistic etcher from Utrecht, is close to that of a group of artists in Nuremberg known as the Little Masters.

Coornhert taught two important reproductive printmakers of the following generation—Hendrick Goltzius and Crispijn de Passe I. Hendrick Goltzius moved in 1577 to Haarlem, where he established the first internationally significant reproductive printmaking business in the Northern Netherlands. Goltzius brought a technical virtuosity, influenced by Mannerism, into the vocabulary of engraving and combined it with highly intellectual subjects. The engravers trained in his shop—Jacob Matham, Jan Saenredam, Jacob de Gheyn II, and Jan Muller— all established successful printmaking careers for themselves. De Passe moved in 1612 from Cologne to Utrecht with his family and prolific reproductive printmaking business. His print shop expanded internationally as his children, trained in their father's engraving style, went to work in foreign cities.

The early years of the seventeenth century saw a proliferation of printmakers in the United Provinces. A large number of artists had fled to Holland following the capture of Antwerp by the Spanish in 1585. These artists were not only professional engravers, such as Crispijn de Passe I and Hendrick Hondius, but also designers of reproductive prints, such as David Vinckboons and Hans Bol. For the first time, a large number of printmakers, many specializing in one particular subject or technique, flourished simultaneously in the United Provinces. Prolific reproductive printmakers, such as Claes Jansz. Visscher in Amsterdam and Hendrick Hondius in The Hague, were active at the same time as small-scale printmakers, such as the painter Gerrit Pietersz. in Haarlem, who produced only six etchings. In Amsterdam and The Hague, Werner van den Valckert, Jacob de Gheyn III, and

Simon Frisius all etched in individualistic styles influenced by Mannerism. In Utrecht, Hendrick Goudt engraved from 1608 on several strong *chiaroscuro* landscapes after paintings by Adam Elsheimer.

The most significant center for the development of landscape in the early years of the seventeenth century was Haarlem. Esaias van de Velde, Willem Buytewech, and Hercules Segers, the greatest innovators in the production of landscape prints, all joined the artists' guild in Haarlem in 1612. As early as 1614, Esaias van de Velde, Jan van de Velde II, and Buytewech began to produce series of naturalistic landscape etchings influential for the development of landscape in the seventeenth century. Small landscape series were etched in Amsterdam as well by Claes Jansz. Visscher, who produced several series of views of the countryside around Haarlem. Hercules Segers took landscape prints in a different direction; his experiments with techniques stretched the medium of printmaking to its most expressive ends. His work influenced Johannes Ruisscher, known as "the young Hercules," and Rembrandt van Rijn. The number and variety of landscape prints in Holland grew during the mid-seventeenth century. Their development paralleled in many ways that of landscape painting because many landscape printmakers were also painters. At the same time, certain genres became the domain of printmaking—specifically, the encyclopedic print series, which brought together different depictions of one theme or place. The tradition of the Italianate landscape, which had begun in the sixteenth century with Hieronymus Cock's etchings of ruins, was carried on by Bartholomeus Breenbergh in about thirty small atmospheric Italian scenes with ruins. Jan Both and Herman van Swanevelt followed Breenbergh with larger idealized Italianate landscapes showing peasants among ruins. Thomas Wijck etched about twenty-five small and subtle Italian scenes in which architecture dominates. Jacob van Ruisdael's twelve etchings made a great impact among those artists who did not travel to Italy. His abundant forest scenes with dense foliage were influential for the prints of Anthonie Waterloo, Adriaen Verboom, and Herman Naiwincx. Allart van Everdingen etched rocky Scandinavian views inspired by a trip to Norway and Sweden around 1644. Late in the century, Isaac de Moucheron etched more elegant landscape scenes.

Topographical prints and city views also became popular in Holland, internationally renowned for its thriving production of maps, atlases, and globes centered along the Kalverstraat in Amsterdam. At the beginning of the century, Pieter Bast engraved a number of large multiplate views of Dutch cities. A few years later, Claes Jansz. Visscher continued the tradition with large panoramic views of foreign cities. Later in the century, series of topographical views became a popular way of reproducing the local scenery. Roeland Roghman and Johannes Leupenius both etched topographical series depicting well-known buildings in the Dutch countryside.

Around 1625 in Leiden, two young painters were getting their start: Rembrandt van Rijn and his friend Jan Lievens. Their earliest attempts at etching were published in Haarlem by Jan Pietersz. Berendrecht. Lievens' printed work consists primarily of etched portraits. For a brief period, Rembrandt engaged Jan Jorisz. van Vliet to produce prints after his paintings. Rembrandt himself eventually etched about three hundred prints, the largest and most stylistically varied body of prints of his time. His experiments with the technique of printmaking reached their height in the 1640s in his large drypoint of *The Three Crosses*, creatively inked and printed on various types of paper so that many impressions are unique works of art. Rembrandt's followers include Ferdinand Bol, Salomon Koninck, and Karel de Moor, but his influence was even more significant among Dutch nineteenth-century etchers.

During the seventeenth century, several new types of subject matter were introduced into prints, and many artists began to etch only one type of subject—for example, Adriaen van Ostade; Cornelis Bega, Van Ostade's student; and later Cornelis Dusart, who specialized in peasant scenes. Animal prints also became subjects for specialization, such as the encyclopedic series of single animals by Paulus Potter and Pieter van Laer. Nicolaes Berchem, Karel du Jardin, and Adriaen van de Velde all etched primarily Italianate peasant scenes. Reinier Nooms, called *Zeeman*, and Ludolf Bakhuizen produced only prints of ships.

Portrait prints also composed a large percentage of the seventeenth-century print market. The most notable of the prints depicting members of the House of Orange and other court figures were produced by Willem Jacobsz. Delff after the paintings of Michiel van Mierevelt. The Visscher brothers, Cornelis, Johannes, and Lambert, as well as Crispijn van Queboren, were also prolific portrait engravers.

Toward the end of the century, a new technique became particularly popular among portrait engravers: mezzotint. Abraham Blooteling, Cornelis Visscher, and Gerard Valck printed large numbers of mezzotint portraits, genre scenes, and reproductions of paintings. Wallerant Vaillant probably learned the technique from Prince Rupert, Count Palatine, who perfected the process he learned from the inventor Ludwig von Siegen, in Brussels in 1654, but Abraham Blooteling was the first to begin engraving large numbers of mezzotints. Blooteling's two main competitors in Amsterdam in the production of mezzotints were Jan van Somer and Jan Verkolje. Cornelis Troost was one of the few eighteenth-century producers of mezzotint, by which time the technique was fading from the Dutch print market.

By the end of the seventeenth century, the great diversity of printmakers who had been active in the middle part of the century had diminished. The small original etchings of the *peintres-graveur* became less of a fixture on the print market. In the final years of the century, a few prolific professional printmakers were active, such as Jan and Caspar Luyken, best known for their innumerable book illustrations and their series showing the trades. Romeyn de Hooghe recorded the period's historical events with hundreds of etched broadsheets, book illustrations, and topographical views.

The eighteenth century witnessed a change in the taste for prints among the Dutch influenced by French artistic trends. The subject matter for prints during this period shifted toward the elegant; *fête* scenes and court subjects became common print topics, as did views of elegant palaces and country houses. In addition, the production of single prints gave way to an abundance of book illustrations. Jacob Houbraken, Jan Punt, and Simon Fokke produced large quantities of historical prints, portraits, title pages, and book illustrations. Jan Punt's student Reinier Vinkeles produced hundreds of history prints characterized by strong effects of lighting. From 1710 on, Abraham Rademaker, Abraham de Haen, and Hendrick Spilman specialized in turning out thousands of small topographical prints. Paulus Constantijn La Fargue in The Hague etched several series of large city views intended for hanging on walls.

In the 1760s, the art collector Cornelis Ploos van Amstel invented a printmaking technique for simulating and reproducing drawings. Ploos van Amstel and his shop experimented with various color printing methods, as well as etching, mezzotint, and woodcut, in order to make faithful reproductions of the seventeenth-century drawings in his collection.

During the final quarter of the eighteenth century, printmakers began to take a new interest in the art of the Dutch Golden Age. The work of artists such as Rembrandt and Potter gained in popularity, and original etching rose to the forefront of printmaking. The leading etchers of this seventeenth-century revival included Jacob van Strij in Dordrecht, whose work was influenced by Aelbert Cuyp, and Strij's brother Abraham, who etched Oriental heads reminiscent of Rembrandt. Wijbrand Hendriks produced Van Ostade–inspired etchings, and P.G. van Os and Jan Baptist Kobell II produced animal etchings influenced by Potter, as did two Amsterdam printmakers, Anthony Oberman and Wouter Johannes van Troostwijk. Jacob Ernst Marcus, primarily a lithographer and book illustrator, produced many images of peasant figures, as did A.H.W. Nolthenius de Man, the first printmaker in Holland to etch on zinc, around 1825.

Only sixteen years after its invention in Germany, lithography came to Holland, and in 1812 J.A. Weiland in Rotterdam became the earliest Dutch lithographer. Lithography came into greater use in Holland around 1820. At that time in Rotterdam, a group of about five artists began to create lithographs; the best among them was Johannes Bemme Adriaensz. When J.Z. Mazel, and Nolthenius de Man, military men by profession in The Hague, took an interest in the new technique, The Hague began to supercede Rotterdam as the Dutch center for lithography. In Amsterdam, Cornelis Kruseman made sketches in lithography, and J.A. Daiwaille, director of the Koninklijke Academie van Beeldende Kunsten (Royal Academy of Arts) in 1820, set up a lithography press in the school where he produced drawing books and other model books.

The technique of wood engraving, dominated by the British, reached a high technical level in Holland between 1845 and 1870. A.C. Verhees in 's Hertogenbosch was the first Dutch wood engraver whose skill rivaled that of foreign colleagues.

In 1848, a second nineteenth-century revival of etching took place in Holland, begun this time by a group of nine artists, among them Jan Weissenbruch, Lambertus Hardenberg,

Johannes Adrianus van der Drift, Jacob van der Maaten, Joseph Hartogensis, and Reinier Craeyvanger, known as The Hague Etching Club (De Haagse Etsclub). The members of the club, which existed until 1860, primarily produced small editions of landscape etchings intended for a limited group of print lovers. Etchers were also active in other Dutch cities, such as Pierre Dubourcq in Amsterdam, and Charles Rochussen in Rotterdam. The Hague School artists made less of a contribution to printmaking than they did to painting. Several artists in their midst did produce many etchings, however—Willem Roelofs etched the polders; J.C. Greive, port scenes; and C.N. Storm van 's Gravesande, landscape and water scenes. They tried to bring painterly effects of tone and atmosphere to their prints. Jozef Israëls in the 1870s chose, in contrast, to portray a less idealized view of the landscape than The Hague School, in addition to poor interior scenes.

In 1885, another group of artists formed a more established society called the Dutch Etching Club (Nederlandsche Etsclub), which printed portfolios containing the work of its members. Among the participants were Jan Veth, who etched portraits; Willem Witsen, known for his cityscapes (Fig. 104); and Marius Bauer, the author of fantastic representations of exotic lands. Competing with the original etchers in the Nederlandsche Etsclub was a group of reproductive etchers headed by Carel Dake called De Distel (The Thistle). They produced portfolios of reproductive prints after paintings by contemporary as well as seventeenth-century artists. Other reproductive etchers were Willem Steelink Jr. and Philip Zilcken.

Nadine Orenstein

See also Amateurs, art academies, and art associations before the nineteenth century; Atlas, atlases; Bellaert, Jacob; Bol, Ferdinand; Bosch, Hieronymus; Cartography; Coornhert, Dirck Volkertsz.; Dupont, Pieter; Goltzius, Hendrick; Graphic design; Hague School, The; Humor, satire; Israëls, Jozef; Kruseman, Cornelis; La Fargue, Paulus Constantijn; Lievens, Jan; Master IAM of Zwoll; Matham, Jacob; Paper, used for prints; Potter, Paulus; Prints, collecting; Prints, early printed books and Bible illustration; Prints, modern graphic arts 1840–1945; Prints, modern graphic arts after 1945; Prints, publishers; Rembrandt van Rijn; Rochussen, Charles; Roelofs, Willem; Van de Velde, Jan II; Van der Valk, Maurits Willem; Van Leyden, Lucas; Van Ruisdael, Jacob; Veth, Jan; Vinckboons, David; Watermarks; Witsen, Willem

Bibliography

Ackley, Clifford S. *Printmaking in the Age of Rembrandt.* Boston: Museum of Fine Arts, 1981.

Blom, Ad van der. *Tekenen dat het gedrukt staat: 500 jaar grafiek in Nederland.* [Amsterdam]: Kosmos, [1978].

Freedberg, David. *Dutch Landscape Prints.* London: British Museum Publications, 1980.

Groot, Irene de. *Landscape Etchings by the Dutch Masters of the Seventeenth Century.* London: Gordon Fraser, 1979.

Groot, Irene de, and Robert Vorstman. *Maritime Prints by the Dutch Masters.* London: Gordon Fraser, 1980.

Hind, Arthur M. *A History of Engraving and Etching from
the Fifteenth Century to the Year 1914.* 3rd ed. Boston
and New York: Houghton Mifflin, 1927.

Hollstein, F.W.H. *Dutch and Flemish Etchings, Engravings,
and Woodcuts, ca. 1450–1700.* Amsterdam: Menno
Hertzberger: 1949– .

Moulijn, S. *De eerste jaren der lithografische prentkunst in
Nederland.* The Hague: Nijhoff, 1927.

Prints, publishers

The large percentage of prints produced in Holland from the
mid-sixteenth century on were carried out to some extent
under the auspices of a publisher. The publisher brought together the designer, engraver, poet, and printer, and arranged
for the financing of the print and its sale. Some publishers were
engravers themselves; others were more businessmen than
artists who would print and sell impressions of other artists'
work. Dutch prints often displayed a publisher's address,
which identified the name of the person who published them
by the Latin words *excudit, divulgavit, caelavit, formis,* or the
Dutch *ten huyse van.*

The first print publishers in the Netherlands, primarily
reproductive printmakers, were centered in the South in
Antwerp around 1550. In the North, a few publishers were
active, such as Jan Ewoutsz. Muller in Amsterdam, but many,
such as Muller's son Harmen, routinely sent plates down to
Antwerp publishers for printing and international distribution. The first print publisher to shift some of the international
glory toward the North was Hendrick Goltzius in Haarlem.
He changed the concept of the reproductive-print publishing
house from a publisher hiring various artists to engrave the
work of different designers to one geared exclusively toward
producing and disseminating the publisher's own stylistic inventions and designs. The 1590s saw a large influx of engravers
and print publishers to the North, which changed the face of
publishing for seventeenth-century Holland. Many small
print-publishing houses now proliferated throughout the
United Provinces. Some followed the model of the large and
varied reproductive houses in Antwerp, such as Hendrick
Hondius in The Hague, while others specialized in producing a limited type of print, such as Jan Pietersz. Berendrecht
who published primarily small etchings by *peintre-graveurs*
such as Rembrandt van Rijn and Esaias van de Velde. By mid-
century, the types of print publishers active in Holland had
very much narrowed, and this remained the case until the
end of the eighteenth century—a few large publishers in
Amsterdam, such as Nicolaes Visscher, the Danckert Dan-
ckerts, and Clement de Jonghe, bought up the stock of the
many smaller ones. These publishers primarily took over the
market for reproductive prints and secondhand plates—that
is, plates passed on from one publisher to another. Another
force on the print market at this time were the *peintres-
graveur*—the painters, mainly landscapists, who published
their own work—such as Allart van Everdingen and Karel du
Jardin. Their products were etchings and small-scale original
works. By the end of the seventeenth century, the *peintres-
graveur* had all but disappeared, and they did not reappear

until the end of the following century with the revival of etching. By the eighteenth century, a shift in printmaking toward
book illustration was reflected as well in print publication, but
many of the book illustrators, such as Bernard Picart, Simon
Fokke, and Pieter Tanjé, all based in Amsterdam, also published prints.

    Nadine Orenstein

See also Calligraphers and calligraphy (1550–1650); Cartography; Goltzius, Hendrick; Humanism, humanist themes; Paper, used for prints; Prints, early printed book and Bible illustration; Prints, printmaking, and printmakers (ca. 1500–ca.
1900); Protestant Reformation; Watermarks

Bibliography
Briels, J.G.C.A. *Zuidnederlandse boekdrukkers en
boekverkopers in de Republiek der Verenigde Nederlanden
omstreeks 1570–1630.* Nieuwkoop: B. de Graff, 1974.

Orenstein, Nadine et al. "Prints and Publishers in Holland
between 1580 and 1620." In *Dawn of the Golden Age.*
Amsterdam: Rijksmuseum, 1993.

Waller, F.G. *Biographisch Woordenboek van Noord
Nederlandsche Graveurs.* The Hague: Nijhoff, 1938.
Reprint. Amsterdam: B.M. Israel, 1974.

Pronk, Cornelis (1691–1759)

Cornelis Pronk, who was born in the North Holland village of
De Rijp, received drawing lessons from Jan van Houten while
he was still young. Afterward, under the guidance of Arnold
Boonen, he became a skilled portrait painter in Amsterdam.
Shortly after, he applied himself to *naar het leven* (after nature)
drawings of village and town views, churches, castles, town halls,
ruins, and other monuments. For this purpose he made several
trips through the Dutch provinces and beyond them after 1724.
During these trips, often in the company of the artist Abraham
de Haen and the amateur historian Andries Schoemaker, Pronk
recorded topographical motifs in sketchbooks for the purpose
of expanding on them later. (Four of these sketchbooks are
preserved in the Rijksprentenkabinet in Amsterdam.) A great
number of Pronk's drawings were engraved on copper to be used
as illustrations in topographies or print editions. In 1733 he
moved to Zaandam, but in 1742 he returned to Amsterdam.
Pronk was the most important topographical draftsman in the
first half of the eighteenth century and also one of the most important teachers in this genre. He taught Jan de Beijer, Abraham
de Haen, Hendrick de Winter, Hendrick Spilman, Jacobus
Buijs, Paulus van Liender, and Gerrit Toorenburgh. Pronk's
topographical work is characterized by a great measure of reli-
ability, a sharp observation, and a great feeling for detail. Besides *topographica* Pronk also drew designs for memorial medallions, and in 1734, in a commission from the Verenigde
Oostindische Compagnie (United East India Company), he
drew designs for porcelain that was made and painted in China.

    Charles Dumas

See also Architectural painting; Atlas, atlases; Drawings, uses
and collecting; Townscapes

Bibliography

Dumas, Charles. *Het verheerlijkt Den Haag: Achttiende-eeuwse aquarellen en tekeningen door de familie La Fargue en haar tijdgenoten.* The Hague: Nijgh and Van Ditmar, 1984. (English summary).

Gevers, A.J., and A.J. Mensema. *Over de hobbelde bobbelde heyde: Andries Schoemaker, Cornelis Pronk, en Abraham de Haen op reis door Overijssel, Drente en Friesland in 1732.* Alphen aan den Rijn: Canaletto, 1985.

Jörg, C.J.A. *Pronk porselein: Porselein naar ontwerpen van Cornelis Pronk.* Groningen: Groninger Museum, 1980.

Protestant Reformation

In contrast to Germany, where Lutheranism played an important role in political developments and in popular prints, the Reformation in the Netherlands was inconspicuously manifested in the visual arts. Because the Reformation movement was harshly suppressed from the start, popular prints caricaturing the pope and clergy as propaganda for the new Protestant faith were rarely seen in the Netherlands. Most satirical representations were made after 1566, when the political and religious opposition to Spanish rule grew more resolute. Mainly they were prints of a political character, directed against the duke of Alva, whose troops were occupying the Netherlands, and the Catholic faith that he was there to enforce.

After around 1520, however, the cultural climate underwent far-reaching changes under the influence of humanism and the Reformation. Belief in the power of relics, miracles, and saints declined as greater interest developed in the original Bible text. This change is also apparent in the themes of works of art. There is less emphasis on depicting the suffering, death, and resurrection of Christ and portraying the Madonna and the saints, and there were more representations of the earthly life of Jesus Christ, parables, and biblical stories with a moral aspect. Avowedly Protestant views—for example, predestination, salvation by faith alone, or Christ's redemption of humankind from death (Fig. 111)—were an exception and were limited to drawings and prints that were made for private use only. It is true that one can find Reformational ideas in, for example, the prints of Cornelis Anthonisz. and the drawings of Jan Swart and Dirck Crabeth, but there is no proof of a Protestant background for these artists. On the other hand, in the Southern Netherlands in the first half of the sixteenth century, the works of artists who we know were persecuted by the Inquisition—Bernard van Orley, Jan and Cornelis Massys, Jan Ewouts, and Cornelis Bos—show hardly any Protestant influence.

In 1566 the great Iconoclasm took place in the Netherlands, and many of the art objects in churches and monasteries—stained glass windows, altarpieces, and statues—were destroyed or damaged. After the arrival of the duke of Alva and the formation of the Council of Blood in 1567 (as the Spanish Inquisition in the Netherlands was called), the Anabaptists, Calvinists, and Lutherans were forced to emigrate to England or Germany. Among them were the artists Adriaan de Weert, Frans Hogenberg, Lucas de Heere, Marcus Gheeraerts, and Joris Hoefnagel. After 1585, following the fall of Antwerp to the Spanish and the beginning of the Counter-Reformation in the South, many Protestant painters fled to the Northern Netherlands, which gave a new stimulus to the arts there.

In the Northern Netherlands after 1572, Calvinism was the acknowledged religion. The Reformed service was the only one that was allowed publicly. Other religions were officially forbidden, but this was not enforced. At first the Calvinists were a minority of the population, a large part remained Catholic, and a smaller part was Baptist or belonged to the less-orthodox Protestant congregation of the Remonstrants. In the Calvinist Church, altarpieces and other devotional works of art were not allowed, in part because of the Second Commandment's prohibition of worshipping graven images. Calvinists did, however, place tablets with Scriptures on them—called Sacrament panels and Ten Commandment panels—in the churches. Religious devotional works that were spared during the Iconoclasm were transferred to other places like the town hall. In many works of art, like the stained glass windows of Sint Janskerk (St. John's Church) in Gouda or in the *Last Judgment* by Lucas van Leyden (1526–1527; Leiden, Stedelijk Museum De Lakenhal), the image of God the Father was replaced by the tetragram, which had been used in Reformation circles in Germany since early sixteenth century.

The Reformed Church strove to strengthen the influence of the gospel and used biblical pictures as an appropriate tool. Protestant publishers of prints like Claes Jansz. Visscher brought many biblical prints onto the art market. Thus, while it is true that the Church ceased to be a patron for painters and other artists, the Calvinist citizens of the Netherlands continued to commission paintings for their private use. Particularly preferred were paintings of stories from the Old Testament or parables from the New Testament. The decline of devotional art in the Northern Netherlands, without a doubt, promoted the rise of so-called cabinet art and its specializations. Seventeenth-century genres such as still life, landscape, or portraiture do not always have to be viewed as evidence of an extreme secularization. In *Vanitas* paintings—for example, those by Edward Collier, a suspected Protestant—the beauty of the material world is emphasized, but also, unambiguously, there are references to mortality and to life after death.

Ilja M. Veldman

See also Allegorical traditions; Churches; Devotional images; Didactic images; Gouda; History painting; Humanism, humanist themes; Last Judgment; Religion of artists; Rhetoricians' chambers; Roundels; Stained glass; Utrecht; *Vanitas, vanitas* still life

Bibliography

Duke, Alastair. *Reformation and Revolt in the Low Countries.* London: Ronceverte, 1990.

Freedberg, David. "Art and Iconoclasm, 1525–1580: The Case of the Northern Netherlands." In *Kunst voor de beeldenstorm: Noordnederlandse kunst 1525–1580.* Edited by W. Th. Koek, W. Halsema-Kubes, and R.J. Baarsen, 69–84. Amsterdam: Rijksmuseum; The Hague: Staatsuitgeverij, 1986.

Gelder, H.A. Enno van. *Erasmus, schilders en rederijkers: De religieuze crisis der 16e eeuw weerspiegeld in toneel- en schilderkunst.* Groningen: Noordhoff, 1959.

Parshall, Peter W. "Kunst en reformatie in de Noordelijke Nederlanden: Enkele gezichtspunten." *Bulletin van het Rijksmuseum* 35 (1987): 164–175. (English summary).

Zijp, R.P. "De iconografie van de reformatie in de Nederlanden, een begripsbepaling." *Bulletin van het Rijksmuseum* 35 (1987): 176–192. (English summary).

Public housing

Between 1870 and 1890, after a long period of economic stagnation, the Netherlands again began to thrive with commercial activity and manufacturing. The opening of the Suez Canal in 1869 reduced the cost of merchandise from the Far East while, through great engineering feats, the ports of Amsterdam and Rotterdam, connected to the Rhine, were able to host the new large vessels. With the return of commerce came a strong economic free trade that stimulated the shipping and manufacturing industries. In counterpoint to this expansion was the crisis in the agricultural sector, which drove farmers to abandon the countryside and seek refuge in the cities, where industrialization offered new opportunities for work and where, as a consequence, the first concentrations of workers from the country were created. Population density increased in the major cities owing to local governments that were unprepared to respond to the new phenomena and to outdated legislation. For reasons of security, until 1874, a national law forbade the expansion of cities outside the limits of their old walls. The result was the use of spaces for housing that were completely inappropriate to that function, such as basements and old warehouses, which worsened the living conditions in the cities by creating serious problems of public hygiene.

Once the restrictions on building outside the walls were removed, private developers began constructing new speculative buildings of rental apartments. These buildings were usually of modest size, but in large cities, where immigration was greatest and the housing situation most serious, three- and four-story complexes were crowded together in minimal spaces.

Other ideas were tried in an attempt to remedy the precarious housing situation. In the second half of the century, building societies were formed whose objective it was to create rental housing for their own members. Inspired by the English building societies, they were promoted by builders with philanthropic goals or by trade associations, such as the railway workers in Haarlem in 1872.

Equally interesting are the solutions found by industries for housing their workers. Among the most remarkable examples was the garden quarter Agneta Park in Delft, built beginning in 1884 for the workers in the local grocery business. The urban plan for the area was designed by Louis Paul Zocher, son of the more famous Jan David Zocher Jr., also a landscape architect, who envisioned the little neighborhood in a picturesque manner with curved streets, abundant vegetation, and a small lake. The workers' residences were built side by side in groups of three or four, while in the center of the quarter was the villa of the owner of the business.

Agneta Park demonstrated that it was possible to have quality buildings at reasonable cost when the production process was taken out of the hands of speculators. But despite several exemplary achievements, the housing situation remained extremely serious, as pointed out by various public investigations carried out during the final years of the nineteenth century. Moreover, because of the rising costs of land suitable for building, the private construction of rental lodgings also fell into crisis.

In this climate of crisis and the need for reform, the *woningwet* (housing law) was promulgated in 1902. The law, created by a liberal, middle-class government, was the most advanced of its kind in Europe at the beginning of the twentieth century. It attempted, above all, to combat the serious housing shortage by creating a mechanism to give government loans to the cities and building societies to construct low-cost housing. But it also proposed to regulate urban development in cities of more than ten thousand inhabitants; these cities were required to develop expansion plans and to control the cost of land suitable for building through expropriation.

The *woningwet*, promoting the production of a great deal of public housing, encouraged the formation of an intense awareness of the role of the different workers involved. Cities and building societies (*woningbouwvereeniging*) on the one hand, and architects on the other, saw in it the driving force of urban construction. The SDAP (Sociaal Democratische Arbeiders Partij), the Social Democratic Workers' Party that at the beginning of the 1910s governed several important cities, including Amsterdam, made it the main thrust of its political action.

The first years of the law's application were difficult, however, since the financing actually available was scarce and the structures called for to manage the new course of action still had to be formed. In order to measure the new law's effects, it was necessary to wait until after World War I, when the economic recession caused by the disruption of exports led again to a standstill of construction by the private sector. In this crisis, public financing became more consistently available and the amount of housing produced with the aid of government loans was remarkable.

The public housing produced through public financing and at contained costs was not marked by univocal typological models. In Rotterdam, Marinus Jan Granpré Molière (1883–1972), together with J.H. de Roos and W.S. Overeynder, created the garden village Vreewijk between 1916 and 1919, which was a synthesis of the spirit of the *woningwet*, aimed toward building for the masses, and the idea of the garden city movement, very much alive in rural areas.

But the most widely spread typology was the one planned by H.P. Berlage in 1915 (Fig. 138) for the new Amsterdam South expansion. This plan, approved by the municipal authorities in 1917, consisted of large urban blocks placed around a courtyard green space. It was, in fact, the planning of these large blocks that diffused among young architects creative ways with a distinctly Romantic flavor that would be known by the name of the Amsterdam School, and that marked the new quarters of the city with a precise identity. Aiming to give their creations a strong expressiveness, the Amsterdam School architects always built in brick of the most varied colors, animating their constructions with organic forms, highly decorated wooden fixtures, and sculpture in stone, terra-cotta, and cast iron, with the chief purpose of transforming modest public housing into true "workers' palaces" (Fig. 112). Amsterdam, where the municipal authorities vigorously supported this very expressive planning, was called in the 1920s the "Mecca of Public Housing."

The major exponent of the creativity of the Amsterdam School with regard to public housing was Michel de Klerk, whose remarkable works survive in the buildings of Eigen Haard in the Spaarndammerbuurt (1913–1921; Fig. 35) and in the complex De Dageraad (1920–1923), built with his friend Piet Kramer (1881–1961). The latter is a combination of approximately three hundred apartments and shops distinguished by two curvilinear towers with a surprising variety of residences placed around them.

If the orientation of the Amsterdam School was toward enrichment in the aesthetic sense of apartment-block living, the construction of Spangen in Rotterdam in 1921, designed by Michiel Brinkman (1873–1925), represented a decisive reconsideration of this typology. Spangen, a large block around a courtyard, is enriched with a vast gallery at the height of the third story, which, in addition to giving access to the duplex apartments on that level, functions as an elevated street where children play and neighbors can converse.

By the end of the 1920s the emotionalism of the architecture of the Amsterdam School had its counterpoint in a radical tendency to simplify the language and progressively abandon the use of closed blocks. A sign of the new times, for example, was the experimental Betondorp project in Amsterdam, promoted by the city, where a new construction technology for building in concrete at low cost was attempted. This was achieved by Johannes Bernardus van Loghem (1881–1940) and other young architects, who combined an urban garden-quarter plan with rhythmically repetitive geometric forms.

The most famous purist experiment was conducted in Rotterdam by Jacobus Johannes Pieter Oud, chief architect of that city from 1918 to 1933. After having designed several public-housing projects that combined traditional elements with formal motifs of Neo-Plasticism, Oud produced his first fully modern work in the workers' residences in Hoek van Holland (1924–1927)—a line of white houses two stories high, marked by cylindrical glass volumes that contain the shops. Oud's masterpiece, however, is the Kiefhoek quarter (1925–1929), consisting of two-story row houses with a small garden for each unit (Fig. 113). Painted white, with continuous horizontal fenestration along the entire façade, organized according to families' minimal lodging requirements, the Kiefhoek quarter represents the quintessence of the new concept of living. Since the moment of its realization, it has been considered a manifest experience of the new modern European architecture.

At the end of the 1920s, the theoretical debate inspired by the modern movement proposed the construction of isolated buildings in lines and with galleries, placed among green zones, in opposition to the type of compact and continuous row housing along the streets. In 1933–1934 one of the first examples of this new trend in public housing was constructed in Rotterdam. It is the Bergpolder Flats (Fig. 48), a high-rise building with an iron framework and an elevator, by Johannes Andreas Brinkman (1902–1949), Leendert Cornelis van der Vlugt (1894–1936), and Willem van Tijen (1894–1974).

In urban construction after World War II, extensive use was made of open apartment blocks, repeated in parallel lines, above a green plain containing the infrastructures. This type follows the lesson learned by the modernists in the period between the World Wars and was first applied on a large scale in the expansion plan for Amsterdam (Fig. 139) devised in 1935 by a team led by Cornelis van Eesteren (1897–1988).

This way of constructing the new residential quarters continued until the mid-1970s, when seeing the urban environment in these terms began to be questioned. Following the creation of a satellite area for one hundred thousand inhabitants to the south of Amsterdam, the Bijlmermeer, consisting entirely of huge open blocks in semihexagonal shape, the national debate turned severely critical. The anonymity of these grand-scale modern interventions was seen as being opposed to the strong identity and quality of the historic cities.

In this context, public housing, which until the 1970s was carried out exclusively in new projects on the outskirts, now is increasingly a part of urban renewal, taking the form of restoring vacant buildings such as warehouses to be used as residences, or constructing new buildings in established urban contexts. The works of the 1980s, therefore, were marked by a return to low-rise buildings, often in brick, sometimes with inclined roofs, with great attention paid to traditional values. Among the results of this discontinuous quality, the works of Aldo van Eyck (born 1918) in the historic center of Zwolle or in the Jordaan in the heart of Amsterdam are outstanding.

For forty years of the postwar period, there was an immense vitality in public construction, with almost four million apartments built or renovated through public subsidies of various kinds. But economic difficulties at the end of the 1980s brought on a progressive reduction of public financing for residential building, accompanied by new, rather restrictive, regulations that aimed at reducing the cost of construction. These new regulations are contested because they limit expressive possibilities. However, they also encourage the interesting work of some young architects, such as the Mecanoo Group (F. Houben, E. van Egeraat, H. Döll, R. Steenhuis, and C. de Weijer) of Delft, who—with reference to the purist experience of Dutch modernism—are experimenting with a language both minimalist and strongly expressive.

Maristella Casciato

See also Amsterdam School; Berlage, Hendrik Petrus; De Klerk, Michel; Functionalism in architecture; Kramer, Pieter Lodewijk (Piet); Oud, Jacobus Johannes Pieter; Postmodernism; Urban planning, from 1750 to the present

Bibliography
Grinberg, Donald I. *Housing in the Netherlands, 1900–1940*. Delft: Delft University Press, 1977.
———. "Modernist Housing and Its Critics: The Dutch Contribution." *Harvard Architectural Review* 1 (Spring 1980): 147–160.
Searing, Helen E. "Amsterdam South: Social Democracy's Elusive Housing Ideal." *VIA: Architectural Journal of the Graduate School of Fine Arts, University of Pennsylvania* 4 (1980), 58–77.
———. "With Red Flags Flying: Housing in Amsterdam." In *Art and Architecture in the Service of Politics*. Edited by Henry A. Millon and Linda Nochlin, 230–269. Cambridge, MA: MIT Press, 1978.
Stieber, Nancy. "A Tradition of Commitment: Housing Design in the Netherlands." *CRIT* 20 (1988): 22–29.

Public monumental sculpture (ca. 1550–1795)

Public monumental sculpture in the Netherlands is largely a phenomenon of the nineteenth and twentieth centuries. Following the restoration of Dutch independence in 1813, renewed feelings of patriotism or national consciousness were expressed in commissions for statues honoring those individuals who had played a significant role in the country's political or cultural history. That this had not happened during the early modern period (the fifteenth through the eighteenth centuries), under a similar set of circumstances, was largely due to the combined forces of three unrelated factors.

First, the absence of a preexisting tradition of large-scale public sculpture in the Netherlands appears to have precluded spontaneous initiatives of this type. Secondly, the widespread acceptance among Dutch Protestants of the Old Testament prohibition against "graven images," coupled with their association of sacred sculpture with "Papish superstition," raised strong reservations about the advisability of three-dimensional art more generally. Thirdly, the instability of a political system that periodically shifted from Orangist to Republican regimes created a reluctance to acknowledge members of a hereditary elite (the House of Orange or local noble families) in terms of public statues. Likewise, there was little support for honoring demotic figures who might be associated in the public's mind with particular political or religious factions.

Nevertheless, there were commissions for public sculpture during the early modern period, which, in some cases, established important precedents for later projects. First, propagandistic programs of architectural or decorative sculpture had been mounted on the exteriors and interiors of Dutch churches and secular buildings (including city gates, town halls, belfries, weigh houses and storehouses, guild halls and schools) from the Middle Ages. While on one level these constituted unexceptional displays of civic pride, on another they were also self-serving celebrations of a town's political, judi-

cial, and economic institutions and the political and social order for which they were responsible. Secondly, important examples of monumental sculpture appear in seventeenth-century Dutch sepulchral art, namely in tombs, mounted in honor of those who had performed exemplary service to the Republic, which mark the transition from the traditional funeral monument to the modern public memorial. Hendrick de Keyser's imposing mausoleum of Willem I of Orange (1614–1621; Delft, Nieuwe Kerk; Fig. 34) was portrayed in paintings, prints, and guide books as the nation's foremost patriotic shrine. A similar status was accorded the monuments commissioned by the Republic's national assembly and the regional assemblies and admiralties in honor of the country's naval heroes. These *heldengraven* (tombs of heroes), produced by De Keyser, Rombout Verhulst (Color Plate 9), Bartolomeus Eggers, and other regional sculptors, not only paid respect to officers who had valiantly served the Republic from the Revolt through the English and French Wars, but they were also intended to inspire future generations of Dutch youth to emulate these heroes' patriotism.

Finally, in contrast to the apparent popularity of the *heldengraven*, nonsepulchral statues honoring other notable Nederlanders were extremely rare. De Keyser's bronze figure of *Erasmus* (1618–1622; Rotterdam, Markt Plein), the object of fierce political debate among political and religious groups in Rotterdam, was the only public statue erected in the Republic during the seventeenth century. It was not until 1722 that another Dutch citizen, the Haarlem typographer Laurens Jansz. Koster, was similarly honored. By the second half of the eighteenth century, and even more commonly from the nineteenth century, public monuments commemorating those renowned for their public or patriotic service, or honoring the "heroes of the spirit" celebrated in the Enlightenment cult of genius, were increasingly erected throughout the Netherlands.

Cynthia Lawrence

See also De Keyser, Hendrick; Eggers, Bartolomeus; Nationalism; Sculpture (1550–1795); Tomb sculpture: early modern and later sepulchral art; Tomb sculpture: medieval effigial monuments; Town halls; Verhulst, Rombout

Bibliography
Becker, J. "'De Rotterdamsche heyligh': Seventiende-eeuwsche echo's op het standbeeld van Erasmus." In *Vondel bij gelegenheid 1679–1979*. Edited by L. Roose and K. Porteman, 11–62. Middelburg: Merlijn, 1979.
———. "Een ketter in heiligenkleed—Erasmus in Rotterdam." In *Beelden in de Gouden Eeuw: Kunst Schrift* 91 (1991): 42–47.
Jimkes-Verkade, E. "De ikonologie van het grafmonument van Willem I, prins van Orange." In *De stad Delft, cultuur en maatschappij van 1572 tot 1667*, 214–230. Delft: Culturele Gemeenschap van Delft, 1981.
———. "Het heldengraf." In *Beelden in de Gouden Eeuw: Kunst Schrift* 91 (1991): 32–41.
Jongh, E. de. "De schaduwen van Daedalus." *Beelden in de Gouden Eeuw: Kunst Schrift* 91 (1991): 10–15.

Kersbergen, A.T.C. *Rotterdamse Standbeelden, Monumenten en Gedenktekens.* Rotterdam and Antwerp: A.D. Doncker, 1948.

Lawrence, C. "Hendrick de Keyser's Heemskerk Monument: The Origins of the Cult and the Iconography of the Dutch Naval Heroes." *Simiolus* 21 (1992): 265–295.

"Monumentale Beeldhouwkunst in Nederland." Theme volume. *Nederlands Kunsthistorisch Jaarboek* 34 (1983).

Neurdenburg, E. *De zeventiende eeuwsche beeldhouwkunst in de Noordelijke Nederlanden: Hendrick de Keyser, Artus Quellien, en Rombout Verhulst en tijdgenoten.* Amsterdam: Meulenhoff, 1948.

Swigchem, C.A. van, T. Brouwer, and W. van Os. *Een huis voor het Woord: Het protestantse kerkinterieur in Nederland tot 1900,* 264–265. The Hague: Staatsuitgeverij, 1984.

Public monumental sculpture (1795–1990)

The Netherlands never had a particularly pronounced sculptural tradition. Calvinist fear of imagery and a Republican form of government permitted honoring heroes of the nation only in monumental grave markers, with two memorable exceptions: the memorials to the intellectual giants Desiderius Erasmus and Laurens Jansz. Koster.

Even though monumental sculptures were eventually created to celebrate the important events of revolution and liberation, they were, as a rule, less conspicuous and aroused more public controversy than in other European countries. Aside from the classically inspired obelisk to commemorate the victory of Napoleon (Soestdijk, A. van der Hart, 1814) and the romanticizing historical monument to the poet Jacob Cats (Brouwershaven, Philippe Parmentier, 1829), public monuments were created only after the independence of Belgium in 1831. These monuments were often in competition with foreign memorials in the attempt to portray the nation's self-confidence as well as to reflect its influence in the European community of nations.

These sentiments were also expressed in commemoration of the past, most notably the Golden Age of the seventeenth century, and especially in regard to the prominent artists of that time. The history of the Netherlands as a naval power in the seventeenth century is commemorated in the memorial to Admiral Michiel de Ruyter (Vlissingen, Louis Royer, 1841). The birth of the nation as a result of the conflict with Spain is remembered in two monuments—created almost at the same time—that pay homage to the "father of the country," Willem I. These monuments show the contrast between international aristocratic ambition and the Dutch middle class: The equestrian statue (1845) that the king commissioned from the French Comte de Nieuwerkercke is a study of action; Louis Royer designed the statue (1848) on the Plein in The Hague whose influence can still be seen in the monument to Count Jan von Nassau (Utrecht, J.Th. Stracké, 1888). Connected to the last two works are romantic historical monuments for heroes of the fight for freedom against Spain, such as J.Ph. Koelman's memorial to Burgomaster Van der Werff (Leiden, 1884).

More recent history is immortalized in the somewhat wooden statue of King Willem II (Tilburg, E.F. Georges, 1853) and the Thorbecke Memorial (Amsterdam, F. Leenhoff, 1876), but especially in the monuments that are thematically more ambitious. An example is the memorial created in 1865 commemorating the spirit of the nation in 1830–1831 (Amsterdam, H.M. Tétar van Elven and Louis Royer); this was the Dutch response to the Brussels Monument to the Martyrs (namely, those who died in the revolution of 1830), which had been unveiled in 1835. Another example is the Monument to 1813 (The Hague, W.C. van der Waaijen Pieterszen and J.Ph. Koelman, 1869; Fig. 124), a memorial comprised of several figures. This marker was intended as a response to Brussels' Congress Column, which commemorates the legislative congress after the separation from France in 1813. Typical for the Netherlands is the lighthouse in Egmond, influenced by architecture of the French Revolution, that commemorates the heroic death of Lieutenant Van Speyck at Antwerp in 1831 (J.D. Zocher, 1841).

After World War I, a stylistic renewal—that is, memorials based on architectural concepts—is apparent in the monuments for the Boer War General Christiaan de Wet (De Hoge Veluwe National Park, J. Mendes da Costa, 1922; Fig. 82); for the first wife of Willem I, Juliana van Stolberg (The Hague, B.A.M. Ingen Housz. and D. Roosenburg, 1930); and for General J.B. van Heutsz. (Amsterdam, G. Friedhoff and F. van Hall, 1936), whose portrait shows him being crowned by an allegorical figure representing the Dutch Indies in front of an abstract backdrop of triumphal architecture. Characteristic of the ambivalent sentiments in the Netherlands is the fact that this monument has been the target of political actions that finally resulted in the removal of the portrait. In comparable style are the monuments of Hildo Krop and Lambertus Zijl, both of whom created important architectural sculptures (for example, Zijl's work for H.P. Berlage's Amsterdam Stock Exchange) (Fig. 125).

A great number of monuments were created immediately following World War II. Of the approximately one thousand monuments commemorating the war, resistance, and destruction, only a few manage to evoke the unspeakable suffering they were supposed to consecrate. The numerous inscriptions are possibly part of the Protestant tradition, as in the monument for H.M. van Randwijk (Amsterdam, Gerda van der Laan, 1970). Exemplary depictions of combatants or, more often, victims rely on older figurative sculpture. Most impressive is the powerful sculpture of *The Dockworker* commemorating the February Strike of 1941 against German occupation (Amsterdam, Mari Andriessen, 1952), as well as the sculpture of Anne Frank, which conveys the fragility of this anti-heroine (Utrecht, Pieter d'Hont, 1960). Among the allegorical works, the Rotterdam image *The Destroyed Town* (1953), created by the Russian-born artist Ossip Zadkine, has received particular attention. In addition, two abstract monuments are especially notable: the memorial by A. Carasso commemorating the merchant navy (Rotterdam, 1957; with an unnecessary figural group added in 1965); and the *Monument to the Women of Ravensbrück* (Amsterdam, J. van Santen, G. Eckhardt, F. Nix, 1975).

The national monument in the center of Amsterdam combines the previously mentioned stylistic elements: a tall pylon with allegorical figures against a backdrop whose features include a poem (J.J.P. Oud and John Raedecker, 1956). The simplest of pictorial media—a broken mirror exposed to the sky—was used by the writer and sculptor Jan Wolkers to create the forceful Auschwitz Monument (Amsterdam, 1977).

Besides the themes mentioned, sculptors have created numerous public works, but only a few impressive monumental sculptures. One modern version is the monumental sculptural image of the river *Maas* by Auke de Vries (Rotterdam, 1982).

Jochen Becker

See also Andriessen, Mari; Krop, Hildo; Mendes da Costa, Joseph; Monuments to artists; Nationalism; Oud, Jacobus Johannes Pieter; Raedecker, John; Royer, Louis; Sculpture (1795–1945); World Wars I and II; Zijl, Lambertus

Bibliography

Adrichem, Jan van et al. *Sculpture in the City Rotterdam: The City As Stage.* Utrecht: Veen/Reflex, 1988.

Beerman, Mirjam, Frans van Burkom, and Frans Grijzenhout, eds. *Beeldengids Nederland.* Rotterdam: 010, 1994.

Bionda, R.W.A. et al. *Monumentale beeldhouwkunst in Nederland.* Weesp: Fibula-Van Dishoeck, 1984.

Daalen, P.K. van. *Nederlandse beeldhouwers in de negentiende eeuw.* The Hague: Nijhoff, 1957.

Quacksalvers, quack doctors

The *kwakzalver*, or quack doctor, as he appears in Dutch art may be defined as a medical practitioner who performs diagnostic or therapeutic procedures outside of either an office or a domestic setting. Often associated with scenes of markets or *kermissen* (the annual open fair), this figure occurs primarily in low-life genre painting and prints and is generally presented as a comic character. While the *kwakzalver* is related to the figures of the charlatan physician, like those depicted by Jan Steen in his genre scenes of lovesick maidens, or the barber-surgeon familiar from works by the Flemish painter David Teniers, he represents a category distinct from them, deriving from different sources and revealing different pictorial and iconographic concerns. The theme is treated in art from the sixteenth through the eighteenth centuries, but it reaches its greatest popularity in the middle years of the seventeenth century.

Quack doctors are portrayed in Dutch art engaged in a variety of activities: They pull teeth, cut stones from their patients' heads, operate on peasants' feet and legs, perform uroscopy, and sell patent medicines. Among the most important iconographic sources for images of quack doctors is folly imagery, such as Hieronymus Bosch's *Stone of Folly* (1470–1490) and Pieter Bruegel's prints *The Lithotomists (Dean of Renaix)* (1557) and *The Sorceress of Malleghem* (1559), all of which depict the surgical excision of a stone from a patient's head as a cure for foolishness. Representations of operations to the head in sixteenth- and seventeenth-century art, even when they do not clearly show the removal of the stone of folly, are nonetheless associated with the notion of transforming or civilizing the gullible, boorish patient. Lucas van Leyden's woodcut of an *Operation on the Ear of a Peasant* (1524), for example, which stems from the iconography established in Bosch's painting, omits the stone. This print, along with Lucas' *Toothpuller* woodcut of 1523, provided a thematic source for countless later images of *kwakzalvers* at work, including genre paintings by Jan Miense Molenaer, Jan Victors, and Steen, and illustrations by Adriaen van de Venne.

In addition to the fifteenth- and sixteenth-century pictorial sources for the subject of the *kwakzalver* in seventeenth-century art, literary sources contributed to the development of the theme as well as to the viewing public's understanding of it. A number of sixteenth- and seventeenth-century popular farces center on the character of a quack doctor in the market, whose primary goal is to trick naive peasants into buying his ineffective remedies or submitting to his dangerous and painful surgical treatments. It seems clear that these theatrical characterizations of the quack strongly informed the seventeenth-century interpretation of the quack doctor in paintings and prints. While earlier representations focus on the foolishness of the patient, in the 1600s the emphasis shifts to the practitioner himself, who becomes the deceitful protagonist of the implied narrative. The character of the *kwakzalver* also occurs in three of the most important literary descriptions of *kermissen* published in the 1600s and early 1700s, and is illustrated by Adriaen van de Venne in his comic account of the fair in The Hague, *Tafereel van de Belacchende Werelt*, published in 1635. Jan Steen's *Quack at the Kermis* (1656–1660), which portrays a theatrical stonecutter on a stage at a fair, combines several of these iconographic traditions in a single work.

One of the best-known examples of quack doctors in genre painting is Gerrit Dou's *The Quacksalver* (1652; Fig. 114), which has received considerable scholarly attention. Dou presents a typical quack doctor, who has set up a make-shift table on the outskirts of Leiden in order to market his patent medicines. A sign posted beside the window in the building at the right of the composition notifies the viewer that the scene takes place at *kermis*-time; this information implies that the *kwakzalver*'s presence has been sanctioned, since the fair permitted the relaxation of social and professional regulations. Forbidden from practicing legally throughout most of the year, the quack was allowed to take part in the festivities associated with the annual open market. His motley costume was designed to attract a clientele as quickly as possible, and at the same time it alludes to the theatrical sources for the quack doctor.

Similarly, the peasant audience that surrounds him recalls the belief, perpetuated in farces, that only the uneducated classes of Dutch society were susceptible to the quack's deceitful promises. At the same time, however, it has been shown that several of these figures were quoted directly from illustrations in seventeenth-century Dutch emblem books, specifically from emblems concerning deception, and that they should be seen to refer to the quack's cunning persona. The inclusion of a self-portrait of Dou in the window at the right forces a comparison between the practice of the quack and that of the painter, both of whom aim, in different ways, to trick the client.

The moralizing interpretations often given to images of quack doctors are based largely on literary and emblematic evidence. Both medical and social historical sources, however, offer new perspectives into the study of *kwakzalver* imagery, in particular helping to distinguish it from depictions of officially approved practitioners such as surgeons and physicians. *Kwakzalvers* were excluded from the rigidly structured medical hierarchy in Holland in the early modern period, and yet they were often well-educated and highly experienced practitioners. They performed a number of essential services for the towns and cities that periodically allowed them to practice: In particular, they specialized in difficult surgical procedures such as cataract and hernia operations, and the removal of bladder stones. Thus, many of them gained genuine respect from the public and medical professionals. This apparent disjunction between the potentially elevated status a *kwakzalver* could achieve and the sometimes satirical pictorial representations of them indicates that the theme, especially in the seventeenth century, was considerably more complex than has been supposed. Future research into these images should take into account the wide range of attitudes toward these practitioners in Dutch culture and the multiple symbolic meanings depictions of them might convey.

Carol J. Fresia

See also Bosch, Hieronymus; Comic modes; Emblems and emblem books; Genre painting, seventeenth century; Steen, Jan Havicksz.; Theater and theatricality

Bibliography

Bax, D. *Hieronymus Bosch: His Picture-Writing Deciphered.* Translated by M.A. Bax-Botha. Rotterdam: A.A. Balkema, 1979.

Brand Philip, Lotte. "The *Peddlar* by Hieronymus Bosch: A Study in Detection." *Nederlands Kunsthistorisch Jaarboek* 9 (1958): 1–82.

De Jongh, E. *Tot Lering en vermaak: Betekenissen van Hollandse genrevoorstellingen uit de zeventiende eeuw.* Amsterdam: Rijksmuseum, 1976.

Emmens, J.A. "De kwakzalver: Gerard Dou (1613–1675)." In *Kunsthistorische Opstellen.* Vol. 2, 163–168. Amsterdam: Van Oorschot, 1981.

Fresia, Carol J. "Quacksalvers and Barber-Surgeons: Images of Medical Practitioners in Seventeenth-Century Dutch Genre Painting." Ph.D. diss., Yale University, 1991.

Gaskell, Ivan. "Gerrit Dou, his patrons, and the art of painting." *Oxford Art Journal* 5 (1982): 15–23.

Vandenbroeck, Paul. *Jheronimus Bosch: Tusen volksleven en stadscultuur.* Berchem: EPO, 1987.

Vries, Lyckle de. "Jan Steen 'de kluchtschilder.'" Ph.D. diss., Rijksuniversiteit Groningen, 1977.

Quellinus, Artus I (1609–1668)

One of the most prominent sculptors of the Flemish Baroque, Artus I Quellinus (alternatives: Quellin, Quellien) studied with his father in Antwerp before undertaking an Italian trip (after 1634) during which he came under the influence of François Duquesnoy and Gianlorenzo Bernini. His works present an inventive reconciliation of the polarized tendencies presented by these artists—the classicism of Duquesnoy, and the high-baroque drama of Bernini. However, in contrast to other Flemish sculptors, such as Rombout Verhulst, Quellinus remains more classicizing.

Quellinus returned to Antwerp in 1639 and became a master in the Guild of St. Luke the following year. From 1650 through 1664 he was active in Amsterdam, producing sculpture and decoration for the new town hall, the most impressive Baroque sculptural ensemble in the Netherlands (and perhaps in Northern Europe), that was in large part designed by Jacob van Campen, the building's architect. Quellinus was responsible for executing the pediment reliefs (the *Seas Pay Homage to Amsterdam* and *Amsterdam Supreme*) and figures (*Justice, Prudence, Peace,* and *Atlas*), as well as the reliefs (the *Judgment of Solomon, Justice of Zaleucus,* and *Justice of Brutus*), caryatids and figures (*Justice*) for the *vierschaar* (public high court); the Burgerzaal (the citizens' hall); and the galleries (reliefs of *Diana, Cybele, Mars, Apollo,* and *Jupiter*).

Numerous terra-cotta studies, models and copies by Quellinus, as well as by his collaborators and assistants (including Verhulst and Bartolomeus Eggers), are in the Rijksmuseum in Amsterdam. Even before he arrived in Amsterdam, Quellinus was represented in Dutch collections, including that of Frederik Hendrik, who commissioned statues of *Mars* and *Venus* (now lost) as early as 1634. Other works from his Amsterdam period include the relief portraits (1660; Amsterdam, Rijksmuseum) of *Cornelis de Graeff* and *Catherina Hooft,* as well as busts of *De Graeff* (1661), *Nicholaes Tulp* (workshop, ca. 1654–1656), and *Johann de Witt* (Dordrecht). He is also credited (Fremantle; and Leeuwenberg and Halsema-Kubes) with the figure called *Frenzy* (ca. 1650; Amsterdam, Rijksmuseum), executed for the courtyard of the Amsterdam Dolhuis (lunatic asylum). In 1665 Quellinus returned to Antwerp, where he was active until his death three years later.

Cynthia Lawrence

See also Eggers, Bartolomeus; Sculpture (1550–1795); Tomb sculpture: early modern and later sepulchral art; Town halls; Van Campen, Jacob; Verhulst, Rombout

Bibliography

Fremantle, K. *The Baroque Town Hall of Amsterdam.* Utrecht: Haentjens, Dekker, and Gumbert, 1959.

Fremantle, K., and W. Halsema-Kubes. *Beelden Kijken: De Kunst van Quellien in het Paleis op de Dam.* Amsterdam: Koninklijk Paleis, 1977.

Gabriels, J. *Artus Quellien de Oude, "kunstrijk belthouwer."* Antwerp: De Sikkel, 1930.

Hoozee, R. "Artus I Quellinus." In *De Beeldhouwkunst in de Eeuw van Rubens*, 142–157. Brussels: Museum voor Oude Kunst, 1977.

Kulturmann, U. et al. "Artus Quellinus d. A." In *Europäische Barockplastik am Niederrhein: Grupello und seine Zeit*, 238–247. Dusseldorf: Kunstmuseum, 1971.

Leeuwenberg, J., and W. Halsema-Kubes, eds. *Beeldhouwkunst in het Rijksmuseum.* The Hague/Amsterdam: Staatsuitgeverij; The Hague/Amsterdam: Rijksmuseum, 1973.

Neurdenburg, E. *De zeventiende eeuwsche beeldhouwkunst in de Noordelijke Nederlanden: Hendrick de Keyser, Artus Quellien, en Rombout Verhulst en tijdgenoten.* Amsterdam: Meulenhoff, 1948.

Rosenberg, H., S. Slive, and E.H. ter Kuile. *Dutch Art and Architecture, 1600–1800.* Baltimore: Penguin, 1966.

Quinkhard, Jan Maurits (1688–1772)

Jan Maurits Quinkhard was one of the most sought-after portrait painters in Amsterdam during the second and third quarters of the eighteenth century. Born in Germany as the son of a painter, he settled in Amsterdam in 1710. There he continued his education with Arnold Boonen and Nicolaas Verkolje, among others. His career as an independent painter likely did not start until after 1723. By around 1730 Quinkhard was the leading portrait painter in Amsterdam; his most important competitors were, originally, Cornelis Troost and, later, Tibout Regters. Over the next forty years he made hundreds of portraits, mostly in life-size bust and half-length formats, which are characterized by a somewhat dry, sometimes arid, manner of painting. In many of his portraits a certain vitality is still achieved by the gestures of the figures. His commissioners were not only from Amsterdam, but also from other Northern Netherlands cities, in particular Utrecht. For the governments of Amsterdam and Utrecht, he made a dozen group portraits of regents. Like his portraits of individuals, these regent portraits are not particularly surprising in composition or design, but a threatening boredom is avoided because the sitters are gesturing and appear active most of the time. In addition to painting life-size portraits, Quinkhard was also in the forefront as a maker of miniatures in oils. Some family groups in a rather small format belong among his most attractive works; they show a greater vitality than his more official portraits and make a contribution to the development of the Dutch conversation piece. His few history and genre paintings fall behind in quality to his portraits. Some of Quinkhard's students were Tibout Regters, Jan de Beyer, and his own son Julius Quinkhard.

Rudolf E.O. Ekkart

See also Conversation piece; Portraiture; Regters, Tibout; Troost, Cornelis

Bibliography

Mandle, R. *Dutch Masterpieces from the Eighteenth Century: Paintings and Drawings, 1700–1800.* Minneapolis: Minneapolis Institute of Arts, 1971.

Staring, A. *De Hollanders thuis.* The Hague: Nijhoff, 1956.

R

Raedecker, John (1885–1956)

The sculptor John Raedecker received his first lessons in carving wood and modeling from his father. As a youth, he worked in furniture factories and in a stone-cutter's firm in his native city of Amsterdam. In 1906 he went to the Rijksacademie, where, for only a short time, he took a sculpting class from Bart van Hove, but he stayed on to take the evening class in drawing for four years. For several months in 1910 he drew the models at the Antwerp Academy. From 1911 until World War I he made several trips to Paris, where he came under the influence of Cubism. Later he developed his own style, which is characterized by expressive round forms that often radiate a dreamy, slightly surrealistic atmosphere.

Raedecker produced many small-scale works of sculpture, mainly in bronze and wood, but he also sculpted various larger forms in stone. An example of the latter is the monument to Jan Toorop in The Hague (1931–1937). Occasionally he made sculpture for architecture (for example, for De Bijenkorf department store in The Hague, 1926). He made a great many drawings during his life, and, especially before 1940, he painted.

After World War II Raedecker spent most of his time on his best-known work, the National Monument (a memorial to all of the Dutch victims of the war) on the Dam in Amsterdam (1947–1956), a project that he carried out in cooperation with the architect J.J.P. Oud. He also created a war monument for the town of Waalwijk (1949). His works can be found in all of the major art museums in the Netherlands.

Mieke van der Wal

See also Monuments to artists; Oud, Jacobus Johannes Pieter; Public monumental sculpture (1795–1990); Sculpture (1795–1945); Van Hove, Bart

Bibliography

John Rädecker, 1885–1956: Beeldhouwwerken, schilderijen, en tekeningen. Haarlem: Teylers Museum, 1985.

Wiessing, H.P.L. *John Raedecker.* Amsterdam: Meulenhoff, 1962.

Regters, Tibout (1710–1768)

In portraiture of the eighteenth century and the history of the conversation piece in particular, Tibout Regters is one of the most interesting artists. After a time training with some little-known painters, Regters completed his education with Jan Maurits Quinkhard in Amsterdam. He settled in that city as an independent artist around 1740 and remained working there until his death. His earliest works, small individual portraits, still betray strongly the influence of his teacher, but he soon developed his own style, in which genre elements play an important role.

Shortly before the middle of the century, Regters started to do small family groups, in which a seeming nonchalance in the arrangement and poses of the figures is characteristic. Dozens of surviving works of this kind are among the best examples of the Dutch conversation piece. After 1751 the artist also made some life-size group portraits of Amsterdam regents boards; however, they lack the vitality and charm of his small family groups. A number of the individual portraits that Regters made for patrons from Amsterdam and other places closely connect with the conversation pieces and show in a rather small format the person portrayed in his surroundings. Regters also made individual portraits in a life-size format; during the last years of his life he made only such likenesses.

Besides his portraits, he is also known to have made a few genre paintings of market scenes. He also made mythological pictures, but none of these has been found.

Rudolf E.O. Ekkart

See also Conversation piece; Portraiture; Quinkhard, Jan Maurits

Bibliography

Mandle, R. *Dutch Masterpieces from the Eighteenth Century: Paintings and Drawings, 1700–1800.* Minneapolis:

Minneapolis Institute of Arts, 1971.
Praz, M. *Conversation Pieces*. London: Methuen, 1971.
Staring, A. *De Hollanders thuis*. The Hague: Nijhoff, 1956.

Religion of artists

Notable stylistic and iconographic differences distinguish the works of Protestant and Roman Catholic artists in the Northern Netherlands during the seventeenth century. Although denominational distinctions did not affect much of the work produced for the open market, religious beliefs often determined the selection, interpretation, and appearance of religious themes for specific patrons. In order to recognize the influence of religious affiliations on Dutch art, one must first establish the religious orientations of seventeenth-century artists and then compare the religious and nonreligious works of artists of different creeds to reveal distinctions.

Biographical facts gleaned from the civic and religious records of birth, baptism, marriage, and death can verify religious persuasions. The absence of this data in seventeenth-century Dutch civic lists indicates that the religious rite, if it occurred at all, did so outside the Reformed Church. Marriage banns, for example, were published in two categories in the town halls of the Netherlands: in one category for the Reformed Church members and in another series for non-Calvinists. This source of information has aided in ascertaining the Roman Catholicism of renowned painters, such as Johannes Vermeer and Gabriel Metsu. Burial accounts can also determine religious orientation. Although Roman Catholics and non-Calvinists were occasionally buried in Dutch Reformed churches, certain conventions were followed for each denomination. The tolling of bells after interment, which was clearly annotated in church records, was associated with the Roman Catholic faith. A marginal note indicating the ringing of bells after Gabriel Metsu's burial in the Protestant Nieuwe Kerk attests to his Roman Catholicism.

In addition to the primary biographical data based on contemporary documents, less authoritative evidence, such as baptismal names, friendships, and neighborhoods, can also indicate specific religious orientations. As John Michael Montias has pointed out, Vermeer's christening name, "Johannis," is a form of "Jan" preferred by Roman Catholics and upper-class Protestants. Although it is unlikely that Johannes Vermeer was born and raised a Roman Catholic, by the time he named his son, Ignatius, presumably in honor of the Jesuit founder, the Dutch genre painter had married a Roman Catholic woman and converted. The name Gabriel, after the annunciate angel, supports, along with the biographical documentation, Metsu's Roman Catholic orientation.

Montias and others have also considered personal relationships as indicative of specific religious affiliations. Vermeer's documented associations with the fellow Delft painter Leonaert Bramer, and his purported training with Abraham Bloemaert in Utrecht, substantiate the Dutch genre painter's ties with Roman Catholicism. Living at the Papist's Corner in Delft, close to a Jesuit *schuilkerk*, or hidden church, provides further evidence of Vermeer's religious convictions.

Inventories may reveal ownership of goods associated with one faith. According to Montias, the presence of a crucifix or a rosary in a list of household goods is a conspicuous sign of Roman Catholicism, while the possession of the Dutch Reformed *Statenbijbel* (version of the Bible authorized by the States General, the governing body of the Netherlands), points to a Calvinist owner. Paintings of saints, priests, and Roman Catholic sacraments would logically appear more often in the collections of Roman Catholics, while Protestant collectors favored Old Testament themes and New Testament stories of grace and baptism.

Determining the faith of seventeenth-century Dutch artists increases one's understanding of their religious and nonreligious art. Vermeer and Metsu did not openly profess their faith in their depictions of everyday life, yet, when dealing with religious subject matter, both artists followed iconographic and stylistic patterns associated with Roman Catholicism. In doctrinal images such as Vermeer's painting of the *Allegory of Faith* (Fig. 115) or Metsu's less familiar representation of the *Adoration of the Real Presence*, the Dutch artists depended on Roman Catholic textual sources and on the likely advice of a learned patron. When depicting traditional themes, such as the Crucifixion, both painters relied on Roman Catholic pictorial prototypes associated with the Counter-Reformation.

Nonreligious works, such as genre imagery, portraiture, and even landscape, may also present religious meaning. For example, by ascertaining Metsu's Roman Catholicism, one can reconsider his depiction of a *Sick Child* (Fig. 85) as a Dutch Pietá or his painting of a woman playing the viola da gamba in San Francisco as a representation of St. Cecilia, the patron saint of musicians.

Recognition of the specific denominational concerns that may have influenced the selection and interpretation of religious and nonreligious subject matter has increasingly interested scholars of Dutch art history. In 1980 Christian Tümpel argued that, in general, no differences exist between the pictorial and stylistic choices of Protestant and Roman Catholic artists. Since that publication, however, studies by David R. Smith, Barbara Haeger, Valerie Lind Hedquist, Pieter J.J. van Thiel, and others have identified distinctions in religious art that reflect sectarian beliefs.

Valerie Lind Hedquist

See also Alberdingk Thijm, Josephus Albertus; Flanders, Flemish School; Metsu, Gabriel; Neo-Gothic; Pre-Rembrandtists; Protestant Reformation; Religious orders and their patronage; Rhetoricians' chambers; Utrecht; Vermeer, Johannes

Bibliography

Haeger, Barbara. "Barent Fabritius' Three Paintings of Parables for the Lutheran Church in Leiden." *Oud Holland* 101 (1987): 95–114.

Hedquist, Valerie Lind. "The Passion of Christ in Seventeenth-Century Dutch Painting." Ph.D. diss., University of Kansas, 1990.

Montias, John Michael. *Vermeer and His Milieu: A Web of Social History*. Princeton, NJ: Princeton University Press, 1989.

Slive, Seymour. "Notes on the Relationship of Protestantism to Seventeenth-Century Dutch Painting." *Art Quarterly* 19 (1956): 3–15.

Smith, David R. "Towards a Protestant Aesthetics: Rembrandt's 1655 Sacrifice of Isaac." *Art History* 8 (1985): 290–302.

Swillens, P.T.A. "Roomsch-Katholieke Kunstenaars in de 17de Eeuw." *Katholiek Cultureel Tijdschrift* 1, part 2 (1945/1946): 416–419.

Thiel, Pieter J.J. van. "Catholic Elements in Seventeenth-Century Dutch Painting, Apropos of a Children's Portrait by Thomas de Keyser." *Simiolus* 20 (1990/1991): 39–62.

Tümpel, Christian. "Religious History Painting." In *Gods, Saints, and Heroes: Dutch Painting in the Age of Rembrandt*. Edited by Albert Blankert et al., 45–54. Washington, DC: National Gallery of Art; Detroit: Institute of Arts; Amsterdam: Rijksmuseum, 1980.

Religious orders and their patronage

Religious foundations in the Netherlands, from cathedrals to charitable institutions, received their ornamentation mostly through gifts. The donors, individuals or groups, belonged to both the laity and the clergy. The patronage of religious orders, active before the Reformation, forms part of this larger pattern.

Often individual members of orders commissioned works for the institutions they served. Those in positions of power and authority might order large altarpieces reflective of their status. Less-affluent members commissioned smaller works, which perhaps decorated secondary or side altars. Sometimes a few members—perhaps two to four—jointly contributed to a commission. The Franciscans' emphasis on poverty may have led them to favor paintings on canvas, less ostentatious and less costly than works on panel. Donor portraits might appear in the altarpieces on the predella (base), on the wings, or discreetly placed at the edge of the sacred scene. Like other patrons, members of religious orders sometimes purchased existing works on the open market, which they might customize in some way.

Members of orders also commissioned small paintings for private devotional use. Carthusians appear in a number of surviving small devotional panels from the Netherlands (Fig. 73).

Lay ascetic communities such as the Devotio Moderna (Brothers and Sisters of the Common Life) and the Beguines also occupied an important place in the culture of the Low Countries. Their members lived communally under rules based on those of regular orders, but they took no vows and were free to leave. Espousing poverty, they did not exhibit much interest in large-scale, expensive works of art. The primary artistic significance of these communities lies in the broad impact of the contemplative life and devotional practices they promoted. These spread far beyond their members and contributed to the elaboration of Passion imagery and the rise of the "dramatic close-up." The Beguines have been linked with sculptural representations of the Pietà. The Devotio Moderna also promoted the cult of St. Jerome, who came to occupy a prominent position in painting.

Popular lay confraternities drew members from a variety of occupations and walks of life. Members maintained their independent lives, but met regularly, celebrated religious occasions, performed charitable acts, and provided for the burial of deceased members and for memorial masses. Some brotherhoods were strictly local organizations. Others, such as the Confraternity of Our Lady in 's Hertogenbosch to which Hieronymus Bosch belonged, attracted aristocratic members from a broad area. The communities might be consecrated to the Virgin or St. Anne, to the Holy Sacrament or the Holy Blood, or to the Rosary. The Knights of St. John of Jerusalem, of which Geertgen tot Sint Jans was a member, evolved from a military order established during the Crusades. Active patrons, confraternities commissioned numerous decorations for their chapels, including altarpieces. Members or leaders of the group often appeared as donor-participants in the central scene (Fig. 62). Members also commissioned small works for personal use, with subjects tied to the devotional focus of the brotherhood.

Portraits of confraternity members played an increasingly prominent role in their altarpieces, heralding a new direction in their patronage. Group portraits without religious scenes appeared in two works for the Jerusalem Brotherhood (pilgrims to the Holy Land) done by Jan van Scorel in the late 1520s. These are the direct forerunners of the great group portraits of the seventeenth-century Golden Age of the Netherlands.

Janey L. Levy

See also Contemplative life, contemplative virtues; Devotional images; Donor portraits; Group portraiture; Last Judgment; Tomb sculpture: medieval effigial monuments; Utrecht

Bibliography
Huvenne, Paul. *Pierre Pourbus, Peintre brugeois, 1524–1584*. Bruges: Memling Museum; Bruges: Crédit Communal, 1984.

Post, R.R. *The Modern Devotion: Confrontation with Reformation and Humanism*. Leiden: E.J. Brill, 1968.

Snyder, James. *Northern Renaissance Art: Painting, Sculpture, the Graphic Arts, from 1350 to 1575*. New York: Harry N. Abrams, 1985.

Ziegler, Joanna E. *Sculpture of Compassion: The Pietà and the Beguines in the Southern Low Countries, ca. 1300–ca. 1600*. Brussels: Institute historique belge de Rome, 1992.

Rembrandt research
History of Rembrandt Research

Rembrandt's work attracted attention as early as 1629 when his contemporary Constantijn Huygens praised the artist's *Judas Returning the Thirty Pieces of Silver*, saying that it could be favorably "placed against all the tasteful art of all time past." By the time Rembrandt died in 1669, however, taste had changed. Writing in 1681, Andries Pels described the artist as "the first heretic of painting." By the fourth quarter of the seventeenth century, Rembrandt's art was being linked with his life and character, an assumed connection that has underlain much subsequent scholarship. Eighteenth-century authors explained Rembrandt's low-life subject matter as stemming from the modest origins of this miller's son and the class of individuals with whom he chose to spend his time. Moreover, his free brushwork, interpreted as his desire for speed in execution, was linked to his avarice. As demonstrated by J.A. Emmens (1968), traditional literary formulas of artistic biography were being applied to Rembrandt by art theorists for the purpose of furthering the classicistic style they espoused. Rembrandt was singled out not because he and his work were particularly unappreciated, but because he had been so influential: Several generations of students and followers had imitated his subjects, his expressive poses and gestures, his picturesque accessories, and his free handling of paint.

In the eighteenth century, a much larger audience was exposed to Rembrandt's art through both his own prints and reproductive prints after his paintings. Already in 1718, Arnold Houbraken noted the widespread admiration for Rembrandt's etchings. The first *catalogue raisonné* devoted to any artist was that of Rembrandt's etchings published by Edme-François Gersaint in 1751. This circulation of his images in graphic form contributed to an appreciation in some circles of the artist's "manner," or style, rather than a concern for attribution or a serious attention to his biography. Toward the end of the century, as Romanticism replaced a taste for classicizing art, the characteristics for which Rembrandt had been criticized were reevaluated in a positive light.

By the nineteenth century, professional art historians joined a dialogue that had previously been dominated by collectors, connoisseurs, and artists. As artists and their work were being grouped by styles and periods, the focus of inquiry shifted from Rembrandt's manner to the man and his work. In 1828 the first documents relating to Rembrandt were published by the Amsterdam print dealer Evert Maaskamp, and in 1836 the first *catalogue raisonné* of his paintings was produced by the Englishman John Smith. A close connection between his art and his life continued to be assumed. But instead of his life explaining his choice of subject matter and style, his paintings—considered literal transcriptions of contemporary observations—were employed as documents for his biography. In addition, the valuation of the man and his work took yet another turn. While eighteenth-century admirers had celebrated the picturesque style of his work to promote the individualistic ideal of the inspired genius, in the nineteenth century Rembrandt's subject matter brought him admiration for democratic sentiments and insight into universal human qualities. The ideals for which he stood transformed him into a touchstone for nationalistic sentiments not only in the Netherlands but also in France and Germany.

By 1900 the growing number of paintings that were accumulating around Rembrandt's name lacked stylistic consistency, and the historical man thought to have produced them was no longer definable. Scholars thus began to restore balance to an *oeuvre* that had become swollen out of all proportion, and perspective to a man characterized as a creative genius with an insight into the human condition beyond that of most mortals. Particularly since 1970, investigations have become more focused and approaches have proliferated. These range from concentrating on the biographical facts and/or human character of the man and the creative personality of the artist, to identifying works produced by his hand, to locating both the thematic and stylistic sources and meanings of those works. Each of these investigations is based on different assumptions concerning the relationship of art, biography, and visual sources and social contexts: Some view Rembrandt's art through his life; some, his life through his art; others investigate both his life and his art within his social and cultural milieu; and one study considers his history paintings in relation to their source images and texts.

While a handful of documentary fragments had been published in 1828, the first comprehensive publication of all known archival discoveries—numbering four hundred thirty-seven entries—was assembled by Cornelis Hofstede de Groot in 1906. Since then, new and important documents in the Amsterdam Municipal Archives have been discovered by I.H. van Eeghen, S.A.C. Dudok van Heel, and others. These not only correct earlier inaccuracies, they have also added to our knowledge about his life, the subjects of his portraits, his patrons and collectors, and the world in which he lived. A new and enlarged transcription of known documents (numbering four hundred ninety-three) was published by Water L. Strauss and Marjon van der Meulen in 1979.

In 1985 Gary Schwartz published the most ambitious project to date to utilize these and other documents. His richly detailed study sought to disentangle Rembrandt the man from romantic generalizations about his works, and his works from attributions based upon stylistic analyses alone. Drawing inferences from the documented relationships of Rembrandt with his contemporaries, Schwartz illuminates the relations between Rembrandt, his patrons, their contemporaries, and the social, political, religious, and literary ideas that concerned them. In contrast to the inherited characterization of Rembrandt as a man who stood apart from his time—a creative genius with an extraordinary insight into the human condition—Schwartz creates an unsympathetic picture of a deeply flawed man, self-centered, manipulative, and avaricious.

It has been Rembrandt's paintings, however, that have continued to receive the largest share of both scholarly and popular attention. From the beginning of the twentieth century, a series of reevaluations of Rembrandt's *oeuvre* have been undertaken. Up to the middle of the century, the corpus had gradually grown, as new paintings were added and others removed. Smith had listed six hundred fourteen paintings; subtracting duplicate entries and those known only from engravings and entries in sales catalogs, the total number stood at about four hundred sixty-five. In 1897–1906 Wilhelm Bode and Hofstede de Groot published an eight-volume work of five hundred ninety-five paintings (plus twenty-one known only through prints). Hofstede de Groot's catalog of 1915 included every reference to a painting by Rembrandt known to him; this monumental list stood at nine hundred eighty-eight entries, roughly six hundred forty-five of which he felt confident.

Wilhelm Valentiner's list published in 1922 had swollen to over seven hundred paintings. In 1935 Abraham Bredius rejected about one hundred of those accepted by Hofstede de Groot, adding others to reach about six hundred thirty. Horst Gerson's 1969 reworking of Bredius' list contained about four hundred thirty unquestionable works, with an additional one hundred that were unsure.

The Rembrandt Research Project

The most extensive reevaluation of Rembrandt's *oeuvre* has been that of the Rembrandt Research Project (RRP). Funded by the Netherlands Organization for the Advancement of Pure Research, the project was established in 1968 in anticipation of the three-hundredth anniversary in 1969 of the master's death. A team of seven Dutch scholars was assembled: Bob Haak, Josua Bruyn, Ernst van de Wetering, P.J.J. van Thiel, S.H. Levie, and J.G. van Gelder and Jan Emmens (the last two of whom have since died).

The RRP is unprecedented in two aspects. First, it is the project not of a single scholar but of a group of men. Second, while the growing body of documents provides increasing circumstantial evidence for the identification and attribution of paintings, it is notable that most documentary entries are too brief or vague to be linked with certainty to known paintings and thus have not proven very useful in evaluating attributions. In addition to the methods of traditional connoisseurship, therefore, the project has turned to scientific data generated by the most sophisticated technical analyses available, including autoradiography and infrared reflectography. Three volumes of *A Corpus of Rembrandt Paintings* have appeared (1982, 1986, 1990), covering works thought to have been produced in the eighteen years between the beginning of the master's career through *The Nightwatch* (Color Plate 5) and 1642. Subsequent volumes will cover the remaining twenty-seven years of the artist's life.

The first volume took as its starting point the catalog by Bredius; subsequent volumes are restricting themselves to Gerson's slightly smaller list. The paintings are arranged chronologically in three categories: A, undoubtedly by Rembrandt; B, no decision has been reached; C, deattributed or rejected. Of the paintings considered by the RRP through 1642, nearly half have been questioned or rejected. The first three volumes consider two hundred eighty paintings attributed to Rembrandt by Bredius/Gerson, plus copies. Of these, one hundred forty-six are accepted, twelve are placed in the B category as of uncertain attribution, and one hundred twenty-two are rejected. A few paintings have been added to the Bredius/Gerson list, including the *Baptism of the Eunuch* dated 1626 and discovered in 1974. The artist who emerges from this investigation is no longer considered the author of several traditional touchstones of the master's style. While the RRP has yet to publish its findings on these two famous works, the *Man with the Golden Helmet* in Berlin has already been deattributed and the so-called *Polish Rider* in the Frick Collection in New York (tentatively reassigned to Willem Drost) is certain to be so as well.

As with the reevaluation projects before them, the RRP has generated controversy, protest, and criticism. Some agree with the goals of the project but criticize their execution. These include scholars who disagree with the specific findings of the team (such as the controversy that arose after the deattribution of five paintings in the collections of the Metropolitan Museum of Art in New York, the Boston Museum of Fine Arts, and the Isabella Stuart Gardner Museum, also in Boston, that led to a conference in Boston in February 1987), as well as those who are troubled by its methods: the lack of consistency in the technical data employed, the potential inconsistency in group decisions (the team is now sometimes registering minority opinion), and the basing of connoisseurship on intuition or technical analysis rather than on documents. Others question the larger aims of the project: the validity of the concept of "author/artist," and of restricting research to a single artist, arguing that this fails to characterize the context that gives meaning to his accomplishments. In the spring of 1993, four of the five remaining members of the RRP retired. The remaining member, Ernst van de Wetering, has assembled a new group of younger scholars who are continuing the work of the project.

While the primary goal of the RRP has been to establish whether or not a work was painted by Rembrandt, the *Corpus* includes an extraordinary compendium of supporting information that is an invaluable resource for future research in a wide variety of other areas. Jan Emmens was originally slated to undertake original iconographic research and investigations into the formal and thematic sources of Rembrandt's paintings. His premature death reduced this study in the first three volumes to a careful assembly and evaluation of existing research, a nonetheless valuable enterprise that has itself resulted in productive observations. Important iconographic studies by others have, however, illuminated genres of paintings as well as individual works. A series of articles by Christian Tümpel has identified precedents for Rembrandt's approach to narration in religious imagery of the late fifteenth and sixteenth centuries (1968–1971). H. Perry Chapman (1990) locates Rembrandt's self-portraits within a variety of approaches to the construction of self in seventeenth-century Holland. Rembrandt's landscapes have been explored by Cynthia P. Schneider in both a book, and an exhibition of his landscape drawings and prints (1990). Egbert Haverkamp-Begemann produced an important and comprehensive study of Rembrandt's *Nightwatch* (1982); William Heckscher (1958) and William Schupbach (1982) have both written exhaustive studies of *The Anatomy Lesson of Dr. Tulp;* and Julius Held (1969) and H. van de Waal (1974) have published important collections of essays on the master. An impressive number of other scholars have published important essays on individual works, to be found in the bibliographies of the RRP entries and catalogs of exhibitions of Rembrandt's paintings in 1991 (Brown, Kelch, and Van Thiel) and 1992 (Cavalli-Bjorkman and Snickare).

The most extensive new information generated by the RRP, however, has been in the material aspects of Rembrandt's creative process. While Rembrandt the man is not the primary focus of inquiry, a much clearer picture of the master's artistic personality (as opposed to his biography) is evolving as a by-product, indeed a prerequisite, of the project. In addition to the findings of the RRP, extensive technical analyses of Rembrandt paintings have also been published by the National Gallery in London (Bomford et al., 1988), the Mauritshuis in The Hague (De Vries et al., 1978), the Metropolitan Museum in New York (Ainsworth et al., 1982), and the Louvre in Paris (Foucart 1982). Because technical analyses had never been so systematically applied to an artist's *oeuvre*, initially the RRP optimistically declared that attributions based on their conclusions would be more definitive than earlier investigations. This has not proved to be the case for two reasons. First, the researchers have investigated these paintings under widely varying conditions over an increasingly long period of time, and they do not have strictly comparable technical data for all works. Second, even when a painting can be dated to the seventeenth century and located with some certainty within Rembrandt's studio, it cannot be concluded that the painting was produced by Rembrandt's hand. Nonetheless, the information generated by these investigations is continuing to provide valuable new insights into seventeenth-century painting techniques.

Inventories indicate that paintings by the master were distinguished from copies by the 1630s. By the eighteenth century, engravings were naming Rembrandt as the author of paintings today no longer believed to be by him. Complicating matters, Joachim von Sandrart, the seventeenth-century Frankfurt painter and biographer of artists, reported that Rembrandt sold students' works. Moreover, Rembrandt may not only have signed his students' works, his students may have placed the master's signature on the works they produced in his studio. A highly productive dimension of RRP research has thus been to clarify the artistic identities of other artists whose works have been confused with Rembrandt's, from such shadowy figures as Isaac de Jouderville, a Rembrandt pupil in Leiden in 1629–1630, to well-known masters like Govaert Flinck.

Current Research on Rembrandt

A number of other authors have also addressed various aspects of Rembrandt's studio practice and the identities of his students, including Svetlana Alpers (1988), Albert Blankert (1992), Ben Broos (1983), Josua Bruyn (1990), Paul Huys Janssen (1992), Werner Sumowski (1983–1990), and Ernst van de Wetering (1986). It has been generally assumed that Rembrandt worked on his paintings and his students on theirs, with little collaboration—indeed a necessary assumption for the categories into which the RRP locates works. The kinds of works produced in the studio range from student exercises, some retouched by the master, to copies after Rembrandt's works, and original paintings by students sold by Rembrandt and perhaps even signed by the master. Evidence for the former comes from inscriptions on etchings, drawings, and paintings, and for the latter from Joachim von Sandrart and recent investigations by the RRP into the signatures on works attributed to Rembrandt. The question of workshop collaboration is beginning to be raised. Bruyn

(1990) has already suggested, for example, that an unknown workshop assistant is responsible for the horse in Rembrandt's *Frederick Rihel on Horseback* in the National Gallery, London, of about 1663. Albert Blankert (1992) has argued that Rembrandt may have collaborated with students more than is currently assumed. In several cases, the RRP attributes one panel or canvas of a pair portrait to Rembrandt, the other (usually the woman) to another hand. Reconsideration of some of these in light of collaboration may be fruitful.

Broos (1983) attempted to give some order to the ever-expanding list of Rembrandt pupils by carefully listing the source of evidence for the connection: in a list of fifty-five names of artists associated with Rembrandt as pupils, only thirty are documented by seventeenth-century documents or mentioned in Houbraken; seven more are circumstantially plausible. Werner Sumowski has compiled a five-volume catalog of paintings by artists who at one time or another have been considered Rembrandt students (1983–1990). It has become increasingly clear that Rembrandt's studio was comprised of artists with a variety of relationships with the master, from apprentices to mature artists who served as workshop assistants. Based on a comment by Von Sandrart, it has been assumed that there were also amateurs, or children of wealthy parents who may have taken lessons in the shop as part of a humanistic education, a point now plausibly disputed by Blankert. Finally, there are those artists who never had a formal relationship with the master but who seem to have followed certain recognizable aspects of his style.

It is the latter aspect of Rembrandt's work, the continued popularity of his style and the problems this has posed for attribution, that is addressed in a recent book by Svetlana Alpers (1988). She asks why these misattributed paintings have fooled us for so long? Examining Rembrandt's characteristic free paint handling and what we have learned about Rembrandt's studio practices, she argues that he was what she calls a *pictor economicus*, who conceived and produced art in terms of the marketplace. He created an artistic personality that he promulgated through his studio and his followers, a personality that created an "aura" of individuality rather than individuality itself.

While the study and reevaluation of Rembrandt paintings have received the most publicity, an important study of his etchings by Christopher White appeared in 1969. A reevaluation of Rembrandt's drawings, which were most recently brought together in the *catalogue raisonné* by Otto Benesch of 1954, is being undertaken by Peter Schatborn and Martin Royalton-Kisch. A preview of the latter appeared most recently in 1991 as an exhibition in the British Museum. Werner Sumowski has published 10 volumes cataloging drawings by Rembrandt pupils (1979–1992).

Finally, a recent study by a literary theoretician has productively approached Rembrandt as a cultural phenomenon. Employing feminist theory, rhetoric, narratology, psychoanalysis, and, above all, semiotics, Mieke Bal (1991) addresses Rembrandt and his work from the point of view of reception. Pointing out that the "artist" (the man and/or his work) is a constructed category produced over time by the "works and the responses to them," she examines in minute detail the mental processes that we undergo to construct meaning from visual information. Among the most familiar issues she examines are those raised by the iconography of history painting. Pointing out that a representational image is always in complex tension with competing interpretations, she argues that meaning becomes possible, in fact, only in the creative tension between the image and its pre-text(s), from literary texts, cultural mis-rememberings or mis-interpretations of those texts, visual precedents, and the real world. To those who are uncomfortable with what critics term her ahistoricism, she points out that invoking "history" is an ideological move, perpetuating a limited set of "permitted readings." Including the perspective of the viewer in the study, in this case the twentieth-century student of Rembrandt, recognizes competing interpretations, their processes, and their functions in art historical discourse.

Ann Jensen Adams

See also Art history, history of the discipline; Rembrandt School; Rembrandt van Rijn

Bibliography

Ainsworth, Maryan et al. *Art and Autoradiography: Insights into the Genesis of Paintings by Rembrandt, Van Dyck, and Vermeer.* New York: Metropolitan Museum of Art, 1982.

Alpers, Svetlana. *Rembrandt's Enterprise: The Studio and the Market.* Chicago: University of Chicago Press, 1988.

Bal, Mieke. *Reading "Rembrandt": Beyond the Word-Image Opposition.* Cambridge: Cambridge University Press, 1991.

Bevers, Holm, Peter Schatborn, and Barbara Welzel. *Rembrandt: The Master and His Workshop, Drawings and Etchings.* London: National Gallery; New Haven: Yale University Press, 1991.

Blankert, Albert. "Rembrandt, His Pupils and His Studio." In *Rembrandt and His Age.* Edited by Görel Cavalli-Björkman and Marten Snickare, 41–70. Stockholm: National Museum, 1992.

———. "Rembrandt's Pupils and Followers in the Seventeenth Century." In *The Impact of Genius: Rembrandt, His Pupils and Followers in the Seventeenth Century.* Edited by Albert Blankert et al., 13–34. Amsterdam: Waterman, 1983.

Blankert, Albert et al., eds. *The Impact of Genius: Rembrandt, His Pupils and Followers in the Seventeenth Century.* Amsterdam: Waterman, 1983.

Bomford, David, Christopher Brown, and Ashok Roy. *Rembrandt: Art in the Making.* London: National Gallery, 1988.

Broos, Ben. "Fame Shared Is Fame Doubled." In *The Impact of Genius: Rembrandt, His Pupils and Followers in the Seventeenth Century.* Edited by Albert Blankert et al., 35–58. Amsterdam: Waterman, 1983.

Brown, Christopher, Jan Kelch, and Pieter van Thiel. *Rembrandt: The Master and His Workshop, Paintings.* London: National Gallery, 1991. New Haven: Yale University Press, 1991.

Bruyn, J. "An Unknown Assistant in Rembrandt's Workshop in the Early 1660s." *Burlington Magazine* 132 (1990): 715–718.

———. "Rembrandt's Workshop: Function and Production." In *Rembrandt: The Master and His Workshop, Paintings.* Edited by Christopher Brown, Jan Kelch, and Pieter van Thiel, 68–89. London: National Gallery, 1991. New Haven: Yale University Press, 1991.

Bruyn, J. et al. *A Corpus of Rembrandt Paintings.* 3 vols. The Hague: Nijhoff, 1982–1990.

Cavalli-Björkman, Görel, and Marten Snickare, eds. *Rembrandt and His Age.* Stockholm: National Museum, 1992.

Chapman, H. Perry. *Rembrandt's Self-Portraits: A Study in Seventeenth-Century Identity.* Princeton: Princeton University Press, 1990.

Emmens, J.A. *Rembrandt en de regels van de Kunst.* Utrecht: Van Oorschot, 1968.

Foucart, Jacques. *Les Peintures de Rembrandt au Louvre.* Paris: Éditions de la Réunion des Musées Nationaux, 1982.

Haverkamp, Begemann, E. "The Present State of Rembrandt Studies." *Art Bulletin* 53 (1971): 88–104.

———. *Rembrandt: "The Nightwatch."* Princeton: Princeton University Press, 1982.

Heckscher, William S. *Rembrandt's "Anatomy of Dr. Nicolaas Tulp": An Iconological Study.* New York: New York University Press, 1958.

Held, Julius. *Rembrandt's "Aristotle" and Other Rembrandt Studies.* Princeton: Princeton University Press, 1969.

Huys, Janssen Paul. "Rembrandt's Academy." In *Rembrandt's Academy,* 20–33. The Hague: Hoogsteder and Hoogsteder; Zwolle: Waanders, 1992.

Rosenberg, Jakob. *Rembrandt's Life and Work.* Cambridge, MA: Harvard University Press, 1948. Rev. ed. London: Phaidon, 1964.

Royalton-Kisch, Martin. *Drawings by Rembrandt and His Circle in the British Museum.* London: British Museum, 1991

Schneider, Cynthia P. *Rembrandt's Landscapes.* New Haven: Yale University Press, 1990.

Schneider, Cynthia P. et al. *Rembrandt's Landscapes: Drawings and Prints.* Washington, DC: National Gallery of Art, 1990.

Schupbach, William. *The Paradox of Rembrandt's "Anatomy of Dr. Tulp."* Medical History, Supplement no. 2. London: Welcome Institute for the History of Medicine, 1982.

Schwartz, Gary. *Rembrandt, His Life, His Paintings.* New York: Viking Press, 1985.

Slive, Seymour. *Rembrandt and His Critics 1630–1730.* The Hague: Nijhoff, 1953.

Strauss, Walter L., and Marjon van der Meulen, eds. *The Rembrandt Documents.* New York: Abaris Books, 1979.

Sumowski, Werner. *Gemälde der Rembrandt-Schüler.* 5 vols. Landau, Pfalz: Edition PVA, 1983–[1994].

———. *Drawings of the Rembrandt School.* 10 vols. Edited and translated by Walter L. Strauss. New York: Abaris Books, 1979–1992.

Tümpel, Christian. "Ikonographische Beiträge zu Rembrandt: Deutung und Interpretation seiner Historien." *Jahrbuch der Hamburger Kunstsammlungen* 13 (1968): 95–126.

———. "Ikonographische Beiträge zu Rembrandt." *Jahrbuch der Hamburger Kunstsammlungen* 16 (1971): 20–38.

———. *Rembrandt: All the Paintings in Color.* New York: Harry N. Abrams, 1993.

———. "Studien zur ikonographie der historien Rembrandt's." *Nederlands Kunsthistorisch Jaarboek* 20 (1969): 107–198.

Vries, A.B. de, Magdi Toth-Ubbens, and W. Froentjes. *Rembrandt in the Mauritshuis.* Alphen aan de Rijn: Sijthoff and Noordhoff, 1978.

Waal, H. van de. *Steps toward Rembrandt: Collected Articles 1937–1972.* Edited by R.H. Fuchs. Translated by P. Wardle and A. Griffiths. Amsterdam: North-Holland, 1974.

Wetering, E. van de. "Problems of Apprenticeship and Studio Collaboration." In *A Corpus of Rembrandt Paintings.* Edited by J. Bruyn et al., vol. 2, 45–90. The Hague: Nijhoff, 1986.

White, Christopher. *Rembrandt As an Etcher.* 2 vols. University Park: Pennsylvania State University Press, 1969.

Rembrandt School

Rembrandt van Rijn was active as a teacher from his earliest years in Leiden (ca. 1625–1631) until his death in Amsterdam in 1669. Throughout his career, he trained students to copy and absorb his style, and some were so successful that their paintings and drawings are only now being separated from Rembrandt's own, with many unclear cases remaining. But no one style characterizes the works of Rembrandt's pupils and associates, which follow the trajectory of his own evolution melded with outside influences. Rembrandt's first recorded pupil, Gerrit Dou (1628), developed the lessons of his master's meticulous early paintings into the Leiden school of *fijnschilderij* (fine painting). His latest, Aert de Gelder (ca. 1660), carried the broad, impastoed handling of his last works into the eighteenth century.

Early sources like Joachim von Sandrart, the Frankfurt painter and biographer of artists (1675) who worked in Amsterdam around 1640, and Arnold Houbraken, who studied with Rembrandt's pupil Samuel van Hoogstraten and published a treatise on Dutch art in 1718, already describe Rembrandt as an influential and prolific teacher. Their information, derived partly from firsthand experience and partly from hearsay, and the international appeal of Rembrandt's style in the second quarter of the seventeenth century have led to the association of a wide range of artists under the rubric "Rembrandt School." Some are recognized today as among the most significant Dutch painters of their time. Others remain mere names whose work has yet to be identified. Some are clearly documented as students of Rembrandt, while others came under his influence by less direct means.

At present, at least forty artists are known as pupils of Rembrandt from seventeenth-century sources and Houbraken's treatise. Among the most important of these are Ferdinand Bol, Jacob and Philips Koninck, who were brothers, Gerrit Dou, Willem Drost, Heiman Dullaert, Carel Fabritius, Govaert Flinck, Aert de Gelder, Isaac de Jouderville, Gerbrand van den Eeckhout, Samuel van Hoogstraten, Nicolaes Maes, Christopher Paudiss, Constantijn Daniel van Renesse, and Dirck van Santvoort. Most of them followed Rembrandt's preference for history painting and portraiture, but there are notable exceptions. Gerrit Dou and Nicolaes Maes were pioneers of domestic genre painting, while Philips Koninck developed a specialty in panoramic landscapes.

A further assortment of artists are connected with Rembrandt either by circumstantial association or by stylistic influence. For some, signed copies of Rembrandt's works are preserved, while others are mentioned in legal transactions as witnesses or in other documents. And some simply absorbed aspects of his style by studying his paintings and prints. Among the artists associated with Rembrandt in these ways are Jacob Backer, Leendert van Beyeren, Gerard de Lairesse (portrayed by Rembrandt, 1665; New York, Metropolitan Museum), Lambert Doomer, Barent Fabritius, Jan Lievens, Willem de Poorter, Roeland Roghman, and Jan Victors. Other artists, notably the landscapists Hercules Segers, Jan Asselijn (portrayed by Rembrandt in an etching of ca. 1647), and Jan van de Cappelle, are known as acquaintances or collectors of Rembrandt but were relatively untouched by his style.

In Leiden, Rembrandt and Lievens worked closely together, but neither can be considered master to the other. After 1631, Lievens went to England, while Rembrandt settled in Amsterdam as principal artist and business partner to the art dealer Hendrick Uylenburgh. With Rembrandt's style as a basis and a stable of pupils and assistants, artist and dealer ran a productive workshop that contributed to the rise of Amsterdam as a leading art center, surpassing Utrecht, Haarlem, and Leiden. In 1639 Rembrandt established a separate studio in his new home on the Anthonisbreestraat in Amsterdam.

Under Uylenburgh and Rembrandt, artistic training did not follow the traditional guild apprenticeship system but was conducted according to academic principles already employed by the Carracci in Bologna, by Hendrick Goltzius and Karel van Mander in Haarlem, and by Gerard van Honthorst in Utrecht. Students and associates in varying degrees of proficiency gathered to draw together from the nude model and from casts after antique sculpture, as evidenced in a drawing by an anonymous Rembrandt pupil (Darmstadt, Hessisches Landesmuseum) and by groups of drawings from the 1640s and 1650s that appear to represent the same model from different angles and by different hands. This practice follows the traditional method of learning by copying from the great works of the past and from nature. Rembrandt sometimes sketched the same figure directly onto a copper plate—*(Nude Man Seated and Another Standing)*—and some of these etchings may, in turn, have served as models for students. As Von Sandrart observed, Rembrandt profited handsomely from fees paid by participants who ranged from young beginners, to accomplished professional artists, to amateurs of all ages who considered lessons in painting and drawing to be a requisite component of the gentleman's education.

While Italian draftsmen often employed figure drawing for the study of anatomy according to ideals of beauty laid down in antiquity, Rembrandt taught students to represent models naturalistically, emphasizing light and shade and the rendering of human individuality. Yet, like classicist artists, Rembrandt stressed figure drawing to train his students as practitioners of history painting. A further step in this preparation was the execution of quick sketches designed to establish composition and content. An *Annunciation* in red chalk, pen and wash, drawn by a pupil and corrected by the master, demonstrates Rembrandt's instructional method and displays his emphasis on dramatic effects of light and narrative content (Berlin, Staatliche Museen, Kupferstichkabinett; Fig. 116). Like Rembrandt, pupils would often make several such drawings of the same subject before settling on the most satisfying compositional arrangement. Students may also have staged *tableaux* from which compositions for history paintings were worked out. Their works frequently employ the colorful fabrics, antique armor, and other paraphernalia gathered in Rembrandt's curio cabinet to lend a historical atmosphere to biblical and mythological scenes.

The term "academy" often connotes a loosely organized, collegial group and carries associations with the movement to establish painting as an intellectual, liberal art. Like the old guild workshops, however, Uylenburgh's academy, and later Rembrandt's own, were commercial enterprises as well as aesthetic training grounds. A young artist's works were the property of the master until he earned independent status. Students learned Rembrandt's manner by painting and drawing copies after his works, beginning with *troniën* (individual bust or figure studies, often in historical or exotic costume), and progressing to commissioned portraits and history paintings. There was a ready market for such copies, which were sold by Rembrandt himself, by Uylenburgh, and through the Frisian painter/dealer Lambert Jacobsz. in Leeuwarden, at a fraction of the price paid for a Rembrandt original. This procedure emulates the production methods employed by Pieter Paul Rubens in Antwerp, although Rembrandt seems to have involved assistants in his own works less frequently than did Rubens. The most likely exceptions lie among the many portraits executed in the 1630s, when specialists may have contributed to the painting of lace and other fine effects of costume.

In some cases, Rembrandt apparently signed a work painted by an associate and sold it as his own, sometimes after touching it up. The most important piece of evidence for this is the large *Abraham's Sacrifice* now in the Alte Pinakothek, Munich, a variant of a painting of the same theme by Rembrandt now in the Hermitage, St. Petersburg. The Munich version was probably painted by Flinck but is inscribed "Rembrandt. verandert. En overgeschildert. 1636" ("Rembrandt changed and overpainted. 1636"). Both works are indebted, in turn, to a composition (grisaille, Amsterdam, Rijksmuseum) by Rembrandt's teacher, Pieter Lastman. Each artist captures the dramatic moment of divine intervention as the faithful old patriarch prepares to offer up his only son to God. Lastman's approach to history painting continued to influence Rembrandt's work and that of many of his pupils, notably Gerbrand van den Eeckhout.

Students came from all over the Netherlands and Northern Europe to study with Rembrandt in Amsterdam, and many returned to their native cities to educate others. Bol, Maes, Van Hoogstraten, De Gelder and others came from Dordrecht. Flinck came from Cleves to Jacobsz.'s studio in Leeuwarden, and moved from there to Amsterdam with Jacob Backer, who was already an independent artist but associated with Rembrandt's circle. Several German artists studied with Rembrandt or came under his influence, notably Paudiss, Johan Ulrich Mayr and Jurriaen Ovens. Von Sandrart is sometimes listed as a Rembrandt pupil, but he was more of a rival for aristocratic portrait commissions. The Danish artist Bernhard Keil went from Rembrandt's studio to Italy, where he gave information to the Florentine writer Filippo Baldinucci, whose treatise of 1686 contains a biography of Rembrandt and a reference to "Uylenburgh's famous academy."

As a teacher of printmaking, Rembrandt was far less prolific. Contemporary accounts describe his complex blend of etching, drypoint, and burin as inimitable. Lievens developed his etching style concurrently with Rembrandt's. Jan Joris van Vliet made reproductive prints after some of Rembrandt's early paintings in Leiden and evidently followed him to Amsterdam around 1631. Among later pupils, Bol, the Konincks, and Van Renesse were most active as etchers.

Around 1636, Flinck took over as Uylenburgh's shop manager. From the 1640s on, both Flinck and Bol enjoyed more successful careers than did Rembrandt, garnering major commissions for portraits of the urban *élite* and public projects such as the decoration of the new Amsterdam Town Hall. Their style moved away from the earthy palette and broad handling of Rembrandt's mature work toward a brighter, clearer, more decorative and refined approach stimulated by the work of Anthony van Dyck and Rubens and by the importation of Flemish and Italian paintings into Amsterdam.

Many of Rembrandt's associates, indeed, evolved highly individual manners, from the meticulous *fijnschilderij* (fine painting) of Gerrit Dou (Color Plate 8) to the Flemish-inspired classicism of the late Flinck, Bol, and Lievens, the quiet genre paintings and fashionable portraits of Maes, and the colorful, Lastmanian history paintings of Van den Eeckhout (Fig. 120). It is often said, as a result, that Rembrandt's pupils were profoundly influenced by his work at first, but then abandoned him for more fashionable trends. But this interpretation devalues the continuing impact of Rembrandt's sensitive approach to characterization and vivid narrative, and the unshakable example of his drawing style. Ironically, the most influential theoretical texts written in Holland in the classicist period were all by artists associated in some way with Rembrandt: Van Hoogstraten (1678), De Lairesse (1707), and

Houbraken (1718–1721). While the theory of creative idealization they advocate reflects international academic doctrines, many of the anecdotes and technical tips they provide may well derive from practices employed in Rembrandt's studio.

Stephanie S. Dickey

See also Backer, Jacob Adriaensz.; Bol, Ferdinand; Dordrecht; Dou, Gerrit; Drawing clubs; Drawing practices and techniques; Drawings, uses and collecting; Flinck, Govaert; France; History painting; History portraits; Huygens, Constantijn; Koninck, Philips; Koninck, Salomon; Landscape; Leiden; Maes, Nicolaes; Portraiture; Prints, printmaking, and printmakers (ca. 1500–ca. 1900); Rembrandt research; Rembrandt van Rijn; Roman history; Self-portraiture; Subjects, subject categories, and hierarchies; Van den Eeckhout, Gerbrand; Writers on art, eighteenth century

Bibliography

Blankert, Albert. "Rembrandt's Pupils and Followers in the Seventeenth Century." In *The Impact of a Genius: Rembrandt, His Pupils and Followers in the Seventeenth Century*. Edited by Albert Blankert et al., 13–34. Amsterdam: Waterman, 1983.

Broos, Ben. "Fame Shared Is Fame Doubled." In *The Impact of a Genius: Rembrandt, His Pupils and Followers in the Seventeenth Century*. Edited by Albert Blankert et al., 35–58. Amsterdam: Waterman, 1983.

Brown, Christopher, Jan Kelch, and Pieter van Thiel. *Rembrandt: The Master and His Workshop, Paintings*. London: National Gallery; New Haven: Yale University Press, 1991.

Haverkamp-Begemann, E., J.R. Judson, and A.M. Logan. *Rembrandt after Three Hundred Years: An Exhibition of Rembrandt and His Followers*. Chicago: Art Institute, 1969.

Huys, Janssen Paul, and Werner Sumowski. *Rembrandt's Academy*. The Hague: Hoogsteder and Hoogsteder; Zwolle: Waanders, 1992.

Liedtke, Walter et al. *Rembrandt/Not Rembrandt in the Metropolitan Museum of Art: Aspects of Connoisseurship*. New York: Metropolitan Musuem of Art, 1995.

Sumowski, Werner. *Drawings of the Rembrandt School*. 10 vols. Edited and translated by Walter L. Strauss. New York: Abaris Books, 1979–1992.

———. *Gemälde der Rembrandt Schüler*. 5 vols. Landau, Pfalz: Edition PVA, 1983–[1994].

Wetering, Ernst van de. "Problems of Apprenticeship and Collaboration." In *A Corpus of Rembrandt Paintings*. Edited by J. Bruyn et al. Vol. 2, 45–90. The Hague: Nijhoff, 1986.

Rembrandt van Rijn (1606–1669)

Rembrandt Harmensz. van Rijn is one of the most famous of all Dutch artists, renowned as a maker of paintings, prints and drawings and as a teacher. Rembrandt specialized in history painting and portraiture, but he also produced landscapes, genre scenes, and figure studies. His painting style evolved from a refined, jewel-like technique with bright local colors in his early years to broad, painterly brushwork in a simple, earthy palette at the end of his career. His etchings vary in effect from the airy linearity of a sketch to pictorial density anticipating the tonal effects of mezzotint.

Rembrandt's long, well-documented life has been the subject of biographies, novels, and films. While he achieved a level of fame and skill unmatched by any other Dutch artist of the seventeenth century, and lived in a manner that favored personal independence over conformity to convention, the legend of Rembrandt as a lonely, isolated genius is no longer accepted by scholars. For over forty years, Rembrandt enjoyed the patronage of prominent collectors in Amsterdam and elsewhere and attracted pupils from throughout the United Provinces and abroad. Before the end of his lifetime, he had achieved an international reputation for both his paintings and his prints.

In the late seventeenth century, Rembrandt's unidealized, humanistic approach to form and subject matter was criticized by connoisseurs who preferred artists to follow prescribed rules based on the monuments of ancient Greece and Rome, and when his dark canvases no longer suited the frivolities of Rococo decor, Rembrandt's work became less fashionable. But his genius, especially in the field of printmaking, was never totally forgotten. The nineteenth century witnessed a revival of appreciation for Rembrandt's evocative brushwork and empathetic approach to subject matter, and many works painted by members of his school were labeled as his own by eager collectors and dealers.

Over the past century, archivists have uncovered many details of Rembrandt's life, loves, and financial dealings, while numerous publications and exhibitions have explored the style, content, and context of his art. Today, scientific research attempts to sort out the masterworks from the imitations and adaptations produced by his many followers.

Rembrandt (one of the few Dutch artists to follow the Italian convention of signing his works with his first name), was born on June 15, 1606, in Leiden, where his parents were successful mill owners and members of the Reformed Church. He attended the Leiden Latin School from 1618 to 1619. On May 20, 1620, he enrolled at Leiden University, probably to study law or to train for the ministry, but he never matriculated. Instead, he took up painting under the tutelage of the history painter Jacob van Swanenburgh (ca. 1571–1638), with whom he worked from around 1621 to 1623.

More formative for Rembrandt's early years was the period of six months in 1624 spent in the Amsterdam studio of Pieter Lastman and Rembrandt's subsequent close association in Leiden with Jan Lievens, who had trained with Lastman in the years 1618–1621. Lastman's work had a lasting impact on Rembrandt's painting style and on his approach to historical subject matter, in which the composition is often organized around a central action and the reaction of observers.

Rembrandt and Lievens were in close contact from 1625 to 1631, sharing interests in biblical subject matter, portraiture, and the study of human expression. They may have shared a studio, and their early works are very close in spirit and style—for example, various versions of *The Raising of Lazarus*, including etchings. The autobiography of Constantijn Huygens, connoisseur and secretary to *stadholder* Frederik Hendrik, records a visit to Rembrandt and Lievens in Leiden and one of the earliest appraisals of their respective skills (ca. 1630). Huygens admired Rembrandt's skill in painting on a small scale, his ability to translate historical texts into pictorial terms, and his depiction of the passions of the soul. Huygens took as his primary example Rembrandt's *Judas Returning the Thirty Pieces of Silver* (1629; England, private collection), which vividly conveys the conflicting emotions of the repentant Judas.

Huygens was disappointed that Rembrandt and Lievens had no plans to visit Italy (a requisite trip for all students of the classical tradition), but the young artists claimed that they could see all they needed to see right at home. This attitude does not imply lack of interest, but presumes access to the wealth of Italian, Flemish, and other works of art imported and exhibited in the markets and collections of Amsterdam and other prosperous Dutch cities during this period, as well as the widespread availability of reproductive prints. Indeed, as far as we know, Rembrandt never left his native Holland, yet his art demonstrates an awareness and creative adaptation of the work of Rubens, Titian, and other artists. Throughout his career, Rembrandt also drew inspiration from the objects in his own collection, which served as a curiosity cabinet, a dealer's stock, and a resource for the training of students. An inventory taken in 1656 includes prints and paintings by students, contemporaries, and past masters like Lucas van Leyden, Raphael, and Anthony van Dyck, natural and historical artifacts, and casts of antique sculpture.

Huygens was influential in securing commissions for Rembrandt from Frederik Hendrik and his court at The Hague, notably the series of paintings of the Passion of Christ (ca. 1633–1646; now Munich, Alte Pinakothek). But Rembrandt was not destined to become a court painter. Early sources (Roger de Piles, *Abregé la vie des peintres*, 1699; Arnold Houbraken, *De Groote Schouwburgh der Nederlantsche konstschilders en schilderessen*, 1718) quote him as stating that he preferred freedom to honor. And the flourishing mercantile culture of Amsterdam, with its growing population of wealthy burghers eager to adorn their new homes with works of art, offered irresistible attractions.

In 1631, while still working in Leiden, Rembrandt invested a substantial sum of money (one thousand florins) with the Amsterdam painter and art dealer Hendrick Uylenburgh and began to receive portrait commissions from Amsterdam citizens—for example, *Nicolaes Ruts* (1631; New York, Frick Collection); *Marten Looten* (1632; Los Angeles County Museum of Art). In 1632, he painted his first group portrait, the *Anatomy Lesson of Dr. Nicolaes Tulp* (The Hague, Mauritshuis). This painting, which depicts Dr. Tulp demonstrating the anatomy of the hand to fellow members of the Amsterdam Surgeons' Guild, secured Rembrandt's reputation by introducing to the staid genre of group portraiture some of the anec-

dotal interest and narrative action of a history painting, an innovation that culminates in Rembrandt's most famous work, *The Militia Company of Capt. Frans Banning Cocq and Lt. Willem van Ruytenburch (The Nightwatch)* (Color Plate 5), now in the Rijksmuseum, Amsterdam, but originally installed in the Kloveniersdoelen (banquet hall of the Kloveniers militia guild) in 1642.

As a portraitist, Rembrandt soon surpassed established masters like Thomas de Keyser and Nicolaes Eliasz. Pickenoy in his ability to animate traditional portrait conventions with human warmth and character. The rapid success of his earliest years in Amsterdam was built on portraits of well-to-do merchants and their wives, such as *Maerten Soolmans* and *Oopjen Coppit* (1634; Paris, private collection) and *The Shipbuilder Jan Rycksen and His Wife Griet Jans* (1633; London, Buckingham Palace). He also portrayed several prominent theologians, including the Reformed minister *Johannes Wtenbogaert* (1633; Amsterdam, Rijksmuseum; etched portrait, 1635) and the Mennonite preacher *Cornelis Claesz. Anslo with His Wife Aaltje Gerritsdr. Schouten* (1641; Berlin, Staatliche Museen, Gemäldegalerie; etched portrait, 1641).

Throughout his life, Rembrandt made studies of his own likeness, adopting a variety of roles and guises that comment on the nobility of art and the nature of human expression. His etched *Self-Portrait Leaning on a Stone Sill* (1639) and painted *Self-Portrait at the Age of Thirty-four* (1640; London, National Gallery) borrow from Renaissance portrait conventions displayed in the works of Titian, Albrecht Dürer, and others to represent the artist at the height of his creative power and commercial success.

By 1633 Rembrandt had established himself in Amsterdam as principal artist of Uylenburgh's workshop, where many artists over the next few years were trained to paint and draw in Rembrandt's style and to produce paintings for sale. Contrary to the usual guild practice of the time, Rembrandt taught whole groups of students and apprentices simultaneously and arranged study sessions in which they drew together from the nude model or sketched out compositions for history paintings. From the mid-1640s on, Rembrandt's own fortunes waned, but his pupils Govaert Flinck and Ferdinand Bol became among the most successful artists in Amsterdam.

On June 22, 1634, Rembrandt married Saskia van Uylenburgh, a young Frisian relative of his business partner. In the same year, he joined the Guild of St. Luke and became an official citizen of Amsterdam, where he lived and worked for the rest of his life. Rembrandt and Saskia lived with Uylenburgh at first, then in rented lodgings, and on May 1, 1639, they moved into an elegant house on the Sint Anthonisbreestraat, at the center of a prosperous middle-class neighborhood of artists and merchants. There Rembrandt maintained his own studio, where he continued to train students and to deal in works of art while producing his own paintings, drawings, and etchings. Saskia bore several children, but only one, Titus, lived to adulthood. He followed his father's profession but died in 1668 at the age of twenty-seven. Saskia died in June 1642, when Titus was less than a year old. Because of stipulations in her will, Rembrandt did not marry again, but he entered into a liaison with Titus' nursemaid, Geertge Dircx, and later with his housekeeper, Hendrickje Stoffels, who remained his companion for the rest of his life and bore him a daughter, Cornelia, in 1654.

The 1640s and 1650s mark the culmination of Rembrandt's career as a printmaker. His complex method of combining etching, burin, and drypoint, sometimes radically altering a composition in progress, mystified critics and gained international acclaim. Connoisseurs have long appreciated the delicacy of his atmospheric sketches on the copper plate—for example, *Christ Disputing with the Doctors* (1652 and 1654), and the rich tonal effects of more highly finished works, such as *Annunciation to the Shepherds* (1634), and have especially prized the rarest early impressions and preliminary states. The famous *Hundred Guilder Print* (ca. 1647/1649) demonstrates the breadth of Rembrandt's technique and synthesizes passages from the Gospel of Matthew to depict the compassionate ministry of Christ. The magisterial *Three Crosses* (1653) and *Christ Presented to the People* (1655) reflect his creative adaptation of the native graphic tradition that originated with Lucas van Leyden and Rembrandt's incomparable mastery of the difficult medium of drypoint. His landscape etchings, some of which may have been executed on the spot, record the native scene with concision and sensitivity—for example, *Six's Bridge* (1645); *Three Gabled Cottages beside a Road* (1650; Fig. 117); *View of Haarlem and Bloemendaal (The Goldweigher's Field)* (1651).

As a history painter, Rembrandt chose primarily Old and New Testament subjects that comment on human emotion and behavior: the stories of Joseph, Abraham and Isaac, heroines like Susanna (for example, 1647; Berlin, Staatliche Museen, Gemäldegalerie), Bathsheba (1654; Paris, Louvre), and Lucretia, Tobit (from the Apocrypha), the apostles (*Denial of Peter*, 1660; Amsterdam, Rijksmuseum), and the life and Passion of Christ. He also painted and etched many images of hermit saints and other scholarly figures, such as *St. Paul at his Desk* (ca. 1629; Nuremberg, Germanisches National Museum); *St. Jerome beside a Pollard Willow*, etching (1648); and *Aristotle Contemplating the Bust of Homer* (1653; New York, Metropolitan Museum). In the mid-1630s, Rembrandt showed a preference for violent, dramatic themes consistent with prevailing Baroque trends—for example, *The Blinding of Samson* (1636; Frankfurt, Gemäldegalerie); and *Belshazzar's Feast* (ca. 1635; London, National Gallery). But Rembrandt is best known for the meditative grandeur and quiet emotion of his later works, such as *Jacob Blessing the Sons of Joseph* (1656; Kassel, Gemäldegalerie; Fig. 118) and the so-called *Jewish Bride*, probably depicting Isaac and Rebecca spied upon by Abimalech (ca. 1668; Amsterdam, Rijksmuseum).

Following Saskia's death and the completion of his most important public commission, *The Nightwatch*, Rembrandt's meteoric rise in fame reached a plateau. In 1656, saddled with debts incurred in the purchase of his house and some unwise speculations in shipping and works of art, Rembrandt went bankrupt and was forced to sell off his collections and to cease doing business in his own name (a legal penalty for the financial and moral transgression of insolvency). Hendrickje and

Titus quickly formed a corporation to employ him, and in 1658 Rembrandt reestablished his family and his business in the Jordaan, a less-prestigious artists' quarter.

Rembrandt's change in fortunes was once attributed to dissatisfaction with *The Nightwatch*, but scholars have since recognized that this painting was much admired in its own time, and that the impropriety of Rembrandt's living arrangements probably had more to do with the decrease in his patronage by the *élite* of Amsterdam. Meanwhile, he continued to be active as a teacher and to be supported by a liberal, intellectual clientele. He portrayed several of his acquaintances in etched portraits that are a brilliant visual equivalent of the verbal eulogies frequently exchanged among humanist friends and colleagues—for example, *Jan Wtenbogaert (The Goldweigher)* (1639); *Jan Six* (1647; also a painting, 1654; Amsterdam, Six Collection); *Abraham Francen* (ca. 1658); and *Dr. Arnout Tholinx* (ca. 1656).

The ascendancy of classicism in the later seventeenth century was another contributing factor to Rembrandt's decline in popularity. Especially in his etchings and drawings, Rembrandt followed the principle of *naer het leven* (after life) essential to the indigenous pictorial tradition. His mistake, according to academic principles, was in transferring this unadulterated naturalism to the higher plane of historical and mythological subject matter. One critic (Andries Pels, in *Gebruik en misbruik des toneels*, 1681, a kind of manifesto for the classicist movement) poked fun at the garter marks visible on the legs of one of his female nudes. But it cannot be said that Rembrandt's art entirely rejects the lessons of the Italian Renaissance. The most profound influence on the broad, scumbled brushwork and ruddy, luminous color of his late work is the art of the Venetian master Titian.

Hendrickje Stoffels died in July 1663; Rembrandt's son Titus, in September 1668; and the artist himself, on October 4, 1669. His last *Self-Portrait* (ca. 1669; Cologne, Wallraf-Richartz Museum) adopts the guise of the ancient painter Zeuxis, laughing in the face of death. Eclipsed by his pupils and financially drained by his bankruptcy, Rembrandt was buried in a rented grave in the Westerkerk in Amsterdam. His remains have long since disappeared, but the hundreds of works displayed in museums throughout the world and the house in the Anthonisbreestraat, now the Museum Het Rembrandthuis, remain the most tangible testaments to his memory.

Stephanie S. Dickey

See also France; Group portraiture; History painting; Huygens, Constantijn; Italy; Leiden; Lievens, Jan; Non-Western cultural influences; Pre-Rembrandtists; Prints, printmaking, and printmakers (ca. 1500–ca. 1900); Rembrandt research; Rembrandt School; Roman history; Self-portraiture; Theater and theatricality; Underdrawings, underpaintings

Bibliography

Alpers, Svetlana. *Rembrandt's Enterprise: The Studio and the Market*. Chicago: University of Chicago Press, 1988.

Benesch, Otto. *The Drawings of Rembrandt*. Edited by Eva

Benesch. 6 vols. New York: Phaidon, 1973.

Bevers, Holm, Peter Schatborn, and Barbara Welzel. *Rembrandt: The Master and His Workshop, Drawings and Etchings.* London: National Gallery; New Haven: Yale University Press, 1991.

Bredius, A. *Rembrandt: The Complete Edition of the Paintings.* Revised by Horst Gerson. London: Phaidon, 1969.

Brown, Christopher, Jan Kelch, and Pieter van Thiel. *Rembrandt: The Master and His Workshop, Paintings.* London: National Gallery; New Haven: Yale University Press, 1991.

Bruyn, J. et al. *A Corpus of Rembrandt Paintings.* 3 vols. The Hague: Nijhoff, 1982–1990.

Chapman, H. Perry. *Rembrandt's Self-Portraits: A Study in Seventeenth-Century Identity.* Princeton: Princeton University Press, 1990.

Haverkamp-Begemann, E. *Rembrandt: "The Nightwatch."* Princeton: Princeton University Press, 1982.

Schwartz, Gary. *Rembrandt, His Life, His Paintings.* New York: Viking Press, 1985.

Strauss, Walter L., and Marjon van der Meulen, eds. *The Rembrandt Documents.* New York: Abaris, 1979.

Tümpel, Christian, and Astrid Tümpel. *Rembrandt: All Paintings in Colour.* New York: Harry N. Abrams, 1993.

White, Christopher. *Rembrandt.* London: Thames and Hudson, 1989.

———. *Rembrandt As an Etcher.* 2 vols. University Park: Pennsylvania State University Press, 1969.

White, Christopher, and Karel G. Boon. *Rembrandt's Etchings: An Illustrated Critical Catalogue.* 2 vols. New York: Abner Schram, 1969.

Renaissance architecture (1500–1625)

The earliest introduction of the building forms of the Italian Renaissance to the Netherlands are found in the architecture in the backgrounds of various paintings around 1500. The first Renaissance-style buildings actually constructed were the honor gates that were erected of wood and cloth as temporary structures for festive inaugurations, like the triumphal arches of the Joyful Entries of Charles V in 1515 and 1520 in several Dutch cities. In the Southern Netherlands, especially in cities like Ghent, Bruges, and Antwerp, the temporary festival buildings were clearly inspired directly by Italian examples. The real world of architecture in the Netherlands, however, remained largely oriented to the late-Gothic style until well into the sixteenth century.

The new forms from Italy arrived in the North in three ways: first, through loose, single-sheet ornament prints; second, through Italian artists and engineers who worked at the different courts in the North; and third, through Italian architectural treatises. During the first decade of the sixteenth century, the ornament prints of Raphael and his students, among others, found their way to the Netherlands and were used by painters, joiners, and architects in the design of decorative details. In architecture, these Renaissance ornaments were at first made a part of the late-Gothic building forms without understanding the nature and the background of the style to which they belonged. This can be seen, for example, in the façade decorations of the castles De Cannenburg (Vaassen) and Twickel (Delden), which are both from the mid-sixteenth century.

At the invitation of prominent Dutch nobles, several Italians remained in the region during the first half of the sixteenth century and provided a firsthand introduction to the formal idiom of the Italian Renaissance. After 1529 Thomas Vincidor da Bologna worked on the renovation of the castle of Breda for Hendrik III of Nassau, adding a square court enclosed by an arcade of classical Doric columns. Alexandro Pasqualini came to the Netherlands as a military engineer for the counts of Buren, and in 1532 he designed the tower of the Gothic church in IJsselstein. He devised an imposing arrangement of three triumphal arches one above the other with Doric, Ionic, and Corinthian pilasters, following Italian examples precisely.

The architectural treatises were, however, very important for transmitting the new style from Italy in the Netherlands. The ample pictorial material offered direct examples to sculptors and architects, and the accompanying text explained the backgrounds, the striving for absolute harmony, and the design on the basis of pure mathematical proportions. In 1537 in Venice, Sebastiano Serlio published his treatise on the correct use of the orders. Two years later, in 1539, this Italian book was already translated and published in several languages, one of which was Dutch, by Pieter Coecke van Aalst in Antwerp. In this way the classical orders became accessible to every carpenter who could read a little. From Antwerp these books—and with them the Renaissance—spread to the distant corners of the Netherlands. Hans Vredeman de Vries later wrote in the introduction to his own model book that he had first become acquainted with the work of Serlio in 1545, while a student in a joiner's workshop in Kollum (Friesland). Within ten years Serlio's treasury of forms apparently had penetrated into the remotest corner of Western civilization.

The town hall of Antwerp, situated on the border between the Southern and Northern Netherlands, is very important for the development of architecture in the North in the second half of the sixteenth century. In the period 1561–1565, this new town hall was built after the design of Cornelis Floris de Vriendt (1514–1575). In a monumental and pure way Serlio's orders were used for the pilasters. The middle bay of the façade, which is crowned with a great gable in place of the traditional watchtower, is very unlike the Italian, however. Direct influence of this composition, even though on a much more modest scale, can be found several years later in the town hall of The Hague from 1564–1565 (Fig. 136). In the treatment of the ground floor, some classical elements have been carefully applied—namely, very unobtrusive pediments above the windows. Above this, however, is a powerful order of Doric pilasters crowned with an entablature wholly patterned after Serlio. Above the roof cornice is a gable in which the Ionic and Corinthian orders have been applied one above the other.

The model books of the engraver and publisher Hans

Vredeman de Vries (1527–1606) were very important for disseminating Cornelis Floris de Vriendt's style. From 1565 until his death in 1606, Vredeman de Vries published many series of prints and books, which were dispersed over the whole of Northern Europe. In his adaptations of the treatises of Vitruvius and Serlio, Vredeman de Vries did not give a pure definition of the proportions of the orders but rather a scale of variations, in which the decorative and inventive aspects played a large role. He also gave imagined applications for these new inventions—for example, to the decoration of the façades of traditional small-scale dwellings. In the second half of the sixteenth century, the houses of the middle class were, after all, the important part of architecture in the Northern Netherlands. After the outbreak of the Revolt against Spain in 1568, the Court and the Church ceased to give commissions for architecture so that only middle-class and civic buildings remained. At the end of the sixteenth century, the transition to stone façades had been generally implemented in Dutch towns. Since most of the time the crest of the roof was perpendicular to the front façade, these façades usually had a top gable, joining the wooden roof construction behind it, that became narrower as it went higher. On these narrow, high-gabled façades it was not always possible to apply the architectural forms of the Italian Renaissance, as these were calculated on the basis of a monumental breadth. The lack of fixed proportions gave Vredeman de Vries a flexible pattern of decoration that could be applied without problems to the modest houses.

By 1600 civic buildings and the houses of prominent citizens were extravagantly decorated with all sorts of variations of the orders and ornaments. The patrons and their architects apparently found great pleasure in providing the façades with a richness of sculptural adornment. With this splendor of decoration, the façade, which was itself articulated by the windows into bays, was forged into one decorative network. The door bay and the gable on top of the façade could locally give one another accent. Most of the houses in the town were built on small lots, and they practically all had gables. Around 1600 the gable had become a refuge for inventive and playful ornamentation with pilasters, herms, volutes, and scrollwork obelisks or cartouches. These rich crownings of façades were so popular that they were also applied to broader, laterally placed houses and civic buildings.

From the end of the sixteenth century, monumental municipal buildings, like town gates, weigh houses, and town halls, were erected next to middle-class houses. How much the whole architectural tradition, which had been slowly created in this style, was grafted on the houses, is shown, for example, in the new façade for the town hall of Leiden from 1593–1598 (Fig. 74). The final design was the result of cooperation between the Leiden executor Claes Cornelisz. and the Haarlem town architect Lieven de Key, while the stones were provided by Luder van Benthem from Bremen. It has an elongated façade, on which the entrance is marked by an independent, richly decorated gable only three bays broad. The central bay with the staircase has freely juxtaposed strictly architectural and imaginative elements, like the taut pilasters and columns of the main floor and the luxurious scrollwork, herms, and obelisks on the gable above. During the expansion of 1604, additions were made to the gable on both sides so that the façade gives the impression of several connecting, narrow façades.

The two most important architects at the end of the sixteenth century and in the first decade of the seventeenth century were Lieven de Key (ca. 1560–1627) in Haarlem and Hendrick de Keyser (1565–1621) in Amsterdam. In the work of these architects can be seen the transition from sixteenth-century playful Mannerism to the more rigorous architecture of the seventeenth century. The many residences that De Keyser built along the new canals in Amsterdam give a first impression that the busy, decorative style from the sixteenth century has been continued: for example, the Huis Bartolotti (Herengracht 170) or the Huis met de Hoofden (House with the Heads) (Keizergracht 123). Hidden behind the abundance of decorative elements, however, there is a façade of very deliberate proportions. In 1631, ten years after De Keyser's death, a book of prints of his work, entitled *Architectura Moderna*, was published. In it, De Keyser is called the most important renewer of Dutch architecture because he was the first to have mastered "*konstige bouwen*" (artful building), meaning that he took the mathematical regularity of the ancients to be the foundation for his architecture. By emphasizing the mathematical foundation, the point was made that architecture is not a trade but a science. Thorough knowledge of this science is required to harmonize the trades that are involved. The architect has to have thought out everything beforehand in one total plan.

As the official stone mason of Amsterdam, Hendrick de Keyser was actually in charge of the town's building trades, the "*stadsfabryck.*" In this office, he designed a number of important public buildings in Amsterdam, such as the Beurs (Stock Exchange, 1608) and three new Protestant churches in the new town expansions: the Zuiderkerk (1614), the Noorderkerk (1620), and the Westerkerk (1621; Color Plate 2). In these churches, which were designed specifically for Protestant services, he introduced new types of centralizing floor plans. The Noorderkerk (North Church) has a Greek cross (a cross in which all of the arms have the same measurements) as a floor plan. In the Zuiderkerk (South Church) and even more in the Westerkerk (West Church), he made use of two connected Greek crosses in the floor plan. These rigorously mathematical church floor plans would find great following in the Netherlands in the course of the seventeenth century.

K.A. Ottenheym

See also Classicism in architecture; De Keyser, Hendrick; Italy; Leiden; Sculpture (1550–1795); Tomb sculpture: early modern and later sepulchral art; Town halls

Bibliography

Meischke, R. De gothische bouwtraditie. Amersfoort: Bekking, 1988.

Neurdenburg, E. *Hendrick de Keyser: Beeldhouwer en*

bouwmeester van Amsterdam. Amsterdam: Scheltema and Holkema, 1930.

Vermeulen, F.A.J. *Handboek tot de geschiedenis der Nederlandsche bouwkunst.* Vol. 2, *Kentering en Renaissance.* The Hague: Nijhoff, 1938.

Vos, R., and F. Leeman. *Het nieuwe ornament: Gids voor de renaissance-architectuur en-decoratie in Nederland in de 16de eeuw.* The Hague: Staatsuitgeverij, 1986.

Zantkuijl, H. *Bouwen in Amsterdam: Het woonhuis in de stad.* Amsterdam: Architectura and Natura, 1993.

Reputation of Dutch art abroad

The foreign reputation of Dutch painting in the Golden Age of the late sixteenth and seventeenth centuries was generally negative. Sixteenth-century critics held the opinion that the Northerners (meaning Dutch, Flemish, and German artists) excelled in landscape painting, but that they limited themselves too much to the mere imitation of visible nature. The serious reproach from foreign critics that Dutch painters were not capable of doing more than mimicking what they saw in reality and that, as a result, their paintings did not conform to the classical rules of beauty, would continue to be heard during the entire seventeenth century and a good part of the eighteenth century. In the milieu of the Académie des Beaux-Arts in Paris during the years 1660–1700, Charles Alphonse du Fresnoy and André Félibien, especially, passed harsh judgment upon Dutch artists who did not comply with the classical standards that were set by Raphael and Poussin.

Only after the "victory" of the Rubénists over the Poussinists in the French Academy was there more official appreciation for the use of color and for the picturesque quality of the Dutch school. The *balance des peintres* that Roger de Piles published in 1708 created much discussion. On this scale, which ran from 0 to 20, Raphael received an ideal score: a 17 for invention, an 18 for drawing (the classical *disegno*), a 12 for coloring, and an 18 for expression. Poussin earned 15, 17, 6, and 15 points, respectively. Rembrandt got 15, 6, 17, and 12 points. Rubens, whom De Piles most admired, received 18, 13, 17, and 17 points in the same categories.

In England, Dutch art became originally and primarily known through the gifts of paintings that the States General made to English kings in 1610, 1629, and 1660. After the Restoration of 1660, the love for Dutch painting was really launched. This trend was considerably strengthened with the arrival of the king-*stadholder*, Willem III of Orange, in 1688. Many Dutch artists, among them the father and son Willem van de Velde the Elder and the Younger, traveled to England at that time. However, in the first half of the eighteenth century, after the death of Willem III in 1701, Dutch painting fell into disfavor with English critics. In 1747 the influential literary figure Horace Walpole could not find anything in Dutch art but "drudging Mimics of Nature's most uncomely coarseness."

Later in the eighteenth century, Sir Joshua Reynolds did not find much to like about the Dutch school either. The Dutch never give "a general view of human life," said Reynolds in the fourth of his *Discourses* (1771). He went on to say that "the painters of this school are excellent in their own way; they are only ridiculous when they attempt general history on their own narrow principles, and debase great events by the meanness of their characters."

But, in both France and England, the doctrine of classicism turned out not to be strong enough to keep collectors from buying Dutch art. Works by Northern Netherlandish artists appeared in several prominent French collections, especially works by the *fijnschilders* (fine painters) like Gerrit Dou and by Italianate landscape painters Bartholomeus Breenbergh and Nicolaes Berchem. Even the name of Rembrandt, who is criticized so much by the academic classicists, is mentioned many times in the catalogs of paintings auctioned in the eighteenth century.

After around 1740, Dutch paintings were also gladly bought by English dealers, and the art market in Germany became more active as well. The most spectacular buy of Dutch art in Germany was made by the estate of Count Wilhelm VIII of Hessen. In 1750 he purchased the complete collection of Valerius Röver from Delft for forty thousand guilders. The collection consisted of sixty-four paintings, almost all of which were of the highest quality: eight paintings by Rembrandt, a waterfall by Jacob van Ruisdael, the *Bonenfeest* (Bean Feast) by Jan Steen, six paintings by Philips Wouwerman, works by the flower still-life painter Abraham Mignon, by the *fijnschilder* (fine painter) Frans van Mieris the Elder, by the cattle painter Paulus Potter, and by Jan van der Heyden. All of these paintings are today in the Gemäldegalerie in Kassel.

In the course of the eighteenth century, foreign appreciation for Dutch painting steadily increased. In England, philosophers and art theorists of all stripes distanced themselves expressly from the French academic ideal of beauty while the first efforts were made to formulate a new aesthetic ideal. The old hierarchy of subjects in painting, which had placed history painting at the top and landscape, portraiture, and still life at lower levels, became completely uninteresting, and that was favorable for Dutch art. In several eighteenth-century writings (for example, Richard Payne Knight, *The Landscape: A Didactic Poem*, 1794) supporting the merits of the picturesque in the arts of gardening, architecture, and painting, Dutch seventeenth-century painters like Meindert Hobbema, Adriaen van Ostade, and Jacob van Ruisdael were held up to be an example to the English. Around 1790 there was even a serious rage for Aelbert Cuyp in England, and an artist like John Constable was deeply influenced by Dutch painting of the seventeenth century.

The English ideas also reached the Continent. In Germany they caught on early with the director of the museum in Dresden, C.L. von Hagedorn, as his defense *Betrachtungen uber die Mahlerey*, influenced by Edmund Burke, of the qualities of the Dutch school in 1762 shows. Around 1790, France also was ready for a reevaluation of Dutch art because of the cult of following nature, truth, and *sensibilité* preached by Diderot. J.B.P. Lebrun in the *Galerie des peintres Flamands, Hollandais et Allemands* (1792) praised the "*sites pittoresques*" (picturesque sites), the *"vérité"* (truth), and the *"imitation fidèle de la nature"* (faithful imitation of nature) of Jacob van Ruisdael, as well as of the landscapes of Meindert Hobbema and the work of Johannes Vermeer, who was then only known to a few.

In France, Dutch genre paintings were also looked at with new eyes. Where nothing was seen before but the reprehensible imitation of nature, now the ideals of middle-class virtue were seen. After the French Revolution of 1789, Dutch paintings were awarded great moralizing value. In 1795, the collection of the *stadholder* Willem V, which the French had confiscated, was triumphantly carried into the Musée National in Paris. The collection consisted mainly of Dutch paintings, one of which was the famous *The Bull* by Paulus Potter.

German Romanticism brought about a decisive upturn in the estimation of Dutch art. The cult of genius during the late eighteenth-century *Sturm und Drang* period, the romantic glorification of nature, of the middle-class, the religious, and the autochthonous as the traits of great art, favored the appreciation of certain branches of Dutch painting of the Golden Age. Seventeenth-century Dutch genre painting became very popular in the course of the nineteenth century. In the wake of developments in England and France at the end of the eighteenth century, people appreciated more of the qualities of the work of Van Ruisdael and Hobbema. In portraiture of the seventeenth century, the German art historians thought they recognized in the most complete sense the national character of the Dutch people. On the other hand, the sixteenth-century artists who went to Italy, the seventeenth-century history painters, and the academicians like Adriaen van der Werff and Gerard de Lairesse received heavy criticism.

The French painters of the Barbizon School found artistic inspiration in the works of the great Dutch landscape painters of the Golden Age. In French writing about art in the nineteenth century, Dutch painting began to play a role as a historical example for timely ideologies. This is best shown in the work of journalist, art historian, and art dealer Théophile Thoré. Under the name of William Bürger, he published an influential series of articles about the Dutch art of painting, *Musées de la Hollande* (1858–1860). Thoré considered this art, in its naturalism, as unique in Europe, as the expression of a struggle for democracy and civil liberty, and as an onset of the realism of Gustave Courbet that he admired. (Courbet had, indeed, studied the work of Frans Hals.) Thoré's advocacy of Frans Hals and Johannes Vermeer contributed to the fame of these two artists, who were not yet famous at the time. After the uncontested master, Rembrandt, they have been considered second and third of the great Dutch painters ever since.

Frans Grijzenhout

See also Drawing theory; France; Genre painting, seventeenth century; Italy; Nationalism; North American art, Dutch influences; State and municipal art collecting and collections; Subjects, subject categories, and hierarchies

Bibliography

Brown, Christopher. *Scholars of Nature: The Collecting of Dutch Paintings in Britain, 1610–1857*. Hull and London: Ferens Art Gallery, 1981.

Chu, P. ten Doesschate. *French Realism and the Dutch Masters: The Influence of Dutch Seventeenth-Century Painting on the Development of French Paintings between 1830 and 1870*. Utrecht: Haentjens, Dekker, and Gumbert, 1974.

Eliel, C.S. "Genre Painting during the Revolution and the *Goût hollandaise*." In *1798: French Art during the Revolution*. Edited by A. Wintermute, 47–61. New York: Colnaghi, 1989.

Gerson, H. *Ausbreitung und Nachwirkung der holländischen Malerei des 17. Jahrhunderts*. 2nd ed. Amsterdam: B.M. Israel, 1983.

Grijzenhout, F., and H. van Veen, eds. *Gouden Eeuw in perspectief: Het beeld van de Nederlandse zeventiende-eeuwse schilderkunst in later tijd*. Nijmegen: SUN, 1992.

Haskell, F. *Rediscoveries in Art: Some Aspects of Taste, Fashion, and Collecting in England and France*. 2nd ed. Oxford: Phaidon, 1980.

Jowell, F.S. *Thoré-Bürger and the Art of the Past*. New York: Garland, 1977.

Reverse painting

An unfired painting applied to the back side of a piece of white glass is called reverse painting. The decoration must be viewed from the opposite side as a reversed image. Reverse painting applied to sheet glass has been practiced in the Netherlands from the end of the fifteenth century until well into the nineteenth, and again in the twentieth century, producing independent pictures with a shiny, opaque surface, mounted in wooden frames. Extant examples are scarce, due to the vulnerable character of the support and to the fact that any break is irreparable.

Reverse painting is frequently, though wrongly, equated with *verre eglomise* (after Jean Baptiste Glomy, a late-eighteenth-century Parisian who made picture frames embellished with reverse—gilded and black—painted glass panels) since it covers several methods of applying reverse decoration. The earliest extant examples date from the first half of the sixteenth century, the most important piece being the triptych *The Last Supper* from the circle of Jacob Cornelisz. van Oostsanen from Amsterdam (ca. 1525; Amsterdam, Rijksmuseum). Other centers of production seem to be Leiden and Haarlem, and the province of Gelderland. The pictures are in general small, up to 34 cm square, because it was difficult to obtain large sheets of glass. They are all executed in a very cumbersome technique, painting "backward"—that is, putting down highlights and deep shadows first and then applying colors. Additional modeling and highlights achieved by scratching away the first layer of pigment are similar to the methods of glass painters. Reverse-painted images follow the iconography of easel paintings and must have functioned likewise.

By the end of the sixteenth century the vogue for reverse

paintings in black or brown shades and gold must have developed. The inner drawing is scratched out of the first layer of transparent varnishes, and the painting is backed with gold leaf. The artists were probably stained glass painters, like Gerhard Janssen (1636–1725) from Utrecht, who worked in Vienna from 1662 on. The pastoral landscapes of Leendert Overbeek (1752–1815) from Haarlem are late examples in the same technique.

During the seventeenth century more color gradually appeared in reverse paintings. The subjects follow contemporary Dutch painting (landscape, marine, still life, genre scenes, and portraits, sometimes in the center of mirrors), and some painters, like Jan van der Heyden (1637–1712) from Amsterdam, worked in both mediums. The formats grew larger at this time, although miniature paintings occur as well. Special mention must be made of Jonas Zeuner (1727–1814), born in Kassel, Germany, and for sixty years active in Amsterdam. His *oeuvre* consists of about one hundred works, mostly signed and dated: portraits in reverse foil engraving on gold or silver leaf with black backing, based on contemporary engravings; and river and cityscapes in a combination of foil engraving and painted details. The practice of reverse painting on glass was discontinued in the later nineteenth century until the German artist Heinrich Campendonk (1889–1957), who learned the technique from members of Der Blaue Reiter in Bavaria, passed it on to his students at the Rijksakademie in Amsterdam after 1935. Only one of them, Marianne van der Heijden (born 1922), seems to have exploited reverse painting extensively. Her later work from the 1960s and 1970s shows a personal, abstract organic style in an experimental technique, combining acrylic paint and scratching with pieces of foil. The history of reverse painting in the Netherlands has hardly been investigated as yet. Systematic research should locate more objects and clarify the connections to stained glass, roundels, and easel painting.

Zsuzsanna van Ruyven-Zeman

See also Roundels; Stained glass; Van der Heyden, Jan

Bibliography
Eswarin, Rudy, ed. *Reverse Paintings on Glass: The Ryser Collection.* Corning, NY: Corning Museum of Glass, 1992.

Ritz, Gislind M. *Hinterglasmalerei: Geschichte, Erscheinung, Technik.* Munich: Callwey, 1972.

Thiel, Pieter J.J. van. *All the Paintings of the Rijksmuseum in Amsterdam: A Completely Illustrated Catalogue.* The Hague: Staatsuitgeverij, 1976.

Rhetoricians' chambers
From their heyday in the sixteenth century through their gradual decline in the seventeenth, the amateur performance societies known as chambers of *rederijkers* (rhetoricians) had significant connections with artists. Dutch painters were members of their local chambers, designed *rederijker* decorations, used *rederijker* themes, or represented chambers in action.

The first *rederijker* chambers in the Southern Netherlands were founded in the fifteenth century on the model of French associations. The chambers owe their name to the rhetorical function of their productions, which aimed to persuade the audience of moral issues through instruction and entertainment, frequently with considerable rhetorical skill. By the early sixteenth century, many towns had at least one chamber, each with a board of prince, deacon, chief author, declamator, and fool. Most members were artisans, shopkeepers, and merchants, sufficiently educated to write and perform complicated verse and three genres of plays: the *spel van sinne* (allegorical play), the *esbattement* (farce, also called *factie* or *clucht*), and the *tafelspel* (table play for festive meals). The chambers contributed plays, poems, and floats to festivals or joyous entries and organized contests in which chambers from other towns were invited to compose plays in answer to a given question.

The situation in Antwerp, where in 1480 the oldest chamber joined with the Guild of St. Luke, making every artist a *rederijker*, was exceptional, but many Dutch artists were *rederijkers*. The two Haarlem chambers included among their members Karel van Mander, Hendrick Goltzius, Frans and Dirck Hals, Salomon de Bray, Adriaen Brouwer, Gerrit and Job Berckheyde, Richard Brakenburg, and earlier probably Maerten van Heemskerck, who designed the printed device of the Haarlem chamber the *Wijngaardranken* (the vineyard shoots). Painters also supplied chambers with wooden blazons, costumes, sets, and illustrations for publication.

The most valued part of *rederijker* output in the sixteenth century was allegorical, and several visual representations sound related themes. Cornelis Anthonisz.'s woodcut series *Sorgheloos* (Careless, 1541) illustrates a Prodigal Son narrative written by an Amsterdam *rederijker*, and his *Misuse of Prosperity* (1546) presents a cycle from rich to poor and back, a favored *rederijker* issue. Van Heemskerck's treatment of the same topic, the *Circulus vicissitudinis rerum humanarum* (Cycle of the Vicissitudes of Human Affairs, engravings, published 1564), follows the program for the Circumcision procession held at Antwerp in 1561. His *Bel and the Dragon* series (engravings, published 1565) includes two diminutive participants partly indebted to the stock *sinnekens* (seductive personifications of evil traits) of the *rederijkers*.

By the mid-sixteenth century, *rederijkers* lamented the antagonism of secular and religious authorities. Some chambers had Reformed leanings, and several in the Southern Netherlands were censored for their incendiary potential. From 1585, Southern exiles significantly strengthened Dutch chambers, and some organized separate *rederijker* associations. But soon afterward *rederijkers* came under fire for aesthetic as well as religious reasons. Calvinists polemicized against immodest leisure activities, including *rederijker* performance, and *rederijkers* themselves complained that members overinterpreted the maxim that Bacchus, god of Wine, inspires poetry. More influential on the decline of the chambers was the development of professional theater, in part out of the old chambers. A well-educated public favored the newly classicist tragedies and comedies, professionally produced in Amsterdam, and the farces that followed each performance filled the need for bawdier entertainment, as did the simpler professional performances at the fairs.

Seventeenth-century representations of *rederijkers* register these developments. David Vinckboons painted *rederijker* performance as fair festivity (ca. 1602–1612), and Frans Hals portrayed the *rederijker* fool *Piero* as a salty wit (1616). Later paintings, however, show absurd religious sectarianism (Anonymous, *Haarlem Rederijkers Disputing*, 1659, Haarlem, Frans Hals Museum) or boozing and bantering. Jan Steen's *Gathering of Rederijkers* (ca. 1663–1667) resembles a dissolute household, a rough verse identifying them as Bacchus' poets, writing verse dry and loose. Steen also painted two views of *Rederijkers at a Window* (ca. 1655 and ca. 1662–1666; Fig. 119), squinting at vague texts and brandishing tankards. Adriaen van Ostade drew and etched similar compositions in which the *rederijkers* take on a milder rusticity (1660s). His works, and a contemporaneous painting by Job Berckheyde of a serious *Rederijker Rehearsal*, indicate the extent of Steen's parody. As similarly parodic references appear in both "serious" comedies and cheaper jokebooks, the ridicule of *rederijkers* must have cut across the broad middle class. Nevertheless, the robust scale of Steen's *rederijker* "portraits" and the rustic joviality of their activities in his and Van Ostade's representations seem to present a nostalgic, urban vision of *rederijkers*. The theater critic Andries Pels expressed similar ambivalence in his assessment of their literary and social contributions (*Gebruik en misbruik des tooneels* [Use and Abuse of the Stage], 1681).

Mariët Westermann

See also Allegorical traditions; Comic modes; Dutch history; Haarlem; Humanism, humanist themes; Protestant Reformation; Steen, Jan Havicksz.; Theater and theatricality; Writers on art, sixteenth and seventeenth centuries

Bibliography

Briels, J.G.C.A. "Reyn genuecht: Zuidnederlandse kamers van rhetorica in Noordnederland 1585–1630." *Bijdragen tot de geschiedenis* 57 (1974): 3–89.

Gibson, Walter S. "Artists and *Rederijkers* in the Age of Bruegel." *Art Bulletin* 63 (1981): 426–446.

Heppner, Albert. "The Popular Theatre of the Rederijkers in the Work of Jan Steen and His Contemporaries." *Journal of the Warburg and Courtauld Institutes* 3 (1939/1940): 22–48.

Hummelen, W.M.H. "Sinnekens in prenten en op schilderijen." *Oud Holland* 106 (1992): 117–142.

Mak, J.J. *De rederijkers*. Amsterdam: P.N. van Kampen and Zoon, 1944.

Veldman, Ilja M. "The Artist among the Rhetoricians of Haarlem." In *Maarten van Heemskerck and Dutch Humanism in the Sixteenth Century*. Maarssen: Gary Schwartz, 1977.

Robertson, Suze Bisschop (1855–1922)

Born in The Hague, Suze Robertson entered that city's Academie voor Beeldende Kunsten (Academy of Arts) in 1874, at the same time as Willem de Zwart and George Hendrik Breitner. Later she was a student of the painter Petrus van der Velden (1837–1915) in The Hague, and she took evening classes at the Rotterdam Academy. In 1882 Robertson registered at the Rijksacademie in Amsterdam, and, to support herself, she gave drawing lessons. She returned to The Hague in 1883 to devote herself entirely to painting. She became a member of the Pulchri Studio, a society of artists, and the Nederlandsche Etsclub (Dutch Etching Club). Robertson worked mostly in The Hague and its environs, Het Gooi, and Brabant. She painted mainly still lifes, views of villages, and interiors with farmers' wives and children. She would explore and repeat these themes all of her life. Her early paintings are marked by a somber use of colors and a vigorous brushwork.

In 1892 Robertson married the painter Richard Bisschop (1849–1926), and in 1894 a daughter was born. Her art production virtually ceased until around 1900 as she devoted herself to her family. The work she created after this is more expressionistic in color and in the handling of the paint.

The first large retrospective of her work was organized by the Rotterdamsche Kunstkring (Art Circle) in 1905. After 1914 she painted less and less because of sickness and depression; however, she still made various pastels and drawings. Much of Suze Robertson's work is owned by the Suze Robertson Foundation, which is managed by the Gemeentemuseum (Municipal Museum) in The Hague.

Rieta Bergsma

See also Amsterdam Impressionists

Bibliography

Bionda, Richard, and Carel Blotkamp, eds. *The Age of Van Gogh: Dutch Painting, 1880–1895*. Zwolle: Waanders, 1990–1991.

Wagner, Anna, and Herbert Henkels. *Suze Robertson*. The Hague: Nijgh and Van Ditmar, 1984.

Rochussen, Charles (1814–1894)

After an education in business and several years in an office, Charles Rochussen began studying to be a painter when he was twenty-two years old; he studied first with W.J.J. Nuyen and, after this teacher's death, with A. Waldorp. From 1839 until 1846 he attended The Hague Drawing Academy; afterward he made several trips to Belgium, Germany, France, and Italy. Rochussen was a prominent figure in the art world, especially from 1849 to 1869, when he lived in Amsterdam and was several times chosen to be the chairman of the artists' society Arti et Amicitiae. After he settled in Rotterdam in 1869, he led a retired bachelor's existence (Fig. 146).

Rochussen was mainly known as a history painter. He contributed to the Historical Galleries of J. de Vos Jacobsz. and Arti et Amicitiae in Amsterdam. His historical representations were painted with much knowledge about the subject; he always put the historical event ahead of the human drama. He tried to make the portrayal as accurate, instructive, and entertaining as possible. Early in his career, Rochussen also painted various views of the society life and sporting life of his time.

84. Hendrick Willem Mesdag. Sunset at Scheveningen, *ca. 1895.*
Oil on canvas, 157 cm. × 134 cm. Museum Mesdag, The Hague.

85. Gabriel Metsu. The Sick Child, *ca. 1663-1664.*
Oil on canvas, 32.2 cm. × 27.2 cm. Rijksmuseum, Amsterdam.

86. Piet Mondrian. Composition with Red, Blue, Yellow and Black, *1929. Oil on canvas, 45.1 cm. × 45.3 cm.*
Collection Solomon R. Guggenheim Museum, New York. Copyright © 1995 ABC/Mondrian Estate/Holtzman Trust/Licensed by ILP.
(Photo: David Heald. Copyright © The Solomon R. Guggenheim Foundation, New York.)

87. *Jan Miense Molenaer.* Musical Company, *ca. 1640. Oil on panel,*
62.5 cm. × 81 cm. Frans Hals Museum, Haarlem.

88. Gerard Ter Borch. A Music Party, *ca. 1675. Oil on panel.*
Cincinnati Art Museum, Cincinnati, Ohio. Bequest of Mary E. Emery.

91. Pieter Oosterhuis. The Herengracht near the Leliegracht, Amsterdam, *1859. Albumen print.*
Half of a stereo photograph. Gemeentearchief (Topografisch-historische atlas), Amsterdam.

92. Pier Pander. Mother and Child, *1905. Marble.*
Stedelijk Museum, Amsterdam.

93. *Paulus Moreelse*. The Beautiful Shepherdess, *1630.*
Oil on canvas, 82 cm. × 66 cm. Rijksmuseum, Amsterdam.

94. *Jan Mijtens*. Portrait of a Couple as Granida and Daifilo, *1660s.*
Oil on canvas, 112 cm. × 143. 5 cm. Rijksmuseum, Amsterdam.

96. *Julius Perger.* View of the digging through the Hoek of Holland, taken from the light structure on the Northern Dam,
1875-1878. Albumen print. Koninklijk Huisarchief, The Hague.

97. Johan Huijsen. Road-worker with an asphalt oven, *ca. 1925. Oil print, 16.8 cm. × 11.9 cm.*
Prentenkabinet der Rijksuniversiteit, Leiden.

98. *Piet Zwart*. Machine Forms, *ca. 1932. Silver gelatine print, 13.1 cm. × 18 cm.*
Prentenkabinet der Rijksuniversiteit, Leiden. Copyright © 1995 Piet Zwart/Licensed by VAGA, New York, NY.

99. Thomas de Keyser. Portrait of Constantijn Huygens and His Clerk, *1627.*
Reproduced by courtesy of the Trustees, The National Gallery, London.

101. Woodcut from Le Chevalier Délibéré *(Gouda: Collaciebroeders, 1489.) Reproduced from F. Lipmann,* Le Chevalier Délibéré by Olivier de la Marche (1425–1500), *London, 1898. (Photo: Bart A. Rosier. Courtesy of the Bibliotheek Vrije Universiteit, Amsterdam).*

102. Jan Swart. Woodcut from Den Bibel *(Antwerp: Willem Vorsterman, 1528). Bibliotheek Vrije Universiteit, Amsterdam. (Photo: Bart A. Rosier. Courtesy of the Bibliotheek Vrije Universiteit, Amsterdam.)*

103. Master I.A.M. of Zwolle. St. George, 1475-1500. Engraving. The Metropolitan Museum of Art,
New York. Harris Brisbane Dick Fund, 1933.

104. *Willem Witsen.* Winter, *ca. 1887. Etching. The Metropolitan Museum of Art,*
New York. Harris Brisbane Dick Fund, 1927.

105. Willem Witsen. Waterloo Bridge, *ca. 1890. Etching. Museum Boymans-van Beuningen, Rotterdam.*
(Photo: Tom Haartsen Studio, Oudekerk aan de Amstel.)

106. Pieter Dupont. Workhorses *(L'Outillage), 1901. Engraving. Museum Boymans-van Beuningen, Rotterdam.*
(Photo: Tom Haartsen Studio, Oudekerk aan de Amstel.)

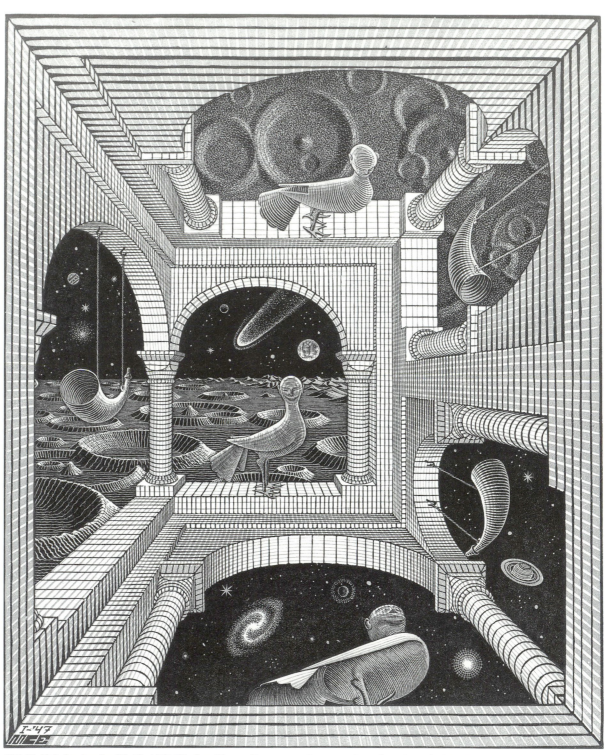

107. M. C. Escher. *Another World, 1947. Woodcut. Museum Boymans-van Beuningen, Rotterdam. Copyright © 1995
M.C. Escher/Cordon Art, Baarn, Holland. All rights reserved. (Photo: Tom Haartsen Studio, Oudekerk aan de Amstel.)*

108. *Bob Bonies.* Untitled, *1969. Silkscreen. Museum Boymans-van Beuningen, Rotterdam. Copyright © 1995 Bonies/Licensed by VAGA, New York, NY. (Photo: Tom Haartsen Studio, Oudekerk aan de Amstel.)*

109. Harry van Kruiningen. De Winkel van Poesjkins Doodkistenmaker *(The Workshop of Pushkin's Coffin Maker), ca. 1970. Etching and aquatint. Museum Boymans-van Beuningen, Rotterdam. (Photo: Tom Haartsen Studio, Oudekerk aan de Amstel.)*

110. *Co Westerik.* Chemicus *(The Chemist), 1968. Etching. Museum Boymans-van Beuningen, Rotterdam. Copyright © 1995 Co Westerik/Licensed by VAGA, New York, NY. (Photo: Tom Haartsen Studio, Oudekerk aan de Amstel.)*

UBI TVVS
O MORS ACVLEVS
VBI TVA INFERNE
VICTORIA.
1.cor.15.

ihs

xps

Ecce Deus noster iste, expectauimus
enim et saluabit nos * esaie.25.

ABSORPTA EST MORS
IN VICTORIA.

A·De·Weert

Inventor·

15

77

Wy waeren kinderen, des torens duer de sonde.
Dies ons thantschrift des doots, bracht in suyants gewelt.
Maer duer christum verlost, die de doot verslonde.
Serpent vertreden heeft, ons in genaede gestelt.

Enfans d'Ire estions nous par peché qui a mort
Obligez nous tenoit, et liurez a l'effort
De sathan, mais par Christ qui le serpent terrasse,
Et abisme la mort, sommes remis en grace.

Ioannes sadeler fecit et excudit.

111. Johannes Sadeler after Adriaan de Weert. Christ Redeeming Humankind, *1577.*
Engraving. Rijksprentenkabinet/Rijksmuseum, Amsterdam.

112. *J.F. Staal. Housing block for De Samenwerking, Amsterdam, 1922-1923. Perspective view along Joh. M. Coenenstraat. Collection Netherlands Architecture Institute, Rotterdam. (Photo: Retina.)*

113. *J.J.P. Oud. Public Housing, Kiefhoek Quarter, Rotterdam, 1925-1929. (Photo: Maristella Casciato.)*

114. *Gerrit Dou*. The Quacksalver, *1652. Oil on panel, 112 cm.* × *83 cm. Museum Boymans-van Beuningen, Rotterdam.*

115. *Johannes Vermeer.* Allegory of Faith, *ca. 1670. Oil on canvas, 114.3 cm. × 88.9 cm.*
The Metropolitan Museum of Art, New York. The Friedsam Collection, Bequest of Michael Friedsam, 1931.

116. Anonymous Rembrandt Pupil (Constantijn Daniel van Renesse ?). The Annunciation, ca. 1645-1650. Drawing in red chalk. Kupferstichkabinett, Staatliche Museen zu Berlin PK. (Photo: Jörg P. Anders.)

117. Rembrandt van Rijn. Landscape with Three Gabled Cottages beside a Road, *1650. Etching.*
The Metropolitan Museum of Art, New York. H.O. Havemeyer Collection. Bequest of Mrs. H.O. Havemeyer, 1929.

118. *Rembrandt van Rijn.* Jacob Blessing the Sons of Joseph, *1656.*
Oil on canvas, 175.5 cm. × 210.5 cm. Staatliche Museen, Kassel.

119. Jan Steen. Rederijkers (Rhetoricians) at a Window, *ca. 1662-1666. Oil on canvas, 73 cm. × 59 cm.*
The Philadelphia Museum of Art, John G. Johnson Collection.

120. Gerbrand van den Eeckhout. The Continence of Scipio, *ca. 1665. Oil on canvas, 138.1 cm. × 161.5 cm. The Toledo Museum of Art. Toledo, Ohio.*

121. Adriaen van der Werff. Self-Portrait with the Portrait of His Wife Margareta Rees and Their Daughter Maria, *1699.*
Oil on canvas, 81 cm. × 65.5 cm. Rijksmuseum, Amsterdam.

122. Adriaen van Wesel. Virgin and Child, ca. 1475. Oak. Rijksmuseum, Amsterdam.

5

*124. J. Ph. Koelman and W.C.
van der Waaijen Pieterszen.
National Memorial to 1813,
1869. The Hague. (Photo: Mieke
van der Wal.)*

125. Lambertus Zijl. Gijsbrecht van Amstel, 1903-1907. Façade sculpture on the Stock Exchange, Amsterdam. (Photo: Drents Museum, Assen.)

126. Dirck Crabeth. Spectators at the Baptism of Christ, 1555. Detail of a stained-glass window in St. Janskerk, Gouda. (Photo: Courtesy of Stichting Fonds Goudse Glazen, Gouda.)

127. Willem Heda. Still Life with a Gilt Goblet, *1635.*
Oil on canvas. Rijksmuseum, Amsterdam.

128. Rachel Ruysch. Fruit Still Life with Stag Beetle and Chaffinch's Nest, *1717.*
Staatliche Kunsthalle, Karlsruhe.

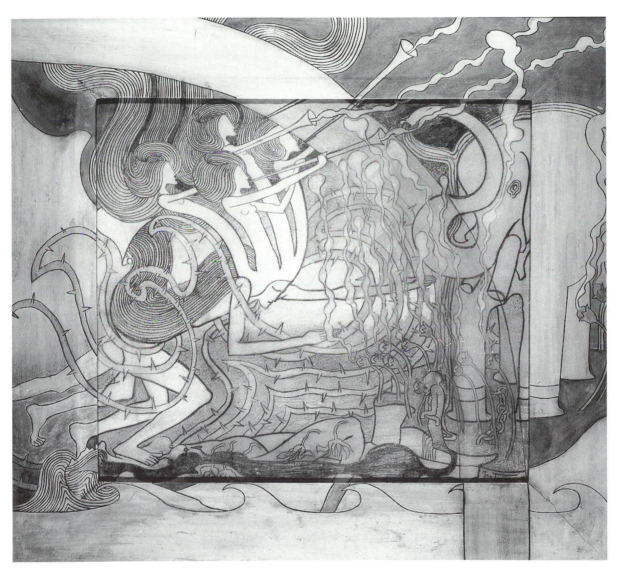

129. Jan Toorop. Play of Lines: Ascendancy, with Opposition, of Modern Art, *1893.*
Collection Haags Gemeentemuseum, The Hague.

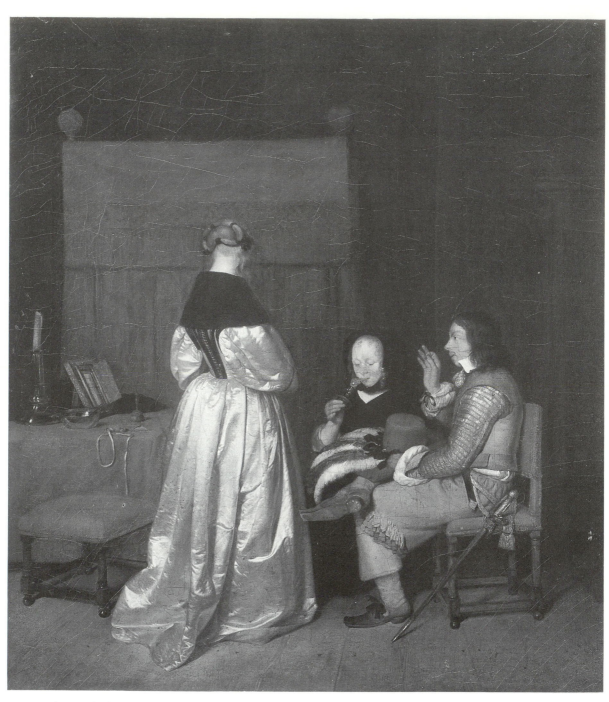

130. Gerard Ter Borch. The Paternal Admonition, *ca. 1654-1655. Oil on canvas, 70 cm. × 60 cm. Gemäldegalerie, Staatliche Museen zu Berlin PK. (Photo: Jörg P. Anders.)*

131. *Hendrick Terbrugghen.* The Calling of St. Matthew, *1621.*
Oil on canvas, 102 cm. × 137.5 cm. Centraal Museum, Utrecht.

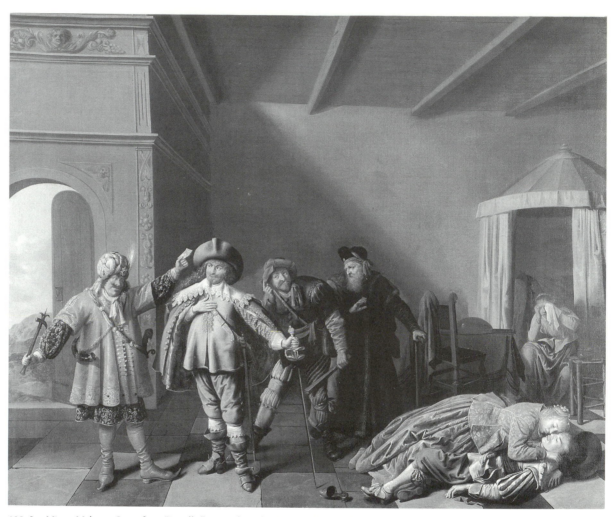

132. Jan Miense Molenaer. Scene from "Lucelle," a tragedy with a happy ending by the Dutch playwright G.A. Bredero (1614), after a French drama by Le Jars, who derived the material from Boccaccio's "Decamerone," *1639. Oil on canvas. Collection Theater Instituut Nederland, Amsterdam.

133. Child Playing with a
Hoop. *Painted ceramic tile,*
middle of the seventeenth-century.
Courtesy of Tegelmuseum,
Otterlo.

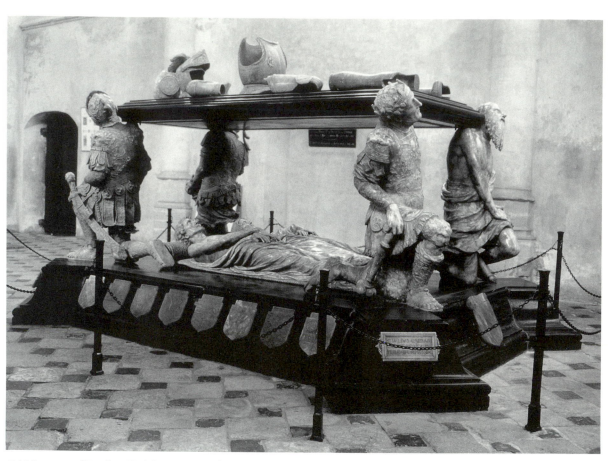

134. Monument of Engelbert II of Nassau, *ca. 1526-1538.*
Breda, Grote Kerk. (Photo: David Lawrence.)

135. *Rombout Verhulst*. Monument of Willem van der Zaan, 1670. *Amsterdam, Oude Kerk. (Photo: Cynthia Lawrence.)*

136. Town Hall, The Hague, 1564-1565. Photograph, end of the nineteenth century.
(Photo: Rijksdienst voor de Monumentenzorg, Zeist.)

137. *Cornelis Troost*. Twelfth Night/Star Singers. *ca. 1740.*
Pastel on paper, 56 cm. × 74 cm. Mauritshuis, The Hague.

138. Hendrik Petrus Berlage. Second and Final Extension Plan for Amsterdam South, 1915.
Gemeentearchief, Amsterdam.

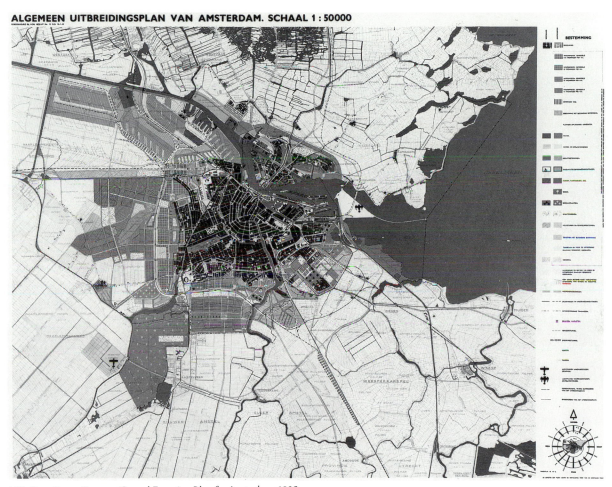

139. *Cornelis van Eesteren. General Extension Plan for Amsterdam, 1935.*
Gemeentearchief, Amsterdam.

140. Gerard van Honthorst. The Denial of St. Peter, *ca. 1618-1620. Oil on canvas.*
The Minneapolis Institute of Arts, Putnam Dana McMillan Fund.

141. Bartholomeus van der Helst. Double Portrait of Abraham del Court and Maria Keersegieter, *1654.*
Oil on canvas, 172 cm. × 146.5 cm. Museum Boymans-van Beuningen, Rotterdam.

142. *M.W. van der Valk.* Pollard Willow in a Meadow, *ca. 1898. Etching. 278 mm. × 198 mm.*
Museum Boymans-van Beuningen, Rotterdam.

143. *Vincent van Gogh.* Self-Portrait, *ca. 1887. Wadsworth Atheneum, Hartford.*
Gift of Philip Goodwin in memory of his mother, Josephine S. Goodwin.

144. *E.M. van Ojen.* Amelandsestraat, The Hague, *1926. Modern print from original negative.*
Dienst Ruimtelijke Ordening, The Hague.

145. *Johannes Vermeer.* View of Delft, *1658-1660.*
Oil on canvas, 98.5 cm. × 118.5 cm. Mauritshuis, The Hague.

146. Maurits Verveer. Portrait of the Painter Charles Rochussen, *ca. 1875. Albumen print.*
Collection Theater Instituut Nederland, Amsterdam.

147. *Carel Visser.* Vier dicte paraplu's *(Four Closed Umbrellas), 1979. 58 cm. × 82 cm. × 35 cm.*
Collection of Carel Visser, Rijswijk. Copyright © 1995 Carel Visser/Licensed by VAGA,
New York, NY. (Photo: John Stoel, Haren.)

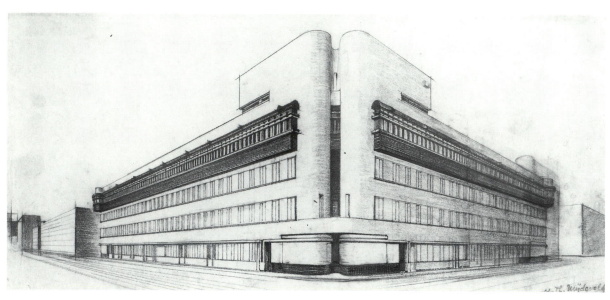

148. H. Th. Wijdeveld. Housing block on the Insulindeweg, Amsterdam East, 1920-1930.
Perspective view of the corner. Collection Netherlands Architecture Institute, Rotterdam. (Photo: Retina.)

149. Meinard Woldringh. Pattern of Sand and Water, *1968.*
Silver gelatine print, 17.6 cm. × 22.3 cm. Rijksuniversiteit Leiden.

150. Geertruyd Roghman. Woman Scouring Metalware, *ca. 1650.*
Etching. Rijksmuseum, Amsterdam. (Photo: Alison Kettering.)

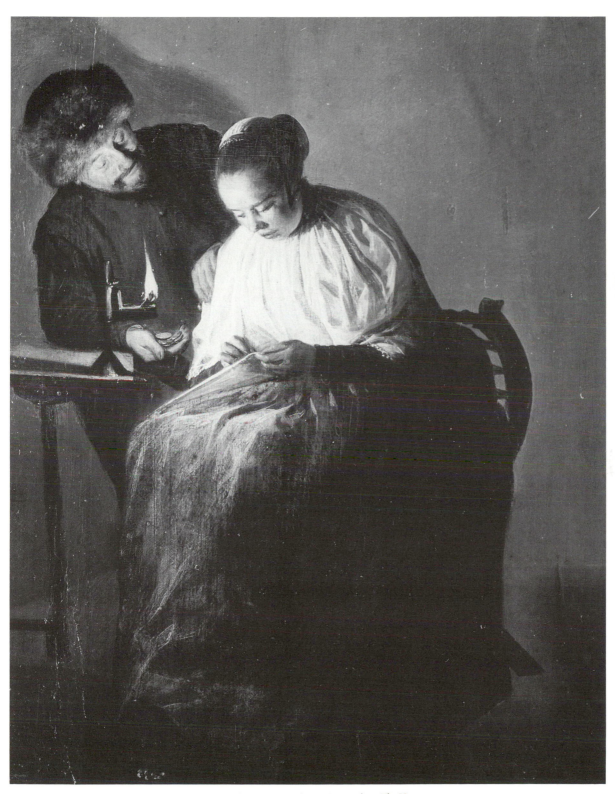

151. Judith Leyster. The Proposition, *1631. Oil on panel, 30.9 cm. × 24.2 cm. Mauritshuis, The Hague.*

152. Philips Wouwerman. Army Camp, *1660s. Mauritshuis, The Hague.*

Moreover, he had a strong preference for soldierly subjects (through which the painter G.H. Breitner grew greatly to admire him). Rochussen also made many drawings and exercised great skill in graphic techniques. His fluency in drawing and excellent feeling for anecdotal detail are well expressed in his numerous book illustrations, which contributed especially to his fame.

Alexandra W.M. van Smoorenburg

See also Belgium; Breitner, George Hendrik; History painting; Nuyen, W.J.J.; Rotterdam; Verveer, Maurits; War and warfare

Bibliography

Bionda, Richard, and Carel Blotkamp, eds. *The Age of Van Gogh: Dutch Painting, 1880–1895*, 203–204. Zwolle: Waanders, 1990.

Hoenderdos, P. *Ary Scheffer, Sir Lawrence Alma Tadema, Charles Rochussen of de vergankelijkheid van de roem.* Rotterdam: Rotterdamse Kunststichting, 1974.

Roelofs, Willem (1822–1897)

The landscape painter Willem Roelofs, who was born in Amsterdam, received his early training in Utrecht from an amateur painter. In 1839–1840, he was registered as a student at the Academie voor Beeldende Kunsten (Academy of Arts) in The Hague along with Johannes Bosboom, Charles Rochussen, Samuel Verveer, David Bles, Jan Frederik van Deventer, Laurens Hanedoes, Johan Philip Koelman, Jan Weissenbruch, and Lambertus Hardenberg. His education also included a year of study with the animal painter Hendrikus van de Sande Bakhuyzen, who took his pupil outdoors to work *en plein air*. After his year with Bakhuyzen, Roelofs worked on his own in Utrecht. From 1838 onward, he regularly entered his works in exhibitions. In 1846 Roelofs again settled in The Hague, and the next year he founded with his friends from the academy the artists' society Pulchri Studio, which later was considered to be the cradle of The Hague School.

In September 1847, Roelofs went to Brussels in Belgium; he became successful very soon and stayed for forty years. In 1848 he was awarded a gold medal at the Brussels exhibition and one of his Dutch landscapes was bought by the king of Belgium, who later would purchase more works by Roelofs.

In Brussels, Roelofs came under the influence of the French Barbizon School, and he went several times to Fontainebleau to work after 1851. By then he was using intense colors that the critics called "unconventionally bright." In 1855, after five years of painting Belgian and French landscapes, Roelofs returned to Dutch subjects. By the end of the 1870s, his works had become slightly more impressionistic.

Although Roelofs lived in Brussels, he, along with Johannes Bosboom and J.W. Bilders, are considered the forerunners of The Hague School (Fig. 58). Belgian art critics, who until the 1870s placed him among the Belgian school of landscapists, were the first to note his new and modern vision. In a book published in 1881, recounting fifty years of Belgian art, the progressive Belgian art critic and writer Camille Lemonnier considered Roelofs a painter who, together with Théodore

Fourmois and François Lamorinière from Belgium and the Dutch artist Martinus Kuytenbrouwer, had fundamentally renewed Belgian landscape painting around 1850 by exact and personal observation of nature. Other Belgian authors, like Henri Hymans, took over this point of view. In his famous review of the Brussels salon of 1866 (in De Bodt, 1995), Lemonnier characterized Willem Roelofs in a way that Dutch critics would not do for at least another decade. "Mr. Roelofs," he wrote, "put emotion in his canvasses and sometimes, in his misty parts where you can feel the north, he pushes it unto melancholy." He went on to observe that "the greens of Roelofs are incredibly strong." In contempory Dutch art criticism—for instance, that written by J. van Santen Kolff—Roelofs became an example of an artist who understood nature the way the great Dutch masters of the seventeenth century had understood it. The striking exception to this view is to be found in the first survey of Dutch nineteenth-century art (1903) by the painter and critic Gerharda Hermina Marius, in which Roelofs is considered scarcely interesting for the development of Dutch art because, in the author's opinion, he was "too much a stranger" (that is, too French) in his work.

During his long stay in Brussels, Roelofs was important as an intermediary between the Belgian and the Dutch art worlds. From 1849 on, he was an active member of the multidisciplinary Brussels art society, the Cercle Artistique (Artistic Circle), and for several years served on the advisory board. In 1856 Roelofs was one of the founders of the Société Belge des Aquarellistes (Belgian Society of Watercolorists) (in De Bodt, 1995). Roelofs' most important students were P.J.C. Gabriël, H.W. Mesdag, C.N. Storm van 's Gravesande, and Frans Smissaert.

Saskia de Bodt

See also Belgium; Bosboom, Johannes; Drawings, uses and collecting; France; Gabriël, Paul Joseph Constantin; Hague School, The; Mesdag, Hendrik Willem; Rochussen, Charles

Bibliography

Bodt, Saskia de. "Hendrik Willem Mesdag en Brussel." *Oud Holland* 95 (1981): 59–87.

———. *Halverweg Parijs: Willem Roelofs en de Nederlandse schilderskolonie in Brussel 1840–1890.* Ghent: Snoek-Ducaju, 1995. (English Summary.)

Bremmer, H.P. *Willem Roelofs, 100 Lichtdrukken naar zijn werken.* Amsterdam, 1909.

Jeltes, H.F.W. "Brieven van Willem Roelofs aan Mr. P. VerLoren van Themaat." *Oud Holland* 42 (1925): 86–96, 131–140.

———. *Willem Roelofs: Bizonderheden betreffende zijn leven en zijn werk.* Amsterdam, 1911.

Leeuw, Ronald de, John Sillevis, and Charles Dumas, eds. *The Hague School: Dutch Masters of the Nineteenth Century.* London: Royal Academy of Arts in association with Weidenfeld and Nicholson, 1983.

Lemonnier, Camille. *Histoire des beaux-arts en Belgique.* Vol. 3, *Cinquante ans de Liberté.* Brussels: M. Weissenbruch, 1881.

Marius, G.H. *De Hollandse schilderkunst in de negentiende eeuw.* 1903. 2nd rev. ed., The Hague: Nijhoff, 1920.

——. *Dutch Painters of the Nineteenth Century.* 1903. Translated by Alexander Teixeira de Mattos. Edited by Geraldine Norman. Woodbridge, Suffolk: Antique Collectors Club, 1973.

Smissaert, H. "Willem Roelofs." In *Het Schildersboek.* Edited by Max Rooses. Vol. 1, 62–80. Amsterdam: Elsevier, 1898.

Roland Holst, Richard N. (1868–1938)

Richard Roland Holst was admitted (after a second attempt) to the Rijksacademie in Amsterdam in 1885. After leaving the academy, he lived for several years outside the city (1888 in Breukelen; 1888–1889 in Hattem; and after that in Heerde) and worked from nature. After returning to Amsterdam his interest shifted from Impressionism to the more literary Symbolism. Roland Holst was at that time strongly under the influence of Jan Toorop and Vincent van Gogh. In his work, he suppressed the picturesque and atmospheric elements and placed the linear aspect in the foreground. After 1892 he produced mainly drawings and prints. Impressed by the theories of Sâr Péladan, Roland Holst became a member of the mystic movement Rose + Croix in 1892. In the course of the 1890s, however, Roland Holst moved from a religious to a more socially engaged view of the arts, as supported by Antoon Derkinderen and others in the Netherlands. Foreign influences on Roland Holst included Maurice Denis in France, and William Morris and Walter Crane in England. During his stay in London in 1893, Roland Holst made a thorough study of Egyptian and Assyrian art.

Roland Holst, who wrote art criticism for the periodical *De Nieuwe Gids* and often communicated his ideas through lectures, articles, and books, married the poet Henriëtte van der Schalk in 1896. Both were supporters of socialism and joined the Social Democratic Workers' Party (SDAP) in 1897. After 1900 Roland Holst developed a geometric-based monumental style, which he applied in wall paintings, leaded glass windows, posters, costumes, and scenery. In 1918 Roland Holst was appointed a professor at the Rijksacademie in Amsterdam; he succeeded Derkinderen as director in 1926. He resigned honorably in 1934.

Alexandra W.M. van Smoorenburg

See also Derkinderen, Antoon J. ; Graphic design; Huizinga, Johan; Stained glass; Symbolism, Symbolists; Toorop, Jan

Bibliography

Blotkamp, Carel et al. *Kunstenaren der Idee: Symbolistische tendenzen in Nederland, ca. 1880–1930.* The Hague: Staatsuitgeverij, 1978.

Polak, Bettina. *Het Fin-de-Siècle in de Nederlandse Schilderkunst: De symbolistische beweging 1890–1900.* The Hague: Nijhoff, 1955.

Saam, Hedwig. "Roland Holst als reclamekunstenaar: Opdrachten voor de Nederlandsche Oliefabriek." *Jong Holland* 3 (1987): 48–55.

Roman history

The figures, deeds, and events from ancient Roman history were depicted primarily by Dutch painters of the seventeenth century. The greatest number of paintings depicted subjects from Republican Roman history, with relatively few from the Imperial period. The largest group of Republican Roman images was produced in Amsterdam from approximately the middle to near the end of the seventeenth century when their numbers declined. The artists responsible for creating Republican Roman paintings included Rembrandt, his pupils and followers, and other prominent painters also active in Amsterdam. Paintings depicting Republican Roman history were created for both public and private viewing. The newly constructed Amsterdam Town Hall provided the greatest number of public commissions. A significant number of paintings were also produced ostensibly for private residences. It is probable that the increase in the number of images produced for private viewing during the middle of the century was stimulated by those commissions produced for the Town Hall. A second factor that stimulated the sudden increase in Republican Roman images, both public and private, was a reinvigorated humanist tradition in Amsterdam, which promoted a didactic reading of such images based on the view that figures and events from Republican Roman history represented the highest ideals of civic and personal virtue.

The depiction of various Republican Roman political and military heroes constitutes an important category of subject matter, from their initial appearance during the late sixteenth century in Haarlem, to an increase in their numbers during the middle of the seventeenth century in Amsterdam. During the late sixteenth century, the prolific Haarlem printmaker Hendrick Goltzius produced a series of historical prints, *The Roman Heroes* (1586), in which full-length images of Republican Roman leaders are depicted in exaggerated poses. Latin inscriptions underneath each single print explain the heroic deed of the figure portrayed. During the middle years of the seventeenth century, the image of the Roman leader functioned in the more specific context of *exempla virtutis* (model of virtue), within public buildings such as the Amsterdam Town Hall. For example, Govaert Flinck's *Marcus Curius Dentatus Prefers Turnips to the Presents of the Samnites*, placed within the burgomaster's council room of the Town Hall, functioned as a visual reminder to the Amsterdam leadership of ideal comportment in public service. The figure of Dentatus was presented as a model of moderation in the face of the temptation of greater riches. The burgomasters of Amsterdam should, like Dentatus, avoid bribery while they carry out their public duties. The use of classical figures as examples of model behavior in public buildings follows a well-established humanist tradition prevalent during the Renaissance in Italy and later, to some degree, in Northern European countries.

While the function of the image of the Republican Roman political or military hero is recognizable when examined within its original public context, as in the case of the Amsterdam Town Hall, it is more difficult to uncover the meaning and function of similar works produced in Amsterdam for the open market or private patrons. However, given the tradition of humanist literature and art theory of the period, which generally promoted the Republican Roman hero as *exempla virtutis*, it is possible that similar ideals were associated with privately commissioned or publicly purchased paintings. As with most of seventeenth-century Dutch literature on art, however, there is no extant written evidence in which the private citizen specifically refers to the meaning or function of his purchased work of art.

A second subject from Republican Roman history that enjoyed great popularity in seventeenth-century Amsterdam was the history of Lucretia, the sixth-century B.C. heroine and wife of Collatinus, the nephew of the tyrannical Roman king Lucius Tarquinius Superbus. Although several episodes from Lucretia's life were rendered throughout the history of art, the depiction of her suicide was by far the most popular subject for seventeenth-century Amsterdam artists. Rembrandt produced three large canvases of this subject, two of which are extant. Various meanings were associated with the image of Lucretia's suicide during the seventeenth century, including her uncompromising virtue (she chose death rather than stand as an example of dishonor after her rape) and, to a lesser extent, patriotism, because the Dutch sometimes equated her suicide with the establishment of the Roman Republic (the Dutch saw parallels between their own struggles for freedom from Spain and the Roman revolt from Lucius Tarquinius Superbus). Rembrandt's depictions of Lucretia, however, seem to present the dramatic choice the Roman heroine made between virtue in death or shame in life, not any patriotic message. A significant amount of seventeenth-century Dutch literature exists that promotes Lucretia's choice of suicide as the correct action, as a model of virtue (although extreme), for the seventeenth-century woman.

The deeds of Publius Cornelius Scipio Africanus constitute the third subject most represented by seventeenth-century Dutch artists in Amsterdam. As a paradigm of continence or self-restraint, Dutch artists favored an episode from the famous Republican Roman general's life in which he returns a captured young woman to her fiancé. Most Dutch artists depicted the moment at which Scipio, standing in front of the young woman, her fiancé, and her parents, reunites the couple. There is very little variation from this standard format among the extant seventeenth-century Dutch depictions. For example, Rembrandt's pupil Gerbrand van den Eeckhout produced four very similar canvases of the subject (Fig. 120). The continence of Scipio falls into the category of *exempla virtutis*, within the tradition of those depictions of other Republican Roman political and military leaders discussed above, but, through the sheer numbers produced, it deserves a category of its own.

The unifying thread among the three major subject groups depicted by seventeenth-century Dutch artists, particularly those artists active in Amsterdam from mid-century onward, is the didactic nature of the particular works, both within and outside the context of the public commission. This didacticism, in turn, was rooted in a humanist tradition that viewed classical figures, such as those from Republican Roman history, as paradigms upon which contemporary human be-

havior should be modeled. During the seventeenth century, Amsterdam nurtured humanist thought, which furthered traditional didactic readings of Republican Roman subjects. The evidence for such an assertion is found in the extant literature that promoted the humanist concept of *exempla virtutis*.

Steven Golan

See also Active life, active virtues; Bol, Ferdinand; Classicism in architecture; Flinck, Govaert; Goltzius, Hendrick; History painting; History portraits; Humanism, humanist themes; Literature, poetry: analogues with the visual; Rembrandt School; Subjects, subject categories, and hierarchies; Van den Eeckhout, Gerbrand

Bibliography

Blankert, Albert et al. *Gods, Saints and Heroes: Dutch Painting in the Age of Rembrandt*. Washington, DC: National Gallery of Art, 1980.

————. *Kunst als Regeringszaak in Amsterdam in de 17e Eeuw: Rondom Schilderijen van Ferdinand Bol*. Lochem: De Tijdstroom, 1975. (English summary).

Fremantle, K. *The Baroque Town Hall of Amsterdam*. Utrecht: Haentjens Dekker and Gumbert, 1959.

Waal, H. van de. *Drie Eeuwen Vaderlandsche Geschieduitbeelding, 1500–1800: Een Iconologische Studie*. 2 vols. The Hague: Nijhoff, 1952.

Wheelock, Arthur. *Rembrandt's Lucretias*. Exhibition brochure. Produced by the Editor's Office. Washington, DC: National Gallery of Art, 1991.

Ronner-Knip, Henriëtte (1821–1909)

Henriëtte Ronner-Knip, daughter of J.A. Knip, was a successful scion of the Knip family of painters. As a child she led a traveling existence, since her father took his family with him whenever he had major wall-painting commissions to execute. From 1823 until 1827 the family lived in France. In the Netherlands, they lived in The Hague (1827–ca. 1832), Vught (1833), Beek (1833–?), and Berlicum (ca. 1840–1850). After her marriage in 1850, Ronner-Knip lived in Brussels.

Henriëtte Ronner-Knip was, like her brother A. Knip, trained to be a painter by her father. At first she painted nearby rural subjects, particularly scenes in and around farmyards. After 1850 she specialized in the depiction of dogs, and after 1870 she made paintings—or stronger still, she made portraits—of cats exclusively. Ronner-Knip's skillfully executed anecdotal animal scenes sold well, not least because of the sudden phenomenon, which has never faded, for increasing numbers of middle-class households to have pets.

Alexandra W.M. van Smoorenburg

See also Animal painting; Knip, Josephus Augustus

Bibliography

Knotter, Mirjam. *Salonkatjes en Pronkpoezen van Henriëtte Ronner-Knip*. Amsterdam: Kattenkabinet; Amsterdam: Art Promotion Amsterdam, 1991.

Kuyvenhoven, Fransje, and Ronald Peeters. *De familie Knip: Drie generaties kunstenaars uit Noord-Brabant.* Zwolle: Waanders, 1988.

Rooskens, Anton (Joseph Antoon Rooskens) (1906–1976)

A self-taught painter in the 1930s, Anton Rooskens was influenced by works of Van Gogh, Jan Sluijters, and the Flemish Expressionist Constant Permeke. Shortly after the Liberation in 1945, he was impressed by an exhibition of ethnographic art from New Guinea, and for several years he painted mask-like primitivistic compositions. By 1947 his work also reflected his interest in African art and Pre-Columbian textile designs. His association from 1946 with the painters Eugène Brands, Karel Appel, and Corneille drew the much older Rooskens into the circle that formed the Dutch Experimental Group and the Cobra Movement in 1948. In November 1949, irritated by theoretical wrangles and tensions within Cobra, he left the movement to pursue his own development of an increasingly abstract but still primitivistically inspired art. In 1954 he fulfilled an old ambition by making a trip to Kenya, Uganda, and the Belgian Congo, and though he was disappointed to discover an Africa that was more Westernized than he had expected, paintings he made after his return included abstract compositions based on African motifs and painted in striking contrasts of blacks and ochres. After a series of somewhat turbulent abstractions made in the early 1960s, Rooskens finally turned to painting mainly simplified bird and mask motifs in vibrant colors. This last phase in his *oeuvre* unmistakably recalls the festive, uncomplicated style and imagery of the Cobra years.

Graham Birtwistle

See also Cobra Movement

Bibliography

Duppen, Leo, ed. *Anton Rooskens: Het jungle-avontuur.* Amstelveen: Gemeente Amstelveen, 1993.
Wingen, Ed. *Anton Rooskens.* Venlo: Van Spijk, 1976.

Rotterdam

A rather modest image is often what remains after reading about the contribution of Rotterdam to Dutch culture. The qualification that Rotterdam was and is, in the first place, a working city evidently dictated the persistent vaunting of a nineteenth-century observation that "*te Rotterdam het fortuin wordt vermeerd, te Amsterdam beheerd en te 's Gravenhage verteerd*" (fortune is increased in Rotterdam, managed in Amsterdam, and spent in The Hague). This image has been revealed in the twentieth century to be partly unjustified.

The city is not known for playing a pioneer role in the area of artistic trends. This does not mean that Rotterdam was subject to an ongoing erosion in artistic respects, or that most artists born in Rotterdam went looking for their livelihood elsewhere. Of course there were those—the artists who without help from their birthplace celebrated international triumphs: Pieter de Hooch (1629–1683), George Hendrik

Breitner (1857–1923), Kees van Dongen (1877–1968), and even later Willem de Kooning (born 1904).

Rotterdam may have developed into the second-largest mercantile city in the country during the seventeenth century, but one will look in vain to find a Vermeer or a Rembrandt. If art meant anything at all in Rotterdam, it remained the custom to point to the applied arts, and, in the eighteenth century particularly, to majolica. At that time the city could still claim that it was the largest producer of this earthenware in the Netherlands, with a specific sort of green as a Rotterdam contribution.

Remarkable among the local painters was the great variety of subject choices. The reason supposedly was that Rotterdam lacked a competitive spirit as a non-leading art center, and, as a result, specialization did not occur. Willem Buytewech (1591/1592–1624) and Adriaen van der Werff (1659–1722) mark the beginning and the end of the Golden Age in Rotterdam. Both are exponents of a time of transition: Buytewech worked in a period when the evolution from the academic-fantasy tradition to naturalistic representation stood central; Van der Werff, as a senior citizen during the last phase of the Golden Age, developed into a zealous classicist. Although Buytewech lived in Rotterdam for most of his life, this pioneer of Dutch drawing and etching hardly influenced Rotterdam painters. Buytewech's paintings of elegant companies in bright colors form only a small part of his *oeuvre*. He depicted a range of subjects: genre scenes, landscapes, religious scenes, and studies of figures whom he knew how to capture in just a few strokes. He was never inclined to join in the specialty of some Rotterdam painters, the stable interior, which his student Hendrick Martensz. Sorgh (1609/1611–1670) had patented. Besides the country interior, Sorgh excelled in market scenes. Together with Cornelis Saftleven (1607–1681), Pieter de Bloot (1601–1658), and Egbert van der Poel (1621–1664), he belonged to the representatives of the Rotterdam stable interior with a peasant company or still life. While Sorgh gave an intimacy to his work through restrained coloring and refined drawing, Saftleven, who became famous as an animal painter, frequently larded his robust paintings with moralizing undertones.

Other genres were represented by Jacob Ochtervelt (1634–1682), the preeminent church painter Anthonie de Lorme (ca. 1620–1673), and Jan Porcellis (ca. 1584–1632). The latter rigorously broke away from the romantic interpretation of the sea as a stormy phenomenon in harsh green tints; his marine paintings were dominated by atmospheric grays. His direct followers were Simon de Vlieger (ca. 1600–1653) and Jacob Bellevois (1621–1676); more so than Porcellis they integrated ships into their sea views. Lieve Verschuier (ca. 1630–1686), also a sea painter, appeared more sensitive to the powerful interpretation of the Amsterdam marine painters, which resulted in daring combinations of brick-reds and blue-grays. Ochtervelt became a specialist in the middle-class figure piece, in which the refined representation of drapery shows a relationship to De Hooch and Frans van Mieris the Elder.

A pivotal figure to appear halfway through the seventeenth century was the genre and portrait painter Ludolf de

Jongh (1616–1679). He had influence on the younger artists from Rotterdam such as Ochtervelt and De Hooch with his figure pieces depicting the middle class. De Jongh's prominence grew during the 1670s with his exquisite representations of the life of the aristocracy. It happened that a number of his unsigned works, due to similarities in style and theme, were credited to his renowned fellow citizen De Hooch, a fact that has hindered the deserved appreciation of his *oeuvre*. De Jongh was also the painter of one of the finest shooting-company group portraits that Rotterdam has possessed. It was destroyed in the fire of 1864 in the Schielandshuis, which was then serving as the municipal museum. This mansion, designed by town carpenter Jacob Lois (?–1677), is the only architectural inheritance from the seventeenth century that Rotterdam still possesses. The famous architect Pieter Post would have been the adviser for this showpiece that was built in the period 1662–1665 for the administrators of the Schieland dikes and waterways; it has continued to function as a museum since 1849.

Around 1680, when the artistic current was subsiding in Rotterdam as elsewhere, an artist appeared who would go down in history as the Rotterdam knight—Adriaen van der Werff (Fig. 121). As a virtuoso *fijnschilder* with a sharp eye for the nuances of brocades, he responded to the taste of very rich patrons. His fabulous technique was reason for the German Elector Palatine Johann Wilhelm to appoint Van der Werff as court painter and to raise him to the nobility in 1703. The pictorial richness of his classicist-theatrical history paintings is remarkable in contrast to the sober architectural designs by his hand, such as the Rotterdam Stock Exchange, completed in 1736, and the premises of the Rotterdam Banking Society.

In the eighteenth century, Rotterdam began a prosperous period. Van der Werff and the tradition of fine painting yielded to the Van Nijmegen family of artists and decorative wall painting. In this period, in which amateur art societies and the assembling of art collections soared, the Van Nijmegens set the tone. Together with his son Dionijs (1705–1798), Elias van Nijmegen (1667–1755) headed a thriving decoration studio. The commissions varied from ceiling paintings and door pieces to salon decorations in merchants' houses. Leading the choice of subjects were allegorical and mythological representations, often freely executed in outline with thin watercolor tints. Except for one decorated reception hall and a series of design sheets, which are in the Rijksprentenkabinet in Amsterdam, the entire estate of the Van Nijmegens was destroyed in the war bombing of Rotterdam in 1940.

The cultural life of the eighteenth century took place mainly in the merchant houses on the Leuvehaven and Wijnhaven and, particularly, in the house of the Bisschops, who were collectors. Their collection comprised over two hundred paintings by seventeenth- and eighteenth-century Dutch and Flemish painters, and etched glassware. Undoubtedly represented were the products of Frans Greenwood (1680–1763), the great master of glass etching, as the Bisschops were the only glass collectors of their time. Greenwood, who was from England, was the inventor of stipple engraving, and he worked in Rotterdam until at least 1726.

He adapted his reproductions from Dutch seventeenth-century paintings, particularly from Van der Werff.

Among the numerous societies, including Natura et Arte and the Bataafsche Genootschap (Batavian Society), was the drawing society Hierdoor tot Hooger (Higher through This), established in 1773 by the artist Hendrik Kobell. Its most important objective was to promote the production of the visual arts by encouraging competitions and purchases. One of the teachers in this forerunner of the present-day Rotterdam Academy of Fine Arts was Nicolaas Muys (1740–1808), whose exercises in drawing after Dutch masters were a typical eighteenth-century practice. Muys excelled in the precious conversation piece, in which middle-class people of means had themselves portrayed with all of their possessions.

Midway through the nineteenth century, the germ of what is today the internationally famous Museum Boymans-van Beuningen was laid. In 1847 the Utrecht collector F.J.O. Boymans decided to bequeath his collection to the city of Rotterdam because all of his works of art could be properly housed in the above-mentioned Schielandshuis. Although landscapes by Salomon van Ruysdael and Meindert Hobbema were included in the bequest, a portion of the twelve hundred paintings was of doubtful value. It would take almost a century before a museum (1935) especially built for that purpose would do justice to the holdings of the Boymans collection. The museum received its present status through a later expansion with the collection of the Rotterdam shipowner D.G. van Beuningen (1958).

One of the few artists to achieve distinction in Rotterdam around 1850 was Charles Rochussen (1814–1894). As a Romantic, he prospered, on the one hand, as a chronicler of nineteenth-century society life and, on the other, as an exceptional history painter. The crystalline coloring, so peculiar to Rochussen's park views, shows a great relation to the fresh, quick stroke of the French Impressionist Alfred Sisley. Exhibitions of Rochussen's work were rare; one was held in 1904, ten years after his death, by the Rotterdamsche Kunstkring.

This society—the Rotterdamsche Kunstkring (Rotterdam Art Circle)— compensated for the lack of a contemporary-art section in the Museum Boymans with regular exhibitions surveying recent developments in painting. The initiative for this, taken by nonartists in 1893, was prompted by Rotterdam's deteriorating reputation as a cultural center while world interest in its port was growing. The Art Circle was not alone in bringing attention to modern art; the Oldenzeel art gallery, which opened in 1859, was a pioneer, and it would go down in history as the place where appreciation of Vincent van Gogh was present at an early stage (1893). On account of this, Rotterdam steadily gained the reputation of being more openminded than other cities with regard to the latest artistic expressions. The public was treated to the work of the Italian Futurists, Kandinsky, Van Gogh, the Belgians Ensor and Van Rijsselberghe, and the French artists Émile Bernard and Odilon Redon. This function of signaling the new in art was later taken over in part by the Museum Boymans-van Beuningen when it received an annex in 1923.

A recurring criticism was that the exhibition halls had

little space for local artists. A nurturing soil from which a possible Rotterdam movement could grow was lacking. For purely practical reasons a number of artists entered into co-operative associations: De Branding, De X (The Ten), and the Rotterdammers. De Branding (The Surf), with Herman Bieling as leader, had been started in 1917 by young artists hoping to change their isolated position. The common bond was not style but the will to bring forth a new art. A minority painted figurative representations; the rest made abstract works. Ultimately, under the influence of theosophy and anthroposophy, De Branding would become known in the Netherlands as a group of artists oriented toward the occult. The scarcely homogenous society did not confront fellow citizens with just its own members' work, but also with the work of foreign artists. Through De Branding exhibitions, Rotterdam had the first showings in the Netherlands of the works of Kurt Schwitters and Constantin Brancusi.

Around World War II, the city would develop into a graphic arts center, in which color lithography would take off in new directions. Rotterdam graphic artists—especially members of the De Venster group and Argus experimenting with color lithography—gained a vanguard position in their own country. Jan Bezemer (born 1907), Daan den Dikkenboer (1918–1979), Wally Elenbaas (born 1912), and Wout van Heusden (1896–1982) attracted national attention for themselves. That Rotterdammers saw to the expansion of the graphic arts was greatly due to their teachers at the Rotterdam Academy of Fine Arts and Techniques, Antoon Derkzen van Angeren and Simon Moulijn; these educators gave their students a thorough knowledge of the craft that opened the way to a multitude of experiments.

The German bombing on May 14, 1940, left Rotterdam a city without a heart; barren plains had to be developed again. Contemporary architecture was given great opportunities as a result. The first traffic-free shopping precinct, the Lijnbaan (1953), by the architectural firm of Van den Broek and Bakema, became a model for shopping centers all over the world. Before the war, the international ideological movement of Het Nieuwe Bouwen (The New Construction) found adherents in Rotterdam in architects such as L. van der Vlugt, J.A. Brinkman, and W. van Tijen. This resulted in, among other things, the transparent Van Nelle factory (1926–1930; Fig. 49) and the Bergpolder apartment building (1933–1934; Fig. 48), which was conceived as the prototype of affordable public housing.

A Rotterdam tradition that came into being in connection with World War II monuments was to place the statues in a municipal context. Meanwhile, in the works of Gabo, De Kooning, Moore, Couzijn, Zadkine, and later Rickey and Coop Himmelblau, the port city has the evidence of international sculptural development at its disposal.

The number of artists who have settled in Rotterdam since the 1960s has increased dramatically as a result of a more benevolent cultural climate, in which attention to studios and exhibition possibilities stands as the number one priority. Keeping track of things is the Rotterdam Arts Foundation (RKS), which was established after the war to stimulate the

arts. At the same time five exhibition halls offer Rotterdam artists such as Mathieu Ficheroux, Kees Franse, Daan van Golden, Klaas Gubbels, Wim Gijzen, and Gust Romijn space to exhibit their work. Initiatives like the annual Poetry International and Film International, for which the RKS provided early support, have in the meantime expanded into well-known events. The fact that Rotterdam felt unfairly treated in a cultural sense by the government for a long time occasioned a change during the 1980s. In the attempt to produce a more balanced distribution of art institutions throughout the country, the government assigned to Rotterdam not only the National Photo Institute but also the Netherlands Architecture Institute (NAI). The headquarters of the latter, designed by the architect J. Coenen and opened in 1993, forms the approach to the spacious Museum Park, containing the Museum Boymans-van Beuningen, the Chabot Museum, dedicated to the Rotterdam artist Hendrik Chabot (1894–1949) and opened at the end of 1993, and the Kunsthal (Art Hall) designed by the architect Rem Koolhaas for major exhibitions (Fig. 70). More than in the past, the municipal government understands that it is advantageous for Rotterdam to have a favorable cultural climate.

Ida Jager

See also Amateurs, art academies, and art associations before the nineteenth century; Animal painting; Applied arts; Breitner, George Hendrik; Ceramics; Chabot, Hendrik; Commerce and commercial life; Conversation piece; Couzijn, Wessel; De Branding; De Kooning, Willem; Drawing practices and techniques; Films, filmmaking; Graphic design; Koolhaas, Rem; Kromhout, Willem; Marine painting; Post, Pieter; Prints, modern graphic arts 1840–1945; Prints, modern graphic arts after 1945; Public housing; Public monumental sculpture (ca. 1500–1795); Public monumental sculpture (1795–1990); Rochussen, Charles; Rural life and views; Sculpture (1945–1990); State patronage, public support; Urban planning, from 1750 to the present; Van Dongen, Kees; Van Golden, Daan

Bibliography

Adriaen van der Werff, 1659–1722: Hofmaler des Kurfürsten Johann Wilhelm van der Pfalz. Munich: Alte Pinakothek, 1972.

Adrichem, J. van. *Beeldende kunst en kunstbeleid in Rotterdam 1945–1985.* Rotterdam: Museum Boymans-van Beuningen, 1987.

Brinkman, E. *De Branding 1917–1926.* Rotterdam: Stichting Kunstpublicaties Rotterdam, 1991. (English summary).

Bruijn, H.C. de. "Charles Rochussen, 1814–1894, als chroniqueur van het societyleven uit het midden der negentiende eeuw." *Antiek* 6 (1981): 471–484.

Daalder, R., ed. *Een paleis in Rotterdam: Historische verzamelingen in het Schielandshuis.* Rotterdam: Stichting Vrienden van het Schielandshuis, 1986.

Dijk, H. van. "Architectuurgids Rotterdam." Theme number. *Wonen/TABK* 19 (May/June 1980).

Fleischer, R.E. *Ludolf de Jongh, 1616–1679.* Doornspijk: Davaco, 1989.

Hannema, D. "Rotterdamsche schilders de zeventiende eeuw." In *Gedenkboek in Rotterdam, 1328–1928.* Edited by E.O.H.M. Ruempol. Rotterdam: Wyt, 1928.

Haverkamp Begemann, E. *Willem Buytewech.* Amsterdam: Hertzberger, 1959.

Hazewinkel, H.C. *Geschiedenis van Rotterdam.* 3 vols. Amsterdam: Vondel, 1940–1942. Reprint. Zaltbommel: Europese Bibliotheek, 1974–1975.

Hecht, P. *De Hollandse fijnschilders: Van Gerard Dou tot Adriaen van der Werff.* Maarssen: Gary Schwartz; The Hague: SDU, 1989. (English summary).

Huyts, J. *De Venstergroep.* Rotterdam, 1977.

Meyerman, A., N.I. Schadee, and C. Thiels. *Aangenaam gezelschap: zes conversatiestukken van Nicolaas Muys.* Abcoude: Uniepers, 1992.

Niemeijer, J.W. "De ateliernalatenschap van het Rotterdamse schildersgeslacht Van Nijmegen." *Bulletin van het Rijksmuseum* 17 (1969): 59–67.

Schadee, N.I. *Zilverschatten: Drie eeuwen Rotterdams zilver.* Rotterdam: Historisch Museum Rotterdam, 1991.

Snoep, D.P., and C. Thiels. *Adriaen van der Werff (Kralingen 1659–1722 Rotterdam).* Rotterdam: Historisch Museum Rotterdam, 1973.

Spaan, G. van. *Beschryvinge der Stad Rotterdam en eenige omliggende dorpen.* 1698. Reprint. Amsterdam: Facsimile Uitgaven Nederland, 1969.

Thiels, C. *Mooi van Kleur: Rotterdamse kunstenaars in de jaren '50.* Rotterdam: Historisch Museum Rotterdam, 1987.

Roundels

The term refers to any unipartite panel of white glass that is painted with black or brown vitreous paint and then fired. Roundels must have been produced on a large scale from the late fifteenth century until the end of the seventeenth century, and again on a lesser scale at the end of the nineteenth century. Although they were originally round, rectangular, square, and oval shapes became common in the sixteenth century. Their dimensions, limited by the size of available sheets of glass, does not exceed 30 to 34 cm. Roundels were glazed into the windows of relatively small rooms, where they could be seen at close quarters. They performed the function of small-scale stained glass and were destined predominantly for secular buildings (hospitals, alms houses, private dwellings), and for cloisters and cells of monasteries. Their advantages over stained glass, which consists of several leaded panels of pot metal glass (colored throughout), were twofold: They were significantly cheaper, and they allowed in more light.

The earliest known extant roundels from the Northern Netherlands date from about 1500, starting the greatest period of production, which lasted until about 1560. Roundels from this date all show additional paint in silver stain that becomes yellow on firing. Another pigment occurring in later work is sanguine, a rose-to-red-brown tint for flesh color and ornamental details. The production of roundels seems to have been concentrated primarily in or around the principal artistic centers of Leiden, Amsterdam, Haarlem, and Gouda. The style is related to paintings and drawings by, and prints after, leading artists of the period: Lucas van Leyden (ca. 1494?–1533); Jacob Cornelisz. van Oostsanen (ca. 1472–1533) from Amsterdam; Maerten van Heemskerck (1498–1574) from Haarlem; and Jan Swart (ca. 1500–1560) from Groningen.

Division of labor between designer and executor was more common than not. Several designs for roundels, drawn to scale by known artists and lesser hands, have survived. The glass painters tend to remain anonymous, except for some outstanding personalities like Dirck Crabeth (active ca. 1540–1574) from Gouda. The production of roundels seems to have been integrated in most cases within the stained glass workshop. The repertory of subjects consisted mainly of religious narratives from the Old and New Testaments and some iconic images of saints. In the later sixteenth century, Reformist and humanist thought influenced both secular—that is, allegorical—and religious imagery. Although many roundels were commissioned, a considerable share—fashionable narratives and moralistic allegories—must have been produced for market sale. The existence of several roundel types like replicas and variants with minor or major compositional or stylistic changes might serve as an indication.

Today no roundels are documented to have survived in their original secular settings. Information on the way roundels were incorporated into the window is provided by paintings and prints. In the fifteenth and early sixteenth centuries, a single roundel, surrounded by a colored border, inscriptions, or foliated running ornament, was set in the upper fixed transom that was glazed in leaded, white diamond panes. Later in the sixteenth century, the entire aperture was glazed and conceived as a decorative whole. The nucleus was formed by the roundel, and the surroundings by decorative stained glass, consisting mostly of Italianate architectural motifs, executed in black paint and silver stain on pieces of white glass.

The violence of Iconoclasm in the sixteenth century did interrupt, but could not eradicate, the production of roundels and stained glass. Through the dissemination of prints, designs by leading Mannerist artists like Hendrick Goltzius (1558–1616) from Haarlem and Abraham Bloemaert (1564–1651) from Utrecht were known and reappear on a small number of oval or rectangular panels. Contrary to earlier roundels, these are monochrome, painted exclusively in black paint.

The designs of Van Heemskerck also continued in use as models to be copied by glass painters into the first quarter of the seventeenth century. They are modernized only with regard to their ornamental surroundings, which are made up of delicate symmetrical compositions employing cartouches or grotesque ornamentation, enlivened with realistic representations of birds, insects, and fishes. The decorative border is executed in translucent enamel paints, an invention from the sixteenth century. Additional cartouches with lengthy inscriptions in calligraphic cursive script commenting on the scene in the roundel, and giving the name of the owner and the date, are standard elements found in the few remaining complete glazings of secular windows.

The subjects that commonly appear in seventeenth-century roundels range from allegories to biblical and mythological scenes. The proportion of genre scenes increased toward the middle of the seventeenth century. Another typical production in this country of seafarers and merchants was the representation of ships of numerous kinds. Enamel paints were now used to decorate both the roundel and its ornamental surrounding of stained glass. The same treatment applies to heraldic roundels. This previously constant but relatively unimportant aspect of roundel production was elevated by the end of the seventeenth century to becoming the sole subject of stained glass and roundel production. (Formerly, coats of arms were integrated in the ornamental surroundings or depicted in the roundel with or without the arms bearer.) In time, heraldic panels set among plain, white rectangular panes became the staple product of the glazier's shop and contributed to the decline of skill in the medium.

Another, lesser-known fashion in later seventeenth-century roundel production concerns the independent use of a realistic representation of the flora—especially tulips—and fauna characteristic of former Dutch ornamental borders. These small, rectangular panes, executed in colorful enamels, were distributed at regular intervals in the window among plain white panes. Representations of figures of tramps in the manner of Pieter Quast (1606–1647), grotesque comedians, or small groups of contemporary genre figures are treated the same way. Some figurative roundels were produced again at the end of the nineteenth century by the workshop 't Prinsenhof of Jan Schouten in Delft. They were executed in a technique and with a style of ornament characteristic of the late Renaissance and Baroque. Research on roundels is complicated by their widespread location. In the late eighteenth and early nineteenth centuries, when there was a drop in appreciation for stained glass in the Netherlands, many pieces were sold abroad.

Zsuzsanna van Ruyven-Zeman

See also Reverse painting; Stained glass

Bibliography
Cole, William. *A Catalogue of Netherlandish and North European Roundels in Britain.* Corpus Vitrearum Medii Aevi, Summary Catalogue 1. London: British Academy and Oxford University Press, 1993.
Filedt Kok, Jan Piet et al. eds. *Kunst voor de beeldenstorm: Noordnederlandse kunst 1525–1580.* The Hague: Staatsuitgeverij, 1986.
Husband, Timothy B. *Stained Glass before 1700 in American Collections: Silver-Stained Roundels and Unipartite Panels.* Corpus Vitrearum, Checklist 4. Washington, DC: National Gallery of Art; distributed by University Press of New England, 1991.
Husband, Timothy B. *The Luminous Image: Painted Glass Roundels in the Lowlands, 1480–1560.* New York: Metropolitan Museum of Art, 1995.
Rackham, Bernard. *A Guide to the Collections of Stained Glass.* London: Victoria and Albert Museum, 1936.

Royer, Louis (1795–1868)

Within the impoverished field of Dutch nineteenth-century sculpture that was strongly defined by foreign or foreign-educated sculptors, Louis Royer was one of the most important figures. He had studied in Mechelen and Paris. After winning the Prix de Rome (1823), he left for Italy. Back in the Netherlands (1828), Royer knew how to procure a prominent position quickly: In 1834 he became sculptor to the king and, in 1837, director of sculpture at the Rijksacademie in Amsterdam.

With his monumental rendering of national heroes, Royer gave form to the strong nationalism rising after the end of the French occupation. Examples of this are the statues of *Michiel De Ruyter* (Vlissingen, 1841), *Willem of Orange* (The Hague, 1848), *Rembrandt* (Amsterdam, 1852), *Laurens Jansz. Koster* (Haarlem, 1856), and especially *Joost van den Vondel* (Amsterdam, 1867). He also made many salon portraits, allegorical representations, and religiously tinged works, among them a number of reliefs for the St. Francis Xavier Church in Amsterdam.

Royer worked mainly with marble, terra-cotta, earthenware, and plaster. His work, based on the classical, has an idealizing character, and it is a clear exponent of the French and Southern Dutch academism with which he was well acquainted through his ancestry and education.

Geraart Westerink

See also Alberdingk Thijm, Josephus Albertus; Monuments to artists; Nationalism; Neo-Gothic; Public monumental sculpture (1795–1990); Sculpture (1795–1945)

Bibliography
Becker, Jochen. "'Justus ex fide vivit': Over het Vondelbeeld (Amsterdam, 1867)." *Nederlands Kunsthistorich Jaarboek* 34 (1983): 132–193.
Daalen, P.K. van. *Nederlandse beeldhouwers in de negentiende eeuw.* The Hague: Nijhoff, 1957.
Wal, Mieke van der. "'Krijgsman of Staatsman?' De oprichtings-geschiedenis van de twee standbeelden voor Willem de Zwijger in Den Haag." *Nederlands Kunsthistorisch Jaarboek* 34 (1983): 39–72.

Rural life and views

Until the sixteenth century, images of peasants and the activities of the countryside were confined to the backgrounds of altarpieces and to the margins and calendar pages of manuscripts. Scenes of peasants and the rustic countryside as the primary subjects of prints and paintings began during the mid-sixteenth century with Pieter Bruegel's *Kermis at Hoboken* (original drawing 1559; London, Courtauld Institute) and his series of paintings of the seasons (New York and Vienna). Typically, these works drew their vocabulary from the seasonal imagery of fifteenth-century Netherlandish manuscripts, such as the famous *Très Riches Heures du Duc de Berry* (Chantilly, Musée Condé) and the *Da Costa Gebetbuch* by Simon Bening (New York, J. Pierpont Morgan Library). This shift in the treatment of these humble subjects reflects a general shift in the political and philosophical outlook of the Netherlands.

Paintings of the rustic countryside were probably enjoyed on a number of levels, which reflect the needs and ideals of patrons. At least part of this appreciation came from an ethnographic curiosity suggested by the presence of sophisticated observers within many paintings of this genre. Karel van Mander noted that Bruegel himself often attended village festivities dressed as a peasant. This curiosity about the ways of the peasant, the "domestic noble savage," as well as the new interest in the native Dutch landscape, were at least partially stimulated by travelers' reports of primitive, "naive" cultures, and their descriptions of the flora and fauna of distant lands. Coincidental with this was, as Margaret D. Carroll has pointed out, the desire to define a distinct ethnic and political identity for the Netherlands as a rallying point during the war with Spain.

The interest in the rustic peasant was also related to the ideological search for a utopian society. Distressed by the political and religious unrest of the sixteenth century, many educated Netherlanders sought solace in the philosophy of the ancient Stoics, adjusted to incorporate Christianity. Among the formulators of this "Christian Stoicism" were Justus Lipsius, professor at the University of Leiden, who believed that man's ultimate goal should be to lead a good and ethical life. Lipsius defined virtue as living according to nature, which he equated with God, supreme reason. To understand nature, one must study the real world. Virtue alone was considered sufficient for a happy life without the necessity of outward goods and fortuitous events. The peasant, who lived according to the earth's cycles, was considered the virtuous exemplar for sophisticated men and women, who had strayed from nature and been corrupted by the "artificiality and backbiting" of the cities.

In the late Middle Ages and early Renaissance, the humble plowman had been associated with industriousness, moderation, and integrity and was often represented in allegorical images of peace, diligence, and hope. Paintings of the village *kermis* (fair) from the sixteenth and early seventeenth centuries, typically depict the rowdy, uncontrolled peasant drinking, fighting, or freely celebrating with dance and romance, the character of the peasant immortalized in literature by Gerbrand Adriaensz. Bredero in *Boerengeselschap* (1622). In recent years, scholars have debated whether, as Hessel Miedema and Keith P.F. Moxey have argued, these images were meant as moralizing examples of negative behavior and foils for civilized society, or, as Svetlana Alpers has countered, intended as comic images to entertain sophisticated audiences. If one considers the peasant an example of the man of nature, however, these images can be understood in a different light in which the misbehavior of the peasants was neither promoted nor condemned. The inclusion in many prints of village *kermissen* of variations of the expression, "Let the peasants have their *kermis*," suggests that this behavior was both recognized as characteristic of the peasant and condoned within the context of the yearly celebration. These images were meant to inform and to entertain in the same way that prints and paintings representing the costume or various areas of the

Netherlands or prints and paintings of peasants and animals in different postures, including defecation, served as documents of "natural behavior." As such, these images of the rustic countryside were enjoyed as something separate from the experience of the citified patron, who responded with curious bemusement rather than contempt.

By the mid-seventeenth century, paintings and prints tended to emphasize the peaceful, inwardly controlled, and moral character of the peasant rather than his bawdy excesses. This important shift in emphasis is particularly clear in the *oeuvre* of Adriaen van Ostade (1610–1685), whose early paintings depict the brawling, rough peasant derived from the example of Adriaen Brouwer. By the 1640s, however, Van Ostade shifted his emphasis to the virtuous peasant in scenes involving the family and peaceful gatherings of respectable farmers and villagers. In contrast to contemporary paintings of Arcadian shepherds, the peasants in these georgic images are not scrubbed clean but are coarse and "natural." In the paintings of Paulus Potter from the late 1640s, the close connection of the men and women to the earth and its cycles is stressed by the dirt on their clothes and faces. Women, often barefoot, appear either as nursing mothers or as milkmaids. Men care for animals or relax; rarely do they engage in strenuous work.

This shift in emphasis reflects the widespread association of the countryside with health, liberty, and pleasure, in part a response to the new security of the Dutch countryside following the initiation of the Twelve-Years' Truce in 1609, when the country became a popular retreat for the Dutch burghers. Their sentiment toward the country is expressed in contemporary *hofdicten*, country-house poems inspired by the *Georgics*, the Roman poet Virgil's practical book on farming (translated into Dutch by Karel van Mander in 1597), which emphasizes the rustic rather than the idealized Arcadian world of Virgil's *Eclogues*. In the *hofdicht*, the poet, the owner of the estate, takes his reader on a walk through his property and out into the countryside. As they walk, he points out distant views, comments on the farmers and their animals, and on the prosperity of the land during times of peace—images reminiscent of contemporary paintings of landscapes and still lifes as well as animals and farmers. In *Farm Near The Hague* of 1648, for example, Paulus Potter represented a well-dressed couple strolling along a line of trees that divides a cow pasture from a farmyard, where a woman milks a cow while a farmer talks to her and other animals rest in the shadows of a late summer afternoon. As the poet of the *hofdicht* described the sounds and sights of the countryside, Potter represented the details of delicate grasses, flowers, and butterflies. This is not an Arcadian scene but a realistic scene of the Dutch countryside. Rather than idealized in terms of perfect forms and actions, the rustic farmers in the paintings of Potter, Van Ostade, and others are idealized by stressing their very close ties to nature, which the artist stressed through realistic details. This attitude toward the farmer, whom Constantijn Huygens compared to Adam before the Fall, was also applied to animals. In his country-house poem *Hofwijck*, Huygens compared the master to the "wise and moderate cow," the traditional emblem of earth and specifically of the prosperity of the Netherlands; unlike the master, the cow knows enough when to stop eating and drinking.

During the second half of the seventeenth century, the rustic farmer was gradually refined and, in many ways, merged with the image of the Arcadian shepherd. In paintings and prints by Karel du Jardin and Adriaen van de Velde, the farmers, animals, and environment are scrubbed and simplified. The details of texture and context found in Potter's work, for example, give way to purity of form. It is this image, based on the earlier part of the century, that survives into the eighteenth and nineteenth centuries.

Amy L. Walsh

See also Animal painting; Comic modes; Country houses and gardens; Eighty-Years' War; Flanders, Flemish School; Huygens, Constantijn; Landscape; Pastoral; Potter, Paulus; Van Mander, Karel

Bibliography
Alpers, Svetlana. "Realism As a Comic Mode: Low-Life Painting Seen through Bredero's Eyes." *Simiolus* 8 (1975/1976): 115–144.

Carroll, Margaret D. "Peasant Festivity and Political Identity in the Sixteenth Century." *Art History* 10:3 (1987): 289–314.

Miedema, Hessel. "Feestende boeren—lachende dorpers: Bij twee recente aanwinsten van het Rijksprentenkabinet." *Bulletin van het Rijksmuseum* 29:4 (1981): 191–213.

———. "Realism and Comic Mode: The Peasant." *Simiolus* 9 (1977): 206–219.

Moxey, Keith P.F. "Sebald Beham's Church Anniversary Holidays: Festive Peasants As Instruments of Repressive Humor." *Simiolus* 12:2/3 (1981/1982): 107–130.

Raupp, Hans-Joachim. *Bauernsatiren: Enstehung und Entwicklung des bäurlichen Genres in der deutschen und niederländishchen Kunst ca. 1470–1570.* Niederzier: Luca-Verlag, 1986.

Walsh, Amy L. "Paulus Potter: His Works and Their Meaning." Ph.D. diss., Columbia University, 1985.

Ruysch, Rachel (1664–1750)

Rachel Ruysch ranks among the most renowned Dutch painters of still life. She was born in The Hague, daughter of the anatomist and botanist Frederick Ruysch. She was apprenticed at age fourteen or fifteen to the renowned still-life painter Willem van Aelst in Amsterdam. Dated paintings are known onward from 1682, when she was eighteen. In 1693 she married the portraitist Jurriaen Pool (1665–1745); they had ten children. In 1701 Ruysch and Pool entered the painters' guild in The Hague. In 1708 they were appointed court painters to the Elector Palatine at Düsseldorf, whom they served until his death in 1716. Subsequently they lived in Amsterdam, where Ruysch died at age eighty-six; her late works are usually inscribed with her age.

Apart from numerous still lifes of flowers—from small posies to lavish bouquets—Ruysch painted a number of fruit pieces, usually in a forest setting (Fig. 128). Her early work clearly shows the influence of Van Aelst, Abraham Mignon, and also of Jan Davidsz. de Heem, but she readily developed her own elegant style. It is characterized by a meticulous attention to detail, a warm and often bright coloring, and compositions that frequently show the S-curve adopted from Van Aelst. The development of her work is exemplary of the transition from seventeenth-century Baroque to eighteenth-century rationalism. A Ruysch family portrait (ca. 1716) by Pool is in the Düsseldorf Historical Museum; a later portait by him is in the Boymans-van Beuningen Museum in Rotterdam.

Fred G. Meijer

See also Still life; Women artists

Bibliography
Berardi, Marianne. "The Nature Pieces of Rachel Ruysch." *Porticus* (Bulletin of the Memorial Art Gallery of the University of Rochester, New York) 10/11 (1988): 2–14.

Grant, Maurice H. *Rachel Ruysch, 1664–1750.* Leigh-on-Sea: F. Lewis, 1956. (NB: strongly in need of revision).

S

Sandberg, Willem

See Art criticism, critical issues in the twentieth century; Graphic design; Prints, modern graphic arts after 1945; State patronage, public support; World Wars I and II

Schelfhout, Andreas (1787–1870)

Andreas Schelfhout was regarded as one of the most important Dutch landscape painters of his time. His career as a painter began in 1815, after he had worked for four years in the studio of J.H.A.A. Breckenheimer, a painter of stage scenery. With his typical Dutch subjects, especially detailed winter scenes, he appealed to the strong nationalistic feelings of the time. Schelfhout exhibited his work with great success both in the Netherlands and abroad. He produced a great many works and repeated himself often, but his best pieces are fresh in conception, giving evidence of technical refinement and a feeling for anecdotal detail. His paintings were executed in a careful manner until the end of his life, but in studies and drawings he could be, especially later, unexpectedly loose. Schelfhout's moderately Romantic style had a great following. His most important students were W.J.J. Nuyen and J.B. Jongkind.

In the mid-1990s, W. Laanstra in the Netherlands is conducting a thorough scholarly investigation of this painter.

Alexandra W.M. van Smoorenburg

See also Jongkind, Johan Barthold; Koekkoek, B.C.; Landscape; Nuyen, W.J.J.; Weissenbruch, Jan Hendrik

Bibliography

Kramm C. *De levens en werken der Hollandsche en Vlaamsche kunstschilders, beeldhouwers, graveurs en bouwmeesters.* Vol. 5, 1470–1471. Amsterdam: Gebroeders Diederichs, 1861.

Sillevis J., and A. van Smoorenburg. *Licht, lucht en water: De verloren idylle van het riviergezicht*, 100–101, 134–135. Zwolle: Waanders, 1993.

Schoonhoven, J.J. (1914–1994)

Jan Jacob Schoonhoven has been recognized since the late 1950s as a remarkable artist, whom art critics and art historians alike consider to be a leading figure in postwar Dutch art. His work is represented in the collections of important museums in the Netherlands and abroad. By their clear structure, his white reliefs and black-and-white drawings appear simple, but they nevertheless have great expressiveness. Schoonhoven was a member of the Dutch Informal Group (1958–1960), together with Armando (born 1929), Kees van Bohemen (born 1928), Jan Henderikse (born 1937), and Henk Peeters (born 1925), as well as a member of the Nul-group (1961–1965).

Schoonhoven was born in Delft, where he lived and worked until his death on July 31, 1994. From 1930 until 1934 he received a secondary education in drawing at the Koninklijke Academie van Beeldende Kunsten (Royal Academy of Arts) at The Hague. His early works from the 1940s and 1950s—figurative and semiabstract drawings in ink and watercolor—reveal the influence of Paul Klee. But in the mid-1950s he went his own way. The first reliefs, for which he would become known as an artist, are shallow constructions of cardboard and papier-mâché with an irregular structure and painted in dark, brown ocher or reddish monochromatic colors. In 1957 he began to glue pieces of newspapers on cardboard and to paint it all with enamel paint. His working method did not change after that.

The first white relief, made out of ribbed cardboard and toilet paper tubes, originated in 1959. At the time, Schoonhoven was a member of the Dutch Informal Group, whose adherents sought an aesthetic of formlessness and monochromy in which individual emotions had to make room for a more aloof attitude. His work in series and white monochrome became his trademark. After that time his reliefs had a very regular structure and emphasized horizontal and vertical order. He built them up out of almost identical elements—ribs, with the concavities either straight or in an angle—that continue until the edge. The use of series resulted in a nonhierarchical structure, without a center, that gives the relief its air of distance and provides it with a high degree of anonymity. Around 1960 he became acquainted with the "Achromes" of the Italian experimental artist Piero Manzoni, and he also saw the catalog of the exhibition *Monochrome Malerei* (with works by contemporary German artists Ludwig Hirschfeld Mack, Otto Piene, and Günther Uecker) that was held in Leverkusen, Germany. Both experiences played a crucial role in his work, although that from the 1980s is sometimes also more capricious in form.

The fascinating effects of light and shadow are intrinsically connected with the reliefs; because of the number, width, and depth of the concavities, the lightfall from the ribs is bent differently every time. Schoonhoven's drawings have similar elements, such as stripes, squares, hatching, dots, and lozenges, which through the subtle changes yield an unmistakable desired effect.

The work of Schoonhoven was, especially during the 1960s, an important source of inspiration for Dutch poets such as J. Bernlef and K. Schippers; they recognized themselves in Schoonhoven's regard for the minimal. His influence on visual artists has been limited, with the exception of a few such as Ad Dekkers (1938–1974). Nevertheless, many artists have felt an affinity with his work. In 1984 Jan Schoonhoven received the David Röell Award for works on paper.

Peter de Ruiter

See also Armando; Art criticism, critical issues in the twentieth century; Nul-group

Bibliography

Beeren, W.A.L. *Schoonhoven.* Amsterdam: Stedelijk Museum, 1973.
Bool, Flip, and Enno Develing, eds. *Jan Schoonhoven retrospectief: Tekeningen en reliëfs / Jan Schoonhoven Retrospektiv: Zeichnungen und Reliefs.* The Hague: Haags Gemeentemuseum; Weesp: Openbaar Kunstbezit, 1984.
Schoonhoven, J.J. "Zero." In *De nieuwe stijl: Werk van de internationale avant-garde,* 118–123. Amsterdam: De Bezige Bij, 1965.
Wesseling, Janneke. *Schoonhoven: Beeldend kunstenaar / Visual artist.* The Hague: SDU, 1990.

Schouman, Aart (1710–1792)

The painter, draftsman, and engraver Aart (or Aert) Schouman was born in Dordrecht. His teacher was Adriaan van der Burg. In 1736 he was admitted to the Dordrecht Guild of St. Luke. From the beginning of his career, Schouman was a versatile artist. He painted not only religious, mythological, and allegorical subjects, but also portraits of members of distinguished families in Dordrecht and Middelburg. However, his paintings on wall hangings of birds are his most famous. In them he shows himself to be a follower of Melchior de Hondecoeter, like his fellow townsman Abraham Busschop, who was forty years older. Schouman did not imitate De Hondecoeter, however, but gave the genre of bird painting his own eighteenth-century decorative and airy character, in which his use of bright colors is especially striking. In the royal palace Huis ten Bosch in The Hague there are still a great number of bird pieces by his hand.

In 1748 Schouman became a member of The Hague's painters' fraternity, Pictura. From then on he lived alternately in Dordrecht and The Hague, until finally settling in The Hague in 1753. He also worked regularly in Middelburg. Schouman was also versatile as a draftsman. He made numerous watercolors of birds and other, often exotic, animals; topographical views, portraits, and sea views are also among his drawings. His watercolors are bright and fresh in color. His graphic work includes both etchings and mezzotints. In the latter technique, he showed a preference for dramatic lighting with candles. He also copied the old masters. Schouman played a major role in the art world of The Hague through both the drawing academy there and Pictura. His most famous student in The Hague was the flower painter Jan van Os.

Christina J.A. Wansink

See also Amateurs, art academies, and art associations before the nineteenth century; De Hondecoeter, Melchior; Dordrecht; House of Orange-Nassau

Bibliography

Bol, Laurens J. *Aart Schouman: Ingenious Painter and Draughtsman.* Doornspijk: Davaco, 1991.

Schwartze, Thérèse van Duyl (1851–1918)

Thérèse Schwartze was trained to be a portrait painter by her father, Johann Georg Schwartze. When he died in 1874, she was already excellently prepared to become the breadwinner of the family. Still, she took a year of lessons (1875–1876) at the academy in Munich from F. von Lenbach and thoroughly studied the work of Rubens and Velazquez in the Alte Pinakotheke.

After 1878 Schwartze annually visited the Paris Salon, which caused her taste and judgment to ripen; she also studied the old masters in the Louvre and in the Palais du Luxembourg. In 1880 she was asked to teach Princess Hendrika at Soestdijk. A well-executed portrait of *Queen Emma with Princess Wilhelmina* from 1881 brought her numerous portrait commissions from the well-to-do.

Thérèse Schwartze made herself be noticed, which was rather unusual for a woman in those days. She fulfilled, for example, administrative functions in the artists' societies Arti et Amicitiae and St. Lucas, and she was a jury member for the international painting exhibition in Amsterdam in 1883. Together with another woman painter, Wally Moes, she worked for several months in Paris in 1884 and won an award at the Salon. Due to her participation in exhibitions in Munich, Barcelona, and Chicago, Schwartze built up an international reputation.

In 1890, her fame consolidated, she was honored with a solo exhibition in the Panorama building in Amsterdam. Afterward, however, the criticism started. Her work was judged not to have enough feeling, not to be artistic enough, and to be too much aimed at saleability. Thérèse Schwartze continued undisturbed, however, and owing to her virtuoso technique, she was able to hold on to her position as a much-in-demand portrait painter until her death in 1918.

Alexandra W.M. van Smoorenburg

See also Women artists

Bibliography

Hollema, C., and P. Kouwenhoven. *Thérèse Schwartze, 1851–1918: Portret van een gevierd schilder.* Zeist: Zeister Stichting voor Kunst en Cultuur, 1989.

Sculpture (ca. 1400–ca. 1550)

The dominance of Utrecht as the great artistic center in the Netherlands in the late-medieval period (ca. 1400–ca. 1525) also applies to sculpture. The works produced there in stone and especially in wood were of more than regional importance. There was also sculptural activity to the north, in the present-day province of Holland, and to the south, around the town of 's Hertogenbosch. Wood sculpture of high quality was also made in the former Duchy of Guelders. A derivative of the latter style is found at the end of the fifteenth century and beginning of the sixteenth century in the region that is today the Dutch province of Limburg.

The late-medieval period for sculpture can be said to begin at the end of the fourteenth century with architectural sculpture on the Sint Janskerk, or Grote Kerk (Great Church), in 's Hertogenbosch (for example, the famous straddling figures on the flying buttresses) and new tomb sculpture at Breda that is a stylistic forerunner to Claus Sluter (The Sculptor from Haarlem who was in the service of Philip the Bold in Burgundy. His works like the *Well of Moses* [1395–1406] in Dijon show an expressive handling of form and innovative realism of detail). The real center of sculptural activity, however, was Utrecht. The building of the Domkerk (cathedral), which was begun in 1287, received new stimulus under the direction of the architect Jacob van der Borch around the middle of the fifteenth century. Utrecht was also at this time an important center for manuscript illumination, with the Master of Catherine of Cleves as the greatest artist in this field, and of a flourishing industry in the mass production of clay figures of saints. The most influential sculptor was Adriaen van Wesel (ca. 1417–ca. 1490), who was the head of a large workshop producing altar retables in wood for Utrecht and other towns (Fig. 122). The competitor of Van Wesel was the anonymous Master of the Emmerich Saints—his figures aiming at a more monumental impact and having a higher finish in details. Another sculptor, Jan Nude (active ca. 1455–ca. 1494), worked in wood and stone. Five stone statues in particular, from the interior of the Domkerk (ca. 1455), are connected with his name. They are broad figures in ample, flowing drapery that still shows the influence of the Sluterian style. In later wood statues—for example, a *St. Ursula* in Amsterdam (Begijnhof) and a *Virgin and Child* (Paris, Musée du Louvre), he shows a somewhat drier style.

The decoration of the funerary chapel of Bishop Rudolf von Diepholt in the Domkerk (1456–1464) is another demonstration of the high standard of sculpture in Utrecht in the late-medieval period. The spandrel reliefs of the wall arcade show finely sculpted figures of angels holding the Passion attributes. The typical heads with curly hair remind one of Van Wesel's work.

Another prolific sculptor working at the turn of the century was Jan van Schayck. The expressive and well-executed bosses from the library in the Domkerk (preserved in Utrecht and London) have been proved recently to be his.

Typical for Utrecht are, in addition, a group of stone epitaphs for canons of the cathedral. The composition mostly shows a bust of the Virgin Mary with the donor and his patron saint, thus going back to the type established in Strasbourg by Nicolaes Gerhaert of Leiden. Hardly any of these epitaphs survives intact, and it is probably because of their damaged state that they are not very well studied. This is undeserved, as they form a separate and attractive group among late-medieval epitaphs in general. A similar style, especially as far as the representation of the Virgin is concerned, is seen in a number of mantelpiece friezes with figurative roundels.

The Middle Ages in Utrecht may be said to have ended with the Master of the Stone Head of the Virgin (so called after a sandstone head of Mary in the Museum Het Catharijneconvent in Utrecht) who worked around 1500 to 1530. His main work is in wood; the only surviving altar retables produced by his workshop are the ones that were exported to Norway.

In Holland proper, the region to the west and northwest of Utrecht, we know of sculptural activity in the towns of Amsterdam, The Hague, and Haarlem. There were, for example, the anonymous master who produced the fine wood figures (four of them surviving) from the tribunal of the old town hall in Amsterdam, and Joost Janszoon working in The Hague in 1511 (fourteen shield-bearing animals from a balustrade). Yet it is the anonymous Master of Joachim and Anna, so called after a group sculpture of the *Meeting of Joachim and Anna* (Amsterdam, Rijksmuseum), who attracts the most attention. A contemporary of Van Wesel, he shows the same intimacy in the representation of the figures but lacks the Utrecht sculptor's artistic virtuosity.

Some sixty names of woodcarvers from about 1425 to about 1525 in the Southern town of 's Hertogenbosch and the neighboring region of the present-day province of North Brabant are known from archival sources, yet not one of them can be connected with still-existing wood sculptures. On the other hand, stylistic analysis by art historians has recently brought to light three distinctive personalities. First, there is the Master of the Statues of Coudewater. Coudewater is the name of a former nunnery near the town of 's Hertogenbosch that is known to have possessed a number of related wood statues of Sts. Catherine and Barbara, and the Archangel Michael. These statues show a static pillar-like form imposed by the block of wood. Eleven works are now attributed to the Master himself, fifteen to his workshop, and about twenty-seven to his followers. Two woodcarvers showing some influence by him in the first quarter of the sixteenth century are now known as the Master of Soeterbeeck, with seven works, the most important being a *St. Augustine* in the convent of Soeterbeeck, near Ravenstein; and the Master of Leende, with thirteen works, four of them surviving in the parish church of Leende, near Eindhoven.

The Grote Kerk in 's Hertogenbosch still possesses impressive choir stalls with carved bench ends and misericords. They date from about 1430–1460, but their maker is unknown. The stalls were taken as an example by Jan Borchmans for his famous stalls at Oirschot of 1505–1510, which, unfortunately, were destroyed during World War II. The oldest choir stalls in the present-day Netherlands are a few pieces found at Zaltbommel and Sittard (ca. 1430). Those at Breda are of about the same date. Later ensembles of some importance are found at Bolsward (from the end of the fifteenth century), Venlo (ca. 1500), and Haarlem (by Jasper Pieterz., 1512).

Some artistic activity is manifested for the Northern region around Zwolle and Kampen. It consists mainly of console and shaft figures in wood showing a lively realism in a provincial style. The wood vaults of many Dutch church buildings in other regions also show a large number of such figures. The present-day provinces of Gelderland, Overijssel, North Brabant (the eastern part), and Limburg (the northern part) in the Netherlands made up, in the late Middle Ages, the Duchy of Guelders. Together with the Duchies of Cleves, Julich, and Berg in nearby Germany, they formed the single cultural region of the Lower Rhine. In the field of sculpture Kalkar was the artistic center, and the altar retables, statues of saints, and other wood sculptures produced there and at other places are known as the products of the Cleves/Guelders style or the School of Kalkar.

An important sculptor of this region in the fifteenth century was Arnt van Kalkar (also called Arnt van Zwolle), who worked in Kalkar up to 1484, and from then until his death in 1492 at Zwolle. In Kalkar he apparently headed a large workshop that produced dozens of works for a great number of parish churches in the region. Works by him or his workshop can still be found in several parish churches in the Netherlands, as at Venray (Fig. 123), Horst, and Eibergen, and in museums in Utrecht and Amsterdam. Of his pupils and followers who apparently produced work for the Dutch parts of the region the most important are Dries Holthuys, the Master of Varsseveld (named after a Marianum, a rosary with the Virgin Mary, formerly in the village of Varsseveld but now preserved partly in Silvolde and partly in Anholt), and Kerstken Woyers. The best known of Master Arnt's successors, indeed the greatest of the Lower Rhine sculptors, is Hendrik Douvermann (ca. 1480–1530). Some of his works, too, seem to have been made for Dutch clients.

In Roermond there probably existed a large workshop comprising at least two generations from about 1490 to 1540 and producing hundreds of statues. Its greatest sculptor is still anonymous but is known by the name of the Master of Elsloo. A recent suggestion that he was Jan van Oel, known from archival records as having worked at Roermond, has not yet been generally accepted. Influenced by Gelderland/Lower-

Rhine sculpture, the Master of Elsloo and his pupils go even further than Arnt van Kalkar in the modeling of sharply gesturing figures in a rather graphic style.

From the first quarter of the sixteenth century we know the name of Jan van Steffeswert, who signed several statues among a total output of forty works. As has recently been established, his workshop was located in the town of Maastricht in Limburg. He is clearly a different master from the woodcarvers of the Elsloo workshop, appearing to have been influenced by the metal engraver Israhel van Meckenem. He is also a sculptor on the threshold of the new period of the Renaissance.

Harry Tummers

See also Tomb sculpture: medieval effigial monuments; Utrecht; Van Wesel, Adriaen

Bibliography

Bouvy, D.P.R.A. *Middeleeuwsche Beeldhouwkunst in de Noordelijke Nederlanden.* Amsterdam: A.A. Balkema, 1947.

Ceulemans, C., R. Didier, and J. Gerits. *Laatgotische Beeldsnijkunst uit Limburg en Grensland.* Sint Truiden: Provinciaal Museum voor Religieuze Kunst; Provincie Limburg Culturele Aangelegenheden, 1990.

Leeuwenberg, J., and W. Halsema-Kubes. *Beeldhouwkunst in het Rijksmuseum: Catalogus.* The Hague: Staatsuitgeverij, 1973.

Lemmens, G. et al. *Beelden uit Brabant: Laatgotische kunst uit het oude hertogdom, 1400–1520.* 's Hertogenbosch: Noordbrabants Museum, 1971.

Meurer, H. *Das Klever Chorgestühl und Arnt Beeldesnijder.* Düsseldorf: Rheinland Verlag, 1970.

Williamson, P. "Roof bosses from Utrecht and Jan van Schayck, beeldensnijder." *Oud Holland* 105 (1991): 140–151.

Sculpture (1550–1795)
Overview

The history of sculpture in the Netherlands prior to 1550 indicates an ambivalence toward the medium, especially in terms of large-scale works, which, in turn, prevented the creation of a strong indigenous tradition. These phenomena, as well as their reciprocal relationship, persisted throughout the early-modern period (the fifteenth through the eighteenth centuries) where they continued to affect the stylistic and technical development of Dutch sculpture as well as its local market. In contrast to the demand for painting in the Republic from 1550 to 1795, that for sculpture was of a significantly lesser magnitude. Furthermore, in comparison with the structure of demand for sculpture in other European countries during the same period, that in the Netherlands presents a different pattern, one that reflects the attitudes and tastes of Dutch patrons, as shaped by their political, religious, and social milieu.

Whereas the scarcity of monumental sculpture (for example, church portals) in the Northern Netherlands during the Middle Ages is often attributed to the scarcity of suitable local materials as well as the country's climate ("no stone, no sun"), this tendency was reinforced during the early-modern period in two ways. First, the widespread acceptance among Dutch Protestants of the Old Testament prohibition against "graven images" created a negative reaction to the presence of sculpture in the church interior, which extended to the medium more generally. Second, the instability of the nation's political system (which vacillated between monarchical and Republican tendencies) led to a reluctance to erect monuments honoring either members of a hereditary *élite* (the House of Orange as well as local noble families) or even those exemplary citizens who had performed exceptional service to the Republic or who had made important contributions to its intellectual or cultural life.

In a major break with tradition, the Catholic Church was no longer the major patron of sculpture in the Netherlands after 1600; however, that commissions for sacred figures and church furniture began to increase dramatically in Flanders at just this point (and would remain at a high level until the middle of the century) later proved to be significant for the subsequent history of sculpture in its northern neighbor. The eclipse of the Church, together with the more active role of other traditional patrons (civic authorities and institutions, the court, and the emerging middle class), meant that the majority of commissions from the seventeenth and eighteenth centuries were for secular works—architectural sculpture and decoration, sepulchral monuments, portraiture, small-scale statuettes, garden figures and vases, and interior furnishings (chimneypieces, furniture, and frames).

In general, the evolution of sculpture in the Netherlands continued to parallel that of Flanders, if slightly later, and in a more casual manner. The stylistic vocabulary of Dutch sculpture after 1550 indicates the persistence of local traditions as well as the influence of new developments in Italy and France. The creative interplay of these diverse vocabularies produced a unique Mannerist hybrid that combined an indigenous tendency toward realism with a highly ornamental decorative style. By the first quarter of the seventeenth century, this treatment had evolved into the Baroque, expressed either in classicizing terms or, somewhat later, the more pictorial style of Rubens and the sculptors of his studio that led to the emergence of the Rococo (from the last quarter of the seventeenth century).

The low level and sporadic pattern of demand during the last half of the sixteenth century provided few opportunities for the training or employment of native sculptors; this accounts for the large number of Dutch expatriates who enjoyed successful careers in Italy, Scandinavia, and Central Europe. Ironically, just at those points when local demand began to increase, there were few sculptors in the Republic capable of producing satisfactory work. Consequently, the most important commissions usually fell to well-trained foreigners, primarily Flemings, who dominated the field of sculpture in the Netherlands into the eighteenth century.

1550–1600
A survey of Dutch church furniture and sepulchral art produced during the second quarter of the sixteenth century in-

dicates that by 1550 the formal vocabulary of the Italian Renaissance had been firmly established in the Northern Netherlands. Sculpture from the second half of the sixteenth century continued to rely less on indigenous innovations than on the inspiration of international developments, especially the continued influence of Italy that entered the Republic via Antwerp. Flemish artists such as Pieter Coecke van Aelst (1502–1550), his student Cornelis Floris de Vriendt (1514–1575), and Hans Vredeman de Vries (1527–1606) produced ornamental prints and pattern books, as well as works for export, that provided models for Dutch sculptors. Also significant for the formation of later sculpture in the Netherlands were Jean Mone (ca. 1485–1550) and the members of his Mechelen studio, as well as the Cambrai master Colijn de Nole (died 1554/1558), who settled in Utrecht (ca. 1530) and introduced an elegant decorative style that appears in his tombs (in Arnhem and Vianan) and in his chimneypiece for the town hall in Kampen (1543–1545), as well as in works by his frequent collaborator Willem van Noort (before 1524–1556) and his son Jacob Colijn de Nole (died 1601), who took over his father's shop after his death.

The need to replace church furniture and decoration destroyed during periodic outbreaks of Iconoclasm between 1566 and 1580 accounts for commissions for choir screens, organ cases, pulpits, and benches or stalls, executed in wood or stone, as well as for table tombs and epitaphs (Breda) and grave slabs (Utrecht). Civic commissions from this period include figures and decoration for the façades of town halls (Franeker, 1591–1594; Leiden, 1593–1598), as well as city gates and portals. The façades of private houses were also redecorated in a rich Renaissance style (the House of Charles V, Zwolle, 1571; the Penninckhuis, Deventer, 1590).

During this period a number of Dutch sculptors studied in Italy. While some of these, such as Willem Daniëlsz. van Tetrode (died before 1588), eventually resettled in the Republic, others continued to work outside the Netherlands: This group includes Jan Gregor van der Schardt (ca. 1530–after 1581); Elias de Witte (Candido) and his son Peter (1548–1628), who were active in Florence; Hubert Gerhard (1550–1622/1623); Paulus van Vianen (ca. 1570–1613); and Adriaen de Vries (1546–1626), who produced elegant decorative works for the courts of Copenhagen, Munich, Prague and Vienna and for the merchants of Augsburg and Nuremberg. These sculptors, who as a group were more international in orientation than their peers who remained at home, had little contact with artists in the Republic and, consequently, do not appear to have exerted significant influence on their work.

Seventeenth Century: First Quarter
The beginning of the Twelve Years' Truce (1609–1621) marked the introduction of a period of peace and growing prosperity that provided a catalyst for commissions for sculpture in the Republic. With the exception of Hendrick de Keyser (1565–1621), indigenous sculptors, many of whom were actually stone masons, can scarcely be considered as more than competent craftsmen. This explains the virtual monopoly of De Keyser

(who, in comparison with international figures such as De Vries, appears more provincial). After De Keyser's death, there were no significant native sculptors in the Republic. In terms of style, this period marks the transition from Mannerism to the Baroque, as indicated in De Keyser's *Tomb of Willem I of Orange* (1614–1621; Delft, Nieuwe Kerk; Fig. 34).

In spite of the reservations by Dutch Protestants, there were numerous commissions for those items of church furniture that served the particular needs of the cult: These included pulpits, organ cases, baptismal fonts, choir screens and walls, choir stalls, and stalls for church elders. Sepulchral art, which was cautiously tolerated in most parishes, was, for the most part, limited to grave slabs and epitaphs: Among the latter is De Keyser's commission from the States General for the memorial of *Jacob van Heemskerk* (1609; Amsterdam, Oude Kerk; Fig. 33). Architectural sculpture was much in demand, especially for the façades of town halls (Bergen op Zoom, 1611; Bolsward, 1613–1617; Delft, 1618; Haarlem, 1630) and for the decoration of institutional headquarters, palaces, and private houses (De Keyser's Bartolotti House, 1617; the House of Heads, 1621/1624; and decorative gable stones, all located in Amsterdam). Sculpted portraits, which follow the same conventions as contemporary painted examples, include busts (such as those by De Keyser), both in the round and in relief, as well as full-length statues and effigies.

Seventeenth Century: Second Quarter

Dutch sculpture from the period between the end of the Twelve Years' Truce (1621) and the Treaty of Munster (1648) is marked by three significant developments. First, Baroque classicism began to emerge as the dominant style of the Republic, as in the Monument of *Piet Hein* (after 1638; Delft, Oude Kerk). Second, there was a greater interest in sculpture at the court of the *stadholder*, especially under Frederik Hendrik, who commissioned portraits, decorative works, and garden sculpture (for example, Pieter Adriaensz. 't Hooft's figures of *Fortuna*, ca. 1637). Other commissions from members of the Orange court include sculpture for the pediments of the Mauritshuis (ca. 1631) and the Oude Hof at Noordeinde (ca. 1645), both attributed to 't Hooft (1610–1650). That in both instances 't Hooft worked after sketches by Jacob van Campen is typical of the frequent collaboration of Dutch sculptors with architects and painters. Third, the Flemings became more active in the Republic during this period. These well-trained sculptors, who increasingly filled that vacuum created by a lack of local talent, may have initially been lured north by commissions from the *stadholders:* Artus I Quellinus (1609–1668), an Antwerp sculptor who was a personal favorite of Frederik Hendrik, executed a series of mythological figures (ca. 1634) for the palace of Honselaarsdijk, and François Dieussart (ca. 1600–ca. 1663) later created statues of the princes of the House of Orange (ca. 1646) as well as portraits for Willem II.

Seventeenth Century: Third Quarter

The ratification of the Treaty of Munster in 1648 ushered in a quarter-century that saw the dramatic expansion of Dutch cities, accompanied by increased demand for architectural sculpture and decoration. The period is also marked by the ascendancy of the Flemings, without whose involvement these projects would not have been achieved. The availability of these proficient sculptors, who were increasingly drawn to opportunities in the Republic when the Counter-Reformation offensive in Flanders began to wind down during the second half of the century, may have discouraged the development of local talent. As in the past, Flemish sculptors continued to provide a conduit for new developments from Italy and France.

The most important of the expatriate artists was Quellinus, who was active at the new town hall (now the Royal Palace) in Amsterdam from 1646 to 1663; there he and his assistants produced figures and reliefs, often based on designs by Van Campen, for the pediments, *vierschaar* (public high court), and galleries. Although Quellinus' workshop included Dutch sculptors, such as Bartolomeus Eggers (ca. 1630–before 1692) and Willem de Keyser (1603–1674), it also depended on a large contingent of Flemings, including Artus Quellien the Younger (1625–1700) and Rombout Verhulst (1624–1698). Verhulst introduced a new style in which Quellinus' classicizing tendencies were tempered by a picturesque naturalism analogous to that of Rubens and the sculptors associated with his studio. After the departure of Quellinus in 1663, Verhulst became the most important sculptor in the Netherlands. In addition to his contributions to the town hall project, he executed numerous tombs, including several memorials honoring the country's naval heroes (Maerten Tromp [Color Plate 9], Willem Joseph van Ghendt, and Michiel de Ruyter), as well as the reliefs for Pieter Post's weigh house in Leiden (1662). Among his students was the Dutch sculptor Johannes Blommendael (died 1703), who later worked for the *stadholder* Willem III. Other Flemish sculptors active in the North during the second half of the century include Pieter Xavery (ca. 1647–traceable to 1683), François van Bossuit (1635–1692), and Jan Claudius de Cock (1667–1735), who also received commissions from Willem III (decoration for the Prinsenhof, Breda, in 1692). Verhulst's only significant competitor was Eggers, the most prominent of the native sculptors active during this period, whose most important commissions include the *Wassenaar Monument* in The Hague (1667) and reliefs for the weigh house in Gouda (1669) and for the Amsterdam Stock Exchange (1670).

The majority of private commissions called for portraits (busts, relief medallions, full-length figures, and effigies), which continued to follow the formal and iconographic conventions of contemporary two-dimensional likenesses. With the exception of those by Flemish sculptors (especially Quellinus and Verhulst), the majority of these works are disappointing in terms of their technique as well as their failure to convey a sense of personality or character. Statuettes of mythological figures, executed in alabaster, terra-cotta, or bronze, were also popular, as were genre subjects by Pieter Xavery and Albert Vinckenbrink (1604?–1664/1665). Garden sculpture was also much in demand by both Dutch and foreign patrons: Eggers received commissions from Johan Maurits van Nassau (from 1668) as well as Friedrich Wilhelm of Brandenburg (from 1662).

Seventeenth Century: Fourth Quarter
In spite of sporadic activity in certain cities (Alkmaar, Haarlem), there was a marked decline in the demand for sculpture in the Netherlands from 1672 (the beginning of the war with France, as well as the year in which Willem III reclaimed his title as *stadholder*) through the end of the century. Although Amsterdam maintained its dominant role, The Hague, newly revitalized as the site of the *stadholder*'s court, began to emerge as a significant center of activity.

Eighteenth Century
The low level of demand for sculpture in the eighteenth century produced a limited number of significant works in the Netherlands; many of these have not survived, and of those that have, most are of indifferent quality. Commissions were primarily for portraiture, sepulchral monuments, and decorative pieces (church furniture and decoration, as well as chimneypieces and garden sculpture) executed in a Rococo style. Orders for architectural sculpture, which had earlier produced some of the country's most renowned monuments, were largely limited to the opulent decoration of the gables of private houses.

Although their numbers, as well as the quality of their work, decreased over the course of the century, Flemish sculptors continued to be a significant presence. Antwerp sculptors active in the North include Jan Pieter van Baurscheit (1669–1728), known primarily for his garden figures and vases, and Jan Baptist Xavery (1697–1742), who produced a wider range of works: These include his allegorical figures for the façade of the town hall in The Hague (ca. 1733) and for the *Allegory of Faith* in the Haarlem Grote Kerk (1753), portrait busts, commemorative monuments, chimneypieces, and garden sculpture. He was also the teacher of his son Jacob Mattheus (1734–1794). A lesser number of French sculptors were also in residence in the Netherlands during this period. Jacob Cressant, who worked in Utrecht (from 1728) and Amsterdam (from 1742), is known for his portrait busts, religious figures, and garden sculpture (*Vases with Reliefs of the Four Seasons*, 1714; Amsterdam, Rijksmuseum). Étienne-Maurice Falconet (1716–1791) settled in The Hague (beginning 1778) for several years, together with his daughter-in-law, Marie-Anne Falconet-Collot (1748–1821), who produced busts of the *stadholder* Willem V and His Wife. Anthonie Ziesenis (1731–1801), from Hanover, became the city sculptor of Amsterdam as well as the official sculptor of the East India Company.

The Republic's few native sculptors were predominantly active in Amsterdam. These include Ignatius van Logteren (1685–1732), best known for his chimneypieces and garden sculpture, and his son Jan (1709–1745), who produced garden figures and vases with mythological subjects. Willem Hendrik van de Wall (1716–1790), a Utrecht sculptor who had studied with Xavery and Cressant, executed sacred, mythological (*Mars* and *Neptune*, 1757; Amsterdam, Rijksmuseum), and allegorical figures (including his *Faith, Hope,* and *Charity*, 1775–1776; Amsterdam, Rijksmuseum) in wood and terra-cotta. Also active in Amsterdam were Frans Blancard (1704–1744), who executed a wooden gable with a bust of Grotius for a house on the Kalverstraat (before 1742; Amsterdam, Rijksmuseum), and Michiel Emanuel Shee (died 1739/1740), who produced decorative and garden sculpture. Johann Heinrich Schepp (1736?–after 1791), originally active in The Hague and, after 1788, in Leiden, was a medalist and gem engraver employed (1772–1787) by the *stadholder* Willem V, for whom he produced a number of portrait medallions (Amsterdam, Rijksmuseum).

Cynthia Lawrence

See also Classicism in architecture; Coins, medals; De Keyser, Hendrick; Eggers, Bartolomeus; Flanders, Flemish School; Nationalism; Post, Pieter; Public monumental sculpture (ca. 1550–1795); Quellinus, Artus I; Renaissance architecture; Tomb sculpture: early modern and later sepulchral art; Van Campen, Jacob; Verhulst, Rombout; Xavery, Jan Baptist; Xavery, Pieter

Bibliography
De Beeldhouwkunst in de Eeuw van Rubens. Brussels: Museum voor Oude Kunst, 1977.
Fremantle, K. *The Baroque Town Hall of Amsterdam.* Utrecht: Haentjens, Dekker, and Gumbert, 1959.
Gelder, H.E. van. *Beeldende kunst en bouwkunst in Nederland.* The Hague: Staatsdrukkerij, 1954.
Halsema-Kubes, W. "De Noordnederlandse beeldhouwkunst in de 17de eeuw." *Beelden in de Gouden Eeuw: Kunst Schrift* 91 (1991): 16–25.
Jonge, C.H. de. "Noordnederlandse beeldhouwkunst in de zeventiende eeuw." In *Kunstgeschiedenis der Nederlanden.* Edited by H.E. van Gelder et al. Vol. 5, *Renaissance, Barok en Klassicism.* Zeist: W. de Haan, 1963–1965.
Jongh, E. de. "De schaduwen van Daedalus." *Beelden in de Gouden Eeuw: Kunst Schrift* 91 (1991): 10–15.
Kloek, W.T., W. Halsema-Kubes, and R.J. Baarsen, eds. *Art before Iconoclasm: Northern Netherlandish Art, 1525–1580.* 2 vols. The Hague: Staatsuitgeverij, 1986.
Kulturmann, U. et. al. *Europäische Barockplastik am Niederrhein: Grupello und seine Zeit.* Düsseldorf: Kunstmuseum, 1971.
Leeuwenberg, J., and W. Halsema-Kubes, eds. *Beeldhouwkunst in het Rijksmuseum.* Amsterdam: Rijksmuseum; The Hague: Staatsuitgeverij, 1973.
Neurdenburg, E. *De zeventiende eeuwsche beeldhouwkunst in de Noordelijke Nederlanden: Hendrick De Keyser, Artus Quellien en Rombout Verhulst en tijdgenoten.* Amsterdam: Meulenhoff, 1948.
Rosenberg, J., S. Slive, and E.H. ter Kuile. *Dutch Art and Architecture, 1600–1800.* Baltimore: Penguin, 1966.
Vos, R., and F. Leeman. *Het Nieuwe ornament: Gids voor de renaissance architectuur en decoratie in Nederland in de 16de eeuw.* The Hague: Staatsuitgeverij, 1986.

Sculpture (1795–1945)
At the start of the nineteenth century, there was barely a tradition of sculpture in the Northern Netherlands. The chief

reason was that major patronage for sculpture was lacking in the eighteenth century: No royal family prominently displayed itself, and the Protestant churches rejected decoration. If there was a sizable commission, it often went to a foreign sculptor. The few sculptors from the Northern Netherlands working around 1800 aspired to establish themselves abroad, particularly in France. After the Netherlands came under French rule in 1795, Paris became the city where many Dutch artists completed their education. Therefore, their work was strongly oriented toward classicism, even though some traces of the Baroque tradition remained visible in the Southern provinces.

The most important classicist Dutch sculptors are Matthias Kessels (1784–1836) and Paul Joseph Gabriël (1785–1833). Kessels, who was born in Maastricht, was educated in Paris, St. Petersburg, and Rome, where he worked for a while in the studio of the Danish sculptor Bertel Thorwaldsen (1768–1844). Kessels' *oeuvre* consists of free-standing figures, allegorical images, and some grave monuments, in a style that for the most part resembles well-known ancient models. In his late work, after about 1830, more emotion is visible, betraying influence from Romanticism. Because he stayed in Rome, he had few followers in the Netherlands.

Gabriël, from Amsterdam, had more influence. He also was educated in Paris and Rome, where he worked in the studio of Antonio Canova (1757–1822). Later, when Gabriël had almost settled in Paris, his appointment as royal sculptor by Willem I forced him to return to the Netherlands in 1814. His *oeuvre* consists almost entirely of portraits and grave monuments in an uncompromising classical style. It is typical of the times that he was never given the opportunity to execute a large statue in a public location. In 1820 he became the first teacher of sculpture at the newly opened Royal Academy of Arts (Koninklijke Academie van Beeldende Kunsten) in Amsterdam. This was the first academy—and for a long time the only one—where sculpture was fully part of the curriculum; however, this did not lead to a great increase in the number of sculptors.

Another institution that was important for sculpture was the Royal Institute of Sciences, Literature, and Fine Arts (Koninklijk Instituut van Wetenschappen, Letterkunde, en Schone Kunsten) established in 1808 in Amsterdam. The department known as the Fourth Class (Vierde Klasse) looked after the interests of the visual arts and held competitions in sculpture; it also mediated in the procurement of scarce commissions. In 1833 Louis Royer (1795–1868) became a member of the Fourth Class, which got him commissions for two statues in the 1840s: *Michiel de Ruyter* (1841, Vlissingen) and *Willem of Orange;* (1848; The Hague). Royer had worked in Rome for several years, undergoing influence from Canova and Thorwaldsen, after an earlier education in his birthplace of Mechelen (Southern Netherlands) and in Paris. After his return, he settled in the Northern Netherlands in 1828 and remained there after Belgium became a separate kingdom. In 1835 he became sculptor to the king, and in the next year he succeeded Gabriël at the Amsterdam academy. Despite the fact that he remained connected with the academy until his

death more than thirty years later, he had only a few notable students.

Royer had a large *oeuvre*, a part of which was the representation of allegorical and biblical themes. At the beginning of his career he worked in a classical style, but his attachment to classical models loosened over the years and he began to give his figures more natural poses. His fame rests on the fact that he made as many as five public statues, including *Rembrandt* (1852) and *Vondel* (1867), both in Amsterdam. He also worked on two other major monuments, so that half of all the public monuments erected around the mid-nineteenth century bear his name.

After Royer's death, the few monumental commissions were carried out mainly by members of the Stracké family, originally from Germany. Johann Theodor Stracké (1817–1891) was responsible for three statues, among them *Jan van Nassau* (1888; Utrecht); his younger brother Frans (1820–1898) made two, including *Alcmaria Victrix* (Victorious Alkmaar; 1876; Alkmaar). The only native Dutchman whose contribution was significant was Ferdinand Leenhoff (1841–1914), who made the statues of *J.R. Thorbecke* (1876; Amsterdam) and of *Jan Pietersz. Coen* (1893; Hoorn). He, too, was educated outside the Netherlands; he had grown up in Paris and was trained by his brother-in-law Joseph Mezzara (sculptor of the *Ary Scheffer* statue in Dordrecht in 1862). The two Strackés and Leenhoff also were educators: Johan Theodor Stracké taught at the Rotterdam academy and at the art school in 's Hertogenbosch; Franz Stracké was a professor at the Amsterdam academy after 1870 (the year that it was reorganized to become the Rijksacademie—the State Academy—and was no longer known as the Koninklijke Academie—the Royal Academy); he was succeeded by Leenhoff in 1890. Their work is in the neoclassical tradition, which lasted a long time in the Netherlands; it is often rather static and sober and does not express much emotion. Only a few of their students achieved any artistic level.

After 1850 there were still few Dutch sculptors with sufficient experience to work on a monumental scale. This is demonstrated in the events surrounding the *National Memorial to 1813*, the largest nineteenth-century monument in the Netherlands (Fig. 124). The winners of the competition in 1863 were sculptor and painter J.Ph. Koelman (1818–1893) and architect W.C. van der Waaijen Pieterszen (1819–1874) with their design of classically inspired forms. Since Koelman was viewed as incapable of executing the great images himself, two Belgian artists, Joseph (1822–1898) and Jacques Jaquet (1830–1898), were brought in, to the great discontent of some critics.

This monument has become historically important more because of the great controversy surrounding it than for its aesthetic qualities. Many at the time would have preferred to see the Neo-Gothic design of architect P.J.H. Cuypers (1827–1921) carried out; it received second prize. The main objection was that the Neo-Gothic style was Catholic and did not fit the Protestant character of the Netherlands. The dispute between Neo-Gothic and classical styles played an important role during the entire second half of the nineteenth century, and not just in this case.

Despite his "loss" in this affair, the Catholic Cuypers, educated at the Antwerp academy, became a leading figure in the Dutch art world. After the restoration of the episcopal hierarchy in the Netherlands in 1853, new construction by the Catholic Church soared and Cuypers took a great part in it. These building activities created a great demand for church furnishings, statues of saints, and altars. Since there were too few artists capable of making such objects, Cuypers established his own studio in 1852 in Roermond, modeled after a medieval workshop, in which students were trained in various, mainly outdated, trades. Other sculpture studios, making primarily religious works, opened in other locations. In 's Hertogenbosch, for example, were the studios of the Goossens brothers (established 1846), the Donkers brothers (1848–1859), and Hendrik van der Geld (established 1872). In Amsterdam was the firm of Van den Bossche and Crevels (established 1882), and in Haarlem the studios of Frans Stracké (established 1882) and J.P. Maas (established in 1893).

Only after 1875 were some large secular buildings designed to include decorative sculpture. The two most important are the Rijksmuseum (1876–1885) and the Centraal Station (1881–1889) in Amsterdam, both designed by Cuypers. A competition was held for the front façade of the Rijksmuseum that led to commissions for sculpture by Jean François Vermeylen of Leuven and Bart van Hove (1850–1914) from The Hague. Vermeylen also made several large reliefs for the Centraal Station in collaboration with Ludwig Jünger (1856–?) and Eduard Roskam (1854–?), both educated in Belgium.

Van Hove took a different direction after the completion of the Rijksmuseum and turned to free-standing work. Soon he was much in demand for portraits, for example, of members of the royal family, and toward the end of the century he was one of the best-known Dutch sculptors. In 1900 he succeeded Leenhoff as professor at the Amsterdam Rijksacademie. He remained very productive, designing five public statues that were executed in the first decade of the twentieth century, among them *Monseigneur F.H. Hamer* (1902; Nijmegen) and *Count Willem Lodewijk* (1906; Leeuwarden). Van Hove worked in an academic style that, notwithstanding some controlled elegance, is completely in the nineteenth-century tradition. His influence on the younger generation of sculptors, who were looking for a new formal idiom, was therefore slight.

By 1900 the Rijksacademie played only a minor role in the development of Dutch sculpture despite its prominent status in art education. As at other older educational institutions in the country—the academies in The Hague and Rotterdam, and the Koninklijke School voor Nuttige en Beeldende Kunsten (Royal School for Useful and Fine Arts) in 's Hertogenbosch—the education consisted mainly of modeling lessons; the cutting of stone was left to skilled stonecutters. At the end of the nineteenth century several new courses oriented toward practical training gained more influence for that reason. In 1877 in Haarlem a school of arts and crafts *(Kunstnijverheidsschool)* was founded, and two years later the

Quellinus School opened in Amsterdam, founded by Cuypers. When construction of the Rijksmuseum began, there was again a lack of capable craftsmen and, therefore, a construction workshop was erected that soon became the Quellinus School (named after Artus I Quellinus, the seventeenth-century sculptor in charge of the decoration of the Amsterdam town hall). The direction came from the sculptor E.C.E. Colinet (1844–1890), who had been attracted to the Netherlands by Cuypers, and his assistant, P.E. van den Bossche (1849–1921), both from Belgium. In 1881 the Rijksmuseum also became the home of the National School for Arts and Crafts (Rijksschool voor Kunstnijverheid); it provided a secondary education in which Cuypers was again involved. Many of the younger Dutch sculptors active around 1900 were trained in the basics of their profession at one of these institutions.

Making sculpture for buildings continued to be the main activity of the younger generation, but a few artists, such as Henri Teixeira de Mattos (1856–1908) and Pier Pander (1864–1919), made free-standing sculpture. After a short time in Rome, Teixeira de Mattos became especially skilled in working in marble. From about 1890, when he moved to London, he made animal sculpture that was strongly influenced by the French Romantic sculptors Antoine Louis Barye (1796–1875) and Emmanuel Fremiet (1824–1910). Pander, educated at the Quellinus School and the Rijksacademie, went to Rome after winning the Prix de Rome in 1885 and stayed. His figures, reliefs, and portraits are in an elegant classical style (Fig. 92); in 1898 he modeled the portrait of Queen Wilhelmina for a new ten-guilder gold coin. Because both artists lived abroad for a long time, they had little influence in the Netherlands.

Two sculptors who did have great influence at the turn of the century are Lambertus Zijl (1866–1947) and Joseph Mendes da Costa (1863–1939). They became acquainted while students at the Quellinus School and the Rijksschool voor Kunstnijverheid in Amsterdam, and they later formed a company together for several years.

Zijl was one of the most prominent architectural sculptors in the Netherlands and worked with such well-known architects as H.P. Berlage, K.P.C. de Bazel, and A.J. Kropholler. Zijl's sculptural contribution to the Stock Exchange (Beurs) designed by Berlage in Amsterdam (built 1898–1903) was especially important for the development of architectural sculpture in the Netherlands. The sculpture on this building is not just a decorative addition, but, for the first time, it is completely integrated into the whole; the statue of *Gijsbrecht van Amstel* is not placed against the wall but has been sunk into the wall in such a way that it forms a unity with the corner line of the building (Fig. 125). This introduced the concept of architectural sculpture as "sculpture that joins in the character of the building." Zijl's later work was a little freer and plastic, as in his only large free-standing statue, *Queen Mother Emma* (1938; Amsterdam). Zijl made many small sculptural works during his career. Even though often described as Impressionistic because of their lively surface treatment, these little sculptures have a pronounced monumental character, and for that they were greatly appreciated by many younger colleagues.

The term *Impressionistic* is also used to characterize the work of Zijl's younger contemporary, Charles van Wijk (1875–1917), who was one of the first sculptors to go into nature to study humans and animals—just like many painters from his time. His portrayals of fishers and farmers, male and female, are often seen as a sculptural equivalent of the paintings of The Hague School.

Mendes da Costa—a cousin of Teixeira de Mattos—was the first and immediately the most important representative of a second important trend that connects directly to Art Nouveau. His designs are strongly stylized, with emphasis on linearity. At the beginning of the 1890s, he modeled Impressionistic images, but around 1900, affected by his study of Egyptian and Assyrian art, his forms became tighter and more stylized to the point that outward similitude was of secondary interest. Like Zijl, Mendes da Costa also made architectural sculpture, chiefly in Amsterdam, and only one statue, the South African Boer War general *Christiaan de Wet* (commissioned by the art collector Hélène Kröller-Müller and placed in De Hoge Veluwe National Park in 1922; Fig. 82). Mendes da Costa consciously took the surroundings into account when he designed this statue, which was something new to do at the time. The most important part of his *oeuvre*, however, are his small-scale sculptures, which have been much imitated (Fig. 83).

J.C. Altorf (1876–1955), who was educated at The Hague academy, is known for mostly small-scale sculpture that is often compared with Mendes da Costa's work. It is somewhat more angular and tighter, however, and there is not the same anecdotal element.

Another important representative of this stylized tendency is Tjipke Visser (1876–1955), educated at the Rijksschool voor Kunstnijverheid and the Rijksacademie in Amsterdam. He also made small-scale sculpture in different materials, such as bronze, silver, and several kinds of wood, in which he makes refined use of the structure and the color nuances of his material.

The *oeuvre* of W.C. Brouwer (1877–1993), another representative of stylization, is quite extensive although restricted to ceramics. In his pottery, founded in Leiderdorp in 1901 to produce functional ceramics, many terra-cotta garden ornaments and earthenware for buildings, such as gable stones, friezes, crowning statues, and other decorative elements, were made after 1906. An important building for which Brouwer delivered the terra-cotta sculpture is the Vredespaleis (Peace Palace) in The Hague (1909–1911).

The influence of the stylized linear tendency of Mendes da Costa continued for a fairly long time, especially in animal sculpture as seen in the work of Françoise Carbasius (1885–1984), Gra Rueb (1885–1972), Bertha Thoe Schwartzenberg (1891–1993), and Jaap Kaas (1898–1972).

In addition to the artists who worked in an impressionistic and linear style, there were others after 1900 who continued in the traditional academic style, such as Toon Dupuis (1877–1937) and August Falise (1878–1936), and as a consequence they received many important commissions for portrait busts and statues. Dupuis, a student at the Antwerp academy and a teacher at the Rotterdam academy from 1900 to 1914, designed statues of the *De Witt Brothers* (1918; Dordrecht), the equestrian statue of *King and Stadholder Willem III* (1926; Breda), and a statue of *Queen Mother Emma* (1936; The Hague). Falise, educated in Amsterdam at the Rijksschool voor Kunstnijverheid and the Rijksacademie, and a teacher in 's Hertogenbosch from 1921 until 1936, produced several statues, among them *Dr. H.J.A.M. Schaepman* (1927; Tubbergen), *P.J.H. Cuypers* (1930; Roermond), and *Jeroen Bosch* (the painter Hieronymus Bosch; 1930; 's Hertogenbosch).

There was also a new development in sculpture around the time of World War I that was related to changes in architecture at the turn of the century. In connection with the buildings of the expressionistic Amsterdam School, architectural sculpture became less "serving" in character, the design became less linear, and the emphasis on volume greater. The Scheepvaarthuis in Amsterdam, designed by J.M. van der Mey, with contributions by Michel de Klerk and Pieter Lodewijk Kramer, is considered the first completely realized building in this new architectural style (Fig. 4). The sculpture was under the control of H.A. van den Eijnde (1869–1939) in 1913. Van den Eijnde specialized in sculpture made for an architectural setting; other works of his can be found in the post offices in Haarlem and Utrecht (both designed in the 1920s by the architect J. Crouwel). In the blocky construction that characterizes a lot of his work, one can see the influence of the German sculptor Franz Metzner, who worked on the *Memorial to the Battle of Leipzig* (1898–1913; Leipzig).

In 1914 Hildo Krop (1884–1970), who had been a student of Van Hove at the Rijksacademie between 1908 and 1911, became Van den Eijnde's assistant in executing the sculpture for the Scheepvaarthuis. Two years later Krop began working for the Amsterdam municipality, a position he would hold for many decades. He made decorative sculpture, in his characteristically compact and sober style, in which can be seen the influence of German Expressionist sculpture, for a great many of Amsterdam's bridges and buildings. John Raedecker (1885–1956), in contrast to Krop, concentrated on free-standing sculpture and made very little in the way of architectural sculpture. In 1906 he studied at the Amsterdam Rijksacademie with Van Hove for a short time, but Van Hove's way of working did not appeal to him. His work, executed in bronze, wood, and stone, is characterized by expressive round shapes, which often radiate a dreamy, light, surrealistic atmosphere. His most monumental work he made only after World War II: the *Nationaal Monument* (1947–1956), a memorial to all of the Dutch victims of the war, that stands on the Dam in Amsterdam, a collaboration with architect J.J.P. Oud.

Krop and Raedecker were by far the two most important sculptors of the period between the World Wars; some sculptors who are stylistically related to them are Leendert Bolle (1879–1942), Joop van Lunteren (1882–1958), Theo van Reyn (1884–1954), Gijs Jacobs van den Hof (1889–1965), and Johan Polet (1894–1971). These artists' *oeuvres* consist mainly of architectural sculpture and small-scale sculptural works.

Next to Krop and Raedecker, a third artist of importance for twentieth-century sculpture is Jan Bronner (1881–1972). Between 1914 and 1947 he was a professor at the Rijksacademie, where he trained more than one hundred forty sculptors, many of whom would later become very well known. He spent the limited time that he had for his own work carrying out his design for the *Hildebrand Monument* in Haarlem, which had won the prize in a competition in 1914. The execution and placing of the monument took almost fifty years, during which time the style of the statues changed from anecdotally detailed to more austere and stylized, so that they became more unified with the architectural forms. In his teaching Bronner also emphasized monumentality and thinking in volumes. Moreover, he urged his students to cut into the stone themselves, something that only skilled stonecutters did at that time. He stressed study of the art of sculpture from earlier periods, a lesson that is noticeable in some of his students' work.

In contrast to the stylized sculptors who followed the example of Mendes da Costa, the sculptors who were Bronner's students display a treatment of the surface that is looser, more impressionistic, and on which the traces of the modeling and cutting are very visible. Because of this their work has more links to Zijl's manner, which Bronner very much respected. Bronner's students produced primarily free-standing sculpture; with the arrival of functionalism in architecture in the 1920s and 1930s there were fewer and fewer commissions for architectural sculpture.

Among Bronner's first students were Mari Andriessen (1897–1979), Frits van Hall (1899–1945), and Bertus Sondaar (1904–1984). Before World War II, Andriessen made many religious works, but after 1945 he became particularly well known for his war monuments depicting the experiences and deprivations of ordinary people. His manner was often still close to Impressionism. In 1924 Van Hall won the Prix de Rome, and afterward he remained for several years in Italy and France. During the 1930s he carried out several monumental commissions, such as the *Van Heutsz Monument* in Amsterdam (1934), that show strong inspiration from classical antiquity. During the war he was captured as a member of the resistance and executed by the Germans. Sondaar completed his education in France as a student of Charles Despiau (1874–1946), whose influence is strong in the Renaissance-like portrait busts that make up the lion's share of his *oeuvre*. In fact, Despiau impressed many of Bronner's students. As a student himself, Bronner very much admired the work of Auguste Rodin (1840–1917), but his students also appreciated the younger French sculptors—namely, Aristide Maillol (1861–1944) and Antoine Bourdelle (1861–1929)—as well as Despiau. In the 1930s their works could be seen at exhibitions in the Netherlands, but most young Dutch artists visited France for some length of time. Some were almost entirely educated there, such as Han Wezelaar (1901–1984), who began at the arts and crafts school in Amsterdam, and Charlotte van Pallandt (born 1898), who first applied herself to drawing but turned to sculpture at the end of the 1920s. The major part of their *oeuvre* came, however, just as with most of Bronner's students, after World War II.

Mieke van der Wal

See also Amsterdam School; Andriessen, Mari; Architectural competitions; Architectural restoration; Bronner, Jan; Coins, medals; House of Orange-Nassau; Krop, Hildo; Mendes da Costa, Joseph; Monuments to artists; Neo-Gothic; Pander, Pier; Public monumental sculpture (1795–1990); Raedecker, John; Royer, Louis; State and municipal art collecting and collections; State patronage, public support; Van Hove, Bart; Van Pallandt, Charlotte; World Wars I and II; Zijl, Lambertus

Bibliography

Beerman, Mirjam, Frans van Burkom, and Frans Grijzenhout, eds. *Beeldengids Nederland.* Rotterdam: Uitgeverij 010, 1994.

Braat, L.P.J. *Uit de werkplaatsen der beeldhouwers.* Amsterdam: De Spieghel, n.d.

Daalen, P.K. van. *Nederlandse beeldhouwers in de negentiende eeuw.* The Hague: Nijhoff, 1957.

Hammacher, A.M. *Beeldhouwkunst van deze eeuw en een schets van haar ontwikkeling in de negentiende eeuw.* Vol. 14, *De schoonheid van ons land.* Amsterdam: Contact, 1955.

Huebner, F.M. *Nieuwe Hollandsche Beeldhouwkunst.* Amsterdam: Van Munster, n.d.

Knuttel, W.G. "De beeldhouwkunst (de negentiende en twintigste eeuw." In *Kunstgeschiedenis der Nederlanden.* Edited by H.E. van Gelder, 519–552. Utrecht: De Haan, 1955.

Koopmans, Ype. "De rehabilitatie van de steenhouwer: Het ambacht als voedingsbodem voor de emancipatie van de Nederlandse beeldhouwkunst sinds de eeuwwisseling." *Jong Holland* 9 (1989): 18–27, 27–45.

———. *Fixed and Chiselled: Sculpture in Architecture 1840–1940.* Rotterdam: NAI, 1994.

Reijn, Theo van. *Nederlandse beeldhouwers van deze tijd.* Amsterdam: Bibliotheca artis Elseviriana, 1949.

Teeuwisse, J. "De Nederlandse beeldhouwkunst in het jaar 1913." In *Nederland 1913: Een reconstructie van het culturele leven.* Edited by J. De Vries, 231–239. Amsterdam: Meulenhoff/Landshoff, 1988.

Teeuwisse, Jan et al. *Er groeit een beeldhouwkunst in Nederland: Het vrije beeld 1900–1960.* Haarlem: Frans Hals Museum; Ghent: Snoeck-Ducaju, 1994.

Wal, M. van der. "Dierbeeldhouwkunst in Nederland vanaf 1800 tot heden." In *150 jaar monumentale animalierscuptuur,* 62–75. Antwerp: Esco, 1993.

Self-portraiture

Throughout the Renaissance and Baroque periods, artists made likenesses of themselves and of their fellow artists. Self-portraits served a variety of purposes, public and private. While almost every artist recorded his own image at least once in his career, some made a regular practice of it. The most significant contributor to the genre was Rembrandt van Rijn, who made self-portraits throughout his life in etching, drawing, and painting.

For history painters, it was important to represent human emotion convincingly. An artist working from a mirror could study the effect of various emotions and moods on the facial features. This practice was advocated by Samuel van Hoogstraten in his treatise on the art of painting (1678) and probably practiced in Rembrandt's studio, where Van Hoogstraten trained. Rembrandt's own earliest self-portrait etchings capture the expressive mobility of his youthful face.

Self-portraits could also remain in the studio as useful samples of the artist's work. For the professional portraitist, the achievement of a convincing likeness took precedence over the representation of emotion. A self-portrait (or a likeness of the artist's wife) kept on hand could testify to the painter's competence, since a client could easily compare it with the original. These samples could also serve as models from which students could learn by copying, another practice frequent in Rembrandt's workshop.

Artists sometimes represented themselves together with their wives or family, often playing wittily with levels of reality by including a portrait within the portrait—for example, Jacob Cornelisz. van Oostsanen, *Self-Portrait Painting a Likeness of His Wife* (1538; Toledo, Ohio, Museum of Art) or Adriaen van der Werff, *Self-Portrait with the Portrait of His Wife Margareta Rees and Their Daughter Maria* (1699; Amsterdam, Rijksmuseum; Fig. 121). Self-portraits could also commemorate an important personal experience such as travel. Maerten van Heemskerck visited Italy in 1532 and painted himself in front of the ruins of the Roman Colosseum (Cambridge, Fitzwilliam Museum).

Self-portraits were sometimes given as gifts to friends or clients, or circulated as personal advertisements. The German painter and printmaker Albrecht Dürer, who portrayed himself in several paintings, gave a self-portrait (1498; Madrid, Prado) as a gift to his native city of Nuremberg; the city fathers, in turn, presented it to Charles I of England. Duke Cosimo de' Medici of Florence amassed a substantial collection of artists' self-portraits, still housed in the Uffizi, that included works by Gerrit Dou, Rembrandt, Frans van Mieris the Elder, and other Netherlandish painters.

In many self-portraits, artists represented themselves seated before an easel (Fig. 75) or actively at work in the studio, sometimes with attributes such as musical instruments, tobacco pipes, and skulls that carried symbolic allusions to the transience of life, the futility of earthly experience, or the power of art to capture, manipulate, and immortalize physical appearance (*ars longa, vita brevis*). A number of meticulous self-portraits by Gerrit Dou and his followers demonstrate the artist's illusionistic skill (for example, Gerrit Dou, *Self-Portrait with Book and Pipe*, ca. 1647, Amsterdam, Rijksmuseum; Fig. 45). In works by David Bailly, Vincent Laurensz. van der Vinne, and others, a painted or etched self-portrait itself becomes a component of the still life—for example, David Bailly, *Self-Portrait with Vanitas Still Life* (1651; Leiden, Stedelijk Museum De Lakenhal).

There are an equal number of self-portraits, however, in which all reference to the artist's profession is absent. This is an important distinction in the typology of the genre, for self-portraiture played a significant polemical role in the drive, initiated during the sixteenth century, to raise painting from the status of a menial craft to that of an intellectual liberal art. Representations of artists in gentlemanly attire, sometimes in engraved portrait series of a type usually devoted to likenesses of prominent leaders in the military and political spheres—for example, Hieronymus Cock (1572; Antwerp), Hendrick Hondius (1610; The Hague), and Anthony van Dyck's *Iconography* (begun ca. 1632)—did much to solidify the image of the artist whose lifestyle and accomplishments equaled those of his patrons. In a famous self-portrait painted in 1558 (Florence, Uffizi), Antonis Mor combines this imagery with that of the studio by representing himself, in gentlemanly dress, before a blank easel, the *tabula rasa* that depends upon the creative power of his intellect to give it form, and to which is attached a note, written in Greek, claiming Mor's superiority to the ancient painters Apelles and Zeuxis.

Artists sometimes assumed historical and symbolic roles in self-portraits. Among the earliest are representations as St. Luke—for example, Rogier van der Weyden (ca. 1435; Boston, Museum of Fine Arts)—who, according to legend, had painted a portrait of the Virgin and Child as they appeared to him in an apparition. Rembrandt later represented himself as the apostle Paul (1661; Amsterdam, Rijksmuseum) and, with his wife, Saskia, as the Prodigal Son in the tavern (1636; Dresden, Gemäldegalerie; see also Gabriel Metsu, *Self-Portrait with His Wife*, ca. 1660, in the same museum). Jan Steen dispensed with the biblical overtones and repeatedly included his own features among tavern low-lifes and drunken revelers—for example, *Drunken Pair in a Tavern* (1660; St. Petersburg, Hermitage); and *Rederijkers at a Window* (ca. 1662–1665; Philadelphia Museum of Art, Johnson Collection; Fig. 119). Gerrit Dou, too, places himself in a suggestive genre context, when he looks out through a window behind a quack doctor hawking his spurious remedies, perhaps commenting on the deceptive power of art (1652; Rotterdam, Museum Boymans-van Beuningen; Fig. 114).

Such role-playing is related to the tradition, already employed by Italian artists like Raphael, for the artist's self-inclusion as witness to a historical event. Again, Rembrandt provides several examples, notably in presenting himself as participant in the *Raising of the Cross* and the *Descent from the Cross*, painted for the *stadholder* Frederik Hendrik (ca. 1633; Munich, Alte Pinakothek). By assuming the role of intermediary between viewer and subject, the artist adds contemporary relevance to an ancient theme and proclaims his power to envision and re-create the past.

Stephanie S. Dickey

See also Berckheyde, Job Adriaensz.; Dou, Gerrit; Drawings, uses and collecting; Italy; Portraiture; Prints, printmaking, and printmakers (ca. 1500–ca. 1900); Rembrandt School; Rembrandt van Rijn; Steen, Jan Havicksz.; Still life; Van Gogh, Vincent; *Vanitas, vanitas* still life; Women artists

Bibliography
Campbell, Lorne. *Renaissance Portraits: European Portrait Painting in the Fourteenth, Fifteenth and Sixteenth Cen-*

turies. New Haven: Yale University Press, 1990.

Chapman, H. Perry. *Rembrandt's Self-Portraits: A Study in Seventeenth-Century Identity.* Princeton, NJ: Princeton University Press, 1990.

Kris, Ernst, and Otto Kurz. *Legend, Myth, and Magic in the Image of the Artist.* New Haven: Yale University Press, 1979.

Popper-Voskuyl, N. "Self-Portraiture and Vanitas Still-Life Painting in Seventeenth-Century Holland in Reference to David Bailly's Vanitas Oeuvre." *Pantheon* 31 (1973): 58–74.

Raupp, Hans-Joachim. *Untersuchungen zu Künstlerbildnis und Künstlerdarstellung in den Niederlanden im 17. Jahrhundert.* Hildesheim/Zurich/New York: Georg Olms Verlag, 1984.

Wittkower, Rudolf, and Margot Wittkower. *Born under Saturn: The Character and Conduct of Artists: A Documented History from Antiquity to the French Revolution.* New York: Norton, 1963.

Sins and punishments

Explicitly labeled depictions of the Seven Deadly Sins occur in a handful of fifteenth- and sixteenth-century paintings. These anecdotal and genre scenes differ from the traditional medieval allegorical female figures of vices. They arose in a period of ecclesiastical emphasis on penance and offered pictorial counterparts to a flourishing literature of sin.

Hieronymus Bosch's *Tabletop of the Seven Deadly Sins and the Four Last Things* (ca. 1470–1490); (Color Plate 1) provides one of the best-known examples. A central medallion resembling both the all-seeing eye of God and a mirror contains compartments with genre scenes enacting the sins. Corner roundels of the Four Last Things (death, judgment, hell, and heaven) remind the viewer of the consequences of sin, and inscriptions carry admonitions. The work expresses traditional Catholic doctrine. Circumstances gave the doctrine new significance.

The Church increasingly stressed the importance of penance in the wake of more than a century of turmoil and challenges to its spiritual and secular authority. The sacrament became important because it offered a powerful means of controlling the faithful—it provided the doorway to participation in the Eucharist and hence to salvation. The requirement that a valid confession be thorough generated a vast body of literature for both clergy and laity, often called "mirrors," since they were meant to provide penitents with mirrors of their souls. Like Bosch's painting, the texts translated abstract notions of sin into terms of daily human activities.

Related to these treatises is the *Ars Moriendi* (Art of Dying; 1464), a popular handbook to assist the clergy in the care of the dying. The book describes and illustrates the sins that tempt the dying and provides guidance on overcoming them and securing salvation.

Related literary traditions include treatises on the Four Last Things, descriptions of the pilgrimage of life, and accounts of visionary journeys to the Other World. The second type tells of the two roads through life; the pilgrim on the road

to hell encounters personifications of the sins. Accounts of voyages to the Other World include the *Visions of Tondal* (or Tundale), which records the journey undertaken by a knight's soul during a seeming death of the body. The soul saw the hideous physical torments inflicted on sinners, and the joys of the blessed.

Since visionary texts draw explicit connections between sins and types of punishments, one might expect to find similar associations in hell images, and this does occur occasionally. The hell roundel on Bosch's *Tabletop* labels the sins being punished. Scholars have attempted similarly to identify sins and torments in other images of hell by Bosch, though the artist himself did not provide labels.

Other paintings may deal with the theme of sin in a less diagrammatic way. Bosch's *Ship of Fools* (ca. 1495–1500) and *Death of a Miser* (ca. 1495–1500) may be fragments of a larger work depicting all seven sins. His *Garden of Earthly Delights* (ca. 1510–1515) denounces lust, while the *Haywain Triptych* (ca. 1500–1505) condemns avarice. Early sixteenth-century paintings of the Fall of the Rebel Angels may address pride. Landscape backgrounds in the works of Joachim Patinir have been interpreted as allegories of the pilgrimage of life. Humanist allegorical interpretations of sin occur in works such as Pieter Bruegel the Elder's *Two Monkeys* (1562) and Maerten van Heemskerck's *Cycle of the Vicissitudes of Human Affairs* (1564). The variety and number of sixteenth-century images testify both to the significance of the theme and the impact of new modes of thought such as humanism.

Janey L. Levy

See also Active life, active virtues; Allegorical traditions; Bosch, Hieronymus; Carnal life, carnal vices; Contemplative life, contemplative virtues; Devotional images; Didactic images; Genre painting, seventeenth century; Humanism, humanist themes; Last Judgment; Manuscript illumination; Prints, early printed book and Bible illustration; Women's worlds

Bibliography

Bloomfield, Morton Wilfred. *The Seven Deadly Sins.* East Lansing: Michigan State College Press, 1952.

Gibson, Walter S. "Hieronymus Bosch and the Mirror of Man: The Authorship and Iconography of the *Tabletop of the Seven Deadly Sins.*" *Oud Holland* 87 (1973): 205–226.

Kren, Thomas, and Roger S. Wieck. *The Visions of Tondal from the Library of Margaret of York.* Malibu, CA: Getty Museum, 1990.

Tentler, Thomas N. *Sin and Confession on the Eve of the Reformation.* Princeton, NJ: Princeton University Press, 1972.

Sluijters, Jan (1881–1957)

Jan Sluijters, born in 's Hertogenbosch in 1881 and educated at the Rijksacademie in Amsterdam, is regarded as one of the pioneers of modern painting, although he turned his back on modernism as early as 1916. After three years abroad (1904–1907) he returned to Holland to encourage the innovation of artists such as Leo Gestel and Piet Mondrian with his paintings from 1906 and 1907 that were themselves influenced by the Parisian avant-garde. The interaction between Mondrian and Sluijters resulted in Luminism, a coloristic, disciplined way of painting. Because of his later joining of Expressionism with realism Sluijters, who painted for a time in Bergen, Laren, and Staphorst (Overijssel) as well as in Amsterdam, was considered to be *the* representative of the Dutch painting tradition during the 1920s and 1930s.

Winning the Prix de Rome in 1904 was important for his development as an artist. After Rome, Sluijters used a grant from the Rijksacademie, contrary to policy, to become acquainted with modern art in Paris in 1906; this action made him subsequently lose the grant. Sluijters' most famous paintings, *Femmes qui s'embrassent* (1906) and *Bal Tabarin* (1907), were influenced by contemporary French Fauvism. Sluijters' rendering of the electric light effects and the celebrating masses in *Bal Tabarin* can be compared especially to the *Moulin de la Galette* (1906) by Kees van Dongen. Van Dongen was also a source of inspiration for Sluijters' later work (the female nudes of 1911–1912). The landscapes that Sluijters painted in Laren, *Octoberzon* (1910) and the series *Maannacht*, I–IV (1912), reveal his interest in the work of Vincent van Gogh. After Sluijters had been under the influence of Futurism and the Cubists of Montparnasse (1913–1916), he worked once again in a figurative Expressionist style that eventually won him distinction as a true Dutch painter.

Anita Hopmans

See also Avant-garde; Bergen; Gestel, Leo; Laren; Mondrian, Piet; Toorop, Jan; Van Dongen, Kees; Van Gogh, Vincent

Bibliography

Haveman, Mariëtte et al. "Jan Sluijters, 'een vooze perversiteit.'" *Kunstschrift* 37 (1993): 10–47.

Hopmans, Anita. *Jan Sluijters 1881–1957: Aquarellen en tekeningen.* 's Hertogenbosch: Noordbrabants Museum; Zwolle: Waanders, 1991.

Juffermans, Jan, and Noortje Bakker. *Jan Sluijters: Schilder.* Mijdrecht: Tableau, 1981.

Soldiers

With the advent of war in the Netherlands during the late sixteenth century, the Dutch had to support and tolerate the presence of troops in their provinces. Early images of soldiers often reflected a negative perception engendered by the cruelties of the occupying Spanish forces during the initial stages of the Eighty Years' War (1568–1648). When the fighting moved farther south during the seventeenth century, the soldiers usually encountered by civilians were those hired by the United Provinces and garrisoned in the major cities. This army of the States General consisted mostly of English, Scottish, German, and French troops, a mixture of mercenary and professional soldiers typical of European armies at the time. After the Twelve Years' Truce (1609–1621), improved relations between the military and civilians altered the image of the soldier from one of brutality and vanity to one of refinement and gallantry, although the images still conveyed a sense of someone on the periphery of the general populace.

The depiction of soldiers as an independent subject for art was introduced into the Netherlands through sixteenth-century German and Swiss prints that represented many aspects of the soldier's life, from the campsite to the battlefield. Initially, early-sixteenth-century Netherlandish artists such as Lucas van Leyden produced very similar images of soldiers, but with the outbreak of war in the Dutch provinces, representations began to reflect the contemporary situation. Hendrick Goltzius' prints of flamboyant officers arrogantly posing in their finest attire do show an influence from the earlier German tradition, but now the soldiers are pictured before recognizable Dutch towns with encampments in the background.

During the early stages of the Eighty Years' War, a type of painting depicting the violent treatment of peasants by soldiers developed in the Southern Netherlands and soon appeared in the North. Images of the plunder of villages and the abuse of civilians are found in the art of Esaias van de Velde, Pieter de Molijn, and Philips Wouwerman after 1620, but the severity of the violence had greatly diminished compared with Flemish examples. In the North, the atrocities of Spain's Army of Flanders were mostly in the past, although by no means forgotten. Reforms instituted by Prince Maurits to impose discipline and inspire faithful service through regular pay were quite effective for the Dutch army and decreased the fearful or scornful perception of soldiers by civilians.

Typical Dutch images of the soldier are *cortegardjes* (guardroom scenes), produced by artists such as Pieter Codde and Willem Duyster in Amsterdam and Jacob Duck in Utrecht during the 1620s and 1630s. These paintings depict soldiers playing cards, gambling, smoking, and drinking, often with women camp followers, which were common aspects of the tedious life in garrisons. Some of these images appear to be satirical or comical, but for the most part they are uncritical representations of the life of the soldier, which was entirely different from that of the ordinary citizen. Artists seem to have taken an interest in describing ways of living and manners of dress unlike their own.

By the 1640s, attitudes toward soldiers had changed to a more sympathetic view, and an increased desire for an end to the war was expressed in most Dutch towns. It was also at this time that the soldier appeared more frequently in genre paintings by Gerard Ter Borch and Pieter de Hooch, often depicted as a gallant and sophisticated officer in the presence of well-dressed women. This type continued to be seen until the end of the century and into the next, growing in refinement as French tastes influenced Dutch society. In the nineteenth century, an interest in depicting famous heroic officers within battle scenes and interiors emerged in art. At the same time, however, a revived interest in the Golden Age led artists such as Herman Frederik Karel ten Kate to paint guardroom scenes with seventeenth-century soldiers.

Since the time of the Eighty Years' War, Dutch artists had created a specialty of images focused on the more intimate and common aspects of a soldier's existence. Despite the fact that the art eventually represented a figure moving within society, the very nature of his foreign status, different manner of dress, and pursuit of alternate activities kept the soldier in a position as a fascinating outsider.

J.M. Kennedy

See also Bramer, Leonaert; Eighty Years' War; Genre painting, eighteenth century; Genre painting, seventeenth century; Goltzius, Hendrick; Nationalism; Ter Borch, Gerard; Van Leyden, Lucas; War and warfare; Wouwerman, Philips

Bibliography

Deursen, A.T. van. *Plain Lives in a Golden Age: Popular Culture, Religion, and Society in Seventeenth-Century Holland.* Cambridge: Cambridge University Press, 1991.

Schama, Simon. *The Embarrassment of Riches: An Interpretation of Dutch Culture in the Golden Age.* New York: Alfred A. Knopf, 1987.

Sutton, Peter C. *Masters of Seventeenth-Century Dutch Genre Painting.* Philadelphia: Philadelphia Museum of Art, 1984.

Stained glass

The term in English derives from one specific glass painting technique, silver stain, invented in the early years of the fourteenth century to color white glass yellow. In general the term is used for leaded windows, whether they are colored or not. Stained glass must have risen by 1450 in the Northern Netherlands to a position of preeminence among forms of monumental painting. Production has continued ever since with minor interruptions, even though the significance accorded to stained glass has not always stayed the same. Monumental stained glass is predominantly destined for public edifices—first of all, churches and prominent civic buildings.

Fifteenth and Sixteenth Centuries

The basic practice in this period was to follow the medieval technique of making stained glass—that is, pieces of colored glass were put together with strips of lead to fit the forms of windows. An indispensable component is pot metal glass, colored throughout by the addition of metallic oxides to the molten glass during manufacture. Another type of window glass is flashed glass, a basically white glass with a thin layer of color, mostly red or blue. Modeling used on figures is achieved by black or brown ferrous paint that has to be fired like the above-mentioned silver stain and by the sanguine colors known since the fifteenth century.

The loss of medieval and early Renaissance stained glass is understandably catastrophic. The only fifteenth-century remnants *in situ* are heraldic devices (Leiden, St. Annahofje). Some fragments are preserved from the church of St. Walburg in the city of Zutphen in Gelderland (ca. 1475; Amsterdam, Rijksmuseum). There is not much left from the first half of the sixteenth century either—only fragments (ca. 1530; Breda, Our Lady's Church), and much-restored windows (ca. 1530, Gouda, St. John's Church; 1541 and 1547, The Hague, St. Jacob's Church).

The golden age of glass painting is connected with the activity of the glass painter Dirck Crabeth (active ca. 1540–1574) from Gouda, and with the glazing campaign of St. John's there after the fire of 1552. This church is the only one in the Netherlands that still possesses its complete Renaissance glazing (1555–1572, 1594–1603). Crabeth executed the largest share, sometimes assisted by his workshop. His strength lies in his technical mastery and his sensitive rendering of the Dutch landscape, populated with small genre figures (Fig. 126). Among the other contributors were Dirck's younger brother Wouter (documented between 1559–1589), Willem Tybaut (ca. 1524–1597) from Haarlem, and Antwerp glaziers. They worked from designs by Lambert van Noort (ca. 1520–1570/1571) from Amersfoort, whose innovative painted architectural backgrounds give immense depth to the windows. Stained glass had become by this time a transparent easel painting, where the whole window is treated as an unbroken pictorial space, and where leading no longer serves the artistic purpose of accentuating the painted lines. The proportion of pot metal glass was slowly diminishing to make way for rectangular panes of white glass painted in black and silver stain, a technique much applied in secular glazing in combination with roundels. The remarkably homogeneous glazing of St. John's was due to the church wardens who firmly directed the iconographic program and the overall composition. The large windows are all divided in half horizontally, the compartments above showing biblical scenes, and those below portraying donors with their patron saints. The windows are due to ecclesiastical, royal, noble, and middle-class patronage.

Since the glazing campaign continued, after an interruption, in the initial years of the Republic, St. John's possesses the earliest surviving cycle of post-conversion stained glass in the country. In spite of a different patronage (civic and from political organizations), there is a certain insistence on figural representation, and to some extent even on biblical events, to harmonize with the earlier windows. Only the work of Tybaut shows considerable difference in technique, as compared to his pre-conversion window, in his preference for monochrome shades in black paint enlivened with heraldic details in pot metal glass. The same is true of his extensive series *The Counts of Holland*, made for the new assembly hall of De Doelen, the headquarters of the militia company of Leiden (1587–1588; Leiden, Stedelijk Museum De Lakenhal).

More sixteenth-century glass can be seen in St. Nicholas' Church in Amsterdam (by Dirck Crabeth and Antwerp glaziers, the latter working from designs by Van Noort, 1555) and in the town hall of Emden, Germany (by the Amsterdam glass painter Jan Janssen, 1576). All of this is only a fraction of what had been produced in the second half of the sixteenth century, as documents and numerous *vidimus* drawings for monumental glass prove. Such designs serve as a visual record of what the window was to look like. Exceptional is the survival of many sixteenth-century glass cartoons or full-size working drawings—in some cases, the only evidence of the former existence of a window. Cartoons are the result of the transfer of the small-scale *vidimus* to the scale of the window. Unique in the world is the virtually intact ensemble of cartoons of the Gouda windows, deliberately preserved with an eye to future repairs.

Seventeenth and Eighteenth Centuries

Stained glass of this period shows remarkable changes in technique, due to the development of enamel glass painting in the sixteenth century. Enamels are vitreous colorants applied onto white glass with heat. Enamel glass painting is alien to the medieval craft in that it removes the necessity of cutting out the shapes from sheets of pot metal glass. Now the picture was painted on clear glass of regular shape, mostly rectangular panes, and leading became purely utilitarian. Work from the first half of the seventeenth century often shows a mixture of pot metal (especially in coats of arms) and enamel painted techniques, but the proportion of the latter was increasing. In addition, the late-sixteenth-century vogue for predominantly monochrome windows in black paint continued. An important change in composition is implied by the growing tendency to leave large parts of the window plain and to restrict the stained glass panels to the middle of the window space.

The tradition of donating windows for churches was maintained by the Calvinists until the beginning of the eighteenth century. Despite serious losses, there is more glass preserved from this period than from the Renaissance, with a concentration in the present province of North Holland. Exceptional cycles of intact church glazings from the seventeenth century are located in Edam (1606–1608, 1624–1625), De Rijp (1655–1657), and Oudshoorn (1666–1671), along with still-substantial parts of extant glazing found in Egmond aan den Hoef (1634), Schermerhorn (1634–1636), and Zaandam (1686–1688, 1701, Oostzijderkerk).

Most glass painters tend to remain anonymous, although the proportionate number of signed windows later is larger than in the sixteenth century. They seem to have worked, with few exceptions, from their own designs; one of them, Pieter Jansz. (1606–1672) from Amsterdam, was also a prolific designer of prints and illustrations for books and maps. Some of the best artists were active in the north of Holland: in Haarlem, Nicolas Abrahamsz. Delft (active until ca. 1618) and Pieter Holsteyn (ca. 1580/1589–1662); in Alkmaar, Jan Maertensz. Engelsman (died 1654) and Cornelis Jansz. Sparreboom (died 1713); in Hoorn, Josef Oostfries (1628–1661); and in Amsterdam, Pieter Jansz. and Gerard van Houten (died 1706).

Stained glass formed part of a new order of church decoration of distinct character. Religious subject matter, in general, had ceded to historical, allegorical (frequently concerning historical events), and mainly heraldic subjects, although it did not disappear completely. An important motif concerns the glorification of Dutch history and rights. Lengthy inscriptions are standard elements within windows in this period. The change in iconography is connected with changes in patronage. In the Republic, patronage shifted from the ecclesiastical field to the secular one, whereby individual patronage was replaced by patronage of corporate bodies. The commissions came from political and civic organizations and from such important persons as the *stadholder* and wealthy owners of country estates. As before, the political importance of the patron corresponds to the prominent placement of his window in the church.

There are fewer windows extant from the eighteenth century, and two-thirds of these are located in the province of Friesland. When commissions dried up elsewhere, stained glass continued to be made there throughout the century. The most important glass painters of the period are Ype Staak (last mentioned 1794), burgomaster of Sneek, and his brother Jurjen. By the eighteenth century the heraldic window, executed in black paint and enamel colors, had claimed exclusive rights. Since the majority of those practicing this simplified technique were less-able craftsmen, the reputation of the medium declined in time. Stained glass had been relegated to the position of a minor art.

Nineteenth and Twentieth Centuries

The revival of stained glass in the second decade of the nineteenth century is due to the experiments of amateur artists in Nijmegen and Rotterdam in a style and technique inspired by seventeenth- and eighteenth-century examples. The revival of the Gothic style that began as late as 1840 led to a more widespread use of pot metal glass, including medieval painting and leading techniques. It was, however, the church building boom of the Catholics, after the restoration of the episcopal hierarchy in 1853, in Neo-Gothic style that led to a quickly expanded production.

The oldest and most important glass workshop is that of Frans Nicolas (1826–1894), established in Roermond, in the province of Limburg, in 1855. He maintained close contact with the architect P.J.H. Cuypers (1827–1921), who had a preference for French Gothic of the Île-de-France of the thirteenth and fourteenth centuries. Other favorite models for style and composition were the late-Gothic achievements of the Rhineland, imitated by the workshops of Utrecht since the last quarter of the nineteenth century. In all of these foreign examples, medieval weak points in anatomy and perspective were corrected and represented in a detailed, realistic manner. Only few church glazings from before 1880 have survived. After 1960 many windows were removed for reasons that included a lack of finances to restore them, a need for more light, and a new Vatican policy stressing simplicity in church decoration.

After 1890 there was an increase in the use of colored stained glass for secular use. The first workshop to meet this need is 't Prinsenhof of Jan Schouten (1852–1937), founded in Delft in 1891. After initial works in the style of Renaissance and Baroque secular glazing, and after some copies of old-master paintings for screen decoration, Delft glass work was influenced by Art Nouveau. In the houses built for the well-to-do in the bigger cities, there was a true explosion of domestic decorative glazing at the turn of the century and in the 1920s. Products from The Hague have the most stylistic affinities with international Art Nouveau: The designs of flora, fauna, landscapes, and decorative females represented with sinuous lines use leading and color to full effect. The material is a most common type called cathedral glass, industrially made.

Decorative stained glass from Amsterdam follows the idiom of Nieuwe Kunst (New Art—the Dutch interpretation of the Art Nouveau aesthetic) and shows mainly spidery, linear forms in soft colors. Ornamental stained glass connected with the Amsterdam School from about 1915, on the other hand, is executed in strong, glowing colors and represents whimsical, organic forms, mollusks being a favorite. This glass is made with more expensive material (pot metal, mouth-blown, and flashed glass) and painted in black and silver stain. Famous works are the windows of Tuschinski Theater, Amsterdam (1921), and the glazing of the Scheepvaarthuis (Navigation Office, 1912–1916). This last work, atypical for its light colors, was executed by the workshop of Willem Bogtman (1882–1955), which was founded in Haarlem in 1912, and ever since has been one of the leading workshops in the country.

The two-dimensional, flat design of decorative glazing is also characteristic of most ecclesiastical and some secular commissions with figurative symbolism. These windows from the first half of the twentieth century were meant as a continuation of the wall surface and are subordinated to the architecture. It was the official style propagated by the Amsterdam Rijksacademie, first under Antoon Derkinderen (1859–1935), who designed the windows for the conference room of the Stock Exchange building (1898–1903) of architect H.P. Berlage, and later under the influential Richard N. Roland Holst (1868–1938), who was a professor there from 1918 until 1934. While the more conventional figures of Derkinderen show links with the Neo-Gothic style, Roland Holst expressed himself in a more modern, angular idiom that shows awareness of medieval art, particularly in the use of strong colors and the artistic purpose assigned to leading. In the period 1925–1940, developments in the province of Limburg constitute a counterpole to the Amsterdam style, accentuating a painterly "Baroque" approach in which the window works by virtue of its contrast with the wall. The initiator of this movement was Joep Nicolas (1897–1972) from Roermond, grandson of Frans Nicolas. Characteristic of his work is the ample use of black paint. Since the leading in his work lives a life of its own, his figural scenes seem to hover against a background of light colored glass. Nicolas is one of the few stained glass artists who have been both designer and executor of their work. The division between art and craft has been an issue in most cases since the second half of the nineteenth century.

Post–World War II reconstruction meant numerous commissions for stained glass from church authorities and the state. According to law, 1.5 percent of the total building costs of any representative state building had to be spent on design (1951), and 1 percent in the case of schools (1953). The duality between the Amsterdam and Limburg school of glass painters remained for a while. The German artist Heinrich Campendonk (1889–1957), who began teaching at the Rijksacademie in 1936, continued the monumental, two-dimensional style of his predecessors, although his language was more graphically lead-based. Instead of figurative symbolism, he focused on motifs of flora and fauna, and used light, cool colors. A change in style in Limburg at the end of the 1940s toward an eclectic manner influenced by some neo-styles (Byzantine, Romanesque, Early Gothic) and by contemporary French work put an end to this long controversy.

Monumental stained glass in the Netherlands failed to remain in touch with the modern movement in painting and, as a consequence, to become part of the language of modern architecture. Theo van Doesburg (1883–1931), one of the leading participants of De Stijl, designed some abstract windows, but the architects and the other artists of his group showed no interest for this medium. Johan Thorn Prikker (1868–1932) evolved his truly modern language for stained glass in Germany, where he lived and worked after 1904.

A greater degree of stylistic experimentation occurred after 1945 in combination with innovative techniques: *dalle de verre* (implying chunks of colored glass bonded together with cement or epoxy), glass bonded with steel, or sheets of glass glued together. The last technique, a Dutch specialty, free of religious context and of any limitations by supports in lead, concrete, or steel, opens the door to free painting in glass. Since the end of the 1960s stained glass in the Netherlands has been perceived as an artistic backwater. State patronage practically ceased to exist due to shifting interest from monumental to environmental art. Church commissions have dried up as well, a notable exception being the commission given in 1991 to Jan Dibbets (born 1941) for thirty-one windows in the cathedral of Blois in France. The few remaining workshops concentrate mainly on restoration of old glass, a task that has always been part of the work of glass painters. Research on stained glass before 1700 is being carried out by the author and others for publication in the international series *Corpus Vitrearum* (supported by the International Committee Corpus Vitrearum, which holds international colloquia of its members and publishes results of their research).

Zsuzsanna van Ruyven-Zeman

See also Amsterdam School; Applied arts; Architectural restoration; Churches; Dutch history; Gouda; Neo-Gothic; Reverse painting; Roundels; State patronage, public support; Van Doesburg, Theo

Bibliography

Bogtman, Rutger W. et al. *Glans der Goudse Glazen: Conservering 1981–1989. Een geschiedenis van behoud en beheer*. Gouda: Stichting Fonds Goudse Glazen, 1990.

Bogtman, Willem. *Nederlandsche glasschilders*. Amsterdam: Allert de Lange, 1944.

Boom, A. van der. *Monumentale glasschilderkunst in Nederland*. The Hague: Nijhoff, 1940.

Boon, Karel G. "Sixteenth-Century Cartoons for Church Windows." *Apollo* 117 (1983): 437–442.

Filedt Kok, Jan Piet et al. eds. *Kunst voor de beeldenstorm: Noordnederlandse kunst 1525–1580*. Amsterdam: Rijksmuseum; The Hague: Staatsuitgeverij, 1986.

Harten-Boers, Henry van, and Zsuzsanna van Ruyven-Zeman. *The Stained-Glass Windows in the Sint Janskerk* at Gouda: The Glazing of the Clerestory of the Choir and the Former Monastic Church of the Regulars. Corpus Vitrearum Netherlands, vol. 1. Amsterdam: The Koninklijke Nederlandse Akadamie van Wetenschap, 1996.

Hoogveld, Carine, ed. Glas in lood in Nederland 1817–1968. The Hague: SDU Uitgeverij, 1989.

Rijksen, A.A.J. Gespiegeld in kerkeglas. Lochem: De Tijdstroom, 1947.

Ruyven-Zeman, Zsuzsanna van. "Some Drawings Attributed to Wouter Crabeth, the Glass Painter from Gouda." Master Drawings 23/24 (1985/1986, published 1987): 544–551.

Ruyven-Zemen, Zsuzsanna van et al. Edam: De glazen van de Grote Kerk. Edam: Kerkvoogdij, 1994.

Swigchem, C.A. van. "Glazen en borden in de protestantse kerken in de periode van de Republiek." Bulletin van de Stichting Oude Hollandse Kerken 14 (1982): 3–24.

State and municipal art collecting and collections

Introduction

The national art museums in the Netherlands were created at the beginning of the nineteenth century. The Rijksmuseum (founded in 1800) in Amsterdam and the Mauritshuis (founded in 1816) in The Hague originally concentrated on showing their own collections, in contrast to today when the accent seems to have shifted to temporary exhibitions. These museums also then had holdings of contemporary art. The two national art museums showed Dutch art (primarily paintings) and the Rijksmuseum especially, Dutch history. As in the rest of Europe, however, classical sculpture and French and Italian paintings of the sixteenth and seventeenth centuries were considered to be the apex of artistic achievement; consequently, more than half of the paintings acquired for the Mauritshuis between 1816 and 1830 were of foreign origin. For several reasons the Mauritshuis was not especially fortunate collecting in this field.

The municipal museums started somewhat later with art and historical objects that often go back to the sixteenth century as the basis for their collections. Their second field of interest was contemporary Dutch art.

The Batavian Republic, 1795–1806

In 1795, as French troops invaded the Netherlands, the *stadholder* fled to England leaving behind his art collection. The most important part was taken to the Louvre in Paris, where the trophies of Napoleon's conquests were displayed. What remained was merged with art objects from some former public institutions to form the first national museum, which opened its doors in The Hague in 1800. The collection consisted of historical objects and Dutch, Flemish, and some French and Italian paintings. As a national museum, it was a break with Dutch tradition: Before 1795 only cities and private individuals had possessed art collections. In accordance with tradition, however, was the fact that the museum was taking care of paintings that had been left behind and exhibiting them, just as formerly the cities had done with the pos-

sessions that were relinquished by churches, cloisters, civic guards, and guilds after the conversion to Protestantism and other events.

It can be said the establishment of state museums was not a Dutch custom but an inspiration from the French. After the French Revolution, the national museums in France exhibited the confiscated art treasures of the former monarch, the nobility, and the churches. The difference in the Netherlands was that the state museum was chiefly a historical museum, for two reasons. First, the authorities wanted the general public to see the economic and political development of the Dutch Republic in the sixteenth and seventeenth centuries as an example to be followed—the catchword in this was patriotic education. The second reason was that portraits—in other words, history—predominated in this collection.

In the paintings that were collected during this period the historical emphasis is very apparent. There were also artistic reasons for buying Dutch or foreign paintings, as in the case of the acquisition of a Rembrandt, that turned out to be a Carel Fabritius, and later not even that. In the modern works acquired (only six in this period), we see the same mixture of history and art.

The Kingdom of the Netherlands and the French Occupation, 1806–1813

King Louis Napoleon (1806–1810) renamed the national art museum the Royal Museum and moved it into the former town hall of Amsterdam that recently had been transformed into a royal palace. Seven of the largest and most important paintings owned by the city of Amsterdam (among them Rembrandt's *The Nightwatch*, painted in 1642; Color Plate 5) were incorporated into this museum. Louis Napoleon spent large sums of money buying approximately two hundred seventeenth-century Dutch and Flemish paintings. These included some marine battles, but most were still lifes, interiors, and landscapes. With these acquisitions, the collection of the museum began to resemble those of eighteenth-century private collectors; however, the king was not successful in buying the international collection of his brother Lucien Bonaparte. In a significant way modern Dutch art also was furthered by the acquisitions Louis Napoleon made for the Royal Museum. After this prosperous time under Louis Napoleon, the first national museum barely survived the annexation of the Netherlands by France (1810–1813).

Willem I, 1814–1840

Willem of Orange, son of the last *stadholder*, maintained all of the art institutions of Louis Napoleon. The Royal Museum now became 's Rijksmuseum (the museum of the nation). From 1815 until the Belgian Revolt in 1830, King Willem I governed a territory that included the Netherlands, Belgium, and Luxembourg. In 1816 a series of new museums were founded, among them the Royal Cabinet of Paintings. This is now better known as the Mauritshuis, named after the building in which the Cabinet was housed in 1821. The king was more interested in this museum than in the Rijksmuseum, in part because the collections of his father and grandfather were placed in the Mauritshuis after they were brought back from Paris. Thus, the collection of the *stadholders* tacitly came into the possession of the Dutch nation.

Art objects were acquired for the museums for various reasons. Much of the art collected was for art's sake. "One good piece by every known old or modern Dutch or Flemish master" was the guiding principle of the handbook. Second was the historical significance—an argument that was used only when an art object was not important enough artistically. For contemporary paintings, sometimes a social justification was used—for example, the need to support older artists or encourage younger ones.

Generally the museums' directors formulated the acquisition policy for Dutch and Flemish works of art, while the minister or the king responded to their suggestions. In most cases the king decided which museum should receive the acquired works, and often he decided in favor of the Mauritshuis. His most disagreeable act toward the Rijksmuseum was assigning Rembrandt's *Anatomy Lesson of Dr. Nicolaes Tulp* (1632) to the Mauritshuis in 1828; the largest part of the money for this acquisition had been raised from the auction of duplicate paintings from the Rijksmuseum that same year. In the case of foreign—often Italian and Spanish—paintings, the initiative to acquire seems to have been the king's, but he was too thrifty to build an international collection. Because those involved did try to make the national collections (at least the painting collection of the Mauritshuis and the print collection of the Rijksmuseum) representative of international developments in art, one cannot call the acquisitions policy of the state museums nationalistic.

Willem I spent the same amount of money acquiring old masters as did Louis Napoleon, but what the latter accomplished in only four years took Willem I twenty-seven years. When the origins of the acquired works are compared, no other conclusion is possible than that Louis Napoleon was more of a chauvinist for the Netherlands and Willem I more an internationalist.

Most of the contemporary art acquired by both national museums in the period 1814–1840 was purchased from the Dutch salons. Government commissions were not given, with a few exceptions. The purchases were evenly divided among the several genres and Northern and Southern artists. Modern portraits—in most cases, private commissions—were not bought, and neither were large scenes of Dutch history. The museums did not have enough money to buy, and not enough space to install, those expensive paintings. Some large scenes of Dutch, ancient, and biblical history were in this period acquired by the king and given to the museums. Since the last quarter of the nineteenth century the Rijksmuseum has acquired a great many nineteenth-century portraits and scenes of Dutch history. Only from that time have such works been thought of as belonging in a national collection. In the time of Willem I, they were made for private individuals.

The Belgian Revolt in 1830 ended the relatively prosperous state of affairs in the Dutch national museums. Political and economic circumstances prevented any acquisition of art objects until 1839. But Willem II (1840–1849) again stopped all art acquisitions for the museums. While Willem II was the most art-loving of all the Orange princes, he had a fatal effect on nineteenth-century museum policy. The new king clearly thought that art collecting was a private and not a public matter.

Stagnation, 1840–1870

In this period of stagnation for the national museums, several municipal art collections were transformed into museums and moved into their own, mostly historic, buildings. In this way museums were founded in Utrecht (Centraal Museum, 1838) and in Haarlem (Frans Hals Museum, 1862). In other cities individual bequests were the starting point, as in Rotterdam (Museum Boymans, 1847). All kinds of societies were founded to collect contemporary art or objects pertaining to local or national history. Those collections found their place in museums like the Haags Gemeentemuseum (Municipal Museum of The Hague) and the Amsterdam Stedelijk Museum (Municipal Museum).

Normally in the Netherlands a collection was auctioned after the death of its owner, as happened to the private collection of King Willem II. Through this process many important old-master and modern paintings left the country. Only in the nineteenth century did Dutch collectors begin to act to ensure the continuity of their collections. At first they donated them to the cities, as did Van der Hoop (1854) and Fodor (1860) to Amsterdam. The first important bequest to the nation was that of Dupper (1870). Bequests and donations became the chief means of enlarging the public collections, as the museums were involved in only very meager buying. The Rijksmuseum began purchasing old art again only after 1852, and contemporary art after 1860. Between 1831 and 1874, the Mauritshuis acquired only four paintings, all of them donations.

New Enthusiasm, ca. 1870–1940

One sign of the beginning of a new era was, in 1872, when the government decided that a new Rijksmuseum should be built. When the building opened its doors in 1885, it was a conglomerate of different museums for old and contemporary art, history, decorative arts, and a print room. Victor de Stuers, who as a civil servant (1875–1901) had reorganized the state museums, played an important part in the formation of this new museum. De Stuers bought art objects for the Mauritshuis and the Rijksmuseum that were not always to the liking of the directors, who made the critical objection that the historical element got the better of the artistic.

In this period the first new art historians became museum directors, among them Abraham Bredius of the Mauritshuis. This meant a major change of acquisition policy. Scholars like Bredius were no longer satisfied with "one good piece by every known old or modern Dutch or Flemish master." They preferred to show unknown aspects of artists who were already represented in the museums, and in the archives they discovered "new" old masters whose works they made an effort to acquire.

Contemporary works at the same time disappeared from

the national museums because a gap was growing between traditional and modern art. Since the end of the nineteenth century the Rijksmuseum has been devoted to collecting only the art of the past, as the Mauritshuis had been since 1838. The collecting of contemporary art became the task of municipal museums.

Most municipal museums were aggregations of historical material, old art, and contemporary art. Amsterdam's was different, however, because the largest part of the city's collection of old art was gathered in the Rijksmuseum. That meant that the Stedelijk Museum of Amsterdam held some historical material and contemporary art but no old art. In the beginning this museum was primarily a building to hold exhibitions; the modern art collection of the city of Amsterdam was started only in 1909.

Also in this period a series of new national museums were established with private donations or bequests as the basis for their support. The most important of these is the Rijksmuseum Kröller-Müller at Otterlo (1937), with its international collection of modern art (works by Van Gogh, Seurat) and some older art as well. In the 1920s the director of the Rijksmuseum in Amsterdam tried again to build an international collection—for example, a Goya portrait was acquired—but too little money was available to spend on developing a representative international collection. In 1883 a society was formed to stop the export of Dutch art. The Rembrandt Society, as it is called, still exists and is still supporting national, provincial, and municipal museums with its acquisitions.

After 1945

During World War II and the German occupation (1940–1945), museum acquisitions were scaled down, and they continued to be during the years it took to reconstruct the Netherlands. Nevertheless, Willem Sandberg, director of the Stedelijk Museum in Amsterdam from 1945 to 1963, laid the foundation for the most important international collection of modern art in the Netherlands—a collection that was at first European and later included American art. Sandberg acquired a series of paintings by Kasimir Malevich (1878–1935) and brought into the Stedelijk the private collection of Regnault with works of Marc Chagall.

The Dutch economy started to revive in the middle of the 1950s. Since that time there has been an explosion in the number of new museums. Cities that did not before have a museum established one. Several provincial capitals founded or enlarged their museums, among them Assen (in Drente) and 's Hertogenbosch (in North Brabant). The emphasis in collecting shifted to modern art, in part because old masters became too expensive. The collections of the largest municipal museums became international in character: This is the case with the Van Abbe Museum (Eindhoven), the Groninger Museum (Groningen), the Haags Gemeentemuseum (The Hague), and the Museum Boymans-van Beuningen (Rotterdam). Most of the smaller municipal museums restrict themselves to Dutch contemporary art.

Because the original Kröller-Müller collection was not to be enlarged, that museum started a collection in a new field—international modern sculpture. The last national museum formed in the Netherlands, the Vincent van Gogh Museum in Amsterdam (1972), collects the nineteenth-century French art that inspired Van Gogh. The Rijksmuseum in Amsterdam and the Mauritshuis collect steadily in their own field of old Dutch art. The Museum Boymans-van Beuningen is the only Dutch museum that is also buying old-master paintings from foreign schools.

Conclusion

In the last two centuries of national art collecting in the Netherlands there has been a shift from making a historical collection through art in general to making a collection of the art of the past. One thing, however, has stayed the same—every museum director since 1800 has welcomed a painting by Rembrandt.

Creating financial support for the national and municipal collections was, at first, a matter for state and local governments. From 1850 to 1940, however, donations and bequests became the chief means of enlarging the collections. After 1945 it was again primarily government money that was spent on the collections. In spite of several attempts to collect international old art, the national art collections have stayed predominantly Dutch. The same is true for the municipal museums with collections of old art.

The only national museum for modern art, the Rijksmuseum Kröller-Müller, has an international orientation, as do the larger municipal collections. The overall international development of twentieth-century art can be studied in these several collections. The smaller municipal and provincial museums are mostly as they started—collections of objects of art and history, and local or Dutch contemporary art. All collect slowly but steadily in their own fields of interest, and in the acquisition of important works they are helped by the private Rembrandt Society or by local or central government.

Ellinoor Bergvelt

See also Art history, history of the discipline; Hammacher, A.M.W.J.; House of Orange-Nassau; Kröller-Müller, Hélène E.L.J.; Nationalism; State patronage, public support; World Wars I and II

Bibliography

Bergvelt, Ellinoor. "Tussen geschiedenis en kunst. Nederlandse nationale kunstmusea in de negentiende eeuw." In *Verzamelen: Van rariteitenkabinet tot kunstmuseum.* Edited by Ellinoor Bergvelt, Debora J. Meijers, and Mieke Rijnders. Heerlen: Openuniversiteit; Houten: Gaade, 1993.

Duparc, F.J. *Een eeuw strijd voor Nederlands cultureel erfgoed.* The Hague: Staatsuitgeverij, 1975.

Hinterding, Erik, and Femke Horsch. "'A Small but Choice Collection'": The Art Gallery of King Willem II of the Netherlands (1792–1849)." *Simiolus* 19 (1989): 5–122.

Kempers, Bram. "Aandelen in onsterfelijkheid. Museaal

mecenaat, particulier initiatief en overheid." In *De hulpbehoevende mecenas: Particulier initiatief, overheid en cultuur, 1940–1990*. Edited by C.B. Smithuijsen, 72–129. Amsterdam: Boekmanstichting; Zutphen: Walburg, 1990.

Knoef, J. "De verzamelaar A. van der Hoop." *Jaarboek Amstelodamum* 42 (1948): 50–72.

Oxenaar, R.W.D. et al. *Kröller-Müller: Honderd jaar bouwen en verzamelen*. Haarlem: J. Enschedé, 1988.

Pieters, Din. *Uit de collectie*. Amsterdam: Stedelijk Museum, 1989.

Thiel, P.J.J. van. "Chronological History of the Rijksmuseum Painting Collection." In *All the Paintings of the Rijksmuseum in Amsterdam: A Completely Illustrated Catalogue*, 10–47. Amsterdam: Rijksmuseum; Maarssen: Gary Schwartz, 1976.

Vries, A.B. de. "Koninklijk Kabinet van Schilderijen." In *150 Jaar: Koninklijk Kabinet van Schilderijen; Koninklijke Bibliotheek; Koninklijk Penningkabinet*, 51–90. The Hague: Staatsuitgeverij, 1967.

State patronage, public support

The policy of the Dutch government—on the municipal, provincial, and national levels—regarding the visual arts in the nineteenth and twentieth centuries continued to build on what had been general practice during the time of the Republic—namely, the commissioning of works from artists and the purchasing of works of art on the market by *stadholders*, regents, citizens, churches, and administrative institutions. Policy is a continuation of earlier forms of mediation: There is patronage in the sense of commission-granting; and there is an art market in the sense of purchasing without a client–commissioner relation. But the differences in the later centuries will gradually become clearer.

A Framework for Government's Intervention in Culture, 1795–1810

Dutch patriots and the French King Louis Napoleon used foreign examples in setting up a unified Dutch state. New regulations that provided for a separation of church and state and rights for established citizens indirectly influenced cultural life and provisions favorable to the arts. The constitution and the "enlightened" thoughts with which it was related embraced ideas about civilization that were implemented by measures affecting education, sciences, and art. The central government reserved funds for art and for organizations in which officials and advisers could formulate rules, procedures, and objectives. In imitation of the national museums in France, a museum was founded in the Netherlands. In this way the state took care of the inheritance of the House of Orange. The collection was expanded, and after 1808 there were exhibitions of living masters. After the example of the Institut de France and the Paris Académie, plans were created for Dutch institutions; in 1808 the Koninklijk Instituut van Wetenschappen, Letterkunde, en Schone Kunsten (Royal Institute of Sciences, Literature, and Fine Arts) was founded. Young artists received grants for study and travel.

Many of the greatest plans, like the one for a national monument in 1879, remained unexecuted, and mainly the contributions were nonfinancial, like the confiscated properties of closed monasteries and guilds and then the buildings and the collections of the House of Orange. Small budgets were reserved for their upkeep and presentation and for adding to the existing collections. This money was used by officials, whose task or partial task it was to look after art in the public interest.

A Long Series of Expansions Alternated with Cutbacks, 1810–1950

Under King Willem I, who returned in 1813 and was crowned king in 1815, came institution of a Prix de Rome in 1817, implementation of plans for a Royal Academy in 1820, and, in spite of several interruptions, creation of a Department for Education, Arts, and Sciences within the Ministry of Domestic Affairs. Willem I made an effort to finance purchases for the museums (which, by the way, did not have a clear nationalist accent), and he commissioned state portraits and some historic pieces (which did propagate a national symbolism). He supported the existing organizations but did not bring about the formulation of a coherent policy. There were also cutbacks and reorganizations. After 1830 the conflict with Belgium led to stagnation in the purchase of paintings; the ardor diminished because ambitious plans turned out to be difficult to implement. The establishment of the monarchy perpetuated central decision making, which went further than the incidental commissions and purchases, but the small size of the state apparatus stood in the way of systematic expansion and greater independence in the fostering of culture.

The government's limited intervention in art and its fragile character were shown clearly in 1850 at the auction of the private collection of King Willem II, where the government did not interfere; they also were shown in 1851 at the abolishment of the Vierde Klasse (Fourth Class) of the since 1816 re-named Koninklijk *Nederlandsch* Instituut van Wetenschappen, Letterkunde en Schone Kunsten (Royal Dutch Institute of Sciences, Literature, and Fine Arts), which had special responsibility for art. Increasingly, it was societies and cities that devoted themselves to museums, monuments, and living masters; following in their footsteps were private collectors, who, after 1860 especially, left their collections to the government for the benefit of a public museum.

In the process of formulating objectives, many thoughts were expressed that would be later elaborated, refined, and become firmly fixed in an organizational sense: strengthening national identity, preserving the cultural inheritance, civilizing the people, contributing to the education of artists, and stimulating the economy. What was new was the connection of these thoughts, coming partly from an older time and partly from the sphere of enlightened thinkers, with public administration. But the political thinking at the time stood in the way of further expansion of government. During the political debates of 1862, the influential liberal jurist Johan Rudolph Thorbecke influenced thinking in the Tweede Kamer (Lower House of the States General [comparable to the U.S.

House of Representatives]) with his statement that government should not interfere in the forming of opinions about art. The representatives of religious denominations, using other arguments, limited the influence of the central government: The anti-revolutionaries (a group of Protestants, united in a party under that name) wanted limitation in the name of "sovereignty in one's own circle"; the Catholics held this opinion on the basis of the "principle of subsidiariness" (sub-sidiariteitsbeginsel)—namely, that higher government institutions must refrain from intervention where lower ones can provide for the wants of citizens. According to liberals, Protestants and Catholics, the government had to keep its distance when the free market, churches, and "social middle ground" were active.

Thanks to the Catholic lawyer Victor de Stuers there was to be in the context of the Catholic emancipation an expansion of care for existing cultural assets, of commissions for the decoration of public buildings, and of purchases of art. De Stuers knew how to combine his part in shaping public opinion on a national level with political influence and his official power. The revival he helped to start around 1870 resulted in the opening of the new Rijksmuseum in Amsterdam in 1885. Between 1918 and 1925, there was a formalizing and bureaucratizing of the earlier initiatives, which were now connected to a general trend. The oversight for culture became lodged in public administration. This can be seen in the growing number of museums and advisory committees, among them the Rijkscommissie voor de Monumentenzorg (National Committee for Monument Preservation, 1918), and the Rijkscommissie voor het Museumwezen (National Committee for Museum Regulations, which two years after its inauguration in 1921 produced its report), as well as the Archive Law (1918), the Museum Law (1925), and the subsidy regulation for libraries (1921). In addition, some budgets on the state level and some municipal budgets for support to artists were increased.

Commissions, purchases of works of art, and support to artists increased and sometimes succeeded one another. Financing for the arts remained marginal and incidental, but granting commissions for public buildings was given more structure, and in 1931 a special budget was reserved and control of it was given to a state advisory committee on commissions to artists. Between 1910 and 1940, major commissions for sculpture, stained glass windows, and murals were given by the national government, municipalities, or institutions like universities and the Nederlandse Spoorwegen (Dutch Railroad). Many of these commissions were given for works of art to decorate important works of architecture: the Beurs (the Stock Exchange building designed by H.P. Berlage), the Academiegebouw of the University of Groningen (where the young professor Johan Huizinga put himself forward, without much success, as critic of the government's architect), the town hall of Amsterdam, the Amstel railway station there, and the building of the Hoge Raad (Supreme Court) in The Hague.

All of the initiatives together gave rise to the first systematic reflection with learned pretensions. The socialist alderman of Amsterdam, Emanuel Boekman, wrote history profusely

critical of the neglect of culture by the government in the period after 1840. His dissertation *Overheid en Kunst in Nederland* (Government and Art in the Netherlands) from 1939 shows an increasing historical awareness and a more learned tendency than existed with previous generations, but the polemical strain has not disappeared: The government neglects culture and must give more care to it. In reaction to the German invasion of the Netherlands, the Jewish social-democrat Boekman committed suicide.

The German occupiers guaranteed a structural revival of government oversight of culture. The Germans established the Kultuurkamer, a public agency with a collecting policy focused on figurative art, and required artists to join it if they wanted to continue to practice their profession. As early as November 1940 there was a reorganization: The Ministry of Education, Arts, and Sciences was dissolved into a Department of Education, Science, and the Protection of Culture and a Department for Peoples' Education and Arts. Political propaganda was planned more than ever before, and Dutch artists were used in the plans.

The relationships formed in resistance movements were used to create the Federatie van Kunstenaarsverenigingen (Federation of Artists' Societies) in 1945 and, shortly after that, the Raad voor de Kunst (Council for the Arts). The first postwar minister of the reunited Ministry of Education, Arts, and Sciences, the socialistic theologian Gerardus van der Leeuw, promoted the concept of a general, unrestricted cultural policy. He attracted advisers from the art world, started a move toward administrative independence for the arts as a national policy, and published the book *Nationale Cultuurtaak* (National Task with Respect to Culture) in 1947 after his short term as minister. The scarcity and frugality of the years between 1945 and 1952 meant a financial slump compared to the years during the war, but organizational and ideological conditions were created then for what would come to bloom in the next decade.

Systematic Expansion, Independence, and Rhetoric of an Art Policy, 1950–1980

The establishment of the welfare state was coupled with the rise of an art policy. The weakening of the "pillars"—the interconnected political parties, broadcasting corporations, unions, and other organizations that shared the same basic beliefs—removed a barrier for the further development of a central art policy. The artists themselves took an active part in this; it was they who were among the very few who had organized as a group in the struggle against the German occupation during World War II. Then came the period of boom and the steady increase of taxation income, followed by an enormous growth in the number of institutions and a growth of existing institutions in a financial, organizational, and ideological context. The Voorlopige Raad voor de Kunst (Provisional Council for the Arts), created in 1947, became permanent in 1955, and achieved legal status in 1977. The Contra-Prestatie Regeling (Counter-Performance Regulation) from 1949, which was aimed at providing support to living artists and became known as the Beeldende Kunstenaars

Regeling (Visual Artists Regulation), underwent alterations and name changes in 1956 and again in 1969 and 1975. The Ministry of Public Housing, the Ministry of Education and Sciences, and several municipalities continually increased the "percentage regulations" that provided for commissions to artists as part of the budgeted expense for new buildings.

Art policy grew along with the general increase of government and obtained a somewhat larger place in it—depending on budget appropriations—of approximately one-tenth to one-half percent. From 1919 until 1965, the Afdeling Kunst (Department of Art) fell under the jurisdiction of the Ministry of Education, Art, and Sciences; after that it came under Directie Kunsten (Arts Management) in the Ministry of Culture, Recreation, and Social Work. The clearest exponent of what, after 1970, was called "art policy" is the policy memorandum: For international policy it is the *Nota betreffende de Internationale Culturele Betrekkingen* (Memoranda regarding International Cultural Relations) of 1970; for national policy it is the *Discussienota* (Discussion Memorandum) of 1972 and the *Nota Kunst en Kunstbeleid* (Memorandum on Art and Art Policy) of 1976. Memorandums became the nucleus of a widespread opinion making in official explanations, budgets, parliamentary debates, community discussions, public polemic (in newspapers, magazines, trade journals, and later on television), protest actions by artists, research reports, and scientific studies. New objectives—social relevance, horizontal and vertical spreading of culture—were formulated, criticized, and adjusted. A rhetoric with its own dynamics was created. The policy domain was visibly independent, and a cycle was formed that could only be followed by experts: formulation of objectives; their implementation; judgments by advisory committees, factions, official work groups, and researchers; adjustment; and reformulation. This policy cycle expanded with new phenomena: cultural education; art lending (which developed in several forms after its introduction in 1951 and grew tremendously between 1972 and 1980); several subsidy regulations for the purchasing of art by private collectors and later also by museums; and contributions to artistic education and amateur practice of art.

Reorganizations, Redistribution, and Reconsideration Since 1980

The perception that there were limits to economic growth intensified a political and official review that also involved the arts sector. In 1982 the central part of art policy came under the protection of the Ministry of Welfare, Public Health, and Culture, where, after some reorganization, the Main Department of Visual Arts, Architecture, and Design was created. In 1985 the media policy came under what is today called the Directoraat-Generaal Culturele Zaken (General Directorate of Cultural Affairs). In 1989 the libraries were added to this entity, which already included the arts, museums, monuments, archives, and the media. Because of these organizational mergers, it seemed that budgets were increasing, but financial growth was stagnating.

The most radical policy measure was the decision, made in 1984, to abolish by 1987 the Beeldende Kunstenaars Regeling (Visual Artists Regulation), abbreviated BKR. Given the size of the budget (one hundred thirty million guilders), the number of artists supported (expanded from two hundred in 1960 to thirty-eight hundred in 1983), and the quantity of art works acquired, the effects were far-reaching. The BKR's position within the Ministry of Social Services disappeared, and eighty million guilders were transferred to the Ministry of Welfare, Public Health, and Culture, which allocated this money for implementation of policy by provinces and the four largest cities as part of "decentralization." The lower governments used this money for different purposes, dividing it among art-lending programs (there was also a national organization for this, which has had different names), projects, exhibitions, publications, purchases, and commissions. But generally there was a tendency to unite all of these activities in a Center for Visual Arts with its own staff, office, exhibition space, and official policy memorandum or paragraph in a municipal cultural document. In spite of retrenchment, the field of policy continued to become more independent.

The state museums also underwent changes. They became more independent, just like the Rijksarchiefdienst (National Archive Service), the Rijksdienst voor de Monumentenzorg (National Service for Monument Preservation), and the Rijksdienst voor het Oudheidkundig Bodemonderzoek (National Service for Archeological Soil Research) with whom they are related in the area of cultural preservation. This independence means that the staff lose their status as government officials, that the form of management becomes like a foundation or related corporation, and that the institution is allowed more elbowroom than was already possible through "budget-financing," which had replaced the supply of operational shortages. In contrast with the largely subsidized theater companies, which saw themselves faced with declining numbers of customers, the museums (their number reaching almost nine hundred, of which about ten percent have an art collection) could generate much of their own income because they received an increasing number of visitors—from over two-and-one-half million in 1950 to twenty-two million in 1990. Foreign tourists account for part of the rise in ticket sales (about forty percent since 1980), but visiting museums is also an important part of the national recreation.

The establishment of funds—that is, subsidized institutions with their own budgets and their own corporate identities—is part of the process—like decentralization and becoming more independent—of striving for smaller government. Politicians and officials want again to concentrate on core tasks and be able to delegate the implementation of policy to autonomous organizations. Founded in 1987, the Fonds voor de Beeldende Kunsten, Bouwkunst en Vormgeving (Fund for the Visual Arts, Architecture, and Design), which grants a wide range of individual subsidies, is part of a still broader fund system for the creative arts that forms a general administration. The subsidies for exhibitions, presentations, and purchases by museums, and for commission grants are, with the endorsement of the Raad voor de Kunst, administered by the Mondrian Stichting (Mondrian Foundation), which dispenses about twenty-five million guilders a year.

The endeavor to reduce the central government does not lead to simplification in organizations, legislation, and rhetoric. There exists a multiplicity of institutions, with new or changed objectives, each with its own budget and personnel: among them are the "thinned-down" Rijksdienst Beeldende Kunst (National Service for the Visual Arts); the Nederlands Architectuur Instituut (Netherlands Architecture Institute) in Rotterdam: the Nederlands Vormgevings Instituut (Netherlands Design Institute) and the Rijksacademie voor Beeldende Kunst (National Academy of Fine Arts) in Amsterdam; and the Jan van Eyck Akademie in Maastricht and Ateliers '63 in Haarlem. Operating at some distance from the government-subsidized research institutions, such as the Boekmanstichting (Boekman Foundation), are the academic departments (Art and Art Policy, Cultural Studies, and Art and Culture Science) at the universities in Groningen, Amsterdam, and Rotterdam, respectively and commercial research offices, which sometimes also give organizational advice and provide interim managers. The expertise of the mediators is expanded with expertise from the business world, of which marketing and public relations are a part, a trend that is strengthened by the emergence and growth of art-sponsoring by companies.

Reorganizations and changed rhetoric cannot cover up the fact that some policy dilemmas are permanent. Since 1974 the Sociaal en Cultureel Planbureau (Social and Cultural Planning Agency) has published a report every two years with cultural statistics furnished by the Centraal Bureau van de Statistiek (Central Bureau of Statistics). This data supports the conclusion that participation in culture is divided unevenly among the population and that people with a higher status, good education, and coming from a milieu where culture is valued are strongly represented. For those attempting to legitimize an art policy in a democratic society, where the dissemination of culture—albeit under different names—has remained a policy ideal, this finding points to a dilemma. Must the government guarantee a supply of culture that its advisers regard as of a high level artistically or should it take the interest of the public into consideration?

The striving for continuing government control is also permanent, as evidenced by the Kunstplan (Art Plan) phenomenon after 1988. This is a policy document that is drawn up for four years, with a recommended procedure attached. The *Nota Cultuurbeleid 1993–1996* (Culture Policy Memorandum) from 1992 shows less enthusiasm than the documents from the 1970s and in that sense builds on the *Notitie Cultuurbeleid* (Cultural Policy Notice) of 1985. There is striving for a practical division into sectors—arts, cultural administration (including museums), media, literature, and libraries—and for putting policy on a legal basis, with a fixed relationship between the state, provinces, and municipalities in the form of a law about specific policy with respect to cultural administration—"specific" because there will remain policy areas for other ministries.

Conclusion

The bond between artist and public has become stretched because of the rise of all sorts of organizations. Intermediaries are burdened with financing on the basis of earmarked budgets raised from taxes, with making decisions and advising according to official regulations, and with implementing decisions in the light of general objectives that are put forward to become law. The independence of the world of art policy finds expression in the expansion of the required expertise and the further branching out on a lower managing level, where large, medium, and even small municipalities issue cultural memorandums that together with the memorandums, notices, and reports of the national government form the substance of art policy in the Netherlands.

Bram Kempers

See also Alberdingk Thijm, Josephus Albertus; Architectural competitions; Architectural restoration; Art history, history of the discipline; Berlage, Hendrik Petrus; Churches; France; Huizinga, Johan; Nationalism; Public housing; Public monumental sculpture (1795–1990); State and municipal art collecting and collections; Town halls; World Wars I and II

Bibliography

Advies cultuurwetgeving: Cultuurbeleid in historisch beleidsanalytisch en juridisch perspectief. Rijswijk: Sociaal en Cultureel Planbureau, 1986.

Akkerman, H.J.M. et al. *Handboek Cultuurbeleid.* The Hague: VUGA, 1989–1993.

Bevers, A.M., ed. *In ons diakonale land.* Amsterdam: Van Gennep, 1988.

Duparc, F.J. *Een eeuw strijd voor Nederlands cultureel erfgoed.* The Hague: Staatsuitgeverij, 1975.

Fenger, P. "Government and the Arts: The Netherlands." In *The Patron State: Government and the Arts in Europe, North America, and Japan.* Edited by Milton C. Cummings Jr., and Richard S. Katz, 105–135. New York: Oxford University Press, 1987.

Hoogenboom, A. "De Rijksoverheid en de moderne beeldende kunst in Nederland 1975–1848." In *Kunst en belied in Nederland.* Vol. 1, 13–79. Amsterdam: Boekmanstichting; Amsterdam: Van Gennep, 1985.

Kempers, B. "Symboliek, monumentaliteit en abstractie: Het beeld van de staat en het beroep van kunstenaar na 1789." *Amsterdams Sociologisch Tijdschrift* 14 (1987): 3–62.

Knulst, W. *Van vaudeville tot video.* Rijswijk: Sociaal en Cultureel Planbureau, 1989.

Mulder, H. *Kunst in crisis en bezetting: Een onderzoek naar de houding van Nederlandse kunstenaars in de periode 1930–1945.* Utrecht: Het Spectrum, 1978.

Oosterbaan Martinius, W. *Schoonheid, welzijn, kwaliteit: Kunstbeleid en verantwoording sinds 1945.* The Hague: Gary Schwartz/SDU, 1990.

Zoest, Rob van, ed. *Generators of Culture: The Museum as a Stage.* Amsterdam: AHA, 1989.

Steen, Jan Havicksz. (1626–1679)

With a surviving production of about three hundred history, genre, and portrait paintings, Jan Steen was one of the most prolific and versatile Dutch painters of the seventeenth century. His early works suggest he was trained in Haarlem by Adriaen and Isaack van Ostade. Jacob Campo Weyerman's claim in *De Levens-beschryvingen der Nederlandsche Konst-schilders en Konst-schilderessen* (*Biographies of Dutch Painters*, 1729) that Nicolaus Knüpfer was his teacher may be substantiated by his history and brothel paintings. In 1648 he joined the new Leiden Guild of St. Luke, and he was to spend most of his career there. He also worked in The Hague (ca. 1649–1654), where he married the daughter of the landscape painter Jan van Goyen; probably in Delft (ca. 1654–1656), where he unsuccessfully operated a brewery; and in Haarlem (1661–1670), where he produced his most ambitious works. Steen painted for the open market and for some well-off collectors, and copies of his work were recorded in his lifetime.

In his best-known paintings of proverbs, festivals, and dissolute households, Steen transformed the Bruegelian peasant tradition to present undesirable behavior of the burgher class as comic. His raucous history paintings and his portraits often apply conventions of genre painting. In many works Steen included his self-portrait, as theatrical fool (Fig. 119), head of a disorderly household, or laughing drunk inviting the viewer to join. Through such posturing and through his witty play with the boundaries of the genres, he identified himself as comic painter. These and other strategies are analogous to contemporaneous conventions of comic literature and performance.

Mariët Westermann

See also Comic modes; Commerce and commercial life; Genre painting, seventeenth century; History painting; Rhetoricians' chambers; Self-portraiture; Theater and theatricality

Bibliography

Chapman, H. Perry et al. *Jan Steen: Painter and Storyteller.* Washington, DC: National Gallery of Art; Amsterdam: Rijksmuseum; Zwolle: Waanders, 1996.

Kirschenbaum, Baruch D. *The Religious and Historical Paintings of Jan Steen.* Montclair, NJ: Allanheld and Schram, 1976.

Sutton, Peter C. "Jan Steen: Comedy and Admonition." Theme volume. *Philadelphia Museum of Art Bulletin* 78 (1982/1983).

Westermann, Mariët. "Jan Steen, Frans Hals and the Edges of Portraiture." *Nederlands Kunsthistorisch Jaarboek* 46 (1995): 298–331.

Still life

The painting of still-standing, mostly inanimate objects as pictorial subjects in their own right first came into its own as a fully independent genre of easel painting in Europe at the beginning of the seventeenth century. Dutch painters played a major role in this development, inventing many distinctive variations on the theme over the course of the century. Surviving inventories of Dutch households confirm that still life enjoyed growing popularity among the Dutch public during this period despite the fact that art theory, from the ancient Greeks through Leon Battista Alberti in the Italian Renaissance, had relegated it to the lowest rung in the hierarchy of subjects for art. In the absence of narrative, still life instead showcases the rendering of various textures and materials, a skill highly valued in the North, known in Dutch as *stofuitdrukking*.

The careful observation and masterful depiction of nature that characterized Dutch still life had a long precedent, from details in prayer books and manuscripts as early as the 1400s and 1500s to the scientific naturalism of period herbals and zoological works. "Scientific" interest extended as well to collecting for *Kunstkammern* and *Wunderkammern* (collections of art and curiosities), and it was probably for such collections that some of the first Dutch still lifes were painted, mostly of flowers and fruit, by masters such as Jacob de Gheyn II (1565–1629), Ambrosius Bosschaert the Elder (1573–1621), his most important follower Balthasar van der Ast (1593/1594–1657), and Roelandt Savery (1576/1578–1639), who worked in Prague for Rudolph II. The *bloemstuk* (flower piece) assembled a vase full of blossoms sometimes even from various seasons, depicted in such detail that botanists today have been able to precisely identify their myriad species. The bouquet was often enlivened with insects, butterflies, or lizards, also exactly rendered. Exotic shells, themselves popular collector's items of the day, sometimes further adorned the tabletop or stone niche, or they could form the sole subject of a scene. The *fruitagie* (fruit piece) employed the same vivid contrast of intense local color against a dark background to display a dish or basket of fruit; flowers and fruit could also be combined in one painting.

The international character of this early style owed partly to the flight of Flemish artists north to the newly proclaimed United Provinces of the Netherlands during the ongoing hostilities with the Spanish, who still ruled the Southern Netherlands. In the opening decades of the seventeenth century, artists working in Haarlem, Antwerp, Frankfurt-am-Main, and (to a lesser extent) Amsterdam simultaneously developed a characteristic format for another type of still life: the *ontbijtje* (breakfast piece) or *banketje* (banquet piece). Looking down over a tabletop neatly laid with a spread of food and drink, painters depicted the discrete elements of a meal clearly and with minimal overlap, again with close attention to detail and strong local color. In Haarlem, Floris van Dyck (1575–1651), Nicolaes Gillis (ca. 1580–after 1632), and Floris van Schooten (active ca. 1610–1655) painted many similar works on this pattern.

The next generation of Haarlem painters, led by Pieter Claesz. (1597/1598–1661) and Willem Claesz. Heda (1593/1594–1680/1682), took up the banquet piece and modified its format. Lowering his viewpoint so that forms overlapped more, Claesz. began in the late 1620s to draw objects together into more unified compositions, tipping glasses and rumpling tablecloths to further animate the arrangements. In the 1630s he and Heda honed their palette toward the neutral tones of the monochrome style employed also in landscape and other painting at this time; for the next few decades the prolific pair worked so closely together that it is often difficult to distinguish which of the two initiated a given innovation. Heda's banquets did tend to be more richly appointed as, for example, his *Still Life with a Gilt Goblet* (1635; Amsterdam, Rijksmuseum; Fig. 127). While Claesz. often focused on simpler foods such as herring, beer, and bread, and less expensive tableware of stoneware or pewter, Heda favored costlier pieces such as the Renaissance-style *tazza* (cup), tipped to highlight the pattern of its emboss, or an elaborately chased guild cup. *Still Life with a Gilt Goblet* displays Heda's masterful deployment of the monochrome palette across a play of surfaces, from the cool polish of the dented pewter jug to the hallmark detail of the lemon, characteristically presented with its dangling spiral of nubby peel.

A host of painters followed suit to produce banquets in the monochrome style, rendering many current attributions uncertain. Besides his own early breakfast pieces, Roelof Koets (1592/1593–1655) sometimes collaborated to add a flourish of grapes and leaves to a composition by Claesz. Heda's best pupils were his own son Gerrit (ca. 1622–1702?), who called himself "*Jonge* (young) Heda," and Maerten Boelema (1611–after 1664), called "*De Stomme*" (the Mute). Jan Jansz. van de Velde III (1619/1620–1663 or later), born in Haarlem, modeled himself after Claesz. before he went on to Amsterdam, where he adopted the color of Willem Kalf, joining a circle of still-life painters in Amsterdam that included Jan Jansz. den Uyl (1595/1596–1640) and his pupil and brother-in-law Jan Jansz. Treck (ca. 1606–1652).

Probably the most versatile and most influential painter of still life in the entire century was Jan Davidsz. de Heem (1606–1683/1684). He is variously claimed as either Flemish or Dutch: Born in Utrecht, De Heem worked in Leiden, Antwerp and Utrecht before the French invasion of Holland forced his return to Antwerp, where he remained until his death. As a result he forged a hybrid between the distinctively Dutch intimacy of his earliest works and the more flamboyant Flemish style, trying his hand at nearly every kind of still life. Under the influence of Flemish painters such as Frans Snyders and Daniel Seghers, his banquets became much larger and more extravagant, his garlands and flower pieces similarly profuse. De Heem's followers ranged far and wide: Besides his own sons Cornelis and Jan, they included Simon Luttichuys and Maria van Oosterwyck in Amsterdam, Jacob Marrel and his pupil Abraham Mignon from Frankfurt, and a troupe of Flemish painters. Disciples in Leiden alone included Pieter de Ring, Johannes Hannot, Jan Potheuck, Johannes Borman, Nicolaes van Gelder, Matthijs Naiveu, and Jan Mortel, all favoring the splendid, copious arrangements that became known as *pronkstilleven* or *pronk* still lifes (from *pronken*, to show off).

A different strain of *pronkstilleven* was created by the Rotterdam-born master Willem Kalf (1619–1693). He began by painting rustic peasant kitchens and farm scenes, then spent several years in Paris on still lifes of gold and silver vessels reminiscent of work of François Ryckhals, who may have been his teacher. When Kalf returned to Holland at mid-century, he settled in Amsterdam, where he created the mature works that won his fame: more restrained compositions of sumptuous objects, typically consisting of only a few fine vessels of glass or porcelain or a nautilus-shell goblet, with a Turkish carpet and some citrus fruit, dramatically highlighted against a dark background. The polished rendering, rich colors, and exotic subject matter appealed to the wealthy burghers of the cosmopolitan city. Among the many artists inspired by Kalf were Willem van Aelst, Juriaen van Streck, Nicolaes van Gelder (Fig. 90), Gillis Jacobsz. van Hulsdonck, Georg Hinz, and Barend van der Meer.

Unlike Kalf or De Heem, Abraham van Beyeren (1620/1621–1690) did not realize career success within his lifetime, though later connoisseurship has singled out his work. He moved constantly, in debt and getting little for his pictures. Born in The Hague, he lived and worked in Leiden, The Hague, Delft, Amsterdam, Alkmaar, and Overschie. Nonetheless, his banquets were lavish, making exuberant use of a flowing brush and often including a tiny self-portrait reflected on a shiny object in the composition—a fascinating note of self-assertion found as well in earlier still lifes by Clara Peeters of Antwerp, Claesz., and others. Van Beyeren also painted fruit, flower, fish, game, and *vanitas* still lifes, and even a few seascapes.

Like still lifes of game and other foodstuffs, pictures featuring raw fish originated within the context of large kitchen scenes painted in the sixteenth century by Pieter Aertsen and Joachim Beuckelaer. The fish specialist Pieter de Putter (died 1659) was thought to have taught Van Beyeren in this area; Isaac van Duynen (died 1677/1681) was Van Beyeren's only follower in the painting of fish. Pieter van Noort and Harmen Steenwijck also painted small, natural arrangements of fish on a table, while Jacob Gillig and Willem Ormea heaped them on a beach against a seascape.

Another exclusively Dutch invention was the *tabakje* (tobacco piece): The long-stemmed white clay "churchwarden" pipes for which Gouda was known were laid out along with a square packet of tobacco or other smoking paraphernalia such as an oval-shaped tobacco box, a brazier of glowing coals, and a length of hemp or the sulfurated nettle-stems known as *zwavelstockjes* used to light the pipe. Smoking requisites frequently appeared in the type of still life known as *vanitas*—alluding to the vanity of life, here by invoking the Latin motto *vita fumus est* (life is smoke)—but the *tabakje* could focus on the popular pleasures of tobacco and beer without overt cues supporting symbolic import. Claesz. and others did monochromes on the theme, sometimes integrating it into larger banquets. Van de Velde, Den Uyl, Treck, and Jan Fris cast it in the more dramatic lighting favored in Amsterdam, while in Dordrecht, Hubert van Ravesteyn (1638–before 1691) produced rich *tabakjes* bearing a strong resemblance to these Amsterdam works.

Scholarly opinion has long been divided over how all of these images should be understood. Many have read in the sensory delight of Dutch still life an implied critique against sinful excess. Ingvar Bergström's seminal work traced details in Dutch still life to earlier Netherlandish religious scenes, arguing that Erwin Panofsky's visual signification of "disguised symbolism"—which the renowned art historian theorized in the 1950s as the invention of early fifteenth-century Flemish painters—lingered on in still life; thus, for instance, the pocket watch that often appears in the midst of a feast was deciphered by Bergström as an admonition to temperance. Sam Segal similarly defines transience and temperance as the key themes of Dutch still life, relating the symbolic vocabulary abounding in emblems, biblical, and other literature. In *vanitas* still life many signs conspire to make the reference to human mortality obvious, but as Eddy de Jongh cautions, most still lifes leave symbolism to speculation. Other scholars have objected altogether to moralizing interpretations, granting greater significance to the sheer powers of description exercised in these works, as in N.R.A. Vroom's straightforward view of the painters of the monochrome *banketje* as "writers of the annals of daily life."

Certainly the tables laid in these images exhibited the booming prosperity of the new Dutch Republic in a display of refined material culture: damask tablecloths and Persian carpets, Chinese porcelain and delicate *façon de Venis* (Venetian style) glass, finely wrought objects of silver and gold such as an ornate saltcellar or an intricately sculpted *bekerschroef* (holder for a green glass *roemer*, a studded wine glass). Commodities both domestic and foreign bore witness to the maritime trading prowess central to the economic success of the United Provinces. While early banquets frequently topped a stack of large cheeses with a dish of butter pats, products of the prized Dutch dairy commerce, a wealth of imported goods betokened the global network established by the great Dutch trading companies that dominated world markets throughout the seventeenth century. Trade and colonization enriched the Dutch diet as much as it did the economy as a whole, overcoming the natural limitations of this tiny, cold, wet country to bring fruits such as lemons and olives from the warmer climes of the Mediterranean, pepper and other spices from the Indies, tobacco and sugar from the New World, and, later, tea from China; the crowded populace even relied for the very grain in their daily bread upon vast fields in the Baltic region. Amsterdam was renowned as the "warehouse of the world"; with the exploitation and violence that also figured in this trade history conveniently excluded from these representations, Dutch viewers could feel both pride and keen appreciation for the power and affluence they registered.

Moreover, luscious as they were, these painted meals comply remarkably with period opinions on healthy diet. Medical treatises differed from moralizing interpretations in their estimation of various foods: Many considered tobacco healthful; physicians recommended wine for all sorts of applications, esteeming it as the healthiest of drinks; and in contrast to emblem literature, in which the lemon represented false friendship, doctors hailed its miraculous powers against poison. Pictured banquets bear out the most minute rules of proper eating and drinking as recorded in these texts, right down to the condiments required for particular foods: To cite but one of countless instances, Heda's banquet (Fig. 127) supplies the pepper (in the curl of paper at right), salt (in the cylindrical saltcellar at rear), and lemon (at left) that doctors advised must temper the cold nutrition of the oysters served there.

Coupling such evidence with the celebratory devotion with which these painters depict the material world, one cannot simply dismiss these pictures as moralizing sermons on what not to do. Even if the strictest Calvinists read them as condemning the luxuries they portray, at the same time these pictures were disseminating a certain "vision of the good life." In reflecting Dutch wealth back to its consumers (Bryson), even in mediating Dutch anxiety over prosperity (Schama), these still lifes do posit that it is somehow possible to consume luxury in moderation—a proposition the Dutch clearly found decidedly to their taste.

By the late seventeenth century, artists were refining their technique to ever-greater virtuosity, finding markets for their skills throughout Europe. Otto Marseus van Schrieck (1619/1620–1678) painted butterflies and reptiles, flowers and fruit, in England, France, and for some years for the grand duke in Florence, before returning to the Netherlands with his pupil Willem van Aelst (1625/1626–after 1683). Van Aelst, working in Delft, Tuscany, and then Amsterdam, gave his own distinctive stamp to flower, fruit, game, and breakfast pieces. Haarlem-born Willem Frederik van Royen (1645–1723) painted flowers, fruit, and game in Amsterdam, Berlin, and as court painter to the Elector Palatine Frederich Wilhelm in Potsdam.

As it began, so it ended: Only flower and fruit pieces continued to be widely popular in the eighteenth century, based on the example of De Heem but shaped also by Van Aelst. Adriaen Coorte (active 1685–1723) of Middelburg silhouetted a bunch of asparagus or a few berries against a dark background in small striking paintings on paper. Meanwhile in Amsterdam, a grander scale had become the norm: Fruit and flower paintings in the style of De Heem by Jacob Walscapelle (1644–1727) fetched high prices. The last great Dutch painters of flowers and fruit were Rachel Ruysch (1664–1750) and Jan van Huysum (1682–1749), both born in Amsterdam. Van Huysum was popularly considered the greatest of all flower painters, but Ruysch, the best of Van Aelst's pupils, surpassed her master to stand second to none in achieving a natural feeling to her renderings (Fig. 128). Conraet Roepel (1678–1748) and others did successful flower pieces perpetuating the smooth style of Ruysch and Van Huysum. The heyday of Dutch still life was over, but its technical achievements and its fascination with observation and description left a vital legacy as the genre of still life thrived into modern times as the "painter's painting."

Julie Berger Hochstrasser

See also Commerce and commercial life; Emblem's and emblem books; Exotica; Gamepiece; Haarlem; Leiden; Natural history illustration; Non-Western cultural influences; Ruysch, Rachel; Subjects, subject categories, and hierarchies; Trade, exploration, and colonization overseas; Van Huysum, Jan; *Vanitas, vanitas* still life; Women artists

Bibliography
Bergström, Ingvar. *Dutch Still-Life Painting in the Seventeenth Century*. Translated by Christina Hedström and

Gerald Taylor. London and New York: Faber and Faber, 1956.

Bryson, Norman. *Looking at the Overlooked: Four Essays on Still-Life Painting.* Cambridge: Harvard University Press, 1990.

Hochstrasser, Julie Berger. "Life and Still Life: A Cultural Inquiry into Seventeenth-Century Dutch Still-life Painting." Ph.D. diss., University of California, Berkeley, 1995.

Jongh, Eddy de. "The Interpretation of Still-Life Paintings: Possibilities and Limits." In *Still Life in the Age of Rembrandt.* Edited by Eddy de Jongh et al. Auckland: Auckland City Art Gallery, 1982.

Schama, Simon. *The Embarrassment of Riches: An Interpretation of Dutch Culture in the Golden Age.* New York: Knopf, 1987.

Segal, Sam. *A Flowery Past: A Survey of Dutch and Flemish Flower Painting from 1600 until the Present.* Amsterdam: Gallery P. de Boer; 's Hertogenbosch: Noordbrabants Museum, 1982.

———. *A Fruitful Past: A Survey of the Fruit Still Lifes of the Northern and Southern Netherlands from Brueghel till Van Gogh.* Amsterdam: Gallery P. de Boer; Brunswick: Herzog Anton Ulrich-Museum, 1983.

———. *Jan Davidsz. de Heem und sein Kreis.* Utrecht: Centraal Museum; Brunswick: Herzog Anton Ulrich-Museum, 1991.

——— *A Prosperous Past: The Sumptuous Still Life in the Netherlands, 1600–1700.* Delft: Stedelijk Museum Het Prinsenhof; Cambridge: Fogg Art Museum; Fort Worth: Kimbell Art Museum, 1988–1989.

Sterling, Charles. *Still-Life Painting from Antiquity to the Twentieth Century.* 2nd rev. ed. New York: Harper and Row, 1981.

Stilleben in Europa. Münster: Westfälisches Landesmuseum für Kunst und Kulturgeschichte; Baden-Baden: Staatliche Kunsthalle, 1979–1980.

Vroom, N.R.A. *A Modest Message As Intimated by the Painters of the Monochrome Banketje.* 2 vols. Schiedam: Interbook International, 1980.

Struycken, Peter (born 1939)

Peter Struycken attended the Koninklijke Academie van Beeldende Kunsten (Royal Academy of Arts) in The Hague from 1956 to 1961. Until 1962 he painted figurative works, after that changing to geometric series and arrangements in which he experimented with shape and color relations. From 1966 to 1976 he was at the Academy of Arts and Crafts in Arnhem, teaching design, both two- and three-dimensional, and in relation to architecture. Since 1963 he has carried out numerous major commissions for government and business. Struycken's first retrospective was in the Stedelijk Museum in Amsterdam in 1966. He began his research into the relation between image and sound in 1968, making a "light machine" in 1969 (Amsterdam, Stedelijk Museum).

Struycken began composing structures in black and white by means of accident: with the help of dice, as in the Dutch pavilion of the World Exposition in Osaka, Japan, in 1967–1968, and with a computer after 1968. The computer structures have been realized with varnish on perspex, and as "tile *tableaux*" in monumental commissions. In 1972–1974 he made his first drawings with the help of a computer program (*Linarc*). Since 1972 he has made color series of computer drawings and paintings—for example, *Cluster* (1974), *Change* (1979), and *Dots* (1980). In 1973 he used a computer-driven color television to visualize shape and color changes in time. His experiments with film are *Afstra* (1973–1974) and *Ras* (1974–1975). Monumental commissions after 1975 on the basis of a computer program are *Blocks* (1976) and *Line* (1977).

In 1976–1977, Struycken designed a two-dimensional color structure for the auditorium of the Rijksmuseum Kröller-Müller in Otterlo. In 1978–1979 he was at the Center for Advanced Visual Studies at MIT in Cambridge, Massachusetts, experimenting with projections of the sixteenth dimension. Some of the many monumental commissions he has carried out are the installation of computer-driven dimming lamps in the ceiling of the town hall opera in Amsterdam (1985–1986) and a light sculpture for the Netherlands Architecture Institute in Rotterdam (1993). His other designs include interiors, graphics, and postage stamps.

John Steen

See also Contemporary art; Films, filmmaking; Graphic design; Postage stamps

Bibliography

Struycken, Peter. "Complexity, Change, Structure." In *Contemporary Art from the Netherlands.* Edited by John H. Neff. Washington, DC: Smithsonian Institution Traveling Exhibition Service (SITES); Amsterdam: Visual Art Office for Abroad, 1982.

———. "Description of the Colour-Programme WAVE." In *Pier and Ocean: Construction in the Art of the Seventies.* London: Hayward Gallery; Otterlo: Rijksmuseum Kröller-Müller, 1980.

———. *Linarc.* Utrecht: Utrecht University, 1975.

Subjects, subject categories, and hierarchies

Dutch artists have depicted a wide variety of subjects in painting from the fifteenth to the twentieth century, ranging from the religious, to the secular, to the abstract. Despite such a wealth of varied imagery, however, there is relatively little known about how the Dutch viewed their own subjects, subject categories, and subject hierarchies. This situation is more typical of the fifteenth, sixteenth, and seventeenth centuries when artistic production did not manifest a modern sense of self-consciousness and self-reference toward the creative process, characteristics more often associated with the nineteenth and twentieth centuries.

Religious subjects dominated the artistic production of a highly devout fifteenth-century Netherlands. Altarpieces were produced in the single-panel, diptych, triptych, and polyptych formats and attest to the veneration of Christ, saints, and the Virgin. Within such an otherworldly, spiritual context, landscape, still-life, and genre elements appeared that later developed as subjects independent of the religious setting. Portraiture took the form of devotional images in which the sitter was depicted in the company of the Virgin or various saints, or in the bust-length format, employing a three-fourths-profile view.

Sixteenth-century Netherlandish art witnessed a general continuation of the subject matter of the previous century. The emerging power of humanist thought, however, allowed artists to reexamine the place of religion in their own physical world. As a consequence, such mundane concerns as a landscape view, once relatively insignificant during the fifteenth century, gained a visual dominance in many essentially religious works and was regarded as a worthy and often independent subject in its own right. In addition, artists such as Pieter Bruegel the Elder (1525–1569), a master of various subjects, including landscape painting, brought genre, or the depiction of scenes from everyday life, into prominence.

During the seventeenth century, a wide variety of subjects was depicted in Dutch painting to satisfy the demands of a burgeoning middle class. The modern classification of these works into the categories of history, landscape, portrait, genre, and still life is often inaccurate with regard to how the seventeenth-century Dutch perceived them. Under the category of history, for example, the Dutch would include scenes from literature, the Old and New Testaments, mythology, and classical history. The term *genre*, or scenes from everyday life, was not used in the seventeenth century, and probably developed from an eighteenth-century French source. Assorted, vague adjectives were used during the seventeenth century to describe genre paintings, including *cortegardje* (guardroom scene), "pleasantry," "drollery," and "peasant" scene. In general, the Dutch in the seventeenth century were quite informal in designating the subjects and subject categories of painting.

With the explosion in numbers of the types of images depicted in seventeenth-century Dutch paintings came some discourse on the hierarchy of subject matter. The artist, biographer, and theoretician Karel van Mander, in his 1604 treatise on painting, *Schilder-Boeck*, placed history at the top of his list of subjects most suitable for the aspiring artist. Other categories, such as landscape or flowers (still life), were regarded as suitable, but to a much lesser degree than history painting. In 1678 Samuel van Hoogstraten elaborated on Van Mander's hierarchy by classifying subjects into three groups, with history painting at the pinnacle, the cabinet piece in the second tier, and still life on the lowest rung. Such a theoretical estimation of subjects in painting was based upon Italian art theory of the fifteenth and sixteenth centuries. Contrary, however, to the vaunted estimation of the history piece, most seventeenth-century Dutch artists chose to create works depicting the "lesser" subjects of landscape, still life, genre, and portraits for the lucrative open market and private patrons.

Dutch artists of the eighteenth century continued to produce works of art with their subjects taken from the established categories of the seventeenth century. Genre, portraiture, landscape, still-life, and history painting continued to attract the attention of painters. However, a lack of innovation in the depiction of subjects was also characteristic of this period. Eighteenth-century Dutch artists looked to the achievements of the past century for inspiration but were often unsuccessful in moving beyond mere imitation. Many scholars agree that the eighteenth century was a period of decline after the monumental achievements of the seventeenth century.

Subjects depicted by nineteenth- and twentieth-century Dutch artists generally followed trends established throughout the rest of Europe. Nineteenth-century artists were engaged with aspects of Realism, Romanticism, and Impressionism. Artists such as Vincent van Gogh expressed a very personal vision of what they created and expressed thoughts about their own work through their own writings. Qualities of abstraction and Expressionism influenced the two most important groups of twentieth-century Dutch artists, De Stijl and Cobra. A one-time member of De Stijl, Piet Mondrian, sought a greater and greater abstraction of the subject until he arrived at a balance of colored, geometric shapes. Cobra artists were influenced by a variety of movements, perhaps the greatest of which was Expressionism.

The subjects produced by Dutch artists from the fifteenth through the twentieth century reflect both an allegiance to, and an independence from, the categories of subjects created by other European artists during these same periods. Arguably, seventeenth-century Dutch painters made the most unique contribution to the iconography of their time. No other European country produced such an immense number of paintings or depicted such a wide variety of subjects. Fifteenth- and sixteenth-century Dutch painting, although in step with the religious concerns of the rest of Europe, fashioned an intense style of Realism that remains its most recognizable characteristic. The eighteenth and nineteenth centuries did not seem to define their particular eras through their art. Dutch painters, with the exception of Van Gogh, were content to follow trends in painting developed elsewhere. Twentieth-century Dutch painting contributed significantly to the modern reassessment of the canvas as a traditional window on the visible world and helped establish the place of Expressionism in the history of world art.

Steven Golan

See also Cobra Movement; De Stijl; France; Genre painting, eighteenth century; Genre painting, seventeenth century; History painting; Humanism, humanist themes; Italy; Landscape; Magic Realism; Mondrian, Piet; Nationalism; Portraiture; Reputation of Dutch art abroad; Still life; Symbolism, Symbolists; Townscapes; Van Mander, Karel; Van Gogh, Vincent; Writers on art, sixteenth and seventeenth centuries

Bibliography

Blankert, Albert et al. *Gods, Saints and Heroes: Dutch Painting in the Age of Rembrandt*. Washington, DC: National Gallery of Art, 1980.

Fuchs, R.H. *Dutch Painting*. New York: Oxford University Press, 1978.

Haak, Bob. *The Golden Age: Dutch Painters of the Seventeenth Century. New York: Harry N. Abrams, 1984.

Mandle, R. Dutch Masterpieces from the Eighteenth Century. Minneapolis: Minneapolis Institute of Art, 1977.

Marius, G.H. Dutch Painters of the Nineteenth Century. 1903. Translated by Alexander Teixeira de Mattos. Edited by Geraldine Norman. Woodbridge, Suffolk: Antique Collectors Club, 1973.

Panofsky, Erwin. Early Netherlandish Painting. 2 vols. New York: Harper and Row, 1953.

Surrealism

Before World War II, Dutch Surrealism flourished especially in Utrecht. The ideas of Sigmund Freud were known there early through the presence of the Willem Arntz psychiatric institution. The psychiatrist Johan Stärcke, a brother-in-law of Pyke Koch, translated one of the primary sources of Surrealism, Les chants de Maldoror by Isodore Ducasse, in 1917.

Surrealism was introduced in Utrecht by Willem Wagenaar, who became acquainted with the style in 1924–1925 in Paris. Wagenaar started the bookshop and art gallery Nord in 1927. He sold Charlie Chaplin movies, jazz records, primitive art, furniture by Gerrit Rietveld, and Surrealist magazines like Variétés, Sélection, La Révolution Surréaliste and Le Surréalisme au Service de la Révolution, which were read enthusiastically by Pyke Koch and a number of younger artists, among them J.H. Moesman, Gerrit van 't Net, and Louis Wijmans. Wagenaar also met with the younger artists at the "drawing club" of Willem van Leusden. By combining academic nude models and classical plaster casts with objets trouvés (found objects), the first Surrealistic drawings were spontaneously created. Van Leusden later imitated the Surrealism of his students. The exhibition of Utrecht Surrealists, which Wagenaar organized in Paris in 1933, did not meet with much response. Kristians Tonny and Kor Postma remain the only artists from the Netherlands who had direct contacts with the Surrealist Movement in Paris, where both of them lived for a long time.

In the mid-1930s Wagenaar organized exhibitions and the Utrecht Free Academy, where he taught a second generation of Surrealists, among them Hendrik Poesiat and Fedde Weidema. Another Utrecht group gathered from 1941 to 1944 around the magazine De Schone Zakdoek (The Clean Handkerchief), started by Theo van Baaren. Contributors included Gertrud Pape, the photographer Emile van Moerkerken, and the poets Cees Buddingh and Chris J. van Geel.

Before the war, Surrealism generally met with little appreciation from the critics and the public in the Netherlands. It was mainly a few foreign contacts who supported the artists. In 1930 they included entries by Belgian and French Surrealists in the exhibition of De Onafhankelijken (The Independents) in the Stedelijk Museum in Amsterdam. The reactions of the press and public to the Exposition Internationale du Surréalisme, which Kristians Tonny and Georges Hugnet organized in the Robert Gallery in Amsterdam and the Royal Art Gallery Kleykamp in The Hague in 1938, were overwhelmingly negative. This exhibition with works by André Breton, Giorgio de Chirico, Max Ernst, René Magritte, Pablo Picasso, and many others—shown earlier in London (1936), Tokyo (1937), and Paris (1938)—was met with special appreciation by the artists. Pieter Ouborg, who had just returned from Indonesia, visited the exhibition. Younger artists such as Eugène Brands and Jan Elburg were inspired to work as Surrealists. To protest the fact that, except for Tonny, there were no Dutch participants, Van Geel and Van Moerkerken organized a Surrealist shadow exhibition displaying their own work.

After the war, Surrealism influenced the Experimental Group in Holland and Cobra. Both groups tried to free the unconscious by means of spontaneity, and they strove for an ideal world in which people can give in to their fantasies, where dream and reality become one. From 1959 until in the 1970s, the artists' group "Bureau de Recherche Surréalistes en Hollande" (Bureau to Research Surrealists and Holland) arranged activities. In 1961 the Bureau, in the person of artist Her de Vries, brought Moesman's work to the attention of André Breton, who was very enthusiastic and invited him to international exhibitions. The public's late appreciation for Surrealism is reflected in the collecting activities of Dutch museums. Around 1970 the Museum Boymans-van Beuningen in Rotterdam set out to collect works of Surrealism; it organized a retrospective of the art of Salvador Dalì and afterward obtained important works from the collection of Edward James. Since that time, Dutch Surrealists have also been brought into public collections, although in limited numbers.

John Steen

See also Brands, Eugène; Cobra Movement; Koch, Pyke; Moesman, Johannes Hendricus (Joop); Ouborg, Pieter; Tonny, Kristians; Utrecht

Bibliography

Grondman, Agnes et al. De automatische verbeelding: Nederlandse surrealisten. Amsterdam: Meulenhoff/ Landshoff, 1989.

Vovelle, José. "La Diffusion du surréalisme dans les pays néerlandophones, 1920–1950." Ph.D. diss., Université de Paris, Pantéon-Sorbonne, 1984.

Symbolism, Symbolists

Two major roles emerge for the Dutch Symbolist artist of the last decade of the nineteenth century: the isolated artist pursuing a form of personal or transcendental Symbolism in search of a higher truth, and the socially concerned artist searching for a new and meaningful role in a society to which he can offer a vision for the future. Often both ideals were combined in some form. Its heyday spanning only the short period between 1892 and 1896, Dutch Symbolist art developed within an international context, characterized by a myriad of connections that existed between artists and writers not only in Holland, but in Belgium, France, and England as well.

In 1885 the periodical De Nieuwe Gids (The New Guide)

was founded, around which a young literary circle formed, including such poets as Willem Kloos and Albert Verwey, the prose writers Lodewijk van Deyssel and Frederik van Eeden, as well as artist and art critic Jan Veth. The journal was international in orientation, eschewing Holland's earlier provincialism. By 1891 naturalism in literature had been declared dead (Van Deyssel) and admiration for foreign and domestic Impressionist schools of art was on the wane. During the early 1890s the pioneering role of *De Nieuwe Gids* was relinquished to a number of other journals: the *Tweemandelijksch Tijdschrift* (Bimonthly Journal), established by Van Deyssel and Verwey in 1894; the Brussels-based magazine *Van Nu en Straks*—whose first volume of 1893 devoted an issue to Vincent van Gogh—which was of great importance for artists as well as literators and addressed the question of a communal art; and P.L. Tak's *De Kroniek* (The Chronicle) of 1895, which continued the debate about the role of the artist in society.

A unifying principle was the quest for a new art that would distinguish itself from that of its predecessors: The rendering of visible reality, as the Amsterdam Impressionists and the artists of The Hague School in Holland had done, was abandoned for a modern art that purported to be antimaterialist and to reflect the essential truth behind the world of appearances, harking back to the Idea discussed in Plato's *Republic*. In 1886 the French poet Jean Moréas had published a manifesto on Symbolism in the newspaper *Le Figaro*, in which he defined the Symbolist approach as an attempt to cloak the Idea in tangible form, through reference and analogy. The theory of correspondences, originated by Swedenborg and propagated by Baudelaire's sonnet *Correspondances*, in which connections between the visible and the invisible world were suggested by indirect means, became an important part of art theory as well. The comparison between the formal elements of painting and the suggestive properties of music also assumed a new significance toward the end of the nineteenth century, in association with the increased importance attached to the theory of synesthesia, according to which stimuli received through one sense elicit a response through others. The theories of expression of the Dutch draftsman and theoretician D.P.G. Humbert de Superville, popularized in the writings of Charles Blanc, may also have been of influence, especially where the evocative powers of line are concerned.

Dutch Symbolist artists in particular turned to the expressive qualities of the formal elements of art, such as form, line and color, stylization and deformation, to render a higher reality in visual form. In addition to Idealist philosophies, interest in Christian and Eastern mysticism and the occult also arose among artists attempting to probe the secrets of the universe. Such themes as fate, death, good and evil, seduction and sensuality, innocence and purity, and the material versus the spiritual world formed the visual vocabulary of the Dutch Symbolists. The subjects they chose were from the imagination, the symbols borrowed from literature, mythology, Christianity, and other belief systems.

In 1891 the ideas generating from the group of French Symbolist poets including Baudelaire, Mallarmé, and Verlaine were applied to a painter, Gauguin, and some of his colleagues in the Pont-Aven group, by the painter and critic Albert Aurier, who wrote in the *Mercure de France* about the new idealist tendency in painting. Aurier's ideas had been applied to Vincent van Gogh the previous year, the year of Van Gogh's death, and soon afterward Dutch critics as well, including the literator Frederik van Eeden of the group called *De Tachtigers* ("of the 1880s"), began to discuss the expatriate artist from the Symbolist point of view. Aurier's own definition of Symbolism later came to include members of the Salon de la Rose + Croix of Sâr Péladan as well as Nabis like Paul Sérusier and Maurice Denis. Two Dutch painters had joined the Nabis, Jacob Meyer de Haan and Jan Verkade, the latter of whom kept in contact with painters in Holland. Late in 1891 Verkade and Sérusier traveled to Holland, where they visited Jan Toorop and Richard N. Roland Holst. Another important connection during the late 1880s was Theo van Gogh in Paris, who often entertained visiting artists and critics from Holland. The activities of the Les Vingt group in Brussels, where Van Gogh had exhibited and to which Toorop was admitted in 1884, also led to the international exchange of ideas. In 1892, a banner year in the history of Dutch Symbolist art, the work of Van Gogh was introduced in Holland in a major exhibition held first at the newly founded Haagse Kunstkring (Hague Art Circle) and later in the year at the Panorama building in Amsterdam, both important meeting places for avantgarde artists of the time. Toorop and Roland Holst were among the young Symbolist artists who admired the work of Van Gogh and helped organize the exhibitions of his work. Roland Holst designed the cover of the catalogue to the Amsterdam Van Gogh exhibition of 1892, representing the artist in the form of a wilting sunflower, surmounted by a halo, against the background of a setting sun, thus conferring sainthood upon him.

During that same year, 1892, the French poet Paul Verlaine and the Rosicrucian leader Péladan visited Holland and held lectures attended by the most important artists, poets, and writers of the day. Péladan, who convinced Toorop, Johan Thorn Prikker, and Roland Holst to join his society, disseminated in Baudelaire's footsteps the notion of the artist as a priest and a prophet, a medium of the true world in the mundane world. It was also the artist's task to point society toward a new and better social order. An intermediate period of anarchy, in which emphasis was placed on individual freedom, seemed to a number of artists a prerequisite. In his talks, Verlaine had remarked, "When you are an artist, it's obvious that you must be an anarchist," as Thorn Prikker reported in a letter to Henri Borel, a theosophical writer on aesthetics and an interpreter of Hindu and Chinese literature and philosophy into Dutch. In addition to Thorn Prikker, Toorop also revealed a predilection toward anarchism, which is reflected among other works in his drawing *Anarchy of 1895*. The architects and graphic artists J.L.M. Lauweriks and K.P.C. de Bazel shared his sympathies in this respect. Others, like Roland Holst, were more attracted to the socialist side of the workers' movements.

The perceived crisis in newly industrialized society was

also connected to the theme of the spirit of the times. Both Toorop's drawing *Song of the Times* (1893) and Thorn Prikker's *Fin d'un ère* (1895) fall into this category. Toorop's drawing represents the battle between the material and the spiritual world (including material and spiritual anarchy) in which, in his view, contemporary society was involved. The evil powers, as usual on the left-hand side of his work, are enveloped in jagged, capricious lines, which move back downward toward the earth; the positive powers, at the right, are surrounded by more fluid, undulating ones, which move upward toward the celestial sphere. Thorn Prikker's work emphasizes form and color in its symbolization of "the misery of the present order of things," as he himself stated. Good, in the form of a mystical "all-encompassing love" would one day profit the society of the future.

Jan Toorop is by far the most famous of the Dutch Symbolists. A manifesto in visual form of his aspirations and his art theory is encountered in the drawing *Play of Lines: Ascendancy, with Opposition, of Modern Art* (1893; Fig. 129). As in the *Song of the Times* the representation extends to the frame, enhancing the work's decorative and abstract qualities. The odor emanated by the flowers turning to face the new art and the sound of the trumpets and the ringing bell are all indicated visually by curvilinear, upward-flowing lines and forms, a reflection of the concept of synesthesia. Sharp thorny branches move back downward, surrounding the body of a dead woman, who symbolizes the older, now vanquished, naturalistic art. Fighting a path through the thorns is a militant sylph from whose head four smaller sylphids in the form of Javanese *wayang* puppets spring, each of whom sounds a trumpet to herald the coming of the new art. The sylph tramples the dead body in the earth, which together with the goblin may also symbolize worldly passions, while the hair of the four sylphids flows upward into the celestial region. The sound lines of the bell, ringing in the new era, also serve as the hair of the sylph. The message brought by the new art is intended for an entrenched and helpless society, here symbolized by the white elephant, chained to the earth, with legs as immovable pillars and broken tusks. A further barrier to her goal is formed by the "arch of hell" that also appears in the drawing *O Grave Where Is Thy Victory?* of the previous year. Toorop's choice of four sylphids and four legs for the personification of modern art is unclear and perhaps came from his reading of Edouard Schuré's *Les Grands Initiés*, which spoke of four great religious traditions whose priests interpreted the word of God for humanity.

Where Toorop is eclectic in his choice of imagery, Christ and Christianity figures more prominently in Thorn Prikker's work. *The Bride of Christ* (Otterlo, Rijksmuseum Kröller-Müller), dating from 1892–1893, is one of the most famous of his Symbolist drawings. In representing a virginal, innocent, spiritual bride, Thorn Prikker chooses a subject also treated by Toorop and a number of others. His bride is merely an insubstantial veil, delineated as a flat silhouette, as is the crucified Christ next to her. The two are joined by heavy black lines encircling the bride, the flowers, and her groom. The myrtle branch of the bride's wreath is transformed into the crown of thorns on Christ's head, suggesting the misery and treacherous sensuality lying in wait in the future. The bride and her flowers are also separated coloristically, enveloped in a soft, luminous purplish-gray against the duller hues of the crucified Christ and the mostly Christian symbolism in the background. Thorn Prikker's explorations of the expressive powers of color and line are described in detail in his extensive correspondence with Henri Borel (1892–1897). Toward 1893 Thorn Prikker developed a style in which the entire picture plane became filled with parallel lines arranged in geometrical and curvilinear patterns, from which figures indicated by only contour lines emerge. By 1895, under the influence of his friend Henry van de Velde, the artist had also turned his interest to the applied arts, including batik and furniture design.

Toward the end of the nineteenth century, many artists looked to the future for a new social order that would be charged with public spirit and in which art would form an integral part. This hoped-for role for the artist indeed resulted in the rise of the applied and monumental arts as democratic forms: Toorop, Thorn Prikker, Roland Holst, and Antoon Derkinderen were among those who turned their hands to the making of tile *tableaux*, wall paintings, book illustrations, posters, and designs for stained glass. In 1892 Roland Holst defended Derkinderen's so-called *Eerste Bossche Wand* (a mural symbolizing the communal ideal of the Middle Ages, to be placed in the town hall of 's Hertogenbosch) in *De Nieuwe Gids* by stating that it rendered the abstract idea behind the reality of the founding of the town of 's Hertogenbosch. Jan Veth, who published a brochure on this work that same year, employed the term *Gemeenschapskunst* (communal art) for the first time. Influenced by his teacher at the Amsterdam Academy, J.A. Alberdingk Thijm, Derkinderen had developed specific ideas about an art anchored in the society from which it sprang. Partly under the influence of Derkinderen and the English Arts and Crafts Movement, the socialist Roland Holst, who was an essayist and a teacher as well as an artist, and who played an important role in the debate on art and society, also turned his interest toward monumental art by the mid 1890s. He made murals for H.P. Berlage's Stock Exchange in Amsterdam (1898–1903) and for two rooms in the building of the Dutch Diamond Workers' Union (1905 and 1912), and during the 1930s he designed stained-glass windows for the cathedral and the post office of Utrecht. Roland Holst proposed an art that was not one of individual expression, but rather of ideals put into service of the community. Like many artists of his day, he admired the supposedly unified society of the Middle Ages, with its handmade artifacts.

Toward the mid-1890s Roland Holst and Derkinderen protested against the depiction of such phenomena as sound lines and the decorative use of line and color, which were the trademark of Toorop and Thorn Prikker. A tendency arose to cloak the Idea in mathematical form, in the belief that this reflected cosmic beauty and harmony. Willem van Konijnenburg, a later follower of Symbolism, built up his large compositions of basic geometrical forms to render what he saw as the true laws of the cosmos in his art. He published a number of writings on art and aesthetics, of which the most important is *De aesthetische idee* (The Aesthetic Idea) of 1916. The influence of theosophy, which propounded a doctrine that purported to combine the truths of all religions and philosophies throughout history, was also of seminal importance in this respect. The theosophical architects De Bazel and Lauweriks employed mathematical imagery in their illustrations for the magazine *Licht en Waarheid* (Light and Truth), and it became an important designing principle in architecture as well. Piet Mondrian, who had long been preoccupied by matters of spirituality and the occult, joined the Dutch branch of the Theosophical Society in 1909. It was upon mathematical notions relating to the underlying unity of reality that both Mondrian and Theo van Doesburg based their theorization of the art of De Stijl. To Mondrian the absolute was to be found in the resolution of antitheses and could be given visual form in the representation of carefully balanced horizontal and vertical lines as well as in the contrasts between the primary colors.

By the turn of the century the initial phase of Dutch Symbolism had died out. Its legacy of mystical beliefs pertaining to a higher truth and its emphasis on the autonomous value of the pictorial media were of great influence on the development of the applied arts and architecture as well as a generative force in the emergence of abstract art.

Andrea C. Gasten

See also Alberdingk Thijm, Josephus Albertus; Applied arts; Avant-garde; Belgium; De Stijl; Derkinderen, Antoon J.; Graphic design; Humbert de Superville, D.P.G.; Mondrian, Piet; Roland Holst, Richard N.; Stained glass; Thorn Prikker, Johan; Toorop, Jan; Van Doesburg, Theo; Van Gogh, Vincent; Van Konijnenburg, Willem; Veth, Jan

Bibliography

Antoon Derkinderen. 's Hertogenbosch: Noordbrabants Museum, 1980.

Bionda, Richard, and Carel Blotkamp, eds. *The Age of Van Gogh: Dutch Painting, 1880–1895.* Zwolle: Waanders, 1990–1991.

Blotkamp, Carel. "Annunciation of the New Mysticism: Dutch Symbolism and Early Abstraction." In *The Spiritual in Art: Abstract Painting, 1890–1985,* 89–111. Los Angeles: Los Angeles County Museum of Art, 1986–1987.

Blotkamp, Carel et al. *Kunstenaren der Idee: Symbolistische tendenzen in Nederland, ca. 1880–1930.* The Hague: Haags Gemeentemuseum, 1978.

Gerards, Inemie, and Evert van Uitert. *In de lijn van Jan Toorop: Symbolisme in de kunst.* The Hague: SDU, 1994.

Hefting, Victorine. *Jan Toorop, 1858–1928.* The Hague: Haags Gemeentemuseum, 1989.

———. *Jan Toorop, 1858–1928: Impressioniste, Symboliste, Pointilliste.* Paris: Institut Néerlandais, 1977.

Joosten, J.M. *De brieven van Johan Thorn Prikker aan Henri Borel en anderen, 1892–1904.* Nieuwkoop: Heuff, 1980.

Nachtigäller, Roland, ed. *Symbolismus in den Nederlanden: Von Toorop bis Mondriaan.* Kassel: Museum Fridericianum, 1991.

Polak, Bettina. *Het fin-de-siècle in de Nederlandse schilderkunst: De symbolistische beweging 1890–1900.* The Hague: Nijhoff, 1955. (English summary).

Rijnders, M.L.J. *Willem van Konijnenburg, 1868–1943.* Utrecht: Centraal Museum, 1990.

Siebelhoff, Robert. "*The Three Brides*: A Drawing by Jan Toorop." *Nederlands Kunsthistorisch Jaarboek* 27 (1976): 211–261.

Siebelhoff, Robert, and Augustinus P. Dierick, eds. *The Low Countries: Fin de Siècle. Journal of the Canadian Association for the Advancement of Netherlandic Studies* 9:2–10:1 (1988/1989).

Spaanstra-Polak, Bettina. *Symbolism.* Amsterdam: Meulenhoff, 1967.

Steen, John. "Symbolism." In *Van Gogh tot Cobra: Nederlandse schilderkunst 1880–1950.* Amsterdam: Meulenhoff/Landshoff, 1980.

Le symbolisme en Europe. Brussels: Musées Royaux des Beaux-Arts, 1976.

Tibbe, Lieske. *R.N. Roland Holst: Arbeid en schoonheid vereend: Opvattingen over Gemeenschapskunst.* Amsterdam: Architectura–Natura, 1994.

Uitert, E. van. "Een kortstondige kentering: Beeldende kunst tijdens de eeuwende." In *Eeuwende 1900: Geschiedenis en Kunsten,* 185–209. Utrecht: Bureau Studium Generale, 1993.

T

Tavenraat, Johannes (1809–1881)

Johannes Tavenraat and Wijnand Nuyen are very likely the only wholehearted Romantics in nineteenth-century Dutch painting. During his life, Tavenraat was not very successful; quite the contrary, he was even reviled. His Romantic, dramatic-idyllic landscapes and hunting scenes were thought to be exaggerated in character. But Tavenraat did not let himself be led from his course. He painted out of inner necessity and hardly for the money, as he was in well-to-do circumstances and could afford it.

From 1827 until 1830, Tavenraat had taken drawing lessons in the evenings with the Rotterdam society Hierdoor tot Hooger (Higher through This), but he first decided in 1839 to apply himself entirely to painting and began studying with W.H. Schmidt. In 1840 he traveled with Schmidt along the Rhine in Germany. The next year he took a trip along the Maas in Belgium with the Belgian artist Felix Bovie. From 1841 until 1843 Tavenraat studied with Eugène de Block in Antwerp; afterward he continued to live there for another three years. In 1846 Tavenraat settled in Materborn near Cleves in Germany. The well-known landscape painter B.C. Koekkoek also lived there. From Cleves, Tavenraat undertook various journeys through Germany and Austria. He returned to Rotterdam in 1860, remaining there until his death. Only in the twentieth century has the work of this "forgotten Romantic" gained an appreciation, and Tavenraat has, after all, been honored with a number of exhibitions.

Alexandra W.M. van Smoorenburg

See also Koekkoek, B.C.; Nuyen, W.J.J.; Rotterdam

Bibliography

Leeuw, Ronald de. *Johannes Tavenraat, 1809–1881*. Cleves: Städtisches Museum Haus Koekkoek, 1981.

Technical investigations

The application of scientific methods of examination to the study of painting techniques and materials is a growing area of research. Various laboratory methods are used to analyze the working methods and materials of the artist. Since the first painting was x-rayed at the end of the nineteenth century, the field of technical studies has expanded considerably. The examination of Netherlandish paintings began with the study of Hubert and Jan van Eyck's *Adoration of the Mystical Lamb* (1432; Ghent, St. Bavo) carried out by Paul Coremans and his team in the 1950s at the Laboratoire Central des Musées de Belgique. These first technical studies opened a new area of knowledge, and in the decades that followed a considerable body of research has been collected.

No comprehensive treatises on technique, like Cennino Cennini's *Il Libro dell'Arte* written in late-fourteenth-century Italy, exist for the Early Netherlands. Karel van Mander's *Schilder-Boeck* of 1604, one of the earliest works devoted to painting practices in the Netherlands, is too late in date to shed light on painting processes in the early decades of the fifteenth century. Rather, our knowledge of techniques rests primarily on direct examination of the paintings.

The Northern easel painter working in the fifteenth century may well have derived his technique from the illuminator. By the adoption of a mixed medium that encompassed the unified tones of tempera painting with the translucency of oil painting, artists successfully transferred the beauty and jewel-like quality of the illuminated manuscript to a monumental scale.

The Netherlands was a crossroads of artistic exchange with the South, and luxurious fabrics and other precious materials came into the area from many countries. The courtly fascination with jewels and sumptuous textures stimulated artistic production. Jewel-like paintings became a visual manifestation of the power and prosperity of the Burgundian princes. The acquisition of fine paintings was a way of displaying wealth and good taste. The organization of the artist's corporation set high standards of quality and techniques.

Artists working in the Northern and Southern Netherlands used virtually the same painting techniques and materials. Generally, a thin layer of white chalk bound with animal glue was applied to a wood panel, usually of oak, and polished until the surface was smooth. A preparatory sketch was applied to the ground after an isolating material, sometimes a layer of oil, was applied to the ground to prevent the above-lying layers of paint from penetrating the ground. Occasionally, a thin layer of lead white priming was brushed above the ground.

Many styles of underdrawings executed with black chalk or paint have been observed. Ink heightened with wash was occasionally used. Some underdrawings are very detailed with sophisticated modeling. The study of underdrawings yields important information concerning copies, replicas, and collaboration on panels and has resulted in a separate area of study.

The paint layer is composed of pigments dispersed in a binding medium, usually based on linseed oil and egg tempera mixtures. The choice of pigments remained fairly constant. Those most often used were ultramarine, azurite, lead white, vermilion, and copper resinate green.

The artist applied transparent colors or glazes over regular, carefully applied opaque layers of paint and, with this combination, was able to obtain striking and saturated colors. The glazes were made of pigments bound in oil; the underlying layers generally were composed of pigments in a tempera medium. The use of this mixed technique distinguished the Netherlandish painters, and their mastery of the complex mixed oil medium techniques was well known and admired throughout Europe. Several Italian documents and treatises praise the skills of these painters during the fifteenth century for their mastery of the depiction of reality.

The presence of Netherlandish paintings in Italy is well documented. Pictures, commissioned by Italian merchants residing in the Netherlands, were shipped south. These paintings had a profound effect on the local artists. While the paintings traveled south in the fifteenth century, by the sixteenth century Netherlandish artists themselves journeyed to Italy to paint. Venetian artists such as Giorgione and Titian influenced Netherlandish painting considerably. The fifteenth-century artistic traditions of intricate colors, smooth surfaces, and profound luminosity gradually led to new techniques. The Northern artists became fascinated by the range of color and mood in Italian paintings. Artists began to prefer the fluid oil medium, which remained wet longer and was less laborious than tempera. By this time visible brushwork and a looser paint handling were adopted. Underdrawing, too, was transformed. A rapidly executed underpainted sketch gradually replaced the detailed preparatory drawing of the previous century.

By the beginning of the sixteenth century, oil painting virtually replaced the earlier methods. Oil paint responded to a direct method of painting application. This technique allowed the greatest spontaneity, and painters could develop a myriad of pictorial effects ranging from thick impasto to thin washes.

Canvas as a support also began to be used more frequently during the sixteenth century. Canvas paintings were flexible, much lighter than wood panels, and they could be easily transported. In addition, as the cost of materials rose, canvas was chosen as an inexpensive and easily obtainable painting support. While paintings on fine linen canvas, called *tüchlein*, were made throughout the fifteenth and sixteenth centuries, fabric supports in increasingly larger dimensions and coarse textures such as hemp and jute came into use. *Tüchlein* paintings were generally painted very thinly, with the matte appearance of tempera painting.

Painting on linen was never completely abandoned as painters experimented with the new, rough surfaces of cloth, which could add vibrancy and strength to their work. The earlier chalk grounds were not pliable enough or suited to a canvas support. The oil technique on a flexible support required a ground layer that also contained oil. Frans Hals is known to have used chalk ground on canvas, but Theodore Turquet de Mayerne in his manuscript (ca. 1620) cautioned against this practice.

The lower layers in the paint structure also underwent transformation. Artists invariably chose to color the ground layer. Chalk grounds were still in use on wood panels but were now usually colored in tones that ranged from gray or red to deep brown. These grounds were sometimes left exposed and incorporated into specific compositional features of the painting. When a white chalk ground was used, a colored priming or imprimatura was painted on top. Maerten van Heemskerck and Jan van Scorel used colored grounds and/or priming layers. In the work of both of these artists who traveled south, a combination of Netherlandish and Italian painting techniques can be seen.

As artists explored the possibilities of the new medium and the expressive nature of thick mounds of paint, surface treatment and texture became more exuberant. Painting was now seen as a whole, and the stunning effects of masses of light and decoration were explored to the fullest. The fluidity of the oil medium allowed the artist to work over extended periods of time, and changes in the composition could readily be made.

Whereas the Early Netherlandish artist worked from a white, reflective ground, building up layers of paint to rich saturated color, by the middle of the sixteenth century this configuration changed. Artists began to work from dark to light—that is, from dark underpainted layers up to brilliant surface highlights. These underpainted layers also included a stage referred to in treatises and documents as "dead coloring," a first paint layer in a more or less unified dull tone. This first stage of painting could also have modeling. In the seventeenth century, colored underpainting became an inherent part of technique. The importance of the underlying colored layers of paint is documented in seventeenth-century sources. The use of texture and thick impasto, highly characteristic of the period, can be seen particularly in the works of Rembrandt.

Seventeenth-century paintings have been examined extensively by laboratory methods. One of the most comprehensive studies to date of an artist's style and technique is being carried out by the Rembrandt Research Project. The project began in the 1960s and brings together specialists in the field of art history and science. In addition, the technical research on paintings by Rembrandt was presented at an exhibition in London at the National Gallery entitled *Art in the Making: Rembrandt* in 1988–1989. And the graphic style of the underpainted sketch was an important part of another study of seventeenth-century artists conducted at the Metropolitan Museum of Art in New York from 1976 to 1980. Autoradiography was used to uncover information from deep beneath the painting surface. Autoradiography is a technique in which the painting is exposed to neutrons. Some elements in the painting become radioactive and emit beta particles that sensitize radiographic film. A progression of images is produced at fixed intervals. By this procedure, evidence of the early sketch and layers of underpainting in works by Rembrandt, Van Dyck, and Vermeer were revealed for the first time.

The early techniques of meticulous painting on a smooth surface gradually changed to a looser method of paint manipulation as artists began to adopt new materials. The tempera medium was gradually abandoned and replaced with painting in oils. Artists chose a wide range of color effects and texture. From the early fifteenth century artists worked from a light ground up to dark glazes; this configuration was gradually reversed as painters began to build up their pictures from dark lower layers to bright highlights. Smooth oak panels, while always in use, were used along with canvas as a painting support. Noticeable brushwork became a desired effect. Technique was important and always an integral part of an artist's style.

Ingrid C. Alexander

See also Art history, history of the discipline; Paper, used for prints; Rembrandt research; Underdrawings, underpaintings; Watermarks

Bibliography

Ainsworth, Maryan et al. *Art and Autoradiography: Insights into the Genesis of Paintings by Rembrandt, Van Dyck, and Vermeer*. New York: Metropolitan Museum of Art, 1982.

Asperen de Boer, J.R.J. van, and J.P. Filedt Kok, eds. *Scientific Examination of Early Netherlandish Painting: Applications in Art History*. Bussum: Fibula-Van Dishoeck, 1976.

Bomford, David, Christopher Brown, and Ashok Roy. *Art in the Making: Rembrandt*. London: National Gallery, 1988.

Groen, Karin, and Ella Hendriks. "Frans Hals: A Technical Examination." In *Frans Hals*. Edited by Seymour Slive. Munich: Prestel, 1989; distributed by Neues Publishing.

Mayerne, Theodore Turquet de. *Le manuscrit de Turquet de Mayerne (1620–1646?): Pictoria, Sculptoria, en Quae Subalternarum Artium*. Edited by M. Faidutti and C. Versini. Lyon: Audin, 1967.

Schoute, Roger van, and Hélène Verougstraete-Marcq, eds. *Art History and Laboratory: Scientific Examination of Easel Paintings*. PACT. Strasbourg: Council of Europe, 1986.

———. *Le Dessin sous-jacent dans la peinture.* 10 vols. Louvain-la-Neuve: Université Catholique de Louvain, 1975–.

Wetering, E. van der. "The Invisible Rembrandt: The Results of Technical and Scientific Examination." In *Rembrandt: The Master and His Workshop: Paintings*. Edited by Christopher Brown, Jon Kelch, and Pieter van Thiel. London: National Gallery; New Haven: Yale University Press, 1991.

Wolfthal, Diane. *The Beginnings of Netherlandish Canvas Painting: 1400–1530*. Cambridge: Cambridge University Press, 1989.

Ten Compe, Jan (1713–1761)

Jan ten Compe, born in Amsterdam and orphaned at a young age, grew up in the orphanage of the Reformed Church in Amsterdam. He was a student of Dirk Dalens III, a painter of wall hangings and landscapes, and afterward he seems to have worked under the supervision of Jacob de Wit. He painted and drew townscapes and country views almost exclusively, and only rarely did a portrait. He was also an art dealer. Except for the period 1745–1755, when he regularly worked in The Hague, he was chiefly active in Amsterdam. Known to be by him are townscapes of Amsterdam, Haarlem, Alkmaar, Utrecht, Leiden, The Hague, Delft, and Rotterdam. Ten Compe, who was much influenced by the work of seventeenth-century painters Jan van der Heyden and Gerrit Adriaensz. Berckheyde, is considered one of the best artists of his generation. His paintings, which are generally quite frugal in the decorative sense, are characterized by a high measure of detailing, a rather cool and light color palette, and a well-balanced composition, which is determined in great part by the fall of light. For a long time, the artist was in the service of the collector Frans van de Velde, who paid him a small daily retainer; he also worked on commission from the collectors Gerrit Braamcamp and Jan van Rijneveld. Ten Compe, who was the teacher of the topographical draftsman Gerrit Toorenburgh, was very popular in his time and often received large sums of money for his paintings. Much of his work can be found in The Hague Historical Museum and the Amsterdam Historical Museum.

Charles Dumas

See also Architectural painting; Berckheyde, Gerrit Adriaensz.; De Wit, Jacob; Townscapes; Van der Heyden, Jan

Bibliography

Dumas, Charles. *Haagse stadsgezichten 1550–1800: Topografische schilderijen van het Haags Historisch Museum*, 138–209. Zwolle: Waanders, 1991.

Ter Borch, Gerard (1617–1681)

Gerard Ter Borch's refined genre scenes and portraits established him as one of the most prominent Dutch painters of the seventeenth century. His reputation rested primarily on the combination of a virtuoso technique with psychological penetration. The reserve, subtlety, and ambiguity of many of his genre interiors have prompted numerous contradictory interpretations of these pictures over the years.

Born in Zwolle in the province of Overijssel, Ter Borch received his first artistic training from his father, Gerard Ter Borch Sr., a public official who had earlier practiced as a painter. In his youth Ter Borch Jr. produced numerous drawings that the elder Ter Borch annotated and kept with the family possessions. Because of his father's efforts, we know more about Ter Borch's *juvenilia* than about the early work of any other seventeenth-century artist. After a short apprenticeship to the Haarlem landscapist Pieter de Molijn, Ter Borch embarked on a series of journeys throughout Europe that made him one of the best traveled of Dutch artists. In 1648 he represented the signing of the Treaty of Munster (London, National Gallery), a rare depiction of a contemporary historical event. In 1654 he married and moved permanently to Deventer.

With his return home to Overijssel, Ter Borch came into his own as a genre painter. His compositions drew their strength from an intimate knowledge of middle-class rituals and concerns; his figures gained expressiveness from a nuanced use of his own family's features. (His sister Gesina became his favorite model.) These genre works are understated, gentrified scenes set in refined surroundings, populated by dignified, contemplative figures. One of the most provocative is the so-called *Paternal Admonition* (ca. 1654–1655; Berlin, Gemäldegalerie, Staatliche Museen; Fig. 130). The eighteenth-century engraver J.G. Wille attached this title to his print of the painting, providing an interpretation accepted by many at the time, including Johann Wolfgang von Goethe. In the mid-twentieth century the painting came to be seen not as a family narrative, but as an enactment of bought love, involving a high-class courtesan, a procuress, and a visiting officer, who possibly once held a coin (now effaced) in his hand. Yet if this were indeed his theme, Ter Borch deviated from the usual treatment of a bordello scene, by emphasizing the luxurious nature of the milieu, by highlighting the protoganist's gleaming satin attire, and especially by creating a delicate and psychologically nuanced exchange among the figures. More recently this work and a number of similar genre paintings from the 1650s and early 1660s have been understood as representations of young people of marriageable age engaged in courtship rituals (among them *The Suitor's Visit*, ca. 1658, Washington, National Gallery of Art; and *The Introduction*, ca. 1662, Polesden Lacey House, Surrey, The National Trust). Although most of Ter Borch's other interiors are less problematic to interpret, they are no less formally rich and psychologically acute. These include his depictions of solitary women writing or reading letters, his representations of refined and contemplative military figures who are, paradoxically, placed in similar domestic settings and similarly involved with love letters, and his renderings of musical groups (*A Music Party*, ca. 1675; Cincinnati, Cincinnati Art Museum; Fig. 88).

Ter Borch produced relatively few genre paintings after the mid-1660s. He concentrated instead on elegant, small-scale, full-length portraits of well-to-do people from Overijssel and Holland placed in austere interiors. These portraits usually focused less upon the sitters' status than upon their individuality and sobriety.

Despite living in Overijssel, Ter Borch maintained an active relationship with the Holland art market. As a result, his genre paintings became widely known. They were especially influential on such artists as Gabriel Metsu, Pieter de Hooch, Frans van Mieris the Elder, and Johannes Vermeer.

Alison McNeil Kettering

See also Drawings, uses and collecting; Genre painting, eighteenth century; Genre painting, seventeenth century; Group portraiture; Musicians, musical companies, musical performers; Textiles, textile industry; Vermeer, Johannes

Bibliography

Gudlaugsson, S.J. *Gerard Ter Borch*. The Hague: Nijhoff, 1959–1960.

Hoetink, H.R. et al. *Gerard ter Borch*. Amsterdam: Rijksmuseum; Münster: Landesmuseum, 1974.

Kettering, Alison McNeil. *Drawings from the Ter Borch Studio Estate in the Rijksmuseum*. The Hague: Staatsuitgeverij, 1988.

———. "Ter Borch's Ladies in Satin." *Art History* 16 (1993): 95–124.

Sutton, Peter C. *Masters of Seventeenth-Century Dutch Genre Painting*. Philadelphia: Philadelphia Museum of Art, 1984.

Terbrugghen, Hendrick (1588–1629)

Though not the most famous of the Utrecht Caravaggists, Hendrick Terbrugghen is now regarded as the most important representative of this group of painters from the beginning of the seventeenth century. Terbrugghen influenced Dutch painting in the development from Mannerism to Caravaggistic realism.

After a period of training in the studio of the Utrecht history painter Abraham Bloemaert, Terbrugghen left for Italy around 1605. No paintings are known from his Italian period, which lasted about ten years. However, that he was impressed by the art of Caravaggio (whom he may have met personally) can be clearly seen in his work after his return to the Netherlands in 1614. What particularly interested Terbrugghen were the expressive possibilities of the realism advocated by Caravaggio. In 1620, after the return from Italy of two other Utrecht painters, Gerard van Honthorst and Dirck van Baburen, Terbrugghen's art received a new stimulus. The refreshed orientation appears in his *Calling of Matthew* (1621; Utrecht, Centraal Museum; Fig. 131). The subject has been taken from Caravaggio's *Calling of Matthew* (1599–1600; Rome, Church of San Luigi dei Francesi), as has the ingenious lighting from an unseen light source. Important, however, is Terbrugghen's own revived addition: the daring abrupt cutting off of the figures at the edge of the painting. This amputation creates a great immediacy of the action.

With Terbrugghen's early death in 1629, an important stimulus for the Caravaggistic painting style was lost.

Terbrugghen's known works are mainly genre, biblical, and mythological scenes. A characteristic of his is the somewhat charged and restless atmosphere that emanates from his work. In his genre paintings as well there is not a genuine cheerfulness.

Eugenie Boer

See also Bloemaert, Abraham; History painting; Italy; Utrecht; Utrecht Caravaggists; Van Baburen, Dirck Jaspersz.; Van Honthorst, Gerard

Bibliography

Blankert, A. et al. *Gods, Saints and Heroes: Dutch Paintings in the Age of Rembrandt*. Washington, DC: National Gallery of Art, 1980.

———. *Nieuw Licht op de Gouden Eeuw: Hendrick ter Brugghen en tijdgenoten*. Utrecht: Centraal Museum; Brunswick: Herzog Anton Ulrich-Museum, 1987.

Klessmann, R. *Hendrick ter Brugghen und die Nachfolger Caravaggios in Holland*. Brunswick: Herzog Anton Ulrich-Museum, 1988.

Nicolson, B. *Caravaggism in Europe*. 3 vols. 2nd ed. rev. and enl. Turin: Allemandi, 1990.

———. *Hendrick Terbrugghen*. The Hague: Nijhoff, 1958.

Stechow, W., and L.J. Slatkes. *Hendrick Terbrugghen in America*. Dayton, OH: Dayton Art Institute, 1966.

Terwesten, Mattheus (1670–1757)

A painter of decorative works, such as wall hangings, chimneypieces, and overdoor paintings, Terwesten was born in The Hague. He was a student of his brother Augustinus Terwesten I, Willem Doudijns, and Daniel Mijtens. In 1695 he traveled via Berlin, where Augustinus was a painter at the court, to Rome to finish his studies. He became a member of the *Bentvueghels* and received the *Bent* name "Arend." In Rome, Terwesten mainly made drawings after ancient art and *naer het leven* (after life). An album with these drawings from 1697 is kept in the Prentenkabinet in Leiden.

Again traveling through Berlin, where in 1698 he received a royal commission to design two ceilings for Charlottenburg Castle, he returned to The Hague in 1699. There he soon received major commissions from important regents to decorate both their houses in town and their country estates. For the secretary Fagel, Terwesten, in collaboration with the flower painter Gaspar Pieter Verbrugghen, painted his most ambitious project: the ceiling of the dome of a pavilion designed by the architect Daniel Marot, in which painting and painted stucco work are combined. In 1710 Terwesten traveled once again to Berlin, where he was appointed a court painter and a professor at the royal art academy. Back in The Hague, he married at the end of that same year. Two of his children from this marriage, Pieter and Augustinus, also became painters.

Terwesten's large paintings for wall hangings, ceilings, and chimneypieces have mostly mythological or allegorical subjects. He is also known for some famous religious works. In addition, he painted many pictures of playing children or *putti* for the open market that were very popular in his time. Terwesten's style is very decorative; his early works especially are loosely painted and elegant. His later works—Terwesten kept painting until an advanced age—are stiffer in execution and often appear routine. His whole life Terwesten was active in the artists' fraternity Pictura and The Hague Academy.

Christina J.A. Wansink

See also Display; Drawing theory; Italy

Bibliography

Schapelhouman, Marijn. "Een album met tekeningen, vervaardigd door Mattheus Terwesten te Rome in 1697." *Nederlands Kunsthistorisch Jaarboek* 33 (1982): 21–48. (English summary).

Wansink, Christina J.A. "De decoratieve schilderkunst van Mattheus Terwesten, een Haagse meester uit de achttiende eeuw." *Oud Holland* 104 (1990): 270–292. (English summary).

Textiles, textile industry

Textile production and textiles were featured in a broad range of seventeenth-century Dutch pictorial contexts. Paintings of textile workers actively engaged in their tasks were produced by artists from Leiden and Haarlem, cities to which the textile industries had brought economic prosperity and international fame. Other images continued the long tradition of depicting textile production as an avocation—women spinning, winding, lace making, embroidering—a private, female world (Color Plate 8). Depictions of the Haarlem linen-bleaching fields commemorated the textile industry in landscape imagery. Textiles as acquired commodities were depicted in paintings of sumptuous finery reflecting the long-standing fascination of Dutch artists with the description of textures.

Three groups of paintings showing various stages of cloth manufacture were produced in Holland's greatest textile production centers, Leiden and Haarlem. The paintings of textile production responded to a demand for imagery that celebrated the lucrative say (a fine-textured cloth, partly silk, partly wool) production in Leiden and linen weaving and bleaching in Haarlem. All three industries were praised in city histories and in travelers' chronicles. Although the cloth-making images were self-congratulatory, they differed strikingly from each other. This difference was clearly due to the local circumstances, the organization of the industries, and the relationship of the images to iconographic precedents.

In Leiden, the strong, centralized say guild commissioned a series of paintings by Isaac van Swanenburgh illustrating the textile-production steps from beginning to end. The unprecedented project reflected the guild's pride in the industry's success, as well as its significant role in Leiden's political and economic well-being.

In Haarlem, the decentralized linen production prompted a different, but no less celebratory response to the industry's success and international reputation. A large group of genre paintings depicting weavers at their looms was produced only by Haarlem artists, or artists living in Haarlem, around the middle of the century. Although the images presented a rustic or humble environment, as did many other depictions of trades and professions, the Haarlem weavers were depicted seriously and respectfully as industrious workers. Other tradesmen were most often shown in a comic light or not actively engaged at their tasks.

The singular interpretation of genre weaving scenes was paralleled by the unusual reworking of the Dutch cartographic/topographic tradition reflected in the depictions of Haarlem linen-bleaching fields by Jacob van Ruisdael, his followers, and by Rembrandt. Like the scenes of weavers' workshops, the many paintings of the linen-bleaching fields satisfied a proud market for civic images.

Although the relationship of these paintings to the Leiden and Haarlem cloth industries is clear, additional factors were influential in creating a market for the paintings. Other economically lucrative industries in both cities were never or rarely depicted. The social and political status of the cloth producers, versus nonskilled handworkers, contributed, therefore, to the unprecedented Leiden- and Haarlem-produced imagery. Cloth workers and merchants were often wealthy, politically powerful members of their communities.

Other aspects of cloth production—spinning, winding, lace making, and embroidering—were also popular subjects for seventeenth-century Dutch artists, such as Gerard Ter Borch and Johannes Vermeer, although such activities were depicted in the context of domestic interiors rather than in the industrial work place. Such images presented handwork as a female avocation rather than as a male vocation and were based on long-standing iconographic precedents, such as the spinning Virgin. The seventeenth-century Dutch images of female handwork reflected contemporary social expectations of the virtuous woman as expressed in treatises and in emblems. The status of the social order, rather than the economic order, was also suggested in spinning and winding imagery in which males rather than females performed the tasks. Such depictions represented the folly of the world-turned-upside-down and often featured men winding in spinning rooms, the traditional domain of women who had the upper hand.

Besides the cloth-production images, paintings by Gerard Ter Borch (Fig. 130) and other *fijnschilders* (fine painters), in which cloth itself was prominently described—fashioned into women's clothing—attest to the major role that textiles played in seventeenth-century Dutch society.

Linda Stone-Ferrier

See also Applied Arts; Dutch history; Genre painting, eighteenth century; Genre painting, seventeenth century; Haarlem; Leiden; Non-Western cultural influences; Still life; Ter Borch, Gerard; Townscapes; Van Gogh, Vincent; Van Ruisdael, Jacob; Women's worlds

Bibliography

Heppner, A. *Wevers Werkplaatsen Geschilderd door Haarlemsche Meesters der 17 Eeuw, A. van Ostade, C. Decker, G. Rombouts, C. Beelt, J. Oudenrogge, Th. Wijck.* Haarlem: De Erven F. Bohn NV, 1938.

Ponting, K.G. "Sculptures and Paintings of Textile Processes at Leiden." *Textile History* 5 (1974): 128–151.

Posthumus, Nicolaas Wilhemus. *De Geschiedenis van de Leidsche Lakenindustrie.* 4 Vols. The Hague: M. Nijhoff, 1910–1922.

Stone-Ferrier, Linda. *Images of Textiles: The Weave of Seventeenth-Century Dutch Art and Society.* Ann Arbor, MI: UMI Research Press, 1985.

Wilson, Charles. "Cloth Production and International Competition in the Seventeenth Century." *Economic History Review* 2nd ser., 13 (1960): 209–221.

Ysselsteyn, G.T. van. *Van Linnen en Linnenkasten.* Amsterdam: P.N. van Kampen en Zoon, N.V. 1946.

Theater and theatricality

Throughout the seventeenth and eighteenth centuries, theatrical literature and practice informed Dutch artistic production in myriad ways. Some painters represented narratives from actual plays; others portrayed actors or illustrated printed plays; many employed theatrical types, costumes, and settings; and a few, it has been argued, turned the production of art itself into a theatrical endeavor.

Around the year 1600 artists such as David Vinckboons limited theatrical representation to rhetoricians' activities at fairs, and in this tradition Adriaen van de Venne illustrated typical fair performers in his *Tafereel van de Belacchende Werelt* (1635). But as theatrical activity in Dutch cities diversified in the seventeenth century, theatrical representation followed suit. The comic playwright Gerbrand Adriaensz. Bredero was a painter, and perhaps not coincidentally his characters and scenes have especially pictorial zest. His comedies are probably the first seventeenth-century plays from which artists represented scenes.

Willem Buytewech designed the title page of Bredero's complete plays, engraved by Jan van de Velde II (1622), showing one scene from each of the plays. He also etched a title engraving for Bredero's *Lucelle* (1616), in which the servant Ascagnes woos the wealthy heroine during a music lesson, overheard by the wily Leckerbeetje. Jan Steen twice represented this episode as a genre scene (1667 and ca. 1667), in which he suggested its theatrical source only by Ascagnes' old-fashioned costume, which was used for romantic and comic stage characters, and by Leckerbeetje's demonstrative gesture.

Jan Miense Molenaer painted two versions of the final crowd scene of *Lucelle* in a more theatrical vein, with fancy costumes and exaggerated gestures and facial expressions (1636, 1639; Fig. 132). The set of the first painting probably resembles the stage of the Nederduytsche Academie, the main Amsterdam theater before 1637. Steen and Molenaer significantly varied their versions of the same scenes, suggesting that they dramatized episodes taken from a text, using visual traditions available, rather than representing actual performances. Such negotiations between text, performance, and pictorial tradition were to remain characteristic of theatrical representation.

This procedure is evident in the works of Pieter Quast. In

two paintings of *The Fool Brutus Suppressing the Masses before Tarquin* (1643 and ca. 1640–1645), Quast reinterpreted an engraved record of a *tableau vivant* ("living picture" staged by silent, motionless actors) written by Pieter Cornelisz. Hooft, which had been enacted in 1609. The painting of 1643 is set on a stage like that of the new Amsterdam Theater of 1637, but the other is more casually arranged. Quast's painting and drawing of *The Marriage of Achilles and Polyxena* (1636 and 1645) are imagined stagings of a scene from Hooft's *Achilles and Polyxena* of 1614. Quast also designed three illustrations engraved for Mattheus Gansneb Tengnagel's *Het Leven van Konstance* (1643), set outdoors without obvious reference to the stage. His drawings of grotesque figures in loose clothing, some of them for engravings, interpret Jacques Callot's prints of *Balli di Sfessania* and *Gobbi* (1621 and 1622), Italian fair actors and dwarfs whose performance in the Netherlands is hardly documented before the late seventeenth century.

Claes Cornelisz. Moeyaert's painting *Mooy-Ael* (ca. 1638) succinctly restates Bredero's play *Moortje* (1615). Moeyaert grouped together four characters who never appear together on stage, but whom Bredero had singled out in his own summary of the play. The resulting painting is a new variant on the well-known pictorial theme of the choice between a rich old lover and a young but destitute gallant. Moeyaert and others are also known to have painted sets for the Nederduytsche Academie.

Although many comic genre paintings appear theatrical, few actually represent scenes from comic plays, although some deal with themes such as marriage, childbirth, and money management in analogous ways. Such themes are as familiar in comic literature as they are in theater. The farcicality of genre scenes by Buytewech, Frans Hals, Judith Leyster, Frans van Mieris, and Steen arises primarily from fanciful, outmoded costuming, immodest laughter, and exaggerated facial expressions, strong gestures, direct appeals to the audience, and bawdy or drunken motifs. All of these strategies are common to the traditions of both rhetoricians' farce and genre painting.

In his many weddings, fairs, rhetoricians' meetings (Fig. 119), and folkloric festivities, Steen represented old genre subjects as well as traditional locales for theatrical activity. His genre and history paintings alike employ stock comic characters, familiar from the fair stage and from prints of actors of the Italian masked comedy (or *commedia dell'arte* in its eighteenth-century designation). Steen developed types such as the arrogant, bamboozling doctor by recombination of pictorial and theatrical conventions, including the long nose, shaggy beard, old-fashioned costume, and hunched or swaggering posture. Some of Steen's comic figures and farcical festivities were represented also by "fine painters" such as Caspar Netscher and Matthijs Naiveu. Naiveu painted some genre scenes that appear staged, and he occasionally represented outdoor performances with scenes from known plays (ca. 1708?). Around the year 1700 Michiel van Musscher also painted three actual scenes, taken from the popular Jan Claasz. comedies by Thomas Asselijn (1682–1685).

Dutch pastoral painting, introduced around 1600 and developed especially in Utrecht, The Hague, and Amsterdam, was specifically enriched by theatrical motifs. The pastoral plays *Il Pastor Fido* by Guarini (1589) and its distant heir *Granida* by Hooft (1605, published in 1615) yielded a new repertoire of meetings between shepherds and courtiers. The meeting of Granida and Daifilo, first painted on the scale of history painting by Dirck van Baburen in 1623, provided couples with a new attribute for marriage portraiture: the shell from which Daifilo offers her water. Neither these pastoral portraits nor the narratives give other evidence of their theatrical origin. Virtually the same holds for similarly romantic paintings derived from *Het Spaensch Heydinnetje* (The Spanish Gypsy Woman), a versification by Jacob Cats of a novella by Cervantes, subsequently dramatized by several playwrights. Scenes from these plays are usually structured like history paintings, although in Jan van Noordt's *The Meeting of Don Jan and Pretiose* (1660s) the hero wears the costume of the stage Spaniard.

Even more connections with contemporary theater might be expected for history painting, given that tragedies and paintings represented many of the same narratives. According to playwright Joost van den Vondel, the ancient dictum that painting is mute poetry, and poetry speaking painting, was specifically applicable to history painting and theater. On his own testimony, Vondel had written his *Jozef in Dothan* (1640) after seeing a painting by Jan Pynas. The *tableaux vivants* shown in most tragedies must have derived their efficacy from pictorial conventions. Nevertheless, there is little evidence that artists represented scenes from tragic performances, as has been argued for Rembrandt's *Nightwatch* (1642; Color Plate 5) and his *Joseph, Potiphar, and Potiphar's Wife* (1655), and for several of Steen's rambunctious history paintings.

Both Rembrandt and Steen, however, seem to have used theatrical principles in staging their historical and other scenes, even if their approaches were rather different. Both painters frequently included themselves in their paintings, in a direct address to the public that seems indebted to a joint pictorial and theatrical tradition. In their self-portraits they appear to engage in deliberate role-play, Steen mostly experimenting with comic roles and Rembrandt taking on guises from the beggar and the lout to the gentleman and the genius. Rembrandt's earliest drawn and etched self-portraits record various emotions, in keeping with the later prescription of his pupil Samuel van Hoogstraten that, to learn the passions necessary to history painting, the painter should practice their expressions "especially before a mirror, to be actor and spectator at the same time" (1678).

Svetlana Alpers (1988) has argued that for Rembrandt theatricality was a central principle of studio production and teaching. Several studio drawings show different approaches to the same narrative groups, perhaps indicating that Rembrandt would stage small acts in the studio, another practice recommended and apparently used by Van Hoogstraten. Van Hoogstraten also suggested, however, that artists should be capable of visualizing narrative scenes in their heads as if enacted there, and Rembrandt indeed seems to have had such a vividly performative imagination.

Whatever his studio practice, Rembrandt's involvement with theatrical procedures is evident in his drawings of actors in comic or tragic costumes, in drawings of a theatrical rehearsal, in the title etching for the *Medea* written by Jan Six (1647), and in the structuring of his history scenes and group portraits. The fanciful costuming and concentrated clarity of gesture and posture appear related to theatrical practice. His contemporary Andries Pels tacitly acknowledged the theatricality of Rembrandt's methods when, in his treatise on proper classicizing theater (*Gebruik en misbruik des toneels*, 1681), he attacked Rembrandt for his outrageous costumes and unidealized physiques, features of the type of theater Pels wished to reform.

More fundamentally, Rembrandt's frequent choice in his earlier works of an instance at which a change of fortune is effected resembles the classical principle of *peripeteia* (sudden, momentous reversal of circumstances) that structures Vondel's tragedies. But rendering the transitional moment is also a pictorial convention, employed by his teacher Pieter Lastman and by Rembrandt's followers alike, which allows the painter to imply in one scene the preceding and following moments in the narrative. Rembrandt's history paintings of the 1650s and 1660s present more condensed narratives, in which characters such as Rebecca (in *Jacob Blessing the Sons of Joseph;* Fig. 118), Lucretia or the father of the Prodigal Son appear in contemplation, perhaps akin to the *agnitio* (recognition of one's situation) of classical tragedy. Ironically, Rembrandt's critic Pels was a leading advocate of the principles of *peripeteia* and *agnitio*.

Steen's engagement with performative strategies, already noted for genre painting, was similarly extensive. His history paintings, too, present moments of change: Cleopatra about to consume her pearl earring, or Esther revealing Haman's treachery. His gestures, postures, and facial expressions are explicit and often exaggerated to comic effect, as if to emphasize the fictionality of the tale. Most of his history paintings sacrifice the concentrated gravity of Rembrandt's work for a dispersal of attention, in which subsidiary figures and vignettes provide comic entertainment, a practice encountered in the new genre of tragicomedy developed in the seventeenth century by Abraham de Koning, an Amsterdam playwright and art dealer, and others. Steen's balconied and curtained settings for festive crowds have been linked to the Amsterdam Theater, but they seem more directly indebted to the pictorial tradition of Venetian feast scenes.

If the acting experiences of Rembrandt, Van Hoogstraten, and Steen must remain a matter of inference and speculation, those of Cornelis Troost are well attested. After a relatively successful career as an actor on the Amsterdam stage he became a full-time painter in 1724, producing portraits (some of theatrical personalities) and scenes from actual comedies. In most of these paintings he showed a few main characters in conversation. As in the seventeenth-century precedents, these moments look like genre scenes without clear reference to the stage. In perhaps deliberate irony, some of his history and genre narratives that are unrelated to plays suggest the appearance of a stage set, especially the "Nelri" series of scenes that chronicle a drunken evening (ca. 1740; Fig. 66). For both theatrical genres, the works of Quast, Steen, and Naiveu provided some models, but no artist before or after Troost specialized in them to the same extent.

The works of Troost and other eighteenth-century artists appear more directly engaged with the theater than had been the case before. Troost's pupil Jacobus Buijs painted similar scenes from plays and, like Troost, decorated a full set for the Amsterdam Theater. Portraits of actors, rare before 1750, were produced more frequently in the second half of the eighteenth century, presumably because of the gradually enhanced social status of actors. The painter Pieter Barbiers operated a miniature theater for the *stadholder* as well as a tavern public (1756). The production of engravings for published plays, in the seventeenth century a side activity for many artists, now became a specialization for engravers such as Pieter van den Berge. All of these activities seem to have registered, and perhaps contributed to, the increasing popularity and professionalization of the theater itself.

Mariët Westermann

See also Comic modes; Dada; Gestures; History painting; Humor, satire; Leyster, Judith; Literature, poetry: analogues with the visual; Molenaer, Jan Miense; Pastoral; Rembrandt van Rijn; Rhetoricians' chambers; Steen, Jan Havicksz.; Troost, Cornelis

Bibliography

Albach, Ben. "Rembrandt en het toneel." *Kroniek van het Rembrandthuis* 31 (1979): 2–32.

Alpers, Svetlana. "The Theatrical Model." In *Rembrandt's Enterprise: The Studio and the Market*. Chicago: University of Chicago Press, 1988.

Blankert, Albert. "Peripeteia." In *Ferdinand Bol: Rembrandt's Pupil*. Doornspijk: Davaco, 1982.

Brink, Peter van den et al. *Het Gedroomde Land: Pastorale schilderkunst in de Gouden Eeuw*. Utrecht: Centraal Museum; Zwolle: Waanders, 1993.

Gudlaugsson, S. J. "Bredero's *Lucelle* door eenige zeventiende eeuwsche meesters uitgebeeld." *Nederlandsch Kunsthistorisch Jaarboek* 1 (1947): 177–195.

———. *The Comedians in the Work of Jan Steen and His Contemporaries*. Translated by James Brockway from the 1945 Dutch edition. Soest: Davaco, 1975.

———. *Ikonographische Studien über die holländische Malerei und das Theater des 17. Jahrhunderts*. Würzburg: Dissertations-Verlag Karl J. Triltsch, 1938.

Hummelen, W.M.H. *Amsterdams toneel in het begin van de Gouden Eeuw: Studies over het Wit Lavendel en de Nederduytsche Academie*. The Hague: Nijhoff, 1982.

Kettering, Alison McNeil. *The Dutch Arcadia: Pastoral Art and Its Audience in the Golden Age*. Montclair, NJ: Allanheld and Schram, 1983.

King, Peter. "Dutch Genre Painting and Drama in the Seventeenth Century." In *Standing Clear: A Festschrift for Reinder P. Meijer*. Edited by Jane Fenoulhet and Theo

Hermans, 173–196. London: Centre for Low Countries Studies, 1991.

Niemeijer, J.W. *Cornelis Troost, 1696–1750*. Assen: Van Gorcum, 1973.

Stanton-Hirst, B.A. "Pieter Quast and the Theatre." *Oud Holland* 96 (1982): 213–233.

Thiel, Pieter J.J. van. "Moeyaert and Bredero: A Curious Case of Dutch Theatre As Depicted in Art." *Simiolus* 6 (1972/1973): 29–49.

Tholen, Willem Bastiaan (1860–1931)

W.B. Tholen grew up in an artistic environment in Kampen, where many artists like Paul Joseph Constantin Gabriël were regular visitors. Together with the painter Jan Voerman (1847–1941) in 1876, Tholen took lessons for one year at the Rijksacademie in Amsterdam. He afterward obtained his diploma in the teaching of drawing in Delft. In 1879 he went to Brussels, where he received an education in painting from Gabriël, who initially influenced him greatly. Tholen gave lessons to earn his living, and in his spare time he worked directly after nature in, among other places, Kampen and Giethoorn. After 1885 he was regularly a guest at Ewijkshoeve, the country house of his friend Willem Witsen. There he had his own studio and came in contact with the circle of the *Tachtigers*. After that experience, Tholen developed a style that was very much his own. In his views of beaches and sand dunes, he no longer concerned himself with the cloudy sky or the sea but chose to focus on the human activity on the shore. His choice of subjects for paintings became diverse and original, including such rarely seen motifs as slaughterhouses and paper factories, which were greatly appreciated by the younger generation in Amsterdam. At the same time he was active as a portrait painter and also worked in drawing, etching, and watercolor. After 1895 he directed his attention once again to nature and painted mainly harbor and sea views. He then used lighter colors applied very thinly on the canvas so that, as a medium, it began to play a role as well.

Harry J. Kraaij

See also Amsterdam Impressionists; Gabriël, Paul Joseph Constantin; Hague School, The; Witsen, Willem

Bibliography
Bionda, Richard, and Carel Blotkamp, eds. *The Age of Van Gogh: Dutch Painting, 1880–1895*, 214–217. Zwolle: Waanders, 1990–1991.

Knuttel, G. *W.B. Tholen*. The Hague: Boucher, 1955.

Jong, Anneke de. *Willem Bastiaan Tholen*. Assen: Drents Museum; Museum and Museum Het Catharina Gasthuis, 1993.

Thorn Prikker, Johan (1868–1932)

After taking lessons at The Hague Academy from 1881 to 1887, Johan Thorn Prikker was turned away because of disorderly conduct. From around 1890, after a naturalistic beginning, he began creating abstract-looking landscapes and figure pieces in which influence from Jean-François Millet and Matthijs Maris can be seen. Color in these works plays a strong connecting role, in which humans and nature are almost dissolved into one another. Around 1892, however, Thorn Prikker went to the other extreme and made expressive line the means of connection. He identified his sources of inspiration: the fifteenth-century Flemish painters and art from the Far East. Thorn Prikker's knowledge of Eastern art was acquired through his friend Henri Borel, who had been to China.

Like Richard Roland Holst and Jan Toorop, Thorn Prikker became fascinated by the mystic theories of Sâr Péladan when he visited the Netherlands in 1892. Thorn Prikker, too, became a member of the Rose + Croix. He used Christian iconography as well as the contemporary literature of Émile Verhaeren and Charles Baudelaire in his attempt to portray the mystical idea of unity. In 1893 he became a member of Les Vingt (The Twenty) in Brussels and l'Association pour l'Art in Antwerp, and he exhibited there with great success—in contrast to the Netherlands.

After 1896 Thorn Prikker became more and more interested in the applied arts that served the people, and he began to create batiks, furniture, and book bindings. In 1898 he became artistic director of the interior design gallery Arts and Crafts in The Hague. In 1904 he moved to Germany, where he allied himself as a teacher of monumental art with various academies in Krefeld (1904–1909), Hagen (1910–1919), Ueberlingen (1919–1920), Munich (1920–1923), Düsseldorf (1923–1926), and Cologne (1926–1932). His specialties were textile design, leaded glass windows, and wall mosaics. Through his former student H. Campendonk (successor of Roland Holst as Director of the Rijksacademie), Thorn Prikker still influenced, although indirectly, the monumental art in the Netherlands.

Alexandra W.M. van Smoorenburg

See also Applied arts; Belgium; Roland Holst, Richard N.; Stained glass; Symbolism, Symbolists; Toorop, Jan

Bibliography
Bionda, Richard, and Carel Blotkamp, eds. *The Age of Van Gogh: Dutch Painting, 1880–1895*, 218–222. Zwolle: Waanders, 1990–1991.

Grinten, H. van der. *Johan Thorn Prikker, 1868–1932: Glas-in-lood vensters 1912–1932*. Nijmegen: Nijmeegs Museum, 1983.

Joosten, J.M. *De brieven van Johan Thorn Prikker aan Henri Borel en anderen, 1892–1904*. Nieuwkoop: Heuff, 1980.

Tiles

In the seventeenth and eighteenth centuries, Dutch wall tiles were produced on a large scale and became popular throughout Europe. This development was a direct result of the economic prosperity of the Golden Age. In the Middle Ages, wall tiles were rarely used in Dutch cities. Only after 1580 did the middle class have the means to have their houses decorated in this relatively expensive way. Over time techniques and designs changed. At first tiles were colorful and mainly decorated with large flower or bird motifs. Around 1625 Dutch tiles acquired their distinct character. Most tiles were now painted in one color, usually blue, on a white background. This change in taste was influenced by the growing popularity of Chinese blue-and-white porcelain; Chinese influences also surfaced in the decoration. The flourishing of the Dutch tile industry and the originality of the decoration are connected with the general development of painting in the same period. There was an increase of motifs taken from daily life: trades, children's games (Fig. 133), ships, and landscapes. These designs were—like many contemporary genre paintings—related to popular prints and emblem books.

Changes in techniques improved the quality of the tiles. In the second half of the seventeenth century, tiles were made more and more in large workshops. The actual painting was routine work, mostly done by young men using stencils. Rotterdam, Harlingen, and Makkum became centers of production. Stylistic development in this period was characterized by a steady shrinking of the painted area, a decrease in ornamentation, and the abandonment of the frame. Tiles now also became popular in rural areas, where farmers favored old-fashioned, colorful, and more richly decorated tiles, especially with biblical scenes. In the eighteenth century, the use of tiles virtually ended in the cities, but they remained popular in the country. After the end of the seventeenth century, the decoration showed increasing French influence.

Between 1670 and 1800 tiles became an important export product. Tiles with Catholic saints were produced for Spain and Portugal. The success of Dutch tiles was confirmed by the fact that manufacturers in other countries started to imitate them.

In the nineteenth century, handmade tiles nearly disappeared. If tiles were used, they were machine made and often imported from England. The use of wallpaper, cheaper and easily adaptable to fashion changes, supplanted tiles more and more. Between 1890 and 1910 the Dutch tile industry enjoyed a brief revival, under influence of the Nieuwe Kunst (Art Nouveau) style. Today traditional tiles still are produced in Makkum, mainly for tourists. In recent years, some individual artists, like Bea Peters, have returned to designing tiles, which some hope may lead to more than a brief revival. Important collections of Dutch tiles are in Museum Het Princessehof in Leeuwarden and in the Philadelphia Museum of Art.

Rudolf Dekker

See also Applied arts; Ceramics; Emblems and emblem books

Bibliography

Dam, J.D. van. *Nederlandse tegels*. Utrecht: Veen/Reflex, 1988. (English summary).

Jonge, C.H. de. *Dutch Tiles*. Translated by P.S. Falla. New York: Praeger, 1971.

Korf, Dingeman. *Dutch Tiles*. Translated by Marieke Clarke. New York: Universe Books, 1964.

Pluis, Jan. 1994. *Bijbeltegels/Bibelfliesen: Biblische Darstellungen auf Niederländischen Wandfliesen vom 17. bis zum 20. Jahrhundert*. Forthcoming.

———. *Kinderspelen op tegels*. Assen: Van Gorcum, 1979.

Poensgen, Albert. *Niederländische Fliesen, 16.–19. Jahrhundert*. Düsseldorf: Hetjens Museum, 1983.

Schaap, Ella et al. *Dutch Tiles in the Philadelphia Museum of Art*. Philadelphia: Philadelphia Museum of Art, 1984.

Tomb sculpture: medieval effigial monuments

Up to the end of the fourteenth century, funerary sculpture in the present-day Netherlands involved products brought in from other regions. Next to a number of thirteenth-century figural coffin slabs of Bentheimer stone from nearby Westphalia, it was the effigial monuments made of Namur and Tournai stone from the Meuse and the Scheldt areas that dominated the fourteenth century. A dozen of these great effigial tombs to bishops and knights have survived. Impressive examples are found at Utrecht (Bishop Guy d'Avesnes, died 1317), at Gorinchem (Jan III van Arkel, died 1324, and his wife), and at Ysselstein (Gijsbrecht van Aemstel, died 1342, and his wife; his son and his wife, of 1375–1380).

The medieval church at Breda houses some funerary monuments from around 1400 and later that are the first to deviate from the traditional works in Tournai and Namur stone. Two of them deserve special attention. The first is a rectangular tomb chest with the figures of Jan van Polanen, Lord of Breda (died 1384), and his two wives, and sculptural decoration on the sides consisting of niches with figures, the middle one showing the Coronation of the Virgin. Most striking are the fashionable clothes of the lady effigies and the niche figures. The latter seem to represent individual family figures, a remarkable deviation from the tradition of uniform *pleurants* (weeping mourners) just before Claus Sluter produced his expressive tombs with *pleurants* at Dijon (ca. 1404, finished by 1414).

The second monument is a retable structure with the kneeling figures of Engelbrecht I of Nassau (died 1442), his son and their wives, each of them with a patron saint. The eight persons are grouped round a statue of the Virgin and Child. The original monument (heavily restored in 1859–1864) was probably put up in 1470–1480, the only vaguely similar retable tombs being found in Spain, the kingdom to which the Netherlands still belonged at the time.

The breakthrough of the full Renaissance style in sculpture manifests itself from about 1525 onward—for example, in the imposing double-decker tomb to Engelbrecht II van Nassau and his wife at Breda (Fig. 134) and in the works of Colijn de Nole. But before that, in the first quarter of the sixteenth century, signs of the Renaissance are already to be seen in the early examples of two extensive series of tomb slabs found in the Northern provinces of Groningen and Friesland and in the Western province of Zeeland. These early examples are important because they belong to a period when everything else was still done in the late-Gothic manner. The new style probably came to these regions via Flemish graphic works. In the former series, it is the use of acanthus, *putti*, festoons, and masks among other decorative details that is distinguishing; in the Zeeland examples, it is the free and conscious representation of the figures that catches the eye.

Harry Tummers

See also Donor portraits; House of Orange-Nassau; Sculpture (1400–1550)

Bibliography

Tummers, H. "Medieval effigial monuments in the Netherlands." *Journal of the Church Monuments Society* 7 (1992): 19–33.

———. "Recente vondsten betreffende vroege grafsculptuur in Nederland. Dertiende en veertiende eeuw." *Bulletin van de Koninklijke Nederlandse Oudheidkundige Bond* 92 (1993): 28–32. (English summary).

———. "Laatmiddeleeuwse figurale grafsculptuur in Nederland." In *Beelden in de late middeleeuwen en re-naissance/Late Gothic and Renaissance Sculpture in The Netherlands*. Edited by Reindert Falkenburg et al., 236–269. Nederlands Kunsthistorisch Jaarboek 45; Zwolle: Waanders, 1994. (English summary.)

Tomb sculpture:
early modern and later sepulchral art

Tomb sculpture in the Netherlands is largely a phenomenon of the early-modern period (the fifteenth through the eighteenth centuries). From the Renaissance through the end of the French occupation (1813), Dutch churches provided a quasi-public setting for displays of sepulchral art, which count among the country's most important public monumental sculpture. Unlike Flanders, where the private donation of memorials (sometimes indistinguishable from traditional sacred art) was encouraged as a solution to the problem of funding the (re)building and decoration of Catholic churches following the iconoclastic fury of 1566 that led to the Revolt of the Northern Netherlands against Spanish rule in 1568, sepulchral art played a more minor role in the Dutch Protestant church interior. Flemish monuments frequently include sacred figures and scenes, Dutch monuments from the same period indicate a preference for a more secular iconography and more restrained ornamentation.

From a stylistic point of view, the evolution of tomb sculpture in the Netherlands parallels that of other forms of sculpture. In spite of differences in their typology and decoration, Dutch monuments from the early-modern period include inscriptions (biographical sketches, verses from the Bible, and poems or rhymes, in both Latin and Dutch); heraldic displays (a coat of arms or an achievement); an effigy (a portrait bust, sometimes presented in relief, or a standing or reclining figure); and allegorical figures and symbols.

The decision to admit a monument into a particular church, as well as the determination of its location, typology, and iconography, was dependent on the attitudes of the denomination, as interpreted and enforced by the local church authorities. Sepulchral art was cautiously tolerated after 1600 in most Dutch parishes because of its didactic potential—it confirmed the transience of life while reaffirming Christ's promise of salvation. At the same time, monuments also reflected the tastes of their patrons (usually the deceased's family, or an organization or institution with which he was associated). Although tombs dating from the beginning of the seventeenth century are for the most part restrained (Fig. 33), later examples increasingly signified the deceased's wealth and/or social status in terms of their size and the lavishness of their iconographic displays (Fig. 135).

The most common type of sepulchral art was the *rouwbord*, a commemorative wooden plaque containing a coat of arms, which was hung on a column or wall near a grave. A more elaborate version, a *wapenbord* or *wapenkast*, included the deceased's armor, weapons, and banner(s). By the eighteenth century the *rouwbord* had grown to immense proportions (some even included wings as well as sculpture). There are few extant examples of these memorials since most were removed and burned following a ban in 1795. Stone grave slabs (*grafzerken*) were mounted above individual or family crypts excavated in the church floor. Crypts, which were considered private property, were priced according to their proximity to the choir or pulpit (those in the western part of the church were the least costly). In addition to an inscription, and sometimes the insignia of a guild or professional association, each stone was marked with an inventory number (so that those buried beneath the stone could be identified in church records). Grave slabs from the sixteenth and seventeenth centuries sometimes include effigies and/or elaborate decoration carved in high relief. The epitaph *(epitaaf)*, an inscribed plaque mounted in a frame and hung on a column or wall, varies significantly in size and decoration. Although some congregations found its emphasis on the deceased's worldly accomplishments inappropriate, the epitaph became the most popular type of sepulchral monument in the Netherlands during the seventeenth century. Many epitaphs employ a format that divides the façade into three zones, one of which is devoted to an armorial display and another to an inscription. Table and wall tombs *(grafmonumenten)*, which were usually erected in honor of members of the nobility, include a table (to support the effigy), which either stands alone (sometimes covered by a canopy) or is set within an architectural frame (usually set into a wall).

Wall tombs, as well as epitaphs, were commissioned in a series of elaborate mausoleums *(praalgraven* or *eretomben)*, erected from the beginning of the seventeenth century in honor of national heroes, which became the country's foremost patriotic shrines. These works, which mark the transition from the traditional sepulchral monument to the modern secular memorial, include the tombs of Willem I of Orange (1614–1621, by Hendrick de Keyser; Delft, Nieuwe Kerk; Fig. 34) and the country's naval heroes (the admirals Heemskerk, Hein, Tromp (Color Plate 9), and de Ruyter) executed by De Keyser, Rombout Verhulst, Bartolomeus Eggers, and other regional sculptors. Monuments honoring heroes *(heldengraven)*, especially victorious seamen, have continued to be commissioned and mounted in Dutch churches into the present century.

By the end of the seventeenth century, the demand for tombs in the Netherlands, just as for other forms of monumental sculpture, began to decline. Relatively few major monuments were commissioned after 1800; burial outside the church, which had been promulgated since 1750, became law under the French occupation in 1804, and was later officially recognized by a Dutch government in 1811. With burial now transferred from the church to the church yard or cemetery (*begraafplaats*), traditional tomb types, and decoration, were no longer appropriate or practical. The demands of the outdoor monument, as well as Neoclassical taste, were reconciled in memorials in which a column or obelisk (*gedenkzuilen*) was mounted on an inscribed socle placed adjacent to the grave slab. More common during the nineteenth century were modest inscribed stone or cast-iron markers (*grafteken* or *gedenktekens*) mounted directly in the ground or on a low base or socle. Due to the increased frequency of cremation during the twentieth century, the use of cemeteries has also declined. Furthermore, with the current preference for cemeteries designed to provide an open park-like setting, with individual monuments vastly reduced in size, or eliminated altogether, tomb sculpture has ceased to be a viable art form in the modern Netherlands.

Cynthia Lawrence

See also De Keyser, Hendrick; Donor portraits; Eggers, Bartolomeus; Flanders, Flemish School; Last Judgment; Marine painting; Nationalism; Public monumental sculpture (ca. 1550–1795); Sculpture (1550–1795); Verhulst, Rombout

Bibliography

Alkemade, C. van. *Inleidinge tot he ceremonieel, en de plegtigheden der begraavenissen, en der wapenkunde.* Delft: Andries Voorstad, 1713.

Bosch, R.P. van den. *Neerlands verleden uit steen en beeld, gedenkteekenen en grafgestigten uit den vroegeren en lateren tijd.* Schiedam: H.A.M. Roelants, 1901.

Dael, P. van. "Graven in kerk en hof." *Graven en begraven in Overijssel: Jaarboek Overijssel* (1981): 41–77.

"De Dood Verbloemen?" Begraven en cremeren in Amsterdam; gedentekens spreken. Amsterdam: Nieuwe Kerk, 1982.

Dood en Begraven: Sterven en rouwen 1700–1900. Utrecht: Centraal Museum, 1980.

Ekkart, R. "Epitafen in Hollandse kerken." *Bulletin van de Stichting Oude Hollandse Kerken* 10 (1980): 3–12.

Jimkes-Verkade, E. "De ikonologie van het grafmonument van Willem I, prins van Orange." In *De stad Delft, cultuur en maatschappij van 1572 tot 1667*, 214–230. Delft: Culturele Gemeenschap van Delft, 1981.

———. "Het heldengraf." *Beelden in de Gouden Eeuw: Kunst Schrift* 91 (1991): 32–41.

Lawrence, C. "Hendrick de Keyser's Heemskerk Monument: The Origins of the Cult and the Iconography of the Dutch Naval Heroes." *Simiolus* 21 (1992): 265–295.

Swigchem, C.A. van, T. Brouwer, and W. van Os. *Een huis voor het Woord: Het protestantse kerkinterieur in Nederland tot 1900*, 254–267. The Hague: Staatsuitgeverij, 1984.

Van Intocht tot Uitvaart: Feesten en plechtigheden in de prentkunst 1500–1800. Rotterdam: Museum Boymans-van Beuningen, 1976–1977.

Vos, R., and F. Leeman. *Het Nieuwe ornament: Gids voor de renaissance-architectuur en-decoratie in Nederland in de 16de eeuw.* The Hague: Staatsuitgeverij, 1986.

Tonny, Kristians (1907–1977)

An active participant in the international movement of Surrealism, Kristians Tonny lived and worked in Paris after 1913. At the beginning of the 1920s he learned a transfer technique from Jean Pascin that he would use until 1960. In 1925 he was part of the first *Exposition Surréaliste* in the Galerie Pierre, his Parisian art gallery. He had contact with Antonin Artaud, Louis Aragon, André Breton, René Crevel, Georges Hugnet, and Benjamin Péret, among others. He belonged to the circle of friends of Gertrude Stein, whose portrait he painted; she wrote a portrait of him that is included in her *Dix Portraits* (1930). She collected his drawings and paintings, as did many other American collectors, among them Alfred Barr, James Thrall Soby, George Platt Lynes, Henry Russell Hitchcock, Mary Harriman, and Carl van Vechten.

From 1930 to 1932, Tonny resided in Tangier with the writer Paul Bowles and others. In 1936–1937 he was part of the exhibition *Fantastic Art, Dada, and Surrealism* at the Museum of Modern Art in New York. In 1937 he had his first American solo exhibition at the Julian Levy Gallery in New York. Also in that year, he traveled with Bowles to Mexico. Tonny was commissioned by director A. Everett Austin to make the wall paintings in the Avery Memorial Auditorium of the Wadsworth Atheneum in Hartford, Connecticut. In 1938, Tonny, together with Georges Hugnet, organized the *Exposition Internationale du Surréalisme* in the Robert Gallery in Amsterdam and the Royal Art Gallery Kleykamp in The Hague. During World War II, he lived in Southern France. After his move to Amsterdam in 1949, he worked and exhibited in turn in the Netherlands and in France. In addition to drawings and paintings, he also illustrated books and book covers.

John Steen

See also North American collecting; Surrealism

Bibliography

Bowles, Paul. *Without Stopping: An Autobiography.* New York: Putnam, 1972.

Jong, Frida de, and Laurens Vancrevel. *Kristians Tonny.* Amsterdam: Meulenhoff, 1979.

Soby, James Thrall. *After Picasso.* New York: Dodd, Mead, 1935.

Stein, Gertrude. *Dix Portraits.* Paris: Editions de la Montagne, 1930.

Toorop, Charley (Annie Caroline Pontifex) (1891–1955)

The daughter of Jan Toorop, Charley Toorop started to paint around 1909, first in a Luminist style, after 1912 in a Cubist and, later, an Expressionist idiom. She painted landscapes in Bergen (North Holland), where she settled in 1912, and Zeeland; she also painted figures (often her children) and self-portraits. She moved to Laren (North Holland) in 1915. In 1916–1917 she lived in Utrecht; in 1917, in Amsterdam. Between 1919 and 1921 she regularly visited Paris, where she was in contact with Piet Mondrian. In 1922 she built a studio-house, De Vlerken, in Bergen with architect Piet Kramer. During this period she developed a social realism. In 1922 she took a trip to the Borinage, where she made drawings in the style of Vincent van Gogh. Her portraits of psychiatric patients are from 1924–1925.

Charley Toorop lived in Amsterdam from 1926 until 1930, where, in addition to circus and *kermis* scenes, a "big-city theme" of night cafés, jazz, and film entered her work. She was a cofounder of the Filmliga (Film League) and had contacts with Joris Ivens. In 1928 and 1929 she and architect J.J.P. Oud organized exhibitions of architecture, painting, and sculpture in the Stedelijk Museum in Amsterdam. A visit to Paris in 1930–1931 strengthened her contacts with the international avant-garde movement. In 1932 she settled permanently at De Vlerken, which she had remodeled by Gerrit Rietveld.

In her work of the 1930s, Charley Toorop revised the traditional Dutch group portrait—for example, *Maaltijd der vrienden* (Meal of friends; 1932–1933) and the *Bremmergroep* (1936–1938). Her *Cheese Porters at the Cheese Market in Alkmaar* (1932–1933; Color Plate 15) is another example of this, with response also to Van Gogh. After 1935 she painted a tree with blossoms and one with fruit every year. Between 1940–1945 her work was a response to the war. She also created many self-portraits and still lifes. From 1941 to 1950 she worked on the *Drie Generaties* (Three Generations) in which she portrayed her father, herself, and her son Edgar Fernhout.

John Steen

See also Avant-garde; Bergen; Fernhout, Edgar R.J.; Films, filmmaking; Kramer, Pieter Lodewijk; Laren; Toorop, Jan

Bibliography

Bosma, Marja. *Charley Toorop, 1891–1955.* Utrecht: Centraal Museum; Stuttgart: Württembergischer Kunstverein, 1982.

Brederoo, Nico J. *Charley Toorop.* Amsterdam: Meulenhoff/Landshoff, 1982.

Toorop, Jan (1858–1928)

Along with Piet Mondrian and Jan Sluijters, Jan Toorop led the modernist movement in painting in the Netherlands in the first decade of the twentieth century. His daughter, Charley Toorop, and his grandson, Edgar Fernhout, were important artists as well.

Born in the Dutch East Indies, Jan Toorop departed for the Netherlands in 1869 to attend school. In 1875 he had drawing lessons from H.J. van der Weele in The Hague, and in 1876–1878 he studied at the Polytechnic School in Delft. After 1880 he was at the Rijksacademie in Amsterdam, where he studied with August Allebé and became friends with Jan Veth and Antoon Derkinderen. With Derkinderen, Toorop moved to Brussels in 1882 to study at the Academy of Fine Arts. In 1883 he exhibited there with the gallery L'Essor. From 1885 to 1893 Toorop exhibited annually with Les Vingt (The Twenty), and afterward with La Libre Esthéthique (The Free Aesthetic), both groups in Belgium. His early works show the influence of Gustave Courbet; James Ensor inspired him to adopt a form of Impressionism. While visiting in England in 1883–1885 he made contact with James McNeill Whistler and Matthijs Maris. In Paris in 1885 he saw the Pointillist canvases of Georges Seurat, whose painting technique he took over. After his marriage in 1886 to an Englishwoman, Annie Hall, he set himself up in Brussels. In 1889 he lived a longer time in England, where he met William Morris. From 1890 to 1892 he lived in Katwijk, where he created Symbolist paintings such as *Venus der Zee (Hétaire)* (Venus of the Sea—Hetaera) in 1890. His daughter, Charley Toorop, was born in 1891.

In these years Toorop had much contact with the writers of the *Tachtig* movement, among them Albert Verwey, and the composer Alphons Diepenbrock. In 1891 he cofounded the Haagse Kunstkring (The Hague Art Circle) through which he and Richard Roland Holst organized the first exhibition of the art of Vincent van Gogh in the Netherlands. At the same time he arranged a reception of friendly writers for Paul Verlaine and Sâr Péladan, the organizer of the Salon de la Rose + Croix in Paris. After 1891 Toorop created important Symbolist drawings such as *The Sphinx* (1892–1897), *O Grave, Where Is Thy Victory?* (1892), and *The Three Brides* (1893), which gave him European exposure. His *Play of Lines: Ascendency, with Opposition, of Modern Art* (1893; Fig. 129) is a manifesto of his aspiration and art theory. In 1900 and 1902 he exhibited his drawings with the Vienna Secession, which the work of the Austrian Symbolist painter and designer Gustav Klimt (1862–1918) had influenced.

Toorop carried out many monumental commissions, among them a *tableau* in tiles for the Beurs (Stock Exchange building) of H.P. Berlage, book jackets, and posters. From the late 1890s on, he spent his summers in Domburg (Zeeland) as the central figure in a group of painters that included Ferdinand Hart Nibbrig, Jacoba van Heemskerck, and, after 1906, Piet Mondrian. During the rest of the year he lived successively in The Hague, Amsterdam, Nijmegen, and, after 1916, in The Hague for good. In 1898 Toorop began again to work in a Pointillist style; after 1907 the touches of paint widened and developed into Luminism. In these years, he, Mondrian, and Jan Sluijters were the leaders of modernism in painting. In 1911 he became chairman of the Moderne Kunstkring (Modern Art Circle) in Amsterdam. After his conversion to Catholicism in 1915, he painted portraits of Roman Catholic priests in an expressive style at the same time that he made drawings in a stylized realism. These were followed by works of mystical religious themes. Under the influence of Catholicism, Toorop became a supporter of Mussolini's fascism; however, he recanted on his deathbed.

John Steen

See also Allebé, August; Avant-garde; Belgium; Berlage, Hendrik Petrus; Derkinderen, Antoon J.; Fernhout, Edgar R.J.; Maris, Matthijs; Mondrian, Piet; Roland Holst, Richard N.; Sluijters, Jan; Symbolism, Symbolists; Toorop, Charley (Annie Caroline Pontifex); Van Gogh, Vincent; Veth, Jan

Bibliography

Hefting, Victorine. *Jan Toorop, 1858–1928.* The Hague: Haags Gemeentemuseum, 1989.
Siebelhoff, Robert. "The Early Development of Jan Toorop." Ph.D. diss., University of Toronto, 1973.
———. "*The Three Brides*: A Drawing by Jan Toorop." *Nederlands Kunsthistorisch Jaarboek* 27 (1976): 211–261.

Town halls

Before the fourteenth century the town hall (*stadhuis*) as a separate building for administration was almost nonexistent in the Netherlands. The bailiff and the aldermen (*schout en schepenen*) used to meet in a chapel or in an ordinary urban dwelling. Originally, they governed the town by order of the count, the noble ruler, but in the course of the fifteenth century their function was limited to the local administration of justice. The governmental power came to be exercised by the burgomasters and the town council.

Since the fifteenth century most towns have had their own town hall. Some of them still exist—for example, the lavishly decorated Gothic town hall in Middelburg (1452–1520) and the free-standing town hall at Gouda (1448–1459). In general these buildings contained a bailiff's or sheriff's courtroom, a room for the council, and another for the burgomasters, a clerk's office *(de vierschaar, later this term would refer to a tribunal)*, a treasury room, meeting rooms for the guilds, for the trustees of the town's orphanage, for the civic guard, and rooms for the overseeing and levying of excise taxes on trade. For the last of these functions, separate weigh houses were built after the fifteenth century. One of the last town halls in the Gothic style was built in Culemborg (1534) by Rombout II Keldermans.

Although the Gothic style never died out completely, the Renaissance style became the favored vehicle for the expression of civic pride in municipal buildings. A famous example was the town hall in Utrecht (1546) by the architect Willem van Noort, which had a stone façade with superimposed orders of pilasters, pediments over the windows, and a colonnade on the ground floor with semicircular arches. It was a close imitation of an Italian Renaissance *palazzo*, with the exception of the bell tower, which had been a necessary feature since the Middle Ages. In contrast to most town halls, there was no perron before the main entrance. This façade was replaced in 1824 by a Neoclassical town hall.

Very different in composition is the Renaissance town hall at The Hague (1564–1565; Fig. 136). The building is entirely medieval in structure with steeply pitched ridged roofs and stepped gables, but the ornamentation is in Renaissance style. All of the classical apparatus of pilasters, cornices, brackets, busts, statues, and pediments was applied in stone to the brick façades.

More moderate town halls in the sixteenth-century Renaissance style are to be found in Oudewater (1588), IJsselstijn (1557), and Woudrichem (1592); each one is a simple rectangular brick building with a steep ridged roof and stepped gable-ends. In the more important city of Leiden, the new town hall (Fig. 74) was given an elaborate stone façade in 1597–1598 by the town mason and master builder of Haarlem, Lieven de Key. It has an impressive perron with two flights of stairs in front of the entrance and abundant decorations in the style of the model books of Hans Vredeman de Vries (1527–1606). In Leiden, as elsewhere, the façade is decorated with the symbols of good government—statues of Justice and Peace.

A rather late example of this sixteenth-century Renaissance style, which could better be described as Mannerism, characterized by conspicuous strapwork, rustication, and many sculptural details like obelisks, balusters, herms, lions, and statues, is the town hall in Bolsward (1613–1617) in Friesland. It was built by the architect Jacob Gijsberts.

The arrangement of the town hall in Bolsward was still medieval, but a few years later a new classicism was introduced by the renowned Dutch architect Hendrick de Keyser (1565–1621) in the town hall of Delft (1619). It was built on a square plan incorporating the medieval bell tower. Symmetry reigned in the design of the plan and elevation. The great central hall (*burgerzaal* or citizens' hall) is composed of two squares and its height is one third of the length, conforming to the classical pattern books. In terms of architectural history, this building heralds a new development in Dutch classicism, although the exterior decoration is still influenced by the Mannerist-style Antwerp Town Hall of Cornelis Floris de Vriendt (1561).

The next and final step in the development of classicism was taken by Jacob van Campen (1595–1657) when he built the Amsterdam Town Hall (1648–1665), which became a royal palace in 1808. It is a huge block-like building of darkish stone with a clear ordonnance of the two-tiered pilastered façades. The design is strongly influenced by the works of the Italian architectural theorist Vincenzo Scamozzi. The glory of Amsterdam and its powerful position in the world are the bases for the iconography of the pedimental sculpture executed by Artus I Quellinus and his workshop.

Dutch classicism with the obligatory ordonnance of pilasters and pediments entered a new phase with the work of Philips Vingboons (1607–1678) in the second half of the seventeenth century. Good examples of the new tendency toward almost flat façades without pilasters and pediments are the town halls of Enkhuizen by Steven Vennekool (1688) and Deventer by Jacob Roman (1693).

During the eighteenth century the great changes in architecture were mainly limited to interior decorations, following French fashions, like the town hall in Weesp by Jacob Otten-Husley (1762).

Not many new town halls were needed in the nineteenth

century, but in some cases the old buildings had to be replaced by new ones. In the beginning of the nineteenth century, an austere Neoclassicism, as favored in France, was preferably adopted for these new town halls, as in Dordrecht (1835). In the second half of the century, when architecture was in the grip of the Neo-styles, it was the Neo-Renaissance that seemed to express the proper aspect of civil authority, reminiscent of the proud city fathers of the Netherlands' Eighty Years War (1568–1648) against Spain.

Wim Denslagen

See also Classicism in architecture; De Keyser, Hendrick; Leiden; Quellinus, Artus I; Renaissance architecture; Roman history; Sculpture (1550–1795); Van Campen, Jacob; Verhulst, Rombout; Vingboons, Philips

Bibliography

Fremantle, Katharine. *The Baroque Town Hall of Amsterdam.* Utrecht: Haentjens, Dekker, and Gumbert, 1959.

Kuyper, W. *Dutch Classicist Architecture: A Survey of Dutch Architecture, Gardens, and Anglo-Dutch Architectural Relations from 1625 to 1700.* Delft: Delft University Press, 1980.

Rosenberg, Jakob, Seymour Slive, and E.H. ter Kuile. *Dutch Art and Architecture, 1600 to 1800.* Baltimore: Penguin, 1966.

Townscapes

In his seminal study of seventeenth-century Dutch landscape painting, Wolfgang Stechow posed the question: "When does a picture which contains the view of a town cease to be a landscape and become a cityscape or a town view proper?" The fact that scholars such as Stechow have struggled to answer this question points up the problems associated with establishing a classification of townscape as a pictorial form with its own conventions and tradition. Jacob van Ruisdael (1628/1629–1682) and Johannes Vermeer (1632–1675) are acknowledged to have painted townscapes in the second half of the seventeenth century, but works made earlier, even those with views of towns or buildings, are usually characterized as landscapes. Stechow chose the year 1650 as the line of demarcation: He defined as landscapes works made earlier than 1650 containing some sort of town view; works made after 1650 he saw as part of the evolution of townscape painting (Stechow, 1966: 124–125).

The town as an element or motif in landscape was frequently seen in the background of fifteenth- and sixteenth-century Netherlandish paintings with biblical, mythological, or historical content. Characteristically, artists combined elements or motifs from several different studies or drawings into their paintings of landscape so that the features only appeared real. The image of Paradise on the interior of the *Ghent Altarpiece* (1432; Ghent, St. Bavo) by Hubert and Jan van Eyck culminates in an exalted view of a Gothic city on the horizon; the multitude of church spires blending into atmospheric perspective is a metaphor for the transformation of the world

of man into the City of God. Even earlier, Jan van Eyck had achieved a union of foreground (the Crucifixion) and background (the city of Jerusalem) landscape views by showing the holy figures elevated on a plateau and soldiers riding down the slope into a valley with the city (Meiss, 1976: 41). Sixteenth-century artists such as Pieter Bruegel the Elder (1525–1569) continued to paint and draw landscapes that on occasion contained town or village views set within a wider panorama.

A later sixteenth-century artist from Haarlem, Hendrick Goltzius (1558–1617), is now recognized as a force in the development of early realism in Dutch landscape painting. Included in Goltzius' various panoramic views are recognizable locations or villages in the Dutch countryside. A contemporary, Claes Jansz. Visscher (1587–1652) of Amsterdam, who shared Goltzius' even, uniform tonality, executed a drawing in 1607 of *The Road to Leiden* (Amsterdam, Rijksprentenkabinet) that could be seen as a shift toward the tradition of townscape, as he strove to record accurately the features of the small village as more than just a part of the country landscape. Esaias van de Velde (1587–1630) from Haarlem made drawings and etchings after nature of the village of *Spaerwou* (ca. 1615–1616) that included figures and animals. Van de Velde's painting of a *View of Zierikzee* (1618; Berlin, Staatliche Museen) shows his developing naturalism: The realistic, documentary portrayal of the town, seen from the far side of a river and reflected in the water, includes three figures in the foreground to establish the scale of the town. Jan van Goyen (1596–1656) of Leiden trained with Van de Velde in Haarlem beginning in 1616–1617, and his works show the influence of Van de Velde's innovations. Van Goyen was obviously interested in the depiction of towns, as he drew, etched and painted several—for example, a *View of Leiden from the Northeast* (1650; Leiden, Stedelijk Museum De Lakenhal; Color Plate 6). Although Stechow credited the origin of townscape painting to stylistic change in the Delft school around 1650, and denied any coincidence with the Haarlem landscape tradition, there is ample evidence of a move toward town description in landscape painting in Haarlem earlier than mid-century.

Most scholars of townscape define it as a view of a town or part of a town that could be seen in one glance, thereby ruling out panoramic views in which a town may appear as only a part of a larger landscape. Views of single buildings are also generally discounted as townscapes. Dutch townscape painters usually came from the growing urban areas of Amsterdam, Haarlem, and Delft, where the intricacies of the town as a motif were coincident with the increase of the population and the emergence of town planning and expansion during the seventeenth century. The artistic possibilities of documenting urban life became increasingly rich.

By the mid-seventeenth century, Dutch painters were notably varied in the ways they executed views of Dutch towns. In Delft, Carel Fabritius, whose *View of Delft with a Musical Instruments Seller's Stall* (London, National Gallery; Fig. 41) is dated 1652, probably studied his view through a lens whose distortions he intended to correct by mounting the canvas on a curved surface inside a perspective box. In Jan

Steen's *The Burgher of Delft and His Daughter* (1655; British private collection), a quiet canal-side exchange between wealthy and poor citizens of the town is shown before a townscape of buildings identified with the development and historic defense of municipal and economic life in Delft. One of Job Berckheyde's earliest works, the *Oude Gracht in Haarlem* (1666; The Hague, Mauritshuis), shows a view of seventeenth-century urban life: A small vessel filled with people and market goods straddles the Haarlem canal as an oarsman works to turn it around; sturdy trees and residences line each side of the canal. Job's brother Gerrit could make his views appear even more unpremeditated: In *The Flower Market in Amsterdam* (ca. 1660–1670; Amsterdam, Rijksmuseum), he chose to concentrate on the canal-side market instead of the new town hall, which was the focal point of so many other paintings at this time. Gerrit shows the town hall from the side and partly obscured by row houses and trees, instead of the traditional frontal view. In *The Market Place and Great Church of St. Bavo in Haarlem* (1674; London, National Gallery; Fig. 13), Gerrit paints the busy town center from a vantage point under the shadow of the town hall.

The independence of the Netherlands as a country was officially recognized in 1648, giving the people a new infusion of the civic and national pride that informs the emergence and/or florescence of several subject categories of seventeenth-century Dutch painting. As the Dutch delighted in describing and interpreting the world of their own making, views of towns appeared in increasing numbers in the backgrounds of marine paintings, genre scenes, and portraits, linking these subjects and their environment. Burgeoning civic pride and the Dutch tradition of descriptive painting helped also to legitimize the townscape as an independent subject.

Discussion of townscape painting continues to be complicated by the casual way in which terms and criteria are usually applied; many scholars make interchangeable references to townscapes and cityscapes, town views, and topographical views. The catalog of the 1977 exhibition *The Dutch Cityscape in the Seventeenth Century and Its Sources* sidestepped the issue by broadly surveying all of these developments. In spite of the fact that this is, indeed, an art that is difficult to classify, it may be useful to offer some general definitions here. Townscape (*stadsgezicht*, literally town-view in Dutch) is a partly stylistic designation (noting changes in the coloring and composition) of the subject that became prevalent around 1650, in which civic pride in the Dutch towns' growing social importance and economic prosperity is combined with a continuation of genre painters' interest in recording the details of daily life. Townscapes (or cityscapes, when the town has grown large and important) are historically correct descriptions in which the town is the primary subject or motif. The term is used for views usually from the outside, such as Jacob van Ruisdael's *View of Haarlem* (ca. 1670; The Hague, Mauritshuis), an accurate portrayal of the town's many buildings, churches, and windmills as seen from a slightly elevated position on the dunes to the northwest, and overlooking the workers' cottages and linen-bleaching fields on the town's outer edge.

Town views (a semantic distinction that is possible in English) are those works that show an interior or intimate view of town life, such as *The Haarlem Lock in Amsterdam* (ca. 1660–1661; London, National Gallery) by Van Ruisdael's disciple Meindert Hobbema (1638–1709). This view of the busy harbor of Amsterdam, seen "from-the-inside-out," shows in the foreground the canal lock with drawbridge where several figures are working to let small boats pass. The distinction between townscape as "outer-city" and town view as "inner-city" is clearly demonstrated by Johannes Vermeer, who painted only one of each. Vermeer's *Het Staatje* (Street in Delft; ca. 1660; Amsterdam, Rijksmuseum) is, as the diminutive ending given to *straat* in the popular Dutch title indicates, a small and intimate view from the street of some houses inside the town. His *View of Delft* (ca. 1662; The Hague, Mauritshuis; Fig. 145), in which the town is seen from across an outside canal with its skyline reflected in the water and sunlight breaking through a cloudy sky overhead, is a dazzling achievement that has helped convince scholars that townscape painting began in Delft. Indeed, stylistic changes have occurred in the more than forty years since the tonal *View of Zierikzee* by Esaias van de Velde; Vermeer in the *View of Delft* uses light to establish the town as the subject and bring it to the center of the viewer's attention.

Topographical views are a third category of town depiction: These more or less exact recordings of the features of a place played a greater part of the domain of printed books and maps, and their profusion might be linked to the developing science of surveying in the sixteenth and seventeenth centuries. Even when topographical views are rendered into painting, they are redolent of those other means of reproducing and communicating information about specific places. As such they may introduce an element of complexity or tension to the painted image, by calling attention to the artifice that exists in every manner of making pictures of the world.

In the second half of the seventeenth century, Jan van der Heyden (1637–1712), who may have become interested in townscape through the works of Pieter de Hooch in Delft, executed a large number of Dutch townscapes and town views and extended the conventions of the theme to Brussels and the German Rhine towns as well. His work generated a small following of townscape painters in the eighteenth century, including Jan Ten Compe (1713–1761) and Paulus Constantijn La Fargue (1729–1782), who were concerned, as was Van der Heyden, with simplicity and clarity of detail, although these eighteenth-century Dutch townscape painters did not expand on the innovations of their predecessors in the seventeenth century. Isaac Ouwater (1748–1793) also concentrated on town views, executing exact renderings of specific buildings, such as his 1779 *Bookshop and Lottery Office of Jan de Groot on the Kalverstraat in Amsterdam* (Amsterdam, Rijksmuseum). These artists were mostly content to stay within the guidelines set forth by seventeenth-century masters, and even to copy them, such as the precise copies made by La Fargue of many of the works of Jacob van Ruisdael and Jan van der Heyden.

In the nineteenth century, under the influence of artistic innovations in France and developments among the painters of The Hague School in the treatment of landscape, a group of artists in Amsterdam applied the approach and technique of Impressionism to the townscape legacy, producing a gritty urban realism. Isaac Israëls (1865–1934), son of The Hague School painter Jozef Israëls, painted some town views—for example, *A Shop Window*; ca. 1887–1900, Amsterdam, Rijksmuseum) along with recording late-nineteenth-century street life in Amsterdam. Willem Witsen (1860–1923) painted many street scenes in an Impressionistic way, using a primarily brown color scheme. His *Warehouses on an Amsterdam Canal in the Uilenburg Quarter* (ca. 1887–1900, Amsterdam, Rijksmuseum) is a modern echo of Hobbema's *Haarlem Lock*.

The best known and most prolific of the Amsterdam Impressionists was George Hendrik Breitner (1857–1923). His 1896 painting of *The Bridge over the Singel at the Paleisstraat, Amsterdam* (Amsterdam, Rijksmuseum) is reminiscent of photography, a medium in which he was also interested. The painting shows a realistic view of the busy intersection in the center of Amsterdam in winter, with multiple figures moving in and out of the fixed frame of the painting. This technique gives the impression that the street is an empty frame waiting for the figures to pass through, very much like street photography of the time. His many other town-view paintings of the Rokin and Dam in Amsterdam (for example, *The Rokin in Amsterdam at Night* in 1895; Amsterdam, Stedelijk Museum; Fig. 3), also strive to capture the ambience of the city. Breitner captured the quality of movement in his paintings and photographs, a goal that exceeded many of his contemporaries. He also took numerous photographs of Amsterdam that were Impressionistic in quality, with their close cropping and blurred images. Breitner was also interested in documenting the demolition of old houses to make way for new streets, as well as buildings and construction sites showing partly standing walls to record the emergence of the modern city.

In the twentieth century, photography emerged as a realistic and favorable way to depict Dutch city life. Some cities, such as The Hague, employed photographers to document their public works projects in the 1920s, and the photographers turned them into modernist town views (Fig. 144). A group of documentary photographers after World War II recorded the devastating effects of the war on Dutch cities and citizens. In the 1950s photographer Kees Scherer became well known for his photographs of Amsterdam city life. The town remains an important motif in Dutch art, as a prominent element in photographs.

Wendi Miller

See also Amsterdam Impressionists; Architectural painting; Atlas, atlases; Berckheyde, Gerrit Adriaensz.; Berckheyde, Job Adriaensz.; Breitner, George Hendrik; Cartography; Commerce and commercial life; Delft; Drawing practices and techniques; Drawings, uses and collecting; Flanders, Flemish School; Goltzius, Hendrick; Israëls, Isaac; La Fargue, Paulus Constantijn; Landscape; Ouwater, Isaac; Paintings-within-paintings; Photography, modern and contemporary; Prints, printmaking, and printmakers, (ca. 1500–ca. 1900); Pronk, Cornelis; Ten Compe, Jan; Urban planning, before 1750; Van der Heyden, Jan; Van Goyen, Jan; Van Ojen, E.M.; Van Ruisdael, Jacob; Vermeer, Johannes; Witsen, Willem

Bibliography

Broude, Norma, ed. *World Impressionism: The International Movement, 1860–1920*. New York: Harry N. Abrams, 1990.

The Dutch Cityscape in the Seventeenth Century and Its Sources. Amsterdam: Amsterdam Historisch Museum, 1977; distributed by Landshoff.

Fuchs, R.H. *Dutch Painting*. London: Thames and Hudson, 1978.

Meiss, Millard. "'Highlands' in the Lowlands." In *The Painter's Choice: Problems in the Interpretation of Renaissance Art*, 36–59. New York: Harper and Row, 1976.

Muller, Sheila D. "Jan Steen's *The Burgher of Delft and His Daughter*: A Painting and Politics in Seventeenth-Century Holland." *Art History* 12:3 (September 1989): 268–297.

Rosenberg, Jakob, Seymour Slive, and E.H. ter Kuile. *Dutch Art and Architecture, 1600 to 1800*. Baltimore: Penguin, 1966.

Stechow, Wolfgang. *Dutch Landscape Painting of the Seventeenth Century*. London: Phaidon, 1966.

Trade, exploration, and colonization overseas

Overseas trade was of great importance to the Dutch Republic's economic well-being as well as an inspiration for many Dutch artists, particularly in the seventeenth century. Dutch trade with exotic lands was primarily divided between two companies, the United East India Company (Verenigde Oostindische Compagnie, or VOC, chartered in 1602) and the West India Company (the WIC, chartered in 1621). The VOC traded in countries east of Africa's Cape of Good Hope, and the WIC traded in the Western Hemisphere and on the west coast of Africa. The commerce in which these companies engaged affected paintings and prints of shipping scenes, landscapes, still lifes, genre, allegories, and even portraiture.

Dutch art reflects the Dutch interest in aspects of trade that they could personally experience. While trade territories were places that few Dutch would ever see and were, therefore, infrequently the subject of paintings, the exotic goods imported to the Netherlands and the ships on which they were transported were a strong presence in the Republic that grew as overseas trade increased. The impressive shipping fleets of both trade companies were a source of pride and thus a frequent subject of paintings and prints by artists such as Hendrick Cornelisz. Vroom (1566–1640; Fig. 80) and Ludolf Bakhuizen (1631–1708). Merchantmen were shown in waters at home and abroad and in many different weather conditions. Wherever they were, their prowess, and by extension that of the Dutch Republic, was always celebrated.

Exotic trade goods also appear in many contexts, including still lifes, allegories, genre, and portraiture. In these paintings, objects from the East are usually the most prominent and numerous, reflecting the amounts in which they were traded. Although overtly moralizing paintings containing exotic items can be found throughout the seventeenth century, there was an increase over time in paintings that demonstrate ambivalence regarding the morality of owning such items, as well as an increase in paintings that were clearly celebratory of the beautiful wares. As the objects became more common due to the increased trade, the Dutch became less wary of them. For example, *pronk* (meaning "show" or "ostentation") still lifes like those by Willem Kalf (1619–1693) and Nicolaes van Gelder (ca. 1625 or 1635–1675/1677; Fig. 90) are unabashed displays of many of the exotica available to the prosperous populace of the wealthy Dutch Republic. Allegories like Jacob van Campen's (1595–1657) painting *The Triumphal Procession with Gifts from the East and West Indies* (ca. 1648–1649; The Hague, Huis ten Bosch, Oranjezaal) show trade goods without apology or any hint of moralizing. In this painting, exotic natives bestow a mixture of Asiatic, African, and American objects like trophies upon the Dutch. This type of general exoticism, or combining of objects from all over the world, was often used and continued into the eighteenth century.

Painted images of the foreign lands from which these goods came were more rare. Few landscapes of Eastern locales exist. Those that do emphasize the Dutch presence in the East and were probably commissioned by the VOC itself. Painted representations of territories in which the WIC traded are more common than those of the East, perhaps because one powerful patron, Count Johan Maurits van Nassau-Siegen, governor of Brazil from 1637 to 1644, included the artists Frans Post (1612–1680) and Albert Eckhout (active 1637–1664) on his exploration of that country. While in Brazil from 1637 to 1644, Post made some paintings and many drawings. When Post returned to Haarlem he continued to paint Brazilian landscapes from his drawings. Although Post concentrated on landscapes, Eckhout painted full-length, life-size portraits of Indians and some still lifes. Post was the only artist who painted a relatively large number of overseas landscapes.

No large market for painted landscapes of overseas trade territories seems to have existed, perhaps because the two companies colonized only to the extent necessary to carry out their trading goals. Since colonization goals were modest, relatively few Dutch men and women went to these faraway lands, and Dutch citizens knew few people there. Thus, the average Dutch person did not have much invested emotionally in these lands. On the other hand, during the seventeenth and eighteenth centuries, travel books with printed illustrations of these foreign lands and peoples were extremely popular. These cheaper printed images seem to have adequately satisfied the Dutch curiosity and any demand for images of those trade territories.

The Dutch artistic response to its overseas trade and exploration was diverse and of long duration, but the ships conducting the trade and the exotic goods brought home were of the greatest interest to the Dutch populace and artists.

Gretchen D. Atwater

See also Commerce and commercial life; Exotica; Landscape; Marine painting; Non-Western cultural influences; Still life

Bibliography

Atwater, Gretchen D. "The Impact of Trade by the Dutch East India Company on Seventeenth-Century Netherlandish Art." Ph.D. diss., University of Kansas, 1991.

Bogaart, E. van den, and F.J. Duparc. *Zo wijde de wereld strekt: Tentoonstelling naar aanleiding van de 300ste sterfdag van Johan Maurits van Nassau-Siegen op 20 dec 1679*. The Hague: Johan Maurits van Nassau Stichting, 1979.

Boxer, C.R. *The Dutch Seaborne Empire, 1600–1800*. New York: Alfred A. Knopf, 1965.

Davies, D.W. *A Primer of Dutch Seventeenth-Century Overseas Trade*. The Hague: Nijhoff, 1961.

Pott, P.H. *Naar wijder horizon: Kaleidoscoop op ons beeld van de buiten wereld*. The Hague: Mouton, 1962.

Troost, Cornelis (1696–1750)

As easy as it is to name the famous Dutch artists from the seventeenth century, it is as difficult to do this for the eighteenth century. One artist has escaped this relative obscurity—Cornelis Troost. He is without a doubt the most famous and the most appreciated eighteenth-century artist.

Born in Amsterdam, he died a valued painter in the same city. He never took long journeys abroad. His whole being was focused on his immediate surroundings; likewise, the subjects he dealt with in his art. However, Troost started his career as an actor in the Amsterdam theater. In 1720 he married the actress Susanna Maria van Duyn. Four years later, Troost became a student of the painter Arnold Boonen (1669–1729) in Amsterdam. The relation with acting, however, would remain all of his life, initially through painting stage scenery. Later he became a specialist in representing theater scenes.

The first paintings that we know from Troost are portraits; in this subject matter he found immediate success. Fragments remain of huge group portraits; his *Anatomy Lesson of Professor Willem Roëll* (1728; Amsterdam, Rijksmuseum), shows an affinity of design and composition with the *Anatomy Lesson of Dr. Nicolaes Tulp* (1632) by Rembrandt.

The connection to the seventeenth century is typical for the art of the first half of the eighteenth century. Troost has given shape to this transition in an original way—for example, in his numerous genre scenes. The pictures of street musicians, domestic parties, doctors' visits, tavern scenes, and *cortegardjes* (guardroom scenes) are in a certain sense a continuation of the seventeenth century. The humor and the moralizing content remind one of Jan Steen, but Troost often made original changes. Where Steen portrayed Twelfth-Night festivities indoors, Troost chose a scene on the street (*Twelfth Night*, ca. 1740; The Hague, Mauritshuis; Fig. 137). Troost also incorporated contemporary, foreign influences; in his *Blindeman-netje* (Little Blind Man, ca. 1735; Rotterdam, Museum Boymans-van Beuningen), the frivolity of Watteau can be recognized in a more moderate form.

Unique is the so-called Nelri series (ca. 1740; The Hague,

Mauritshuis), five gouaches that go together in which the increasingly disorderly gathering of a little group of gentlemen is portrayed with sparkling humor (Fig. 66). Troost's sharp observations have compelled some art historians to compare him with the English artist William Hogarth (1697–1764). Next to Hogarth's biting viciousness, however, Troost's view is light-stepping and mild.

Typical for the eighteenth century is the conversation piece, but the subject most associated with Troost is the theater. In the seventeenth century, theater scenes were chosen only incidentally as a subject; Troost takes the subject to great fruition. Many versions exist of scenes from *Jan Klaasz. of de gewaande dienstmaagd* (Jan Klaasz., or The Pretended Maid) and of David Lingelbach's *De ontdekte schijndeugd* (Pretended Virtue Unmasked), which Troost painted chiefly as commissions.

Cornelis Troost used several techniques but reached his highest level in the mixed-pastel technique (pastel combined with gouache). Troost had only a few students; besides his daughter Sara (1732–1803), he taught Jacobus Buijs (1724–1801). There has always been much interest in the work of Cornelis Troost; because of his sharp insight, he was held to be an excellent chronicler of his time. His paintings, pastels, and gouaches have been frequently translated into prints by, for example, Jacob Houbraken, Jan Punt, Simon Fokke, Pieter Tanjé, and Abraham Delfos.

Eugenie Boer

See also Conversation piece; Genre painting, eighteenth century; Humor, satire; Steen, Jan Havicksz.; Theater and theatricality

Bibliography

Buijsen, E. et al. *Cornelis Troost and the Theater of His Time: Plays of the Eighteenth Century.* The Hague: Mauritshuis; Zwolle: Waanders, 1993.

Grijzenhout, F. *Cornelis Troost: De Nelri-serie.* Paletseries. Bloemendaal: Becht, 1993.

Niemeijer, J.W. *Cornelis Troost, 1696–1750.* Assen: Van Gorcum, 1973.

Wagenberg-Ter Hoeven, Anke A. van. "The Celebration of Twelfth Night in Netherlandish Art." *Simiolus* 22 (1993/1994): 65–96.

Underdrawings, underpaintings

The terms refer to a preparatory sketch artists made beneath the paint surface. The underdrawing was usually executed on a smooth white ground with black paint or chalk. This sketch reveals the artist's early ideas as well as his graphic style. *Pentimenti*, or alterations, and changes in composition made by the painter can be found in underdrawings. The study of underdrawings can show to what extent the artist followed the preliminary drawing in the paint layer. Underdrawings can also elucidate collaboration and other workshop practices.

During the fifteenth and most of the sixteenth centuries, artists worked in a systematic fashion developed within the strict guild traditions of the period. Few drawings exist from Northern Europe when compared to those from Italy; thus the study of underdrawings is particularly important. A vital area of study has resulted. Biannual colloquia devoted to the study of underdrawings have been organized by the *Laboratoire d'étude des oeuvres d'art par les méthodes scientifiques* of the Catholic University of Louvain since 1975.

Occasionally an underdrawing is revealed when the paint layer becomes transparent. Sometimes we can see underdrawing with the naked eye. When the technical examination of paintings began in the 1930s, underdrawings were captured in photographs using film sensitive to infrared radiation, which revealed layers normally hidden beneath the painted surface. However, only parts of the underdrawing were made visible. With the discovery of infrared reflectography in the late 1960s by Dutch physicist J.R.J. van Asperen de Boer, more information could be extracted. In this technique, infrared light is absorbed by carbon-containing pigments and reflected back from the white ground layer. Infrared light penetrates some colors better than others. The resulting image appears on a television monitor, where it can be photographed and mounted in mosaic-like fashion or assembled by computer.

During the fifteenth century, painters used a broad range of styles in underdrawing. Some were meticulously executed, fully worked out compositions, with outlines carefully defined and shadows drawn with hatched strokes that are quite dense at times. Others reveal only summary indications of the composition.

The expressive underdrawings, dating from around the turn of the sixteenth century, of the Master of the Amsterdam Cabinet, are characteristic of the type of detail prevalent at that time. Later artists, like Jan van Scorel and Lucas van Leyden, demonstrated a more fluid underdrawing technique. These artists used the same materials and adhered to similar traditions of the previous century.

It was not until the latter half of the sixteenth century that a significant change can be seen in the underdrawing techniques. Later painters, while not entirely abandoning white grounds, adopted colored ones. A well-planned undersketch was executed on the ground. The first lay-in of the principal forms of the composition was painted in grayish or brown paint. This preliminary sketch ranged from detailed thin lines of paint to broad, very free washes of color.

Since no carbon-containing material is present in this preparatory stage and paint layers are often thick and applied on a nonreflecting ground, infrared light is usually unable to detect any underdrawing. However, the pigments contain elements that can be observed using neutron-induced autoradiography. This method has been used to study the preliminary sketches beneath numerous paintings of the seventeenth century.

Preliminary layers of color are called underpainting. The first layer of color or underpainting that the artist applied is sometimes called "dead coloring." Although in early treatises and documents the term referred to a monochromatic layer of paint beneath the surface color, dead coloring has come to mean any dull area of color laid-in before the final layers of paint. These areas could be modified with modeling.

Once the rapid first sketch was applied to the ground, the artist could choose a variety of pigments to lay-in the principal areas of color. Frans Hals, for example, used thin washes of brown or grayish paint beneath the black clothing in many of his paintings. Rembrandt often used a fluid sketch in bone black before applying a muted and usually dark layer of underpainting.

Underdrawing at first was a well-defined method of laying-in the preparatory sketch on a white ground. By the sixteenth century, painters preferred a more fluid and rapid method of underdrawing creating a free underpainted sketch. Colored grounds and underpainting were frequently used during the sixteenth and seventeenth centuries as artists adopted a more expressive brushwork to achieve particular pictorial effects.

Ingrid C. Alexander

See also Drawing practices and techniques; Hals, Frans; Rembrandt van Rijn; Technical investigations; Van Leyden, Lucas

Bibliography

Ainsworth, Maryan, and Molly Faries. "Northern Renaissance Paintings: The Discovery of Invention." *Saint Louis Art Museum Summer Bulletin*. Theme volume. 1986.

Asperen de Boer, J.R.J. van. *Infrared Reflectography: A Contribution to the Examination of Earlier European Paintings*. Amsterdam: Central Research Laboratory for Objects of Art and Science, 1970.

Miedema, H., and B. Meijer. "The Introduction of Coloured Ground in Painting and Its Influence on Stylistic Development, with Particular Respect to Sixteenth-Century Netherlandish Art." *Storia dell'Arte* 35 (1979): 79–98.

Schoute, Roger van, and Hélène Verougstraete-Marcq, eds. *Le Dessin sous-jacent dans la peinture*. 10 vols. Louvain-la-Neuve: Université Catholique de Louvain, 1975– .

Urban planning, before 1750

A number of traditions can be identified in the history of the planning and layout of towns during the Republic. In the first place, there was the tradition of the "ideal city"—that is, the tradition of literary, philosophical, and politically tinged conceptions that developed in Italy in the mid-fifteenth century and found their way, through the writings of Simon Stevin (1548–1620), into the formulation of theories about the layout and functioning of towns in the Netherlands at the end of the sixteenth century. Simon Stevin was the author of the only treatise on town planning in the Netherlands in the pre-industrial era.

A second identifiable tradition in the theory and practice of town development was that of military and, particularly, surveying practice. As early as the sixteenth century, the great embanking and drainage schemes in Holland developed into large-scale, planned projects that, in their form of legal organization, structure, management, and exploitation, may rightly be regarded as the unique Dutch variants of the Italian ideal city. The same applies to developments within the military profession: An independent training course was established for engineers and surveyors in Leiden in 1600 that also paid attention incidentally to the technical, hydrological,

and architectural principles of town development. It was particularly through this "Nederduytsche Mathematique" that Dutch ideas about the planning and layout of towns achieved a wide international diffusion. Besides the ideas about the ideal city published by Stevin and the technical, military, and hydrological practices of land development and subdivision developed by engineers and surveyors, there was a third tradition. This was associated with the political situation in the individual cities, with demographic developments, and with the various economic, military, and theoretical considerations that formed the basis for deciding whether or not to proceed with town extensions in Amsterdam, Leiden, Utrecht, and Haarlem.

Simon Stevin's *Van de Oirdeningh der Steden*

In the years 1604–1605, the physicist, mathematician, and military engineer Simon Stevin was planning a treatise on *Huysbou* (House-Building), of which only a few fragments were published in his lifetime as part of other writings. Not until 1649 were important sections, including long extracts from the town-planning treatise *Van de Oirdeningh der Steden* (On the Planning of Towns), published by his son Hendrik Stevin. This is a theoretical source that has been almost totally neglected in the urban history of the Netherlands, and its importance has only gradually become clear since the studies by C.M.J.M. Van den Heuvel. Stevin's ideas about the planning and layout of the town were not only derived from the concepts of the ideal city inherited from Vitruvius, Alberti, and other civil and military treatises, but also were largely determined by contemporary military, surveying, and hydrological practice as applied to the improvement and extension of towns around 1600.

Surveying Rationality

Recent research into the technical, military, and scientific aspects of Simon Stevin's *oeuvre* and, in particular, of his treatises on *Huysbou* and *Van de Oirdeningh der Steden*, has shown that Stevin's primary intention was a didactic one. He wrote his books in a comprehensible language and used surveying as an instrument and experimental method for expounding, in absolutely clear and unambiguous terms, on questions relating not only to the technical and technological fitting out of a house (ventilation, drainage, water supply, heating), but also to the development, subdivision, and land use of a town.

Stevin's theoretical contribution to the planned layout of towns in the Republic must be related to the great surveying tradition in the Northern Netherlands. This is traceable from the mid-sixteenth century in the large-scale land development projects (such as the embanking of De Zijpe around 1550 and the schemes for draining De Schermer, Beemster, and similar locales in the first half of the seventeenth century), and also in the various military projects for the layout of army camps (Castrametatio) and ideal fortress towns (Bourtange, Coevorden).

The rectilinear plans made by surveyors for polders, army camps, and fortress towns have previously been regarded as purely technical projects, as forerunners of the great urban concepts of the humanist tradition developed for Amsterdam, Leiden, Utrecht, and Haarlem in the course of the seventeenth century. Recent research, however, not only into Stevin's *Castrametatio* (1617), but also into survey-based projects between 1550 and 1565, has shown that this "descriptive" manner of land development, subdivision, and management of the water infrastructure is also tied to a specific rationality and represents a specific ethic and idea about the relationship between the division of space and the ordering of urban and rural society.

The central position occupied by surveying on both a civil and a technical level in the early years of the Republic is confirmed by the establishment of the Nederduytsche Mathematique, a training course for engineers that was given at the Leiden Academy (1600). The plan, worked out by the *stadholder* Prince Maurits of Orange and Stevin for the establishment of a practically oriented training institute for engineers and surveyors, must be seen as part of the total reorganization of the contemporary art of warfare that Maurits and Stevin had in view, and that found its inspiration in the philosophical and historical studies of humanists attached to the Leiden Academy such as Justus Lipsius. During the early decades of the seventeenth century, the Leiden engineering school was an international center for surveying and military architecture, as appears not only from the various fortification and surveying treatises published in the Netherlands around that time, but also from the presence in Leiden of many Danish and Swedish engineers, who were employed by Christian IV and Gustavus Adolphus in the establishment and enlargement of numerous towns in Scandinavia.

Town Extensions in the Netherlands

In the first half of the seventeenth century, plans were made in the Northern Netherlands for the extension and enlargement of a great many towns. There were various reasons for this of a military, economic, and general political kind—for example, control of taxes and urban rivalry. This development has two striking features: first, the emergence of the "architectural plan form"—that is, the growing contribution of classicist architects to the design and implementation of town-extension plans—and second, the slow pace at which the new urban neighborhoods were built up. In general, hesitation—in infilling as well as in the making of decisions—is an essential characteristic of town-extension schemes in the Netherlands. Recent research into the laying out of the famous Amsterdam canal girdle, for example, has further unmasked several other urban myths, such as the view developed by Lewis Mumford in his influential *The City in History* (1961) of the Amsterdam canal plan as a grandiose town-planning concept. Detailed archive study of the decisions taken in relation to the Amsterdam extension plan leads to the unavoidable conclusion that Amsterdam did not have an overall extension plan in the seventeenth century; there was no master plan. The so-called canal plan of 1613 was never made and discussed in the form of a town-planning design. The reasons for the seventeenth-century extension are to be found in the need to provide the city with a new and militarily adequate

fortification system. Within the generously designed circumvallation, the merchant patricians themselves devised the mathematical concept for what is now called the canal girdle.

Study of the various phases of such typical industrial towns as Haarlem (1642–1671) and Leiden (1611, 1644, 1659), or of a medium-size market town like Utrecht (1624, 1664) yields the same picture of a great deal of reluctance on the part of the town authorities to adopt a well-organized town-extension scheme. Town extension in the Republic was less a task with an architectural and propagandistic appeal than an economic and military necessity, directly aimed at the prosperity of the town. Town extension must be viewed as the spatial outcome of the striving to increase the population as much as possible, in order both to benefit urban consumption and to create the largest possible reservoir of cheap labor. From the economic point of view, complex designs, such as that made by the humanist architect Salomon de Bray for the general extension of Haarlem (1661), stood little chance of being implemented; but the ideal, mathematical designs by surveyors, such as that made for Leiden by Pieter Dou (1611), were also either not implemented or were stripped down and reduced on economic grounds.

Ed Taverne

See also Classicism in architecture; Commerce and commercial life; Humanism, humanist themes; Renaissance architecture; Town halls·

Bibliography

Burke, G. L. *The Making of Dutch Towns: A Study in Urban Development from the Tenth to the Seventeenth Centuries*. New York: Simmons-Boardman, 1960.

Heuvel, C.M.J.M. van den. *"Papiere bolwercken": De introductie van de Italiaanse stede-en vestingbouw in de Nederlanden (1540–1609) en het gebruik van tekeningen*. Alphen aan den Rijn: Vis, 1991. (English summary).

Morris, A.E.J. *History of Urban Form: Before the Industrial Revolutions*. 2nd ed. New York: Wiley, 1979.

Roding, J. *Christiaan IV van Denemarken, 1588–1648: Architectuur en stedebouw van een Lutherse vorst*. Alkmaar: Cantina Architectura, 1991. (English summary).

Taverne, E. *In 't Land van belofte: In de nieue stadt: Ideaal en werkelijkheid van de stadsuitleg in de Republiek 1580–1680*. Maarssen: Gary Schwartz, 1978.

Taverne, E., and I. Visser, eds. *Stedebouw: De geschiedenis van de stad in de Nederlanden van 1500 tot heden*. Nijmegen: SUN, 1993.

Urban planning, from 1750 to the present

Although the Netherlands lagged behind England and Germany in industrialization and consequently in the development of modern urbanization, the Dutch have played a leading role in urban and regional planning during the twentieth century. A consistently high level of public and professional discussion has exemplified modern planning practice in the Netherlands.

Dutch economic decline in the eighteenth century was followed by a gradual recovery in the nineteenth century that made the modernization of urban infrastructure both possible and necessary. Within cities, water and sewer lines as well as gas lighting were introduced. Canals, roads, and trains formed a network connecting cities. Following the French model, defensive ramparts were dismantled, opening urban expansion to the surrounding countryside. On the site of demolished city walls, parks in the style of romantic English landscape gardens appeared, such as those designed in Haarlem and Utrecht by the landscape architect J.D. Zocher (1791–1870). Under the Municipal Act of 1851, municipalities enjoyed considerable autonomy, but local *laissez-faire* policies resulted only in piecemeal efforts to introduce planning to the city, and the law of 1874 permitting new construction on former defenses yielded no coordination. Toward the end of century, the need for housing and industrial development drove cities to adopt general plans for extension, although government leadership remained minimal. In Amsterdam, the plan of 1877 projected a periphery of gridiron neighborhoods, a plan conducive to private, speculative housing development. The first major urban park in Amsterdam, the Vondel Park (1865), was developed by private interests, as was the Maaspark in Rotterdam (1853). A greater degree of public intervention was eventually invoked to serve the collective requirements of hygiene and transportation. Acknowledgement of the economic and health costs of inadequate housing led in 1902 to passage of a far-reaching Housing Act. This required that every city with a population above ten thousand prepare an extension plan, a requirement further strengthened by the laws of 1908 and 1921.

Amsterdam had anticipated the Housing Act by commissioning H.P. Berlage (1856–1934) to prepare a plan for the southern expansion of the city. His plan of 1904 was largely inspired by the Austrian theorist Camillo Sitte, who had rejected the prevailing engineer's approach to urban planning in favor of an aesthetic approach based on knowledge of the history of urban design. Berlage's 1915 revision of the plan (Fig. 138) reflected more-recent international trends in urban planning, notably the influence of the English Garden City Movement and of the German planners A.E. Brinckmann and W.C. Behrendt from whom Berlage derived a grander, more Baroque-inspired model and the concept of shaping the city with blocks of housing. Elsewhere, the influence of the Garden City Movement was felt in the suburban development of garden villages, such as 't Lansink outside Hengelo (1911) and Heyplaat (1914) in Rotterdam. Vreewijk (1916–1920), a garden suburb in Rotterdam planned by Berlage with housing designed by M.J. Granpré Molière (1883–1972), became a prototype for suburban enclaves imitating the small scale and architectural intimacy of the rural village through the use of traditional images and materials. In the larger cities, such as Rotterdam and Amsterdam, calls arose for coordinating the many new neighborhood plans in the central city and the scattered plans for garden villages in the periphery.

There was also a growing perception for the need to expand urban planning beyond physical planning to encompass economic and social planning. Dirk Hudig (1872–1934) spearheaded the professionalization of Dutch urban planning, founding the Dutch Institute of Housing and Urban Planning in 1918. In 1924 the annual International Planning Conference was held in Amsterdam; discussion there of the coordination of garden city, landscape architecture, and urban planning in a scientific regional planning process influenced Dutch urban planning in the following decade.

Th.K. van Lohuizen (1890–1956) emerged as one of the important leaders of the scientific planning process. Van Lohuizen's research was vital to the development of the General Extension Plan for Rotterdam (1928) by W.G. Witteveen. In 1928 an urban planning office was established in Amsterdam's Public Works Department. There Van Lohuizen provided the survey that formed the basis for the General Extension Plan (1935) designed by Cornelis van Eesteren (1897–1988). This plan (Fig. 139) provided a vision of the city in its regional context, examining traffic, recreation, demographics, and industrial development. The plan integrated the existing older city and Berlage's extensions into a total vision of the city, including harbors, residential districts, transportation routes, and nature areas. Van Eesteren, earlier a collaborator in De Stijl, abandoned the closed city block in favor of slab housing. As the chairman of CIAM, the international congress of modern architects, he contributed to the European debate on the functional city.

Dutch postwar reconstruction polarized designers between the modernist proponents of Het Nieuwe Bouwen (The New Construction), who applied standardization and abstract aesthetics, and the traditionalists of the Delft School led by Granpré Molière, who favored historic forms and materials. Van Eesteren's 1935 plan provided guidance for Amsterdam's postwar development. There and elsewhere the rational formula of open space combined with low- and high-rise residential construction provided the basis for suburban development. An outstanding example is Pendrecht in Rotterdam (1953), designed by the architect Charlotte Stam-Beese (1903–1988). Taking social structure as the basis for design, this introduced the neighborhood concept of urban planning. It was a modern variation on the garden village in which suburban districts were to be linked to the central city by green buffers. A larger extension of this idea was the planning concept for a megalopolis, the Randstad, consisting of the agglomeration of the major cities in the west of the Netherlands, with a green heart at its center.

Postwar reconstruction also involved the planning of new towns in the newly created polder lands in the former Zuider Zee, the IJsselmeer. While most settlements were designed by Delft School planners and architects, the modernists created a city of abstract rationality and geometry at Nagele (1948–1962). In central cities, a similar contrast between modernity and tradition appeared. De Lijnbaan (1951–1953), a modern pedestrian mall designed by J.H. van den Broek (1898–1978) and J.B. Bakema (1914–1981) in the bombed-out center of Rotterdam, emphasized the composition of plastic building masses rather than the creation of street walls. In The Hague, areas destroyed in the war were replaced by plans designed by Willem M. Dudok (1884–1974), whose closed blocks followed Berlage's precedent. In cities such as Groningen and Middelburg, reconstruction was dominated by Delft School traditionalists.

During the 1960s, Dutch urban planning turned to the large-scale modernization of the city. Transportation issues dominated, with the introduction of highways and improvement of rail linkages into the city. Typical of the era was a combined office building, conference hall, shopping mall, and railroad station in the center of Utrecht, the Hoog-Catherijne (1962). Outside Amsterdam arose the Bijlmermeer (1965), a suburb linked to the city by highway and public transportation, in which high-rise apartment complexes formed in a honeycomb pattern around open space. Plans were made for similar construction within the city to replace slums slated for renewal. However, a citizen movement began to protest such projects, emphasizing the values of the old city fabric, historic preservation, and citizen participation. In 1975 protests in Amsterdam against the destruction of an old neighborhood to make way for a subway tunnel inaugurated a new period of urban renewal in which the fabric of the city was respected with infill housing and maintenance of existing street patterns. The 1978 plan for Rotterdam typifies the new aim of preserving the housing function of urban centers. Small-scale, neighborhood-oriented construction replaced the city of the future as the ideal. In Groningen, the automobile was banned from the center of the city in a comprehensive plan.

During the 1980s, a faceless zone of industrial parks and shopping centers along highways developed on the periphery of Dutch cities. As urban sprawl appeared for the first time in the Netherlands, the issue of urban identity became a focus of discussion. City governments searched for means to attract higher-income residents and businesses back to the city; public–private partnership appeared to offer possibilities for encouraging new investment in the city. Disused infrastructure such as old harbor sites was viewed as possible locations for new intensive use. Ambitious plans were developed in Rotterdam for the Kop van Zuid and in Amsterdam for the banks of the IJ. A former wharf area north of the IJ River was converted into a residential area (1980–1982) according to the plans of Rem Koolhaas (born 1944). At the end of the century, despite continued high public standards of urban planning, the Dutch were facing daunting problems of defining urban identity in an era of the automobile and electronic communications.

Nancy Stieber

See also Amsterdam school; Architectural criticism; Architectural restoration; Berlage, Hendrik Petrus; De Stijl; Dudok, Willem Marinus; Functionalism in architecture; Koolhaas, Rem; Landscape architecture; Postmodernism; Public housing

Bibliography
Rossem, Vincent van. *Het Algemeen Uitbreidingsplan van Amsterdam: Geschiedenis en ontwerp*. Rotterdam: Nederlands Architectuur Instituut, 1993.
Ruijter, P. de. *Voor volkshuisvesting en stedebouw*. Utrecht: Matrijs, 1987.
Taverne, Ed, and Irmin Visser, eds. *Stedebouw: De geschiedenis van de stad in de Nederlanden van 1500 tot heden*. Nijmegen: SUN, 1993.
Woud, Auke van der. *Het lege land: De ruimtelijke orde van Nederland, 1798–1848*. Amsterdam: Meulenhoff, 1987.

Utrecht

At the time of the Romans, Utrecht was already a center of some importance, but in an artistic sense it did not have much significance. During the later Middle Ages, Utrecht's first efflorescence in the arts was coincident with the appointment of David of Burgundy as bishop of Utrecht in 1456. Utrecht bishops were also secular authorities over the largest part of what was then the Netherlands. Inside this territory Utrecht was the most important city and would remain so until the second half of the sixteenth century.

The most important surviving artistic evidence from the time of David of Burgundy is the Domkerk (the Cathedral). True, Bishop Hendrik van Vianen laid the first stone of the choir in 1254, and construction would continue until 1517; however, the most important phase of building took place while David of Burgundy was bishop. Leading the operation was the architect Jacob van der Borch.

The building and the decorating of Utrecht's cathedral led to an enormous artistic productivity. The archives offer extensive information about the artists and their works, but they also reveal that only a fraction of the original output has survived. Furthermore, some documents have been misinterpreted; for example, the *oeuvre* of Adriaen van Wesel (ca. 1417–ca. 1490), one of the most important late-medieval Dutch sculptors (Fig. 122), was at one time wrongly attributed to Jacob van der Borch.

Van Wesel and Van der Borch belong to the elite group of medieval artists whose names can be connected with their works. The majority of works, however, remain anonymous, despite the many names the archival sources have to offer. In a number of cases certain works or a body of works are given names out of necessity. This is true in particular for artists who illustrated manuscripts, an art that flourished on a high level in Utrecht. The name that is given often refers to an important patron, such as (the Master[s] of) Otto van Moerdrecht, Zweder van Culemborg, Gijsbrecht van Brederode, Catherine of Cleves, and Evert Zoudenbalch. These miniaturists are also connected with wall paintings, representative examples of which have survived in the Domkerk, the Buurkerk, and the St. Jacobskerk, and with panel paintings. The Master of Evert Zoudenbalch, for example, painted a portrait of his patron on a panel. Research comparing miniatures with frescoes and panel paintings has been made more difficult by the fact that while many works in the first group have survived rather few from the second group have.

A good example of identification problems is the so-called Master of the Amsterdam Cabinet. This name was given to the artist whose almost complete *oeuvre* is kept in the Amsterdam Cabinet—that is, the print room of the

Rijksmuseum. His hand was later observed in a large portion of the illustrations of the Housebook, a manuscript of drawings of medieval household effects and other subjects; this led to a new name, Master of the Housebook. After this same artist was also labeled the Master of 1480, he was eventually identified as Erhard Reuwich from Utrecht, illustrator of Bernhard von Breydenbach's report of his journey to Jerusalem. The necessary question marks have been placed even on this identification.

Reuwich was one artist from Utrecht whose success was mainly abroad. He was active in Heidelberg and Speyer, and especially in Mainz, during the 1480s. The sculptor Nicolaas van Leyde, who was also from Utrecht, made a name for himself in Strasbourg in the second half of the fifteenth century.

Regional influences from the Rhineland and Burgundy are united in the architecture of the Domkerk. This is true also for Utrecht sculpture of the late Middle Ages. The historical connections are not surprising; the artists were part of the world of David of Burgundy and his court, following him as he moved from south to north for longer or shorter periods. The suffragan bishops of Utrecht were the ecclesiastical subordinates of the archbishops of Cologne, which explains the connections with the Rhineland, and there were close commercial, intellectual, and artistic contacts between the two cities. It is now assumed that some artists, once considered to be from Cologne, were actually from Utrecht or at least received their training there (for instance, the Master of the Bartholomeus Altar). The mobility of some members of the monastic orders—even austere ones like the Carthusians—was one of the ways in which the International Style was spread.

David of Burgundy died in 1496; he was succeed by Frederik van Baden, related to the House of Burgundy. In 1517 Frederik relinquished his bishop's seat to the artistic Philip of Burgundy, half brother of David. The relatively short time that Philip was bishop of Utrecht (he died in 1524) was enough, however, to give the Renaissance a foothold in Utrecht. The tone of the new style was set by artists who were foreigners: Jan van den Eynde from Mechelen was commissioned by the clerical Chapter to make a copper choir screen in Renaissance style for the cathedral; Gregorius Wellemans from Antwerp was asked to make a wooden model. Jan Gossaert, called Mabuse after his birthplace of Maubeuge, played a primordial role. He became a master in the guild in Antwerp in 1503 and left for Rome five years later, following his patron, Philip of Burgundy. After his return from Italy, where he had seen the legacy of antiquity, Gossaert became a protagonist of the Renaissance in the Netherlands. After the death of Philip of Burgundy, Gossaert worked for Adolf of Burgundy, count of Veere, until the end of his life in 1541.

In 1517, when Gossaert followed his patron, Philip of Burgundy, to Utrecht, the young Jan van Scorel (1495–1562) also decided to move there and become a student of Gossaert. Soon afterward, Van Scorel went to Italy, passing through Germany and Austria, and then on to Jerusalem. In Rome in 1522, he entered the service of the newly elected Pope Adriaan VI, who was from Utrecht. As court painter to the pope, Van

Scorel was a successor to Raphael, in whose Vatican studio he worked. After the pope's death, Van Scorel returned to Utrecht in the autumn of 1524, and except for a visit to Haarlem (1527–1529) he remained there.

Jan van Scorel is prominent in the history of Dutch painting. One of the first commissions he accepted after his return from Italy was for a triptych with the *Entry of Christ into Jerusalem* (1526–1527; Utrecht, Centraal Museum). The work is a testimony to his great mastery: an exact topographical rendering of Jerusalem; tempered coloring; responsible use of perspective; a dynamic composition; special attention to the human figure, also in regard to anatomy and proportion; and a smooth painting technique. The superiority of his work is best observed in comparison with the work of a contemporary, Jacob van Utrecht (alias Jacobus Trajectensis). The paintings by Jacob van Utrecht are very refined, but the atmosphere they radiate is entirely that of the late Middle Ages. It is assumed that Jacob van Utrecht was from Utrecht. In the period 1506–1520 he was active in Antwerp, while in the years 1520–1524 he can be traced to Lübeck.

Two of Van Scorel's students, Maerten van Heemskerck from Haarlem and Antonis Mor from Utrecht, equal their teacher in fame because of the high quality of their work. Mor (1519–ca. 1575) was active almost exclusively as a portrait painter. He spent a major part of his life as court painter to King Philip II in Spain, where he was called Antonio Moro and influenced Spanish art of his time.

With Van Scorel began the period in which an ideal art is based on classical antiquity and on contemporary Italian art. A trip to Italy such as Gossaert, Van Scorel, Mor, and Van Heemskerck made became a requirement for every self-respecting Dutch artist. The marks of such a study trip are clear not only on style and technique but also on iconography—mythology would receive special attention in history painting.

The artist Anthonie Blocklandt (1534–1583) lived in lordly style on the eve of the Dutch Golden Age and enjoyed a great reputation in his time. He was a student of Frans Floris in Antwerp, and in Rome in 1572. In his *oeuvre* there are traces of a harsh Mannerist style like Floris' as well as of the more refined style of Italians like Parmigianino. After Italy, Blocklandt first settled in his birthplace of Montfoort and later in Utrecht, where he was an eyewitness to the Iconoclastic fury in 1566. In spite of the Reformation he continued to make altarpieces. He made a most impressive triptych of *The Ascension of the Virgin* for a Utrecht church in 1579; today it can be found in a Catholic church in Bingen am Rhein.

For sculptors, even more than for painters, the Iconoclastic fury (*beeldenstorm*) meant literally and figuratively a breaking point. Before the Reformation, the many churches, monasteries, and charitable organizations in Utrecht supported the work of sculptors as well as painters. It is important to remember that the greater part of these commissions came from laymen who donated the art objects to particular institutions; with the Reformation this came to an end.

During the sixteenth century, the De Nole family had the greatest influence on sculpture in Utrecht and the surrounding area. Colijn de Nole arrived from Cambrai in Northern

France to settle in Utrecht around 1530. His work was continued by his son Jacob and his grandson Willem, who married a sister of the painter Paulus Moreelse; Willem's brothers left for Flanders.

The most important works by Colijn de Nole that survive are the tomb of Reinhout van Brederode and his wife, Philippote van der Marck, in the Dutch Reformed Church in Vianen (1540–1541) and the mantelpiece in the aldermen's hall of the town hall in Kampen (1543–1544). Colijn de Nole also played an important role as an importer and disseminator of the so-called grotesque style in the Netherlands.

In 1565 Hendrick de Keyser was born in Utrecht. He was also trained there by the sculptor Cornelis Bloemaert, father of the painter Abraham Bloemaert. At age twenty-six, De Keyser moved to Amsterdam, where he resided until his death in 1621 and where he enjoyed great success as a sculptor and an architect (Color Plate 2). When De Keyser left Utrecht, it meant the end of Utrecht's reputation as a center for sculpture. The cathedral city would never again witness so high a level of achievement as in the past, and it would not even be able to compete with smaller cities like Delft and Haarlem. In architecture, too, Utrecht had no major talents during the seventeenth century. Ghijsbert Thönisz. van Vianen and the painter Paulus Moreelse are among the few architects who had any reputation in Utrecht during the seventeenth century. Their *oeuvre*, however, has little more than local significance and is overshadowed by the work of Hendrick de Keyser, who was their great model.

With painting, it was an entirely different story in the seventeenth century. In the first half of the century especially, the art of painting flourished in Utrecht. At the beginning of this development are three celebrities: Abraham Bloemaert (1564–1651), Joachim Wtewael (1566–1638), and Paulus Moreelse (1571–1638). They started their careers when Mannerism was rampant in the Netherlands. Wtewael would hang on to it the longest, except in his portraits, while Bloemaert, who lived into his eighties, was much more open to new stylistic options.

The versatile and talented Abraham Bloemaert was teacher to a considerable number of artists, some of whom came from abroad to study with him in Utrecht. Bloemaert's sons Hendrick, Adriaen, Cornelis, and Frederick also belonged to his group of students. The latter two were exclusively printmakers, Frederick working mainly after designs and paintings by his father. Cornelis was well known in Rome, where he lived. Adriaen was active as a landscape painter, while Hendrick worked in the same style as his father without ever achieving the same level.

Among Bloemaert's students were Hendrick Terbrugghen (1588–1629), Gerard van Honthorst (1592–1656), and Jan van Bijlert (1598–1671), who, like the followers of the Italian painter Caravaggio, caused a furor. These so-called Utrecht Caravaggists achieved a top level artistically and, at the same time, initiated one of the most important episodes in Dutch painting. Following Caravaggio, the Caravaggists of Utrecht did not portray people in an idealized way, but in a naturalistic way, mostly life-size. They limited themselves to essentials in an organized composition and stayed away from elaborate treatment of the background. Light plays an important role in accentuating the figures and the action.

Hendrick Terbrugghen is the most important; the refined coloring and forceful expression of his works are striking (Fig. 131). Terbrugghen was in Italy from 1604 until 1614, but Caravaggism did not take hold in the Netherlands on his return. This had to wait until Gerard van Honthorst returned to Utrecht from Italy in 1620. Van Honthorst was a celebrated master in Italy, where he was called Gherardo della Notte (Gerard of the Nights) because of his paintings with strong light-dark effects (Fig. 140). His reputation would continue to grow both in his own country and abroad—a feat unequaled by any other artist from Utrecht in the seventeenth century. He was a court painter in The Hague and also worked for the kings of England and Denmark and for the Elector of Brandenburg. The very productive artist Jan van Bijlert was also appreciated; however, his artistic qualities were inferior to those of Terbrugghen and Van Honthorst.

Other Utrecht Caravaggists were Dirck van Baburen (1595–1624; Color Plate 3) and Jan Gerritsz. van Bronchorst (1603–1661). The latter was originally a glass painter, but under the influence of Cornelis van Poelenburch he turned to painting and engraving. After 1647 he was a very popular artist in Amsterdam. In the *oeuvre* of Van Bronchorst, Van Bijlert, and Van Honthorst, one can clearly see the development from Caravaggism to a more idealized classicism. This is not the case with the talented Van Baburen, who died in 1624 at the age of thirty-four.

Dirck van Baburen did not study with Abraham Bloemaert, but with Paulus Moreelse. Both older masters made Caravaggistic works under the influence of their students (Fig. 68). Although Paulus Moreelse painted religious, mythological, and allegorical genre scenes, he is known primarily as a superior portrait painter. The same is true for Joachim Wtewael. Moreelse also worked as an architect in Utrecht, and together with Joachim Wtewael he was a member of the city council.

The Italianates in Utrecht, some of whom were the most important representatives of this style, also attracted attention in the seventeenth century. Their works consist of landscapes and townscapes that are invented views but almost always contain Roman buildings or ruins under bright, southern sunlight. The views include a religious, mythological, or simple genre scene. Figures are usually represented as animated and refined; lucid color is preferred.

In front of the line of Italianates is Cornelis van Poelenburch (1594/1595–1667), who after studying with Abraham Bloemaert traveled to Italy. He worked both in Rome and in Florence, where he was in the service of the grand duke of Tuscany. In 1626 Van Poelenburch returned to Utrecht and, except for a few trips to England, lived there until his death in 1667. Well-known in the Netherlands and abroad, Van Poelenburch's works commanded high prices; not surprisingly he had many followers as well as students.

In the second generation of Italianates was Jan Both (ca. 1615–1652). He left for Rome with his brother Andries

(1612/1613–1641) after both had studied with Abraham Bloemaert. Andries Both is reported to have drowned in Venice in 1641, and afterward Jan returned to Utrecht. Like Van Poelenburch, Jan Both was much appreciated as a painter and had many followers.

Jan Baptist Weenix (1621–1660/1661) belonged to the same generation of Italianates as Jan Both. Born in Amsterdam, he was also a student of Abraham Bloemaert in Utrecht before he left for Italy. After four years in the South, he settled in Utrecht, where he developed into one of the most important painters of the time. He was also well known in Rome, where he had worked for Cardinal Giovanni Battista Pamphili, the later Pope Innocent X. Jan Baptist Weenix painted portraits and still lifes as well as harbor views and other Italianate themes. His son and student Jan (1640–1719) followed him as a still-life painter. From 1702 to 1714 Jan was a court painter to Johann Wilhelm, the Elector Palatine, for whom he decorated Castle Bensberg with the painted wall hangings that are now in museums in Munich and Augsburg.

The representatives of the third and last generation of Italianates, who were active in the last quarter of the seventeenth century, continued to work in the tradition of artists such as Jan Both. This is the case with praiseworthy Utrecht painters Jacob de Heusch (1656–1701) and Johannes Glauber (1646–1726).

The Italianates are often mentioned, unjustifiably, in the same breath with the *Bamboccianti*, followers of the painter Pieter van Laer from Haarlem who worked in Italy. A physical deformity earned him the nickname *Bamboccio*, which means something like clumsy doll. After Van Laer, whose most important creative period was in the 1630s, his followers were called *Bamboccianti* and their work *Bambocciate*. In their paintings these artists preferred to represent vulgar scenes of daily life in Italy, including utterances from the fringes of society. One of the most important representatives of this group was Andries Both. Before he left for Italy, Andries Both painted low-life genre scenes that can be placed in the same category as those of Adriaen van Ostade, David Teniers, and Adriaen Brouwer. As a genre painter, Andries Both was surpassed by Jacob Duck (1600–1667), also from Utrecht.

Besides the Italianates, a number of other Utrecht artists were active as landscape painters. This is another area in which Abraham Bloemaert made a ground-breaking contribution. Roelandt Savery (1576/1578–1639) did also, bringing his own accent with heroic landscapes. Savery found a follower in this genre—namely, Gilles Claesz. de Hondecoeter (?–1638), who was from Flanders. More idyllic and a prelude to the Romantic are the real and imaginary Rhine and Mosel River valley landscapes of Herman Saftleven (1609–1685).

Savery is known also as a painter of flower still lifes and animals, credited with having introduced the animal piece to Dutch art. He may have been the first master in the Netherlands to paint independent flower still lifes; the earliest works that survive in this genre date from 1603 and are by his hand (Utrecht, Centraal Museum; American private collection). Besides Savery, Ambrosius Bosschaert the Elder (1573–1621) and his sons Ambrosius (1609–1645), Abraham (1612/1613–

1643), and Johannes (1610/1611–1628); his son-in-law Balthasar van der Ast (1593/1594–1657) and later Jan Davidsz. de Heem (1606–1683/1684), Jacob Marrel (1614–1681), and Abraham Mignon (1640–1679)—the last two from Frankfurt—made Utrecht into an internationally renowned center of flower, fruit, and *pronk* still-life painting. During the 1640s, Jan Davidsz. de Heem took the profuse and elaborate *pronk* still life to an unprecedented high. In the category of the animal piece, Melchior de Hondecoeter (1636–1695), who left a sizable *oeuvre*, would achieve great fame. He was a grandson of Gilles Claesz. de Hondecoeter (?–1638), son of Gijsbert Gillesz. Claesz. de Hondecoeter (1604–1653), and cousin of Jan Weenix (1640–1719).

A remarkable fact is that a number of painters in Utrecht applied themselves to fish still lifes, even though the city is inland and not by a river. Marcus Ormea (?–1664) and his son Willem (?–1673) were the first to practice this genre, and in doing so they brought something new to Dutch painting. More important, however, were Jan de Bont (?–1653) and Jacob Gillig (ca. 1636–1701).

Utrecht also had some marine painters. Adam Willaerts (1577–1664) and his sons Abraham (1603–1669) and Isaac (1620–1693) were the most prominent. Their love for water and ships is not so strange when it is known that the Willaert family came from the port city of Antwerp. Savery was also from Flanders; he was born in Kortrijk about 1576/1578 and left with his family for the Netherlands while he was still very young. At the invitation of Rudolf II he went to Prague in 1605. After Rudolf died in 1612, Savery stayed on as a court painter until 1614. He returned to the Netherlands, moving first to Amsterdam and then in 1619 to Utrecht, where he remained until his death.

When Savery was working in Prague, Paulus van Vianen (ca. 1570–1613), who was also from Utrecht, was active there as a gold and silversmith. Before Van Vianen went to Prague in 1603, he had worked at the court of Bavaria in Munich since 1596. In 1613 or 1614 he was back in Utrecht. He, his older brother Adam (ca. 1569–1627), and Adam's son Christiaan (ca. 1600–ca. 1667) are counted among the most famous silversmiths of their time. In 1637 Christiaan, who was also an engraver and a publisher, entered the service of Charles I of England. In 1639, he made the church silver for the St. George Chapel at Windsor.

Most of the artists introduced here, including the metalsmiths, were also skilled draftsmen. Some were also printmakers. In addition to Cornelis and Frederick Bloemaert, a number of members of the De Passe family had a special reputation as graphic artists. Crispijn de Passe I was born in Arnemuiden around 1560 and worked in Utrecht from 1612 until 1637, the year of his death. However, he also worked in Antwerp, Paris (where he was a teacher at the academy of Antoine de Pluvinel), Aachen, Frankfurt, and Cologne. His children Crispijn II (1594/1595–1670), Willem (ca. 1590–?), Simon (1593?–1647), and Magdalena (1600–1638) were all born in Cologne; they would all apply themselves to engraving, some more skillfully than others. They worked not only in Utrecht, but also in Copenhagen, London, and Paris.

Because of this they gained international fame, but they also assured that Dutch art became widely known through the prints they made after paintings.

Somewhat of an outsider in the Utrecht art world of the seventeenth century was Hendrick Goudt (1582/1583–1648), who applied himself particularly to printmaking but also produced a few paintings. His remarkable and surprising *oeuvre*, made so through his own peculiar handling of *chiaroscuro*, had a great influence on his contemporaries.

The celebrated architectural painter Pieter Saenredam (1597–1665) was not really from Utrecht; he did not stay longer than a few months in 1636. The cathedral city was not a vital center of townscape, topographical, and architectural painting, making Saenredam's activities more noticeable. His paintings and drawings of the exteriors and interiors of churches fill a special place in art history.

The death of Abraham Bloemaert in 1651 is symbolically the end of Utrecht's artistic effulgence. The initiating role that artists had played in the first half of the seventeenth century stops, while the level of artistry does not rise to the earlier level either. In the second half of the seventeenth century, Utrecht lost forever the character of a first-rate artistic center. Typically, a number of artists left Utrecht and looked for work elsewhere. Paulus van Liender (1731–1797), for example, went to Haarlem, where he developed more into a merchant than a painter and draftsman of landscapes and townscapes. His older brother Pieter Jan (1727–1779) stayed in Utrecht, where he made painted wall hangings. Both brothers were trained by their uncle Jacob van Liender (1696–1759), whose real profession was a physician.

A Utrecht painter who knew how to attract attention in the second half of the eighteenth and the beginning of the nineteenth century was Louis François Gérard van de Puyl (1750–1824). From 1785 to 1788 he lived in London, occupying himself with painting portraits that clearly show the influence of the local English production. From 1804 to 1807 he was director of the Utrecht Drawing Academy, into which he tried to breathe new life. Afterward he disappeared to France, where he seems to have worked mainly in the North. The sculptor Jacob Cressant (?–ca. 1765), on the other hand, left Abbeville in Northern France to settle in Utrecht at the end of the 1720s; later he left Utrecht to go to Amsterdam. He had a worthy successor in his student Willem Hendrik van de Wall (1716–1790), who was born and reared in Utrecht.

In the nineteenth century, Pieter Christoffel Wonder (1780–1852), a painter of portraits and interiors, achieved some regard. From 1802 to 1804 he studied at the academy in Düsseldorf. In 1807 he founded an art appreciation society (Het Genootschap Kunstliefde) with the landscape and animal painter Jan Baptist Kobell II (1778–1814); from 1823 until 1831 Kobell worked in London. Wonder's student Christiaan Kramm (1797–1875) should be mentioned as an architect, painter, and graphic artist, who also gained a reputation as a biographer of artists. A painter of imaginary townscapes, Jan Hendrik Verheijen (1778–1846), also acquired a name. Verheijen, Wonder, and Kobell were chiefly inspired—as were many of their Dutch contemporaries—by the work of their seventeenth-century predecessors.

Johannes Warnardus Bilders is of major importance as a Romantic landscape painter; the members of The Hague School considered Bilders their teacher. Bilders was born in Utrecht in 1811, although he would work there only for a limited period in his life. During 1839–1844 he was busy working in the area of Wiesbaden, caught in the grip of Romantic landscape painting of the Düsseldorf School. Afterward Bilders settled in Oosterbeek, where he formed a center of Dutch Romantic painting; he died there in 1890.

The artistic slumber in Utrecht continued until the 1920s; it was interrupted only by a driven advocacy of the Neo-Gothic style; the St. Bernulphus Guild in Utrecht, founded in 1869, was essential in the development of the Neo-Gothic style in the Netherlands. There were roughly two movements: The Utrecht movement, which held on very tightly to the historic past; and the Amsterdam movement, which interpreted the Gothic style liberally. Three individuals left an indelible mark on the Utrecht movement of the Neo-Gothic style: the architect Alfred Tepe, the sculptor Friedrich Wilhelm Mengelberg, and the silversmith Gerard Brom. The last, the progenitor of two generations of Utrecht metalsmiths, came from Amersfoort. Tepe was originally from Amsterdam; he settled in Utrecht in 1872. He was educated in Berlin, following which he was involved in finishing the cathedral in Cologne from 1865 until 1867. Mengelberg was born in Cologne in 1837. Originally a Protestant, he converted to Catholicism out of an enthusiasm for the Middle Ages. Tepe and Mengelberg worked together a great deal. Tepe's architecture is striking because of its taut simplicity, while the decoration of the interiors, taken care of by Mengelberg, was much more elaborate.

Since the 1920s there have been three artists of special significance from Utrecht: Pyke Koch (1901–1991), Johannes Moesman (1909–1988), and Erich Wichmann (1890–1929). Koch, born in Beek near Nijmegen, came to Utrecht to study law, but under the influence of Wichmann he started painting. His work, which is striking because of a refined technique and a merciless realistic expression, is part of Magic Realism. Moesman, with his erotically charged work, is the only true Dutch Surrealist. Wichmann, who lived in Amsterdam from 1914 until 1921, was a writer and critic as well as a painter, sculptor, graphic artist, and designer. After 1913 his paintings became abstract; his work shows a relation to that of Kandinsky and the Futurists.

The architect and designer Gerrit Rietveld (1888–1964) had to wait a long time for recognition, but now he enjoys international fame. His Schröder House, designed in 1924 and named after the Mrs. Schröder who commissioned it, is world famous (Color Plate 12). Rietveld was a furniture maker who developed into an extremely original designer and architect. In his view, the form had to be the materializing of the function. Rietveld has had great influence, in design (Fig. 39) as well as in architecture.

Rietveld had close contact with the members of De Stijl, and he became a member in 1919. He had a particularly good relationship with Theo van Doesburg (1883–1931) and with

Bart van der Leck (1876–1958), both of whom were born in Utrecht. Another architect of importance is Sybold van Ravesteyn (1889–1983). At first he worked in a functional style, but later he opted for a more playful, more elegant design.

Until the middle of the seventeenth century Utrecht was one of the most important artistic centers in the Netherlands and Europe. Later other cities stepped into the foreground, in particular Amsterdam. This is the way it is today.

Jos de Meyere

See also Bloemaert, Abraham; De Hondecoeter, Melchior; De Keyser, Hendrick; De Stijl; History painting; Italy; Koch, Pyke; Landscape; Magic Realism; Mannerism, Mannerists; Manuscript illumination; Moesman, Johannes Hendricus (Joop); Neo-Gothic; Pastoral; Sculpture (ca. 1400–ca. 1550); Surrealism; Terbrugghen, Hendrick; Utrecht Caravaggists; Van Baburen, Dirck Jaspersz.; Van Doesburg, Theo; Van Honthorst, Gerard; Van Schurman, Anna Maria; Van Wesel, Adriaen

Bibliography

Defoer, H.L.M., and W.C.M. Wüstefeld, eds. *L'art en Hollande au temps de David et Philippe de Bourgogne: Tresors du musée national Het Catharijneconvent à Utrecht.* Zwolle: Waanders, 1993.

Landscap in Utrecht. Utrecht: Centraal Museum, 1974.

Meyere, Jos de. *Jan van Scorel 1495–1562: Schilder voor prinsen en prelaten.* Utrecht: Centraal Museum, 1981.

———. *Roelant Savery 1576–1639.* Utrecht: Centraal Museum, 1985.

———. *Utrecht op Schilderijen: Zes eeuwen topografische voorstellingen van de stad Utrecht.* Utrecht: Kwadraat, 1988. (English summary).

Meyere, Jos de et al. eds. *Jan van Scorel in Utrecht: Altaarstukken en schilderijen omstreeks 1540.* Utrecht: Centraal Museum, 1977.

Rosenberg, J., S. Slive, and E.H. ter Kuile. *Dutch Art and Architecture 1600–1800.* 1966. 2nd Rev. ed. Harmondsworth: Penguin Books, 1977.

Utrecht Caravaggists

In the first half of the seventeenth century a concentration of painters in the town of Utrecht in the Northern Netherlands were influenced by the Italian painter Michelangelo Merisi da Caravaggio (1571/1572–1610). With all of the differences among them, they are regarded as one group—the Utrecht Caravaggists. The most important are Hendrick Terbrugghen, Dirck van Baburen, and Gerard van Honthorst. Also included are Jan van Bijlert, Paulus Bor, Jan Gerritsz. van Bronchorst, and Hendrick Bloemaert. Some had been students of the Utrecht history painter Abraham Bloemaert before travel to Italy brought them in contact with the works of Caravaggio. The first painter to return from Italy was Terbrugghen in 1614; six years later, Van Honthorst and Van Baburen returned. With these three painters back in Utrecht there was a breakthrough of Caravaggism and the start of a new phase in seventeenth-century Dutch painting. Until then, the leading style in Utrecht had been Mannerism.

It should not be surprising that the intense realism of Caravaggio received so much approval from the Dutch since it was connected with artistic traditions already present in the North. For several centuries realism had been one of the mainstays of Netherlandish painting. The strong contrast of light and dark that Caravaggio used to increase the dramatic power of his paintings was a part of Northern art; night scenes, often related to elements from daily life, had been known in the Flemish tradition since the fifteenth century. The Dutch Caravaggists, in fact, sharpened the light–dark effect through the frequent use of an artificial light source, such as a candle or a torch, often cunningly concealed behind a figure or an object in the painting (Fig. 140). The artists from Utrecht had a good eye for striking details. The old man wearing conspicuous pinch-nose eyeglasses in Caravaggio's *Calling of Matthew* (1599–1600; Rome, Church of San Luigi dei Francesi) is a type that can later be seen again in religious pictures by Van Baburen and Terbrugghen (Fig. 131). In Caravaggio's *Calling of Matthew* are also some young men who are wearing brightly colored clothes. Such young men went on to lead a life of their own in Dutch art; they were set apart and portrayed at half-length, given wine glasses to hold, musical instruments to play, or young women of easy virtue to consort with (Color Plate 3). In this way, the Italian painting was transformed into a genre scene. The reasons for the changes have to do with the different working situation that artists faced in the Northern Netherlands. In Catholic Italy, the commissions given to Dutch painters had been for the better part religious in nature. In the officially Protestant Netherlands, the market for religious works was more limited; commissions for church decorations did not exist. Painters worked mainly for the open market, and paintings of cheerful young men enjoying a drink and making music (especially if there was a moral message attached) were very welcome there. In the 1620s, paintings of theatrically costumed young men—and a few women—were made in large numbers in Utrecht.

Even though Caravaggism also occurred in other towns of the Netherlands, it did not find anywhere else the degree of response it had in Utrecht. In Delft, there was Leonaert Bramer; in Gouda, Pietersz. Crabeth; in Amersfoort, there were Matthias Stom and Simon Hendrixz. The bloom of Dutch Caravaggism lasted about ten years; by 1630 it had lost its vitality. The death of two important exponents of the style, Van Baburen and Terbrugghen, in 1624 and 1629, respectively, surely accelerated the decline. But by that time there was also a new trend developing in painting—classicism. The influence of Caravaggio had made its impact in a short time and would remain evident long into the seventeenth century, even in the works of great masters such as Johannes Vermeer, Frans Hals, and Rembrandt.

Eugenie Boer

See also Bloemaert, Abraham; Bramer, Leonaert; Delft; Dordrecht; Frames, painted; Framing devices within pictures; Genre painting, seventeenth century; Hals, Frans; History painting; Italy; Mannerism, Mannerists; Musicians, musical companies, musical performers; Rembrandt van Rijn; Terbrugghen, Hendrick; Theater and theatricality; Utrecht; Van Baburen, Dirck Jaspersz.; Van Honthorst, Gerard; Vermeer, Johannes

Bibliography

Blankert, A. et al. *Nieuwe Licht op de Gouden Eeuw: Hendrick ter Brugghen en tijdgenoten.* Utrecht: Centraal Museum; Brunswick: Herzog Anton Ulrich-Museum, 1987.

Eck, Xander van. "From Doubt to Conviction: Clandestine Catholic Churches As Patrons of Dutch Caravaggesque Painting." *Simiolus* 22 (1993/1994): 217–234.

Haak, B. *The Golden Age: Dutch Painters of the Seventeenth Century.* Translated and edited by E. Willems-Treeman. New York: Harry N. Abrams, 1984.

Houtzager, M.E., ed. *Caravaggio en de Nederlanden.* Utrecht: Centraal Museum, 1952.

Huys Janssen, P. *Schilders in Utrecht, 1600–1700.* Utrecht: Matrijs, 1990.

Mai, E. *Die Utrechter Malerschule: Caravaggisti des Nordens.* Cologne: Wallraf-Richartz Museum, 1984.

Nicolson, B. "Caravaggio and the Netherlands." *Burlington Magazine* 94 (1952): 247–252.

Van Baburen, Dirck Jaspersz. (ca. 1595–1624)

During his short life Dirck van Baburen was able to become an important representative of the Utrecht Caravaggists; he was the first to introduce the dramatic Caravaggistic *chiaroscuro* in the Netherlands. After a brief period of training with the Utrecht painter Paulus Moreelse (1571–1638), the young Van Baburen left for Rome, where he was influenced by the art of Caravaggio and his follower Bartolommeo Manfredi. During his six-year stay in Italy (ca. 1615–1621), Van Baburen received important commissions from Cardinal Scipione Borghese, the marquis Vincenzo Giustiniani, and the grand duke of Tuscany. For the Church San Pietro in Montorio in Rome he painted three large canvases that are still hanging there: *The Entombment of Christ, Christ on the Mount of Olives,* and *Christ Carrying the Cross.* After his return to Utrecht, he developed a type of young male musician that shows the inspiration of Caravaggio. The *Jongen met mondtrommel* (Boy Playing a Jew's Harp) of 1621 (Utrecht; Centraal Museum) is one of the earliest works that he made after Italy. These half-length portrayals of single figures grew very popular in the Northern Netherlands in just a short time. During the three years before he died from the plague in 1624, Van Baburen probably worked in the same studio as Hendrick Terbrugghen.

Van Baburen also received important commissions in the Netherlands. He worked with Terbrugghen, Pieter Paul Rubens, and Jacob Jordaens from Flanders in making a series of portraits of Roman emperors for Prince Frederik Hendrik. Van Baburen painted chiefly religious and mythological subjects with large figures; in execution he strove for great immediacy of effect. His Caravaggio-inspired naturalism was sometimes stretched far in the emphatic commonness of his models. His figures are often recognizable by their rude physiognomy and their big, red noses. This is very apparent in his *Bound Prometheus* (1623; Amsterdam, Rijksmuseum) as well as in his genre paintings, such as *The Procuress* (1622; Boston, Museum of Fine Arts; Color Plate 3).

Eugenie Boer

See also House of Orange-Nassau; Terbrugghen, Hendrick; Utrecht; Utrecht Caravaggists; Women's worlds

Bibliography

Blankert, A. et al. *Gods, Saints, and Heroes: Dutch Paintings in the Age of Rembrandt.* Washington, DC: National Gallery of Art, 1980.

———. *Nieuw Licht op de Gouden Eeuw: Hendrick ter Brugghen en tijdgenoten.* Utrecht: Centraal Museum; Brunswick: Herzog Anton Ulrich-Museum, 1987.

Nicolson, B. *Caravaggism in Europe.* 2nd ed., rev. and enl. Turin: Allemandi, 1990.

Slatkes, L.J. *Dirck van Baburen, ca. 1595–1624: A Dutch Painter in Utrecht and Rome.* Utrecht: Haentjens, Dekker, and Gumbert, 1965.

Van Brekelenkam, Quirijn Gerritsz. (ca. 1620/1625–ca. 1668/1669)

A painter from Leiden, loosely associated with the Leiden *fijnschilders* (fine painters), Van Brekelenkam may have been trained by Gerrit Dou, although his style is looser and less meticulous. He was a prolific painter, whose *oeuvre* includes several hundred works of varying quality. His specialty was scenes of simple domestic life, but he also produced images of domestic economy, such as housewives at market or craftsmen in their home workshops. His pictures of tailors and shoemakers at work are Van Brekelenkam's most unique achievement. As a Catholic, he also did paintings of praying hermits, which were popular with a Catholic clientele.

Elizabeth Alice Honig

See also Commerce and commercial life; Dou, Gerrit; Leiden; Religion of artists

Bibliography

Lasius, Angelika. *Quiringh van Brekelenkam.* Doornspijk: Davaco, 1992.

Sutton, Peter C. *Masters of Seventeenth-Century Dutch*

Genre Painting. Philadelphia: Philadelphia Museum of Art, 1984.

Van Campen, Jacob (1595–1657)

Jacob van Campen was the leading artist in the introduction of an Italian classical formal idiom in the Northern Netherlands. In the beginning of the seventeenth century, Van Campen was trained as a painter along with Pieter Saenredam in the Haarlem studio of Frans de Grebber. Arnold Houbraken in 1721, and Filippo Baldinucci in a work about artists' lives written earlier and published in 1728, told how Van Campen made a trip to Italy to study during his youth and how he came into contact with classical architecture. However, a stay in Italy has not been documented. If he was there, he probably worked only as a painter. The few known paintings by Van Campen show some influence of the school of Caravaggio, comparable to the work of the Utrecht Caravaggists. Around 1648–1650, Van Campen, together with Constantijn Huygens, planned the program for the cycle of paintings in honor of the late *stadholder*, Frederik Hendrik, in the Oranjezaal of Huis ten Bosch in The Hague. Several artists from the Northern and Southern Netherlands were commissioned to execute the cycle. Van Campen himself painted two of the lower parts and a part of the ceiling and also had the task of coordinating the execution of the remaining parts.

His most important architectural creations, the Mauritshuis in The Hague and the Amsterdam Town Hall, led the way for the further development of Dutch architecture, which, chiefly because of their example, remained inspired by classicism until the end of the seventeenth century. Begun in 1633, the town palace of Johan Maurits van Nassau-Siegen, called the Mauritshuis, signaled the definitive breakthrough of the new, more rigorous classical style inspired by the ideas of the Italian architectural theorists Palladio and Scamozzi. Van Campen's masterpiece is the new town hall of Amsterdam, which was started in 1648 after the Treaty of Münster; the bare structure was completed in 1665. This monumental building measures 200 x 280 feet. The front and rear façades have powerful corner pavilions and projecting centers and are articulated with pilasters in the Composite order placed above pilasters in the Corinthian order, conforming to instructions in the treatise *L'idea dell 'architettura universale* (1615) by Scamozzi. The tympanum on the front façade shows clearly the ambitions of this merchant city: Represented allegorically are the world's oceans paying tribute to the Maid of Amsterdam. Above this is the personification of Peace, a reference to the successful end of the Eighty Years' War (1568–1648). Just inside, there are also numerous allegorical figures and mythological scenes in marble reliefs, executed by Artus I Quellinus and his studio; the reference is always to the function of the rooms of government, which lie in the back.

K.A. Ottenheym

See also Classicism in architecture; Country houses and gardens; House of Orange-Nassau; Huygens, Constantijn; Nationalism; Post, Pieter; Quellinus, Artus I; Town halls; Writers on art, eighteenth century

Bibliography

Bogaart, E. van den et al., eds. *Johan Maurits van Nassau-Siegen, 1604–1679: A Humanist Prince in Europe and Brazil*. The Hague: Johan Maurits van Nassau Stichting, 1979.

Fremantle, K. *The Baroque Town Hall of Amsterdam*. Utrecht: Haentjes, Dekker, and Gumbert, 1959.

J. Huisken, K.A. Ottenheym, G. Schwartz, eds. *Jacob van Campen: Het klassieke ideaal in de Gouden Euw*. Amsterdam: Architectura en Natura, 1995.

Swillens, P.T.A. *Jacob van Campen: Schilder en bouwmeester, 1595–1657*. Arnhem: Gysbers and Van Loon, 1979.

Van de Velde, Jan II (1593–1641)

A prolific draftsman, painter, etcher, engraver, and publisher of prints, Jan van de Velde II was one of a group of artists in Haarlem who developed a new concept of naturalistic landscape representation in the early seventeenth century. He was born in Delft or Rotterdam, son of the prominent writing master Jan van de Velde I, an immigrant from Antwerp. In 1613 Jan II became apprenticed to the engraver Jacob Matham in Haarlem, where he entered the Guild of St. Luke in 1614. He married Christina Non of Enkhuizen in 1618. Until this time he had been engraving and etching after his own designs, but after his marriage he worked from designs of others, while continuing to be active as a draftsman. From 1636 until his death he resided in Enkhuizen. His son, Jan van de Velde III, became a still-life painter.

In his early years in Haarlem, Jan II was closely associated with other young artists, including his cousin Esaias van de Velde and Willem Buytewech. Together they produced innovative work in the genres of landscape and upper-class leisure scenes. Jan's contribution was in developing a graphic formula for conveying characteristics of an idealized but "local" landscape, and in popularizing this imagery through hundreds of etchings. Although the scenes are imaginary they convey an effect of reality, showing the Dutch countryside as an idyllic site for pleasure and visual enjoyment. His prints after other artists—Esaias van de Velde, Buytewech, Pieter Saenredam, Frans Hals, Pieter de Molijn, and others—include peasant scenes, costume series, character types, and topographical views.

Elizabeth Alice Honig

See also Commerce and commercial life; Haarlem; Landscape; Matham, Jacob; Prints, printmaking, and printmakers (ca. 1500–ca. 1900); Townscapes

Bibliography

Freedberg, David. *Dutch Landscape Prints of the Seventeenth Century*. London: Colonnade Books/British Museum, 1980.

Gelder, J.G. van. *Jan van de Velde, 1593–1641: Teekenaar-Schilder*. The Hague: Nijhoff, 1933.

Luijten, Ger, and Christiaan Schuckman, comps., and D. de Hoop Scheffer, ed. *Hollstein's Dutch and Flemish Etchings, Engravings, and Woodcuts, ca. 1450–1700*. Vols. 33 and 34. Roosendaal: Koninklijke van Poll, 1989.

Van den Eeckhout, Gerbrand (1621–1674)

Gerbrand van den Eeckhout is recognized primarily as a productive Amsterdam history painter who created scenes derived from the Bible, ancient history, and mythology; yet he also made genre and portrait paintings. After an apprenticeship with Rembrandt of approximately five years, Van den Eeckhout produced his first dated canvas in 1641. He began depicting genre interiors and guardroom scenes in the middle of the seventeenth century. His history paintings from later in his career tended toward a large-scale format. Van den Eeckhout never married and died a bachelor in Amsterdam.

Van den Eeckhout's earliest paintings are generally small in size and display a formal debt to both Rembrandt and Rembrandt's teacher, Pieter Lastman. Van den Eeckhout incorporated the immediacy of Lastman's narration with the subtlety of Rembrandt's *chiaroscuro* effects. Van den Eeckhout's mature painting style ranges from the consistently Rembrandtesque qualities of his history paintings to the refined elegance of his portraits, often associated with a Flemish influence.

As a prolific history painter, Van den Eeckhout depicted scenes from a variety of historical periods. The majority of the subjects of his paintings are taken from the Bible, particularly from the Old Testament. A large number of landscape drawings evolved out of his interest in the incorporation of the landscape as background to his religious works. However, there exists only a very small number of landscape paintings. A significant portion of Van den Eeckhout's *oeuvre* was also devoted to the depiction of figures and deeds from ancient history, especially Republican Roman history, a popular source of subject matter for Amsterdam artists from the middle to late seventeenth century. One manifestation of the popularity of history painting in Amsterdam was the emergence of the history portrait in which the sitters commissioned artists to portray them as famous historical figures. Van den Eeckhout produced several history portraits, the subjects of which were taken from Republican Roman history.

One of the most popular Republican Roman subjects chosen by Dutch artists or their patrons was the magnanimity of Scipio Africanus, a famous general of the late third century B.C. Van den Eeckhout depicted the magnanimity of Scipio in four canvases. Of these four canvases, three are probably history portraits based on the portrait qualities of the figures represented (Fig. 120). Scipio's great deed of returning the captive bride to her fiancé was traditionally viewed as a paradigm of virtuous behavior, or *exempla virtutis* (model of virtue), a humanist concept evident in seventeenth-century Dutch thought.

More research needs to be done on the life and work of Gerbrand van den Eeckhout, one of the most accomplished Dutch painters of the middle to late seventeenth century. In addition to an updated monograph, there needs to be a further assessment of Van den Eeckhout's works in relationship to Rembrandt's studio and output, and iconographical studies on the categories of history painting produced by the artist.

Steven Golan

See also History painting; History portraits; Humanism, humanist themes; Portraiture; Rembrandt School; Roman history

Bibliography

Blankert, Albert et al. *Gods, Saints, and Heroes: Dutch Painting in the Age of Rembrandt*. Washington, DC: National Gallery of Art, 1980.

Brown, Christopher et al. *Rembrandt: The Master and His Workshop: Paintings*. New Haven: Yale University Press, 1991.

Haak, Bob. *The Golden Age: Dutch Painters of the Seventeenth Century*. New York: Harry N. Abrams, 1984.

Roy, R. "Studien zu Gerbrand van den Eeckhout." Ph.D. diss., Vienna, 1972.

Sutton, Peter. *Northern European Paintings in the Philadelphia Museum of Art*. Philadelphia: Philadelphia Museum of Art, 1990.

Van den Eijnde, Hendrik Albertus (1869–1939)

H.A. van den Eijnde is particularly important as an architectural sculptor. In collaboration with Hildo Krop (1884–1970), he created the sculpture for the Scheepvaarthuis (1912–1916) of architect J.M. van der Mey (1878–1949), the first important building of the Amsterdam School (Fig. 4). From 1917 to 1923 he worked for the national government with several architects, among them J. Crouwel (1885–1962) and J.M. Luthmann (1890–1973), on university and PTT (Post, Telegraph, and Telephone) buildings. Interesting is the early application of concrete sculpture on the Luthmann radio station in Kootwijk (1922).

With the fading of the Amsterdam School caused by, among other things, the influence of De Stijl and the Nieuwe Zakelijkheid (New Objectivity, or Functionalism in architecture), he began working with J. Wils (1891–1972) and W.M. Dudok (1884–1974). In cooperation with Dudok, he created the austere sculpture on De Bijenkorf department store in Rotterdam (1929–1930) and the monument to the controversial *General Van Heutz in Batavia* (1927, destroyed in 1953).

From about 1913 until the end of the 1920s, when Van den Eijnde worked in the style of the Amsterdam School, he was under the influence of archaic sculpture (Egypt, Babylonia, Assyria) and the work of the Germans F. Metzer (1870–1919) and B. Schmitz (1856–1916). This is expressed in strong stylizing and a preference for the use of freestone. In the following period, his work was influenced by international tendencies to realism and classicism in art, with the result that his stylization decreased and sculpture began to take a more independent position. In addition to architectural sculpture, Van den Eijnde produced tomb monuments, applied art work (in silver among other materials), and a modest amount of uncommissioned work.

Geraart Westerink

See also Amsterdam School; Applied arts; Dudok, Willem Marinus; Krop, Hildo; Nationalism; Public monumental sculpture (1795–1900); Sculpture (1795–1945)

Bibliography

Boterenbrood, Helen, and Jürgen Prang. *Van der Mey en het Scheepvaarthuis*. The Hague: SDU, 1989.

Koopmans, Ype. "Een cultus van lelijkheid: Duitse invloeden op de Nederlandse bouwsculptuur." *Archis* 8 (1987): 30–37.

———. *H.A. Van den Eijnde*. Assen: Drents Museum, 1994.

———. "Hendrik Albertus van den Eijnde, 1869–1939: Op de grens van beeldende kunst en kunstnijverheid." Ph.D. diss., Rijksuniversiteit Leiden, 1984.

———. "Stenen des aanstoots: Van Heutsz-monumenten in Nederland en het voormalig Oost-Indië." *Jong Holland* 2 (1986): 27–45.

Van der Aa, Dirk (1731–1809)

Painter of decorative works and carriages, Dirk van der Aa (who was baptized Theodorus van der Ha) was born in The Hague. In 1755 he became a member of the Guild of St. Luke, and in 1768 he was made a master painter. He was a student of Johann Heinrich Keller, a painter born in Zurich who received his training in Germany and Paris before establishing himself in The Hague in 1726. Van der Aa also traveled to Paris to study. Keller introduced to the Netherlands the overdoor piece *à la française*, in which groups of small figures are placed in a mythological, allegorical, or idyllic context. This type was developed further by Van der Aa, who made children his subject. He painted them in color as well as in different monochromes: in grisaille like the *witjes* made famous by Jacob de Wit, also in nuances of white and pink. In these scenes with children and *putti* he represented a later, more French-oriented, phase of the genre. He can, therefore, be considered more a follower of François Boucher than of De Wit. Some examples of his work are still preserved in The Hague in the palace on the Lange Voorhout and a few other places.

Van der Aa was also a prominent decorator of carriages. He was trained in this by Gerard Mes in The Hague, and he managed the business for some time after Mes' death. Van der Aa's students included Jan Evert Morel I and Louis Moritz.

Christina J.A. Wansink

See also Bas-relief painting; De Wit, Jacob; France; Leiden

Van der Helst, Bartholomeus (1613–1670)

Bartholomeus van der Helst was one of the most successful painters in Amsterdam in the second half of the seventeenth century. Like many Dutch artists of his time, he devoted himself to a single subject specialty: portraiture. His style is characterized by technical precision and clarity of lighting, color, and expression.

Van der Helst was born in Haarlem in 1613. By the time of his marriage in 1636, he had settled in Amsterdam, where

he lived and worked until his death on December 16, 1670. His first works built on the conservative, unidealized portraits of the previous generation (Thomas de Keyser, Werner van den Valckert, and Nicolaes Eliasz. Pickenoy, who was probably Van der Helst's teacher). In 1639 Van der Helst's fame was launched with the commission for *The Militia Company of Capt. Roelof Bicker and Lieutenant Jan Michielsz. Blauew* (Amsterdam, Rijksmuseum), which hung beside Rembrandt's *The Nightwatch* (Color Plate 5) in the Kloveniers militia guild hall (Kloveniersdoelen) and was described by Sir Joshua Reynolds in 1781 as "comprehending more of those qualities which make a perfect portrait than any other I have ever seen." For the rest of his career, he enjoyed the patronage of the leading families of Amsterdam, received more commissions for group portraits, and portrayed more reigning burgomasters than any other artist of his generation.

It is not surprising that Van der Helst's slick manner and formal clarity appealed more to the classicist Reynolds than did Rembrandt's shadowed masterpiece. While Van der Helst's earliest works—for example, *Portrait of a Preacher* (1638; Rotterdam, Museum Boymans-van Beuningen); and *Andries Bicker* (1642; Amsterdam, Rijksmuseum)—are simple in format and trenchant in character, his mature portraits follow the developing trend toward ostentation in costume, comportment, and setting, emphasizing superficial description of rich fabrics and other attributes of privilege, sometimes at the expense of psychological depth. His *Double Portrait of Abraham del Court and Maria Keersegieter* (1654; Rotterdam, Museum Boymans-van Beuningen; Fig. 141) exemplifies his talent for glittering effects of drapery, voluminous life-size figures in elegant poses, and a ritual display of affection between marriage partners. Other examples are the *Portrait of a Young Couple Walking in a Landscape* (1661; Karlsruhe, Staatliche Kunsthalle); and *Anthonie Reepmaker and Susanna Gomaerts with Their Children* (ca. 1669; Paris, Louvre).

The evolution in Van der Helst's portraiture, and that of his contemporaries (Ferdinand Bol, Govaert Flinck, Nicolaes Maes), owes much to the Flemish artist Anthony van Dyck, whose works were known through travel, importation, and circulation of reproductive prints. But innovations like the introduction of landscape and classical architecture into portrait backgrounds, a rhetorical vivacity in poses, and a general air of elegance and wealth derive not only from Van Dyck but from international trends brought to the Netherlands by traveling artists like Joachim von Sandrart, who worked in Amsterdam from 1637 to 1645 after a long sojourn in Italy, and Adriaen Hanneman (1601–1671), who picked up the Van Dyckian mode in England and brought it to The Hague in 1637. Furthermore, the shift toward aristocratic pretension in portraits reflects a more general cultural evolution in social aspirations and taste among the new generation of upwardly mobile urban *élite*.

In addition to portraits, Van der Helst produced a few genre paintings that present individual, life-size figures in evocative settings, often engaging the viewer with a dramatically direct pose and glance—for example, *Woman behind a Green Curtain* (1652; Dresden, Gemäldegalerie). Such works are related to the historicizing character studies, or *troniën*, produced by the Rembrandt School.

Van der Helst's principal follower was Abraham van den Tempel (Leeuwarden 1622/1623–Amsterdam 1672). His son, Lodewijk van der Helst (Amsterdam 1642–after 1682), also followed his father's profession—for example, *Posthumous Portrait of Admiral Aucke Stellingwerf* (1670; Amsterdam, Rijksmuseum).

Stephanie S. Dickey

See also Bol, Ferdinand; Flinck, Govaert; Group portraiture; Marriage and family portraits; Portraiture; Self-portraiture

Bibliography

Gelder, J.J. de. *Bartholomeus van der Helst*. Rotterdam: W.L. and J. Brusse, 1921.

Dickey, Stephanie S. "Bartholomeus van der Helst and Admiral Cortenaer: Realism and Idealism in Dutch Heroic Portraiture." *Leids Kunsthistorisch Jaarboek* 8 (1989): 227–245.

Haak, Bob. *The Golden Age: Dutch Painters of the Seventeenth Century*, 290–291, 371. New York: Harry N. Abrams, 1984.

Rosenberg, Jakob, Seymour Slive, and E.H. ter Kuile. *Dutch Art and Architecture: 1600 to 1800*. 1966. 2nd rev ed. Harmondsworth: Penguin Books, 1977.

Van der Heyden, Jan (1637–1712)

Most of Jan van der Heyden's paintings, prints, and drawings are skillfully rendered townscapes, though he also produced refined rural landscapes and a few interiors with still lifes. In addition to being an accomplished artist, he was also the inventor and administrator of Amsterdam's advanced and innovative systems of firefighting and street lighting near the end of the seventeenth century.

His precise, clear pictures, particularly his *stadsgezichten* (townscapes or cityscapes), leave modern viewers with the impression that they are seeing almost photographic views of actual locations. In many instances, the buildings and locations are identifiable and the views seem to be topographically accurate, as with his painting *The Dam in Amsterdam*, located in the Amsterdam Historical Museum. But at other times, Van der Heyden used artistic license in adjusting viewpoints, moving buildings, or fabricating whole scenes, which may include both real and fantasy elements. Of his six known views of Nijenrode Castle, for instance, only three seem to show the country residence in its true environs (as in the Amsterdam Rijksmuseum version), while in the other three variations, the castle is transplanted to other locales. A work in the National Gallery of London has Nijenrode set on an urban square with the sacristy of Utrecht Cathedral looming in the foreground.

The only thorough monograph of the artist is the 1971 German publication by Helga Wagner. The fairly reliable illustrated catalog of the artist's extant paintings is particularly useful. (The book's strengths and weaknesses are fully assessed in Egbert Haverkamp-Begemann's review of the work.) Biographical information and discussions about specific works can be found in the exhibition catalogs listed in the bibliography below. For an interesting discussion of the artist as self-promoter, the relationship between artist and patron, and art as propaganda, see the article by Gary Schwartz.

Diane E. Cearfoss Mankin

See also Architectural painting; Country houses and gardens; Landscape; Townscapes

Bibliography

Haverkamp-Begemann, Egbert. "Review of H. Wagner, *Jan van der Heyden, 1637–1712*." *Burlington Magazine* 115 (1973): 401–402.

Schwartz, Gary. "Jan van der Heyden and the Huydecopers of Maarsseveen." *J. Paul Getty Museum Journal* 2 (1983): 197–220.

Sutton, Peter C. et al. *Masters of Seventeenth-Century Dutch Landscape Painting*, 342–345. Boston: Museum of Fine Arts; distributed by University of Pennsylvania Press, 1987.

Wagner, Helga. *Jan van der Heyden, 1637–1712*. Amsterdam and Haarlem: Scheltema and Holkema, 1971.

Wattenmaker, Richard J. et al. *Opkomst en bloei van het Noordnederlandse stadsgezicht in de 17de eeuw/The Dutch Cityscape in the Seventeenth Century and Its Sources*. Amsterdam: Amsterdams Historisch Museum, 1977.

Van der Meer, Hans (born 1955)

Hans van der Meer is a documentary photographer who is aware of the fact that events take on an assumed importance when photographed. Much contemporary documentary photography, which aims at showing how things are going somewhere nearby or far away, is produced with a single-mindedness of purpose that has led to the content of the photograph, not its form, being considered of paramount importance. These photographs serve a firm objective of informing the public about political and social problems and injustices, yet photographers seldom approach their subjects without a thought to composition. One action or look, however brief, can summarize tensions, relationships, or feelings. These momentary encounters meet the documentary photographer's need to make general statements or to express things that cannot easily be concluded from external appearances. As a consequence, a meaning has been imposed upon these situations.

Hans van der Meer seeks to avoid the pitfalls (that is, the deceptive suggestions) that can transform documentary photographs into symbolic moments. When he traversed the streets of Budapest, Hungary, between 1984 and 1986 and photographed people walking there, he wanted to avoid the obvious subjects and ways of showing them. His photographs, collected in the book *Quirk of Fate* (1987), give the sense that Van der Meer has walked around in Budapest with amazement and distance, not fully understanding other people's actions. What struck him—and also strikes the viewer of his photographs—is the introverted, unself-conscious nature of people in the street, as if it is perfectly normal behavior to carry a soccer ball or an inner tube every time one goes out.

Hans Rooseboom

See also Photography, modern and contemporary

Bibliography

Meer, Hans van der. *Quirk of Fate*. Amsterdam: Bert Bakker, 1987.

Van der Valk, Maurits Willem (1857–1935)

Maurits Willem van der Valk was a student along with Jan Veth and Willem Witsen from 1878 to 1883 at the Rijksacademie in Amsterdam, where their teacher was August Allebé. Van der Valk's first dark paintings of still lifes and landscapes were in the style of Amsterdam Impressionism. During the years 1886–1889, Van der Valk's studio on the Amsteldijk in Amsterdam was a meeting place not just for many artists, but also for most of the writers of the circle calling itself *De Tachtigers* ("of the 1880s"), to which Herman Gorter and his longtime friend Willem Kloos belonged. During this period, Van der Valk, Veth, and Witsen collaborated in writing art criticism for the periodical *De Nieuwe Gids* (The New Guide).

In 1891 Van der Valk moved to France for two years. Living in Auver-sur-Oise, he painted Impressionistic landscapes using clear, light colors and, for the first time, also made several sketch-like etchings of the landscape. During these years he exhibited his prints at the Nederlandsche Etsclub (Dutch Etching Club), and three times he was represented by one of his etchings in the album of the etching club. The prints and paintings of the flat Dutch landscape that he made after he returned to Amsterdam in 1893 are characterized by a more detailed realism (Fig. 142). Nevertheless, his work still shows moderate austerity under the influence of Japanese art, for which he had a great interest. Because of a lack of financial success, Van der Valk was forced to teach. His most famous students were Pieter Dupont, Gerhard Haverkamp, and Samuel Jessurun de Mesquita. Dupont, especially, acquired an enduring interest in the graphic arts from Van der Valk.

Maartje S. de Haan

See also Allebé, August; Art criticism, critical issues in the nineteenth century; Dupont, Pieter; Prints, modern graphic arts 1840–1945; Veth, Jan; Witsen, Willem

Bibliography

Bionda, Richard, and Carel Blotkamp, eds. *De schilders van Tachtig: Nederlandse schilderkunst 1880–1895*. Zwolle: Waanders, 1991.
Blotkamp, Carel. "Art Criticism in *De Nieuwe Gids*." *Simiolus* 5 (1971): 116–136.
Giltay, Jeroen. "De Nederlandsche Etsclub, 1885–1896." *Nederlands Kunsthistorisch Jaarboek* (1976): 91–125.
Vries, R.W.P. de, Jr. *Nederlandsche grafische kunstenaars uit het einde der negentiende eeuw en het begin van de twintigste eeuw*. The Hague: Oceanus, 1943.

Van Doesburg, Theo (1883–1931)

Best known as the founder and editor of the journal *De Stijl*, Theo Van Doesburg was also a versatile artist (painter, designer, architect, typographer) and writer of short stories, poems, and essays about art. Because of his versatility in combination with a dynamic personality, Van Doesburg acted as a catalyst within the European avant-garde. He knew everybody, from El Lissitzky to Hans Richter, from Tristan Tzara to Filippo Tommaso Marinetti, and corresponded with many avant-garde artists. He gave lectures and organized exhibitions. In addition to *De Stijl*, he devoted himself to several other journals and artists' groups. Van Doesburg's importance lies in the totality of his activities, even though they did not always agree with one another. For example, his editorship of *De Stijl* was difficult to reconcile with his interests in Dada. Therefore, Van Doesburg used the pseudonyms I.K. Bonset for his Dadaist work and Aldo Camini for a philosophic text tinged by Futurism, *Het andere gezicht* (The Other Face, ca. 1913).

Van Doesburg was not even his real name. On August 30, 1883, he was born in Utrecht as Christiaan Emile Marie Küpper. He renamed himself after his stepfather, Theodorus Doesburg. The young Van Doesburg wanted to become a painter and a writer but did not receive any schooling. His early paintings are conservative, but Van Doesburg admired Vincent van Gogh and Matthijs Maris; after 1909 he focused on the artistic expression of emotions. In the spring of 1913 he gained an admiration for abstract painting. Through reading Kandinsky's *Das Geistige in die Kunst* (The Spiritual in Art), he realized that the moderns and he shared a striving for a spiritual art.

In 1915 Van Doesburg met Erich Wichmann, Janus de Winter, Vilmos Huszár, and Piet Mondrian. These new contacts pushed him to an explosive activity: He wanted to gather the forces of the Dutch moderns into a society of artists and started a magazine in which new ideas could be expressed. In 1915 Van Doesburg never got around to do any painting; however, he did make drawings and pastels and he wrote poetry. The paintings from 1916 reveal the influence of De Winter and Huszár. From his friend the architect J.J.P. Oud, Van Doesburg received his first commission to design a leaded glass window.

The first issue of *De Stijl* appeared in October 1917. Van Doesburg's supporters were Mondrian, Huszár, Bart van der Leck, the Belgian painter and sculptor Georges Vantongerloo, and the architects J.J.P. Oud, Jan Wils, Robert van 't Hoff, and Gerrit Rietveld. *De Stijl* was devoted to a new form of art in a new and better world. The equal cooperation of painters and architects was, therefore, an important goal. Mondrian formulated the characteristics of the new art of painting: straight crossing lines and primary colors plus black, white, and gray. Together, De Stijl painters examined the practical possibilities of these visual means. The abstraction of a motif and the illusion of a foreground and background were issues that were expressly discussed. Although after 1918 one can no longer recognize the point of origin in Van Doesburg's paintings, later studies show that they are based on visible reality, such as a woman's portrait or a dancing couple. In his designs for leaded glass a year earlier, Van Doesburg had already reached a high level of abstraction in that his motif varied through reflection and rotation.

Van Doesburg grasped every opportunity to work with the architects of De Stijl. Oud and Wils found him commissions for leaded glass windows, tiled floors, and color schemes for interiors. In the beginning, Van Doesburg's designs were merely additions to the architecture and there was yet no mention of equal contributions. In 1919 he colored the surfaces of walls, doors, and ceilings in a house in Katwijk so that they seem to come loose from their foundation and actually change the character of space. The furniture for the rooms was designed by Rietveld.

The relationships with his associates in De Stijl were difficult. Huszár, Wils, and Van 't Hoff terminated their collaboration in 1919. Mondrian was still a participant but had returned to Paris. After the isolation caused by World War I, Van Doesburg felt a great need for the international exchange of ideas. He focused more and more on disseminating abroad the underlying ideas of De Stijl. Early in 1920 he traveled to Brussels, Paris, Milan, and Berlin. A year later he again made a major trip abroad with his future third wife, the pianist Nelly van Moorsel, to settle in Weimar in April 1921. There he stayed until November 1922. In his studio he gave a course on De Stijl, which was attended by students from the Bauhaus. He was at the same time active as a Dadaist. With the help of Tristan Tzara, he published the journal *Mécano* and, in September 1922, he organized a meeting of Constructivists and Dadaists in Weimar.

In the beginning of 1923 there was a Dada campaign in the Netherlands. Van Doesburg gave a lecture, *What Is Dada?*, Kurt Schwitters read poetry, Huszár performed with his *Mechanical Dance Figure*, and Nelly van Doesburg played the piano. At the time of the campaign, László Moholy-Nagy, a Hungarian avant-garde artist who had moved to Berlin by 1920 and was headed toward Constructivism, was appointed a teacher at the Bauhaus. Van Doesburg, who had hoped for this appointment, returned in April 1923 to Weimar to pack his suitcases in preparation to move again.

Van Doesburg had hardly painted since 1920. He no longer considered the art of painting adequate to express his views of reality. He became interested in perception as a phenomenon dependent upon place and time through reading popular scientific literature based on the work of Einstein. Architecture seemed especially suitable to express those kinds of ideas. A quarrel with Oud in 1922 over the application of color in architecture gave him more reason to become engrossed in architecture, along with the young architect Cornelis van Eesteren.

In May 1923 Van Doesburg moved to Paris, and soon thereafter he was given the opportunity to work out his ideas. Léonce Rosenberg made his Galerie L'Effort Moderne available for an exhibition of De Stijl architecture. The exhibition was held in October and November 1923. Van Doesburg and Van Eesteren presented three designs: a gallery addition to a house for Rosenberg, a private home, and an artist's home. The designs were asymmetrical and eccentric. The spaces openly connected with one another, and no distinction was made among the front, sides, and back of the house. Color was also part of the design and not a later addition.

It was a major disappointment for Van Doesburg that the exhibition did not lead to an architectural commission, and in 1924 he went back to painting. At first he and Mondrian were in close contact, but soon disagreements of opinion and character arose that had not been important in their correspondence. As a result of the architectural drawings that Van Doesburg called contra-constructions, there came into being the so-called contra-compositions. The slanting lines of these compositions emphasized the difference between Mondrian, who believed in universal truth, and Van Doesburg, who thought that motion was essential.

In 1927 and 1928 Van Doesburg worked with Hans Arp and Sophie Taeuber-Arp as painter-architect at the reconstruction of the Aubette amusement complex in Strasbourg. The walls and ceiling of the main festivity hall were divided into rectangles of different sizes and colors. In the dance hall annexed to the movie theater, the surfaces were slanted, as in contra-compositions. The project became a disappointment, especially since Van Doesburg had to make concessions in the use of materials. The interior was changed soon after the Aubette was first opened for use in February 1928. The Aubette still exists, and the restoration of the interiors as designed by Van Doesburg and Arp was completed in April 1994.

From 1929 until his death on March 7, 1931, Van Doesburg exhibited regularly, but Surrealism ran rampant at the time and success eluded him. He did, however, receive close attention from a younger generation of artists. He organized, with four young artists (Otto Gustav Carlsund, Jean Hélion, Leon Tutundjian, Marcel Wantz), the group Art Concret in January 1930. Of these four signers of the group's manifesto, only the French-born Hélion later received substantial recognition for his art of geometric abstraction. At the end of his life, Van Doesburg lived in a studio residence in Meudon that he designed. Like the Van Doesburg archive, this house is now the property of the Dutch national government and every year is home to a different Dutch artist.

Els Hoek

Natalie Kamphuys

See also Avant-garde; Dada; De Branding; De Stijl; Mondrian, Piet; Oud, Jacobus Johannes Pieter

Bibliography

Baljeu, Joost. *Theo van Doesburg*. London: Studio Vista, 1974.

Blotkamp, Carel. "Theo van Doesburg." In *De Stijl: The Formative Years, 1917–1922*, 3–37. Cambridge, MA: MIT Press, 1986.

Doesburg, Theo van. *Principles of Neo-Plastic Art*. Translation of *Grundbegriffe der neuen gestaltenden Kunst*, a volume in the Bauhausbücher series, 1925. London: Lund Humphries, 1969.

Doig, Allan. *Theo van Doesburg: Painting into Architecture, Theory into Practice*. Cambridge: Cambridge University Press, 1986.

Hedrick, Hannah. *Theo van Doesburg: Propagandist and Practitioner of the Avant-Garde, 1909–1923*. Ann Arbor, MI: UMI Research Press, 1980.

Straaten, Evert van. *Theo van Doesburg: Painter and Architect*. The Hague: SDU, 1988.

Troy, Nancy J. *The De Stijl Environment*. Cambridge, MA: MIT Press, 1983.

Van Dongen, Kees (1877–1968)

The artist Kees van Dongen, of Dutch origin (he became a French citizen in 1929), received fame mainly through his contributions to French art: the Fauvist paintings of 1905–1906 and his later paintings, after 1907–1908, of prostitutes, circus artists, and dancers, in which he often, in a very confrontational way, accentuated the sensuality of his models. He was at the height of his reputation from 1916 to 1930. In this period Van Dongen painted chiefly realistic, partly stylized, portraits, sometimes in an uncompromising style and at other times submitting to the taste of the worldly Parisian *élite* (for example, the portrait of *Anatole France*, 1917). Van Dongen's later success overshadowed his beginning as an avant-garde painter, resulting in a position among the avant-garde that is still in dispute. Van Dongen's start as a draftsman and illustrator and his contact with the Netherlands, which he maintained until 1910, have faded completely into the background.

After his education at the Academie van Beeldende Kunsten en Technische Wetenschappen (Academy of Fine Arts and Technical Sciences) in Rotterdam (1892–1894), Van Dongen spent several months in Paris during 1897–1898. In 1899 he settled in Paris permanently. Until 1904, the year that he made his debut at the Salon des Indépendants, Van Dongen worked mainly as a draftsman and illustrator. His model for this work was, most certainly, Th. A. Steinlen. Like this artist, Van Dongen drew primarily street scenes; workhorses, street workers, and prostitutes reoccur often as subjects. Van Dongen worked as an illustrator for ideological reasons; in those days he considered painting as work for the capitalist *élite*. His illustrations for *L' Assiette au Beurre, Gil Blas*, and *L'Indiscreet* are well known; sometimes using the very same sketches, Van Dongen made a series of independent drawings during this time. His habile and fluent style of drawing became the basis for his later painting.

After a youthful period characterized by a Rembrandt-esque style (1895–1897), Van Dongen again devoted himself to painting from about 1903 on. In a loose, Impressionistic style he began painting primarily views of the city and the sea (Paris, Trouville). In 1905 he followed with a more neo-impressionist technique, painting landscapes in Fleury-en-Bière and, with more pronounced patterns of color, the well-known scenes of Parisian entertainment, such as the first electric carousels and the audience reveling in the Moulin de la Galette. With these works Van Dongen joined the avant-garde. In 1904 and 1905 he had solo exhibitions at the Vollard and Druet galleries. In the Indépendants and Autumn exhibitions of 1906 his works were grouped with those entered by Matisse and other Fauvist painters. In 1905 and 1906 he was shown with these artists in several Parisian art galleries. Therefore, the recent placing of Van Dongen on the periphery of Fauvism is not at all correct (Freeman et al., 1990: 13–16). It is true, however, that Van Dongen already was moving away from Fauvist circles by 1907—a development that was reinforced by a long stay in the Netherlands during that same year. Later Van Dongen worked mostly in a style of Fauvist realism, and he increasingly opted for an individual, independent position as an artist. After 1908 his work was presented at the important international exhibitions of modern art.

Anita Hopmans

See also Avant-garde; France; Rotterdam; Sluijters, Jan

Bibliography

Adrichem, Jan van et al. *Kees van Dongen*. Rotterdam: Museum Boymans-van Beuningen, 1989.

Chaumeil, Louis. *Van Dongen: L'homme et l'artiste: La vie et l'oeuvre*. Geneva: Pierre Cailler, 1967.

Derouet, Christian et al. *Van Dongen: Le peintre 1877–1968*. Paris: Les Amies du Museé d'art moderne, 1990.

Freeman, Judi et al. *The Fauve Landscape*. New York: Abbeville, 1990.

Van Gogh, Vincent (1853–1890)

Introduction

The name of Vincent van Gogh has become legendary, the embodiment of the Romantic notion of the suffering, unappreciated artist. In the wake of the Romantic concept of artistic geniality, this artist has become the typical representative of the passionate, irrational, mentally unbalanced and *thus* inspired creator. Because of the special nature of Van Gogh's renown, a great deal of scholarship—and popular literature—has been devoted to every aspect of his life and work, attracting not only art historians, but also such disparate specialists as social and cultural historians, physicians and psychiatrists, and even demographers and astronomers, who have attempted to elucidate every detail of the personal, physical, social, and medical circumstances surrounding the creation of Van Gogh's art. The many letters preserved for posterity have been an invaluable source of information for art-historical research, as well as grist for the mill of those authors who wished to interpret the artist's *oeuvre* through the knowledge of his life and character. Throughout the century since his untimely demise, many critics have seen evidence of mental disturbance and torment, if not a specific pathology, reflected in Van Gogh's *oeuvre;* art historians as well, even one of the stature of writer and teacher Meyer Schapiro, whose ideas have influenced numerous twentieth-century artists, art historians, and critics, have often given analyses of the symbolism and formal qualities of works that purported to see Van Gogh's state of mind directly reflected in his paintings.

Modern research—the best of which attempts to temper the excesses of the past and to render a more accurate representation of Van Gogh's importance as an artist—concentrates not only on such traditional aspects of the works as style and iconography (too many authors to possibly mention here), but also on the influences on the artist and the history of his reception, his importance in the development of modern art and the force of his inspiration on his contemporaries and artists of younger generations, the history of the exhibition and marketing of his works, and problems relating to connoisseurship and authenticity as well as technical studies. Theories as to the true nature of Van Gogh's mental troubles also continue to be put forward. More exact dating of the letters and the analysis of documents and information of all kinds have led to a better overall picture of Van Gogh's artistic production. Recent tendencies in art history have emphasized consideration of the works within the larger framework of Van Gogh's *oeuvre* as a whole, as well as the social and historical context in which they were made.

Biography and Brief Sketch of the Artist's Career

Vincent van Gogh was born the first living son of a Protestant pastor in the Southern Dutch town of Zundert. During his short period of activity he made about nine hundred canvases and thousands of drawings, some eleven hundred of which are extant. His entire *oeuvre* was created during the short space of time between his twenty-eighth and thirty-seventh year, during which time he furthermore underwent several major changes in style.

After failing at several professions, including art dealer, teacher, bookseller, and evangelist, Van Gogh made the decision to become an artist. The traditional placing of this event, following the lead of his sister-in-law, Johanna van Gogh-Bonger, was in March of 1880, after his walking journey to the studio of Jules Breton, a painter of peasant subjects whom he greatly admired, in Courrières. Van Gogh researcher and document expert Jan Hulsker, in contradistinction, believes on the basis of certain passages from the letters that Van Gogh had decided on his real calling as early as July of 1879. In any event, it is certain that he drew regularly from that time forward. Van Gogh was mainly self-taught but studied art in the academic manner during the early 1880s. He later studied drawing with the aid of examples and read the publications of, among others, Charles Blanc, president of the French Académie des Beaux-Arts.

In 1881 he moved to the town of Etten to stay with his parents. There he practiced mainly figure drawing. His first teacher was his cousin by marriage, Anton Mauve, whom he approached for instruction late in 1881 in The Hague, in those years the center of The Hague School of painters whose sober, muted palette so influenced the art of Van Gogh's Dutch period (Color Plate 10). In 1883 Van Gogh settled for several months in the Eastern Dutch province of Drenthe and painted and drew in its environs. Late in 1883 he returned to his parents, who were now living in Nuenen. In emulation of one of his greatest painter-idols, J.F. Millet, Van Gogh had decided to become a painter of peasant life, and to this end he again began to practice the rendering of the human figure. He painted and drew a great many studies after peasants at home and at work and a series of weavers (Color Plate 11), as well

as the landscape in and around Nuenen. In 1885 he painted his first masterpiece, *The Potato-Eaters*, in which his ambition was to achieve the caliber of a true history painting. Traditional precedents for his peasants' meal include seventeenth-century regent portraits and numerous renderings of the Supper at Emmaus. Van Gogh retained his identity as a painter of peasant subjects throughout his life. Nuenen was also the period of the artist's first display of interest in color theory and the ideas of the French painter Eugène Delacroix.

In November of 1885, Van Gogh left Holland, never to return. He first went to Antwerp, where, beginning in Jannuary 1886, he attended the academy for several months in order to study drawing from life and plaster casts, and later he continued his formal training at Fernand Cormon's studio in Paris. In Paris dramatic changes occurred: Van Gogh's palette had until then been quite somber. In Paris he was exposed to the art of Adolphe Monticelli, who had just died in Marseilles in 1886 but who, until the end of the Second Empire (1871) had been Napoleon III's favorite painter of portraits and still lifes in a bright and lyrical style. He was also exposed to the Impressionists, whose last group exhibition took place in the year of his arrival, 1886; and to the Post-Impressionists, among others the Pointillists Paul Signac and Georges Seurat, and a lesser-known group, including Émile Bernard and later Paul Gauguin, who experimented with the use of flat, decorative local areas of color. Van Gogh experimented widely in the use of a brighter palette and rapidly assimilated the more avant-garde styles. A further significant influence was that of Japanese prints, which he had begun to collect in Antwerp. During his Paris period Vincent painted many still lifes, landscapes, and cityscapes, and, perhaps for lack of a better model, a series of self-portraits. Interesting in this respect is that he never painted a portrait of either his brother Theo, or later of Gauguin. An original contribution of Van Gogh's was his conception of the modern portrait, which he developed fully in 1888. It involved the use of color, line, stylization, physiognomy, and attributes, among other things, to express some essential aspect of the character not only of the sitter, but also of the era in which he lived. Theo and Gauguin figured prominently as individuals in Van Gogh's life, presumably rendering him incapable of abstracting and generalizing their personalities in this fashion.

In February of 1888 Van Gogh left Paris for Arles in the South of France. There he painted orchards in bloom, still lifes, subjects from the seaside village of Saintes-Maries-de-la-Mer, self-portraits, portraits of local people, including the postman Roulin and his family, still lifes of sunflowers and other blooms, and town views and interiors, among them his famous *Night Café* and several versions of *The Bedroom*. In preparation for Gauguin's arrival he invented a program of decoration for the yellow house he had rented. Unfortunately, Van Gogh's fond dreams of collaboration came to nothing, and the ensuing argument and hospitalization are well known. In May of 1889 Van Gogh voluntarily entered the asylum at St. Rémy for treatment, and between bouts of illness he painted views of the hospital and its gardens, the surrounding landscape, including the olive groves and cypress trees, as well as his famous *Starry Night,* and he made translations in color of the compositions of a number of his most admired predecessors, such as Millet, Delacroix, and Rembrandt. Van Gogh later abandoned any flirtation with traditional religious themes and painting from memory and returned to his grounding in the real world. In Auvers, where he went upon his release from St. Rémy in May of 1890, Van Gogh continued to make portraits; he also painted and drew the town hall and the local church and spent time with his easel in the vast wheatfields nearby. He died by his own hand on July 29 of that year at the age of thirty-seven.

The *Oeuvre*
One of the most interesting types of research to come out in recent years is the insights of Evert van Uitert (first put forward in his 1983 dissertation) into Van Gogh's own preconceived ideas about his *oeuvre* as an entity. The idea of a cohesive *oeuvre* originated in the nineteenth century and had to do with the notion of art as the expression of the artist's personality. Van Gogh had indeed wanted to make his mark on the world in this way. General criteria that aid us in reconstructing Van Gogh's intended *oeuvre* include his practice of collecting works into groups and series, the designing of decorative programs, his practice of repeating works, of designating them in old-fashioned academic terms as, respectively, studies or finished compositions, their size, the giving of titles, the signing of works, and whether or not particular paintings were intended for exhibition. Peasant pictures, which Van Gogh saw as equal in stature to religious and history painting, remained at the core of his *oeuvre.* The literary and symbolic allusions in many of Van Gogh's works often become evident only through knowledge of his letters. An avid reader throughout his life, Van Gogh constantly drew links between painting and literature, which was a major source of inspiration for his ideas. His intended meaning of many works can only be discovered when these chains of connection are revealed.

Van Uitert, in collaboration with Louis van Tilborgh and Sjraar van Heugten of the Van Gogh Museum in Amsterdam, presented his ideas on Van Gogh's intended *oeuvre* in the catalog to the 1990 commemorative exhibition held in that city. Van Gogh's *oeuvre* had portraits and figural works at its core; other associative works, including the *Night Café, The Bedroom,* and landscapes with figures at labor, were secondary in significance; and there was an outer circle of the more ambitious still lifes, landscapes, and townscapes. Van Uitert and Van Tilborgh conclude that Van Gogh, in fact, failed to accomplish his heart's greatest desire: great figure paintings in the peasant genre. His reputation, however, never suffered for it.

This type of research into Van Gogh's own intentions was only possible once the authenticity and chronology of the works and the letters had largely been established by other means. As early as 1928, J.B. de la Faille's pioneering *catalogue raisonné (L'oeuvre de Vincent van Gogh)* of Van Gogh's works appeared. This served as the basis for further study and refinement of the data, which were carried out in a number of *catalogues raisonnés* of portions of the *oeuvre*

during the 1930s, and many monographs and journal articles thereafter. In 1970 a new edition of De la Faille was brought out, now in English, by a Dutch team of scholars. It included works discovered after the original publication and took advantage of the new data that research had yielded in the meantime. The texts of all of the available letters were now studied in conjunction with the works and used to solve problems of chronology and authenticity. In his comprehensive introductory essay to the 1970 edition, A.M. Hammacher surveyed Van Gogh research and reception up to that time, for the first time bringing some real historical objectivity into what until then had been almost cult worship of the artist. In 1977 Jan Hulsker also published a *catalogue raisonné,* in which all of the works are illustrated, and arranged in chronological order rather than separated according to their media. Hulsker also introduced a new system of numbering, with a concordance to De la Faille.

Other avenues of research regarding the authenticity of Van Gogh's works involve a thorough study of their provenance and of the art market. Roland Dorn and Walter Feilchenfeldt are among the most prominent recent scholars to tackle problems of attribution and forgery. They question the attribution of, among other works, a *Self-portrait* of Van Gogh's (F268; Fig. 143) included as an autograph work in the catalogs of De la Faille and Hulsker and call for further investigation of its early provenance; few genuine self-portraits of Van Gogh's are historically unaccounted for.

Physical analysis of Van Gogh's pigment and his application of the paint has been undertaken by, among others, Cornelia Peres of the Vincent van Gogh Museum. Such technical research is quite expensive as well as an intrusive procedure to the priceless canvases, so that such studies have been carried out only to a limited extent, but they promise interesting results.

The Letters
Vincent van Gogh was a prolific letter writer: in addition to his brother Theo he corresponded with his parents and sisters as well as with a number of artist friends, including Gauguin, Émile Bernard, and Anthon van Rappard. There is no doubting the fact that the letters were a major factor in the reception of his art and the growth of his fame, providing as they do a wealth of information on Van Gogh's ideas on art and artists as well as on such matters as his attitude toward society, religion, and literature, his relationships with others, and his hopes and ambitions. The letters and the sketches drawn in or included with them provide a key to the interpretation of the works of art and shed light on questions of chronology and authenticity. Selections from Van Gogh's letters were published in periodicals within a few years of his death. Theo's widow, Johanna, undertook the mammoth task of arranging the generally undated letters into chronological sequence and translating them into English. The first edition of the letters in book form (three volumes) appeared in 1914 in the original Dutch and French and included an extensive biographical introduction by Johanna, who undoubtedly realized their importance in furthering her brother-in-law's reputation.

Editions of the letters were published in German and English during the 1920s. A more complete edition in the original languages, including letters from Vincent to his sister Wil and reminiscences by personal acquaintances of the artist, appeared in 1953, on the one-hundredth anniversary of Van Gogh's birth. In 1958 the New York Graphic Society first published an American edition of the *Complete Letters*, which is still the standard in the English-speaking world in spite of numerous inaccuracies. When the Vincent van Gogh Museum opened in Amsterdam in 1973, the original letters, including a number of unpublished letters written by Theo to family members, became available for study. Jan Hulsker, a prolific documentalist who has published profusely, has been able to throw light upon many important problems concerning the chronology of the letters themselves and of the works to which they refer, and to point out certain deletions in the 1953 and earlier editions. Johanna van Gogh, for instance, tended to omit segments relating to disagreements among family members. A facsimile edition of the manuscripts of Van Gogh's letters written in French, which was published in 1977, allowed scholars to uncover some of the many errors that had been made in transcription (and translation). In 1990 *De brieven van Vincent van Gogh* was published, a Dutch-language edition of the letters in which all of them appear in chronological order for the first time, building on all of the research of the last decades, especially that of Jan Hulsker and Ronald Pickvance. For the first time, the 1990 edition also provides an index to the material. In 1992 *Van Gogh Indices*, a German-language index of subjects and proper names, was published by a seminar group at the Johann Wolfgang Goethe-Universität (Frankfurt am Main), based on the 1974 Amsterdam and the six-volume German editions. The Vincent van Gogh Museum is preparing to publish before the end of the 1990s an annotated unabridged edition of the letters in English.

Reputation

Van Gogh holds a special place in the history of art: His fame is equaled by that of only four or five other great artists, like Picasso, Michelangelo, and Rembrandt. This is the result of the legends that have formed around him, typifying him as a misunderstood artist who toiled relentlessly, sick, abandoned and desperate, for truth in his art. Both the publication of the letters and the double burial of Vincent and Theo, also arranged by Johanna van Gogh in 1914, fanned the flames of incipient mythology accruing to the artist. Elements of Van Gogh's life, such as his repeated failures in love, his incessant travels, and his suicide, underscored the image of the creative madman on a quest. The artist's first biographer, Julius Meier-Graefe, expressed an exalted view of Van Gogh, whom he characterized in 1921 as a "God-seeker." The publication in 1934 of Irving Stone's novel *Lust for Life*, made into a motion picture starring Kirk Douglas in 1956, greatly increased the artist's public acclaim. Van Gogh's renown also gave rise to a great many monuments and commemorative plaques, located in virtually all of the places he had ever lived or worked and culminating in the plans for the Vincent van Gogh Museum

in Amsterdam. It was at about this time that scholars began actively to counterbalance the legends. Hammacher's 1970 essay had put the previous writings on Van Gogh into historical perspective; a 1977 essay by Evert van Uitert explained the typology that had emerged in the legends surrounding Van Gogh's life, characterizing the artist, among other things, as a saint, a martyr, a pilgrim, a prophet, and a second Christ. Carol M. Zemel analyzed the Van Gogh criticism of the period 1890–1920 and how it served to promote the formation of a mythology. One specific instance of the Van Gogh story, that of the supposedly superhuman devotion between the two brothers Vincent and Theo, was tackled by Jan Hulsker, whose dual biography, first published in 1985, places this relationship in a more realistic perspective. In 1993 a large anthology bearing the title *The Mythology of Vincent van Gogh* was published under the editorship of the Japanese scholar Tsukasa Kodera and Yvette Rosenberg. It deals with many of the manifestations of Van Gogh's fame, including film, theater, painting, literature, and the commercial exploitation of his art.

Illness

A great deal has been written about the state of Van Gogh's health and the nature of his illness. Interest in his mental problems, in particular, is connected with the question of their relationship to his creativity as an artist. Since the Romantic era, "madness" in particular has been directly related to artistic genius. More specific diagnoses have resulted in a plethora of suppositions about a direct relationship between the alleged illness and the development, style, subject matter, and symbolism in Van Gogh's art.

Various hypotheses have been advanced to explain his affliction. A complete list was compiled by Elmyra van Dooren in 1993. One of the first was that of epilepsy, suggested by Van Gogh himself in his correspondence and adopted by his doctors, Rey and Peyron, who treated him in 1889. The more precise diagnosis of psychomotor epilepsy was put forward in the mid-1950s. This theory has been the subject of debate as well, and a diagnosis of psychomotor or temporal lobe epilepsy enjoys a consensus among many modern scholars. Other diagnoses have included various types of psychosis, including manic depression and schizophrenia (first suggested by Karl Jaspers in 1992), venereal disease, physical ailments such as brain tumors and Ménière's disease, and alcoholic or chemical poisoning. Wilfred N. Arnold and L.S. Loftus have (1991) put forward a case for the hereditary metabolic disease acute intermittent porphyria, which often presents both physical and psychiatric symptomatology, to which they relate not only Vincent's various complaints, but Theo's as well.

This theory as well is quite problematic, but Arnold (1992) is surely correct in emphasizing the fact that Vincent's attacks of mental derangement were interspersed among periods of lucidity, during which the artist's genius manifested itself. As prudent scholars—Carl Nordenfalk (1953), among others—have been pointing out for years, Van Gogh was a brilliant artist in spite of, not on account of, his mental troubles. This insight has existed side by side with the view of others who misguidedly insist upon seeing evidence of psychosis in the works themselves. Still others, including the psychiatrist A.J. Lubin (1972), have contended that the exact nature of Van Gogh's illness is not important; significant is the way Van Gogh's psychological conflicts were played out in the service of his art. The creative rivalry described by Van Uitert in 1983, while grounded in the literary tradition of *aemulatio* (formulated in the nineteenth century as "doing something different from one's predecessors"), may also be viewed as a psychological process that facilitated Van Gogh's artistic production.

History of the Collections

The Netherlands boasts the two largest collections of Van Goghs in the world. The Rijksmuseum Kröller-Müller in the town of Otterlo, whose collection of Van Goghs resulted largely from the efforts of a single collector, Hélène Kröller-Müller, and her adviser, H.P. Bremmer, contains two hundred seventy-four paintings and drawings. The only larger collection in the world is that of the Vincent van Gogh Museum in Amsterdam, containing many of the works brought back to Holland by Theo's widow, Johanna. In 1960, during the lifetime of her son, the engineer Vincent van Gogh, these works entered a foundation set up to keep them from being sold for inheritance taxes. The permanent loan from the Vincent van Gogh Foundation to the museum, built in 1973 to house and display the collection, includes more than two hundred paintings and five hundred eighty drawings, seven sketchbooks and six hundred original letters from Vincent to Theo. The museum also has hundreds of reproductions collected by the artist himself, a great deal of original correspondence and other documentary material relating to Van Gogh, including the archives of Marc Edo Tralbaut, and a particularly well-organized and comprehensive library relating to the art of Van Gogh and his time. Since 1988 the museum has published a scholarly series entitled *Cahiers Vincent* as well as a quarterly *Van Gogh Bulletin*.

The remaining two-thirds of Van Gogh's *oeuvre* has been dispersed to museums and private collectors the world over.

Andrea C. Gasten

See also Belgium; France; Hague School, The; Japonisme; Mauve, Anton; Van Gogh, Vincent: diverse views

Bibliography

Arnold, Wilfred N. *Vincent van Gogh: Chemicals, Crises, and Creativity.* Boston: Birkhauser, 1992.

———, and L.S. Loftus. "Vincent van Gogh's illness: Acute intermittent porphyria?" *British Medical Journal* 303 (1991): 1589–1591.

The Complete Letters of Vincent van Gogh. 3 vols. Greenwich, CT: New York Graphic Society Books, 1958. Boston: New York Graphic Society, 1978.

Cooper, Douglas, ed. *Paul Gauguin: 45 lettres à Vincent, Theo, et Jo van Gogh: Collection Rijksmuseum Vincent van Gogh, Amsterdam.* The Hague: Staatsuitgeverij, 1983.

Crimpen, Han van, and Monique Berends-Albert, eds. *De brieven van Vincent van Gogh.* 4 vols. The Hague: SDU, 1990.

Dooren, Elmyra van. "Van Gogh: Illness and Creativity." In *The Mythology of Van Gogh.* Edited by Tsukasa Kodera and Yvette Rosenberg, 325–345. Tokyo: Asahi; Amsterdam: Benjamins, 1993.

Dorn, Roland, and Walter Feilchenfeldt. "Genuine or Fake: On the History and Problems of Van Gogh Connoisseurship." In *The Mythology of Van Gogh.* Edited by Tsukasa Kodera and Yvette Rosenberg, 263–307. Tokyo: Asahi; Amsterdam: Benjamins, 1993.

Faille, J.B. de la. *The Works of Vincent van Gogh: His Paintings and Drawings.* Amsterdam: Meulenhoff, 1970.

Hulsker, Jan. *The Complete Van Gogh: Paintings, Drawings, Sketches.* New York: Harry N. Abrams, 1980, 1984. Translation of *Van Gogh en zijn weg.* Amsterdam: Meulenhoff, 1977.

———. *Vincent and Theo van Gogh: A Dual Biography.* Ann Arbor, MI: Fuller, 1990.

———. *Vincent van Gogh: Een leven in brieven.* Amsterdam: Meulenhoff, 1984.

Kodera, Tsukasa, and Yvette Rosenberg, eds. *The Mythology of Vincent van Gogh.* Tokyo: Asahi; Amsterdam: Benjamins, 1993.

Lubin, Albert J. *Stranger on Earth: A Psychological Biography of Vincent van Gogh.* New York: Holt, Rinehart, and Winston, 1972.

Meier-Graefe, Julius. *Vincent.* Munich: R. Piper, 1921.

Nordenfalk, C. *The Life and Work of Vincent van Gogh.* Translated by Lawrence Wolfe. London: Elek, 1953.

Schapiro, Meyer. *Vincent van Gogh.* New York: Harry N. Abrams, 1950.

Stein, Susan A. *Van Gogh: A Retrospective.* New York: Hugh Lauter Levin, 1986.

Uitert, Evert van. "De legendevorming te bevorderen: Notities over Vincent van Gogh." In *Rond de roem van Vincent van Gogh*, 15–27. Amsterdam: Rijksmuseum Vincent van Gogh, 1977.

———. *Vincent van Gogh in Creative Competition.* Ph.D. diss., Zutphen: Nauta, 1983.

Uitert, Evert van, Louis van Tilborgh, and Sjraar van Heugten. *Vincent van Gogh: Paintings.* Amsterdam: Rijksmuseum Vincent van Gogh, 1990.

Uitert, Evert van, and Michael Hoyle, eds. *The Rijksmuseum Vincent van Gogh.* Amsterdam: Meulenhoff, 1987.

Van Gogh Indices: Analytischer Schlüssel für die Schriften des Künstlers. Frankfurter Fundamente der Kunstgeschichte, Band 8. Frankfurt am Main: Johann Wolfgang Goethe-Universität, 1992.

Vincent van Gogh on Film and Video: A Review, 1948–1990. Amsterdam: Stichting Van Gogh, 1990.

Wolk, Johannes van der. *The Seven Sketchbooks of Vincent van Gogh: A Facsimile Edition.* New York: Harry N. Abrams, 1987.

Wolk, Johannes van der, Ronald Pickvance, and E.B.F. Pey. *Vincent van Gogh: Drawings.* Otterlo: Rijksmuseum

Kröller-Müller, 1990.

Zemel, Carol M. *The Formation of a Legend: Van Gogh Criticism 1890–1920.* Ann Arbor, MI: UMI Research Press, 1980.

Van Gogh, Vincent: diverse views

In the century following Vincent van Gogh's death, his work has been examined by scholars in disciplines other than art and art history, including, most recently, medicine, the social sciences, and literature. These approaches expand the conventional analyses that took as a first task the placing of Van Gogh and his works in an identified stylistic development. Correlating with Sigmund Freud's early publications in psychoanalytic theory, traditional art-historical studies were augmented by an emergent interest in psychological studies of creative personalities. Fostered and perpetuated by subsequent biographies, histories, films, and novels, the development of the Van Gogh myth explained the artist's unique style from a perspective intriguing and entertaining to a general audience. The result is an artist who has been inadequately and incorrectly characterized as an untutored genius who substituted art for a thwarted religious calling, who was misunderstood by family and associates alike, and whose distinctive style was seen as pictorial documentation of insanity, addiction, and illness. The diversity of recent scholarship, which has included restoration and conservation of Van Gogh's work, study of the major recurring themes (constellations, isolated figures, men digging) explored via electronic technology, and searching literary sources for his paintings, has effectively diminished the myth of the mad genius, revealing a purposeful artist who innovatively reinterpreted avant-garde trends. Furthermore, a determination to tailor subject and style to attract an emerging taste in the market was a goal identified early, but it is an aspect of his career so obscured by the Van Gogh legend that it remains largely unexamined.

There is still little agreement about interpretations of Van Gogh's work, which continue to interest scholars who represent a wide range of research methodologies. Exegesis of the collection of letters, the most complete and augmented version of which was published after World War II, has led to myriad theoretical ideas that seem most effectively explored by scholars in fields other than art history.

Background

Nearly thirty years old when he began to paint, Vincent van Gogh's career ended with his death on July 29, 1890, at thirty-seven, the same age at which Raphael, Watteau, and Caravaggio died. That he has been elevated to the highest level in the elite pantheon of artists credited with initiating major directions in modern art is incontrovertible. His paintings, particularly those of the Arles and St. Rémy periods, rarely available for auction, have sold for the highest prices ever recorded in the history of art marketing. Public attention has focused largely on biographical details, but art critic Robert Hughes advises that Van Gogh's paintings should be seen carefully, by an unhurried eye, to "receive their energy, pathos and depth of conviction." Careful examination does indeed reveal an artist who was consistently, but never recklessly, experimenting and whose work was not precipitated by irrational emotion but sustained by a deliberate development toward a defined purpose. Yet, because Van Gogh research has been influenced by persistent, although belated, medical and psychiatric diagnoses of pathological masochism, bipolar personality disorder, emotional imbalance, and temporal-lobe epilepsy complicated by venereal diseases and severe dental problems, there is an almost irresistible tendency to interpret his art as a record of his emotional and physical traumas.

The idea, probably introduced in 1891 by author and playwright Octave Mirabeau (Hulsker, 1990), that Van Gogh's style derived from an excessive psychopathology was perpetuated by the self-serving Paul Gauguin who described Van Gogh as a martyr deranged by the intense social and religious conflicts that tormented him. Gauguin therefore discredited Van Gogh's paintings as uncontrolled products of a "disorderly brain" incapable of forming a logical critical judgment (in Hulsker, 1990). In a later 1903 entry in his memoir, *Avant et Après* (published as *Paul Gauguin's Intimate Journals*), Gauguin dramatically, but with questionable accuracy, described events surrounding the episode of the mutilated ear.

Education

That Van Gogh's art training was more formally structured than is generally acknowledged in early biographies is noted in recent literature. At the age of thirteen, he was sent to the King Willem II State Secondary School in Tilburg, where, in addition to mathematics and language, four hours a week of art were required. The teacher, C.C. Huysmans, was compelled to cut short a promising career as a painter in Paris for compassionate family reasons. Devoting his energies to art education, he created a drawing curriculum that far exceeded the art requirement established by the Dutch Education Law of 1863. Familiar with current French movements in art, Huysmans held classes outdoors to teach his students to draw directly from nature.

In 1880 Van Gogh sought and received willing critical feedback from Willem Roelofs and Anthon van Rappard in Brussels, both of whom advocated working from nature. Determined to acquire the skills necessary for figure drawing, he turned to his cousin Anton Mauve in The Hague. Mauve advised him to abandon pen and ink in favor of brush and paint, introduced him to the descriptive properties of color, and taught him fundamentals of figure drawing. In addition, Van Gogh drew from the model two evenings a week at the Pulchri Studio and asked Jan Weissenbruch, well known for his own paintings and for his sharp criticism of the work of other artists, to make critical comments. Weissenbruch encouraged his efforts and advised him to continue spontaneous pen-and-ink drawing as his painting developed. In 1886 Van Gogh spent two unproductive months at the Antwerp Academy, then under the direction of Charles Verlat, who, committed to an obsolete classicism, required students to draw from draped male models and antique casts.

Convinced that Paris would offer the instruction in figure drawing as well as provide the market he needed, Van Gogh joined his brother Theo there in 1886 and again attempted academic study, this time at Fernand Cormon's atelier. Lessons at Cormon's were disappointingly similar to those at the Antwerp academy, with emphasis on drawing from casts. He was, however, determined to improve his figure-drawing skill and dutifully made literal copies of assigned casts.

Psychoanalytic Perspectives

Recent studies of Van Gogh's contributions demonstrate the use of methodologies usually reserved for sociological and psychological research. Such research often includes investigation of how the artist's emotional complexities may have shaped construction of his highly personal iconography.

Because a brother, stillborn precisely a year before his own birth, was also named Vincent Willem, some psychologists have classified Van Gogh a substitute, or replacement, child who had no choice but to compete with an idealized parental image of the dead brother. Psychobiographical accounts of an unhappy childhood, during which he was deprived of genuine maternal affection and paternal approval, proliferated as modern psychologists attempted to understand and explain the behavior of creative individuals. Theorizing that the emotional deprivation suffered during his childhood caused separation anxiety that led to depression, homesickness, and a succession of failed attempts to find a lifelong companion, psychoanalytic studies have created the universally familiar portrait of an artist beset with agitated depressive episodes.

Psychological research methods have also yielded alternative assessments of the affinity between the brothers Vincent and Theo, long seen as one of financial and emotional dependence by Vincent on the strong, tolerant Theo who received nothing in return for his support. Alternative opinions include divergent analyses that range from psychic masochism on Vincent's part to theorizing a symbiotic dyad in which Theo depended equally on the maintenance of a stable relationship.

Sociological Inquiry

In contrast, sociological histories suggest an alternative account of how Van Gogh's choice of vocation is rooted firmly in the history of his middle-class Dutch family of clergymen, art dealers, and civil servants. His paternal grandfather and his father both completed theological studies and became Calvinist ministers in the Dutch Reformed Church, the oldest Protestant denomination in the Netherlands. His maternal grandfather, a craftsman, was a bookbinder at the royal court in The Hague. His newly ordained father, Theodorus, had assumed a compromise position in a Church divided between traditionalists and modernists, a decision that resulted in his assignment to a country parish in Zundert in Dutch Brabant near the Belgian border. The region was known as Catholic Brabant, meaning that the Protestant population was a minority consisting mainly of peasant farmers scattered over a wide area. Van Gogh accompanied his father on the long walks visiting parishioners and developed an interest in nature by studying and cataloging plants and animals. Industrial progress had not invaded the Brabant countryside, and its

agricultural life affirmed Van Gogh's romanticized view of nature, which he retained as subject matter for his paintings. His mother, Anna Cornelia Carbentus, stretched the family budget to allow for an indoor servant, leaving her free to engage in such genteel activities as reading and painting watercolor floral studies. Surviving drawings, including one of a snarling dog made when he was nine years old, are evidence that she encouraged Vincent to sketch along with her. There is no doubt that Van Gogh wanted, and was expected, to emulate his father and grandfather by entering the clergy, although the fact that three of his uncles were art dealers was a significant early influence and raises a question about the depth of Pastor van Gogh's disappointment when Vincent later demonstrated he was not suited to the ministry. Art dealing was a respectable option in Holland and in the Van Gogh family.

Sociological studies challenge the replacement-child theory, noting that both Vincents were named, in accordance with Dutch custom, for an uncle, Vincent Willem van Gogh, a successful art dealer who lived in Paris and was known to the Van Gogh children as "Uncle Cent."

Shrewd and perceptive in his assessment of public taste in art, Cent van Gogh had successfully introduced Barbizon paintings to Holland and encouraged young Dutch painters to paint directly from nature as French artists were doing. Furthermore, inasmuch as Barbizon School paintings were popular in Holland, he correctly assumed there was a corresponding market in France for Dutch painters. In 1861 he entered into an active partnership with Adolphe Goupil, who had galleries in Paris, London, Berlin, and The Hague. By reinforcing the French fervor for art from the same "North" that had produced Rembrandt and Vermeer, Cent van Gogh became Goupil's valued, wealthy associate, and the Dutch artists he represented enjoyed a wide market for their work. In the hope that Vincent would become his successor, Cent devoted long periods of time, during visits to Brabant, teaching his nephew art history, criticism, and gallery management. Following two brief apprenticeships, beginning in 1873, first at Goupil and Company in The Hague and, later, its London office, which specialized in reproductions, it was clear that Vincent's destiny was not in the art trade. In 1875, when Vincent requested financial support for his new interest in studying theology, Cent van Gogh severed their relationship. In 1873 Theo began work at the Brussels branch of Goupil's; he was transferred to The Hague office, then finally employed permanently by the Paris branch in 1880.

Curiously, sociological research has not examined Van Gogh's sojourn in the Borinage region of Belgium with the community of coal miners to whom he intended to minister. It was his identification with conditions there, and the need to record his impressions, that is fundamental to the persistent realism of his figures throughout his career.

Art-Critical Studies

The two-year period during which he worked in Paris was crucial in shaping and refining Van Gogh's goal to work from nature producing "inhabited landscapes" that would appeal to the new generation of collectors. Because the two brothers lived together until Vincent departed for Arles in 1888, the resultant insubstantial amount of correspondence during this period has caused most scholars to avoid it, thinking it undocumented and difficult to study. However, Van Gogh's letters, never intended as autobiographical, are unreliable as explanations of his work. The more than two hundred paintings and fifty drawings, including most of the familiar self-portraits, produced while he was in Paris record his evolving style in a visual language that has best been interpreted by art critics.

Although at the time few foresaw him as an innovative genius, it was during the Paris period that Van Gogh constructed a solid foundation for his later, mature style of the Arles and St. Rémy periods. Sweetman quotes A.S. Hartrick, writing in 1916, and Émile Bernard's commemorative tribute *Vincent Van Gogh* (1891) as noting an obsessive devotion in Vincent to his work, an observation confirmed in retrospect by fellow artists Suzanne Valadon and Paul Signac (Sweetman 1990, 223–227, 233–235). His compulsive efforts were directed toward a single-minded exploration of expressive pictorial forms. Albert Aurier later described this purpose in a critical essay, "Les Isolés" (January 1890) written shortly before Van Gogh's death, as investing formal elements such as line, color, and shape with intensely original symbolic significance.

In Aurier's essay (the only published critical response to his work that Van Gogh ever read), published in the first issue of *Mercure de France*, he defined Les Isolés (The Isolated Ones) as those troubled artistic visionaries who are separated from their contemporaries precisely because of that vision. Basing his interpretation on aesthetic factors, Aurier concluded that Van Gogh's art was devoid of social content and described him as an artist whose eccentric vision separated him from a contemporary culture so conformist in its aesthetic attitudes that few could comprehend the meanings implicit in the visual language he was introducing. By acknowledging that Van Gogh's singular vision derived from an inner intensity that manifested itself in his need to create a pictorial description of the struggle within, Aurier unintentionally suggested that the eloquence of Van Gogh's work may have been due to an emotional depression caused by disappointing social experiences. Unlike critical essays written by Mirbeau, Émile Bernard, and Paul Gauguin, Aurier's analysis was a coherent application of a systematic theoretical position. By clearly charting the creative process that underlies Van Gogh's body of work, Aurier's theory remains a relevant decoding of Van Gogh's work.

Carol M. Zemel's comprehensive study of the criticism in France, Germany, and the Netherlands from 1890 until 1920 has added an important dimension to an understanding of the variety of responses to Van Gogh's work and the context in which it was first reviewed.

Literary Sources for Van Gogh's Work

Particularly interesting and informative are recent studies that acknowledge Van Gogh's wide-ranging literary tastes and identifiable connections of verbal and visual imagery. A voracious reader, Van Gogh read English, French, German, and Dutch and was familiar with Latin and Greek. Included among the authors he most admired were Charles Dickens, Harriet Beecher Stowe, and the French naturalist literature of Emile Zola, Jean Richepin, and Alphonse Daudet. Reading Guy de Maupassant and Zola seemed to sustain him during the Arles and St. Rémy periods, leading some researchers to speculate that his own idiosyncratic vision may have been affirmed by their naturalist precepts.

Constructing the Legend

As manager of the Montmartre branch of Boussod, Valadon and Company, which had purchased Goupil and Company, Theo attempted a replication of their uncle's astute perception of the changing taste of European buyers and collectors. The shift in taste, also predicted by the Post-Impressionist innovations of Camille Pissarro and Georges Seurat, confirmed Van Gogh's purpose. During the two years he lived in Paris, he began exploring the expressive properties of color in at least fifty impasto floral studies and numerous tentatively colored street scenes, including *Montmartre*, *Hill of Montmartre*, *Stone Quarry, Montmartre*, *La Moulin de la Galette* and *Aux Confins de Paris*, all painted in 1886. Although Theo worked assiduously to sell these and works by other contemporary artists, the managers of Boussod, Valadon and Company were less enterprising, insisting on safe and familiar marine studies and landscapes by Édouard Manet and Auguste Renoir. Not until 1887, when he began to acquire works by Degas, Sisley, Gauguin, and Pissarro, could Theo acquaint his clients with contemporary art, but while Claude Monet's Antibes landscapes found a modest market, sales in general were not brisk.

While it is true that letters that document the brothers' perceptions and experiences are scarce, other evidence suggests that the conditions of their partnership were forged by the combination of Vincent's visionary exploration of color and Theo's acute awareness of the changes in the art market. Their financial arrangement was based on the shared conviction that Theo would be amply repaid when Vincent's potential was realized and recognized. This joint venture, rooted in Cent van Gogh's teaching and shaped during the two years Vincent spent in Paris, formed the basis of a plan to develop a wide audience, and eventual market, for his work. Convinced that his brother's work would be appreciated by future collectors, it was Theo's wish, recorded in his sparse correspondence, that Vincent should be free to work without worry. Production was Vincent's part of the bargain, and, despite his deteriorating physical and emotional health, the last three years of his life were his most productive. He worked incessantly, often completing six canvases in two weeks. Paintings of the Arles and St. Rémy periods are internationally familiar images mercilessly reproduced on postcards, posters, and in art appreciation books intended for a general audience. Yet, immediately after Vincent's death, Theo had no trouble persuading the other members of their family that he should legally acquire his brother's estate; they had no interest in either the paintings or the artist's belongings.

When Theo died tragically on January 25, 1891, less than six months after Vincent's death, their arrangement to protect the work and, at the same time, familiarize the public with it was carried on by Theo's widow, Johanna van Gogh-Bonger (1862–1925) and her son, also named Vincent Willem (1890–1978). Less than a year old, Vincent Willem was named sole heir to Theo's estate and, therefore, to Vincent's estate, which consisted of five hundred fifty paintings, hundreds of drawings, and the more than 600 letters, finally released for publication in Amsterdam in 1914 when Van Gogh's reputation as an artist was securely established. By then Johanna van Gogh-Bonger had arranged for several minor exhibitions of Vincent's work in Amsterdam, Rotterdam, and The Hague and a major exhibition at the Stedelijk Museum in Amsterdam. Roger Fry's 1912 Post-Impressionist exhibition in London had included twenty-one Van Goghs, affirming him as one of the group of artists whose work differed distinctively from Impressionism, and the German Sonderbund exhibition in Cologne in the same year included one hundred eight Van Goghs, associating him with emerging Expressionism.

Mary F. Francey

See also Avant-garde; Belgium; France; Hague School, The; Mauve, Anton; Symbolism, Symbolists; Van Gogh, Vincent; Weissenbruch, Jan

Bibliography

Auden, W.H. *Van Gogh: A Self-Portrait*. New York: Paragon House, 1989.

Baneke, Joost et al. *Dutch Art and Character: Psychoanalytic Perspectives On*. Amsterdam: Swets and Zeitlinger, 1993.

Gedo, John E. *Portraits of the Artist: Psychoanalysis of Creativity and Its Vicissitudes*. New York: Guilford, 1983.

Hughes, Robert. *Nothing If Not Critical*. New York: Penguin, 1990.

Hulsker, Jan. *Vincent and Theo van Gogh: A Dual Biography*. Ann Arbor, MI: Fuller, 1990.

Kodera, Tsukasa. *Vincent van Gogh: Christianity versus Nature*. Amsterdam: Benjamins, 1990.

Lubin, Albert J. *Stranger on the Earth: A Psychological Biography of Vincent van Gogh*. New York: Holt, Reinhart, and Winston, 1972.

Mathews, Patricia Townley. *Aurier's Symbolist Criticism and Theory*. Ann Arbor, MI: UMI Research Press, 1984.

Paul Gauguin's Intimate Journals. Edited by Van Wyck Brooks. Bloomington, IN: Indiana University Press, 1958.

Sund, Judy. *True to Temperament: Van Gogh and French Naturalist Literature*. Cambridge: Cambridge University Press, 1992.

Sweetman, David. *Van Gogh: His Life and Art*. New York: Crown, 1990.

Welsh-Ovcharov, Bogomila. *Van Gogh in Perspective*. Englewood Cliffs, NJ: Prentice-Hall, 1974.

Zemel, Carol M. *The Formation of a Legend: Van Gogh Criticism, 1890–1920*. Ann Arbor, MI: UMI Research Press, 1980.

Van Golden, Daan (born 1936)

Gold, the symbol for light, is not unimportant in the closely connected life and work of Daan van Golden. His frequent travels, especially, have left their traces in his work. In Japan, where he lived from 1962 to 1964, Van Golden began to paint copies of textile squares *(Furoshiki)* with the utmost precision. These manipulations of reality—through their as-true-as-possible imitation—came to be named *Zakdoeken* (Handkerchiefs). The impersonality that often goes together with a very refined technique was elevated by a palpable concentration. The works thus transcended the material.

The works were frequently exhibited in the 1960s. After that was a quiet period, which lasted until 1978. Van Golden, however, worked steadily through it. In 1973–1974 he made, for example, *Fats Domino*, a painted copy of a newspaper photograph, so much enlarged that the screen dominated the image. Van Golden has treated photography as an independent medium since 1966. After 1978, the year his daughter Diana was born, he made a series of color photographs during his trips to Mexico, India, and Nepal, among other places, as well as in Europe.

The coherence between life and art that comes out in his works also comes out in the way they are exhibited; Van Golden composes his separate works into installations where the preconceived meets the unarranged.

His attitude toward life as well as his work has been found to be of great importance for young artists, who often share his preference for the reuse of materials. The artist makes high demands on ideas as well as the execution of his works, which results in a small production. Van Golden makes conscious use of chance and association because they stimulate the imagination. In this way an Abstract Expressionist painting by Jackson Pollock served as the source for *Pollock* (1991). The artist selected a detail in which he recognized figures and faces and magnified it. In this manner a literal quotation from an abstract painting produced a figurative image. *Studie* (1986) also balances on the boundary line between abstraction and figuration. A magnified detail from a picture postcard of a Greek temple yielded a silhouette of a sharp-beaked bird. Notions of abstraction and figuration lose their relevance in a work such as this one.

In 1987 Van Golden colored the gravel of the Amsterdam Botanical Garden azure blue and quoted the Norwegian painter Edvard Munch: "Art is the opposite of nature." In 1990 he was awarded the PC Prize for his art by the PC foundation, an Amsterdam funeral cooperative. On this occasion the artist gave a speech titled "De kunst is geen wedstrijd" (Art Is No Contest), a pronouncement of the Dutch author A. Roland Holst. This collage of statements from artists and philosophers offers an impression of Van Golden's view of life. He concluded his address as follows: "Speech is silence, silver is gold, I have spoken."

Brigitte van Mechelen

See also Contemporary art

Bibliography

Blotkamp, Carel. *De wereld als troost*. Amsterdam: Stichting PC Kunstprijs, 1991.

———. *Keuzen: Beschouwingen over hedendaagse Nederlandse kunstenaars*, 53–67. Utrecht: Reflex, 1985.

———, Marion Busch, and Daan van Golden. *Daan van Golden: Overzichtstentoonstelling 1963–1982.* Rotterdam: Museum Boymans-van Beuningen, 1982.

Dippel, Rini, and Daan van Golden. *Daan van Golden: Werken 1962–1991.* Amsterdam: Stedelijk Museum, 1991.

Golden, Daan van. "Shivaratri Pasupatinath, Nepal (1983)." *Museumjournaal* 23 (1987): 154.

Raay, Stefan van, ed. *Imitation and Inspiration: Japanese Influence on Dutch Art.* Amsterdam: Art Unlimited Books, 1989.

Van Goyen, Jan (1596–1656)

Jan van Goyen is one of the most important Dutch landscape painters from the Golden Age. He is credited as the most prominent exponent of the so-called tonal style that had a great following in the second quarter of the seventeenth century. There are over twelve hundred paintings and more than a thousand drawings known to be by him, and almost all of them have the Dutch landscape as their subject.

Van Goyen was born in Leiden in 1596, the son of a shoemaker. During his youth he had six teachers, of whom the last—Esaias van de Velde from Haarlem—influenced him the most. After finishing his education, he married Annetje Willemsdr. van Raelst in Leiden in 1618. In 1632 he moved from Leiden to The Hague. In 1651 Van Goyen was commissioned by the magistrate in The Hague to make a panoramic view of the city. For this he received six hundred fifty guilders, more than ten times the amount he usually received for his works. Despite his great production, he always needed money. Without much success, he speculated in tulip bulbs and real estate. When he died in The Hague in 1656, he left great debts.

Van Goyen's early work shows the strong influence of his last teacher, Esaias van de Velde; however, between 1626 and 1629 his style underwent a thorough change. His multicolored palette made way for a sober one of totally harmonized tints. The human figure was given a subordinate role, and nature in its simplest-appearing forms became central. He strengthened unity of the composition through a system of double diagonals: two slanted lines that run toward each other and lead the viewer's glance into depth. In this way all of the parts of the composition were "captured" in one great diagonal movement. This new landscape type is known in the art-historical literature as "tonal landscape." Even though Van Goyen was not the first one to apply it, he did become the most important representative of it. Until his death he continued to work in the tonal style, although he let color and clear skies return in his landscapes every now and then (Color Plate 6).

Within the limitations of the Dutch landscape, Van Goyen painted a great variety of subjects, such as country roads, dune landscapes, river views, beach scenes, panoramic views, town skylines, and winter landscapes. He knew how to catch the atmosphere of the flat Dutch land like no one else.

With a minimum of colors and shapes, he achieved a maximum effect. Van Goyen used his brush in an easy and unforced way. His high productivity could lead to endless variations on one theme; he painted more than thirty versions of the Valkhofburcht in Nijmegen and used almost the same compositional scheme every time.

Van Goyen was also a very active draftsman, who liked to work in open nature. He took trips, for example, to the Southern Netherlands and along the Rhine to Emmerich and Cleves. His numerous sketchbooks were taken apart at a later time to sell the pages separately. Only the *Bredius-Kronig Sketchbook* (1644–ca. 1650; on loan to the Museum Bredius, The Hague) is still intact. Back in his studio his sketches served as memory support when he made elaborate drawings and painted landscapes. In the process he transferred in an imaginative way his spontaneous nature studies into carefully thought-out compositions.

Around the middle of the nineteenth century, appreciation for Jan van Goyen hit a low point. Partly due to the rise of Impressionism, his easy conception of nature attracted new interest around the turn of the century. Today Jan van Goyen's work is in practically every collection of Dutch seventeenth-century painting.

Edwin Buijsen

See also Country houses and gardens; Drawing theory; Haarlem; Landscape; Leiden; Townscapes

Bibliography

Beck, Hans-Ulrich. *Jan van Goyen, 1596–1656: Ein Oeuvre-verzeichnis.* 2 vols. Amsterdam: A.L. van Gendt, 1972–1973.

———. *Jan van Goyen, 1596–1656: Ein Oeuvre-verzeichnis.* Vol. 3, supplement. Doornspijk: Davaco, 1987.

Buijsen, Edwin et al. *Between Fantasy and Reality: Seventeenth-Century Dutch Landscape Painting.* Baarn: De Prom, 1993.

———. *The Sketchbook of Jan van Goyen from the Bredius-Kronig Collection.* The Hague: Stichting Bredius Genootschap, 1993.

Stechow, Wolfgang. *Dutch Landscape Painting of the Seventeenth Century.* London: Phaidon, 1966.

Sutton, Peter C. et al. *Masters of Seventeenth-Century Dutch Landscape Painting*, 317–332. Boston: Museum of Fine Arts, 1987.

Waal, H. van der. *Jan van Goyen.* Paletserie. Amsterdam: Becht, 1941.

Wright, Christopher et al. *Jan van Goyen, 1596–1656: Poet of the Dutch Landscape: Paintings from Museums and Private Collections in Great Britain.* London: Alan Jacobs Gallery, 1977.

Van Honthorst, Gerard (1592–1656)

This most famous representative of the Utrecht Caravaggists is also called Gherardo della Notte (Gerard of the Nights) because of the nightly atmosphere that he created in many of his works (Fig. 140). The nickname was first applied in Rome, where he worked for about ten years and was attracted to the dramatic *chiaroscuro* lighting effects in works by Caravaggio. By introducing a torch or candle as the only light source in the picture, Van Honthorst was able to provide a rational explanation for Caravaggistic darkness. The effect can be well seen in his *Christ before the High Priest* (1617; London, National Gallery), a painting that was commissioned by the Roman marquis Vincenzo Giustiniani. The flickering candle light in the middle of the picture illuminates only the faces of Christ and Caiaphas, while the other persons in the scene remain in partial darkness. Because of works like this one, the painter was very successful and popular in Italy. After his return in 1620, there was a burst of enthusiasm for Caravaggism in the Netherlands. It had already been developing since the return of Hendrick Terbrugghen in 1614. Van Honthorst even influenced his teacher, Abraham Bloemaert, to include Caravaggistic elements in his works for a while (Fig. 68).

In 1630 Van Honthorst abandoned his Caravaggistic style to begin working in a more elegant, classical style. He also applied himself more to allegorical and mythological themes and became much in demand as a portrait painter. Van Honthorst already had worked for prominent patrons in Italy, and back in the Netherlands he was one of the few painters able to build an international reputation during that time. He worked for the *stadholder*, Prince Frederik Hendrik (Fig. 32), on the decoration of several of his palaces and also carried out commissions for the English and the Danish royal courts. Possibly his success made him somewhat lazy; during his life the criticism was made that too great a smoothness had crept into his style.

Eugenie Boer

See also Bloemaert, Abraham; Court and official portraiture; House of Orange-Nassau; Italy; Pastoral; Terbrugghen, Hendrick; Utrecht; Utrecht Caravaggists

Bibliography

Blankert, A. et al. *Gods, Saints, and Heroes: Dutch Paintings in the Age of Rembrandt.* Washington, DC: National Gallery of Art, 1980.

Judson, J.R. *Gerrit van Honthorst: A Discussion of His Position in Dutch Art.* The Hague: Nijhoff, 1959.

Nicolson, B. *Caravaggism in Europe.* 2nd ed., rev. and enl. Turin: Allemandi, 1990.

Van Hove, Bart (1850–1914)

One of the most prominent and productive sculptors in the Netherlands in the period around 1900, Bartholomeus Johannes Wilhelmus Maria ("Bart") van Hove was the son of the painter J.H. van Hove. He was educated at The Hague Academy under Eugène Lacomblé, and after that at the "Higher Institute" in Antwerp (1870–1874), where he studied under Jozef Geefs. From there, with a grant from Prince Hendrik, he went to Paris for five years (1874–1879) to study at the École des Beaux-Arts under P.J. Cavalier. He received his first large commission in this period for two allegorical fe-

male figures of *Waarheid* (Truth) and *Spaarzaamheid* (Thrift) (ca. 1877) for the side façade of the Ministry of Justice building in The Hague. He completed his training in Italy with a grant from the government (1881–1882).

Back in the Netherlands, Van Hove was awarded, through a competition, the commission to make several of the sculptures for the Rijksmuseum in Amsterdam, which had been designed by P.J.H. Cuypers (1882–1885). His other early works include the sculptural group crowning the façade of the Teylers Museum in Haarlem (*Science and Art Crowned by Fame*, 1884–1886) and a strikingly similar group with Minerva for the Barlaeus Gymnasium, a grammar school, in Amsterdam (1885). Between 1885 and 1902, he worked in the Quellinus School in Amsterdam, where he was the director after 1889. From 1900 until his death he was a professor of sculpture at the Amsterdam Rijksacademie. Van Hove was also active in the Amsterdam artists' society Arti et Amicitiae and was several times named its chairman. He worked in an academic style, although in his later work one can sometimes see the influence of Art Nouveau.

Later in his career, Van Hove designed several public statues, among them the ones for *Monseigneur F.H. Hamer* (1902; Nijmegen), *Jan van Schaffelaar* (1903; Barneveld), *J.P. Minckelers* (1904; Maastricht), *Adriaan van Bergen* (1904; Leur), and *Count Willem Lodewijk van Nassau* (1906; Leeuwarden). The greatest part of his *oeuvre* consists of portraits of famous contemporaries, among them King Willem III, Queen Emma, and their daughter, Wilhelmina. The Rijksmuseum and the Stedelijk Museum in Amsterdam, the Teylers Museum in Haarlem, the Bonnefanten Museum in Maastricht, and the Centraal Museum in Utrecht have works of Bart van Hove in their collections.

Mieke van der Wal

See also Public monumental sculpture (1795–1900); Sculpture (1795–1945)

Bibliography

Daalen, P.K. van. *Nederlandse Beeldhouwers in de negentiende eeuw.* The Hague: Nijhoff, 1957.

Hulk, John F. "Bart van Hove." *Elsevier's Geïllustreerd Maandschrift* 9:17 (January/June 1899): 1–11.

Van Huysum, Jan (1682–1749)

Painter and draftsman of still lifes and landscapes, Jan van Huysum was one of the most important still-life painters of the eighteenth century, with a long-lasting influence on Western flower painting. Van Huysum was born in Amsterdam, where he was a pupil of his father, Justus I, whom he assisted in his workshop. He married in 1704. His reputation soared after his father's death in 1716; his greatest success was due to the lavish bouquets with a bright background he developed in the years before 1720. Dated works survive from 1714 onward, but two flower pieces by him are already recorded in an Amsterdam inventory of 1701. Still some degree of confusion exists between works of Justus I and II, Jacob and Jan van Huysum, to whom a vast number of works by others also have been wrongly attributed.

Besides his meticulously executed still lifes of flowers and fruit, often made in pairs and ranging from simply composed small works to large extravaganzas, Van Huysum painted rather traditional Italianate landscapes, often with classical motifs. Both subjects were rendered in drawings as well: The still-life drawings are usually rather sketchy, serving a studio purpose; the landscapes, often highly finished and intended for the art market. A portrait of Van Huysum by Arnold Boonen (traditionally considered to be a self-portrait) is in the Ashmolean Museum, Oxford.

Fred G. Meijer

See also Still life

Bibliography

Grant, M.H. *Jan van Huysum, 1682–1749, Including a Catalogue Raisonné of the Artist's Fruit and Flower Paintings.* Leigh-on-Sea: F. Lewis, 1954.

White, C. *The Flower Drawings of Jan van Huysum, 1682–1749.* Leigh-on-Sea: F. Lewis, 1964.

(NB: both strongly in need of revision)

Van Konijnenburg, Willem (1868–1943)

Willem van Konijnenburg learned the basics of drawing from his mother, a lady from a noble Limburg family who liked to draw herself. From 1882 until 1884 he took lessons from The Hague illustrator J.C. d'Arnaud Gerkens, and from 1884 until 1886 he attended The Hague Academy, from which he received the intermediate certificate in drawing in 1886. After leaving the academy, Van Konijnenburg visited Paris, where he studied the works of the Barbizon School painters. His own landscapes and portraits from this period are painted in a loose, Impressionistic style, but with a strikingly somber, almost monochrome coloring. At first his work was not well received; he was accused of virtuoso superficiality. The new developments in art took him on another track. In the Haagse Kunstkring (The Hague Art Circle), which he joined in 1894, he became acquainted with the stylized work of Jan Toorop and Johan Thorn Prikker, and he was impressed by Antoon Derkinderen's ideas about monumental art. He began to stylize and design his compositions according to geometrical ordering principles. In the meantime, he used his fluency in drawing for advertising work and illustrations in the magazines *De Kroniek* (1895–1897) and *De Nederlandsche Spectator* (1896–1901). In his independent work of that time Van Konijnenburg occupied himself with the rendering of an unchangeable, ideal reality. According to him, the artist had the task of holding up a mirror to humanity in his work. He sought inspiration for content in religious and mythological themes (the struggle between good and evil, dark and light, male and female) and for form in ancient Egyptian art. His ideas about ethics and aesthetics were fully formulated in the theoretical treatise *De Aesthetische Idee* (The Hague, 1916). His most important proposition in this was that beauty in art contributes to the cosmic harmony.

Alexandra W.M. van Smoorenburg

See also Derkinderen, Antoon; Symbolism, Symbolists; Thorn Prikker, Johan; Toorop, Jan

Bibliography

Rijnders, Mieke. *Willem van Konijnenburg, 1868–1943.* Assen: Drents Museum, 1990.

Van Leyden, Aertgen (Aert Claesz.) (1498–1564)

Aert Claesz., known as Aertgen, was a painter in Leiden whose *oeuvre* is still much disputed. Of the works described by Karel van Mander only one has been identified, a triptych of the *Last Judgment* (Valenciennes) commissioned by the Van Montfoort family and dated 1555. His style was characterized by Van Mander as careless and uneven, "sometimes more clever than serious," and exhibiting an "occasional neglect of proportions."

Further complicating the attempt to sort out the numerous attributions is Van Mander's recognition that Aertgen's work changed according to the dominant stylistic influence, from that of his teacher Cornelis Engebrechtsz., whose workshop he entered in 1516, to that of Jan van Scorel and later Maerten van Heemskerck. Several works are known from Aertgen's late period and are clearly related to the style of Van Heemskerck and Franz Floris, including the *Last Judgment* and two engravings by Bartholomeus Dolendo, a Leiden artist active 1585–1629, representing the *Four Evangelists* and *Shipwreck of Paul* and signed "Aertgen van Leyden."

These late works are not very helpful, however, in clarifying Aertgen's early style of the 1520s–1530s. Bruyn grouped a body of works around the *Church Sermon* in Amsterdam (ca. 1530–1535) and the *Temptation of St. Anthony* in Brussels, although they are now generally given to the Master of the Church Sermon because of the lack of any definitive association with Aertgen's later style. The same difficulty is found with the Kanis family triptych of the *Crucifixion* in Nijmegen (ca. 1526–1530), attributed to Aertgen by Lemmens and Begheyn, and the *Raising of Lazarus* in Amsterdam (ca. 1530–1535), recently associated with Aertgen but now acknowledged as being by an unknown Leiden artist. Scholten's scientific investigation of the *Sermon*, the *Temptation of St. Anthony*, and the *Raising of Lazarus* confirmed the need to separate what was earlier seen as a coherent body of works attributable to Aertgen into several independent, although at times interconnected, groups of paintings with which no names can be securely associated.

Elise Lawton Smith

See also Engebrechtsz., Cornelis; Leiden; Van Mander, Karel

Bibliography

Bruyn, Joos. "Twee Antonius-panelen en andere werken van Aertgen van Leyden." *Nederlands Kunsthistorisch Jaarboek* 11 (1960): 36–119.

Kloek, W. et al. *Kunst voor de Beeldenstorm.* 2 vols. Amsterdam: Rijksmuseum; The Hague: Staatsuitgeverij, 1986.

Lemmens, G.Th.M., and P.J. Begheyn. *Het drieluik van de familie Kanis: Een werk van Aertgen van Leyden in*

Nijmegen? Nijmegen: Nijmeegs Museum, 1975.

Mander, Carel van. *Dutch and Flemish Painters.* Edited and translated by Constant van de Wall. New York: McFarlane, Warde, McFarlane, 1936.

Scholten, Frits. "Technische aspecten van de *Kerkprediking* en twee andere werken uit de Aertgen van Leyden-groep." *Nederlands Kunsthistorisch Jaarboek* 37 (1986): 53–74.

Van Leyden, Lucas (ca. 1494–1533)

Lucas van Leyden was a remarkably versatile painter, print-maker, and draftsman working in Leiden in the early sixteenth century. His early fame was primarily due to his skill as a printmaker; his painting production was more limited, consisting of only seventeen extant originals, although that *oeuvre* is increased by the later copies of now-lost works.

Karel van Mander described him as a child prodigy "who seemed to be born with brush and burin in hand." Various attempts to push the birth date of 1494 cited by Van Mander back to 1489 have not been entirely successful, and in any case Lucas' early work would still reveal an unusually precocious talent. According to Van Mander, Lucas studied first with his father, Huygh Jacobsz., who has been tentatively identified as the Master of the St. John Panels, and then with Cornelis Engebrechtsz., although there is little apparent influence from the latter.

Only four of Lucas' paintings are securely dated, all from the 1520s, so the chronology of his early panels is established by comparison with the dated engravings. This endeavor is complicated, however, by the fact that Lucas was exploring different issues as he worked in different media. He experimented with the representation of expansive space and volumetric form in such prints as *Mohammed and the Monk Sergius* (1508), whereas his early paintings are closely framed, half-length narratives concentrating on the psychological interaction among the characters portrayed, as seen in the *Chess Players* (ca. 1508; Berlin) and *Potiphar's Wife Accusing Joseph* (ca. 1510–1511; Rotterdam). Lucas' more loosely constructed compositions of the *Card Players* in Lugano and Wilton House (1513–1517) are still not as spatially bold as such panoramic engravings of the second decade as *Ecce Homo* (1510; Fig. 63) and the *Crucifixion* (1517).

In 1521 Lucas traveled to Antwerp, which had a profound impact on his style. The work of Albrecht Dürer, also in Antwerp 1520–1521, inspired his portrait drawings and prints (such as the *Small Passion* series, 1521), and for several years after this trip he concentrated on devotional images under the inspiration of Dürer, Quinten Massys, and Joos van Cleve. Lucas' *Virgin and Child with Mary Magdalene and a Donor* (1522; Munich) also reveals his increasing concern with the representation of solid, robust forms.

During his late period (ca. 1526–1531), Lucas again concerned himself with different issues in his paintings and prints. His engravings are now limited to a few closely framed, volumetrically conceived Renaissance nudes represented in a relatively hard and schematized technique, seen in *Adam and Eve* (ca. 1530). Most of his late paintings, however, like *Christ Healing the Blind Man* (1531; Leningrad), are panoramic compositions filled with skillfully interwoven groupings of full-length figures set within an atmospheric setting and are characterized by looser brushwork and a subtle, complex use of color.

Despite these essential differences, the broad, fluid compositional rhythms of a painting like the *Dance Around the Golden Calf* (ca. 1529–1530; Amsterdam) are similar to the easy, undulating lines in engravings from the same period (for example, *Murder of Abel*, 1529). Also, in both media the figures are increasingly corporeal and monumental, exhibiting a powerful plasticity inspired by his study of the work of Marcantonio Raimondi and Jan Gossaert. Although Lucas never went to Italy, his *Last Judgment* (1526–1527; Leiden) is full of figures related to poses by Raimondi. The style of Gossaert also became an important factor in the development of Lucas' late style, as seen in his *Virgin and Child* (ca. 1528; Oslo).

Lucas can perhaps best be characterized as an experimenter, an artist aware of the distinct possibilities presented by different media, but there are common concerns that underlie both his graphic and painting production. Certain iconographic themes were approached repeatedly in his prints and paintings, especially those dealing with the relationship between the sexes (Fig. 26) and the fundamental issues of sin and faith. Another unifying element throughout his career was his exploration of narrative meaning, his search for the moment of greatest dramatic impact, and his often unconventional approach to the representation of that moment.

Elise Lawton Smith

See also Comic modes; Engebrechtsz., Cornelis; Flanders, Flemish School; History painting; Last Judgment; Leiden; Prints, early book and Bible illustration; Prints, printmaking, and printmakers (ca. 1500–ca. 1900); Roundels; Soldiers; Underdrawings, underpaintings

Bibliography

Filedt Kok, J.P. "Underdrawing and Other Technical Aspects in the Paintings of Lucas van Leyden." *Nederlands Kunsthistorisch Jaarboek* 29 (1978): 1–184.

Jacobowitz, Ellen S., and Stephanie Loeb Stepanek. *The Prints of Lucas van Leyden and His Contemporaries.* Washington, DC: National Gallery of Art, 1983.

Kloek, Wouter. "The Drawings of Lucas van Leyden." *Nederlands Kunsthistorisch Jaarboek* 29 (1978): 425–458.

Mander, Carel van. *Dutch and Flemish Painters.* Edited and translated by Constant van de Wall. New York: McFarlane, Warde, McFarlane, 1936.

Parshall, Peter W. "Lucas van Leyden and the Rise of Pictorial Narrative." Ph.D. diss., University of Chicago, 1974.

Smith, Elise Lawton. *The Paintings of Lucas van Leyden.* Columbia, MO: University of Missouri Press, 1992.

Vos, Rik. *Lucas van Leyden.* Bentveld: Andreas Landshoff; Maarssen: Gary Schwartz, 1978.

Van Looy, Jacobus (1855–1930)

The painter and writer Jacobus van Looy grew up in the city orphanage in Haarlem. From 1877 until 1884 he studied at the Rijksacademie in Amsterdam, where with other students he founded the artists' society St. Lucas. In 1883 he also became a member of the literary society Flanor. The next year Van Looy won the Prix de Rome and began a two-year journey to study in Italy, Spain, and Morocco. After he returned to the Netherlands, Van Looy kept in close contact with the *De Tachtigers*, as the young painters and writers of the 1880s called themselves. He gave lessons in painting and drawing, and he published and exhibited regularly. In 1888 he became a member of the Nederlandsche Etsclub (Dutch Etching Club). Van Looy preferred figure painting with a narrative character. During this period in Amsterdam, his manner of painting became much more Impressionistic, but his palette remained dark and heavy.

Van Looy married the elocutionist Titia van Gelder in 1892, and two years later the couple moved to Soest, where Van Looy created brightly colored paintings of gardens in bloom that strongly recall French Impressionism. In 1901 there was a retrospective of his work in Amsterdam. Because the press constantly judged Van Looy as having double talents, and rated his qualities as a writer higher, he decided not to exhibit anymore as an artist. His literary career soared from then on, especially after he moved back to Haarlem in 1907. From 1925 until his death in 1930, Van Looy painted regularly. A large collection of his work is in the Frans Hals Museum in Haarlem, as a long-term loan from the Stichting Jacobus van Looy (Jacobus van Looy Foundation), which was founded in 1949.

Rieta Bergsma

See also Amsterdam Impressionists

Bibliography
Bionda, Richard, and Carel Blotkamp, eds. *The Age of Van Gogh: Dutch Painting, 1880–1895*, 23–35, 175–178. Zwolle: Waanders, 1990–1991.

Will, Chris, and Peter J.A. Winkels. *De dubbelbegaafdheid van Jacobus van Looy.* Haarlem: De Vriesseborch, 1988.

Van Mander, Karel (1548–1606)

Painter, draftsman, poet, and rhetorician, Karel van Mander achieved fame as author of the *Schilder-Boeck* (Book on Picturing, 1604), the first history of Dutch and Flemish painting, which is also the first sustained attempt to offer a theory of Netherlandish painting, drawing, and printmaking.

Born to a landed family in the West Flemish village of Meulebeke in 1548, Van Mander matriculated at the local Latin and French schools before entering the Antwerp workshop of Lucas de Heere, the distinguished painter, poet, and Calvinist partisan, whose *Hof en boomgaerd der poësiën* (Court and Orchard of Poesy, 1565) contains several art-theoretical poems and whose now lost verse lives of Northern masters were a spur to Van Mander's art-historical efforts. Having studied with De Heere between 1566 and 1567, Van Mander then spent a year in the workshop of Pieter Vlerick of Kortrijk, an epigone of Tintoretto, who perhaps instilled his abiding interest in Venetian painting. In 1573 Van Mander traveled to Italy, visiting Florence en route to Rome, where he stayed until 1576. Active in the circle of Federico Zuccaro, he particularly admired the Lombard Girolamo Muziano and the Emilian Lorenzo Sabbattini. Having returned to Flanders in 1577, he migrated to Haarlem in 1583, driven by the religious troubles associated with the Revolt of the Netherlands. In Haarlem he established himself as a painter of histories for collectors' cabinets, and he became closely associated with the engraver Hendrick Goltzius and the painter Cornelis Cornelisz. From the late 1580s he was a major supplier of *modelli* (models) to the reproductive engravers Zacharias Dolendo and Jacob de Gheyn II, and he encouraged the revival of interest in the prints of Albrecht Dürer and Lucas van Leyden. He moved to Amsterdam in 1604, soon after finishing the *Schilder-Boeck*, and died there in 1606, his funeral cortege comprising the most celebrated masters and collectors of his day.

Although Van Mander was a Mennonite by 1588, his most important surviving works include two Catholic commissions: the *St. Bartholomew's Night Massacre* (ca. 1575), painted in Rome for a papal dignitary, and the *Martyrdom of St. Catherine* (1582), the centerpiece of a triptych painted for the newly furnished chapel of the Guild of Linen Weavers in St. Martin's, Kortrijk. Among his most ambitious cabinet pictures are the *Amor Omnibus Idem* (ca. 1600), an allegory of love as the font of artifice, and the *Passage Through the River Jordan* (1605), commissioned by the Amsterdam wine merchant Isaac van Gerwen, in which Van Mander portrays himself as one of the carriers of the ark. Toward the close of his career, Van Mander also explored various specializations, painting peasant festivities, *predicaties* (sermons, usually featuring John the Baptist), and *bloemstukken* (flower pieces).

Published after nearly ten years of research and writing, the *Schilder-Boeck* is Van Mander's answer to Giorgio Vasari, whose *Vite* (Lives, eds. 1550 and 1568) traces the history of Italian art but ultimately claims the superiority of Tuscan pictorial diction above all other vernaculars. By chronicling the lives of Northern practitioners of art, Van Mander established the canon of fifteenth- and sixteenth-century masters that continues, and he set forth critical categories such as *teyckenconst* (also spelled *tekenkonst;* drawing or the art of delineation) and *reflexy-const* (the art of depicting reflections), through which local pictorial excellence could be discerned and exemplified. He also strongly supported contemporary masters such as the portraitist Michiel van Miereveld and the painter of *perspectiven* (perspectives) Hans Vredeman de Vries, specialists who had chosen to concentrate on subject categories other than history. Every subsequent Dutch art-theoretical text—Philip Angel's *Lof der schilder-konst* (Praise of Painting) of 1642, Samuel van Hoogstraten's *Inleyding tot de hooge schoole der schilderkonst* (Introduction to the Elevated School of Painting) of 1678, Gerard de Lairesse's *Groot schilderboek* (Great Book of Picturing) of 1707, and Arnold Houbraken's

Groote schouburgh (Great Theater) of 1718—derives from Van Mander's.

Walter S. Melion

See also Amateurs, art academies, and art associations before the nineteenth century; Flanders, Flemish School; Goltzius, Hendrick; Haarlem; Italy; Mannerism, Mannerists; Subjects, subject categories, and hierarchies; Van Leyden, Lucas; Writers on art, eighteenth century; Writers on art, sixteenth and seventeenth centuries

Bibliography

Melion, Walter S. *Shaping the Netherlandish Canon: Karel van Mander's Schilder-Boeck.* Chicago: University of Chicago Press, 1991.

Miedema, Hessel. *Karel van Mander: Den grondt der edel vry schilder-const.* 2 vols. Utrecht: Haentjens, Dekker, and Gumbert, 1973.

———. *Karel van Mander's Leven der moderne, oft dees-tijtsche doorluchtighe Italiaensche schilders en hun bron.* Alphen aan den Rijn: Canaletto, 1984.

———. *Kunst, kunstenaar en kunstwerk bij Karel van Mander: Een analyse van zijn Levenbeschrijvingen.* Alphen aan den Rijn: Canaletto, 1981.

Muylle, Jan. "'Pier den Drol'—Karel van Mander en Pieter Bruegel: Bijdrage tot de literaire receptie van Pieter Bruegel's werk ca. 1600." In *Wort und Bild in der niederländischen Kunst und Literatur des 16. und 17. Jahrhunderts.* Edited by Herman Vekeman and Justus Müller Hofstede, 137–144. Erftstadt: Lukassen Verlag, 1983.

Reznicek, Emil K.J. "Het Leerdicht van Karel van Mander en de acribie van Hessel Miedema." *Oud Holland* 89 (1975): 102–128.

Van Ojen, E.M. (1886–1964)

Evert Marinus van Ojen is best known for his architectural views, especially of buildings by modern architects like J.J.P. Oud, J.A. Brinkman, and L.C. van der Vlugt. He also used as subject a much wider range of works of art, such as paintings, tapestries, sculptures, glass, furniture, and interiors. His photographs appear in many books on interior decoration and furniture. In addition, he worked on assignment for the city of The Hague between about 1922 and 1930, documenting its building activities.

In the 1920s Van Ojen, who had started as a pictorialist, turned to New Photography. Many others had done so, too, including the pioneers of New Photography from outside the Netherlands. Those who had introduced New Photography in the Netherlands—Gerrit Kiljan (1891–1968), Paul Schuitema (1897–1973), and Piet Zwart (1885–1977)—had not been photographers before they became interested in using photographs in their graphic designs. Thus, they skipped over a pictorialist phase in their work.

By its sharpness and clarity, Van Ojen's picture of the Amelandsestraat in The Hague (1926; Fig. 144) is exemplary of New Photography. For a while pictorialism and New Pho-

tography existed side by side in his *oeuvre;* his architectural photography may have marked the transition to New Photography. In the *oeuvre* of Bernard Eilers (1878–1951), one of the foremost pictorialists, the architectural views stand out as the most progressive part. A remarkable effect of depth, achieved through the well-considered use of shadows, can be seen in that part of the pictures by Van Ojen, Eilers, and Johan Huijsen (1877–1959) that are at the division of pictorialism and New Photography.

Hans Rooseboom

See also Functionalism in architecture; Oud, Jacobus Johannes Pieter; Photography, modern and contemporary; Townscapes

Bibliography

Venetië, Robbert van, and Annet Zondervan. *Geschiedenis van de Nederlandse architectuurfotografie.* Rotterdam: 010, 1989.

Van Pallandt, Charlotte (born 1898)

Charlotte Dorothée, Baroness of Pallandt, born in Arnhem, was already drawing while in boarding school in England (1913–1914). When she returned to her family in The Hague, she took lessons in painting from Albert Roelofs. After World War I she moved to Switzerland, where for a while she worked at a free academy in Lausanne. In 1926 she moved to Paris, where she studied with the Cubist painter André Lhote and also met the Russian sculptor Akop Gurdjan, who advised her to start sculpting. In 1928 she was back in The Hague, using Toon Dupuis' studio and receiving advice from Oswald Wenckebach and later also from Albert Termote. Until the outbreak of World War II, she paid regular visits to Paris, where she had contact with the French sculptors Charles Despiau and Aristide Maillol; she also worked for a time in 1935–1936 at the Académie Ranson in Paris under the direction of sculptor Charles Malfray.

Van Pallandt primarily made small sculptures and portraits, which are conceived very plastically and have a strongly monumental character. On the one hand, she molded clay sculptures that were cast in bronze; on the other hand, she also carved directly in stone and wood. Often she made preliminary studies, in which she showed the volumes only schematically, in order to better judge the working of light. In the many preparatory drawings she made, one can see clearly how she built up her sculptures from loose geometric shapes. One of her few monumental commissions is the freestone statue of *Queen Wilhelmina* in Rotterdam (1966–1968). In 1984 a bronze cast of this statue was placed in The Hague.

In 1992 Van Pallandt was awarded a prize for her life's work from the Stichting Fonds van de Kunsten, Vormgeving, en Bouwkunst (Foundation Fund of the Arts, Design, and Architecture). Her works are widely available for viewing in state and municipal museums and public collections in the Netherlands.

Mieke van der Wal

See also Public monumental sculpture (1795–1990); Sculpture (1795–1945)

Bibliography

Koning, Marijn de, and André Kraayenga. *Wilhelmina monumentaal.* Zwolle: Waanders; Heino: Stichting Hannema-De Stuers Fundatie, 1987.

Tegenbosch, Lambert, and Marian Koekkoek. *Charlotte van Pallandt. Beelden en tekeningen.* 2nd ed. Zwolle: Waanders, 1994.

———. *Charlotte van Pallandt: Tekeningen.* Venlo: Van Spijk, 1981.

Van Ruisdael, Jacob (1628/1629–1682)

Considered the foremost Dutch landscape specialist of the seventeenth century, Jacob van Ruisdael was a prolific painter, etcher, and draftsman. He is noted for the multiplicity of landscape subjects he produced, his heroic characterizations of trees, and his powerful evocations of atmospheric conditions. Despite the rarity of documents concerning this Haarlem-born artist's life, informative biographies of Van Ruisdael are included in monographs on the artist by Seymour Slive and E. John Walford. Few of Van Ruisdael's works are dated; however, Jakob Rosenberg, in his 1928 monograph, established the still widely accepted canon for the stylistic development of the artist. Van Ruisdael's prints, primarily images of vigorous trees and forests, all date from the early part of his career.

Unlike most landscapists of the time, who tended to specialize more narrowly, Van Ruisdael was the master of nearly all of the categories of landscape painting identified by Wolfgang Stechow in his 1966 survey of the genre. Many typical Dutch locales, such as dunes, beaches, woods, rivers, canals, the sea, and winterscapes, as well as imaginary and foreign scenes, were executed by the artist. He rendered some of the most memorable images of the Dutch countryside, such as *The Windmill at Wijk* (Amsterdam, Rijksmuseum) with its monumentalized mill silhouetted against a heroic sky. During his lifetime, however, his Alpine and Scandinavian scenes of mountains, pines, and waterfalls (inspired by fellow artist Allart van Everdingen, because Van Ruisdael himself probably never visited such regions) were more lucrative, since paintings of foreign locales garnered higher prices than scenes of the flat and familiar domestic lands.

While Slive and Rosenberg concentrated mainly on connoisseurship issues, scholars such as Hans Kauffmann, Josua Bruyn, Linda Stone-Ferrier, and Walford have written about the levels of meaning within Van Ruisdael's works. Since the painter often manipulated, altered, or invented topographical elements and whole scenes, art historians have assumed he did this for more than just aesthetic reasons. Bruyn found religious and moral symbolism, not only in overtly allegorical paintings like *The Jewish Cemetery* (two versions, Dresden and Detroit), but also in works such as the 1651 *View of Bentheim Castle* (English private collection). For Bruyn, Bentheim Castle, set on a much-exaggerated hilltop, represented the heavenly Jerusalem on Mount Zion (In Sutton, 1987: 98–100). In analyzing *The Windmill at Wijk*, Kauffmann asserted that Van Ruisdael used direct emblematic associations to imbue his works with meaning. Walford, employing a semiotic approach, contended that components

such as light beams falling on bleaching fields would have generally been understood by seventeenth-century viewers as indications of man's dependence on God's providence. Focusing more specifically on several of Van Ruisdael's panoramic views of Haarlem, called *Haarlempjes,* Stone-Ferrier suggested, instead, that the highlighting of the city's linen-bleaching fields was meant as a celebration of an economically strong industry that was a source of local civic pride. No matter how Van Ruisdael's works are interpreted, they are representative of the rich variety and strength of the seventeenth-century Dutch landscape tradition, of which Van Ruisdael was one of the best assets.

Diane E. Cearfoss Mankin

See also Country houses and gardens; Landscape; Prints, printmaking, and printmakers (ca. 1500–ca. 1900); Textiles, textile industry; Townscapes

Bibliography

Kauffmann, Hans. "Jacob van Ruisdael: 'Die Mühle von Wijk bei Duurstede.'" In *Festschrift für Otto von Simson zum 65: Geburtstag.* Edited by L. Grisebach and K. Renger, 379–397. Frankfurt am Main: Propylaen Verlag, 1977.

Rosenberg, Jakob. *Jacob van Ruisdael.* Berlin: Bruno Cassirer, 1928.

Slive, Seymour. *Jacob van Ruisdael.* New York: Abbeville, 1981.

Stechow, Wolfgang. *Dutch Landscape Painting of the Seventeenth Century.* London: Phaidon, 1966.

Stone-Ferrier, Linda. "Views of Haarlem: A Reconsideration of Ruisdael and Rembrandt." *Art Bulletin* 67:3 (September 1985): 417–436.

Sutton, Peter C. et al. *Masters of Seventeenth-Century Dutch Landscape Painting,* 437–465. Boston: Museum of Fine Arts; distributed by University of Pennsylvania Press, 1987.

Walford, E. John. *Jacob van Ruisdael and the Perception of Landscape.* New Haven: Yale University Press, 1991.

Van Schurman, Anna Maria (1607–1678)

Born in Cologne, Anna Maria van Schurman was the daughter of Frederik van Schurman, an emigrant from Antwerp, and his noble wife, Eva von Harff de Dreiborn. Besides ancient and modern languages, she studied the natural sciences, music, and crafts of all kinds. Around 1616 the family moved to Utrecht, where Anna Maria attracted the interest of the preacher Gisbertus Voetius, who was to teach her theology and various Oriental languages. In Utrecht she also took lessons in drawing and engraving from Magdalena de Passe, daughter of the well-known engraver Crispijn de Passe I.

By 1625 Jacob Cats had addressed some verses to her in his book entitled *Houwelyck* (Marriage), and it was the lawyer and archeologist Arnout van Buchell who informed Caspar van Baerle (Barlaeus), a professor at the University of Leiden, of her exceptional genius, erudition, and assiduity. Around 1630 Barlaeus introduced her to the poet and diplomat Constantijn Huygens. In 1637, on occasion of the elevation of Utrecht's famed Latin school to the status of a university, she was invited to write a poem to celebrate the opening. In the same year a separate box was prepared in the theology lecture theater from which she could, as the first female university student in the Netherlands, attend the lectures. Also in 1637 Jacob Cats dedicated his book *Trou-Ringh* (Wedding Ring) to her; opposite the frontispiece appears a print of a self-portrait designed by Van Schurman.

Van Schurman's correspondence with the Huguenot theologian André Rivet on the question of the education of women led to the publication of the *Dissertatio, de ingenii muliebris ad doctrinam, & meliores litteras aptitudine* (Leiden, 1641); it was translated into English and published in London in 1659 under the title *The Learned Maid, or, Whether a Maid May Be a Scholar?* Anna Maria van Schurman not only defended the thesis that women have a particular vocation in the arts, she had put it into practice from her youth. She developed her natural manual skill in the direction of specifically dilettante and more professional arts. Convincing artistic quality is to be found in a number of her portrait engravings and portrait miniatures executed in charcoal, gouache, oils, or pastels. Besides these, she made wax moldings, designs for medals, and paper cutouts with scissors, and practiced embroidery, calligraphy, and the art of whittling wood and ivory. Only a few specimens of these minor arts have been preserved (in Franeker, 't Coopmanshuis; in Utrecht, Centraal Museum; and in Amsterdam, Rijksmuseum). Accordingly, it is not surprising that she is included in the register of the Guild of St. Luke in Utrecht for the year 1643 as a "painter, sculptor, and engraver."

In 1648 Van Schurman's *Opuscula*, mainly a collection of letters, appeared in Leiden. From 1653 to around 1655 Van Schurman lived in Cologne, and afterward she withdrew for some years to the countryside near Vianen. By 1660 at the latest she was back in Utrecht, where she became interested in the former Jesuit and preacher Jean de Labadie. De Labadie had acquired by 1669 a large following who lived a communal life with him in Amsterdam, and Van Schurman did not hesitate to move into the Labadist house. At the end of 1670 the Labadist community left the city, and a temporary residence was found first in Herford in Westphalia and later in Altona, where the first volume of Van Schurman's religious apologetic autobiography (*Eukleria*, 1673) was published. Van Schurman died on May 4, 1678, in Wieuwerd, a village in Friesland, where the Labadist community next found a stopping place.

Katlijne Van der Stighelen

See also Huygens, Constantijn; Utrecht

Bibliography

Baar, Mirjam de et al., eds. *Anna Maria van Schurman, 1607–1678: Een uitzonderlijk geleerde vrouw.* Zutphen: Walburg, 1992.

Birch, Una. *Anna Maria van Schurman: Artist, Scholar, Saint.* London: Longmans, 1909.

Van der Stighelen, Katlijne. *Anna Maria van Schurman of "Hoe hooge dat een maeght kan in de konsten stijgen":* *Symbolae Facultatis Litterarum et Philosophiae Lovaniensis.* Series B, vol. 4. Louvain: Universitaire Pers, 1987.

Van Wesel, Adriaen (ca. 1417–ca. 1490)

The most important woodcarver of the Northern Netherlands in the fifteenth century, Adriaen van Wesel lived and worked in Utrecht, where he produced altar retables for the great churches of Utrecht and several other towns in the region. He was born around 1417 and died around 1490, yet his known carvings all date from after around 1470. His works included an altar retable for the high altar of the Mariakerk, dating from before 1484, the same year in which he was asked to make the high-altar retable for the Nieuwe Kerk in Delft. In 1487 he made a retable for the St. Agnes convent near Zwolle, and in the same year he delivered three saints' figures for the high altar of the Buurkerk in Utrecht. His last known commission, from 1489, was a group of seven saints for the predella, or base, of the high altar in the Domkerk in Utrecht.

All these retables have been lost. But of the great altar retable he made for the fraternity of Our Lady in 's Hertogenbosch between 1475 and 1477, several fragments have survived, as well as quite a number of documents related to its origin and later history. Eleven pieces of woodcarving out of twenty-three now considered to be work by Van Wesel may be said with some certainty to have belonged to this retable.

The retable was commissioned for three hundred fifty Rhenish guilders, but at the end Van Wesel was paid thirty-six guilders extra. In 1488–1489 two outer wings were added, painted by Hieronymus Bosch, now lost. The polychrome finish of the woodcarvings, intended from the start, was only added in 1508–1510 and cost four hundred sixty-two Rhenish guilders. In 1629, when the great church in which the retable stood was handed over to the Protestants, it must have been taken apart and stored away. Most of the fragments were dispersed at the end of the nineteenth century.

The retable probably consisted of three compartments with a higher middle part. The two sculpted wings of this upper part, showing the Emperor Augustus with the Sibyl of Tibur and St. John on Patmos, have always been in the possession of the fraternity, whose association was never discontinued. The other reassembled pieces show scenes from the life of Mary as the mother of Jesus (Fig. 122).

Van Wesel's style is characterized by the expression of human emotion. His great virtuosity in carving is not used to produce minute details or violent emotions, but to give a rapid and telling story. As a result, there is a certain carelessness in the execution, but the general effect is simple and direct. Thus, his faces do not show ideal beauty or grotesque caricature, but are rather childlike and gentle.

Sixteenth-century Iconoclasm has not left us one single altar retable intact in the Netherlands itself. The pieces preserved from the important 's Hertogenbosch retable by Van Wesel show us what a Netherlandish retable may have looked like. Van Wesel's work may be seen as the prototype of Northern Netherlandish woodcarving in the fifteenth century.

Harry Tummers

See also Devotional images; Sculpture (ca. 1400–ca. 1550); Utrecht

Bibliography

Halsema-Kubes, W. "Der Altar Adriaen van Wesels aus 's-Hertogenbosch: Rekonstruktion und kunstgeschichtliche Bedeutung." In *Flügelaltäre des späten Mittelalters*. Edited by H. Krohn and E. Oellermann, 144–156. Berlin: D. Reimer, 1992.

Halsema-Kubes, W., G. Lemmens, and G. de Werd. *Adriaen van Wesel: Een Utrechts beeldhouwer uit de late middeleeuwen*. The Hague: Staatsuitgeverij, 1980.

Vanitas, vanitas still life

Meditation upon the passage of time and the vanity of earthly endeavor in the eternal scheme of things constituted a familiar theme in seventeenth-century painting. Certain Dutch still lifes made reference to this theme with objects that could be interpreted as reminders of human mortality: most commonly, a human skull; perhaps a candle or an oil lamp sometimes with its wick still smoking, an hourglass, or a pocket watch; or emblematic or biblical references such as soap bubbles or fading flowers. Various worldly pursuits were represented by a range of other objects: wealth by coins and purses, gold, and jewelry; power by crowns and scepters, weapons and armor; knowledge by books, globes, scientific instruments, and attributes of the various arts; other diversions by smoking and drinking requisites, musical instruments, playing cards, and dice. Frequently Latin inscriptions were incorporated: *memento mori* (remembrance of death); or the excerpt from Ecclesiastes 1:2, *vanitas vanitatis et omnia vanitas* (vanity of vanities, all is vanity). While such imagery had appeared within earlier Netherlandish representations, independent still lifes composed of it became popular in the late 1620s and took various forms throughout the century.

Vanitas (Latin for "vanity") still life first flourished in the university town of Leiden. Consciousness of death was surely heightened by the ending of the Twelve Years' Truce with Spain in 1621; and in 1624–1625 and again in 1635, Leiden was struck with plague. The earliest known Dutch *vanitas* had been a skull in a stone niche inscribed *humana vana*, painted in 1603 by Jacob de Gheyn II (1565–1629). David Bailly (1584–ca. 1657), said to have studied with De Gheyn in Leiden, may have been the influence uniting a whole circle of painters producing similar *vanitas* still lifes there around 1630, including his pupils Harmen and Pieter Steenwijck as well as Pieter Potter (ca. 1600–1652) and the young Jan Davidsz. de Heem (1606–1683/1684); a generation later, the Leiden *vanitas* of Jacques de Claeuw (1620–after 1676) still recalled Bailly's precise rendering and scattered compositions. Rembrandt's Leiden-period genres (1606–1631) incorporate details such as books and candlesticks commonly found in still lifes from this group; his pupil Willem de Poorter (born 1608) painted unique scenes of armor and weapons recognizable from Rembrandt's studio. Gerrit Dou (1613–1675), who also studied under Rembrandt in Leiden and worked there all of his life, frequently employed *vanitas* details such as skulls and

hourglasses in his genre scenes, especially of hermits; he also painted several *bedriegertjes* (illusionistic or *trompe l'oeil* works) of such objects.

Elsewhere, too, painters tried their hand at *vanitas*. In Haarlem, some of Pieter Claesz.'s and Willem Claesz. Heda's early monochromes featured skulls; later Vincent Laurensz. van der Vinne (1629–1702) specialized in *vanitas* there, assembling some compositions around portraits of Charles I of England. Pieter van Roestraeten (1630–1700) found a successful market in London painting costly objects; his pupil Edwaert Colyer (ca. 1640–ca. 1706) returned to Leiden to specialize in *vanitas*. Matthias Withoos (1627–1703) created *vanitas* landscapes with skulls and urns in Italy that are indebted to Salvator Rosa; and Jan van der Heyden (1637–1712), better known for his townscapes, did some unusual interiors with rich accoutrements.

Ingvar Bergström traced *vanitas* iconography to earlier Netherlandish painting: scholarly paraphernalia in the study of St. Jerome, purses and coins in Marinus van Reymerswaele's paintings of tax men, riches in pictures of dying men tempted by the devil, certain flowers or foods in images of the Madonna and Child or the Last Supper, skulls and hourglasses on the backs of portrait diptychs. Bergström saw *vanitas* in particular—and still life in general—as gradually becoming emancipated from this context, but he acknowledged it is unclear where in Dutch still life moralizing symbolism fades and description takes over.

More recent scholarship has explored other connotations to the theme. Svetlana Alpers locates *vanitas* in the act of representation itself: In replicating fine or elaborately handwrought objects in paint, Dutch painters asserted their ability to outcraft the craftsmen of these precious objects. The many other ways artists called attention to their own role—clever signatures, painters' tools included in the composition, even tiny self-portraits reflected in depicted objects—lend further credence to this view. In the poignant context of the painter's own mortality, *vanitas* highlights the immortality of painting: As another Latin motto quoted in such still lifes declares, *ars longa, vita brevis* (art is long, life is brief). In Jan Vos' 1652 poem *Strijd Tussen Doodt en de Natuur* (Battle between Death and Nature), Painting comes to Nature's rescue by vanquishing Time and Death with her enduring images. Yet after all, of course, a picture is not life, but only a representation, and, as Ernst Gombrich pointed out, that remains the ultimate *vanitas*.

Julie Berger Hochstrasser

See also Didactic images; Dou, Gerrit; Exotica; Gamepiece; Still life

Bibliography

Alpers, Svetlana. "'With a Sincere Hand and a Faithful Eye': The Craft of Representation." Chap. 3 in *The Art of Describing: Dutch Art in the Seventeenth Century*. Chicago: University of Chicago Press, 1983.

Bergström, Ingvar. "The Masters of the *Vanitas* Still Life." Chap. 4 in *Dutch Still-Life Painting in the Seventeenth Century*. Translated by Christina Hedström, and

Gerald Taylor. London: Faber and Faber, 1956.

Gombrich, Ernst. "Tradition and Expression in Western Still Life." *Burlington Magazine* 103 (1961): 175–180.

Tapié, Alain. *Les Vanités dans la Peinture au XVIIe Siècle.* Caen: Musée des Beaux-Arts; Paris: Musée du Petit Palais, 1990–1991.

Wurfbain, M.L. *Ijdelheid der Ijdelheden: Hollandse Vanitas voorstellingen uit de zeventiende eeuw.* Leiden: Stedelijk Museum De Lakenhal, 1970.

Verhulst, Rombout (1624–1698)

A Flemish sculptor who worked in stone, wood, and ivory, Rombout Verhulst studied with Rombout Verstappen and Frans van Loo in his native Mechelen before moving to Amsterdam in 1646. As a member of Artus I Quellinus' workshop at the new town hall, he executed reliefs of *Venus* (before 1658), *Fidelity*, and *Silence* for the galleries, and terracotta studies (ca. 1655; Amsterdam, Rijksmuseum) for the bronze doors of the *vierschaar* (public tribunal). Although the classicizing tendencies of these works attest to the influence of Quellinus, their greater warmth and delicacy also indicate Verhulst's similarities with Rubens and the sculptors of his circle. Verhulst's reputation as the foremost marble carver of the century is based on his sensitive modeling and subtle rendering of surfaces. By 1658 he was resident in Leiden where he executed reliefs (the *Butterseller*, 1662) and decoration for Pieter Post's *waag* (weigh house); by 1663 he was active in The Hague, where he became a member of the guild in 1668 and the painters' fraternity Pictura in 1676. Following Quellinus' return to Antwerp in 1665, Verhulst became the most important sculptor in the Netherlands.

Verhulst produced a number of terra-cotta portrait busts (Amsterdam, Rijksmuseum; and Malibu, California, J. Paul Getty Museum) in which his sensitive handling of the physiognomy and subtle evocation of the sitter's personality and character create a vital living presence. A somewhat more refined expression of Baroque verisimilitude appears in the effigies of his funeral monuments, which are located in churches throughout the Netherlands. While the majority of these commissions were for private family tombs—for example, those of *Johan Polyander Kerkhoven* (1663; Leiden, Pieterskerk); *Willem van Liere and Maria van Reygersberg* (1663; Katwijk); *Adrian Clant* (ca. 1665; Stedum); and *Carel van In-en-Kniphausen* (ca. 1665; Midwolde)—Verhulst also designed and/or executed monuments for several of the nation's naval heroes, including those of *Jan van Galen* (1654; Amsterdam, Nieuwe Kerk), *Maerten Tromp* (signed and dated 1658; Delft, Oude Kerk; Color Plate 9); *Willem Joseph van Gendt* (1676; Utrecht, Domkerk) and *Michiel de Ruyter* (1677–1681; Amsterdam, Nieuwe Kerk). As most sculptors from this period, Verhulst is also credited with several garden statues (Amsterdam, Rijksmuseum).

Cynthia Lawrence

See also De Keyser, Hendrick; Eggers, Bartolomeus; Flanders, Flemish School; Leiden; Post, Pieter; Quellinus, Artus I; Sculpture (1550–1795); Tomb sculpture: early modern and later sepulchral art ; Van Campen, Jacob; Xavery, Pieter

Bibliography

Fremantle, K. *The Baroque Town Hall of Amsterdam.* Utrecht: Haentjens Dekker and Gumbert, 1959.

Freemantle, K., and W. Halsema-Kubes. *Beelden Kijken: De Kunst van Quellien in het Paleis op de Dam.* Amsterdam: Koninklijk Paleis, 1977.

Hoozee, R. "Rombout Verhulst." In *De Beeldhouwkunst in de Eeuw van Rubens*, 254. Brussels: Museum voor Oude Kunst, 1977.

Kulturmann, U. et al. "Rombout Verhulst." In *Europäische Barockplastik am Niederrhein: Grupello und seine Zeit*, 273–276. Dusseldorf: Kunstmuseum, 1971.

Leeuwenberg, J., and W. Halsema-Kubes, eds. *Beeldhouwkunst in het Rijksmuseum*, 311–320. The Hague: Staatsuitgeverij, 1973.

Mulder, T.R. "Rombout Verhulst's monument voor Johannes van Gheel in de Nederlands Hervormde Kerk van Spanbroek." *West-Friesland oud en nieuw* 25 (1958): 48–52.

Neurdenburg, E. *De zeventiende eeuwsche beeldhouwkunst in de Noordelijke Nederlanden: Hendrick De Keyser, Artus Quellien, en Rombout Verhulst en tijdgenoten.* Amsterdam: Meulenhoff, 1948.

Notten, M. van. *Rombout Verhulst, beeldhouwer 1624–1698: Een overzicht zijner werken.* The Hague: Nijhoff, 1907.

Rosenberg, J., S. Slive, and E.H. ter Kuile. *Dutch Art and Architecture, 1600–1800.* Baltimore: Penguin, 1966.

Scholten, F.T. *Rombout Verhulst te Groningen.* Utrecht: Matrijs, 1983.

Staring, A. "Het laatste werk van Rombout Verhulst." *Oud Holland* 85 (1970): 134.

Vermeer, Johannes (1632–1675)

The pictures of Johannes Vermeer bring to a culmination key developments that occurred in Delft painting in the mid-seventeenth century. The artist's light-filled interiors depicting women engaged in quiet domestic pursuits, his *View of Delft* (The Hague, Mauritshuis; Fig. 145), and *Street in Delft* (Amsterdam, Rijksmuseum), demonstrate the preoccupation among artists in Delft with the domestic townscape, both interior and exterior, and their accompanying concern in optics and perspective. At the same time, the elusive qualities of Vermeer's painting technique and the compelling sense of mystery evoked in his pictures give the artist a special status within Dutch art.

Little is known about Vermeer's life and personality, though the recent archival work of J. Michael Montias has revealed an abundance of data on the artist's family and social network. Vermeer was born in Delft on October 31, 1632. His father, Reynier Vos, was at one time a silk worker, owned a tavern, and dealt in pictures. Leonaert Bramer, an important figure in the artistic milieu of Vermeer's youth, has been postulated as a possible teacher of the artist; more recently it has been suggested that the young Vermeer may have received his training in Amsterdam and/or Utrecht, possibly spending time in the atelier of Abraham Bloemaert. In April, 1653, Vermeer married Catharina Bolnes, the daughter of a prominent Catholic family from Gouda; the couple had eleven children. At some point the artist converted to Catholicism. Eight months after his marriage, Vermeer was enlisted in the painters' guild in Delft, and in the autumn of 1662 he was elected to its governing board. Vermeer supplemented his income by dealing in pictures. Though he never traveled to Italy, the artist was a recognized authority on Italian art; in 1672 he and Hans Jordaens I were asked to judge a disputed art collection that was being sold to the Elector of Brandenburg. Vermeer's strained financial situation in his later years was largely due to the economic crisis prevailing then in the Netherlands.

Only about thirty paintings by Vermeer are known; no drawings by the artist have been identified. While he consistently signed his paintings, only three works are dated. *The Procuress* (Dresden, Staatliche Gemäldegalerie) is signed and dated 1656, *The Astronomer* (Paris, private collection) is signed and dated 1668, and *The Geographer* (Frankfurt, Städelsches Kunstinstitut) is signed and dated 1669. His earliest paintings (ca. 1654–1659) are marked by a vigorous brushwork and deep colors, displaying an Italianate workmanship that differs sharply from Dutch painting of the period, while the paintings of the 1660s may be distinguished by their refined optical qualities suggesting the use of the *camera obscura*. Vermeer's late paintings (1670s) exhibit a technical virtuosity that has been labeled as "mannered."

Vermeer's paintings appear to have been produced for an exclusive circle of enlightened connoisseurs. Pieter van Ruijven, a man of independent means who held a small municipal post in Delft, owned twenty pictures by the artist in the seventeenth century. Vermeer's paintings were considered rare and especially praiseworthy in the eighteenth century, judging from comments in contemporary sales catalogs. However, broader public exposure of his art occurred only in the late nineteenth century, when the French politician and critic Théophile Thoré (alias William Bürger) published the first comprehensive overview of his work, dubbing the artist "the sphinx of Delft."

Vermeer's pictures demonstrate a variety of artistic influences. Two history paintings assigned to his early years are related to the works of Erasmus Quellinus and Jacob van Loo, both active in Amsterdam at mid-century, while his early *Woman Asleep at a Table* (New York, Metropolitan Museum of Art) is inspired by the Dordrecht painter Nicolaes Maes. Vermeer's paintings of the 1660s are closely related to works by Pieter de Hooch (for example, *Woman Drinking a Glass of Wine*; Berlin, Staatliche Museen, Gemäldegalerie), and later the artist appears to have also absorbed the influence of Frans van Mieris the Elder (*The Art of Painting*, Vienna, Kunsthistorisches Museum). While the famous *View of Delft* has been connected with city and town views by other Dutch painters (Daniel Vosmaer, Egbert van der Poel), this picture and the maps that appear consistently in his work have suggested an interest in contemporary cartography and cartographic imagery.

The Art of Painting and the *Allegory of Faith* (New York, Metropolitan Museum of Art; Fig. 115) are the only clear-cut instances of allegory in Vermeer's *oeuvre*. Yet there have been repeated attempts to provide allegorical and/or moralistic interpretations for his domestic interiors. Examples of this are the *Woman Asleep at a Table*, which has been interpreted as an allegory of "sloth," and the *Woman Weighing Pearls* (Washington, DC, National Gallery of Art), which has been interpreted as an allegory of "vanity." The inscription ("Music: Companion of Joy, Balm of Sorrow") written in capitals on the cover of the harpsichord in the *Music Lesson* (London, Buckingham Palace) has helped underscore the possible meaning latent in Vermeer's images of the Dutch "everyday" world. There has also been a tendency to see Vermeer's preoccupation with women in his paintings and with amorous subject matter as an expression of "repressed" feelings regarding women and sexuality or as a more basic comment on the problematic nature of seeing as a means of grasping the world (see Berger, 1979; Brusati, 1993; Gowing, 1970; and Snow, 1979).

Vermeer's "realism" and the related issue of the artist's technique have been a constant element in the critical appreciation of his paintings. Montias has suggested that many of the people and objects that inhabit Vermeer's painting are derived from the artist's immediate surroundings. More fundamentally, however, it is the artist's way of recording the world that has inspired the greatest interest. What have been described as the "photographic" qualities of his pictures have strongly suggested the use of a mechanical device—namely, the *camera obscura*. At the same time, it has also been shown that the *camera obscura* as well as pictorial conventions were employed by the artist as a means of rearranging reality and providing his own imaginative re-creation of it. There has also been discussion of Vermeer's realism in relationship to important scientific developments of the period, such as Dutch seventeenth-century cartography, the optical inquiries of his Dutch contemporary Anton van Leeuwenhoek, and the findings of Sir Francis Bacon and Johannes Kepler.

Vermeer's extraordinary painting technique, which appears to record optical stimuli rather than tactile presences, has been viewed by some as an anticipation of nineteenth-century French Impressionism and by others as evidence of the artist's use of the *camera obscura*.

Jane ten Brink Goldsmith

See also Bloemaert, Abraham; Bramer, Leonaert; Cartography; Delft; France; Genre painting, eighteenth century; Genre painting, seventeenth century; Maes, Nicolaes; Religion of artists; Reputation of Dutch art abroad; Townscapes; Women's worlds

Bibliography

Berger, Harry. "Some Vanity of His Art: Conspicuous Exclusion." *Salmagundi* 44/45 (Spring/Summer 1979): 89–113.

Blankert, Albert. *Vermeer of Delft: Complete Edition of the Paintings*. Oxford: Phaidon, 1978.

Brusati, Celeste. *Johannes Vermeer*. New York: Rizzoli, 1993.

Gaskell, Ivan. "Vermeer, Judgment, and Truth." *Burlington Magazine* 126 (September 1984): 557–561.

Gowing, Lawrence. *Vermeer*. New ed. New York: Harper and Row, 1970.

Montias, J. Michael. *Vermeer and His Milieu: A Web of Social History*. Princeton, NJ: Princeton University Press, 1989.

Snow, Edward A. *A Study of Vermeer*. Berkeley: University of California Press, 1979.

Salomon, Nanette. "Vermeer and the Balance of Destiny." In *Essays in Northern European Art Presented to Egbert Haverkamp-Begemann on His Sixtieth Birthday*. Doornspijk: Davaco, 1983.

Welu, James. "Vermeer: His Cartographic Sources." *Art Bulletin* 68 (1975): 263–267.

Wheelock, Arthur K., Jr. *Jan Vermeer*. New York: Harry N. Abrams, 1988.

Wheelock, Arthur K., Jr., ed. *Johannes Vermeer*. Washington DC: National Gallery of Art; The Hague: Mauritshuis; New Haven: Yale University Press, 1995.

———. "St. Praxedis: New Light on the Early Career of Vermeer." *Artibus et Historiae* 7 (1986): 71–89.

Wheelock, Arthur K., Jr., and C.J. Kaldenbach. "Vermeer's *View of Delft* and His Vision of Reality." *Artibus et Historiae* 3 (1982): 9–35.

Verster, Floris (1861–1927)

Floris Hendrik Verster van Wulverhorst is known primarily for his flower still lifes. At the age of seventeen he took lessons at Ars Aemula Naturae in Leiden for one year when George Hendrik Breitner was a teacher there. From 1879 until 1882, Verster attended The Hague Academy, followed by a half-year of study at the academy in Brussels. He shared a studio with the painter Menso Kamerling Onnes (1860–1925) for ten years, and in 1892 he married Menso's sister. Verster had close contacts with the circle of the Amsterdam Impressionists, but he lived a fairly secluded life in his country house outside of Leiden. Until about 1885 he was clearly influenced by the painters of The Hague School. This changed in the second half of the 1880s when he made his first flower still lifes. These gigantic, Impressionistic bouquets of wild plants and flowers caused quite a stir in the circle of the *Tachtigers*. During this time Verster experimented a great deal with color and light effects, and he developed into a colorist almost non-Dutch in manner. Between 1895 and 1900 he made mainly pastel and crayon drawings, in which he called more attention to the line and form. Then followed a number of paintings in subdued colors with simple subjects like tin cans or a napkin with eggs, which create a still, sometimes strongly spiritual impression. After that he created a series of flower pieces in which the paint was applied in short, forceful touches in a very expressive and impasto way. From 1912 on, Verster painted more modest flower still lifes, and around 1918 a new period of stillness appeared. Verster also made portraits and etchings. In the Netherlands, works by Verster are in the collection of the Stedelijk Museum de Lakenhal in Leiden and the Rijksmuseum Kröller-Müller in Otterlo.

Harry J. Kraaij

See also Amsterdam Impressionists; Breitner, George Hendrik; Hague School, The; Symbolism, Symbolists

Bibliography

Bionda, Richard, and Carel Blotkamp, eds. *The Age of Van Gogh: Dutch Painting, 1880–1895*, 235–240. Zwolle: Waanders, 1990–1991.

Hammacher, A.M. *Floris Verster*. Amsterdam: Becht, n.d.

Scherjon, W., ed. *Floris Verster: Volledig geïllustreerde catalogus van zijn schilderijen, waskrijt en waterverfteekeningen, en grafisch werk*. Utrecht: Scherjon, 1928.

Verveer, Maurits (1817–1903)

The career of Maurits Verveer sheds light on those many photographers who earned their living after about 1860 by making portraits on *cartes-de-visite* (visiting cards, approximately 9 x 6 cm) and in slightly larger formats. As capable as Verveer must have been, and as successful as he was, his portraits are typical in lacking the distinction of character in pose or facial expression. There is little variation in the settings and props he used, and the small format of *cartes-de-visite*, combined with the custom of depicting the sitter at full-length or half-length, limited the expressive possibilities.

Made in large quantities, *cartes-de-visite* constitute a considerable part of nineteenth-century portrait photography produced in the Netherlands and elsewhere; this fact should be kept in mind when judging the quality of the small portraits and the ability of their makers. Usually they bear the name of the maker, in contrast to many other kinds of photographs, and many have been well preserved. For these reasons, their low quality can too easily give a distorted view of the history of nineteenth-century photography.

In contrast, Verveer's portrait of the painter Charles Rochussen (ca. 1875; Fig. 146) is a rare example of a more intimate kind of nineteenth-century photographic portrait. This portrait has been printed in several ways, both photographic and nonphotographic. A common albumen print on cardstock is reproduced here. A variant in which the hands and the sketchbook are left out served as an illustration to Carel Vosmaer's *Onze hedendaagsche schilders* (Our Contemporary Painters) of 1881–1882. The beautiful woodburytype technique was used for that. An expensive photomechanical reproduction technique, the woodburytype was not the final solution to the problem of printing photographs in ink. Graphic techniques already in existence at the time of the invention of photography were also used. For example, a hand-drawn wood engraving after the portrait of Rochussen was published in the popular magazine *Eigen Haard* in 1876.

Hans Rooseboom

See also Photographers, anonymous; Photography, early; Photography, modern and contemporary; Rochussen, Charles; Vosmaer, Carel

Bibliographic Note

There is no bibliography on Maurits Verveer. His works can be found in the collections of the Rijksprentenkabinet of the

Rijksmuseum in Amsterdam and in the Prentenkabinet of the University of Leiden.

Verwey, Kees (1900–1995)

As a painter, working in Haarlem, Kees Verwey expressly continued in the Dutch figurative painting tradition. His early work is based on Amsterdam Impressionism; only after 1945 did he follow more contemporary art. Verwey achieved general recognition with his watercolor still lifes of flowers. More important are his drawings of the poet of the De Stijl group Antony Kok (1953–1954) and the monumental paintings of his own studio interior that he made after the early 1970s.

In spite of growing up in a "modern" artistic milieu, created by his uncles the architect H.P. Berlage and the writer Albert Verwey, Kees Verwey revealed himself early as a traditional realistic painter. He was trained in Haarlem by the painter H.F. Boot, for whom the realistic rendering of actual surroundings was the single most important feature of Dutch painting. Stylistically, Verwey's early work (particularly the still lifes and figure pieces) is, like that of his teacher Boot, related to the painting of George Hendrik Breitner. Verwey thought of Breitner's angular style as typically Dutch. "A curve provides its horizontal and vertical surfaces to be analyzed," Verwey said. Another source of inspiration considered to be Dutch was the detailed lyrical prose of Lodewijk van Deyssel (*De Adriaantjes; Uit het leven van Frank Rozelaar*, 1920). Challenged by the developments in modern art, Verwey experimented in the 1950s and 1960s with a decorative-surface, abstract style of painting, following the example of the later work of Georges Braque especially. These divergent elements are integrated in Verwey's later style; the series of paintings of the interior of his own studio (1971–1990) are an important example of this. Verwey died in the Netherlands in July 1995.

Anita Hopmans

See also Amsterdam Impressionists; Berlage, Hendrik Petrus; Breitner, George Hendrik; De Stijl

Bibliography
Hopmans, Anita. "Kees Verwey: The Painter in His Domain." *Dutch Heights* 2 1990: 16–19.
———. *Kunst is spiegeling: Kees Verwey, een studie naar zijn oeuvre*. Dordrecht: Dordrechts Museum; Haarlem: J. Enschedé 1989.
Jaffé, Hans L.C. et al. *Kees Verwey: Het Atelier van de schilder 1971–1978*. Amsterdam: Stedelijk Museum, 1978.

Veth, Jan (1864–1925)

Jan Pieter Veth became known primarily as a portrait painter and an art critic. In his birthplace of Dordrecht, he received drawing lessons from A.J. Terwen (1841–1918) and was a member of the drawing society Pictura. In 1880 Veth moved to Amsterdam to attend the Rijksacademie. With Willem Witsen and Antoon Derkinderen, he founded the Nederlandsche Etsclub (Dutch Etching Club) in 1885. Veth was also an ardent spokesman for the Amsterdam Impressionists. His views on art and art criticism published in *De Nieuwe Gids* and other journals had great influence on his contemporaries. In 1888 Veth married Anna Dirks and moved to Bussum, where he gave up his original plans to be a landscape painter and devoted himself entirely to portraiture. Among the many contemporaries who sat for him were the poet Albert Verwey and the painter and critic Maurits van der Valk. He also made a large series of lithographs portraying well-known contemporaries for magazines and weeklies. After 1890 Veth shifted his attention from Amsterdam Impressionism to the Symbolism of Derkinderen and Richard Roland Holst. In 1894 he translated into Dutch *The Claims of Decorative Art* by the English designer and illustrator Walter Crane (1845–1915), who was an advocate of the Arts and Crafts Movement. A number of Veth's portraits from this period show by their conscious stylizing a direct influence of this new trend in the visual arts. Veth was appointed professor of portraiture at the Amsterdam Rijksacademie in 1913.

Harry J. Kraaij

See also Amsterdam Impressionists; Applied arts; Derkinderen, Antoon J.; Huizinga, Johan; Roland Holst, Richard N.; Symbolism, Symbolists; Van der Valk, Maurits Willem; Witsen, Willem

Bibliography
Bionda, Richard, and Carel Blotkamp, eds. *The Age of Van Gogh: Dutch Painting, 1880–1895*, 82–94, 241–242. Zwolle: Waanders, 1990–1991.
Bijl de Vroe, Fusien. *De schilder Jan Veth 1864–1925: Chroniqueur van een bewogen tijdperk*. Arnhem and Brussels: Rap, 1987.

Vinckboons, David (1576–1632)

A prolific and popular painter and draftsman in Amsterdam, David Vinckboons contributed to the development of realism in Dutch landscape and genre painting. Vinckboons was born in Mechelen in the Southern Netherlands on August 13, 1576, to a watercolor painter, Philips Vinckboons, and his wife, Cornelia Querry or Carré. The family lived in Antwerp from 1580 to 1586. They then emigrated with other Protestant families, first to Middelburg and then to Amsterdam, where Philips is listed as a citizen in 1591. On October 8, 1602, David married Agneta van Loon, daughter of a prosperous notary from Leeuwardin and widow of the painter Philip Loemans. Agneta's brother was the painter Willem van Loon. David and Agneta had ten children, six boys and four girls. Of the six boys, five continued in the flourishing art business begun by David, becoming painter, engraver, mapmaker, or architect. Besides teaching his sons, David is mentioned as the teacher of Jacob Kina and Guiliame Helming. Claes Jansz. Visscher, Hessel Gerritsz., Gillis Claesz. de Hondecoeter, and Esaias van de Velde were probably also his pupils.

According to Karel van Mander, David's earliest paintings were, like his father's, watercolors on canvas. These works were a specialty of Mechelen and were used as inexpensive wall hangings that imitated tapestries. None of these "imitation tapestries" has survived. Van Mander mentions that David soon abandoned watercolor in favor of small works done in oil. Vinckboons' paintings known today are on panel, canvas, and copper supports. Many are dated and signed with the monogram "DvB."

Vinckboons painted panoramic landscapes and scenes of everyday life. In the landscapes, towering trees and extensive vistas nearly overshadow groups of small, animated foreground figures. The figures enact biblical stories and participate in scenes of hunting, wedding celebrations, banquets, and brigands attacking travelers.

In the genre scenes, Vinckboons emphasized the figures by making them larger and having them fill the foreground space. These paintings can be divided into two types: peasant scenes and portrayals of the upper class enjoying their leisure. Some have obvious moralizing content. The peasant scenes are set in a village with houses, churches, inns, and a few towering oak trees. Peasants walk to market with their goods, dance, fight, drink, or make music. Vinckboons' figures remind one of those painted earlier by Pieter Bruegel the Elder: brightly garbed, robust, clumsy peasants. With the peasant genres, Vinckboons introduced new subjects into Dutch painting: the wretched beggar, the blind hurdy-gurdy player, and the tooth puller. Vinckboons' outdoor banqueting scenes depict elegantly dressed figures who observe courtly manners while they drink wine, converse, make music, or dance. This theme of the merry company grew out of sixteenth-century love gardens and moralizing works, based on the idea of The Life of the Prodigal Son and Mankind Awaiting the Last Judgment. Some of Vinckboons' banquets appear to be garden parties with no moral intended—works similar to the Venetian garden scenes of the Amsterdam artist Dirck Barendsz. The outdoor-banqueting theme was exploited later by Esaias van de Velde and Dirck Hals.

As a draftsman, Vinckboons favored pen and ink. He provided models for a stained-glass window and perhaps for tapestries. Although some drawings were independent works, most were designed as vignettes to ornament maps (Fig. 18) and title pages or embellish literary and musical books of the time. Jan van Londerseel, Claes Jansz. Visscher, and Pieter Serwouters were among those who frequently engraved or etched after Vinckboons' designs. Vinckboons etched only a few sheets himself at the beginning of his career.

Shirley K. Bennett

See also Cartography; Commerce and commercial life; Hals, Dirck; Landscape; Prints, printmaking, and printmakers (ca. 1500–ca. 1900); Stained glass; Theater and theatricality; Vingboons, Philips

Bibliography
Bennett, Shirley K. "Drawings by David Vinckboons As Models for Ornamenting Bible Maps." *Hoogsteder-Naumann Mercury* 10 (1989): 15–25.
Goossens, Korneel. *David Vinckboons.* 1954. Reprint.
Soest: Davaco, 1977.
Lammertse, Friso. "David Vinckboons, 1576–1632: Schilder en tekenaar in Amsterdam." In *Het Kunstbedrijf van de familie Vingboons: Schilders, architecten en kaartmakers in de gouden eeuw.* Amsterdam: Koninklijk Paleis; Maarsen: Gary Schwartz; The Hague: SDU, 1989.
Wegner, Wolfgang, and Herbert Pée. "Die Zeichnungen des David Vinckboons." *Münchner Jahrbuch der Bildenden Kunst* 31 (1980): 35–128.

Vingboons, Philips (1607–1678)

Son of the prodigious painter and draftsman David Vinckboons (1576–1632), Philips Vingboons (who chose to use the slightly shorter spelling of the name) became the most influential and sought-after architect in Amsterdam during the middle years of the seventeenth century. He was mainly known for his distinctive, austere classicizing townhouses, including the still-extant Poppenhuis (Kloveniersburgwal 95), built in 1642. Vingboons also designed country villas for his urban patrons and public buildings in Amsterdam and other locations.

The architect set a standard for elegant building not only through his executed structures, but also with the publication of many of his designs in the two-volume *Afbeelsels der voornaemste gebouwen uyt alle die Philips Vingboons geordineert heeft* (Representations of the Principal Buildings of All Those Designed by Philips Vingboons), which appeared in Amsterdam in 1648 and 1674 (Ottenheym, 1989: 185–270, for reproductions). His designs helped define the cubic block structure that dominated Dutch seventeenth-century architectural fashion, with its perfect symmetry, hipped roof, and reserved use of classical elements. Fortunately, several Amsterdam townhouses, besides the Poppenhuis, also survive to give an indication of his style. His son, Justus (1620/1621–1698), carried on the tradition, too, with such works as the innovative Trippenhuis (Kloveniersburgwal 29), 1660–1662, which is actually two houses united behind one monumental façade.

Though none of the country houses or public buildings Vingboons built survive in their original form, they were based upon the design standards he established with the Amsterdam townhouses. Besides being reproduced in plan and elevation in his own publications, at least two of his villas are represented in paintings: Westwijck, in a family portrait by Cornelis Holsteyn (location unknown); and Driemond, in a bird and landscape painting by Melchior de Hondecoeter (Munich, Alte Pinakothek). The Amsterdam *Schouwburg* (Theater), built in 1664–1665 and destroyed by fire in 1772, must have also exhibited the traits characteristic of this architect, although little evidence of its original appearance still remains.

Diane E. Cearfoss Mankin

See also Architectural painting; Classicism in architecture; Country houses and gardens; Vinckboons, David

Bibliography
Kuyper, W. *Dutch Classicist Architecture: A Survey of Dutch Architecture, Gardens, and Anglo-Dutch Architectural*

Relations from 1625 to 1700, 103–144, 221–224. Delft: Delft University Press, 1980.

Ottenheym, Koen. *Philips Vingboons, 1607–1678: Architect*. Zutphen: Walburg, 1989. (English summary).

Visch, Henk (born 1950)

Originally a graphic artist, Henk Visch made his first work of sculpture *Getimmerde Tekeningen* (Carpentered Drawings) in 1981. It is composed of fragile architectonic constructions manufactured out of thin slats and represents objects like a house, a high-tension power pole, or a boat. A few years later he made massive wooden human and animal figures that seldom wear a facial expression. The visible reality serves less and less frequently as motive or grounds for associations; the sculpture itself becomes an experience. Gradually, an *oeuvre* is developing that is distinguishing itself through a great range of plasticity, spatiality, and choice of materials.

Brigitte van Mechelen

See also Contemporary art

Bibliography

Hefting, Paul. *De eigen ruimte: Beeldhouwkunst in Nederland na 1945*. Amsterdam: Elsevier, 1986.

Tuyl, Gijs van et al. *Henk Visch*. The Hague: Rijksdienst Beeldende Kunst, 1988.

Visser, Carel (born 1928)

Carel Visser is considered to be the most important Dutch sculptor after World War II. After two uncompleted efforts to study architecture and art at The Hague Academy, he established himself as an independent artist in Amsterdam in 1952. The starting points of his work are natural motifs from visible reality that he interprets in a strongly abstract formal vocabulary. In his early work he was inspired by twentieth-century sculptors Julio González, Constantin Brancusi, Alberto Giacometti, and Marino Marini. Until the end of the 1970s he worked mainly in iron, creating works that are variations on a number of principal themes, mostly in series in which one image is often the starting point of the next. Visser makes much use of stacking, rotation, reflecting, and linking of similar forms. Until 1963 most works were constructive in character; the welding seams connecting the iron forms are clearly visible. Around 1963 destruction entered; forms were divided into parts or burned out of plates. New connections with leather and stacking of loose plates were applied.

Besides his sculpture, Visser makes drawings and graphics (especially woodcuts) both as independent works and as studies. Possibly inspired by his new surroundings (of dams, locks, and bridges) while living in the Netherlands' river region, and the application of collage and the "paper images" that came out of that, he began at the end of the 1970s to use "unknown" materials in his sculpture and even concrete objects. The outward appearance of his work was boldly changed in character. The role of color increased, and the new work is freer, more direct, and has more associations (Fig. 147). The starting points for the image, the accent on connections, and the stacking,

rotations, and symmetry remain essentially present, however.

Geraart Westerink

See also Prints, modern graphic art after 1945

Bibliography

Blotkamp, Carel. *Carel Visser*. Utrecht: Veen/Reflex, 1989.

Hefting, Paul. *De eigen ruimte: Beeldhouwkunst in Nederland na 1945*, 59, 68–69, 91–94, 131. Amsterdam: Elsevier, 1986.

Locher, J.L. *Carel Visser: Beelden-tekeningen-grafiek*. Vlaardingen: Van Dooren, 1972.

Visser, Carel. *Enige opmerkingen over mijn beelden*. Amsterdam: Eén op één, 1987.

Voogd, Hendrik (1768–1839)

The painter Hendrik Voogd was born in Amsterdam and began his education at the Stadstekenakademie (City Drawing Academy) in 1783. Later he became a student of the wallpaper painter J. Andriessen (1742–1819). In 1788 he left for Rome to become more skilled in the art of landscape painting. His colored drawings in typical eighteenth-century linear style are dated from this period until around 1800. Lacking a group of Dutch fellow professionals in Rome, Voogd stayed mainly in the Franco-Flemish and German artists' colonies. From his preserved correspondence, it appears that Voogd made a lot of topographical drawings of Rome and its environs. These drawings in pencil and black chalk consist of pure nature motifs and *vedute* (views). Voogd's Dutch origin is evident from his attention to special light effects and abundant leaves on trees. Around 1805 he became interested in drawing animals, which took on an increasingly important role in his work.

Voogd left only a few graphic works; around 1800 he created some classicist etchings and a series of eight engravings after seventeenth-century paintings by Claude Lorrain, Nicolas Poussin, and Gaspar Dughet, among others. Various lithographs with landscape scenes date from the years 1818–1823; these can be considered as still the incunabula of this printmaking technique. They probably satisfied the need of travelers on the Grand Tour for souvenirs. In composing his work, Voogd used a usual working method. First, he made preparatory studies, sometimes preceded by a preliminary sketch. For the animal *staffage* he also made separate preparatory drawings. He copied these studies accurately, sometimes in mirror image, in the final work. In doing this he repeated himself several times by copying his own motifs and using them again in different groupings. This mechanical technique was probably the consequence of his position as an established artist. There are no known colored drawings by his hand after the turn of the century, only oil paintings, for which he asked high prices.

Biographical data about Voogd are scarce. Except for a short visit in 1828, he never again returned to the Netherlands. He did not marry and did not leave any children. He died in Rome on September 4, 1839; from his obituary it appears that he died an old-fashioned, forgotten artist. Interest in him was revived in 1959 when about two hundred of his drawings were found in the Castle Duivenvoorde (South Holland).

Fransje Kuyvenhoven

Bibliography

Bruyn Kops, C.J. de. "Hendrik Voogd: Nederlands landschapschilder te Rome, 1768–1839." *Nederlands Kunsthistorisch Jaarboek* 21 (1970): 319–369.

Kuyvenhoven, Fransje. "De Leidse collectie tekeningen en grafiek van Hendrik Voogd." In *Achttiende-eeuwse kunst in de Nederlanden*. Edited by Carla Sheffer et al., 269–286. *Leids Kunsthistorisch Jaarboek*, no. 4. Delft: Delftsche Uitgevers Maatschappij, 1987. (English summary).

———. "Lady Devonshire, an English Maecenas in Post-Napoleonic Rome: Her Publication of Virgil's *Aeneid* and Hendrik Voogd's Contribution to It." *Mededelingen van het Nederlands Instituut te Rome. Nova Series 11*, 46 (1985): 145–154.

Vosmaer, Carel (1826–1888)

The literary critic and archeologist Carel Vosmaer was originally a lawyer: He studied law at the University of Leyden, where he received his doctor's degree in 1851. He worked until 1873 as a substitute clerk in The Hague—first at the Provincial Court of Justice and from 1866 on at the Dutch Supreme Court. He was also at the same time very active in the field of literature and art. He published in leading journals and newspapers such as *Kunstkronijk*, *De Banier*, and *Het Vaderland*. He was co-founder of the monthly magazine *De Tijdstroom* and the versatile, intellectual weekly magazine *De Nederlandsche Spectator*, which he edited and contributed to until his death. He provided critical commentaries on the political and literary scenes of the day with his cartoons and his "Vlugmaren" (Nimble Tidings), which he wrote under the pseudonym Flanor. He also studied and wrote reviews on art and literature.

Vosmaer resisted naturalism in art and literature; he preferred the classical tradition. This helps explain his friendship with Laurens Alma Tadema and Vosmaer's admiration for Tadema's classical paintings. In 1880 he published *Amazone*, an "aesthetic novel." Its main character, the painter Aisma, was based on Alma Tadema. This novel was a great success and was soon translated into French, German, and English. He wrote several other novels: *Londinias* (1873), *Nanno* (A Greek idyll, 1883), and *Inwijding* (1888; published posthumously). In 1878–1880 Vosmaer published his translation of Homer's *Iliad*.

Vosmaer's interest in art is also shown by the two books he wrote about the work of Rembrandt (1863 and 1868) and in the serial *Onze hedendaagsche schilders* that appeared during the years 1881–1885, in which he discussed in detail the work of contemporary Dutch painters. Vosmaer collected drawings from the seventeenth century and later and was a fairly good draftsman himself.

Hanna Pennock

See also Alma Tadema, Laurens; Architectural restoration; Art criticism, critical issues in the nineteenth century; Verveer, Maurits

Bibliography

Heijbroek, J.F., ed. *De verzameling van Mr. Carel Vosmaer, 1826–1888*. Amsterdam: Rijksprentenkabinet; The Hague: SDU, 1989.

Maas, Nop et al. *De literaire wereld van Carel Vosmaer: Een documentaire*. The Hague: Haags Historisch Museum; The Hague: SDU, 1989.

War and warfare

The most important situation dominating the latter part of the sixteenth century and much of the seventeenth century was the Eighty Years' War (1568–1648), which resulted in the independence of the Dutch Republic. It was at this time that a significant number of military images appeared in prints and paintings. These images, depicting actual events or scenes inspired by the presence of the military in the Netherlands, established the foundation for a tradition of representations of warfare that continued long past the seventeenth century. Artists in later centuries revised earlier pictorial models to accommodate contemporary conflicts and also reworked previous subjects to incorporate new interpretations.

The early images of battles and episodes from the Eighty Years' War were possibly influenced by Flemish works produced by artists such as Sebastian Vrancx and Pieter Snayers. Another significant influence upon Netherlandish artists came from German woodcuts and engravings of descriptively rendered individual soldiers as well as highly schematized battle scenes. Dutch artists used similar conventions when depicting battles and sieges, placing the main area of conflict in the middleground with details of armor, weapons, and fallen soldiers scattered in the foreground. Depictions of famous battles and sieges, such as the Battle of Nieuwpoort in 1600 or the Siege of 's Hertogenbosch in 1629, would be recognized from the town fortifications in the background. Such notable events obtained popularity and were portrayed repeatedly, probably due to the great accessibility of news and illustrated reports. Histories, travel accounts, personal journals, and pamphlets related information about the progress of the Eighty Years' War in both text and image. Although paintings of some famous events were produced in considerable numbers, they never exceeded those that were merely generalized references to warfare.

More characteristic of Dutch art dealing with aspects of war were representations of limited cavalry skirmishes and infantry clashes. These types of images were more indicative of the actual nature of warfare as it had developed in the seventeenth century. Full-scale battles were rarely fought. Advances in fortification and siegecraft as well as the difficulty of the marshy terrain of the Netherlands made siege warfare marked by periods of skirmishes, ambushes, and raids the norm. Images of these small-scale conflicts were popularized by Esaias van de Velde in the 1620s and continued in the art of Philips Wouwerman even after the cessation of the war. Typically, these works omit any reference to a specific historical incident and may often lack indications as to the allegiance of the soldiers. Artists intended to convey the spirit of contemporary armed conflict rather than the particulars of some episode.

Part of the explanation for this interest in only the general aspects of war may derive from the fact that those who fought for the Dutch Republic were primarily foreign mercenaries. Furthermore, although the major cities had garrisons of soldiers, experiences of actual warfare were mostly limited to the Southern Netherlands and the frontier areas, especially after the Twelve Years' Truce (1609–1621). Scenes of violence and plunder were depicted, but by the time images of war achieved popularity as cabinet pieces for collections early in the seventeenth century, the severity and brutality of such depictions had diminished.

Although works dealing exclusively with land war and warfare are not as numerous as other themes in Dutch art, including war at sea, artists did frequently include military elements or figures within their paintings of other subjects. Soldiers, weapons, or armor were incorporated within scenes of daily life, still lifes, portraits, and landscapes. Such elements either allude to the idea of war or simply reveal a fascination with military figures, activities, or dress. Artists could consult the various military manuals of the time in order to learn about the appearance, discipline, duties, and equipment of the common soldier. Jacob de Gheyn II created the most influential of these manuals, *The Exercise of Arms*, in 1607. Produced in response to the military reforms initiated by Prince Maurits, the handbook furnished detailed illustrations and instructions for the use of firearms and pikes by foot soldiers.

A focus on the process of war, evident in de Gheyn's manual, rather than on the glories of war, became the defining characteristic of Dutch paintings of military conflict. Perhaps the absence of a monarch, court, and large aristocratic class of patrons led artists to depict those aspects of war most familiar to them: The life of the ordinary soldier. In the 1620s and 1630s, a number of Dutch painters created a specialty of views of soldiers in a guardroom or tavern, playing cards, gambling, smoking, and drinking, sometimes in the company of women. These scenes, by artists such as Jacob Duck, Willem Duyster, Pieter Codde, and, later, Gerbrand van den Eeckhout, do not glorify war nor do they create a heroic conception of the soldier or his life. Occasionally, a satiric message may be conveyed, but the majority of these paintings simply record the actions of a group on the fringes of society. For the officer, a dashing representation was limited to late genre works, but even in these, intimacy and refinement predominated rather than military greatness.

Even when the *stadholders* Maurits or Frederich Hendrik were depicted on horseback before the site of a famous siege, the heroic conception was often subverted by their placement to the side of the composition. These portrayals reflect the pragmatic approach to warfare taken by the military commanders of the Netherlands at the time. Instead of seeking glory in war, these leaders attempted to prevent defeat.

Works of the eighteenth century continued this generally unheroic, unglorified conception of war. Artists such as Dirk Langendijk who depicted contemporary events from the invasion of French revolutionary forces in 1795, adopted the earlier conventions for representing sieges, military conflicts, and encampments. It was not until the following century that the sense of glory and heroism in war, in addition to a greater sense of patriotism, pervaded the art. Jan Willem Pieneman's depiction of the *Prince of Orange during the Battle of Quatre Bras* (1817–1818; Amsterdam, Rijksmuseum) and the subsequent *Battle of Waterloo* in 1815 (1824; Amsterdam, Rijksmuseum) focused on his heroism. Unlike the earlier works by Esaias van de Velde, the action of battle is no longer the focus. Dramatic light on prominent individual leaders in large-scale works served to glorify their military accomplishments and indicated the historical importance of the event for the Kingdom of the Netherlands. Furthermore, artists such as Charles Rochussen depicted the Siege of Haarlem and other events of Dutch military history, however the interpretation had changed. Interest in the heroic actions of particular citizens and an emphasis on historic events charged with patriotic significance replaced the earlier focus on the process of war.

Despite the changes that occurred in the depictions of war from the descriptive aspects of warfare in seventeenth-century images to the more emotional aspects in nineteenth-century paintings, a consistent approach remained. Although the violence of war was represented on occasion, a harsh and critical response to the existence of war was rarely shown. History and human nature had taught the Dutch that war was an inevitable part of life.

J.M. Kennedy

See also Eighty Years' War; Genre painting, seventeenth century; History painting; House of Orange-Nassau; Marine painting; Nationalism; Public monumental sculpture (ca. 1550–1795); Public monumental sculpture (1795–1990); Rochussen, Charles; Soldiers; Still life; Tomb sculpture: early modern and later sepulchral art; *Vanitas, vanitas* still life; World Wars I and II; Wouwerman, Philips

Bibliography

Hale, J.R. *Artists and Warfare in the Renaissance.* New Haven: Yale University Press, 1990.

Kist, J.B. *Jacob de Gheyn: The Exercise of Arms.* New York: McGraw-Hill, 1971.

Mandle, Roger. *Dutch Masterpieces from the Eighteenth Century: Paintings and Drawings, 1700–1800.* Minneapolis: Minneapolis Institute of Arts, 1971.

Tallett, Frank. *War and Society in Early-Modern Europe, 1495–1715.* London: Routledge, 1992.

Watermarks

Important for the study of the history of prints, a watermark is the trace left in laid paper by a wire design sewn into the mold from which the paper is formed—less paper pulp accumulates in the areas covered by the wires, thus the resulting paper is thinner in those areas, which are then visible when held against the light. Sometimes an additional watermark, known as a countermark, would also have been sewn into another section of the paper mold. Typically, watermarks were given simple, recognizable shapes: animals, objects, coats of arms, or intertwined letters—the Gothic P is often found on fifteenth-century Netherlandish prints, the foolscap on seventeenth-century Dutch prints, and the beehive on eighteenth-century Dutch prints. In the seventeenth century, more elaborate designs began to be created, such as the Pro Patria, which shows the Dutch Maid and the Batavian Lion occupying the Garden of Holland. Primarily, watermarks and countermarks indicated that a particular sheet of paper was produced by a particular factory. Sometimes one paper mill's watermarks also varied according to the market for which the paper was intended or the particular agent responsible for marketing the paper abroad. Around 1635 certain French papermakers began to produce paper especially for the Dutch market with an Arms of Amsterdam watermark; eventually, the Dutch papermakers also started to produce paper with the Arms of Amsterdam.

Watermarks are of only limited use for dating an impression of a print because they can give only an approximate date for when a sheet of paper was made and thus a possible date *ante quem* for when an impression was printed. One watermark could be used on different molds over a long period of time, so paper with closely related watermarks may have come from the same paper factory, but not necessarily from the same period. In addition, paper could be stored and used over a period of many years. In general, watermarks can indicate whether an impression of a print is "early" or at least "of the period." The precise recording of watermarks is of the utmost importance for making an accurate comparison. Slight differences in size and appearance can make the difference among several watermarks of the same type. For example, among Rembrandt's etchings dated between 1633 and 1655, forty different foolscap watermarks have been identified. Beta-radiography and x-radiography have in recent years become the most effective techniques for recording watermarks. Catalogs of watermarks—for example, Briquet, Churchill, and Heawood—are still essential tools for the comparative dating of watermarks. These catalogs compile hand tracings of watermarks found in archival documents, printed books, and other material for which a secure date and place can be established. In addition, some detailed *oeuvre* catalogs of the work of particular artists have recorded watermarks for particular impressions of prints. While more specific than the large watermark catalogs, these kinds of catalogs are useful references because the paper used for writing was in many cases not the same as that used for printmaking.

Nadine Orenstein

See also Paper, used for prints; Prints, printmaking, and printmakers (ca. 1500–ca. 1900); Technical investigations

Bibliography

Ash, Nancy, and Shelley Fletcher. *Watermarks on Rembrandt Prints.* New York: Abaris, 1995.

Briquet, C.M. *Les Filigranes: Dictionnaire historique des marques du papier dès leurs apparition vers 1282 jusqu'en 1600.* 4 vols. Facsimile. Edited by Allan Stevenson. Amsterdam: Paper Publications Society, 1968.

Churchill, W.A. *Watermarks in Paper in Holland, England, France, etc., in the Seventeenth and Eighteenth Centuries and Their Interconnection.* Amsterdam: Menno Hertzberger, 1935.

Heawood, Edward. *Watermarks Mainly of the Seventeenth and Eighteenth Centuries.* Vol. 1 of *Monumenta Chartae Papyraceae.* Hilversum: Paper Publications Society, 1950.

Hunter, Dard. *Papermaking.* 2nd ed. New York: Alfred A. Knopf, 1967.

Laurentius, Theo et al. "Het Amsterdamse onderzoek naar Rembrandts papier: Radiografie van de watermerken in de etsen van Rembrandt." *Bulletin van het Rijksmuseum* 40 (1992): 353–384.

Weissenbruch, Jan (1822–1880)

Jan Weissenbruch, cousin of the famous master of The Hague School Jan Hendrik Weissenbruch, painted mainly townscapes in an unadorned, realistic manner. Still, they are not always topographically correct. From 1839 to 1847, Weissenbruch took lessons at The Hague Drawing Academy along with S.L. Verveer (brother of the photographer Maurits Verveer) and A. Waldorp. In 1846 he took a trip to Belgium. Besides being an excellent and respected painter and art restorer, Weissenbruch was also a skilled lithographer and etcher. He won many awards and was cofounder of Pulchri Studio in The Hague (1847) and The Hague Etching Club (1848). After 1870, when the artistic tide began

to turn and the recording, realistic style was exchanged for a poetic vision, Weissenbruch virtually retired from public life. He then suffered from agoraphobia. He hardly painted in the last ten years of his life, creating only twelve more paintings.

Alexandra W.M. van Smoorenburg

See also Architectural painting; Prints, printmaking, and printmakers (ca. 1500–ca. 1900); Weissenbruch, Jan Hendrik

Bibliography

Laanstra, W. *Jan Weissenbruch: Schilder, graficus, 1822–1880.* Amsterdam: Tableau, 1986.

Weissenbruch, Jan Hendrik (1824–1903)

Jan Hendrik Weissenbruch was only two years younger than his cousin Jan Weissenbruch, but in a stylistic sense it seems that the two painters had a whole generation between them. Where the older Weissenbruch can be seen as the exponent of Dutch realism, the younger developed into one of the most important protagonists of The Hague School. Until around 1870 Jan was considered *the* great Weissenbruch; after 1875 Jan Hendrik became more visible.

Jan Hendrik Weissenbruch was a student of J.J. Löw, and afterward, from 1843 until 1850, he took evening lessons at The Hague Drawing Academy. In all probability he was working in the studio of B.J. van Hove during the day at that time. He exhibited his works after 1847. At first they were fairly accurately painted landscapes, mostly panoramas, in which the influence of Andreas Schelfhout is clearly evident. Gradually, however, his brushstroke became looser and his use of color bolder, creating landscapes that were full of atmosphere yet also brighter. In addition to good and original paintings, Weissenbruch also made splendid watercolors. In 1866 he became a member of the Société Belge des Aquarellistes, and ten years later he joined the Hollandsche Teeken-Maatschappij (Dutch Watercolor Society).

Public appreciation of his work came slowly: only after about 1880, with his impressions of the landscape near Nieuwkoop and Noorden. The appreciation by colleagues starter earlier; they especially praised his marvelous compositional talent. Weissenbruch traveled abroad only once; in 1900 he visited Barbizon and Fontainebleau, bringing back from there a number of beautiful studies.

Alexandra W.M. van Smoorenburg

See also Hague School, The; Schelfout, Andreas; Van Gogh, Vincent: diverse views; Weissenbruch, Jan

Bibliography

Laanstra, W., and S. Ooms. *J.H. Weissenbruch, 1824–1903.* Amsterdam: Tableau, 1992.

Leeuw, Ronald de, John Sillevis, and Charles Dumas, eds. *The Hague School: Dutch Masters of the Nineteenth Century,* 274–288. London: Royal Academy of Arts, in association with Weidenfeld and Nicholson, 1983.

Wendingen (1918–1931)

In the earliest years of the twentieth century a theoretical debate over the nature of modern architecture took place among a group of architects, designers, and devotees of architecture known as the Genootschap Architectura et Amicitia. This society, founded in 1855, was very active organizing exhibitions, conferences, evening courses, and competitions, as well as promoting the publication of pamphlets and magazines. In this atmosphere, the young architect Hendricus Theodorus Wijdeveld proposed to the society the creation of an illustrated monthly magazine that might contribute to the efflorescence of modern art.

The first issue of *Wendingen* (Turnings), printed in only one hundred fifty copies, appeared in 1918. The year before, Theo van Doesburg had launched *De Stijl*, a publication by a group of artists identifying themselves with the international avant-garde movement in painting; the cover of *De Stijl* was gray with a logotype by Vilmos Huszár (Fig. 38) and graphics that were mostly traditional. In contrast, the appearance of *Wendingen* was sensational: The large square format, the typography, and the binding had nothing in common with the current graphic style.

The animator, as well as chief editor until 1925, was Wijdeveld; he identified himself totally with the magazine, and his Romantic attitude fully determined its cultural motivation. All typographical decisions were Wijdeveld's: format, page layout, pages printed only on the front side, folded double and bound in flax with the knots on the outside adding to the decorative appearance of the cover. The covers, printed in lithography or woodcut, were different each time and represent a remarkable iconographic repertory of twentieth-century Dutch art. The tendency was to favor artists who were part of the current Symbolist movement or Nieuwe Kunst. The most active of these were Richard N. Roland Holst, Hildo Krop, Samuel Jessurun de Mesquita, Jan Toorop, Joseph Mendes da Costa, and J.L.M. Lauweriks. But there were also artists of a completely different orientation, such as El Lissitzky, who designed the cover for the issue devoted to Frank Lloyd Wright's Imperial Hotel in Tokyo; this demonstrates the nonpartisan, profoundly international attitude with which Wijdeveld ran the magazine.

The spirit animating Wijdeveld is evident in the editorial with which he opened the first issue: "Here may be found the changes that affect all artistic expression . . . . Here, together with architecture in its new conception of pure structure, is manifest the full splendor of appearances by persons filled with imagination . . . . Here one may find the atmosphere which transforms rigid wall masses into flexible architectural sculpture, full of movement which joyfully follows the rhythm of space."

The editorial staff of *Wendingen* consisted of architects as well as artists in order to underline the importance of the interrelationship between architecture, painting, sculpture, and the applied arts. There were many international contributors whose entries were often published in their original languages. In 1931 publication of the magazine was interrupted after thirteen years and a total of one hundred sixteen issues,

half of them monographs on architecture.

Architecture was, in fact, the subject of major attention. Other topics considered were the theater (often commented on by the English producer Edward Gordon Craig), dance, stage design, applied arts (with much attention paid to the design of furniture and urban fixtures), sculpture, graphic arts (one issue was entirely devoted to Gustav Klimt), Middle Eastern and Far Eastern art. The aim of this multiple approach toward the world of art was to achieve the complete connection between the figurative and applied arts necessary for the creation of a work that the viewer may fully enjoy in its figurative, symbolic, and spiritual dimensions.

Wijdeveld turned *Wendingen* into the main sounding board for the works of the Amsterdam School, although he also published monographs on famous international architects such as Josef Hoffmann of Austria, Eric Mendelsohn and Emil Fahrenkamp of Germany, Eileen Gray, who was born in England but became a French citizen, and Wright, on whose work eight issues were published. The development of modern architecture outside the borders of the Netherlands was also well documented.

If the major interpreters of the Amsterdam School wrote little for *Wendingen* themselves, it was Wijdeveld who directly described their works, promoting and broadcasting their designs. During the magazine's first year, the architectural projects illustrated were almost entirely by members of the Amsterdam School: Johan Melchior van der Mey (1878–1949), Michel de Klerk (1884–1923), Cornelis Jonke Blaauw (1885–1947), Jan Frederik Staal (1879–1940), Pieter Lodewijk Kramer (1881–1961), and Wijdeveld himself. *Wendingen* was, at the same time, advocate for the motivations that were the basis of the movement; during the first years especially, the magazine favored projects strongly artistic in concept, highly individual in expression, and destined to be translated into productions of predominantly sculptural effects—only in this way, it was felt, is architecture elevated to the rank of a work of art. Within the pages of *Wendingen*, the ideal references for this way of building were proposed: Repeat the same perfection expressed in the growing process of organic forms. As shown in beautiful photographs, seashells and crystals, in their perfect essential forms, became natural metaphors for creating architecture.

Maristella Casciato

See also Amsterdam School; Applied arts; Architectural criticism; De Klerk, Michel; De Stijl; Kramer, Pieter Lodewijk; Symbolism, Symbolists; Wijdeveld, Hendricus Theodorus

Bibliography

Fanelli, Giovanni et al. *Wendingen, 1918–1931: Documenti dell'arte olandese del Novecento.* Florence: Palazzo Medici-Riccardi, 1982; distributed by Centro Di.

Oldewarris, Hans. "Wijdeld Typografie." *Forum voor architectuur en daarmee verbonden kunsten* (Genootschap Architectura et Amicitia) 1 (1975–1976).

Pehnt, Wolfgang. *Expressionist Architecture.* Translated by J.A. Underwood and Edith Kustner. London: Thames and Hudson, 1973.

Werkman, Hendrik Nicolaas (1882–1945)

Hendrik Werkman was a painter, printer, and graphic artist who, from his relative seclusion in Groningen, made contact thorough his work with the international avant-garde. He moved to Groningen in 1894. In 1896 he saw an exhibition of the work of Vincent van Gogh. He worked in photography after 1898 and as a journalist from 1903 to 1907; in 1907 he opened a printing shop. The same year he started drawing and painting, originally in an Expressionist–realistic style that calls to mind Vincent van Gogh, later in a way that connects with the Expressionism of De Ploeg (The Plow), a group he joined in 1920. By combining painting with printer's techniques and materials, he produced what he called his *druksels*. Werkman's printing shop failed in 1923, but he continued to print with a small business. Besides commercial work, he produced posters and programs for De Ploeg and a magazine, *The Next Call*, through which he reached the entire international avant-garde. In 1929 he traveled to Cologne and Paris with Jan Wiegers. Until 1929 his printed work consisted of abstract geometric shapes, letters, and numbers in which can be seen the influence of De Stijl and Constructivism. After that he also used a stamp technique in which figurative and abstract elements alternate. After 1934 he used stencil plates—mostly in combination with other printing techniques.

In 1939 Willem Sandberg of the Stedelijk Museum in Amsterdam visited Werkman in Groningen. In 1940, after the beginning of the German occupation of the Netherlands, Werkman's printing was interrupted and so he returned to drawing and painting. At the end of that year, he did his first work for the resistance: the printing of contemporary writer Martinus Nijhoff's poem *Het jaar 1572*, recalling the first Dutch victory in the Revolt against Spain. In May 1941 Werkman visited Sandberg in Amsterdam and resumed printing. In the autumn of 1941 he created the first series, followed in 1943 by the second series, of *Hasidic Legends*. These were followed by further portrayals of an earthly paradise, such as *Vrouweneiland* (Island of Women, 1942). On March 13, 1945, Werkman was arrested, and on April 10 he was executed by the Gestapo. A large part of his work was confiscated and burned.

John Steen

See also De Ploeg; Graphic design; Wiegers, Jan; World Wars I and II

Bibliography

Bromberg, Paul, ed. *Werkman*. Arnhem: D. Brouwer, 1947.

Martinet, Jan. *"Hassidic Legends": A Suite by H.N. Werkman*. Groningen: Wolters-Noordhoff, 1985.

Martinet, Jan, ed. *Hot Printing: Catalogue of the "Druksel" Prints, and Interim Catalogues of General Printed Matter, Lithographs, Etchings, Woodcuts, Typewriter Compositions, and Paintings by Hendrik Nicolaas Werkman*. Amsterdam: H.N. Werkman Foundation and Stedelijk Museum, 1963.

Westerik, Co (born 1924)

The work of Co (Jacobus) Westerik is characterized by a very private form of realism that is open to prevailing art trends of the past as well as of the present. The artist, who began in the mid-1940s making paintings, drawings, and graphic works, is interested in historical painting techniques and traditions of composition. His work was hardly acknowledged in the late 1960s. His striving for perfection as well as the modest formats were long characteristic of his art (Fig. 110). Since the 1980s, however, the drawings, especially, have become increasingly larger. Human life is always central in the work. The apparently single theme often contains several layers of meaning. The carefully chosen titles frequently offer a key to the riddle. Westerik does not attempt to achieve a literal rendering so much as the sensation of the experience in his work. To that end he often uses abstract as well as figurative elements in a work. Themes such as death or the carnal body come and go through the years.

In the 1990s Westerik's work has become more and more radical. By means of a searching observation he has attempted to reveal the mysteries of the body and spirit.

Brigitte van Mechelen

See also Prints, modern graphic arts after 1945

Bibliography

Beeren, W.A.L. "Co Westerik: Een markante bijdrage aan de naoorlogse schilderkunst." *Kunstbeeld* 3 (1980): 14–20.

Mignot, Dorine, ed. *Co Westerik: Schilderijen en tekeningen 1946–1991*. Amsterdam: Stedelijk Museum, 1991.

Jitta, M.J., and C. Wiethoff. *Co Westerik: Grafiek 1945– 1984*. The Hague: Haags Gemeentemuseum; Weesp: Openbaar Kunstbezit, 1984.

Wiethoff, C. *Westerik en Van Gogh*. Amsterdam: Stichting Van Gogh, 1990.

Wiegers, Jan (1893–1959)

Educated to be a sculptor and painter in Groningen, The Hague, and Rotterdam, Jan Wiegers made early contact with modernism on a visit to the separatists' exhibition in Cologne in 1912. He traveled with his teacher from Rotterdam, the Belgian A.H.R. van Maasdijk, through Germany and Switzerland working as a church painter. In 1918 Wiegers cofounded the Expressionist artists' group De Ploeg (The Plow) in Groningen. During this period his work was under the influence of the Expressionists of the Bergen School, particularly of Henri Le Fauconnier and Leo Gestel. In 1920–1921 Wiegers traveled to Davos in Switzerland for health reasons, and there he came in contact with Ernst Ludwig Kirchner, one of the founders of the German Expressionist group Die Brücke, who had an obvious influence on his themes. Wiegers also copied Kirchner's graphic style and painting technique: Oil paints with bee wax dissolved in benzine are applied on unprepared linen so that the surface consists of only dry colors without a shine. Back in the Netherlands, Wiegers used this technique to paint Expressionist color portraits of the painters of De Ploeg—for example, *Hendrik Werkman* (1922)—and the Groningen landscape, *Landschap met rode bomen* (Landscape with Red Trees, 1924; Color Plate 13). Beyond this, Wiegers's *oeuvre* is comprised of interiors and a rare female nude. Wiegers also made drawings and woodcuts, etchings among which is a portrait of *Ernst Ludwig Kirchner* (1925), and sculpture, including a bust of *Hendrik Werkman* (1926). In 1934 he moved to Amsterdam, where he was a cofounder of the magazine *Kroniek voor Kunst en Kultuur* (Chronicle for Art and Culture). After 1945 and a long interruption, Wiegers returned to the Expressionist style of the 1920s. In 1953 he became a teacher at the Rijksacademie in Amsterdam. He died in 1959.

John Steen

See also Bergen; De Ploeg; Gestel, Leo; Werkman, Hendrik Nicolaas

Bibliography

Jaffé, H.L.C. *Jan Wiegers*. Amsterdam: Stedelijk Museum, 1960.

Welling, Dolf. *The Expressionists: The Art of Prewar Expressionism in the Netherlands*. Amsterdam: Meulenhoff, 1968.

Wijdeveld, Hendricus Theodorus (1885–1987)

A romantic spirit, an exuberant protagonist of Dutch architectural culture, and an eclectic designer animated by a pronounced utopian sentiment, Hendricus Theodorus Wijdeveld played an important role as spokesman for his country's modern architecture in international circles.

Wijdeveld, born in The Hague, was the son of a building contractor who undertook several projects in South Africa that failed. Due to his family's economic difficulties, he began working at age fifteen, choosing architecture as his field. In 1900 he was employed as a draftsman in the studio of P.J.H. Cuypers, the most famous representative of the Gothic revival in the Netherlands. The working environment was stimulating and there were many apprentices. Two years earlier, two of the most brilliant collaborators had chosen to leave the studio: Karel Petrus Cornelis de Bazel (1869–1923) and Johannes Ludovicus Mattheus Lauweriks (1864–1932), whose anarchic theosophic ideals had come into conflict with the Catholicism of Cuypers. But their ideas were still being discussed, much as Lauweriks' graphic ability was being praised while in the meantime he had become successful as a teacher of design. Wijdeveld was instinctively captivated by these two personalities, sought them out, and struck up a friendship with them; he was seduced by their mystic anarchism as well as the exotic sources that inspired their compositions. Through Lauweriks, Wijdeveld discovered Orientalism and particularly the graphic, painterly, and spatial traditions of Japanese art and architecture that later would play a significant role in his cultural formation. In 1905 he traveled to England, where he was attracted to the developments of the Arts and Crafts Movement and by socialism as applied to the art world by John Ruskin and William Morris. In London he

took evening courses at the school of the British Museum.

Wijdeveld played a leading role in the architectural debate in the Netherlands during the years of World War I and gained an important position in 1918, the year of the first issue of *Wendingen*. First as editorial secretary and later as editor-in-chief, he had a determining influence over the nature of the publication as the organ of the Amsterdam School. He pushed his country's architecture toward a true renewal and accelerated its international diffusion. Artists and architects, even outside national boundaries, unanimously acknowledge this as his merit.

Between 1918 and 1920, Wijdeveld returned to traveling. In Berlin he began a successful working relationship with Eric Mendelsohn, with historian and critic Adolf Behne, and with Max Reinhart and Hans Poelzig, whose Grosses Schauspielhaus (Grand Theater) literally enraptured him. Traces of it may be discovered, together with hints from the glass architecture of the German Gläserne Kette (Glass Chain), in his Expressionist project for the Groote Volkstheater (Great Popular Theater) in the Vondel Park in Amsterdam (1919). In 1920 he was in Paris, where he met painter and writer Amédée Ozenfant. Travel was of great importance for expanding Wijdeveld's cultural horizon: It was a means of gathering knowledge and at the same time a way of exchange for him, a person moved by an unending trust in the sociopolitical value of interrelationships between peoples and cultures.

Wijdeveld was an exemplary architect; more than a builder, he was a driver of architectural culture, interested in architecture's message to the world. With his friend Mendelsohn he traveled to Egypt and Palestine in 1923. In 1931 he went first to the Soviet Union and then to the United States, where he visited Frank Lloyd Wright at Taliesin West and began a project for a workshop, which, however, never became reality. His meeting with writer Lewis Mumford in 1932 strengthened even further his relationship with American culture. Wright invited Wijdeveld for a series of lectures and conferences in the United States during the period 1947–1950.

Public housing and exhibition spaces are the two principal themes at the center of Wijdeveld's career. From the 1920s until the mid-1970s he was continuously occupied with preparing exhibitions and creating single pavilions, such as the Dutch Pavilion for the World Exposition in Antwerp (1930) or the one for the Holland-American Line in the Paris Exposition in 1937.

The public-housing blocks, all in Amsterdam, that Wijdeveld created are characterized by their daring formal solutions that combine the fantasy of the Amsterdam School and certain clear aspects of the dramatic design of German Expressionism. A famous example was the corner of the now demolished apartment building on the Insulindeweg (1920–1930) in which the rectilinear wall masses of the façade curved suddenly in order to form two high towers separated by a narrow fissure (Fig. 148). On the Hoofdeweg, in the new Amsterdam West quarter, he designed the buildings on both sides of the street (1925–1927), making the best of the opportunity to create a fascinating urban stage-wing through accentuation of the horizontal elements of the opposing house fronts. The dynamic thrust imprinted on the buildings by the continuous band of brick work and fenestration is then gathered up in the cylindrical volumes at the end of each block.

Maristella Casciato

See also Amsterdam School; Applied arts; Architectural criticism, issues of style; *Japonisme;* Public housing; *Wendingen*

Bibliography
Stralen, Mariette van. "The country houses of H.Th. Wijdeveld." *Forum voor architectuur en daarme verbonden kunsten.* (Genootschap Architectura et Amicitia) 3/4 (1995).
Tummers, N.H.M. "H.Th. Wijdeveld: De *mise en scène* van de architectuur—'Plan the impossible'—een fundamentele studie." *Bouwkundig Weekblad* 19 (1965): 333–364.

Witsen, Willem (1860–1923)

The painter Willem Arnold Witsen held a central place among the Amsterdam Impressionists. Painters and writers would congregate in his house and studio, the present Witsenhuis in Amsterdam, or they stayed at his country house, Ewijkshoeve. From 1876 to 1884, Witsen attended the Rijksacademie in Amsterdam, and with fellow students he founded the artists' society St. Lucas and the Nederlandsche Etsclub (Dutch Etching Club). He also wrote art criticism for the journal *De Nieuwe Gids* (The New Guide).

Quite noticeable in Witsen's early works is the influence of the French Barbizon painters and the masters of The Hague School, especially Anton Mauve. In this period he produced many landscapes showing figures working. After 1887 he concentrated on urban themes. His city views are characterized by a forceful composition and dark colors. Often he chose to make a snapshot-like, frontal rendition of house walls and bridges in which the presence of the human figure plays a minor role (Fig. 104). His art reached its peak in the paintings, etchings, and watercolors that he made during a period in London (1888–1891; Fig. 105). After 1900 his technique became looser and he applied the paint thinly. Possibly he was influenced in this regard by the American-born painter James McNeill Whistler (1834–1903), who lived and worked in England. Witsen also made still lifes and portraits. He was one of the most important graphic artists of his generation and received posthumous credit for his qualities as a photographer.

Harry J. Kraaij

See also Amsterdam Impressionists; Mauve, Anton; Photography, modern and contemporary; Prints, modern graphic arts (1840–1945); Prints, printmaking, and printmakers (1500–1900)

Bibliography
Bionda, Richard, and Carel Blotkamp, eds. *The Age of Van Gogh. Dutch Painting, 1880–1895*, 249–253. Zwolle: Waanders, 1990–1991.
Vergeer, Charles. *Willem Witsen en zijn vriendenkring: De Amsterdamse bohème van de jaren negentig.* Amsterdam:

Rap, 1985.
Wiel, Rein van der. *Ewijkshoeve, tuin van tachtig.* Amsterdam: Querido, 1988.

Woldringh, Meinard (1915–1968)

After World War II photographers had a much wider range of possibilities for earning their livelihood—advertising, fashion, and illustration were fields that had recently opened to them and provided alternatives to the photographer's mainstay of portraiture. The assignments, however, were not always inspiring. Meinard Woldringh, an introverted, sensitive, and serious man engaged by a publishing and printing firm, was very much aware of this fact. He escaped into nature as much as possible and made a large and impressive body of black-and-white photographs of details from nature. He usually chose complex and capricious forms, focusing on the contrasts that they reinforced: the branches of a tree against a white sky; the structure of rocks; patterns of snow on sand; cracks in a layer of ice; moving water that optically deforms the sand underneath (Fig. 149).

Woldringh was not alone in this. Reinforced contrasts of black and white—leaving out most of the gray tones—were the subject of many photographers in the 1950s and 1960s, Aart Klein among them. The German Subjektive Fotografie (Subjective Photography) Movement had considerable influence in the Netherlands in the 1950s. Woldringh and others took part in its famous international exhibitions (Saarbrücken in 1951 and 1954–1955, and Cologne in 1958). Experiments with photographic means—solarization, out-of-focus adjustment, double exposures, photograms, and the heightened contrast of black and white—constituted the greater part of the aesthetics of Subjektive Fotografie.

Woldringh did not employ all of these techniques since he never intended to go beyond near-abstraction; his love of nature was probably too strong for that. For some photographers, the Subjektive Fotografie aesthetics may have been practiced briefly as fashionable gimmickry. Woldringh, however, made his photographs with so much care and coherency that he cannot possibly be suspected of that.

Hans Rooseboom

See also Nature photography; Photography, modern and contemporary

Bibliography
Leijerzapf, Ingeborg Th., ed. *Geschiedenis van de Nederlandse fotografie.* Alphen aan den Rijn/ Amsterdam: Samsom/Voetnoot, 1984– .

Wolvecamp, Theo (1925–1992)

Painter and graphic artist Theo Wolvecamp was the youngest founding member of the Dutch Experimental Group in 1948 and participant in the Cobra Movement from 1948 to 1951. Born in Hengelo, he studied at the Art Academy in Arnhem from 1945 to 1947 and was attracted to Cubism. After moving to Amsterdam in 1947, he met Corneille and Karel Appel and quickly developed a linear abstract style that suggested influences from Miró and Kandinsky. As an Experimental and Cobra artist, Wolvecamp admired older colleagues such as Appel but pursued his own development of an abstract, elementary sign-language. He was among the Experimental artists who resigned from the Group in November 1949, but was the only one to return; he exhibited at the final Cobra exhibition, held at Liège in 1951. In the early 1950s—a lean period in his production—Wolvecamp spent time in Pont Aven (Brittany) and Paris before returning to the Netherlands in 1954 to settle in his native Hengelo. His paintings of the later 1950s, with their swirling forms and ghostly faces, have been compared to works of Asger Jorn, while his style since the 1960s could vary from Pierre Soulages–like broad slashes of the brush to biomorphic compositions reminiscent of those of Arshile Gorky and Jackson Pollock in the early phase of Abstract Expressionism. Since Wolvecamp destroyed many earlier works and left many others undated, art-historical assessment of his *oeuvre* has proved particularly difficult.

Graham Birtwistle

See also Appel, Karel; Cobra Movement; Corneille

Bibliography

Stokvis, Willemijn, ed. *Informele Kunst 1945–1960: Lyrische Abstractie, Cobra, Materieschilderkunst.* Enschede: Rijksmuseum Twenthe, 1982.

Women artists

During the seventeenth century a number of women successfully pursued artistic careers in the Dutch Republic. Judith Leyster (1609–1660) and Rachel Ruysch (1664–1750), in particular, attained recognition for their paintings. Other artists of note included the painters Maria van Oosterwyck (1630–1693) and Clara Peeters (1594–ca. 1640) and the etcher Geertruydt Roghman (1625–1653/1657). Scores of amateurs, such as Gesina Ter Borch (1631–1690), attained a recognition that extended at least as far as their local communities. Whether professional or amateur, these women were often born to progressive-minded, educated parents who provided the necessary encouragement for their daughters' artistic inclinations; in many other instances the women came from artistic families whose homes were equipped with the materials necessary for their technical training.

A number of social and economic conditions within the Dutch Republic contributed to women's artistic development: increased literacy, changes in family life that allowed women more leisure and independence, the participation by women in businesses, the open art market, and overall prosperity. The production of art was considered a business by many Dutch and was typically conducted out of a craft-based workshop, usually located in the home. Clients for this art came from a middle-class public eager to collect small-scale pictures for domestic decoration. These clients were more inclined to purchase small-scale, ready-made pictures from shops, fairs, and auctions than to commission pictures from specific artists (with the exception of portraits). Still lifes and scenes from everyday life were favored over history paintings. These were just the subjects accessible to women painters, encouraged by the ideology of the time to remain indoors, confined to the domestic sphere. Leyster's main output consisted of genre scenes. Ruysch, Van Oosterwyck, and Peeters practiced still-life painting exclusively. No female landscape painters have been documented, nor history painters. Even portraiture, because of its commissioned nature, seems to have been beyond most Dutch women's reach. Only an amateur such as Ter Borch, who was free of market restrictions and professional conventions, restricted largely to the drawing media, and oriented toward a private, local audience, could explore a somewhat wider variety of subjects.

As for the training of these women artists, nothing indicates that any attained the technical experience and education that would have enabled them to attempt history painting. In some cases, the names of their masters are known: Van Oosterwyck studied with the still-life painter Jan Davidsz. de Heem (1606–1683/1684); Ruysch, with the still-life painter Willem van Aelst (1625/1626–after 1683); and Peeters, with the Antwerp still-life painter Osias Beert (1580–1624). Circumstantial evidence indicates that Leyster may have been apprenticed to Frans Pietersz. de Grebber (1573–1649), perhaps in part because another female, his daughter Maria de Grebber (ca. 1602–1680), was present as a student in his shop. Stylistic similarities with the genre pictures of Frans Hals (ca. 1582/1583–1666) suggest that Leyster may have sought additional training from him or worked as his assistant. No contracts between any of these three artists and their masters, indeed no contracts for any female apprentices, survive.

On the whole, seventeenth-century Dutch girls were rarely encouraged to pursue painting. Boys who exhibited artistic talent were apprenticed to masters between the ages of twelve and sixteen. Girls were instead encouraged to learn embroidery, calligraphy, and lace making within the family home—alongside the usual domestic instruction intended to prepare them for marriage. (Only wealthier girls might occasionally have taken drawing lessons, as dilettantes.) The situation was easier for artistic girls if the family home included a studio, as did the home of Roghman. Her father, Hendrick Lambertsz. Roghman (1600/1601–1647), was an engraver; her mother, a member of the Savery family of artists; and her brother, the landscape painter Roeland Roghman (1627–1692). Both Geertruydt and her sister Magdalena (1637–after 1669) learned printmaking. Likewise, the engraver Magdalena de Passe (1600–1638) got her start working in the family shop.

In the case of Ter Borch, the family's artistic commitment was educational rather than commercial. Her father, Gerard Ter Borch Sr. (1582–1662), previously a painter and draftsman, drew on his early artistic education to train his sons in drawing. One of them, Gerard Ter Borch Jr. (1617–1681), later became a successful painter (Fig. 130). The father offered little encouragement to his daughters, except in calligraphy. Nevertheless, Gesina Ter Borch persisted, essentially learning drawing by the side of her younger brothers. She eventually produced a few oil portraits in the style of her well-known older brother. More important, she filled several ambitious albums with delicately painted, watercolor miniatures, a medium considered at the time more suitable for women, certainly, than portraiture. But without the benefit of the traditional "classic" training that a gifted boy could acquire during his apprenticeship to a professional painter, she remained an amateur, like so many women. Most of the work of these women amateurs has not survived, though the art of the learned Anna Maria van Schurman (1607–1678) provides another exception.

For those women fortunate enough to take that important step to professional training, the open-market system in Holland presented obvious disadvantages, as well as advantages. Competition for clients was stiff, and financing a studio was expensive. Women were more likely to work in a family shop, for both social and economic reasons. Roghman and De Passe are good examples. Roghman executed a number of copies after other artists' portraits, landscapes, and even one history subject. Best known today are a series of five genre prints dating from around 1650 depicting women engaged in such domestic tasks as sewing, spinning, scouring, and baking pancakes. The least stereotypical is *Woman Scouring Metalware* (Fig. 150), because of the unusual presentation from behind of the woman, which suggests her deep engrossment in this ordinary task and her obliviousness to the viewer. De Passe's prints consisted primarily of copies after, or closely related to, the work of Crispijn de Passe I (ca. 1560–1637), her father.

Leyster, however, demonstrated unusual initiative by establishing an independent shop and taking on students. Less surprisingly, her endeavor lasted only a few years (ca. 1629–1636). Once she married the painter Jan Miense Molenaer (1609/1610–1668) in 1636, she largely gave up painting in order to bear and care for their five children and to help administer Molenaer's studio and property. Ruysch and Van Oosterwyck enjoyed financial advantages denied to Leyster, whose father went bankrupt when she was sixteen. Oosterwyck's father and grandfather were Calvinist clergymen near Delft, and Ruysch's father was a well-known professor of anatomy and botany in Amsterdam who had developed a celebrated collection of rarities. No details are known about these women's shops, except that Van Oosterwyck trained her maid to paint. Yet both attained patronage few Dutch male artists could claim. Van Oosterwyck included among her clients William III of England and Holland, Louis XIV of France, and Emperor Leopold I of Austria. Ruysch—along with her husband, portrait painter Jurriaen Pool (1665–1745)—became court painter to the Elector Palatine Johann Wilhelm in Düsseldorf. In these two instances the women's gender seems to have worked to their advantage, for both were celebrated not only for the excellence of their still lifes (Fig. 128), but for their exotic appeal as examples of rare women artists.

Little is known about Peeters, who likely worked in Holland in 1612 and 1617. The rest of her life she spent in Antwerp, producing a variety of still lifes, among them works that included breads and fruits (breakfast pieces), and others featuring costly objects (banquet pieces). Into many of the latter, she incorporated her own self-portrait reflected on the shiny surfaces of metal goblets, as if to identify her own work in painting with the exquisite craftsmanship of the elaborate objects. The still life of 1612 in the Staatliche Kunsthalle in Karlsruhe, for example, represents her facial features eight times on the gold goblet at the right, testimony to her virtuoso skill at perspective and her knowledge of optics.

Only three Dutch women artists are recorded as having joined a guild. Leyster became a member of the Haarlem Guild of St. Luke in 1633. Perhaps her decision was influenced by the need for the social security that the guild could offer. Ruysch joined the painters' guild in The Hague in 1701, for unknown, but certainly different, reasons. One other woman is recorded in the Haarlem guild in the seventeenth century, Sara van Baalbergen, though otherwise nothing is known about her. The rest of the women artists, perhaps because of their families' artistic connections, managed to pursue their art apart from the guilds.

A few other women artists of the time should be mentioned, most of them still life painters. Maria Sybilla Merian (1647–1717), daughter of a Swiss engraver and stepdaughter of a Flemish still life painter, lived many of her years in Holland. She was primarily a botanical and entomological illustrator who published a number of volumes on engravings after her exquisitely detailed drawings. These publications made important contributions to scientific research. Other artists that should be cited include: the still life painters Margaretha de Heer (ca. 1603–ca. 1665) and Maria Schalcken (no dates, the sister of Godfried Schalcken), the genre painter Eva van Marle (active in Zwolle, ca. 1650), the multitalented Adriana Spilberg (born 1650, the daughter of painter Johann Spilberg and the wife of Eglon van der Neer), the celebrated producer of paper cutouts Joanna Koerten (1630–1715), and the needlework specialist Rozee of Leiden (1632–1682). Eighteenth-century painters include Maria Margaretha La Fargue (1743–1813), Catherina Backer (1689–1766), and Margaretha Haverman (no dates), mostly still life and genre painters. In the nineteenth century, women continued to concentrate on still life painting, but not so exclusively as before. Among the most prominent are: Maria Vos (1824–1906), Sina (Sientje) Mesdag-van Houten (1834–1909), Maria Ph. Bilders-van Bosse (1837–1900), Margaretha Roosenboom (1843–1896), Thérèse van Duyl-Schwartze (1851–1918), Suze Bisschop Robertson (1855–1922), Lucie van Dam van Isselt (1871–1949), Coba Ritsema (1876–1961), and Anna Julia de Graag (1877–1924).

A number of seventeenth-century Dutch women painters were celebrated by contemporary writers. Their praise was consistent with a tradition begun in modern times by Giorgio Vasari in the *Lives* (second edition, 1568) of inserting exceptional women artists into publications on artists' biographies. Karel van Mander listed no women in his *Schilder-Boeck* (1604). But Cornelis de Bie's dictionary of artists, *Het*

Gulden Cabinet (1661), included a section on women paint-ers. So did Arnold Houbraken's *De groote schouburgh der Nederlantsche konstschilders en schilderessen* (1718–1721), J.C. Weyerman's *De levens-beschryvingen der Nederlandsche konst-schilders en konst-schilderessen* (1729–1769), and J. van Gool's *De Nieuwe Schouburg der Nederlantsche Kunstschilders en schilderessen* (1750–1751). The latter devoted considerable attention to Ruysch. More typical of the eighteenth century, however, was the disappearance of women's names from criti-cal and scholarly writings, due in part to the changing orien-tation of the publications toward more historical accounts focused on art as individual expression, and, therefore toward masters (for which no female equivalent existed) and their influences. Leyster is a good case in point. Lauded by Theodorus Schrevelius in his history of Haarlem in 1647 as a "leading star," her name was lost entirely by the nineteenth century as her paintings became absorbed into the *oeuvre* of Frans Hals and his school. Her art was only rediscovered by Cornelis Hofstede de Groot in 1893 because of a lawsuit. The women's movement around 1900 stimulated interest in other women artists. Even after Leyster's rediscovery, however, her work was belittled as derivative. In the one monograph (Grant, 1956) devoted to Ruysch, too, condescension toward women occasionally colored the author's descriptions of the painter's still lifes.

More recently, art historians of the first wave of modern feminism in the 1970s began combing the archives in search of long-lost women artists, including the Dutch and the Flem-ish. Exhibitions were mounted and dictionaries and hand-books on women artists published in order to upset negative stereotypes and create a positive and powerful image of women. Even now, however, only two of these women have been given monographic treatment: Ruysch, in the previously mentioned, outdated publication, and Leyster in a book (Hofrichter, 1989) and an exhibition catalog (Welu, 1993) reflecting modern approaches.

Some writers have seen these artists' paintings as assert-ing a specifically female point of view. Hofrichter (Hofrichter, 1975, 1982), for example, analyzed the influence of a femi-nine sensibility on the iconography of Leyster's *The Proposi-tion* (1631; The Hague, Mauritshuis; Fig. 151); in similar terms, Peacock (1993) discussed Roghman's choice of motifs in her engraving series made around 1650. Yet other writers have investigated the various influences exerted by the prevail-ing patriarchal society on women artists, including the ob-stacles they faced, the conditions under which they worked, the subjects they were encouraged to represent (still life most particularly), and the terms in which they interpreted sexual difference. In related fashion, art historians have recently analyzed how seventeenth-century ideologies of femininity functioned in representations of women by male artists (Franits, 1993). Rather few writings on women's art have taken twentieth-century critical theories into account, though one article used viewer response to analyze how viewing was (and is) affected by cultural constructions of gender (Kettering, 1993). Despite the timidity with which art histo-rians and critics of this art have used feminism as a critical tool, feminism has nevertheless asserted a considerable general in-fluence during the 1990s. Discussions of seventeenth-century Dutch art (and to some extent later art) routinely include women as makers of art, and, little by little, writers have be-gun to raise the issue of how sexual difference is registered in representations of women.

Alison McNeil Kettering

See also Andriesse, Emmy; Feminism, feminist issues; Fortuyn/O'Brien; Leyster, Judith; Natural history illustration; Robertson, Suze Bisschop; Ronner-Knip, Henriëtte; Ruysch, Rachel; Schwartze, Thérèse van Duyl; Self-portraiture; Still life; Textiles, textile industry; Toorop, Charley (Annie Caroline Pontifex); Van Pallandt, Charlotte; Van Schurman, Anna Maria; Writers on art, eighteenth century

Bibliography

Franits, Wayne E. *Paragons of Virtue: Women and Domestic-ity in Seventeenth-Century Dutch Art*. Cambridge/New York: Cambridge University Press, 1993.

Grant, M.H. *Rachel Ruysch, 1664–1750*. Leigh-on-Sea: F. Lewis, 1956.

Halbertsma, Marlite. "Vrouwenstudies kunstge–schiedenis." In *Gezichtspunten: Een inleiding in de methoden van de Kunstgeschiedenis*. Edited by Marlite Halbertsma and Kitty Zijlmans, 214–240. Nijmegen: SUN, 1993.

Harris, Ann Sutherland, and Linda Nochlin. *Women Artists: 1550–1950*. Los Angeles: Los Angeles County Mu-seum of Art; New York: distributed by Random House, 1976.

Hofrichter, Frima Fox. *Judith Leyster: A Woman Painter in Holland's Golden Age*. Doornspijk: Davaco, 1989.

———. "Judith Leyster's *Proposition*: Between Virtue and Vice." *Feminist Art Journal* 4 (1975): 22–26. Re-printed in *Feminist and Art History: Questioning the Litany*. Edited by Norma Broude and Mary D. Garrard, 173–182. New York: Harper and Row, 1982.

Kettering, Alison McNeil. *Drawings from the Ter Borch Stu-dio Estate in the Rijksmuseum*. Amsterdam: Rijksprentenkabinet; The Hague: Staatsuitgeverij, 1988.

———. "Ter Borch's Ladies in Satin." *Art History* 16 (1993): 95–124.

Oele, Anneke et al. *Bloemen uit de kelder, Negen Kunstenaressen rond de eeuwwisseling*. Arnhem: Gemeentemuseum; Zwolle: Waanders, 1989–1990.

Peacock, Martha Moffitt. "Geertruydt Roghman and the Female Perspective." *Women's Art Journal* 14 (1993): 1–10.

Russell, Margarita. "The Women Painters in Houbraken's *Groote Schouburgh*." *Woman's Art Journal* 2:1 (Spring/Summer 1981): 5–12.

Welu James A., et al. *Judith Leyster: A Dutch Master and Her World*. Worcester: Worcester Art Museum; Haarlem: Frans Hals Museum; Zwolle: Waanders, 1993.

Women's worlds

In contrast to the epic pictures of classical and biblical heroines that dominate the art produced in other countries, Dutch seventeenth-century paintings of women possess incredible candor. Although Dutch painters imaged women in a somewhat limited number of contexts and situations, all of these seem to be tied to direct experience. Paintings of women range from mothers caring for their children and maids diligently performing domestic tasks to the moral antipode: seductive prostitutes plying their trade in brothels. Yet despite their seemingly straightforward, uncomplicated appearance, these pictures must be recognized as products of a patriarchal culture. As such, paintings of virtuous wives as well as vixens reflected, yet simultaneously contributed to, a firmly established system of beliefs and values toward women that were endorsed by the male-dominated social order of the Dutch Republic.

Following age-old philosophical and "medical" theories, popular wisdom of the seventeenth century considered women physically weak and mentally deficient in comparison to men. Patriarchal ideology held that women, as potential incarnations of vice and disorder, needed to be controlled, both physically and sexually. Therefore, the options available to women in the Netherlands, as in all European countries during this period, were extremely limited. Some women were involved in rather modest occupations, such as selling fish or second-hand clothing. However, given male anxieties concerning the need to control inherently unstable females, exceedingly large numbers of women practiced the two principal offices for which they had been ordained since birth: housewifery and motherhood. In light of this it is probably no mere coincidence that so many Dutch seventeenth-century paintings show women engaged in those tasks that were considered intrinsic to these offices, among them sewing and spinning, the supervision of servants, care for children, and the like.

Literally hundreds of pictures illustrating domestic virtue survive today. A noteworthy example is Gerrit Dou's celebrated *The Young Mother* (1658; The Hague, Mauritshuis; Color Plate 8). The exquisitely crafted surface of this work—its painstaking depiction of numerous objects scattered about the cavernous room—invites our close examination. Therefore, like so many other images of domestic virtue, the pictorial surface of Dou's work provides enjoyment of bold mimetic effects as well as intellectual engagement of the motifs depicted. Dou furnishes the viewer with a veritable catalog of highly conventional motifs that appear in seemingly countless domestic images, including discarded shoes, an overturned lantern, comestibles, and sewing implements. These objects refer to an exemplary woman's tasks and the scope and limitations of her obligations, which, according to contemporary theory, lay exclusively in the home.

The conventionality of Dou's painting and numerous others attests to their popularity, reflecting widespread attitudes and ideas that dictated their production and even their content. Surely the subject formulas that constitute these images of domestic virtue are evidence of what contemporary viewers expected to see and what they deemed significant to see out of a multitude of representational possibilities. These paintings, therefore, express intrinsically wholesome domestic values that can be linked to the underlying interests of the public who bought them, a public whose attitudes toward women were thoroughly conditioned by the patriarchal culture in which they lived. And in this sense, the pictures in question did more than palely reflect the existing gender inequalities—they actively articulated them.

If, on the one hand, the world of women in Dutch seventeenth-century art is a virtuous one, on the other it is a dissolute one, as we encounter an equally prodigious number of paintings that depict unruly servants and prostitutes. Representations of prostitutes were especially popular and, therefore, like images of domestic virtue, thoroughly conventional, even if they illustrated the male nightmare of inherently unstable females unbridled by the strictures of domesticity. Moreover, they were often highly erotic. For example, Dirck van Baburen's *The Procuress* (1622; Boston, Museum of Fine Arts; Color Plate 3), which depicts a young client who offers a coin to a lute-playing whore in the presence of her procuress, is sexually charged. The prostitute's breast is partially exposed, displaying her cleavage as well as a nipple crushed by the top of the bodice of her ill-fitting dress, made all the more palpable by the artist's typically voluminous forms. The titillating, libidinous aspects of this picture, a frequent characteristic of images of prostitution, almost seem voyeuristic and difficult to reconcile with the propensity among art historians to interpret it exclusively as an admonition against morally dubious activities.

In the end, seventeenth-century Dutch paintings of wantons and those of their polar opposite, virtuous housewives, can be considered verisimilitudinous yet fictitious constructs that illustrate male attitudes, perceptions, and theories about women. In other words, they conform to male values and expectations of what were considered appropriate female roles and behavior and what were not. These pictures, therefore, shed further light on the position of women in seventeenth-century Dutch society and on the all-important question of the role that art played in early-modern Europe in espousing and maintaining the male-oriented status quo.

Wayne Franits

See also Commerce and commercial life; Donor portraits; Dou, Gerrit; History portraits; Housewives and maids; Pastoral; Roman history; Textiles, textile industry; Van Baburen, Dirck

Bibliography

Dresen-Coenders, Lene, ed. *Saints and She-Devils: Images of Women in the Fifteenth and Sixteenth Centuries.* London: Rubicon Press; distributed by ISBS, 1987.

Franits, Wayne. "Housewives and Their Maids in Dutch Seventeenth-Century Art." In *Politics, Gender, and the Arts: Women, the Arts, and Society.* Edited by Ronald Dotterer, and Susan Bowers, 112–129. Sellinsgrove, PA: Susquehanna University Press; London and Toronto: Associated University Presses, 1992.

———. *Paragons of Virtue: Women and Domesticity in Sev-*

enteenth-Century Dutch Art. New York: Cambridge University Press, 1993.

————. "'Wily Women?' On Sexual Imagery in Dutch Art of the Seventeenth Century." In *From Revolt to Riches: Culture and History of the Low Countries 1500–1700*. Edited by T. Hermans and R. Salverda, 300–319. London: Center for Low Countries Studies, 1993.

Möbius, Helga. "Die Moralisierung des Körpers; Frauenbilder und Männerwünsche im frühneuzeitlichen Holland." In *Frauen, Bilder, Männer, Mythen*. Edited by I. Barta et al., 69–83. Berlin: D. Reimer, 1987.

Pol, Lotte C. van de. "Beeld en werkelijkheid van de prostitutie in de zeventiende eeuw." In *Soete minne en helsche boosheit: Seksuele voorstellingen in Nederland 1300–1850*. Edited by G. Hekma and H. Roodenburg, 109–144. Nijmegen: SUN, 1988.

Schama, Simon. *The Embarrassment of Riches: An Interpretation of Dutch Culture in the Golden Age*. New York: Alfred A. Knopf, 1987.

————. "Wives and Wantons: Versions of Womanhood in Seventeenth-Century Dutch Art." *Oxford Art Journal* 3 (1980): 5–13.

World Wars I and II

The neutrality of the Netherlands was respected by the embattled powers during the First World War but was brutally ignored in May 1940 when Adolf Hitler's troops began an occupation of the country that was to last five years. Though the Great War of 1914–1918 affected the lives of Dutch artists in many ways, it did not prevent the free exhibition of work, new groups being formed, and important developments in early-modern Dutch art taking place. Under the occupation of 1940–1945, however, any semblance of normality in the Dutch art world quickly vanished. Nazi control and censorship strangled the official art institutions, and artists, no less than other members of the community, were victims of repressive policies and of the devastating persecution that overcame the Jewish population. Some artists collaborated with the Germans while others became renowned for deeds of resistance, and by the later stages of the war most simply had to devote their energies to the basic needs of survival. Commemorative monuments to the tragic events of 1940–1945 have been commissioned throughout the postwar period, but relatively few major artists have chosen to deal explicitly with war themes. Effects of the Second World War on individual artists have often remained private matters, though one of the most commonly shared effects can be noted in the mood of liberation and renewal that swept Dutch art in the later 1940s and 1950s.

The outbreak of a European war in the summer of 1914 caught many internationally oriented artists, both Dutch and foreign, by surprise. Dutch artists who were abroad at the time, such as Peter Alma, Leo Gestel, Adriaan Korteweg, and Otto van Rees, were obliged to return home. Piet Mondrian, on the other hand, happened to be in the Netherlands and was forced by the sudden change of circumstances to stay. The Dutch-domiciled French Cubist Henri Le Fauconnier chose not to return to his native land, while a large contingent of Belgian artists—among them Gustave de Smet, Rik Wouters, and Georges Vantongerloo—sought refuge in the Netherlands, and there was even a Belgian Modern Art Circle founded in Amsterdam in 1917. Uncertainty about whether the Netherlands would be caught up in the conflict meant that the nation initially mobilized its forces. Many artists were among those drafted into military service, but most were demobilized after a year or two when the continuing neutral status of the Netherlands seemed assured. Theo van Doesburg, for example, was drafted in 1914 and discharged from the army in February 1916, while Otto van Rees was discharged as early as 1915 after his submission of a Cubist-inspired collage to an exhibition of soldiers' art had embarrassed the authorities. Van Rees then went to join his wife, Adya, in neutral Switzerland, where they became associated with Hans Arp and Hugo Ball in the emerging Dada movement in Zurich in 1916. For most Dutch artists, on the other hand, the opportunity for international contacts was drastically reduced. The years 1910–1914 had seen particularly strong foreign participation at Dutch exhibitions, and it was this international flavor that was most obviously missing from many exhibitions held during the war.

It has been argued, however, that in the relative isolation of the war years Dutch artists gained a certain independence and became less superficially reliant on foreign influences. Certainly, the years 1914–1918 saw important strides being taken in the development of characteristically Dutch variants of Expressionist and abstract art. In 1915 the half-yearly exhibitions of De Onafhankelijken (The Independents) included several artists' first essays into abstract work, while as a result of other group shows held at the Rotterdamsche Kunstkring (Rotterdam Art Circle) and the Stedelijk Museum in Amsterdam, Mondrian's new paintings drew a considerable amount of attention. The Dutch art world was not completely isolated, however, and 1916 brought a rare injection of international work when artists associated with Herwarth Walden's German gallery Der Sturm (including Wassily Kandinsky and Franz Marc) exhibited at Kunstzalen d'Audretsch in The Hague. Dutch interest in the abstract art and theosophical notions of Kandinsky intensified in 1916–1917 and played a role in the formation of the Rotterdam group De Branding. Kandinsky also influenced the ideas of Van Doesburg, who in founding the magazine *De Stijl* gave rise to the movement of that name, which included Mondrian, Bart van der Leck, and the architect J.J.P. Oud. In one and the same month, October 1917, De Branding had its first exhibition and Theo van Doesburg published the first issue of *De Stijl*. Announcements for *De Stijl* earlier in 1917 promised contributions from leading foreign artists, and while these were not always forthcoming a clear signal was given that the new movement intended to overcome the limitations of the wartime situation and forge the kind of international links that Dutch artists had enjoyed in 1910–1914.

When the war ended in 1918, the two main tendencies in modern Dutch art, represented by De Branding and De

Stijl, were still largely building on the prewar foundations of Expressionism and Cubism. In *De Stijl's* "Manifest 1" of 1918, however, it was proclaimed that the war was destroying the old world and its individualism and making way for a new universalism. And in the contributions of Van Doesburg to *De Stijl*, the influence of Dada was also making its presence felt. With its open assaults on cherished values and its pervasive irony, Dada reflected perhaps more than any other artistic development of the time the breakdown in civilization and the sense of futility brought on by the First World War.

In many important respects, the events of 1940 had their origins in those of 1914–1918. The unsettled economic and political situation of Europe after the First World War, and not least the shift in the international balance of power brought by the emergence of a Communist state in Russia after October 1917, affected the Netherlands in the 1920s and 1930s no less than other European countries. The economic crisis of 1929–1931 coincided with increasing political extremism in the Netherlands, both from Communist and fascist sides. In 1931 the Nationaal-Socialistische Beweging (National-Socialist Movement), or NSB, was founded by Anton Mussert as a Dutch counterpart to Italian fascist and German National Socialist parties. Though various nationalist and fascist groups made their mark on Dutch politics and culture in the 1930s, it was Mussert's NSB that was to survive after 1940 to become the party of collaboration under the German occupation. The NSB proclaimed authoritarian ideals, and, much as in German Nazism, this ideology laid great stress on the values of the *volk* (the people), an emotive term loaded more with nationalist and racialist implications than with socialist ones. Artists were among those charmed by such ideals, and it has been pointed out that self-portraits made in the later 1930s by Pyke Koch show an unmistakable fascination with the heroic iconography of fascism.

On May 10, 1940, after a brief ultimatum and a savage bombardment of Rotterdam, German forces began to occupy the Netherlands. Within a few days, Queen Wilhelmina escaped to Britain to form a Dutch government in exile, and on May 15 the Netherlands officially capitulated. In the summer of 1940, the Austrian Arthur Seyss-Inquart was installed as commissioner for the Netherlands, and in November he instituted the Departement van Volksvoorlichting en Kunsten (Department of Public Information and the Arts,) or DVK, in order to establish control over the cultural life of the nation. Dutch Jews were subjected to discrimination and then increasingly to persecution, and the nation rose up in solidarity with them in the February Strike of February 25–26, 1941. But in the months and years that followed, the net of repression tightened. From July 1941 on, the only Dutch political party permitted was the NSB, and it was one of the party's officials, D. Tobi Goedewaagen (also secretary-general of the DVK), who initiated the Kultuurkamer (Chamber of Culture) on November 25, 1941, with the avowed aim of purifying, disciplining, and "supporting" the arts.

Modeled on the Kulturkammer in Germany, the Dutch Kultuurkamer was given a command structure with Goedewaagen as president at the top, guilds for the different arts in the middle, and artists and their associations at the base. The practice of any art was forbidden outside the jurisdiction of the Kultuurkamer, and heavy fines were threatened for failure to comply. However, the main leverage exerted by the Kultuurkamer was its complete control over access to artists' materials and to public performances or exhibitions; nonmembers were simply deprived of their means of livelihood, and artists' associations were threatened with the closure of their premises and the confiscation of their funds. As a result, not only many individual artists but major artists' associations such as Arti et Amicitiae, St. Lucas, De Onafhankelijken, and Pulchri Studio accepted the terms of the Kultuurkamer. Since those terms included the signing of a declaration of Aryan race, artists' associations dutifully expelled those of Jewish descent before submitting their membership lists. The Kultuurkamer gave accredited artists financial support and the opportunity to show in carefully vetted exhibitions in the Netherlands and Germany. In accordance with Nazi ideology, *entartete Kunst* (decadent art)—which covered most modernist developments as well as non-Western tribal arts—was expressly targeted for attack, while *volksche* values and heroic presentations of manhood and womanhood were advocated as part of a deliberate propaganda campaign to re-educate the Dutch nation and conform it to Aryan ideals. The art presented as admirably *volksch* in the Kultuurkamer's publication *De Schouw* was largely folkloristic or romantic, and stereotypical "Dutch" landscapes, rural scenes, and still lifes were favored. However, if Goedewaagen's brand of National Socialism was particularly pro-Dutch and romantic, other Nazi bodies such as the SS Movement and its publication *Storm SS* took a harder, pro-German line. And within the NSB ranks, Goedewaagen finally clashed with Mussert and, as a result, had to relinquish his leadership of the Kultuurkamer in 1943. Nazi attempts to control the arts were to a degree frustrated by substantial divergences of opinion and by the struggles of individuals and factions for power. After Goedewaagen's departure in 1943, the Kultuurkamer continued but became considerably less coherent in its policy.

Organized artists' resistance against the Kultuurkamer was rather more in evidence among sculptors than among painters: Gerrit van der Veen and many others in the Nederlandsche Kring van Beeldhouwers (Dutch Circle of Sculptors) refused to collaborate with the Kultuurkamer, even to the extent of petitioning Seyss-Inquart about the matter. Other means of resistance used by artists included the publication of clandestine magazines such as *De Vrije Kunstenaar* (The Free Artist), which first appeared in May 1942, and the circulation of graphic works that directly or indirectly challenged Nazi ideas and policies. The hand-printed graphics of the Groningen artist Hendrik Nicolaas Werkman are now among the most-valued artistic results of the resistance, and the names of Werkman and Van der Veen—who both paid for their resistance with their lives—have taken on a special significance in postwar remembrance of the years of occupation. Resistance also took the form of clandestine meetings in which artists and intellectuals began to plan for a postwar organization of the arts: Willem Sandberg, then adjunct-director of the

Stedelijk Museum in Amsterdam, was one of those involved in such discussion groups as early as 1941.

After the liberation of May 5, 1945, several exhibitions served both to remember the tragic events of the preceding years and to mark the new-found freedom of the Dutch art world. In July 1945, the Stedelijk Museum in Amsterdam showed *Kunst in het harnas* (Art in Armor) in commemoration of the fallen and the persecuted, and the Rijksmuseum followed in October with *Kunst in Vrijheid* (Art in Freedom), a massive spectacle with over nine hundred works, many of a kind previously censored by the Nazis. In March 1946, *Weerbare Democratie* (Resistant Democracy) presented a series of large, specially commissioned collective paintings that depicted the most poignant events of the occupation and resistance; this exhibition began in the Nieuwe Kerk in Amsterdam and then traveled throughout the country, but the paintings were not preserved for posterity. At the Stedelijk Museum in November 1946, the Dutch Circle of Sculptors exhibited designs for war monuments; the question of suitable styles was discussed very thoroughly, since the Netherlands had no strong tradition in this area. In subsequent years, and up to the present day, monuments have been commissioned and placed throughout the land, with over a hundred in Amsterdam alone. In many monuments of the 1950s and 1960s, the solution was found in symbol—doves, hands, and broken stones, for example—or in figurative work with realistic or expressionist leanings, such as Mari Andriessen's *The Dockworker* (1952; Amsterdam, J.D. Meijerplein), erected in commemoration of the February Strike of 1941. Since the 1970s, however, there has been a tendency to use modern materials and abstract or architectonic forms, as in the monument to the *Women of Ravensbrück* by Guido Eckhart, Frank Nix, and Joost van Santen (1975; Amsterdam, Museumplein).

Of strategic importance for the postwar renewal in Dutch art was the appointment in 1945 of Sandberg as director of the Stedelijk Museum, Amsterdam. In the mid- and later 1940s, the Stedelijk Museum's exhibitions of prominent artists such as Picasso, Matisse, Klee, and Kandinsky, and major movements such as Expressionism, helped make younger Dutch artists enthusiastic about, and acquaint them with, international developments. And by supporting Experimental/Cobra artists such as Constant (Fig. 25), Corneille, and Karel Appel (Color Plate 16), Sandberg came out openly for a fusion of left-wing, anti-bourgeois politics with progressive attitudes toward art. As Sandberg has made clear in his own writings, this conjuncture maintained the spirit and impetus of wartime resistance; now, however, it was not the Nazi occupying force but Dutch Establishment culture that was the enemy. That spirit of ongoing resistance and artistic liberation had an incalculable effect on postwar Dutch art, since it helped create a climate in which modernist and Experimental developments were favored over more traditional and realist ones. What certainly played a role was the awareness that during the war, rather too many realists and some Magic Realists had been favored by the Nazis or had been known to be Nazi sympathizers, while modernist art had been banned and thus emerged from the occupation as a symbol of resistance. For artists who had indeed been found guilty of collaboration in the war, the judicial processes of the postwar years brought, at the very least, lengthy periods of exclusion from public exhibitions.

Few major Dutch artists went on in subsequent years to thematize the Second World War. The Cobra artist Constant made an impressive war-related *oeuvre* in the years 1950–1952, which betrayed influences from Picasso's *Guernica* and his *Franco Suite* from 1937, as well as from Goya's *Disasters of War*; but though they resonate with experiences of the Second World War, Constant's images were made primarily as a response to the new hostilities brought on by the Cold War and the outbreak of the Korean War. Anton Heyboer, on the other hand, has not dealt with explicit war themes, but he has revealed how crucial his war experiences were for his very career as an artist. As a young man in occupied Holland, Heyboer was sent to work in Germany, but he returned physically and mentally ill; his art, begun in the 1950s and based on a highly personal, quasi-Christian symbolism, became his means for dealing with the trauma of his war years. It is Armando, however, who has most significantly and most consistently dealt with themes of the Second World War. From the mid-1950s to the present, Armando—who is both artist and writer—has concentrated his attention on thematic series, which include battlefields, enemy observations, flags, and death-heads, as an exercise in self-reflection about a youth spent in an occupied country and surrounded by violence.

Students of the history of the Netherlands in the Second World War will inevitably make use of the archives of the Rijksinstituut voor Oorlogsdocumentatie (State Institute for War Documentation), or RIOD, Amsterdam, and the standard multivolume historical study by Dr. Lou de Jong. Arthistorical coverage, which is almost entirely in Dutch, is spread over many smaller and larger publications, and because of the sensitivity of the issues dealt with it continues to be a matter capable of raising controversy.

Graham Birtwistle

See also Andriessen, Mari; Appel, Karel; Armando; Bergen; Cobra Movement; Constant; Corneille; Dada; De Branding; De Ploeg; De Stijl; Koch, Pyke; Magic Realism; Mondrian, Piet; Nationalism; North American art, Dutch influences; Oud, Jacobus Johannes Pieter; Photography, modern and contemporary; Van Doesburg, Theo; Werkman, Hendrik Nicolaas

Bibliography

Dittrich, Kathinka, and Hans Würzner, eds. *Nederland en het Duitse Exil 1933–1940.* Amsterdam: Van Gennep, 1982.

Hammacher, A.M. *Stromingen en persoonlijkheden: Schets van een halve eeuw schilderkunst in Nederland 1900–1950.* Amsterdam: Meulenhoff, 1955.

Imanse, Geurt et al. *Van Gogh tot Cobra: Nederlandse schilderkunst 1880–1950.* Amsterdam: Meulenhoff/Landshoff, 1980.

Jong, Lou de. *Het Koninkrijk der Nederlanden in de Tweede*

Wereldoorlog. Vol. 1. The Hague: Staatsuitgeverij, 1969.

Mulder, Hans. *Kunst in crisis en bezetting: Een onderzoek naar de houding van Nederlandse kunstenaars in de periode 1930–1945.* Utrecht: Het Spectrum, 1978.

Schram, D.H., and C. Geljon, eds. *Overal Sporen: De verwerking van de Tweede Wereldoorlog in literatuur en kunst.* Amsterdam: Vrije Universiteit Uitgeverij, 1990.

Stigter, Bianca. "Beelden om nooit te vergeten: Monumenten ter nagedachtenis aan de Tweede Wereldoorlog in Amsterdam 1945–1991." In *Kunst en beleid in Nederland 6,* 13–62. Amsterdam: Boekmanstichting/Van Gennep, 1993.

Stokvis, Willemijn, ed. *De doorbraak van de moderne kunst in Nederland 1945–1951.* Amsterdam: Meulenhoff/ Landshoff, 1984.

Wouwerman, Philips (1619–1668)

This gifted and prolific artist from Haarlem specialized in military and hunting scenes in which horses assume a prominent role. Eighteenth-century aristocratic collectors highly valued his paintings, and his style influenced many followers. This evidence attests to Wouwerman's accomplishments, but it has been only since the late 1980s that his works have regained much of the recognition that was lost during the nineteenth century.

Wouwerman was the son of the painter Pauwels Joostensz. Wouwerman, from whom he probably received his early training. Early biographical sources mention that he was a student of Frans Hals and that in 1638 or 1639 he worked briefly in the studio of the German history painter Evert Decker in Hamburg. During the remainder of his life in Haarlem, Wouwerman's greatest influence was undoubtedly from Pieter van Laer, whose sketches he is said to have acquired after that painter's death. Even after developing his own style, Wouwerman continually found inspiration in Van Laer's art, incorporating similar stylistic elements as well as figural types into his paintings.

Despite the almost one thousand paintings attributed to Wouwerman, it is difficult to establish a chronology of his paintings with any certainty due to the very small number of dated works. It has been determined, however, that his early works are marked by a somber palette and diagonal elements, while his masterpieces from the 1650s incorporate brighter colors and a more elegant style, often with Italianate elements. A painting such as *Army Camp* (1660s; The Hague, Mauritshuis; Fig. 152) is indicative of his sustained interest in military subjects, hunting scenes, and stables, which include prominently displayed horses, although he was equally adept at painting landscapes, genre scenes, and some religious subjects.

J.M. Kennedy

See also Commerce and commercial life; Eighty Years' War; Haarlem; Soldiers; War and warfare

Bibliography

Duparc, F.J. "Philips Wouwerman, 1619–1668." *Oud Holland* 107 (1993): 257–286.

Sutton, Peter C. *Masters of Seventeenth-Century Dutch Landscape Painting.* Boston: Museum of Fine Arts, 1987.

Writers on art, eighteenth century
Houbraken, Arnold (1660–1719)

Arnold Houbraken is the author of *De Groote Schouburgh der Nederlantsche konstschilders en schilderessen* (Great Theater of Dutch Painters;) Amsterdam, 1718–1721), an indispensable tool for all scholars of Netherlandish art of the sixteenth and seventeenth centuries.

Arnold Houbraken was born on March 28, 1660, in Dordrecht. In 1685 he married Sara Souburg and had several children. His son Jacob built a reputation as an engraver and illustrator. Houbraken was a pupil of Jacobus Leveck (Le Vecq), a painter of fashionable portraits, and Samuel van Hoogstraten. His paintings include landscapes and portraits. Most noteworthy are his mythological and biblical works. He moved to Amsterdam in 1710 and traveled to England in 1713 to illustrate a historical work on Charles I.

Houbraken wrote *Philaletes Brieven* (Philaletes' Letters, 1712) and *Verzameling van Uitgelezen Keurstoffen* (Collection of Selected Samples, 1713) before he started on his *De Groote Schouburgh der Nederlantsche Konstschilders en Schilderessen,* which appeared in 1718 and 1719, in two volumes. He died suddenly on October 14, 1719, and his widow published the third volume in 1721. A second edition with identical text and illustrations by Jacob Houbraken was published in 1753.

Arnold Houbraken regarded his *De Groote Schouburgh* as a sequel to Karel van Mander's *Schilder-Boeck.* Several quotations and opinions can be traced back to his predecessor and to many others who wrote lives of the artists in the sixteenth and seventeenth centuries: in Flanders, Cornelis de Bie (*Het gulden cabinet van de edel vry schilderconst,* 1661); in Germany and the Netherlands, Joachim von Sandrart (*Teutsche Academie der edlen Bau- Bild- und Mahlrey-Kunste,* 1675–1679); in France, Roger de Piles (*Abrégé de la vie des peintres,* 1699), Florent le Comte (*Cabinet des singularitez d'architecture, peinture, sculpture, et graveure,* 1699–1700), and André Félibien (*Des principes de l'architecture, de la sculpture, de la peinture, et des autres arts qui en dependent,* 1676; second edition 1690). Other information came from theoretical works such as those by Philips Angel (*Lof der schilderkonst,* 1642) and Samuel van Hoogstraten (*Inleyding tot de hooge schoole der schilder-konst,* 1678); from Flemish artist Anthony van Dyck's series of engraved and inscribed portraits of artists, *L' Iconographie* (ca. 1645); and from several town chronicles including the ones by Jan Jansz. Orlers (*Beschryvinge der Stad Leyden,* 1642) and Samuel Ampzing (*Beschrijvinge ende Lof der Stad Haerlem,* 1628). Throught Houbraken's *De Groote Schouburgh,* we also find quotations from the poets Joost van den Vondel (1587–1679) and Joannes Antonides (1647–1684).

Houbraken, who relied solely on chance information, has tried to present the painters in chronological order. With so many unknown details, however, he often strays from this approach, putting together family members, or painters from the same town or school. He vented his opinions broadly throughout the text, and several bibliographies are followed by descriptions of ancient coins and sacrificial tools. Houbraken's theoretical opinions are loosely based on (French) classicist rules, as in his principle that the artist should choose the best from the ancients, the most beautiful from the beautiful. He voices this idea in his biography of Rembrandt, which contains many factual errors and topical anecdotes, reducing Rembrandt to a stereotype of frugality and arrogance. Houbraken's view that a person's work and his life are analogous is made obvious by his descriptions of painters like Adriaen Brouwer, Frans Hals, and Jan Steen. Still, the many details and descriptions of the painters' world make this work essential for scholars of Netherlandish art.

Houbraken's friend and successor Johan van Gool followed in his footsteps, corrected mistakes, and added many new names in his *De Nieuwe Schouburg* (1750–1751). Jacob Campo Weyerman used his work extensively in his *De Levens-beschrijvingen* (1729–1769).

Weyerman, Jacob Campo (1677–1747)

Weyerman is the author of *De Levens-beschryvingen der Nederlandsche Konst-schilders en Konst-schilderessen* (Biographies of Dutch Painters), the first three volumes of which were published in The Hague in 1729, and the final volume in Dordrecht in 1769.

Weyerman was born in a military camp near Charleroi (now Belgium) on August 9, 1677. He lived for most of his formative years in Breda, where he was trained by local masters. Later he studied in Delft and Antwerp. He received his classical and literary education in Delft and at the university in Utrecht. From Breda Weyerman traveled frequently to England, where he received commissions from Queen Anne and several noblemen. Although few of his own paintings—mostly of flowers in vases—have survived, they show his versatility.

After an initial attempt to write for the theater, Weyerman made his formal appearance on the literary scene with his publication of *De Rotterdamsche Hermes* (Rotterdam Hermes, 1720). In this weekly journal, he skillfully addressed the idiosyncrasies of his time, mixing politics with anecdotes about his contemporaries, erotic allusions with personal comments, quotations from the classics with ribald songs. Several other journals, with fancy names like *De Ontleeder der Gebreken* (The Dissector of Deficiencies, 1724), *De Doorzigtige Heremyt* (The Visionary Hermit, 1728), and *De Vrolyke Tuchtheer* (The Merry Castigator, 1729), followed in rapid order. In other works he criticized church authorities, publishers, alchemists, art dealers, and quacks.

From the 1720s onward Weyerman traveled throughout Western Europe while maintaining a home in several places in the Netherlands: Breda, Amsterdam, Abcoude, and Vianen. He was arrested in Vianen in 1738, accused of extortion and insulting the authorities, particularly the board of the Dutch East India Company. Sentenced to life in prison, he died after eight years in The Hague on March 9, 1747.

In *De Echo des Weerelds* (Echo of the World, 1725–1726), Weyerman published fragments describing painters' lives, which would culminate in his three volumes of *De Levens-beschryvingen der Nederlandsche Konst-schilders en Konst-schilderessen* (1729). The last volume, with fragments written in prison, was published posthumously in 1769. An edited manuscript of the latter can be found in the Royal Library, Brussels.

Weyerman, whose proficiency for foreign languages was legendary, was a skillful translator (of Swift, Cervantes, and others) and an established writer when he published his *De Levens-beschryvingen*. His extensive borrowing from Arnold Houbraken's *De Groote Schouburgh* (1718–1721), which he justifies as an improvement on Houbraken's poor style, should be seen in light of his other literary works. Using both quotations from antiquity and his own sources, he succeeded in writing his own version, which should not be relied on as an encyclopedia. Accuracy with factual information, like dates of birth and death, was not as important to him as the entertaining and didactic portrayal of a painter's art and life, including vices and virtues. He contended that an author with a witty pen is nevertheless also bound to include useful comments. His own experiences as a painter add to the liveliness of the text. The many anecdotes are used to enhance the description of his characters.

With scant references to theories or schools, it is clear throughout *De Levens; beschryvingen* that Weyerman was no art theoretician. Weyerman's advice to painters in general boils down to this: Be careful with your money, moderate in drinking, cautious with women, and show respect to nobility. He also highly recommends the benefits of travel to young painters: It improves one's knowledge about painting, cultivates the etiquette, and enhances proficiency in languages.

De Levens-beschryvingen is a collection of seven hundred sixty-four biographies, which leans heavily on Houbraken for the majority of his work but adds interesting new information about contemporaries and the seamy side of the art world. Interspersed with personal opinions and amusing digressions, Weyerman's work is still of great importance as a document of early eighteenth-century Dutch life in the arts. His successor in this area was Johan van Gool.

Van Gool, Johan (1685–1763)

Johan van Gool was Jacob Campo Weyerman's successor and the last in the line of biographers modeled after Karel van Mander. He saw himself carrying the torch of Houbraken, whose family he befriended, in his two-volume work *De Nieuwe Schouburg der Nederlantsche kunstschilders en schilderessen* (The New Theater of Dutch Painters, The Hague, 1750–1751). He was a pupil of Simon van der Does and became a cattle painter. As an art dealer and board member of The Hague Art Academy, he was well acquainted with the art world. He wrote his work, at age sixty-three, to improve the image of Dutch art and to stimulate young painters.

Like Weyerman, Van Gool did not refer to art theories but relied on his own judgment, based on personal taste. His research, consisting of personal interviews and visits to private collections and public buildings, resulted in an extensive collection of biographies. Van Gool steered away from the flamboyant literary style of Weyerman, and he lacks his predecessor's imagination. However, the many facts and critical opinions on contemporaries contained in his *De Nieuwe Schouburg* make it an important tool for art-history research. Van Gool's work had an effect on contemporary readers, especially Gerard Hoet, who in a pamphlet defended the art dealers against the accusation that they were the reason for the decline in Dutch art. Hoet furthermore listed many artists who were left out of Van Gool's *De Nieuwe Schouburg*.

Weyerman and Van Gool were the first to engage in art criticism with a distinct personal opinion. They turned away from the classicist approach and did not believe in a strict division of genres in painting, stressing the truth-to-nature that should pervade paintings.

Contrary to later conventional wisdom regarding the effect on art of the rainy Dutch climate, Calvinism, and the ending of the Dutch Golden Age, Dutch art did not decline suddenly in the eye of these eighteenth-century biographers. Gerard de Lairesse, Adriaen van der Werff, Jan van Huysum, and Cornelis Troost were highly praised and held out as examples for the learning youth. Some complained about strict French rules, decorative wallpaper gaining favor over paintings, or criticized *fijnschilders*—fine painters specializing in delicate details—whose art was time-consuming and expensive. The main target of the biographers' condemnation, however, was the world of art dealers, who bought older and foreign art instead of their contemporaries' work and generally exploited the artists. Notwithstanding the validity of their criticism, the Dutch art world had changed in numbers of artists and opinions about taste since the turn of the century.

Ton J. Broos

See also Amateurs, art academies, and art associations before the nineteenth century; Genre painting, eighteenth century; Van Mander, Karel; Writers on art, sixteenth and seventeenth centuries

Bibliography for Houbraken

Emmens, J. *Rembrandt en de regels van de kunst.* Utrecht: Haentjens, Dekker, and Gumbert, 1968.

Hofstede de Groot, C. *Arnold Houbraken en seine "Groote Schouburg" kritisch beleuchtet.* Quellenstudien zur holländischen Kunstgeschichte 1. The Hague: Nijhoff, 1893.

Houbraken, Arnold. *De groote Schouburgh der Nederlantsche Konstschilders en Schilderessen.* Amsterdam, 1718–1721; 2nd ed., 1753. Reprint. Amsterdam: B.M. Israel, 1976.

Bibliography for Weyerman

Broos, Ton. J. *Tussen zwart en ultramarijn: De levens van schilders beschreven door Jacob Campo Weyerman, 1677–1747.* Amsterdam: Rodopi, 1990. (English summary).

Weyerman, Jacob Campo. *De Levens-beschryvingen der Nederlandsche Konst-schilders en Konst-schilderessen.* Vols. 1–3. The Hague: Wed. E. Boucquet, H. Scheurleer, F. Boucquet, and J. de Jong, 1729. Vol. 4. Dordrecht: A. Blussé, 1769.

Bibliography for Van Gool

Gool, Johan van. *De nieuwe schouburg der Nederlantsche kunstschilders en schilderessen.* 2 vols. The Hague, 1750–1751. Reprint. Soest: Davaco, 1971.

Vries, Lyckle de. *Diamante gedenkzuilen en leerzaeme voorbeelden: Een bespreking van Johan van Gools Nieuwe Schouburg.* Groningen: Forsten, 1990.

Writers on art, sixteenth and seventeenth centuries

Published in 1604, Karel van Mander's *Schilder-Boeck* (Book on Picturing) offered the first critical history of Netherlandish painting, drawing, and engraving. Developing art-theoretical categories culled from Latin and vernacular sources, including humanist texts, workshop usage, and Italian treatises, Van Mander embedded them in a historical scheme, using terms such as *inventie* (invention), *teyckenconst* (also spelled *tekenkonst*; drawing or the art of delineation), and *wel verwen* (coloring well) to chronicle the history of Dutch and Flemish painting of the fifteenth and sixteenth centuries. Having consolidated earlier local efforts to write on the visual arts, the *Schilder-Boeck* set the standard for all subsequent theoretical texts on Dutch art.

Before 1604, Latin writers on Dutch art focused on two major figures, the painter-draftsman Maerten van Heemskerck and the engraver Cornelis Cort of Hoorn, both of whom produced images for the print publisher Hieronymus Cock in Antwerp. Circulated at the major book fairs, prints designed by Van Heemskerck soon became known to humanists such as Petrus van Opmeer and Hadrianus Junius, who responded to his draftsmanship by praising him in terms applied by the ancient historian Pliny the Elder to the Greek masters Apelles, Parrhasius, Protogenes, and Zeuxis. In the world chronicle *Opus chronographicum orbis universi* (Chronography of the Entire World, 1569), Van Opmeer compares Van Heemskerck's *lineas formarum* (contour lines) to those of Protogenes, famed for his sureness of hand. In the *Batavia*, the official history of Holland composed between 1565 and 1570, Junius extols several masters—among them the painters Jan van Scorel and Antonis Mor and the engravers Dirck Volkertsz. Coornhert and Philips Galle—but he reserves his highest praise for Van Heemskerck, whose diligence and inventiveness recall Apelles' virtues, and whose landscape panoramas resemble those of the ancient painter Ludius. Junius is also the author of numerous *emblemata*, poems that elucidate printed images, a collection of which, the *Pinaces liber unus* (First Book of Pictures), appeared posthumously in 1598. The notion that prints can distill a master's accomplishments derives from Erasmus, who had eulogized Albrecht Dürer in the *Dialogus de recta latini graecique sermonis pronunciatione*

(Dialogue on the Correct Pronunciation of Latin and Greek Speech, 1528), praising the painterly effects of his *monochromata* (prints) rendered entirely *nigrae lineae* (in black lines).

Domenicus Lampsonius, secretary to the prince-bishop of Liège, writes about Cort in his letters to Titian and Giulio Clovio, dated 1567 and 1570, respectively. Author of the first artist's life published in the Netherlands, the *Lamberti Lombardi apud Eburiones pictores celeberrimi vita* (Life of the Most Celebrated Liègois Painter Lambert Lombard, 1565), and of the first canon of Netherlandish masters, the *Pictorum aliquot celebrium Germaniae inferioris effigies* (Effigies of Some of the Celebrated Netherlandish Painters, 1572), Lampsonius views Cort as a nonpareil whose prints after Titian and the Roman masters are so accurate that they provide a true record of their pictorial manner. Through his powers of imitation, Cort conveys new kinds of visual information that exceed the scope of *ekphrasis* (rhetorical description). His prints are thus the essential currency of canon-formation, for they allow the critic to judge painters whose works are otherwise inaccessible. That Cort is a Dutchman allows Lampsonius to claim his burin-hand as a distinctive invention of the Netherlands, which now controls entry into the canon of great masters even in Italy.

In Holland the author-engraver Dirck Volkertsz. Coornhert produced a series of religious treatises that elucidate his activities as a printmaker. Devoted to allegory as a fundamental exegetical tool, Coornhert defended his literary and pictorial usage in polemical texts such as the *Negentich plaetsen der H. Schriftueren* (Nineteen Passages from Holy Scripture, 1585), which disputes the Calvinist model of biblical exegesis, arguing that he, by using allegory, reads the Bible as did the Church fathers. In *Van de predestinatie* (On Predestination, 1589), he reflects briefly upon the process of imitation, which negotiates between conception and realization, explaining how difficult it is to translate the images generated by his imaginative-discursive faculty. Coornhert's stance on allegory resonates with that of the *rederijkers* (rhetoricians), artisans and merchants who pursued poetry and the dramatic arts as members of civic chambers of rhetoric, performing in *spelen* (plays). As is evident from the *Spelen van sinne* (Allegorical Plays, 1562), published to commemorate the great *landjuweel* (dramatic competition) held in Antwerp in 1561, painting and its sister arts enjoyed high status as expressions of artifice. Asked to respond to the question, "What compels us to the practice of *consten* (the arts)?" the chambers answered by distinguishing between mere labor and skilled artisanship, identifying the latter as an emanation of God's spirit and reflection of God's handiwork. Humankind pursues the visual arts because they, like poetry, rhetoric, and the liberal arts, issue from God and are the means through which we imitate God, the supreme artificer.

These views underlie Van Mander's *Schilder-Boeck* (eds. 1604 and 1618), which aims to canonize *onser consten doorluchtighe oeffenaers namen* (the names of illustrious practitioners of our arts). Alert to Italian theoretical texts, especially to the competing claims of Tuscan *disegno* (manner of line and command of the human figure) and Venetian *colorito*

(coloring), grounded, respectively, in Giorgio Vasari's *Vite* (*Lives*, second edition 1568) and Lodovico Dolce's *Aretino* (1557), Van Mander appropriated Italian critical categories, redefining them to accommodate the distinctive achievements of Northern masters such as Jan van Eyck and Hendrick Goltzius. He also introduced new categories, perhaps based in workshop usage, such as *netticheyt* (neatness, meticulousness, precision) and *reflexy-const* (the art of depicting reflections), exemplifying them in the works of masters whose lives he recounted. The organization of the *Schilder-Boeck* is Van Mander's boldest critical maneuver, allowing him to authorize local pictorial tradition as equal to, yet different from, the distinguished lineages of Florentine, Lombard, Roman, and Venetian art. The text opens with the *Grondt* (Groundwork), Book 1, a long poem divided into fourteen chapters that establish critical categories. There follow three sets of *Levens* (Lives), Books 2–4, which develop terms introduced in the *Grondt*. Organized chronologically, the *Levens* consist of artists' biographies. In effect, Van Mander juxtaposes three parallel histories of art—of the ancient world, of Italy, and of the Netherlands—tracking criteria whose meanings change as they migrate through changes of place and time. Book 4, the Dutch and Flemish *Lives*, concludes with biographies of living masters, many of whom specialize in the *verscheydenheden*, the distinctive subject categories—landscape, portraiture, and still life, among others. Van Mander certifies the pursuit of such subjects, praising Gillis van Coninxloo, whose landscapes engage the eyes, drawing them deep into the image; Hans Vredeman de Vries, whose *perspectiven* (perspectives) deceive the eyes, playing at the threshold between the feigned and the actual; and Hendrick Goltzius, who makes pictorial manner itself his object of imitation, impersonating the representational means of fellow masters with protean fidelity.

Between 1604 and 1650, none of the texts that evince art-theoretical concerns is as comprehensive as the *Schilder-Boeck*. In his manuscript *Autobiography*, composed in Latin between 1629 and 1631, Constantijn Huygens glorifies Rubens as the greatest living painter, yet follows Van Mander in approving masters like Jacob de Gheyn II, who have a universal knowledge of painting but have devoted themselves to still life, especially to flower pieces. Huygens praises Goltzius in terms borrowed from Van Mander, and, playing upon the theme that the highest art is that which conceals art, he praises Michiel van Miereveld, whose portraits are deceptively lifelike because they imitate the artifice of nature, rather than of art. In a famous aside, Huygens observes that the Dutch have surpassed both ancients and moderns in their ability to delineate swiftly the true lineaments of people, places, and things. Indeed, it was his father's wish that he learn to draw so that he might portray the noteworthy things he would see while traveling abroad.

Trained like Huygens in the study of ancient culture, the historian Arnoldus Buchelius shared his admiration for De Gheyn. His notes on contemporary art, compiled in a series of unpublished manuscripts that date between 1583 and 1640, document the contents of many of the most famous *constcamers* (*kunstkammern*, art and curiosity cabinets) of his day. The journal of his third trip to Cologne, which records his purchases of art, is a crucial source on print collecting, as is the catalog of his library, composed in 1620, which includes a list of *prentboeken* (print albums). In his *Diarium* (Diary, begun 1583) and *Res pictoriae* (Notes on Pictures, begun 1591), which rely in part on information gleaned from Johannes de Wit's lost manuscript lives of early Netherlandish painters, Buchelius deploys criteria such as *teneritas* (tenderness) and *venustas* (grace and beauty that incite love) when referring to the pictorial excellence of contemporary masters like De Gheyn.

Published in 1637, Franciscus Junius' *De pictura veterum* (On the Painting of the Ancients) consists of three books, which set forth the doctrine *ut pictura poesis* (as is poetry, so is painting), using it to justify the author's attempt to organize knowledge of ancient painting through rhetorical categories such as *imitatio* (imitation), *phantasia* (fantasy), and *simplicitas* (simplicity). Although Junius aimed to provide a theoretical account of the principles of ancient painting, his exhaustive philological study of ancient texts achieved currency as a thesaurus of classical references to painters. The Dutch translation of 1641, *De schilder-konst der oude*, includes an influential preface by Johan de Brune that develops a *paragone* (comparison) of painting and sculpture, weighing their relative merits. Inverting the shibboleth that sculpture is superior to painting because it actually embodies what painting can only feign, De Brune decides that painting is the more accomplished, precisely because it relies entirely on artifice to achieve the appearance of nature. Moreover, De Brune continues, following Van Mander, painting can imitate transitory effects beyond the sculptor's ken—rain, mist, reflection, and the darkness of night.

De Brune's preface proved crucial to Philips Angel, whose *Lof der schilder-konst* (Praise of Painting, 1642) is the text of a lecture presented on St. Luke's day in 1641 to the assembled painters of Leiden. On behalf of his audience, Angel hoped to convince the city fathers to allow the formation of a local Guild of St. Luke. Following De Brune, he emphasizes that painting is praiseworthy because it consists of *schijn sonder sijn* (appearance rather than matter). Painting, aiming above all to please the eyes, requires diligent attention to nature's visual effects, and the best masters are those who approach life more closely than any previous painters and whose images seem unmediated by any trace of pictorial manner. Their *schijn eyghentlijcke krachte* (feigned yet true force) will overpower the viewer's eyes, and so these painters will find patrons, who will desire to acquire such commodities. In fact, Gerrit Dou, whom Angel considers to be an incomparable painter of materials, has done just that. Although the *Lof der schilder-konst* has neither the metaphorical richness nor historical apparatus of the *Schilder-Boeck*, Angel's belief that painters must specialize and that painting is virtuous because it is salable, deceptive, and pleasing to the eyes derives from Van Mander,

who makes similar points in the *Grondt*. Like Buchelius and Huygens, Angel, therefore, stands in a lineage that acknowledges implicitly the importance of Van Mander's groundbreaking efforts.

Walter S. Melion

See also Coornhert, Dirck Volkertsz.; Drawing theory; Emblems and emblem books; Erasmus, Desiderius; Flanders, Flemish School; Goltzius, Hendrick; Haarlem; History painting; Humanism, humanist themes; Huygens, Constantijn; Literature, poetry: analogues with the visual; Nationalism; Rhetoricians' chambers; Subjects, subject categories, and hierarchies; Van Mander, Karel; Writers on art, eighteenth century

Bibliography

Ellenius, Allan. *"De Arte Pingendi": Latin Art Literature in Seventeenth-Century Sweden and Its International Background.* Uppsala: Almquist and Wiksells, 1960.

Melion, Walter S. *Shaping the Netherlandish Canon: Karel van Mander's "Schilder-Boeck."* Chicago: University of Chicago Press, 1991.

Miedema, Hessel. *Karel van Mander: Den grondt der edel vry schilder-const.* 2 vols. Utrecht: Haentjens, Dekker, and Gumbert, 1973.

———. *Karel van Manders "Leven der moderne, oft dees-tijtsche doorluchtighe Italiaensche schilders" en hun bron.* Alphen aan den Rijn: Canaletto, 1984.

———. *Kunst, kunstenaar en kunstwerk bij Karel van Mander: Een analyse van zijn levensbeschrijvingen.* Alphen aan den Rijn: Canaletto, 1981.

Müller Hofstede, Justus. "'Wort und Bild': Fragen zu Signifikanz und Realität in der Holländischen Malerei des 17. Jahrhunderts." In *Wort und Bild in der niederländischen Kunst und Literatur des 16. und 17. Jahrhunderts.* Edited by Herman Vekeman and J. Müller Hofstede, 9–23. Erftstadt: Lukassen Verlag, 1983.

Schenkeveld, Maria A. *Dutch Literature in the Age of Rembrandt: Themes and Ideas.* Amsterdam and Philadelphia: Benjamins, 1991.

Sluijter, Eric J. "Belering en verhulling? Enkele 17de-eeuwse teksten over de schilderkunst en de iconologische benadering van Noordnederlandse schilderijen uit deze periode." *De zeventiende eeuw* 4 (1988): 3–28.

Veldman, Ilja M. *De wereld tussen goed en kwaad: Late prenten van Coornhert.* The Hague: SDU, 1990.

———. "Maarten van Heemskerck and Hadrianus Junius: The Relationship between a Painter and a Humanist." *Simiolus* 7 (1974): 35–54.

Writers on art, nineteenth and twentieth centuries

See Art criticism; Art history, history of the discipline

Xavery, Jan Baptist (1697–1742)

The *oeuvre* of the Flemish sculptor Jan Baptist Xavery, a student of his father, Albert Xavery, and Michiel van der Voort, shares analogies with those of his Antwerp contemporaries in its shift toward an increasingly Rococo mode. Xavery left Antwerp for Italy in 1719, traveling south to Rome through Vienna. An unusual work from this period, a terra-cotta figure of a *River God* (signed and dated 1720; Amsterdam, Rijksmuseum), suggests his interest in antique art. By 1723 he had moved to The Hague, where he became a master in the Guild of St. Luke in 1725 and court sculptor to Willem IV, Prince of Orange-Nassau. Several signed and dated works from this period would appear to be models for garden sculpture, perhaps for the Huis ten Bosch. Among these is a terra-cotta group (1726; Amsterdam, Rijksmuseum) of three children (who resemble the *putti* of Van der Voort) representing *Summer*, which may have been intended for an allegorical group of the four seasons (such as that dating from the same year in London, Victoria and Albert Museum).

Xavery's portrait busts (Amsterdam, Rijksmuseum) from the 1720s are rather grandiose, with oddly misshapen features and blank expressions. The effigies included in his terra-cotta maquettes for table tombs, such as the reclining figure (1731) of Lieutenant-General *Johan Theodoor, Baron of Friesheim* (Amsterdam, Rijksmuseum), for the monument in Heusden, are more successful. Xavery also executed small-scale works in other media, including ivory (statuettes of *Male and Female Satyrs*, 1729; and busts of *Cleopatra* and *Lucretia*, 1732 and 1734; both Amsterdam, Rijksmuseum), as well as boxwood (*Meleager and Amphitrite*, 1728; The Hague, Gemeentemuseum) and lindenwood (a figure of *Bacchus*, based on an antique model, 1729; London, Victoria and Albert Museum). Xavery was also responsible for an elegant Rococo relief depicting the *Allegory of Faith* (1738–1741), with figures of *Piety*, *Poetry*, and *Music*, placed beneath the organ of the Grote Kerk in Haarlem.

In 1734, following a brief visit to Kassel, Xavery returned to The Hague, where, according to a newspaper notice from September (and another from May 1735), he was selling sculpture, including works by his father as well as by De Kok (the Antwerp sculptor Jan Claudius de Cock?), Van Logteren, (Ignatius or Jan?) and other masters.

Cynthia Lawrence

See also Flanders, Flemish School; Sculpture (1550–1795)

Bibliography

Kulturmann, U. et al. "Jan Baptist Xavery." In *Europäische Barockplastik am Niederrhein: Grupello und seine Zeit*, 289–292. Dusseldorf: Kunstmuseum, 1971.

Leeuwenberg, J., and W. Halsema-Kubes, eds. *Beeldhouwkunst in het Rijksmuseum*, 373–384. The Hague: Staatsuitgeverij, 1973.

Xavery, Pieter (ca. 1647–traceable to 1683)

Little is known about the Antwerp sculptor Pieter Xavery prior to his arrival in Leiden in 1670. His earliest recorded work, a signed and dated terra-cotta relief of the *Flagellation of Christ* (1667; Bruges, Gruuthuis Museum), offers few clues to his background and training. While earlier sources suggest that Xavery may have been brought to Leiden by his fellow Fleming Rombout Verhulst, it is more likely that he was simply Verhulst's successor in that city. Xavery enrolled in the university in 1670 and married later that same year. He was active in Leiden until 1674, when he returned to Antwerp; although ostensibly traceable to 1683, there are no recorded works by him after he left the Netherlands.

Xavery was responsible for a number of monumental commissions in Leiden, including a vestibule (1670) in marbled oak with bronzed terra-cotta (Leiden, Stedelijk Museum De Lakenhal). He also executed figures of *Justice* and *Prudence* for the pediment and gable decoration of the Gravensteen (ca. 1671–1672), the pediment sculpture for the House of the Vergulde Turk on the Breestraat (1673; including the bust of *a Turk*, in a cartouche, between reclining figures of *Mercury* and *Neptune*), and several figures and figural groups for the *vierschaar* (public tribunal) of the town hall, including the *Winning Party* and the *Losing Party* (1672) and the *Hoofd-Schout* (high sheriff) (signed and dated 1673; the last three are terra-cotta maquettes, Leiden, Stedelijk Museum De Lakenhal). Xavery's group of two madmen (the so-called *Orlando furioso*, 1673; terra-cotta maquette, Amsterdam, Rijksmuseum) was probably designed for a lunatic asylum. He is credited with a series of busts of Roman emperors, of which the bronzed plaster series in Leiden are probably copies.

Xavery's small-scale genre subjects demonstrate his talent for picturesque caricature. The scale and spontaneity of these terra-cotta figures, with their oversize heads and prominent features, prefigure Rococo taste: These include the *Bagpipe Player* (1673; Amsterdam, Museum Willet-Holthuysen), *Bacchanale* (The Hague, Museum Meermanno Westreenianun), and *Laughing Jesters, Lady with a Lapdog, Two Madmen,* and *Lady Portrayed As Flora* (1673; Amsterdam, Rijksmuseum). Xavery also worked in ivory (statuettes of *Adam and Eve*, 1671; Amsterdam, Rijksmuseum) and bronze (several male busts and his *Peasant Boy and Girl*, ca. 1675; Amsterdam, Rijksmuseum).

Cynthia Lawrence

See also Leiden; Sculpture (1550–1795); Verhulst, Rombout

Bibliography

Jongh, E. de. "Pieter Xavery, 'De Leidse Vierschaar.'" *Openbaar Kunstbezit* 15 (1971): 21a–21b.

Kulturmann, U. et al. "Pieter Xavery." In *Europäische Barockplastik am Niederrhein: Grupello und seine Zeit,* 286–288. Dusseldorf: Kunstmuseum, 1971.

Leeuwenberg, J., and W. Halsema-Kubes, eds. *Beeldhouwkunst in het Rijksmuseum,* 326–332. The Hague: Staatsuitgeverij, 1973.

Neurdenburg, E. *De zeventiende eeuwsche beeldhouwkunst in de Noordelijke Nederlanden: Hendrick de Keyser, Artus Quellien en Rombout Verhulst en tijdgenoten.* Amsterdam: Meulenhoff, 1948.

Pelinck, E. "Nieuws over den beeldhouwer Pieter Xavery." *Oud Holland* 59 (1942): 102–109.

Staring, A. "De Beeldhouwer Pieter Xavery." *Oud Holland* 44 (1927): 1–15.

Vandenven, M. "Pieter Xavery." In *De Beeldhouwkunst in de Eeuw van Rubens,* 294–296. Brussels: Museum voor Oude Kunst, 1977.

Z

Zijl, Lambertus (1866–1947)

Together with Joseph Mendes da Costa (1863–1939), Lambertus Zijl was chiefly responsible for the renewal of Dutch sculpture around the beginning of the twentieth century. Under the influence of industrial-design instruction directed at reviving the practice of the crafts and new tendencies in architecture, he broke with academic tradition and was inspired by medieval and archaic sculptural approaches. This is clearly apparent in his major commission for architectural sculpture for the Stock Exchange building (1898–1903), designed as a *Gesamtkunstwerk* (total work of art) by H.P. Berlage (1856–1934) in Amsterdam, where the new formal language and the increased stylizing is especially visible in the keystones. In most buildings by Berlage to which he contributed, the sculpture filled a subordinate role in accordance with the architect's convictions (Fig. 125).

In cooperation with K.P.C. de Bazel (1869–1923), Zijl worked on the office of the Nederlandse Handelsmaatschappij (Dutch Trade Society, 1919–1926), among others; he also worked on a number of architect A.J. Kropholler's later, traditional buildings, such as the town halls of Waalwijk and Noordwijkerhout. The Monument to the *Queen Mother Emma* in Amsterdam (1938) is Zijl's most important autonomous monumental work.

In his uncommissioned work, Zijl introduced everyday subjects like human and animal figures, which he executed in an unpretentious manner. He did this in a technique derived from Impressionism in which he paid much attention not only to the surface effects but also to the structure and composition of the statue. In doing this he also set a new trend in his independent work.

An important part of Zijl's *oeuvre* consists of interior decoration for ships, which he made between 1906 and 1938 mostly under the direction of C.A. Lion Cachet. A great part of this work has been lost. As a sculptor Zijl was more concerned with form than content. He was flexible in the execution and interpretation of his commissions, and this made him an artist much in demand.

Geraart Westerink

See also Alberdingk Thijm, Josephus Albertus; Applied arts; Berlage, Hendrik Petrus; Mendes da Costa, Joseph; Nationalism; Public monumental sculpture 1795–1990; Sculpture (1795–1945)

Bibliography

Broekhuis, Madelon. "Ideologie in steen: Het beeldhouwwerk van Lambertus Zijl aan het beursgebouw te Amsterdam." In *Monumentale beeldhouwkunst in Nederland*, 195–226. Weesp: Fibula, 1984. (English summary).

Hammacher, A.M. *Beeldhouwkunst*. Vol. 14, *De Schoonheid van ons land*. Amsterdam: Contact, 1955.

Heij, Jan Jaap, ed. *Lambertus Zijl, 1866–1947*. Assen: Drents Museum, 1990.

Vries, R.W.P. de. *Lambertus Zijl*. Bussum: Kroonder, 1946.

Index

Boldface indicates encyclopedia entry as well as entries under contributor names.